W9-AAN-330

A GENERAL'S LIFE

AN AUTOBIOGRAPHY BY
GENERAL OF THE ARMY

OMAR N. BRADLEY

and Clay Blair

SIMON AND SCHUSTER
NEW YORK

To Kitty, my beloved wife, who saved my life
and filled every day of it with joy.

—OMAR N. BRADLEY

Grateful acknowledgment is made to the following for permission to reprint the materials listed:

The Patton Papers, Vol. II (1940–1945), edited by Martin Blumenson. Copyright © 1974 by Martin Blumenson. Reprinted by permission of Houghton Mifflin Company.

Triumph in the West (Vol. II of The Alanbrooke Diaries), edited by Arthur Bryant. Copyright © 1959 by Arthur Bryant. Reprinted by permission of Doubleday & Company, Inc. and Collins Publishers, London.

The Papers of Dwight David Eisenhower, nine volumes, edited by Alfred D. Chandler and Louis Galambos. Copyright © 1970–1978. Reprinted by permission of The Johns Hopkins University Press.

Memoirs by Bernard Montgomery. Copyright © 1958 by Bernard Law, Viscount Montgomery of Alamein. Reprinted by permission of Collins Publishers, London.

The Eisenhower Diaries (Vol. IV), edited by Robert H. Ferrell. Copyright © 1981. Reprinted by permission of W.W. Norton and Company, Inc.

Published by Simon and Schuster, Inc.
A Division of Simon & Schuster, Inc.
Simon & Schuster Building
Rockefeller Center
1230 Avenue of the Americas
New York, New York 10020

SIMON AND SCHUSTER and colophon are registered trademarks of Simon & Schuster, Inc.
Designed by Eve Kirch
Production by Richard L. Willett
Photo research by Vincent Virga
Manufactured in the United States of America

14 13 12 11 10 9 8 7 6 5
10 9 8 7 6 5 4 3 2 pbk

Library of Congress Cataloging in Publication Data

Bradley, Omar Nelson, 1893–
A general's life.

Includes bibliographical references and index.
1. Bradley, Omar Nelson, 1893– . 2. United States—History, Military—20th century. 3. Generals—United States—Biography. 4. United States. Army—Biography. I. Blair, Clay, 1925– . II. Title.
E745.B693 1983 940.54'21'0924 [B] 82-19404
ISBN 0-671-41023-7

Contents

Picture sections follow pages 192 and 512.

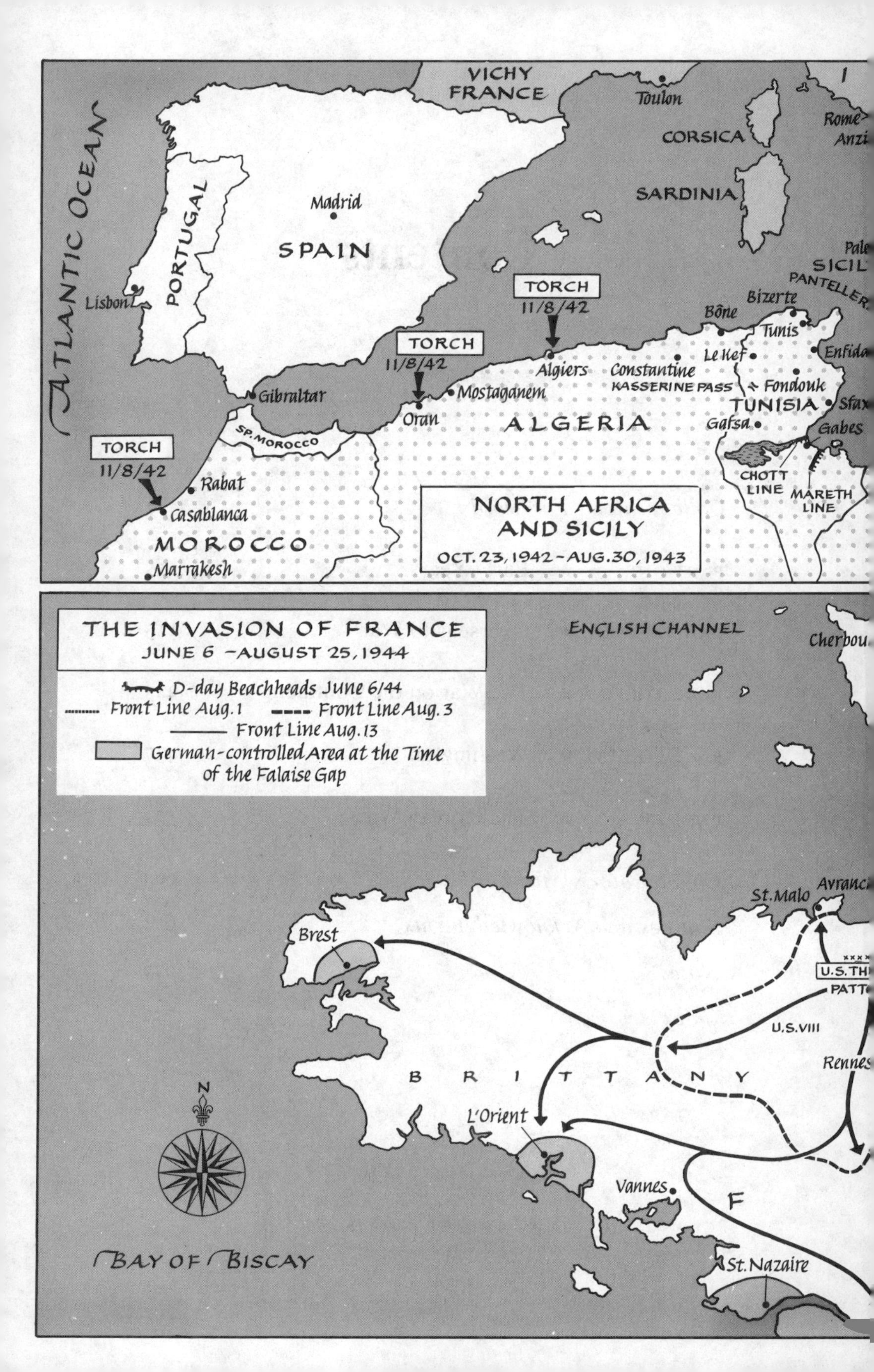
VICHY FRANCE
Toulon
CORSICA
SARDINIA
ATLANTIC OCEAN
PORTUGAL
Madrid
SPAIN
Lisbon
TORCH
11/8/42
Bizerte
Bône
Tunis
Le Kef
Algiers
Constantine
KASSERINE PASS
Fondouk
Gibraltar
Mostaganem
Oran
TUNISIA
ALGERIA
Gafsa
Gabes
SP. MOROCCO
CHOTT LINE
MARETH LINE
Rabat
Casablanca
MOROCCO
Marrakesh
NORTH AFRICA AND SICILY
OCT. 23, 1942 – AUG. 30, 1943
THE INVASION OF FRANCE
JUNE 6 – AUGUST 25, 1944
D-day Beachheads June 6/44
Front Line Aug. 1
Front Line Aug. 3
Front Line Aug. 13
German-controlled Area at the Time of the Falaise Gap
ENGLISH CHANNEL
St. Malo
Brest
U.S. VIII
BRITTANY
L'Orient
N
Vannes
F
BAY OF BISCAY
St. Nazaire

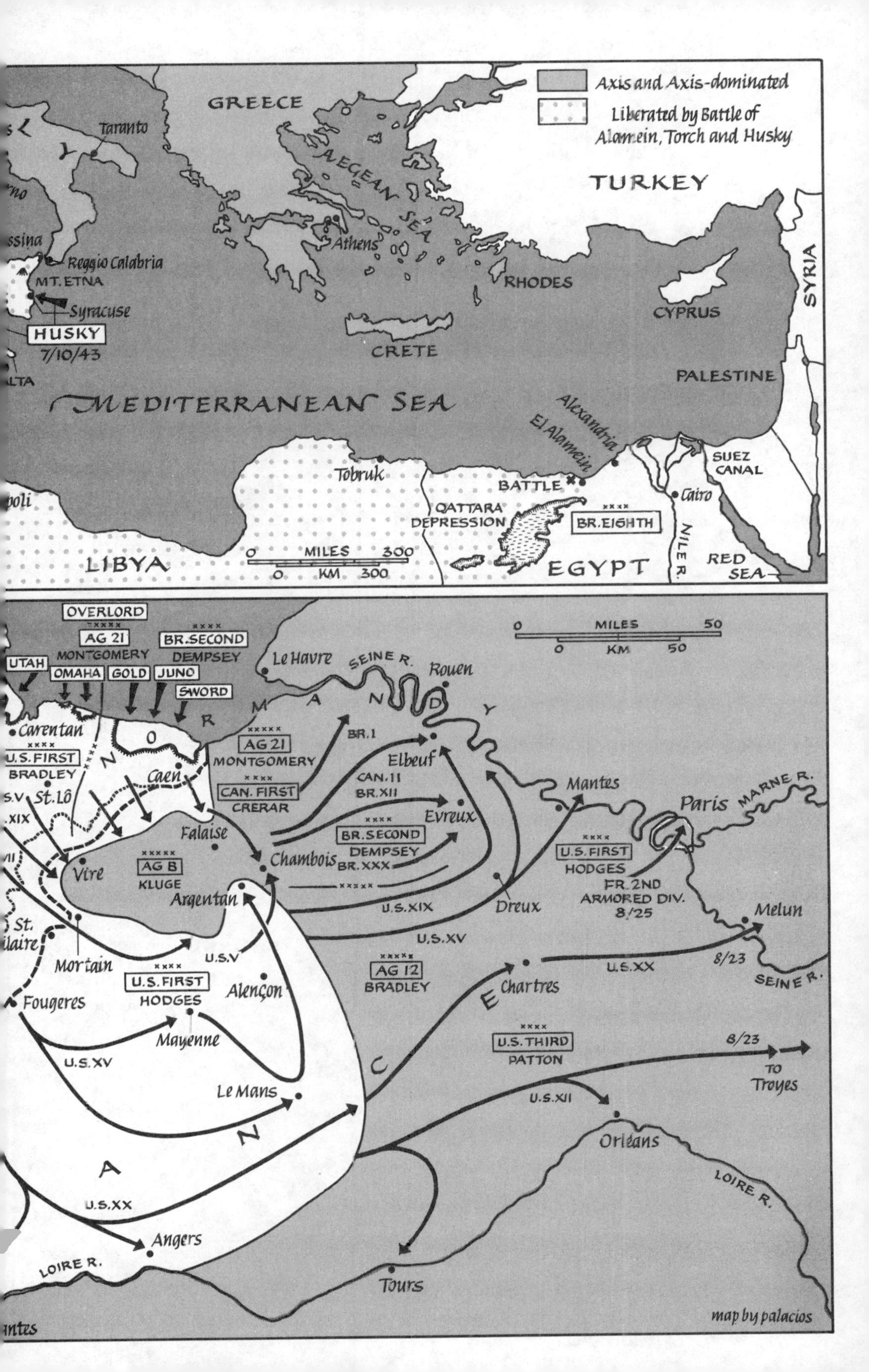

Axis and Axis-dominated
Liberated by Battle of Alamein, Torch and Husky
GREECE
Taranto
AEGEAN SEA
TURKEY
Reggio Calabria
MT. ETNA
Syracuse
HUSKY
7/10/43
Athens
RHODES
CYPRUS
SYRIA
CRETE
PALESTINE
MEDITERRANEAN SEA
Alexandria
El Alamein
Tobruk
BATTLE
SUEZ CANAL
Cairo
QATTARA DEPRESSION
BR. EIGHTH
NILE R.
LIBYA
MILES 300
KM 300
EGYPT
RED SEA
OVERLORD
AG 21
MONTGOMERY
BR. SECOND
DEMPSEY
UTAH
OMAHA
GOLD
JUNO
SWORD
Le Havre
SEINE R.
Rouen
MILES 50
KM 50
Carentan
U.S. FIRST
BRADLEY
AG 21
MONTGOMERY
BR. 1
Elbeuf
CAN. II
BR. XII
Caen
St. Lô
CAN. FIRST
CRERAR
Mantes
Paris
MARNE R.
Evreux
Falaise
BR. SECOND
DEMPSEY
BR. XXX
Chambois
AG B
KLUGE
Vire
U.S. FIRST
HODGES
Argentan
Dreux
FR. 2ND ARMORED DIV.
8/25
U.S. XIX
U.S. XV
Melun
Mortain
U.S. V
AG 12
BRADLEY
U.S. XX
8/23
SEINE R.
U.S. FIRST
HODGES
Alençon
Chartres
Fougeres
Mayenne
U.S. THIRD
PATTON
8/23
TO Troyes
U.S. XV
Le Mans
U.S. XII
Orléans
U.S. XX
LOIRE R.
Angers
LOIRE R.
Tours
map by palacios

Collaborator's Foreword

In his twilight years, General of the Army Omar N. Bradley decided he wanted to write his autobiography. There was much he wanted to say about his family, his youth and the pre–World War II years. He was not altogether satisfied with his excellent World War II war memoir, *A Soldier's Story,* which was ghosted by his aide, Chester B. Hansen, and published in 1951. This memoir was written long before the official World War II documents were declassified or the official and private papers of Eisenhower, Patton and others had been made available. Moreover, when the book was published, Bradley was still on active duty—as Chairman of the U.S. Joint Chiefs of Staff—and while it was not officially "cleared," his prominent public position imposed considerable restraints on what he could write. Finally, there was much Bradley wanted to say about his postwar experiences in Washington as a leading figure in the Truman administration during the Cold War and the hot war in Korea and as one who had counseled Truman to fire MacArthur.

In 1971, when he was seventy-eight years old, Bradley commenced writing the autobiography which he called *As I Remember*. He had never had a way with words; he had a real struggle with English at West Point. Throughout his life almost all his speeches had been written by his aides or others. His personal letters were pedestrian. Thus he found the autobiography tough going. When he reached the World War II section, selectivity and organization defeated him; the work began to sprawl inchoately. After a brief stab at the post–World War II years, he gave up and set the project aside.

General Bradley's second wife, Kitty Buhler Bradley, was a screenwriter with a strong sense of history. Before their marriage, she had interviewed Bradley to gather background for a proposed movie, *Breakout*. After their marriage, she began collecting his disorganized papers and memorabilia and deposited them at the U.S. Army Military History Institute, Carlisle Barracks, Pennsylvania, where the Omar N. Bradley Foundation and Omar N. Bradley Museum are situated, and at the U.S. Military Academy at West Point, where the Omar N. Bradley Library is located. The Institute also arranged to elicit General Bradley's recollections and reflections on his distinguished career. These were recorded in a massive taped and transcribed Oral History, which Lieutenant Colonel Charles K. Hanson of the Institute conducted in 1974–5. All the while, Kitty Bradley encouraged her husband to continue with the autobiography. When she finally realized this was not possible, she began looking for a professional writer with a military history background to serve as collaborator.

I joined the enterprise in the fall of 1979, when Bradley was eighty-six years old. He was not a total stranger. I had met him—and reported on his doings—in 1950–53, when I was a Pentagon correspondent for *Time* and *Life* magazines. As collaborator, I began from scratch. Utilizing what Bradley had already written, the Hanson oral history, his personal papers and hundreds of other documents, books and other transcribed interviews (more fully described in the back of this book under "Sources and Acknowledgments"), I taped some forty-eight hours of interviews with General Bradley over the period February 1 to February 13, 1980. Mrs. Bradley fully participated in these interviews and was very helpful at prodding out long-forgotten episodes. She was named "research editor and coordinator" of all Bradley documents, letters and biographical material for this project.

Paralleling these interviews, my wife Joan and I started researching Bradley's life as though we were writing a biography. We visited the scenes of his childhood and dug through records in Missouri courthouses, archives, cemeteries and family Bibles. With the assistance of Missouri state officials, genealogists and archivists, we were able to construct a heretofore nonexistent Bradley family tree. We interviewed school classmates and friends and searched through hundreds of back issues of local newspapers. Subsequently, we reconstructed his official Army and personal life with the help of Bradley's papers and diaries, official government papers, published memoirs and interviews with his daughter, Elizabeth Dorsey, and scores of contemporaries. In tracking down all these people—and some obscure documents and books—we were invaluably assisted by Mrs. Bradley and by Bradley's aides Allan G. Little, Courtney M. Rittgers, Thomas A. Hansen and Ricardo P. Mosqueda, with whom we remained in almost daily touch by telephone or mail.

I began writing in June of 1980. By fall I had completed the pre–World War II section. Bradley read it and was delighted. "He knows more about me than I do" was his comment to Mrs. Bradley. I then began the World War II section, an immense job inasmuch as I had made the decision to survey all extant important scholarship, including the recent official disclosures on Ultra—the valuable output from breaking the German military codes. In the war section, I was greatly assisted by the monumental daily diary of Bradley's aide Chester Hansen, which was only selectively used in *A Soldier's Story,* and by the recently published nine volumes of Eisenhower papers, two volumes of Patton papers, numerous memoirs and interviews and, not least, by the magnificent official American and British histories of the European war.

Bradley died in April 1981, before I completed the World War II section. This development naturally posed no small dilemma. Could one proceed with and publish an "autobiography," part of which Bradley had never seen? Should I not now shift gears and turn it into a biography? After prolonged consideration, I decided to proceed in the autobiographical mode. By that time my own mind was so deeply immersed in Bradley's that I *thought* like Bradley. I had at hand literally thousands of pages of Bradley's transcribed words. By confining myself to these words or to official documents or correspondence, and introducing no views or opinions that I knew Bradley did not positively hold, I could reconstruct the war virtually in his own words. So I proceeded with painstaking care, double- or triple-checking other sources for every word I wrote. I feel certain that had Bradley lived to read the result he would not have made any substantial alterations or changes in emphasis.

A similar technique was utilized for the postwar period, when Bradley served as chief of the Veterans Administration, then as Chief of Staff of the U.S. Army and finally as Chairman of the Joint Chiefs of Staff. Here I was invaluably assisted by the prodigious work of the historical division of the Joint Chiefs of Staff, which has recently produced in manuscript form some 2,600 pages of JCS history, covering the years 1945–52, and by Bradley's postwar speeches, magazine articles, interviews and testimony before congressional committees, which have been collected, photocopied and bound. In addition, I also had available Bradley's official papers and correspondence from the National Archives, plus memoirs and numerous secondary works. Bradley's recollections of the postwar period were less distinct than his memories of his youth and World War II. Nonetheless I have conscientiously endeavored not to impute any view or opinion to him that I could not verify from at least two sources.

Owing to the unusual way in which this book was ultimately carried to completion, I asked a number of distinguished American military historians to read it before publication. The entire book was carefully scrutinized for factual accuracy by the Army's Chief of Military History, Brigadier General James L. Collins, Jr., and his staff of historians. In addition, the World War II historians Charles MacDonald, Martin Blumenson and Forrest Pogue closely read the World War II sections, as did Chester Hansen. JCS historians Robert J. Watson, James F. Schnabel, Kenneth W. Condit and Walter S. Poole read the Cold War and Korean War sections, as did Dr. Pogue, who has recently covered the same ground in the forthcoming fourth volume of his George C. Marshall biography.

The final result, then, is the story of Bradley's life from birth to 1953, when he stepped down from official government service. In a sense the book is probably best described as half Bradley, half Blair. To Bradley's recollections, earlier and later, I have provided solid historical underpinning, as a competent collaborator should. While all of it did not get Bradley's official approval, I am confident that it faithfully carries out his original design.

CLAY BLAIR

Washington Island, Wisconsin
September 1982

Throughout the war he was not only an outstanding commander, but he was my warm friend and close adviser. I think I may claim some right to at least a casual recognition in the field of strategy, organization, and in developing Allied teamwork. Bradley was the master tactician of our forces and in my opinion will eventually come to be recognized as America's foremost battle leader.

—DWIGHT D. EISENHOWER

PART ONE

★★★★★

EARLY YEARS

ONE

Let me begin my story with a few words about my family. They were all plain Missouri farmers, proud, honest, hardworking and poor. Desperately poor.

According to family legend, my Bradley ancestors immigrated from the British Isles sometime in the mid-1700s to Madison County, Kentucky. In the early 1800s they migrated west to what would become the State of Missouri. They settled on small, hard farm parcels in Randolph County in the central part of the state near Clark, a farm village, and Higbee, a coal-mining town.

My grandfather, Thomas Minter Bradley, still in his teens, served as a private in the Confederate Army during the Civil War. When he came home, he married Sarah Elizabeth Lewis, the daughter of a poor Clark farmer. They had nine children. My father, John Smith Bradley, born February 15, 1867, was the eldest.[1]

Like all the Missouri Bradleys, my father began life as a sodbuster. But he became the first Bradley to break out of the mold. At age nineteen, and until then largely self-educated, he entered one of the rural schools near Clark. He was a quick study. Two years later he had advanced far enough to qualify as a teacher in the rural school system and about 1888 he launched his life's work.[2]

My father was a curious blend of frontiersman, sportsman, farmer and intellectual. Powerfully built and fearless, he was a superb hunter and shot —indisputably the best in Randolph County. A pioneer in baseball, he carved his own bats, taught himself to pitch curve balls and organized and starred on local teams. In the months when school was not in session, he usually hired out to farmers or sharecropped to earn enough money to survive. At the same time, he was an omnivorous reader and lover of books. Everywhere he taught, he encouraged his students to read and created small libraries for them.

Owing to his strength and fearlessness, my father was one of the few rural teachers able to discipline the older, sometimes unruly farm boys. When a difficult situation arose, he was sought after. As a consequence, he taught at nearly a dozen different rural schools, none more than fifteen or twenty miles from Higbee, and all within the same school district. His peak salary was about forty dollars a month.

In his fourth year as a teacher, age twenty-five, my father fell in love with one of his pupils at the Fairview School, Sarah Elizabeth (Bessie) Hubbard, one of five children of Henry Clay and Mary Elizabeth Spurling Hubbard. Henry Clay Hubbard had served briefly in the Union Army during the Civil War. He and his wife were then farming a poor forty-acre tract about three miles west of Clark and lived in a crude three-room log house. Bessie, born April 18, 1875, was then only sixteen.[3]

My father and Bessie Hubbard were married on May 12, 1892, at the Hubbard home. Nine months later, to the day, February 12, 1893—Lincoln's birthday—I was born, without complications, in that same house. My mother, Bessie, was still only seventeen. They named me Omar Nelson Bradley—Omar from Omar D. Gray, a local newspaper editor my father admired; Nelson from the name of a local doctor.[4]

When I was about three and a half years old, my mother's older, married sister, Emma Jane Bogie, died of tuberculosis, leaving two daughters, Nettie, seven, and Opal, six. A few months later, my grandmother Hubbard also died. Since there were no other Hubbard women to care for little Nettie and Opal, my parents took them into our home. Thus my two first cousins became instant "older sisters," who remained with us, off and on, many, many years. Our family grew further in February 1900, when mother had another son, Raymond Calvert. But, to our great sorrow, Raymond died of scarlet fever on January 18, 1902, a few days before his second birthday. My parents had no more children.[5]

As my father moved from school to school, I grew to boyhood living in a variety of primitive wood frame houses in the countryside outside Higbee. In the fall of 1899, age six, I commenced my schooling at Pemberton, ten miles southwest of Higbee. The next year we moved again and I attended the Locust Grove School in nearby Howard County. In 1903, I entered the Baldridge School, ten miles south of Higbee in Harrisburg. Each of these schools consisted of one room and my father was the sole teacher.[6]

We could not afford a horse and buggy, so my father and I walked to and from school each day carrying our lunch baskets, down dirt roads that were either dusty, muddy or icy, depending on the weather. Father set a hearty pace—seventeen minutes to the mile. This was quite a daily hike for a young lad, especially on bitter cold days, but having those hours alone each day with my father was spiritually reinforcing to a very great degree.

In school we sat in the one large room, more or less grouped by age and grade. My father moved from group to group, assigning lessons, teaching. He was, without doubt, a brilliant man. I idolized him. He taught us youngsters individual words—sight reading—before we learned the alphabet. I learned to read very quickly. Perhaps it was because my father was the teacher. When your father is the teacher, there's added incentive to do your homework! He was a strict disciplinarian and stricter on me than the others. Even when I climbed in bed with him to get warm at night, he would give me math problems to work out in my head.[7]

He succeeded very quickly in inculcating in me a love for books. After I could read fairly well, I devoured books such as Sir Walter Scott's *Ivanhoe,* Kipling's *Jungle Books,* and the like. I was particularly fascinated by history—tales of the French and Indian Wars, the Revolutionary and Civil wars. I would act out many of these battles on the living-room rug, using dominoes to build forts and empty .22 cartridges to represent lines of soldiers. I made "heavy artillery" from hollow elderberry reeds or brass tubing and would bombard the domino forts with navy beans. In my mock wars, the Americans always won.[8]

Almost all the meat mother put on the table was game that father bagged with his 12-gauge L. C. Smith double-barrel shotgun: rabbit, squirrel, quail, coon, duck, deer. When I was about six, he gave me a pump-action BB rifle and took me hunting with him. Of course I could not kill game with BB's, but it was excellent training. He taught me to walk quietly behind him, taking care not to step on sticks or rustle leaves, and to focus my vision close in and ahead. I learned a great deal by simply watching my father in action. And, of course, he taught me all the safety precautions in using a weapon. Occasionally I would go off on my own, down near a lake, and kill frogs with my BB rifle. I was proud to contribute these frogs to our table.

When my father judged me qualified for a real weapon and gave me a single-shot Stevens .22 rifle, I felt I had achieved manhood. I shall never forget the humiliation I experienced the first time we went squirrel hunting. I saw a squirrel in the top of a tree and signaled to my father. He went to the opposite side of the tree, forcing the squirrel to my side. As carefully as I knew how, I shot three times. The squirrel never moved. My father came over and examined my rifle. Both the front and rear sights were out of line. He adjusted them and said, "If I don't knock his eye out, something is very wrong with the sights." He aimed and got off one shot. The squirrel fell to the ground—dead. When I picked it up, I saw that father had shot him in the right eye. That was the last time I ever fired a rifle with the sights out of line.[9]

I worked hard to live down that humiliation. In those days a box of fifty .22 short shells cost only fifteen cents. I killed and dressed rabbits and sold them for five cents apiece. Almost all the money I made went for more shells. In time, and with practice, I became as good a shot as my father. One time, one of my cousins came over to play. I got him to throw an egg high into the air for a target. He threw it straight up and cupped his hands to catch it, not believing for a second that I could hit it and not wanting to waste the egg. I cut the egg straight in half and my cousin got an omelet on his head.[10]

My mother, blue-eyed, strong-minded and entirely gray-haired before she was twenty, was an unfailingly cheerful and resourceful woman. She was a strict, attentive, though far from doting, mother and a superb cook. She would usually stew the squirrels and fry the rabbits, after dressing the hind legs and back saddle. Like everyone else, we had a large vegetable garden. She did the canning in the fall and, of course, the baking all year long. She was an excellent seamstress. Father gave her a foot-operated Singer sewing machine which she used with growing skill for years, making all of her own clothes.[11]

Neither of my parents was strongly opinionated or emotionally demonstrative. Politically, my father was, like many in the Midwest in those days, a Populist in the tradition of the "Boy Orator," William Jennings Bryan. He sided with the farmers, particularly the poor farmers, against the railroads and big trust interests, whom he believed were exploiting the little man. He approved of the Sherman Anti-Trust Act, the Interstate Commerce Act and other measures of the day designed to curb the "robber barons." But he was no soap-box orator, no political activist. When he spoke his views, it was in a quiet, reasoned tone, usually at the supper table in the privacy of our home.

Nor were my parents demonstratively religious. Father was raised in the Church of Christ, baptized by immersion at about age fifteen and called a "Christian." Mother, like all the Hubbards, was a Baptist, but she converted to the Christian Church. We walked to the Church of Christ every Sunday, wearing our finest clothes. But in our home, there was no grace at mealtime, no Bible reading or other religious overtones. However, both my parents were clearly devout and their faith was strong. They lived a Christian life in every sense of the phrase, and by their example imparted a strong faith to me.[12]

In 1905, when I was twelve, we moved into Higbee itself, primarily so that I could attend its excellent public school. This was a hardship on my father, forcing him to walk as much as seven miles each way every day in order to continue teaching in the outlying rural schools where he was needed. My parents bought a small house at a sheriff's auction for $515—$65 down with a $450 mortgage. To help carry the payments, my mother and I and Nettie and Opal took turns operating the switchboard for a rural telephone line of about ninety telephones. The switchboard was located in one of our bedrooms, and we alternated standing "watch" at night.[13]

After reviewing my school records and giving me rudimentary tests, the Higbee School principal skipped me ahead a year and placed me in the eighth grade. This was a new experience for me. I had never before been in a school where all my classmates were in the same grade; and, of course, at twelve, I was the youngest in the class of twenty-two boys and girls. Even so, I did well. My average grade for all courses for that eight-month school year was 94 and ranked me at the top of my class.[14]

During this time I did not see much of my father except on weekends. The following year, when I was thirteen, he bought a new pump-action shotgun and gave me his old double-barrel 12-gauge L. C. Smith, which had a powerful kick. Father and I found good quail hunting at a place about five or six miles outside Higbee. By this time, I was fairly skilled with a gun. I'm proud to say I killed the first quail I shot at.[15]

I also became quite proficient with a slingshot. I made lead pellets for it in a bullet mold, so my pellets were always uniform in size and weight, an important factor in achieving maximum accuracy. I killed rabbits, squirrels and sparrows—sparrows because they would nest in our gutters and stop them up. Once a friend challenged my accuracy. We stuck a penny in the ground. I moved back to a range of twenty feet. I hit the penny with my second shot.

In spite of our two incomes, we were poor—very poor. Father would, of necessity, conceive all sorts of schemes to make extra money and often I helped in these projects. We laid a trap line, but it yielded only one mink for which we got $1.25. We gathered honey from hollow trees, even collecting about 240 pounds on one memorable occasion. But gathering honey, I found, was a hazardous undertaking. One of our most profitable schemes was digging for roots of goldenseal, commonly known as yellowroot, which in those days was used in making medicine. Father knew of a place near Burton where we could find yellowroot. We'd take the train down in the morning, gather roots, then walk the twelve miles back to Higbee. Then we'd dry the roots and sell them by the pound for a pretty fair price.[16]

In Higbee during the summers, following in my father's footsteps, I played baseball with a passion. We boys would gather at the baseball diamond about nine in the morning. We played until lunch, then, after lunch, walked about a mile out in the country for a swim in a lake, then back to the baseball diamond until suppertime. When I wasn't out on the diamond, I played catch, often with my cousin Fred Bradley. He recently recalled: "We'd go down to the railroad track. The rails were thirty feet long, so you could measure very accurately how far you were throwing. Both of us got to where we could throw the ball ten rails. That's three hundred feet, or a hundred yards, the length of a football field."[17]

In my second year at Higbee School, there were only twelve of us in what was called the "sophomore class." As a consequence, the teacher was able to give us very close attention. My final average grade of 98.66

again led the class. I must have been a very well behaved young man. In both semesters that year I received a perfect grade in deportment.[18]

The winter of 1907–1908 was an especially harsh one in Higbee. It was hard on my father, who was teaching at Ebenezer School, a six-mile round-trip walk each day. In January he came home one day very ill. His illness was soon diagnosed as pneumonia. After several days in bed, at 4:00 A.M. on the morning of January, two weeks shy of his forty-first birthday, he died in our home.

It was an indescribably shattering blow for Mother, for me, for the relatives, for all his many friends and the community. His obituary in the *Higbee Weekly News* in part:

> No death in recent years has cast such a gloom over the community. That such a good man who, a week ago, was in the vigor of his manhood, should now be lying so low, is a fact that his friends and acquaintances can not yet realize. . . .
>
> No better citizen ever lived among us. He was absolutely honest in all things with himself and with those with whom he came in contact and was for anything and everything that tended to elevate humanity. The world is better for his having lived in it, and although he is gone from among us, his life was such that it will have influence for good for years to come. As a tribute of respect to the memory of such a good citizen, we suggest that every business house be closed during the funeral services and that all who are not prevented by sickness attend. It is his due.[19]

At the time of father's death, I, too, was sick in bed with a cold. Mother thought it better that I not leave my bed. I did not see my father in death. I was still sick on the day of the funeral service at the Christian Church and the burial at Log Chapel Cemetery, where Raymond was buried. The *Higbee Weekly News* described some of the events of that sad day:

> The large crowd that faced the bitter cold wind to attend the funeral of John S. Bradley at the Christian Church last Saturday morning was a fitting tribute to his memory. Notwithstanding the fact that it was the coldest and most disagreeable day of the winter, and that the hour for the services had been changed without notice, late arrivals could scarcely find seats. The discourse, preached by W. W. Boatman, while brief, was forceful and practical. At the request of the family, the casket was opened, that John's friends might look upon his face the last time. No matter how hard they had tried to suppress their emotions, the strongest among the large crowd turned from the casket with tears in their eyes. To die universally regretted is a privilege accorded but few.[20]

My beloved father was gone; I was but a few days short of fifteen. He left no estate, of course, only the heavily mortgaged house, which my mother and I were in no position to carry. But he left me with a priceless legacy. Thanks to father, I was determined, no matter how poor we might be, to continue my education all the way through college; to make something of myself; not to squander my time or intellectual gifts; to work hard. He had given me much else as well. A love of and appreciation of the out-of-doors, hunting and sports. A sense of justice and respect for my fellow man and his property, especially the less fortunate. Integrity. Sobriety. Patriotism. Religiosity. No son could have asked more of his father, nor been more grateful for his example.[21]

TWO

In the months following my father's death, Mother decided to move from Higbee to Moberly, a big new city about fifteen miles north, home of the Wabash Railroad workshops and the Brown Shoe Company. To support us she would become a professional seamstress and take in boarders. She rented our Higbee house to cover the mortgage payments, and we loaded our few possessions in a horse-drawn moving wagon and set off on a new life.[1]

Mother rented a house on South Fourth Street in Moberly, found two paying boarders and launched her new career. I got a part-time job delivering the *Moberly Democrat* and that fall entered the new and magnificent red brick Moberly High School. To my dismay, the school authorities decided to put me "back" one year to the class of 1911. Since it was a four-year school, that made me a lowly sophomore once more, facing three long years of studies before I could graduate.[2]

By now I was even more keenly interested in sports. Moberly High School had no formal athletic teams, but there were informally organized track and baseball teams. I signed up for both, but my primary interest was baseball. By that time I was a baseball nut. We players provided our own equipment and arranged games with other schools. As I recall, we had a pretty fair season. I played in the field and, owing to many long hours of practice, could catch well and throw the ball long and hard. The editor of the 1909 yearbook wrote of me: "A good ball player, if he doesn't look like one."[3]

Although mother was not a devout woman, she was a regular Sunday churchgoer, as was I. We joined the Central Christian Church, an impressive new stone structure with a soaring steeple and a large congregation. On February 14, 1909, two days after my sixteenth birthday, I was baptized by immersion in a tank in the church basement.[4]

I seldom missed Sunday School. My teacher—Eudora (Dora) Quayle, a widow with two teenage daughters, Mary Elizabeth, born July 25, 1892, and Sarah Jane, two years younger—lived across the street from us. Dora's husband, Charles Quayle, who had been the highly esteemed elected marshal of Moberly (equivalent of police chief), had died of tuberculosis in 1902, age thirty-five, leaving a modest estate, including two small houses. Dora and the two girls lived in one house and rented the other to make ends meet.

I was attracted to Mary Quayle, but she was six months older than I and, owing to my having been "put back," a year ahead of me in school. When I first met her she had a beau, an older boy who had already graduated from high school. I was shy around girls, a stranger in town, busy with my paper route, sports and chores and did not date the whole time I was in high school. However, as they were neighbors and members of the same church, I came to know all the Quayle women quite well.[5]

In the fall of 1909 I re-entered the Moberly High School for my junior year. It was then realized that I had been wrongly put back a year. At midterm I was jumped ahead a full year into the senior class of 1910, to graduate the following June. This was Mary Quayle's class, a closely knit, clannish group that had been together since grammar school days. Except for Mary and the boys on the baseball team, I did not get to know any of them well. I remained the "loner" or "outsider" from Higbee who, bafflingly, kept jumping back and forth in grade.[6]

In the winter, when the lake in Forest Park was frozen hard, ice skating was extremely popular. I had been skating for years and did it well. But that winter I suffered an absolutely catastrophic accident on the ice, a bone-shattering collision with another boy one dark night. His head smashed into my teeth, knocking almost every one of them loose and severely damaging my gums. Had we the money, I would have gone to a dentist for braces or whatever might be required. But we had no money for such luxuries and, to my eternal regret, I did nothing. For years thereafter, my teeth and gums were a source of trouble and occasionally caused great pain. I never smiled when my picture was taken, but rather closed my lips tightly to avoid there being any permanent record of that jumbled mess. Eventually I would have all my teeth pulled at a very early age.[7]

We graduated in May 1910. My grades during my two years at Moberly High School were good but not the highest. Generally, I did better in science (96) and math (94) than in English (90) or history (85). My overall average grade was 91.4. In our yearbook, each of us seniors was described with a single adjective, designed to sum up our personalities or attributes. Mary Quayle, who stood third in the class, was described as "linguistic" because she was good at languages. I was labeled "calculative," I hope because I was good at math. By a curious coincidence, Mary's senior picture and mine were randomly paired at the bottom of the same page.[8]

By graduation, I had decided that I wanted to be a lawyer. But I did not have enough money to put away to go to college, and I was concerned about how Mother might fare without my help. The plan I arrived at was to return to a job I had had the previous summer at the Wabash Railroad, work a full year and try to save several hundred dollars, enough to keep me going at the University of Missouri in Columbia until I could find a job there. Accordingly, in the summer of 1910, I went back to work for the Wabash, first in my old job in the supply department, later in the boiler shop, where I made a better salary helping to repair the steam engines. I worked nine hours a day, six days a week, and was paid seventeen cents an hour, or about forty dollars a month.[9]

Mary Quayle's favorite aunt, Papita, was a teacher at the State Normal School, St. Cloud, Minnesota. Mary decided that she would join her in St. Cloud and do her first two years of college there, and later, finances permitting, go on to the University of Missouri. This was arranged, and in the fall of 1910 Mary moved to St. Cloud. I did not see much of her for the next several years.[10]

That summer and fall, my mother, who was then thirty-five, began to take interest in a man, John Robert (Bob) Maddox. He was a poor farmer, very hard of hearing. His wife, Mary, had recently died, leaving him to raise his two young sons, David Russell, age seven and Charles William, age two. My mother apparently felt no qualms over the prospect of raising two more boys not her own. On Christmas Day 1910 they were married, and I now had a stepfather and two little stepbrothers. All three Maddoxes moved into our house; the boarders moved out. A month later, Mother let our house in Higbee go by default. It was sold at sheriff's auction for $441.20, sufficient to satisfy the mortgage, removing that burden from her shoulders.[11]

Mother's decision to marry Bob Maddox relieved me of any misgivings about going away to college and leaving her to cope alone. My goal now was to enter the University of Missouri in the fall of 1911. But a talk one day with my Sunday School superintendent, John Cruson, drastically changed my plans. He said: "Why don't you try for West Point?"[12]

I knew a little about West Point from my study of history. I replied, rather naively, "I couldn't afford West Point."

He put me straight. He told me that not only was West Point free, but that the cadets were paid a small monthly salary while there. He went on to explain how one got an appointment to West Point through one's congressman, competing against other candidates.

I discussed the idea with my mother. She was not too enthusiastic. West Point, New York, was a long, long way from Moberly, Missouri. But the more I thought about it, the more convinced I became that West Point was made to order for my financial circumstances. I wrote a carefully composed letter in longhand to our congressman, William M. Rucker, who lived about thirty miles away in Keytesville.

Not long afterwards I received a reply from the congressman. He was sorry to report that he had no vacancies to fill at that time. Under existing law, each congressman and senator could only provide one cadet for West Point every four years. Rucker's current appointment was in his third year, with one more year to go. This meant that I would have to wait a full year before I could apply. That seemed too long a time. I would settle for the University of Missouri as originally planned.

As it happened, that very spring Congress amended the law concerning appointment of cadets to West Point. Congressmen and senators could now appoint a new cadet every three years. That meant Rucker would now have a late-starting opening for 1911. On June 27, I received a letter from Rucker explaining the change and informing me that his principal candidate was a Keytesville boy, Dempsey Anderson, and that if I so desired, I could be an alternate candidate. This meant that if Dempsey Anderson failed his mental or physical examinations and I passed both, I would become the appointee. The examinations would be held at Jefferson Barracks in St. Louis on July 5, only eight days from then.

I mulled this letter over for quite some time. I had previously received some West Point literature and knew the subjects in which I would be examined. They included geography, geometry, algebra, and one of my weaker areas, English. I had been out of school a full year and I was a bit rusty. I had not looked at an algebra book since Higbee High School, three years back. It seemed imprudent to quit work to cram for the exams; I could only study at night, after a long hard day's work in the boiler shop, and then for only six days. Dempsey Anderson had probably been preparing himself for a long time. It seemed foolish to spend hard-earned, much-needed money on a round-trip ticket to St. Louis with the odds stacked so heavily against me.

Assailed by these doubts, I sought advice and counsel from the superintendent of Moberly schools, J. C. Lilly, who had been a friend of Father's. He weighed the difficulties and the odds and, after his usual careful deliberation, he advised me to go ahead and try for it. Even if it came to naught, he said, the experience would be worthwhile. I had to agree, but with one reservation. I still thought it imprudent to gamble the cash outlay involved. If the Wabash would give me time off and a free pass to St. Louis, I would go for it.

The Wabash generously gave me time off and the free pass. On July 4, I boarded a train for St. Louis with a small suitcase and an armload of books. This was my first trip to the big glittering metropolis of St. Louis, but I had little time for sightseeing. I crammed all the way on the train and on the streetcar to Jefferson Barracks.

About a dozen West Point candidates, both principals and alternates, reported to Jefferson Barracks from various congressional districts, including my direct competition, Dempsey Anderson. He was the son of

Orville Bradley Anderson (no kin), a former sheriff of Keytesville, who had been a close friend of Congressman Rucker's. Anderson was a year older than I, and I was appalled to learn he had been prepping for the exams a full year.[13]

The exams stretched over four days, four hours for each of the subjects. I had a terrible time with the algebra. At the end of two hours, I had solved no more than 20 percent of the necessary 67 percent of the problems required to pass that subject. That was it, complete failure. There was no way I could finish or pass. Utterly discouraged, and not a little angry at myself for coming all the way to St. Louis, I gathered up my papers and walked up to the officer in charge to turn them in and go back to Moberly and go to work. I saw he was deeply engrossed in a book. Not wishing to disturb him, I returned to my desk thinking I might as well give it one more try. Then, almost magically, the theorems started to come to me. I fell to work eagerly. At the end of the four hours, I thought I had completed a bit more than the necessary 67 percent, but not by much. However, this experience encouraged me, and I hung on through the rest of the exams, all of which I found very, very tough.

I returned to Moberly and my job in the Wabash boiler shop without the slightest hope of going to West Point. On July 27, I was absolutely astonished when I received a telegram stating that I had been appointed to West Point and that I should report on August 1, before noon. I was so certain a mistake had been made, I telephoned Dempsey Anderson in Keytesville. But there had been no mistake. He had just received a telegram informing him he had failed.

A day or so later, I received a letter of congratulations from Congressman Rucker officially informing me that Dempsey Anderson had failed "some" of the examinations, that I had made the "required grade" in all of them, and that therefore I was the "successful contestant." He added: "I wish to congratulate you heartily upon the rather remarkable showing made by you in this test. In view of the limited notice given and the short time in which preparation could be made, your grades reflect great credit upon yourself as a student. I am especially gratified by this showing for it is an indication of the work that you are sure to do at the Academy and of the fact that you will take high rank there in that work."[14]

I felt a twinge of guilt about Dempsey Anderson, as though I had taken away something that was his. I offered to decline the appointment, thinking he might somehow regain it, but he said, "Indeed not. You have won."

All this happened so quickly that I barely had time to pack and make my farewells. I put the bulk of my clothes in a steamer trunk and shipped them to West Point, keeping one change in a small suitcase. On the afternoon of July 30, I went to the Moberly railroad station alone and departed on the Wabash Railroad, carrying my suitcase and my entire fortune, one hundred dollars, in cash in my wallet. Twenty-four hours later, I debarked at Highland Falls, New York, a small town just outside the gate of West Point. I spent that night in a hotel sleeping soundly, and on the following day, August 1, reported to the post headquarters before noon, as ordered. There was a sergeant on duty. I said, "Sir, Candidate Bradley reporting for duty."[15]

THREE

The four years I spent at West Point were among the most rewarding of my life. I loved every minute of it. For a young boy who had lost his father and might have unconsciously been in search of a surrogate, it was the ideal place. West Point was a rigidly structured, highly disciplined all-male society with no end of strong "father figures" to emulate. For a young boy who was a sports nut it was edenic. In those days, West Point was sports-oriented to a feverish degree. The most esteemed cadets in the society were star athletes. For a young boy who had a natural intellectual bent for math and science, West Point was academically tailor-made. It was essentially a narrow-gauge engineering school, with a smattering of liberal arts and social sciences thrown in for seasoning.[1]

The Corps of Cadets in 1911 was small—a mere 600 men. Our plebe class—1915—which numbered 265 at the outset, was the largest ever to enter the Academy and comprised 44 percent of the corps. It had officially reported for duty on June 14, and had been in summer camp, living in tents on the northeast corner of what is still today known as the "Plain" for almost seven weeks.

The fourteen of us who reported late owing to the change in the law were forever stigmatized as "Augustines" because we had been mercifully spared seven weeks of intense "crawling" (hazing) in "beast barracks." The school authorities apparently held our lateness against us, too. We Augustines were always "behind." None of us was promoted to cadet noncommissioned officer or officer until our senior, or first class, year.

We Augustines spent several days double-timing from one somber gray granite building to the next, getting indoctrinated to military life. We filled out endless forms, drew our uniforms, bedding and furniture, had our hair cut short and took a physical exam. My uniform bill came to $160. I turned in the hundred dollars in cash I had (cadets were not allowed to have cash) for uniforms, making arrangements to pay off the balance from my monthly salary of fifty dollars. My physical turned up no defects. The records show that I was tall and skinny: 5 feet 11¼ inches, a mere 145 pounds. Like my mother, I became prematurely gray and even then—age eighteen—I had some gray hairs.

The roommate assigned me turned out to be a trial. He was Benjamin W. Mills, a lackadaisical Southerner, born in Georgia and raised in Florida. He was not too bright and seldom applied himself seriously to his studies. Against all rules, he smoked and continued to smoke throughout his four years at West Point. Had I not spent countless hours coaching him in math and science, Bennie Mills would not have made it through the first year.

We soon joined the rest of our class on the Plain. Among these young men were fifty-nine who, because of World War II, would become general officers. One of those, a smiling golden-haired Kansan, Dwight D. Eisenhower, would wear five stars and become President of the United States. Two would wear four stars: Joseph T. McNarney and James A. Van Fleet. Seven would wear three stars, among them Joseph M. Swing and George E. Stratemeyer. In time, we would be known as "The Class the Stars Fell on."

Summer camp was a purely military exercise. There, on the Plain, almost in the shadows of the granite buildings of West Point, and overlooking the Hudson River, officers of the department of tactics schooled us in rudimentary field problems. We lived in tents, hiked with packs, stood guard duty, set up fields of fire and the like. We also got in some target practice on the range. My long years of hunting in Missouri stood me in good stead. I did well, scoring many bull's-eyes. In spite of the unrelenting hazing by the upperclassmen, I found summer camp fascinating and was genuinely sorry that I had come late.

The hazing, so often criticized, had several positive by-products. It was a great leveler. There were among us many pampered boys, campus heroes and heartthrobs, prep school snobs and even a few bullies. Hazing knocked the wind out of their sails in a hurry. It impressed upon us the sense of rank and privilege and taught us to unquestioningly and quickly obey orders, fundamental grounding for any soldier. At the same time, we were learning basics: how to make a bed and clean and care for our rooms and rifles, when to shave, when to shine our shoes, and always, always, always to say "sir" to our superiors.

We learned, too, about the West Point honor code and the Academy's stirring motto "Duty, Honor, Country." These were not hollow trappings. It was impressed upon us that in all official matters, truth was overriding, mandatory, absolute. We were to report any official violation, even if we had to report ourselves. Lying or cheating would bring instant dismissal.

That summer, and thereafter, we were encouraged to engage in a wide variety of intramural and varsity sports. These included wrestling, boxing, riding, fencing, swimming (all cadets had to pass a tough swimming test), football, basketball and baseball.

One afternoon some of us plebes turned out for organized baseball. I played left field, as usual, and was lucky enough to get some good long throws to home plate and to make a home run. Looking over the plebes was the West Point baseball coach, Sam Strang Nicklin, an ex-Giant and a legendary character who spent his weekends in New York on benders with his old baseball buddies.

After the game, he approached me and complimented me on my performance, remarking that one of my throws to home plate was the longest he had ever seen. (No one measured the distance, of course; over the years legend exaggerated it beyond reason.) He noted on a card bearing my name and class: "Bats right, throws right, hits curve, fine arm." He indicated that I might be able to help the West Point varsity baseball team the following spring. Nothing could have pleased me more.[2]

The Corps of Cadets was organized, administratively, into a battalion of six hundred-man companies, A through F. Cadets were assigned to companies according to their height, so that when the corps marched as a group the lines of our hats, rifles and greatcoats would not be jagged. The tallest cadets, including most of the athletes, were assigned to A and F companies, which marched on the flanks and were thus called "flankers." The smaller men, called "runts," were assigned to B, C, D and E companies, which marched in the middle, between the flankers. Because I was nearly six feet tall, I spent my plebe year in A Company and, following a corps reorganization in 1912, my last three years in F Company.

That first winter passed quickly, a blur of feverish, rigidly organized routine. Reveille at 0600. Company roll call outside. Breakfast at 0630 (excellent food served by hired waiters). Room clean-up. Classroom work from 0800 to noon. Lunch (more excellent food). Classroom work from 1300 to 1600. Athletics or "free time" from 1600 to 1800. Then dinner (still more excellent food). After dinner, study or "free time." Taps at 2000. We marched to meals or classrooms by company or academic "sections." Weekends were likewise closely supervised with inspections, compulsory chapel and so on. We were not allowed to leave the Academy grounds except for a few organized sporting events such as Army-Navy games.

Discipline was enforced in part by the administration of demerits or "skins." We were allowed nine demerits a month. Any demerit beyond that had to be "walked off" in the "Area," with rifle, one hour per demerit, a humiliating—and boring—punishment. The first month after returning from the Plain, I racked up sixteen demerits, for such dumb things as twice knocking my hat off with my rifle and not having my collar properly adjusted at dinner. Walking off those seven hours had the desired effect on me. Thereafter I remained well below the allowable nine demerits.

Academically, we cadets were grouped into twelve-man sections, numbered 1 to 28, according to our grades. The top men were in Section

1; those with the worst grades ("goats") in 28. Based on my test scores at Jefferson Barracks, I started off near the bottom: Section 24 in math, Section 27 in English and history. However, by dint of hard study, I moved up throughout the year and by June my overall class standing was 49. Had it not been for English—my toughest course—I would have stood even higher.

In the spring of 1912 I turned out for varsity baseball. I made the squad but not the first team. There were marvelous advantages to being on varsity athletic squads. We plebes were "recognized" by the upperclassmen. We did not have to say "sir" each time we spoke to them and we were spared hazing on the athletic fields and at mealtimes. We sat at a special training table in the dining hall where discipline was loose, almost nonexistent. I was inducted into a completely illegal secret Greek fraternity, Omicron Pi Phi, composed mostly of star athletes and student athletic managers. The membership included many cadets who would someday be world-famous generals. (The fraternity was abolished in the 1920s.)[3]

By the fall of 1912, our cow (or sophomore) year, I had gained thirty pounds and weighed in at 178. I went out for varsity football, but owing to my inexperience, I failed to make the squad. However, that fall I earned a place on the junior varsity or "farm" team, Cullum Hall, which played local high schools. Our varsity football team had a winning season (5–3), but to our bitter disappointment, we lost to Navy (0–6) at Franklin Field in Philadelphia. Early in the season, our star running back, Ike Eisenhower, so badly injured his knee he had to give up his place on the squad. He became a cheerleader. Ike's knee injury was so persistent and severe it nearly cost him his commission two and a half years later, and it continued to trouble him the rest of his life.[4]

The following spring, 1913, I was immensely pleased to make the varsity baseball team as left fielder. We had an outstanding season (16–6) and beat Navy 2–1 at home.

The class of 1915 was granted its first furlough that following summer, 1913. I went home to Moberly and spent a leisurely two and a half months living with my mother, stepfather and two stepbrothers. I played baseball three times a week with a semi-pro Moberly team, refusing pay so that I would not become ineligible to play for West Point. Mary Quayle had finished two years at St. Cloud Normal School and had graduated. She was then teaching at a school in Albert Lea, Minnesota, and was home for the summer. We began dating—going on picnics with friends and relatives, to Christian Church functions, to the Bijou, or sitting alone on her front porch. Mary planned to teach in Albert Lea for one more year, saving money for further college study. By that time, her younger sister, Sarah Jane (who now preferred to be called merely Jane), would have graduated from Moberly High School. The plan was for Mrs. Quayle, Mary and Jane to move temporarily to Columbia so that both girls could attend the university as day students. After that summer, Mary and I began a correspondence, exchanging letters once a week.[5]

In my yearling (or junior) year and in my first class (or senior) year, I became almost obsessively absorbed in athletics. In the fall of 1913 I won a slot on the varsity football team as a substitute center, playing in one game. We had a sensational season—eight wins including a 22–9 rout of Navy. The following year, 1914, our football team achieved a perfect season—nine wins, no losses. I played in five games including our 20–0 win over Navy. I earned a football letter but like Ike I sustained a knee injury that would plague me the rest of my life. During those same two years I held my place in left field on the varsity baseball team and earned two more letters. Our 1914 won-loss record (10–5) was middling but we beat Navy. Our 1915 baseball team, which scored eighteen wins (including one over Navy) and only three losses, was officially described as "the best team that has ever represented the Academy."[6]

In our final year, 1914–15, some of us remaining Augustines were finally promoted to cadet officers and noncoms. I was made first sergeant of F Company and was later promoted to cadet lieutenant.

In early fall of 1914 World War I erupted in Europe. The conflict seemed remote from our cloistered world. We received no official documents or reports on the war. Everything we knew about it—and that was very little—came from newspapers and periodicals. None of the new tactics or technology employed in Europe caused the slightest change in the curriculum at West Point. We continued to study the men and campaigns of the Civil War for the most part and, as first classmen, spent three days at Gettysburg, thoroughly grounding ourselves in that battle.

Unfortunately my athletic activities during my four years at West Point had a pronounced impact on my grades and academic class standing. From my plebe year class standing of 49, I slipped to 53 at the end of my cow year. I pulled that up sharply in my yearling year to 43, but my final standing in June 1915 slipped back to 44 out of 164 who graduated. Had I not given so much time and effort to athletics, I believe I could easily have graduated about twentieth.

However, I have never regretted my sports obsession for a moment. It is almost trite to observe that in organized team sports one learns the important art of group cooperation in goal achievement. No extracurricular endeavor I know of could better prepare a soldier for the battlefield. West Point sports also gave me an excellent opportunity to take the measure of many men who would serve with, or under, me in World War II. It is noteworthy, I think, that all the men on our 1914 baseball team who remained in the Army went on to become generals.

Now, after four years at West Point, we were ready to take our places as second lieutenants in the small regular Army, which then consisted of about 5,000 officers and 100,000 men.

Owing to the more rapid promotions, the most sought after branches were the corps of engineers and field artillery. I applied for engineers, artillery, and infantry in that order. I did not stand high enough to make engineers or artillery and wound up in the infantry, along with cheerleader and yearbook editor Ike Eisenhower, who stood 61, and Jim Van Fleet, a football star, who stood 92. My roommate, Bennie Mills, who stood five from the bottom, chose the aviation section of the signal corps.

At first I was a trifle disappointed and half regretted squandering so much time on athletics. But quite soon I got over my mild disappointment. Only a year after we graduated, the Army abolished "branch" promotions, and we all found ourselves on an equal footing in that regard. Moreover, we in the infantry soon learned that it is in that branch more than any other that a soldier learns the art of leadership and command and, ultimately, has the best chance of reaching the topmost positions.

Ike Eisenhower wrote the brief portrait of me in our yearbook, *Howitzer,* setting it off with a flattering anonymous quotation: "True merit is like a river, the deeper it is, the less noise it makes." He noted my "greatest passion" was baseball, followed by "football and F Co." His conclusion was highly flattering. "His most promising characteristic is 'getting there,' and if he keeps up the clip he's started, some of us will some day be bragging to our grandchildren that, 'Sure, General Bradley was a classmate of mine.' "[7]

FOUR

When we graduated from West Point in June 1915, all of Europe was bleeding from the ghastliest war in the history of the world. The United States was not yet openly involved. Rather, we were caught up in trouble, or in today's jargon, a "limited war" in Mexico. Aside from a brief combined Army-Marine action in Vera Cruz, most of the skirmishing took place along the border.[1]

Most of us shavetail lieutenants in the infantry who stood high in our class had a choice of duty stations. Few of us elected duty on the Mexican border. As Eisenhower recalled: "This service was disagreeable. Usually, it separated a man from his family. Living conditions were rough. Anything was better to most officers than the border." Eisenhower chose duty in the Philippines but was sent to the border anyway! Several others and I chose the 14th Infantry Regiment based in the Pacific Northwest. It was one of the few outfits that had not been skeletonized for Mexican border duty, and I preferred to begin my career in a "normal garrison" atmosphere. We packed and made our farewells. Among my belongings were three new items: a .45 Colt pistol, which I had adjusted to a three-pound trigger pressure; a sword; and a pair of six-power field glasses.[2]

We were granted a three-month "graduation leave," from June 12 to September 12. I spent that summer in Moberly, living with my mother and stepfather on a farm north of town. Mary Quayle, who had completed her junior year at the University of Missouri, often came up to visit her best friend, Rose Richardson. Mary and I began to see more and more of each other, picnicking, going to the Bijou, or for long walks. I also played right field on the semi-pro Moberly baseball team, the Moberly Athletes, again without pay.[3]

I had not dated in high school, had "dragged" only one girl to a hop in my four years at West Point, and was thus deplorably inexperienced in matters of the opposite sex. But Mary was endlessly fascinating to me. She was pretty, bright, ambitious and domineering, like my mother. She did not hesitate to order Second Lieutenant Bradley around. She had strong likes and dislikes about people. Those she liked, she could not do enough for. Those she disliked got an icy shoulder. Her college and teaching experience in Minnesota and a year at the University of Missouri, where she and Jane had joined the Kappa Alpha Theta sorority, had considerably matured and broadened her. She was no longer dependent on her Moberly roots and friends. She wanted to expand her horizons still more.

We soon realized we were deeply in love. Before the summer was out, I gave her a white gold ring with a small solitaire diamond and we became officially engaged. We were to be married in June 1916, upon her graduation.[4]

The 14th Infantry Regiment to which I reported on September 12, 1915, was commanded by Colonel R. H. Wilson. It was composed of three scattered battalions, all at about half or two-thirds strength. The First Battalion was on detached service in Alaska, lending a military presence to that barren frontier. The Second Battalion was stationed at Fort Laughton, near Seattle, Washington, and the Third Battalion was at Fort George Wright, outside Spokane, at the western foot of the Rocky Mountains. I was assigned to the Third Battalion in Spokane, commanded by Captain A. J. Harris, then to K Company, commanded by Wilbur A. McDaniel, a onetime schoolteacher who had been commissioned seventeen years earlier in the Spanish-American War and, owing to the Army's glacial promotion system, had not advanced beyond the rank of captain. He was a good soldier: I liked him immediately. The first sergeant, Ernest M. Johnson, was a man of uncommon ability. (He held a reserve commission of major.) In time, I would learn much from him, including typing.[5]

Like most Army units in those days, K Company was understrength —only sixty or seventy men. Most of the enlisted men had long years of service. Why any of them joined the Army almost defies explanation. In those days, a man was considered a "recruit" until he had completed one year in the Army. As a private he was paid thirteen dollars a month. He put in countless years before he became eligible for promotion to corporal. (We had one outstanding private in our company, and later, when a corporal's vacancy occurred, I unhesitatingly recommended him. But McDaniel turned him down because he only had five years' service!) The Army placed great emphasis on marksmanship, even to the extent of financial incentives. An enlisted marksman earned an extra three dollars a month; an expert marksman five dollars a month. That helped a little, but obviously such low pay and slow promotion seldom attracted higher caliber personnel.

Fort George Wright, located at the end of a Spokane trolley line, three miles out of town, was only several years old. Its buildings were brick, the parade ground gravel. Two other new lieutenants and I were assigned to quarters in a three-bedroom brick duplex. We hired a black cook and established a mess to which we invited two other bachelor officers. One of us served as mess officer, buying the food, paying the cook; and at the end of the month, we split the cost five ways. It was quite reasonable, easily within our salaries of $141.67 a month.

The other half of our duplex quarters was occupied by a man of rare wit, ability, intelligence and professionalism, twenty-nine-year-old Edwin Forrest Harding of the Class of 1909, who after six years in the infantry, was still a second lieutenant. Forrest Harding was a serious student of history, a fine writer and a compulsive teacher. Soon after we arrived, Forrest organized an unofficial weekly gathering in his home to which he invited about six of the lieutenants on the post. For several hours under his guidance we would discuss small-unit tactics, squads and platoons in attacks on a variety of terrains and so on. These meetings were immensely stimulating and educational, often turning to broader discussions of military history. No single person in my early Army career had a more salutary influence on me than Forrest Harding. He instilled in me a genuine desire to thoroughly learn my profession.[6]

In those days, garrison duty could not have been more pleasant or less demanding. We reported for duty about 7 A.M. Then for about four hours we worked with the men on close order drill (squads right, squads left, etc.) or went to the rifle range or, very occasionally, conducted simulated attacks on the platoon or squad level. Because I was a West Pointer with extensive experience in drilling, Captain McDaniel was content to let me handle these daily chores most of the time. At 11 A.M., we had "officers' call," an assembly of all officers to discuss various post problems or new regulations. After the noon meal, the remainder of the day was our own. I spent these languorous fall afternoons hiking or going to the movies in Spokane. I also signed up for dancing lessons. In the fall, I bought a 12-gauge Winchester pump-action shotgun for forty dollars and hunted grouse with Sergeant Johnson.

Winter soon set in, bringing sub-zero arctic blasts from the north. Almost predictably, the AWOL's, preferring the warm food and lodging of the guardhouse to the cold outside, began to straggle in. Since Wright was the only Army installation in the area, our guardhouse was soon fully occupied. Each of the AWOL's, of course, faced a court-martial, some on multiple charges. I was detailed as defense counsel for the first man to come to trial. He had also been accused of stealing a suitcase. I boned up on the rudimentary law we had been taught at West Point, and by creating a doubt as to the man's true identity on the stealing charge, I managed to have him acquitted. When this news reached the guardhouse, all thirty-three remaining AWOL's urgently requested that I serve as their defense counsel. For several weeks I was the busiest man at Fort Wright, a poor man's Clarence Darrow, almost overwhelmed with my heavy case load. I was ultimately relieved of this interesting but onerous responsibility when my superiors transferred me to the opposite side of the bench and appointed me a member of the court.

The bitterly cold winter curtailed our drills and field exercises. As was customary at Fort Wright, organized indoor athletic competitions between the four companies of the battalion substituted for outdoor activity. There were four events: boxing, wrestling, high jumping and basketball. Knowing that I had actively participated in sports at the Academy, Captain McDaniel gave me the mission of coaching K Company. This was no light responsibility. As James Jones has depicted so graphically in *From Here to Eternity,* such matches were taken very seriously in the peacetime Army. A winning season reflected great credit on the commanding officer of a unit. Often the results were noted in his official Army record, and could help with a promotion someday.

I gladly accepted this assignment and others like it as I climbed the ladder of the peacetime Army. In fact, for the next twenty-odd years I usually coached or played on Army athletic teams. I was determined to keep myself in top-notch physical condition. Athletics also proved to be a good way to get to know the men in my outfit and let them get to know me. Besides that, it was good clean fun.[7]

All this time, the civil war in Mexico raged on. President Wilson had recognized a de facto government headed by Venustiano Carranza; but he was not acceptable to many rebels, notably his most powerful rival Francisco (Pancho) Villa, who had established himself, in effect, as the governor of northern Mexico. It was Villa's soldiers who were carrying out most of the organized raiding on the border. On January 10, 1916, his men attacked a train near Chihuahua, Mexico, and executed sixteen Americans in cold blood. On the night of March 9, 1,500 Villa troops raided Columbus, New Mexico, two miles north of the border, looting and killing. A small U.S. Army force fought back fiercely and gallantly, driving the invaders back across the border. They killed about forty of Villa's troops and wounded many more. Villa's men killed eight soldiers and nine civilians and seriously wounded many others.

The entire nation was shocked and enraged by this murderous attack. Public pressure forced President Wilson and his new Secretary of War, Newton D. Baker, to take decisive action. They ordered Brigadier General John J. Pershing to form an expeditionary force of about 5,000 men to cross the border and capture Villa. President Carranza gave tacit approval to the mission, thereby transferring, temporarily at least, the onus for eliminating his chief rival to the United States.

Nine days later, Pershing and his troops (which included a flamboyant young cavalry officer, Lieutenant George S. Patton) crossed the border. His force included three innovations: six airplanes, several automobile staff cars and trains of motorized trucks, the first time the U.S. Army had employed trucks in combat. (All six airplanes eventually crashed; the cars and trucks in that rough terrain proved less than satisfactory.) Pershing had to fight a "limited war" with severe political restrictions: Carranza, playing both sides against the middle, would not permit the general to use the Mexican railroads or enter any town. Even with these handicaps, not to mention many other shortcomings in his forces and the difficulty of the terrain, Pershing achieved a notable success, breaking up a half-dozen of Villa's best bands and killing or capturing a dozen of his top officers. It is interesting to note that in one skirmish that gained him much publicity as a "hero," George Patton utilized three automobiles, the first instance in U.S. Army history of motorized assault.

Then Carranza decided enough was enough. The Pershing expedition was, to say the least, not popular with the Mexican populace as a whole. Traditionally, "gringos" had come to Mexico only to conquer or take its resources. On April 12, when Pershing's forces were attacked by some of Carranza's forces, Carranza demanded Pershing's immediate withdrawal. The United States agreed to withdraw its troops—gradually—provided Carranza could assure the United States that his troops would keep Villa under control. While these increasingly belligerent talks were proceeding, Villa's men arrogantly raided Glenn Springs, Texas. The talks broke down; in the confusing aftermath, Carranza threatened total war against the United States.[8]

The crisis was grave indeed; a war seemed close at hand. On May 9, the War Department called up the National Guard of Texas, New Mexico and Arizona. Most Regular Army combat units, including our 14th Regiment, were ordered to proceed to the border at once. In the growing tension, we had anticipated these orders, and on May 11, at 12:45 A.M., we boarded a long troop train with all our gear—including horses, mules, wagons, weapons—and headed south in a high state of excitement and anticipation.[9]

The impending war could not have come at a more awkward time for me personally. Mary and I were to be married in about a month in Moberly, upon her graduation. I had already arranged my leave. Now, an indefinite postponement was mandatory. Before I could get my wits together and write her a proper letter of explanation, the *Moberly Democrat,* having somehow learned of our orders to the border, telephoned and asked me one too many questions. Thus, Mary found out about the postponement in a story in the *Democrat* with these headlines: "WAR ORDERS DELAY MARRIAGE/LT. OMAR BRADLEY CALLED TO BORDER/WAS SOON TO WED MISS MARY QUAYLE."[10]

The way the story was written, it appeared that *I* was making the announcement that the wedding was to be postponed. Since that is customarily the prerogative of the bride-to-be, Mary was justifiably annoyed. But our love survived this misunderstanding. We would marry when conditions permitted.

It may well have been fortunate that the wedding was postponed. Only a few days after her graduation, Mary was stricken with typhoid fever and was hospitalized. She was gravely ill and very weak for months. All her hair fell out; she was skinny as a rail. From my distance, I could only offer sympathy and encouragement by mail. Many months passed before she recovered her health.

Our destination on the border was Douglas, Arizona. It took about five full days to get there because, by law, we had to stop and exercise the horses four hours out of twenty-four. We were joined in Douglas by the Second Battalion of our regiment (the First Battalion remained in Alaska), and the regimental staff, including our regimental commander, Colonel Wilson. We pitched our tents in the sandy desert east of Douglas, alongside the 11th and 18th Infantry regiments. An artillery battalion, a cavalry squadron and an Arizona National Guard regiment soon joined the group. In our border sector, there were in all literally thousands of men; the greatest congregation of military might I had ever seen. We represented only one sector of the border. There were similar concentrations in Texas and eastern New Mexico. Truly, we were ready for total war with Mexico.[11]

While we were thus deployed, momentous events were taking place in Washington. In the warlike atmosphere, Congress passed the National Defense Act (June 3, 1916), which, among other features, provided for a gradual (five-year) increase in the strength of the Regular Army to 175,000 men, almost double our 1916 size, and to include sixty-five infantry regiments. (This was the law that abolished branch promotion, putting us infantrymen on an equal footing with the engineers.) It also further strengthened the federal government's control over the National Guard. As soon as President Wilson signed the bill into law, he called up the entire National Guard—some 130,000 men. Most of these units were sent to the border. Within a month, there were a total of 159,000 soldiers assigned to the Southern Department, most on border duty—48,000 Regulars and 111,000 Guardsmen. Not since the Spanish-American War had so many Americans been under arms. Meanwhile, as enemy faced enemy across the border, diplomatic talks proceeded.[12]

After a time, tensions ebbed and the possibility of war with Mexico receded. We soldiers, living in absolutely miserable circumstances, settled into more peaceful routines. I ran a target range, coached a 14th Infantry baseball team, participated in an epic experimental 200-mile "motorized hike" with a convoy of trucks, and took a great many photographs with a camera I had acquired while at West Point.[13]

On September 20, our regiment was ordered to move from Douglas to Yuma, Arizona, a no less disagreeable outpost.[14]

The border war soon cooled completely, but I benefited from the scare it caused in an unexpected way. Owing to the provisions of the National Defense Act of 1916, and the doubling in size of the Army, in October my classmates and I were automatically promoted to first lieutenant—after only seventeen months' service! Other much-longer-termed officers in the regiment, such as Forrest Harding with seven and a half years' service, also moved up a rank. On October 21, I took my oath. My pay increased to the handsome sum of $206 a month.[15]

By this time, Mary had mostly recovered from her typhoid fever and we had set our wedding date for December 28. I applied for a month's leave, December 7 to January 7. I met Mary in Kansas City, where she was visiting cousins. She was still pale and a trifle weak and her hair had not grown out, but it was a grand reunion. We had not seen each other for fifteen months.

The Quayles were still living in Columbia; Mary's sister Jane still had another half-year to go before graduating. So it was decided that we would marry in Columbia, not Moberly. Mary and I took a train to Columbia, where I stayed with the Quayles for a few days, making plans for the wedding, which was to be a simple affair in the home of good friends, Professor and Mrs. F. P. Spalding. Then I went to Moberly to see my mother, stepfather and stepbrothers Russell and Charles, Nettie, Opal and friends. Mother was still poor as a churchmouse, but in very good spirits, happy with her life and happy about my forthcoming marriage.

Mary and I were married on the afternoon of December 28 in the Spalding home. My mother and stepfather did not attend because of the expense involved. Nor did the maid of honor, Jane Quayle. She had been visiting in Moberly and missed a train connection for Columbia and was furious that we had gone ahead without her. The Reverend Madison Ashby Hart of the Columbia Christian Church performed the ceremony. Mary's hair was still so short she could not wear the veil her Aunt Papita had sent her. (My hair was short, too, and completely gray.) She wore a hat and a lovely calf-length afternoon frock. Her mother gave her away; I stood alone. Afterward we left for Kansas City, Missouri, where we honeymooned in a suite in the Muehlebach Hotel. Later, Mary's mother sent out the announcements, which stated we would be "at home" in Yuma, Arizona, after January 20, 1917. We laughed uproariously over that. We did not expect many of our Missouri friends or relatives to call.[16]

From Kansas City we took a Pullman car to El Paso, Texas, where a West Point friend, Jo Hunt (Spec) Reaney, was serving with an infantry unit. On New Year's Eve morning, we checked into the historic Pasa del Norte Hotel, then went to see Spec for lunch in his tented mess—Mary's introduction to Army life. He welcomed us warmly and gave us a Navaho rug for a wedding present. That afternoon we watched a high-scoring service football game.

Ever westward by Pullman. We stopped briefly in Yuma to pick up my December pay and continued on to Los Angeles, where two of Mary's aunts, Papita and Maud, were then living. We spent several happy days with the aunts sightseeing in Los Angeles. While there, I saw an ad in the newspaper for a female English setter. I looked up the man and traded my old .22 rifle for the dog, whose name was Birdie. She was a good and lovable companion, but not well trained; she was always running away.

We returned to Yuma on January 11, 1917, and rented a small furnished house on a hill—two rooms and a screened porch. (The kitchen and bedroom were on the porch.) Mary perked the place up with some curtains and the Navaho rug Spec Reaney had given us. And so we began forty-nine years of married Army life.

Duty at Yuma was miserable. Clearly there was to be no war with Mexico; the situation had developed into endless verbal wrangling. Our official camp duties were routine and boring. Yuma was primitive and dusty. Our major diversion was the tedious round of formal calls on superiors for tea or coffee. A few weeks after Mary and I settled in, I applied for a transfer to our First Battalion, which was still on duty in Alaska at Tanana, five or six hundred miles up the Yukon River, in absolute wilderness. In time, my request was approved—to take place the following summer. We were thrilled. Any place seemed preferable to Yuma, Arizona.[17]

FIVE

We were still in Yuma when the United States declared war on Germany April 6, 1917. A few weeks later, May 18, Congress enacted the most sweeping manpower mobilization act in the history of the country. All males between the ages of twenty-one and thirty were subject to registration and draft. (Though many were to be "exempted" for various reasons.) The Regular Army was to expand to its wartime strength of 175,000 men, the National Guard would be fully mobilized, federalized and expanded to 500,000 men. An additional 500,000 men would be drafted into a "National Army" for use as the President saw fit—replacements for the Regular Army, National Guard or as special forces. Tens of thousands of qualified men would be commissioned from civilian life and in a period of ninety days be trained to lead combat troops. In all, it would amount, more or less, to a million-man Army![1]

Two days after the mobilization act was passed by Congress, our outfit was relieved by a battalion of the 35th Infantry. The two battalions of our 14th Regiment were ordered back to the Pacific Northwest, to Vancouver Barracks, Washington, for duties as yet unspecified. Mary and I were profoundly happy to be leaving miserable Yuma. I gladly turned over most of my Yuma post jobs to my relieving officer, leaving me only one main responsibility: regimental supply company commander. At the same time, my orders to join the First Battalion in Alaska were canceled.[2]

As a professional soldier and a West Pointer, my overwhelming desire at that time was to go to France and prove my mettle in a real war. I immediately perceived that I would not make it there with the 14th Infantry. Word had come down from higher headquarters that our First Battalion would remain indefinitely in Alaska. We knew they would never send the 14th to France lacking a battalion. The 14th was doomed to a fate worse than death—or so I thought at the time: processing an endless stream of recruits.

The next sixteen months were, professionally, the most frustrating of my early Army career. I tried every possible scheme I could dream up to get out of the 14th Infantry and into an outfit bound for France. I sincerely believed that if I did not get to France I would be professionally ruined. Nothing worked. By the luck of the draw, it appeared that I was doomed to sit out the war in the Pacific Northwest.

In mid-January 1918, whatever waning hopes I had were thoroughly dashed. The War Department ordered the 14th Infantry Regiment to special duty: policing the copper mines and utilities in various places in Montana. Copper was vital to the war effort. There was labor unrest—agitation and strikes—at many of the Montana mines. Talk of sabotage was rife. Accordingly, small detachments of the 14th were sent to Anaconda, Great Falls and elsewhere. In the shuffle, I was assigned to command Company F, consisting of five officers and eighty-six men, and ordered to take it to Butte, Montana.[3]

By this time Mary was seven and a half months pregnant. I went ahead to Butte with Company F (and our dog, Birdie) to arrange suitable barracks for the men and living quarters for the officers. When I reached Butte on January 26, 1918, it was forty degrees below zero! Mary arrived shortly thereafter as did her mother, Dora, who wanted to be on hand when Mary had the baby.

Butte was still very much a wild and rough frontier town. Almost everyone packed a gun. It was also the principal hotbed of labor unrest in Montana. The Industrial Workers of the World (IWW) had located their headquarters in Butte. We believed the leaders of IWW to be anarchists whose aim was to shut or slow down the Anaconda copper mines. The inglorious assignment of Company F was to guard the mines and the workers from IWW agitators.

Not long after we settled in Butte, Mary went into labor. The baby, a boy, was stillborn, perhaps an aftermath of Mary's siege of typhoid fever. We were deeply grieved. For me, it evoked depressing memories of my little brother Raymond's death and my father's untimely death. Mary's mother escorted the body back to Moberly and buried him in the Quayle plot in Oakland Cemetery, alongside Mary's father. Dora placed a small tombstone to mark the grave. It was inscribed "Infant son of O. N. and Mary Bradley."[4]

At about this same time, the IWW attempted to stage an all-out riot to shut down the Anaconda mines. They chose St. Patrick's Day, March 17, 1918. Main Street was soon teeming with literally thousands of agitators, many armed with brass knuckles and knives. Forewarned, I deployed the entire company with loaded rifles and bayonets fixed throughout the town. This show of force had a decisive impact, and except for a few random incidents of violence we were able to maintain peace and order. Thereafter we had no serious problems with the IWW leadership.[5]

That summer of 1918, while the great climactic battles raged in

France, I continued to do my bit on the home front. I gave patriotic speeches for the Liberty Loan drives. The company personnel fought forest fires and voluntarily helped train prospective draftees in rudimentary close order drill. I organized a company baseball team, which played local semi-pro teams. On August 14, the tedium was relieved somewhat when I received the news that I had been routinely (and temporarily) promoted to major.[6]

A month later, we received electrifying news: the 14th Infantry Regiment, including the battalion in Alaska, had been ordered to Camp Dodge, near Des Moines, Iowa. The regiment was to be a cadre for the newly forming 19th Infantry Division, which was destined for the front in France. I would have a chance to fight after all! Our new regimental commander, Armand I. Lasseigne (Class of 1886), appointed me commander of the regiment's Second Battalion. On September 25, the 14th Infantry Regiment arrived at Dodge and merged into the 19th Division.[7]

We immediately went into intensive field training, coached by officers recently returned from combat in France. However, within a week or so, the great and dreaded influenza epidemic of 1918 hit Camp Dodge. Hundreds of men collapsed; many died. Our hospitals were jammed with the sick. The epidemic drastically curtailed our training schedule and decimated our ranks. On top of that came rumors from France that the Kaiser was extending peace feelers. Once more my hopes of getting into combat evaporated.[8]

During the height of the epidemic, we received a letter from Mary's sister, Jane, stating that she was going to be married in Moberly on October 12. The groom was Wayne Case Stewart, a well-to-do rancher from Dayville, Oregon, whom Jane had met while teaching school in Dayville. Although we were only 150 miles from Moberly, neither of us made the wedding. I was "in the field" and not eligible for furlough. It seemed imprudent for Mary to travel on crowded trains in the midst of the flu epidemic. As Jane had missed Mary's wedding, so Mary missed Jane's.[9]

A month later, November 11, 1918, Mary and I were in downtown Des Moines. There had been several premature "armistices," but now came the real thing. We heard whistles blowing all over town; people surged into the streets wildly celebrating. The war to end all wars was over. I was glad the carnage had stopped, but I was now absolutely convinced that, having missed the war, I was professionally ruined. I could only look forward to a career lifetime of dull routine assignments and would be lucky to retire after thirty years as a lieutenant colonel.[10]

The U.S. Army, which had grown to 3.6 million men, demobilized in a great rush. By early December, the rapid demobilization had virtually reduced Camp Dodge to a ghost town. Our 19th Infantry Division was one of the first to be mustered out, leaving only our greatly depleted Regular Army 14th Regiment and a few miscellaneous housekeeping units. We soon received orders to move on December 11, to Camp Grant, Illinois, near Rockford, to assist in closing that camp and taking custody of government property. Before leaving Camp Dodge, we bought our first automobile, a new four-door Dodge touring sedan. We paid cash—$1,067.00 from savings—and drove the car for the next six years.[11]

Camp Grant was no less chaotic than Camp Dodge. Men by the thousands were being discharged as rapidly as possible. My battalion was soon little more than a skeleton force. Since I was hard put to muster two or three squads for close order drill, any sort of military training or routine was pointless. Mary and I rented a house in Rockford, where one of her Quayle cousins lived, and spent a bitterly cold, inactive winter, reading a great deal and discussing what duty I should request next. We decided I had been with troops long enough (going on four years) and that I should attempt to return to the Pacific Northwest—which we loved—perhaps as a military instructor in a college ROTC unit.

In March 1919, I was appointed a member of a general court-martial. It was a serious, complicated and touchy case. Sixteen black soldiers had been indicted for the gang-rape of a white woman. The lurid testimony and legal maneuvering dragged on for months—until August. Although it was distasteful duty, I was extremely lucky to have been appointed to that particular court. On July 11, near the conclusion of the case, I received dispatch orders from the War Department to proceed without delay to Columbus Barracks, Ohio, and take charge of a 1,000-man Army unit that would sail from San Francisco to Vladivostok, Russia, on August 15, for "duty in Siberia." I was appalled. Siberia was the last place on earth I wanted to go. Fortunately for me, the War Department had previously issued orders that no member of that court could be transferred until the case was concluded. I immediately telegraphed the War Department pointing out the conflict, stating I would not comply with the orders unless otherwise advised. The Vladivostok orders were revoked—thank God—and I was spared what was sure to be another miserable and unhappy assignment.[12]

In the meantime, I had applied, through routine War Department channels, for a position as a military instructor at a college with an ROTC unit. In a box on the application designating location preferred, I typed in "Northwest," assuming that to mean the states of Washington and Oregon. My request for ROTC duty was granted, but unknown to me, in those days the states of Washington and Oregon were designated "Pacific Northwest." My choice, "Northwest," denoted the area of North and South Dakota. As a result of this misunderstanding, on August 25, I was assigned to be assistant professor of military science and tactics at the South Dakota State College (of Agriculture and Mechanic Arts) in Brookings, a small city in the eastern part of the state.[13]

Our year at Brookings was a bitterly cold one, but the work turned out to be interesting and challenging. During my year there, Washington was engaged in a bitter debate over the future of the Army. The Army Chief of Staff, Peyton C. March, wildly misjudging the public mood, proposed a regular standing Army of 500,000 men, backed up by a huge reserve of men trained through a compulsory universal military training program and a National Guard of 435,000 men. General of the Armies John J. Pershing, a national war hero, perhaps more in tune with the people and Congress, countered with a proposed standing Army of 280,000, plus a trained Reserve and National Guard. Congress, now in a retrenchment mood, sided with Pershing and (on June 4, 1920) amended the National Defense Act to embody most of Pershing's concepts, although abjuring a draft or any form of military training.

The revised National Defense Act held promise of providing the United States with a reasonable military posture. But in practice, it turned out to be pure blue sky. In the ensuing years, Congress adamantly—and consistently—refused to give either the Army, the Reserves or the National Guard anywhere near reasonable support. Only one year after amending the Act, in 1921, Congress slashed the Regular Army by almost half, to 150,000 men, forcing one thousand qualified officers to resign. As the Roaring Twenties blew on and a pacifist devil-may-care mood seized the country, Congress relentlessly whittled away at the Regular Army. Its average strength in the years 1922 to 1929 was 137,300 officers and men. All attempts to maintain a viable enlisted Reserve failed because there was no draft or universal military training program to fill and sustain it. Similarly, Congress whacked away at the National Guard until it was barely able to maintain half its 435,000-man authorized strength. In sum, in the 1920s, we reverted to an absurdly inadequate Army attempting to scrape by in a nation that had grown hostile to anything "militaristic."[14]

After ROTC summer encampment in Michigan and a lovely three-week leave camping and fishing on lakes in Minnesota, Mary and I returned to Brookings in late August prepared for another school year. I was soon astonished to receive a telegram ordering me to duty at West Point "without delay," as an instructor in the math department. I was asked to suggest a relief at Brookings. I chose my classmate James Van Fleet, who had won a Silver Star and Purple Heart in France. My recommendation was accepted. On September 11, 1920, we loaded the Dodge and drove to West Point. Our dog Birdie had again wandered off and had to be left behind. We never saw her again.[15]

SIX

World War I had thrown the routine of West Point into turmoil and drained off virtually the entire Corps of Cadets. By the spring of 1919, there was no established Corps of Cadets as I had known it, and utter confusion reigned within the academic and tactical staffs. Declaring West Point to be not only a mess but also "forty years behind the times," Army Chief of Staff Peyton March hand-picked thirty-nine-year-old Douglas MacArthur, a handsome, dashing, unorthodox war hero, to be superintendent and bring order out of chaos.

MacArthur instituted drastic—and highly controversial—reforms. He greatly broadened and liberalized the academic curriculum. He introduced compulsory intramural athletics for those cadets not on varsity squads: football, baseball, basketball, track, wrestling, soccer, lacrosse, tennis, golf, polo. He abolished hazing, summer camp on the Plain; he relaxed discipline and granted more off-post leaves and furloughs. He drew up visionary plans to expand the Corps of Cadets from 1,300 to nearly 3,000 —comparable to the Naval Academy midshipman population. However, these plans did not carry in Congress, which was then in a pacifist mood and paring the Army budget.[1]

By September 1920, when I reported for duty at the Academy, heroic efforts had been made to get the life back to normal. The upper classes were still a mixed bag of men graduating after an optional three or four years. But the entering plebes of the Class of 1924 were back on a normal four-year schedule. The class was huge: some 400 men, many veterans of the fighting in France. Living quarters for the plebe class were in such short supply that men had to double up, four to a room. To further confuse matters, the entire plebe class (dubbed the "Thundering Herd") had been forced to report two weeks late owing to a nationwide poliomyelitis epidemic. It was because of this huge class—and the urgent need for plebe math instructors—that I and others had been summoned to West Point at the very last minute.[2]

This sizable increase in the teaching staff—there were thirty-seven of us in the math department alone—created a severe staff housing shortage. There was a scramble for available on-post quarters, with rank—and often date of rank—deciding. Many were forced to live off-base at the Highland Falls Hotel, or in whatever temporary quarters they could find. Mary and I drew quarters in a somber four-story stone building adjacent to Cullum Hall. Once exclusively quarters for bachelor officers, its apartments had been crudely converted to accommodate married officers, some with children. Despite the temporary inconveniences of the quarters (in time we moved to a lovely small house), I was overjoyed to be back at West Point. It was like coming home again.[3]

There were many classmates and old friends at West Point. Among them was a standout from the class of 1917, Matthew B. Ridgway. As a cadet, he had been in my company for two years and was manager of the football team and a member of the secret fraternity Omicron Pi Phi. He had been ordered back to the Academy to teach Spanish and went on to serve as Superintendent MacArthur's manager of athletics, an important job for so young a captain. Son of a West Point graduate, Ridgway was a soldier of impressive military bearing who, like me, had not gotten to France and was deeply disappointed. During this tour we became frequent hunting companions and learned to play golf together. Ridgway took his golf casually but I became an instant golf nut and pursued the game relentlessly for the rest of my professional career and after. In 1929, at the top of my form, I managed to take second place in the annual Army-wide Golf Championship.[4]

Had Mary and I been so inclined, we could have enjoyed a zestful social life at West Point. Although Prohibition was in force, there was no shortage of bathtub gin or beer or bootlegged whiskey, and every night there was an informal party someplace on the post. But neither Mary nor I drank or smoked. It did not concern me that our friends did (some heavily), but contact with even a slightly inebriated person sent Mary into a towering rage, and cigarette smoke greatly discomfited her. The result was we led a rather quiet social life compared to most of our friends. Mary found diversion in an officers' wives bridge group; I played poker with the boys. Occasionally we drove down to New York for dinner and the theater.

Nobody had much money to throw around. After the war, I had been routinely demoted to captain, repromoted to major and demoted again to captain. In the spring of 1924, I was repromoted to major and stayed a major for the next twelve years! Our income was about $300 to $350 a month, depending on the whims of Congress. Those of our friends who had no family wealth went heavily into debt buying automobiles and having children, but Mary and I, having developed strict habits of frugality in childhood, got by quite well. I helped not a little with poker winnings. I was a conservative player who folded a hand unless I saw a 70 percent chance of winning. As a result, I was a consistent winner.[5]

Mary and I wanted children, but again we had difficulties. Not long after our arrival at West Point, she miscarried, another depressing personal setback for both of us. In March 1923, she again became pregnant. This time there were no serious problems and on December 3, 1923, a very healthy daughter, Elizabeth, was delivered at the West Point hospital. Owing to the difficulties Mary had experienced, we did not attempt to have any more children.[6]

The head of the West Point math department was a fine gentleman, Colonel Charles P. Echols, West Point Class of 1891. He had been teaching math at West Point since 1904—had taught me math, in fact. He had chosen me for this assignment, he said, because I had done well in math, standing 32 in my first class year. He assigned me to teach plebe math—geometry and algebra—the easiest courses. I taught all morning six days a week. In the afternoons, five days a week, I attended a math refresher course given by Echols or one of his assistant professors. In the evenings, I studied the work I would teach the plebes the following day, making certain I could answer all the obscure—and theoretical—questions they would inevitably ask. It made for a full day.

As time passed and my grasp of mathematics improved markedly, I thoroughly enjoyed my work, perhaps unconsciously emulating my father. Whatever the case, I know I benefited from this prolonged immersion in math. The study of mathematics, basically a study of logic, stimulates one's thinking and greatly improves one's power of reasoning. In later years, when I was faced with infinitely complex problems, often requiring immediate life-or-death decisions, I am certain that this immersion in mathematics helped me think more clearly and logically.

The junior officers assigned to the academic department were recruited to coach in MacArthur's new intramural athletic program. I was assigned to coach a company in soccer. I knew nothing about soccer, not even the rules. One of the staffers, a classmate, Lehman W. Miller, had been assigned to coach the same company football. He had never played football *or* soccer. Since I knew football, he suggested we trade coaching jobs so that the company would receive expertise in at least one sport. It turned out to be a good idea. Our company won both the football and soccer championships.

MacArthur, as in his later, more famous years, was an aloof, reclusive figure. Still a bachelor, he lived in the superintendent's quarters with his aged, ailing mother who served as his official hostess. Except for sporting events, or an occasional official ceremony, I seldom saw him, even from a distance. I cannot recall a single exchange with him. I was but a lowly captain in the math department, he a legendary general. The gulf between us was vast indeed.

On the whole, I approved of MacArthur's revitalization and liberalization of West Point academics, even if it did somewhat curtail the study of my specialty, mathematics. I also applauded his new emphasis on physical fitness and athletics. However, I did not fully approve of the way he relaxed cadet discipline. I was one of the many who deplored the abolition of summer camp on the Plain, since I believed it provided the first classmen with a rare opportunity to exercise command, however limited or artificial.

On one matter I was sorely disappointed by MacArthur. He backed the varsity sports squads to the hilt, often appearing at practices, offering suggestions and exhorting the men to do their utmost. Among the 1920 plebes there was a standout athlete, Walter E. French, who starred in both football and baseball. French was a borderline student: it was doubtful he would make it academically. MacArthur deemed French so vital to West Point athletics that he passed the word to the academic department that French would be "found" over his—MacArthur's—dead body. This act of favoritism was a blatant, even outrageous, corruption of West Point tradition and honor, and it more than rankled the academic department. In our eyes, it was "relaxing" the high standards at West Point a bit too far.

MacArthur's reign at West Point continued to be controversial, especially among the Old Grads, who were now more than wringing hands over the new "permissiveness." They were writing angry letters and drafting acidulous reports castigating MacArthur and his policies. In 1921, when General of the Armies John Pershing relieved Peyton March as Chief of Staff of the Army, he took a hard look at the administration of West Point. He did not like what he saw. Like most of the Old Grads, Pershing (who was not one of MacArthur's admirers) demanded the new permissiveness be abolished, the clock turned back. In January 1922, we learned that MacArthur would not serve out the customary four-year tour of duty, merely three. In June of that year, he was relieved by Fred W. Sladen, Class of 1890, a noted disciplinarian, who wrenched the clock hands back with alacrity.[7]

To his credit, General Sladen promptly dealt with the controversial case of our star athlete, Walter E. French, whom MacArthur had been shielding academically. French was properly "found" and forced to resign.[8]

Our second two years at West Point passed swiftly. In my third year I hoped to escape the afternoon refresher sessions with Echols or his assistants, but a new course—descriptive geometry—was added to the curriculum and we teachers had to learn that. In my fourth year I was named an associate professor in the department and had to *conduct* the afternoon refresher course for the new teachers. So there was never a moment's respite.

In the spring of 1924, as my four-year assignment was drawing to a close, Mary and I again held prolonged discussions on our preference for my next assignment. After nine consecutive years of duty Stateside, I was overdue for an overseas assignment with troops, but the choices were limited: Puerto Rico, Panama, Hawaii, the Philippines. After we had put in for an infantry regiment scattered around posts in Puerto Rico, I learned that Matt Ridgway, who had high connections in the War Department, had obtained orders to the Infantry School in Fort Benning, Georgia. Inasmuch as it was not customary for an officer to go directly from one school to another without intervening troop or overseas duty, Ridgway had "set a precedent." Since I believed it would help me professionally to take a course at the Infantry School before going back to the troops, I (and several others on the West Point staff) took advantage of Ridgway's "precedent" and applied for the school. I was delighted when I was accepted for the one-year senior officers' advanced course.[9]

That summer of 1924 we were due ten weeks' leave. Owing in part to some stock market losses and in part to the added expense of our new child, we felt we could use some extra money. We decided that we would spend our leave in our West Point quarters and that I would take a job on the construction of the Bear Mountain Bridge, a few miles south of West Point. Construction of this privately financed structure (by a Harriman family conglomerate) spanning the Hudson River, was well under way, and the daily pay was good for those days: ten dollars for twelve hours.

The bridge was to open Thanksgiving Day 1924. By that summer, the two 350-foot towers had been built and enough cable had been strung between the towers to lay a 2,400-foot temporary wooden workmen's footbridge across the river 187 feet above the water. The wind whistled through this narrow neck of the river with alarming force, swaying the cables and the temporary footbridge. One day in a high wind, one of the smaller wires in one of the big cables snapped. This deadly whip hit my wristwatch and razored it off cleanly. I thought, What if it had hit my neck? I would have been decapitated!

When I got home that night, I discovered from my broker that I had made ninety dollars that day on a rise in Western Railroad stock. That was the equivalent of nine days' pay on the bridge. I had taken out an insurance policy after Elizabeth was born, but we decided finally that bridge work was too dangerous for the return. I spent the rest of the summer playing the stock market to good advantage and fly-casting in the many lakes in the area.[10]

Our four years at West Point had been beneficial to me professionally in several ways. Being on the teaching staff had not only sharpened my wits, it had broadened and matured me considerably. In these years, I began to seriously read—and study—military history and biography, learning a great deal from the mistakes of my predecessors. I took a particularly keen interest in one Civil War general, William T. Sherman, who, despite his infamous reputation in the South, was probably the ablest general the Union produced. Among other talents, he was a master of the war of movement. In the 1920s, the U.S. Army was dominated by men who had won their laurels in static trench warfare in France, but I still believed that rapid, sweeping massed movement of forces deep into the enemy's heartland was the best way to destroy an enemy army. Studying Sherman, to the exclusion of World War I battle reports, reinforced that belief.[11]

Fort Benning—the Infantry School—was then a mere six years old. It had been established during the war, initially as a home for the School of Musketry, which had been pushed out of Fort Sill, Oklahoma, by the expanding School of Artillery. Conceptually, Benning (named for Confederate General Henry L. Benning) soon grew far beyond musketry training. It evolved into the "home" of the U.S. infantry, a broad-gauge school dedicated to the task of producing the best-trained infantry leaders in the world. In 1922, Congress decreed Benning a "fort," and authorized limited funds for some facilities: fifty brick officers' quarters, quartermaster warehouses, a school headquarters building, a hospital, bakery, printing plant and the like.

When we arrived two years later, a massive construction program was under way: three-story brick and stucco barracks for the enlisted men, a stadium, swimming pool, theater. The reservation itself was enormous—some 97,000 acres, about half of that in valuable yellow pine, the rest open area suitable for military maneuvers. The main garrison was situated on a beautiful bluff on the east bank of the Chattahoochee River, where the stately antebellum John Woolfolk plantation had once stood. So vast was the reservation that post personnel had been compelled to construct twenty-seven miles of narrow-gauge railroads in order to commute to the outlying ranges and maneuver areas.[12]

That fall, as was then customary, two groups reported for the nine-month course of instruction, one for the advanced course, one for a lower-level company officers' course. There were seventy-three of us in the advanced class (senior captains, majors, lieutenant colonels), which was composed of twenty-three West Pointers, forty-eight non–West Pointers and two Marines. Among the West Pointers were three of my classmates, all still senior captains and soon to be repromoted to major: Charles W. (Doc) Ryder, Harold W. James and Tom Fox. Among the non–West Pointers I was delighted to find an old friend, my first company commander at Fort George Wright, Wilbur A. McDaniel, now a permanent lieutenant colonel. In the company officers' course, in addition to Matt Ridgway, there was another standout from his 1917 class: Mark Wayne Clark, whom I knew at West Point (and whom we addressed as Wayne rather than Mark).[13]

In those days, "student" housing at Benning was almost nonexistent.

Only the most senior of our class drew post quarters. The rest of us—and all those in the company officers' course—had to find housing in nearby Columbus. Mary and I rented a modest frame house that appeared to suit our needs. I noted there was no central heating, merely a coal-burning stove in the living room. The landlord assured us that there was no cause for concern; the Columbus winters were "mild," and the stove was more than adequate to heat the entire house. That proved to be the case until Christmas. But for the next several months, it was far from adequate. Night after night I huddled in the frigid kitchen reviewing my studies in extremely uncomfortable circumstances, silently cursing the landlord.

Transportation between Columbus and Benning was primitive. A modern two-lane concrete road was then under construction but far from finished. One result was that the old dirt washboard road had suffered extreme neglect. Two classmates—Doc Ryder and Tom Fox—another officer, Alexander W. (Sandy) Chilton, Class of 1907, and I formed a car pool. We commuted over that ghastly road ("The Daily Risk") five days a week. It took one hour each way to negotiate the nine miles. Thus our days were long—6:30 A.M. to 6:30 P.M. We deeply envied those who lived on post.[14]

There were two regiments of troops stationed at Fort Benning in direct support of the school. The 29th Infantry, which had been denied service in France because of crippling losses in the influenza epidemic, was maintained at "war strength" (two of three battalions on active status). The 29th was utilized by the teaching staff in the field during our many-leveled war games. The other regiment was the 24th Infantry, a far-under-strength, all-black unit which was utilized in housekeeping duties on the post. Some members of this black unit organized a chorus and sang gospel and Negro spirituals in concerts on Sunday afternoons, an unforgettable experience for all who attended.[15]

Even though Benning was a relatively new school, its standards were of the highest caliber. Much of the credit for this excellence must be given the remarkably able Colonel Frank S. Cocheu (West Point 1894), the assistant commandant responsible for the academic department. Having missed the fighting in France and having been away from troops for five years, I learned a great deal at Benning. When I arrived, I knew nothing about machine guns, mortars, automatic rifles or the workhorse 37-mm gun. The weapons section was ably staffed by a group of sergeants who were determined that we students leave Benning fully qualified in every standard-issue weapon in the Army's arsenal. In my case, they succeeded. The knowledge I gained under the guidance of the weapons section personnel would be forever valuable, and five years later, it would help me stage the most important exercise of my peacetime years.

On a higher level—in classroom study of tactics and strategy—it slowly dawned on me that my failure to get to France had not ruined me professionally after all. The emphasis at Benning was on open warfare or "war of maneuver," General Sherman's specialty. The trench warfare of France was not only not relevant, it was disdained. My classmates who had served in France had great difficulty adjusting to these concepts. They had fixed, inflexible ideas, whereas I, who had been denied that experience, still had an open mind and I grasped the theories under discussion more easily.

I immensely enjoyed my brief tour at Fort Benning. Probably 70 percent of our work was out-of-doors, working with the 29th Infantry demonstration troops on tactical problems from platoon to brigade level. (At any unsuspecting moment I might be told, "Major Bradley, the enemy has seized X hill. Take command of the battalion and recapture it.") I preferred being in the field with troops to any other duty. Tactics and terrain, "fire and movement," became my specialties.

Ever since the formalization of the Army's advanced peacetime school system, it had become common knowledge that one must do well in one school in order to advance to the next higher school—in my case Command and General Staff School and then the Army War College—and that a good record in these successive schools could be an important factor in promotions. Thus, at Benning, most of us applied ourselves with extraordinary diligence, and the work gradually became fiercely competitive. While I was certainly not among the promotion-hungry, I was fully caught up in the competition, doing my utmost. When the final grades were posted in May 1925, I was pleased to see that I stood number two in the advanced course, just below Leonard T. (Gee) Gerow, a regular officer who was a 1911 Virginia Military Institute (VMI) graduate.[16]

There were shortcomings in the curriculum at Benning which I see with twenty-twenty hindsight. There was far too little emphasis on the tank and the airplane. There was a tank battalion at Benning, but its equipment was utterly obsolete and our contact with the unit was limited to watching rolling demonstrations—mere parades—in the boondocks. We did not actually integrate tank deployments or movements into our infantry problems, a regrettable lapse. One of the Air Corps' major installations, Maxwell Field, Alabama, was only a hundred miles away—an hour-and-a-half flight in a Jenny—but we seldom saw aircraft of any type, and much too much time would pass before the visionary concept of utilizing aircraft for close support of infantry units would become a reality.

SEVEN

Now, after ten years of Stateside duty, it was time for the Bradleys to go overseas. We drew duty in Hawaii, considered *the* choice assignment. We could not have been more pleased.[1]

That summer we shipped our furniture ahead to Hawaii, traded the Dodge in on a new 1925 Buick and drove to Moberly to spend a few weeks visiting our relatives and friends. My mother and stepfather were well, although life was still a hard struggle financially. Dora Quayle, who was now renting both her houses on South Fourth Street, had been living alternately with us and the Stewarts. She would spend a prolonged visit with us in Hawaii.[2]

We departed from Brooklyn in the Army transport *Chateau Thierry* on August 11, 1925. We sailed via the Panama Canal to San Francisco, where we had a delightful week's layover for sightseeing. We arrived in Honolulu on September 8 to the traditional welcome of a dockside band, hula girls and orchid leis. After brief temporary duty in the 19th Infantry Regiment, I arranged a swap of jobs with another major and wound up in the 27th Infantry Regiment as commanding officer, First Battalion. We moved into large, beautiful quarters on the main post at Schofield Barracks.[3]

The Hawaiian Division, then commanded by Major General William R. Smith (Class of 1892), was a "square" division, composed of two brigades, each with two regiments. Our 22nd Brigade commander, Brigadier General Stuart Heintzelman (Class of 1899), had served in France. The 27th Regiment, to which I was assigned, consisted of fifty-seven officers and about one thousand enlisted men. The commanding officer was a classmate of Heintzelman's, Colonel Laurence Halstead, who had also served in France. Both Heintzelman and Halstead were keen on tactical training. That suited me fine because I was anxious to pass on to my battalion the many new ideas I had learned at Fort Benning.[4]

Over the past decade our relationship with the Japanese had deteriorated. Japan had become a first-class military power and appeared increasingly belligerent. In return for siding with the Allies in the war, she had been given several island groups in the Pacific region (the Marshalls, the Carolines) which strengthened her militarily. In Washington, Army and Navy war planners devised a strategy—called Plan Orange—to defeat Japan should she attempt military excursions in the Pacific. Our naval base at Pearl Harbor, Hawaii, was a key bastion in Plan Orange, the major staging base for counterattack against the Japanese. The primary function of the Hawaiian Division, together with air and coast artillery units, was to protect Pearl Harbor and to prevent a Japanese attack on or invasion of the island of Oahu. Accordingly, all our war planning, tactical exercises and maneuvers and training were conducted with this remote threat uppermost in mind.

Peacetime garrison life in Hawaii for a major and his family was pleasant indeed. We worked only half-days and seldom on weekends. Colonel Halstead was a fine officer who knew how to delegate authority. He allowed me to make up my own battalion training schedule. I had four able company commanders, and I gave them a free hand, even to the extent of requiring no more than one half-hour of close order drill per week—provided it was snappy. My primary concern was tactical training in the field on terrain my battalion was assigned to defend. I improved our overall familiarity with this terrain by constructing intricate scale-model "sand tables" for the officers and noncommissioned officers to study.

The official work schedule left me ample time for recreation and family life. I played golf on Schofield's fine eighteen-hole golf course four or five afternoons a week and whittled my handicap to a four. After one match on a newly opened course near Honolulu, I stopped in at the "nineteenth hole" and, at age thirty-three, had the first drink of whiskey in my life—some kind of Hawaiian rotgut. I found it pleasantly relaxing and thereafter made a habit of having a bourbon and water or two (but never more) before dinner. Mary remained a staunch teetotaler.

We had many family outings. Often we put on our bathing suits and drove ten miles to the beach at Waianae to swim in the surf. On Sunday afternoons, Mary and I sometimes drove thirty miles to Waikiki Beach outside Honolulu to listen to authentic Hawaiian musicians and watch the fabled hula dancers at the Moana Hotel. Our pay was still only about $300 a month, but that was sufficient to hire a domestic who made Mary's life easier and gave us considerable freedom.

In the quarters across the street from us lived one of the most extraordinary men—military or civilian—I ever met. He was George S. Patton, Jr., then a major and G-2 (chief intelligence officer) of the Hawaiian Division. In Hawaii, we hardly knew the Pattons at all. We were not inclined toward the heavy social life they led. Besides that, Patton was a dedicated horseman, always playing polo or off with a ladies' riding class he taught.

Since I had little use for horses, we had not much in common. Our one close contact occurred when Patton decided to organize a trapshooting team. He had heard that I was a fair shot and invited me to try out for the team. I missed the first two, then hit the next twenty-three in a row. He said laconically, "You'll do." I was not certain I wanted to be on the team; Patton's style did not at all appeal to me. But I signed on for the sport of it.

I served with the 27th Infantry Regiment for twenty months. I look back on those months as the most fulfilling and rewarding of my early career. It is rare that an infantry officer can find an assignment with troops in an area and climate ideal for field training together with the fine living quarters and other amenities Schofield Barracks had to offer. Professionally, I grew and assumed larger responsibilities. In late May 1926, when Colonel Halstead was temporarily detached to division headquarters, I had the high honor of serving as acting commander of the 27th Regiment for two months.[5]

Then came—as it must to all career Army officers—a sudden and unexpected shift in assignment. On June 9, 1927, I was relieved of my duties with the 27th Regiment and appointed officer in charge of National Guard affairs (and Reserve and ROTC matters) for the Hawaiian Department. In effect, I became the liaison officer between the U.S. Army and the Hawaiian National Guard, responsible for training standards and a wide variety of administrative duties, none of them overly taxing or challenging. Duty called; I responded, but not happily.[6]

The normal tour of duty in Hawaii was three years. Some officers requested extensions, which were freely given, and remained in the islands for four or five years. However, my National Guard assignment seemed a dead end, and I requested a return to the States for other duty. On April 8, 1928, I was quite pleased to find that I had been ordered as a student to the Army's Command and General Staff School at Fort Leavenworth, Kansas. This was an honor. I knew that if I successfully completed the course and subsequently discharged my duties competently, I was virtually certain to be promoted to colonel before retirement. We packed, traded the Buick in on a new Hudson (to be delivered Stateside) and on May 28, 1928, embarked on the Army transport *Cambria*.[7]

We had taken no leave in Hawaii. By regulation, I had more than three months owing me. We again decided to spend the summer in Moberly with family and friends. While there, I took a train to Detroit, picked up the new Hudson, literally at the end of the assembly line, and drove it back to Moberly at break-in speed of fifteen miles per hour. We passed many lazy weeks in Moberly, visiting friends, going on picnics, playing golf, swimming (Elizabeth could not understand why the water was not salty), reading, buying and selling stocks (at a good profit) on the volatile, skyrocketing New York Stock Exchange. In early September, we reported to

Fort Leavenworth. We drew student quarters—a frame house—facing on the golf course and polo field.

Since the days of the Indian Wars, Fort Leavenworth had been one of the Army's primary training centers for officers. In the earlier days it had been hit or miss, but during the reforms of Secretary of War Elihu Root in the early 1900s, it was formally established as the Command and General Staff School, a postgraduate course for senior officers to prepare them for battlefield management of large-scale units, such as divisions and corps. In sum: a classroom for future generals. Over the years the school had grown enormously in prestige. Whether it deserved its high reputation was debated in Army circles.

When I arrived, the school was in a transition period. The War Department had decreed that the course should be increased from one year to two, the first year devoted to division and corps study, the second (wisely, I think) to logistics in support of corps, armies or army groups. Our incoming class was divided evenly into men who would study one year or two. I drew the one-year course.

Since the assumption had taken root that a high grade at the Command and General Staff School would almost insure promotion to colonel or general, for too long the competition at the school had been literally killing. Some students who failed to score high had nervous breakdowns or committed suicide. When we assembled on our first day, the commandant, Brigadier General Edward L. King (Class of 1896), who had fought in the Philippines and in France, pointedly announced that henceforth no grades —no class standings—would be publicly posted at year's end. My old friend and car-pooler from Fort Benning, Sandy Chilton, who had just finished the course, advised me: "Brad, don't take this thing too seriously. Study until 10 o'clock, then go to bed. It's much more important to stay awake in class lectures than to study all night and go to class sleepy." I followed his advice to the letter.[8]

The problems—and solutions—presented to us in the lectures were trite, predictable and often unrealistic. If you closely followed the undertones of the lectures, you could fairly easily predict what lay ahead and what to do. One day after a lecture, I said to a classmate, Gilbert S. (Doc) Brownell, "Pretty soon we are going to get a problem where we are marching in a column—or two columns—and we are going to be caught by the enemy astride a river. The proper solution is to show aggressiveness, go on the attack." About two weeks later, sure enough, that exact problem came up on a test. When I got home that night, Doc Brownell called and said, "Brad, have you got time to come over and kick me in the tail? I went on the defensive!"[9]

We students were officially required to exercise two hours a week to stay in shape. This presented no problems for me. During fair weather, I played golf almost every Saturday and Sunday. When the inclement weather drove us indoors, I got my real exercise once a week in the riding hall on a horse a cavalry officer had left in my care. The horse was a dedicated, obsessive jumper. I'd point him down the middle of the hall and let him have his head for an hour. He'd take every jump in sight—a very strenuous routine for me and certainly the equivalent of two hours' normal exercise. However, officially I needed one more hour per week, so I'd go to the gym and hit golf balls in a driving cage for another hour. By springtime, I had my swing pretty well grooved and my golf game improved substantially.[10]

That winter at Leavenworth, I had two serious medical problems. The first was my teeth. Ever since my ice-skating accident at age seventeen, my teeth had been a mess. Off and on I had severe gum infections, the result of abscesses. The infections recurred at Leavenworth. They were so discomforting I reported to the hospital. An Army physician told me that poisonous bacteria from abscessed teeth could settle on the heart valves and cause heart disease—even a fatal heart attack. He urged that I have all my teeth pulled and replaced by a full set of dentures. I was naturally hesitant to become toothless at age thirty-five, but even more reluctant to die of a heart attack. All my teeth were pulled in two sessions, two days in a row, and dentures were fitted and installed.

The second medical problem was an attack of influenza, still a dreaded disease. There was a minor epidemic at the school and, unluckily, I became a victim in early December. I went to bed in my quarters. When my temperature rose above 104 degrees, Mary became gravely concerned and called the hospital. An insensitive medic informed her that the hospital was full, the doctors were too busy to make house calls, and "not to worry," because a temperature of 104 was "quite common" among the influenza victims. Fortunately, my fever broke in a few days and by Christmas I was fully recovered. Mary was justifiably outraged at the hospital personnel for their disregard of me and she never forgave them.[11]

On the whole, I profited from my year at Fort Leavenworth. It was a good intellectual experience, good mental discipline. I was introduced to a new level of war planning and management. Although the teaching methods and solutions to problems left a great deal to be desired, the exposure stimulated my thinking. When the "conventional" solution to a complex military problem is already well known by rote, unconventional—and often better—solutions are more likely to occur.[12]

Again it was time to move on, to put in for new duty. Two choices came my way. My former division commander in Hawaii, General Smith, then superintendent at West Point, wrote asking if I would be interested in returning to West Point as treasurer of the Academy. At the same time, I was offered a position as an instructor at the Infantry School at Fort

Benning. Mary much preferred the comforts and atmosphere of West Point. I much preferred the informal outdoor atmosphere of Benning and thought a tour there would be more beneficial to my career. We chose Benning, the most fortunate decision of my life.[13]

EIGHT

We were pleasantly impressed by the physical changes that had taken place at Benning in the four years we had been away. The extensive construction that had been in progress during my year as a student in the advanced course was finished—and more had begun. Benning now had the solid comfortable look of a permanent Army post. We drew quarters in an on-post duplex unit, conveniently located to everything, including the new nine-hole golf course. Again we had to watch our pennies: in the terrible stock market crash of 1929 we had lost about $5,000 and had to take out a loan to cover our losses.[1]

Not only had the Fort Benning Infantry School changed for the better physically, it had changed spiritually and intellectually. The architect of the latter changes was the most impressive man I ever knew, one of the greatest military minds the world has ever produced: George Catlett Marshall, then a lieutenant colonel and assistant commandant in charge of the academic department at the school. My association with Marshall began during this tour at Fort Benning and, with brief gaps, continued for more than two decades. No man had a greater influence on me personally or professionally. No man served his country more nobly or perfectly, or sought so little public credit.

Born in Uniontown, Pennsylvania, in 1880, Marshall was a VMI graduate (1899) who had played tackle on the varsity football team. Commissioned in the Regular Army in 1902, Marshall may well have been the most brilliant, level-headed and imperturbable officer the Army ever had. Within four years he was a student, then instructor, at the Command and General Staff School in Fort Leavenworth. During the war he became one of General Pershing's chief war planners in France, and afterward he remained with Pershing as a sort of unofficial chief of staff and general factotum. Few junior officers in the history of the U.S. Army had ever had such rapid rise and so much high-level exposure and responsibility for so long a period. Few gained so much in terms of personal and professional growth.

In 1924, Marshall, age forty-four and a lieutenant colonel, was assigned to troop duty in Tientsin, China, where he became executive officer of the 1,000-man 15th Infantry Regiment. This outfit was assigned to protect American officials in China and report on the fighting Chinese war lords and other dissident and insurgent groups. This was an electrifying time in Far Eastern history, and Marshall became well aware of its far-reaching impact. While serving in the 15th Infantry, he grew to admire two of its majors, my old mentor, cohort at West Point and classmate at Leavenworth, Forrest Harding, and a feisty, iconoclastic intelligence officer, Joseph W. Stilwell, whom Marshall had known at GHQ in France.

Marshall had found that the officers of the 15th Regiment were adept in handling weapons, target and bayonet practice, and paperwork, but, he wrote, "When it comes to simple tactical problems, the actual duty of troop leading, they all fall far below the standards set in other matters." One tactical exercise especially galled him. He came upon a bright officer who had graduated first in his class at Fort Benning completely "stuck" because he could not draft a written order for his men in the cumbersome and "absurd" manner required by Army Regulations and as taught at Benning. "I then and there formed an intense desire to get my hands on Benning," Marshall wrote.

Upon returning to the States, Marshall was detailed to lecture at the War College in Washington, D.C. A few weeks into that duty, his wife, Elizabeth Coles (Lily) Marshall, who had been in frail health all her married life (and had had no children) died of heart disease. Lonely and devastated by grief, unable to lecture, Marshall asked to be sent to Fort Benning. In November 1927, he relieved Colonel Frank Cocheu as assistant commandant, in charge of the academic department. He now had his "hands on Benning" and, perhaps to help overcome his grief, threw himself into the job compulsively.

By the time I came on the scene almost two years later, Marshall had gradually wrought a minor revolution in the academic department. He had undertaken an almost complete revamping of the instruction and technique. He believed—on the basis of his experience in France and China—that "our equipment, administrative procedure and training requirements are all too complicated for anything but a purely professional Army." In sum: Army doctrine was too cumbersome and complicated for the citizen Army we would train and lead in wartime. His credo was "I insist we must get down to the essentials, make clear the real difficulties, and expunge the bunk, complications and ponderosities; we must concentrate on registering in men's minds certain vital considerations instead of a mass of less important details. We must develop a technique and methods so simple and so brief that the citizen officer of good common sense can readily grasp the idea."

To assist in this gradual revolution, Marshall had recruited his own team in the academic department. During my tour there were four basic sections. The first, tactics, was headed by Joseph Stilwell; the second, logistics, by Lieutenant Colonel Morrison C. Stayer (a physician, no less!); the third, weapons, by Lieutenant Colonel Ralph W. Kingman; and the fourth, military history and publications, by Forrest Harding. Each of these section leaders had common traits: keen analytic intelligence, outspokenness, ingenuity. In sum, they were, like Marshall, highly creative. The subordinates they had chosen for their sections, such as my good friends Harold R. (Pink) Bull for logistics and Charles T. (Buck) Lanham for history and publications, J. Lawton (Joe) Collins in weapons and others too numerous to list, were, in a later phrase, the Army's "best and brightest."

Dean Acheson has written of Marshall: "The moment he entered a room, everyone in it felt his presence. It was a striking and communicated force. His figure conveyed intensity, which his voice, low, staccato, and incisive, reinforced. It compelled respect. It spread a sense of authority and calm. There was no military glamour about him and nothing of the martinet."

Even in those far-off days, that was true. Outwardly, Marshall was austere, cold, aloof, succinct, prudish. There was an impenetrable glass shield around him. He had no intimate friends. Except for George Patton, whom he had known well in France, he never addressed anyone by his first name; and I never knew anyone, except his wife, who called him by *his* first name. (He was notoriously poor at remembering even last names.) He frowned on excessive drinking, silly behavior, off-color stories and marital infidelities. And yet, off duty Marshall had a discernible warmth and moderate sense of fun. He loved to ride, to fox-hunt, to stage elaborate pageants and parades, to gather his officers and their wives for tea and cakes, to entertain and write to children he knew.[2]

In the first of my four years at Benning, I had the good fortune to be assigned to Joe Stilwell's first section, tactics. My specific duties were to teach senior officers "battalion in the attack." This was useful review for me—and a heavy responsibility—but what I valued most was the close contact with Stilwell, one of the most challenging, difficult and interesting personalities I ever encountered and a prime mover in the revolution at Benning.

In later years, when Stilwell became a famous four-star general, the media would nickname him "Vinegar Joe." It was apt. There was a strong streak of sourness in his character. He was, as one officer put it, "pretty close to a misanthrope." In an essay to his family, he harshly described himself as "unreasonable, impatient, sour-balled, sullen, mad, hard, profane, vulgar." I would not disagree with any of those adjectives. But I would hasten to add several others: brilliant, professional, visionary, ingenious, aesthetic, athletic (at forty-six, he still ran several miles a day). I found to my delight that he despised horses. He wrote, "If there is a woodener, less intelligent animal on earth than a god-damned hammer-headed horse, show him to me. All prance and fart and no sense."[3]

Much of my work in tactical instruction was carried out in the classroom with blackboards, terrain maps, lectures. Mostly lectures. Heretofore, it had been the custom for a Benning instructor to prepare written notes for lectures. But when Marshall and Stilwell threw the book away, the notes went with it. No one could lecture from notes. The lectures had to be delivered extemporaneously—and succinctly. This was not an easy adjustment for me. I had never been, nor would I ever be, a gifted orator. I was so edgy at my first lecture that I cheated. I made several cards with subject matter headings in large letters and placed them on the floor at my feet![4]

The high points in tactical instruction were the field exercises, with the units of the 29th Infantry Regiment serving as demonstration troops. Before such exercises, I would spend the weekends going over every foot of the terrain, committing it to memory. When I was a student at Benning, the exercises had been conducted with standard by-the-book rules and solutions—the cumbersome, complex procedure Marshall and Stilwell were determined to eradicate. They preached simplicity and common sense and improvisation. Marshall decreed that "Any student's solution of a problem that ran radically counter to the approved school solution, and yet showed independent creative thinking, would be published to the class." Stilwell welcomed any "screwball idea" to test, and often proposed them himself. In field exercises, both Marshall and Stilwell would deliberately create disorder and confusion during the problems, throwing in the wholly unexpected in order to encourage almost instantaneous clear, correct, improvised solutions. One of the student officers in tactics that year, Matt Ridgway, who was subjected to one of these contrived confusions, profited by it and declared that that sort of "mental conditioning" was "more important to a combat officer than any number of learned techniques."[5]

There was a larger purpose behind the radical change in training. Both Marshall and Stilwell were strong advocates of open warfare or "war of movement." Such perceived warfare demanded simplicity, improvisation, ingenuity, speed. There could be no long delays while battalions or smaller units drafted requests or waited for detailed orders from higher headquarters, as they had in the trenches and during the great set-piece battles in France. If an unexpected advantage arose, an officer was to instantly seize the prize. If an unexpected setback occurred, he was to work his way out of it by his own resourcefulness. The paperwork could come later.

Our family life at Fort Benning was pleasant. Our quarters were properly heated, and in the colder months—in contrast to the house in Columbus—we were snug. We hired a black domestic who was an excellent cook, but she and Mary had now to be careful about what I ate. After my teeth were pulled (perhaps coincidentally), I had developed allergies to certain foods—corn, wheat, seafood, chocolate—and if I ate any of those I broke out in painful hives and my face swelled grotesquely. Elizabeth, now six, entered first grade in the post school. Mary was busy running the house, playing bridge and quilting, an activity she took up at Fort Leavenworth and continued with skill for many years. I joined a poker club, which met one night a week and, continuing my conservative style of play, was a consistent winner.[6]

Fort Benning was a hunter's paradise. It abounded with quail and pheasant. In October, I stored my golf clubs and got out my guns. I bought a young liver-colored, white-spotted purebred English setter for sixty-five dollars and named him "Tip." With the help of a trainer, Sergeant Thomas Tweed, and his assistant, Sergeant Sinclair, Tip quickly became one of the finest bird dogs in Georgia, if not the whole United States. I teamed with another Fort Benning hunter, Master Sergeant Charles B. Copass, bought an ancient Model A Ford and converted it to a hunting wagon for hauling dogs, guns, camping gear and game, and we relentlessly hunted over most of South Georgia, seldom failing to get the generous legal daily bag of twenty birds.[7]

At the conclusion of my first year at Benning, I received the highest possible personal honor. George Marshall selected me to relieve Ralph Kingman as chief of the weapons section. I was thus elevated in status (but not rank) to a level with Joe Stilwell, Forrest Harding and Dr. Stayler, and became one of Marshall's four chief assistants at the Infantry School. Joe Stilwell wished me well. As I departed his section, I was somewhat apprehensive about how he would grade my efficiency report. He was notoriously restrictive, seldom grading any but the most outstanding officers "Superior," a cause of much resentment then—and throughout his later career. I felt lucky when I received an "Excellent."[8]

Our fifteenth Academy class reunion was scheduled for June 1930. I took accumulated leave, and Mary and I drove to West Point for the occasion. It was our first major class get-together, and a high percentage of the Class of 1915 managed to attend with wives in tow or towing. Owing to the vagaries of assignments—the Army life—I had not laid eyes on most of my classmates since graduation. We all had a grand time getting reacquainted, meeting wives, seeing and/or hearing about children.

It was not a happy time in the nation or the U.S. Army. The Depression was full upon us, with all its misery and tragedy. The greatest nation on earth had been brought to its knees. In Washington, the cry was "economize in government." The Army, as usual, suffered in the budget cutting. Force levels were held to about 138,000 officers and men, and funds for aircraft, mechanized vehicles (tanks, armored cars), ammunition and new weapons were almost nonexistent. In those dark days, when almost every family in America was struggling to survive, and the possibility of war seemed as remote as the moon, money for a standing army seemed an absurd luxury.

Some of our reunion talk was speculation about who would be the new Chief of Staff of the Army, replacing the retiring chief, Charles P. Summerall. Douglas MacArthur, then serving in the Philippines, was frequently mentioned. But he appeared to have too many strikes against him: he was too young (fifty), he had been involved in a highly publicized divorce, he was not favored by Pershing—and Pershing was still a power behind the scenes. However, a few months later, President Herbert Hoover chose MacArthur. Our classmate Ike Eisenhower, then serving in the War Department, was detailed to be MacArthur's amanuensis—secretary and ghostwriter for speeches and reports.[9]

Back at Benning, I took over my new duties as chief of the weapons section, feeling the cold blue eyes of George Marshall on the back of my neck. He said little or nothing to me about my new duties—when he gave a man a job, he let him alone—but I was inspired to do my absolute utmost.

Traditionally, when the school term opened, the other three sections (tactics, logistics, history and publications) spent a day briefing the other staff instructors on the functions of the sections and what each intended to achieve with the students in the school year. The weapons section had always been excluded from these sessions because it was assumed that weapons, being second nature to all Army officers, required no elaboration, it was all old hat, and the firing ranges were not easily accessible. I disagreed with this concept and forthrightly told Marshall. My section had much that was new to show off, and I thought it would be worthwhile to stage an outdoor demonstration for the staff. He agreed and allotted my section one morning—four hours—for a comprehensive outdoor show.

The plan I conceived and the decision I made with respect to that demonstration were among the soundest and most important of my peacetime career. We planned to stage fourteen separate "events" within the allotted four hours, busing the staff from one range to the next. It would be a very tight squeeze: about ten minutes for each event, including travel time. I calculated that if each individual weapons expert gave a briefing, it would take too much time. I decided I would introduce the expert, give the briefing myself and invite questions of the expert.

When the big day came, my section staff of thirteen officers and dozens of enlisted men was primed and ready. The instructors—and Marshall —climbed aboard the buses and we sped off to the events: direct and indirect laying of machine-gun fire, firing at a moving target with a 37-mm field gun, mortar firing, Browning automatic rifle demonstration, and so on. As we drove from event to event, I conducted the briefing and when we arrived at a new event, I introduced the expert on the weapon, inviting questions. (There were none.) The exercise was carried out without a single discernible flaw in a mere two and a half hours! When Marshall debarked from the bus he said, "Bradley, that's the best demonstration I ever saw. I want you to give it to every class that comes to Fort Benning."[10]

I made at least one other favorable impression on George Marshall that fall. One of the students in the advanced class was a standout, Walter Bedell Smith. Born in Indianapolis in 1895, Smith had attended Butler University in Indianapolis, but when his father fell ill, he was forced to withdraw to help support the family. He had joined the National Guard at a young age. When the United States entered World War I, he rose to first sergeant and later, after specialized training, was commissioned a second lieutenant in the infantry. He fought with the 4th Division in France and was wounded and hospitalized. After the war he elected to remain in the Regular Army.

At Benning I had organized a trapshooting range. Bedell Smith had come out to shoot and we became friends. I was quite taken with this young captain; he had an absolutely brilliant and analytical mind. Outwardly he was brittle, like Stilwell, a bit of a Prussian, and brutally frank. Offstage, he was genuinely modest, shy, humorous and kind. After I got to know him fairly well, I concluded he would make a fine instructor and I put in a formal request with the front office that, upon graduation, Smith be assigned to my section.

One day Marshall dropped into a classroom (as was his habit) while student Smith was presenting a monograph on an assigned subject. It was a brilliant presentation; Smith could express himself easily and well, both orally and in writing. Marshall returned to his office, where I happened to be, and said of Smith: "There is a man who would make a wonderful instructor and I'll bet no one has asked for him." By that time, my official request for Smith had reached Marshall's office and when he looked into the matter that day, he found it. No words were exchanged between us, but I was elated. I had "discovered" Smith before he had![11]

In mid-October of that year, 1930, an event occurred that we hoped would mellow and "humanize" Marshall: he remarried. His new wife was Katherine Boyce Tupper Brown, the widow of a businessman, Clifton S. Brown, who had been murdered two years before by an associate. Katherine, who had once been an aspiring actress, had three children. Marshall met her at a friend's house in Columbus the year before and was instantly smitten. On October 15, they were married in her home town, Baltimore. General Pershing was Marshall's best man.[12]

After the Marshalls returned to Benning, there were a number of social occasions to introduce Katherine Marshall to the post and to Army life. We were all very pleased to find that Marshall had made an outstanding choice. Katherine was charming and gracious; it was obvious that they were deeply in love. But the hoped-for mellowing in the colonel did not occur. He remained his same formal, aloof self. After the initial festivities, we seldom saw the Marshalls socially.

Toward the end of the school year, in early May 1931, I received news from my stepfather that my mother had had a stroke. On May 22, I was granted a ten-day leave "under exceptional circumstances" and took a train to Moberly. Mother—then fifty-six—was very ill and seemed unlikely to recover. I remained in Moberly as long as possible—visiting mother, relatives and friends—then returned to Fort Benning by bus on June 2. Mother died at home a few weeks later of another stroke, on June 23. She was buried in Log Chapel Cemetery alongside Father and Raymond. Subsequently, my stepfather moved from Moberly and I never saw him again.[13]

By that summer of 1931, George Marshall had served four years as assistant commandant at Benning. By regulation, it was time for him to move on to troop duty. But his presence at Benning was so manifestly valuable that special arrangements were made to extend his tour through the school year 1931–32. Administratively he was detached to the all-black housekeeping 24th Infantry Regiment at Benning, but he continued to serve as assistant commandant of the Infantry School, an arrangement profitable to all concerned. At the end of that school year, 1932, he was relieved as assistant commandant by Colonel C. W. Weeks.[14]

Marshall served briefly as commanding officer of a 400-man infantry battalion at Fort Screven, Georgia, near Savannah, and was then appointed senior instructor of the Illinois National Guard in Chicago. This last assignment came about on the personal recommendation of Chief of Staff Douglas MacArthur, who wrote: "He has no superior among Infantry colonels." Marshall believed (as did many of us) that this assignment would be a serious setback to his chances of moving up the ladder to high command. He appealed directly to MacArthur for reconsideration, but MacArthur let the orders stand, assuring Marshall that the job, owing to problems facing the Illinois National Guard, was of great, perhaps critical, importance to the Army.

In my opinion, Marshall should have been promoted to general and assigned to Washington to serve the Army in some high capacity on the General Staff. But there was no love lost between Pershing and MacArthur, and Marshall was a "Pershing man." Moreover, MacArthur, then and later, had a penchant for surrounding himself with low-caliber sycophants and yes-men. Marshall, ever candid and forceful, would not have suited MacArthur.

Many believe that Marshall's assignment to the Illinois National Guard was a slight that planted the seeds of a Marshall-MacArthur feud that would increase in intensity over the years. I am not in a position to know firsthand whether this is true or not. Marshall never confided to me his innermost thoughts on MacArthur or anything else. The assignment may have rankled more than Marshall let on, he may well have resented MacArthur on a personal basis. But he was not a man to harbor a personal grudge. I feel certain that no "feud" developed between them that colored Marshall's conduct of World War II to the extent of deliberately denying MacArthur men and supplies (as some MacArthur adherents claimed) or, later, led to Marshall's decision to recommend that Truman fire MacArthur during the Korean War.[15]

As we commenced my last year at Benning (1932–33), I had to give serious consideration to my next assignment. My record as a student at Benning and at Fort Leavenworth qualified me for consideration as a candidate for the Army War College, the last—and highest—rung on the Army's peacetime school ladder. Secretary of War Elihu Root had initially established the Army War College to serve the General Staff, providing it various war plans and studies for consideration. There was a growing belief that if another war came along, War College graduates would be assigned as headquarters or field staff officers rather than line officers, or troop commanders. When I discussed the matter with Joe Stilwell, who had refused to put in for the War College, preferring troop duty to staff duty, he said, "Brad, why would you go to school and prepare yourself for a job you don't want?"

He had a good point. Not only that, I knew that George Marshall had been relegated to staff duty and denied a troop command in France in part because of his extended staff education at Fort Leavenworth. Often Marshall had expressed to me—and others—his deep regret over not having a troop command in combat. But Forrest Harding advised going to the War College. No matter what the future held, it was good background and was beginning to carry weight in the selection of general officers. Harding was applying for the course. Thus for some weeks I was torn. Finally I decided to apply. I had grown professionally with each of the Army schools I had attended. I felt certain that if a war came I could wrangle my way back to troop duty. Colonel Weeks approved my application.[16]

Upon completion of my tour at Benning, Mary and I looked forward to a long summer leave in Moberly. But our plans were dashed by a program of the new President, Franklin D. Roosevelt. As part of his effort to put people to work and get the country back on its feet, he persuaded Congress to create the Civilian Conservation Corps. This was a program to employ thousands of idle young men in forestry work—planting trees and protecting certain land from floods and erosion. The Army was assigned to mobilize, organize and administer the 250,000-odd men who were expected to enter the CCC. All leaves were canceled. Joe Stilwell could not even get a short furlough to see his son graduate from West Point. The Army was not happy at being saddled with the CCC.

Men signed up for the CCC in droves, in the end, about 300,000. They were organized into 1,330 Army-like companies. Fort Benning became a focal point of CCC activity; the base was flooded with CCC applicants, almost all black. I was placed in command of six all-black companies, men who had arrived from the poorest farm areas of Georgia and Alabama. We organized them, issued clothing, established pay accounts (the CCC men were paid thirty dollars a month, in contrast to the twenty-one dollars a private in the Army received), gave them physicals and a couple of weeks "training," then shipped them to camps in the field. Some of these men had not had a square meal for at least a year.

The Army's magnificent performance with the CCC in the summer of 1933, undertaken so reluctantly, was one of the highlights of its peacetime years. It all ran with clockwork precision; the CCC itself was judged first rate. It was a good drill for us, like the rapid mobilization of 1917—and another rapid mobilization that, unknown to us, lay only seven years ahead. It also helped our budget crisis. Roosevelt and Congress were dead set to slash the Army's budget 33 percent. After a heroic defense on MacArthur's part, in which he emphasized the Army's role in the CCC program, overall the Army budget was cut by only 11 percent. Even so, this was a tough reduction. It all but halted new aircraft, tank and weapons development and drastically curtailed training within the Regular Army, the National Guard and the Reserves. In terms of combat readiness, the Army was reduced to the lowest ebb in its modern history.[17]

By this time, the banks had closed and we had reached the pits of the Depression. As one money-saving measure, Roosevelt decreed that all Army personnel must take one month on "payless furlough." In other words, our annual pay would be docked by one month; we were expected to continue working through the "payless furlough." The pay cut was spread through the twelve months of the year. My monthly paycheck was reduced to $290, but we were fortunate compared to the vast majority. With the various benefits provided by the Army—housing, medical and dental care, discounted groceries and other items at the commissary and the PX—our standard of living was not substantially curtailed. Our one great financial inconvenience and restriction was the payback on the loan to cover our stock market losses.

We prepared to leave Fort Benning with a mild feeling of disquiet and loss. These had been four wonderful and constructive years. I had not only participated in a revolution but had made or renewed and cemented many friendships with infantry officers who would play leading roles in the years ahead: George Marshall, Joe Stilwell, Bedell Smith, Joe Collins, Matt Ridgway, Pink Bull, Buck Lanham, Forrest Harding and scores of others. The Marshall years at Fort Benning have been flippantly described as his "nursery school" for the generals of World War II. One industrious historian has calculated that no less than two hundred of the students and staff during Marshall's reign at Benning became generals in World War II. Equally important, I think, was the imaginative training Marshall imparted to the countless hundreds of junior officers who passed through the school during his time and who would lead—often brilliantly—the regiments and battalions under the command of those generals.[18]

NINE

In 1933, Washington was a sleepy, distinctly Southern city. The Army War College was located at Fort Humphreys (later renamed Fort Lesley J. McNair), a sylvan setting on the Potomac River. There were no student quarters at the War College. Mary and I rented an apartment in the northwest section of the city within an easy streetcar commute of the college.[1]

The War College only faintly resembled a "school." It was more like a graduate seminar or a contemporary think tank. We eighty-four students were divided into teams of about a half-dozen men and assigned specific broad-gauged topics to research. When we had mastered the material, we then made a formal presentation on our topic to the whole class, which was then invited to respond critically. Between these presentations, we were treated to general lectures on a variety of topics (economics, diplomacy, etc.) by visiting government luminaries or civilian experts from industry or academe.

There was very little pressure. We were not graded on our work; there was no class standing to be achieved, no one of importance to impress. There was little distinction between students and faculty. Many in our class did not take the work seriously, and often the quality of the presentations reflected that attitude. The War College no longer supplied real war plans to the General Staff, nor were we permitted access to actual plans the General Staff generated. We had to content ourselves with composing theoretical or hypothetical war plans with whatever "intelligence" we could glean from open sources, such as newspapers, periodicals and books. It was not very realistic, and often I thought I was wasting my time.[2]

The student reports ranged far and wide. One group was assigned to study Hitler, then rising to power in Germany. In its presentation, the group told us Hitler could be discounted because he was mentally unstable. Another group war-gamed the operation of a half-million-man field army in the Philippines. I found that lecture valuable background later in the European war. Our group drew a series of unglamorous topics relating to mobilization of the U.S. Army in time of crisis. I chose to give one presentation Fort Benning style, without notes.

As part of a well-intentioned but largely futile effort to keep the War College students physically fit, authorities organized a softball team, which played during the lunch hour. Classmate Ernest N. Harmon remembered that it was a "champion" team, with many future military celebrities: Bradley, pitcher; Navy Captain William F. (Bull) Halsey, shortstop; Jonathan M. (Skinny) Wainwright, umpire. I pitched only briefly. When the authorities saw how few hits I was allowing (thus defeating the goal of exercising the men) I was barred from the mound.[3]

So we passed a quiet, uneventful year in the nation's capital. We went sightseeing—visiting the Capitol, Washington Monument, Arlington Cemetery, Smithsonian Institution, Mount Vernon and other historical points of interest. On February 6, 1934, we were invited to a large reception for senior Army officers in the area at the White House and met President and Mrs. Roosevelt in a receiving line. We ourselves entertained very little, but Mary often played bridge with the Army wives. Elizabeth, now ten and enrolled in the nearest public school, was so good a student she was moved ahead a half-grade.[4]

While my War College cohorts and I played at mythical war games, Roosevelt and his brain trust launched the radical New Deal economic recovery programs. Although I had never voted and like most Army officers considered myself apolitical, I was in sympathy with most New Deal measures because, like my father, I always pulled for the little man, worker or farmer. Of course, I faulted Roosevelt in one area. He had been Assistant Secretary of the Navy in Woodrow Wilson's administration and was still blatantly pro-Navy. While slashing the Army budget, he launched a new Navy shipbuilding program that grew ever larger through the Depression years. Meanwhile, the Army remained static.

In the spring of 1934, when Mary and I were discussing what duty I should request upon completion of the War College, an old friend and skeet-shooting companion from my teaching tour at West Point, Colonel Simon B. Buckner, contacted me in Washington. He had just been named commandant of cadets at West Point. He asked if I would be interested in a job—a senior position in the tactical department. The suggestion appealed to the teacher in me. It would be an opportunity to influence a large number of cadets over a long period of time. Mary had always preferred duty at West Point to any other post. The post elementary school and the recreational facilities would be excellent for Elizabeth. As a senior major (ten long years in grade), I would be assured of fine quarters.

We said yes.

West Point had grown considerably since our last tour in 1924. There were big new academic buildings and cadet living quarters, a huge new cadet mess hall, an ice skating rink, a new hotel (the Thayer) and a post school for staff dependent children. Other new buildings were under construction. The new gothic structures of gray granite had been carefully designed to blend with the old. West Point has often been criticized for looking like a grim, gray penitentiary with gray-clad inmates. To me, it was—and is—a place of unparalleled beauty and solidarity. I again felt like I was coming "home."[5]

In the ten years I had been gone, West Point had slowly swung away from the reactionary regime of Fred Sladen toward a more liberal outlook. To help insure the swing in that direction, Chief of Staff Douglas MacArthur had appointed Major General William D. Connor superintendent. This is not to say the Academy was now a hotbed of political liberalism or socialism. To the contrary, it was still, by the standards of the New Deal 1930s, staunchly conservative and still basically an engineering school. But the curriculum was manifestly far broader than it had been in my cadet days and in much closer touch with the realities of the world outside.[6]

The mission of the department of tactics, to which I was assigned, remained the same as it always had been. It was "to develop character, soldierly manhood, loyal discipline, gentlemanly conduct; to build physical strength, stamina and the coordination necessary for prolonged and arduous field service and to instruct every cadet in combat principles . . ." In sum, we were to discipline the cadets and teach them to be soldiers.

During the scholastic year, we "tacs" had of necessity to confine our military indoctrination of the cadets to classroom, drill or riding halls. We taught them fundamentals: weapons, small-unit maneuver and the like. Drawing on my long experience at Fort Benning in the weapons section, I made certain the cadets in my charge received a thorough indoctrination in all weapons, including machine guns, mortars and artillery. I introduced sand tables, similar to those I had made in Hawaii, to help them better visualize and understand terrain problems.

But our best work was done in the summer months with the new first classmen. The War Department (perhaps MacArthur himself) had decreed that first classmen would spend most of the summer touring real military installations where maneuvers were conducted and weapons were fired for their benefit. This junket included several weeks at Fort Benning and Fort Monroe, Virginia, a center for coast artillery and anti-aircraft study and development, and two weeks at an Army Air Corps base for indoctrination into the mysteries of military aviation. These summer tours were not universally approved, because they took the first classmen away from summer camp and beast barracks, and left the hazing to the yearlings. They were discontinued in 1939.[7]

During these four years at West Point, we graduated about 1,100 cadets. These were men who would serve as junior officers in World War II and Korea. Some of them rose to high rank later, in the Vietnam era.

To name only the most prominent, all of whom reached four-star rank: William C. Westmoreland, Creighton W. Abrams, Jr., Bruce Palmer, Jr., Andrew J. Goodpaster, Jr., John L. Throckmorton. Westmoreland and Abrams rose to be Chief of Staff of the U.S. Army, successively, during the years 1968 to 1974. Goodpaster became superintendent of the Military Academy.[8]

I knew these outstanding cadets well. It pleases me to know that I had some influence on them. In his memoirs, Westmoreland (who was cadet first captain in the class of 1936) recalled:

> For any commander, trying to anticipate the enemy's moves is an essential preoccupation. The need had been stamped indelibly on my mind during my cadet days by a tactical officer, a major with quiet, sympathetic manner, patient in counseling his young charges, who later became one of the nation's few five-star generals: Omar Bradley.
>
> As a first classman-to-be on summer maneuvers, I commanded a battalion defending a hill. Against my ill-conceived defenses, the opposing troops succeeded. As the cadet battalion continued the maneuver, the umpire, Major Bradley, waited for me beside the road on horseback. As acting battalion commander, I too was riding. As I came abreast, he summoned me to join him.
>
> "Mr. Westmoreland," he said, "look back at that hill. Look at it now from the standpoint of the enemy."
>
> Turning, I became aware for the first time of a concealed route of approach that it was logical for an attacker to use. Because I had failed to cover it with my defense, he as umpire had ruled for the attacking force.
>
> "It is fundamental," Major Bradley said calmly but firmly, "to put yourself always in the position of the enemy."[9]

As in any Army outfit, there were constant changes in the tac department—departures, new arrivals, promotions. In 1936, Commandant Simon Buckner moved on to other duty, and the next-senior man, Dennis E. McCunniff, routinely moved up to be commandant of cadets. That same year, in July, I was promoted to lieutenant colonel, having been a major for twelve long years. As second in command of the department under McCunniff I assumed additional duties as training officer.[10]

I made one significant change in the training of the cadets from which I am certain they benefited. That was to abolish some of the absurdly close by-the-book supervision they were heretofore compelled to endure from tac officers. I put more responsibilities on their shoulders. For example, once when the first classmen were ready to pack and leave a summer camp, one of my officers brought me an elaborate plan for this operation, detailing how each company tac officer would supervise the dismantling of camp, storage of tents and so on. I tore up the plan and said, "No. I don't want a single officer in that camp. Turn it over to the cadet officers. You can go over later and see if they did it right. Let them learn to make decisions for themselves." Of course, the cadet officers carried out this simple task properly, perhaps better than with strict supervision. I would hope that the tac officer who drew up the plan also learned a lesson that helped him later in his career.[11]

Shortly after my promotion, I noted that George Marshall—still serving with the Illinois National Guard in Chicago—was promoted to brigadier general, a long overdue recognition for his services to the Army. There was more to this promotion than met the eye. Under the Army's complicated promotion, seniority and retirement system for senior officers, it meant that Marshall had just made it under the wire for eligibility for further promotion and, someday perhaps, consideration as Chief of Staff.

I wrote him a letter of congratulations. His reply is one of my most prized possessions:

> I found your letter of congratulations on my return from leave. Thank you very much for writing as you did. I especially appreciate what you had to say, because you rank at the top among my Army contacts who have displayed the highest efficiency.
>
> I very much hope we will have an opportunity to serve together again; I can think of nothing more satisfactory to me.[12]

In my last year at West Point, 1937–38, McCunniff, who had served out his four-year tour, moved on to other duty. In the normal course of events I would have moved up, as McCunniff had, to be commandant of cadets. But the commandant's job was somewhat "political," a special niche, often sought by ambitious officers. Our superintendent, General Connor, was retiring in midyear, and a new man—Brigadier General Jay L. Benedict—would be taking over. It turned out that Benedict preferred to name his own commandant of cadets.

That appointee was my classmate Doc Ryder, who was also a lieutenant colonel and senior to me by five files. There was some natural resentment among the younger tac officers who were loyal to me and felt that I deserved a shot at the job, even if briefly. But I honestly didn't care. I was perfectly happy to be number two. I thought Ryder a good choice. He was a handsome, dashing figure, a hero of the war in France, still carrying the shell fragments imbedded in his back.[13]

During these four years at West Point—1934 to 1938—there were ominous developments abroad. The comically pompous Benito Mussolini, dictator of Italy, successfully "invaded" Ethiopia. Adolf Hitler, assuming dictatorial powers in Germany, had launched a massive rearmament program—land, sea and air—and in the following year, 1936, his troops occupied and annexed the Rhineland and then blatantly supported fascist forces in the Spanish Civil War. In the Far East, the bellicose government of Japan, also arming at an alarming pace, made no secret of its designs on China, ravaged by prolonged civil war, and seemingly ripe for plucking. These military adventures abroad gave the Army a little more clout in the halls of Congress. In 1936, legislators increased the Army in size to about 167,000 men, a very welcome addition, although still terribly inadequate. The West Point Corps of Cadets expanded proportionately to about 1,800 men.[14]

In the spring of 1938, when Hitler staged his bloodless coup and absorbed Austria into the Third Reich, and the Japanese rampaged through China, the Bradley family faced yet another move. There was not much choice this time. I had had four years with "troops" (as the West Point tactical department was classified); there were no more schools for me to attend. My "mobilization assignment" was the War Department General Staff. I had never served on the General Staff. Inasmuch as my superiors had deemed me "ideal" for such an assignment, that was where we were ordered: Washington.[15]

In later years some writers would observe that I had the air of a schoolteacher. Perhaps this was not without good reason. Counting my one year at Brookings in South Dakota, my four years on the Fort Benning School staff and my two four-year tours at West Point, I was in fact officially a teacher for thirteen of my first twenty-three years of commissioned service. I might add that it is not a bad way to learn your profession thoroughly.

TEN

That summer of 1938, the War Department and the General Staff were a minefield of political intrigue. On the very highest level, the Secretary of War, Harry Woodring, and his number two, Assistant Secretary of War Louis Johnson, were at swords' points. Woodring, onetime Democratic governor of Kansas, was a dovish Midwest isolationist. Louis A. Johnson, a big gruff West Virginia lawyer with powerful roots in the American Legion, was a bull-in-the-china-shop hawk with unbounded political ambition. Those two rarely agreed on anything and had no personal relationship. Caught in no man's land was the Army's lame-duck Chief of Staff, General Malin Craig, who had replaced MacArthur in 1935 and who would retire on September 1, 1939.

One of the pressing internal political issues was who would replace Craig as Chief of Staff. The question was complicated by various Army Regulations and laws regarding age, seniority and remaining length of service before mandatory retirement. One of the five possible candidates was George C. Marshall, who had been ordered to the General Staff at the same time I was ordered to Washington. Marshall was then serving as chief of the war plans division, but was already being groomed to succeed General Stanley D. Embick as deputy chief of staff. In a moment of rare accord, both Woodring and Johnson agreed that Marshall was the most qualified man for Chief of Staff. But Marshall's appointment was far from a foregone conclusion; he had competition in other quarters. Woodring and Craig were hesitant to bring him on too quickly—to jump Marshall over generals senior to him. However, Louis Johnson typically resolved all that. One day in Woodring's absence, he ordered Craig to relieve Embick and to promote Marshall to deputy chief of staff.[1]

Although I cannot say I approved of the insensitive way Johnson handled the matter, I was pleased to see that Marshall had at long last received the recognition he had earned and so richly deserved. As deputy chief of staff, he was still responsible to the outgoing General Craig (as well as Woodring and Johnson), but he was now in position to apply his talents to the major issues confronting the Army, and it appeared that he now had the inside track to Chief of Staff.

We rented a very comfortable two-story brick and frame house in the northwest section of Washington. It was within an easy commute to the War Department, which was then in process of moving into the rambling old World War I "temporary" Munitions Building on Constitution Avenue, near the Lincoln Memorial. It was also convenient to Western High School, where Elizabeth enrolled as a junior that fall. The house had a large fenced backyard where Tip and one of his offspring, Mollie, whom Elizabeth had adopted as a pet, could exercise and bury bones.[2]

I was assigned to what ordinarily would have been the least glamorous and taxing of the General Staff divisions, G-1 (personnel). However, owing to the ever-worsening world situation, the long-standing, long-ignored questions of the size and makeup of the peacetime Army were once again arising, this time with a sense of urgency. My new boss, Brigadier General Lorenzo D. Gasser, one of the finest administrators I have ever known, was then attempting to deal with these formidable and politically delicate questions for Craig. I was detailed to become one of Gasser's principal assistants.[3]

As we have seen, beginning in 1936, the fortunes of the U.S. Army took a modest turn for the better. In the following year, 1937, after Japan had launched full-scale war against China, and Roosevelt had been inaugurated for a second term, the Army grew to 178,000 men. In the spring of 1938, after Hitler annexed Austria and threatened Czechoslovakia, the Army expanded slightly again—to 185,000 officers and men. When I reported to G-1 in June 1938, General Gasser, at General Craig's request, was refining plans to increase the Army by another 40,000 men in 1939—to a total of 225,000. (That was still 55,000 men short of our legal authorization by the National Defense Act of 1920.)[4]

In September 1938, three months after I reported for duty in Washington, Hitler, allied with Italy's Benito Mussolini, launched his political takeover of Czechoslovakia. The first step was a demand that a portion of German-speaking Czechoslovakia, the Sudetenland, be turned over to the Third Reich. Meeting in Munich with Hitler and Mussolini, Britain's Prime Minister Neville Chamberlain and France's Premier Edouard Daladier, linked by military treaties but powerless to stop Hitler, not only agreed to his infamous demand but also helped persuade the Czechoslovakian government to accept the settlement. Chamberlain returned to England and declared that the Munich Pact had brought "peace in our time." The free world—the U.S. Army General Staff in particular—was shocked and shaken by this act of appeasement. I personally believed that a European war with Hitler was now inevitable, merely a matter of time.[5]

More than any other single factor, Munich jarred Washington into a realistic reappraisal of U.S. military forces and provoked our mobilization for World War II. During the next month, and continuing all through the fall of 1938, President Roosevelt conferred frequently with his principal military advisers, assuming a hawklike stance. From the outset, what worried Roosevelt most (as it had Chamberlain and Daladier) was Hitler's superior—and rapidly growing—air power. In fact, Roosevelt dramatically opened this series of meetings by demanding the United States gear up to produce 24,000 planes a year! This unreasonable and militarily lopsided demand was deflected—or indefinitely deferred—but out of these secret talks at the White House emerged an unequivocal message: Military mobilization, with the heaviest emphasis on air and sea power, was to proceed without delay. The decisions reached were not altogether satisfying to General Craig (and his deputy, Marshall, who attended the White House meetings), but at least the work had begun.[6]

One direct result of these meetings was that our G-1 office, already thinly staffed, was buried in paperwork. For one solid year my cohorts and I responded to ever-changing requests from General Craig or Marshall for this personnel mobilization plan or that. We drafted proposed new congressional legislation for force levels and money, and dealt with a hundred other related items. Through it all, General Gasser was clear-headed and unflappable. From him I learned a great deal about how to properly organize and deal with a Niagara of paperwork. I also learned a great deal more than I cared to know about military manpower legislation.[7]

In the spring of 1939, as Hitler predictably enlarged his hold on Czechoslovakia to include the whole nation, rumors about who would succeed General Craig as Chief of Staff were flying thick and fast. It was said that Woodring was vacillating on Marshall and looked with equal favor on a well-qualified contender, General Hugh Drum. Rumor had it that Marshall had not endeared himself to Roosevelt in the White House meetings by forthrightly opposing the President's lopsided aircraft production proposals and that the President might not find Marshall acceptable. There were further rumors that Marshall's health might disqualify him; he had an old thyroid condition that caused an irregular pulse and fatigue. Craig himself seemed to be torn between Drum and Marshall, or at least unable to recommend one man over the other.

The White House ended the suspense on April 27, 1939, when the President announced his selection: George C. Marshall. Some of the senior generals were not pleased, but among the officers of my rank and age (I was then forty-six) there was universal agreement that Marshall was by far the best possible man for the job.[8]

Marshall officially took over the duties of Chief of Staff on July 1, 1939, while Craig went on terminal leave. A week later he walked down the hall to see my boss, General Gasser. Within my hearing, Marshall said to Gasser, "I'm sorry, but you've got one man in your section I want." Gasser looked at Marshall and said, "I suppose you mean Bradley?" Marshall replied, "Yes."

I cleaned out my desk and moved down the hall to an outer room in the Chief of Staff's office. Typically, Marshall had not previously discussed the transfer with me, nor did he ever mention it thereafter. Of one point I was certain. This would be the most challenging opportunity of my career. If I did well, I could almost certainly count on a bright future in the rapidly expanding Army.

General Marshall was in the process of reorganizing the entire General Staff—abolishing sections, weeding out dead wood—to make it a tauter, more efficient administrative machine. One of his early steps was to name my former boss, General Lorenzo Gasser, deputy chief of staff. Gasser, as Marshall later said, assumed about 75 percent of the routine or "normal business," leaving Marshall free to concentrate on the pressing problems of mobilization and rearmament.

Within his own small inner office, there was what was known as a "secretariat," a mini-staff whose job it was to receive the massive upward flow of staff studies and papers, decide what Marshall should see or what should go to Gasser, then distill the papers for Marshall to a single typed page and present them orally each day for decision or action. The senior man on the secretariat was Colonel Orlando Ward (Class of 1914), whom I had known at West Point, a fellow Missourian who had served with Pershing in Mexico and in France as a cavalry officer and had become a tank expert. Officially, Ward—scholarly, intelligent, reserved—was *the* secretary of the General Staff.

Ward was authorized two assistants. One was Lieutenant Colonel Stanley R. Mickelsen, an anti-aircraft artillery expert who had entered the Army from St. Paul, Minnesota, in 1917 as a Reserve second lieutenant and had made the Army a career. He was a graduate of the Command and General Staff School and the Army War College. Among other talents, Mickelsen was a whiz at statistics.

I was the other assistant. Technically Mickelsen and I were designated assistant secretaries of the General Staff. In practice, we and Colonel Ward functioned as an interchangeable team, with no distinction as to rank or job; and, when feasible, all three of us were on hand for the presentations to Marshall.[9]

I had worked closely with Marshall at Fort Benning for three years. I knew his wife, Katherine, and his stepchildren. I knew he valued my judgment and professionalism. And yet I was still in awe and some fear of the man. I was never at ease when I made a presentation. No matter how well I knew my subject, he was apt to ask pertinent questions on something

I didn't know. I was almost certain to be tripped up every time. Often he would become angry at my failings. Never shouting-angry, merely icy cold and withdrawn. He kept all of us keyed up to a nerve-racking degree.[10]

At the end of our first long, busy week on the job, Marshall asked the three of us—Ward, Mickelsen and me—to report to his office. He said coldly, "I'm disappointed in all of you." We were stunned and dismayed. Orlando Ward, ashen-faced, managed to utter, "*Why,* sir?" Marshall replied, "You have not disagreed with anything I've done all week." I assumed the role of defense counsel. I assured Marshall that nothing had come through the office that week we disagreed with and, if it had, we surely would have pointed it out to him. Still he seemed vaguely dissatisfied.

Several days later, a staff study arrived which all of us thought had glaring weaknesses, and in our presentation we pointed them out. Marshall seemed pleased. He almost smiled when he said, "Now, *that's* what I want. Unless I hear all the arguments for or against an action I am about to take, I don't know whether or not I'm right. If I hear all the arguments against some action and still find in favor of it, I'm *sure* I'm right."[11]

The mounting flow of paper in Marshall's office soon became so heavy the three of us were not able to digest all of it and confer before our presentations. That meant I had to pay very close attention when Ward or Mickelsen was presenting a matter foreign to me. Once, after such a presentation by Mickelsen, Marshall turned to me and said, "Bradley, what do you think of that?" Based only on what I had heard from Mickelsen, I fired from the hip. "I don't like it, sir." There was a pause. I held my breath, and then Marshall said, "I don't either." I had never been one to make snap judgments, but the pressure of the work now demanded it.[12]

Daily we generated a large number of outgoing letters for Marshall's signature. I was not any better at letter writing than I was at speech making. Neither was Ward or Mickelsen. The result was that Marshall rewrote our letters with his pen at his desk. Not once did we manage to get a letter by him unedited. The three of us agreed that this was not only humiliating but a great waste of our time and, more important, the Chief of Staff's time. What we needed was a man who could put words together in a way that satisfied Marshall.

I remembered Bedell Smith, the bright young captain I had "discovered" at Fort Benning. Ward and Mickelsen agreed with me that Smith would be the perfect man for the job—and he was available. I was nominated to suggest to Marshall we take on Smith. After I had made my case, Marshall said, "Smith? I don't know him." This was another example of Marshall's most glaring weakness: his inability to remember people's names. As tactfully as possible, I reminded the general about Smith—how impressed he had been with him at Fort Benning—but I'm not certain he remembered him. In any case, Bedell Smith was ordered to the secretariat on my recommendation. But he never did carry out the letter-writing job he was recruited for. Marshall appointed him a liaison officer to the White House and Treasury Department and to other duties. Smith would soon go on to far greater responsibilities.[13]

Marshall often delegated to the three of us confounding and difficult problems to solve—and he wanted the solutions instantly. One day he called me into his office, handed me a great sheaf of papers and said, "Fix this." I left, scanning the top sheet, which summarized the problem. Raw rubber, a vital war material, was already in critically short supply. To help alleviate the shortage, a scheme had been arranged to ship rubber seeds from Southeast Asia to Brazil, a "good neighbor," where they would be planted. The gist of the problem was that the shipment of seeds had been stalled in Panama and they were about to go bad. Marshall had succinctly scrawled the solution at the bottom of the page: "Fly them to Brazil in B-17 bombers."

A tall order, I thought, a *very* tall order. It was so tall I knew routine channels would be wholly inadequate. I carried the paper down the hall to the office of the newly appointed deputy chief of staff for air, Major General Henry H. (Hap) Arnold, my classmate at Fort Leavenworth. As usual in those days, Arnold's outer office was jammed with people waiting to see him on urgent business. I went through a back door directly into his inner office. As luck would have it, Arnold was in conference with Juan T. Trippe, a Pan American Airways founder and executive. Knowing that Trippe had pioneered commercial aviation in South America and might well know the location of Brazilian airfields that could accommodate B-17s, I interrupted the conference and laid out the problem to both men. Trippe, of course, was immensely helpful, and within no time at all the matter was settled. Arnold gave the necessary orders to get the B-17s in motion, and he resumed his talks with Trippe. Proud as a peacock, I returned to Marshall's office to report the problem solved. Only twenty minutes had elapsed since he gave it to me. My reward for this performance was a grunt and a nod. He expected no less of us.

As we grew accustomed to our jobs, Marshall directed us not only to make recommendations but also to assume responsibilities and make independent decisions. Some of these turned out to be quite delicate. One night he handed me the service record of a major who had served under him and said, "If it does not violate Army policy, I would like this man to go to the War College. But study his record. The decision is yours." I took the record home that night. On the whole, it was poor, not good enough to qualify him for the War College. But there was one "Superior" rating, signed by Marshall! Clearly the officer had greatly impressed the general at some point in his career and Marshall wanted to bring him along. Nonetheless, I decided he was not War College material and I would so tell Marshall. I was so troubled I had nightmares all night—I was pursued by wildcats. The next day I said to Marshall, "Sir, I have studied this man's record and I recommend he not be sent to the War College." Marshall's face clouded in anger. He fixed me with his steely blue eyes and snapped, "What are you doing coming in here making a *recommendation?* I told you the decision was yours!" I hesitated a moment, gathered my courage and said, "Yes, sir. He does not go."[14]

Although there were days when we believed we might drown in the trivia of the chief's office, Marshall himself kept his mind clearly focused on the overriding problems facing the U.S. Army. Despite a little gain here, a little gain there, the Army (which then included the Air Corps) was still absurdly small and ill-equipped. Marshall was firmly convinced that Europe would soon erupt in a war with Hitler and that the United States would ultimately be drawn into the conflict. Given free rein and a blank check, he would have ordered all-out (but orderly) manpower mobilization and war production in the summer of 1939.

But, of course, Marshall had no such powers. To the contrary, there seemed to be days when he had no power at all and the Army still had too few friends in the right places. Roosevelt's growing hawkishness expressed itself in terms of sea and air power: more ships, more planes. Marshall's repeated requests within the administration for building up the Army, the National Guard and the Reserves fell on deaf ears. Funds for tooling up to produce new weapons (the Garand semi-automatic rifle, medium tanks, artillery pieces, for example) were denied. The Regular Army, the National Guard and the Army Reserves hobbled onward, producing exquisitely detailed expansion plans for the files.

Then suddenly war came in Europe. On August 23, 1939, less than two months after I had assumed my new duties in Marshall's secretariat, Hitler signed a nonaggression pact with Russia's Joseph Stalin. A week later, September 1, Hitler's forces invaded Poland, followed shortly thereafter by Stalin's troops advancing into Poland from the east. Great Britain and France declared war on Nazi Germany. The French Army, believed by many (including the U.S. General Staff) to be the finest in the world, mobilized behind the "impregnable" Maginot Line. Britain made hasty preparations to send an expeditionary force to the Continent. And so began the greatest conflict in the history of the world.[15]

Washington was stunned by the swiftness of the onset of war and by the crushing power and brutality of the Nazi blitzkrieg in Poland. On September 8, Roosevelt declared an equivocal "limited" state of national emergency; Marshall sent out an "alert" to our pitiful far-flung Army. In the days and weeks thereafter, Roosevelt, assuring the nation that "I hate war," that U.S. armies would not be sent to Europe, and that the United States would remain strictly a neutral (as required by the Neutrality Act), grudgingly authorized minor increases in Army ground forces: the Regular

Army to 227,000 men (still 53,000 short of the 1920 authorization); the National Guard to 235,000 (215,000 short of the 1920 authorization).[16]

Then, abruptly, anticlimax. Hitler appeared satisfied with the conquest of Poland, Stalin's forces invaded then bogged down awkwardly in Finland. The "phony war" set in and the tension in Washington ebbed.[17]

Mary's mother, Dora Quayle, who had been living with us or the Stewarts for the last two decades, died at age sixty-nine on the day Great Britain and France declared war on Germany—September 3, 1939. She was visiting the Stewarts in Dayville, Oregon, when she passed away. Mary's sister, Jane, accompanied her body to Moberly. The service was conducted by the Reverend C. W. Cornn, of the Central Christian Church. She was interred in the Quayle plot at Oakland Cemetery alongside the grave of her husband, Charles, whom she had survived for thirty-seven years, and our infant son. Owing to the pressures in Washington, neither Mary nor Elizabeth nor I was able to attend the funeral service. She left a small inheritance (her two houses in Moberly and some stocks), which was divided equally between Mary and Jane.[18]

In the fall of 1939, while the uneasy "phony war" settled over Europe, the U.S. Army General Staff hammered out our budget for 1940. It was assumed that the lid was off, that for the first time in twenty years the Army might be given manpower and hardware commensurate with the threats facing the country. The staff was unrestrained in its internal demands: More, more, more. Perhaps never in the history of the U.S. Army had so many officers labored so long with typewriters and charts. Each day an Everest of paper rose on our desks. We worked deep into the nights, digesting and analyzing, preparing our presentations for Marshall.

The Chief of Staff walked a tightrope. There was a widespread isolationist sentiment in the nation, with powerful representation in the Congress. Almost every day this element of our society demanded assurances that the United States would not be dragged into a European war, "phony" or real. It was possible that if the Army demanded too much too soon, the isolationist bloc in Congress might be provoked into cutting our budget to shreds, leaving us in a more vulnerable position than ever. Besides that, the Army still lacked support in the White House. While he was unstinting in support of the Navy and the Air Corps, which was gradually becoming semi-autonomous, Roosevelt seemed unwilling or unable to face up to the urgent needs of the foot soldier.

There was another significant political problem. The Woodring-Johnson feud had steamed to a boiling climax. Louis Johnson tried to oust Woodring and take his job, utilizing anonymous press "leaks" to discredit Woodring and enhance his own image. The overall effect of the leaks was to make a mockery of the Army's civilian leadership at a critical moment in its history. It was an embarrassment to us and to the White House. And yet Roosevelt, quixotically, refused to resolve the conflict. One result was that the full load of Army leadership fell on Marshall's shoulders, when he himself did not yet have the full confidence of the President and was still an unknown quantity on Capitol Hill.

Marshall's decision on the Army budget was not one he liked, but under the circumstances he had no other choice. The Army would not now seek large-scale mobilization. It would keep its profile and requests reasonably low. Marshall's primary objective was to get enough money from Roosevelt and Congress to fully equip the modest force levels already authorized (227,000-man Regular Army; 235,000-man National Guard) and lay the groundwork for further industrial expansion later in the year. He correctly believed that after winter Hitler would make another move in Europe; and when he did, both the President and Congress would be more amenable to further expansion of the Army. The dollar figure finally settled on within the administration was $853 million.

As was customary, Marshall presented the budget first to the House Appropriations Committee on February 23, 1940. I accompanied him to provide facts and figures for his testimony, but my presence was unnecessary. Marshall had total and magnificent grasp of the Army's military posture and needs. He frankly told the members of the committee that he believed the budget to be inadequate, but he did not ask for further increases. He hoped that Congress would let the budget stand as it was. He warned that further requests might come in the near future with this oft-quoted metaphor: "If Europe blazes in the late spring or early summer, we must put our house in order before the sparks reach the Western Hemisphere."

The House cut the budget only 10 percent, but before the document reached the Senate, Europe blazed. On April 9, Hitler unleashed his blitzkrieg to the west, overrunning Denmark and invading Norway. A month later the Nazi juggernaut smashed through the Low Countries and into France, going around the Maginot Line and hounding down a dispirited and shockingly inept French Army. The Dutch fell in five days; the Belgians, despite British and French help, in nineteen days. On May 27, the badly mauled British Expeditionary Force began evacuating in small craft from Dunkirk, leaving its equipment on the beaches. On June 10, Italy invaded France from the south and the Germans occupied Paris. On June 22, France capitulated and signed an armistice. In a mere two and a half months, Hitler's Luftwaffe, panzers and infantry had conquered Western Europe and now threatened an invasion of Great Britain.[19]

Militarily, the Nazi forces had operated with awesome efficiency. The coordination between air and ground, tanks and motorized infantry, exceeded anything we had ever dreamed of in the U.S. Army. We were amazed, shocked, dumbfounded, shaking our heads in disbelief. Here was modern open warfare—war of maneuver—brought to the ultimate. To match such a performance, let alone exceed it, the U.S. Army had years of catching up and little time in which to do it.

I saw that with my own eyes in May, as the Nazis crunched through the Low Countries and France. That spring, the small standing U.S. Army, mobilizing into the new "triangular" divisions, staged various corps-level infantry maneuvers, the first in years. Marshall designated me to escort Senators Henry Cabot Lodge, Jr., of Massachusetts and Rufus Holman of Oregon to the maneuvers in Louisiana, May 19 to May 22. Apart from the undistinguished and unimaginative leadership displayed by the generals conducting the maneuvers, we saw the urgent need in infantry divisions for more tank and anti-tank units, armored vehicles, more powerful and mechanized artillery (including anti-aircraft weapons) and a dozen other major items. The "close air support" by Air Corps fighters was a joke. Of thirty-four air missions requested by the ground commanders, only two were carried out.[20]

My work had now become so demanding I only gradually realized that in two brief years Elizabeth had all but grown to womanhood. After her junior year at Western High School, she had transferred to a private girls' school in Washington, Holton Arms, for her senior year. I got back from the Louisiana maneuvers just in time for her high school graduation ceremony. I was very proud of her. She was now a striking, tall blue-eyed blonde, with exquisite manners, a becoming modesty and a deep Christian faith. She had decided she would go away to college in the fall, to Vassar. Ordinarily that would have overburdened a lieutenant colonel's budget, but Mary and I had had considerable luck on the stock market over the past ten years. We had paid off our 1929 debts and had netted much beyond. Vassar seemed a prudent investment in Elizabeth's future.[21]

A few days after Elizabeth's graduation, Mary and I took three days' leave, June 8 to June 11, to attend an important school event of our own: the twenty-fifth reunion of the West Point Class of 1915. When we gathered, the Germans were in Paris and the French capitulation was only twelve days away. Winston Churchill had replaced Chamberlain as Prime Minister of Great Britain and was exhorting his countrymen with magnificent oratory to prepare for and throw back an invasion, while he pled with Roosevelt, privately and publicly, for help. It was the darkest of times; it seemed inevitable that we lieutenant colonels of the Class of 1915 would soon be moving up to positions of higher responsibility, leading forces against Hitler on the battlefields. But none of us dreamed that we would go as high or be saddled with as much responsibility as that which shortly befell many of us.[22]

Later in the summer of 1940, while Hitler launched an all-out air and U-boat war against England, hoping to force surrender without invasion, the public mood in the United States shifted strongly in favor of the Army

—as Marshall had predicted. The modest budget Marshall had submitted to the House emerged from the Congress almost three times greater in size. Each day major new bills were introduced to provide us more aircraft, tanks, vehicles, guns, ammunition. There was growing sentiment to call up the National Guard and establish a Selective Service System—the draft. Marshall wisely decided to lie low on the manpower mobilization and let others champion the Guard call-up and draft. He concentrated his energies instead on meeting the equipment deficiencies that the spring maneuvers and the Nazi conquests had brought to light and which would have to be urgently remedied in the event of a rapid mobilization.

To the vast relief of the entire Regular Army, Roosevelt finally took action with respect to the Army's civilian leadership. He first eased out Woodring, then Louis Johnson, and brought in a whole new team. He named Colonel Henry L. Stimson Secretary of War. Stimson, who had held the same post under William Howard Taft eons past, was then seventy-two years old, but his mind was still tack-sharp, and he brought immense prestige and long experience in government service to the office. To replace Johnson, Stimson named Judge Robert P. Patterson assistant secretary. Within a few months, Patterson would be retitled Undersecretary of War, to make room for two new assistant secretaries, John J. McCloy, a New York lawyer who was an expert on intelligence matters, and Robert A. Lovett, a Wall Street banker who had been a Navy pilot in World War I and who would concentrate on Air Corps procurement matters. In time, I came to know all four men well. The Army could not have asked for better civilian leadership.[23]

We in the secretariat were privy to many top-secret matters that crossed Marshall's desk. Among the most secret and intriguing were the daily hand-carried documents from the Army signal corps. These were—I learned to my utter astonishment—decryptions of encoded Japanese military and diplomatic radio traffic. During the 1930s, U.S. Army and Navy codebreakers, working in a rare display of interservice cooperation, had broken several Japanese codes. In the early years, the work accomplished was fairly primitive, but as time went on the geniuses involved became more proficient and their output more meaningful and useful.

In the late summer of 1940, as I later learned, the codebreakers, led by the Army's Colonel William F. Friedman, probably the world's leading expert in the field, achieved a major scientific triumph. They broke the high-level Japanese diplomatic code "Purple." It took some time to properly organize sufficient radio intercept stations, train Japanese translators and other personnel, but we soon had a continuous and incalculably valuable "ear" into the highest levels of the Japanese government.

The output from Purple was the Army's most closely held secret. Each day a signal corps officer delivered copies of decoded Purple messages to Stimson and Marshall and three other top-level men in the War Department. After Marshall had read these messages (and we underlings had quickly scanned some of them) they were collected by the signal corps and burned. Much of the information in these raw messages was obscure and, to me, almost meaningless and often confusing. At times, there was almost too much to digest. But, here and there were clear, priceless nuggets of Japanese military and diplomatic future plans, extraordinary insights for Marshall and others who read them. However, time and events —notably Pearl Harbor—would prove that the Army failed to properly exploit Friedman's remarkable achievement. That would be rectified in due course; and the output of Purple and other codebreaking would play a vital role in the defeat not only of Japan but of Nazi Germany.[24]

Europe continued to blaze furiously in the summer and fall of 1940. Hitler maintained the aerial blitz and U-boat war against England and absorbed Hungary and Rumania into the Third Reich. The Russians gobbled up the Baltic States: Lithuania, Latvia, Estonia. There was fear in the General Staff that Hitler had designs on Latin America, which was virtually defenseless and a constant source of worry. In late September, Japan joined Nazi Germany and Italy in a Tripartite Pact, becoming a full partner in the Axis.[25]

In Washington, outside pressure to call up the National Guard, Army Reserves and to institute a draft continued to mount. Although Stimson was publicly committed to conscription, Marshall continued to lie low, still leery that the anti-draft isolationist bloc in Congress might succeed in emasculating the Army's budget by one legislative device or another. But Marshall—and Roosevelt, now committed to running for a third term—had badly misjudged the public mood. The fires in Europe had kindled a martial spirit at home. In late August and September, Congress, responding to public sentiment, enacted legislation to call up the National Guard and Army Reserves and to begin inducting men through the Selective Service System.

A gigantic mess ensued. Despite all the years of planning—the files bulging with mobilization plans—the Army was simply not prepared to assimilate such vast numbers of new manpower. There were no organized basic training camps for draftees. Recruits were sent directly to existing or organizing Regular Army units for basic training, even though those units might be engaged in maneuvers. The Guard units—organized on paper into eighteen divisions—were ill-equipped and in some instances so ill-trained that the officers in charge had not the slightest idea of their jobs or how to train the men in their units. There was as yet no equipment for the newly recruited men. The much-publicized photos of recruits carrying broomsticks for rifles or using stovepipes to simulate artillery—and the slogan "Hurry up and wait"—were all to the point.[26]

When I reflect on those frenetic days in the summer and fall of 1940,

I often shudder at some of the antiquated precepts that underlay our thinking. The quaintest by far was the notion that after we had trained a force of four field armies (over a million soldiers), Marshall himself would lead it, perhaps to Europe, as Pershing had led the American Expeditionary Force to France in 1917. In fact, on July 26, 1940, we actually established a Pershing-like GHQ at the Army War College (which was closed for the war), bestowing a second hat on General Marshall as commanding general. He had been stuck in a staff job against his will in World War I, but this time he would command troops in the field, as a proper general should.

We proceeded on a limited basis to staff the GHQ. As his chief of staff to be, Marshall named one of the Army's finest officers, Brigadier General Lesley J. McNair (Class of 1904). McNair was an artilleryman who had served with Pershing on the Mexican border and on his GHQ staff in France. Most recently, he had been commandant of the Command and General Staff School at Fort Leavenworth. McNair had a razor-sharp mind and was much respected throughout the Army. He was ideally placed as chief of staff of GHQ. McNair brought in Mark Wayne Clark as one of his chief assistants.

As the war expanded worldwide and the U.S. Army grew to millions upon millions of men, the quaint GHQ concept soon faded away. McNair's outfit was converted to the main headquarters for training American soldiers and renamed Army Ground Forces, General McNair commanding. In this way, McNair was given responsibility for the training of every ground soldier in the U.S. Army in World War II. A genuine unsung hero of the war, he inherited a mess in the fall of 1940 and performed magnificently right up to the day he met a tragic fate in Normandy. Thanks to McNair, the GI of World War II was far better trained than the doughboy of World War I, or any previous war in our history.[27]

ELEVEN

With Europe blazing out of control and our Army expanding, however shakily, I began to get itchy feet. I was an infantryman, not a staff officer, and I was determined not to get stuck in a staff job for the duration of the war. I was loath to leave Marshall's staff. Each day, however hectic or demanding, was a fascinating challenge and education, but I had now been in the War Department two and a half years. It was time to think about moving on to a troop command, where professionals were desperately needed.

One day we had a visit from Brigadier General Robert L. Eichelberger (Class of 1909), whom Marshall had recently appointed superintendent of West Point. Our careers had briefly overlapped at West Point in 1934–35, when Eichelberger was adjutant to the superintendent and secretary of the academic board. He was not only an outstanding infantry officer but also a broad-gauge intellectual. (He had preceded Orlando Ward as secretary of the General Staff.) As he waited in the outer office to see Marshall, we chatted briefly. Then he said, "How'd you like to be commandant of cadets?"

I thought that over carefully. There was no promotion in it; it was a lieutenant colonel's slot. I would be relieving my classmate Doc Ryder, which might be considered a step backwards, or at least sideways. On the other hand, it was a one-way ticket out of staff duty and back to command of troops (the tactical department and Corps of Cadets), as well as a considerable honor and an opportunity to influence men who would probably soon be company commanders in combat and the future leaders of the Army. I said to Eichelberger, "Yes, sir. I would like that." During his meeting with Marshall, Eichelberger asked for me, and I was delighted when Marshall approved my new assignment.

Several days later, Marshall said to me, "Bradley, are you sure you want to go to West Point?" I gave him my reasons for accepting the job. He glanced idly out the window and then said, "How'd you like to have Hodges' job?"

My heart went to my throat. Courtney H. Hodges was now a brigadier general and commandant of the Infantry School at Fort Benning. I did not hesitate a second. I said, "Sir, that's a new situation. I would much prefer Hodges' job." Marshall said, "All right. Bring in Bryden and we'll fix it up."

Bryden—Major General William Bryden—was deputy chief of staff of the Army, having relieved General Gasser. I fetched General Bryden and escorted him to Marshall's office, walking on clouds. Marshall thereupon directed that Bryden put the incumbent chief of infantry, George A. Lynch (whose tour was drawing to an end), on terminal leave, promote Courtney Hodges to major general and chief of infantry and issue orders for me to relieve Hodges at Benning. Neither man said a word about promoting me. I assumed that would be discussed after I left the office. But I had no idea what new rank I would receive.

Two days later, on a Sunday, I awoke at home from a nap with a severe earache. I telephoned the duty officer at Walter Reed Army Medical Center to ask what I might do to relieve the pain. The duty officer turned out to be an old friend from West Point and (as I knew) an ear specialist. He strongly suggested I get in my car and come at once to Walter Reed so he could have a look at my ear. I did. He diagnosed mastoiditis, gave me some drops and ordered me to check into the hospital the following day.

I was dismayed. Mastoiditis! Did that mean an operation? A mastoidectomy? No, it did not. The doctor gave me a new drug, sulfa. It turned out I was allergic to sulfa and I came down with severe hives. My face swelled like a balloon. Day after day dragged by. I began to seriously worry about my new assignment to Fort Benning. They would not order a sick man to the job. There was a good chance I might lose everything.

On the thirteenth day—February 15, 1941, three days after my forty-eighth birthday—I finally talked my way out of the hospital, promising to work only half a day. A week later, February 23, I was ordered to Fort Benning to be both commandant of the post and commandant of the Infantry School. By then, I felt fine again, and Mary and I, Tip and Mollie (Elizabeth was at Vassar) set off in the Hudson. When we reached Benning two days later, there was a telegram from the War Department waiting. It said I had been promoted to brigadier general (temporary) and the promotion had been duly approved by the U.S. Senate. I had half suspected this honor, but the reality of it floored me. Five years a lieutenant colonel, never a colonel, now a general, and the first man in my class to make it![1]

What seemed equally hard to believe was that I—until that day a mere lieutenant colonel—was relieving Courtney Hicks Hodges. For countless years Hodges had been to me an august figure like Marshall and a man I admired almost equally. From this point forward in my story, our careers would be closely intermingled; ultimately Hodges would command one of my armies in the defeat of Nazi Germany. As such, he was on a par with

George Patton, but owing to his modesty and low profile, he has been all but forgotten.

Born on January 5, 1887, in the hamlet of Perry, Georgia, Hodges had entered West Point in 1904 at the age of seventeen. He was not well grounded academically and after one year he was "found" in math and compelled to resign. He was so devoted to the Army that he re-entered as a private on November 5, 1906. Hodges was so clearly a natural soldier and leader that in 1909—only one year behind his former West Point classmates—he was commissioned a second lieutenant from the ranks, a singular honor and achievement in those pre–World War I Army days. He served in the Philippines and then with Pershing in Mexico, chasing Pancho Villa.

Like MacArthur, Hodges was a hero of World War I in France. He shot up through the chain of command to command a battalion in the 5th Division, with the temporary rank of lieutenant colonel. As such, in the waning days of the war, he boldly led a scouting expedition across the Meuse River and punched into the main German defense lines. His outfit, pinned down for forty grueling hours, became the spearhead of an attack which put the Americans across the Meuse in force. For his "fearlessness and courage," Hodges was awarded the Distinguished Service Cross, as well as the Silver Star and the Bronze Star with three battle stars.

I first met Hodges during my tour at West Point, 1920–24. He was then a major serving in the tactical department; and as such, ironically, he was a profound inspiration for the very corps that had earlier rejected him. He may well have been the first non–West Point graduate ever to teach tactics to the cadets. He was my idea of the quintessential "Georgia gentleman" and the most modest man I had ever met. A crack shot from childhood, he was then—and for years thereafter—the Army's star in the national rifle matches. We served together again at Fort Benning in the early 1930s during the Marshall regime, Hodges as a member of the infantry board. Marshall had enormous regard for Hodges. In 1933–34, Hodges and I were classmates at the Army War College. Thereafter, Hodges returned to the Philippines for another tour as a senior commander with Douglas MacArthur (and his assistant, Ike Eisenhower), who was military adviser to the Philippine President Manuel Quezon.[2]

That day at Fort Benning when I relieved him, Hodges could not have been more courteous or helpful. He arranged my swearing-in ceremony to brigadier general, standing aside as Mary pinned the one-star insignia on my collar. After a change-of-command ceremony and parade, he left for his new—and important—job as chief of infantry in Washington. Fort Benning with all its headaches and opportunities was mine.

By the time I assumed my duties at the Fort Benning Infantry School in early March 1941, the U.S. Army, augmented by draftees, the National

Guard and the Reserves, had grown to well over a half-million men. The existing mobilization plan called for an Army force level of 1.4 million men by June 30, a figure that was, in fact, met. The total number would include about 100,000 officers of all ranks.

It had long been assumed by the Army planners that there were sufficient numbers of well-trained junior officers in the National Guard and Reserves (mostly ROTC graduates) to meet the requirements of large-scale mobilization. It was further assumed that after these officers had received concentrated training in small- and large-unit maneuvers and a refresher course at the Fort Benning Infantry School, they would be "seasoned" and ready. But Marshall had never really believed any of this. He correctly foresaw that too many National Guard junior officers would be inadequately trained or otherwise unfit, too many Reserve officers would be siphoned off for the Air Corps or other non-infantry duties, and the infantry—and other branches as well—would find itself with a severe shortage of junior officers.

Early in the mobilization planning, Marshall had proposed that the Army establish special schools for the rapid training of junior commissioned officers recruited from the existing enlisted ranks or from the ranks of draftees with six months of basic training. They were to be called Officer Candidate Schools—or OCS. Marshall believed, correctly, that the draft would net many men qualified in leadership and other abilities to warrant commissioning. Moreover, he argued, it would be salutary for the morale of the draftees to know that officers were being chosen from their ranks. But his G-1 (personnel) section on the General Staff and the chief of infantry, George Lynch, had adamantly opposed OCS for a variety of reasons and disbelieved Marshall's contention that a critical shortage of junior officers would occur in the infantry.

By the time I reached Benning, a sort of gold-plated prototype OCS had been established by Courtney Hodges, mainly to pay lip service to Marshall. There were only two classes, and these were poorly organized and instructed. The men taking the course were elitist draftees or volunteers, graduates of Ivy League colleges, many of the students scions of distinguished or wealthy American families. Courtney Hodges, who also was cool to the OCS concept, had told me that it was pointless to think in terms of expanding OCS, that not another man could be shoehorned into Fort Benning's badly overcrowded facilities.

I shared Marshall's view that an OCS, or some form of it, would be essential to fill the junior officer ranks in the expanding Army. For several weeks I studied the problem, then I drew up a sort of assembly-line plan that would enable us to expand the Benning OCS program twenty-fourfold without exorbitant expense or the need for large numbers of skilled instructors, who were everywhere in critically short supply. I took my plan to Washington and presented it to Hodges—now chief of infantry—and to

G-1. Because of the widespread underlying prejudice against OCS in general (the graduates had already been derisively tagged "ninety-day wonders"), I got nowhere until I decided to go over everybody's head and take the plan directly to Marshall. He was impressed—and pleased—and promptly gave the plan a green light.

The Fort Benning OCS became the model, or prototype, for all future OCS's, carefully studied and copied by representatives from the other branches. The school turned out countless thousands of junior officers who went on to fill the infantry ranks in Europe and the Pacific. I consider the founding of the Fort Benning OCS my greatest contribution to the mobilization effort. I'm happy to say it still exists.[3]

There were two other major activities afoot at Fort Benning that interested me enormously and which, as post commander, I supported to the fullest extent possible. These were the formation and training of new tank and airborne combat units, which were very nearly revolutionary in character.

As we have seen, tanks had been tragically neglected by the U.S. Army between the wars, owing principally to severe budgetary limitations. Following the Nazi blitzkrieg in the Low Countries and France, in July 1940 Marshall established the armored force at Fort Knox, Kentucky, founded with two paper divisions, the 1st Armored, based at Fort Knox, and the 2nd Armored, based at Fort Benning. The 2nd Armored Division was commanded by Charles L. Scott, a fifty-seven-year-old cavalryman (and superb equestrian) from the Class of 1905. His 2nd Armored Brigade —the "Iron Fist" or "Sunday Punch"—of the division went to Colonel George S. Patton, who, like other old tankers, had rushed to the new command.

Patton was the driving force and spirit behind the creation of the 2nd Armored Division. He began with a cadre of ninety-nine officers and 2,200 men and fleshed out the division with draftees. One man Patton tried hard to recruit into the division was Lieutenant Colonel Dwight D. Eisenhower, an erstwhile tanker in World War I who had met Patton then but did not get overseas. Ike was eager to serve with Patton, but he was trapped in a staff job at Fort Lewis, Washington, and shortly thereafter moved to another staff job. I have often wondered how Ike's life might have turned out had he been available at this point to answer Patton's call.

By the time I came on the Benning scene, six months later, the 2nd Armored Division was a going concern. Patton and I were closely associated at Fort Benning for a period of almost one year. It was during this time I first got to know him well. Thereafter our professional lives would become interwoven in war. He would be my boss; then in a kind of Greek drama, I his. As a result I probably knew Patton as well as any man.

Patton was the scion of rich and aristocratic forebears. His father's ancestors were Scots who settled on large estates in Virginia in the late 1700s. His great-grandfather had been a governor of Virginia. His grandfather—a VMI graduate—commanded a regiment in the Confederate Army and died of battle wounds. His widowed grandmother and his father —also a VMI graduate—moved to California, where his father, a lawyer-businessman-politician, managed vineyards and wineries and made a fortune. On his maternal side, Patton descended from an officer who fought in the Revolutionary War and later became speaker of the Tennessee House of Representatives. His maternal grandfather, Benjamin D. Wilson, migrated to California, married a wealthy Mexican, and became one of the founders of the orange industry, planted the first large vineyards, and also amassed a fortune. Upon the death of his first wife, Wilson remarried, and a daughter of this second marriage married Patton's father, merging the two large California fortunes. George, born in California on November 11, 1885, was raised by cultured, educated parents and sent to private schools. He vacationed on the various family ranches, where he became as proficient on a horse as any cowboy.

There was never any doubt about what George Smith Patton, Jr., would be in life: an Army officer. At eighteen, he entered VMI. A year later, in 1904, he received an appointment to West Point. No cadet was ever more ambitious to excel, to be a great soldier. He was cadet corporal, sergeant and adjutant. He tried out for football but failed to make the team. He won a letter in track and field. He was set back one full year for academic failures and graduated in about the middle of the Class of 1909. He naturally chose the cavalry. He married Beatrice Ayer, daughter of a wealthy Boston businessman; they had two daughters and a son. The incomes from the Patton and Ayer families probably made George the richest officer in the U.S. Army. The Pattons had horses for riding, racing and showing, and a string of thoroughbred polo ponies. Everywhere, they had the highest social connections.

As a soldier, a professional officer, Patton was the most fiercely ambitious man and the strangest duck I have ever known. He appeared to be motivated by some deep, inexplicable martial spirit. He devoured military history and poetry and imagined—in the spirit of reincarnation—that he had fought with Alexander the Great, Genghis Khan, Caesar, Napoleon. He dressed as though he had just stepped out of a custom military tailor shop and had his own private bootblack. He was unmercifully hard on his men, demanding the utmost in military efficiency and bearing. Most of them respected but despised him. Although he could be the epitome of grace and charm at social or official functions, he was at the same time the most earthily profane man I ever knew. I sometimes wondered if this macho profanity was unconscious overcompensation for his most serious personal flaw: a voice that was almost comically squeaky and high-pitched, altogether lacking in command authority.

Like Douglas MacArthur, Patton was a born publicity hound, a glory seeker. Before the war, he participated in horse shows, racing and polo because, as he wrote, it was "the best sort of advertising." In 1912, he amassed newspaper clippings by entering the Olympic Games in Stockholm, competing in a pentathlon of pistol shooting, swimming, fencing, steeplechasing and cross-country foot racing. (He finished fifth against forty-three contestants.) He wrote obsessively candid self-congratulatory (or self-abnegating) letters and diaries, which have recently been edited and published in two volumes. Reading these volumes was one of the most astonishing literary experiences of my life. It would seem that no thought George ever had in his life—however trivial or magnificent—went unrecorded, that his sense of greatness and destiny demanded a full accounting to the public.

On the Mexican expedition, Patton had made a deep and favorable impression on General Pershing. When Pershing left for France, he recruited Patton as a headquarters aide. George chafed in this rear-area assignment. His destiny demanded he be at the front, facing the enemy and death. Pershing offered him command of an infantry battalion, but instead, Patton asked for—and got—command of our embryonic tank corps, being fielded with the help of British and French tankers. Patton led this glamorous new force—out front all the way—in the battles of St. Mihiel and Meuse-Argonne, achieving conspicuous success, much publicity, a Distinguished Service Cross and Medal, a battle wound which temporarily hospitalized him and a battlefield promotion to full colonel.

Patton returned a hero, convinced that the tank had revolutionized warfare. He urged a separate corps for tankers and other grandiose schemes. But the amended National Defense Act of 1920 put the tank corps under the infantry, and it fell into disarray. Then Congress reduced appropriations for tank research and development to a pittance, and for too long a time the Army completely neglected tank warfare. Discouraged by these developments, reduced in rank like all of us, Major Patton returned to the cavalry and spent the peacetime years in schools and routine assignments, such as that in Hawaii when we first met. The outbreak of war in Europe and the creation of the armored command in 1940 saved Patton—then going on fifty-five years old and still only a colonel—from retirement.

That year, Patton's division, staging out of Benning, participated in two major maneuvers: Carolina-Tennessee in the spring, Louisiana in the fall. In both maneuvers, Patton broke all the old-fashioned rules, smashing his mechanized forces ever onward with dazzling speed and surprise. He was criticized by the umpire-generals for his unorthodoxy, for leaving his command post and prowling the "front line," for running his division "roughshod" over the "enemy." But it was clear to anybody in the U.S. Army with the eyes to see that we had on our hands one of the most extraordinary fighting generals the Army had ever produced. He was not much concerned with details—logistics were and would remain a mystery to him, and he improvised war plans as he went along—but if you wanted an objective or a favorable headline, Patton was clearly the man for it.[4]

After the Louisiana maneuvers, Patton was named to the biggest tank combat job in the Army, commander of I Armored Corps. He moved his tank corps to a desert training center out west. I was sorry to part company. In our year together at Fort Benning I had learned a great deal about mechanized warfare from him. After his departure, he wrote me: "Dear Omar . . . During our service together I never was associated with anyone who more whole-heartedly and generously cooperated with everything we worked on together."[5]

Equally impressive to me during my tour at Fort Benning were the experiments in airborne warfare. The Germans had utilized this revolutionary concept—"vertical envelopment"—in the Low Countries with remarkable success, landing both paratroopers and glider-borne troops with complete surprise. Their extraordinary success (especially the capture of key bridges over the Maas and Waal rivers) spurred the British and the U.S. Army to create airborne units. In June 1940, the U.S. Army established an airborne test platoon (some forty-eight men) at Fort Benning. The platoon set up a tent camp near Lawson Field and used an abandoned corrugated iron hangar for training and parachute packing. Great emphasis was placed on physical fitness: one full hour per day of calisthenics, tumbling, hand-to-hand combat, plus forced marches and a daily three-mile run. Three months later, this unit was increased from platoon to battalion size. A noted Army athlete, forty-two-year-old Major William M. (Bud) Miley, a champion gymnast from the Class of 1918, who had served with me in the West Point tactical department, was placed in command of the battalion, known officially as the 501st Parachute Infantry Battalion.

When I was still working in Marshall's office in Washington, Bud Miley had appeared one day looking somewhat gloomy. He needed help from the quartermaster corps—all kinds of supplies and equipment—to get his battalion in operation; and he was getting nowhere, mired in red tape. Knowing that Marshall was very much in favor of the experiment, I said, as Miley later recalled, "Well, Bud, let's see what we can do to help." I took him to see the proper people, and he left the War Department "with twice as much" as he needed. In this small way, I helped push along our fledgling airborne unit.

By the time I arrived at Benning, several months later, Miley had done wonders. He had built two 250-foot parachute towers, based on the amusement rides at the 1939 New York World's Fair. He had erected double-decked wooden barracks for his all-volunteer force (mostly athletes) and scratched out a jump field. Three Air Corps C-47 aircraft had been assigned to Lawson Field to be utilized for training jumps. The War

Department had authorized two additional battalions, the 502nd and 503rd, for 1941. Miley's men, whom I inspected shortly after my arrival, were a breed apart—the toughest, best-trained infantry I had ever seen.

Later in the year, spurred by the larger German airborne operations in Greece and on Crete, the Army established at Benning what was known as the "Provisional Parachute Group"—in effect, a substantial expansion of Miley's embryonic facility. It was the Army's first "jump school," to train paratroopers for the rapidly expanding airborne forces of three battalions. Lieutenant Colonel William C. Lee, who had been pushing the airborne concept in the General Staff and who is generally conceded to be the "father" of the Army's airborne forces, came to Benning to command the group. His plans and training officer was Major James M. Gavin, a brilliant young officer who had joined the Army as a private in 1924 at age seventeen, and who subsequently had gone from the ranks to West Point, Class of 1929.

By the fall of 1941, Lee's outfit had activated a fourth battalion and established a full-fledged parachute school. Hundreds of volunteers reported to the school and the individual battalions. The sudden influx of men imposed a nearly fatal strain on the facility. There was a critical shortage of everything: housing, aircraft, jump fields, ammunition, communications gear, even parachutes. Lee survived the expansion by resourcefulness and cunning. Wherever possible, we—the Fort Benning staff—gave him support, whether authorized by the War Department or not. I took great pride in pinning on the parachute insignia of the school graduates. In my association with Miley and then Lee, and other officers at the facility, I suffered through the airborne's growing pains and, in the process, learned a great deal about its promise—and limitations.

The limitations were severe. Aircraft had to be obtained from the Air Corps, which was not overly enthusiastic about transporting soldiers around, especially behind enemy lines. Drop zones had to be chosen with extreme care and the indifferent Air Corps pilots indoctrinated on the correct approach and precise point of drop. Since paratroopers could not bring in heavy weapons or large amounts of ammunition or food, they had no "staying power." They could only be utilized in special situations where the main forces could smash through and link up in a matter of a day or so, otherwise they would be chewed to pieces or forced to surrender. In violation of all military precepts, tradition and training, paratroopers would be expected to fight and act individually and independently, not as small cogs in a huge machine.

For these reasons, and others, the War Department staff at first could only visualize airborne operations on the smallest possible scale. For example, seizing key bridges ahead of an advancing army before the retreating enemy could destroy them. Hence the initial limitation of airborne units to battalion size. But after the German operations on Crete—where 13,000 men, almost the equivalent of a division, had jumped—Lee, Miley, Gavin and others began to think in much larger terms: airborne regiments, airborne divisions. I shared their enthusiasm.[6]

Marshall visited Fort Benning several times while I was commandant. Fort Benning held a special place in his heart, as it did for me and all infantrymen. At Benning, Marshall could get away from the pressures of his desk in Washington, ride, hunt, and otherwise take his leisure. At the same time, he could cast an appraising eye on our production of young officers for his expanding Army. He was evidently pleased with our progress; at least he did not find fault.

On one of these visits, Marshall typically jolted me with this stark question: "Bradley, do you have a man to take your place when you leave here to command a division?"

I caught my breath. Heretofore, I had not the slightest hint that I—or any of my classmates—was anywhere near eligible for command of a division. Divisions then were going to much more senior men, the Classes of 1909 to 1912, or non–West Pointers equivalent in terms of seniority. Command of a division—the epitome for an infantry officer—also meant another star, a promotion to major general. I had only been a brigadier for six months!

Choking down my exhilaration, I managed to say, "Not yet, sir." Earlier, I had tried to recruit Lieutenant Colonel Leven C. Allen to be my number two at Benning, but the War Department turned me down. I explained that problem, adding, "Lev Allen would have been the man." Marshall nodded, saying nothing more. Not long afterwards, Lev Allen reported to Fort Benning for duty and I began preparing him to take my place.[7]

On the afternoon of Sunday, December 7, 1941, Mary and I were working in the yard pruning a flower bed. An old friend, Pink Bull, then stationed at Benning as an instructor in logistics, and his wife Betty passed by, stopped and asked if we had heard the news: Pearl Harbor had been bombed by the Japanese. Like all Americans that day, we were stunned. I immediately put on my uniform and hurried to post headquarters, where my staff was already gathering, speaking in hushed, somber tones.

In event of war, we at Fort Benning had a special duty to perform. The War Department assumed that the enemy would attempt to sabotage key facilities throughout the State of Georgia—electrical generating plants, bridges, dams—and we had orders to protect these facilities. One of my post planning officers, Lieutenant Colonel Truman C. (Tubby) Thorson, a big, tough, lean man of Scandinavian extraction, with a gift for detail and getting things done, had drawn up a document known as "Emergency Plan White" to cover this contingency. I ordered Plan White executed, and by four the following morning our troops were deployed statewide guarding the key facilities.

I realized, of course, that there was little likelihood of sabotage in the State of Georgia, that what we all of us now faced was far larger: total war with the Axis powers. The U.S. Army was far from ready for that war. Our weaknesses were still many. But when I finally got to bed and closed my eyes, I thought how lucky we were to have George Catlett Marshall as Chief of Staff. In his two and a half years in command, he had laid the necessary groundwork for us to go to war.[8]

TWELVE

In the dark days of late December 1941, when the Japanese were overrunning the Western Pacific and Southeast Asia with shocking efficiency, I received a telephone call from the War Department. The caller was Lieutenant Colonel George van Wyck Pope in G-1, whom I had first met—and admired—when I was a math teacher at West Point and Pope was in the tactical department.

Pope had long-awaited news for me. The Army was activating three new divisions from scratch: the 77th, the 82nd and the 85th. Robert Eichelberger, superintendent of West Point, would command the 77th; Wade H. Haislip, Class of 1912, then on the General Staff, would command the 85th; and I would command the 82nd. We would all receive temporary promotions to the two-star rank of major general. Of the three, I was by far the junior man—the second in my class to make two stars, the first to command a division. I could not have been more elated.

Working with Pope, I gradually pulled together my division staff. For my number two, assistant division commander, I was assigned Matt Ridgway, probably at Marshall's suggestion. Ridgway was then a colonel working in the war plans division, a specialist in Latin American affairs, but first and foremost one of the most charismatic and able young infantrymen in the Army. He was absolutely delighted to be sprung from Washington; I was lucky to get him. For my chief of staff, I asked for Richard R. Coursey, but he was deemed indispensable in his job as director of the Fort Benning OCS. It turned out that Pope himself was available for that job, and he got it. A classmate, Joseph M. Swing, a crusty disciplinarian, was available to be my artillery commander. For my adjutant and G-1, I received Ralph P. (Doc) Eaton, an enlisted stretcher bearer in France in World War I who later went to West Point (Class of 1924) and wisely chose the infantry. He and Ridgway had served together in the past and were good friends. For my G-2, I drew George E. Lynch, another West Pointer and son of the recently retired chief of infantry. For my G-3 and G-4, I was able to bring two close and able associates from Fort Benning: Willis

S. Matthews (who had been serving as my aide and alter ego) and Tubby Thorson.[1]

I now needed a new aide. I had heard about a likely candidate, Lewis D. (Lew) Bridge, who was then in the April 1942 OCS class at Benning. Bridge, son of a California grape grower, was a graduate of the University of California, an athlete who played tennis and golf well. I asked Richard Coursey, who was running the OCS operation, to look him over for me. Coursey reported that Bridge was first-rate, a fine young officer with outstanding leadership qualities. But he also recommended that I take another excellent man from the same class, Chester B. (Chet) Hansen, a Syracuse University graduate who had been editor of the university daily and who had worked for a newspaper in the summers. Both Bridge and Hansen had been drafted about the same time and had received extensive basic and advanced infantry training before going on to OCS. I gladly accepted both men, and each in his own way proved to be outstanding. Among other fine qualities, Hansen proved to be an artist at putting words together, thus filling a much-needed gap in the "old man's" skills.[2]

In late February and early March 1942, we assembled in dribs and drabs at Camp Claiborne, a new Army post outside Alexandria, Louisiana, on the Red River. My Fort Benning driver, a Louisiana Cajun, twenty-two-year-old Sergeant Alex Stoute (whom I had recruited from the school library staff), drove me down in an Army staff car. We took three dogs: Tip, Mollie and a new hunting dog I had acquired, Pete. Mary came later in a new 1941 blue and white Buick we had bought at the Detroit factory to replace the aging Hudson. When she arrived, we rented an unfurnished house in Alexandria. Since gas rationing had been imposed, I commuted to Camp Claiborne in a car pool. On base, Stoute drove me around in a fancy new division staff car, a plush Packard Clipper.[3]

The 82nd Division had first been created in World War I. It had served in France with extraordinary distinction, having spent more consecutive days in the front lines than any other American division. It fought in all the major battles: Lorraine, Saint-Mihiel, Meuse-Argonne. My War College classmate Skinny Wainwright, who was now fighting for his life with MacArthur's forces on Bataan, had been a staff officer with the division in France. But its most famous World War I soldier had been the Tennessee sharpshooter Sergeant Alvin C. York, who had single-handedly broken up an entire German battalion, for which he won a Medal of Honor. He became world famous when Gary Cooper portrayed him in the 1941 film *Sergeant York*. After World War I, the 82nd had been deactivated.

The reborn 82nd was to be a new experiment in mobilization. Heretofore, draftees had been sent directly to existing Regular Army or National Guard divisions, trained and integrated into the units. The 82nd would spring to life full-blown, almost overnight, composed of an experienced 10 percent cadre (700 officers and 1,200 enlisted men, mostly from the 9th Division at Fort Bragg, North Carolina) and about 16,000 draftees who would come to us directly from the reception centers. The challenge was large; the danger of failure, or even disaster, lay everywhere.

We knew, of course, that an army draftee's most desolate hours occurred on arrival. Only a few days away from home, family and loved ones, cast into a strange, impersonal and wholly unfamiliar world, senselessly ordered to "hurry up and wait" for this seemingly stupid reason or that, it was no wonder that depression and homesickness were commonplace. With an entire division of new draftees reporting to an organization that did not even exist except on paper, there was real danger that we might experience devastating morale problems, delaying our training and readiness, or generating the usual flood of accusatory letters to Congress, Drew Pearson and other columnists, and even to Marshall himself.

I conceived the notion—radical at the time—that we would do everything within our ability to make the draftees feel they were coming to a "home" where people really cared about their welfare. This is not to say we intended to coddle the recruits. In fact, we intended to be tough as hell on them, but in an intelligent, humane, understanding way. At the same time, we would evoke and build upon the 82nd's illustrious history, giving our conscripts the impression that they were not only coming to a home, but a famous, even elitist, one.

Most of our draftees came from Southern states—Georgia, Alabama, Mississippi, Tennessee. When the time came, Doc Eaton sent teams of men from G-1 ahead to the reception centers to greet, interview, classify and assign each draftee to a specific paper unit and duty, according to his civilian background (cook, truck driver, clerk, lineman, carpenter, plumber, etc.). When the trains backed into Camp Claiborne, we greeted each with a brass band, formed the men into their preassigned units and marched them to preassigned tents, where they found their equipment on a cot with bedding. A hot meal waited in the mess tent. We even instituted rush cleaning and laundry so that the draftees could refurbish travel-stained uniforms. This system worked so well, I'm proud to say, that General McNair gave us a hearty pat on the back and recommended that all new divisions adopt it.

The rudest shock we experienced with the draftees was the discovery that they, the prime youth of America, were generally in appallingly poor physical condition. After the war, I read many disturbing analyses about this—that a third or more of all inductees were found to be in physically poor condition. If our own experience was typical, then the analyses were valid. Some of our draftees could not walk a mile with a pack without keeling over. Most were overweight and soft as marshmallows. Only a very few were capable of the hard sustained physical exertion that we knew they would experience in combat.

We forthwith instituted a rigorous physical fitness program. Over and above daily calisthenics and sporting events, we erected an extremely difficult obstacle course, with high walls, deep ditches, log barriers, culverts, rope swings and the like. All men in the division, including staff officers and even myself, were required to participate in the fitness program, including the obstacle course. I had always prided myself on keeping fit. You can imagine my humiliation when, a month after my forty-ninth birthday, my hands slipped on the rope swing and I fell, very un-Tarzan-like, into a stinking raw sewage drainage ditch beneath it. Ridgway recalled that the "sight of a two-star general in such a predicament was a vast delight to all ranks" and that "the incident became one of the memorable highlights of the training period."[4]

In every possible way, we evoked the history of the division to build morale and fighting spirit. In this connection, it occurred to me that we ought to invite Sergeant York down to talk to the men. He readily agreed. We laid out the red carpet and staged a division review—the whole division on parade—for him. There was intense media interest in his visit. He addressed the troops and his simple, unpretentious yet inspiring words were carried live on a nationwide radio hookup.

Sergeant York was my house guest during the visit and I served as his personal escort a large part of the time. During the interludes between official events, I queried him closely on his experiences in France. One important fact emerged from these talks: most of his effective shooting had been done at very short range—twenty-five to fifty yards. As a result of these talks, I had the staff set up a short-range firing course in the woods with partially concealed cans for targets. The men had to traverse this wooded course, spot the cans and shoot quickly. It was a radical departure from the standard static long-distance firing range. When our IV Corps commander, Oscar W. Griswold, an old friend with whom I had served at West Point in the early 1920s, had a look at the course, he inquired, "Whose idea was this?" When told it was mine, he said, "I should have known that." He approved wholeheartedly.

Sergeant York's visit was a tremendous morale builder for the troops. But he surely deflated me. On his departure he told me in his candid hill-country way that I would not get very far in this world because I was "too nice."

We made good progress with the division, adhering closely to or exceeding McNair's seventeen-week training schedule. He and Griswold and others who inspected our work from time to time drafted glowing reports. I was proud of the division and looked forward to leading it into battle whenever and wherever it might be sent—Europe or the Pacific.[5]

That hope was utterly dashed when, four months after mobilizing the division, I received a personal and confidential letter from McNair. He wrote that Marshall had made the decision that I would take command of the 28th National Guard Division, an outfit that "needs help badly." McNair realized that the change would "be a disappointment" for me personally, but he reassured me that "your ability is going to be recognized in due course." I didn't know whether to laugh or cry.[6]

Command of my pride and joy, the 82nd Division, went to the best possible choice: Matt Ridgway. He brought in a young artillery officer, Maxwell D. Taylor, Class of 1922, to be his chief of staff. A month or two later, the 82nd—owing largely to its fine state of training and high morale—was designated to be the first full-scale airborne division in the United States Army and was moved to Fort Bragg for specialized training. Bud Miley, the paratrooper pioneer, became its assistant division commander. One of its new parachute regiments was commanded by James Gavin. Cadres from the 82nd Airborne Division were utilized to form our second airborne division, the 101st. We would all meet again—under far different circumstances.[7]

The mobilization of the eighteen National Guard divisions, commencing in the fall of 1940 and continuing on a gradual basis through 1941, had not been satisfactory. The Guard was shot through with state-level politics. Almost without exception, the senior commanders—the generals and colonels—were political appointees who were militarily incompetent. A high percentage of the junior officers were over-age and physically unfit. (In June 1941, a study found that 22 percent of all Guard first lieutenants were over forty.) Competent regimental and battalion commanders were almost impossible to find. McNair, who was responsible for training the Guard divisions, had to fire almost every officer in the Guard from major general through colonel, and a large percentage of the lower-ranking officers.

The situation was so bad that in June 1941 Marshall himself felt compelled to write a "frank" (but tactful) letter to all Guard division commanders, pointing out some of the grave weaknesses in the discipline and training.

McNair's experience with the training of National Guard divisions was eventually to lead him to some rather drastic conclusions. Much later in a blistering memorandum to Marshall, drafted in the spring of 1944, McNair wrote that the Guard had "contributed nothing to National Defense," that its history since mobilization "was one of unsatisfactory training, physical condition, discipline, morale and particularly leadership." He bluntly recommended that "the National Guard be dispensed with as a component of the Army of the United States."[8]

The 28th National Guard Division, to which Marshall had consigned me in June 1942, was plagued with all the faults of most Guard divisions. It was based at Camp Livingston, ten miles north of Alexandria, Louisiana, only thirty-eight miles from our own camp, part of Oscar Griswold's IV Corps, to which the 82nd Division was assigned. Griswold and I had often discussed its problems in private. It was a Pennsylvania outfit, known as the "Iron Division" or the "Keystone." A less fitting epithet than "iron" could not be imagined.[9]

The 28th had been called up in January 1941; and after several months of basic training, outfitting and organization at Indiantown Gap, Pennsylvania, it had been shipped to Camp Livingston. Its commanding general on activation had been a powerful Pennsylvania politician, Edward Martin. In January 1942, after a full year on active service, Martin had been retired, officially for being "over-age in grade." Actually, he went home to run for governor of Pennsylvania and won. McNair had replaced Martin with a classmate of Patton's, James G. Ord, but Ord was simply not up to the job. After eighteen months in training, the 28th was still not far from square one. Marshall found Ord a sinecure in Brazil, and I became the 28th's third commanding general in the space of six months, not an easy pair of shoes to fill.[10]

Marshall, sensitive to National Guard politics, had long ago decreed that there would be no wholesale substitution of Regular Army officers for Guard officers on the staff level. Even if there had been enough available Regulars, a wholesale substitution would have caused a counterproductive public furor in the home state, destroyed the "state" character of the division and unfairly blocked the promotion of qualified Guardsmen to higher rank. The policy was for a Regular Army commanding general to move in with as few assistants as possible, find the qualified men in the Guard division and promote them into positions of responsibility.

I moved over to the 28th Division on June 26, 1942, taking only six men from the 82nd Division: my chief of staff, George Pope; my G-3 (responsible for training), Willis Matthews; my G-4, Tubby Thorson; my two aides, Chet Hansen and Lew Bridge; and my driver, Alex Stoute. I inherited two other Regular Army staffers, both West Pointers: Basil H. Perry (Class of 1917), artillery commander, and Forrest Caraway, the G-1 (Class of 1931). There was one outstanding senior Guard officer in the division, Kenneth Buchanan. I promoted him to assistant division commander.[11]

My staff and I spent four intense weeks in the field researching the problems of the 28th Division. They were legion. Owing to errors or mismanagement on the staff level, the division had been riddled of manpower, reduced in effect to a replacement center or personnel pool. Over 1,600 noncoms had left for OCS and upon graduation gone to other outfits. Hundreds more had left to become aviation cadets. Still others had been siphoned off as cadres for other divisions. On one of my field tours I noted that there was only one officer at a 105-mm battery, assisted by a buck sergeant. When I inquired into this preposterous situation, the officer told me that twelve of his senior noncoms had gone to OCS and the buck sergeant, who was the thirteenth-ranking noncom in the battery, was now number one. We put an immediate stop to this drain of manpower, and I requested that Oscar Griswold send me a new cadre of officers from the next OCS classes.

There was another grave problem endemic to all Guard divisions: home-townism. A unit commander from Podunk would have in his outfit, let us say, sons of his home-town banker on whom he was professionally dependent in civilian life. He might be hesitant to properly discipline the sons out of fear that they would complain to the father and he would lose his line of credit. Moreover, home-townism inevitably bred back-scratching cliques which excluded the new replacements, making it impossible to mold the division into a solid, unified organization.

I was determined to wipe out this practice. At the end of four weeks, I assembled all officers and noncoms in one of the camp theaters. I explained my views and told the assemblage that within twenty-four hours all officers and noncoms (except the supply and mess sergeants) would be transferred to a new infantry company or field artillery battery and that no two noncoms would go to the same outfit. A stunned hush fell over the theater, and I left the stage not knowing what to expect—meek compliance or mutiny. To my surprise, my innovation was roundly approved by all. One junior officer walked up to me and said, "General, this is the best thing that ever happened to this division."

Not enough stress had been placed on physical fitness. We enforced daily calisthenics, encouraged outdoor sporting events and built a tough obstacle course patterned on that in the 82nd Division—but no sewer under the rope swing! One tough physical test all divisions had to pass was a twenty-five-mile hike, with equipment. My regiments worked up to it by stages, first an eight-mile hike, then a twelve, then a sixteen. My aides tactfully suggested that I participate in the work-up hikes, but I declined. I knew very well I was in good enough shape to hike twenty-five miles.

When the Big Day came, the twenty-five-mile hike, we staffers joined the 109th Regiment. It was staged at night to avoid the broiling summer sun. Men were advised not to gulp water from their canteens, to drink only sparingly, but many disregarded this advice, and by the first hour they had fallen out, canteens empty. The ambulances picked them up, and later they were forced to repeat the hike. I walked along with the men, wearing fatigues, unrecognized. One soldier said to me, "Who the hell ordered this march?" I replied, "I don't know, but they ought to hang the S.O.B." Other than a little pain in my football knee, I completed the march without difficulty, drinking only one cup of coffee. I arrived at the finish line laden with the packs and rifles of several men who barely made it.

The division made rapid progress in its training. In August we were sufficiently advanced to stage a full-scale parade for Griswold, and shortly thereafter we went into the field for division maneuvers, augmented by our new cadre of OCS graduates. It was clear in these exercises (regiments "fought" regiments with supporting artillery) that we had come a long way in a short time, that what had been a hodgepodge was now shaping into a tough fighting unit.

The media were ever present, on the lookout for "color" and anecdotes, always hoping, I suppose, to discover a new Patton. I think they found me disappointing. One journalist wrote, "He is not showy enough to become legend. He is not mystic enough to cause wonderment. He is tough but not cussed enough to provide narrative. In a service where personal conspicuousness is regarded with awe and something of disfavor, Bradley appears solid and stable. He'll take his Army straight, thank you, and leave the color to the sideburn boys. But don't confuse glamour with leadership. Bradley is preeminently a leader. . . . The general doesn't only command respect: he wins devotion. That, perhaps more than anything else is responsible for the heated loyalty to his command. That more than anything else is the key to his character."

After our early fall field maneuvers, I was quite pleased to hear from McNair and Griswold that the division was deemed fit for final training exercises: simulated amphibious assault. A new amphibious training base, Camp Gordon Johnson, had been established at Carrabelle, Florida, near Apalachicola, in the Panhandle. The entire division and all its equipment would move there by train, the fourth such division to utilize the base.

Upon completion of the amphibious training, the division would be sent overseas. Whether or not I would remain in command was doubtful. On December 23, Marshall wrote me, saying that he "felt rather badly" about keeping me in command of the 28th Division. "I think they have asked for you five or six times to command a corps," he wrote, "each of which I disapproved because I thought we must not have such rapid changes in National Guard units we are trying to build up." He indicated that in due course he would move me to a more interesting assignment.[12]

Assuming that I would soon be heading overseas in one capacity or another, Mary and I decided to prepare for that eventuality. We packed our household goods and shipped them to Moberly for storage, each of us keeping one footlocker for our personal effects. When and if I was ordered overseas, Mary would move to the Thayer Hotel at West Point, where many wives of senior officers were living out the war. Elizabeth was entering her junior year at Vassar in Poughkeepsie only thirty miles from West Point. She was now seriously dating a West Point cadet, Henry S. (Hal) Beukema, son of my classmate Herman (Dutch) Beukema, who was a renowned West Point professor of government, history and economics. Elizabeth could spend her weekends at the Thayer Hotel with her mother and see Hal at the same time.[13]

Before we moved the 28th Division to Carrabelle for amphibious training, there was one important change in the top command. My chief of staff, George Van Wyck Pope, was promoted to brigadier general and assigned as assistant division commander of another division. William B. Kean, Class of 1919, became my new chief of staff. I had known Kean in prewar days in the War Department, when I was in G-1 and Kean was serving in the personnel section of the chief of infantry. He was a hard taskmaster and a perfectionist, curt and abrasive with his underlings, but an able, professional infantryman.[14]

The move to Camp Gordon Johnson in Carrabelle, by train and private automobile, took place just after the New Year (1943) when Christmas leaves expired. Following tight security rules regulating troop movements, all men removed shoulder patches and painted over insignia on the vehicles, an absurd time-wasting procedure, since everyone in Alexandria knew exactly where we were going. Mary and I found temporary quarters in a hotel in Wakulla Springs, fifty miles inland from the camp. I spent most of my time with the troops and saw Mary only on Sundays.[15]

Camp Gordon Johnson was the most miserable Army installation I had seen since my days in Yuma, Arizona, ages past. It had been hacked out of palmetto scrub along a bleak stretch of beach. We were forced to scatter our three infantry regiments miles apart and thus could never train as a complete division. Moreover, it was bitterly cold in that northern leg of Florida. Every training exercise in the landing craft was a numbing experience. The man who selected that site should have been court-martialed for stupidity.

Day after day, our various divisional units practiced "assaulting" a small island off the coast held by the "enemy." It was a new experience for all of us. I had studied amphibious warfare in schools and on my own read a great deal about the British World War I amphibious debacle at Gallipoli in the Turkish Dardanelles, but I had never actually "stormed a beach" in an LCVP (landing craft, vehicle and personnel) or the other small craft produced for this purpose since Pearl Harbor. The training imbued in all of us a healthy new respect for the tactical and logistical problems involved, especially the logistical ones, which, I saw, could become nightmares in a twinkling.

This training was the final precombat phase for the 28th Division. By that time, McNair had made it clear that any day I would be promoted to corps commander and the division would go to someone else. On Friday, February 12, 1943, I celebrated my fiftieth birthday. At noon, a TWX arrived from George Marshall:

> It is only fitting that your birthday should precede by only a few days your transfer to command a corps which comes as a long-delayed acknowledgment of your splendid record with the 28th Division. Congratulations and best wishes.[16]

On the following Tuesday, February 16, secret orders arrived assigning me to command X Corps, based at Temple, Texas, near Austin. I had scarcely finished reading the message when I received a telephone call from McNair's G-1, Alexander R. Bolling. He said cryptically, "We're cutting orders for you today, Brad. You're going overseas on extended active duty. Not the division—just you."

I was understandably flabbergasted. I said, "I've just received orders to Temple, Texas, to—" Bolling broke in, "Oh, that was yesterday." I composed my voice and said, "Well, what kind of clothes? Which way do I go?" I meant Africa or the Pacific, holding my breath, devoutly hoping it would be Africa. It was against regulations to discuss troop movements (in this case, me) on an open telephone. Cagily, Bolling said, "Remember your classmate? You're going to join him."

Eisenhower! Africa.

"How soon can you leave?" Bolling said curtly. "You'll have to be briefed in Washington."

"Tomorrow," I replied.

In further guarded talks with Bolling I divined that I was not being ordered to a specific troop command in Africa but rather to some nebulous, unspecified job which permitted no staff of my choice, not even my driver, Alex Stoute. I was allowed only my two aides, Chet Hansen and Lew Bridge. This was disquieting news. Had Marshall taken away my corps to relegate me to a rarefied staff job in Ike's headquarters (as Marshall had served in Pershing's headquarters in World War I)? I certainly hoped not.

Because I was now moving under classified orders, I made the overcautious decision, to my lasting regret, to slip away from the division with as little notice as possible, forgoing the customary farewells and thanks for a job well done to staff and unit commanders. To my knowledge, only Bill Kean, Willis Matthews and Alex Stoute (to whom I was compelled to confide) knew of my sudden departure. I promised each of these men that if it proved possible in my new assignment, I would send for them. By early afternoon I was gone. In subsequent days, command of the division went to Major General Lloyd D. Brown, whom I would meet later in Normandy under circumstances which proved to be difficult and awkward.

My aides and I flew to Washington the following day, February 17. Since wartime air travel limited us to seventy-seven pounds of baggage each, I took only one footlocker and a Val-pac suitcase. I sent a second footlocker containing a fine waterproof L. L. Bean tent and a down bedroll to Africa by ship, but months would pass before that gear caught up with me. Mary and Marjorie Hansen, Chet's wife, drove our Buick to West Point, taking Mollie, who was then about eleven years old and feeling her age. Mary checked into the Thayer Hotel for a very long stay. An old hunting cohort of mine, a sergeant in the West Point band, took over the care and feeding of Mollie, who died a year or so later.

Now, for the first time in thirty-one and a half years of active Army service, I was on my way to a real war.

PART TWO

★★★★★

OVERSEAS TO WAR

THIRTEEN

The war Hitler started had now been raging for almost three and a half years. The United States had been at war with the Axis—Germany, Italy, Japan—for fourteen months. British and American leaders had agreed on a strategy of beating Germany and Italy first and then Japan, but they disagreed about how to defeat Germany and Italy. Generally, the British leaned toward what we called an "indirect" or "peripheral" strategy. They argued that while Hitler exhausted Germany in his vast land war with Russia, the United States and Britain should defeat Hitler's U-boats, which had almost paralyzed the Allies; smash the German war production base to smithereens with massive air bombardments; and chip away at the periphery of the Axis empire in the Middle East, the Balkans and the Mediterranean—Churchill's famous "soft underbelly" approach. American strategic planners, notably George Marshall, generally leaned to a direct approach: an early invasion across the English Channel into France and Germany, striking straight at the heart of the German empire. This underlying difference in strategic thinking would keep the American and British staffs at loggerheads for nearly three years.

The indirect strategy had led the British into a deep and costly involvement in the Mediterranean–North African theater of war. It began in 1940, when Mussolini's inept army in Libya launched a wobbly invasion of Egypt. Determined to hold Egypt and the Middle East at any price, Churchill committed a large share of his available military forces to the area. Thereafter, the British—the "Desert Rats"—routed the Italians so completely that Hitler was forced to come to their rescue. He sent Erwin Rommel, a blitzkrieg expert and a hero of the battle of France, to Libya with a small force, the Afrika Korps. The British then had the military power to clear North Africa of all Axis forces, but Churchill unwisely stripped his desert force in a visionary scheme to help the Greeks eject Italian invaders and then create a "Balkan Army" to strike Hitler in his underbelly. Hitler responded to that threat by invading Greece, then Crete, inflicting devastating defeats on the British in both places, while Rommel, with slimmest resources but no lack of gall, attacked the weakened British desert army, driving it back into Egypt.

For the next year the desert war, highly romanticized in novels and films, see-sawed back and forth across Egypt and Libya. A few weeks before Pearl Harbor, the Desert Rats, reinforced and properly dignified with the title British Eighth Army, attacked Rommel in overwhelming strength and drove him back on his heels into Libya. A few weeks after Pearl Harbor, Rommel, the aptly nicknamed "Desert Fox," unleashed a blinding series of offensives that sent the Eighth Army reeling back into Egypt, ultimately to El Alamein, where Rommel finally outran his supply lines. Concurrent with the see-saw desert battles were relentless air and sea battles in the Mediterranean, each side attempting to cut the other's supply lines. British losses on land, in the air and at sea were severe.[1]

As has recently been officially disclosed, the British had an intelligence advantage in the desert war and elsewhere. British codebreakers had deciphered the Enigma machine codes utilized by the German Air Force and some other German Army and Navy codes using certain versions of the Enigma machines. The decodes were known as "Ultra," after their high classification, "ultra secret." Ultra provided the British with priceless insights and information on German strategy and tactics, Rommel's supply situation, force levels and, often, specific orders and battle plans. The British used this information to good advantage, particularly in interdicting Rommel's sea supply lines by air and submarine attack. The British Eighth Army commander, Claude Auchinleck, expressed the opinion that without Ultra, Rommel "would certainly have got through to Cairo," imperiling the Suez Canal and the whole Middle East.[2]

Soon after the United States entered the war, Churchill began pressing his indirect strategy on Roosevelt. At their first wartime "Big Two" meeting in Washington in December 1941, when the British were doing well in the desert, Churchill proposed that the Allies make an amphibious landing (Operation Gymnast) somewhere in French Northwest Africa at Rommel's rear, with the idea of trapping Rommel between those forces and the British Eighth Army, destroying the Afrika Korps once and for all. Roosevelt was intrigued because it appeared to be a relatively safe and easy way of introducing American soldiers into combat, which he was eager to do, and at the same time to satisfy Russia's unrelenting demand for an Allied "second front."

Secretary of War Stimson and George Marshall vehemently disagreed with Churchill and Roosevelt. They viewed the Mediterranean–North African theater as peripheral and diversionary, a bottomless hole down which Allied resources would endlessly and uselessly pour.

By this time Marshall had chosen my classmate Ike Eisenhower for an important job in the war plans division. Until then the two men had not been close; they had never served together. Ike had first come to Marshall's attention during the 1941 Louisiana maneuvers, when Ike had done some outstanding staff planning. Ike was further helped along the way by McNair's chief of staff, Mark Wayne Clark. Clark had earlier served with and impressed Marshall. Since McNair was hard of hearing, he often sent Clark to Marshall's office in his place for conferences. Marshall became so impressed with Clark that he jump-promoted him from lieutenant colonel to brigadier general—as he had me. During one meeting, when Marshall asked Clark to suggest a list of candidates for the job of war plans chief, Clark, who had also earlier served with Ike, replied, "I can give you one name and nine dittos." Clark's choice was Eisenhower. After Pearl Harbor, Marshall had brought Ike into war plans as a Far East specialist, to help MacArthur in the Philippines. On February 14, Marshall promoted Ike to major general and two days later named him chief of the division. Several weeks later its name was changed to the operations division (OPD).[3]

Eisenhower was an early disciple of Marshall's concept of a cross-channel invasion strike at Hitler's heartland. Soon after taking over as chief of OPD, Ike and his assistants drew up formal plans for such a strike, code-named "Roundup." It was to be carried out as soon as possible, perhaps in late 1942 or, at the latest, the spring of 1943. Marshall sent Ike to London to plan the buildup and to command forces for Roundup. To assist him in this job, Ike pried two valuable men out of Washington: Mark Clark to serve as tactical commander of the Roundup invasion forces (then designated as II Corps), and Bedell Smith, who would become Ike's chief of staff.

The British were cool to Roundup. In June 1942, when Rommel drove Auchinleck back to the El Alamein line, threatening Cairo, Churchill, under severe criticism at home, again pressed Roosevelt to consider a North African invasion—Gymnast. At the same time, the British military advisers, in particular Marshall's counterpart, General Alan Brooke, Chief of the Imperial General Staff, faulted Marshall's cross-channel invasion plan as poorly conceived, much too premature and possibly disastrous. Roosevelt, already predisposed to a North African invasion, overruled Stimson and Marshall and ordered that Gymnast, renamed "Torch," be carried out as swiftly as possible. Marshall still opposed Torch, but when Roosevelt made the final decision, Marshall worked faithfully to carry it out.

When Roundup was shelved in favor of Torch, the U.S. military forces designated for Roundup became the nucleus of Torch. Since Torch was then conceived as largely an American operation, Ike was named commander in chief; Clark was elevated to serve as his deputy, Bedell Smith became Ike's chief of staff. I didn't know it until years later, but in one preliminary command proposal to Marshall, Ike listed me as one of four possibilities to lead the Torch forces ashore.[4]

French Northwest Africa—composed of Tunisia, Algeria and Morocco—was a vast area, over one thousand miles across, populated by 16 million people, some loyal to French rule, but many hostile. Under terms of the German-French armistice, the area, like the French fleet, had been "neutralized." It was governed by emissaries of Vichyite Marshal Henri Philippe Pétain and an ill-equipped French Colonial Army and Air Force of about 135,000 men. They were under orders from Pétain to defend the territories against any invader, Axis or Allied. However, Torch advocates hoped that the French military would defect to the Allies and welcome the invaders with open arms, and thus the landings would entail minimum risk. An Allied lodgement in Northwest Africa threatening Rommel's rear might be had at little or no cost and, in the bargain, enlist a French Army and Navy that could be turned against the Axis.

The Allied military planning for Torch was helter-skelter. Too much was attempted too soon with too little. For weeks the planners could not even agree on the landing sites. British air and naval leaders and some ground generals urged a major landing closest to Rommel's rear in Tunisia. If Tunisia were not quickly seized, they argued, the Axis would occupy it, driving a wedge between Torch and Rommel's forces, defeating one vital purpose of Torch.

But Marshall opposed Tunisian landings or any landings inside the Mediterranean as too risky. He insisted Torch operations be confined to Casablanca, French Morocco, outside the Mediterranean on the Atlantic coast, one thousand miles from Tunisia. The British believed a single Casablanca landing to be self-defeating. It would provoke the Axis into seizing Tunisia without any commensurate Allied gain. Brooke agreed that a Tunisia landing was too risky but argued that at the least the Allies had to seize Algeria. Ultimately Churchill and Roosevelt had to be drawn into the debate to resolve it. Roosevelt again overruled Marshall. Torch forces would land at Casablanca and two sites inside the Mediterranean—Oran and Algiers. A subsidiary force, mostly British, would then "dash" from Algiers to Tunisia to seize that place before the Axis could take it. The conquest of Tunisia, by all odds the key military objective of Torch, would thus become a race between the Allies and the Axis. Torch D-day was set for November 8, 1942.

In the summer of 1942, while Roosevelt, Churchill and the Combined Chiefs debated Torch, Rommel and the British Eighth Army were stalemated at El Alamein. In the lull, the British recaptained and revitalized the Eighth Army. Churchill picked Sir Harold R. L. G. Alexander as overall commander in the Middle East. Alexander, a solid, thoroughgoing professional, was a low-profile soldier of vast and varied combat experience in World War I and II. Command of his Eighth Army went to Bernard L. Montgomery. "Monty" was the antithesis of "Alex" in character and temperament: flamboyant, eccentric, strident, difficult, demanding and—in a GI term of the time—a glory hound. Monty, in turn, had picked for his chief of staff Francis (Freddie) de Guingand, who had no peer in the British Army as a planner. The brilliant, suave and diplomatic de Guingand would pull Monty's fat out of the fire more than once before the war was over and, on one momentous occasion, save Monty from certain professional ruin.

Ultra intelligence revealed that Rommel's long pursuit to El Alamein had exhausted both the general and his army. It also revealed that Rommel had one more trick up his sleeve: a final desperation attack at Alam Halfa. When the attack came at the end of August 1942, Alexander and Montgomery knew Rommel's exact plan of action and laid a trap. Monty's G-2, Brigadier E. T. Williams, subsequently wrote: "It became obvious from Ultra that Rommel intended his final drive to Alexandria in the full moon of August by a sweep through the southern flank. The Army Commander accepted the evidence and made his arrangements . . . a day or two later everything happened according to plan." In the ensuing battle, the Desert Fox was stopped cold and his army fatally shattered. Overnight the British press lionized Monty as a general of uncanny prescience: he could read Rommel's mind! Churchill urged Monty to follow up the victory swiftly, to annihilate the German-Italian forces. But Montgomery, an exasperatingly methodical general, would not be hurried. For the next seven weeks he worked out the details of a classic set piece counteroffensive reminiscent of the frontal assaults of World War I, meanwhile amassing overwhelming strength in tanks (including 300 Shermans stripped from American divisions), artillery and aircraft.[5]

Monty's planned counteroffensive against Rommel and the Torch invasion were not, in the strictest sense, integrated into a single interlocking military plan. They were, however, designed to be mutually supportive psychologically, politically and militarily. It was believed that a decisive, annihilating victory by Monty over Rommel, followed shortly by the Torch landings, would be a show of force sufficient to impel the French holdouts and fence straddlers into the arms of the Allies. This was one reason Churchill had strongly urged Monty to follow up his victory at Alam Halfa swiftly.

For a while, it appeared that Monty might delay so long that the anticipated psychological advantage would be lost. But finally, on October 23, a mere two weeks before Torch forces were scheduled to land, he jumped off. By that time his Eighth Army outnumbered Rommel's army by about two to one in men and tanks (195,000 men and 1,000 tanks vs. 104,000 men and 500 tanks). Monty preceded the jump-off with a shattering artillery barrage employing over 1,000 guns, the greatest concentration of artillery in the desert war to date. Rommel was not present; he was in Germany on sick leave (fatigue, low blood pressure, dizzy spells, chronic digestive problems). His armies were temporarily commanded by General Georg Stumme.

The ensuing battle—famous as El Alamein—was Monty's finest hour.

Again taking good advantage of Ultra intelligence and a clever deception plan based on that intelligence, Monty's tanks, superbly supported by thunderous air, smashed headlong into the Axis defensive positions. General Stumme fell dead of a heart attack. The next senior general, Ritter von Thoma, was captured. German and Italian tankers and soldiers fought tenaciously and bravely, but they were simply overwhelmed. Rommel left his sick bed and rushed back to Africa to save what he could of his routed and decimated army.

Having knocked his opponent senseless, Monty failed to deliver the coup de grace. He let the remnants of Rommel's force slip away into the desert, westward toward Tunisia. Monty's caution caused some dismay in official London. Even Rommel was professionally contemptuous. He wrote that the "British command continued to observe its usual caution and showed little evidence of ability to make resolute decisions." Monty blamed his failure to pursue, trap and annihilate Rommel on the onset of desert rains, which mired his tanks and trucks. British military historian Liddell Hart, in his masterful *History of the Second World War,* blamed Monty's generalship:

> After the event, the rain formed the main excuse for the failure to cut off Rommel's retreat. But, in analysis, it becomes clear that the best opportunities had already been forfeited before the rain intervened—by too narrow moves, by too much caution, by too little sense of the time factor, by unwillingness to push on in the dark, and by concentrating too closely on the battle to keep in mind the essential requirements of its decisive exploitation.

In due course, I would become closely associated with Monty, fighting in harness with him in Northwest Africa, Sicily and Europe. While Liddell Hart's judgment was meant to apply only to Monty's conduct of El Alamein, it actually characterizes every battle he fought thereafter of which I have direct knowledge. His failure to annihilate Rommel when the opportunity was there, coupled with the Torch decision to relegate the seizure of Tunisia to a race, set the stage for very difficult times ahead in Africa for Ike and the Allies.

While Monty methodically prepared to pursue Rommel's fleeing forces, the Torch landings proceeded on schedule on November 8. Inasmuch as Roosevelt believed the French would be more receptive to American than British forces * and the majority of Torch troops were American, he insisted that Ike's assault force commanders for the three major landings should be American generals. George Patton, commanding about 25,000 American troops, went ashore at Casablanca. Lloyd R. Fredendall

* Sometime previously, the British had bitterly antagonized the Vichy French in several land and sea attacks elsewhere.

commanded about 18,000 American troops at Oran. Fredendall, fifty-eight, had originally been a member of the West Point Class of 1905. After washing out twice, he enlisted in the Army and was commissioned in the infantry in 1907. He had been urged on Ike for the Torch job by Marshall. My classmate Doc Ryder, commanding a force of about 18,000 troops of which about half were British, landed at Algiers—Americans first.

The French did not, as hoped, rush into the arms of the Allies. The political situation became extremely complex. Some French remained loyal to Pétain, others defected to the Allies, still others straddled the fence. Torch forces met moderate to strong French resistance in the Casablanca and Oran areas; weak to no resistance at Algiers, where a pro-Allied Frenchman commanded. After vexing political negotiations, on the third day of operations Mark Clark was able to work out a general cease-fire by arranging a "deal" with Pétain's deputy, Admiral Jean F. Darlan. The "Darlan Deal" was universally denounced in the Western media, but Darlan had temporarily served Clark's military purpose and stopped the fighting. Although he tried, Darlan did not, however, deliver the French fleet; it was scuttled by its crews in Toulon.

Meanwhile, the crucial race for Tunisia had begun. After Doc Ryder led his Torch forces ashore and secured Algiers, he stepped aside, as planned, and a British general, Kenneth A. N. Anderson, took command of the race. It was to be run mostly by a small force of well-trained but green British troops. Anderson made a noble, even heroic, effort to win the race, but he had to run some four hundred miles over narrow, clogged roads with little air support and faltering communications. As feared, the Germans and Italians quickly seized Tunisia, immediately began a massive air and ground buildup, and soon deployed to attack the oncoming Anderson force, which was somewhat bolstered by French Army defectors from Tunisia. Some advance elements of Anderson's force actually got within fifteen miles of Tunis. But by that time, Anderson's momentum was spent, his supply lines overextended, his troops punch-drunk with fatigue and his modest air support overwhelmed by the Luftwaffe. The Germans checked Anderson's advance and counterattacked, pushing him back. Anderson's noble effort had proved to be too little too late.

Ike had established an Allied headquarters in Algiers. Well knowing the strategic value of Tunisia, he had exhausted himself mentally and physically in an ever more futile and depressing effort to back Anderson with supplies, air support and additional troops, including American units, some brought overland from Fredendall's force in Oran. But Ike was overwhelmed by a logistical nightmare: jammed seaports and clogged roads, poor communications and seasonal rains which mired everything on wheels. By Christmas, Ike, in a "bitter decision," conceded defeat, canceled further offensive operations and ordered Anderson to withdraw to defensive positions in western Tunisia to wait out the two-month rainy season. It was now clear that the capture of Tunisia would be a prolonged struggle requiring a substantially revised strategy. Moreover, the hope of trapping Rommel between Torch forces and Monty's Eighth Army had been irretrievably lost.

The decision to relegate the seizure of Tunisia to a secondary or even tertiary military objective would later generate much heat and controversy. Many of the British admirals and generals involved in Torch and the official and unofficial British military historians have criticized the decision, in some cases harshly. Samuel Eliot Morison judged the decision one of the rare provable instances of an important "strategic mistake" and wrote that had we adopted the British proposal for a landing directly in Tunisia at Bizerte, it would have saved "both time and precious lives." Ike and Mark Clark, Ike's chief planner for Torch, felt the same way. Ike skirted the issue in his war memoirs, but according to his aide, confidant and private diarist, Captain Harry C. Butcher, after the fact Ike conceded the landing at Casablanca had been a "mistake." Clark wrote that he and Ike had been "unquestionably timid (although far less so than Washington) in the scope of our original invasion of Africa," and had they landed forces in Tunisia "we almost certainly would have been successful."[6]

The defeat in Tunisia eroded Ike's confidence and temporarily dampened his inborn optimism and cheerfulness. He became ill with what he diagnosed as "walking pneumonia." His British driver, Kay Summersby, recalled that he was "feverish" and had "great puffy bags under his eyes." He was so depressed, his aide Butcher recalled, that he repeatedly stated: "Anyone who wants the job of Allied Commander in Chief can have it." Bedell Smith, who had become a grimly abrasive person, perhaps owing to the discomfort inflicted by a bleeding ulcer, "blistered anyone who came within range," according to Ike's biographer Stephen E. Ambrose. Butcher dismissed Smith as "a neurotic with an aching ulcer." These poor attitudes sifted down to the staff. "The tone in the office was bad," Ambrose wrote. "Morale had dropped measurably." The American, British and French Allies fought among themselves, each one blaming the other two for the failures.

The Allied front in Tunisia, stretching north-south along some 250 miles of mountainous terrain, was militarily chaotic. Allied forces—American, British, French—had been rushed to the front and committed piecemeal in small units, and they were now all mixed together with confused chains of command, communications and supply lines. There was no battle plan; there were no reserves to commit should the Germans try to punch through the thinly held line. The ill-equipped but gallant and proud French refused to take orders from the British and had to be reinforced with American and British artillery and armor. There was no overall front-line commander; Ike tried to manage the battlefield from distant Algiers.

When that didn't work, he established an "advanced command post" halfway to the front at Constantine, Algeria, run by an outstanding American general, Lucian K. Truscott, Jr., who had led some of our forces ashore at Casablanca. But that didn't work either. All the while, Rommel was retreating toward Tunisia in the face of Monty's ponderously oncoming Eighth Army.

It appeared to the British that the loss of the race to Tunisia had paralyzed Ike, that he was incapable of managing the Tunisian war. General Ian Jacob, deputy to Churchill's personal chief of staff, Hastings Ismay, visited Algiers and judged Ike "far too easily swayed and diverted to be a great commander in chief." British Admiral Andrew Cunningham, a salty veteran of the Mediterranean fighting, and commander of Torch naval forces, cabled London that Ike's Air Force organization and operations were "chaotic." In London, the Imperial General Staff drafted a blistering criticism of the confused, dangerous and nonaggressive situation on Ike's Tunisian front for Marshall, but it was not sent. Alan Brooke wrote in his diary that "unfortunately" Ike "had neither the tactical nor strategical experience required" for the war in Africa.

Marshall was worried, too. He advised Ike to stop spending so much time on the French political and diplomatic situation, writing long reports justifying his actions, and "give your complete attention to the battles." He followed these suggestions with concrete actions and proposals. He had Roosevelt assign State Department troubleshooter Robert Murphy to Ike's headquarters to carry the burden of civil and diplomatic matters. He suggested that Ike bring Patton (recently glorified in a big *Life* magazine article and champing at the bit for action) from Morocco to serve as Ike's "deputy" to run the Tunisian battlefield. Ike replied that he was happy to have Patton's "great mental and physical energy in helping me through a critical period" and informed Marshall that he would name Patton "Deputy Allied Commander for Ground Forces." In the meanwhile, he brought Lloyd Fredendall and the old II Corps staff to Tunisia to command the American sector of the front.

In the midst of all this, Roosevelt, Churchill and the Combined Chiefs of Staff met at Casablanca to plan worldwide war strategy. The British came prepared to achieve two important goals: to persuade American leaders to continue the war in the Mediterranean following the anticipated victory in Tunisia by invading Sardinia or Sicily with the aim of knocking Italy out of the war at the earliest possible date; and to kick Ike upstairs and insert experienced British air and ground generals under him to run the war in Tunisia.

On the first issue, both Marshall and Chief of Naval Operations Ernest J. King vigorously opposed any further Mediterranean operations for all the old reasons. Torch had already delayed Roundup. Further Mediterranean operations would delay Roundup well into 1944. King argued that invading Sicily (which he preferred to Sardinia) would be "merely doing something just for the sake of doing something." But Roosevelt favored the Sicily invasion. It would keep American troops in Europe busy and battle-honed until Roundup. Once again he overruled Marshall and King.

On the second issue, the British put the case tactfully—without criticism of Ike. They pointed out that in a few weeks Monty's Eighth Army, still ponderously pursuing Rommel, would be approaching Tunisia. Under the circumstances, it would be advisable to coordinate the ground and air operations of that army with those of Torch forces in Tunisia by single overall air and ground commanders reporting to Ike. Since the majority of the combined air and ground forces would be British, those commanders should be British. Marshall, who had come to the conference convinced the British would demand that Ike be replaced by a Britisher for the combined operations, readily agreed. Whereupon the British named Alexander to be Ike's ground commander and Alexander's Royal Air Force counterpart, Air Chief Marshal Arthur Tedder, to be Ike's air commander. With Admiral Andrew Cunningham already serving as Ike's naval deputy in the Mediterranean, this command decision meant that the British would hold all important commands under Ike: sea, air, land.

Brooke gloated in his diary: "We were pushing Eisenhower into the stratosphere and rarefied atmosphere of a Supreme Commander, where he would be free to devote his time to the political and inter-Allied problems, whilst we inserted under him one of our own commanders to deal with the military situations and to restore the necessary drive and coordination which had been so seriously lacking."

The command decisions reached at Casablanca stimulated Ike to clarify the command muddle on the Tunisian front. Marshall's suggestion of naming Patton Ike's "deputy" for ground operations had to be shelved. That job was now Alexander's. On January 26, Ike placed all Allied forces on the Tunisian front under formal command of Anderson, who, in turn, would report directly to Alexander when the latter assumed his new duties. For a while, Lucian Truscott remained on the scene in his nebulous advanced command post, but eventually he was ordered away to command an infantry division designated for the Sicily invasion. In full charge at last, Anderson issued various orders designed to reorganize his forces by nationality and to take up improved positions. But these measures came too late to forestall the disaster that lay ahead.

By the time the Casablanca meetings were over, Rommel, commanding a force of 78,000 men (30,000 Germans), had reached southern Tunisia. He turned about and dug in to face Monty's Eighth Army at some French-built fortifications known rather too grandly as the Mareth Line. Here Rommel encountered some unexpected command problems of his own. Hitler and Mussolini had lost faith in Rommel's magic. Hitler had plucked another general, Jürgen von Arnim, from the Russian front and sent him to Tunisia to take overall command of operations from Rommel. On the same day that Ike gave Anderson formal command of Allied forces in Tunisia—January 26, 1943—Hitler ordered Rommel to consolidate his forces on the Mareth Line and then turn over his command to an Italian general who would report to von Arnim. Rommel was to return to Germany for extended sick leave.

Hitler left it up to Rommel to choose his date of turnover and departure. Perhaps hoping to regain some of his lost prestige, Rommel decided to hang on for a while and fight. He conceived a plan to exploit his central position between the Torch forces and Monty's slowly oncoming Eighth Army. He would first hit the Allies at his rear, then turn back and hit Monty. At the same time, von Arnim planned to strike at Anderson's positions farther north. Fortunately for the Allies, the von Arnim and Rommel attacks were only very loosely coordinated and the two German generals had to compete for the limited panzer divisions available to them in Tunisia. Both men were also bedeviled at times by conflicting orders from higher German and Italian headquarters.

German preparations for the offensive against Torch forces generated a Niagara of Ultra intelligence. The pertinent messages were decoded in England and relayed to Ike's G-2 in Algiers, British Brigadier General Eric E. Mockler-Ferryman, a skilled analyst of Ultra intelligence. Mockler-Ferryman deduced from the evidence that the main thrust would come in the middle of the line at Fondouk. Accordingly, Anderson, convinced that the Ultra was accurate, even though his own front-line G-2 had reported German concentrations at Faid, laid a trap at Fondouk. But Mockler-Ferryman had drawn the wrong conclusion from the Ultra data. Von Arnim's main thrust came on February 14, farther south at Faid Pass, directly against the American positions. On the following day, elements of Rommel's Afrika Korps struck the extreme southern American flank near Gafsa and rolled on toward Feriana.[7]

Aware from Ultra that the offensive was coming, Ike had toured the American front lines the day before the attack. He was dissatisfied with almost everything he saw. Some of the French had been pulled out of the line for rest and refit. The British and Americans had moved south and north to fill the middle gap. The ninety-mile II Corps front was overextended, paper-thin along its entire length. The as-yet-unblooded, inadequately trained American troops were complacent and poorly deployed. The main punch of II Corps, the 1st Armored Division, had been split into two widely separated units, one at Fondouk, one near Faid. The armored commanders were uncertain as to who was in charge. Communication between all units was less than satisfactory.

Nor was Ike entirely happy with II Corps commander Lloyd Fredendall. He was not an inspiring commander. Lucian Truscott has described him well: "Small in stature, loud and rough in speech, he was outspoken in his opinions and critical of superiors and subordinates alike. He was inclined to jump at conclusions which were not always well founded. He rarely left his command post for personal reconnaissances and visits yet he was impatient with the recommendations of subordinates more familiar with the terrain and other conditions than he was. General Fredendall had no confidence in the French, no liking for the British in general and General Anderson in particular, and little more for some of his own subordinate commanders." His "command post" was an embarrassment to every American soldier: a deep underground shelter dug or blasted by two hundred engineers in an almost inaccessible canyon far to the rear, near Tebessa. It gave the impression that, for all his bombast and bravado, Fredendall was lacking in personal courage.[8]

When the Germans struck the American lines, complete disaster ensued. There were notable pockets of gallantry, but for the most part our soldiers abandoned their weapons, including tanks, and fled to the rear like the frightened young boy in *The Red Badge of Courage*. Uselessly shouting slogans and exhortations over the radio to units gone amok, Fredendall lost complete control of the battlefield. Even these many years later, it pains me to reflect on that disaster. It was probably the worst performance of U.S. Army troops in their whole proud history.

FOURTEEN

That was the situation in North Africa when my aides and I reported to the Pentagon on the morning of February 18. We went directly to Operations (OPD), where we were thoroughly briefed and read Ike's dispatches. It was not a happy time. There was an air of crisis mixed with gloom.

There was also no little criticism of the British—and Ike. The British "indirect" strategy had prevailed over Marshall's "direct" strategy; and now the United States, against all common sense, was becoming deeper and deeper involved in the Mediterranean at the expense of Roundup and the war in the Pacific. The commitment had been extended at Casablanca to include Sicily. Not only that, Ike's land, sea and air commanders were now all British and they were calling the military shots. OPD was bitter. One of its chief planners, Albert C. Wedemeyer, had written from Casablanca: "We came, we listened, and we were conquered." There was a growing feeling in OPD that Ike had "sold out" to the British—caved in on his commanders, caved in on Sicily. Ike had recently written the new chief of OPD, Thomas T. Handy, a patronizing letter admonishing him and his planners not to be so anti-British in their thinking. "One of the constant sources of danger to us in this war," Ike had written, "is the temptation to regard as our first enemy the partner that must work with us in defeating the real enemy." The letter had naturally incensed Handy and his subordinates.[1]

Rommel correctly sensed that he was on the threshold of a complete rout. Playing it largely by ear, he conceived a plan to drive on Tebessa, then swing north behind the entire Allied lines to Bone. Had he been in sole command of all Axis forces, there is no doubt in my mind that he could have achieved this objective—or even conquered Algiers—well before Monty could reach the Mareth Line in force to threaten his rear. But fortunately for the Allies, Rommel's own comrades and superiors defeated him. Berlin and Rome favored his plan to a point, but von Arnim did not. Von Arnim cautiously restrained his panzers while the matter was debated.

Rome ultimately directed Rommel to go north not by a wide westward sweep through Tebessa but rather by a narrower sweep toward Thala and Le Kef. As Liddell Hart wrote, that order was the real "turning point" in the battle. It would lead Rommel directly into Anderson's strength, not to the rear of it. Rommel, realizing his plan was doomed, rightly denounced the orders as "an appalling and incredible piece of shortsightedness."[2]

Rommel's narrower northward swing would lead him up through a key Allied defensive position, Kasserine Pass. Early on the morning of February 19, his tanks pushed into the pass. Green American forces—augmented by a small, seasoned, gallant British detachment—checked Rommel that first day and night. But on the next afternoon, February 20, Rommel brought up reinforcements and broke through, inflicting another severe and humiliating defeat on the Americans. U.S. Army historian George Howe wrote: "The enemy was amazed at the quantity and quality of the American equipment captured more or less intact." Probing northward toward Thala over the next two days, Rommel ran into the heavy Allied resistance he had anticipated. On the afternoon of February 22, he reviewed the situation and decided to break off the offensive, withdraw and prepare to face Monty's oncoming Eighth Army. As Rommel withdrew, the Allies bungled an opportunity to stage a counterattack.

Alexander had rushed to the Tunisian front on February 19, the day Rommel launched his assault on Kasserine Pass, to take command of operations. He was "frankly shocked." He signaled Brooke in British understatement: "General situation is far from satisfactory. British, American and French units are all mixed up on the front, especially in the south. Formations have been split up. There is no policy and plan of campaign. The air is much the same. This is the result of no firm direction or centralized control from above." In a follow-up report to Churchill and Brooke, he repeated: "Real fault has been lack of direction from above from very beginning resulting in no policy and no plan." Alexander pointed the finger at Anderson, who he doubted was "big enough for the job." But the British historian, Major General I. S. O. Playfair, judged that Alexander was "too hard" on Anderson, that Anderson had not been in charge long enough, that the fault had to lie with Eisenhower.

Ike had now been defeated twice in Africa—in the December race for Tunis and the February German offensive. The latter had cost 6,300 American casualties—300 killed, 3,000 wounded, 3,000 missing, most of these captured. Ike led an extraordinarily charmed life. Had the British not already engineered his elevation into the "stratosphere" one month before at Casablanca and brought Alexander into his command, I feel certain that after Kasserine Pass he would have been fired. Ike was a political general of rare and valuable gifts, but as his African record clearly demonstrates, he did not know how to manage a battlefield.

While in the Pentagon, I was more than a little curious to find out what job Ike had in store for me. All I learned then was that I was to serve in some vague capacity on the Tunisian front. Years later, when Ike's official papers were published, I learned the background of my selection. During the Casablanca meeting, or shortly thereafter, when Marshall had suggested bringing Patton to Tunisia to serve as Ike's ground deputy, he apparently also suggested orally that Ike choose a personal representative to send to the front to serve, in his phrase, as Ike's "eyes and ears." Since Lucian Truscott was already there more or less in that capacity and Patton was then under consideration as ground commander, I cannot imagine why Marshall proposed yet another man on the battlefront, and the record is not clear on the point. Perhaps Marshall was tactfully seeking a way of reinforcing Ike on the battlefield with professional generals skilled in infantry tactics, without actually saying so.

In any case, in response to Marshall's suggestion, Ike, just prior to Rommel's offensive, responded favorably to the suggestion and sent Marshall a list of thirteen names, including mine. From this list, Marshall chose me, and on February 15 cabled Ike: "I propose General Omar N. Bradley for the detail in question. . . . If this meets with your desires he will be sent immediately . . . [and] would remain on detail as long as you desire him." Ike replied on the following day: "Please dispatch General Omar Bradley by first available air transport."[3]

Before leaving the Pentagon, I paid Marshall a brief courtesy call. Despite the mammoth load he carried on his spare shoulders, he appeared fit—his keen blue eyes and sharp sensibility missing nothing, however mundane. He was deeply concerned about the Kasserine setback, the failure of our troops in their first real test against the Germans. He briefly discussed my forthcoming assignment, wished me well and appointed me a courier to carry to Ike two top-secret letters regarding Husky, the code name for the Sicily invasion. He said, "Read the letters, commit the contents to memory and if your plane is forced down, destroy the letters and orally report the contents to Ike." These letters, one of which specified the Husky D-day—one of the most closely held secrets we had—burned a hole in my pocket all the way to Algiers.[4]

My aides and I traveled the newly created "southern route" on more-or-less scheduled Air Transport Command aircraft, some comfortable but others cold and merely fitted with bucket seats. We flew to Miami; Georgetown, British Guiana; Natal, Brazil; across the Atlantic to Dakar; then on to Marrakech, Casablanca and Algiers. In all, it was a numbing ninety-hour trip, counting the refueling stops and changes of planes. We arrived at the cold, windy, muddy airport at Algiers on February 24. Ike's aide Ernest (Tex) Lee met us in Ike's bulletproof Cadillac, a vehicle so heavy and unwieldy that it had been relegated to ceremonial use only.[5]

We went directly to Ike's headquarters at the sprawling St. George

Hotel on a hill overlooking the city and the harbor jammed with shipping. The St. George was like a miniature Pentagon, manned by a huge staff of British, American and French officers in their varied uniforms. At Ike's suite of offices, I was greeted by Ike's chief of staff, Bedell Smith. By this time, Rommel and von Arnim had withdrawn and the crisis on the front had subsided, at least temporarily. But it had been a disastrous, humiliating defeat; and no one on Ike's staff claimed otherwise. The atmosphere was somber, even grim.

I spent the rest of the afternoon and evening with Ike. In a way it was a "get to know each other" session as much as anything else. Although we had known each other at West Point thirty years before, serving in the same company, we had not been close. We had seen little or nothing of each other in the intervening years. We had never served together; we had exchanged few letters. In all those years I had only seen Ike a few times, fleetingly, at class reunions or Army-Navy football games, usually with Mamie and Mary in tow. Since Mary and Mamie did not—and never would—take to each other, these occasional social meetings had not rekindled our earlier acquaintance into any sort of flame. However, as I learned later from his book *At Ease,* Ike held me in high regard.[6]

Ike was wearing his brand-new four stars and his custom-made "Eisenhower jacket." He greeted me warmly and effusively, like a long-lost brother, and instantly made me feel at home—and needed. After the amenities, he took the time to brief me personally (map, pointer and all) on the recent German offensive. I was impressed with his detailed tactical grasp of the battlefield situation and his clear, concise manner of describing what had happened. Ike had matured into a charming man with a first-class mind. During the briefing, I noted, he studiously avoided any personal recriminations, save one. He laid heavy blame on his Ultra specialist and G-2, Brigadier Mockler-Ferryman, who had called the shots wrong. He had already asked Alan Brooke for Mockler-Ferryman's relief, but "without prejudice." Otherwise, Ike took full personal responsibility for every aspect of the defeat.[7]

From my days in Marshall's secretariat, I had known that the United States was reading certain Japanese codes. But until I reached North Africa, I had had no idea that the British were reading Enigma codes, nor that an elaborate, closely held organization had been established to pass the data along to Army and Air Force commanders in the field. Ultra was very secret and glamorous, and its distribution was extremely limited. In the U.S. Army, to be "put in the Ultra picture," as the British phrased it, was like being admitted to a small elite society or club. But coming into the Ultra picture on the heels of Mockler-Ferryman's wrong call, I was very cautious. I did not then or later embrace Ultra as the Oracle of Delphi, but rather as a marvelous source of intelligence to be evaluated and used tactically with utmost care.

Later, over dinner at Ike's villa nearby, I noted another aspect of Ike new to me: a deep-seated, barely controlled anger. The public perceived him as smiling and genial. But I saw that he had very thin skin, a short fuse and an explosive temper. The conversation unfortunately strayed to his "Darlan Deal." Thereupon Ike's anger welled up and for a very long time—overly long, I thought—he defended the deal, for which he had been severely criticized in the media worldwide. Media criticism was a new experience for Ike, as it was to all of us who had grown up in the obscurity of the peacetime Army. It was not easy for any of us to cope with it.

While my aides scoured about acquiring proper battlefield dress and small arms for us (I chose a Springfield .30-06 rifle over an automatic weapon), I spent two days in Ike's headquarters going over reports, getting acquainted with the men assigned to the mammoth joint staffs. I learned that Ike brooked no American criticism of the French or British—especially the British. Any American who criticized the British stood a very good chance of being busted and sent home. I came away with the opinions expressed back in Tom Handy's OPD: In his efforts to achieve harmonious "coalition warfare," Ike had become excessively pro-British in his attitudes and thinking. Even his sometime driver and bridge companion, Kay Summersby, was British. I believe his close association with Kay and her family likewise contributed to Ike's pro-British attitudes, that her influence over him was greater than is generally realized.*

When I concluded my indoctrination at Ike's headquarters and received my formal orders, I was not overjoyed at my assignment. I was not only to act as Ike's eyes and ears on the Tunisian front, reporting back to him directly, I also had authority to make "suggestive changes" (as Ike put it) to American commanders at the front. Inevitably, I would be regarded as an odious spy for Ike, carrying tales outside the chain of command. Any suggested corrections from a rank newcomer from an exalted rear-echelon headquarters would be bitterly resented and probably ignored or laughed at behind my back. I decided my best policy was to keep a very low profile, eyes and ears open, mouth shut.

By this time, Alexander had established headquarters and staff in Constantine. On February 27, Ike, Bedell Smith and I flew there in Ike's

* Their close relationship is quite accurately portrayed, as far as my personal knowledge extends, in Kay's second book, *Past Forgetting*. Ike's son John published his father's personal letters to Mamie, in part to refute Kay's allegation that she and Ike were deeply in love. Many of these letters are obviously Ike's replies to probing letters from Mamie about his relationship with Kay. To my mind, Ike protests too much, thus defeating John's purpose. ("If anyone is banal and foolish enough to lift an eyebrow at an old duffer such as I am in connection with WAACS—Red Cross workers—nurses and drivers—you will know that I've no emotional involvements and will have none.") However, I do not believe the story Harry Truman allegedly told Merle Miller for his book *Plain Speaking* that Ike wrote Marshall that he wanted to divorce Mamie to marry Kay.[8]

personal armed B-17. (My aides rode up in a sedan and two jeeps we would need at the front.) Alexander proved to be all that I had heard: a patient, wise, fair-minded, shrewd, utterly charming professional soldier with a firm strategic grasp of the whole Mediterranean–North African Theater. His combat experience was intimidating to all American officers: four years in World War I, two years in Russia, one year on the frontier in India, three years in World War II. He had been thrust into a difficult position in Tunisia, a job requiring utmost tact, diplomacy, tolerance and discretion. He was clearly the man for the job and he bore the responsibility with disarming modesty. He was already sizing up his subordinates and realigning his forces and formulating a plan to crush the Axis in Tunisia and lead our victorious armies into Sicily in July.[9]

Alexander was not pleased with the senior army commanders in Tunisia. He believed both Anderson and Fredendall should be replaced. He asked Montgomery if he could spare one of his generals, Oliver Leese, to relieve Anderson. However, Monty refused to transfer Leese and Alexander left Anderson in place, but closely watched. Alexander judged Fredendall "dithering" and had said to Ike, "I'm sure you must have better men than that." However, at this point Ike was reluctant to relieve anyone of combat command—a professional disaster for the man concerned. (He would soon change that attitude.) Fredendall, moreover, was a special problem. He had been Marshall's hand-picked choice for the Oran invasion, which had gone well under Fredendall's direction. Consequently, Ike dragged his feet and left Fredendall in place.

Anderson had come to Constantine from his front-line headquarters. I found him to be one of the more difficult personalities in the British Army. His countryman Admiral Cunningham described him thus: "A Scot, very direct and outspoken, he was not everybody's man; but I liked and thought a lot of him." Ike found Anderson gallant, devoted to duty, absolutely selfless, honest and straightforward, but "blunt, at times to the point of rudeness," and thus "not a popular type." Lucian Truscott judged Anderson "personally bold and fearless," but "reserved and reticent," a man "not easy for Americans to know and understand, nor was his personality one to inspire them with confidence." Anderson, Truscott recalled, "usually took a pessimistic view of military operations." Unfortunately his chief of staff, C. V. O'N. McNabb, a "dour, silent kilt-clad Scotsman," was almost a carbon copy of his boss and had the same relentlessly pessimistic view of things. At the very least, the selection of Anderson and McNabb insured poor communications with the Americans; at the worst, as it developed, gross misunderstanding and heated antagonism. I thought that as an army commander, Anderson was in over his head.

Alexander had put a heavy head of steam behind Anderson's existing orders to "tidy" up the Tunisian battlefront, to restore it to normal organization and operation by nationality and division. Anderson would command the British First Army (actually, it was merely a corps in size) in the northern sector. The French, being re-equipped with American arms and reorganized as XIX Corps under overall command of Alphonse P. Juin (who also commanded French air forces) and holding the center of the line, had finally agreed to take orders from the British and would serve under Anderson's First Army. In the south, Fredendall's II Corps, in process of being reconstituted to consist of four normal American divisions—1st Armored and three infantry divisions—would fight as a separate entity, like a small army, reporting directly to Alexander.

From Constantine, Bedell Smith, my aides and I jeeped to Fredendall's new II Corps headquarters at Djebel Kouif, about fifteen miles north of Tebessa. It was freezing cold in Tunisia, but Fredendall's reception was colder than the weather. He lived in a comfortable home and, by military custom, should have invited me to share it. Instead, I was banished to a shabby windowless "hotel" with no amenities, quarters unsuitable even for a second lieutenant. Fredendall and his II Corps staff were rabidly, if not obscenely, anti-British and especially anti-Anderson. They blamed Anderson for everything that had gone wrong during the February offensive. Bedell Smith reached the conclusion, I believe, that Fredendall was incompetent or crazy or both and went back to Algiers and recommended to Ike that he relieve him immediately.[10]

Over the next several days, in cold rainy weather, I visited the four American divisions of II Corps. Orlando Ward, my friend from West Point and my former boss on Marshall's secretariat, commanded the 1st Armored Division. We knew one another sufficiently well to talk frankly. Ever since coming to Africa, Ward's division had been split up among the Americans, French and British. It had never fought as an integrated unit. During Rommel's offensive, Fredendall took personal command of some of Ward's units, bypassing Ward completely. When those units failed, Fredendall demanded Ike relieve Ward of command. Ike declined that drastic step. Instead, he rushed one of Patton's tank division commanders, my War College classmate, Ernie Harmon, to the front to serve in the nebulous capacity of "useful senior assistant" for tank operations. Harmon, a profane tornado like Patton, arrived at the tail end of Rommel's withdrawal. Fredendall turned over the entire battlefront to Harmon and went to bed. Harmon, in effect acting corps commander, took over Ward's tank operations and directed the battle in Fredendall's name for several days, while Ward looked on from a distance. When the dust settled, Harmon returned to Algiers and recommended Fredendall be relieved and later told Patton that Fredendall was a "physical and moral coward."*

* From Patton's diary and papers. Patton was hot-tempered and impetuous and blew off steam in the privacy of his diary. Frequently his notes are shallow, unconsidered and brutally critical of his fellow officers. In many cases that I am familiar with, Patton's comments are unjustified and not to be taken at face value. Had he lived to write his autobiography, I feel certain that he would have been more reflective and less extreme in his comments.

The various units of the 1st Armored Division had been decimated and many tanks lost. The men, including Ward, were understandably a little skittish and most, including Ward, had lost all confidence in Fredendall.[11]

Next I visited the three infantry divisions. Doc Ryder was now back in command of his full 34th (National Guard) Infantry Division, which had also been committed and fought piecemeal under various commanders and had suffered extremely heavy losses. Ryder, too, had come under severe criticism from Anderson and Fredendall. Ryder, an expert tactician, had his faults. In trying too hard to be a nice guy, he was too easy on his subordinates, some of whom were incompetent. As a result, the division suffered. He blamed the poor showing of the division on Fredendall, who, Ryder claimed, had ordered him to take the wrong positions—low ground rather than high. In this case, I had to side with Ryder.

An old friend, Terry de la Mesa Allen (Class of 1911), commanded the 1st Infantry Division, the "Big Red One." His second in command was Theodore Roosevelt, Jr., son of the late President. Teddy was an Army Reservist and a spirited martial character like his father. Owing to arthritis, he had to walk with a cane. The 1st Division had also been committed piecemeal, but blessedly had been spared heavy casualties. Neither Allen nor Roosevelt had any confidence in Fredendall, but I weighed their comments with a grain of salt. Both men were exceptional leaders revered by their men, but both had the same weakness: utter disregard for discipline, everywhere evident in their cocky division. It was clear that the division needed firm discipline and intensive training. I was not certain that Allen or Roosevelt had the inner toughness to impose the discipline and training or the willingness to take orders from and play on the same team with higher command.

The third infantry division, the 9th, commanded by Manton S. Eddy, was only just arriving to take up position in the line. I did not know Eddy, but I was impressed with his bearing and professionalism. He was a good leader and a well-schooled tactician but, as it developed, inclined to be cautious. His division was unblooded and, like the other three, badly in need of training, not only in basics but in large-scale maneuvers.[12]

A few days after I arrived at the front, Ike returned, on March 5, for a visit to II Corps. By that time, Alexander, Anderson, Bedell Smith, Lucian Truscott and Ernie Harmon had recommended that Fredendall be relieved of command. The pressure was mounting, and Ike, owing to his proclivity for writing endless letters, was really on the spot. Twice during Rommel's offensive he had commended Fredendall in writing for his "stout-hearted" leadership against the enemy. Only two days before, he had written Fredendall another commendation in which he cautioned him that he must trust subordinates and delegate authority but added, "There is no question at all in my mind of you having proved your right to command a separate and fairly large American force on the battlefield." Now

Ike had come for a final face-to-face confrontation and appraisal that could only result in Fredendall's relief.[13]

Fredendall had been alerted to Ike's arrival but discourteously had not informed me. That morning I rode off to Eddy's command post, a cold one-hour ride. When I arrived, Eddy informed me Ike was at II Corps and wanted to see me urgently. After my useless two-hour jeep ride, I arrived back at II Corps frozen to the marrow. Ike drew me aside for a private chat. He had only one question on his mind, a big one. "What do you think of the command here?" I suppose he wanted the assurance of one more negative opinion from a man he knew and respected. "Pretty bad," I replied. "Thanks, Brad," he said with what appeared to be relief. "You've confirmed what I thought."[14]

He had already selected George Patton to relieve Fredendall, a choice entailing considerable complications. Patton had been recently named to command the newly organized U.S. Seventh Army. It and Monty's Eighth Army were to spearhead the invasion of Sicily a mere 120 days hence. Patton was deeply involved in creating his army and planning the invasion. It would be highly disruptive to that effort to bring him to Tunisia. Moreover, Patton was, in the best of times, a bull in the china shop. Only a month before, Ike had been compelled to write Patton a letter advising him in no uncertain terms to keep his big mouth shut, that his braggadocio was hurting his standing with his Allied superiors. "You are quick-witted and have a facile tongue," Ike had written. "As a result you frequently give the impression that you act merely on impulse and not upon study and reflection. People who know you as I do are quite well aware of the fact that much of your talk is a smoke-screen, but some of those in authority who have a chance to meet you only occasionally do not have this knowledge." Patton was a notorious and outspoken Anglophobe, worse even than Fredendall, if that were possible. The II Corps job demanded a man of tact, reason and diplomacy. Ike was concerned that Patton could not—or would not—get along with the British.[15]

Ike had important personal news for me, as well. He confided that he would recommend to Patton that I be appointed deputy commander of II Corps. Ike's plan was that Patton would serve in Tunisia only a very short time, long enough to kick II Corps in the butt and lead it into its initial battles as a corps. Then he would send Patton back to Morocco to continue the Sicily planning. If, as Patton's understudy, I proved my battlefield mettle, I would replace Patton as II Corps commander. When Patton arrived at II Corps headquarters on March 6, these arrangements were confirmed and I was officially designated II Corps deputy that day.[16]

Only two days later, March 8, Ike called to say that Marshall had proposed a different duty for me. Ike would be flying up to talk it over with Patton and me. However, foul weather grounded Ike in Algiers. Patton, absorbed with his new responsibilities at II Corps, suggested that I go to Algiers and find out what it was all about. I flew to Constantine in a Piper Cub, then traveled by sedan to Algiers—a fourteen-hour motor trip![17]

The following day, March 10, I conferred with Ike and Bedell Smith all day and late into the night. This was the problem: On March 7, Marshall had cabled Ike suggesting that rather than serve as deputy commander of II Corps, I should go to Morocco and temporarily take over the Sicilian planning in place of Patton. On the following day, March 8, in a cabled reply to Marshall, Ike had proposed his own ideas. He would keep Patton at the Tunisian front only briefly—three weeks or so—then turn over II Corps to me about April 1, sending Patton back to Morocco to continue with the Sicilian planning. "So far as Bradley's personal and professional abilities are concerned," Ike had told Marshall, "he could do this [take over II Corps] at once, but I think it is most desirable that he be given an opportunity to learn the conditions here and become acquainted with terrain and personnel, including the British."[18]

Ike laid out the conflicting proposals to me, stating his own preference—that I remain with II Corps—and asked me for my opinion. I thought his own idea made more sense. Patton's staff in Morocco was his own; they might resent a temporary outsider who had yet to give a single thought to Sicily. Moreover, I preferred the combat job to a planning job and believed I could serve Ike better at the Tunisian front. We all agreed Ike's idea was the better one and on the very same day, March 10, Ike cabled Marshall: "After a full discussion of command problem with Bradley and my staff, all of us believe it best to adhere to original plan of giving Bradley command of II Corps but probably at earlier date than first contemplated."[19]

On return to II Corps the following day, March 11, I candidly discussed with Patton the options, my own opinions and Ike's decision in the matter. Patton fully concurred, noting that day in his diary: "I accepted this as best." Patton knew his assignment to II Corps was merely temporary and extremely limited in scope, that quite soon he would be returning to Morocco for the much more important task of commanding an army in the Sicily invasion. He much preferred to have me as his understudy in Tunisia than as his stand-in in Morocco.[20]

I have taken some pains to lay out the facts about this sequence of events owing to the fact that in my war memoir, *A Soldier's Story,* inexact writing led me to inadvertently create a wrong impression. In that version, I erroneously stated that Ike asked me if I thought Patton should remain with II Corps for "the rest of the Tunisian campaign" or return soon to Morocco for the Sicily planning. My response in *A Soldier's Story* was: "Well, I think that George should go back and resume the Sicilian planning." This has given some readers and historians—notably Patton's biographer Ladislas Farago—the impression that I, because of my "professional rivalry" with Patton, was trying to undercut him and railroad him back to Morocco so that I could get command of II Corps as quickly as possible. Nothing could be further from the truth. As I have shown in the Marshall-Ike exchanges, Ike had already made up his mind that Patton would remain at II Corps only a brief time and that, unless I fell on my face, I would replace him when he returned to Morocco. I was never asked how long I thought Patton should stay in Tunisia, and I regret the error.[21]

The fact of the matter is that not in Tunisia, nor ever, did I feel a "professional rivalry" with George Patton, or any sort of jealousy, as Farago implies. It is obvious from the foregoing that I enjoyed the complete confidence of both Marshall and Eisenhower.

Later, in a private memorandum for his personal files, Ike put down his impressions of Patton:

> *George S. Patton, Jr.* A shrewd soldier who believes in showmanship to such an extent that he is almost flamboyant. He talks too much and too quickly and sometimes creates a very bad impression. Moreover, I fear that he is not always a good example to subordinates, who may be guided by only his surface actions without understanding the deep sense of duty, courage and service that make up his real personality. He has done well as a combat corps commander and I expect him to do well in all future operations.

Patton was a superb field general and leader—perhaps our very best—but a man with many human and professional flaws. Those flaws held the potential for danger, even disaster, so much so that Marshall and Ike felt Patton had to be continuously watched and tethered. I was aware of these reservations about Patton on the higher level and, in fact, I shared them.[22]

FIFTEEN

George Patton's arrival at II Corps has been vividly depicted in many books and the film *Patton*. His primary task was to shape the corps quickly into a tough, highly disciplined, battleworthy outfit. He laid heavy emphasis on externals, such as dress codes (ties, leggings, helmets at all times), saluting, salty pep talks and sudden dramatic appearances in unlikely places with his bone-handled pistols, shiny helmet and glaring countenance. For my taste, it was all excessively harsh; but intentionally or unintentionally, excess was Patton's style. A firm but more mature and considerate discipline would no doubt have achieved the same results. But he was the boss, the stage was his.

Together, that first week, we inspected the four divisions of II Corps. During one of those inspections, Patton conducted himself in a manner I have not seen depicted or described elsewhere. Terry Allen had established a command post in a small oasis. He and his staff lived in tents. Since the Luftwaffe was extremely active in our sector, there were many slit trenches in the area. Patton strode about eyeing these slit trenches with utter contempt, as though they were cowardly retreats. In his squeaky tenor, he said, "Terry, which one is yours?" When Allen pointed out his slit trench, Patton strode over, unzipped his fly and urinated into the trench. Imperiously rezipping his fly, Patton sneered at Terry: "Now try to use it." With this earthy GI gesture, Patton had virtually labeled Allen a coward in front of his own men. I was no less shocked than Terry, and I had to wonder if this was indeed good leadership.[1]

By the time Patton and I took over our duties at II Corps, the Allies were assured of victory in Tunisia. Montgomery had reached the Mareth Line and rebuffed a Rommel attack. Our own lines in Tunisia were at last unscrambled and militarily precise. Allied air and sea power had virtually isolated von Arnim and Rommel within the Tunisian peninsula. In the lull since the February rout, we had been stockpiling enormous quantities of ammunition and gasoline; and now Monty, resupplied through Tripoli, had vastly shortened his supply tail. The Axis forces, denied supplies and reinforcements, were growing weaker every day with every patrol skirmish. Our military problem was relatively simple: to defeat a hopelessly trapped Axis force with minimum Allied casualties in the fastest possible time, without allowing any of the enemy to slip out of Tunisia to fight again.[2]

Rommel perceived the utter hopelessness of the situation. "A great gloom settled over us all," he wrote. "For the Army Group to remain longer in Africa was plain suicide." He urged Rome and Berlin to organize a plan—a Dunkirk—to evacuate his soldiers. But neither Hitler nor Mussolini would hear of it. He urged a pullback from the Mareth Line to a better defensive position farther north, the Chott Line. No luck—at least not then. Rome and Berlin ordered the Axis forces in Tunisia to fight to the death, thereby tying down for as long as possible Allied armies that could be employed elsewhere. On March 9, Rommel turned over his command to von Arnim and left Tunisia for good, belatedly going home on extended sick leave. Not for a long while did Ultra reveal his departure and until then we believed we were still up against the champ.[3]

Alexander had two fundamental strategic choices for the defeat of the Axis in Tunisia. He could boldly drive a wedge between von Arnim in the north and the Afrika Korps in the south at the Mareth Line, encircling and destroying the two forces separately; or he could cautiously squeeze the Axis forces together into a smaller and smaller beachhead in northern Tunisia until they had no more usable airfields or room to maneuver and would finally be compelled to fight to the last man or surrender. He chose the second, more cautious, approach. He was strongly influenced in this decision by his complete lack of faith in the American soldier. The way the Tunisian front was laid out, if he chose the bolder "wedge" concept, it would fall to II Corps to spearhead the wedge. Patton or no Patton, Alexander did not believe II Corps had the skill or verve to pull it off. The wedge was certain to invite brutal, slashing counterattacks from the veteran panzer divisions of the Afrika Korps. Alexander doubted we could withstand those counterattacks.

Montgomery's Eighth Army would carry the weight of the attack in the "squeeze" strategy. Monty would break through the Mareth Line, driving the Afrika Korps northward along the coastal plain back into Tunis. Anderson's First Army (now 170,000 troops, including 50,000 re-equipped French) would aggressively hold the north and central Tunisian front. In the southern sector, the U.S. II Corps (90,000 troops) would "demonstrate" and "make noise" with limited feinting attacks eastward out of the mountains, drawing the Axis off Monty's front and threatening the Axis right flank. We were specifically prohibited from making any major thrusts into the coastal plain, let alone a bold wedge that would split the Axis.

Patton would lead the corps through these feinting actions, then, about April 1, would return to Morocco, at which time I would replace him as commander.

Some authors have described Patton as being bitter that II Corps was assigned so limited a role. That is certainly an exaggeration. We were both disappointed, but we took it with good grace. Alexander was right, II Corps was not then ready in any respect to carry out operations beyond feints. Patton and I would have only ten days in which to prepare the corps for action, not nearly enough time to shake it down and shape it up. Better, I thought, that we learn to walk before we ran, and I believe for all his tough talk Patton believed that, too. At any rate, in the privacy of his diary, he appears philosophical. After Alexander came to II Corps on March 14 to give us our orders, Patton noted almost laconically: "Alexander is O.K., though naturally selfish for his side [i.e., the British] just as I would be in his place."[4]

Monty prepared for his Mareth Line breakout with his usual maddening thoroughness. Several times he postponed its date to amass more men and supplies. Monty was not finally satisfied until (as at El Alamein) he outnumbered the Axis on his front by about two to one in men and guns and four to one in tanks (160,000 men, 1,410 guns and 610 tanks vs. 80,000 men, 680 guns and 150 tanks). At the time, these delays were exasperating. But, upon reflection, I am glad they occurred. Each delay gave us a day or so longer in which to hone II Corps troops to a finer edge.

II Corps jumped off on March 17, three days prior to Monty's offensive. Our major objectives were two. Terry Allen's Big Red One would take Gafsa and, if conditions were right, El Guettar, where Allen would establish a fuel dump for Monty. Then, Orlando Ward's 1st Armored Division would drive eastward through Kasserine Pass to Station de Sened, east northeast of El Guettar and, if conditions were right, push on to the heights around Maknassy. Manton Eddy's green 9th Infantry Division would contribute forces to both Allen and Ward. Doc Ryder's 34th Division, farther north, was held in reserve to make a third feint when the Axis retreated its way.[5]

Both Alexander and Eisenhower were on hand at II Corps' advanced CP at Feriana to watch our jump-off. Patton and I joined the troops at the front. Patton went with Terry Allen on the push to Gafsa; I joined Orlando Ward's outfit thrusting toward Station de Sened, with elements of Eddy's 9th Infantry Division in the assault. This was my first taste of battle, and I was very nearly killed in the first few hours. The area was thick with enemy land mines. The wheel of my jeep rolled over one of these nasty weapons —an Italian model with eight sticks of dynamite. For reasons no one could fathom, the mine failed to explode. I was unnerved by this close call and it required considerable effort not to show it. Later, on reflection, I concluded that God must have spared me for more important duties.

Alexander's air counterpart, Arthur Tedder, had by now brought some order out of the chaos in Ike's Mediterranean air forces, creating command and supply organizations which were more efficient than their predecessors. Control of tactical aviation in close support of the various Allied armies had been delegated to a British general, Arthur ("Mary," from "Maori") Coningham. Like most airmen, Coningham believed less in "close support" than in "strategic" air strikes deep at the enemy's rear bases and airfields, and dogfights to achieve air superiority. Consequently, he was opposed to maintaining an air umbrella at all times over ground troops. Also, the air power he had available for close support was disproportionately assigned to Monty. The air doctrine and the disposition of the available close air support were imperfectly understood in II Corps, to say the least. We had expected full close air support. At no time did we get it. One result was that throughout our mission in support of Monty's Mareth Line breakout we were continually harassed by Axis air, which not only significantly impeded our operations but also led to bitter feelings on our part toward Mary Coningham and his staff.[6]

Both II Corps feints were at first successful. Our enemy along this sector of the front was Italian. He had already begun a gradual withdrawal to shrink and tighten up his lines. Terry Allen took Gafsa with ease and struck off down the road to El Guettar—Patton exhorting him every yard of the way. Ward's infantry took Station de Sened with equal ease. But when Ward ordered his armor to roll through toward Maknassy, he encountered difficulty. Heavy rains had turned the terrain into a quagmire. His tanks and trucks bogged down. Patton was furious, blaming not the rain but Ward. The thoughtful, quiet-spoken, colorless Ward was not Patton's idea of a combat leader. Patton impulsively concluded that Ward and the 1st Armored Division, still skittish from the defeat at Kasserine Pass, were lacking in aggressiveness. Nothing I said would change Patton's mind. I saw then that Ward's days were numbered, that his career was seemingly dogged by bad luck.[7]

Monty jumped off on March 20 with a thunderous frontal assault and a feint on the left side of the line. The enemy fought tenaciously, and the frontal assault, Liddell Hart wrote, was "a failure." After one full bloody day's fighting, Monty wired Alexander: "Enemy obviously intends to stand and fight and I am preparing a dogfight." He thereupon proposed a greatly expanded role for II Corps to assist his breakout: a "strong eastward thrust of the U.S. Armored Division," all the way to the sea to "cut Sfax-Gabès Road." But Alexander quashed this proposal: "The role you suggest for II Corps is too ambitious at the moment." Indeed it was.[8]

Nonetheless, on the following day, March 22, with Monty smashing his head against a stone wall, Alexander envisioned a substantial step-up in our operations. He ordered II Corps to *prepare* a plan to send a small fast armored force to Maharès (on the coast between Sfax and Gabès) to disrupt the enemy rear and strike at his supply dumps. This was clearly meant to be a harassing attack, not an all-out II Corps offensive to drive a wedge to the sea. But, of course, the proposal vastly appealed to Patton's offensive spirit, and I could almost see him licking his lips in anticipation. The problem was, however, that the armor required for this proposed mission—Ward's—was still bogged down in the mud and had not even captured the assigned heights at Maknassy. Ward was holding everything up, a harsh reality encroaching on Patton's John Wayne fantasy of a cavalry dash to the sea! Red-faced with rage, Patton blistered Ward by telephone and, in his diary, bitterly regretted that he had not personally led the assault on Maknassy.[9]

Terry Allen's feint toward El Guettar had worked better than Alexander or Monty had expected. Von Arnim ordered the veteran (though depleted) 10th Panzer Division to counterattack Allen at El Guettar. Our front-line codebreakers picked up and decoded the order, giving us a full day's notice, and Terry Allen prepared excellent defensive positions. A second decoded message provided us further valuable details of the attack. When the two Axis divisions struck on the afternoon of March 23, Allen was very well prepared and mauled the Germans and Italians, destroying thirty-two tanks. This victory was doubly sweet. Not only had the feint worked as designed, it was the first solid, indisputable defeat we inflicted on the German Army in the war. Kasserine Pass had now been avenged.[10]

I was not present for this American triumph. I was in Algiers conferring with Ike on a matter of grave importance both to me and to II Corps.

Two days after our jump-off, on March 19, Alexander's chief of staff, Richard L. McCreery, came to our CP to lay out the long-range plan for the final conquest of Tunisia. As drawn, Monty's Eighth Army and Anderson's First Army would conduct a converging attack toward Bizerte and Tunis, squeezing the Axis into its final bridgehead. Eddy's 9th Infantry Division would be assigned to Anderson's army, otherwise II Corps would play no role whatsoever in the final victory. We would be left behind in the desert. When McCreery had finished outlining his plan, both Patton and I were speechless with rage. But since we were under strict orders from Ike to do what Alexander told us to do, we raised no objections. That night, Patton confided to his diary: "I kept my temper and agreed. There is nothing else to do, but I can't see how Ike can let them [the British] pull his leg so. It is awful. I hope I will be back in Morocco on the other job before we are pinched out. . . . The more I think about the plan of pinching us out, the madder I get, but no one knows that except me." These were my sentiments exactly.[11]

We were both too busy at the front over the next two days to give the Alexander plan much time or attention. But every time I thought about it, I seethed with anger—I more so than Patton, because he was going back to Morocco and II Corps would no longer be his responsibility. On March

22, three days after Monty's Mareth Line breakout fizzled, I obtained Patton's approval to fly to Algiers to carry our objections to Ike about the future role of II Corps. As I had suspected, Ike did not know that II Corps was to be pinched out of the final victory. I was disappointed to find him taking so little interest in II Corps, but I tried not to show it. I forcefully urged that the plan be changed, that II Corps be included in the final kill, making these major points: that it was tactically foolish to forgo the use of three divisions that had had as much combat experience as any in Anderson's army; that to split off our 9th Division and give it to Anderson was a reversion to the original error in Tunisia of mixing up nationalities (and incompatible supply lines); that all our divisions needed the battle experience to harden them for operations that lay ahead and for providing combat veterans to train the new divisions coming up; and that our troops had won the right, and we owed it to the American people, to share in the final victory.

None of the foregoing had apparently occurred to Ike. He heard me out patiently, nodding in agreement at each point I made. When I was finished, he was in complete agreement. He then asked me how I would fit II Corps into the final plan. I had been mentally working that out for several days. I proposed that the entire corps (including Eddy's 9th Division) be shifted to the north of Anderson's First Army, giving it the mission of mounting an independent drive on Bizerte. It was a radical and complicated idea. I'm not sure Ike agreed with my specific plan or even fully grasped it, but I had sold him on the concept that II Corps should be in on the final victory as a separate entity with a meaningful task.

In *Crusade in Europe,* Ike credits himself, Patton and others with the idea. Farago implies I stole the idea from Patton. But in fact it was my idea alone. Ike wrote in *Crusade* that "I had a personal interview with Alexander to insist upon the employment of the entire II Corps as a unit," misciting documents to back up his claim. In fact, as Ike's published papers now reveal, he first broached the matter with Alexander at the tail end of a letter, March 23, the day I was in Algiers. He reinforced the suggestion with the same arguments I had just used to convince him. Ike did not specifically order that Alexander use II Corps, but his words were tantamount to an order: "I would consider it unfortunate if the developments of the campaign were such that participation by American troops, in an American sector, was deliberately eliminated as the crisis of the campaign approaches."[12]

I flew back to the front. Time would elapse before Alexander and McCreery would come around to my view, but at least I had swung the commander in chief.

Montgomery, meanwhile, had got nowhere at the Mareth Line with his frontal assaults. In mid-battle, he completely changed his plan. He enlarged the feint on the left side of his line into the major thrust. On March 26, he broke through. The Afrika Korps, fighting stubbornly, slowly fell back to the north toward the Chott Line above Gabès.[13]

Our II Corps had materially assisted Monty's breakthrough by initially drawing off the 10th Panzer Division, some Italian troops and considerable Axis air. But our follow-up operations were unimpressive. Allen's Big Red One, having checked the 10th Panzer attack, ran out of steam and dug in, fending off savage but minor assaults. Ward's 1st Armored Division remained bogged down near Maknassy, unable to complete its mission of taking the heights near the town—a failure that so infuriated Patton that he ordered Ward personally to lead an attack. Ward did so and was slightly injured by a ricocheting rock, but he failed to take the hills. After that, any hope of pushing across to Maharès had to be abandoned. Farther north, Doc Ryder's 34th Division, ordered to "make noise" toward Fondouk but not to run grave risks, encountered unexpectedly heavy resistance, broke off the attack and withdrew without having accomplished anything of consequence.[14]

These inconclusive operations had done nothing to enhance the image of the American soldier in British eyes. Alexander and his staff continued to hold us in low esteem. The British were especially critical of Ward and Ryder and their divisions. They freely criticized us to the war correspondents, who in turn relayed these criticisms back to II Corps. Since Alexander had not officially expressed any reservations to Patton, me or II Corps staff, we were justifiably enraged at these backbiting leaks which served no purpose other than to sow bitter dissension between allies. What made it especially galling was that all U.S. personnel were under strictest orders from Ike not to criticize the British in any way. Why didn't Ike impose the same muzzle on the British? He was well aware of the British leaks. His failure to stop them contributed to our growing paranoia that Ike was so pro-British he didn't much care what happened to II Corps.[15]

Meanwhile, Montgomery had once more failed to exploit a breakthrough. After cracking through the Mareth Line, he had the opportunity to dash ahead, to encircle and annihilate the Afrika Korps. But, as at El Alamein, he let them slip away—to dig in at the Chott Line. British Army historian I. S. O. Playfair put it this way: "The British could take full credit for what they had achieved but, as at El Alamein . . . they had not produced the quality of being what pugilists call 'good finishers.' "

Anticipating a tough battle at the Chott Line, and typically massing forces for another brutal frontal assault, Monty again asked Alexander for help from II Corps. "If that corps could come forward even a few miles," Monty wrote Alexander, "it would make my task very simple." Thus was born a scheme to substantially enlarge the role of II Corps operations: an armored thrust out of El Guettar down the Gabès Road. This was not to be a major assault—a wedge to divide the Axis or drive to the sea—but rather a harassing attack on the enemy near the Chott Line. We were specifically ordered not to incur a major tank battle.[16]

For Patton—chafing under Alexander's tight restrictions on II Corps—here was a heaven-sent opportunity to show his dash and verve. I have no doubt that he secretly believed he could punch through to the sea, divide the Axis and upstage Monty. He moved Eddy's full 9th Division to El Guettar to join Allen's 1st Division for the infantry push that would open the way for the armor. He went up to Maknassy to see Ward—whose armor would carry the weight of the attack—and told him that if his division failed again he would relieve him of command. He designated Clarence C. Benson, a tanker who had served under Patton in the glory days in France in World War I, to command the armor, which was called "Benson Force."[17]

I went to the front on April 1 to observe the jump-off of Benson Force. The slow, slugging advance of Eddy and Allen's infantry had alerted the Axis and attracted very heavy enemy air attacks. That morning, a flight of a dozen twin-engine Junker bombers hit our observation CP, and for the second time in Tunisia I was very nearly killed. We took cover in slit trenches, but the heavy bomb blasts killed three men, including Patton's aide Richard N. Jenson (fifteen feet from me), one of our jeep drivers and a tanker and wounded several others, including a British liaison officer, Charles A. L. Dunphie, and my aide, Lew Bridge. The bomb fragments had riddled my jeep and my .30-06 Springfield rifle. I treated Dunphie and Bridge—years of Army first aid drill finally put to good use—and loaded Dunphie, who was severely hit, into a command car and drove him back to an evacuation hospital. Bridge, who made his own way to the rear, was out of action for a month. My other aide, Chet Hansen, quickly recovered from the shock and remained on full duty.[18]

Patton, deeply moved by Jenson's death, frustrated by Benson's slow start, angry that Monty had been allotted the lion's share of local air support, imprudently took this opportunity to vent his long pent-up rage at the British. He impulsively added his personal signature to a II Corps situation report that circulated throughout Alexander's command and which that day was harshly critical of Mary Coningham's air support. "Forward troops have been continuously bombed all morning," the report stated. "Total lack of air cover for our units has allowed German air forces to operate almost at will." When Coningham saw this official document publicly criticizing him and his aviators, he in turn seized the opportunity to publicly vent his—and the British—contempt for our GI's. He denounced II Corps for a "false cry of wolf," demanding that such "inaccurate and exaggerated reports should cease." He sarcastically and superciliously hoped that II Corps was not adopting "the discredited practice of using air force as an alibi for lack of success on the ground.'' Then the knife: ''If SITREP [Situation Report] is in earnest and balanced against . . . facts it can only be assumed that II Corps personnel are not battle-worthy in terms of present operations.''

At his headquarters, Arthur Tedder, Coningham's boss, read this exchange in stunned disbelief. He later recalled: ''I knew this was dynamite with a short, fast-burning fuse, and the situation could well have led to a major crisis in Anglo-American relations.'' Tedder telephoned Ike to assure him that he had already ordered Coningham to ''withdraw and cancel the signal'' and to immediately fly to II Corps headquarters and apologize to Patton. Ike apparently took the incident very, very hard. Tedder wrote that afterwards he learned ''that Ike had actually drafted a signal to Washington referring to this incident, and saying that since it was obvious he could not control his Allied commanders, he asked to be relieved. That signal never went.'' Ike's biographer Stephen Ambrose wrote that Bedell Smith ''talked him out of sending it.''[19]

Even though Patton had ignited the furor with the SITREP, Coningham's riposte stung him to the quick, and for days he was in a towering rage. When Coningham came to II Corps to apologize, a shouting match ensued. But in the end Patton accepted a grudging official apology from Coningham. As part of the détente, Patton in turn sent a letter of ''appreciation'' to Coningham ''for your more than generous signal,'' and regretting ''the misunderstanding for which I am partially responsible.'' But privately Patton continued to seethe, directing much of his anger at Ike for permitting British criticism—this time official—of our GI's to continue. ''It is noteworthy that had I done what Coningham did, I would have been relieved,'' he wrote.[20]

Ike, after coolly considering the matter for some days, blamed Patton for the furor and wrote him a chiding letter: ''I realize how chagrined you were and why you felt that some public retraction or apology was indicated. However I realize also that the *great purpose of complete Allied teamwork must be achieved in this theater* and it is my conviction that this purpose will not be furthered by demanding the last pound of flesh for every error, when other measures should suffice. . . . I am since informed that there was a certain amount of unwise distribution of your SITREP.'' He advised Patton that if in the future he felt critical of another service it should be expressed in a ''confidential report to the next military superior *only*.'' This letter was further proof to us that in Ike's eyes the British could do no wrong.[21]

Benson Force bogged down in the face of stubborn enemy resistance and, for a time, got nowhere. Alexander blamed Ward and suggested to Ike that Ward be relieved of command. Ike agreed, but insisted that Alexander write Patton and take up the matter directly. By that time, Patton had already made up his mind to relieve Ward, but he resented the Alexander letter, viewing it as more British criticism of our GI's, and refused to use it as "a cloak for my act." In fact, Ward's relief was not Patton's "act." This bravest of all battlefield warriors could not summon the personal courage to confront Ward face-to-face. Instead, he asked if I would do it![22]

This was one of my most difficult assignments in the war. Ward was a close friend. I had often visited him at Maknassy and thoroughly understood his situation and the problems in his division. It was my opinion that Ward was a victim of bad luck (heavy rains, for example) and circumstance and that the decision to relieve him was unfair and unwise. But Ward had lost the confidence of both Alexander and Patton and it was impossible for me at that stage to reverse the decision and probably not in the best interests of II Corps. Grudgingly, I went to Maknassy and gave Ward his walking papers. He was not surprised. He took the decision with grace. On his return to the States, Marshall gave him command of another armored division, which he led with distinction.[23]

Patton summoned Ernie Harmon from Morocco to replace Ward in command of the division. Meantime, he tried to kick or drag Benson Force down the Gabès Road. He fearlessly drove right into the front lines and told Benson he was "disgusted" with his slow progress. He exhorted Benson "to push on until he got into a big fight or hit the ocean . . . keep pushing for a big fight or a bath." Soon afterwards, on April 7, advance elements of Benson Force linked up with advancing troops of Monty's Eighth Army. This made good media copy, but the truth was that Benson Force failed in its mission to close the Chott Line and harass the enemy.[24]

The rapidly retreating Axis forces, in fact, merely paused at the Chott Line, then slyly resumed the northward withdrawal. Monty gave them a good stiff blow, but then he dallied and again missed a golden opportunity to encircle and annihilate; the enemy slipped out of his grasp. Historian Playfair lamented: "Once again the Eighth Army had won its battle and had given the enemy a severe mauling. Yet once again it had failed to finish the enemy off."[25]

Alexander, meanwhile, had set in motion a scheme to strike the enemy in his right flank farther north and partly impede his retreat. For the purpose, he hastily formed the IX Corps, commanded by British General John T. Crocker. The corps, which like II Corps would report directly to Alexander, was composed of forces from Anderson's First Army and, we discovered with a jolt, Doc Ryder's 34th Division, which was summarily detached from our command. Patton and I were unhappy. We didn't like the plan and we did not like the idea of Ryder's division being incorporated into a British command. But short of raising another disruptive furor, there was nothing we could do.

The IX Corps jumped off on April 8. Ryder's 34th Division, together with British infantry, spearheaded the attack to break a path for the British armor. The attack failed abysmally. Owing to a faulty battle plan, and an unavoidable delay, Ryder's men got trapped in the open with little or no flank support and were blistered by enemy artillery and forced to break off the assault. Later, Crocker blamed Ryder for the failure and bitterly castigated the 34th Division to Allied war correspondents. Because of a misguided censorship policy at Ike's headquarters, the correspondents' stories were allowed to pass untouched and were printed worldwide.* Ike fired his censor for his "inexcusable action," held a press conference to refute criticism of U.S. troops, prodded Alexander into issuing a statement in praise of II Corps—but did not censure Crocker. No words can describe Patton's rage and fury at Ike. He wrote in his diary that Ryder had failed because the 34th Division was assigned "an impossible mission." He went on: "Ike is more British than the British and putty in their hands. . . . God damn all British and so-called Americans who have their legs pulled by them. . . . I would rather be commanded by an Arab. I think less than nothing of Arabs."[26]

Alexander and his staff, influenced by Crocker, now reached a drastic decision: The 34th Division should be withdrawn from the line, sent to the rear and retrained, the junior officers under supervision of the British. There was little indication that Ike cared, so Patton and I undertook to avert what would surely have been the destruction of the division and professional ruin of Doc Ryder, a valuable tactician. Patton drew up a letter strongly advising against withdrawing the 34th Division, and I flew to Alexander's headquarters in Haidra to present the letter and to make the case orally. We stressed that the 34th was a National Guard division, the first into combat in Africa. To withdraw and humiliate it could have far-reaching consequences, not only throughout our whole National Guard system, but also in the U.S. domestic political arena. I gave Ryder high marks and faulted Crocker's battle plan. What the 34th needed most, I stressed, was a victory to restore its self-confidence. "Give me the division," I pleaded, "and I'll promise you they will take and hold their very first objective." Alexander was amused at my earnestness, but he weighed the pros and cons and thereupon overruled his staff: "Take them, they're yours."[27]

The Crocker IX Corps fiasco concluded the first phase of our final operations in Tunisia. The Axis fell back to a strong defensive position at

* One result of these stories, and some earlier ones, was that the American public was completely misinformed about the mission of II Corps in support of Monty's offensive. The public was led to believe that our mission had been to break through to the sea and split the Axis forces. When we "failed" to do so, we had been "outwitted" by Rommel. The misconception was largely our fault. We had not yet learned how to deal with war correspondents or to fully trust them. We were still feeling our way with censorship policies.

Enfidaville, and Monty moved up and paused to catch his breath. In the meantime, I had obtained grudging approval from Alexander for my II Corps thrust at Bizerte in the north, and we began the complex job of shifting the corps behind Anderson's lines and setting up an independent supply line along the Mediterranean coastal roads. Patton had remained in Tunisia two weeks beyond the original schedule and was anxious to return to Morocco and the Sicily planning. I relieved him as II Corps commander at midnight April 15. The turnover was kept secret so that the Axis would think Patton was still in Tunisia and not preparing to strike elsewhere. His final diary comment from Tunisia on Ike: "What an ass."[28]

As he took leave of II Corps, Patton drew me aside for a private chat. He was warm and flattering in his praise. I returned the compliment, but I cautioned him to button his lip, to stop criticizing Ike and the British. A few days after he returned to the rear he dropped me a personal letter which said, in part: "I have continued to take your advice and say nothing. . . . I want to repeat that I never enjoyed service with anyone as much as you and trust that some day we can complete our warlike operations."[29]

Patton's forty-two-day tour in Tunisia had gained him much notoriety, contributing to his growing legend, but it had not been his finest hour. It was no fault of his. He had been thrust into Fredendall's job with no warning and had to make do with Fredendall's staff and a deputy corps commander also new to the scene. He had restored discipline to the corps and to a large extent its self-confidence. But Patton, severely tethered because of Alexander's lack of faith in our soldiers, had little opportunity to show his battlefield prowess. II Corps had not done particularly well even in its limited role. For all Patton's bravado, the American GI had yet to prove himself in combat. There had been many isolated noteworthy achievements and acts of valor, but on the whole we had merely learned to walk.

As Patton's understudy, I had grown on the job. I had learned much, in terms of men and machines, about what was possible and not possible on a battlefield. But the most revealing and at times fascinating learning aspect had been the close-hand observation of the personal interplay between the generals and their often conflicting views on strategy and tactics. I shared Patton's misgivings about Ike, though I was less harsh in my private judgments and never criticized him before others. Ike was too weak, much too prone to knuckle under to the British, often, as I have shown, at our expense. If I were to continue to serve as one of his battlefield lieutenants, it was clear that I must be much, much firmer in advancing American interests and strategy.

The British had fought a long, hard, costly battle across North Africa, and I admired their courage and battlefield expertise. But I was not convinced that they were infallible or as good as their press notices. On the whole, Monty's pursuit of Rommel lacked vigor and imagination; it was more akin to moving trench warfare than the fast, open maneuvering of

Sherman, or the German blitzkrieg personified by Rommel himself in his better days. Military historians will argue the point forever, but I thought Alexander might well have brought the fighting in Tunisia to a swifter conclusion by the wedge strategy—a bold, strong thrust to the sea to divide the Axis while Monty held fast at the Mareth Line. Alexander's IX Corps attack toward Fondouk might have succeeded in splitting the Axis had it been more carefully conceived and launched earlier and with far greater strength. On the whole, I concluded, British generalship was too slow and too cautious.

SIXTEEN

The final battle of Tunisia was a classic set piece. Churchill aptly compared it to the great German defeat at Stalingrad. It engaged the utmost energies of well over half a million men on the ground and probably half that number in the air and on the sea. The Allied victory was inevitable, but it was no easy victory. The trapped enemy was the elite of the German and Italian armies, tough, desert-hardened young men who, as the official British historian wrote, "fought with the desperation of men who knew they could not retreat."[1]

By the time I assumed command of II Corps, April 16, we knew from Ultra that Rommel had gone. Our opposing senior general was Jürgen von Arnim, who had orders to fight to the last man. There would be no "Dunkirk" for the Afrika Korps and the other Axis units sent over since the Torch landings—in all some 250,000 men. But von Arnim had little to fight with. Tedder's 3,000-plane air force had achieved air superiority over the combat zone and Cunningham's navy had imposed a tight maritime blockade. Nothing could reach or leave Tunisia. Von Arnim was reduced to about a hundred serviceable tanks and was critically short of gasoline, ammunition, medical supplies and food.

Our situation, conversely, could scarcely have been better. Facing the enemy along the hundred-mile perimeter, we had amassed some twenty divisions—well over 300,000 men—with some 1,400 tanks and an equal number of artillery pieces. Mary Coningham's tactical air force now had the use of abandoned Axis airfields below Enfidaville in the coastal plain. His fighter aircraft could range at will along the whole of the perimeter, and—blessedly!—we no longer had to dive for slit trenches to save our skins from Luftwaffe bombs and machine-gun bullets. By then, too, our ragged, uncertain supply lines had been shaped into a well-oiled machine, delivering more than adequate stocks. Only Monty's Eighth Army, still dependent on a long supply tail to Tripoli, suffered from spot shortages, and these were not severe.

On the day I took over my II Corps duties, Alexander published battle orders for the final assault, which was called "Vulcan." Basically, his strategy called for a giant squeeze all around the perimeter. Since the terrain and supply situation favored Anderson's First Army, Alexander designated him to make the major assault. Monty's Eighth Army would merely exert pressure at Enfidaville, making what gains he could without excessive risks. The French XIX Corps, in the mountains to Monty's left (and Anderson's right), would put on pressure and exploit opportunities as Anderson and Monty squeezed forward. My II Corps, positioned to the north of Anderson's First Army, would cover Anderson's left flank, draw off the enemy and advance eastward to the high ground at Chouigui and further north along the coast toward Bizerte. In the final phase we would assist Anderson in capturing Bizerte.[2]

Administratively, Alexander placed II Corps under Anderson's command. This outraged Patton, but I was not at all concerned. Alexander had outlined the II Corps mission in such fine detail—in which I was in complete accord—there was little likelihood that Anderson would attempt to alter it. Moreover, Alexander told me privately that if at any time I received an order, suggestion or request from Anderson to which I objected, I was to feel free to contact Alexander directly. I was not to be boxed in or hamstrung by a British Army command.[3]

That same day, Ike sent me my first official letter as II Corps commander. It was very long, patronizing in tone, and it contained some specific tactical suggestions which were dangerously ill-conceived and proof to me (if further proof were needed) that Ike had little grasp of sound battlefield tactics. He expounded at length about how important it was that American troops make a good showing—as if I needed to be reminded of that! He concluded with "one item" of advice, which, coming from Ike, was somewhat amusing: "You must be tough with your immediate subordinates and they must be equally tough with their respective subordinates. . . . We have reached the point where troops *must* secure objectives assigned by commanders and, where necessary, we must direct leaders to get out and *lead and to secure the necessary results*." I filed the letter, unanswered, dismissing it as so much grist for the historians.* [4]

I established my II Corps headquarters under canvas on a hillside outside Bedia. By this time, I had sent for my chief of staff at the 28th Division, Bill Kean, and my driver, Alex Stoute. Kean arrived promptly but Stoute became "lost" in Army red tape in Oran and did not join us in time for the campaign. I kept all the key men of the original II Corps staff

* Ike's written output, beginning at West Point and continuing throughout his professional career, was astounding. His severely edited and published papers for his three years of wartime service in Africa constitute four thick volumes plus a separately published volume of letters to Mamie.

in place: G-1, Francis A. Markoe; G-2, Benjamin A. (Monk) Dickson; G-3, Robert A. Hewitt; G-4, Robert W. Wilson; artillery, Charles E. Hart; ordnance, John B. (Bruce) Medaris; engineers, William A. Carter, Jr.; quartermaster, Andrew T. McNamara. Kean ruled this staff with an iron fist. Hart recently recalled that Kean was irreverently known (behind his back) as "Captain Bligh."[5]

My command of II Corps was far less flamboyant than had been Patton's. I administered with a firm but more compassionate hand. I relaxed some of Patton's more drastic edicts, such as one that compelled nurses working in evacuation hospitals to wear heavy, cumbersome steel helmets. I coaxed rather than ordered, and I encouraged my staff and subordinate commanders to solve most problems themselves. It seemed to me that II Corps was soon working smoothly, as a good team should.[6]

Now the great climactic battle for Tunisia began. To deceive von Arnim into believing the Eighth Army would make the main thrust, Monty jumped off first on the night of April 19-20. Although this was primarily a feint, Monty's forces ran into a bloody buzz saw and suffered heavy casualties. The main offensive, Anderson's First Army—which consisted of two corps, V Corps, commanded by C. W. Allfrey and IX Corps, commanded by John T. Crocker—jumped off on April 22. Both Allfrey and Crocker, pushing off after murderous artillery barrages, soon bogged down, checked by fanatical well-dug-in veterans of the Afrika Korps who skillfully utilized the handful of tanks and the precious liters of gasoline at their disposal. The upshot was that the main British offensive failed and Alexander had to substantially modify his plan.[7]

My II Corps was deployed along a forty-mile front lying between Anderson's First Army and the Mediterranean coast, facing due east, toward Bizerte. The three infantry divisions were disposed as follows: Manton Eddy's 9th (plus a mixed unit of French, including some fierce Berber tribesmen) on the left, or north; Doc Ryder's 34th moving up into the center; and Terry Allen's 1st on the right, or south, adjacent to Anderson's First Army. I held the tanks of Ernie Harmon's 1st Armored Division in reserve, to exploit the holes punched through by the infantry.

In his letter to me, Ike had said that he expected me to make my main effort in the initial stages by attacking with tanks along the Tine River Valley in the southern sector. After a careful study of the terrain—and Monk Dickson's intelligence—I concluded that such an attack would lead to a disaster. Here, as elsewhere along my front, the Germans held the high ground and had zeroed in anti-tank guns. Had I followed Ike's suggestion—it was tantamount to an order—I feel certain we would have suffered another Kasserine Pass. As an ever-present reminder to ourselves, we labeled that route "Mousetrap Valley."

My simple, straightforward orders to my division commanders can be summed up in a few words. I told them to stay off obvious routes of approach such as macadam roads and Mousetrap Valley and first take the high ground. When we held the high ground, then I would bring up Harmon's tanks. These orders entailed some hard, sweaty hacking through rough terrain, but I believe they were the best solution to the problem.

We jumped off one day after Anderson's First Army—on April 23. My II Corps headquarters was crowded with visiting firemen looking over our shoulders: Ike and his retinue, which included my old friend Pink Bull, who had replaced me as Ike's eyes and ears, and Lesley McNair and his retinue. Our infantry proceeded cautiously but steadily along the entire front. It was a tough fight every yard of the way, and our casualties—especially in Allen's 1st Division—were not light. As we moved forward, rooting the fanatical enemy out of the high ground, he fell back slowly and methodically, shrinking his lines, digging in again on the high ground. Everywhere in his retreat he laid enormous numbers of land mines (we found 600 in one area 50 by 100 feet), and his artillery was deadly effective. Lesley McNair, observing in the front lines of Allen's 1st Division, sustained head and shoulder wounds and was evacuated to the rear, escorted by Pink Bull.[8]

I gave my division commanders broad objectives but usually left the details of achieving these objectives up to them. Nonetheless, I kept in very close touch. We had excellent telephone communications, and every morning before getting out of bed I called all four commanders to find out firsthand the situation on each division front and to ask for ideas. (We spoke in a prearranged code that Terry Allen never did seem to fully grasp.) Until they learned about these calls, my staff wondered how on earth I was so well-informed at the morning briefings. Later in the day, I visited each division commander at his CP and usually went up to the front with him to study the terrain and enemy positions firsthand, and to show the GI's that their commander was no rear-echelon tent hog. On one such visit I was very nearly killed—the third time in Tunisia—by "timed" enemy artillery fire on a road junction.[9]

By the third day, April 26, we had slugged forward about five miles, but then we bogged down. The enemy had dug in atop a stark, rugged peak, Hill 609, so named for its height in meters on our French maps. The hill—the highest terrain in the whole II Corps sector—dominated Allen's routes to the east, making them impassable.[10]

It occurred to me that here was a good opportunity for Doc Ryder to display his fine tactical skill and redeem the reputation of his division. "Get me that hill," I told Ryder, "and no one will ever again doubt the toughness of your division."

It was no easy task. Ryder drew up his plans with care and launched his attack. He painstakingly pried the enemy out of the lower hills, then, with help of a massive barrage from Charlie Hart's artillery, assaulted 609.

Once, twice, thrice, his troops bravely stormed the peak only to fail. I then proposed a novel suggestion: tanks employed as mobile artillery. It was novel because to my knowledge no one had ever attempted to storm an objective like 609 with tanks.[11]

At about this point, I received two separate, infuriating messages from Anderson. First he ordered me to give up the assault on Hill 609, bypass the citadel and "get behind the enemy." Secondly he proposed that I transfer to his First Army one of my infantry regiments. I could not in good conscience obey either order. The first was absurd; the second was a violation of the agreement that U.S. troops would remain under U.S. command. I determined to get the orders countermanded, intending, if need be, to appeal directly to Alexander or, failing that, Ike. After hearing me out on both points (on separate occasions), Anderson backed down. These encounters with Anderson served to confirm my original judgment that he was in far over his head as an army commander, and I well understood why his own "main thrust" had bogged down.[12]

On the morning of April 30, Ryder's infantry, reinforced by seventeen tanks, once more stormed Hill 609. The tanks, approaching on the flank and from the rear, slammed shell after shell at the enemy positions. By afternoon, Ryder's men captured the summit. During that night and the following day, May 1, they fended off several counterattacks, and finally at nightfall the enemy gave up and withdrew. The Germans we captured conceded that our use of tanks had swung the victory. They had not expected tanks and had not prepared countermeasures. One POW actually told us that the use of tanks had been unfair!

I was immensely pleased by this victory at Hill 609. It cleared away the main obstacle in our paths to the east, enabling me to bring up Ernie Harmon's armor for a fast punch through to Mateur. I was pleased, too, for Doc Ryder's 34th Division. As I had expected, the victory restored self-confidence to the division, and no one ever again would question its courage. In fact, it went on to become one of the finest infantry outfits of World War II.[13]

When Anderson's "main thrust" failed, Alexander was compelled to modify his strategy. He ordered Monty to hold fast, "borrowed" what amounted to an understrength corps from the Eighth Army (the crack 4th Indian Infantry Division, the 7th Armored Division and the 201st Guards Brigade), brought it around to Anderson's front and attached it to Crocker's IX Corps. Crocker, meanwhile, had been badly injured while demonstrating a mortar. To replace him, Alexander chose one of Monty's ablest corps commanders, Brian Horrocks. The swollen IX Corps (two infantry divisions, four battalions of infantry tanks, two armored divisions, plus attached units), led by veterans of the Eighth Army, would now make a new main thrust for Tunis on a narrow front, supported by Allfrey's V

Corps, an immense weight of artillery and most of Mary Coningham's tactical air force. Alexander set the new jump-off for May 6.[14]

I drew new plans to coordinate our offensive with Anderson's May 6 jump-off. Beyond Mateur the flat—though well-defended—terrain seemed to offer an opportunity for a rapid two-pronged tank thrust that might rip into the enemy's rear and thoroughly disorganize him. Harmon—a brazen, profane, yet superbly aggressive and well-organized division commander—thought my plan would cost fifty tanks, but agreed it was worth the risk. I coordinated the forward movement of the three infantry divisions to take best advantage of Harmon's expected breakout and to continue in support of Anderson's left flank.[15]

On May 6, the entire British-American front jumped off with murderous artillery and close air support. The Axis reeled back in stunned confusion. On my front, Harmon moved forward and took his objectives—losing forty-seven tanks. On the left sector, Manton Eddy, always meticulous and cautious, advanced more slowly than I wished; but with firm prodding and assurances from me, he picked up steam and closed on Bizerte. Doc Ryder, assigned a complex crossover maneuver with Allen's 1st Division, carried it out with skill and verve and seized Chouigui, our primary objective in support of Anderson's First Army. Only one episode marred an otherwise perfect operation: Terry Allen foolishly ordered his division into a completely unauthorized attack and was thrown back with heavy losses. From that point forward, Terry was a marked man in my book. I would not permit him or his division to operate as a separate force, ignoring specific orders from above. Had we not been on the threshold of our first important U.S. Army victory in Africa, I would have relieved him—and Teddy Roosevelt—on the spot.[16]

The British main thrust moved out with a bang. The infantry pushed ahead three miles on its narrow front. The armor roared through and advanced another three miles, for a total gain of six miles. But here the British cautiously paused to tidy up the battlefield. "There was no reason for such caution," Liddell Hart wrote. The artillery and air had pulverized the Axis defenses, and von Arnim had no gasoline to bring up his decimated panzer reserves. The British could have punched through to Tunis that day with little risk or cost. As it was, the final all-out push was postponed to the following day, May 7. On that same day, Manton Eddy's 9th Division troops entered Bizerte, without any help from the British.[17]

Tunisia, at long last, was ours. On May 9, von Arnim ran up the white flag. Over the next week, about 250,000 demoralized Axis military personnel (including 100,000 Germans) laid down their arms, far more than had surrendered at Stalingrad. About 40,000 of these surrendered to II Corps, including a number of generals. No other single incident of the war brought me more satisfaction—indeed, elation—than that long procession of abject Axis POW's. The vaunted Afrika Korps that had bloodied our nose at

Kasserine Pass had ceased to exist. The U.S. II Corps had substantially assisted in bringing about its demise. On May 9, I took immense pride in drafting a two-word cable to Ike: "Mission accomplished."[18] *

My superiors were pleased by my performance in command of II Corps; my name was released to the media, and a flood of encomiums and Stateside publicity came my way. I think it is fair to say that none of this publicity turned me into a household name at home. Ike made an effort to rectify that when, according to his aide Harry Butcher, he told war correspondent Ernie Pyle to "go and discover Bradley." In time, Pyle followed that advice. Locally, however, I apparently became well known. On what had to be a very slow day, an OSS agent in Morocco filed a report to Washington stating that the Arabs, believing my Christian name, Omar, to be Moslem, were "proud to believe that a man of their own religion" was rising to high command in the U.S. Army. So much for fame![19]

Amidst all the Allied public back-slapping, there was a single—and galling—sour note. Monty claimed full credit for the final strategic plan and the victory in Tunisia and contrived, with considerable success, to manipulate the British media to give him full credit. Anderson was furious and telegraphed Ike that all ranks in his First Army "deeply resent reference by BBC in news bulletin . . . to present operations as 'left hook by Eighth Army.' Cannot this pernicious rivalry be stopped? We are all in one Army working for one cause." Ike, equally furious, held a press conference to clear up the misconception, but the truth never really caught up with the lie. Even in his memoirs, Monty persisted in his claim that it was his idea for Anderson to make the main thrust on Tunis and that "Alexander agreed." Subsequently, Alexander's biographer Nigel Nicolson unearthed and published the correspondence between Alexander and Monty proving beyond a shadow of a doubt the plan was conceived by Alexander. But the myth dies hard.[20]

A last word on North Africa. A year earlier, Marshall and Ike had been passionately committed to an early direct invasion of France—Roundup. The invasion of North Africa, Torch, had been a British concept reluctantly undertaken by Marshall and Ike. On reflection, I came to the conclusion that it was fortunate that the British view prevailed, that the U.S. Army first met the enemy on the periphery, in Africa rather than on the beaches of France. In Africa we learned to crawl, to walk—then run. Had that learning process been launched in France, it would surely have—as Alan Brooke argued—resulted in an unthinkable disaster.

* The cost in Allied casualties—killed, wounded, missing—of defeating the Axis in Tunisia had been high: British First Army since the November 8 Torch landings and British Eighth Army after reaching Tunisia on February 9: 35,940; the French since Torch landings: 16,180; the United States: 18,221. Total: 70,341. The United States lost 2,715 killed, 8,978 wounded and 6,528 missing.

SEVENTEEN

Operation Husky, the British proposal to invade Sicily, approved by Roosevelt, Churchill and the Combined Chiefs at Casablanca, was originally envisioned as a stiff jab that might achieve four main objectives: knock Italy out of the war; clear the central Mediterranean of Axis forces, securing the Allied sea lanes; divert German pressure from the Russian front to help satisfy Stalin; and keep busy and further sharpen and temper Allied forces for the main United States objective in Europe—Roundup.

Since both Marshall and King had opposed first Torch, then Husky, and looked with disfavor on further peripheral operations, the British tactfully left future Mediterranean strategy hanging in the air. There were no decisions reached about how to exploit a victory in Sicily—such as an invasion of Italy, which Churchill and other British had in mind. It was an egregious error to leave the future unresolved. It led to misguided planning for and a cloudy conclusion to the Sicily operation and to costly mistakes beyond Sicily. Liddell Hart upbraided the Chiefs for the lapse in these words: "Tactical deferment is apt to result in strategic unreadiness."[1]

The Combined Chiefs named Ike commander in chief for the Sicily operation. But Ike had no direct command responsibility for planning and executing the operation. The Combined Chiefs delegated this responsibility to Ike's three deputies for ground, air and sea: Alexander, Tedder and Cunningham. Ike had become, in his own description, "chairman of the board," presiding over a committee of three to run the war. Since Alexander, Tedder and Cunningham were then utterly absorbed in fighting the war in Tunisia from three widely dispersed headquarters, responsibility for planning Sicily was further delegated to lower level staffs. The upshot was that there was no single man "who could conceive the operation as a whole, impose on it his own imprint, see it through in practice and accept responsibility for the consequences."[2]

Sicily is a lopsided triangular island, roughly 170 miles on the side, located a mere two and a half miles from Calabria in the toe of Italy. It is rugged and mountainous, dominated by the famous 10,000-foot Mount

Etna. In 1943, its road system was primitive—narrow lanes winding along the coastlines or through the mountains. Its principal ports—famous from antiquity—were Messina on the northeast corner, Palermo on the northwestern coast and Syracuse on the southeastern corner. One could not imagine a more difficult place to assault with the mobile road-bound Allied armies of 1943, or conversely, an easier place for the Axis ground troops to defend.

Until our Allied armies converged in Tunisia, the Axis had made scant defensive preparations in southern Italy or Sicily. But now, Hitler and Mussolini had to face the possibility that either or both of those places might soon become an Allied invasion target. This prospect led to some devious talks and footwork between the dictators and their military planners. Mussolini had lost the cream of his armed forces in Greece, Russia and North Africa. What was left in Italy could not possibly repel an Allied attack. Yet, out of vanity and fear of becoming another occupied German territory, the Duce was hesitant to ask Hitler to send German divisions to defend southern Italy. For his part, Hitler was reluctant to send divisions. For some time he had distrusted Mussolini. He feared the Duce might defect to the Allies and attack or entrap any German divisions in southern Italy.

The outcome of these discussions was a series of uneasy compromises engineered by Hitler's military representative in Rome, the able Field Marshal Albert Kesselring. In the spring of 1943—as the Allied armies closed on Tunisia—Hitler authorized five German panzer divisions for the defense of southern Italy. Three came from France and Germany; two were created on the spot from replacements bound for Tunisia but unable to get there. Kesselring decided he would send one of these divisions to the island of Sardinia, two to Sicily, and keep the other two in southern Italy. Later, in June, on Kesselring's advice, two other German panzer divisions were alerted for movement to southern Italy. Ultra informed us of these various German plans and reinforcements.[3]

While these discussions were in progress, the Italians were compelled to look seriously at the defenses of Sicily. The island's main military force was the 200,000-man Italian Sixth Army, organized into about ten or twelve divisions, under command of sixty-six-year-old General d'Armata A. Guzzoni. There were four "mobile" divisions and six "coastal" divisions, two "coastal" brigades and one "coastal" regiment. The four mobile divisions, the American Army historian wrote, were "none too good." Only one of them—Livorno—was at full strength and had its own transportation. The others were "poorly trained" and ill-equipped. The coastal units, made up largely of discontented Sicilian conscripts, were also poorly equipped and had virtually no transportation. Some Allied intelligence officers believed the Italian Sixth Army would bolt at the first shot; but others believed that on "home soil" the Italians would resist fiercely.[4]

Owing to Sicily's peculiar geography—its proximity to Italy's toe—

there were two basic ways to capture the island: by encirclement and isolation, with a primary amphibious assault in the Strait of Messina and Calabria combined with a secondary assault on the island to draw Axis power from the strait area; or by a direct frontal assault on the island itself, followed by a hard fight across its length and breadth, with the possibility of the bulk of the enemy escaping through Messina to Calabria.

Option one, encirclement and isolation, offered the best possible solution. We now had freedom of naval movement in the Mediterranean, giving us flexibility to strike almost where we pleased. Calabria—Italy's toe—was only lightly defended by ill-equipped and uncertain Italian troops and by one or, at most, two German divisions of uncertain quality and strength. The German and Italian air forces had been mauled in Tunisia. We had two British aircraft carriers for the Sicily operation, *Indomitable* and *Formidable,* an air base on Malta (180 miles from Calabria), which could have served as a refueling and rearming stop for the bulk of our fighter aircraft staging from Tunisia (300 miles from Calabria); and our heavier aircraft in Tunisia were within easy range of Calabria.

Option one seems never to have received the serious consideration it warranted and was dismissed early. One reason, it appears, was the failure of the Chiefs at Casablanca to come to grips with operations beyond Sicily. In the strictest sense, a landing on Calabria constituted "an invasion of Italy," even though its limited purpose was the capture of Sicily. An "invasion of Italy" far exceeded the strategic guidelines agreed upon at Casablanca. Thus the planners were forced to view Sicily as an isolated island, as though it sat in the middle of nowhere. Another reason was the undue caution that marked all our Mediterranean operations, beginning with Torch. The planners exaggerated in their minds such factors as the capabilities of the shore guns protecting the Strait of Messina and Axis air power in southern Italy, meanwhile grossly underestimating our own air and naval capabilities.

The German generals in Italy could never understand why we dismissed option one. General Heinrich von Vietinghoff, who commanded the German Tenth Army in southern Italy, said after the war that "from a German standpoint it is incomprehensible that the Allies did not seize the Strait of Messina, either at the same time as the landing [in Sicily] or in the course of the initial actions, just as soon as the German troops were contained. On both sides of the strait—not only in the northeast corner of the island but in southern Calabria as well—this would have been possible without any special difficulty." His superior, Albert Kesselring, said that "a secondary landing on Calabria would have turned the landing in Sicily into an annihilating victory" for the Allies.[5]

After the fact, Ike himself conceded that it had been a "mistake" to dismiss option one. In mid-August, after a talk with Ike, Harry Butcher wrote: "Ike now thinks we should have made simultaneous landings on both sides of the Messina Strait, thus cutting off all Sicily and obtaining wholesale surrender and saving time and equipment."

American naval historian Samuel Eliot Morison wrote: "I cannot avoid the conclusion that the entire Husky Plan was wrong; that we should have attacked the Messina bottleneck first . . . the enemy, whose dispositions had been made to meet landings elsewhere, would have been completely surprised and his communication with the mainland severed. His forces could then have been rolled up into western Sicily and forced to surrender, and in less time than it took to push them out of Sicily into Italy, where they 'lived to fight another day.' "[6]

Thus, with little guidance from the top—no one man exerting a firm hand—the staff planners settled on the less desirable option, a frontal assault, and devoted all their energies to its details. Their planning was slow, cautious and conservative in the usual military tradition. In one sense they should not be blamed. Sicily was to be the first major Allied amphibious assault against a hostile beachhead in Europe. The planners had to assume the worst possible case, that the ragged Italian troops on Sicily would fight defiantly. Their solution was pure Leavenworth textbook: a giant pincer movement. Monty's Eighth Army would land in the southeast corner of the triangle that was Sicily, near Syracuse; Patton's Seventh Army would land on the northwest coast near Palermo. The two armies—supplied through the ports of Syracuse and Palermo—would both quickly strike along the coastlines toward Messina, enveloping the island defenders and preventing a Dunkirk across Messina Strait to Calabria by air and sea interdiction.[7]

From the outset George Marshall sensed that this massive frontal assault might not be the best way. Shortly after he gave his grudging approval to Husky at Casablanca, he suggested to Ike that a better solution might be a small quick thrust to grab the island on the heels of a Tunisia victory, while the Axis forces were still reeling in confusion and before they could properly reinforce Sicily. Ike agreed that this was a scheme worth serious consideration, and when he later broached the possibility with Tedder and Cunningham they both agreed the idea had merit. Marshall and Tom Handy's OPD planners continued to raise this possibility all through March and April. But Ike and his deputies, impressed by the tough Axis defense of Tunisia, gradually lost their enthusiasm for that scheme. It never did receive the study it deserved.[8]

In fact, it appeared for a time that Ike was losing his enthusiasm for any kind of Husky. Ultra revealed the Kesselring plan to send two German panzer divisions to Sicily. The news sent a chill through Ike's headquarters. On March 20, Ike (reflecting the views of Alexander) cabled the Combined Chiefs, stating that "if substantial German ground troops should be placed in the region [Sicily] prior to the attack, the chances of success become practically nil and the project should be abandoned." He iterated this caution on April 7, in another cable to the Combined Chiefs, in which he stated that if more than two German divisions were posted to Sicily "the operation offers scant promise of success."[9]

This timidity and caution absolutely outraged Winston Churchill, Alan Brooke and the other British Chiefs. Churchill, in what the official British historian described as "one of his most memorable minutes of the war," exploded:

> If the presence of two German divisions is held to be decisive against any operation of an offensive or amphibious character open to the million men now in North Africa, it is difficult to see how the war can be carried on. Months of preparation, sea power and air power in abundance, and yet two German divisions are sufficient to knock it all on the head. I do not think we can rest content with such doctrines. . . . It is perfectly clear that the operations must either be entrusted to someone who believes them, or abandoned. . . . I trust the Chiefs of Staff will not accept these pusillanimous and defeatist doctrines from whomever they come. . . . I regard the matter as serious in the last degree. . . . We have told the Russians that they cannot have their supplies by the northern convoy for the sake of Husky and now Husky is to be abandoned if there are two German divisions (strength unspecified) in the neighborhood. What Stalin would think of this, when he has 185 German divisions on his front, I cannot imagine.[10]

The British Chiefs cabled a sizzling bill of complaints to Washington. They stated they were "opposed resolutely" to canceling Sicily merely because there might be two German divisions present, especially since Sicily had a "relatively undefended shoreline manned by Italians primarily," and the two German divisions could not possibly attack everywhere at once. The JCS relayed these views to Ike, stressing that Washington was in "complete agreement." A much-chastened chairman of the board replied to both sets of Chiefs on April 12: "Operation Husky will be prosecuted with all means at our disposal. . . . There is no thought here except to carry out our orders to the ultimate limit [of] our ability."[11]

Monty, fighting in Tunisia, was kept abreast of the Sicily planning. He did not at all like the shape it was taking. He believed the planners were grossly underestimating the difficulties his Eighth Army would face in the landing near Syracuse, typically demanding greater strength and concentration of his forces. On April 24 he signaled Alexander, in part: "Planning to date has been on the assumption that resistance will be slight and Sicily will be captured easily. Never was there a greater error. Germans and Italians are fighting well in Tunisia and will repeat process in Sicily. If we work on the assumption of little resistance, and disperse our effort as is being done on all planning to date, we will merely have a disaster. We must plan for fierce resistance, by the Germans at any rate, and for a real dog fight battle to follow the initial assault. . . . I am prepared to carry the war into Sicily with the Eighth Army but must really ask to be allowed to make my own plans."[12]

This lugubrious pronouncement knocked all the Sicily planning to date into a cocked hat. In the following week there were new, urgent and acrimonious Allied meetings all across North Africa, culminating in an emergency meeting of the board in Algiers May 2 to hear a new plan conceived by Monty. Montgomery, Cunningham and Tedder made it, but Alexander and Patton were grounded by bad weather. Monty buttonholed Bedell Smith in the men's room and "sold" his plan with little difficulty. Basically, Monty proposed that Patton's landing at Palermo be canceled and his Seventh Army shifted across the island to land adjacent to Monty's Eighth Army on the south coast near Gela. In sum: a massive concentration of Allied strength in a single area, rather than the dispersed pincer concept.

When the full board finally got together in Algiers in subsequent days, Ike and Alexander fully endorsed Monty's radical changes. Tedder and Cunningham voiced many grave reservations. Basically, they did not want to forgo the pincer concept and thought Monty's plan too conservative. However, in the end, they yielded, Cunningham very reluctantly. Throughout the discussions, Patton, though he disapproved of Monty's plan, was untypically reserved and closed-mouthed. He assumed the pose of a loyal soldier who would follow whatever orders were given him.[13]

In these various meetings, which for the first time brought Monty into close association with the Americans, he came across as pompous, abrasive, demanding and almost insufferably vain. Ike summed up his opinion of Monty in a letter to Marshall:

> Montgomery is of different caliber from some of the outstanding British leaders you have met. He is unquestionably able, but very conceited. For your most secret and confidential information, I will give you my opinion which is that he is so proud of his successes to date that he will never willingly make a single move until he is absolutely certain of success—in other words, until he has concentrated enough resources so that anybody could practically guarantee the outcome. . . . Unquestionably he is an able tactician and organizer and, provided only that Alexander will never let him forget for one second who is the boss, he should deliver in good style.

Everybody felt that Alexander was much too inclined to give in to Monty. Patton wrote that "Monty is a forceful, selfish man, but still a man. I think he is a far better leader than Alexander and he will do just what he pleases, as Alex is afraid of him." Even his British compatriots turned on Monty. Cunningham cabled the First Sea Lord in London: "I am afraid Montgomery is a bit of a nuisance; he seems to think that all he has to do is to say what is to be done and everyone will dance to the tune of his piping. Alexander appears quite unable to keep him in order." According to Patton, Tedder confided to him: "It is bad form for officers to criticize each other, so I shall. The other day, Alex, who is very selfish, said of General Anderson, 'As a soldier, he is a good, plain military cook.' The remark applies absolutely—to Montgomery. He is a little fellow of average ability who has had such a build-up that he thinks of himself as Napoleon —he is not."[14]

What none of the board members quite realized at the time was that Montgomery had set a stage on which he meant to be the principal actor. Sicily would merely become a larger-scale version of Monty's Mareth Line breakout, with Patton's Seventh Army playing a supporting role, just as our II Corps had played a supporting role to the Eighth Army in Tunisia. In part, Alexander had ceded this leading role to Monty because of his lingering distrust of the American GI.

Informed of these shifts in plans and aware of the imminent Axis collapse in Tunisia, George Marshall still thought the Husky plan too cumbersome and timid. His mind was still fixed on the idea of a quick grab of Sicily before the Axis could firm up defensive plans. He cabled Ike that "your planners and mine may be too conservative in their analyses." A quick grab, with the element of surprise working in Allied favor, "may justify your accepting calculated risks." Planners were notoriously orthodox, Marshall said. They lacked the boldness and daring "which won great victories for Nelson and Grant and Lee." The plans for Sicily "suggested a lack of adaptability." But even after the sudden massive Axis collapse in Tunisia, Ike could not extemporize. He did not have sufficient landing craft for a quick grab; there was no way he could talk Alexander or Monty into drastically moving up the schedule.

No one was really happy, least of all Mark Clark. On April 28, he summed up his feelings in his diary:

> It is inexcusable that high planning on an overall scale is not taking definite form. Planners should project themselves forward and set up a grand-scale strategic plan for the Allied forces. We can't win a war by capturing islands [Sicily-Sardinia]. This coming move [Sicily] in the Mediterranean will be no great move. In reality, we will get no place by doing it and the result will not be commensurate with the effort and losses involved. We are going to have to attack the continent proper and we should decide now how we are going to do it. We are losing time to plan and train for a specific goal.[15]

Meanwhile, in mid-May Roosevelt, Churchill and the Combined Chiefs held another global strategy meeting. It took place in Washington, D.C., and was called Trident. Churchill and his advisers arrived with plans for all kinds of aggressive schemes, including an invasion of the Italian mainland to insure Mussolini's capitulation. Roosevelt, Marshall and the rest of the American contingent absolutely opposed an invasion of Italy as yet another peripheral operation draining men and supplies from Roundup. The Americans believed that a victory in Sicily, together with intensive aerial bombardment of the Italian mainland, would suffice to insure Italian capitulation. Marshall and his planners, now seriously doubting the British resolve for Roundup, spent most of the conference pressing for a solid commitment. In the end, Churchill yielded and agreed that Roundup should be mounted—on May 1, 1944. In return, he received no assurances on the invasion of Italy. The Combined Chiefs merely agreed that Ike could "plan such operations in exploitation of Husky as are best calculated to eliminate Italy from the war." But final discussions on those plans would rest with the Combined Chiefs.[16]

Churchill would not let go of his scheme to invade Italy. With George Marshall in tow, he flew to Algiers with the idea of enlisting Ike and his British war directors to his views. In a series of meetings with Ike, Alan Brooke, Marshall, Alexander, Cunningham, Tedder, Smith and others, Churchill expounded his views, dramatically painting the "capture of Rome" as a "very great achievement for our Mediterranean forces." Ike was sold. If Sicily proved to be easy—say within a week—he would at once cross the strait and establish a bridgehead in Calabria. But if Sicily proved difficult, he would be forced to reconsider. Churchill thought he had also sold Marshall, but he was wrong, a victim of wishful thinking. Marshall did not agree. Marshall would go no further than to approve a general study for a proposed invasion of Sardinia or Corsica or both—and possibly southern Italy. Any final decision by the Combined Chiefs would have to await the outcome of Sicily.[17]

Montgomery, on leave in England, arrived late for these meetings in Algiers. At once, he made an egotistical presentation of his plan to invade Sicily. Marshall's biographer Forrest Pogue reports that Marshall, perhaps influenced by Ike's earlier criticism of Monty, "was not impressed by his manner." Marshall, Pogue wrote, would have agreed with much of what Alan Brooke wrote about Monty in his diary that day: "He requires a lot of educating to make him see the whole situation and the war as a whole outside the Eighth Army orbit. A difficult mixture to handle, brilliant commander in action and trainer of men, but liable to commit untold errors, due to lack of tact, lack of appreciation of other people's outlook. It is most distressing that the Americans do not like him, and it will always be a difficult matter to have him fighting in close proximity to them."[18]

This then was the extent of the strategic considerations about Sicily and its follow-up operations. Seldom in war has a major operation been undertaken in such a fog of indecision, confusion and conflicting plans. It is little wonder that Ike could later tell Butcher that the Sicily plan had been a "mistake"—that the Allies should have landed simultaneously in Sicily and Calabria. Much of the blame for the mistake could be attributed to the unresolved conflicting views of the Combined Chiefs—the inevitable compromises of coalition warfare. But Ike must also share a large part of the blame. Though he had been kicked upstairs to chairman of the board, he was nonetheless in name and fact the commander in chief for the operation. Inasmuch as his three deputies were absorbed in the Tunisia fighting, it seems to me it was all the more important that Ike give the Sicily operation his utmost care and attention. He was the logical man to conceive the operation as a whole, impose his imprint, see it through and accept responsibility for the consequences. But Ike did not rise to the challenge.

EIGHTEEN

The principal military force in Patton's Seventh Army for the Sicily invasion was to be VI Corps, commanded by Major General Ernest J. (Mike) Dawley, a field artilleryman from the Class of 1910, who had fought with distinction in World War I. Dawley and I had served together at West Point in the 1920s, when I taught math and Dawley was on the staff of the tactical department. More recently, Dawley had commanded and trained the 40th Division in the States, then VI Corps, which he brought to Africa about the time I took over II Corps. Ike thought Dawley "a splendid character, earnest, faithful and well informed."[1]

At first meeting Patton wrote that Dawley "seems O.K." But later he changed his mind. It really did not make sense to assault Sicily with an inexperienced corps commander and staff when II Corps and I were on the spot and available. Ike and Patton discussed the situation, and on May 15 Ike informed Marshall that he was sending me and II Corps to Patton and shifting Dawley and VI Corps to Clark's Fifth Army in Morocco. Ike explained to Marshall that "[Bradley] has done so remarkably well that I simply cannot afford to take a chance on a green corps commander and staff although Dawley is a splendid officer."[2] *

My key staff officers, aides and I left Tunisia on May 13. We spent a day or so in Algiers with Ike and his staff going over the Husky invasion plans and discussing the lessons we had learned in Tunisia. We then flew west to Patton's headquarters at Mostaganem, a cool seaside city about fifty miles east of Oran. Patton met our plane with a guard of honor, then held a champagne luncheon in my behalf, during which he grandly toasted me as "the conqueror of Bizerte."[4]

The festivities and celebrations went on for several days more. Ike called to invite Patton and me to a "victory parade" in Tunis on May 20.

* Later, in Italy, Dawley did not prove out in combat. He was relieved of command, reduced in rank to colonel and returned to the States.[3]

We flew there in a B-25 medium bomber, passing close to Hill 609, which now looked strangely mute and remote. Ike and Kay Summersby were at the Tunis airport greeting the legions of dignitaries who were mostly British and French: including Alexander, Anderson (Monty was on home leave in England), Tedder, Cunningham and Juin. Ike was so busy, Patton recalled, that "we had no time to talk to him." The British and French dignitaries joined Ike on the main reviewing stand. Patton and I, after Ike the principal American generals, were relegated to a minor reviewing stand some distance away, occupied by minor French bureaucrats and officers. The effect was to give the British overwhelming credit for the victory in Tunisia. For Patton and me, the affair merely served to reinforce our belief that Ike was now so pro-British that he was blind to the slight he had paid to us and, by extension, the American troops who had fought and died in Tunisia.[5]

I had assumed that we would establish II Corps headquarters in Mostaganem, alongside Patton's Seventh Army headquarters for ease of communication. But Patton had other ideas. For reasons I have never understood, he banished II Corps to a fetid, fly-infested, unbearably hot town, Relizane (literally, "City of Flies"), some thirty-two miles south of him in the desert. Perhaps it was sheer vanity. My promotion to the three-star rank of lieutenant general—Patton's rank—had been approved by Marshall, Roosevelt and the Senate, to become effective June 2. Perhaps Patton resented the presence of another general of equal rank. We made the best of our miserable quarters at Relizane, but I had a hard time forgiving Patton for inflicting this petty, demeaning and wholly unnecessary discomfort on my men.[6]

After scrubbing and cleaning the entire town of Relizane, we established II Corps headquarters in a set of school buildings surrounded by a barbed-wire fence. Bill Kean and I found rooms in the home of an elderly French couple across the street. By this time I had an orderly, Frank J. Cekada, and my driver Alex Stoute had been "liberated" from the clutches of Army red tape in Oran. With my two aides Chet Hansen and Lew Bridge we five constituted a small "family" which would remain together for the duration of the war.[7]

From Relizane my II Corps staffers and I commuted to Patton's headquarters in Mostaganem. In spite of Relizane, I was pleased to be working again in close harness with Patton. By now we understood one another perfectly and professionally we worked in complete harmony, although my combat-hardened II Corps staff tended to look down its nose at the "untried" Seventh Army staff. Patton, as always, was impatient with planning. His mind was fixed on the attack and not the logistics, and he was content to leave the details to his deputy army commander, Geoffrey Keyes, and the rest of us.

By that time, six U.S. divisions comprising some 80,000 men had been earmarked for Husky. Three reinforced infantry divisions would spearhead the assault on the beaches. Two of those three (numbering 45,000 men) would be my direct responsibility: Terry Allen's Big Red One and the 45th National Guard Division commanded by Troy H. Middleton. The other, Lucian Truscott's reinforced 3rd Infantry Division (numbering 27,000 men), would operate independently, reporting directly to Patton. A regiment of Matt Ridgway's 82nd Airborne Division, the 505th, commanded by Jim Gavin, would parachute beyond the beaches in my II Corps sector and then link up with Allen's 1st Division. Held in Seventh Army reserve off the beaches would be the 2nd Armored Division, commanded by Hugh J. Gaffey, and other infantry forces. Manton Eddy's 9th Infantry Division would be held in reserve in North Africa, should this additional force be required.[8]

My two division commanders for the assault, Allen and Middleton, were a mixed bag. I was not happy with Terry Allen. I had already expressed my misgivings about Allen several times with Ike, and he had decided the best solution would be to return Allen to the States, without prejudice, recommended as a corps commander. But Patton valued Allen's battlefield swagger and insisted on keeping him "at least until the initial phase of the operation is consummated." I agreed—reluctantly—meanwhile persuading Patton to tone down a commendation he was writing for Allen's service in Tunisia with a warning: "He's a very poor disciplinarian."[9]

I did not know Troy Middleton except by reputation, which was very, very good. He had entered the Army in World War I and had twice been promoted on the same battlefield in France to become the youngest regimental commander in the U.S. Army. Later, he had been a classmate of Patton's at the Command and General Staff School in Fort Leavenworth. He retired from the Army in 1937 and subsequently became dean of administration at Louisiana State University. After being recalled to active service in 1942, he was named commanding general of the 45th Division, a National Guard outfit from Oklahoma-Texas, which was, in the words of the official Army historian, "probably one of the best-trained divisions in the American Army." The 45th was entirely green to combat and, in fact, was still back in the U.S. It would embark from the States "combat-loaded," disembark for a few days near Oran (leaving its gear aboard ship) to limber up the troops, then re-embark for Sicily. I had considerable misgivings about introducing the 45th to combat over an enemy beach in the first major amphibious landing of World War II, but if it had to be done that way, there was probably no better group of guinea pigs.[10]

Beyond that, I was deeply concerned about the fighting spirit of all our GI's, whether green or bloodied. In the II Corps drive to Bizerte, I had observed two flagrant weaknesses: an unwillingness or reluctance to reconnoiter, maintain contact with and aggressively close the enemy; and an unwarranted tendency to surrender when outnumbered. The former problem I attributed to a general lack of aggressiveness on the part of our junior officers; the latter to unrealistic training exercises in the States. In responding to Marshall's message of congratulations to me on the Tunisia campaign, I took that opportunity to convey to him my feelings on the second point:

> It seems to me that our large-scale maneuvers [in the States] are partially responsible for creating one frame of mind which must be corrected by special methods. In maneuvers, when two forces meet, the umpires invariably decide that the smaller force must withdraw, or if greatly outnumbered, it must surrender. And while the umpires deliberate, the men simply stand or sit about idly. No means are provided for giving proportionate weight to the many intangibles of warfare, such as morale, training, leadership, conditioning. There have been many cases where, in my opinion, forces have surrendered unnecessarily. According to the umpire rules, they were probably justified. I believe that very few circumstances arise where surrender is actually justified. A greatly outnumbered force can accomplish wonders by vigorous and aggressive action.[11]

Another serious problem with our GI's had arisen immediately after our victory in Tunisia. An inexplicable rumor spread like wildfire that those divisions that had fought in Tunisia had "done their share" and would be returned to the States. For them, "the war was over." New divisions would come over to take their place for future operations. When the men were told emphatically that this was not true, there was widespread rebellion. Lucian Truscott described it as "an intense reaction among them that required stringent measures to control." Many cases of self-maiming were reported.

The "rebellion" centered primarily in Allen's 1st Division and in Truscott's 3rd Division, which had been beefed up with battle-hardened units drawn from Ryder's 34th Division, now on "occupation duty" in Tunisia. Truscott took proper disciplinary and leadership measures. But Allen let his division get completely out of hand. The Big Red One literally ran amok along the entire coast of North Africa from Bizerte to Oran. In Algiers, cocky veterans of the fighting hunted down and assaulted the rear area troops, touching off widespread rioting. It became so grave a matter that Ike's headquarters sent orders to me to get all of Allen's men out of town at once.

In part, I was at fault. If I had thought to inform the Tunisian veterans that their war was not yet over, the rumors would never have started. I should also have made arrangements for the divisions returning from the front to be bivouacked in seaside rest camps where they could blow off steam before resuming the training for Sicily. However, this incident (and others too numerous and trivial to mention) convinced me that Terry Allen was not fit to command, and I was determined to remove him and Teddy Roosevelt from the division as soon as circumstances on Sicily permitted.[12]

By the last week in May, we had corralled the Sicily-bound divisions into bivouac for a full month of intensive training. In addition to the normal routines, we imposed mandatory exercises with live ammunition, including house-to-house "fighting" of the type we would face in Sicily's cities. Patton himself participated in one of these drills and wrote Marshall: "The bullets pass extremely close to the people's heads. . . . When I went through it personally, it frightened me to death." When I visited the divisions in our immediate area—the 1st and 9th Infantry and the 2nd Armored —I talked to the men in groups, on battalion level. I stressed two points: the need to beware of enemy mines (which had been so troublesome to us in Tunisia), and the need to be aggressive in patrolling and keeping close to the enemy, surrendering only when the situation was absolutely hopeless.[13]

Patton likewise visited our troops, flamboyantly staging his earthy pep talks, though never quite so dramatic as the galvanizing opening scene by George C. Scott in the movie *Patton.* The language Patton actually employed would not be suitable for a family film. Jim Gavin recently recalled one of Patton's talks on the eve of Sicily and found a way to describe it:

> Patton went on to discuss the tactics that we should employ in fighting the Germans and Italians, stressing the Italians. The point that he wanted to make was that we should avoid a direct assault on an enemy position but seek to envelop his flanks. However, in doing so, the general used terms applicable to sexual relations. He did so in a very clever manner, emphasizing the point that when one arrived in the rear of one of their positions, the Italians would invariably quickly try to switch to a new position to protect themselves, and at that moment would become vulnerable to our attack from the rear. It was not so much what he said as how he said it that caused us to remember the point he wanted to make—though I did feel somewhat embarrassed at times, and I sensed that some of his troops felt a bit embarrassed too. . . . Yet the general made his points, and the troops remembered them as much for the very language he used as for their content.[14]

When Monty forced his new plan for Sicily on everyone—canceling our landing near Palermo—it caused a radical change in our vital logistical setup. There was no seaport of consequence in our assault area. This meant that in the early stages of the campaign we would have to resupply our assault troops "across the beaches." Everything would come to us courtesy of the U.S. Navy, which had the responsibility for delivering it to the beaches, where our own troops would then unload and distribute. This had never before been done in combat, and the planning for it was literally mind-boggling.

Fortunately, by that time the British and American navies—and the United States' arsenal of democracy—had produced a variety of new shallow-draft naval craft for landing and resupplying troops on beaches. The biggest (and scarcest) of these craft was the boxy LST (landing ship, tank) with its clamshell doors in the bow. Next in importance was the LCI (landing craft, infantry), followed by the smaller bow-ramped boats: the LCT (landing craft, tank) and the LCVP (landing craft, vehicle or personnel). In addition, the U.S. Army had produced its own remarkable vehicle, the DUKW, or as we naturally called it, the "duck." It was a two-and-a-half-ton truck converted to amphibian, propelled in the water by a boat screw and on land by wheels. The duck could carry twenty-five men with gear or five thousand pounds of cargo. It proved to be very efficient for unloading the ships.[15]

Much of our pre-Sicily training was devoted to rehearsing with these craft and vehicles. The naval vessels were manned by reserve personnel, many of whom, in the words of naval historian Morison, "had never even smelled salt water before 1943." In our rehearsals, the young seamen fouled up so many times that I almost despaired. They rarely landed us on the right beach at the right time. Sometimes they were off-target as much as ten or twelve miles.[16]

While in Algiers with Winston Churchill, George Marshall flew over to pay us a visit on June 2. Ike and Pink Bull accompanied him. No one in Algiers had invited me to the meeting—an oversight I'm sure—and Patton was kind enough to call me in Relizane and ask me to hurry over to his headquarters. Marshall was flattering in his private, personal remarks to me about my performance in Tunisia and wished me well in Sicily.

That day, for Marshall's benefit, we staged a landing rehearsal on a beach at Arzew, outside Oran. When the first wave of Big Red One soldiers tumbled ashore, we were within spitting distance. Patton noticed the soldiers had failed to fix bayonets. He ran to the water's edge, lost his temper and raged up and down before the men, cursing as only Patton could curse. Ike stood by in embarrassed silence. I could scarcely believe my own eyes and ears. Pink Bull nodded toward a stony-faced Marshall and whispered to me, "Well, there goes George's chance for a crack at high command. That temper of his is going to finish him yet."[17]

Middleton's 45th Division was scheduled to arrive from the States toward the end of our training, June 23. As an exercise, we ordered the division to "assault" the beaches of North Africa directly from the combat-loaded ships that had brought them. Bill Kean and I watched as the huge convoy anchored off Arzew in darkness and discharged its armada of landing craft. The Navy put one regiment on the proper beach, but the other two regiments came ashore several miles off-target. I said to Kean, "Good Lord! Suppose they miss it by that much in Sicily?" Kean said nothing. It was too grim to contemplate—unthinkable.[18]

The British, meanwhile, had gone to extraordinary lengths to deceive the Germans as to our next move, to divert attention from Sicily. Operation Mincemeat is the most famous of those deception efforts. A body, fictitiously made out to be that of Major William Martin of the Royal Marines, was launched from the submarine *Seraph* off the coast of Spain with a courier's briefcase chained to its wrist, as though it had washed up from a plane crash at sea. Ingeniously drafted high-level documents and personal letters were planted on "Martin" indicating that our next attacks would come against Sardinia, Corsica and Greece and that to disguise them, an apparent feint at Sicily would become the cover plan!

The whole unlikely scheme worked as designed. The Spanish found the body, as they were supposed to, passed copies of the documents to German spies in Madrid, and they in turn forwarded the information to Berlin and Hitler, who swallowed the bait. On Hitler's personal orders, defensive preparations in Corsica and Sardinia and in Greece were intensified. He sent Rommel to Greece to command the Axis forces. The British codebreakers listened closely and knew from decoded Ultra dispatches that the deception was working as planned.* [19]

In Rome, neither Albert Kesselring nor the Italian high command was deceived. Against the possibility that Sicily was probably the real target, Kesselring, in June, proceeded with his earlier plan to send two German panzer divisions there. These were the Hermann Goering and the 15th Panzer Grenadier divisions, reconstituted from some 30,000 stranded Tunisia-bound German replacements. Both divisions were well trained and stocked for twenty days of combat, although short of tanks (in total, perhaps 120). In a very lucky piece of work, the codebreakers temporarily penetrated a tough version of German Army Enigma known as "Playfair," and were thus able to provide details on the dispositions of these two divisions. The Italian commander in Sicily, General Guzzoni, believing our attack would come where it did, argued to hold both divisions poised to counterattack us in the southeastern part of the island. But Kesselring, believing western Sicily to be vulnerable, insisted on moving most of one division, the 15th Panzer, there. He left the Hermann Goering Division in the southeast, along with the best of the Italian "mobile" divisions.[20]

Those of us "in the Ultra picture" greeted the intercepts with mixed feelings. The presence of two German panzer divisions in Sicily—however hastily mobilized and short of tanks—would make our job much tougher. For one thing, their presence was certain to put more spine in the Italian Sixth Army. We were gratified to learn that Kesselring had ordered the

* The deception was first described by its clever originator, British intelligence specialist Ewen Montagu, in the 1953 best-selling book *The Man Who Never Was*, but without the Ultra aspect. Montagu's more recent book, *Beyond Top Secret Ultra*, includes the role Ultra played in the scheme.

15th Panzer "to the wrong side of the island," but that still left the Hermann Goering Division in an ideal position to counterattack the American landing beaches. Owing to the extreme secrecy of Ultra, we were not allowed to pass this information on to the lower echelons or include it in our circulated intelligence summaries. If we were asked if there were Germans on the island, we had to lie and say, "There may be a few technicians." This was a cruel deception on our own forces, but necessary in order to protect the secrets of Ultra.[21]

The final days of planning passed in a blur. On June 27, we closed our command post in Relizane and moved to Oran to make preparations for debarkation. We were housed in a closely guarded villa on a cliff overlooking the sea we would soon be crossing. On July 4, we drove to the French naval base Mers El Kebir, five miles west of Oran. There we boarded our amphibious forces command ship, the *Ancon,* a 493-foot prewar luxury liner in the Caribbean trade, commissioned AGC-4 by the U.S. Navy in 1942. I settled into my comfortable quarters and ordered a dish of ice cream.[22]

NINETEEN

The battle for Sicily had already begun—in the air. This campaign was directed by Tedder, Coningham and the chief American air general in our theater, Carl (Tooey) Spaatz. All three were fiercely committed to the theory that "strategic" air warfare was more efficacious than "tactical" air warfare, and in the Sicily operation each was apparently determined to prove his case. The result was that the air war for Husky was carried forward virtually independently of our operations.

The air generals set two primary strategic goals: the destruction of the German and Italian air forces not merely on Sicily and Calabria but as far up the boot of Italy as they could reach; and the destruction of enemy seaports, railroads, depots and staging areas that would enable the Axis to prosecute the war in Sicily.

In pursuit of this strategy, the airmen launched several operations designed to move our air striking power closer to Sicily and Italy. They established a dozen new bomber bases on the Cape Bon peninsula in Tunisia. They expanded the facilities on Malta to accommodate a total of twenty fighter squadrons and built a full-scale air base on the adjacent island of Gozo in twenty days. They bombed the small island of Pantelleria —midway between Tunisia and Sicily—into smithereens and surrender and then built an air base on that island for American fighters. These three islands—Malta, Gozo, Pantelleria—provided the airmen with three "unsinkable aircraft carriers" accommodating 670 first-line fighters within 55 miles of Sicily and 150 miles of Calabria.

From this network of bases and others in North Africa, Tedder launched a massive strategic air assault on the Axis. In total, his air forces now had nearly 4,000 first-line combat aircraft. After the mauling in Tunisia, the Axis could muster only about 1,500 planes (900 fighters, 600 bombers) in the Mediterranean area, and Hitler was loath to send more. In the final three weeks of the strategic air campaign, blessed with beautiful flying weather, Tedder focused on the thirty major air bases and satellite airstrips on Sicily. The Americans bombed by day, the British bombed by night. These bases were utterly pulverized and the few surviving aircraft forced to pull back to bases in central Italy or Sardinia. By July 1, the Allies had achieved air superiority over Sicily and southern Italy.

Throughout this aerial blitz, Luftwaffe Ultra flowed in abundance to the Allies. Inasmuch as the Axis was compelled to redeploy its aircraft frequently, these Ultra reports (combined with other intelligence and aerial reconnaissance) were extremely useful in pinpointing the new target areas and avoiding wasteful attacks on abandoned airfields.

All this was a noteworthy achievement, but it was small comfort to us soldiers in the days immediately prior to D-day. In their pursuit of strategic objectives, the airmen had studiously—and arrogantly—avoided the tactical planning for Sicily. We knew little or nothing of their plans or about the success of the strategic air war. Even when pressed, they would tell us nothing about how they would support our landings. At Ike's headquarters, Pink Bull wrote that the air plan was a "most masterful piece of uninformed prevarication, totally unrelated to the Naval and Military Joint Plan." The effect on those responsible for the success of the amphibious landings was pronounced. Lucian Truscott wrote that "when we sailed for the operations, we had no information as to what, if any, air support we could expect on D-day. We had no knowledge of the extent of fighter protection we would have. We sailed ignorant of when, where, in what numbers, or under what circumstances we would ever see our fighter protection. . . . This lack of air participation in the joint planning at every level was inexcusable."

It certainly was inexcusable. We were preparing to assault an enemy beach in darkness, knowing full well that a panzer division was ready to pounce on us. It would have been immensely comforting to know positively that our massive air power would be overhead to help us if we needed it. In southern Tunisia, I had seen what could happen to ground forces when the airmen pursued strategic rather than tactical objectives. The Luftwaffe pasted the hell out of our men on the battlefield and nearly killed me. Moreover, on the rare occasion when Tedder and Coningham deigned to provide our soldiers "close support," the lion's share usually went to the British troops.

We were soon to discover that our fears were not groundless. The air support provided us on Sicily was scandalously casual, careless and ineffective.[1]

Our vast invasion armada set sail from a dozen or more ports in North Africa. In all, we numbered 1,411 seagoing vessels of all types. It was by far the greatest aggregation of sea power the world had ever seen.

The British Navy provided the big-ship "covering force," consisting of the aircraft carriers *Indomitable* and *Formidable,* six battleships, plus cruisers and destroyers. Part of the covering force, including the two carriers, made a feint toward Greece, to foster the deception planted by the fake documents on the Man who Never Was. Later these ships swung around and stood off Sicily during the invasion, vainly hoping to lure the six battleships of the Italian Navy out to fight. To the acute embarrassment of Admiral Cunningham, a single old Italian torpedo-bomber hit the carrier *Indomitable* and forced her to return to Gibraltar for repairs.[2]

Our command ship, *Ancon,* got under way in the late afternoon of July 5. We led a vast armada of attack transports, each towing a barrage balloon. Allied aircraft patrolled overhead, a comforting sight. We, like the covering force, followed a deceptive eastward course to further the impression that our target was Greece. The weather was good, the seas moderate. Nonetheless, I was queasy with a touch of seasickness.

Our circuitous route to Sicily took five days. During the voyage, I developed a physical malady worse than seasickness: hemorrhoids. The pain was excruciating and no painkiller seemed to relieve it. Knowing that if the pain continued I would be incapacitated on D-day and beyond, I consulted *Ancon*'s physician. He recommended local surgery. As our vast flotilla approached the darkened beaches of Sicily, in mounting seas and high winds, I stumbled along *Ancon*'s pitching decks to sick bay. After the operation, I returned to my cabin feeling worse than I had ever felt in my life. Unknown to me, my aide Chet Hansen had begun a personal diary. That night he discreetly logged: "The general is ill in his room, confined there by an inopportune local operation. Compelled to lie in bed, he soon became quite ill in the pitching sea. Chafed because he has been confined to his quarters and is unable to view the start of this campaign."[3]

The assault on Sicily proper began with an airborne drop, the first such large-scale Allied operation in World War II and the first for any army at night. The plan was worked out by British General Frederick (Boy) Browning, a noted paratrooper assigned to Ike's headquarters. He drew units from the British 1st Airborne Division and Matt Ridgway's 82nd Airborne Division. The 1,500 British paratroopers would go in towed by gliders; the 3,400 American troopers would jump from transports. The operation required 366 aircraft—331 of them United States C-47s, 35 of them British Albemarles. The American unit chosen for this mission was Jim Gavin's 505th Parachute Regimental Combat Team, reinforced with an extra battalion from the 504th Regiment. The British glider troops were to land south of Syracuse and seize a key highway bridge; Gavin's troopers were to seize the high ground immediately inland from Allen's 1st Division landing beach.

The airborne forces left from Tunisia in darkness on the evening of July 9, flying a complicated route over the sea. The pilots of the 366 planes were green to combat and inexperienced in airborne and over-water operations. None had ever approached an enemy-held position at night. The planes were thrown off course by the high winds. Some planes became lost and turned back or were never heard from again. Some pilots prematurely released the gliders and about fifty landed in the sea. Only fifty-four gliders landed in Sicily, twelve (with about 100 men) on or near the objective. Gavin's paratroopers fared little better. They were dropped not in a neat group near the objective but across a sixty-mile swath of southeastern Sicily, many in the British zone. For a long time, Gavin and others were not even certain they were in Sicily. It was not an auspicious beginning; we would soon feel the loss of the paratroopers.[4]

The British and American amphibious forces landed almost precisely on schedule in the early hours of July 10. Monty's Eighth Army, consisting of four divisions and a brigade organized into two corps,* went ashore along a thirty-five-mile stretch of east-facing beach in the Gulf of Noto. Patton's Seventh Army, consisting of four reinforced divisions, landed along a fifty-mile stretch of south-facing beach in the Gulf of Gela. From west to east: Truscott's 3rd Division assaulted Licata; Allen's 1st, Gela; and Middleton's 45th, Scoglitti. Gaffey's 2nd Armored Division plus an infantry regiment of the 1st Division were held in "floating reserve."

Contrary to Monty's dire forecast in April, there was negligible opposition in both sectors. The discontented Sicilians of the coastal divisions manning thinly spread fortifications showed no heart for a fight, even on home soil. They were fed up with Hitler and Mussolini and the personal and economic privations war had imposed. In both sectors they surrendered in droves or melted into the countryside. In Monty's sector, one observer remarked that the Italian coastal troops "stampeded to the safety of our prisoner of war cages on the beach in such terrific disorder that our troops faced greater danger from being trampled upon than from bullets." Many Sicilian coastal troopers volunteered to work as stevedores for the British rather than go to a POW camp in North Africa.

In our sector, operations moved ahead more or less as planned. Truscott's 3rd Division overwhelmed the weak Italian defense at Licata, and by noon the town and its small port and its airfield were his. In the center, a force of Rangers led by William O. Darby landed directly on the town dock and took Gela after a stiff but brief firefight. By 0800, the town was his. Meanwhile, the bulk of Terry Allen's 1st Division landed on the beaches to the east (or right) of Gela. His men met sporadic fire, but after help from the heavy shore bombardment by the naval vessels standing off shore, opposition diminished rapidly. By 0900, Allen's men had secured Gela and all objectives and had sent out forces to link up with Gavin's paratroopers, who, unknown to Allen, were not at their assigned objective

* XIII Corps commanded by Miles C. Dempsey, and XXX Corps commanded by Oliver Leese. The troops were the 1st Canadian Division, the British 5th, 50th and 51st Infantry divisions and the 231st Infantry Brigade, plus commando units.

on the high ground inland. On the far right, Middleton's 45th Division landed abreast Scoglitti, encountering sandbars and rocky beaches. But by 0900, Scoglitti was Middleton's, and his infantry battalions were pushing inland, striving to maintain the momentum of the assault.

Axis aircraft appeared over our sector at dawn. A Stuka sank the U.S. destroyer *Maddox* well offshore; another just missed the British beacon submarine *Safari*. A U.S. minesweeper was sunk inshore. In the afternoon, there were two bombing attacks on the transports at Gela which inflicted minor damage on a destroyer. Near sundown, a lone Me-109 attacked the beaches and blew up LST 313. Later that day, there were high-level bomber attacks on our naval forces but no serious damage. These attacks were hit-and-run; there was no well-organized Axis air assault on our invasion forces, and except for the nuisance of repeated air raid alarms (real and false), the Seventh Army was not seriously interfered with. Nonetheless, it was immensely disturbing not to know the details of our air plan.

Not all had gone as smoothly as I might have liked. The sand bars had grounded scores of landing craft short of the beaches. Owing to these obstructions, the sporadic air attacks and the soft sand ashore, Terry Allen had not been able to get his artillery and armor ashore. Middleton had had similar problems. One of Allen's regiments had been held in floating reserve and though he had Darby's Rangers attached, the absence of the paratroopers left him with no immediate reserves ashore to call on. Allen's sector was thus a potential weak link in the beachhead chain.

And yet I counted our blessings. All our forces had got ashore with negligible casualties and were displaying remarkable aggressiveness. Surveying the chaotic beaches with binoculars from the bridge of the *Ancon,* I offered a silent prayer of thanks to God. The Allies had returned to Europe—to stay.[5]

TWENTY

The Axis forces on Sicily were not in the least surprised by our assault. As soon as the paratroopers began landing in both sectors, Italian General Guzzoni took immediate offensive action. He ordered the 15th Panzer Division in the western end of the island to come rapidly east. He deployed a panzer brigade to block Monty's move northward along the east coast highway toward Augusta. He ordered the Hermann Goering Division and two of the best mobile Italian divisions to throw our Seventh Army back into the sea.

The counterattack on the Seventh Army hit us about noon on D-day. The full weight fell on Terry Allen's understrength 1st Division. Gavin's scattered paratroopers and Darby's Rangers helped significantly to blunt the attacks, but everyone was hard-pressed owing to the lack of armor, artillery, anti-tank weapons and communications. Patton immediately ordered the floating reserve to go ashore to buttress the 1st Division, but it became bogged down in the unloading process and did not play a significant role in repulsing the attack. Patton ordered another night airborne drop into the 1st Division area but then postponed it to the following night, owing in part to the confusion on the beachhead.

The second—and strongest—attack came on the second morning, July 11. The panzers simply rolled right through our lightly armed forces. At the same time, Axis air hit us with full fury, causing chaos in our landing zone. The enemy air was incessant and unrelenting. It blew up an ammunition ship off the beach and forced the other ships to up-anchor and scatter. Bombs straddled the cruiser *Boise,* our command ship, *Ancon,* and several destroyers. The sky was a confused mass of Axis and Allied planes. Anti-aircraft weapons ashore and afloat blazed away at everything with wings, friend or foe. So much for "strategic" air warfare.* [1]

* The official Army historian wrote that the Axis "committed 198 Italian and 283 German planes against the various Allied beaches on July 11." Most of these attacks were mounted from bases on Sardinia.

Both Patton and I went ashore in separate LCVP's that morning, July 11. I was still in agony from my hemorrhoid surgery. On the beach I picked up a tubular inflatable life jacket to use for a pillow. I hitched a ride on a duck to our hastily organized II Corps command post in Middleton's 45th Division area at Scoglitti. The pillow provided some comfort as we bounced across the beaches and stone roads. But for two weeks of the Sicily campaign, I suffered severely—and finished each day with bloody shorts.

Our CP, initially located in the Scoglitti police station, was moved to an almond orchard two miles north of the town. I found personal quarters in the home of a colonel in the coastal command—and slept on a bed with springs but no mattress.[2]

That day, for many hours, the issue was in grave doubt. The German tanks crunched down to within a mile of the beaches. On every hand heroism was commonplace. Jim Gavin approached to within ten feet of a Tiger tank and fired at it point-blank with our newest portable anti-tank weapon, the bazooka. The shell—far too small—simply bounced harmlessly off the tank. Bill Darby turned some captured Italian guns against the tanks and blazed away. But none of this heroism was sufficient. It was the U.S. Navy that saved the day. The cruisers *Boise* and *Savannah* and a host of destroyers finally stopped the tanks with relentless, well-directed salvos of eight- and five-inch shells. Late that afternoon, the Germans fell back, the attack defeated. In vain we searched the skies for close air support from our airmen.

I saw little or nothing of Patton that day, but an incident arose that put a severe strain on our relationship. The full details are too complicated to relate here. In brief, Patton brashly countermanded an order I had given for a unit to hold fast until we could clear out a threatening pocket of Germans, and instead told the unit to go on the attack. He did not consult me but gave the order directly to Terry Allen. It soon developed that the order was a mistake and the unit found itself in serious jeopardy. Later when I sharply confronted Patton for bypassing me, he apologized. The matter might have rested there had not Patton later complained to Ike that I was "not aggressive enough." This naturally infuriated me. On the battlefield there is a great difference between recklessness and aggressiveness, but the distinction was blurred in Patton's mind.[3]

That night, July 11, Patton ordered up the postponed airborne drop. Ridgway, who was ashore in the beachhead, chose the 504th Regimental Combat Team, commanded by Reuben H. Tucker. Ridgway had established elaborate and highly specific safeguards to prevent our men from firing at our own planes. But that night the 144 C-47s carrying the 2,008 men of the 504th arrived over the beachhead in the dark only fifty minutes after the last Axis air raid. The gunners were edgy. One gunner on a naval vessel opened fire on a low-flying C-47. Then, as we all looked on in helpless fury, seemingly every gun ashore and afloat blazed away at the formation. The planes careened wildly in evasion. Many crashed in flames. Panicked and wounded paratroopers frantically bailed out. Some were cut down as they floated to earth. In all, twenty-three planes were lost and thirty-seven badly damaged. The airborne force suffered 318 casualties: 88 dead, 162 wounded, 68 missing.[4]

These airborne fiascos on Sicily seriously jeopardized the future of airborne operations. Many of my infantry cohorts declared the paratrooper a dead dodo. There was soon a strong move in Washington to abolish the force. But I disagreed. In spite of the foul-ups, Gavin's scattered force had caused great confusion and distraction among the enemy on D-day. However, it was clear to all of us that successful employment of airborne forces in the future would require the utmost care and control and far greater training for the pilots of the troop transports.[5]

Ike, meanwhile, had been champing at the bit in a command post in Malta. Reports on our invasion progress from Patton were thin to nonexistent, and Ike was unable to tell the Combined Chiefs what was going on. Early on the morning of July 12, he boarded the British destroyer *Petard* to visit our sector and get his own impressions. He arrived at Patton's command ship, *Monrovia,* anchored off Gela, at 0630 to find Patton in the midst of shifting his CP to the beach.

The meeting lasted only forty-five minutes, but I believe it was one of those turning points historians like to pinpoint. I think it marked a distinct cooling of the relationship between Ike and Patton, a sudden loss of faith by the commander in chief in his army commander. That loss of faith would have a distinct bearing on my own future, so the meeting was a turning point in my life as well as Patton's. I was not present at the meeting, but, of course, I heard about it later and can reconstruct it from my memory of the recollections of those who were present.

Patton led Ike to his map room and briefed him on the situation ashore. In the course of this briefing, Patton described his trip to the "front" the day before, probably in his usual self-glorifying way. He had been machine-gunned, bombed, had personally helped set up some 4.2 mortars at a range of 900 yards from enemy infantry, and had been within 300 yards of exploding enemy tanks. He felt that his presence ashore had helped turn the tide and that (as he had confided to his diary) "this is the first day in this campaign that I think I earned my pay." He probably complained loudly about our lack of air support and may have told Ike on this occasion that I was "not aggressive enough."

But had Patton earned his pay in Ike's eyes? Perhaps not. When Ike sent Patton to take over II Corps in Tunisia, he wrote him: "I spoke to you about personal recklessness. Your personal courage is something you do not have to prove to me and I want you as Corps Commander—not as a casualty. I am quite well aware that in getting ready for the tasks to come, you must see every portion of your troops and of the positions they occupy; but don't forget that in actual battle under present conditions a commander can really handle his outfit only from his Command Post, *where he can be in touch with his commander and with his subordinates.*" (Italics added.)

Patton had left his command post, the *Monrovia,* for a full ten hours in the most critical phase of the Sicily landings. Ashore, at times he had played the role of a heroic company or platoon commander rather than an army commander. Meanwhile, he left Ike—and the Combined Chiefs—in the dark about Seventh Army progress. Patton later told Cunningham: "Admiral, I was no longer in command of an army, but merely a reconnaissance unit." Harry Butcher, who was present, recorded that Ike was angry: "Ike spoke vigorously to Patton about the inadequacy of his reports of progress reaching headquarters in Malta. Because of our inability to know at headquarters of even his impressions of progress, we were unable to determine just what assistance, particularly in the air, he needed. . . . Ike had stepped on him hard. . . . There was an air of tension. . . . When we left General Patton I thought he was angry."

Another who attended the briefing substantiated Butcher's observation. He was Major General John P. Lucas, West Point Class of 1911, Ike's latest "eyes and ears." Lucas was first-rate. In the States, he had trained Truscott's 3rd Division to its high level of efficiency. Lucas was dogging Patton, whom he greatly admired. He was also keeping a diary. He logged:

> Eisenhower was seemingly disturbed by the failure of news of the situation to arrive promptly at [his headquarters]. I didn't hear what he said but he must have given Patton hell because George was much upset. . . . The C in C might have mentioned the fact that a most difficult military operation was being performed in a manner that reflected great credit on American arms.

Patton had good reason to be angry. Not only had Ike failed to congratulate him on his great personal victory, he had spent the meeting criticizing him. Later Patton wrote in his diary: "When I took him to my room to show him the situation, he was not much interested but began to compare the sparsity of my reports with the almost hourly news bulletins of the Eighth Army. I have intercepts of many of them, and they are both non-essential and imaginary in the majority of cases. Furthermore they are not fighting and we are. . . . Ike also told me that I am too prompt in my replies and should hesitate more, the way he does, before replying. I think he means well but it is most upsetting to get only piddling criticism when one knows one has done a good job." *

* Obviously, naval historian Morison was in error when he wrote that Butcher's account of an "altercation" between Ike and Patton was "without foundation."

Ike had two "pool" war correspondents in tow and they and Butcher had urged him to go ashore—put foot on Italian soil—so they would have a better story. Even though he had not long to stay, Ike was "especially hopeful of visiting Bradley and his II Corps headquarters," Butcher wrote. But Patton discouraged a visit to my headquarters, telling Ike it was at least an hour-and-a-half boat ride merely to reach the beach. Thereupon, Ike left the *Monrovia*. Later that morning he briefly went ashore in the Canadian area of Monty's Eighth Army, then returned to Malta.

Shortly after Ike left the *Monrovia,* a full account of the 504th parachute disaster reached Patton. A report was promptly forwarded to Ike at Malta. Since Patton had not known the full extent of the disaster, I do not think he mentioned it at his meeting with Ike, and Ike may have felt that Patton had been covering up. That same day, Ike sent a blistering cable to Patton which seemed to place the blame for the disaster on Patton: "Before the beginning of this operation you particularly requested me to authorize this movement into your area. Consequently ample time was obviously available for complete and exact coordination of the movement among all forces involved. If the cited report is true, the incident could have been occasioned only by inexcusable carelessness and negligence on the part of someone. You will institute within your command an immediate and exhaustive investigation into allegation with a view to fixing responsibility. Report of pertinent facts is desired and if the persons found responsible are serving in your command, I want a statement of the disciplinary action taken by you. . . . This will be expedited."

Patton saw this as a "wire from Ike, cussing me out." He went on to write with some bitterness: "As far as I can see if anyone is blamable it must be myself but personally I feel immune to censure. . . . Perhaps Ike is looking for an excuse to relieve me. . . . Men who get bombed all day get itchy fingers. . . . Ike has never been subjected to air attack or any other form of death. However he is such a straw man his future is secure. The British will never let him go."* [6]

Now that we and the British were firmly established ashore, we had to puzzle out what to do next. Astonishing as it seems in retrospect, there was no master plan for the conquest of Sicily. Nothing had been worked out beyond the limited beachhead objectives. Patton and I had assumed the post-landing strategy would be somewhat as follows. Monty would push quickly up the east coast highway through Catania to Messina, thus blocking any Axis withdrawal to Calabria. Our Seventh Army would push

* The "exhaustive" investigation soon fell by the wayside. Ridgway quite properly wrote: "The responsibility for loss of life and material resulting from this operation is so divided, so difficult to fix with impartial justice, and so questionable of ultimate value to the service because of the acrimonious debates which would follow efforts to hold responsible persons or services to account, that disciplinary action is of doubtful wisdom." However, I believe Ike, in his mind, continued to hold Patton responsible.

quickly north from our beachhead through Enna and Nicosia to the north coast road, where we would turn east to Messina. The defending Axis forces would thus be caught in giant encircling Allied pincers and forced to surrender. But, I emphasize, this was merely an assumption on our part.

In fact, it was Axis reaction that ultimately decided our strategy for Sicily. When the initial counterattack against the Seventh Army failed, Albert Kesselring flew to Sicily to reassess the situation. He concluded that Sicily was ultimately doomed. The best the Axis could possibly do would be to fight a delaying action, tying down as many Allied troops for as long as possible, and then withdraw across Messina Strait to Calabria. In pursuit of this strategy, he recommended that two additional German divisions be rushed to Sicily, and Hitler personally approved. These divisions were the 29th Panzer Grenadiers based in Calabria and the 1st Parachute based in southern France.

Since Monty's threatened push up the east coast highway represented the most immediate threat to Messina, the Axis generals threw the weight of their forces to block him. The Hermann Goering Division facing us began shifting over toward Catania on the night of July 12. That same night, the first elements of the German parachute division, escorted by German fighters, dropped near Catania. The 15th Panzer Division, which came from western Sicily, took up position near Enna to block our way. In the days following, the 29th Panzers crossed the Messina Strait and entered Sicily to join in creating a strong defensive line running roughly from Catania to Enna, southwest of Mount Etna.

I assume that Ultra revealed these plans and movements to Monty. In any case, he did his utmost with Dempsey's XIII Corps to smash through Catania before the Axis could establish the line and block his northward movement. This effort included a combined airborne-commando assault on Catania the night of July 13, the same night that more German paratroopers dropped in the same area. A third Sicily airborne fiasco ensued. Some 145 Allied aircraft (nineteen towing gliders) left Tunisia with 1,900 troopers of the British 1st Parachute Brigade. When the formation approached Sicily in darkness, Allied naval vessels opened fire, shooting down two planes and forcing nine to turn back because of damage or injuries to the pilots. Then the fully alerted German anti-aircraft batteries opened up, forcing ten more planes to turn back. Those who jumped fell amidst the arriving German paratroopers and were immediately engaged. Of the 1,900 paratroopers who set off from Tunisia, only about 200 reached their objective, and that was too few to do the job properly. Other efforts failed, and the coastal highway to Catania and Messina remained solidly blocked.

In the meantime Monty, entirely on his own, had conceived a strategic plan for the Allied conquest of Sicily. Leese's XXX Corps, which had landed in Monty's southern sector and had had a very easy time of it, now stood virtually idle. Blocked at Catania, Monty decided to circle Leese's XXX Corps around the west side of Mount Etna (a left hook), thence northeast toward Messina, breaking the coast highway block. Both British corps would then converge on Messina, entrapping the Axis defenders. In effect, Leese's XXX Corps would displace the role we had assumed for the Seventh Army, using the only good road (Route 124) available for a northward thrust west of Mount Etna. This plan left the Seventh Army in the subsidiary role of protecting Monty's rear and left flank.

What followed was the most arrogant, egotistical, selfish and dangerous move in the whole of combined operations in World War II. Without checking with a soul—not even Alexander—Monty ordered Leese to jump off on the morning of July 13 and head for Enna on our road, Route 124. Since by that time my II Corps forces had advanced to within a thousand yards of the road, it meant that Monty had ordered Leese's XXX Corps directly across our immediate front without any notice whatsoever.

After he had set Leese's corps in motion, Monty then presented his new plan to Alexander—a fait accompli—on the morning of July 13. He demanded that the army boundaries be altered, moving the Seventh Army west to make room for Leese's oncoming corps. Alexander agreed to this plan (so far as I have been able to ascertain) without a single objection and without giving any thought whatsoever to the impact the decision would have on American sensibilities. Alexander then flew over to announce the plan to Patton, interrupting Patton at lunch in Gela.

Here again was a turning point, a truly meaningful one, since the Allied strategy for the conquest of Sicily as well as American honor, prestige and pride and the lives of many soldiers were at stake. We were ready to strike for Messina, the only real strategic prize on Sicily. Now Monty would deny us this role, relegating us (as in southern Tunisia) to the demeaning and inconsequential task of protecting the Eighth Army's rear and flank. Would George Patton sit still for such an outrageous decision?

He would—and did. Like a lamb.

No one has ever satisfactorily explained Patton's position on this decision. It was wholly out of character. By all rights, he could have been expected to roar like a lion. My guess is that at that point, Patton sincerely believed Ike was "looking for an excuse" to relieve him (as he had noted in his diary). In Tunisia Ike had sharply warned him to curb his rampant Anglophobia and "to respond to General Alexander's orders exactly as if they were issued by me." Only the day before, Ike had landed on him hard in person. Ike's accusatory cable about the paratrooper disaster had arrived just that morning, and Patton already felt the blame must rest on him. Patton did not yet grasp British Army protocol—that by tradition, an "order" from a superior was open to challenge, a basis for discussion. He had been trained to obey explicitly an "order" from a superior.* I feel certain that Patton believed that if he caused a ruckus on this day Ike would fire him.

That afternoon Patton brought word of the decision to me at my corps CP. My staff and I were absolutely outraged. We at once perceived the full import of the decision: that Monty had nominated himself for the starring role on Sicily, leaving us to eat his dust. An entire American army that had fought its way ashore was to be wasted. The decision entailed many disappointments and complications for us: giving up Route 124 that we had struggled so hard to take; repositioning the whole 45th Division to the left of the 1st Division; regrouping all II Corps support units (artillery, engineers, etc.); slowing down the driving momentum of our attack—not to mention the deleterious effect on the morale of our troops. I reacted sharply. "My God," I said to Patton, "you can't allow him to do that!" Patton replied with curious lameness that it was too late to change the orders.

My G-2, Monk Dickson, later wrote: "General Bradley executed this preposterous order silently and skillfully, but inwardly he was as hot as Mount Etna." I certainly was. Many times thereafter I questioned my own timidity and obeisance. The orders were so outrageous, so obviously wrong, and so much was at stake, I should have stood my ground even at the risk of incurring displeasure or relief. I now believe that had I done so, the campaign in Sicily would have taken a far different turn, saving many Allied lives and insuring a decisive victory for us rather than the cloudy finish that ensued.

Let me explain further. At that time, D-day plus 4, the Seventh Army was poised to break out. We had secured our beachhead, firmed up our front and got our armor and artillery ashore. Our supply line was running smoothly over the beach, and the enemy air attacks had subsided. Our troops were in marvelously aggressive spirits, all having performed far beyond my wildest expectations. We had reached the main road north. With our superior trucks and self-propelled artillery, we could move much faster than the British. The enemy front before us was soft from his withdrawals; he was concentrating in the main before XIII Corps at Catania, not us. We were in ideal position for a fast run to the north coast—before the enemy could organize his defensive perimeter—and an encircling right turn toward Messina. I feel certain that we could have pulled it off and that with our quick movement, the pressure on Monty would have eased sufficiently for him to break out at Catania. I agree with the British military historian Major General Hubert Essame who wrote in his biography of

* Later Monty would say to Patton: "George, let me give you some advice. If you get an order from [Alexander] that you don't like, why just ignore it. That's what I do."

Patton that had this plan rather than Monty's been adopted, "the campaign in Sicily could have been shortened by weeks." *

General John Lucas, believing the strategic situation was "rapidly becoming very dangerous," flew to Algiers on July 17 to convey his views to Ike and his staff. Ike was away, but Lucas told Ike's G-3, Lowell S. Rooks, that "the British were determined to put us [the American forces] in a secondary role. . . . That this could not be accepted, that the two armies must be treated alike, and that neither we nor the American people as a whole would stand for our being pushed into the background." When Ike returned, Lucas iterated his views to him, adding that "Patton must stand up to General Alexander and fight for what he thought was right." Lucas logged Ike's response:

> He agreed and said, however, that he had never found a case where the British had deliberately tried to put anything over on us. I didn't answer that. He also said that I must try to put myself in Alexander's place. He first came in contact with American troops when the fighting in Kasserine and Gafsa was going on. That they were so inexperienced that the British command completely lost confidence in them as offensive troops. That these same divisions did well in Tunisia but that now, in Sicily, there were two new divisions, one, the 45th, that had no combat experience at all, and the other, the 3rd, with very little. Alexander should not be blamed too much for being cautious. . . . He told me to see that Patton was made to realize that he must stand up to Alexander. He didn't mean he was not to obey orders, of course.

In sum: Ike defended the outrageous Monty-Alexander decision to relegate the Seventh Army to a supporting role. It was up to George Patton to protect American interests in the Sicily campaign. If the role of the Seventh Army were to be enlarged, Patton would have to persuade Alexander on his own. Ike would not come to bat for us.

I cannot leave this subject without calling attention to the sly way in which Monty described this infamous episode in his memoirs. He wrote: "The method by which the campaign would be developed once the armies were ashore, and how the island would finally be reduced, was not decided. In fact there was no master plan. As a result the operations and actions of the two Allied armies were not properly coordinated. The army commanders developed their own ideas of how to proceed and then 'informed' higher authority. The Seventh U.S. Army, once on shore, was allowed to wheel west toward Palermo. It thereby *missed the opportunity* to direct its main thrust northward in order to cut the island in two as a preliminary to the encirclement of the Etna position and the capture of Messina." (Italics added.)[7]

* Monty's chief of staff, Freddie de Guingand, also agreed. He wrote that if Patton had concentrated all his effort toward Messina, "a speed-up of the campaign could have been achieved."

TWENTY-ONE

We regrouped to protect the Eighth Army's flank and give Leese's corps room to maneuver. I side-slipped Middleton's 45th Division to the left of Allen's 1st Division and readjusted corps units accordingly. In the meantime, Patton had received grudging permission from Alexander for limited elements of Truscott's 3rd Division to move a few miles west and take the port of Empedocle, which facilitated our resupply situation.[1]

All the while, we continued driving aggressively inland against the weak Sicilian and Italian defenders. They surrendered by the thousands, often without a fight. They were sick of war, fascism and Mussolini. Some even provided us valuable intelligence. Their attitude led me to the idea of actively encouraging defections. Perhaps violating Roosevelt's ill-advised "unconditional surrender" dictum announced at Casablanca, I declared a local "amnesty" policy: any Sicilian in the Italian Army who wanted to defect was free to go home. In all, 33,000 Sicilians were paroled home, thereby easing our way forward and our POW congestion in the rear.[2]

Denied a role in taking Messina, Patton began to cast covetous eyes on Palermo. The city had no real strategic significance—it lay in the opposite direction from the German defense line around Mount Etna—but it had a legendary and a glamorous history and its capture was sure to make headlines. That would bring much-needed prestige to our troops and our army commander. The city and the territory between it and the Seventh Army beachhead was only lightly held by Sicilian and Italian troops. The operation would thus be a cakewalk. It might also enable Patton to cut loose Gaffey's 2nd Armored Division tanks, giving them meaningful combat experience.

As the plan took shape in his mind, Patton was cagey and secretive, consulting no one outside his staff, including me. He did not want to risk having the scheme disapproved by Alexander on the drawing board. I think he had learned well from Monty's example: launch an operation, then inform Alexander. On paper, he created a provisional corps for the operation consisting of Truscott's 3rd Division, Gaffey's 2nd Armored Division, the two regrouped regimental combat teams of Ridgway's 82nd Airborne Division, Darby's Ranger battalions and a regiment of Manton Eddy's 9th Infantry Division, which had just arrived from Army Reserve in North Africa. He named his deputy army commander, Geoffrey Keyes, to command the corps.

Then came yet another blow from Alexander. On July 16, he issued a formal order spelling out the strategy for the final conquest of Sicily. In effect, it was a codification and elaboration of Monty's plan. Monty's two corps would mount the main drive on Messina. Patton's Seventh Army would protect Monty's left flank by securing the road net to the west of Enna. When that had been achieved, the Seventh Army would drive north to the sea. This order, if explicitly obeyed, would preclude—even prohibit—Patton's scheme to capture Palermo.

This time Patton reacted in character. On the very next day he flew to see Alexander, who was in Tunis for a strategy meeting with Ike, Tedder and Coningham. Patton arrived, Butcher recalled, "mad as a wet hen." But he evidently made his case for Palermo with calm reason, emphasizing that "it was inexpedient politically for Seventh Army not to have equal glory" with the Eighth Army. Later Patton saw Ike and presumably made the same calmly reasoned case. The official Army historian wrote that Alexander "reluctantly agreed and gave his consent to Patton's proposal."[3]

Patton returned to Sicily on July 18 euphoric. He gave orders to Keyes for his provisional corps to jump off for Palermo the very next day. The corps would drive due northwest from our beachhead, leaving my II Corps (of two divisions) to support the Eighth Army up through central Sicily toward Enna. Had I been consulted, I would have advised against this operation. It was taking the main weight of the Seventh Army off in the wrong direction in what was essentially a public relations gesture. But Patton had yet to ask my advice, and I feel certain he would have ignored it. He had the bit in his teeth; there was no stopping him now.

Four hours after the provisional corps jumped off on July 19, Alexander's formal orders came through. What a shock they must have caused in Patton's headquarters! They were far different from Patton's understanding of the oral agreement in Tunis. Alexander now ordered Patton to send the full weight of the Seventh Army directly north to the coast, establishing a firm north-south line through the whole of central Sicily. Only after this had been accomplished was Patton authorized to "exploit" the western end of the island, including Palermo. When he read these orders, Patton's chief of staff, Hobart R. Gay, concealed them from Patton for several days, allowing the offensive to continue, in direct disobedience of Alexander's orders![4]

It thus fell to my II Corps to carry out the assignment Alexander had

1

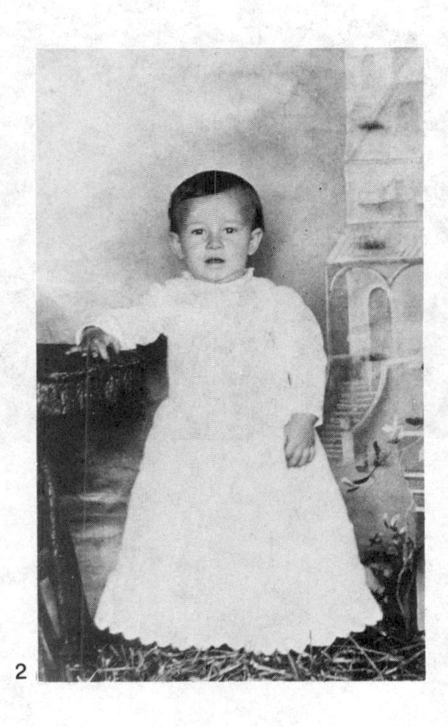

2

One of the small wooden frame houses in Missouri in which I lived as a boy (1). This picture (2) was taken when I was about two years old.

3

A studio portrait of my mother, Bessie, myself, and my father, John Smith Bradley, taken when I was about seven.

4

The Moberly High School baseball team, 1908. I'm on the left in the second row.

5

West Point as it looked when I entered in 1911.

6

As a cadet, next to my locker.

Our 1915 championship baseball team. I'm fourth from right.

7

8

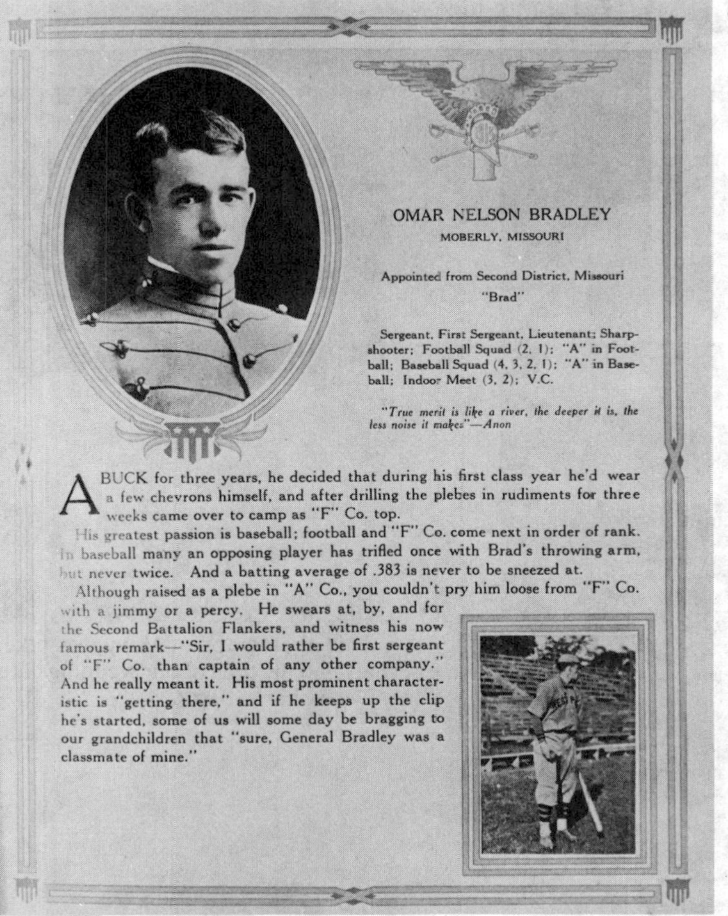

OMAR NELSON BRADLEY

MOBERLY, MISSOURI

Appointed from Second District, Missouri

"Brad"

Sergeant, First Sergeant, Lieutenant; Sharpshooter; Football Squad (2, 1); "A" in Football; Baseball Squad (4, 3, 2, 1); "A" in Baseball; Indoor Meet (3, 2); V.C.

"True merit is like a river, the deeper it is, the less noise it makes"—Anon

A BUCK for three years, he decided that during his first class year he'd wear a few chevrons himself, and after drilling the plebes in rudiments for three weeks came over to camp as "F" Co. top.

His greatest passion is baseball; football and "F" Co. come next in order of rank. In baseball many an opposing player has trifled once with Brad's throwing arm, but never twice. And a batting average of .383 is never to be sneezed at.

Although raised as a plebe in "A" Co., you couldn't pry him loose from "F" Co. with a jimmy or a percy. He swears at, by, and for the Second Battalion Flankers, and witness his now famous remark—"Sir, I would rather be first sergeant of "F" Co. than captain of any other company." And he really meant it. His most prominent characteristic is "getting there," and if he keeps up the clip he's started, some of us will some day be bragging to our grandchildren that "sure, General Bradley was a classmate of mine."

The Academy yearbook for 1915. My classmate, Ike Eisenhower (9), wrote the flattering comments about me.

DWIGHT DAVID EISENHOWER

ABILENE, KANSAS

Senatorial Appointee, Kansas

"Ike"

Corporal, Sergeant, Color Sergeant; A.B., B.A., Sharpshooter; Football Squad (3, 2), "A" in Football; Baseball Squad (4); Cheer Leader; Indoor Meet (4, 3).

"Now, fellers, it's just like this. I've been asked to say a few words this evening about this business. Now, me and Walter Camp, we think—"

—Himself

9

10

On a picnic with Mary Quayle, the future Mrs. Bradley, in 1915.

11

This photograph of Mary was taken around the time of our wedding date, December 28, 1916.

12

In front of my tent in Arizona in the summer of 1916 during the border war with Mexico.

13

Handsome, dashing and unorthodox Douglas MacArthur, Superintendent of West Point when I arrived there to teach math in September 1920.

Mary with Elizabeth (Lee) Bradley, born December 3, 1923, at West Point.

14

15

In my second tour at West Point, 1934–38, where I was an instructor in the Tactics Department.

16

Some of the senior teaching staff at Fort Benning, where I taught in the early 1930s between my two tours at West Point. Seated at center is the most impressive man I ever knew, General George C. Marshall, who revolutionized infantry training at Fort Benning. I'm standing second from left. Seated second from left is General Joe (Vinegar Joe) Stilwell, under whom I taught at Benning and who was a prime mover in the teaching revolution there.

17

Sergeant Alvin York, winner of the Medal of Honor and World War I hero, who told me that I wouldn't get very far because I was "too nice."

18

While I was on General Marshall's staff in the War Department in Washington, Hitler began the Second World War and the bombing of London (19).

19

20

Marshall gave me command of the reactivated 82nd Division shortly after the bombing of Pearl Harbor in 1941. He sent Matthew B. Ridgway to be my assistant commander. We heavily stressed physical training, from which not even the generals were exempted.

Reviewing local troops in French Northwest Africa soon after my arrival there in 1943.

21

Churchill and Ike conferring in Algiers with British General Harold Alexander, the Allied ground commander in North Africa, Sicily and Italy, who is directly behind Ike. Alex was the most able and most friendly of the British generals.

22

23

Our most flamboyant and aggressive front-line general, George S. Patton (23), the master of tank warfare, and his nemesis in North Africa, Field Marshal Erwin Rommel (24), "the Desert Fox." I began my combat service in North Africa as Patton's understudy.

24

26

Three key and controversial generals in the North African campaign. British Air General Arthur C. (Mary) Coningham (25) outraged Patton and me when he failed to provide close air support in difficult situations. My West Point classmate General Charles W. (Doc) Ryder (26), commander of the 34th Infantry Division. Unjustly accused of incompetence by the British, he led his men in the capture of Hill 609, a crucial victory in the Tunisian campaign. General Terry Allen (27), commander of the 1st Division, the fabled "Big Red One." He failed to discipline his division properly, and I had to relieve him of command.

28

In Sicily General Lucian Truscott commanded the 3rd Infantry Division. An underrated general, he went on to more important command in Italy.

29

I spent anxious months in England massing supplies such as these, preparing for the forthcoming invasion of France.

30

While with Ike on an inspection tour of U.S. troops in England preparing for the Normandy invasion, Churchill expressed a desire to try the new American carbines. The targets were twenty-five yards away for Churchill, fifty for Ike and seventy-five for me. All the targets were tactfully removed before anyone could inspect them.

31

The Allied chiefs in charge of planning and executing Overlord, the Normandy invasion, at command headquarters in London. With me in the back row are British Admiral Bertram Ramsay, the Allied naval commander; British tactical air commander Trafford Leigh-Mallory; and Ike's chief of staff, Lt. Gen. Bedell Smith. In front, left to right, are Ike's deputy, British Air General Arthur Tedder; Ike; and General Bernard Law Montgomery, the hero of El Alamein, better known as "Monty."

32

Throughout the war the Chief of the Imperial General Staff, Field Marshal Alan Brooke, was the principal architect of British war strategy, excepting Churchill. A brilliant strategist, he remains the least known of the major figures of the war.

33

34

35

General Miles Dempsey (33), commander of the British Second Army in the Normandy assault, directed British forces at Gold, Juno and Sword beaches. General Clarence (Terry) Huebner (34), 1st Infantry Division (Big Red One) commander, whose troops performed so heroically at Omaha Beach in Normandy and throughout the war. Huebner later commanded V Corps. General Henry Crerar (35), commander of the Canadian First Army in Normandy. General Maxwell D. Taylor (36), commanding officer of the 101st Airborne Division, jumped into Normandy alongside General Matt Ridgway and his 82nd Airborne Division.

36

With General J. Lawton (Lightning Joe) Collins, VII Corps commander, who led the assault of Utah Beach.

37

Mary with Lee and Hal Beukema at their wedding in the West Point chapel on June 8, 1944. I was unable to attend the wedding due to a prior commitment on the shores of France.

Omaha Beach early in the morning of June 6, 1944. The valiant men who died on that beach should never be forgotten. Every man who set foot on Omaha Beach that day was a hero.

40

On the morning of June 7, Monty's destroyer pulled alongside my headquarters ship, the heavy cruiser *Augusta,* and I climbed aboard to confer about the progress of the invasion.

41

With Rear Admiral Alan G. Kirk, commander of the naval task force off the coast of France whose supporting fire saved our hides on Omaha Beach.

42

allotted to the entire Seventh Army: break through to the north coast, meanwhile supporting the Eighth Army's flank. There was little glory in this assignment, rather a lot of brutal, bloody fighting against pockets of tenacious Germans who were conducting a well-organized fighting withdrawal to the Etna Line. Our task was enlarged when Monty—without informing us—constricted Leese's encirclement of Mount Etna and left it to us to take Enna. We were not informed of this abrupt change in plan, and, as a result, our whole right flank was left exposed to enemy counterattack. I fired off a testy letter to Leese, who apologized, quickly corrected the situation, and sent me two bottles of scotch in atonement. On the heels of this exchange, came a BBC broadcast crediting Leese's Canadian division with taking Enna!* [5]

Patton's 100-mile dash to Palermo against spotty opposition was great theater and it generated the headlines he so craved. A large share of the credit should go to Truscott, Ridgway and Darby, whose superbly trained infantry advanced rapidly and mostly on foot. Keyes held Gaffey's tanks in reserve all the way to the outskirts of the city, then turned them loose for a noisy, triumphant procession through the narrow stone streets. Palermo meekly surrendered to Keyes and Gaffey on the evening of July 22. Patton moved into a luxurious palace, ensconced in a regal splendor beyond the wildest dreams of Hollywood.†

So far as I am aware, Patton was never criticized by his superiors for this flagrant disobedience of orders. The victory and the headlines were too sweet. However meaningless in a strategic sense, it was our most dramatic and crowed-about "success" to date. It made our soldiers proud, lifted spirits at home, and impressed Alexander. It also put Patton back in Ike's good graces, temporarily at least. When the word reached Algiers that Palermo had fallen, Butcher wrote that "Patton's great progress gives Ike a warm glow." [8]

After a tough fight in the center of the island, II Corps made good progress toward the north coast. I sent Middleton's 45th Division angling northwestward from central Sicily, toward Palermo, and by the morning of July 22, his patrols reached the outskirts of the city. However, this was Patton's stage and the patrols were ordered away. The main strength of the division reached the coast at Termini Imerese (about twenty miles east of Palermo) in the early morning hours of July 23. Allen's 1st Division progressed less spectacularly. The division had borne the brunt of the hard fighting in the Enna area and had sustained higher casualties. In its push

* This was no isolated journalistic misstatement. Throughout the Sicily campaign, BBC and other British media credited Monty with all the hard fighting while we were depicted as "eating grapes" and "swimming." Since BBC broadcasts were our main source of outside news on Sicily, our men were naturally infuriated.[6]

† The Palermo operation cost 272 American casualties: 57 killed, 170 wounded, 45 missing. Some 2,900 enemy were killed; 53,000 surrendered.[7]

beyond Enna, it encountered more tenacious German units, fiercely rugged terrain and searing summer heat. On July 23, it captured Petralia, then bogged down after two unrelieved weeks of brutal combat.

In the meantime, Monty had got nowhere in his encirclement of Mount Etna and the drive on Messina. Dempsey's XIII Corps was still blocked along the east coast road at Catania. Leese's XXX Corps bogged down in the Adrano area, compelling Monty to bring yet another infantry division, the British 78th, from his North Africa reserve. This gave him a total force of about six divisions against the three German divisions, the German paratroopers and associated Italian units; but the Germans now had the terrain advantage. Monty, typically, had been too slow, too methodical in his post-landing tactics. He had given the enemy too much time to reinforce his line and get well entrenched. In sum, Monty's revised plan for the invasion of Sicily, forced on the Allies in early May—a plan that only Monty really liked—had failed abysmally.[9]

Alexander was thus compelled to alter the strategy. He reverted to a rough outline of the original Sicily plan, which had called for an American landing at Palermo and a thrust to Messina along the north coast road in coordination with Monty's push up the east coast road. On July 23, he issued orders to Patton to throw the full weight of the Seventh Army at Messina, utilizing Palermo as the main supply base and line of communications, curtailing our beach operation on the south coast. The American Seventh Army was now to have equal status with the British Eighth Army. We spoke of the revised strategy, not without justification, as "going to Monty's rescue."[10]

We pivoted II Corps ninety degrees to the right and spearheaded the Seventh Army drive to Messina. Middleton's 45th Division utilized the coast road (113), Allen's 1st Division a parallel road (120), about fifteen miles to the south. The Germans, gradually withdrawing into a narrower defensive position, yielded ground only grudgingly, and we fought hard for every yard. After one week, on August 1, both divisions ran into steely defenses, the 45th at Santo Stefano, the 1st at Troina. Here we paused to regroup and give the 45th and 1st Divisions some much needed rest. Truscott's 3rd Division came up and relieved Middleton's 45th. The remainder of Manton Eddy's 9th Division was landed at Palermo and ordered forward to relieve Allen's 1st Division. But Allen wanted to take Troina before pulling the 1st Division out of the line. Two of Eddy's three regiments joined him in this effort.*

The Germans were not yet ready to abandon Troina. It developed into

* Patton's provisional corps, under Keyes, was disbanded. The 82nd Division returned to North Africa to prepare for other operations. Gaffey's 2nd Armored Division remained in Palermo on "occupation" duty, 75 percent of its tanks with disabled tracks. However, the tanks would have been of little use to us in the rugged terrain where we fought.

our toughest fight in the Sicily campaign. It was during this fight that I finally made up my mind to relieve Allen and Roosevelt.

In the initial assault on Troina, Allen flubbed badly. He miscalculated the enemy's strength and verve and was thrown back with heavy losses. Throughout the seven days of heavy fighting that ensued, he attempted to operate much as he had in the past, as an undisciplined, independent army, unresponsive to my wishes—or in some cases, orders. Without meaning any disrespect to the individual soldiers—who fought with great valor—the whole division had assumed Allen's cavalier attitude. I personally took over the tactical planning, and at the end of the Troina battle (the Germans finally withdrew to another line), when Eddy's 9th Division replaced the 1st, I relieved both Allen and Roosevelt, one of my most unpleasant duties of the war. Clarence R. Huebner, a flinty disciplinarian who had just been fired as an "American adviser" to Alexander for being too outspoken, replaced Allen as division commander. This controversial decision was mine and mine alone. Patton merely concurred. Allen returned to the States without prejudice, and both men would serve me again with distinction in Europe.

It was in Troina, too, that George Patton came to personal and professional grief as a result of the first of the two infamous "slapping incidents." During the heat of the Troina battle, on August 3, Patton visited the wounded at an evacuation hospital near Nicosia. While there, he encountered one of Allen's privates, Charles H. Kuhl, who apparently had no wounds. When Patton asked why Kuhl was in the hospital, Kuhl replied, "I guess I can't take it." The doctors had diagnosed him as being in a "psychoneurosis, anxiety state, moderately severe." It was the third time Kuhl had been evacuated for the same reason.

Patton flew into a rage, cursed Kuhl, slapped him across the face with his gloves, then grabbed him and threw him out of the tent, shouting, "I don't want yellow-bellied bastards like him hiding their lousy cowardice around here, stinking up this place of honor." In Patton's view, the man was simply a coward with no right to leave the front, a rotten apple who could contaminate the whole barrel. It later developed that Kuhl suffered from chronic diarrhea, had malaria and a fever of 102.2 degrees. He was sent back to a North Africa hospital by sympathetic medical personnel who had been shocked and outraged by Patton's loss of self-control and abuse of a patient.

This particular incident caused no immediate repercussions. Patton, the medical personnel and everybody else got on with the war at hand. Patton noted it in his diary: "In the hospital I also met the only arrant coward I have ever seen in this Army. . . . I gave him the devil, slapped his face with my gloves, and kicked him out of the hospital." On the following day, August 5, Patton sent out a memo to corps, division and separate unit commanders, ordering us to court-martial at unit level "for cowardice in the face of the enemy" the "very small number" of soldiers who were attempting to go to hospitals "on the pretext that they are nervously incapable of combat." I was too busy at Troina to give this order proper thought or wonder at the reason behind it. I had heard nothing about the slapping incident. But a fuse had been lit on a time bomb.[11]

Truscott's progress toward Messina along the coast road in the face of strong German resistance was slow. The Germans were fighting a skillful delaying action in mountainous terrain, blowing bridges behind them, sowing thousands of mines. Our slow progress was most disconcerting to Patton because he had now become determined to "beat Montgomery to Messina." I confess that while no strategic purpose would be served by it, I was equally anxious to beat Monty to Messina, if it were possible without recklessness or undue casualties. For a long time now, our men had been ridiculed and abused by the British media in Sicily. It seemed fitting revenge to rob Monty of the triumphant march into Messina.[12]

My tactical discussions with Patton led me to the idea of utilizing the small U.S. naval force at Palermo to make limited "leapfrog" or "end run" amphibious attacks around the strong enemy positions on the north coast road. Patton seized upon this idea with such unabated enthusiasm that I became gravely concerned. The danger, as always with Patton, was possible excess, that he would order us to bite off more than we could chew and suffer a disastrous reverse. To avert that possibility, I insisted on tight control over the operations. Historians Samuel Eliot Morison and Martin Blumenson have criticized our caution, raising the question of why we had not utilized amphibious end runs sooner and on a larger scale. Perhaps some of the criticism is justified. But it should be borne in mind that we had not before attempted such intricate maneuvers, that we were dependent on extremely limited naval backup, which could and did draw enemy air attack, that the Germans had proven themselves wily and tenacious fighters at every encounter.[13]

Our first end run took place on the night of August 7-8. We landed a reinforced battalion at Sant' Agata. At the same time, Truscott opened a combined frontal assault and flanking movement on the high ridges inland. The Germans were caught by surprise but the results were not all we could have wished for. The 29th Panzer Division had already begun a withdrawal, and while we inflicted some casualties, we had landed too late to trap the Germans in strength.[14]

The second end run was carried out after one postponement on the night of August 10-11 at Brolo. Regrettably, Patton, in his excessive enthusiasm for this new form of warfare, had arranged for a large number of war correspondents to witness the operation. Because his land-based forces were meeting very heavy resistance, Truscott requested a second postponement of twenty-four hours. The official Army historian wrote that because Patton "did not relish" having to tell the correspondents the operation would be delayed (possibly incurring "unfavorable publicity" for the Seventh Army), he denied Truscott's request. Truscott then appealed to me to deal with Patton. I backed Truscott all the way, warning Patton that unless Truscott's land-based units could link up quickly, the amphibious assault might turn into a disaster. In spite of the fact that he had previously assured me tight control over this operation, Patton arrogantly overruled me, demanding that the Brolo operation proceed as scheduled. I had no alternative but to comply with his order, but I was very angry. For the sake of a favorable headline, Patton was placing the lives of many men in jeopardy.[15]

This was the second time in Sicily that Patton, in effect, ignored or bypassed my authority and dealt directly with my troops, ordering an ill-advised operation, in this instance, for its publicity value. I believe that in this case, as in the instance on the Gela beachhead, Patton later told Ike I was "not aggressive enough" and had therefore overruled me. The Brolo operation, led by Lieutenant Colonel Lyle A. Bernard, turned into a complete fiasco, suffering 27 percent casualties: 177 out of 650 men killed, wounded or missing. The Germans evaded the "trap" and pulled back with negligible losses.* [16]

On the same fateful day—August 10—that Patton overruled me on Brolo, he visited another evacuation hospital, this one in Truscott's rear near Sant' Agata. Here Patton found another unwounded soldier, Paul G. Bennett, suffering a severe case of "shell shock." He was huddled shivering on his bunk. What then ensued was almost an exact replay of the Nicosia slapping incident. When Patton asked his problem, Bennett replied: "It's my nerves. I can hear the shells come over, but I can't hear them burst." Patton again exploded in rage: "Your nerves, hell. Hell, you are just a goddamned coward, you yellow son of a bitch. . . . You ought to be lined up against the wall and shot. In fact, I ought to shoot you myself right now, goddamn you."

Patton pulled his pistol out and waved it in Bennett's face, then hit him in the face with his free hand, shouting to the doctor, "I want you to get that man out of here right away. I won't have these other brave boys seeing such a bastard babied." Patton reholstered his pistol and started to leave the tent, but when he saw Bennett was openly crying he rushed back and hit him so hard his helmet liner flew off and rolled out of the tent. The doctor then interposed himself between the soldier and Patton, who stormed out saying, "I meant what I said about getting that coward out of here. I won't have those cowardly bastards hanging around our hospitals.

* In his biography of Patton, Farago states that the official Army historian praised the operation as a "highly successful landing on the coast." On the contrary, the official historian's detailed account of Brolo makes it clear that the operation failed. The historian's conclusion was that "Bernard's landing accomplished little." [17]

We'll probably have to shoot them sometime anyway, or we'll raise a breed of morons."

After leaving the hospital, Patton came to my CP. He mentioned that he had had to slap a malingering soldier, but his remark was so casual and vague it didn't fully register on me. Two days later I had good reason to recall his remark. Bill Kean handed me an explosive official letter to II Corps from the hospital commander reporting in damning detail the entire incident. I was horrified. Even for George Patton it was excessive conduct. I realized that if word of this incident got out, we might lose Patton's talents forever. I ordered Kean to lock the letter in my safe and say nothing whatsoever about it. Not aware of the first slapping incident, I naively hoped the matter would be forgotten or go away.* [18]

The final chapter in our Sicily operation was not a happy one. By August 10, we had squeezed the Axis into a narrow triangular thirty-mile beachhead with Messina at the apex. Clearly it would be suicidal for the enemy to hold out much longer. Since we enjoyed air and naval supremacy, our final plan should have included a concentrated and coordinated air and sea operation to cut off the Strait of Messina and trap the Axis on Sicily, as we had trapped them in Tunisia. But no such plan evolved, and the Axis staged a clean getaway right under our noses.

This remarkable "Dunkirk" commenced on August 10. It was carried forward over the next six days and seven nights with Germanic efficiency. In total, the Axis evacuated 110,000 men (70,000 Italians, 40,000 Germans), 10,000 vehicles (including 47 tanks) and about 17,000 tons of supplies and equipment. Allied air and sea attacks on the evacuation resulted in negligible losses. The three German divisions (plus the paratroopers) we had fought so bitterly on Sicily survived virtually intact, "completely fit for battle and ready for service." They lived to fight on, taking many Allied lives before the war was over. Military historians have justifiably criticized the Allied failure to block this evacuation. It was an abysmal tactical failure which left our "conquest" of Sicily with a cloud on the title.†

Our role in the final stage of the campaign can be quickly told. Hueb-

* By striking an enlisted man, Patton had technically committed a court-martial offense. Had I forwarded the letter through official channels, as Army Regulations required of me, it would have gone to the Seventh Army, the next stop in the chain of command, probably accomplishing nothing other than to widen the circle of readers. Had I bypassed the Seventh Army and sent it directly to Ike, I would have been guilty of gross disloyalty to my commanding officer.

† Most historians blame the failure on a lack of planning and coordination at the very top. Throughout the Sicily campaign, the board of directors was widely scattered: Alexander in Sicily; Tedder in Tunisia; Cunningham in Malta; Ike in Algiers. Alexander's biographer adds another reason: "Eisenhower would take no initiative." Jim Gavin in *On to Berlin,* commenting on the command failure, wrote: "Remoteness from the battle scene, when critical decisions had to be made, was to prove to be one facet of Eisenhower's type of generalship." [19]

ner's Big Red One, after a full week's rest, was brought up to fight alongside Eddy's 9th Division, and to share the honors for the entry into Messina. Truscott's 3rd Division troops now pushed quickly along the north road, meeting only withdrawing rear-guard defenses. Patton unwisely ordered a third and very large amphibious end run, utilizing a regimental combat team of Middleton's 45th Division. Both Truscott and I opposed the idea, and I asked Patton to cancel it. Truscott was advancing so rapidly there was real danger that Middleton's troops might come ashore in the midst of Truscott's troops and touch off a battle between friendly forces. Again, mainly for publicity reasons, Patton insisted the operation proceed. After we had taken elaborate precautions to prevent unnecessary bloodshed, the landing was carried out on the night of 15-16 August. The force landed amid Truscott's troops. No men were killed by friendly fire, but eleven drowned needlessly in a landing craft accident. Truscott invited one of Middleton's newly arrived battalions to march with his troops into Messina.[20]

Toward the end, Patton became nearly irrational in his determination to beat Monty to Messina. He stopped me on the road and exhorted: "I want you to get to Messina just as fast as you can. I don't want you to waste time on these maneuvers, even if you've got to spend men to do it. I want to beat Monty into Messina." I was shocked. The orders sickened me. I ignored them. I continued to maneuver and refused to waste lives merely for the sake of winning a meaningless race.[21]

General John Lucas visited my CP on August 14 and spent the night. Since his job was to report deficiencies on our battlefield, I was candid. I was especially critical of Seventh Army headquarters. Throughout the Sicily campaign, it had failed us at every hand, particularly with respect to logistics. We had fought the entire campaign with an acute shortage of artillery ammunition, forced on one occasion to stop fighting and send every truck we had to the rear to bring up ammo. We had been compelled to lay our own lines of communication to the Seventh Army, when it was their responsibility to lay lines to us. Army had failed to establish any sort of reliable operating procedures with our air forces. We had had little or no direct air support, had often been bombed or strafed by our own planes, and could not get anyone to carry out proper photo reconnaissance over enemy positions. Patton did not give a damn about these details, and his attitude was reflected by his staff.[22]

On the evening of August 16, thirty-eight days after we landed on the southern beaches, advanced elements of Truscott's 3rd Division entered the city of Messina. The following morning, civil dignitaries came out of the city and attempted to surrender to Truscott, but he declined. Orders had come down from Patton to leave all that for Patton. He was organizing a parade and a surrender ceremony. None of Truscott's units was to enter the city until he arrived to lead them. One result was we had to hold

Truscott's men in the hills and watch helplessly as the last of the Germans fled the city. I was so angry at Patton's megalomania that I was half tempted to enter the city myself and greet him on a street corner when he arrived.

At 1000 hours, Patton rode up in his command car and demanded, "What in hell are you all standing around for?" He led a motor cavalcade into the city, where an official surrender ceremony of sorts was staged in a park. An hour later, a British column clanked into the city. The senior British officer walked over to Patton, shook hands and said, "It was a jolly good race. I congratulate you."[23]

The real estate of Sicily had been purchased at great cost. Total Allied casualties were 22,811—5,532 killed, 14,410 wounded, 2,869 missing. We thought we had killed a great number of Germans, but postwar records showed we were wrong—at most a few thousand. Offsetting our losses, however, were immeasurable gains. We had learned a great deal more about fighting a war. We had conducted our first amphibious and airborne operations. We had fielded our first full-blown army. We had introduced four new divisions (3rd, 45th, 82nd Airborne, 2nd Armored) and the Ranger battalions to combat and provided taut new leadership for the swaggering veterans of the Big Red One. Patton, Truscott, Middleton, Eddy, Gaffey, Huebner, Ridgway, Keyes and I, together with our staffs, had gained invaluable experience in battlefield management.[24]

Beyond that, the conquest of Sicily had done much to achieve one of its primary political goals: knocking Italy out of the war. On July 25, Mussolini was forced to resign and the Berlin-Rome partnership fell into chaotic disarray. Mussolini was replaced by Pietro Badoglio, who almost at once extended secret surrender feelers to the Allies while pretending to Hitler that Italy would continue the fight in order to avert a German occupation of Italy. Neither Hitler nor his generals was fooled. While Badoglio secretly negotiated with the Allies, Hitler ordered massive forces into Italy, literally occupying the country, draining his fronts elsewhere and setting up a battlefield that continued to the end of the war.

A final personal note. As I mentioned earlier, Ike had told columnist Ernie Pyle to "go and discover Bradley." Pyle caught up with me in Nicosia. I was still very leery of publicity, but my aide Chet Hansen convinced me I should cooperate. Pyle was a little leery, too. Up to now, he had written exclusively about GI's and he was not comfortable with the brass. He stuck with me like a shadow for three days. Then he wrote a six-part series (about 5,000 words) that was widely published in the States. The series hardly made me a household name, but it was my first extensive national publicity. Even with all his creative gifts, Pyle had a difficult time making me "colorful."[25]

TWENTY-TWO

The conquest of Sicily was also clouded by the personal disaster that finally overtook George Patton. As we were rolling toward Messina, word of the second slapping incident spread swiftly throughout the Seventh Army. Several respected war correspondents, including Demaree Bess of *The Saturday Evening Post,* thoroughly investigated the rumors and found them to be true. Bess drafted a meticulous report, which he took to Eisenhower in Algiers. Quentin Reynolds of *Collier's* flew to Algiers to tell Ike that there were "at least 50,000 soldiers who would shoot Patton if they had the slightest chance." Charles Daly of CBS News also submitted a report and told Butcher that he thought "Patton had gone temporarily crazy." About the same time, a formal letter of complaint from a medical officer on Sicily—bypassing the chain of command—reached Ike's headquarters. Ike persuaded the correspondents to "bury" the story, assuring them that he would deal harshly with Patton. All agreed that Patton was too valuable a combat leader to be lost.

A day later, August 17, Ike got off a secret anguished letter to Patton, enclosing a copy of the medical officer's report. Ike sincerely hoped that Patton could assure him that none of the allegations was true. He went on: "I am well aware of the necessity for harshness and toughness on the battlefield. I clearly understand that firm and drastic measures are at times necessary in order to secure desired objectives. But this does not excuse brutality, abuse of sick, nor exhibitions of uncontrollable temper in front of subordinates." Ike would not institute a "formal investigation," but if there were any truth to the allegations "I must so seriously question your good judgment and your self-discipline as to raise serious doubt in my mind as to your future usefulness." He admonished Patton to give the matter of his personal deportment "your instant and serious consideration to the end that no incident of this character can be reported to me in the future." Patton was to apologize "to the individuals concerned" before replying, in secret, to Ike.

After receiving Ike's letter, Patton was devastated. He summoned Kuhl and Bennett and the doctors, nurses and medical orderlies who had witnessed the incidents, singly or in groups, to his posh palace. He more or less apologized to all, shaking hands with Kuhl and Bennett. He explained to one and all that he had had a friend on the front in World War I who had shirked his duty and later, out of remorse, committed suicide. He had slapped Kuhl and Bennett in hopes that they would regain their "manhood" and not have to suffer his friend's fate. He expressed regret for his "impulsive actions." (Kuhl said after the apology that he thought Patton "was suffering a little battle fatigue himself.") Then Patton drafted a contrite and humble letter to Ike. He could not find words to express his chagrin and grief "at having given you, a man who I owe everything and for whom I would gladly lay down my life, cause for displeasure with me."

So the matter was laid to rest for the time being. It would surface again with the force of a typhoon three months later when columnist-broadcaster Drew Pearson released a garbled account of the incidents.

In the meantime, Ike was more than willing to keep Patton in his service. On August 24, he wrote Marshall praising Patton's "brilliant successes" on Sicily. However, Ike was unwilling to consider Patton for any job higher than an army commander. "George Patton continues to exhibit some of those unfortunate personal traits of which you and I have always known and which during this campaign caused me some most uncomfortable days. His habit of impulsive bawling out of subordinates, extending even to personal abuse of individuals, was noted in at least two specific cases. I have had to take the most drastic steps; and if he is not cured now, there is no hope for him. Personally, I believe that he is cured—not only because of his great personal loyalty to you and to me but because fundamentally he is so avid for recognition as a great military commander that he will ruthlessly suppress any habit of his own that will tend to jeopardize it. Aside from this one thing, he has qualities that we cannot afford to lose until he ruins himself. So he can be classed as an army commander that you can use with certainty that the troops will not be stopped by ordinary obstacles."[1]

While we had been fighting on Sicily, Roosevelt, Churchill and the Combined Chiefs continued to wrangle over the best strategy for beating Hitler. Although the British had agreed in principle to Roundup (the code name was changed to "Overlord") in May 1944, they were far from enthusiastic about it. Churchill, still pressing his indirect and opportunistic strategy, painted a grim word picture of "a channel full of corpses." He continued to urge a variety of indirect strategies—thrusts at the German heartland through Italy, the Mideast, Greece, the Balkans and Norway. Stimson and Marshall remained firmly opposed to these peripheral schemes, still believing the decisive blow must be a cross-channel invasion.

The indecision compelled yet another meeting of Roosevelt, Churchill and the Combined Chiefs. They met at Quebec, Canada, in mid-August, as we were winding up the Sicily fighting. The conference was code-named "Quadrant." Marshall arrived determined, once and for all, to secure an irrevocable British commitment to Overlord. After much give and take, some of it bitter, he succeeded. It was agreed that Overlord would be the main Allied effort in 1944. Less clearly defined was future Allied strategy in the Mediterranean, especially in Italy. Churchill was still intent on carrying the fight at least as far as Rome. Marshall remained lukewarm to Italy, but he did approve (as did all the Combined Chiefs) Ike's plan to invade southern Italy immediately after the fall of Sicily in order to assure Italy's capitulation and to secure air bases for bombing Germany from the south.

One other important decision was reached at Quadrant. Up until that time, the British had assumed that if Overlord were to be carried out, a British general would lead it. In fact, Churchill had told Alan Brooke that he would be the man. But at Quadrant it became clear that the Americans would be furnishing the preponderance of forces for the operation and that, logically, an American general should lead. It was Churchill who raised the point and when he did, Roosevelt readily agreed. Both men had Marshall in mind for the job and although Marshall was not formally appointed, it was assumed by all that he probably soon would be. Churchill, rather offhandedly, disclosed the change to Alan Brooke. Brooke was naturally shocked, but on reflection thought it "a correct move."[2]

The plan for invading southern Italy involved a two-prong ground attack, commanded by Alexander. Monty's Eighth Army would cross the Strait of Messina into Calabria on September 3. Six days later, September 9, Mark Clark's Fifth Army would land at Salerno, below Naples, at the same time that other British forces invaded the "heel" of Italy's boot at Taranto. While Clark advanced on Naples, Monty's forces would secure the southern area of the boot. There was very little planned coordination between the two landings, nor at first, any scheme to link up the two armies. Monty wrote: "If the planning and conduct of the campaign in Sicily were bad, the preparations for the invasion of Italy, and the subsequent conduct of the campaign in that country, were worse still."

Hanging over the operation were many political uncertainties: Would the Italians surrender? If so, when? Would Hitler make a military stand in Italy? If so, how determined and where?[3]

I was not certain that Mark Clark was the best choice for this rather bold leap into Italy. I had come to know Clark well by now. He had commanded a battalion in combat in World War I and had been wounded in action. But he had not yet commanded large-scale forces in combat in World War II. Moreover, I had serious reservations about him personally.

He seemed false somehow, too eager to impress, too hungry for the limelight, promotions and personal publicity. Patton didn't trust him either. He thought Clark was "too damned slick" and "more preoccupied with bettering his own future than winning the war."[4]

Nor was I certain that Clark's Fifth Army itself was ideally organized. Clark would have two corps—one British, one American. The British X Corps would be composed of two British divisions plus British commandos and U.S. rangers. The U.S. VI Corps (under Mike Dawley) was composed of the untried 36th Division, with Middleton's 45th Division in reserve and the 82nd Airborne Division in Army Reserve. We had never done well in mixing American and British units in the same army. The situation seemed ripe for disaster.

I was drawn into the preliminaries of the Salerno operation at the conclusion of Sicily. Ike had decided that should "anything happen" to Clark, I would replace him as Fifth Army commander. He instructed me to familiarize myself with the Salerno plans at the earliest opportunity. I met with Clark and his chief of staff, Alfred M. Gruenther, at Clark's headquarters in Mostaganem. Gruenther was a superb staff officer and the planning was flawless. But I still came away with misgivings.[5]

In the meanwhile, George Marshall, having obtained an irrevocable commitment for Overlord in Quebec, was anxious that the detailed planning proceed. An American Army would land on the beaches of France in eight months. There was as yet no American army headquarters or an American army commander in Britain. It was decided that the U.S. First Army would be established in Britain as quickly as possible. But who was to get command of this plum? On August 25, Marshall cabled Ike: "My choice has been Bradley. . . . Could you release Bradley for this command?"[6]

That same day I was in North Africa to go over Clark's plan for Salerno. I had stopped at Ike's headquarters for dinner, where I was cordially received. Almost in passing I mentioned to Ike that our heavy artillery was worn out and had to be replaced. Ike was flabbergasted that no one at Seventh Army had called this to his attention before, Butcher recalled. The next day Ike "went after the ordnance problem full tilt." Inasmuch as Marshall's cable had not yet arrived, Ike did not raise the possibility of an Overlord command with me—only my stand-in job for Mark Clark at Salerno.[7]

After I had returned to Sicily, Ike responded to Marshall's cable suggesting me as commander of First Army for Overlord. Ike's reply is curious. While he praised me to high heaven, he also went out of his way to mention Clark as a strong possibility, perhaps in some respects a better choice than I. Bradley, Ike wrote, "has had some little experience in planning amphibious operations, but his function in preparing for the Sicilian show was a subordinate one, especially with respect to all the intricate cooperations with Navy and ground forces." Clark, he wrote, "is the ablest and most experienced officer we have in planning of amphibious operations. He will soon have his battle test in high command and . . . he would then have to be classed as a capable leader of any amphibious operation. In preparing the minute details of requisitions, landing craft, training of troops and so on, he has no equal in our Army." He went on to say: "As you can see, I personally am distressed at the thought of losing Bradley because I have come to lean on him so heavily in absorbing part of the burdens that otherwise fall directly upon me. This has been so in the past even when he was only in corps command. This very reason probably makes him your obvious choice for the other job; but if you should take Clark, I could shove Bradley immediately into command of Fifth Army."[8]

On the following day, August 28, Ike evidently had second thoughts. He cabled Marshall: "I have been thinking over what I told you in my telegram of the other day reference Bradley and other commanders. The truth of the matter is that you should take Bradley and, moreover, I will make him available on any date you say. I will get along. I hope my former telegram did not sound weaseling to you."[9]

On September 1, Marshall responded: "Thanks for your generous attitude regarding Bradley. Have him make preparations to leave for England. . . . Tell him that he will head an Army headquarters and will also probably have to develop an Army Group headquarters in order to keep pace with the British planning and requisitions."[10]

I was aware of none of these exchanges. After the surrender of Messina, II Corps had set up "headquarters" at Camp Felice overlooking a sheltered cove and beach near Palermo for a few days of well-deserved R and R. Patton, meanwhile, was going around to the various divisions attempting to make a speech of vague "apology" to the troops. This was a remarkably touching and humiliating episode in Patton's life. Some units cheered him in this personal ordeal, as depicted in the film *Patton*. Others, however, were contemptuous. Monk Dickson recalled: "When Patton spoke before the 1st Division to apologize for his conduct during the campaign, he ended on a great inspirational note. The massed division, however, remained stonily silent. Not a man applauded and the division was dismissed. It faded away in silence to the great embarrassment of its commander and the total chagrin of Patton."[11]

On Sunday, August 29, the day after Ike cabled Marshall that he should "take Bradley," I was alerted to meet Ike at Monty's headquarters at Catania. The purpose of this gathering was to honor Monty. Ike was to present him with a U.S. Army Legion of Merit medal. I flew to Catania in Patton's C-47 with Patton, Keyes, Kean, Truscott, and some of Patton's senior staff. It was virtually a "public event," and official photographers swarmed about to record it. I had only a moment's chat with Ike, but he gave not the slightest indication that I was being considered for a higher job. I did not know it then, but Patton, in a brief exchange with Ike, handed him his letter of apology for the slapping incident.

After the ceremony, Monty invited us to a large semi-official luncheon. This was the first time I had met Monty and I observed him closely. He was relaxed and entertaining—a general off duty. His famous conceit stood out even in this company. He was the center of attention. Patton, I noted, was unusually subdued, and perhaps just as well. After the lunch, Monty and Ike rushed off to Messina for some sightseeing, and we returned to the airfield for the return flight to Palermo. Later we learned that two rogue German fighters strafed the airfield five minutes after we took off![12]

Monty was preparing to cross the Strait of Messina into Calabria on September 3. Dempsey's XIII Corps would spearhead the attack; Oliver Leese's XXX Corps would provide artillery support from Messina. At the luncheon, Leese invited me to Messina to watch the operation and, of course, I accepted. On the morning of September 2, Bill Kean and I set off for Messina in a two-jeep caravan. Just beyond Brolo, my Piper Cub, *Missouri Mule,* buzzed our jeeps and landed in a nearby field. My aide Chet Hansen debarked from the plane with an urgent message from Patton. I was to return immediately to go on "a short trip."

Completely mystified, I flew back to my CP at Camp Felice and telephoned Patton. He had just returned from Ike's headquarters in Algiers. Ike had told Patton that I was to go to England to form a new army and help plan the Normandy invasion, but Patton gave no hint of it. He merely said that Ike wanted to see me in Algiers the following day. He offered the use of his C-47 and invited me to have breakfast with him in Palermo. I accepted both.

The next day, September 3, I drove to Palermo and saw Patton. He was in fine fettle. After breakfast we received word that Ike was leaving Algiers for Alexander's headquarters at Cassibile, outside Syracuse, and that I should meet him there. At that time Alexander, Bedell Smith, Ike's diplomatic trouble-shooter Robert Murphy and his British counterpart, Harold Macmillan, were in Cassibile secretly negotiating the Italian surrender with Badoglio's emissaries. Later I learned that these immensely complex and delicate negotiations had reached a historic climax that day and Ike was flying to Cassibile to witness the signing of the surrender document.

That afternoon, we flew in Patton's C-47 to an airfield near Cassibile. Ike's aide Tex Lee met the plane and drove us to Alexander's CP, a group of tents in an olive grove. Ike was in a tent in conference when we arrived. I chatted with Alexander and Bedell Smith. The latter, looking somewhat weary after his non-stop negotiations, told me in strictest confidence that the surrender instrument had been signed and that Ike would announce it on September 8, the evening before Clark's troops landed at Salerno. Shortly after that, Ike emerged from his tent, apologized for keeping me waiting and invited me inside for a private conference. I still had not the slightest inkling of what he had to tell me, although I was beginning to gain the impression that it must be something big and urgent.

He came right to the point: "I've got good news for you, Brad. You've got a fancy new job." As I sat in silence he told me what it was. I could not have been more stunned or elated. It was going to grow into the most important combat job in the U.S. Army in World War II. No soldier could have wished for more. I was to leave as soon as possible, first to London, then to the States to recruit a full army staff.[13]

This may have been a difficult moment for Ike personally. Rumors were flying that Marshall would be named commander in chief of Overlord and that Alexander would probably be his ground forces deputy. Further rumor had it that when Marshall moved over to London, Ike would replace him in Washington as Chief of Staff of the Army. This proposed change did not at all suit Ike. He much preferred to remain in some capacity in the European Theater of Operations.[14]

Alexander had business elsewhere, but Ike invited Hansen and me to stay for dinner with him, Bedell Smith, Ike's G-2 Kenneth W. D. Strong, and the various aides. The talk was mostly about the Italian surrender—the effect it would have on Clark's Salerno landings—and Monty's operations in the foot of Italy. Ike was optimistic about the outcome in Italy, but knowing that the Germans were now moving into Italy in great force, I had my private doubts. I foresaw a long, bitter Sicily-like campaign in central Italy with heavy casualties and cloudy results. I was very glad I would not be involved.[15]

During our private talk, Ike had informed me that John Lucas would relieve me as II Corps commander. The corps was slated to participate in future Italian operations, not yet defined. I was free to "raid" II Corps of all personnel I wanted. I initially settled on twenty-five men including Bill Kean, Monk Dickson, Tubby Thorson (who had come over to replace Bob Hewitt as G-3 in the final stages of Sicily), my G-4 Bob Wilson, Bruce Medaris, Bill Carter, Charlie Hart, Andrew McNamara and others. In effect, I cannibalized II Corps to form my new army staff.[16]

After Ike returned to Algiers, Marshall sent along a list of officers he proposed to promote in permanent rank, asking Ike's advice. Since all of us were holding temporary wartime promotions (I was still merely a permanent lieutenant colonel), this list was of great importance to us personally and to our postwar standing in the U.S. Army. I was on Marshall's list for promotion to permanent brigadier general, fourth after our classmate McNarney, MacArthur's Air Force chief, George C. Kenney, and Tooey Spaatz. In commenting on the list, Ike (already promoted to permanent major general) agreed with Marshall that McNarney should head the list but thought I, Tom Handy and Bedell Smith should precede Kenney and Spaatz, in that order. I was promoted to permanent full colonel on November 13, 1943, and to permanent brigadier general five months later, May 31, 1944.[17]

Lucas arrived at II Corps headquarters on September 6. On the following day I drove to Patton's headquarters in the big palace to say goodbye. I found him in a near-suicidal mental state. The day before, Ike had sent him a message which began: "Plan is that Seventh Army will not repeat not continue as an Army." It was to be disbanded. Patton had logged, "I feel like death but will survive—I always have." He had already told his Seventh Army staff personnel that they might be "backing the wrong horse" or might have hitched their "wagons to the wrong star" and had invited them to seek other assignments. None did.[18]

This was an exceedingly awkward time for me personally. This great proud warrior, my former boss, had been brought to his knees. Clark's Fifth Army was en route to Salerno. I was en route to London and the States and First Army command. Patton had not only been passed over for these important jobs, his own creation, the Seventh Army, was to be abolished. But he did not yield easily; he had unbounded faith in his "destiny." He spent much of my visit giving me his "best ideas" for Overlord, to pass along to George Marshall. After I left, he noted in his diary: "Bradley has a chance to help or hurt me with General Marshall. I hope he chooses the former course, but I did not ask him to."[19]

Early on the morning of September 8, I formally took leave of II Corps. It was a moving ceremony for all of us. The day was beautiful, the Tyrrhenian Sea iridescent. The II Corps officers, a large gathering, formed a semicircle, and I bade them goodbye in a few simple words, regretting that I could not take them all. Afterwards the officers formed into single file to shake hands with me. As Bill Kean and I walked to my car, a band struck up "Auld Lang Syne." En route to our airfield, troops lined the road shoulder to shoulder, and as our car passed, they smartly presented arms, dipped guidons or saluted.

Patton had put his plane at my disposal for the first leg of our voyage to Algiers. At 0905 we lifted off.[20]

TWENTY-THREE

Ike had invited me to a farewell lunch at his "advanced" headquarters outside Carthage in Tunisia. We flew there, passing near the Salerno invasion forces churning north across the sea. Looking at that vast armada, I mentally set aside my misgivings about the operation and wished each and every man good luck. In a few hours—at 0330 the following morning—American soldiers would go ashore on the Italian beaches. Many would die.

Ike was in a dither. The Salerno operation had been tied to an announcement of an Italian armistice scheduled for that evening. The 82nd Airborne Division had been alerted to drop at Rome. But Badoglio was now weaseling on his agreement for a simultaneous announcement, leaving everything confused and forcing Ike to cancel the airborne operation. New plans were being drawn to send the 82nd Division to Salerno, where it was sorely needed. I was very happy not to be playing a role in these nerve-twisting proceedings. Ike had gambled on Italian help and lost. Bad luck would continue to dog us in Italy for months to come.

After a late lunch with Ike, we continued our air journey. We spent the night in Algiers, then flew on to Marrakech. There we caught a C-54 for England. Aboard this plane was the British general Brian Horrocks, who had commanded X Corps under Monty. He had been gravely wounded in an air attack in Bizerte on June 1. His X Corps, now commanded by Richard McCreery, had just landed at Salerno. Horrocks was being attended by several nurses in a makeshift hospital ward in the forward end of the cabin. I did not think he wanted visitors, so I staked out a bucket seat and dozed off. Our long flight took us far to the west to avoid German fighters based in France.

At Prestwick, Scotland, we were to catch a shuttle flight for London. As it happened, our newly appointed ambassador to Russia, W. Averell Harriman, was passing through en route to London. He invited our small party to join him on his plush aircraft. This was my first meeting with

Harriman. I found him to be a man of extraordinary energy and discernment. In later years, my contacts with him would be frequent and my admiration for him grew with each encounter. He was a great and selfless man who unhesitatingly devoted most of his long life to public service. On our brief flight he inquired about Patton, with whom he had played polo in his younger years.[1]

At London's Henley Airport, my new boss, Jacob L. Devers, also a lieutenant general, met the plane and drove me to the Dorchester Hotel, where he had arranged rooms. I knew Devers (a classmate of Patton's and thus my senior by six years) fairly well. He had been a math and engineering instructor and manager of the baseball team on which I played three years at West Point and had been in the tactical department when I taught math in the early 1920s. He had caught Marshall's eye in 1940 while commanding the 9th Division at Fort Bragg, North Carolina. Additional barracks were urgently needed to accommodate an incoming National Guard outfit; Devers had them built seemingly overnight, earning him a "can do" reputation. When Ike moved to Algiers for Torch, Marshall had sent an Air Force general, Frank M. Andrews, to London to replace him as commanding general of the European Theater of Operations. But when Andrews was tragically killed in an airplane crash, Marshall sent Devers to replace him. For the past six months, Devers had exercised important responsibilities. He had represented the United States in Overlord planning and overseen the buildup of the U.S. Army forces in the British Isles.

By this time, the assumption that Marshall was to command Overlord was no longer questioned. The speculation now centered on who would be Marshall's chief subordinates to command American forces in the invasion. Ike was not in the running; he would replace Marshall as Chief of Staff in Washington. Rumor had it that Marshall had in mind important jobs for Lesley J. McNair, Courtney Hodges and Jake Devers. McNair might be army group commander with Devers and me commanding armies. But McNair had one drawback, his deafness. If he were ruled out, Marshall might name Devers army group commander with Hodges and me commanding armies under him.

I was not overjoyed at the prospect of Jake Devers being elevated to high command in Overlord. I may have been initially prejudiced against Devers by Ike, who had recently had several long-distance set-tos with him over air power. Ike wanted more heavy bombers shifted to the Mediterranean to assist the Italy operation. Devers refused to release them. The matter had been bucked up to the Combined Chiefs, who backed Devers, making Ike furious. (According to Patton, Ike characterized Devers as ".22 caliber.") Over the next several days I studied Devers closely and formed my own independent opinion of the man. I found him to be overly garrulous (saying little of importance), egotistical, shallow, intolerant, not very smart, and much too inclined to rush off half-cocked.[2]

After a week in England, on September 14 I flew on to the States to choose some more First Army personnel. We traveled via Scotland, Iceland, Maine and New York, concluding the trip at Bolling Field in Washington. Marshall's secretary of the General Staff, Frank McCarthy, had alerted Mary, and she and Lee met the plane. I had only been gone eight months, but it seemed like eight years. We had a warm family reunion. Among other topics, we discussed Lee's future. She was now engaged to Hal Beukema. In early June, upon her graduation from Vassar and his from West Point, they were to be married. Owing to security, I could not tell them that I could not be present for any of the ceremonies.

By this time, George Marshall was so burdened with office routine he had no time to greet visiting firemen. However, on September 21, he invited me to fly with him and Simon Buckner to Omaha, Nebraska, where Marshall and I addressed a national convention of the American Legion. En route I reviewed the Sicily campaign—the mistakes, the lessons learned, the pluses—avoiding personalities insofar as possible. Patton had hoped that I would put in a good word for him with Marshall but I did not. Sicily had soured me on George Patton.

Back at the Pentagon, I received a call from Frank McCarthy who informed me that President Roosevelt wished me to brief him on the Sicily campaign. Most likely George Marshall had suggested this to the President in order that Roosevelt might become acquainted with me. I reported as requested. I had seen Roosevelt at the aforementioned White House social receptions when I was a lowly lieutenant colonel, but I did not really know him. My report was brief and to the point.

When I finished, Roosevelt astounded me with a fairly detailed briefing on our Manhattan Project, the effort to build an atomic bomb, then one of our most secret projects and one I had never heard of. Roosevelt was concerned that the Germans might be leading us in the race to build this revolutionary weapon and that I might be confronted with it in the invasion of France. I was so completely flabbergasted that I did not know what to say in response. I left his office—unrecognized and thus not approached by the White House press corps—in a troubled state of mind. I decided that the President, however well intentioned, had spoken out of turn. Not once during the war did I question Marshall or Ike about the atomic bomb nor did they ever mention it to me. Fortunately for all of us, Hitler's atomic bomb project never got off the drawing boards.

Marshall had made the decision, meanwhile, that a U.S. Army group headquarters staff would also be established in England. In addition to my job as First Army commander, I was also to serve as acting commander of the First U.S. Army Group (FUSAG) until such time as the final decisions were made on our principal Overlord commanders. This meant that I had to select key personnel for both outfits, not an easy task, since good men who could be spared were extremely hard to find, especially those with combat experience.[3]

A First U.S. Army headquarters already existed at Governors Island,

New York. It consisted of about 350 men commanded by General Hugh Drum, who was shortly to retire on account of age. Drum was to be briefly replaced by another aging general, George Grunert, a close friend of Marshall's who had been buried in a tedious Pentagon job and whom Marshall wanted to honor, however briefly, with the prestige of army command. Grunert would bring the First Army staff to England, saving us many headaches. It sailed for Bristol, England, on October 12.[4]

The key men of II Corps—Kean, Dickson, Thorson, Wilson—became the key men of the First Army staff. To these veterans I added one more: Joseph J. (Red) O'Hare, a close friend with whom I had played football at West Point. I found O'Hare serving as G-1 of the First Army at Governors Island and I kept him on the job. He was thoroughly unpopular, imperious and autocratic, capricious in his judgments, and not too bright. But he had a lot of common sense and knew the personnel business. His mule-headedness would serve us well in France and Germany.[5]

Eventually the original First Army staff was thoroughly decimated and restaffed. The official historian relates that of the 361 men who composed the First Army staff on D-day, 37 remained from the original Governors Island group, 38 came from II Corps, 100 joined the First Army before it left the States and 186 came aboard in England. But the II Corps veterans set the tone of the staff: arrogant, combat-wise, infallible. Everybody else in the ETO was considered green, stupid or incompetent.[6]

There was no army group staff in being. It had to be created from scratch. Jake Devers had already begun to assemble the FUSAG staff in England, perhaps hoping he would lead it in Overlord. Marshall handpicked FUSAG's chief of staff: Lev Allen, who had relieved me as commandant at Fort Benning. As far as I was concerned, no finer choice could have been made, and had it been left up to me, I would have picked Allen myself. He was the antithesis of Bill Kean: amiable and accommodating. Allen, with O'Hare's help, began to build the FUSAG staff on the foundation Devers had laid.[7]

I returned by air to England on October 2, retracing my steps on the northern route. We established FUSAG headquarters in London in a strip of West End flats on Bryanston Square, First Army headquarters in Bristol in the gothic buildings of Clifton College. I commuted between my two commands in a Cadillac limousine with Alex Stoute at the wheel. I posted Lew Bridge as aide in London, Hansen as aide in Bristol. In London I lived at the Dorchester Hotel, a brisk ten-minute walk from the office; in Bristol in a spacious country house large enough to accommodate the key staff members of the First Army.[8]

The three-hour commute between London and Bristol was not without its dangers. On November 10, en route to Bristol, we ran into a dense fog near Slough. Stoute slowed to creeping speed behind a long line of trucks. Stoute thought he saw a clear area to pass but when he pulled out, we crunched head-on into a British Army command car. I was thrown against the rear of the front seat, broke my glasses and badly gashed one cheek. Fortunately, no one else was hurt. I was in favor of proceeding on to Bristol, but an ambulance appeared and the doctor insisted that I go to a nearby American hospital. Since I was physically exhausted and had a bad cold, I didn't object and I remained at the hospital five days.[9]

We added a new member to our small official family in London. He was Richard Moberly Dudley, age thirty-six, an MP on duty at our Bristol headquarters, who in civilian life had been a salesman for a printing company. We made Dudley our mess sergeant. He turned out to be the most resourceful scrounger in the ETO, even to the extent of finding a chef from a well-known New York restaurant. The First Army mess soon achieved an enviable reputation for elegance. When I gingerly raised a question about the opulence of the food, Dudley replied, "General, you fight the war and I'll worry about your standard of living."[10]

While we focused on the nuts and bolts of Overlord planning, the question of higher command dangled enticingly. Marshall wanted the top job above all else, Roosevelt had assured him it was his, and Secretary of War Stimson was determined that Marshall have it. But Marshall had not yet been formally appointed and thus the secondary and tertiary jobs were still officially unfilled, adding to our uncertainty. Moreover, a thorny complication soon developed over the proposed Marshall appointment. Word of it leaked to the media and a public uproar ensued. Many people believed —or professed to believe—that the proposed Overlord job was a step down for Marshall, that Roosevelt, for various motives, might be trying to ease Marshall out of the administration or "kick him upstairs." Roosevelt attempted to quiet the uproar with this argument, advanced in a letter to General Pershing: "I want George to be the Pershing of the Second World War—and he cannot be that if we keep him here." But the public furor raged on, the Marshall appointment became a hot political potato and, privately, Roosevelt began to weigh the implications.

No one was more acutely tuned to these debates than Ike. It had been Ike who had drafted the original cross-channel attack plan; Ike had gone to London on Marshall's behalf to implement it. Now Ike was stuck in the Mediterranean backwater with an increasingly sticky and irresolvable battle in Italy on his hands. Moreover, Ike was well aware that when Marshall was named to command Overlord, he, Ike, would be forced to relinquish his Mediterranean job to a British general to balance out the Allied command structure. As a four-star general, Ike would not handily fit into an Overlord commanded by Marshall. This left only one place for Ike to go: Washington, replacing Marshall or serving as a surrogate chief of staff to Marshall. Ike did not want to go to Washington.

What Ike wanted most was command of Overlord in place of Marshall.

His case had merit, in many ways more merit than Marshall's. No one could effectively replace Marshall as Chief of Staff and member of the Combined Chiefs. In this area, Marshall's talents and prestige were unique. Ike did not have the well-developed strategic grasp required for global war planning. On the other hand, Ike had demonstrated an extraordinary diplomatic talent for getting Allied generals and admirals to work in harness. In this chairman of the board capacity, by and large, he had earned the respect of the British. Diplomacy was the overriding talent required of the Overlord commander, and no American general had it in greater abundance than Ike.

Ike could not stand the uncertainty of his future; it was beginning to impinge on the Italy and Mediterranean war planning; he was personally on edge. On October 5, he sent Bedell Smith to Washington to "find the lay of the land." Among others, Smith conferred with Marshall in the Pentagon and Roosevelt at Hyde Park. The news was uniformly bad. Marshall would take command of Overlord on January 1, 1944. He did not think it a good idea for Ike to participate in Overlord (as, say, army group commander) because it would look like a comedown. Roosevelt, Hopkins, Stimson, Marshall and others all felt that Ike should replace Marshall as Chief of Staff in Washington.

There the matter rested until late November. At that time, Roosevelt, Churchill and the Combined Chiefs met at Cairo, Egypt, then later at Teheran, Iran, with Stalin and his military advisers. By then, United States planners had devised a scheme whereby Marshall could have his cake and eat it too: he would both command Overlord and all other Allied forces in Europe and keep his seat on the Combined Chiefs. But the British objected to this plan on the grounds that it diluted the authority of the Combined Chiefs and gave Marshall too much sway in Europe and the Mediterranean. The British were so absolutely adamant on this point that the new plan was quickly dropped. The conferees moved on to Teheran to meet with Stalin, the matter still unresolved.

It was Joe Stalin who finally forced a decision. In Teheran, he asked bluntly who would command Overlord. When he learned that no decision had yet been made, he scornfully suggested that the Allies could not be serious about a second front in France if they had not even agreed on a commander. Back in Cairo, Roosevelt at last made the decision. He could not spare Marshall from Washington or the Combined Chiefs. When George Marshall was out of the country, he could not sleep at night. It had to be Ike. When Churchill readily gave his approval, Roosevelt, on December 6, asked Marshall to take down a letter for Stalin: "The immediate appointment of General Eisenhower to command of Overlord operation has been decided upon. Signed, Roosevelt." Marshall was shocked speechless, but typically he bore his disappointment with good grace. He even generously thought to send Ike the handwritten letter with a note:

"Thought you might like to have this as a memento." On his way back to Washington, Roosevelt stopped in Tunis and broke the news: "Well, Ike, you are going to command Overlord."

In London, the news of Ike's appointment landed like a bombshell. I had mixed personal feelings. On the one hand I was very pleased that Marshall would remain at his vital post in Washington and keep his seat on the Combined Chiefs. It was a winning team; no time to change personnel. On the other hand, I was very sorry that Marshall would be denied the prestige and fame of Overlord, that Ike, not Marshall, would become the "Pershing of the Second World War." [11]

TWENTY-FOUR

Ike arrived in London on January 15, 1944. At that time D-day for Overlord was set for May 1, a mere three and a half months away. Much had been accomplished, but there still remained much to be done.

Ike's first important Overlord task was to establish and staff the high command. Given a free hand, I'm sure he would have duplicated the winning Mediterranean command: Ike, chairman of the board; Alexander, deputy for ground forces; Tedder for air; Cunningham for Navy; Bedell Smith, chief of staff, presiding over an integrated Allied staff. This time, however, there would be one important modification: Ike would not only be chairman of the board but chief executive officer as well. He would return from the stratosphere to which the British had elevated him at Casablanca. He would exercise direct command of the whole vast enterprise, including the armies in the field.

He did not have his way on the principal British subordinates. For ground force deputy, Churchill and Alan Brooke chose Monty over Alexander. By now Monty was a living legend in the eyes of the British, a general "who had never lost a battle." He also enjoyed the confidence of the American public. In contrast, the shy and reclusive Alexander had made only small impact on the British public and almost none on the American public. Monty turned over command of his Eighth Army to Oliver Leese and came to London. Alexander remained in Italy to carry on that frustrating and difficult campaign. He must have been devastated, but he gave no evidence of it, then or later in his memoirs. Both Ike and I were keenly disappointed in the decision. In the future, there were many occasions when we bitterly regretted it.

The Overlord ground force command would evolve as follows. Monty would command all the ground forces for the assault on the beaches. These would include one British army, the Second, commanded by Miles Dempsey, and my First Army. As additional American and British armies came ashore and widened the beachhead, Monty would relinquish his role as ground force commander and assume command of all British forces as head of the Twenty-First Army Group. At that point, the U.S. First Army Group commander—yet to be named—would assume command of all U.S. ground forces, on a par with Monty. Both army groups, in turn, would be commanded by Ike. Then, after the initial assault, the position of overall ground commander would be abolished; Ike would take over direction of the ground campaign himself.

On the naval side, Cunningham was not available. He had replaced Sir Dudley Pound in the exalted position of Britain's First Sea Lord. In his stead, Churchill named Admiral Bertram H. Ramsay, a senior and no less remarkable naval officer, who had been Cunningham's right-hand man in Torch and Husky and earlier had been knighted for his organization of the Dunkirk evacuation. One American admiral who had served with Ramsay remembered him as "quiet, brilliant, intelligent, determined and easy to get on with." Ike, of course, knew Ramsay well. He described him as "a most competent commander of courage, resourcefulness and tremendous energy," a judgment that I readily seconded.

Nor did Ike have his way on the air command, a tedious and complicated story. By that time the hundreds of heavy strategic bombers of our Eighth Air Force and the British Bomber Command had been organized into a semi-autonomous outfit waging a combined bomber offensive against Germany under the general supervision of the Combined Chiefs of Staff. Ike wanted the strategic bombers, as well as all tactical aviation, brought under his direct command for Overlord. At first neither the Combined Chiefs nor the British government would go along with his plans. However, after a long, bitter bureaucratic war, during which Ike threatened to "go home" if he did not have his way, it was finally agreed that strategic air would come under Ike's "direction" (but not command).

At Churchill's suggestion, Tedder was named deputy supreme commander for Overlord. As such, Tedder was in a position to exercise direct command over all Overlord tactical air, commanded by British General Trafford Leigh-Mallory, and "direction" over strategic air. Arthur T. Harris, a notorious prima donna, remained the head of Bomber Command. Ike brought Tooey Spaatz to England to assume overall command of our strategic air. James H. Doolittle (of the Tokyo raid), who had been one of Spaatz's chief deputies in the Mediterranean, was named to command our heavy bombers of the Eighth Air Force.[1]

The U.S. ground force command problems were more easily resolved. As a first step, Ike sought to remove Jake Devers from the scene by sending him to the Mediterranean to serve as deputy allied commander to Ike's British replacement, Henry Maitland (Jumbo) Wilson. Since Devers was a "Marshall man," Marshall was naturally miffed, but he finally agreed, albeit reluctantly, to the transfer. It was a comedown for Devers, and thereafter his relations with Ike were frosty.

The next important decision was to choose the American First Army

Group commander, one of the jobs I was holding down in a temporary capacity. I feel certain that Ike never seriously considered any candidate other than me, but Marshall suggested Courtney Hodges, then commanding the Third Army in the States, as an alternative. He cabled Ike that Hodges "is exactly the same class of man as Bradley in practically every respect. Wonderful shot, great hunter, quiet, self-effacing. Thorough understanding of ground fighting . . ." Other possibilities were George Patton (universally condemned when Drew Pearson revealed the slapping incident), Lesley McNair, or William H. Simpson, then commanding the U.S. Fourth Army in the States. Ike early dismissed Patton as a possibility, writing Marshall that "in no repeat no event will I ever advance Patton beyond Army command." Ike admired and respected McNair "tremendously" (as did we all) but he thought McNair's deafness ruled him out. Neither Hodges nor Simpson had commanded in combat. Early on, Ike cabled Marshall that "my preference for American Army Group Commander . . . is General Bradley."[2]

Shortly after his arrival in London, Ike held a press conference and announced that I would command all American ground troops on the assault under Monty. Patton—relieved of command of the Seventh Army but still in the Mediterranean—received the news bitterly. "I suppose that this means that he will command the American Army Group," he wrote prophetically in his diary. "I had thought that possibly I might get this command. It is another disappointment." Now, for the first time (at least in writing) he turned his venom on me. "Bradley is a man of great mediocrity," he continued, going on to list a half dozen examples of my "timidity" in North Africa and Sicily, all of them distortions or fabrications. "On the other hand," he continued in a sarcastic vein, "Bradley has many of the attributes which are considered desirable in a general. He wears glasses, has a strong jaw, talks profoundly and says little, and is a shooting companion of the Chief of Staff. Also a loyal man." He then concluded with what I believe was intended as a sincere assessment: "I consider him among our better generals."[3]

Although Ike had made up his mind about me, many weeks would pass before he officially named me Army Group commander. Meanwhile, he brought those men who would command armies under me to England. First, Courtney Hodges. He was appointed my understudy at First Army, as deputy commanding general. When I moved up to Group, Courtney would take over the First Army. I had always liked and admired Courtney Hodges, but now, as he became my subordinate, I began to fret privately. Courtney seemed indecisive and overly conservative. I hoped that my veteran First Army staff—Bill Kean in particular—would keep a fire under him. Next came George Patton, hat in hand, eating humble pie. Our roles in North Africa and Sicily were now reversed; I was his boss. Had it been left up to me, I would not have included Patton in Overlord. I did not look forward to having him in my command. He had shown in Sicily that he did not know how to run an army; his legendary reputation (now badly tarnished) was the product of an uncritical media buildup. But Ike insisted on Patton for his undeniable drive. Last, and much later, came big Bill Simpson—steady, prepossessing, well organized, earthy, a great infantryman and leader of men. The army headquarters he brought to England was numbered Eight, but Ike changed it to Nine in order to prevent any confusion with the illustrious British Eighth Army.[4]

At that time, Patton was at loose ends, with no command or Overlord responsibilities. Owing to his rank and notoriety, we chose him to become the figurehead in a gigantic hoax, or military deception, we had launched, called "Fortitude."

By early 1944, Hitler and his generals knew that an invasion of France would come, probably in May or June. We could not hope to completely disguise so vast an enterprise or to trick the Germans into disbelieving their own logical conclusions. The best that we could hope for was to deceive them as to where and when the assault would come, so that they would prepare to meet us in the wrong place. The British were the principal architects of this plan, and Ultra was central to Fortitude's conception and execution and provided a continuous monitor on German reactions to it, telling us whether or not we were really fooling the Germans.

There were countless beaches along the French coast where we could land our assault forces. Early in the game, Fortitude planners discovered through codebreaking that Hitler and most of his Berlin staff believed the most likely spot would be Pas de Calais. This knowledge in part led early Overlord planners to choose Normandy. Thereafter, the aim of Fortitude was to feed Hitler's belief in Pas de Calais as the likely spot, to change the minds of those German generals who believed that Normandy was the likely spot, and to lead all to think that when Overlord took place it was merely a feint. As an additional smoke screen, Fortitude's clever schemers also concocted a fictitious invasion of southern Norway simultaneously with Overlord by a British Army based in Scotland.

Fortitude utilized two principal devices to fool the Germans. The first was the German network of spies and agents in England. Early in the war the British, through Ultra intercepts of Hitler's spy organization, Abwehr, were able to find and capture every German spy in England. Most of these spies were "turned" into double agents, feeding the Abwehr disinformation or harmless truth. As additional spies arrived to join the network, they too were captured and turned against Germany. Through continuing Abwehr Ultra intercepts, the British spymasters were able to judge the success of their enterprise, building up the credibility of certain German "agents." When Fortitude was launched, these carefully nurtured top spies fed false information to Germany pointing to Pas de Calais as the assault target. Through Ultra intercepts the British spymasters confirmed that the Germans took the bait.*

The second device was the creation of a fictional army group in southeast England as though poised to strike at Pas de Calais. To further confuse the Germans, this group was named First Army Group. It was not, of course, my own real First Army Group, which was kept secret, and which, when activated into battle at Normandy, would become the Twelfth Army Group, leaving the bogus First Army Group behind in England still poised for Pas de Calais. Patton was selected to pose as commanding general of the notional First Army Group, which, to enhance the deception, had attached to it both real and fictional divisions. Dummy headquarters, airfields, tanks, landing craft and so on were fabricated from paper, wood and rubber. Telegraphers from real divisions that had already been in combat against the Germans (and whose "fists" were thus known) flooded the radio channels with fake messages designed to create the impression of an army group preparing for invasion.

The entire Fortitude plan was carried forward with exceptional efficiency. The "leaks" to the turned agents were carefully coordinated with the "activities" of the fictional First Army Group and necessary (and truthful) public disclosures, so that all the information flowing to the Germans appeared plausible and was never in serious conflict. The historians have judged that Fortitude worked as designed—the Germans swallowed the bait—and I believe the deception materially contributed to the success of Overlord. Without Ultra to monitor its intricate and interlocking parts (and to warn of German counterdeception), Fortitude could not even have been attempted.[5]

There was a real—as opposed to the fictional—plan for using Patton's battlefield talents. He was to assume command of Hodges' former command, Third Army, secretly move it to France after the assault forces were firmly established ashore, then, as Third Army commander, participate in the beachhead breakout and the conquest of France. However, during our preparations in England that spring, Patton twice got into serious hot water again and was very nearly relieved as Third Army commander and sent home in disgrace.

The first episode harked back to Sicily. Shortly before the invasion, Patton had given one of his famous "blood and guts" pep talks to Middleton's green 45th Division troops. I was not present, but Albert Wedemyer from OPD was on hand and he recalled: "He admonished them to be very careful when the Germans or Italians raised their arms as if they wanted

* This remarkable intelligence coup is described in the 1972 best-selling book *The Double-Cross System,* by J. C. Masterman. However, existing security restrictions prevented Masterman from describing the role of Ultra in the coup. More recently, it has been alluded to by various British authors, but the definitive correlation remains undescribed.

to surrender. He stated that sometimes the enemy would do this, throwing our men off guard. The enemy soldiers had on several occasions shot our unsuspecting men or had thrown grenades at them. Patton warned the members of the 45th Division to watch out for this treachery and to 'kill the S.O.B.'s' unless they were certain of their real intention to surrender."

Shortly after the 45th Division hit the beach at Scoglitti, two of its men, a captain and a sergeant, in two separate incidents, had lined up and murdered in cold blood a total of seventy-nine German POW's. When I learned of these appalling incidents, I at once reported them to Patton. I do not believe Patton fully grasped the gravity of the matter, or his moral sense had temporarily deserted him. As he recorded in his diary that day, he told me to tell the two men to certify "that the dead men were snipers or had attempted to escape or something, as it would make a stink in the press and also make the civilians mad." I, of course, disregarded these absurd instructions, and general-court-martial proceedings were brought against the two men.

The legal proceedings extended over a period of months. Both men pleaded in their defense that the atrocities had been committed because Patton had encouraged them to wantonly kill POW's. This line of argument led, in turn, to an investigation of Patton by the Army's Inspector General. The investigator arrived in England, and his presence in our theater touched off an angry behind-the-scenes flap in the American high command. I, for one, was more than a little troubled. If the media found out about the court-martial and publicized it, the consequences could be fatal not merely to Patton's reputation (and by extension to the U.S. Army high command) but also for every GI captured on the Continent by the Germans. Recalling Patton's cavalier attitude toward the incident, I inwardly boiled with anger. Patton's big mouth had us dancing on yet another griddle.

Ike invited Patton and me to a dinner in honor of visiting firemen: Assistant Secretary of War John McCloy and my classmate Joe McNarney, who was now Marshall's deputy chief of staff. During the course of the dinner, the subject of the Inspector General's investigation of Patton arose. Ike, who had been briefed on the matter, was furious and jumped on Patton, saying, "You talk too much." Patton replied, "If you order me not to, I will stop. Otherwise, I will continue to influence troops the only way I know, a way which so far has produced results." Ike yielded, saying, "Go ahead, but watch yourself." Patton later let loose more venom in his diary: "As usual Bradley said nothing. He does all the getting along and does it to his own advantage. . . . All of them but me are scared to death. I shall certainly attempt to say nothing which can be quoted." A few days later, he wrote: "I have a feeling, probably unfounded, that neither Monty or Bradley are too anxious for me to have a command. If they knew what little respect I had for the fighting ability of either of them, they would be even less anxious for me to show them up.'' The feeling was not unfounded —on my part, anyway.

Patton had not, of course, encouraged Middleton's men to murder POW's, and the defense—and the investigation—mercifully collapsed with no publicity. Patton was scornful of and completely insensitive to the entire proceedings. He wrote his wife: ''Some fair-haired boys are trying to say that I killed too many prisoners. Yet the same people cheer at the far greater killing of Japs. Well, the more I killed, the fewer men I lost, but they don't think of that. Sometimes I think that I will quit and join a monastery.''[6]

The dust had barely settled on this incident when Patton was back in trouble. On April 25, at the invitation of the British Ministry of Information, Patton addressed a group of ladies who had formed a Welcome Club for U.S. soldiers at Knutsford. In his brief address he said that ''since it is the evident destiny of the British and Americans—and of course the Russians—to rule the world, the better we know each other, the better job we will do.'' This talk was strictly ''off the record,'' not to be reported by the several journalists present. But the British Press Association broke the rules and released the story, omitting the Russian reference, leaving the impression that the United States and Britain would rule the postwar world. The story received little or no play in England, but since it was completely out of line for Patton to be commenting on who would rule the postwar world, it made the front pages all over the States and touched off an immense public political furor.

Had this been an isolated boner, Ike might have let it pass. But it came on the heels of the delicate atrocity investigation, and Ike blew sky high. On April 29, Ike cabled Marshall stating that Patton was apparently ''unable to use reasonably good sense in all those matters where senior commanders must appreciate the effect of their own actions upon public opinion and this raises doubts as to the wisdom of retaining him in high command despite his demonstrated capacity in battle leadership.'' Ike went on to say that ''I have grown so weary of the trouble he constantly causes you and the War Department, to say nothing of myself, that I am seriously contemplating the most drastic action.'' In a cable the following day, Ike added: ''On all of the evidence now available I will relieve him from command and send him home unless some new and unforeseen information should be developed in the case.''

I fully concurred in Ike's decision to send Patton home. I, too, was fed up. But who would command the Third Army? Ike spoke for both of us when he cabled Marshall on April 30: ''I now more than ever regret that I did not, before I left the Mediterranean, arrange to send Truscott to the Overlord command with the expectation that he would be one of the senior ground commanders. He would make an ideal commander of the Third

Army." But Truscott, now commanding VI Corps in the tough campaign in Italy, could not be yanked from that important assignment. We resorted, as Ike told Marshall, to the "next best thing." We selected Courtney Hodges to command the Third Army, leaving open, for the time being, my replacement for the First Army.

Ike got off a tough letter to Patton, ordering him to keep his mouth shut and report at once to "present his case." The meeting took place on May 1. Patton made his case so persuasively that Ike backed off and decided to reconsider. Without further consultation with me, Ike made the decision to keep Patton, in part because there was no hope of getting Truscott; in part because Churchill thought the whole episode a tempest in a teapot. Ike feared that Hodges, separated from First Army staff, might lack drive. And also Ike had a soft spot for Patton. On May 3, he wrote Patton: "I am once more taking the responsibility of retaining you in command in spite of damaging repercussions resulting from a personal indiscretion. I do this solely because of my faith in you as a battle leader and from no other motives."[7]

Overlord planners had assigned my First Army three U.S. Army corps for the Normandy assault: V, VII and XIX. V Corps was commanded by an old and good friend, Leonard T. (Gee) Gerow, four years my senior in age. A Virginian of French extraction (Giraud), he was an honors graduate of VMI (1911) who had served in the Mexican border war and in France in World War I. I first met Gee in 1924, when we were classmates in the advanced class at Fort Benning. (He graduated first in the class, I second.) When Marshall became Chief of Staff, he had picked Gerow to head the war plans division, where he served until Ike relieved him. He was an outstanding gentleman and soldier—cool, hard-working, intelligent, well organized, competitive—clearly destined for high rank and responsibility.[8]

The other two corps commanders were question marks in my mind. One, my West Point classmate and fraternity brother (and our cadet first captain) Roscoe B. Woodruff commanded VII Corps. A noted tanker from the class of 1913, Willis D. Crittenberger, commanded XIX Corps. But we soon lost Crittenberger to Jake Devers, who sent him to command IV Corps in Italy under Mark Clark's Fifth Army.

The Overlord plan specified that Gerow's V Corps and Woodruff's VII Corps would spearhead the assault on France, while the XIX Corps was held in floating reserve to come ashore behind them. Neither Gerow nor Woodruff had commanded large forces in combat or participated in an amphibious landing. This was worrisome. I tried my utmost to get Lucian Truscott, but Devers and Clark made it clear that Truscott would remain in Italy.[9]

The problem was partly solved by the arrival in England of Joe Collins, one of the outstanding members of the Class of 1917. He was fresh from command of the 25th "Tropic Lightning" Infantry Division on Guadalcanal and New Georgia in the Solomon Islands (and had there earned the nickname "Lightning" Joe). Marshall had recommended Collins for corps command. Ike and I interviewed him closely on his combat experiences. Collins spoke lucidly and modestly, emphasizing that in the attack, he always went for the high ground. When the interview concluded, Collins later wrote, I remarked to Ike: "He talks our language." We subsequently made the tough and painful decision to give Collins command of Woodruff's VII Corps.[10]

I placed Woodruff in temporary command of XIX Corps, meanwhile devoutly hoping I would by some stroke of luck get Truscott. However, about that time another Pacific veteran, Charles H. (Cowboy Pete) Corlett (West Point 1913), arrived in England highly recommended by Marshall. Corlett had commanded the 7th Infantry Division in the invasion of the Marshall Islands and had captured Kwajalein by what Ike described as a "nearly perfect" maneuver. I thought, as did Patton, that Ike had gone overboard on Corlett, but we made the decision to give him the XIX Corps and send Woodruff home. Woodruff was naturally bitter, but he was a good soldier and went on to achieve a distinguished record as a division commander in the Philippines under Bob Eichelberger.[11]

Corlett, whom I knew from my cadet days, was not one of my favorite people. He was abrasive, short-fused, and arrived with a chip on his shoulder which was still there thirty years later when he published his memoir: "Many times I made suggestions about amphibious matters, but these ideas of mine were 'brushed off.' I soon got the feeling that American generals in England considered anything that had happened in the Pacific strictly 'bush league stuff,' meriting no consideration. I felt like an expert according to the naval definition: 'a son-of-a-bitch from out of town.' " I think it was Corlett's own personality that got in his way; certainly we did not denigrate Joe Collins' Pacific combat experience. We would come to depend on Collins more than any other corps commander in Europe.[12]

From V and VII Corps, two infantry divisions had been selected to spearhead the assault on our beaches, Omaha and Utah. These were the 29th, commanded by Charles H. Gerhardt (West Point 1917) and the 4th, commanded by Raymond O. Barton (West Point 1912). Though each division was superbly trained, neither had seen combat and this, to say the least, was worrisome. Though I hated to call on them for another brutal assignment, I made the decision to substitute elements of Clarence Huebner's blooded Big Red One for the assault. Two 1st Division regiments and one 29th Division regiment would lead the attack on Omaha. To the 4th Division, which would assault Utah, I added Teddy Roosevelt, whom I had fired from the 1st Division, believing that his presence with the assaulting forces would be an inspiration.[13]

Within the First Army, we approached our planning and training objectives with utmost determination and gravity. There could be no error, no failure, no oversight, no lapse. If Overlord failed, the consequences would be unthinkable. Even if the British could be persuaded to do it again, it would require a full year for another team to organize and mount a second assault. By that time, Hitler might have sufficient "secret weapons" (rockets, jet airplanes, vastly improved U-boats) to decisively repulse us. The Russians, losing all faith in the Allies, might stop at their historic borders and negotiate a peace. Hitler's Festung Europa might go on for a thousand years. For the Allies, it was now or never—everything riding on one throw of the dice.

TWENTY-FIVE

Ike, Monty and I and our chiefs of staff, Bedell Smith, Freddie de Guingand, Lev Allen and Bill Kean, worked in close harness on the plans for Overlord. I saw Ike several times a week at official meetings, lunches, dinners or for private chats, and we talked often on the telephone. In contrast to his chairman-of-the-board role in the Mediterranean, Ike as chief executive officer of Overlord administered with a tight rein. Where in North Africa he had been diverted by time-consuming and frustrating political matters (the French and Italian negotiations), in England he was free to concentrate his considerable energies on the invasion itself. There was never any question about who was in charge. Ike's imprint on Overlord was large and forceful.

We made three substantial changes or additions to the original Overlord plans.

First we increased the impact of the assault force. The initial plan for the assault on France had been drawn by the able British general Frederick Morgan, presiding over a small but dedicated U.S. and British staff. He had chosen the time (May or June, based on the most favorable weather, tidal and moon conditions) and the place (Normandy). None of us had any quarrel with the time or place, but all of us found fault with the assault plan itself. Based originally on a planning assumption that forces available would be severely limited, it was far too conservative. As Ike put it rather simply, "There's not enough wallop in the initial attack." We nearly doubled the size of the assault forces—from three divisions to five—and demanded much heavier supporting naval gunfire. I proposed that the landing be made at night, as on Sicily; but the air generals and the admirals argued for daylight so their men could see the targets and beaches, and their views prevailed.[1]

To further increase the impact of our assault, I, almost alone among the senior commanders, urged the use of airborne troops. On my own front I wanted the 82nd and 101st Airborne divisions to drop behind Utah Beach in darkness, before we landed. As I have shown, our airborne operations on Sicily were less than successful. Thereafter a move had begun to greatly curtail them in size and scope. However, nothing could dissuade me from my view that these two superb divisions landing in full strength could be decisive in seizing the limited egresses from Utah Beach and throwing the enemy into general confusion.

Ike's British tactical air commander, Leigh-Mallory, whose transports would have to deliver the paratroopers and gliders in darkness, was equally adamant in his view that airborne operations were too risky and should be eliminated. He produced absurdly alarmist estimates that showed we would suffer 50 percent casualties among paratroopers and 70 percent among the gliders. I tried without success to change Leigh-Mallory's mind. Ultimately the impasse became bitter and had to be bucked up to Ike, who, after hearing all the pros and cons, ruled in my favor.

I worked closely with the two airborne division personnel in planning their assaults. The 101st Division, commanded by William C. Lee, had not yet jumped in combat. Since Matt Ridgway's 82nd Division was still engaged in combat in Italy, he sent Jim Gavin ahead to London to help plan the division's operation in Normandy. Unfortunately Bill Lee had a severe heart attack and had to be sent home, where he died. I decided to replace Lee with the young but experienced Max Taylor from the 82nd Division. Mark Clark, who had a tough fight on his hands in Italy, was naturally reluctant to give up the superb 82nd Division and finally, much to my anger, insisted on keeping one-third of it (the 504th Regiment) until the very last hour. The regiment arrived in England—one month before D-day—so badly battered and riddled with casualties it could not be used for Overlord. Ridgway had to train a new regiment from scratch to replace it.[2]

The second substantial change in Overlord involved the highly controversial and much-debated operation Anvil, a proposed secondary landing in southern France near Marseilles. The purposes of Anvil were several: to divert and to draw German troops and aircraft from Normandy; to lodge a mutually supporting Allied force on the mainland of Europe; to provide additional seaports for landing supplies; and to create an operation in which French troops could participate, thus contributing to the liberation of their homeland. Marshall, Eisenhower and I believed firmly in Anvil; Churchill, Alan Brooke and Monty did not. The British preferred to use the forces earmarked for Anvil for thrusts in the Balkans—the "soft underbelly." For months Anvil had hung in the air unresolved.

When we expanded the Overlord assault forces from three to five divisions, we imposed an immediate demand for many more LST's and other landing craft. By this time, mostly at Churchill's insistence, Alexander and Mark Clark had enlarged Italian operations to include a landing at Anzio on January 22, 1944, to which the Germans had reacted with astonishing fierceness. The Anzio operation required the diversion of sixty-eight LST's that were earmarked for Overlord and/or Anvil. Owing to this diversion, it soon became obvious that there was not enough sea lift to mount a proper Overlord and a meaningful Anvil. This led to a hard re-examination of Anvil and many new debates about how or if it could or should be retained.

When the full intensity of the German stand in Italy was encountered, the British held that Anvil should be canceled. They argued that the Italy campaign was already serving the main military purpose of Anvil: tying down large numbers of German air and ground forces that otherwise might be used against Overlord. The ground forces earmarked for Anvil could be more effectively utilized in further operations in Italy to reinforce Alexander's main force, or for mounting other small amphibious end runs. Some of the LST's slated for Anvil could be used for Overlord; the LST's in Italy earmarked for Anvil could remain in Italy.

The British argument was appealing but complicated, so much so that the British proposed yet another meeting of the Combined Chiefs to thrash it out. But Marshall deemed the matter one that Ike, as supreme commander of Overlord, should resolve himself, in consultation with the British, and so advised him. In the ensuing debates, the availability of sea lift became a decisive factor in all operations. It led to Churchill's declaration that "the destinies of two great empires . . . seem to be tied up in some Goddamned things called LST's."

The upshot was compromise: Anvil, finally reduced in size and scope, was retained, but had to be postponed weeks beyond D-day so that some Overlord LST's could be used in Anvil. In addition, the Overlord D-day had to be postponed from May 1 to the first week in June in order to accumulate one more month's production of landing craft—about one hundred vessels. The campaign in Italy was reinforced with ground forces, but all further amphibious end runs were discouraged and many surviving LST's in Italy were diverted to Overlord or Anvil.

Throughout these tedious, seemingly endless debates, I was an unyielding advocate of Anvil, subsequently renamed "Dragoon." There were times when Ike, owing to the shortage of LST's and the complexities of utilizing those we had, was sorely tempted to give in to the British view and cancel Dragoon. My stubborn stand undoubtedly influenced him to hold on to the concept. However, then and later, I often wondered why, with our seemingly unlimited industrial production, someone in Washington had not thought to give LST's a higher shipbuilding priority. It was indeed scandalous that the major decisions of history's mightiest military endeavor were determined in large part by a shortage of LST's.[3]

The third Overlord change was that we proposed utilizing many of our "strategic" bombers to help Leigh-Mallory's "tactical" air forces in an all-out assault on the French railway and bridge systems in the weeks before D-day. The purpose of this plan was to utterly destroy the principal means available to the Germans for rushing troops and tanks to reinforce German positions in Normandy. This appeared to me to be a perfectly straightforward and logical use of our heavy bombers, but, as it developed, few proposals during the war generated so much heat and controversy.

Our strategic bomber commanders, Tooey Spaatz and Arthur Harris, were engaged that spring in what they believed to be a "decisive" strategic air war against Germany. The air offensive consisted of massive 1,000-plane raids (Eighth Air Force by day, the Bomber Command by night) against German cities, defense industries, ball bearing plants and so on. These raids were not only inflicting severe damage on the ground but gradually chewing up the German Air Force sent up to shoot down the bombers. Spaatz and Harris were utterly committed to this campaign; they sincerely believed that Germany could be defeated by bombers alone, that Overlord was not even necessary. To them it was unthinkable to interrupt the strategic bombing campaign to tactically knock out the French railway and bridge systems. They had strong support for their views in the British War Cabinet and in the Combined Chiefs of Staff.

A furious bureaucratic battle ensued, the like of which I have seldom seen. Spaatz and Harris were then on the verge of concentrating their bombers on the German oil industry. They argued that an all-out bomber assault on German oil production would not only destroy that vital strategic war-making segment, but most likely the remainder of the German Air Force, since, it was assumed, the Germans would defend the oil industry to the last plane. The destruction of the German Air Force would be far more valuable to Overlord, they argued, than knocking out French trains and bridges. Besides that, they pressed, bombing French cities and bridges was likely to inflict massive casualties (some 80,000, they suggested) on the French population, turning it against the Allies at the most inopportune moment.

For untold years we infantrymen had been subjected to the glib, enticing arguments of strategic air power advocates, who unfailingly promised a quick-easy-cheap victory through air power. But I had seen the reality of air wars in North Africa and Sicily. Air power had not lived up to the glamorous advance billing. It had failed us in Tunisia and in the invasion of Sicily. I did not believe it could knock out the German oil industry or the German Air Force. Least of all could it break the German will to resist and force unconditional surrender, the ultimate air power fantasy. I argued fervently for the destruction of the French transportation system.

The battle was bitter, at times bloody. In the end Ike, who supported the ground forces all the way, declared that if Spaatz and Harris would not concede, he, Ike, would request relief as Supreme Commander. By this dire threat, he got his way.

Commencing in April, a substantial portion of the strategic bombers were diverted to transportation targets in France. A system was set up to warn the French population in advance of the attacks, keeping civilian casualties to a minimum and causing no discernible animosity. In April, the Eighth Air Force flew 33,000 sorties, mostly against French railway and bridge targets. During May, Allied pilots claimed destruction of 16,000 freight cars, 900 locomotives, countless bridges and 1,000 German aircraft. The French transportation system was severely crippled and the German Air Force was virtually destroyed, contributing to the ultimate success of Overlord and saving many lives. I consider this to have been one of Ike's greatest personal achievements in World War II.[4]

As Overlord planning proceeded, and my responsibilities increased, I was drawn closer into the tight little circle of British governmental and military leaders. I came to know King George VI, Churchill, Alan Brooke, Monty, Ismay, Tedder, Ramsay, Leigh-Mallory, de Guingand, Dempsey and members of the War Cabinet quite well.

My first close association with King George occurred on the evening of February 2, when Winston Churchill held a dinner for the Overlord chiefs at Number 10 Downing Street. Ike, Bedell Smith and I represented the Americans. It was a bit stiff at first. I was a trifle awed in the presence of both the King and Churchill, but as the evening wore on rank was outwardly forgotten, an informal air pervaded the gathering, and I thoroughly enjoyed myself. The King seemed to appreciate the informality more than any of us. For the first time I realized how dreadfully lonely and isolated the life of a monarch must be, how difficult it must be for him to have any sort of life outside the royal family. He seemed to take great delight in signing my "short snorter" (an autographed one-dollar bill, one of my prized possessions to this day) and produced his own, as did the others. I did not know until that night that the King stuttered badly; often he seemed in agony when trying to express himself.[5]

Another man I watched closely that evening was Alan Brooke. In company, he was soft-spoken, retiring, self-effacing, a British version of George Marshall. Excluding Churchill, Alan Brooke was the principal architect of British war strategy. I knew that he, like Churchill, had opposed Overlord from the outset, preferring the British "peripheral" strategy—the Mediterranean campaign, indirect approach to the heart of Germany through the soft underbelly. In spite of our differences in strategic outlook, I developed a deep admiration for Alan Brooke. He had a truly brilliant global-ranging mind, sweeping from the Far East to the North Atlantic to the Mediterranean to the Channel with equal facility and a hard-nosed grasp of details and political realities. His common sense, patience and tact kept the impulsive Churchill in rein, a nearly full-time job in itself, as we all learned later from Brooke's published diaries.

Outside military circles, Alan Brooke was virtually unknown in America and remains so today. Churchill and Monty dominated the headlines and, later, the histories. I was pleased to note that in his later writings, Monty, with uncommon modesty, gave Alan Brooke his just due. He wrote that Alan Brooke "was the best soldier produced by any nation during Hitler's war." Monty believed that Churchill and Brooke "between them played a greater part in ensuring that the Allies won the Second World War than any other two men" and that "neither of the two . . . could have done without the other." While I do not completely agree with these judgments—Marshall is my choice of "best soldier"—every aspiring military officer could profit from a close study of the British historian Arthur Bryant's two volumes on Brooke's wartime years.[6]

I next saw Churchill when he and I joined Ike for an extended inspection of U.S. troops on March 23 and 24. We stopped first at Max Taylor's 101st Airborne Division, based at Newbury Race Course. We next visited the 2nd Armored Division, which under Hugh Gaffey had "captured" Palermo. Gaffey had been named Patton's chief of staff; and the division, part of Corlett's XIX Corps, based at Tidworth, was now commanded by Edward H. Brooks. We concluded our inspection at Barton Stacy, where Manton Eddy's 9th Infantry Division was bivouacked. Eddy's division had been assigned to Joe Collins' VII Corps and would follow Barton's 4th Division onto Utah Beach. I was happy to see that all three divisions were in top form.[7]

Churchill was recovering from a recent and severe illness, but you would never have known it. Joe Collins, who joined us on the second day, recalled: "Churchill had had two strenuous days of inspections and had ridden for miles perched on the tonneau of an open car so that he could better see and be seen by the troops. . . . He had insisted on getting out of the car to walk around the honor guards and examine the weapons displayed. That day he had stood through a review of our regiments and delivered a stirring address to the men. In one of the towns through which we had passed he had gotten out of the car to walk with General Eisenhower for a couple of blocks through throngs of cheering townspeople, who pressed about him in their enthusiasm, many with tears streaming down their cheeks."[8]

Everywhere he went, Churchill, wearing his famed black derby, joshed with the American troops and mugged for the photographers. At Eddy's 9th Division, he expressed a desire to try out the new American carbine. Eddy had his men set up targets—twenty-five yards for Churchill, fifty for Ike, seventy-five for me. We each got off fifteen rounds rapid fire. I "pulled" my first shot and am certain I scored fourteen hits, but we never found out because Eddy tactfully moved us on before we could inspect the targets.[9]

We traveled on Ike's special train, which was equipped with posh dining and sleeping facilities. Churchill seemed to abhor sleep. Both nights we had dinner for the local corps and division commanders, and Churchill kept us up late drinking brandy and eloquently advancing his ideas on tactics and strategy. The campaign in Italy was still going badly; Churchill was shockingly frank in his comments on the generalship. The lack of progress there had intensified his desire to cancel Anvil and divert its resources to Italy; but Ike was now committed to Anvil, however reduced in scope, and would not be talked out of it. Happily, Churchill was relaxing his long-standing opposition to Overlord and now was beginning to champion it. In fact, he now talked grandly of going in with the first assault wave! To my mind, the most impressive feature about Churchill was his bulldog determination to win the war.[10]

Churchill was seemingly indefatigable. Collins, who had dinner with us on the train the second night, wrote, "Churchill was fresh as we were and held forth after dinner until eleven o'clock, dominating the conversation, alternately regaling us with stories or stirring us as he spoke feelingly of our common ideals and endeavors. He ended the evening with passages from Kipling and from Bret Harte's *The Reveille,* to each verse of which he added extemporaneously 'The drums! The drums! The drums!' which he rolled forth with obvious relish."[11]

I saw Monty in London frequently. As Overlord ground commander (pro tem), he was technically my immediate boss, and we had many details to discuss. These meetings were invariably stiff, almost formal. Monty was usually coolly aloof, almost withdrawn, and not readily open to suggestions. There was no "chemistry"; our personalities simply did not mesh. He left me with the feeling that I was a poor country cousin whom he had to tolerate. Fortunately his chief of staff, Freddie de Guingand, in every way Monty's opposite, was usually on hand to provide a measure of warmth, affability—and common sense.

What Monty liked most, it seemed to me, was a stage. Perhaps not coincidentally, my most vivid memory of him that spring in London was a stagey mass meeting of senior Overlord commanders on April 7. It took place at Monty's Twenty-First Army Group headquarters at St. Paul's School in Kensington. Those in attendance were Churchill, Ike, Tedder, Ramsay, Leigh-Mallory, de Guingand, Bedell Smith, Patton, Hodges, Miles Dempsey, the U.S. and British corps commanders, and many others.

A large lecture hall had been turned into a fittingly dramatic setting. Monty's staff had constructed a scale model of the Normandy coast we would assault. The model was about thirty feet wide and was mounted in the center of the hall and was tilted up so that all on the tiered seats could see it. On it were displayed the various French seacoast towns and important topographical features. Standing on the model with a pointer, Monty opened the meeting with a two-hour run-through of how the assault would proceed. He spoke without notes, completely in command of the plan, the forces, the enemy dispositions (provided by Ultra) and probable enemy reaction.

In broadest terms the invasion plan was as follows. Dempsey's Second British Army would land on the left, my First Army on the right. Once we were firmly lodged ashore, Dempsey's troops would move ten miles inland and seize Caen, a key road center on the Orne River through which German counterattacking forces would most likely try to pass. My First Army would move inland, cut the Coentin Peninsula, then pivot to the right and seize Cherbourg, which was deemed an essential port for our immense supply line. While we sought these objectives, the Canadian First Army, commanded by Henry D. G. Crerar, would come ashore to reinforce Dempsey. Patton would come ashore to reinforce me, setting the stage for what we called the "breakout."

The breakout was simple in concept. Monty's British and Canadian armies would hold firmly near Caen, like decoys, drawing the main weight of the German counterattack and blocking them from getting at me. My First Army would then wheel in a giant arc as far southeastward as the Loire River. When Patton's Third Army came ashore, it would wheel westward to capture the Brittany Peninsula and its important ports, such as Brest. When all this had been accomplished, the Allied line would then consist of a north-south "front" about 140 miles long, facing east toward the Seine River (and Paris), ahead of which we expected the Germans to make a very firm stand, blocking our way into Germany.

In preparing this plan, Monty, always methodical, had developed a series of "phase lines." These were lines on the map of western France outlining where we hoped our fronts would be on certain days following D-day. For example, by D plus 36, Monty had projected a phase line running north-south through Le Mans. In our planning, I had objected strenuously to the use of phase lines. It tended to cast the plan into a rigid mold which might discourage exploitation among the commanders. Phase lines also could not take into account the unexpected by the enemy—a success, for example. If projected phase lines were not met, it might appear that we were "failing." Ultimately, I persuaded Monty to drop the phase lines—or so I thought.

When we gathered at St. Paul's School that day, I was astonished to find that the model and maps were adorned with phase lines extending all the way to D plus 90, when it was assumed we would face Germans across the Seine River. I was quite put out with Monty. He had unilaterally reneged on an important agreement. I insisted that at the very least the phase lines be removed from the American sector. I did not realize it then, but Joe Collins overheard our testy discussion. Later he wrote, "Monty, somewhat petulantly, finally agreed." This was, Collins recalled, the "first sign, but not the last, of Bradley's irritation with Montgomery."

Monty left the phase lines in the British sector. They clearly showed that Monty's British forces would take Caen on D-day and then, over the next month, advance about ten miles eastward, securely anchoring the hub on which the Americans would pivot. In his oral presentation, Monty, brimming with optimism, exceeded his own phase line. He placed his pointer on the plain south of Caen, almost at Falaise (some thirty-two miles inland from the beach), and said he hoped to "rattle about" or "knock about" down there with his tanks on D-day.

Monty's briefing made a profoundly favorable impression on Ike, Bedell Smith—all of us in fact. Gone was the methodical, conservative set-piece thinking of the Monty of North Africa, Sicily and Italy. Here was a "new," almost recklessly brash Monty. On D-day his tanks would strike thirty-two miles inland to Falaise! The airmen were particularly pleased. They needed the area south and east of Caen for airfields—and the sooner the better. Monty would deliver that area to them on D-day. The airmen could hardly ask for better service than that.

In later years, some confusion would arise in the minds of military historians over the exact role Monty assigned his own forces in Overlord. There was never any confusion about his role at the time. Monty's self-assigned mission was to seize Caen and the area south and east toward Falaise for the construction of Allied airfields and to give his ground forces a lodgement of sufficient size for resupply and maneuver. He did not ever envision a major "breakout" from his lodgement; the major breakout was to be conducted by my forces, wheeling as described; Monty would absorb the main shock of the enemy counterattack, pin down and kill as many of the enemy as possible (keeping them off my forces), providing the solid hub on which we would turn our wheel.

For all Monty's bravado, we were soon to learn through bitter experience that there was a grave weakness in the invasion plan. A great amount of work, thought and intelligence gathering had gone into the assault phase—getting a toehold on the beach. But not nearly enough planning and intelligence gathering had been devoted to the immediate problems of exploitation of the beachhead. Owing to this lapse, we did not fully appreciate the difficulties of the terrain we would face beyond the beachhead in my sector. The terrain is what the French called *bocage* country and we called "hedgerow" country. The farm lands are divided into small square or rectangular-shaped parcels, with formidable tree and hedge embankments on all four sides. This checkerboard of high bushy embankments would provide excellent cover for German defensive deployments and severely impede armored operations. Many military historians have rightly criticized us for failing to reckon more realistically with the French terrain.

It was an all-day session at St. Paul's School. After Monty, Admiral Ramsay gave the naval side—a gloomy talk stressing all the negatives and difficulties, which we already knew so well. Then came Leigh-Mallory, who optimistically assured us that the German Air Force would be well under control by D-day. After lunch, we army commanders followed with a more detailed briefing of our specific missions. The corps commanders followed us with even greater detail. Joe Collins, speaking without notes and walking on the model like Monty, was superb. When he sat down, Bedell Smith whispered, "Done in the best tradition of Fort Benning." De Guingand later wrote, "Collins, I think, would have won a Gallup Poll, and there was no doubt that he lived up to the feeling he then gave us all, as being a forceful and able commander."

Monty was neither a smoker nor a drinker and did not permit smoking in the lecture hall. There were signs all over the place: "No Smoking." Throughout the day he declared short breaks for the smokers. Toward the end of the afternoon, just before Churchill was scheduled to speak, all the signs disappeared and Monty rescinded the no-smoking rule. Churchill gave the final talk—to mixed reviews. Alan Brooke thought that he "was looking old and lacking a great deal of his usual vitality." De Guingand wrote that "he appeared rather tired and grave at first but finished with great strength. . . . He stressed the need to take great risks." Patton thought Churchill's talk was "the best." He recalled that he said, "Remember that this is an invasion, not the creation of a fortified beachhead."[12]

TWENTY-SIX

In North Africa and Sicily, we had been entirely dependent on the British for Ultra intelligence. It was encoded and radioed from the British code-breaking center at Bletchley Park in England to British specialists in the field attached to higher headquarters. However, in the summer of 1943, the British agreed to give the Americans wider access to Ultra. One provision of this agreement specified that our armies and air forces could have American "Ultra representatives" who would receive the raw Ultra data from Bletchley Park, interpret it and brief the top American commanders.

The responsibility for recruiting and training these American Ultra "reps" fell to a hush-hush outfit: Special Branch of Army G-2 in Washington. John McCloy had created the Special Branch after Pearl Harbor to better analyze and distribute the Magic and other intelligence we were getting from breaking Japanese diplomatic and military codes. McCloy chose an able Army intelligence specialist, Carter W. Clarke, to head Special Branch, and he recruited one of his former New York law partners, Alfred McCormack, to serve as Clarke's deputy. McCormack was instrumental in helping Clarke recruit an outstanding staff for Special Branch. Many were lawyers or investment bankers; nine were, like McCormack, Princeton graduates.

Clarke delegated to one of these bright recruits, attorney Telford Taylor (after the war, a chief prosecutor at the Nuremberg war crime trials), responsibility for recruiting and training the American Ultra reps for service in the ETO. Taylor set up a secret headquarters at the American embassy in London through which the Ultra reps were routed from Special Branch, processed and then sent to Bletchley Park for duty and training.

In the spring of 1944, these American Ultra reps (officially, special security officers, or SSO's) began to report to our Army and Air Force headquarters for duty. Since I wore two hats—First Army and Army Group—I became closely associated with two American Ultra teams. At Army Group, the team was headed by William H. Jackson, a brilliant New

York attorney (from the firm of Carter, Ledyard & Millburn), who would later help establish the Central Intelligence Agency and serve as one of its deputy directors. Jackson's chief assistant was Alexander Standish, an astute Boston investment analyst. They were assisted by an electrical engineer, Samuel M. Orr, Jr., and another attorney, Charles R. Murnane. At First Army, the senior Ultra rep was a Philadelphia attorney and active National Guardsman, Adolph G. Rosengarten, who had originally been attached to my 28th Division. These men worked in closest collaboration with my chief G-2s, Edwin L. Sibert (who had served with me in the West Point Tactics Department) at Army Group and Monk Dickson at First Army.

The Ultra teams traveled with considerable top secret baggage: radios, encoding and decoding machines, files, etc. As a consequence, they were given special vans and security guards and would travel with our headquarters. These outfits were naturally the object of intense scrutiny and speculation by our own personnel. Although inevitably some people guessed what the teams were up to, there was not one major security leak in American Ultra operations during the war, and those Americans involved in the enterprise kept the secret until the mid-1970s when British authors began to reveal Ultra's secrets.

After our Ultra teams became operational, my two headquarters began to receive a steady flow of information from Bletchley Park. At first much of this data was presented to me (and others "in the Ultra picture") in raw form. Much of it was fragmentary and difficult to understand or make sense of. But as time passed, my G-2s and Ultra reps became highly skilled at interpreting the important material in the data and thereafter presented it to me daily in far more comprehensible form, either oral or written.

Added to the massive flow of Ultra from the Germans was an additional bonus: a Magic source in the ETO. This was Japan's ambassador in Berlin, General (and Baron) Hiroshi Oshima, who had arrived in Berlin in the early 1930s as a military attaché, had climbed the ladder to ambassador, and was then close to Hitler and the Nazi leadership. He regularly reported to Tokyo in Magic, and most of what he relayed was intercepted and decoded and forwarded through Special Branch to us.

Oshima's unwitting contribution to our ETO intelligence picture has not yet been fully plumbed by the historians. But one on his trail, Carl Boyd, recently wrote: "In late 1943 Oshima made an extensive inspection tour of German fortifications along the coast of France. He sent a detailed message to Tokyo in which the Japanese warrior-diplomat described not only various German military installations, but he also discussed his briefings by the German high command on how the coast would be defended. His details included the names of the German Army, Air and Navy commanders, the number of divisions and men available to defend the coast, and the number of Tiger and Panther tanks in reserve and behind the fortifications."

In addition, of course, Oshima passed to Tokyo the results of his many diplomatic interviews with Hitler and his staff. The importance of Oshima's contribution to our Overlord intelligence picture may be inferred from an excerpt of a letter George Marshall wrote in the summer of 1944: "Our main basis of information regarding Hitler's intentions in Europe is obtained from Baron Oshima's message[s] from Berlin reporting his interviews with Hitler and other officials to the Japanese government."[1]

As a result of information gained from Ultra and Magic, as well as aerial reconnaissance and other sources, we were extraordinarily well informed about the enemy, his probable intentions, his power and weapons and his weaknesses and vulnerabilities. Seldom in history has an opposing army known so much about its opponent.

This was the general picture we had. Hitler was hard pressed on the Russian front; Italy was a drain on his resources. Overlord represented both his greatest danger and his greatest opportunity. If the Overlord forces could be repulsed and trounced decisively on the beaches, Hitler knew it would be a very long time indeed before the Allies tried it again—if ever. A decisive victory on the beaches of France would free fifty German divisions for the Russian front, enough force, perhaps, to check the Soviet drive and turn encroaching disaster into a German triumph. The Third Reich might yet prevail.

Hitler's dream of a decisive victory in the west was based, in part, on exaggerated faith in two new "wonder weapons": the V-1 cruise missile or flying bomb, and the much more sophisticated V-2 ballistic missile. After repulsing Overlord, he would saturate England with these missiles, preventing another cross-channel buildup and sapping our will to continue the war. Foreign agents and Ultra had revealed to British intelligence a good deal about these weapons and where they were being developed and tested. Photo reconnaissance then pinpointed the sites.

Behind the scenes in England, the discovery of these weapons had caused gravest concern. Like Hitler, we greatly exaggerated in our minds their anticipated effectiveness and reliability. Extraordinary measures were taken to stop their development. For example, on a night in August 1943, the British Bomber Command staged a 600-plane raid on the V-2 development site at Peenemünde, an isolated town on the German Baltic coast. When "ski ramp" V-1 launching sites were discovered in the Dieppe-Calais-Cherbourg areas, a great deal of Overlord air power was diverted to destroy them. In all, some 40,000 tons of bombs had been expended against the wonder weapons, delaying operational deployment of both beyond D-day, for which we were all very grateful.

We were not yet done with these weapons, however. We learned from Ultra and other sources that a slew of simplified hard-to-spot V-1 launching ramps had been erected in France and that the V-2 had entered advanced testing. One of our most highly classified Overlord objectives was to overrun as quickly as possible the V-1 launching sites in France so that the weapons could not be utilized against our resupply ports (Plymouth and Portsmouth) in southern England.

My main concern was what lay ahead on the ground—the German Army. The commander in-chief in the west was sixty-eight-year-old Field Marshal Gerd von Rundstedt. Known variously as the "Last Prussian" or the "Grand Old Man," the autocratic von Rundstedt had held large and important jobs during Hitler's early European conquests, and though aging, he was sure to be a formidable opponent. His principal subordinate was the Desert Fox, Erwin Rommel, now also a field marshal, and commanding Army Group B, which consisted of two armies, the Fifteenth (near Pas de Calais) and the Seventh (in Normandy and Brittany). The Russian and Italian fronts had drained off some of von Rundstedt's better divisions, but he still had fifty-eight divisions of varying strength and effectiveness. Rommel's Seventh Army, which we would meet in Normandy, numbered some fourteen divisions including one Panzer division, the 21st.

Fortunately for us, there was a fundamental and important difference of opinion between von Rundstedt and Rommel about how to repulse the invasion. Von Rundstedt favored a mobile defense, a vast war of maneuvers in the heart of France after we had got ashore. He was thus less interested in defending the coastline and more interested in maintaining a massive mobile reserve far from the beaches. Rommel favored the exact opposite strategy. Having been immobilized by the weight of Allied air power in Tunisia and aware that the Luftwaffe could not effectively overcome Overlord air power, he believed a mobile defense was out of the question. In his view, there was only one way to achieve a decisive victory and that was to destroy us at the water's edge, within the first forty-eight hours. He was thus more interested in defending the coastline and less interested in maintaining a massive mobile reserve in the hinterlands.

The upshot was a compromise defensive strategy reflecting the conflicting views. Rommel launched a massive plan to fortify the whole northern French coastline—the Atlantic Wall—with the heaviest defenses in the Calais area, where he originally believed the assault would come. The fortifications consisted of mobile guns, pillboxes, tank traps, mines, underwater obstacles to wreck landing craft implanted on the beaches, and fields of floating mines off the coast. Little by little he moved his divisions forward toward the beaches, establishing nests of resistance. Given free rein, he would have moved all his divisions to within striking distance of the beaches, and brought the reserves forward. But von Rundstedt put his foot down and most of the panzer divisions were kept in reserve. The result was a defensive crust at the beaches that was too thin to destroy us and reserves too small for von Rundstedt's war of maneuver.

In the spring of 1944, Hitler had an intuition that convinced him—despite Fortitude—that our assault would come at Normandy, not Pas de Calais. He insistently telegraphed his views to von Rundstedt and Rommel. Von Rundstedt stubbornly clung to his view that Calais was our target, but Rommel began to side with Hitler. Belatedly Rommel launched a fortification program in Normandy to match that at Pas de Calais, but it was too little and too late, and Allied air attacks severely retarded the construction. However, Rommel succeeded in moving new troops into our assault area—notably the 77th, 91st and the 352nd Infantry divisions. Ultra picked up these movements and put together a fairly reliable German Army Order of Battle. One Ultra historian wrote that of the twenty-eight German divisions manning the coast from Amsterdam to Brest, Ultra had positively identified about fifteen. Ultra had also located and named all the army and corps headquarters. In addition, five weeks before D-day, Ultra detected the arrival of the 91st Infantry Division near St. Lô, where the 101st Airborne was to drop, and that notice led me to shift the drop zone.[2]

As D-day approached, we were frantically busy tying up loose ends, going over war plans, attending meetings, coordinating. One meeting stands out vividly in my mind. This was Ike's "final review" of Overlord, staged at Monty's headquarters at St. Paul's School in London. In addition to all the commanders directly involved, Ike invited the King, Churchill, Field Marshal Jan Christiaan Smuts of South Africa, the British Chiefs of Staff and the War Cabinet. It was the greatest gathering of Allied brass that I saw in World War II.

The conference was held in a Victorian gothic building with a two-story circular arena like a cockpit. We sat on hard narrow curved benches rising in tiers. Black columns supported an overhead gallery packed with admirals and generals. The King, Churchill and Ike sat on a first-row bench. Alan Brooke, Monty, Tedder, Ramsay, Leigh-Mallory and others spread to their left and right. I was assigned to the second tier with Miles Dempsey, Bedell Smith, Tooey Spaatz, Arthur Harris, Courtney Hodges and George Patton. Behind us came the corps commanders and then the division commanders. Admiral Cunningham recalled that he found himself "wondering what might happen if the Germans made a daylight raid in force and landed a bomb on the building."

One U.S. admiral who was present, Morton L. Deyo, later wrote: "As we took those uncompromisingly hard and narrow seats, the room was hushed and the tension was palpable." For the first time we were to hear in detail what everyone else was to do. Deyo continued: "It seemed to most of us that the proper meshing of so many gears would need nothing less than divine guidance. A failure at one point could throw the momentum out of balance and result in chaos. All in that room were aware of the gravity of the elements to be dealt with."

Ike rose to address the gathering, speaking for ten minutes. Deyo recalled: "It had been said that his smile was worth twenty divisions. That day it was worth more. . . . Before the warmth of his quiet confidence the mists of doubt dissolved. When he had finished the tension was gone. Not often has one man been called upon to accept so great a burden of responsibility. But here was one at peace with his soul." Alan Brooke had a different view. He wrote in his diary: "The main impression I gathered was that Eisenhower was no real director of thought, plans, energy or direction. Just a coordinator, a good mixer, a champion of inter-Allied cooperation, and in those respects few can hold a candle to him. But is that enough? Or can we not find all qualities of a commander in one man? Maybe I am getting too hard to please, but I doubt it."

Following Ike, Monty laid out the ground forces' plan. Admiral Ramsay did the same for the naval forces. Leigh-Mallory gave the air plan. Afterward we broke for lunch. Patton, who was clamlike that day, and properly so, sat opposite Churchill at the luncheon. Churchill asked Patton if he remembered him. When Patton replied in the affirmative, Churchill immediately ordered him a glass of whisky.

After lunch we reconvened. The King led off with a few words of greeting. Patton found it "rather painful to watch the efforts he made not to stammer." After the King, a dozen other speakers described their roles in Overlord. I gave my little talk Benning-style, without notes. Patton later wrote: "Bradley and Spaatz made short and good speeches." Churchill gave the final address. Patton thought it "a really great fighting speech, worth all that preceded it." To all of us who knew how much he had resisted Overlord, he now said, "Gentlemen, I am *hardening* to this enterprise."

The King chose that day to confer a great honor on me personally. He presented me with a coveted British decoration: Honorary Companion of the Military Division of the Most Honorable Order of the Bath. The award had been initiated by Alexander for my leadership of II Corps in Tunisia. Later in the year, the King would present me with a higher decoration in the Order of the Bath: Honorary Knight Commander.[3]

Owing to my high position, the media intensified their interest in me, straining as before for "color" and "human interest." I was featured on the cover of *Time* magazine, which called me "The Doughboy's General." *Life* and *Newsweek* also did stories about me.[4]

The torrent of publicity transformed me into a celebrity. This was not at all to my liking, for I was sincerely a private person and wished to remain so. However, I saw that this was impossible. America was at war; the American public, whose sons were serving under me—as my aide Chet Hansen had argued in Sicily—had a right to know a little something about me. The only real satisfaction I derived from these stories was that most of them stressed that I valued the lives of my soldiers and would not spend them recklessly. That, I felt, would instill confidence in the GI's I would send into battle.

In the final days before we embarked, I made a point of visiting as many American units as I could, both to allay the growing rumors that we would suffer heavy casualties and to give the men some final words of encouragement. Lastly, I called my corps and division commanders to Bristol for one final review. In his memoirs, Max Taylor recalled that meeting:

> General Bradley, the old school teacher from West Point and the Infantry School, personally conducted the class of generals. Each of us stepped up to the operation map of France, pointer in hand, and described in detail the scheme of maneuver of his corps or division. When my turn came, I found that Bradley knew as much about what my battalions were supposed to do as I did. I sat down wondering like a cadet how many "tenths" I had lost by my recitation and whether, indeed, I had made a passing mark for the day.

When the review was over, it seemed appropriate for me to say a few words. In the pause that followed, Max Taylor recalled Patton's final review at Mostganem, on the eve of the Sicily invasion. At that time, Taylor remembered, Patton "turned on us with a roar and, waving a menacing swagger stick under our noses, concluded: 'I never want to see you bastards again unless it's at your post on the shores of Sicily.' "

Taylor continued:

> The meeting in Bristol was a study in contrasts with that at Mostganem. . . . When the discussion was over, like General Patton in North Africa, Bradley felt the need to say something appropriate to this occasion, something to rouse these commanders upon whom the success of his Army depended. But General Bradley, although a wonderfully inspiring leader in most ways, is a quiet man of few words and not a fluent speaker. Seeming to sense his rhetorical inadequacies at this critical moment, he folded his hands behind his back, his eyes got a little moist, and in lieu of a speech, he simply said, "Good luck, men." We left without the smart of Patton's blistering farewell but with the feeling that we had a commander worth all we could give.[5]

All was in readiness for mankind's greatest military enterprise. The southern seaports of England were crammed with warships and landing craft of every description. We would assault the shores of France on June 5.

Monty, apparently feeling the need for one last get-together before we boarded our respective command ships, invited the four army commanders —Patton, Dempsey, Crerar and me—to have dinner and spend the night with him at his debarkation headquarters in Portsmouth. In preparation for this visit, Patton drove to my headquarters in Bristol on May 31. My aide

Chet Hansen recalled: "General Patton, of course, is extremely unpopular in this headquarters. Most of our officers have carried with them the punctured legend from Sicily." Nonetheless, we gave Patton the red carpet treatment, including a motorcycle escort.

On the following afternoon, June 1, we flew to Portsmouth. Monty, Patton and I had tea and then retired to Monty's office to go over our plans one final time. Later Dempsey and Crerar and Monty's chief of staff, Freddie de Guingand, and other staffers arrived and we had a fine informal dinner. De Guingand recalled: "Things couldn't have gone better. Everyone was in their best form, and all appeared supremely confident."

Indeed so. That night Monty believed the war would be over by November 1, and was willing to bet on it. I thought he was much too optimistic and bet five British pounds (then about twenty-five dollars) that it would take longer, one bet I would have been happy to lose. Catching some of Monty's optimism, I invited Dempsey to dinner in Paris on August 11, his birthday. When the port was passed, Monty toasted us four army commanders. Patton recalled: "Nobody did anything about it, so I said: 'As the oldest army commander present, I would like to propose a toast to the health of General Montgomery and express our satisfaction in serving under him.' "

It was a most pleasant evening. Patton wrote that "I have a better impression of Monty than I did." It would not take long for this amiability to dissolve. Soon our relationships with Monty would be very much less than pleasant.

Next day, June 2, Patton and I returned to Bristol. There we said our goodbyes at the airport. Patton was emotional. Hansen recalled: "Patton clenched Bradley's hands, hitched up his trousers under the custom-tailored tunic to say, 'Brad, the best of luck to you. We'll be meeting again—soon, I hope.' "[6]

On June 3, some of my key staff and I drove to Plymouth to board the heavy cruiser U.S.S. *Augusta,* our headquarters ship for the invasion. Each of us had a mountain of gear: waterproofed gas masks, Mae Wests, pistols, web belts, helmets, vitamin pills, and so on. I wore a pair of experimental infantry combat boots made by the Brown Shoe Company in Moberly and carried a copy of John Hersey's *A Bell for Adano*. I was assigned to the cabin ordinarily reserved for *Augusta*'s skipper. Courtney Hodges and the rest of the First Army staff boarded the newly commissioned amphibious command ship, U.S.S. *Achernar*. We visited that ship later in the day. Hansen noted that the staff looked "quite warlike" in battle dress; that Hodges, cigarette in a holder pointed at a jaunty angle, "was grinning like a youngster." We had some ice cream and drew some French francs. I added a franc note to my prized short snorter, collecting signatures and giving them out in return. Aboard the *Achernar,* we learned the weather was making up unfavorably for our enterprise.

On Sunday, June 4, the weather in Plymouth harbor was foul: soupy and wet. Bill Kean came into my cabin with bad news: Ike, who was at Portsmouth, had postponed D-day twenty-four hours to June 6. A storm was raking the Channel. The weather forecasts were not encouraging. Later in the evening, I went ashore for a conference with Rear Admiral Alan R. Kirk, U.S. Navy commander for the Western Task Force of Overlord, Major General Ralph Royce, deputy commander of the U.S. Ninth Air Force (our tactical air support), and other officials, to help formulate a recommendation to Ike. We grappled with the many imponderables: tide, moon, weather, daylight hours. Our recommendation to Ike (via Kirk to Admiral Ramsay) was that if we couldn't go on June 6, we'd prefer June 8 or 9 in preference to a longer delay.[7]

When I awoke in my cabin on the *Augusta* on the morning of June 5, there was a teletype message from Ike: "D-day stands as is, Tuesday, June 6." Later in the day the *Augusta* got under way and we steamed out into the channel to assume our position in the escort of the twenty-one convoys headed for Omaha and Utah beaches. We were merely one of an estimated 5,000 ships that would participate in the Overlord invasion. The weather was terrible—seemingly too foul for our purposes. I crawled into my bunk at eleven that evening for four hours of fitful sleep.

As in the Sicily invasion, I was beset by a small but painful physical problem, this time in a different location. A monstrous boil arose on my nose. It was so painful I had to have it lanced in the infirmary. The Navy medic insisted that to prevent further infection I must wear a bandage for several days. I complied, lest this minor problem grow into a serious one that might incapacitate me. But I felt ridiculous with that big bandage on my nose—and told Chet Hansen to ban all photographers from taking my picture.[8]

At 0335, June 6, *Augusta*'s clanging bells called the ship to general quarters. I went to the dimmed-out bridge. Hansen, it seems, recorded my every movement, but tactfully omitted my unsightly nose: "He is now on the bridge—a familiar figure in his OD's, with the Moberly infantry boots, an OD shirt, combat jacket, steel helmet, covered this time by a Mae West that hangs around his shoulders. He smiles very lightly as though it is good to be nearer the coast of France and get the invasion under way. The waiting was difficult, and the moments of decision on postponement were telling on the other commanders. Bradley, however, does not reveal any concern or worry whatsoever. He looks quite optimistic about the entire operation."[9]

Appearances can be deceiving. I was far from optimistic. We were going up against the first team. To make matters worse, last-minute intelligence had revealed that part of that first team—the 352nd Division—had moved into the Omaha Beach area on training maneuvers. Owing to this unlucky turn, Omaha was bound to be bloody.[10]

PART THREE

★★★★★

THE WAR ON THE CONTINENT

TWENTY-SEVEN

The first Allied troops to set foot on French soil were our airborne forces. They came in the dark and early hours by parachute and glider. There were 24,000 of them—16,000 American and 8,000 British—lifted by an armada of 1,000 aircraft. The American 82nd and 101st Airborne divisions were to land behind Utah Beach; the British 6th Airborne Division at key positions near Caen on the Orne River. Owing to the foul weather and the anxiety and inexperience of some transport pilots, most of the American paratroopers were scattered far and wide of their objectives. Only a few units were able to organize and fight as planned. However, the sudden presence of 24,000 paratroopers behind the Atlantic Wall in Normandy created immense confusion and fear among the German defenders, and that alone justified their employment. Many brave roving paratroopers assembled into guerrilla bands and inflicted heavy casualties on the enemy on D-day and thereafter. Some units or bands captured and valiantly held key objectives—bridges, roads, enemy strongpoints—greatly disrupting German countermeasures. Total American paratrooper casualties were 2,500, or less than 15 percent, far less than the disastrous 50 to 70 percent predicted by Leigh-Mallory.[1]

Next came the U.S. infantry at Omaha and Utah beaches. Sunrise was at 0558; H-hour at 0630.

As we faced France, Utah Beach—Joe Collins' VII Corps objective —lay to our right, or west. At 0405, in utter darkness, the men of Ray Barton's unblooded 4th Division began climbing into the landing craft, the gallant Teddy Roosevelt in the lead. Because of our fear of big German coastal artillery, the landing craft were launched eleven and a half miles from the beach! In the vanguard was a wave of eight LCT's transporting thirty-two new "secret weapons" on which we were counting heavily. These were Sherman tanks equipped with flotation gear and a boat screw somewhat akin to our "duck" trucks. They were to be launched at sea and "swim" ashore, to provide our troops instant "artillery" on the beach. Later, additional DD's would be landed directly on the beach by LST's.*

As the landing craft embarked on the long, fearful trip to Utah Beach, air and naval forces commenced a softening up of the beach fortifications. Some 360 American medium bombers attacked Utah Beach, but the heavy overcast thwarted their aim. Official Army historian Gordon A. Harrison reported accurately that "on the whole the bombing achieved little." The naval warships standing off Utah Beach opened fire at 0536 and for fifty minutes blasted the enemy fortifications with every gun that would reach. Rocket-equipped LCT's delivered 5,000 five-inch rockets onto the beaches just ahead of the leading boat wave. The naval bombardment at Utah was highly effective, naval historian Morison wrote. During the remainder of the day, warships continued to fire at targets of opportunity. The aged *Nevada* even destroyed a group of German tanks.

The invasion force at Utah Beach was lucky in one respect. As the landing craft neared the shore, they fell in the lee of Cape Barfleur. Closer to shore, where the DD's were to be launched, the water was less rough. The DD's rolled off the LCT's and plopped into the water without foundering. One LCT struck a mine, blew up and sank with its four DD's, but the other twenty-eight DD's swam ashore without undue difficulty. Swarms of ducks carrying 105-mm artillery also had the advantage of relatively calm water. Thus the assault waves at Utah Beach were backed by both tanks and artillery.

Utah Beach was defended by one regiment of the German 709th Division, a "static" (non-mobile) outfit composed of reservists and foreign volunteers, many of them anti-communist Russians from the Republic of Georgia. American paratroopers inland had cut their communication lines and they were unable to sound an alert. They effectively raked the landing craft that came into their field of fire, but quickly surrendered in close combat. By a lucky accident, the Navy put our infantry ashore on the wrong beach, beyond reach of the most telling enemy gun emplacements. Led by Teddy Roosevelt, the initial waves of infantry quickly readjusted to the mistake, overwhelmed the lackluster defenders and struck inland to link up with some paratroopers who were holding key positions. By the end of the day, 23,000 men had landed at Utah Beach. The 4th Division

* The DD's had been conceived by an engineer, Nicholas Straussler, and enthusiastically embraced by British tanker pioneer Percy Hobart. After Ike and I had tested the DD's, we were also enthusiastic and ordered some 300 new Shermans converted to DD's. Hobart had also conceived and offered to us several other "funny tanks" for special uses: the "crab," equipped with flailing arms to beat paths through minefields; the "crocodile," equipped with a flamethrower; and the ARVE, a multipurpose tank that could be fitted with a mortar or small bridge-laying equipment or fascines for filling tank traps. All the "funnies" except the crab were converted British Churchill tanks. Since accepting the Churchills would require retraining our tank operators and maintenance men and a complicated separate supply chain for spare parts, we declined. Had the "funnies" been conceived earlier, in time to adapt their gadgetry to Sherman tanks, we would have probably made use of them.[2]

had pushed six miles inland. Casualties were gratifyingly light: 197. Utah Beach was a piece of cake.

Omaha Beach, however, was a nightmare. Even now it brings pain to recall what happened there on June 6, 1944. I have returned many times to honor the valiant men who died on that beach. They should never be forgotten. Nor should those who lived to carry the day by the slimmest of margins. Every man who set foot on Omaha Beach that day was a hero.

Fearing enemy shore batteries, our invasion fleet anchored twelve miles off the coast. One of these rumored coastal batteries, on Pointe du Hoe, was of gravest concern. French intelligence agents had reported it consisted of six French 155-mm guns with a range of 25,000 yards (about twelve nautical miles). We had assigned two Ranger battalions under Lieutenant Colonel James E. Rudder, a Texas rancher, to land, scale the high cliffs and destroy the guns. Rudder's men would be supported by destroyers operating close to the beach. His mission was deemed vital. Properly manned, those six monstrous guns by themselves could fatally wreck our invasion forces.

In our open roadstead, we were exposed to the full fury of the boisterous channel weather. Waves three to six feet slapped at the warships and transports. The launching of landing craft in total darkness was difficult and perilous. Climbing into those bobbing craft with heavy gear, our infantrymen were soon miserable: wet, cold and seasick. The sixteen LCT's carrying the sixty-four DD tanks to the east and west beach sectors wallowed heavily and clumsily in the seas. The seamen in charge of landing the west sector's thirty-two DD's wisely decided it was too rough to launch at sea and landed twenty-eight directly on the beach. But twenty-nine of the thirty-two east sector DD's were launched two and a half miles off the beach. All but two foundered in heavy seas. Three others were landed directly on the beach, for a total of five. Most of the dozens of ducks transporting the 105-mm artillery likewise foundered. Result: only half the DD's and a few artillery pieces reached Omaha Beach.

The naval and air forces commenced softening up the beach at 0550. First came the terrific (and reassuring) salvos from the warships. This bombardment went on for a solid thirty-five minutes. During it, commencing at 0600, some 480 U.S. B-24 heavy bombers dropped 1,285 tons (2.5 million pounds) of bombs. Historian Morison judged that the naval bombardment, though brief, was highly effective, probably reducing enemy resistance by "half to three quarters." The aerial bombardment, as at Utah Beach, was completely ineffective. Owing in part to poor flying weather, the 2.5 million pounds of bombs fell inland of Omaha Beach, killing some French civilians and many cattle, but few Germans.

Omaha Beach was normally defended by a regiment of the static 716th German Division, which was no better than the German regiment at Utah

Beach. But, as I mentioned, the 716th had been reinforced by elements of the crack mobile 352nd Division, one regiment at the beach defenses, two regiments only a few miles away at Bayeux. The regiment of the static 716th Division at Omaha Beach had actually been incorporated into the command structure of the 352nd Division. Thus at Omaha Beach we faced better than two regiments of German troops, many of them first-line.

The beach fortifications and terrain were formidable. There were three well-placed rows of underwater steel or concrete obstacles, most of them mined. At low tide—when we intended to land the assault forces—the beach itself was two hundred yards wide with no cover. Then came a low seawall. Beyond that were sand dunes and bluffs, slashed by five widely spaced draws which we intended to use as exit roads from the beach. All the draws were heavily covered by enemy gun emplacements, and the area between the seawall and cliffs and dunes was sown with thousands of mines. In addition, the Germans had cleverly concealed concrete gun emplacements in the bluffs so as to enfilade almost the entire length of the beach.

Omaha Beach, then, was truly an Atlantic Wall. Historian Morison wrote: "Altogether, the Germans had provided the best imitation of hell for an invading force that American troops had encountered anywhere. Even the Japanese defenses of Iwo Jima, Tarawa and Peleliu are not to be compared to these."

At 0630, the first waves of Gerow's V Corps infantry hit Omaha Beach, most in the wrong places. These were assault elements of the 116th Regiment of Charles Gerhardt's 29th Division and the 16th Regiment of Huebner's Big Red One, plus specially trained engineers to blow the underwater obstacles. All men instantly came under a hurricane of enemy machine-gun, mortar and artillery fire. Dozens died or fell wounded, many drowning in the sea. A majority of the demolition engineers became instant casualties, although a few managed to blow several paths through the underwater obstacles. There was no cover. The men lay in the sand or shallow water, unable to return fire, or crouched behind stranded landing craft. Most of the DD's were knocked out. There was no artillery. For several hours, the beach and the water just beyond was a bloody chaos.

We were fortunate in some respects. The Luftwaffe in Normandy had been utterly crushed or forced to retreat to distant bases. We had complete air supremacy. No German aircraft interfered in any significant way with our operations at Utah and Omaha beaches on D-day. Nor did the German Navy. Some U- and E-boats were ordered to attack us, but these were deflected with ease. Nor were the V-1s or V-2s ready in time. None was fired against us. Rudder's Rangers—in one of the great heroic feats of D-day—scaled the Pointe du Hoe cliffs and found the six monstrous guns there were dummies—telephone poles! Later, Rudder's men located four of the six guns in a field behind the point and spiked them with grenades.

Omaha Beach remained a bloodbath for too long. Six hours after the landings we held only ten yards of beach. Not until the principal commanders got ashore did the men begin to move toward the cover of the seawall and bluffs. These gallant officers were Brigadier General Norman D. Cota, assistant division commander of the 29th (a good friend and onetime member of my weapons section at Fort Benning); Colonel Charles D. W. Canham, commanding the 116th Infantry; and Colonel George A. Taylor, commanding the 16th Infantry. Cota was a fearless example to every man on the beach as he calmly strode about giving sensible orders. Taylor shouted to his men, "They're killing us here! Let's move inland and get killed!" Cota yelled, "Two kinds of people are staying on this beach, the dead and those who are going to die. Now let's get the hell out of here." Men who were able dashed for the seawall through murderous fire. Hundreds more soldiers of the 18th and 115th Infantry came behind, disgorging from the landing craft. Everywhere courage and valor were commonplace. Slowly, almost imperceptibly, our foothold increased.[3]

Here I must give unstinting praise to the U.S. Navy. As on Sicily, the Navy saved our hides. Twelve destroyers moved in close to the beach, heedless of shallow water, mines, enemy fire and other obstacles, to give us close support. The main batteries of these gallant ships became our sole artillery. Huebner's chief of staff, Stanhope B. Mason, later wrote, "I am now firmly convinced that our supporting naval fire got us in; that without that gunfire we positively could not have crossed the beaches." When he got ashore that night to establish his V Corps command posts, Gee Gerow's first message to me was emotional: "Thank God for the U.S. Navy!"

The whole of D-day was for me a time of grave personal anxiety and frustration. I was stuck on the *Augusta*. Our communications with the forces assaulting Omaha Beach were thin to nonexistent. From the few radio messages that we overheard and the firsthand reports of observers in small craft reconnoitering close to shore, I gained the impression that our forces had suffered an irreversible catastrophe, that there was little hope we could force the beach. Privately, I considered evacuating the beachhead and directing the follow-up troops to Utah Beach or the British beaches. Chet Hansen recorded that I later remarked to Monty, "Someday I'll tell General Eisenhower just how close it was those first few hours." I agonized over the withdrawal decision, praying that our men could hang on.[4]

They did—barely. Then at 1:30 P.M. I received a heartening message from Gerow: "Troops formerly pinned down on beaches . . . advancing up heights behind beaches." I sent my chief of staff, Bill Kean, and Chet Hansen to the beach for a firsthand look. Their report was more optimistic than I dared hope for. The situation everywhere on the beach was still grave, but our troops had forced one or two of the draws and were inching inland. Based on their report, I gave up any thought of abandoning Omaha Beach.

By nightfall, the situation had swung in our favor. Personal heroism and the U.S. Navy had carried the day. We had by then landed close to 35,000 men and held a sliver of corpse-littered beach five miles long and about one and a half miles deep. To wrest that sliver from the enemy had cost us possibly 2,500 casualties. (No exact accounting has ever been arrived at.) There was now no thought of giving it back.

I had often agonized over assigning green troops to spearhead the Omaha Beach assault: Gerow and his V Corps headquarters, Gerhardt and his 29th Division. That was why I had made the decision to add elements of Huebner's battle-hardened Big Red One. As in the Sicily assault, the Big Red One once more bore the brunt of the enemy's fury. But I thanked God the division was there.

In the British sector, owing to reefs and foul ground, Monty's Second Army under Miles Dempsey had to land on a flood tide an hour to an hour and a half after we landed. This gift of time enabled the warships of the Royal Navy to deliver Monty's beaches a two-hour daylight bombardment, nearly four times as long as the naval bombardment at Omaha. To this was added a massive attack by British heavy bombers. The combined sea and air attacks in the British sector were far more effective than those in the American sector.

Dempsey had three divisions to our two, and thus three landing beaches. These were, from west to east: Gold, Juno and Sword. Each of these three British landings was far less arduous and bloody than Omaha. The British sector was defended by men of the 716th Division, composed of many Poles and Ukrainians. The British 50th Division, landing its DD's on Gold Beach, quickly overran the lackluster defenses, pushed four miles inland, but failed to reach its D-day objective, Bayeux. In the center, the Canadian 3rd Division, at Juno Beach, lost eight DD's in rough seas, but the assault forces overran the defenses and also penetrated about four miles inland. Some Canadian armored patrols reached the vital Bayeux-Caen road. At Sword, the British 3rd Division lost twenty-eight of its forty DD's in pitching seas, but the remaining twelve knocked out German gun positions on the beach, enabling the division to overrun the enemy. The division also pushed four miles inland, linking up with the British 6th Parachute Division along the Orne River, but it failed to take its D-day objective, Caen. In sum, Dempsey landed 75,000 British and Canadian troops and 8,000 paratroopers on D-day. He suffered about 3,000 casualties, one-third of these Canadians.

Fortunately, German reaction to our invasion was confused, indecisive and obstructed by bureaucratic red tape. None of the top German commanders expected an invasion in such poor weather. In fact, Rommel had gone to his home in Germany to visit his wife on her birthday. Most of the German Seventh Army division commanders were at Rennes for war games. Of the senior German commanders, only von Rundstedt was at his command post.

When word of the widespread airborne assault reached von Rundstedt in the early hours, he realized at once that something out of the ordinary was afoot. Whether or not it was the real invasion or a Dieppe-like hit-and-run operation was immaterial to him. He perceived that so large-scale an airborne operation would require a substantial amphibious assault for link-up. He at once placed all German troops in Normandy on "highest alert." He correctly guessed that Caen was the logical target for the amphibious assault. He ordered Rommel's 21st Panzer Division, near Caen, to move up and repulse any attackers.

At the same time, still in the early hours, he ordered two divisions of the 1st SS Panzer Corps near Chartres to prepare to move toward Caen. These were the 12th SS (sixty-five miles from Caen) and the Lehr Panzer Division (eighty-five miles from Caen). These two panzer divisions would give von Rundstedt a total of three to repel the invaders on the beaches. But bureaucratic indifference and stupidity thwarted him. Berlin Army headquarters refused von Rundstedt permission to commit these divisions without Hitler's direct approval. Hitler, away at his Bavarian mountain retreat, Berchtesgaden, had stayed up late the night before. No one dared wake him up. Von Rundstedt had full authority to call Hitler direct, but he declined to do so. Twelve crucial hours ticked by. Not until four o'clock on D-day afternoon did von Rundstedt receive permission to bring up the other two panzer divisions. By that time the skies had cleared and Allied air was overhead in force, compelling the Germans to postpone movement of the divisions until nightfall, when Allied air was blind.

That left only the 21st Panzer Division to deal with the British and Canadian forces advancing on Caen. In Rommel's absence, his chief of staff, Hans Speidel, directed its operations on D-day. He assigned half its infantry to fight the British airborne troops on the east side of the Orne River, the other half to support the 716th Division in beach defense. At noon, he ordered the division to regroup and cross the Orne to the west and position itself due north of Caen to attack the oncoming British and Canadians. Owing to the congestion in Caen and the lack of bridges, the division did not reach attack position until four o'clock in the afternoon. The attack—the only large-scale German counterattack on D-day—was met by the British 3rd Division and it failed. But the panzers dug in and denied the British Caen.

In subsequent days, after I had had an opportunity to study Dempsey's D-day operation, I was keenly disappointed. The British had thrown one airborne and three infantry divisions—83,000 men—at the Bayeux-

Caen objectives, against slight or indifferent opposition, excepting the 21st Panzer Division, which consisted of 15,000 men, and some reserve elements of the 352nd Division, perhaps 3,000 men, which were directed against the British emerging from Gold Beach. Until noon, the 21st Panzer was engaged at the Orne River, leaving the northern and northeastern approaches to Caen virtually wide open. A bolder, faster thrust by the British 3rd and the Canadian 3rd Division would certainly have gained Caen and, with the help of the 6th Parachute Division, might have led to encirclement and annihilation of the 21st Panzer Division. Historian Liddell Hart blamed the missed opportunity on "the excessive caution of the commanders on the spot—at a time when there was hardly anything to stop them."[5]

Even the official British Army historian was critical. In summing up British and Canadian operations for the day, he concluded:

> The operations of all three divisions had made a good start but had subsequently developed too slowly for the main (and perhaps over-ambitious) object to be *fully* realized—namely, the capture of Bayeux and the road to Caen, the seizure of Caen itself and the safeguarding of the Allies' left flank with a bridgehead east of the Orne. Partly this was due to physical cause—the unexpectedly high tide and the resulting congestion on the shore which delayed the start of the advance inland. Partly it was due to the strength of the opposition at certain points and to the fact that the 21st Panzer Division had time to intervene. But partly it was also due to the pace at which the assault divisions' operations were carried out. Caen is eight miles from the coast from which the attack was launched and Bayeux six or seven. There was no possibility of taking them that day unless the advance was made as rapidly as possible, and at times there was little evidence of the urgency which would have to characterize operations if they were to succeed fully.[6]

In sum, the British and Canadian assault forces sat down. They had Caen within their grasp and let it slip away. Weeks would pass before Caen fell. In failing to take Caen on D-day, Monty likewise lost the opportunity of having his tanks "knock about" near Falaise, as he had boasted. Not for a long time was he able to deliver the real estate south and east of Caen to the airmen for airfields. Monty then and later in his memoirs blithely dismissed these failures, but he had severely disappointed Supreme Headquarters and me. The "new" bold Monty of the St. Paul's schoolroom was gone. The old cautious, methodical Monty was back.

In spite of these tactical failures and our own, D-day was, on the whole, an Allied triumph on a magnificent scale. We had smashed through and over the Atlantic Wall to land over 156,000 men on French soil at a total cost of perhaps 8,000 killed, wounded and missing. Our foothold was, in some areas, still precarious; but Rommel's strategy of repulsing us on the beaches had failed abysmally. We were resolved to stay. And behind us came a follow-up force of men and supplies that would insure that resolve.

Hitler and his generals had one last chance to defeat us. The nineteen divisions of the Fifteenth Army in the Pas de Calais (120 miles away) and von Rundstedt's five panzer divisions of armored reserve were still uncommitted. Had Hitler thrown these forces against us within the first few days or within the first week, he might well have overwhelmed us. But Hitler had now rejected his own intuition that Normandy was the likely main invasion area. Like von Rundstedt, he now believed Pas de Calais was the primary Allied objective, that our operation in Normandy was a feint. Perhaps influenced by the Fortitude deceivers, he kept the Fifteenth German Army at Pas de Calais waiting for George Patton's mythical First Army Group to storm ashore.

TWENTY-EIGHT

Early on the morning of June 7, Monty came alongside the *Augusta* in a British destroyer. I went aboard the destroyer for a brief conference. Monty was gravely concerned about our heavy V Corps losses at Omaha, our slim toehold on Normandy and the ten-mile gap that still existed between Gerow's V Corps and Collins' VII Corps at Utah and the gap between American and British forces. A major counterattack through one of these gaps by the Germans could be disastrous. Accordingly, we agreed to a minor modification of the Overlord plan.

The original plan called for Collins' VII Corps to drive southwest across the Cotentin Peninsula, seal it off, then wheel north and take the port of Cherbourg as quickly as possible, ignoring his left flank. Monty and I decided to secure a link-up of V and VII Corps at Carentan as quickly as possible and at the same time a link-up of U.S. and British forces. My deputy army commander, Courtney Hodges, would oversee the V-VII Corps link-up, leaving Collins a free hand to plan and execute the drive on Cherbourg. Monty no longer talked of his tanks knocking about at Falaise; Bayeux would fall that day, but he clearly had a tough fight on his hands for Caen. That morning, the 12th SS and the Lehr Panzer Division had reinforced the 21st Panzer.[1]

After Monty departed, I went ashore on Omaha Beach to confer with Gerow about the modification to the plan. Omaha was still chaotic, littered with the dead and wounded and the horrible wreckage of war. As I hitchhiked my way up the bluffs, I tried my best to smile, to give encouragement to the exhausted, long-faced troops. I found Gerow at Huebner's advanced CP. The Big Red One had mauled the German 352nd Division on the beachhead (mercifully sparing us a counterattack). We were firmly rooted in France and slowly enlarging our toehold, but there was still a grave shortage of artillery, ammunition, tanks and vehicles of every kind. The confusion and jam-up on the beach caused the unloading of Navy supply ships to come to a dangerous standstill. After conferring with Gerow and Huebner, I returned to the *Augusta*.

At 11:00 A.M., Ike arrived alongside in the British minelayer *Apollo*. I went aboard for a conference. A smiling Ike helped me up the boarding ladder. What ensued was an almost exact replay of Ike's D-plus-1 visit with Patton at Sicily. He jumped all over me for not sending him progress reports on D-day. He'd been in the dark again, unable to brief the Combined Chiefs. I was stung—and inwardly boiled—because I had faithfully reported to Ike almost hourly. Later investigation discovered that my frequent messages to Ike, properly routed through Monty's headquarters, had bogged down in Monty's cipher room. The encoded radio traffic had fallen twelve hours behind schedule.[2]

I briefed Ike as fully as I was able on D-day operations and what was happening ashore at that moment. I did not reveal how close I had come to evacuating Omaha Beach. I also told him of the modification in the battle plan Monty and I had agreed to earlier in the day. Ike had little to say beyond the petty carping about the lack of messages from me. I returned to the *Augusta;* Ike went on to visit the British sector and to hold a shipboard conference with Monty. On the whole, Ike's visit had been perhaps necessary for his own personal satisfaction, but from my point of view it was a pointless interruption and annoyance.

In the afternoon, the *Augusta* moved to Utah Beach and I went ashore to visit Joe Collins. I found his command post but, typically, Collins was at the front. His 4th Division had encountered stiff resistance beyond the beachhead; the link-ups with the scattered elements of the 82nd and 101st had not yet been fully realized. I explained the modified plan—the need to join the V and VII Corps at Carentan—to the deputy corps commander, Eugene M. Landrum. I visited Ray Barton at the 4th Division CP, some wounded in an evacuation hospital, then returned to the *Augusta*.[3]

The following day, June 8, I again visited Omaha Beach, but that day my mind frequently turned to my family. That was the day Lee and Hal Beukema (both only twenty years old) were married in the West Point chapel. Hal had graduated high in his class two days before—on D-day—and had chosen the Air Corps. In my absence, an old friend, Colonel Harris Jones, who graduated number one in the Class of April 1917, and who was then head of the West Point mathematics department, gave Lee away. Among those who attended the wedding and reception was the radio broadcaster Mary Margaret McBride, who had been a sorority sister of Mary's at the University of Missouri. She made a special report for me and sent it along through NBC channels.

After the wedding, Mary surrendered her room at West Point's Thayer Hotel and moved to an apartment on Connecticut Avenue in Washington, D.C. Having no need for a car, she loaned our Buick to Lee and Hal for the duration. Hal entered Air Corps flight training and upon completion of the usual preliminary courses was assigned to advanced training in the Air Corps' newest and most powerful aircraft, the B-29 heavy bomber.[4]

German reaction to our Normandy landings now began to intensify. Hitler, von Rundstedt and Rommel remained convinced that Pas de Calais was the main Allied target, that Normandy was a feint, and kept the Fifteenth Army rooted there. But as the growing scale of our "feint" became apparent, the Germans were ever more determined to deny us Caen and Cherbourg and, if possible, to destroy us without a large-scale commitment of forces. Erwin Rommel was the chief architect of the German reaction. Given the limitations, it was skillfully conducted.

In German eyes, Caen became the decisive battleground, literally and symbolically. Caen lay 120 air miles due west of Paris. The terrain between those cities was ideal for tank operations. A breakthrough at Caen might imperil Paris, with all that implied. Thus the three panzer divisions, and later additional infantry, were sent to Caen.

But in Rommel's mind, Cherbourg, too, loomed large. It was the finest port in Normandy, obviously a prime Allied military objective. Denied Cherbourg, the Allies would be forced to carry on the laborious work of hauling supplies in over the difficult and vulnerable beachheads, exposed to weather. Accordingly, Rommel in a bold gamble stripped Brittany of the 17th SS Panzer Grenadiers, the 77th Infantry and the 3rd Parachute Division and hurried them over to block our drive in the Cotentin Peninsula. The movement of these three divisions was slowed by intense Allied air attacks but most arrived substantially intact to join the 91st Infantry Division and surviving elements of the 352nd Division. These five divisions —plus remnants of the static divisions—composed the bulk of our opposition, and tough opposition it would be.[5]

By Friday, June 9, we were sufficiently entrenched on French soil to justify moving First Army headquarters ashore. My staff chose an apple orchard behind Pointe du Hoe. There we set up a small tent city. My living and working quarters were primitive—GI issue for the field. But my headquarters commandant insisted on one amenity: a portable enclosed one-man latrine, about the size of a telephone booth. They would faithfully transport this Chick Sale all through Europe.[6]

Among those at First Army headquarters, few invited more curiosity among the uninitiated than the Ultra specialists. These were the British radiomen who received and sent messages to and from Bletchley Park and the First Army Ultra rep, Adolph Rosengarten, who, in collaboration with our G-2 Monk Dickson, distilled the output from the Park. Utilizing this information, and other intelligence, Dickson briefed me twice daily and kept my German Order of Battle maps continuously updated. The Ultra and G-2 tents (later vans) were closely guarded and off limits to all but a few.

The most important Ultra contribution in the first few days in Normandy, Rosengarten later wrote, "was information indicating the arrival of German reinforcements." Rosengarten went on: "Initially we learned from Ultra of the movement, mostly from Brittany, of formations under control of the German Seventh Army." These were the aforementioned 17th SS Panzer Grenadiers, the 77th and the 3rd Parachute Division. Ultra gave us ample notice of their forthcoming arrival.[7]

I left the *Augusta* and moved ashore on the morning of June 10. That same day Monty called me to his CP near Port-en-Bessin for a conference. By that time, Gerow and Collins had substantially enlarged our beachhead, and forces of both corps were converging on Carentan for a link-up that afternoon. I unfolded my map cases and proudly displayed our position to Monty and his staff. Chet Hansen wrote that Monty's staffers had "never lost their superior opinions of their own arms," but "stood amazed at the incredible progress we have made after the difficulty of those initial landings." Monty told me he was quite pleased with our progress.[8]

Monty's situation before Caen was still about the same: little or no progress. To make matters worse, Ultra had revealed that von Rundstedt had ordered three more armored divisions to Caen (for a total of six). Monty had conceived a plan to encircle or outflank Caen before these reinforcements arrived. In support of this plan, Gerow's V Corps was to push south toward Caumont. The British 7th Armored Division—the famous Desert Rats—would come ashore to spearhead this attack on V Corps' left flank; the British 1st Airborne Division might be lifted from England to join in. It was an impressive plan. However, the Germans resisted fiercely, the plan failed and once again Caen eluded Monty.[9]

On Monday, June 12, American forces overran Carentan; V and VII Corps linked up and closed the gap. Pete Corlett's XIX Corps began to land and reinforce the weak seam between V and VII Corps.

That same day, the Normandy invasion beaches were invaded from the rear by sightseeing dignitaries. Prime Minister Churchill and Alan Brooke came over by destroyer to visit Monty and Dempsey. The U.S. Joint Chiefs—Marshall, King, Arnold—escorted by Ike, came to Omaha Beach in the destroyer *Thompson*. I met them at the beach and escorted them to my CP, where we briefed and fed them a lunch of C rations and hardtack biscuits. Hodges, Gerow, Collins and Corlett were present.[10]

I had a private chat with Marshall. He was flattering in his praise of our operations. At that time we believed that Hitler would be defeated fairly soon—probably before Christmas. I therefore asked Marshall to keep me in mind for a Pacific command, should the war with Hitler fold up in time.[11]

Marshall, King, Arnold and Ike had scarcely left Normandy when we received an Ultra flash from Bletchley Park which caused gravest concern. One of the units Rommel shifted from Brittany, the 17th SS Panzer Grenadier Division (supported by the 6th Parachute Regiment), was moving up swiftly for an attack on Carentan on the following morning. This was one of the rare times in the war when I unreservedly believed Ultra and reacted to it tactically. Carentan had been seized by Max Taylor's 101st Airborne Division. Taylor had few heavy weapons with which to blunt a tank attack. A determined German breakthrough at Carentan would split the new seam at V Corps and VII Corps and perhaps thrust to the beaches, with catastrophic results.

I hurriedly wrote Gee Gerow a two-page note ordering him to shift a battalion of tanks and a battalion of armored infantry, both from the newly arrived "Hell on Wheels" 2nd Armored Division, to the Carentan area, prepared to fight on the following morning. I concluded: "Sorry to have to bother you but consider this highly important." Chet Hansen hand-delivered the message and returned it to my personal files. Gerow was reluctant to denude the 2nd Armored, but he sent an armored task force under Maurice Rose, a veteran of North Africa and Sicily. The Germans attacked Carentan exactly as Ultra had forecast. Max Taylor and Rose were able to throw them back with heavy losses.[12]

This transfer of armor, in turn, seriously weakened our line near Caumont. Huebner's Big Red One had linked up with the British 50th Division at the U.S.-British boundary line and then pushed ahead to support the abortive British 7th Armored Division attack on Villers-Bocage. The failure of that attack and withdrawal of the 7th Armored had left the Big Red One in an exposed position at Caumont. The newly arrived 2nd Panzer Division was moving to strike at the U.S.-British seam and Huebner demanded the full power of our 2nd Armored Division to back him up. However, Monty corrected the weakness by shifting elements of the British 7th Armored Division onto Huebner's immediate left flank, closing the gap and tightening the seam.[13]

These important tactical maneuvers thwarted Rommel's best opportunity to drive a wedge between U.S. and British forces. In the next few days, additional U.S. and British divisions came ashore to buttress the bridgeheads. With their arrival, there was no longer any way Rommel could eject us with the limited German forces committed to Normandy. Ultra had played an important, but not decisive, role in blunting Rommel's best effort.

TWENTY-NINE

Monty's failure to take Caen—let alone stage a tank knockabout at Falaise—was beginning to rankle Ike and his staff, especially the airmen who were anxiously awaiting the gift of land south of Caen for airfields. The failure of the enveloping offensive through Villers-Bocage by the Desert Rats was especially tough to swallow. Now a total of six panzer divisions had massed along Monty's front. Drawing these divisions to Monty had been part of Overlord strategy, leaving me free to wheel. But not *before* Monty had taken Caen and the area south of it. He had been hemmed into much too small a beachhead for proper maneuver and denied the key roads that were essential for modern warfare.

Another cause for concern was that Hitler had at last unleashed his V-1 cruise missiles. On the night of June 12-13, four fell near London, killing four persons and wounding nine. This was not an impressive start, but the attack was renewed, and by June 16, 244 V-1s had been fired at London. The missile assault came as a rude shock to Londoners, who believed the war was all but over. We continued to exaggerate in our minds the potential of the weapon. We became gravely concerned about its possible effectiveness in a congested beachhead like Monty's. A great proportion of Leigh-Mallory's Overlord air power was diverted to attack the V-1 launching sites, which, Ike ruled, would take precedence over everything except the battlefields. It was no time for shilly-shallying at Caen.[1]

Monty conceived yet another all-out drive on Caen to commence on June 17. This struck Ike as a leisurely pace to fight the war. On June 15, Butcher logged: "Last night Ike was concerned that Monty couldn't attack until Saturday. Ike was anxious that the Germans be kept off balance and that our drive never stop. But apparently Monty wants to tidy up his 'administrative tail' and get plenty of supplies on hand before he makes a general attack." Ike was then dismayed to learn that Monty delayed the offensive yet another forty-eight hours, until June 19. The day before, Ike goaded Monty: "I can well understand that you have needed to accumulate reasonable amounts of artillery ammunition but I am in high hopes that once the attack starts it will have a momentum that will carry it a long ways. . . . I thoroughly believe you are going to crack the enemy a good one.''[2]

No such luck. On the morning Monty's offensive was to begin, a gale raked the channel. The thirty-five-mile-per-hour winds wrecked the gigantic prefabricated artificial harbors (mulberries) we had erected and drove some 800 vessels up onto the beaches. The storm greatly disrupted our unloading and supply operations. I was compelled to severely ration ammunition supplies. Monty postponed his Caen offensive until he could be certain of his supply tail and the arrival of a new corps.

The storm damage to our mulberries made it more imperative than ever that we take Cherbourg as soon as possible. With the front at Caumont and Carentan stabilized for the moment, I gave nearly my full attention to the Cherbourg campaign. It turned out to be one of the classic actions of the war.

I assigned four divisions to Collins for the Cherbourg campaign: Barton's 4th, Ridgway's 82nd and two divisions recently arrived from England, Manton Eddy's veteran 9th and Jay W. MacKelvie's 90th. The last division turned out to be one of the worst-trained to arrive in the ETO. I approved Collins' decision to relieve MacKelvie and two of his regimental commanders. MacKelvie, an artillery specialist, had commanded the division only a brief time; its deplorable condition was not his fault. He was relieved without prejudice and sent to Italy. Collins gave the division to his chief of staff, Gene Landrum, a veteran, like Collins, of Pacific combat. Heroic efforts on Landrum's part were unavailing, however. The division remained weak throughout the Cherbourg campaign and later. Collins requested that Ira T. Wyche's newly arrived 79th replace the 90th, and I approved; but the 79th could not be brought into play in time.[3]

Collins jumped off on June 14. His first goal was to drive twenty-five miles west to the Atlantic Coast, sealing off the Cotentin Peninsula. Ridgway's 82nd and Eddy's 9th Division spearheaded the drive, with Landrum's lackluster 90th bringing up the rear. By that time (as we knew from Ultra), Rommel had reinforced the Cotentin with the 77th Division, which joined with elements of the mobile 91st Division and the static 243rd and 709th coastal divisions. At a meeting with von Rundstedt and Rommel near Soissons on June 16, Hitler ordered that the Cotentin and Cherbourg "be held at any cost." But conflicting field orders to the German defenders in the Cotentin resulted in confused and poor defensive deployment. In four days of brilliant maneuver, Joe Collins punched through to the Atlantic Coast at Barneville-sur-Mer.

So far, so good. The second phase of the campaign called for Joe to anchor his line across the Cotentin and swing north to Cherbourg. By that time, a new corps headquarters, the VIII, commanded by a veteran of Sicily and Italy, Troy Middleton, who had so ably served as commander of the 45th Division, had reached France. I gave Middleton's corps the job of holding the anchor line, assigning him the 90th Division and the 82nd and the 101st Airborne. Collins' VII Corps, now consisting of the 4th, 9th and 79th divisions, thrust north from the anchor line on June 19—the day the storm wrecked Omaha Beach. Thereafter, the VII Corps ammunition supply was severely rationed. Because of the shortage, I ordered Troy Middleton to dig in and hold.

Among the regimental commanders in Barton's 4th Division was my classmate James Van Fleet. Van Fleet was another Ridgway, an absolutely superb soldier and leader. He was earning about three Distinguished Service Crosses a day, and I was happy to see that he finally got one, and a British decoration besides. I simply could not understand why Marshall and McNair had not given Van Fleet command of a division; I had to assume that he had a very bad mark in his record or had angered them in some way. In not too long, I found out the answer. Marshall, so forgetful about names, had confused Van Fleet with a man who had a remarkably similar name and a problem with the bottle. Marshall apparently passed the mixup on to McNair. When McNair arrived in France for an inspection, he asked me, "Who's been unusually good?"

"Van Fleet has probably been the most outstanding," I replied.

"It's too bad he has a drinking habit, isn't it?" McNair said.

I exploded in rare profanity. "Jesus Christ! You got the wrong guy. Van Fleet is a teetotaler."

"What!" McNair exclaimed, disbelieving.

"The man you're talking about is ———, not Van Fleet. I know him, too."

I was soon able to right this egregious injustice. I got Van Fleet promoted to brigadier general and later gave him a division. That set him on his way, ultimately to four-star rank.[4]

By the time Collins swung north for Cherbourg, Ultra had given us a good idea of the German Order of Battle. The 30,000 to 40,000 German defenders were in disarray, falling back on Cherbourg helter-skelter. Our best opportunity lay in driving north at such speed as to prevent a consolidation of their defenses. When the Channel storm abated, we launched a massive air and sea bombardment against Cherbourg in support of the VII Corps drive. In four days, Collins was on the outskirts of the city.[5]

On June 24, Ike, delayed by the storm, paid his second visit to France. He came over on the destroyer *Thompson* accompanied by his son Lieutenant John S. D. Eisenhower, who had just graduated from West Point with my new son-in-law Hal Beukema. I met them on chaotic Omaha Beach, which after the storm looked worse than D-day. Ike and John climbed into my jeep. John recalled: "Bradley sounded quite optimistic; I could see why Dad considered him a tower of strength. He was at that time short on artillery ammunition, and every time a C-47 cargo plane flew overhead he would happily remark: 'There come two more tons of ammunition.' "

I had lunch for Ike, another visitor, General Crerar, who would soon land the First Canadian Army in Monty's sector, and Gee Gerow, an old family friend of the Eisenhowers. I was happy to report that Cherbourg would fall within a day or so. But von Rundstedt and Rommel had begun moving in still more reinforcements. There was danger that the Germans might seal us off in the Cotentin Peninsula. Thus our discussions focused on the urgent need to turn Collins around, bring his corps back south to join those of Gerow, Corlett and Middleton, and to launch a massive four-corps American offensive to the south and west—to break out and run.

Ike was moody. Later, privately, he groused about Monty's lack of progress at Caen. Monty's much-vaunted all-out offensive, originally scheduled for June 17, had been repeatedly postponed for various reasons. Now, finally, it was scheduled to commence on the following day, June 25. Ike was most anxious that I take advantage of Monty's thrust to launch an American breakout.[6]

On the following day, as Monty jumped off, Ike wrote me, "I most earnestly hope that you get Cherbourg tomorrow.* As quickly as you have done so we must rush the preparations for the attack to the southward with all possible speed. The enemy is building up and we must not allow him to seal us up in the northern half of the Peninsula. The Second Army attack started this morning and enemy reinforcements should be attracted to that general direction. This gives an opportunity on the West that may not obtain very long. I know that you already have General Montgomery's directive on these matters; all I am saying is that I thoroughly agree with him and know that you will carry out your part of the task with resolution and boldness."

That same day, he wrote Monty: "All the luck in the world to you and Dempsey. Please do not hesitate to make the maximum demands for air assistance that can possibly be useful to you. Whenever there is any legitimate opportunity we must blast the enemy with everything we have. I am hopeful that Bradley can quickly clean up the Cherbourg mess and turn around to attack southward while you have got the enemy by the throat on the east. I am sure that Bradley understands the necessity of hitting hard and incessantly. Again good luck."[7]

Over the years Ike and Bedell Smith have caused historians some confusion—unwittingly, I'm sure. In his final report to the Combined Chiefs, Ike wrote rather carelessly that since "in the east we had been unable to break out toward the Seine" American forces were directed to

* We did.

"smash out" from the west. Bedell Smith, in his book *Eisenhower's Six Great Decisions,* wrote with similar carelessness that since "the massing of opposition against our eastern flank made a breakout at that end of the line improbable" then "changes were needed in the original tactical plan" and that Ike and Monty decided then that "the full weight of the American strength should be used to break out on the right."

These statements foster at least two quite erroneous impressions: That in the original Overlord plan Monty had been expected to "break out" in the east and failed, and after this failure the plan was changed to have me "break out" in the west. I have never been able to understand why Ike and Bedell made those statements. They were both intimately acquainted with the Overlord ground strategy formulated months before. That called for Monty not to "break out" but to hold and draw the Germans to his sector, while I "broke out" in my sector and wheeled to the east. We adhered to that basic concept throughout the Normandy campaign with no major changes in strategy or tactics.[8]

When Monty commenced his offensive, the British sector confronted seven panzer and two infantry divisions. Nonetheless, Monty, exuding confidence, cabled Ike: "I will continue battle on eastern flank until one of us cracks and it will not be us." Monty threw his full weight against the Germans. But it was to no avail. The Germans fought fiercely and even managed a counterattack. Casualties on both sides were heavy. Caen remained in German hands; the British front was becoming dangerously stalemated.[9]

By that time, von Rundstedt and Rommel had concluded that they could not eject the Allies from Normandy with the limited forces at their command. What forces they had—all committed piecemeal—were gradually being chewed up, while the Allied bridgehead continued to swell in numbers of men and equipment. On June 29, von Rundstedt and Rommel met with Hitler at Berchtesgaden to propose a revision in strategy. Generally they favored a withdrawal from the Caen pocket, perhaps as far as the Seine River, and then a regrouping of forces for a war of maneuver, drawing the Allies away from the beachhead (and naval gun support). Hitler adamantly opposed any such withdrawal. His strategy was unchanged: keep the Allies tightly roped into the beachhead by whatever means possible.

When von Rundstedt and Rommel returned to France, they (for reasons never satisfactorily explained) issued orders for their forces to begin a withdrawal according to the plan they had presented to Hitler. When copies of these orders reached Hitler, he instantly countermanded them. He then sent his adjutant to France with a handwritten note to von Rundstedt relieving him of command. On July 3, von Rundstedt was replaced by Field Marshal Guenther von Kluge. Other changes quickly followed, but Rommel retained his command. German defensive strategy in France continued as before.[10]

At the same time, Monty's failure to take Caen had generated terrific heat in London. Both British and American leaders began to express gravest doubts about his generalship. At the forefront of the British scalp hunters was Churchill. Alan Brooke recalled that at a late evening meeting, July 6, Churchill "began to abuse Monty because operations were not going faster, and apparently Eisenhower had said that he was overcautious." Enraged, Alan Brooke leaped to Monty's defense: "I lost my temper and started one of the heaviest thunderstorms that we had had. He was infuriated, and throughout the evening kept shoving his chin out, looking at me and fuming at the accusation that he ran down his generals."[11]

Monty blamed part of his failure on the air forces. He carped that they were "not vigorous enough in support of the immediate battle." This criticism, in turn, infuriated the airmen who were impatiently waiting for Monty to deliver the Caen airfield sites. British Air Chief Marshal Charles Portal, commenting on the British Army's lack of progress, remarked acidly that the problem was Montgomery, who could "neither be removed nor moved" to action. Tedder remarked that "the Army did not seem prepared to fight its own battles," and when Ike asked him what he thought of Monty's plans, he ridiculed them as "company exercises." Tedder recalled that "Mary" Coningham, providing Monty close air support, "continued to be sharply critical of the Army's slow progress."

Ike was "smoldering," Butcher recalled. After conferring with Tedder and Smith, it was agreed that Ike should write Monty a letter telling him, as Tedder recalled, "tactfully to get moving." This long, prodding letter went forward on July 7. In it, Ike said (tactfully): "It appears to me that we must use all possible energy in a determined effort to prevent a stalemate or of facing the necessity of fighting a major defensive battle with the slight depth we now have in the bridgehead." He promised Monty every conceivable backup, including, if necessary, a U.S. armored division.[12]

In the meantime I had been drawing plans for our "breakout" offensive, which I designed to be launched while the enemy was diverted by Monty's June 25 offensive. My plan was bold, ambitious and optimistic. I would employ four corps (V, VII, VIII, IX) composed of about twelve divisions in a massive frontal assault on the enemy lines. My goal was to punch through the crust of enemy defenses, follow up with a powerful fifty-mile blitz southward to Avranches, opening the way for Patton's Third Army to crack into and overrun Brittany, capturing Brest and other seaports. My optimism was reflected by a note in Chet Hansen's diary: "Once the crust goes, we are expected to roll through the stuff easily."

All this was in general accordance with the original Overlord plan. As a courtesy, I submitted the plan to Monty for approval. He suggested no changes.

Unfortunately, my offensive was unavoidably delayed. It took longer to clear up the Cherbourg Peninsula than we hoped, thus delaying the turnaround and redeployment of VII Corps. The 4th Division had sustained 6,000 casualties since D-day; several days were required to infuse its replacements. The storm had delayed the landing of Troy Middleton's VIII Corps divisions. I had hoped to jump off on June 30 but was compelled to postpone the attack to July 3. In explaining the delay, I wrote Ike on June 29: "I am very anxious that when we hit the enemy this time we will hit him with such power that we can keep going and cause him a major disaster. I want to keep going without any appreciable halt until we turn the corner at the base of the Peninsula." Ike was disappointed, but he replied: "I definitely agree with you that your attack must be strong when you start so you can keep going."[13]

Ike was anxious to be on hand for the launching of our breakout but he insisted on a low profile and minimum fuss. He arrived at Omaha Beach on July 1. We housed him in an ordinary field tent near my CP; Chet Hansen had to lend him his shaving kit because Ike's orderly had forgotten his. He slept on a cot garbed in red pajama bottoms, no top, and shaved and bathed like all of us, in cold water. Since we had no special mess as yet, he ate C rations, which were served with a fine bottle of "liberated" French champagne.

The next day Ike and I jeeped to Monty's elaborate CP which he had moved into the U.S. sector, near Bray. Although Caen still lay beyond his grasp, Monty was quite pleased with himself. According to his view of things, everything was "going according to plan." He had drawn the bulk of the German forces into his sector, thus making it easier for the Americans to carry out their task of capturing Cherbourg and launching the wheeling movement. As he saw it, his job now was "to retain the initiative," that is, keep actively punching at the enemy, and "to have no setbacks." His D-day objective, the capture of Caen and the area south, seemed no longer important. He was severely disparaging of the close air support he had been receiving from Coningham.

Ike withheld comment then, but later, in private, he confided to me his disappointment with Monty's progress. He felt the British had sat down again, that Monty should be much more aggressive than he had been. He was much distressed by Monty's criticism of the air support. It was reminiscent of the Coningham–Patton dispute in Tunisia, which had caused Ike so much personal agony.[14]

Another disquieting note arose in this meeting. By that time Hitler was raining V-1s on London, and intelligence was forecasting that the much more formidable V-2s would soon appear. The V-1 casualties were mounting; London officialdom was in near panic. A note in Chet Hansen's diary reflected our concern: "British civilians suffering considerably from results of the things. Communications destroyed. 1500 civilian casualties on June 30 alone. Wearing down on civilian morale, distracting the efficiency of the wartime worker who is bothered by the devices while trying to sleep. Many people now spend their sleeping hours in the shelter. Enormous horizontal blast causes severe breakage in windows, menacing people in buildings and casualties resulting from flying glass are enormous."

Most of the V-1 launching sites were concentrated in the Pas de Calais area. Monty made an offhand proposal—I assume it was offhand—that we, in effect, abandon the Overlord plan and concentrate all our efforts on a drive on Pas de Calais to destroy the launching sites. He would lead the offensive, employing the British Second Army, the U.S. First Army and the Canadian First Army. Ike and I were astonished. Did Monty mean for us to take him seriously?

He did, and on reflection I realized there was far more to the suggestion than met the eye. As Hansen later wrote: "Political considerations are obvious." I did not realize it then, but Monty had made up his mind that he and he alone should command Allied ground forces in Europe. He opposed the approved plan whereby I would soon command U.S. forces on an equal footing with him, and Ike himself would direct land operations through our two army groups.

Monty's suggestion for leading an all-out thrust at Pas de Calais, I believe, grew out of this determination to retain command of all land forces. It meant that I would relinquish command of my First Army to him. When my army group headquarters came ashore, as Hansen so rightly noted in his diary, "we would continue with administrative control while British would retain tactical control." If the thrust at Pas de Calais were successful and the V-1s were wiped out, Monty would probably have been canonized. It would have been difficult if not impossible for me to get back tactical control of the First Army; I would probably have been forced to give Patton's Third Army to Monty as well.

Quite apart from these "political" considerations, the plan was militarily unsound, Pattonesque. Our logistical problems were becoming nearly insurmountable. After August, bad weather would probably prohibit our using our landing beaches for resupply. We desperately needed to take the ports in Brittany; otherwise Cherbourg (when it became operational) would be our sole source of supply. An attack on Pas de Calais would lead to a frontal assault on Hitler's main strength in France, the Fifteenth Army, still rooted there in anticipation of the "main" Allied amphibious assault. Hansen recorded that I was "insistent that we hold to our basic plan." Indeed so. Quite apart from the foregoing considerations, I had drawn one lesson from Africa. American troops should never be placed under direct British control. It had not worked in Africa; it would not work in Europe. I would resist it to my utmost, even to the point of resignation.[15]

Ike was with us for four days, our longest and closest personal association to date. We spent most of that time on ceremonial visits to the four corps headquarters and to seven of the nine divisions then in Normandy. He inspected the captured German defenses at Cherbourg. Elwood R. (Pete) Quesada, the boyish-looking general who so ably commanded our air support, the IX Tactical Air Command, took Ike aloft in a P-51 fighter fixed with a special observer's seat for a sweep over the entire Allied beachhead. Throughout his visit—a much-needed diversion from the pressures of his headquarters—Ike was in high spirits, seemingly having the time of his life.[16]

We launched the breakout on July 3. The four corps were deployed, right to left, facing the enemy: VIII (Middleton), VII (Collins), XIX (Corlett) and V (Gerow). The broad plan was this: Middleton and Collins on the right would deliver the hammer blow in an all-out drive down the west coast of the peninsula toward Avranches; Corlett, operating in more difficult terrain, would take St. Lô in the center; Gerow (at Caumont) would hold at the hub of the wheel, protecting Monty's right flank. If successful, our wheeling movement would threaten the rear of the enemy facing Monty and could lead to encirclement and annihilation of those forces. At the same time, it would provide Patton enough friendly real estate to land his Third Army and crack into Brittany.

Middleton's VIII Corps on the extreme right jumped off first. Middleton commanded three divisions: Ridgway's 82nd, scheduled for imminent withdrawal to England to be replaced by the newly arrived 8th Division, commanded by William C. McMahon; Wyche's 79th; and Landrum's 90th. Ridgway performed magnificently, as usual, but the 79th and 90th divisions were disappointing. When Ike and I visited the 79th Division CP, we found both Wyche and his assistant division commander there. One of them should have been at the front. Hansen noted: "Brad did not like that and it did not set too well with Ike."

Landrum had not yet got the ill-trained 90th Division in fighting trim. He had cleaned house but not enough. I was compelled to relieve him. I thought that Teddy Roosevelt's magnificent performance on Utah Beach had earned him command of a division and decided to give him the 90th. As I was in the process of clearing this appointment with Ike, I learned to my shock and sorrow that Teddy Roosevelt had died in his sleep of a heart attack. In his stead, I gave the division to Raymond S. McLain, a distinguished Oklahoma City banker and longtime National Guardsman. McLain had come to Africa as artillery commander of Troy Middleton's 45th Division. Like Middleton, he was an exceptionally able officer. Under his command, the 90th would become one of our best divisions.[17]

I had high hopes that McMahon's 8th Division would provide the corps the necessary drive. Ike had said, "It's the best-trained division I've seen pass through England." McMahon had been Mark Clark's roommate at West Point and we had served together at Fort Benning. But when the 8th relieved the 82nd, the division fell on its face. McMahon relieved two regimental commanders, but still no progress. When I went up to McMahon's CP, I learned that the assistant division commander had been killed and McMahon seemed mentally paralyzed. He said, "Brad, I think you're going to have to relieve me." I replied, "Well, you haven't been moving. But I'm going to give you forty-eight hours. At the end of forty-eight hours I'm coming back, and if you haven't moved, I may have to relieve you." I returned in forty-eight hours and the division had not moved an inch. I relieved McMahon and gave the division to Donald A. Stroh, who had been Manton Eddy's assistant commander in the 9th. The VIII Corps attack failed to crack the enemy crust and give us a breakout.[18]

To the left of Middleton, Joe Collins and his VII Corps jumped off on July 4. Collins had to go with only two divisions; Eddy's 9th was still redeploying from Cherbourg. The divisions were Ray Barton's 4th, which was also redeploying and in process of assimilating 6,000 replacements (one-third of the division's strength), and the newly arrived 83rd Division, commanded by a tough veteran of Tunisia, Robert C. Macon. The 83rd led the attack into the hedgerows. German resistance in this hedgerow terrain was fierce and the weather was foul. Leadership all through the division was uncertain. It, too, fell on its face. Collins rushed up elements of Barton's 4th Division, but these units, with a high proportion of replacements, fared no better. Nor did Eddy's 9th Division when it reached the front on July 9. The VII Corps attack likewise failed to provide the breakout.[19]

Pete Corlett's XIX Corps jumped off on July 7 with three divisions: Gerhardt's 29th, veterans of Omaha Beach, and two newly arrived divisions, the 30th, commanded by Leland S. Hobbs, and the 35th, commanded by Paul W. Baade. Leland Hobbs was a classmate and close friend, a star of our winning football and baseball teams. Hobbs had not changed in the slightest. At West Point he had a big strong jaw and stubborn streak a mile wide. Nobody could get by him on the football field. His division was a perfect expression of his character. Hobbs was a hard charger. Early in the attack he drove his division across the Vire River and gained an important bridgehead. We attempted to exploit the bridgehead with elements of Leroy Watson's 3rd Armored Division (led by the assistant commander John J. Bohn), but the area was too confined. Corlett, Hobbs and Bohn got into a shouting match arising from conflicting orders and personalities. We met fierce enemy resistance, and as a consequence the XIX Corps attack likewise failed to punch the crust. Corlett became ill and had to be temporarily assisted by Walton H. Walker, commanding XX Corps still in England. John Bohn was relieved for "unsatisfactory performance," busted to colonel and sent home.[20]

Thus my breakout and dream of a blitz to Avranches failed badly, a crushing disappointment to me personally. It failed in part because I bowed to pressure from above and allowed it to go too soon. I should have given Collins more time to redeploy from Cherbourg. It failed in part because of the bad weather. The heavy rains canceled out our air support and mired vehicles and tanks. It failed in part because of the difficult hedgerow terrain. We had not given sufficient forethought to our terrain nor yet learned how best to fight in hedgerows. Joe Collins wrote: "Except for the later Huertgen Forest, it was the deadliest most difficult fighting I experienced in France, with the concealment afforded the enemy by the hedgerows and the tenacity of the Germans making it much like the jungle fighting in the Pacific against the Japanese." It failed in part because of poor leadership and a lack of aggressiveness and experience in some of the divisions. And it failed in part because the Germans reinforced their front with panzers, notably the Lehr Division.[21]

Patton arrived secretly in France on July 6, as our breakout was failing. He was still much under cover, part of the Fortitude plan to keep the Germans thinking he would lead the fictional First Army Group ashore at Pas de Calais. We would endeavor to continue that fiction, even after Patton's Third Army became operational in Normandy. Lesley J. McNair was en route to England to "replace" Patton in command of the fictitious First Army Group.

Patton was, of course, champing at the bit to launch his Third Army, and severely critical of what had so far transpired. He hurled his venom at us in his diary: "Neither Ike or Brad has the stuff. Ike is bound hand and foot by the British and does not know it. Poor fool. . . . Brad says he will put me in as soon as he can. He would do it now, with much benefit to himself, if he had any backbone. . . . Collins and Bradley are too prone to cut off heads. This will make the division commanders lose their confidence. A new man should not be damned for an initial failure with a new division. . . . Bradley and Hodges are such nothings. Their one virtue is that they get along by doing nothing. I could break through [the enemy defenses] in three days if I commanded."[22]

THIRTY

By July 10, we faced a real danger of a World War I–type stalemate in Normandy. Montgomery's forces had taken the northern outskirts of Caen, but the city was not by any means in his control. The airfield sites still lay beyond his grasp. My own breakout had failed. Despite enormous casualties and loss of equipment, the Germans were slavishly following Hitler's orders to hold every yard of ground. We, too, had suffered heavy casualties: about 22,000 in the British sector; over 30,000 in the American sector. The Allied media were becoming increasingly critical.

On that day, Monty and I met for a strategy session at his CP. As always, we were outwardly cordial, but now political undercurrents were causing a strain in our relationship. Monty had become the focus of much of the criticism; it was eroding his invincible public image. He must have realized by then that his overriding personal goal of remaining ground commander was rapidly slipping away. Moreover, the steady American build-up was also working against this ambition. Patton had arrived. When I activated his Third Army, I would move up to army group commander, on a par with Monty. Shortly after that, Ike would move his headquarters to France and become overall ground commander.[1]

By July 10, I had conceived a new plan for a breakout. Rather than mount the second attempt across a broad four-corps front, I would focus the breakout on a very narrow front in the St. Lô area, spearheaded by Joe Collins and his aggressive VII Corps. A key feature of the offensive would be a massive, paralyzing air attack on the Germans in the narrow front. We called our plan "Cobra." We would launch it in nine days, on July 19. When Collins broke through, the whole weight of my growing First Army—some fifteen divisions—would be thrown into the assault.[2]

Over the next several days, Monty began drawing plans for an offensive operation designed to support Cobra. He called his plan "Goodwood," after a well-known English racetrack, suggesting dash and speed. Goodwood was to be launched on July 17, two days prior to our jump-off.

It was by far Monty's biggest and most aggressive plan to date. Its salient feature was an all-out thrust on his left (or east) flank with an armored corps—three tank divisions. It, too, would be preceded by a massive aerial assault.

Much confusion and controversy would later arise about Monty's exact intent in launching Goodwood. At the time, I was led to believe that basic Overlord strategy remained unchanged, that Goodwood was designed principally to draw the Germans to Monty while we broke through and wheeled. Monty's all-out armored thrust on the east flank would very likely fool the Germans into believing *his* was the major breakout attempt rather than mine. If so, the Germans might well shift some of their forces from my front to his, making our task that much easier.

I now believe that Monty had more than one purpose in mind for Goodwood. The first, and most vital, was to draw the Germans away from us so that Cobra had the optimum chance of success. The second purpose —and here I admit to some speculation—might be called public relations or image building. If he were to achieve his goal of remaining ground commander, Monty badly needed a "victory" to reverse the growing official and public criticism of him. A modest thrust in support of Cobra was not enough. It had to be an operation so spectacular and decisive that when we broke out at St. Lô, he could claim the lion's share of the credit. If we failed to break out, he could say that it was no fault of his, that he had given us all he had to give.

There was perhaps a third purpose in the back of Monty's mind. We knew from Ultra that the Germans had incurred grievous losses in men and materiel. Militarily, Hitler's strategy of holding every yard at any expense made no sense and could not go on forever. Anything can happen in war. It was just possible that Monty's armored thrust on his east flank, taking advantage of the good tank country, would prove to be the proverbial straw. Conceivably it could force a general German withdrawal, or even a disastrous disintegration. If so, I believe Monty, for all his inbred caution, was mentally prepared to exploit any gains to the hilt; perhaps with a limited encircling movement to the west, toward us, which would entrap the German forces on our front, combined with a simultaneous dash for Paris—and glory.

For all these reasons, and others, Monty, in my opinion, commenced to oversell Goodwood to his superiors. On July 12, he boasted to Ike: "My whole eastern flank will burst into flames . . . the operation may have far-reaching results." Two days later, he wired Tedder that the Goodwood plan, "if successful, promises to be decisive." That same day he wrote Alan Brooke: "I have decided that the time has come to have a real 'show down' on the Eastern flank and to loose a corps of three armored divisions into the open country about the Caen-Falaise road." An aide he sent to London to explain his plans to the British War Office pronounced that "all is ready to take advantage of any situation which gives reason to think that the enemy is disintegrating."

These messages from Monty were very welcome news to Ike. In two separate replies to Monty on July 13 and 14, Ike said he was "enthusiastic" and "so pepped up" that he or Tedder or both would be glad to come to Monty's headquarters "if we can help in any way." Ike went on: "I am confident it will reap a harvest from all the sowing you have been doing during the past weeks. . . . I am viewing the prospects with the most tremendous optimism and enthusiasm. I would not be at all surprised to see you gaining a victory that will make some of the 'old classics' look like a skirmish between patrols. . . . I am sure, also, that when this thing is started, you can count on Bradley to keep his troops fighting like the very devil, twenty-four hours a day, to provide the opportunity your armored corps will need, and to make the victory complete. . . . May good fortune attend you: I am looking forward to the happy chore of telling about your accomplishments as soon as we have put this one over. I hope you will forgive me if I grow a bit exuberant."

Some historians have seized on these pronouncements, and others, to suggest that at this point there was a radical change in Allied strategy. That owing to lack of faith in the GI and the difficulty of the terrain facing my forces—the hedgerows and marshes—Monty had decided that he, not I, would mount the real breakout in good tank country and that Ike approved this change in strategy. This is not true. Monty's order to Dempsey's Second Army, dated July 15, clearly defines a limited offensive in which "a victory on the eastern flank will help us gain what we want on the Western Front." The aide he sent to the War Office also said, "All the activities on the eastern flank are designed to help the [American forces] in the west while ensuring that a firm bastion is kept in the east."

What happened, I think, is that Monty promoted Goodwood to such a degree that Ike allowed himself to believe that it could develop into something larger than designed. At this point, Ike desperately wanted Monty to *get moving*. Goodwood was the first solid indication that Monty *might* really get moving. In his eagerness to buttress Monty's apparent resolve, Ike got a little carried away himself.

Nor had Monty *misled* Ike into believing that he, Monty, had made a fundamental change in strategy—as some historians also suggest. Ike knew full well that the original Overlord strategy was still the guiding policy, that Goodwood was designed to support Cobra, the main breakout effort, and not the other way around. This is clearly shown, I believe, in an undated letter Ike wrote me on the eve of Cobra. He said, in part:

> General Montgomery's plan calls for a vigorous and continuous offensive by the other armies in the line thus allowing you to pursue every advantage with an ardor verging on recklessness and with all your troops without fear of

> major counteroffensive from the forces the enemy now has on this front. All these attacks are *mutually supporting* [italics added] and if Second Army should secure a breakthrough simultaneously with yours, the results will be incalculable.[3]

Monty launched Goodwood on July 18. It was preceded by a massive air attack. Some 1,700 heavy bombers plus 400 medium bombers dropped nearly 8,000 tons of bombs into the German front. At first the attack went well. The British armored corps advanced three miles into the stunned German lines, and for a time the corps seemed on the point of a clean breakthrough. But Monty's advance was slowed by the thousands of large bomb craters our Air Force had created and the onset of rain. The Germans pulled themselves together and launched a limited counterattack. They gained no ground but inflicted heavy losses on the British, then and over the next forty-eight hours. Rommel was not present; he had been caught on the road by British air, bombed, and severely injured. On the afternoon of July 20, when the rains had turned the battleground into a sea of mud, Monty, declaring himself well pleased with the results of Goodwood, abruptly halted it. He had gained only the rest of Caen and the ground about six miles to the south of the city. The cost had been appalling: 4,000 casualties and 500 tanks—over one-third of all the tanks in Monty's command.[4]

Monty's promoting of Goodwood had extended to the war correspondents at his headquarters. During the early phases of the battle, Monty raised public expectations to a high degree with misleading statements to the media. The *London Times* on July 19 carried these rosy headlines: "Second Army Breaks Through; Armoured Forces Reach Open Country; General Montgomery Well Satisfied." Three days later, when the truth was apparent, the *Times* angrily castigated Monty: "Possibly the offensive was too much boomed when in its initial stages. It is always better to do the booming after complete success has been secured." The *New York Times* correspondent Drew Middleton, until then a staunch Monty supporter, found the "preliminary ballyhoo" and the use of the words "broke through" regrettable. In his memoirs, Monty conceded he had been "too exultant" in his press conference, but implied that he had done so to help trick the Germans into believing Goodwood was the major offensive.[5]

The truth was, I believe, that Monty was "too exultant" both in private and public—and not merely to trick the Germans. He oversold Goodwood. He raised expectations to an almost giddy level and then dashed them. It was a disastrous personal miscalculation. Whatever hopes he had for remaining overall ground commander died with Goodwood.

Ike, Bedell Smith, Tedder—the whole of SHAEF—were furious with Monty. Butcher logged that Ike was "blue as indigo over Monty's slowdown," but as I soon found out, this was vast understatement. Tedder, in a private talk with Air Chief Portal, discussed the British Army's "failure," and "agreed in regarding Montgomery as the cause." Tedder (as he wrote a friend) thought he and Ike had been "had for suckers. I do not believe there was the slightest intention to make a clean breakthrough." He told Ike "that his own people would be thinking that he had sold them to the British if he continued to support Montgomery without protest." Tedder was fed up, demanded decisive action, and if it were not forthcoming, "then we must change our leaders for men who will get us there."[6]

Meanwhile, I had been refining my Cobra plan. Its key feature, the saturation bombing of the German concentrations opposite us, was risky. For all their boasting, the aviators were not skilled in pinpoint bombing. Cobra called for pinpoint saturation bombing of a rectangle three and a half miles wide and one and a half miles deep, south of the St. Lô–Périers road to which Collins' troops would advance prior to the jump-off. There was no room for error; a mistake on the part of the aviators could bring a rain of bombs on our own troops.[7]

To minimize the chances for error, I proposed a plan whereby our aircraft would approach the rectangle on a course *parallel* to the east-west St. Lô–Périers road and, of course, south of it. So directed, our planes would not fly over our own troops. Thus, if the aviators dropped bombs long or short of the target area (as they were wont to do), the misdirected bombs would fall on the German side of the St. Lô–Périers road, not ours.

Owing to the foul weather, Cobra had to be postponed until July 21. On July 19, I flew to Leigh-Mallory's headquarters at Stanmore, a mansion near Harrow, for a final discussion of the bombing. Present were most of the air power top brass: Tedder, Spaatz, Leigh-Mallory, plus a platoon of senior air commanders. I outlined my plan for a parallel approach on the St. Lô–Périers road, which would be the "flank guide" (or boundary line) to avoid hitting our own troops. The airmen raised objections. A parallel approach, they held, would maximize our aircraft's exposure to enemy flak and present the narrowest rather than the widest target, as well as air congestion over the target. I countered that flying parallel to the road would enable our planes to attack out of the rising sun in the morning or the setting sun in the evening, partly blinding the German flak gunners and minimizing flak risk to our planes. In any case, I said unequivocably and frankly, I would not agree to bombing on a course perpendicular to the St. Lô–Périers road that would bring the planes over our own troops on the bombing approach.

In the end, the airmen (less Leigh-Mallory, who was called from the conference) agreed that the bombing runs would be made parallel to the St. Lô–Périers road. At the same time, to further minimize the chances of bombing our own troops, I agreed to withdraw Collins' forces some 1,500 hard-won yards north of the road. It was also agreed that to avoid heavy cratering of the rectangle, the airmen would use no bombs larger than 100 pounds.

Ike flew over to visit us on the eve of the attack, July 20. It was then that I learned that he was more than "blue as indigo" about Monty's failure to press Goodwood. A more accurate color would be red—red as a hot coal. If Ike had had a free hand, I am certain that he would have sacked Monty then and there. But Alan Brooke was firmly in Monty's corner and had swung Churchill to his side; Churchill was pleased that Caen had at last been taken.

In lieu of fruitless talk of sacking Monty, we discussed the early activation of my army group. It was now to be called the Twelfth, so that the fictitious First Army Group under McNair could go on fooling the Germans. We agreed that the Twelfth Army Group would go operational on August 1; that Ike would go operational with SHAEF headquarters in France on about September 1. Thereafter, Ike would take direct control of the land forces. Hansen noted aptly in his diary: "Question of how graciously Monty looks on this." Ike then left to see Monty at his CP.[8]

The next day we received the astonishing news that on July 20 a cabal of German generals had attempted to assassinate Hitler. The Fuehrer himself released the news in a speech on July 21, the day Cobra was to go but did not because of continuing bad weather. Tedder went at once to see Ike and told him "that Montgomery's failure to take action earlier had lost us the opportunity offered by the attempt on Hitler's life." That is, Tedder believed (as did we all for a while) that the news indicated a widespread revolt in the highest echelons of the German Army, and that had Montgomery pressed Goodwood to the utmost it might have found a demoralized and confused enemy and overwhelmed him. Tedder wrote that he asked Ike "to act at once with Montgomery" and said that he intended, if the Supreme Commander would not act firmly, to put "my views in writing to the British Chiefs of Staff."[9]

That same day, Ike drafted a letter to Monty. It was not the blistering assault Tedder had recommended, but another tactful exhortation. He urged Monty once more to get moving: "*Time is vital*. We must not only have the Brittany Peninsula—we must have it quickly. So we must hit them with everything. . . . Now we are pinning our hopes on Bradley's attack. . . . But the country is bad, and the enemy strong at the point of main assault, and more than ever I think it is important that we are aggressive throughout the front. . . . I feel that you should insist that Dempsey keep up the strength of his attack. . . . As Bradley's attack starts Dempsey's should be intensified. . . . We must go forward shoulder to shoulder, with honors and sacrifices equally shared."[10]

When Tedder saw a copy of this letter, he was gravely disappointed.

He told an aide it was "not strong enough. Montgomery can evade it. It contains no order." Later, Tedder wrote: "I could not help fearing that in this dangerous situation, Montgomery, while welcoming the terms of the letter, might fail to carry out its implications."[11]

Monty's failure to put greater push behind Goodwood was a disappointment to us at First Army, but we did not react apoplectically as did those at SHAEF. For one thing, we had not been subjected to the promotion. We viewed Goodwood as a limited thrust in support of Cobra and expected no more. By now, we knew very well that Monty would not take chances. He had drawn the bulk of the panzers to his front, and the Germans were fighting with great determination. A rash move on Monty's part could invite disaster, not only for the British and Canadians, but also us. Tactically, Goodwood helped us. As we saw from Ultra and other intelligence sources, it compelled von Kluge to commit all of his reserves to Monty's front.

Far more disturbing to me were the obvious cracks appearing in the Allied command structure. Monty's failure in Goodwood had infuriated both British and American airmen who had diverted so much of their air power to make it successful. Ike and Monty maintained a barely civil relationship. Monty knew that Ike was running him down at every opportunity and would relieve him if he had the authority. At the same time, Alan Brooke was unstintingly defending Monty. His low opinion of Eisenhower had not changed. In a letter to Monty at this time, Alan Brooke wrote that it was "clear that Ike has the very vaguest conception of war." For the moment, coalition warfare seemed not to be working; everybody was at each other's throat.[12]

Cobra thus assumed vast importance in my mind. If it succeeded, I was certain it would give everybody a much-needed shot in the arm. It would help eliminate the back-stabbing. It would put such momentum in the war that the very speed of it would heal the seams in our rupturing alliance. Conversely, if it failed, it could develop into much more than another military setback. It could bring on dangerous open warfare in the alliance that might lead to Monty's relief and perhaps Ike's and my own. There was a good possibility that the airmen, who still believed Germany could be defeated by air power alone, would emerge in commanding roles, leaving the Allied armies mired in a fruitless Normandy stalemate.

One factor working in our favor was a similar discord in the German high command. In the post-assassination shakeup, Hitler's crony Heinrich Himmler, who was not a professional military officer, was elevated to a leading (though vaguely defined) position in the Fuehrer's war machine. Von Kluge, Rommel (still recuperating from his injuries) and Rommel's chief of staff, Hans Speidel, fell under suspicion. Ultimately, Rommel and Speidel were directly implicated in the plot. Rommel was forced to commit suicide; Speidel was later imprisoned. Thus Nazi politics had removed from our front Hitler's most able general, Erwin Rommel.[13] *

Heavy continuous rains forced us to postpone Cobra day after day. There was little we could do except fret in our tents and go over the plans again and again, making minor adjustments. We waited—and waited and waited. I have seldom been so frustrated and edgy. I could not sleep; Chet Hansen recorded that I somewhat sheepishly asked for sleeping pills. I do not doubt that every commander involved in Cobra suffered the same agonizing frustration.

Finally the weather forecasters promised a break on July 24. Our CP was soon jammed with distinguished visitors: Lesley J. McNair, now heading the fictitious First Army Group; Bill Simpson, commanding the Ninth Army, and his chief of staff, James E. Moore; Leigh-Mallory; Matt Ridgway; others. H-hour for the 2,246 aircraft that would lay the bomb carpet was 1300 hours. To a man, the First Army was primed and ready.[14]

To our dismay, in late morning a heavy cloud cover moved over the target area. Leigh-Mallory sent out a message canceling the attack, but it was too late to stop all the planes. Some 400 bombers reached France and let go. Owing to a mixup in the orders, the bad weather and human error, many bombs fell behind our own lines, killing 25 and wounding 131. One reason for the error was that the planes flew a course perpendicular to our lines rather than parallel to it as I had been assured they would. I have seldom been so angry. It was duplicity—a shocking breach of good faith.

We feared this abortive and unlucky start for Cobra had tipped our hand to the Germans. After the war we discovered our fears were unjustified. Von Kluge suspected a major offensive was afoot, but he wrongly guessed it would come in Monty's sector, where Crerar's fresh Canadian First Army was primed for a limited offensive to coincide with Cobra. Von Kluge joined his panzers there, discounting the Cobra air activity as a feint.

I launched an immediate investigation to find out why the airmen had bombed on a perpendicular course rather than a parallel one as promised. To my astonishment, the Air Force brass simply lied, claiming they had never agreed to bomb parallel to the road. Not only that, they put me over an impossible barrel. They would not mount a second attack except perpendicularly to the road. Fearing the Germans were onto us, I had no

* It is noteworthy, I think, to recall that no American general ever really defeated Rommel. He had left Tunisia before our victory there. We forced his Atlantic Wall in Normandy, but he had thwarted all our efforts to exploit the lodgements. When he recommended withdrawal, he implicitly admitted defeat, but it had not actually occurred. After July 18, Rommel no longer participated in the fighting.

choice but to accept what the airmen offered and we reset the jump-off for the following day, July 25.

That day the weather cleared. Ike hurried over to watch the jump-off. The planes came on schedule: 1,500 heavy bombers, 380 medium bombers and 550 fighter-bombers. In total, these 2,430 aircraft, flying perpendicular to the target, dropped some 4,000 tons of bombs and napalm. To our horror, reports of "shorts" immediately flooded into my CP. Quite soon so many reports had accumulated that we believed our own casualties were devastating, perhaps so great that Cobra would have to be canceled. This proved to be an exaggerated fear, but the final toll was shocking and ghastly: 111 dead, 490 wounded. Among the dead was Lesley McNair, who had been observing in the front lines with a unit of Leland Hobbs's 30th Division.

Hansen recorded: "General Hobbs said afterwards it was horrible. The ground belched, shook and spewed dirt to the sky. Scores of our troops were hit, their bodies flung from slit trenches. Doughboys dazed and frightened. Huebner, who is an old front-line campaigner, said it was the most terrifying thing he had ever seen. . . . A bomb landed squarely on McNair in a slit trench and threw his body sixty feet and mangled it beyond recognition except for the three stars on his collar."*

Meanwhile, Joe Collins had thrown his VII Corps assault troops into the hole. Three trusty infantry divisions led the attack: Eddy's 9th, Barton's 4th and Hobbs's 30th. The GI's—somewhat dazed and demoralized by the "shorts"—charged through expecting to meet little or no opposition. All were shocked to meet heavy resistance. The assault bogged down. I was dismayed. Ike flew off to his headquarters in England completely dejected and furious at the Air Force for killing and maiming so many of our own men and determined never again to use heavy bombers in support of ground forces. Butcher reported Ike was still "glum" and "visibly depressed" when he reached England.[16]

The heavy opposition we initially encountered was, in fact, merely the valiant and instinctive reaction of a few tough Germans. The bombing had done far more damage than we could possibly imagine. Official Army historian Martin Blumenson wrote: "Bombs buried men and equipment, overturned tanks, cut telephone wires, broke radio antennas, sent messengers fleeing for foxholes or the nearest crater. Communications with forward echelons were completely disrupted. The bombardment transformed the main line of resistance . . . into a frightening landscape of the moon.

* Because news of McNair's death might compromise the Fortitude deception plan, I ordered that his funeral in Normandy be held in strictest secrecy. Since we had no coffins, I instructed my quartermaster, Andrew McNamara, to get one from the French civilians. Patton, Hodges, Pete Quesada and his deputy, Ralph Royce, Bill Kean, McNair's aides and I served as pallbearers. "A sad ending and a useless sacrifice," Patton noted in his diary, expressing the sentiments of us all. Subsequently, McNair was replaced in Fortitude by a distinguished older general, John L. DeWitt.[15]

. . . No less than a thousand men must have perished in the Cobra bombardment. About one-third of the total number of combat effectives . . . were probably killed or wounded, the survivors dazed. Perhaps only a dozen tanks or tank destroyers remained in operation. Three battalion command posts of Panzer Lehr were demolished. The attached parachute regiment virtually vanished. Only local and feeble resistance was possible against attacking American infantrymen." [17]

Joe Collins soon sensed the confusion and lack of coordination within the German lines. Accordingly, he called on his reserves and threw Huebner's Big Red One into the fight. He then committed his armor: Ted Brooks's 2nd Division and Leroy Watson's 3rd. Watson—my classmate—disappointed Collins, and Collins relieved him of command. This was one decision I did not believe was correct, but because Watson was under Joe's command, I had to back him up. We gave the division to Maurice Rose.*

Slowly it came to me that Cobra had not failed. It had succeeded; we had broken through. Joe Collins, absolutely justifying our faith in him, enlarged the rupture in the German lines and kept right on moving south, mile after mile. On his right flank, Middleton's VIII Corps, after a wobbly start, likewise broke through and Middleton cut loose his armor: the 4th Division under John S. Wood, and the 6th Division under Robert W. Grow. The armor smashed through thirty-five miles to our long-sought goal, Avranches, at the base of the peninsula. The Germans, now completely routed, retreated in haste or surrendered.

On July 28, I wrote Ike: "To say that the personnel of the First Army Headquarters is riding high tonight is putting it mildly. Things on our front really look good. . . . I'm sorry that you happened to be here the one day when the situation was obscure. While I felt and told you we would still punch through, I believe it would have been much more satisfying to you if you had been here yesterday or today. I can assure you that we are taking every calculated risk and we believe we have the Germans out of the ditches and in complete demoralization and expect to take full advantage of them." [19]

Ike flew over the next day to check on our progress and extend congratulations. (He brought Kay Summersby, raising a few eyebrows.) Gone was the gloom and dejection of a few days past. The world-famous Eisenhower grin was now in evidence. With perhaps some relief, Chet Hansen logged that Ike was "highly elated." Indeed, we all were, even Patton, who had sat out Cobra on the sidelines, grousing in his diary before the jump-off that it was "really a very timid operation." Monty and Dempsey

* Watson took the blow like a man and asked if he could stay in the ETO in any combat capacity. Impressed by his attitude, I reassigned him as assistant division commander of Gerhardt's 29th Division. Ultimately, he moved up to replace Gerhardt as commander of the division and performed well.[18]

had also called at my CP. Hansen noted that both were "pleased" at our progress. Patton wrote Ike: "Bradley certainly has done a wonderful job. My only kick is that he will win the war before I get in."[20]

Cobra would go down in history as the "St. Lô breakout." It was, in fact, a total and smashing breakin, breakthrough and breakout, a major turning point in the war. Seven agonizing weeks had passed since D-day. All that time the terrain, the weather and the tenacious German troops had kept us bottled up in the Cotentin Peninsula. But now at last we were moving out at breathtaking speed. One phase of the war on the Continent had ended, another had begun.

THIRTY-ONE

On August 1, we activated Twelfth Army Group headquarters at Coutances. I relinquished command of the First Army to Courtney Hodges, who then commanded three corps: Gerow's V, Collins' VII and Corlett's XIX. That same day, George Patton activated the Third Army with four corps: Middleton's VIII, Wade H. Haislip's XV, Walton Walker's XX and Gilbert R. Cook's XII. These two U.S. armies comprised, in total, twenty-one combat divisions (five armored and sixteen infantry), nearly 400,000 men. Including the service and supply troops and specialized forces, there were about 903,000 men under my command in France. On that same day, Monty's Twenty-First Army Group consisted of two armies, Dempsey's Second and Crerar's First Canadian, a total of sixteen combat divisions. Monty commanded in all about 663,000 men. Combined, the Allies numbered four armies of thirty-seven divisions—a total of 1.5 million men.[1]

Monty was not at all happy that the Twelfth Army Group had at last gone operational. His chief of staff, de Guingand, wrote: "Now, Montgomery, although he knew and approved of all these preparations for the day when Bradley was to open up his own Army Group Headquarters, never, I believe, thought that day would come so soon. Possibly, as always, he thirsted after simple solutions, and, therefore, hoped that the initial command setup was there to stay for a long time. He was, I think, apt to give insufficient weight to the dictates of prestige and national feelings, or to the increasing contributions of America, in both men and arms, to the European Theater of War."[2]

The modern U.S. Army had had only limited experience with army group command. General Pershing had briefly commanded two U.S. armies on the Western Front in the last two weeks of World War I. In the intervening peacetime years, army group functions had been studied and discussed at the Command and General Staff School and War College, but only in vague and theoretical terms. Published regulations suggested that an army group should direct but not conduct operations, confining itself to broadly stated "mission orders." But these regulations were not binding. I was free, in a tactical sense, to command however I wished. I chose to pattern my administration somewhat on the model set by Alexander, who had commanded Allied army groups in Tunisia, Sicily, and Italy. I would issue broad "missions," but at the same time I would watch the situation very closely and suggest—or order—modifications as I thought required, even to the movement of specific divisions. In sum, I would exercise the very closest control over Hodges and Patton.

It was a personal wrench to leave the veteran combat-wise staff of the First Army. We had been together for some seventeen months. In addition to my personal "family," I took only one man with me: the G-1 (personnel expert), Red O'Hare, whom I felt would be more useful and productive on a higher level and who was not one of the original II Corps gang from Tunisia. We moved over to Group without missing a beat. I had been working with the Group staff since the past October and we were well acquainted.*

Group, code-named "Eagle," had established itself in a vast tent city on a handsome French country estate. It had grown into an enormous, unwieldy organization that could obviously not move quickly. Since I intended to keep up a fast pace and stay close to the front whenever the tactical situation permitted, we formed a smaller highly mobile headquarters which we named "Eagle Tac." Initially composed of about 200 officers and men (G-2, G-3, G-4, engineers, signal personnel, Ultra reps, etc.), Eagle Tac outfitted itself with vans. My aides had a "personal" van built for me with a handsome wood-paneled interior. It could serve both as my office and living quarters. The larger Twelfth Army Group staff "tail," which would follow as conditions permitted, subdivided into two other sections code-named "Eagle Main" and "Eagle Rear."[4]

Until now, I had been hopping about the Normandy battlefield in Piper Cubs. With command of Group came a new amenity, courtesy Tooey Spaatz: a brand-new plushed-up twin-engine C-47 (military version of the workhorse transport DC-3), with a sofa, desk and comfortable seats for passengers. The crew of this plane, which I named the *Mary Q,* was permanently assigned to me. These were the pilot, Alvin E. (Robbie) Robinson, a Texan and veteran of D-day airborne operations; the navigator, Walter M. Lamb; and a crew of two staff sergeants, Leslie (Bud) Wiser and Earl Fisher. Robinson was superb. I have never flown with a pilot in whose judgment and skill I had more confidence.[5]

Upon my assumption of Army Group, Ike believed a promotion of

* The principals, in addition to my chief of staff, Lev Allen, were: Henry B. Lewis, deputy chief of staff, a superb administrator; G-1 O'Hare; G-2 Edwin L. Sibert, who had served under me in the tactical department at West Point in the late 1930s; G-3 A. Franklin Kibler, a high-level planner of rare talent; G-4 Raymond G. Moses. My personal staff remained: Chet Hansen, Lew Bridge, Dick Dudley, Alex Stoute, Frank Cekada.[3]

some kind was in order. Hodges, Patton, Simpson and I all wore three stars, yet I was the ranking officer in terms of responsibility. Four-star rank for me would probably have been appropriate; but that would have put me on a level with Ike, causing all kinds of problems. Ike's solution was to recommend a promotion in permanent rank, which would insure me an important position in the postwar Army, a small increase in pay and retirement benefits, and make me eligible for selection to Chief of Staff of the Army. Six weeks later—September 16, 1944—I was promoted to permanent major general. Patton was appointed permanent major general on September 2, outranking me on the permanent list by two weeks.[6]

When Patton entered combat, he did so initially with a single corps, Middleton's VIII. The Overlord plan called for Patton's full Third Army to first clear Brittany, seizing the major seaports of St. Malo, Brest, Lorient and St. Nazaire. By this time, we knew from Ultra that von Kluge had virtually stripped Brittany of its major German divisions to fight the battle of Normandy. Accordingly, I made the decision, in consultation with Ike, Monty and Patton, to greatly reduce our commitment of forces to the Brittany campaign. We would do it with one corps—Middleton's—rather than the full Third Army as called for in the plan. Patton's other corps could thus be made available to throw against the Germans in the east.[7]

Patton blazed through Brittany with armored divisions and motorized infantry. He conquered a lot of real estate and made big headlines, but the Brittany campaign failed to achieve its primary objectives. The Germans withdrew to the major seaports, organized strong defenses and prepared to carry out Hitler's orders to fight to the death. As it developed, none of these ports could be captured without an expensive siege. By the time we wrested them from the Germans—Brest at great cost in U.S. casualties—the war had moved on and we had little use for them.[8]

Some military historians have roundly criticized me for even undertaking the Brittany campaign. They hold that I should have ignored Brittany entirely; that I inflexibly and stubbornly clung to the original Overlord plan merely because it was there; that Middleton's corps, employed in Normandy against the Germans, might have been the decisive extra weight necessary to insure an annihilating victory rather than the outcome that ensued.[9]

There was one overriding reason why I sent Patton and Middleton to Brittany: logistics. This is the dullest subject in the world, and no writer has ever succeeded in glamorizing it. The result is that logistics are usually either downplayed or ignored altogether. But logistics were the lifeblood of the Allied armies in France. Without ports and facilities we could not supply our armies. We could not move, shoot, eat, land new troops or evacuate the wounded. One division in combat required about 700 tons of supplies a day. The Allies had thirty-seven divisions on the Continent, most in active combat. Thus we needed about 26,000 tons a day, or 780,000 tons (1.5 billion pounds) per month. These facts were very much on my mind. Ever since D-day I had been severely rationing ammunition; it was still being brought in on an emergency basis by aircraft, a very inefficient way to transport supplies.

At the time we launched the Brittany campaign, we still had only a single major port in France, Cherbourg. Owing to an expert German demolition and mining program, it had required several weeks to get Cherbourg operating. Even so, in the whole month of August we brought in only 266,000 tons through Cherbourg—about one-third of our requirements. The deficit was made up by continuing to utilize Omaha and Utah beaches, over which in the same month we brought in an astonishing 537,000 tons. At the beginning of August, no one had dared hope Omaha and Utah could be used to that extent. We had to assume there might be another disastrous storm. In any event, September was sure to bring uncertain weather and a drastic plunge in tonnage figures. Cherbourg would be given to Monty for his supply line; the United States would rely on Brittany ports.

There were two other considerations, neither minor. Our logistical demands in France had created a shipping logjam. American divisions destined for France were backing up in the States, unable to find transport to England, then across the channel to Normandy. If we had the Brittany ports, those divisions could sail directly from the United States to France, bypassing England. In addition, there was a new proposed plan afoot to cancel Dragoon, the landing in southern France, now set for August 15, and bring those troops into France through Brittany, thus eliminating the need for them to storm an occupied beach.

Beyond that, simply ignoring Brittany and "sealing it off" appeared to me militarily imprudent. There were some 50,000 German troops in Brittany. Most of these were attached to the less effective and understrength garrison or static units. However, as we learned from Ultra, the crack 2nd Parachute Division, commanded by Herman B. Ramcke, a tough and skilled soldier, had recently slipped into Brittany. Had Ramcke been ignored, I have no doubt he would have caused us no end of trouble. An airtight seal would have required a 100-mile north-south line, Avranches-Rennes-St. Nazaire. To guard against Ramcke's attacks, the line would have had to be manned by at least three divisions. A limited offensive in Brittany was preferable to a long, vulnerable, possibly troublesome defensive seal.[10]

In Normandy, we kept punching ahead, mile by mile, shoving the Germans back, seeking to widen our breach at Avranches so that we could crowd more divisions through the breakout. Collins' splendidly aggressive VII Corps drove through to Mortain. This gave us room to feed two more of Patton's corps through the breach: Haislip's XV and Walker's XX. Haislip, performing brilliantly, drove through into open country at Laval and was soon on the road to Le Mans. In three days Haislip advanced an astonishing seventy-five miles.[11]

This was a heady time for all of us. After the tedious, bloody yard-by-yard fighting in the hedgerows of Cotentin, the rate of our advances on the right flank was almost dizzying. Ike was exultant: "We are to hell and gone in Brittany and slicing 'em up in Normandy," he crowed to Butcher. Patton, driving his corps to the limit or beyond, wrote a friend: "We are having one of the loveliest battles you ever saw. It is a typical cavalry action, in which, to quote the words of the old story, 'The soldier went out and charged in all directions at the same time, with a pistol in each hand, and a sabre in the other.' "[12]

However, it was still very tough going on the left of our front in Hodges' First Army sector, where Corlett's XIX Corps and Gerow's V Corps were fighting toward Vire. The collapse of the German left flank at Avranches seemed to have small effect on the German units defending Vire. They fought with determination, inflicting heavy casualties on our forces. With one exception, our troops gave a good account of themselves. The exception proved to be an awkward case for me, personally. My former 28th Division, commanded by Lloyd Brown, finally committed to combat in Corlett's XIX Corps, fell on its face. The fault, we judged, was Brown's, and I relieved him of command without delay. I chose a fine officer to replace him, James E. Wharton, assistant commander of Manton Eddy's 9th Division. A few hours after taking command, Wharton, sizing up his front, was mortally wounded. The division then went to another outstanding officer, Norman Cota, assistant commander of Gerhardt's 29th Division and a hero of Omaha Beach. Cota led the division with great distinction. It soon became one of the toughest and most dependable in my command.[13]

Monty's self-assigned Overlord mission was to hold the Caen hub and draw the Germans on him while my armies broke out, wheeled east and also cleaned out Brittany. This had gone more or less according to plan. While Monty's forces had failed to exploit the D-day landings and capture Caen and deliver territory for Allied airfields, his presence and limited maneuvers such as Goodwood had indeed drawn a great weight of German forces to him, thus making our breakout achievable.

However, after I broke out, Ike and I thought that Monty should "hold" the Caen hub in a far more aggressive manner with strong attacks against his front. That is to say, we thought he should aggressively expand his hub, at the least making good on his long-overdue promise to deliver the airmen territory toward Falaise for airfields. He had mounted no offensive of consequence since Goodwood. At a dinner with Churchill and Alan

Brooke on the evening of July 27—two days after our breakout—Ike and Bedell Smith came down very hard on Monty, flatly stating that the British Army "could and should be more offensive." In a letter to Monty the next day, Alan Brooke wrote that Monty should be mindful of the criticism from Ike and that "Dempsey must attack *at the earliest possible moment* on a large scale." [14]

Monty had already ordered Dempsey and Crerar to attack "to the greatest degree possible with the resources available." This included an ambitious six-division offensive by Dempsey on his right front near Caumont—adjacent to Hodges' drive on Vire—to commence on August 2. But Ike feared an offensive of that size would take too long to get going. Instead he urged Monty to order a three-division attack right away. "Now as never before," Ike urged Monty, "opportunity is staring us in the face. . . . Let us not waste an hour in getting the whole affair started. Never was time more vital to us. . . . I am counting on you." [15]

These goads from Ike and Alan Brooke did the trick. Monty responded: "Everything will be thrown in. Gave orders to Dempsey this morning that attack is to be pressed with utmost vigor and all caution thrown to the winds and any casualties accepted and that he must step on the gas for Vire." Dempsey jumped off on July 30. His offensive developed into the most aggressive and sustained British effort since D-day. His forces pushed through difficult bocage country against stubborn German resistance for an average advance of about ten miles. British armored elements approached the northern outskirts of Vire on August 2, about the same time that Gerow and Corlett were closing on the town from the west. At last Monty was moving!

But he was angry—at Ike and Bedell Smith. Until that time, Ike had coddled Monty, catered to his monumental ego, resorting to exhortation rather than direct criticism. Monty wrote in his memoirs that he did not think Ike "had any idea of the trouble he was starting." For Ike to complain to Churchill that "the Second Army was not fighting as it should" was "the greatest disservice that could ever have been done the Allied cause. . . . The trouble which began this way in Normandy was to grow and develop into storms which at times threatened to wreck the Allied ship." [16]

THIRTY-TWO

A key assumption in the Overlord plan was that after we had achieved overwhelming strength in Normandy the German armies facing us would make a gradual withdrawal to the Seine River, a natural defensive barrier. We also assumed that by that time the Germans would have awakened to the fact that Fortitude had been a deception, and the German Fifteenth Army would be shifted from Pas de Calais to the Seine for an all-out defense, the showdown battle for Germany.

These were the prescribed textbook solutions to the German military battle in Normandy. But the Germans were not following the textbook. Hitler, still in pain and agony from the wounds he received in the assassination attempt, and distrustful of von Kluge's loyalty, had taken control of strategy on the Western Front. Against all military advice, he forbade withdrawal to the Seine. Not a foot of ground was to be yielded to the Allies. Not only that, he was hatching plans for a new and visionary counterattack that would shatter the Allies and drive us back into the sea. In preparation for this offensive, he released divisions from the Fifteenth Army at Pas de Calais to move to Normandy. Other units in southern France received similar orders. In all, Hitler committed some seven new divisions. Hitler had made the decision to fight the showdown battle for Germany not at the Seine, as we had anticipated, but in Normandy. It was the worst possible military strategy, one of the great mistakes of World War II.[1]

Contrary to some recent accounts, we had no specific Ultra information on Hitler's forthcoming plans in Normandy. In fact, after our breach in the line at Avranches, Monty's follow-up British Second Army drive on Vire, together with Hodges' intense pressure in the center, we were somewhat mystified by the German reaction. By all rights, our immense ground pressure—together with a terrific pounding from the air—should have forced a general German withdrawal, or at the least a constriction of their lines. But we knew from captured POW's that Hitler was reinforcing his lines with new troops. I remarked to Chet Hansen in puzzlement, "They tell me he's fighting for time, but I'll be damned if I know how time can help him except to enable him to live a few days longer. . . . He'd better straighten out on our front or he'll be terribly embarrassed one of these days."[2]

The failure of the Germans to withdraw in textbook fashion began to suggest to us a fabulous opportunity. We might be able to trap the Germans west of the Seine, giving them no chance to set up a defensive line along the river, and thus annihilate them. Since this opportunity had not been anticipated in the Overlord plan, it required some hasty and rather radical revisions in our thinking. After hearing these ideas of mine, Ike presented them to Marshall on August 2, suggesting the possibility of "aggressive action toward the northeast to destroy the bulk of the German mobile forces, all generally located along our present front and stretching up to include Pas de Calais."[3]

Over the period August 2 to August 6, I began to develop an idea for a vast encirclement—or long envelopment—of the German forces in Normandy. Chet Hansen recorded the general outlines in his diary. Following the conquest of Brittany, we would draw the First and Third armies up to a line Caen–Le Mans and build up supplies. The blitzkrieg offensive would be spearheaded by six U.S. armored divisions—all we had available—followed by motorized infantry. The armor would strike toward Paris. An airborne corps of three divisions would land north of Orléans to block the escape of Germans through the line Paris-Orléans and, later, to give us protection on the southern flank. The armor and infantry would swing southeast around Paris and then east of the Seine, north to Dieppe. (This would cut off Paris, where we expected heavy German resistance and perhaps tragic destruction; we would take the city later.)

This long and vast wheeling movement and envelopment would trap all the Germans in Normandy, prevent a withdrawal to the Seine, block any effort of the German Fifteenth Army to move toward the Seine and isolate Paris. A follow-up thrust from Dieppe to Pas de Calais (eighty-five miles) would encircle and destroy the German Fifteenth Army, leaving nothing to block our path into Germany itself. The thrust at Pas de Calais would also enable us to knock out the V-1 launching sites. Hansen commented: "His . . . plan . . . is the most ambitious yet. He views it calmly, weighs its mathematical chances and plots it deliberately. Worked the entire thing out in a series of definite lines . . . assigning bulk of mission to Third Army . . . armor to strike quickly . . . strike through . . . pour on infantry, burst up to coast, cut off and destroy the German Army in France." He recorded that when I unveiled the plan to my G-2 (Sibert) and G-3 (Kibler) I said, "Let's talk big turkey. I'm ready to eat meat all the way."[4]

Indeed so. I viewed my idea as nothing less than a war-winning drive.

An important feature of my idea was the build-up of supplies behind our Le Mans–Caen line. As Hansen noted in understated shorthand: "Supply may limit the rapidity with which we move towards Paris." The offensive would require *vast* supplies, especially gasoline for our tanks and motorized infantry. To insure the safety of this supply build-up and to gain space for Allied airfields, we hoped Monty would put heavy steam behind an offensive Crerar's First Canadian Army was planning on August 7—a drive on the long-promised Falaise. As Hansen noted: "Attack of First Canadian Army . . . if successful to Falaise, should clean out much resistance and take flanks with it to straighten line, permit us to build supplies without threat of Ger[man] attack on the hinge north of St. Hilaire." That "hinge" was Mortain, the weakest link in our front and, I had to assume, the most likely place should the Germans be so foolish as to counterattack.[5]

At about the time I first conceived this idea, and unknown to us, on August 2 Hitler had ordered von Kluge to mount a counteroffensive against us at our vulnerable "hinge" near Mortain. By that time, von Kluge was reeling from the weight of our ground and air attack. He assumed Hitler meant a limited offensive designed to facilitate a general withdrawal to the Seine and at once he set about planning for this maneuver. Von Kluge shifted several panzer divisions from Monty's front to ours and gave orders for them to jump off early on August 7, strike through Mortain and seize Avranches.[6]

Recently some historians have begun to write that Ultra alerted us to this counterattack almost at inception. These accounts appear to stem from Group Captain F. W. Winterbotham's book *The Ultra Secret,* which was based not on documents but memory. My recollection is in sharp variance. In this instance Ultra was of little or no value. Ultra alerted us to the attack only a few hours before it came, and that was too late to make any major defensive preparations, as we had at Carentan. My recollection is buttressed by the meticulous researches of Ralph Bennett into the official Ultra dispatches. In his recent book *Ultra in the West,* based largely on documents, Bennett states categorically that Ultra "knew nothing" of Hitler's August 2 order and did not detect the offensive until mere hours before it was launched.[7]

On August 6, as von Kluge was on the verge of launching the offensive, Hitler telephoned to discuss it. In this conversation von Kluge learned for the first time that Hitler had a much more grandiose scheme in mind—a massive offensive of "several corps"—to be launched when all the reinforcements had arrived. Hitler asserted that it was a "unique opportunity, which will never return, to drive into an extremely exposed enemy area and thereby to change the situation completely." As official Army historian Martin Blumenson wrote: "The Avranches counterattack . . . was to be the decisive blow sought since the invasion, the master stroke of strategic significance that was to destroy Operation Overlord." Von Kluge was to divide the First and Third armies, isolate Patton in Brittany, roll up the Allies and throw them back "into the sea."[8]

The tactical situation was such that von Kluge could not postpone the offensive. He would launch it; Hitler's reinforcements would be welcomed to exploit it. Only with great reluctance did Hitler approve. According to Bennett, Ultra picked up the first information on the attack that evening, August 6. This information included von Kluge's attack order, with time, place and strength: elements of five panzer divisions. Thereafter, Bennett writes, "These were some of Ultra's most prolific days of the whole war." An unprecedented amount of Enigma traffic was accurately and rapidly made available to us from Bletchley Park over the next week. This included information on the transfer of divisions from the Fifteenth Army and elsewhere to Normandy.[9]

Inasmuch as I had recognized the weakness in our line at Mortain, we were not as vulnerable there as the Germans supposed. It was Joe Collins' VII Corps sector that was weak, and he was also concerned about the possibility of a counterattack. Huebner's 1st Division had occupied Mortain on August 3 without a fight. On August 6, the 1st was replaced by Hobbs's 30th, releasing the 1st to move to Mayenne. Eddy's 9th Division was nearby. Barton's 4th Division was in corps reserve near St. Pois. Part of Rose's 3rd Armored Division was nearby, and by sheer chance elements of Brooks's 2nd Armored Division were passing through the area en route to join the 1st Division at Mayenne. I had no better field generals than Collins, Hobbs, Eddy, Barton, Brooks and Rose. The four divisions and the strong armored elements they commanded were among our best and most experienced.[10]

Nonetheless, upon receipt of the Ultra alerts that night I took certain precautions. I gave Collins Baade's 35th Division, which was near Fougères en route from Gerow's V Corps to Walker's XX Corps. I called Patton to explain this transfer and the reason for it, and also asked him to stop the forward movement of two other of Walker's divisions. The next day, August 7, Patton made an entry in his diary which, I believe, further reinforces my memory that our Ultra was received only at the eleventh hour: "We got a rumor last night from a secret source that several panzer divisions will attack . . . Mortain . . . or Avranches. Personally I think it is a German bluff to cover a withdrawal, but I stopped the 80th, French 2nd Armored and 35th in the vicinity of St. Hilaire just in case something might happen." In addition, we called for all-out air support for the following morning.[11]

The main force of the German attack hit Leland Hobbs at Mortain. Von Kluge could not have chosen a more stubborn opponent. The men of the 30th Division fought—and held—like bulldogs. The weather was good and the Allied air forces tore into the advancing panzers, forcing them off the roads into the woods for cover and camouflage. Although the fighting would continue for several days, it was clear to me after a few hours that the offensive was suicidal, that it could be destroyed by the forces assigned to Collins, which were ideally situated on the German flanks to turn in and chew him to pieces. I agree with James Gavin's judgment: "Hitler could not have played into the hands of the Allies more completely if the Allies had planned it."[12]

That day, August 7, I drove to Patton's CP. Patton briefed me on Brittany; I briefed him on the Mortain counterattack. I was not overly concerned about the latter, but nonetheless I kept a "hold" on Walker's XX Corps in case it would be needed. At the same time, I approved Haislip's thrust to Le Mans. My mind was on the larger picture. I spent most of our meeting outlining to Patton my new idea for the long envelopment around Paris to Dieppe. He appeared to agree with it—he would lead the wide sweep—but he proposed a lesser "pivot" role for Hodges' First Army and questioned the use of the airborne corps. Hansen wrote: "Brad nods but sells his own."[13]

When I got back to my CP, Churchill arrived in the late afternoon. He said, "General Bradley, I came to tell you how magnificently we believe you are doing." In fact, Churchill had launched a campaign to cancel Dragoon, our subsidiary landing near Marseilles, which would take place in eight days. Churchill wanted my support in his campaign to kill Dragoon. He argued that it was foolish to risk a landing on a hostile beach, that the Dragoon forces should be brought in through Brittany ports. He had already conceived an operational plan for deployment of those forces through southern France on our right flank. "Why break down the back door when the front door had already been opened by your magnificent army?" Ike had forewarned me of Churchill's campaign. We both absolutely opposed it for many reasons. Not wishing to become involved in the debate, I courteously listened to Churchill but did not reply—other than "Yes, sir." The Prime Minister soon left for Ike's CP to continue his campaign, which, I was pleased to learn later, came to nought. Ike rightly insisted that Dragoon go forward as planned.[14]

That same night, August 7, the Canadian First Army jumped off on its first major offensive—"Totalizer"—led by the best of the Canadian generals, G. G. Simonds, commanding II Corps. Simonds had a formidable assault force: two armored divisions (including the recently arrived Polish 1st Armored Division), two armored brigades and three infantry divisions. Monty had ordered the Canadians to break through to Falaise, twenty-one miles southeast of Caen. We silently prayed the offensive would go well. If it did, it was bound to take considerable pressure off Joe Collins at Mortain. The Canadians ran into fierce resistance from three German divisions that were dug in well—and deep. Nonetheless, in one day the Canadians drove ahead about six miles, to within about twelve miles of

Falaise. But then they bogged down, and once again Falaise lay beyond Monty's grasp.[15]

By now we had learned from Ultra that von Kluge's offensive at Mortain had been ordered by Hitler himself and that it was intended to be much more than a "bluff to cover a withdrawal" (as Patton put it). On every division front the Germans were fighting hard, a clear indication that Hitler had no intention of withdrawing from Normandy.

It occurred to me that night, August 7, that Hitler's Mortain offensive had set the stage for an Allied coup de main. As I later put it to Hansen: "Greatest tactical blunder I've ever heard of. Probably won't happen again in a thousand years." If the Canadians could push into Falaise and beyond to Argentan, and if I turned Haislip due north from Le Mans toward Argentan, there was a good chance that we could encircle and trap the whole German force in Normandy in a matter of a few days. This short envelopment was far preferable to my grander idea of a blitzkrieging long envelopment around Paris to Dieppe. Because the "wheel" would be much smaller, we could go immediately, without waiting for a logistical buildup.

The next day, August 8, after reviewing the new plan with my staff, I went to Patton's CP to discuss it. He was curiously cool to the idea. He leaned toward my idea of the day before—the deeper and wider envelopment along the Seine—perhaps because it was more dramatic, perhaps because the success of my proposed shorter envelopment was heavily dependent on the Canadian army closing the gap from the north. Typically, the fact that logistical considerations argued for the shorter envelopment carried no weight with Patton.[16]

That same morning, I "arranged hurriedly" to meet Ike, who was touring the battlefields. I found him on a road near Coutances in a Packard Clipper, Kay Summersby at the wheel. I got in the Packard, and while we toured the battlefield and had a roadside lunch of K rations, I sketched the main features of the plan to Ike. He was so enthusiastic about it that he returned to Twelfth Army Group with me to discuss the plan in greater detail with maps.[17]

We could see no flaws in the plan. Tedder later recorded that Ike "approved it then and there." While Ike was still at my CP, I telephoned Patton and told him to alert Haislip to a move north, from Le Mans toward Argentan. Red O'Hare recalled my orders a month later: "You told George to turn north and keep it going." Patton recorded in his diary August 8: "I wrote an order for the attack of XV Corps." Two visitors at his CP, he continued, "said it was historic. I hope so." Later that same day he wrote his wife: "We may end this in ten days."[18]

Ike and I then telephoned Monty at his headquarters to outline the plan. I later recorded that he was "much surprised." To say the least, it was a radical shift in American strategy. Monty expressed some concern about Mortain, but I assured him Hodges and Collins had that situation well under control. To his credit, Monty was flexible in his thinking. Ike wrote in his memoirs that Monty "agreed the prospective prize was great and left the entire responsibility for the matter in Bradley's hands." We drew a "boundary line" through Argentan where we would close the trap. Monty was confident that the Canadians would quickly take Falaise and get to Argentan well before Haislip. Ike and I were not too sure about that; the Canadian offensive had come to a standstill. That night, Butcher recorded, Ike went to Monty's headquarters "to make certain that Monty would continue to press on the British-Canadian front."[19]

There is considerable confusion in the various military histories and memoirs as to whose "historic" idea it was to turn U.S. forces north and encircle the Germans. Monty claims full credit for himself in his postwar battle report: "In view of the Mortain counter stroke I decided to attempt . . . a shorter envelopment with the object of bottling up the bulk of the German forces deployed between Falaise and Mortain. On August 8, therefore, I ordered 12 U.S. Army Group to swing its right flank due north . . . at full strength and with all speed." Butcher attributes the idea to Ike: "Ike was pressing for switch of Patton's forces to the northeast the better to squeeze the enemy into a great pocket against the Seine River." Patton admirers, notably Farago, give him the credit. Farago wrote that when I visited Patton on the morning of August 8, "Patton grabbed the opportunity to tell Bradley about the plan he was working on—turning XV Corps north from Le Mans." And so on.[20]

Let me put it very plainly: it was my idea. Official Army historian Martin Blumenson credits me as the author. So does Ike, in a private memorandum he dictated that day, August 8: "The American right wing on this front should swing in closer in an effort to destroy the enemy by attacking him in the rear. On a visit to Bradley today I found that he had *already acted on this idea*. . . . I believe this will be tactically sound." (Italics added.)[21]

At a press conference on September 7, 1944, a war correspondent asked Patton if the Falaise trap were part of the original Overlord plan or an improvisation. Patton replied: "Improvisation by General Bradley. I thought we were going east and he told me to move north."[22]

THIRTY-THREE

The opportunity that now lay before us was nothing short of fantastic. I could scarcely believe our good fortune. I remarked to Hansen, "The German is either crazy or he doesn't know what's going on. I think he is too smart to do what he is doing. He can't know what's going on in our sector. Surely the professional generals must know the jig is up." Hansen said, "Hitler is your greatest ally, sir?" I replied, "Yes, perhaps he is."[1]

Secretary of the Treasury Henry Morgenthau visited my headquarters the next day, August 9. I outlined our plans and let my enthusiasm run away with me: "This is an opportunity that comes to a commander not more than once in a century. We're about to destroy an entire hostile army. If the other fellow will only press his attack here at Mortain for another forty-eight hours, he'll give us time to close at Argentan and there completely destroy him . . . he'll have nothing left with which to oppose us. We'll go all the way from here to the German border."[2]

On the next day, August 10, Haislip turned his XV Corps due north at Le Mans. From the outset of the maneuver, I privately worried about the troops under Haislip's command, wishing they were more battle-wise. Initially he commanded two armored and two infantry divisions. The armored divisions were our least experienced: the U.S. 5th, commanded by Lunsford E. Oliver, and the newly arrived French 2nd, commanded by Jacques P. LeClerc, who had fought in Africa. His division had been organized and equipped with American tanks in England, but LeClerc was notoriously undisciplined and did not speak English. His sole ambition seemed to be the liberation of Paris; the turn north deflected him from that objective. The infantry divisions were Wyche's 79th and the ill-starred 90th. I have already noted that Ike and I had expressed reservations about Wyche. The 90th was now commanded by the very able Raymond McLain, but he was the third commander in as many weeks and the division had not yet proved itself. The newly arrived and utterly green 80th Infantry Division, commanded by Horace L. McBride, was ordered up to protect the rear of the corps. Over the next several days my decisions would, in part, be influenced by the misgivings I had about these five divisions.[3]

With Haislip pushing north and the Canadians pushing south to close the jaws of the trap, we had to be extremely careful in joining these forces. As Ike put it, "a calamitous battle between friends could have resulted." Allied air was attacking ahead of each force, the "bomb lines" for each moving ever closer. Allied air had already killed or wounded too many Allied troops to suit me. There was grave danger that as the gap between the armies narrowed and closed, the airmen would mistakenly attack one or the other. The same danger applied to the artillery. Without the utmost care, I could foresee our armies accidentally shelling one another. As we saw in Cobra, nothing is more demoralizing to troops than to see their men killed by friendly fire. These considerations tended to add to my caution.[4]

When we turned Haislip north at Le Mans, von Kluge perceived at once that the trap was being set. He wanted to abandon the Mortain offensive, turn about and fight his way out to the Seine before the jaws closed on him. Hitler still hoped to mount a decisive drive on Avranches, but by the end of the day, August 11, even he had to concede another attempt was hopeless and that Haislip's drive north was creating a trap. Hitler ordered a turnabout and attack on Haislip's left flank. Although his divisions had been decimated in the abortive Mortain counterattack and maneuver inside the pocket was difficult in the extreme, von Kluge was only too happy to oblige. An eastward attack on Haislip's flank would set the stage for a fighting withdrawal from the whole dangerous pocket. On the following day, August 12, von Kluge ordered preparations for the offensive; a panzer division moved toward Argentan and remnants of the others were to follow. While we received no explicit notice of this offensive from Ultra, there were sufficient indications from Bletchley Park (such as transfer of the panzer division) to cause me utmost concern for Haislip's exposed position.[5]

Meanwhile the Canadians, so crucial to our trap, were still getting nowhere. On August 12, Hansen reflected the mood in Twelfth Army Group: "British [Canadian] effort from the north is still mediocre with troops at their deepest salient only 12 miles in advance [south] of Caen, which was their D-day objective. . . . The Canadian attack toward Falaise has been disappointingly slow. . . . British effort . . . appears to have logged [bogged] itself in timidity and succumbed to the legendary Montgomery vice of over-caution." The Canadians were still some ten miles north of Falaise.[6]

By this time, Ike had established an advanced SHAEF headquarters in France—code-named "Shellburst"—near Granville and was in full-time residence. He had not yet formally taken command of the ground forces but he was ever-present. I made no major move without consulting him. On the afternoon of August 12, as Haislip's forces closed on the "boundary" near Argentan, Ike came to my CP to monitor Haislip's progress, and he remained through dinner.[7]

I was now gravely concerned about the impending German attack on Haislip's left flank. With Ike's approval, I took steps to reinforce Haislip with the best troops I had in my command: Collins' VII Corps. That afternoon I ordered Collins to go all-out to the northeast, inserting his corps between Haislip and the bulk of the Germans withdrawing from Mortain. Collins put Huebner's Big Red One, Eddy's 9th and Rose's 3rd Armored in the van, with Barton's 4th in reserve. With characteristic speed, Collins had his corps on the way that night. This somewhat eased my concern, but we did not yet know what Collins would encounter on the morrow. Until Collins closed the gap, Haislip's left flank was wide open.[8]

The next day, Sunday, August 13, was one of the most taxing I would ever experience. During the previous night, Haislip's forces had closed to the "boundary" at Argentan. The Canadians were still bogged down six miles short of Falaise; there was thus a gap of about nineteen miles between our forces. Haislip signaled Patton that he had reached his stated objective and, in effect, requested authority to continue *beyond* the boundary. Without consulting me, Patton ordered Haislip to "push on slowly in the direction of Falaise" and when he reached Falaise "continue to push on slowly until contact [with] our Allies" was made. During the early morning hours of August 13, a few of Haislip's patrols drove eight miles beyond the boundary—to within about six miles of Falaise.[9]

When I learned what had happened during the night, I was furious. In ordering Haislip to advance beyond the Allied boundary, Patton had knowingly and willfully violated an Allied agreement. He had placed his troops into "no man's land," where they were exposed to Allied air attack. He had extended Haislip's vulnerable left flank even further, knowing full well Ultra had forecast a German counterattack on that very day. An advance to Falaise would leave Haislip thinly strung out over a forty-mile line with troops that had not yet proven themselves in a difficult situation. Collins was only then beginning to move north to cover Haislip's left; we still had not closed the gap. No formal procedures had yet been arrived at for joining the two armies.

Falaise was a long-sought British objective and, for them, a matter of immense prestige. If Patton's patrols grabbed Falaise, it would be an arrogant slap in the face at a time when we clearly needed to build confidence in the Canadian Army.[10]

I had a sharp telephone exchange with Patton that morning. He further infuriated me with his boastful, supercilious attitude. "Let me go on to Falaise and we'll drive the British back into the sea for another Dunkirk." I replied coldly and firmly, "Nothing doing. You're not to go beyond Argentan. Just stop where you are and build up on that shoulder." I much preferred a solid shoulder at Argentan to the possibility of a broken neck at Falaise. Patton recalled Haislip's patrols to the boundary and his men began to dig in on the shoulder.[11]

Soon after this exchange with Patton, I met Ike and Monty at Monty's CP for lunch and a full afternoon of discussion of the strategic and tactical situation. Monty chose this occasion to unveil a grandiose strategic plan to carry the war beyond Normandy and the Seine. It was a radical departure from the plans we had drawn in England before D-day and (as on Sicily) it subordinated U.S. forces to Monty's to an absurd and unacceptable degree. With our forces poised to close the trap at Falaise-Argentan and Monty's forces falling down on the job, Monty could not have chosen a more inappropriate time to unveil his strategic plan. Ike and I were dismayed—both at the plan and the timing. It was a distinctly uncomfortable afternoon.[12]

Our discussion of the tactical situation—the "Falaise Gap" as we now called it—was preceded by an extensive intelligence briefing which embodied all the latest Ultra intercepts. I cannot recall any specific dramatic dispatches, but the general impression conveyed was that the German commanders, with or without Hitler's authorization, were already carrying out a substantial withdrawal to the east. The German forces still inside the pocket appeared to be in complete disarray, perhaps on the verge of a stampede. Owing to the German chaos inside the pocket, it was no longer possible to present a tidy Order of Battle; no one was then certain how many German divisions had withdrawn or still remained. But the general estimate was that too many had already escaped.*

This news was a shattering disappointment—one of my greatest of the war. A golden opportunity had truly been lost. I boiled inside, blaming Monty for the blunder. We had done our part, set the lower jaws at Argentan and restrained Patton from a brash and foolish overextension. Monty, perhaps too busy with his strategic plans, had turned his part over to the Canadians, an unproven army depending to a great extent on two armored divisions, one Canadian, one Polish, both new to combat. I could not understand why at so crucial a moment Monty had not reinforced the Canadians with some of his battle-hardened British troops, especially the armor. His unrealistic faith in the Canadians had cost us the golden opportunity.†

* Our estimate that afternoon is reflected in several contemporary documents, all written or dated the following day, August 14. Monty wrote me, in part: "It is difficult to say what enemy are inside the ring, and what have got out to the east. *A good deal may have escaped.*" (Italics added.) A Twelfth Army Group operational report stated that "many of the German divisions which were in the pocket have now escaped." Chet Hansen gloomily wrote: "It is now definitely established that our opportunity to close the pincer and trap the German Army has been lost."[13]

† Official Canadian historian Colonel C. P. Stacey wrote: "Had our troops been more experienced, the Germans would hardly have been able to escape a worse disaster . . . less raw formations would probably have obtained larger and earlier results." Chester Wilmot

We now know from the research of the historians that intelligence evaluations were wrong—egregiously wrong. The Germans had not yet withdrawn any substantial numbers of combat troops, merely noncombatants and other nonessential forces. The orders to withdraw the main forces would not be issued for another forty-eight hours and the withdrawal itself would not commence until the evening of August 16. We still had it within our power to close the trap, but we did not know it.[15]

Based on these wrong intelligence estimates, the discussion now focused on how we could still inflict the greatest damage on the "escaping" enemy. We decided on two courses of action. We would continue to close the Falaise Gap, although this now seemed less important; and we would mount a second, larger, encirclement to the northeast, hoping to catch the bulk of the escaped German divisions before they reached the Seine.

Primary responsibility for the first course, closing the gap, would remain Monty's. The Canadians were gearing up for a renewed attack on Falaise the following day, August 14. In support of this effort, Dempsey's Second Army would simultaneously attack toward Falaise from the northwest. Ike and I were frankly dismayed and mystified by these plans. If, as intelligence indicated, the Germans were already withdrawing, Dempsey's attack would amount to aggressive pursuit rather than entrapment. It would tend to hurry the Germans through the gap before the Canadians had closed it. We privately likened it to squeezing the toothpaste from the bottom of the tube with no cap on. A far better plan, we thought, would be to shift part of Dempsey's army around—the armor, for example—to the east of the Canadians, toward Chambois, creating a parallel pincer (firmly screwing the cap on the toothpaste tube). But this was Monty's responsibility, and it would not have been politic for either Ike, who had not yet formally taken command of ground forces, or me to attempt to make radically new suggestions about the deployment of his forces.[16]

Primary responsibility for the second course of action, casting the nets farther northeast to entrap the fleeing Germans west of the Seine, fell on me. This responsibility was restressed by Monty in his above-mentioned letter to me of August 14: "I think your movement . . . should be northeast towards Dreux. Also any further stuff you can move round to Le Mans should go northeast. We want to head off the Germans and [also] stop them breaking out to the southeast." The plan I conceived to carry out my responsibility was, in effect, a modification, a scaling down, of my earlier idea to wheel Patton around Paris toward Dieppe. The essential differences were that the wheel would be severely constricted to turn west of Paris, and that it could be launched at once, without waiting for a

judged that "the evidence suggests that the thrust from the north was not pressed with sufficient speed and strength." The Canadian attack, he went on, was not "as vigorous and venturesome as the occasion demanded." A week later, Crerar sacked the commanding general of the 4th Armored Division.[14]

massive logistical buildup. Hodges' First Army would pivot northeast as an even smaller wheel inside Patton's wheel and release Patton of all responsibility for closing the Falaise Gap.

It was a very long, tedious day during which many vital decisions had been discussed and made at the very highest levels. In the late afternoon, I went back to Ike's CP, Shellburst, for dinner. I cannot say that Ike and I were in the best of spirits. Owing to Monty's wildly misplaced confidence in the Canadians, we thought we had missed an opportunity to annihilate the Germans and that they were escaping through the gap. Monty's plan for finally closing the gap was less than satisfactory. My own plan for casting the nets farther northeastward was more like emergency procedure than careful maneuver. And to top it all off, Monty had unveiled an unworkable long-range strategic plan that was sure to lead to endless debate and acrimony.[17]

All that afternoon, meanwhile, Patton had been stewing over my decision to halt Haislip at Argentan. His chief of staff, Hugh Gaffey, had been on the telephone with my chief of staff, Lev Allen, and others, trying to get the decision overturned so that Haislip could attempt to take Falaise. But while I had been closeted with Ike and Monty, Allen had firmly iterated my orders. Given the complex circumstances and intelligence assumptions that had led to these orders, I believe they were sound—and believe so to this day. Patton, in his diary, blamed Montgomery: "I believe that the order . . . emanated from the 21st Army Group, and was either due to [British] jealousy of the Americans or to utter ignorance of the situation or to a combination of the two." But, in fact, Montgomery had no part in the decision; it was mine and mine alone. Some writers have suggested that I appealed to Monty to move the boundary north to Falaise and he refused, but, of course, that is not true. For all the reasons I have stated, I was determined to hold Patton at Argentan and had no cause to ask Monty to shift the boundary. Ike, as he wrote in his memoirs, "completely supported" me in this decision.[18]

Before dinner with Ike that night, I sought a few moments' relaxation at the bridge table. Butcher came on the scene and later recorded that "Bradley was here playing bridge as calmly and peacefully as if he had just come off the golf course on a Sunday afternoon." From this tidbit some writers—including most regrettably that good soldier and friend James Gavin—have implied or asserted that I spent that day out of touch with my forces and the situation. Gavin wrote that my proper place that day was at Patton's or Haislip's CP, where the "critical action" was taking place. I could not disagree more. My proper place that day was where I spent it, with Ike and Monty.[19]

On the following morning, August 14, as Crerar and Dempsey jumped off for the renewed attack on Falaise and with Haislip halted and dug in at Argentan, I finalized my plans for the northeastward wheeling movement to entrap the "escaping" Germans. Inasmuch as intelligence had led me to believe "many" German divisions had already escaped, and Joe Collins had closed the gap and blazed north twenty miles on Haislip's left the day before against light resistance (seeming to confirm our belief that the Germans had withdrawn), I decided that Haislip's five divisions (including the arriving 80th Infantry) on the shoulder were now excessive. I would split Haislip's corps, giving him two divisions (5th Armored and 79th Infantry) and leaving behind three (French 2nd Armored, 80th and 90th Infantry). Gee Gerow, commanding Hodges' V Corps (which had been pinched out of the action near Vire), would bring his staff around to form a "provisional" corps for the three divisions left at Argentan. This would free Haislip's reduced XV Corps to join in Patton's larger northeastward wheel, and leave the Falaise Gap solely to Hodges' First Army. I would send Haislip to Dreux.[20]

That afternoon Patton, who had been alerted to his new and larger wheeling role, flew back to my CP with a rough "plan" of action. Patton made much of this "plan," writing: "It is really a great plan, wholly my own, and I made Bradley think he thought of it." His plan was for Walker's XX Corps to wheel northeast to Dreux; Cook's XII Corps to wheel northeast to Chartres. Since he was unaware of my plan to send Haislip's reduced XV Corps to Dreux, we were compelled to completely revise his plan, sending Walker to Chartres and Cook to Orléans.[21]

I gave verbal orders to Patton to execute the plan that afternoon. Patton wrote in his diary: "I am very happy and elated. I got all the corps moving by 2030 [hours] so that if Monty tries to be careful, it will be too late." In fact, Patton had no need to fear caution from Monty this time. Our plans and orders were in keeping with Monty's suggestions in his letter to me that day to "go northeast."[22]

Our decision to send Patton wheeling northeast on August 14, as we now know, was not only a poor decision but a distinctly dangerous one. Unknown to us, the major share of German forces were still inside the pocket, still vulnerable to encirclement. Had we known this—had we not been misled by intelligence—we would have held Haislip solidly in place on the Argentan shoulder and most likely would have sent Walker directly north on Haislip's right flank toward Chambois, to help close the gap. With Collins, Haislip and Walker forming a solid eleven-division east-west front along the southern edge of the pocket, we would probably have then requested that Monty pull the boundary back so that our forces could advance on Falaise to link up with Crerar and Dempsey, probably on August 16. Had this been done, we would have trapped most of the German force inside the pocket. But this falls into the nebulous and pointless "what if" category of history. What we had done in splitting Haislip's corps and ordering Gerow to come around to take command of the three divisions Haislip left behind at Argentan had gravely weakened the shoulder at a time when it was most vulnerable.

On the very next day, August 15, intelligence reversed itself. To our astonishment it was now reported that the Germans had not yet withdrawn after all. Elements of at least five panzer divisions were at or approaching Argentan. We knew these divisions had been severely mauled by our ground and air forces, that they were desperately short of fuel, ammo and everything else, but we did not know that the divisions were in fact completely decimated. (Intelligence, including Ultra, consistently overrated German strength.) I had to assume these divisions now posed the gravest threat to our weak Argentan shoulder, where Hugh Gaffey was commanding, pending Gerow's arrival. I went immediately to Patton's headquarters to halt his northwestward wheel and to alert Haislip and Walker for a possible about-face to reinforce Gaffey at Argentan. Having already unleashed his three-corps blitzkrieg to the northeast, Patton was contemptuous: "Bradley came down to see me suffering from nerves. . . . His motto seems to be 'In case of doubt, halt.' . . . I wish I were Supreme Commander."[23]

By the following day, August 16, the Germans had received permission to withdraw. The battered panzer divisions, now desperate to get out, hit McLain's 90th Division on the Argentan shoulder a very hard blow. The Germans, like the trapped Germans in Tunisia, fought desperately. McLain's troops fell back and for a few hours we held our collective breaths. But McLain's superb leadership rallied the division and it held. That same day, elements of Dempsey's and Crerar's armies at long last took Falaise, where Monty had hoped to stage a tank knockabout on D-day. It was D plus 71 days.[24]

There was still a gap of some sixteen miles between the British-Canadian and American forces. The gap was now teeming with Germans who seemed more willing to die than be trapped. There was now no way on earth the British-Canadians could fight their way to Argentan. Nor, conversely, was there any way my weakened Argentan forces could fight through to Falaise. Monty telephoned to suggest we try closing the gap farther east at Chambois. He had already ordered Crerar to turn his Canadians southeast through Trun to Chambois. Could my forces help snap the jaws shut at Chambois?[25]

Monty's proposal could not have come at a more inopportune time. It was too late to turn Patton around. Haislip, Walker and Cook—in some of the most astonishing wide-open sweeps of the entire war—had already reached Dreux, Chartres and Orléans. The best I could promise was to disengage Gerow's provisional corps at Argentan and send it to Chambois. This was an extremely difficult maneuver for Gerow, who was only then taking command from Gaffey and whose forces included LeClerc's undisciplined French Armored Division and McBride's utterly green 80th Infantry Division.

I did not sleep well that night. I was torn with doubts about my own judgment. I had privately sworn never to overrely, tactically, on Ultra.

And yet I had. Because of that mistake, I had imprudently sent Haislip, Walker and Cook far to the northeast. Had I not been so impetuous, Haislip and Walker—and if necessary Cook—would have been available to close the jaws at Chambois and annihilate the Germans in the pocket. What I now had available—Gerow's makeshift corps—was not a proper response to the job I had been asked to do.[26]

The rest of the story is quickly told. The Canadians swung southeast through Trun toward Chambois. Gerow's corps, after losing valuable time during the confusion that arose in the change of command, moved six miles east, then swung north to Chambois. On August 19, a tenuous link was established between our forces and the Canadians at Chambois, encircling elements of perhaps twelve German divisions, half of them panzers. But our "jaws" were too weak to contain what we had encircled. In a truly remarkable feat of arms, on August 20-21, the trapped Germans skillfully organized a breakout and, as on Sicily, all too many—perhaps 40,000 or more—escaped to fight again.[27]

There was still a chance that we might yet cut off the escapees and stragglers before they reached the Seine to organize a defensive line on that natural barrier. Haislip's XV Corps at Dreux was in the best position to close the net. After clearing the plan with Monty, I ordered Haislip to drive farther northeast to Mantes on the Seine, thence north along both sides of the river toward Rouen. At the same time, I ordered Corlett's XIX Corps to swing around Le Mans and go northeast toward Evreux to protect Haislip's left flank. These moves, while expertly executed by Haislip and Corlett, forced the Germans ever northward, where the river was twice as wide and therefore more difficult to cross, but they netted no large bag of prisoners. Most of those Germans who escaped from the Falaise pocket got across the Seine. However, if the Germans had any hope of organizing a defensive line on the east bank of the Seine, Haislip's maneuver dashed it.[28]

So ended the Battle of Normandy. It had raged some eighty days, from Utah, Omaha, Gold, Juno and Sword beaches to Cherbourg and the Seine, with a side excursion into Brittany. Hitler had committed two large armies, the Seventh and the Fifth Panzer, comprising about forty divisions (600,000 men) and 1,500 tanks. Opposing him at the end, we had deployed four armies totaling about forty divisions (600,000 men) and some 3,000 tanks. In addition, we had an air force of perhaps 12,000 planes; Hitler had almost none to employ in France. Both German armies had been destroyed in all but name. Some 10,000 to 15,000 Germans had been killed in the Mortain-Falaise battle alone, another 50,000 had been captured. The Germans had suffered some 500,000 casualties in all of France since D-day. But the victory had cost us dearly: 200,000 Allies killed, wounded or missing, two-thirds of these American.[29]

Our victory in Normandy, together with the Dragoon landing in the south of France on August 15, liberated France. Owing to Hitler's abortive Mortain offensive and our encircling reaction at Argentan-Falaise, however technically imperfect, and Haislip's wheel toward Rouen, the Germans were unable to establish a defensive line along the Seine. The survivors of Normandy were in full flight to the German border, leaving the much-weakened Fifteenth German Army at Pas de Calais out on a limb.

There was wild jubilation in the Allied camp. Nothing of consequence lay between us and Germany. Hitler's vaunted military machine had been irretrievably smashed; the military high command fatally undermined by defeat (von Kluge committed suicide) and the widespread purge in the wake of the assassination attempt on Hitler. German cities lay devastated by Allied strategic bombing, the population demoralized. The economic and industrial bases had been shattered beyond recovery. We had only to cross the rest of France, then Belgium and Holland, then the Rhine into Germany. The war, many thought, would surely be over by the end of September.[30]

There was only one sour note in this sweet symphony of victory: our frustrating Brittany campaign. Under Patton, Middleton's VIII Corps of three divisions had taken St. Malo after a stiff fight, but the Germans had withdrawn into the ports of Lorient, St. Nazaire and Brest, prepared for a long and bitter siege. As each day passed, the prospect of utilizing these ports for supplying our forces (as envisioned in Overlord) seemed to be less and less promising. By the time we took Brest and could get it operational, for example, it seemed likely that we would have advanced so far to the east that the port would be too far to the rear to be of real use.

We might have been well advised at this point to give up the good fight and let Brest remain in German hands, contained by our newly arriving green infantry divisions or by the French Forces of the Interior, which had ably assisted Patton's run through Brittany. We certainly could have used Middleton's corps to better advantage in the forthcoming drive toward Germany. But by then, Brest had taken on a symbolic value far exceeding its utilitarian value and, perhaps imprudently, I was stubbornly determined to capture it. I explained my views in a private talk with Patton, who recorded them in his diary:

> He said to me with reference to the Brest operation, "I would not say this to anyone but you, and I have given different excuses to my staff and higher echelons, but we must take Brest in order to maintain the illusion of the fact that the U.S. Army cannot be beaten." More emotion than I thought he had. I fully concur in this view. Anytime we put our hand to a job, we must finish it.[31]

General Ramcke and his 38,000 well-organized troops at Brest held out until September 19. By that time I had shifted the responsibility for Brest to Bill Simpson's newly arrived Ninth Army, transferring Middleton's VIII Corps from Patton to Simpson. Three U.S. infantry divisions and half of Middleton's 6th Armored Division were committed to the final siege, plus thousands of tons of valuable ammunition and no little scarce air power and transport. Middleton's VIII Corps suffered 9,831 casualties—killed, wounded, missing. That was far too high a price to pay to maintain illusions of invincibility.

Owing to the character of the German resistance in Brittany—Brest in particular—I did not share the general Allied euphoria, the belief that, after the Falaise Gap, Germany was all but beaten. If she could hold out so stubbornly in a lost cause like Brest, what would happen when we reached her own borders or the Rhine River?[32]

THIRTY-FOUR

Long before D-day, Ike, Monty and I had agreed on a broad plan for the defeat of Germany after we were securely ashore in Normandy. Anticipating the Germans would make a textbook retreat to the Seine, we would draw up our combined ground forces opposite the river. There we would pause for several weeks to rest and refit our divisions, fully open our supply ports in Cherbourg and Brittany, create logistical lines to our front and stockpile gasoline, ammunition and food. When all was ready we would cross the Seine and strike toward Germany.

Our primary objective in Germany was the Ruhr industrial complex, the main source of Germany's steel production. We believed that when Hitler perceived our objective, he would commit his remaining ground forces to its defense. We would encircle the Ruhr and in one stroke destroy or capture both his Army and his war production base, bringing the war to an end.

As we envisioned it before D-day, our strike against Germany would consist of two massive, mutually supporting thrusts, one led by Monty, one by me. Monty's thrust, composed of two armies (Dempsey's Second and Crerar's First), would follow a course roughly Amiens-Liège-Aachen, passing north of the Ardennes, a large, densely wooded and hilly area considered unsuitable for tanks and motorized vehicles. My thrust, composed of two armies (Hodges' First and Patton's Third), would follow a course roughly Troyes-Nancy-Metz, passing south of the Ardennes. My forces would destroy or capture the important coal and steel production facilities in the Saar industrial complex, swing northeast to Frankfurt, thence north to the Ruhr, joining Monty's thrust for the coup de grace.

No one had foreseen a quick or easy victory. We expected that the Germans would fight tenaciously at the Seine, retreat slowly to natural defensive barriers at the Somme, Marne, Meuse and Moselle rivers, then finally to the West Wall, or as we called it, the Siegfried Line, a series of interlocking pillboxes along the entire length of Germany's western border. There, and at the Rhine River, we expected another arduous fight, since the Germans would be defending their homeland and their lines of supply would be short and ours very long. We believed it would take us a full year to reach the West Wall, or as the planners put it, D plus 350 days. All logistical planning was based on that estimate.[1]

Several new and unforeseen factors, all major, now compelled us to rethink the "two thrust" strategy. The first was Hitler's decision to fight a showdown battle in Normandy, our great victory and the headlong flight of the Germans beyond the Seine. The second was the intensification of Hitler's V-weapon assault on England. By mid-August, V-1s had killed 5,000, injured 35,000 and destroyed 36,000 dwellings. Ultra and other intelligence sources were predicting that Hitler had no less than a thousand of the more formidable V-2 rockets ready for deployment in mid-September. The third factor in our rethinking was our failure to quickly seize the Brittany ports, especially Brest, causing us to rely on Cherbourg and the invasion beaches for our logistical support. They were not adequate to sustain operations beyond the Seine. At any time, inclement weather could close down the invasion beaches which, as I have stated, constituted our main supply ports.[2]

Even before we developed a revised grand strategy to deal with these new factors, we all agreed on one point. With the enemy reeling in defeat, the planned "pause" at the Seine was clearly inappropriate. Regardless of the logistical limitations, which were growing ever more binding, we would, as Ike put it to Marshall on August 17, "dash across the Seine" without pause, both to prevent the Germans from creating defensive positions on the east bank and to entrap as many stragglers as possible. In the north, Haislip's XV Corps was already across the Seine at Mantes. In addition to that maneuver, I ordered Walker's XX Corps and Cook's XII to advance to and cross the Seine south of Paris at Melun and Troyes.

These spearheads jumped off on August 21. Regrettably, Cook had been hospitalized with "extraordinarily high blood pressure" (he could not walk the length of a football field) and we were compelled to relieve him. Ike, Patton and I agreed that Manton Eddy, who had so ably commanded the 9th Division, deserved a promotion. Eddy replaced Cook. Prodded by Patton, Walker and Eddy achieved their objectives within a few days, notwithstanding an inept performance at Melun by the commander of Walker's 7th Armored Division, Lindsey McD. Silvester. Eddy's 100-mile drive from Orléans to Troyes was one of the most electrifying of the war. His route was in keeping with our pre-D-day strategy for my thrust south of the Ardennes via Nancy-Metz-Frankfurt.[3]

This drive had brought our forces to within a stone's throw of Paris. No city in Europe was more alluring. Everybody, it seemed, wanted to liberate Paris. Everybody, that is, except me. In a tactical sense Paris was meaningless. We were in pursuit of the fleeing German Army, which was leaving Paris behind. It had always been our plan to bypass Paris, isolating whatever garrison troops it might contain, and deal with it after we had destroyed the German Army or, at least, reached the Siegfried Line or the Rhine. Pausing to liberate Paris would not only needlessly slow our eastward drive, but also require the diversion of transport and gasoline to provide the four million Parisians a planned 4,000 tons of food and supplies per day.

However, certain events forced me to alter that plan. On August 19 there was a spontaneous uprising of the Resistance in Paris, encouraged by the French police. The German occupation commander, Dietrich von Choltitz, in order to spare the city from ruin and prevent further useless bloodshed, concluded an armistice with the Resistance forces, which he fully intended to honor. Mistakenly believing the armistice was merely temporary (or a ruse), emissaries of the Resistance sneaked out of Paris into our lines with frantic pleas for help. Reluctantly, I delegated the task to Gee Gerow's V Corps and asked him to send LeClerc's French 2nd Armored Division to accept the surrender. Concerned that LeClerc's forces might be engulfed with champagne-bearing well-wishers and thus diverted and delayed in their mission, I also asked Gerow to send Ray Barton's battle-hardened 4th Infantry Division to help. Goaded by that threat, LeClerc's men, nearly overwhelmed with wine and women, rolled and reeled into Paris on August 25 and took the surrender while Barton's men were entering the suburbs.

Ike could not resist sneaking a quick glimpse of Paris. He invited Monty and me to accompany him. Monty declined; I reluctantly accepted. We drove into the city in his Cadillac (protected by a small armed convoy) the morning of August 27, a Sunday, and met Gee Gerow on a quiet street corner. Gerow escorted us to police headquarters, where Charles de Gaulle, political leader of the Free French Forces, had already established his base.

By this time, LeClerc's men had disappeared into the back alleys, brothels and bistros. De Gaulle imperiously demanded a show of military force—a parade—to nail down the capitulation and to reassure the Parisians. I worked out a plan with Gerow whereby we could redeploy Norman Cota's 28th Infantry Division through the streets of Paris to its jump-off point east of the city without loss of time. In this way, on August 29, de Gaulle got his "parade" down the Champs-Elysées and I got the 28th Division tactically poised for pursuit of the German Army. As predicted, the feeding of the Parisians imposed an enormous strain on our already thinly stretched logistical lines.[4]

These rapid thrusts across the Seine were all to the good, but they were spur-of-the-moment pursuits, not grand strategy. However appealing, logistical restraints would not allow us to pursue the Germans willy-nilly across France on all fronts. We had supported Patton's drive to Melun and Troyes with an emergency airlift of gasoline, but there was nowhere near enough airlift to keep that up. Moreover, our emergency airlift completely immobilized our excellent airborne forces which had now been organized into a three-division corps—the XVIII Airborne—under Ridgway.

Even as we "dashed" across the Seine in hot pursuit, all of us in the Allied high command were simultaneously giving deepest attention and thought to a revised grand strategy. As it developed, Monty and I produced different—and conflicting—plans. Our differences led to disputes, some of the bitterest of the war. Ike was caught in the middle, mediating as always, seeking a compromise. The strategy finally settled on satisfied neither Monty nor me. Some distinguished military historians—Liddell Hart, for one—have asserted that in our deliberations and decisions we threw away an opportunity for an early end to the war. Patton called it "the most momentous error of the war."[5]

Let me begin with Monty's plan. When Ike and I met with Monty on July 2, he made the astonishing proposal that the Normandy campaign be more or less abandoned in favor of his offhand proposal to lead a force of three armies, including my First Army, directly at Pas de Calais. This was the seed, I believe, which grew to become his master plan. The chief feature of this master plan, then and always, was that Monty would lead the major thrust on Germany, leaving the Americans, as he had in Tunisia and attempted to in Sicily, in a distinctly subordinate role. He was also obsessively determined to retain complete control of Allied ground forces, keeping Ike in the role of "chairman of the board," as in the Mediterranean.

Monty had first unveiled his master plan to Ike and me on that busy, vexing Sunday, August 13, when I stopped Patton at Argentan. He proposed—and continued to propose over the next several weeks—that the "two thrust" strategy for operations beyond the Seine be scrapped. In its place he suggested a massive "single thrust," composed of all four Allied armies (forty divisions). The single thrust, commanded by Monty, would sweep northeastward, wipe out the remainder of the German Fifteenth Army at Pas de Calais, establish a powerful Allied airfield network in Belgium, seize Antwerp and Rotterdam (thus solving our logistical problems), destroy the V-1 and V-2 launching sites, capture the Ruhr and then drive straight through to Berlin. All this would be accomplished with utmost speed while the German forces were still in disarray and demoralized. For the thrust to succeed, every resource of the Allied command would have to be placed behind it. If successful, it would end the war by October.[6]

The plan was breathtaking and bedazzling—a panacea. It solved all our problems in a single tidy package. It called to mind Monty's spell-binding performances at St. Paul's School in April. It also called to mind the bravado prior to and in the early stages of Goodwood when Monty had assured everyone of a breakout.

There were any number of weaknesses in the plan. The principal one was that Monty would be in complete charge. We would be putting all our money on a horse that looked good in the paddock but had a tough time getting out of the starting gate and had never shown well on a fast track. We had well noted Monty's ponderous build-ups and long delays before mounting an attack, his apparent reluctance to take risks and pursue and exploit (at El Alamein, the Mareth Line, Chott Line, Sicily, Italy, Caen on D-day, Falaise Gap). Now he was asking us to believe that he could lead us straight through to Berlin in a single quick dash that would be one of the riskiest maneuvers in the history of warfare.

It would give Monty too large a role in the ground command, in effect upstaging or obscuring Ike, who was to assume that role on September 1. Monty would never have more than sixteen British and Canadian divisions; we Americans would soon have three times that number. If Monty's plan were approved, there was no doubt in my mind that all Allied divisions would come under his command. The U.S. public would not any longer accept a single British ground commander, especially not one who was so unwilling to share credit for success. It was a time of extreme jingoism; the American public demanded its own epic-size war heroes, and it wanted them in command at the kill.

This last point was vividly illustrated only a few days later. Owing to a censorship error, the media prematurely released the news that I had assumed command of the Twelfth Army Group and was now the "co-equal" of Monty. The British press was stunned and outraged; in their eyes no American general could be the "co-equal" of the hero of El Alamein. Fleet Street complained insultingly that my promotion amounted to a "demotion" for Monty. The U.S. media, in turn, took sharp exception to the implied insults to me and demanded apologies of Fleet Street. The furor led some American papers to re-examine the entire Allied command setup and to bitterly criticize it for being "too British." Marshall became so concerned about the rising level of criticism of the Allied command that he wrote Ike advising him to assume ground command as soon as possible.[7]

Beyond these political and psychological considerations, there were technical weaknesses in Monty's plan. Complete success demanded utmost speed. That meant that Monty could not, as was his wont, pause to "tidy up the battlefield." Inevitably he would have to bypass strong pockets of German forces which might hole up in ports, as Ramcke had done at Brest. Thus Monty would be compelled to "drop off" divisions as he went along to deal with these pockets and to protect his flanks. No one could predict how many divisions might be dropped off—perhaps as few as ten or as many as twenty. Whatever the number, it would mean that as Monty approached and crossed into Germany, where he could expect to meet the strongest resistance, his force would be ever shrinking in strength and thus most vulnerable at exactly the wrong time and place.

There were other technical weaknesses. Monty's more northeasterly route of advance would lead him across terrain that was far less suitable for armor. The proposed route was laced with canals and waterways, natural barriers for defense, forcing the tanks to move along a few constricted and highly vulnerable roads. It would be like fighting in the bocage again: slow, tedious, bloody. In such country, Patton shrewdly observed, tanks would be "practically useless." Beyond that was the pressing but unanswered question of how Monty intended to move his infantry and artillery forces rapidly. The British and Canadians had no lorry comparable to our workhorse two-and-a-half-ton truck and no efficient artillery tractors.[8]

In my opinion, Monty's basic assumption—that he could strike straight through to the Ruhr and Berlin before the Germans could organize to resist him—was downright crazy. I was sure the Germans could organize at least twenty to thirty crack divisions to defend their homeland. By then, Monty's spearhead would be dangerously weak. There would not be time enough to open Antwerp for supplies; his lines would stretch all the way back to the invasion beaches. His flanks would be exposed to counterattack. In my estimation, there was a good possibility that Monty's diminished spearhead could be utterly destroyed, that a determined German counterattack could drive us all the way back to the Seine.

Nevertheless, certain features of Monty's plan had undeniable merit for the long range. Foremost, militarily, was the early capture of Antwerp and Rotterdam. With these ports in our hands our long-term logistical problems would indeed be solved. They would be much closer to our rapidly advancing front and much closer to England than the Brittany ports. No less important was the capture and destruction of the V-weapon sites. We had by now diverted a substantial proportion of our strategic air power to the destruction of the sites at the expense of raids on German oil refineries, aircraft production plants and the population centers. Moreover, these "super" weapons had become a major psychological tool in Hitler's efforts to rally the German citizenry. In Hitler's maniacal rhetoric, they held promise that Germany would win the war after all. In our revised planning, the capture of Antwerp and the destruction of the V-weapon sites now assumed highest priority.[9]

My plan was far more conservative and conventional. Believing as I did that we would have a tough fight on our hands at the German border, I stood by the original concept of the "two thrust" strategy; Monty's two armies to the north of the Ardennes, my two armies to the south of the

Ardennes through the Saar. I envisioned for both thrusts a "pause" at the western German border—the Siegfried Line and/or the Rhine River—to build up logistics for a final all-out concentrated assault. However, I fully approved Monty's more northeastward course to capture Antwerp and destroy the V-weapon launching sites and agreed that his thrust should be substantially reinforced by U.S. forces. We were already making plans to give him Ridgway's XVIII Airborne Corps of three divisions to help him through the canal country, where the airborne could be particularly useful. In addition to that, I proposed detaching a conventional corps from Hodges' First Army (Collins, Corlett or Gerow) and assigning it to Monty. That would be a total allotment of six divisions, giving Monty some twenty-two divisions, leaving me about fifteen or so for the thrust to the Saar.[10]

My plan did not at all suit Monty. He had convinced himself by now that his plan—his leadership—was the only solution or, as he wrote, "the only possibility of bringing the war to a quick end." Four days after his August 13 presentation to Ike and me, he flew to my headquarters near St. James to enlist my unqualified support for his plan. He later wrote incorrectly and deceitfully that "Bradley agreed entirely with this outline plan." I agreed that Monty should go northeast, capture Antwerp and the V-weapon launching sites and that he should be reinforced at my expense. But I *did not* agree to the salient points of his plan: that he would lead a four-army force directly to Berlin and that my Saar thrust would be dropped.[11]

On the day after Monty's visit, August 18, Ike arrived to discuss Monty's proposed plan. Hansen noted: "Ike feeling lighthearted and gay and is taking active part in determining the strategy—allocating missions to Bradley and Monty. . . . Believe he favors the Brad plan of driving eastward to Germany rather than diverting too much strength up over the northern route to the Lowlands and into Germany from that direction."[12]

Hansen was only partly right. Ike agreed with me that Monty's grandiose forty-division single thrust to Berlin was, for all the reasons I have enumerated, dangerously visionary. But the capture of Antwerp and destruction of the V-weapon launching sites were now highest-priority objectives. To assure Monty's success, Ike, to my dismay, wanted to give Monty a full American army. I contested the point vigorously, insisting that the addition of the airborne corps and one conventional corps was more than sufficient. If we were to allot Monty a full additional army and back this swollen force to the hilt, it would, in effect, immobilize our thrust to the Saar; Patton would have neither the numerical strength nor the gasoline to carry it out. Stopping our biggest ground gainer in favor of reinforcing the British would not be popular with Patton, our troops or the American public. In fact, there might be hell to pay.[13]

I believe Ike left my headquarters fully convinced my plan was the sounder of the two. That very day he wrote Monty that he could be assured of Ridgway's airborne corps but that requests for U.S. ground units "should be kept to a minimum . . . because of the desirability of thrusting quickly eastward."[14]

Monty, meanwhile, had withdrawn into seclusion at his headquarters. He delegated to his amiable and urbane chief of staff, Freddie de Guingand, the job of selling his plan. For that purpose, de Guingand virtually lived at SHAEF from August 20 to August 22. The irony was that de Guingand did not believe in the master plan. He wrote in his memoirs: "This was the only major issue over which I did not agree with my Chief." However, de Guingand did his work well. He helped persuade Ike and Ike's G-3, Pink Bull, that at the very least Monty should be allotted my full First Army in addition to Ridgway's airborne corps. This was a clear-cut political victory for Monty and a stinging defeat for me—and Patton.[15] *

This was Ike's first major decision in the ground war, and, as Monty saw it, the decision had gone against him. Monty must have been blindly enraged. That is the kindest explanation I can find for his next tactless and arrogant move. Via de Guingand, he as much as demanded that Ike renounce his plan to take over the ground forces and leave the planning and leadership to Monty. The notes de Guingand delivered to Ike in Monty's behalf stated, in part: "Single control and direction of the land operations is vital for success. This is a WHOLE TIME job for one man. The great victory in N.W. France has been won by personal command [i.e., Monty]. Only in this way will future victories be won. If staff control [i.e., Ike and SHAEF] of operations is allowed to creep in, then quick success becomes endangered. To change the system of command now, after having won a great victory, would be to prolong the war."[16]

On the following day, August 23, Monty made one final desperate try to put over his master plan. He would not go to SHAEF, but instead arrogantly insisted that Ike come to his headquarters. Before Ike arrived, Monty (for the second time in a week!) flew to my headquarters to make an eleventh-hour appeal for my support. By that time, I had heard about Monty's outlandish demands for Ike to abdicate and I knew that Monty had been falsely stating that I agreed with his master plan. My reception was frosty. Monty deceitfully wrote in his memoirs: "I found to my amazement that Bradley had changed his mind. On the 17th August he had agreed with me, on the 23rd he was a whole-hearted advocate of the main effort of his Army Group being directed eastwards on Metz and the Saar." I had not changed my mind. I had *never* agreed to the main features of Monty's plan.[17]

* The abundant ironies of this situation were not lost on me at the time. I, customarily the most ardent advocate of fast open warfare, was now counseling that the most conservative general in our command be reined in. Patton, customarily regarded with disdain in my headquarters, was now our most useful ally against Ike.

Patton came by shortly after Monty had left. He was like a raging bull. We "losers" commiserated. He accurately reflected my mood in his diary: "Bradley was madder than I have ever seen him and wondered aloud 'what the Supreme Commander amounted to.' " Typically, Patton suggested a melodramatic solution to the debate: "I told Bradley that if he, Hodges and myself offered to resign unless we went east, Ike would have to yield. But Bradley would not agree and said we owed it to the troops to hold on because if we left the pickings were poor. . . . I think other motives activated him. I feel in such a showdown we would win, as Ike would not dare to relieve us."[18]

It was an unthinkable suggestion. I had made up my mind in Africa that, owing to Ike's tendency to favor British plans and generals, often to our detriment, I would do all in my power to vigorously represent the interests of our men. To resign then would have been to abnegate that responsibility, an attitude reflected in a Hansen diary entry of the day before: "It is certain that although Brad is not getting his way on the strategy . . . everyone is confident he will take care of our interests. . . . Interests himself particularly in the American picture and he is certainly our spokesman here, for Ike must essentially be arbiter almost without a nationality. [Ike] inclined to bend over towards Monty, however, where special consideration is given because of the political nature of the arrangement."[19]

Ike arrived at Monty's headquarters with Bedell Smith, whom Monty had not seen since D-day. Monty rudely demanded that Smith be barred from the discussions. When Monty and Ike were alone, Monty made an impassioned plea for his master plan and again suggested that he, Monty, should retain control of the ground forces. The supreme commander, Monty argued, "should not descend" into the details of the land battle but remain "on a very lofty peak" in order to be able to take a "detached view of the whole intricate problem." Ike quietly explained why he would not relinquish ground command to Monty. For the moment at least, Monty set that issue aside. Later he wrote: "Possibly I went a bit far in urging on him my own plan, and did not give sufficient weight to the heavy political burden he bore."

By this time, Monty knew that Ike had committed the First Army to support Monty's northeasterly thrust. That would be a minimum of nine divisions, plus Ridgway's airborne corps. Still Monty was not satisfied. He demanded "an American army of at least twelve divisions." Ike demurred. To provide Monty three more divisions would strip Patton's army to bare bones, grind it to a halt. That he would not do. Public opinion would not tolerate it. Monty and Hodges would get the lion's share of supplies and gasoline, but Patton's drive on Nancy and Metz would be supported, albeit minimally. Monty would have authority to effect "operational co-ordination" of Hodges' army but not "operational direction."[20]

Monty accepted Ike's decision but he and Alan Brooke were bitterly contemptuous of it. Monty wrote: "And so we got ready to cross the Seine and go our different ways. . . . The trouble was we had no fundamental plan which treated the theater as an entity. Our strategy was now to become 'unstitched' . . . I had great misgivings. All my military training told me we could not get away with it. . . . We were throwing overboard the principle of concentration of effort." Brooke wrote: "This plan is likely to add another three to six months to the war. . . . If the Germans were not as beat as they are this would be a fatal move; as it is it may not do too much harm."[21]

I, too, was unhappy with the decision. I did not relish surrendering "operational coordination" of one of my armies to Monty. It occurred to me that the command picture was developing exactly along the lines Monty had offhandedly suggested on July 2. He was now leading a three-army drive on Pas de Calais. In retrospect, I wondered if Monty's "forty-division" master plan had been a mere bluff, a manufactured bargaining position to obtain what he now had. I still wonder. Of one thing I was certain: Monty's plan sprung from his megalomania. He would not cease in his efforts to gain personal command of all the land forces and reap all the personal glory for our victory.[22]

The final decisions satisfied no one, but had the compromise thrown away an opportunity for a quick end to the war, as Liddell Hart and some other historians suggest? Liddell Hart argues that at the time Ike made the compromise, the enemy "had already collapsed" and what was required for early victory was "pursuit without pause," specifically a "rapid, long-range thrust" into Germany, preferably via the Ruhr. Patton argued, similarly, that had we put the bulk of Allied resources behind his Third Army for a rapid armored thrust to the Saar and beyond, he could have brought the war to an early end.[23]

All of us were acutely aware of the need for "pursuit without pause." That awareness led to Ike's early decision to dash across the Seine. I do not believe any appreciable time was lost in arriving at the decision—the compromise—on follow-up grand strategy. As I have stated, even as we debated strategy our troops (Walker and Eddy, for example) were driving across the Seine into France "without pause." I was also bringing Hodges' First Army to the Seine without pause and prepared to go northeast with Monty or directly east with Patton, depending on Ike's final decision.

In truth, Monty's northeast thrust, reinforced by Hodges' army, was designed to be a pursuit without pause. Although at the time I thought it was too large and Monty thought it was too small, in retrospect his twenty-five-division force appears to be exactly what was called for, considering the weight we had given the V-weapon sites and Antwerp and the acute logistical shortages. There were no binding restraints imposed on Monty. Had everything gone according to plan, had the pursuit without pause been successful, the war might well have ended much earlier. But it is incorrect for historians to write that we blindly threw away the opportunity for hot pursuit.

Alternately, what if we had backed Patton in an all-out pursuit without pause? Could he, as he claimed, have brought the war to an early end?

I am not aware that anyone other than Patton has taken this idea seriously. Undeniably Patton had a marvelous talent for gaining ground—and headlines. Without meaning to detract from his extraordinary achievements, Patton's great and dramatic gains, beginning in Sicily and continuing through Brittany and on across the Seine at Mantes, Melun and Troyes, had been made against little or no opposition. Until now Patton had not really had a serious fight on his hands, and I was certain that sooner or later Patton was going to have one. I was not sure how good a tactician he would be in a tough fight. None of his divisions had ever been put to the real test.

Had we backed Patton all-out, it would have been necessary to throw the full weight—all three corps—of Hodges' battle-hardened First Army into the chase with him. That, in fact, had been the original Allied plan on a much slower timetable. The addition of Hodges' army would have imposed a logistical demand so heavy as to preclude pursuit without pause. As I have stated often, Patton gave little or no consideration to logistics. He and Hodges might well have pursued without pause to the German border, but logistical limitations would have halted them there, perhaps for a very long time, with no real gain to us.[24]

On analysis, Ike's decision to substantially reinforce Monty in a pursuit without pause was the correct one. Monty condemned it as a "broad front" strategy, all of us "going our separate ways." But this was not true, far from it. It was, in fact, a single-thrust strategy toward the Ruhr, with Patton's army reduced, in reality, to little more than a supporting force.

If there were to be an early end to the war, everything now depended on how aggressively Monty conducted the pursuit.[25]

THIRTY-FIVE

No time was lost in preparing Monty's massive northeastward thrust. By August 25, the three armies were assembling along a 130-mile stretch of the Seine. Crerar held the left, or Channel, flank with two corps of six divisions. Dempsey was in the center with two corps of seven and a half divisions. (His VIII Corps had been "grounded" to more fully motorize the others.) Hodges held the right flank, abutting Patton's Third Army, with three corps of nine divisions: Corlett's XIX on the left adjacent to Dempsey; Gerow's V in the center; Collins' VII on the right at Melun. Altogether Monty's force comprised twenty-two and a half divisions—eight and a half armored—or about 400,000 men, nearly all of them hardened veterans of the Normandy campaign. Monty's orders were to go flat out for Antwerp.[1]

On Monty's right, I deployed Patton's Third Army, now reduced to a mere two corps, Eddy's XII and Walker's XX. (Middleton's VIII was still in Brittany; Haislip's XV was redeploying from Mantes.) I fleshed out the two corps with two additional infantry divisions: McLain's 90th and McBride's 80th. I had never seen Patton in finer fettle or more optimistic. Even though his mission would be distinctly subordinate to Monty's, Patton was certain that he could win the war. He diaried: "I am sure that if we drive him hard enough now, we will cause the end of the war in a very few days."

Patton's smaller force jumped off from Melun and Troyes, or rather continued unabated in an eastward drive, on August 26. The progress of his two motorized corps through the old battlefields of World War I over the next several days was absolutely breathtaking—pure blitzkrieg. Eddy's XII took Chalon on August 29 and pressed on to St. Mihiel. Walker took Reims on August 30 and Verdun the following day. By September 1, both Walker and Eddy had reached the Meuse River in force and had established bridgeheads on the east bank. The advance placed Patton within sixty miles of the German border.[2]

Monty's massive northeastwardly drive, which finally got off on August 29, was no less electrifying. British forces, spearheaded by the very able Brian Horrocks, recovered from his grave wounds in Africa and commanding XXX Corps from the turret of a tank, smashed ahead with awesome speed. In six days, Monty advanced 250 miles, liberating Amiens, Lille, Brussels. On September 4, his forces entered Antwerp and seized the docks before the Germans could demolish them. On his left, the Canadian First Army took Dieppe, abandoned by the Germans, and isolated German Fifteenth Army forces at Le Havre, Calais and Dunkirk. Hodges' three corps, racing northeast on Dempsey's right flank, performed no less splendidly. In a little-known but brilliantly conducted operation at Mons, Belgium, Collins captured 25,000 German troops, remnants of some twenty-odd disorganized divisions from Normandy and elsewhere.

Having achieved this striking gain, Monty now committed two tactical blunders that must rank among the costliest of the war. Once again he failed to exploit his opportunities—go for the jugular. The Rhine River lay only seventy-five miles beyond Antwerp at Arnhem. Owing to his favorable ration of gasoline allotment, Monty still had ample stocks. There were no significant German forces between Horrocks and the Rhine. But instead of ordering Horrocks onward, on September 4 Monty halted him. The British military historian John North wrote that a "war is won" attitude set in and there was "little sense of urgency among commanders." In his memoirs, Horrocks lamented: "Had we been able to advance that day we could have smashed through . . . and advanced northward with little or nothing to stop us. We might even have succeeded in bouncing a crossing over the Rhine . . . if we had taken the chance and carried straight on . . . the whole course of the war in Europe might have been changed." But the opportunity to force a Rhine crossing was quickly lost; on the very next day hastily forming German troops began throwing up a defensive line behind the Albert Canal at Antwerp.

Similarly, Monty failed to exploit fully the capture of Antwerp. The city lay inland some sixty miles. Between the city and the open sea was the Schelde, an estuary bounded by numerous islands, notably Walcheren, where the Germans had established powerful coastal batteries. On September 3, Ike's naval chief, Bertram Ramsay, in a cable to Ike and Monty, drew attention to the peculiar geography of Antwerp, warning that it was "essential" that the Walcheren coastal batteries be captured; otherwise the Germans could block the port. A quick dash over the Albert Canal to Woensdrecht, then down the Walcheren road and causeway would have captured these batteries and cleared the Schelde. But Ramsay's cable apparently made no impression in Monty's headquarters. In fact, Monty, Dempsey and Horrocks entirely ignored the Schelde, and in the coming days retreating Germans of the Fifteenth Army reinforced the islands and the coastal batteries. It would require a major campaign to dislodge them.

Because of this blunder, Antwerp, captured on September 4 as a matter of highest strategic priority, would not become available to us until nearly three months later—November 28.[3] *

On both fronts an acute shortage of supplies—that dull subject again! —governed all our operations. Some twenty-eight divisions were advancing across France and Belgium. Each division ordinarily required 700–750 tons a day—a total daily consumption of about 20,000 tons. In addition, we were supplying liberated Paris with about 1,500 tons of supplies per day, far less than the planned 4,000 tons daily. We pared our daily divisional consumption to a spartan 500 tons; nonetheless our daily requirements, including Paris, came to about 15,000 tons (30 million pounds). Ike set up a strict allocation schedule for our combat divisions: about 6,000 tons to Monty's British and Canadian forces and about 6,000 tons for Hodges and Patton combined. Hodges was to receive 3,500 tons per day; Patton about 2,500 tons per day.[5]

Since the French railway system had been virtually destroyed by Allied air before D-day, we had to rely primarily on trucks and emergency airlift to bring our supplies forward. We organized the famous Red Ball Express—thousands of trucks running between Normandy and the front on a killing 700-mile round-trip twenty-four-hour schedule. But the Red Ball's 6,000 trucks could only deliver an average 7,000 tons a day. Five trucks were required in the "pipeline" to deliver one truckload at the front, and owing to the brutal schedule, we were wearing out trucks at a fearful rate. An independent British supply system was severely impaired by the discovery that some 1,400 new three-ton trucks had defective pistons and no spare parts to replace them.[6]

As I stated earlier, since D-day we had relied on emergency airlift to alleviate our most critical shortages. With a maximum effort, the Air Force could deliver about 1,000 tons a day directly to our front. Since the same aircraft were utilized to drop our airborne troops, whenever a drop was planned this source of supply was shut down. In his advance on Brussels, Monty planned to drop Ridgway's airborne corps near Tournai. When I saw how fast Hodges' troops were moving, it became clear that they would overrun Tournai before the paratroopers could get there. I urged Monty to cancel the drop and return the aircraft to delivering gasoline. But Monty, ever cautious, waited until the eleventh hour before canceling. The aircraft involved were thus tied up for five or six days, denying us a total of about 5,000 tons.[7]

* Official U.S. Army historian Charles B. MacDonald in his unofficial account of the European campaign, *Mighty Endeavor,* described the failure to sweep the Schelde as "one of the great tactical mistakes of the war." Horrocks frankly conceding it was a "serious mistake," wrote: "My excuse is that my eyes were fixed entirely on the Rhine and everything else seemed of subsidiary importance. It never entered my head that . . . we would not be able to use Antwerp until the channel had been swept and the Germans cleared from the coastlines on either side."[4]

Our greatest logistical problem proved to be gasoline. Each of our armies consumed about 400,000 gallons of gasoline a day. We had no shortage of gasoline in the rear area. We had built a cross-channel gasoline pipeline—Pluto—and by mid-August it was operational. But the Red Ball could not keep up with our enormous thirst. (The Red Ball itself burned 300,000 gallons of gasoline a day.) The tie-up of aircraft for the Tournai drop denied us a million and a half gallons. The upshot was that the American divisions began running out of gasoline on or about September 1. For that reason, I was compelled to order Hodges to stop his advance near Mons and Patton to stop at the Meuse.

Monty was furious that I halted Hodges and accused me of diverting unauthorized gasoline from Hodges to Patton. Of course this was not true. If anything, Patton had gotten the short end of the stick. He had reached the Meuse only because he had captured a million gallons of low-grade but usable German gasoline. Patton's staff believed the gasoline shortage to be a conspiracy engineered by those who were jealous of Patton's spectacular successes. Patton wrote in his diary: "The British have put it over again. We got no gas because, to suit Monty, the First Army must get most of it. . . . If I could only steal some gas, I could win this war." Patton complained to me: "Damn it, Brad, just give me 400,000 gallons of gasoline and I'll put you inside Germany in two days." He might as well have asked for the moon.[8]

On September 1, as planned, Ike took formal command of the ground forces. In order that this would not be perceived as another "demotion" for Monty, Churchill persuaded King George to promote Monty to the rank of field marshal. As previously explained, we considered the British field marshal rank the equivalent of our four-star general. Thus Monty, commanding only one-third the number of men I commanded, now outranked me by one star and was on a par, in terms of rank, with Ike. Patton noted in his diary: "The Field Marshal thing made us sick—that is, Bradley and me."[9]

Ike had not officially decided what strategy we would follow after Monty took Antwerp. He leaned to the original pre-D-day Allied plan of a double thrust at the Ruhr and Saar, skirting the Ardennes to the north and south. On September 2 he came to my headquarters at Chartres to discuss tactics and grand strategy with Hodges, Patton and me. At that time it appeared to us that the Germans had totally collapsed along the entire front. I urged that we exploit the collapse with everything at our disposal without stopping to regroup for supplies—pursuit without pause. I thought that with an all-out effort we could crack through the Siegfried Line, reach the Rhine and establish beachheads on the east bank within a week.[10]

My plan was basically a two-thrust strategy, aimed directly at the Ruhr and Saar, going north and south of the Ardennes. The northern thrust would go due east from Brussels on a line Liège-Aachen-Cologne, establishing a beachhead over the Rhine. It would consist of three corps: Horrocks' XXX, Corlett's XIX and Collins' VII. Hodges' remaining corps—Gerow's V—would swing south to the Ardennes and Luxembourg, filling the wide gap between Patton and Hodges. The rest of Monty's forces would secure the French channel ports and Antwerp, push on to Rotterdam and Amsterdam, seize the V-weapon launching sites and establish a bridgehead across the Rhine near Arnhem.

The southern thrust, led by Patton, would jump off from the Meuse bridgeheads and go directly east to the Rhine through the Saar on a line Metz-Frankfurt. It would consist of three corps: Walker's XX, Eddy's XII and Haislip's XV. By now, Bill Simpson's Ninth Army had relieved Middleton's VIII Corps in Brittany, freeing Middleton to come east to join in the push.[11]

While Ike leaned to a two-thrust strategy, I cannot say that he leaped to embrace my plan. Monty clearly would not be pleased and might even raise a big stink. It would bring a quick end to Monty's single-thrust concept and—no small matter—swing the limelight away from Monty to Hodges, Patton and me. Ike was concerned that owing to the logistical crisis we might be attempting too much too soon. When Patton interrupted to pronounce, rather grandly, that he would "stake his reputation" on his ability to push into Germany with the reduced flow of supplies he was getting, Ike was testy in his reply: "Be careful now, that reputation of yours hasn't been worth very much." Chastened, Patton managed a wan smile and said, "Pretty good now."[12]

It was a long and tedious day. Ike, perhaps feeling a sense of history and need to show us who was now in charge of the land battle, unfortunately (and windily) pontificated and quoted Clausewitz. Patton, in customary exaggeration, wrote his wife that Ike's lectures that day made him, Hodges and me "quite ill." Actually, the lectures were merely boring and irrelevant. Patton noted in his diary that Ike "kept talking about the future great battle of Germany, while we assured him that the Germans have nothing left to fight with if we push on now. If we wait, there *will* be a great battle of Germany. . . . Ike is all for caution since he has never been at the front and has no feel of actual fighting. Bradley, Hodges and I are all for a prompt advance."[13]

Finally Ike approved my plan. No jump-off date was set. That would be contingent on the expected improvement in our logistics following Monty's capture of the channel ports and Antwerp. On the following day, Ike's staff drafted the historic order which was issued on September 4. The key points were that the forces north of the Ardennes were "to secure Antwerp, breach the sector of the Siegfried Line covering the Ruhr and then seize the Ruhr"; and the forces south of the Ardennes were "to occupy the sector of the Siegfried Line covering the Saar and then seize Frankfurt . . . as soon as possible."[14]

After leaving my headquarters that day, Ike suffered an accident. His plane was caught in a sudden storm and forced to land on a channel beach, believed to be heavily sown with old German mines. While helping the pilot pull the plane inland, away from the rising tide and keeping a sharp eye out for mines, Ike severely wrenched his knee—not his old "football knee" but the other, his "good" right knee. He was in such pain that he confined himself to bed for two days, then off and on for a week, his leg encased in a plaster cast. This accident grounded Ike at a most inopportune time.[15]

One result was that it fell to me to unveil the new strategic plan to Monty, face-to-face. I met him and Dempsey at Dempsey's headquarters at Amiens on the following day, September 3. Hodges flew in to join the discussions. Monty must have been shocked and dismayed and he must have resented the fact that I, not Ike, bore the bad news. But he showed no sign of it. He raised some sharp questions about our ability to keep Patton supplied, but otherwise appeared to agree completely with the plan. We drew up the customary army boundaries. That same day Monty issued the necessary instructions to his army and corps commanders. Hodges and I departed, confident that we had Monty's full support.

We could not have been more wrong. Monty's cordial reception that day was an artful deception. He was, in fact, furious.[16]

On the following day, September 4, Monty, rising up in full fury and insolence, fired off a message to Ike which, in effect, demonstrated complete disdain of the new plan. He insisted that we stick to his one-thrust strategy: "I consider we have now reached a stage where one really powerful and full-blooded thrust toward Berlin is likely to get there and end the German war." There were not sufficient supplies for "two full-blooded thrusts," he wrote. Everything should be put behind a single thrust, which should be a "northern one via the Ruhr." If two thrusts were attempted, neither of them "full-blooded," Monty pronounced, "we will prolong the war." Time was vital, a decision "must be made at once." He concluded: "If you are coming this way perhaps you would look in and discuss it. If so delighted to see you lunch tomorrow. Do not feel I can leave this battle at present."[17]

Ike, in severe pain from his wrenched knee, was angry and exasperated with Monty. Later, in a letter to Marshall, he dismissed Monty's proposal for a dash at Berlin as a "fantastic idea" that was based on "wishful thinking." In a memo for the record, he said: "I now deem it important, while supporting the advance on eastward through Belgium, to get Patton moving once again so that we may be fully prepared to carry out the original conception for the final stages of this campaign." To Monty, Ike firmly but tactfully wrote: "While agreeing with your conception of a powerful and full-blooded thrust toward Berlin, I do not repeat not agree that it should be initiated at this moment to the exclusion of all other maneuvers." Ike agreed with me that we must breach the Siegfried Line and draw up to and cross the Rhine "on a wide front" with "all possible speed." He unequivocally disapproved Monty's plan to go immediately for Berlin: "No re-allocation of our present resources would be adequate to sustain a thrust to Berlin." Strategy beyond the Rhine—one or two thrusts—would be decided following the opening of channel ports and Antwerp and the capture of the Ruhr and Saar.[18]

Monty would not let go his obsession. He responded (in part): "I submit with all respect . . . that a reallocation of our present resources of every description would be adequate to get one thrust to Berlin." Even though Monty now knew Ike had hurt his knee, he again suggested that Ike call on him: "It is very difficult to explain things in a message like this. Would it be possible for you to come and see me?"[19]

Following my September 2 meeting with Ike at Chartres, I gave orders to Hodges and Patton to jump off on the two-thrust offensive. These maneuvers were launched with severe handicaps. Our troops had been fighting on the run, almost without pause, since the St. Lô breakout, July 25. They were tired; their tanks and vehicles were wearing out. There was not only a severe shortage of gasoline, but now, owing to the lower priority allotted it, ammunition. Nonetheless, morale was high, as high as I had ever seen it. The men were confident that with one more hard push they could breach the Siegfried Line, reach the Rhine, and perhaps even force the unconditional surrender of Germany.

North of the Ardennes, Hodges realigned his three corps on a north-south front: Corlett northernmost, Collins in the center, Gerow to the south. Corlett's XIX Corps would drive on Cologne; Collins' VII on Bonn; and Gerow's V on Coblenz. Collins and Gerow received highest gasoline priority; Corlett (whose 79th Division was being transferred to Patton) was thus forced to wait, then "bring up the rear." Collins, as customary, performed brilliantly. By September 5, he had gained the Meuse River and two days later he captured Liège. His advance elements planned to bypass Aachen to the south. By September 10, they were in Eupen, a mere ten miles west of the Siegfried Line. Gerow swung south through the Ardennes and Luxembourg on a very wide front, and by September 10 his forces, too, were within ten miles of the Siegfried Line. Corlett, reduced to two divisions (Brooks's 2nd Armored and Hobbs's 30th Infantry) finally got enough gasoline to move forward, and by September 10 he crossed the Albert Canal.

Now facing the Siegfried Line across a wide front, Hodges grew cautious. The Siegfried Line, intelligence reported, was then only thinly held, but could we believe that? Would Hitler not do his utmost to stop our crossing into Germany itself? Heretofore we had been passing through friendly country and the natives were, on the whole, helpful. But the

German population would surely not be friendly and might very well be violently hostile. Before proceeding into Germany, Hodges wanted more ammunition. He ordered a two-day halt so that it could be brought forward.[20]

To the south of the Ardennes, Patton, after stockpiling gasoline, jumped off from his Meuse bridgeheads on September 5. He launched the attack with two corps of six divisions: Walker's XX and Eddy's XII. (Haislip had not yet received his divisions, which were to be LeClerc's French 2nd Armored and Wyche's 79th.) Patton's ultimate objective was Frankfurt, his immediate ones Metz and Nancy on the Moselle River. I was present for the jump-off. Patton was confident that he could smash right through to the Rhine. But he was in for a rude shock. The Germans had stopped the retreat and firmed up their lines. Both Walker and Eddy encountered fierce resistance and made only slow progress. This was the first time in his rush across France that Patton had met serious opposition.[21]

THIRTY-SIX

The airborne forces were still assigned to Monty. A half-dozen operations had been planned and canceled, most owing to the rapid advance of our forces. It was a great waste of a valuable resource and we were all acutely aware of it. At our September 3 meeting at Amiens, Monty, Dempsey and I discussed a plan to employ airborne forces in our eastward advance toward Aachen. But Monty favored a drop near Arnhem to secure the bridges and waterways north of Antwerp. Ike approved a drop at Arnhem for September 7. This time, foul weather forced a cancellation.[1]

On the evening of September 8, the first two V-2 rockets fell on London. British technicians concluded, from a study of the ballistic path and other data, that the V-2s had been launched from the vicinity of Rotterdam or Amsterdam. Churchill and Alan Brooke were then on the *Queen Mary* en route to Quebec for a meeting with Roosevelt and the Combined Chiefs to hash out strategy for the Pacific War. However, those officials left behind in London urged Monty to "rope off those general areas" whence the V-2s were being launched.[2]

The sudden appearance of the V-2s provided Monty a heaven-sent (literally and figuratively) opportunity to mount yet another internal political campaign to have his way with ground strategy. He at once began drawing plans for a new and massively increased air-ground operation against Arnhem. I learned of this plan, code-named "Market-Garden," in an indirect way, via a liaison officer between our headquarters. I was shocked and dismayed that Monty would first agree completely to my strategic plans, then, in a matter of a few days, conceive a wholly new one without personally consulting or informing me. It was either monumental arrogance or a deliberate attempt to sneak it through to approval behind my back.[3]

Market-Garden was enormous in scope. Monty would drop or glider-land three and a half airborne divisions—two on the road to Arnhem and one and a half at Arnhem itself. One other full "air portable" division would be landed near Arnhem when airfields had been secured. At the same time, Dempsey's entire British Second Army would crash through from Antwerp to Arnhem, linking up with the "carpet" of airborne forces in successive stages as he moved northward. Horrocks' XXX Corps would spearhead the land drive with one and a half armored divisions and two and a half infantry divisions. The British XII Corps of one armored division and two infantry divisions would protect Horrocks' left flank. The British VIII Corps of one armored division and one and a half infantry divisions would protect Horrocks' right flank. In sum, the airborne and air portable elements would comprise four and a half divisions of about 50,000 men. The land forces would comprise nine and a half divisions of about 150,000 men.[4]

What became clear to me at once was that Market-Garden was not, as advertised, a minor sideshow but rather an attempt by Monty to almost unilaterally launch a "full-blooded" thrust to Berlin. (The fourteen divisions he would command nearly equaled the combined strength of my First and Third armies—sixteen divisions—then poised at the German border.) If Market-Garden was successful—if it captured a bridgehead across the Rhine—there was little doubt that Monty would keep right on going across the north German plain in an attempt to reach Berlin. Once committed to that objective, no one would dare order him to stop, certainly not Ike. Every resource at our disposal would be finally committed to Monty, including, I was sure, Hodges' First Army, compelling Patton's Third Army to halt again and go on the defensive.[5]

The Market-Garden plan was a dazzler, one of the most daring and imaginative of the war. It seemed wholly improbable that it had sprung from Monty's ultraconservative mind. However, he was desperately, obsessively determined to lead a single thrust to Berlin and this was about the only way left to do it. It was strategy by subterfuge, legerdemain. It was dangerously foolhardy—the wrong plan at the wrong time and the wrong place.

I immediately telephoned Ike to lodge a protest—a violent protest. I described the plan for what it was: a rejection of our two-thrust strategy, an attempt to commit us step by step to Monty's single-thrust strategy and a gravely dangerous run to Berlin. I objected on tactical grounds as well. Monty's massive swing to the north would open a dangerous and ever-widening gap between the British and American armies. If the Germans could quickly pull together sufficient forces, they might attack through that gap, completely isolating Dempsey in Holland, and perhaps drive through to the North Sea, regaining Antwerp. And what about Antwerp, the Schelde? It was vital to all future operations. Intelligence was now reporting that the Germans had reinforced the Walcheren Island coastal batteries and were using the estuary as an escape route for the retreating units of the Fifteenth Army. Monty, I insisted, should be devoting his entire energies to clearing the Schelde and blocking the escape of the Germans.[6]

I could tell immediately by his equivocating response that Ike had approved Monty's scheme. To this day I do not know why. After the event I was too angry to question him. The explanation he gave in his memoir *Crusade in Europe* is inadequate and wrong. He downgrades Market-Garden to "merely an incident and extension of our eastward rush to the line we needed for temporary security." To stop short of a bridgehead over the Rhine at Arnhem, he wrote, would "have left us in a very exposed position." None of this is true. As I have shown, Market-Garden was not "merely an incident" (or sideshow) but a major change in direction of half our available combatant units on the German front. Ike conceded as much when he wrote Marshall on September 14 that "I have sacrificed a lot to give Montgomery the strength he needs to reach the Rhine in the north and to threaten the Ruhr. That is, after all, our *main effort* at the moment." (Italics added.) A Rhine bridgehead at Arnhem, in the manner Monty had chosen to attempt it, *increased* rather than decreased our exposure by splitting our forces and opening a dangerous gap between them.[7]

Surely other reasons and motives led to Ike's decision. For some time he had been under heavy pressure from Marshall and Hap Arnold to utilize our valuable (and expensive) airborne forces. These highly trained elite forces were, as historian Charles B. MacDonald so aptly put it, "like coins burning a hole in SHAEF's pocket." At that moment I had no specific plan for airborne operations. To the contrary, I preferred to use the airlift to bring gasoline forward to my stranded tanks. Monty's Arnhem plan offered Ike a golden opportunity to stage a splashy airborne spectacle. I feel certain, too, that Ike was influenced by London's request to "rope off" the V-2 launching sites. The V-2 was a terror weapon without precedent. The RAF and anti-aircraft units could shoot down the slower, noisy V-1 buzz bombs, but there was absolutely no defense against the V-2 ballistic missile, which arrived with no warning at terrific speed and mounted an awesome thousand-pound warhead. I feel sure that Ike was reluctant to disapprove a plan that might stop the rain of these terror weapons on London. Moreover, at any time these weapons could be directed against our vulnerable supply bases.* Finally, there was the human factor. The force of Monty's personality seemed to mesmerize Ike and befuddle his thinking. I think in this instance Ike succumbed to Monty in part to stroke his ego and keep peace in the family.[9]

Ike, leg still in a cast, flew from his headquarters to confer with me at Versailles on September 9. He spent the night, patiently rehearing all my objections to Market-Garden. By that time, it was clear that Monty's fail-

* The Germans launched a total of 1,190 V's against London and 1,610 against Antwerp.[8]

ure to clear the Schelde estuary was a major blunder. I urged that Ike order Monty to cancel Arnhem and devote all his resources to that urgent matter.[10]

Beyond that—and no less important—were the unusually complete Ultra reports we were receiving from Bletchley Park. These indicated that the Germans were organizing to resist us all along our front with remarkable efficiency. Several specific signals indicated that the Germans were much stronger in the Arnhem area than heretofore believed. The II SS Panzer Corps, which had been falling back as we advanced through northern France and Belgium, had been ordered to stop at Eindhoven and refit three panzer divisions (2nd, 116th and 9th SS). Eindhoven lay directly along Horrocks' route to Arnhem. We knew these divisions had lost almost all of their tanks, that they were exhausted and battered from a long retreat, nonetheless they now appeared to have stopped retreating. Inasmuch as Horrocks' spearhead would be compelled to thread its 20,000 vehicles for some sixty hours along a single causeway from Antwerp to Arnhem, I believed these panzer divisions, however depleted, could prove to be a formidable, if not decisive, obstacle, possibly preventing a link-up between Horrocks and the paratroopers.*

Ike was not much impressed by my arguments. He believed a bridgehead across the Rhine at Arnhem was worth the risk. However, he reassured me on several vital points. Monty's lopsided priority on supplies would obtain only through Market-Garden. He would give Monty specific orders to stop at the Rhine bridgehead. Under no circumstances would he permit Monty to lead a single thrust to Berlin. I would retain control of Corlett and Collins; they would not be integrated into Market-Garden. During Market-Garden, Hodges and Patton would be allowed to advance toward the Rhine as available logistics permitted. After Market-Garden, Monty's primary responsibility would then become clearing the Schelde and opening Antwerp.†

The next day, September 10, Ike flew on to Brussels to see Monty. Owing to Ike's immobility, the meeting was held in Ike's plane at the Brussels airport. Tedder was present. Monty got things off on the wrong foot by requesting that Ike's chief administrative officer, British General Humfrey M. Gale, be barred from the discussion, even though his own, General M. A. P. Graham, would stay. Astonishingly, Ike acquiesced to this insulting demand, as he had in their last meeting when Monty insisted

* Four days later, September 14, Ultra reported that Walther Model, commanding Army Group B, had established his headquarters at Oosterbeek, on the outskirts of Arnhem. An Ultra report of September 16 placed the 9th SS and "probably" the 10th SS Panzer divisions in Arnhem itself. These reports proved to be absolutely accurate.[11]

† Patton confided to his diary: "Brad told Ike that if Monty takes control of XIX and VII Corps . . . as he wants to, he, Bradley, will ask to be relieved. . . . Bradley said it was time for a showdown." This is untrue. I was forceful with Ike but did not threaten to resign.[12]

that Bedell Smith be excluded. That accomplished, Monty, waving a sheaf of their latest messages, began denouncing Ike's strategic decisions and directives in the strongest possible terms. His language was so insubordinate that Ike was compelled to interrupt. He leaned forward, put his hand on Monty's knee and said, "Steady, Monty! You can't speak to me like that. I'm your boss." Monty cooled and said, "I'm sorry, Ike."

As I had suspected, Monty's real aim was far larger than Arnhem. It was Berlin. After taking Arnhem, his goal was to lead Dempsey's Second Army, with the four and a half airborne or air portable divisions attached, around the north of the Ruhr straight across the north German plain to Berlin. Hodges' First Army of three corps (Corlett, Collins, Gerow) would continue east through Aachen to Cologne, encircling the Ruhr from the south, thereafter linking up with Dempsey for the dash to Berlin, forming a full-blooded thrust of some twenty-three divisions. Patton's Third Army and Crerar's Canadian Army would stand in place and go on the defensive, turning over all available transport to Monty.[13]

Years later, Ike recalled to author Cornelius Ryan that he replied to Monty, "What you're proposing is this—if I give you all of the supplies you want, you could go straight to Berlin—right straight to Berlin? Monty, you're nuts. You can't do it. What the hell! If you try a long column like that in a single thrust you'd have to throw off division after division to protect your flanks from attack. . . . Monty you can't do it."[14] *

The discussion was not brief. Monty continued to press, but Ike held firm; a thrust to Berlin was unthinkable, out of the question. Market-Garden would be limited to Arnhem, a bridgehead across the Rhine. Even though he was reluctant to do so, Ike would postpone clearing the Schelde estuary in favor of Arnhem. But after Arnhem, Monty must "turn instantly" to clearing the Schelde. Antwerp *must* be opened as rapidly as possible. Meanwhile, Ike would do his "utmost" to provide the necessary supplies for Market-Garden. Tedder wired Portal in London: "I feel the discussions cleared the air, though Montgomery will, of course, be dissatisfied in not getting a blank cheque."[16]

It had been agreed that Market-Garden would go on September 17. But when Ike returned to his headquarters, he received a message from Monty stating that owing to supply difficulties, it might be necessary to postpone it to September 23 or "possibly" September 26. The problem was in bringing forward Dempsey's VIII Corps, which had been grounded in Normandy to provide transport for the British dash to Antwerp. I was visiting Ike when this message arrived. He was livid—another Monty delay! The next day, September 12, Bedell Smith flew to see Monty, bring-

* At the time, according to Kay Summersby, Ike put it this way in his official diary: "Monty's suggestion is simple, give him everything, which is crazy."[15]

ing Ike's assurance that Monty would receive 1,000 extra tons of supplies a day and in return, Ike wanted Market-Garden started *on time*. To provide the tonnage, three U.S. divisions were to be grounded, stripped of their trucks. (These were my newly arrived 26th, 95th and 104th Infantry divisions.) The trucks were integrated into the Red Ball Express, which in turn sent an equal number of trucks with experienced drivers to the British Red Lion supply route.[17]

While conferring with Monty, Bedell Smith called attention to the Ultra dispatches indicating that the 9th and 10th SS Panzer divisions were now located in Arnhem. Owing to this danger, Smith urged Monty to shift an additional airborne division to drop near Arnhem. But, Smith recalled, "Montgomery ridiculed the idea" and "waved my objections airily aside."[18]

That same day, September 12, I met with Hodges and Patton at my headquarters. I briefed them on Market-Garden, and we reviewed our own operations and supply situation. The gasoline reserves had now improved somewhat. Both Hodges and Patton had sufficient stocks to "carry them to the Rhine." But the ammunition shortage was still severe: Hodges had a five-day supply, Patton four. We were now receiving an average daily supply of 5,800 tons, divided 3,300 to Hodges and 2,500 to Patton. This figure was about one-half of what we required for normal combat operations. Until Market-Garden was over, there was no relief in sight. Monty was to continue receiving highest priority on supplies—plus the 1,000 extra tons a day Ike promised him. It was a bleak picture for the American forces advancing eastward on the Siegfried Line.[19]

Even so, we remained optimistic that we could reach the Rhine. On that day, I told both Hodges and Patton to keep going, to breach the Siegfried Line and not stop. I reported my decisions to Ike by letter and he approved them.[20]

Hodges had released Collins and Gerow on reconnaissance patrols. Gerow's troops were the first Allies to cross the German border. Collins' troops were second—the next day, September 12, south of Aachen. But these were merely symbolic border crossings, having no real military significance. In both areas the Germans fought back tenaciously, blunting Collins and Gerow, forcing them to stop.

Corlett, with only two divisions, moved eastward, preparing to assault the Siegfried Line north of Aachen. By this time, Horrocks had pulled away from Corlett's left flank to prepare for the assault on Arnhem. Monty had assured me his VIII Corps would fill the gap, but as Corlett wrote: "Without a word of notice they [the British] pulled out and opened my left flank for fifty miles." As Corlett continued his advance eastward, the gap grew ever wider and he was justifiably enraged, since he had the grave responsibility of covering the whole left flank of the First Army. Had I known Monty would so expose us, I would have left Wyche's 79th Division with Corlett until the lines were properly drawn.[21] *

To the south of the Ardennes, Patton's XX and XII corps continued to face heavy German resistance on the Moselle River at Metz and Nancy. He described the battle to his wife as "desperate," and now bitterly regretted that he had earlier been forced to stop. On September 15, Eddy took Nancy; and Haislip, going into action on the southern flank with two divisions, took Epinal and, two days later, Luneville. But Walker was unable to capture the key objective, Metz, a heavily fortified city blocking Patton's advance to the Saar. Patton wrote his wife that "for the last three days we have had as bitter and protracted fighting as I have ever encountered." Clearly, too, Patton had bogged down, and not for want of gasoline.[23]

We did not yet realize it, but the long, long pursuit was over. Along the entire length of the Siegfried Line, hastily organized German units were digging in to defend the Fatherland with utmost determination. Our great war of movement which had swept us 325 miles east of St. Lô in two months was, as historian Martin Blumenson put it, "merging imperceptibly into a war of position."[24]

The massive Market-Garden operation proceeded as planned on September 17. It has been well documented in memoirs and popular histories, notably in Ryan's book and the film *A Bridge Too Far*. In essence, it failed. The reasons were several. The ignored Ultra reports proved all too correct. The Germans had gathered in Arnhem and along its southern approaches. Commanded by General Model at the scene, and invaluably assisted by the immediate capture of a Market-Garden battle plan which had been stupidly taken into battle by an American officer, the Germans counterattacked in force, not only at Arnhem but along the land approaches. Horrocks, ably assisted by Max Taylor's 101st and Jim Gavin's 82nd Airborne divisions, pushed north to Nijmegen, but Horrocks could not cross the Rhine bridge at Arnhem. Surrounded and isolated, the magnificently gallant British paratroopers in Arnhem were slaughtered or forced to surrender. The total cost of Market-Garden was appalling: 17,000 Allies killed, wounded or missing. This was far more than we suffered on D-day in Normandy.[25]

The ultimate cost of Market-Garden cannot be measured in casualties alone. It diverted the force, thought and planning required to open Ant-

* Corlett's advance was further confounded by an unforeseen but necessary change in command. Gerow was compelled to leave V Corps temporarily and return to Washington to testify before the Army's Pearl Harbor Board, which had been created by a joint resolution of the U.S. Congress to investigate the Pearl Harbor disaster. In his absence, Ted Brooks of Corlett's 2nd Armored Division was promoted to serve temporarily as V Corps commander. On September 12, Brooks was relieved by Ernie Harmon.[22]

werp at a time when the Schelde could have been cleared with relative ease. It was a massive assault *in the wrong direction* at what was probably the most crucial moment on the German front. Had all the thought and effort it drained away from our eastward thrust been placed behind Hodges and Patton during the period September 10 to September 20, I am certain that both American armies could have maintained momentum and reached the Rhine River. Had this goal been achieved, we would have been in a far superior position to mount our final offensives on the heartland of Germany and would have been spared the tens of thousands of casualties we suffered to achieve that position.

After the fact, both Alan Brooke and Bertram Ramsay agreed with my views on Market-Garden. Brooke noted in his diary on October 5: "I feel that Monty's strategy for once is at fault. Instead of carrying out the advance on Arnhem he ought to have made certain of Antwerp in the first place." Admiral Ramsay, he wrote, "criticized Monty freely." Brooke went on: "Ike nobly took all the blame on himself as he had approved Monty's suggestion to operate on Arnhem."[26]

In permitting Monty to launch Market-Garden, Ike committed his gravest tactical error of the war.

THIRTY-SEVEN

Dragoon forces had landed in southern France near Marseilles on August 15. The American commander was Alexander M. (Sandy) Patch (West Point 1913), an old friend who, like Joe Collins, was a veteran of Guadalcanal. Patch commanded Patton's old Seventh Army headquarters, which had been rescued from the ash heap at Palermo and restaffed. His assault force, VI Corps, commanded by Lucian Truscott, included two veteran divisions from my forces in Sicily: the 3rd and 45th Infantry divisions, which had been fighting in Italy. After Patch's Seventh Army (which included some French units) had got ashore against slight opposition, the First French Army, commanded by Jean de Lattre de Tassigny, was fielded. This imposed the need for an army group headquarters, the Sixth, which was to be commanded by Jake Devers. Initially, Devers' Sixth Army Group forces, which began marching northeastward toward Germany (on Patton's right flank), numbered about 400,000 men.

Thus, by mid-September, Allied land operations on the Continent had grown to enormous proportions. Including Devers' Sixth Army Group, which soon came under Ike's jurisdiction, Ike commanded three army groups comprising eight field armies: two under Monty (British Second, Canadian First), three under me (First, Third, Ninth), two under Devers (French First, U.S. Seventh) and the airborne forces that had been organized as the First Allied Airborne Army. Within these eight armies there were now a total of fifty-five divisions of all nationalities, of which half (twenty-eight) were American. In total, there were about two and a half million men and over half a million Allied vehicles in France.

Even so, it was now quite apparent that we were not going to run through Germany as we had run through France. The German retreat was over. In a near miracle, Hitler had managed to field some sixty-three numbered divisions to oppose us along the Siegfried Line, including fifteen panzer and panzer grenadier divisions. To command this force, Hitler brought von Rundstedt back from the obscurity to which he had been relegated since Normandy. Most of von Rundstedt's divisions were at no more than half strength and lacked guns and vehicles. Some were composed of hastily drafted old men and young boys with only rudimentary training. But what the Germans lacked in manpower and hardware, they made up for in esprit. And von Rundstedt had several advantages over us: vastly shorter supply lines; terrain ideal for the defense; ever-worsening fall weather which impeded both our ground and air operations.[1]

On September 22, while Market-Garden was in its final dismal stages, Ike convened a summit meeting of the Allied commanders at his headquarters in Versailles to review the situation and map out future strategy. This was the most important gathering of Allied brass since the final Overlord review on May 15 at St. Paul's School in London. Monty boycotted the meeting, pleading unconvincingly that he was still absorbed in Market-Garden. In his place, he sent his chief of staff, Freddie de Guingand. The Americans—and not a few British—regarded this as a calculated affront to Ike. Monty explained in his memoirs: "I knew I was not popular at either Supreme Headquarters, or with the American generals, because of my arguments about the conduct of the war; I thought it best to keep away while the matter was being further argued."[2]

In preparation for this meeting, I had already presented Ike my views on our future operations, both orally and in writing. I believed, first, that nothing of consequence could be attempted without the opening up of Antwerp. Antwerp, I wrote Ike, "is essential." Secondly, I believed that any move into Germany had to be made in "great depth," engaging the enemy "on a very wide front in order to keep him from concentrating on the main effort." Thirdly, I declared the Ruhr to be the "number one" territorial objective. I believed it should be taken by a double thrust of "pincer movements from north and south." Monty's army group would form the northern pincer. The "main thrust" of the southern pincer, I believed, should be made by Patton through the Saar to Frankfurt, thence north to join with Monty. Hodges should go east toward Cologne as well, but I thought the rugged terrain he faced (the Huertgen Forest and other obstacles) would make his route much more difficult and thus take longer.[3]

Monty had also conveyed his ideas to Ike in writing. They were, fundamentally, a repetition of his September 4 position: a "full-blooded" thrust on the Ruhr, thence to Berlin "on the northern route," led by him and supported by Hodges' First Army. "It is my opinion," he wrote, "that a concerted operation in which all the available land armies move forward into Germany is not possible." In other words, owing to the shortage of supplies, Patton should be stopped and all the weight thrown behind Monty and Hodges. "I have always said stop the right and go on with left," Monty wrote. "I would say that the right flank of 12 Army Group should be given a very direct order to halt . . . if you want to get the Ruhr you will have to put every single thing into the left hook and stop everything else . . . if this is not done then you will not get the Ruhr."[4]

Ike was thus again faced with conflicting viewpoints from his chief ground commanders. And again he ruled in favor of Monty. Ike decided that Monty's forces, assisted by Hodges' First Army, should seize the Ruhr from his newly gained position in the north, and clear Antwerp as rapidly as possible with his Canadian forces. Dempsey would lead the assault on the Ruhr. Hodges would assist by taking over Dempsey's VIII Corps area on First Army's left flank and by pushing ahead at Aachen. Monty wanted absolute control of the First Army, but Ike would not accede. However, "to save time," Ike decreed that Monty could "communicate his desires directly to Hodges." Patton would go on the defensive.[5]

This was yet another poor decision. Even though he had retained the 82nd and 101st Airborne divisions, which were fighting as regular infantry, Monty did not have sufficient strength to carry out his part of an offensive on the Ruhr. Dempsey's Second Army had just suffered a setback at Arnhem and his troops were tired. Giving the Ruhr attack first priority inevitably meant further delay in opening Antwerp, which was the key to any victory. That job had been relegated to the Canadian Army. I did not think the Canadians had the strength or verve to carry it out. Stopping Patton, a proven ground gainer, to favor Monty, who wasn't, simply did not make any sense at all.

Why the decision? Ike omits any mention of this offensive in his memoirs, implying that immediately after Arnhem Monty turned all his attention to clearing Antwerp. In truth, it was a case of throwing good money after bad, or as my chief of staff aptly observed at the time: "We're putting a lot of money into an unprofitable stock." I believe Ike reasoned that since Dempsey had gained Nijmegen at huge cost, slightly outflanking the Siegfried Line, a thrust from there southeast toward the Ruhr conceivably could succeed, thereby justifying the earlier wrong decision to go for Arnhem.[6]

I was disappointed at the decision. Chet Hansen wrote: "Found that Brad had not slept well and he is beginning to look tired. Disappointed with results of conference they had. It begins to look as though we may be faced with a winter campaign here on the [Siegfried] Line and this is precisely what we are trying to avoid." Patton put it this way: "[Bradley] was feeling very low because Montgomery has again put it over on Ike and demands the assistance of the First Army in a push into the Ruhr. To do this I will have to . . . assume a defensive attitude . . . very discouraging. . . . Bradley and I are depressed. We would like to go to China and serve under Admiral Nimitz."[7]

Monty's proposed offensive compelled a major realignment in my armies. To strengthen Corlett, who would take over British VIII Corps sector on our left, I brought forward Gerhardt's 29th Division and transferred the 7th Armored Division from Patton to Hodges. In addition, I moved Simpson's Ninth Army headquarters and Middleton's VIII Corps headquarters from Brittany and inserted them in the Ardennes and Luxembourg between Hodges and Patton. Finally—and most drastically—to relieve Patton's supply situation, I transferred Haislip's XV Corps of two divisions to Jake Devers, whose well-supplied (from Marseilles) U.S. Seventh Army, under Sandy Patch, had linked up on Patton's right flank. Patton groused: "At the moment I am being attacked on both flanks, but not by the Germans." Patton was so angry and miserable, he wrote his wife, he tried to get drunk—but couldn't.[8]

After all that, Monty's Ruhr offensive never got going. Market-Garden had drawn the enemy to his front in force. Monty was not strong enough; he couldn't move. He became enmeshed in a complicated fight with the Germans in the gap that had opened between his VIII Corps and the U.S. XIX Corps in the Peel Marshes. Hodges was compelled to "lend" Monty the 7th Armored Division, commanded by Lindsey Silvester. Monty suffered heavy casualties without getting much done. In the aftermath, I lost confidence in Silvester and was forced to relieve him of command.[9]

The momentum Hodges had gained in support of Monty's non-offensive carried forward briefly. Corlett, reinforced by Gerhardt's 29th Division, drove east to the Siegfried Line, then angled down under heavy counterattack to join Collins and take Aachen after a bitter fight on October 16. Hobbs's 30th and Huebner's Big Red One jointly encircled the city, reduced it to an utter shambles and compelled its stubborn defenders to surrender on October 21.

Pete Corlett had been under intense strain since D-day. As I said previously, his health was not good. During the Aachen fight, he showed signs of breakdown. Unable to control a red-hot temper, he antagonized Hodges and his staff and, as he recalled candidly in his memoir, even his own loyal staff. On October 19, I relieved him of command, without prejudice, and recommended that he be returned to the States "for rest and a complete physical check-up." I replaced him with Ray McLain, the National Guardsman who had so ably commanded the 90th Division.[10]

These early days in October were a time of utmost frustration in the Allied ground command. Winter was coming on. Owing to logistical problems, ammunition was now in critically short supply. We couldn't move. Every day that passed gave the Germans more time and opportunity to build defenses. I had little or no faith in Monty's plans; he had little or no faith in Ike's or mine. I was increasingly put out by Ike's predilection to favor Monty at our expense. Owing to Monty's failure to take Antwerp promptly, there now loomed before us the very real possibility that we might be compelled to dig in deep for the winter, postponing our major offensives until the spring.

George Marshall arrived on October 6 to pay us an official visit. Ike invited me to Paris to join him and Bedell Smith at Le Bourget Airport to meet the plane. Marshall was bubbling with optimism about the course of our campaign. He believed that if we kept the pressure on the Germans, we could probably wind up the war by Christmas. His optimism was based on overly rosy intelligence reports emanating from the Combined Chiefs of Staff. Even so, Marshall was like a breath of fresh air and, beyond doubt, his visit lifted our spirits and lent impetus to our planning for a November offensive.[11]

Marshall was with us for a full week. He visited extensively with me, Hodges and Patton, the corps commanders, and many of the front-line division commanders. This tour gave him a far more realistic grasp of our situation and our problems, particularly the problem of logistics. I disliked having to puncture his optimism, but I made it quite clear that the war could not be brought to an end by Christmas. We would be lucky to reach the Rhine by Christmas.[12]

On the third day of Marshall's visit, October 8, I flew with him to Monty's tactical headquarters in Eindhoven. Monty insisted on a private talk with Marshall. When they were closeted, Monty made another grave political error. He took this opportunity to denounce Ike. In his own words: "I told him that [ever] since Eisenhower had himself taken personal command of the land battle . . . the armies had become separated nationally and not geographically. There was a lack of grip, and operational direction and control was lacking. Our operations had, in fact, become ragged and disjointed, and we had now got ourselves into a real mess." The thrust of his argument was that Ike's leadership of the ground battle was not satisfactory and that a single ground commander should be appointed.

Marshall remained coolly silent—just barely. He later told his official biographer, Forrest Pogue: "I came pretty near to blowing off out of turn." Marshall recalled that "it was very hard for me to restrain myself because I didn't think there was any logic in what he said but overwhelming egotism."[13]

Monty did not stop there. He was moved at this juncture to reopen the same line of argument with Ike. On October 10, he sent Bedell Smith papers entitled "Notes on Command in Western Europe," which began: "The present organisation for command within the Allied forces in Western Europe is not satisfactory." The gist was that since Normandy, when Monty was overall ground commander, everything had gone to hell. There must be a single land commander for taking the Ruhr, Monty argued, and he must be appointed at once. Either Ike should move his tactical headquarters forward and take complete charge of the battle, or he, Monty, or I should be named overall land commander. If Ike chose me, Monty wrote, he would be "proud to serve under my very great friend Omar Bradley."[14]

This jab from Monty evoked a long, deeply felt letter from Ike. He and Smith cleared it with Marshall before sending it along. Ike began by putting the whole strategic picture in proper perspective: "The questions you raise are serious ones. . . . However, they do not constitute the real issue now at hand. That issue is Antwerp. . . . I have been informed by both the Chief of the Imperial General Staff [Alan Brooke] and the Chief of Staff of the United States Army [Marshall] that they seriously considered giving me a flat order that until the capture of Antwerp and its approaches was fully assured, this operation should take precedence over all others. . . . The Antwerp operation does not involve the question of command in any slightest degree."

As to Ike's competence to serve as overall land commander, Ike reminded Monty that "this is no longer a Normandy beachhead." The "battlefield" extended from Switzerland to the North Sea. Ike's proper job was to oversee the management of the entire battlefield and to delegate specific areas of responsibility to the army group commanders. He agreed that one commander should lead the attack on the Ruhr. His present view was that Monty had so much left undone in the north, including opening Antwerp, that the Ruhr objective would be given to me, with Monty providing support. If, after all this, Monty still felt Ike's leadership was "unsatisfactory," then the matter must be referred to "higher authority for any action they may choose to take, however drastic."[15]

Monty, apparently chastened, replied on October 16: "You will hear no more on the subject of command from me. I have given you my views and you have given your answer. That ends the matter and I and all of us up here will weigh in 100% to do what you want and we will pull it through without a doubt. I have given Antwerp top priority . . . Your very devoted and loyal subordinate . . ."[16]

Monty did not actually give the Schelde campaign his "unqualified support" until October 16, after this sharp exchange with Ike. He reinforced the Canadians with Dempsey's XII Corps. In addition, I provided the newly arrived 104th Infantry Division, commanded by Terry Allen, whom I had relieved of command of the Big Red One in Sicily. Counting the 82nd and 101st Airborne divisions, which Monty had not yet released and which to Ridgway's fury were still fighting as ordinary infantry, and the 7th Armored Division, which had been temporarily absorbed into Monty's VIII Corps, Monty now had four U.S. divisions under his command for the Schelde and other operations in the north. Even so, it took Monty another three full weeks of hard fighting—and a Canadian amphibious operation on Walcheren Island—to clear the Schelde. The Schelde campaign, October 1 to November 8, cost the Allies 13,000 casualties.[17]

Monty wrote in his memoirs: "I must admit a bad mistake on my part —I underestimated the difficulties of opening up the approaches to Antwerp so that we could get the free use of that port. I reckoned that the Canadian Army could do it *while* we were going for the Ruhr. I was wrong."[18]

Following the failure of Monty's Ruhr non-offensive in early October, Marshall's visit, and other events and decisions, on October 18 Ike decided to adopt the strategy I had proposed on September 22: a two-thrust attack to the Rhine by my Twelfth Army Group, with Monty, for the first time since D-day, playing a subordinate role. I would send one thrust eastward from Aachen toward Cologne and Bonn, another through the Saar to Frankfurt, thence north to encircle the Ruhr. After clearing the Schelde, Monty would attack southeast toward the Ruhr from the Nijmegen area. Owing to the logistical problems and the delays in clearing the Schelde, my offensive could not be scheduled until early November.[19]

In preparation for this offensive, I shifted Simpson's Ninth Army from the southern Belgium-Luxembourg area to the area north of Aachen formerly held by Hodges' XIX Corps. This, in effect, inserted the Ninth Army between Monty's forces and Hodges' forces. I did this for two principal reasons. First, I felt there was a good likelihood that at some future date Monty would again attempt to incorporate a U.S. army into his command. The U.S. First Army staffers—those mule-headed, swaggering veterans of North Africa and Sicily—were so bitterly anti-Monty that I feared they might mutiny if they were again compelled to serve under him. Simpson and his staff had not yet been subjected to Monty's megalomania and were, on the whole, more diplomatic and adaptable. Secondly, the Ninth Army was far less experienced than the First Army. If I were again forced to lend Monty an army, I preferred to give him my green troops rather than trusted lieutenants such as Collins, Gerow (who had returned from the Pearl Harbor investigations), Middleton and others.

To accomplish the changes with minimum disruption, I gave Simpson McLain's XIX Corps in exchange for Middleton's VIII Corps, which was in the Ardennes and thereafter reported to Hodges. In addition, Simpson had a new corps, XIII, commanded by Alvan C. Gillem, Jr., which as yet had no troops. (It was slated to get the 7th Armored, the 84th and 102nd Infantry divisions.)[20]

I was very glad to have Simpson in the line. He was a 1909 classmate of Forrest Harding, Patton and Eichelberger. Nicknamed "Simp" because he graduated second from the bottom of his class, he was a quiet but strong-willed Texan—tall, rawboned and bald as a billiard ball. Son of a rancher on the Pecos River, Simpson had arrived at West Point in the summer of 1905 without a high school degree and was only a few days past seventeen when he entered. His whole four years at West Point were a desperate struggle to hang in academically, but he was a born soldier and leader of men and those obvious qualities probably helped pull him through. He served on the Mexican border and in France, rising to lieutenant colonel and chief of staff of the 33rd Division, where he won a Distinguished Service Medal, a Silver Star and other awards. He married, adopted a little girl and spent the peacetime years like the rest of us with troops or at Fort Benning or teaching ROTC. He was a graduate of the Command and General Staff School and the Army War College.

He had spent his time following the mobilization of the Guard in 1940 in straightening out two National Guard Divisions. Marshall had then promoted him to command a corps, then an army.

Simpson had a wonderful earthy sense of humor. He loved to tell this story:

> One night Patton came in with a bottle of brandy and said, "Let's have a nightcap." We drank and talked. Patton said, "Well, here we all are under Eisenhower and Bradley, both six years our junior. Hodges flunked out of West Point Class of ought-eight and had to enlist and now he commands First Army. I was turned back from ought-eight and it took me five years to graduate—with ought-nine—but I command Third Army. You came out second from the bottom in our class in ought-nine and you command Ninth Army. Isn't it peculiar that three old farts like us should be carrying the ball for those two sons-of-bitches?"[21]

As I have said, my forces north of the Ardennes—Simpson's and Hodges'—faced formidable terrain obstacles. One of these was the Roer River. Upstream, on the south end of the Huertgen Forest, opposite the Ardennes, the Germans had built a series of seven imposing dams across the Roer. At first we paid these dams scant heed. Then belatedly it dawned on us that if the Germans demolished the two largest dams, the torrent of water would flood the lower Roer, making our crossing difficult, if not impossible.

Official Army historian Charles B. MacDonald has implied that we did not fully appreciate the strategic significance of these dams and thus neglected them in our planning. This was true—at first. But by mid to late October we were very much aware of the threat they posed, and while they were not specifically set forth in Hodges' or my directives as a key objective, they were a constant source of worry and discussion. This, in turn, led directly to the decision to order General Norman (Dutch) Cota's 28th Division, heavily reinforced with artillery and engineers, to attack the town of Schmidt on November 2. While the Roer dams were not an assigned objective, the whole point was to gain control of the dams and spillways.

In launching Cota, we grossly underestimated both the terrain and the German defenses. The terrain was extremely rugged and the roads mined, as in Sicily. We could not get tanks into the area, whereas the Germans, approaching the battle over more favorable terrain, could. The weather was unfavorable, impeding or wiping out a heavy Allied air attack in support of Cota. The ensuing battle was a disaster. Cota collided with the reconstituted 116th Panzer Division and two other tough German divisions, causing panic in some 28th Division units. Cota suffered appalling losses—6,000 killed, wounded, captured or missing—before he was compelled to withdraw without having achieved his mission.[22]

This tough defeat notwithstanding, we pushed ahead with plans for our November two-thrust offensive to the Rhine. This grew to be by far the largest Allied effort on the Continent to date. My First, Third and Ninth armies combined numbered some twenty-two divisions plus supporting units, comprising about 500,000 men. Hodges, Simpson, Patton and I felt a very heavy responsibility. This would be our last chance to crack through the Siegfried Line before the onset of winter. Moreover, Ike had made it clear that if we had not achieved success by the first of the year, my Ninth Army would be given to Monty for a renewed effort in the north.[23]

Patton got off first, on November 8. He still had only two corps—Eddy's XII and Walker's XX. But each of these corps had gradually swollen in size far beyond normal corps strength. Eddy commanded five divisions plus numerous attached artillery and special units; Walker commanded four divisions plus numerous attached units. In addition, I placed the 83rd Infantry Division on alert for possible transfer to Walker. In all, Patton commanded nine divisions comprising some 220,000 men. Released at long last, Patton recorded that he felt "40 years younger" but had "indigestion and the heaves as I always do before a match." On the eve of battle, he read the late Erwin Rommel's book *Infantry Attacks*.[24]

Patton attacked in grim weather—heavy, cold rain. The rivers were flooding. He had little or no air support. The Germans resisted every muddy inch of the way. Heavily fortified Metz still blocked the path to the Saar. Walker attacked Metz on November 9. After twelve days of bloody fighting, Patton claimed the city, but pockets of Germans in the forts held out until December 13. In three weeks, Patton slugged his way forward some thirty-five to forty miles to the Saar River, crossed it, but was stopped dead at the Siegfried Line. His failure to break through deeper into Germany infuriated him. Moreover, at Eddy's request, he was forced to relieve one of his best friends and front-line generals, John Wood, commanding the 4th Armored Division, who was mentally and physically worn out. In his frustration, he raged at me, Ike and Monty in his diary. When I was compelled to deny him use of the 83rd Division, he petulantly blamed it on my "natural timidity" and added vehemently: "I hope history records his moral cowardice." Patton's drive to the Siegfried Line cost 27,000 casualties.[25] *

The main thrust of the November offensive was to be launched simultaneously with Patton, to the north of the Ardennes, toward Cologne and

* Ike sent Wood home for extended "rest and recuperation," but he did not return to the ETO.[26]

Bonn. This force comprised four corps of about twelve divisions. These were Simpson's XIX (McLain) and XIII (Gillem) and Hodges' VII (Collins) and V (Gerow). As in the St. Lô breakout, Cobra, I named Joe Collins and his VII Corps to spearhead the First Army attack. McLain's experienced XIX Corps was chosen to spearhead the Ninth Army attack. Both spearheads would be preceded by massive air bombardments, à la Cobra, but with improved safeguards to protect our own forces from accidental bombing.

Collins' VII Corps spearhead was beefed up to the equivalent of almost five divisions. These units included Rose's 3rd Armored Division, Huebner's Big Red One, Barton's 4th Infantry Division (replacing Louis A. Craig's 9th Division, badly mauled in recent action) and Allen's 104th Division, brought over from the Schelde campaign. In addition, Collins was given half of Gerow's 5th Armored Division. It was my hope that Collins could duplicate his breakout at St. Lô and dash to the Rhine.

The northern thrust was delayed by poor weather and other factors until November 16. Although the weather was still marginal, some 2,200 U.S. and RAF bombers, escorted by about 1,000 fighters, came through to drop 10,000 tons of bombs in front of VII and XIX corps. Thereafter, some 1,200 artillery pieces along the front opened up with an incessant barrage. The spearheads jumped off as planned, but soon bogged down against fierce resistance in difficult terrain—the Huertgen Forest.

What followed over the next several weeks was some of the most brutal and difficult fighting of the war. The battle—known as Huertgen Forest—was sheer butchery on both sides. In three weeks, Collins advanced a mere six miles in miserable weather and at terrible cost. McLain's forces, advancing through more favorable terrain, reached the banks of the Roer on November 28. Farther south, Gerow reached the river about the same time, but the vital Roer dams remained in German hands. Collins reached the Roer on December 16. In this November drive to the Roer, the First and Ninth armies suffered a total of 35,000 casualties.

To put it candidly, my plan to smash through to the Rhine and encircle the Ruhr had failed. Patton, facing weaker forces, had advanced some forty miles to the Saar, but he could move no further. Simpson and Hodges had bludgeoned their way through heavy German forces some eight or ten miles to the Roer. We had killed or captured tens of thousands of Germans and moved our front to the Saar and Roer, but in both sectors the Rhine River (and hence the Ruhr) lay well beyond our grasp. Between our front and the Rhine, a determined enemy held every foot of ground and would not yield. Each day the weather grew colder, our troops more miserable. We were mired in a ghastly war of attrition.[27]

Monty promptly seized on our failures to position himself for a renewed political offensive inside the high command to have his own way. On November 17, he wrote Alan Brooke a bitterly contemptuous letter about Ike: "He has never commanded anything before in his whole career; now, for the first time, he has elected to take direct command of very large-scale operations and he does not know how to do it. . . . I am getting rather alarmed; I think we are drifting into dangerous waters." He iterated his view that a single land commander should be appointed and that all the Allied ground powers be concentrated in a single "colossal crack" at the Germans in the north. But he wondered if, after telling Ike that he would hear no more from him on the subject, he should again reopen the matter with Ike.[28]

Alan Brooke and the British Chiefs agreed with Monty's fundamental points. "Eisenhower completely fails as Commander;" Brooke wrote in his diary. "Bedell Smith lives back in Paris quite out of touch; as a result the war is drifting in a rudderless condition." But he cautioned Monty to lie low and not reopen the matter with Ike. The failure of my November offensive would provide "sufficient justification" to review the matter on the highest level. However, owing to the preponderance of U.S. forces on the Continent, Alan Brooke saw no hope that Monty could be named overall land commander. Instead, he suggested me: "Do you consider that Bradley is fit for the job? Will he be able to control Patton and Devers? Would he discuss plans with you sufficiently?"

Monty replied: "I have offered in writing to serve under Bradley, but it is no use; Ike is determined to do it himself." Monty went on to suggest the following solution: that the front be divided into two sectors, one to the north of the Ardennes, the other to the south. He would command the northern sector; I would command the southern. We would both report to Ike. In sum: *two* land commanders reporting to Ike. Alan Brooke wrote back that that was a poor solution. "You have repeatedly affirmed that the northern line of advance is the one and only one that has any chance of success. . . . You are therefore proposing yourself for the one and only front that can play any major part in the Western offensive on Germany." There was little possibility that the Americans would find that solution acceptable.[29]

Brooke countered with his own proposal. He wrote Monty on November 24: "Personally I consider Bradley much better suited to carrying out the tasks of land force commander than Ike. . . . I agree that the front could be divided into two groups, and consider a suitable setup to be Bradley Land Forces Commander, yourself Northern Group and Patton Southern Group. With that setup there might be some chance of your being accepted for Northern Group." In response, Monty flew to London on November 26 for a face-to-face chat. Monty agreed that I should be named overall land forces commander; he would propose that to Ike at once. However, he had a different idea as to how the armies on the front should be deployed. He proposed that he command the northern group, which would include, in addition to British and Canadian forces, Patton's Third

Army. He thought Jake Devers should command the southern group, which should consist of Hodges' First, Simpson's Ninth and Patch's Seventh armies. Alan Brooke evidently agreed.

On the following day, November 27, Alan Brooke took the plan to Churchill. Brooke wrote: "Winston said that he was also worried about the Western Front. He agreed with most of what I had said, but was doubtful as to the necessity for a Land Forces Commander." When Brooke again raised the matter with Churchill a week later, December 4, Brooke recorded that Churchill declared "he did not want anybody between Ike and his Army Groups, as Ike was a good fellow who was amenable and whom he could influence. Bradley, on the other hand, might not listen to what he said!"[30]

Having set all this in train, Monty then invited Ike to his headquarters to present the new plan. He got off on the wrong foot again by stating that "we had definitely failed," describing my November offensive as a "strategic reverse." Ike did not agree with that, but he remained silent, and Montgomery wrongly interpreted Ike's silence as full agreement. Monty went on to say that we now needed a new strategic plan which, in place of "attacking all along the front," would "concentrate our resources on a selected vital thrust." He went on to say "it seemed a pity he did not have Bradley as Land Forces Commander" to relieve him of the burden of front-line operations. To that Ike most emphatically "did not agree" and "shied right off it." Monty likewise let the subject drop. That was the end of the British effort to name me overall ground forces commander.[31]

After his meeting with Ike, Monty wrote Alan Brooke: "It is my impression . . . that he thinks Bradley has failed him as an architect of land operations. There is no doubt that he is now very anxious to go back to the old setup we had in Normandy and up to September 1 and to put Bradley under my operational command with both our Army Groups north of the Ardennes. In fact, he now definitely wants me to handle main business but wants Bradley to be in on it and, therefore, he will put him under me."[32]

Here Montgomery was guilty of wishful thinking. At no time did Ike ever express to me, or to my knowledge anyone else, the opinion that I had "failed him." Nor is there a shred of evidence in his correspondence, papers and private diary or those of his closest wartime associates that he felt this way. To the contrary, on every occasion he had to mention me, it was in utmost flattering terms. It is inconceivable to me that Ike said any such thing to Monty, who was bound to use it against me at the first opportunity. Likewise, I do not believe that Ike told Montgomery that he wanted to put me under Monty's "operational command." That was simply out of the question. My view is seconded by official British historian Lionel Ellis, who wrote that Monty misunderstood Ike on this point.[33]

On November 30, Monty—perhaps at Brooke's suggestion—wrote

Ike a letter "to confirm" the main points on which they had "agreed." Monty stated that we had failed and suffered a strategic reverse; we needed a new plan which must not fail; the new plan would concentrate at one point enough strength to assure success; we would divide the land operations into two major fronts, naming one commander for forces north of the Ardennes, one for forces south of the Ardennes; we would put both the Twelfth Army Group and the Twenty-first Army Group north of the Ardennes and "put Bradley under my operational command."[34]

But in the very next paragraph, Monty himself suggested that that point was very much undecided: "I said that Bradley and I are a good team. We worked together in Normandy, under you, and we won a great victory. Things have not been so good since you separated us. I believe to be certain of success, you want to bring us together again; and one of us should have the full operational control north of the Ardennes; and if you decide that I should do that work—that is O.K. by me."

During their meeting, Ike had proposed to Monty a formal conference of all of us at Simpson's headquarters in Maastricht to thrash out the problems of strategy and command. Monty concluded his letter with this arrogant proposal: "I suggest we want no one else at the meeting except Chiefs of Staff, who must not speak."[35]

I knew nothing of all this. On the day that Ike and Monty met, I came down with a severe case of the flu, together with hives, which confined me to my Luxembourg hotel room for a week. Hansen, noting my condition, wrote that I looked "completely exhausted." He went on: "Contrary to his robustness a year ago, he shows the indications of weariness more evidently and bounces back less quickly." I was scheduled to meet Ike at Simpson's headquarters on December 1, but owing to my illness Ike came instead to Luxembourg. He arrived bearing a gift: a Cadillac limousine to ease my way on inspection trips. He also had the letter from Monty summing up their November 28 meeting.[36]

Ike was as angry as I had ever seen him. After talking with me, he dictated a reply to Monty, probably his strongest letter of the war. He took great exception to Monty's statement that "things have not been good" since Normandy. "Bradley's brilliant breakthrough made possible the great exploitation by all forces which blasted France and Belgium and almost carried us to the Rhine." In case Monty missed the point, he added, "If we had advanced from the beginning [i.e., Caen] *as we had hoped,* our maintenance services would have been in a position to supply us during the critical September days when we actually reached the limit of our resources." Strategy would be ironed out at the forthcoming conference but he had "no intention" of stopping Patton and Devers "as long as they were clearing up our right flank and giving us capability of concentration." He avoided the command issue—my serving under Monty—stating, "I am quite sure that you, Bradley and I can remain masters of the situation."

Ike added: "With respect to the Chiefs of Staff attending the conference, it makes no difference to me whether your Chief of Staff attends or whether Bradley's does. Mine will be there unless some unforeseen circumstance prevents. Bedell is my Chief of Staff because I trust him and respect his judgment. I will not by any means insult him by telling him that he should remain mute at any conference he and I both attend."[37]

The conference at Maastricht was set for December 7—Pearl Harbor Day plus three years. Ike and Tedder came to Luxembourg the afternoon before to go over various proposals which had been submitted to Hodges and Simpson. The next day we drove up together. I was still not well, but this was a meeting that I could not afford to miss. The whole future course of the war—and perhaps my professional future—was at stake.[38]

The conference was another long and tedious affair. Monty repeated all the views and arguments he had been making all fall. These now boiled down to three basic points: that the main thrust on Germany should be made with all the force at our disposal, from the north against the Ruhr, then Berlin; that this force and all other forces north of the Ardennes should be commanded by him; and all other armies, including Patton's and Devers', should be halted.

When the interminable discussion was concluded, Ike decided that the main thrust against Germany would now be made, as Monty wished, from the north; that it would be led by Monty; that Monty would be reinforced with a U.S. army of ten divisions (Simpson's Ninth); that I would retain control of Hodges' First and Patton's Third armies (both north and south of the Ardennes); that Hodges, Patton and Devers would continue aggressive operations against Germany; Hodges toward Bonn, Patton toward Frankfurt, thence north to the Ruhr, with Devers protecting Patton's right flank.

This was a classic Eisenhower compromise that left me distinctly unhappy. It tacitly implied that my Twelfth Army Group offensive had failed. Now Monty had been chosen to make the "main effort," and henceforth my operations would be "supporting." Monty would be given my Ninth Army. Ten U.S. divisions would be compelled to serve directly under a British commander who would make certain they never received any credit. Monty would again receive priority on logistics. That situation had improved markedly since Monty had finally opened Antwerp, but owing to an optimistic cutback in production in the States and the demands of the Pacific Theater, we still suffered from a critical artillery ammunition shortage.

Nor was Monty happy. He had failed to ease Ike back into the role of chairman of the board and win his primary goal of being named overall land commander. Ike was still making the big decisions on land operations. Monty had also failed to carry his fall-back positions of having me appointed land commander, or of having two land commanders—Monty commanding all forces north of the Ardennes and me commanding all forces south of the Ardennes. He would command three armies to my two, but I would still command Hodges' First Army north of the Ardennes. Finally, and perhaps worst of all from Monty's point of view, my two armies would continue on the offensive. There would be no single "full-blooded" thrust to the Ruhr or Berlin, but rather a general offensive across a "broad front." Monty wrote Alan Brooke: "I personally regard the whole thing as quite dreadful. . . . We shall split our resources and our strength, and we shall fail. . . . If we want the war to end within any reasonable period you have to get Eisenhower's hand taken off the land battle. I regret to say that he just doesn't know what he is doing. And you will have to see that Bradley's influence is curbed."[39]

That was not the end of it. Brooke had persuaded Churchill to telegraph Roosevelt to urge a meeting of the Combined Chiefs of Staff. Churchill painted the darkest imaginable picture, stating "we have definitely failed to achieve the strategic objective which we gave to our Armies five weeks ago." But Roosevelt—at Marshall's request—declined to convene the Chiefs at that time, stating that "our agreed broad strategy is developing according to plan."[40]

That avenue having been closed off, Brooke then decided to work directly on Ike. He invited Ike and Tedder to London on December 12 for a conference with Churchill and the full British Chiefs of Staff. Here Ike dismayed one and all by stating that there probably could be no all-out decisive Allied ground campaign until May 1, 1945. After Ike explained the new plan, Brooke tore into him with undisguised contempt. "I disagreed flatly with it, accused Ike of violating principles of concentration of force, which had resulted in his present failures. I criticized his future plans and pointed out impossibility of double invasion with the limited forces he has got." To Brooke's astonishment, Churchill leaped to Ike's defense. As a consequence, Brooke was so "depressed" that he "seriously thought of resigning." But the next day, Churchill confessed to Brooke that he had supported Ike only because Ike was "his guest" and was far outnumbered. In truth, Churchill had been deeply impressed by Brooke's savage attack and asked Brooke to prepare a paper attacking Ike's new plan. Brooke's staff got out the knives and set to work with the aim of compiling a document which would compel the Combined Chiefs to overrule Ike and give Monty everything that he sought.[41]

THIRTY-EIGHT

In early September, most men in the Allied high command believed that victory over Germany was imminent. The near-miraculous revitalization of the German Army in October had come as a shock, dissipating some of the optimism. The failure of our November offensive to crack the Siegfried Line and push through to the Rhine had been a further jolt, leading Ike and SHAEF planners to conclude that we would probably be stalemated through the winter, unable to mount a decisive offensive until after the spring thaw in late April or May 1945.

However, in early December, there was a resurgence of optimism in the Allied intelligence community. An analysis of our November offensive found that Hodges' and Patton's armies had captured nearly 60,000 Germans, the manpower equivalent of five or six divisions. Moreover, SHAEF analysts reported, our continuing pressure all along the front was costing the Germans some 9,000 permanent or long-term casualties a day, the equivalent in manpower of five divisions a week.[1]

This was a terrific drain in manpower, which no nation could sustain for long. Most of the German divisions opposing us were only at half strength. Moreover, as we knew, the Germans, simultaneously fighting the oncoming Russians on the Eastern Front, were sustaining even greater losses there. All the while our strategic and tactical air was ferociously pounding the German heartland and military installations immediately behind the front.

Thus, on sober reflection, our intelligence analysts began to paint the general picture in rosier hues. In his weekly summary, dated December 12, my G-2, Eddie Sibert, wrote: "It is now certain that attrition is steadily sapping the strength of the German forces on the Western Front and that the crust of defenses is thinner, more brittle and more vulnerable than it appears in our G-2 maps or to the troops in the line. . . . With continued Allied pressure in the south and in the north, the breaking point may develop suddenly and without warning." Monty's G-2, E. T. Williams, produced an even more sanguine appreciation: "The enemy is in a bad way; he has had a tremendous battering and has lost heavily in men and equipment. . . . [He is] at present fighting a defensive campaign on all fronts; his situation is such that he cannot stage a major offensive operation."[2]

When we launched our November offensive, we knew from Ultra that professional soldier von Rundstedt had reassumed command of Hitler's Western Front. His professionalism was everywhere evident in the manner in which the Germans resisted our offensive. On December 5, when members of the House Military Affairs Committee visited my headquarters, one of the congressmen asked me if I thought Hitler, who had not made a public appearance since the July assassination attempt, was out of the picture owing to the lingering injuries of that episode or some other illness. I replied, as Chet Hansen recorded it, that "he probably is or at least there is an indication that he has returned command of his armies in the west to the German General Staff." I added, "If he is ill, I wish he'd recover and take command again."[3]

What I meant was that if Hitler were directing strategy on the Western Front, he might very well order another desperate and disastrous offensive like the one at Mortain. Such an offensive might enable us to destroy the German armies west of the Rhine, as we had west of the Seine. This would put an end to our stalemate and grinding war of attrition and enable us to cross into Germany as we had crossed into eastern France, Belgium, Holland and Luxembourg, pursuing a mangled and fleeing army in fast-moving open warfare.

However, believing von Rundstedt to be fully in charge of the Western Front, we expected a textbook defense against our offense. Our immediate plan in the northern sector was to continue the pressure, seize control of the Roer dams, then cross the Roer River and strike for the Rhine. We knew from a steady flow of Ultra that von Rundstedt had created a strong panzer reserve near Cologne. This was the Sixth Panzer Army. In addition, we knew from Ultra that the Fifth Panzer Army had been withdrawn from the front lines for refitting and remanning, and we had to assume it could soon be incorporated into the reserves. We anticipated that when we crossed the Roer, von Rundstedt would counterattack us with his panzer reserves (principally the Sixth Panzer Army) in the good tank country between the Roer and Rhine rivers. That was the proper professional solution to the military threat we posed to von Rundstedt.[4]

Our views of von Rundstedt's capabilities and intentions were crystallized by First Army's G-2, Monk Dickson, in his intelligence report of December 10:

> German strategy in defense of the Reich is based on the exhaustion of our offensive to be followed by an all-out counterattack with armor, between the

> Roer and the Erft, supported by every weapon he can bring to bear. . . . It is apparent that von Rundstedt who obviously is conducting military operations without benefit of intuition [Hitler] has skillfully defended and husbanded his forces and is preparing for his part in the all-out application of every weapon at the focal point and the correct time to achieve defense of the Reich west of the Rhine by inflicting as great a defeat on the Allies as possible. Indications to date point to the location of this focal point as being between Roermond and Schleiden [north of the Ardennes opposite Aachen] and within this bracket this concentrated force will be applied to the Allied force judged by the German High Command to be the greatest threat to successful defense of the Reich. . . . [The counterattack] is to be expected when our major ground forces have crossed the Roer River, and if the dams are not controlled by us, maximum use will be made by the enemy of flooding of the Roer in conjunction with his counterattack.[5]

It should be emphasized that none of us, including Dickson, was thinking in terms of a major strategic counterattack. We were thinking in terms of (as a SHAEF intelligence report put it) "a spoiling attack of considerable power" *after* we crossed the Roer River. As quoted above, Monty's G-2 agreed with our thinking: "He cannot stage a major offensive operation." He also agreed with us that von Rundstedt was "unlikely" to commit his panzer reserves "until the Allies advance over the Roer to present a threat."[6]

The assumption that von Rundstedt was in charge and that future operations would more or less follow the textbook was universally held in the Allied high command. I am not aware that a single soul in authority believed otherwise. No one came forward to say, "Hey, watch yourself. Hitler may really be in charge. Anything can happen."

We were all wrong, of course—tragically and stupidly wrong. After the experience of Mortain, it should have occurred to at least one of us that as we pushed Germany to the wall, Hitler might very well do something crazy and desperate again. That was his style.

One major fault on our side was that our intelligence community had come to rely far too heavily on Ultra to the exclusion of other intelligence sources. Ultra had become virtually "infallible." But Ultra depended on radio intercepts. Now that we had advanced almost to the German border, the German Army had less need for radio communications and more often used secure and uninterceptable land lines. Moreover, it apparently did not occur to our intelligence community that the Germans could—or might—plan and launch an operation with complete radio and telephonic silence imposed.

The fallacy that crept into our thinking was that since Ultra had not specifically forecast or suggested a major strategic counterattack, there was no possibility of one. Monty's G-2 wrote later: "We had begun to lean: that was the danger of Ultra." Eddie Sibert was more specific: "As for general intelligence operations . . . it occurs to me that we may have put too much reliance on certain technical types of intelligence, such as signal intelligence . . . upon which we had come to rely too much." The First Army Ultra rep, Adolph Rosengarten, wrote: "Some clues came from open sources but were not heeded as no clue came from Ultra."[7]

The truth was that Hitler was not ill—not in the conventional sense. Nor had he relinquished control of strategy on the Western Front. He was in full charge; von Rundstedt was merely a front man, perhaps deliberately put there to help mislead us. Behind a cloak of utmost secrecy—including absolute radio silence—Hitler was preparing a desperate strategic counter-offensive of massive proportions. Four armies of some forty divisions would blitzkrieg through the Ardennes, spearheaded by seven armored divisions. The armies were to split the Allied forces in two, seize our supply depots, close off Antwerp and then encircle and destroy us piece-meal.[8]

When we launched our November offensive, we were hard pressed for divisions. The earlier fighting in the Huertgen Forest and the Roer dam area had badly chewed up two of our very best, Craig's 9th and Cota's 28th. Owing to Monty's failure to quickly open up Antwerp, I had been compelled to divert seven divisions earmarked for my front to Jake Devers' Sixth Army Group so that they could be supplied via Marseilles. Monty had held on to the 82nd and 101st Airborne divisions until late November, greatly delaying their rest and refit. The result was I had had to commit every division I could lay my hands on, leaving the Ardennes front thinly held and no reserves at army group level. The refitting 82nd and 101st Airborne divisions, placed in SHAEF reserve, constituted our principal backup.[9]

The weakest link in our front was the Ardennes sector, an eighty-five-mile stretch lying between Hodges and Patton. It was held by Troy Middleton's VIII Corps, now attached to Hodges' First Army. Even though we were well aware that Hitler had launched his 1940 attack on France through the Ardennes, we did not then consider it an unusually dangerous area. Ultra told us that it was only lightly manned by transient divisions or the newly created *Volksgrenadier* divisions, composed of sailors and airmen. The area was utilized by the Germans, Monk Dickson wrote, for the "seasoning of newly formed divisions . . . prior to their dispatch to a more active front." We used the "quiet" Ardennes front for much the same purpose.[10]

On November 8, coincident with the launching of our offensive, Ike and I visited Troy Middleton at his headquarters in Bastogne. We had lunch, toured part of the long, desolate front and inspected several of his divisions, including the brand-new 9th Armored and the badly mangled 28th, which had been assigned to VIII Corps for rest and rebuilding. Ike and I decided the sector could be held with four divisions. Subsequently these were, north to south: the newly arrived 106th Division, the 28th Division, the 4th Division (badly chewed up in the November offensive) and the 9th Armored.[11]

There was a calculated risk involved in manning the Ardennes front so thinly with so many green troops, but I thought the gamble was negligible. In the remote event the Germans launched a spoiling attack in this sector, with our great mobility we could quickly cut it off by diverting troops south and north from Hodges' and Patton's armies. Such an attack —another Mortain—would even be welcomed. It would certainly fail, affording us an opportunity to destroy German elements at small loss to us. Later, Ike set forth my views to Marshall:

> I personally discussed this matter with Bradley but his attitude was that it would be an unprofitable region for the enemy to use and if he made such an attack it would subsequently lead to our advantage. At the worst it was a reasonable sector in which to take a risk and risks had to be taken somewhere. With respect to this one point, Bradley and I, and so far as I know, everyone else with whom I have ever discussed the matter, felt about as follows: We did not repeat not believe that the hastily trained *Volkssturm* [he meant *Volksgrenadier*] divisions could be used effectively in an offensive. We did not repeat not consider that in winter time the enemy could supply a major thrust permanently through the Ardennes. In view of the strength we could finally bring to bear, we did not repeat not consider that the enemy could capture, through the tortuous communications lines of the Ardennes, any really vital targets, which were manifestly Liege, Namur, and/or Verdun. Therefore we thought the Ardennes attack would be a strategic mistake for him.[12]

Even so, the calculated risk was not undertaken casually. Ike later wrote that it was a matter of "constant concern" to him. It worried Patton. On November 24, he noted in his diary with uncanny astuteness: "The First Army is making a terrible mistake in leaving VIII Corps static, as it is highly probable that the Germans are building up east of them."[13]

Patton's intuition may have been based in part on the excellent work of his G-2, Oscar Koch. Third Army paid keen attention to the disposition of German armor. From November 20 onward, Koch's daily intelligence reports pointedly noted the re-forming and refitting of German panzer divisions in the Sixth Panzer Army and on several days (November 27, November 30, December 11) raised the possibility of a limited enemy counterattack. For example, Koch's report of December 11 stated: "The massive armored force the enemy has built up in reserve gives him the definite capability of launching a spoiling [diversionary] offensive to disrupt the Allied drive." On the morning of December 16, Koch suggested in his report that the re-formed and refitted panzers were either "available for immediate employment in the event of a serious threat of a major [Allied] breakthrough" or were being amassed "in positions of tactical reserve presumably for a large-scale counteroffensive."[14]

I, of course, did not see these Koch reports. Even if I had, they would not have unduly alarmed me. We—and SHAEF—were also well aware of the panzer build-up. Ike's G-2, Kenneth Strong, at Bedell Smith's suggestion, came to Luxembourg in early December to warn me that, among other possibilities, the German Sixth Panzer Army might launch a "relieving" (or spoiling) attack through the Ardennes against VIII Corps. But at no time did anyone present me with unequivocal or convincing evidence that a massive German attack through the Ardennes at VIII Corps was imminent.[15]

Although I continued to believe such an attack only a remote possibility, I discussed the possibility in detail with Middleton and we made plans to defend against it. If the Germans hit his sector, Middleton was to make a fighting withdrawal—all the way back to the Meuse River if necessary. We chose the specific defensive positions he would hold. Since there were only a few roads through the area, we thought our tactical air forces could interdict them with relative ease, further delaying the Germans. Middleton was to locate no gasoline or food dumps, or anything else of value to the enemy, within that line of withdrawal. If Middleton were forced to withdraw, he would slow the enemy as much as possible, and I would order reserve armored divisions (the 7th from Simpson, the 10th from Patton) and other units to close pincers at the base of the German salient and cut him off.* Lacking the resources to continue our offensive *and* defend the Ardennes in depth, my defensive plan for the Ardennes was broadly based on *mobility,* at which we had proven ourselves unequaled, rather than *concentration*.[16]

These plans, and the carefully calculated risks entailed, were based on the possibility of a limited German "spoiling attack" of four to six divisions. Another Mortain. I believe the plan could have even contained the full weight of the Sixth Panzer Army.

What preoccupied me most professionally on December 16, 1944, was not the possibility of an enemy attack through the Ardennes but rather an alarming crisis in manpower. Not only were we short of divisions, we were also critically short of manpower *within* the divisions. Particularly riflemen. The shortage was due to several factors: inept long-range personnel planning at SHAEF and in the War Department; heavy combat casualties in the October, November and December fighting, combined with a wholly unexpected onslaught of trench foot, caused by late-arriving, ill-designed

* The 7th and 10th Armored divisions were in Ninth and Third Army reserve, respectively. The Big Red One was in First Army reserve. I kept a finger on those reserve divisions. They could not be committed to action without my prior approval.

cold-weather footwear. Trench foot had cost us an additional 12,000 nonbattle casualties.[17]

Our infantry replacement problem had become so grave a matter that I ordered my army group G-1, Red O'Hare, to fly to Washington to demand a speedup. That day, December 16, I accompanied O'Hare by car to SHAEF headquarters in Versailles to lend my weight to his urgent mission. We left early—before the morning briefing—traveled icy roads, stopped at the Ritz Hotel in Paris for lunch, then continued on to Ike's headquarters in Versailles. Ike was in a sunny mood. He had just received word from Washington that he had been promoted to the rank of five-star "General of the Army."[18]

This promotion, ironically, had its roots in the U.S. Navy. Our admirals, historically more rank-conscious than our Army generals, had been pressing for some time to promote four-star Chief of Naval Operations Admiral Ernest J. King to the rank of five-star "Admiral of the Fleet" and Roosevelt's Chairman of the Joint Chiefs of Staff, four-star Admiral William D. Leahy, to the *six*-star rank of "Admiral of the Navy." Roosevelt favored the plan and suggested that the War Department propose a similar rank for the Army. But Marshall adamantly opposed the idea, first because he didn't feel the need for another star, and second because a title such as "General of the Army" might detract from the unique title "General of the Armies" borne by his aged friend and benefactor John J. Pershing.

Owing to Marshall's opposition, Roosevelt shelved the matter for many months. But in the fall of 1944, the President revived it with a will, and pro-Navy legislators in the Congress, notably Congressman Carl Vinson, chairman of the House Naval Affairs Committee, pushed a bill through the Congress. As finally signed into law, the act provided for eight promotions to five-star rank (but none to six): Leahy, King, Nimitz and Halsey in the Navy; Marshall, Arnold, MacArthur and Eisenhower in the Army. To preserve Pershing's unique title, each five-star Army general was to be known as "General of the Army." Each admiral was to be known as "Fleet Admiral of the U.S. Navy," usually shortened to "Fleet Admiral."[19]

These promotions opened the way for promotions for men serving under the five-star Army generals. That day Ike pronounced that he would immediately recommend to Marshall that Tooey Spaatz and I be promoted to the four-star rank of full general. In our eyes, this would put me on a par with Field Marshal Montgomery and one star above Patton and Hodges. I was flattered—and pleased.

Later that afternoon, word reached SHAEF that the Germans had launched counterattacks early that morning at five separate points along the First Army front in Middleton's VIII Corps sector. At that time, Hodges was in process of attacking the Roer dams; Patton was mounting a full-scale attack at the West Wall in the Saar area. My initial reaction to these fragmentary and unclear reports was that von Rundstedt had launched a limited spoiling attack through the Ardennes in an effort to force Hodges and Patton to slow down or pull back. I was not overly concerned.[20]

In the early evening, Ike had an important social obligation. His orderly, Michael (Mickey) McKeogh, had married one of Ike's WAC drivers, Pearlie Hargreaves. Ike made an appearance at the wedding reception in the WAC quarters in Versailles, then returned to his headquarters. Later, we cracked a bottle of champagne to celebrate Ike's promotion. We then played five rubbers of bridge.[21]

During the evening, ever-more alarming reports of enemy attacks at the front poured into SHAEF. At first Ike and I were frankly astonished that the *Volksgrenadier* divisions could mount an offensive. However, it gradually became apparent—Ike sensed it before I did—that this was no spoiling attack by *Volksgrenadier* divisions but rather an all-out offensive by three German armies: the Sixth Panzer, Fifth Panzer and the Seventh, with perhaps as many as twenty-four divisions involved. Bletchley Park began to confirm our suspicions later that evening; but not until dawn of December 17 did we get the intercepted decodes of von Rundstedt's attack order: "The hour of destiny has struck. Mighty offensive armies face the Allies. Everything is at stake. More than mortal deeds are required as a holy duty to the Fatherland."[22]

Bedell Smith said, "Well, Brad, you've been wishing for a counterattack. Now it looks as though you've got it."

I replied gloomily, "A counterattack, yes. But I'll be damned if I wanted one this big."[23]

Urged on by Ike, who had correctly diagnosed the full extent of the danger, I made telephone calls to Patton and my chief of staff, Lev Allen, to order the 10th Armored and 7th Armored to turn north and south, respectively, to close in on the base of the enemy salient. At the same time, I gave orders to Patton and Hodges to stand by to move other available divisions to reinforce the armor. Patton scoffed; he thought (as I had at first) that it was merely a spoiling attack and that Middleton could handle it. I was compelled to give Patton a direct, unequivocal order to get the 10th Armored moving. He did so reluctantly, logging: "Bradley admitted my logic but took counsel of his fears and ordered the . . . move. I wish he were less timid." Patton's intuition appeared to have deserted him.[24]

I finally got to bed around midnight. But I could not sleep. I lay awake most of the night mulling over the impact of this massive attack. We had been caught flat-footed. We had to reorganize our strategy, not only to contain the attack but also to make Hitler pay a high cost for mounting it. If we played our cards right, we had a good chance of destroying the

German Army west of the Rhine. It would mean a radical shift in our thinking and strategic planning. We must break off all offensive attacks, turn the full weight of Hodges south and the full weight of Patton north, closing giant pincers, sealing the Germans off west of the Roer. It would be a "Falaise Gap" on a far grander scale. But this time we would have to act with much greater speed and boldness.[25]

The news on the following morning, December 17, was not good. The green 99th and 106th divisions had been hard hit and were falling back in confusion. The undermanned 28th and 4th divisions were likewise reeling. Ike, Smith and I conferred. It appeared then that the enemy objective was no less than Liège and the Meuse River. We three—and the staff present—agreed that our immediate defensive strategy would be first to hold the north and south "shoulders" of the penetration, second to block the westward rush by holding the road hubs of St. Vith and Bastogne, and third to prepare strong defenses behind the Meuse River. Von Rundstedt might conceivably reach the Meuse, but he would go no farther. Ike gave orders for his reserve 82nd and 101st Airborne divisions to race to the Bastogne–St. Vith area to reinforce units of the 7th, 9th and 10th Armored divisions. In addition, he ordered that the 11th Armored and the 17th Airborne divisions be rushed from England to replace SHAEF reserve and help defend the Meuse River line.[26]

The heavy German pressure on Ray Barton's 4th Division in Middleton's southernmost sector placed my Eagle Tac headquarters in Luxembourg in possible jeopardy. Ike urged me to withdraw Eagle Tac to Eagle Main at Verdun. "I will never move backwards with a headquarters," I said. "There's too much prestige at stake." To retreat would be a sure sign of weakness—to the Germans, the Luxembourgers and my own troops. A panic could ensue.[27]

The weather that day was still miserable. Nothing could fly. I was compelled to return to Luxembourg by car—a long, tedious trip. When I arrived at my headquarters in late afternoon, I found plenty of long faces and all too many panzer divisions pinpointed on the situation maps. I said with quiet anger, "Where in hell has this son of a bitch gotten all his strength?" The full extent of the intelligence failure was now becoming apparent. Hansen logged: "The G-2 section . . . found itself confronted by a situation it did not believe possible." There was now no doubt that the German attack was a massive commitment—the Sixth and Fifth Panzer armies, supported by the Seventh Army. Twenty-five to thirty divisions, plus some 1,000 aircraft and even V-1 missiles.[28]

Patton came to my headquarters in Luxembourg on the following day, December 18, with his principal staff officers. I do not believe it is generally known, but Patton thereafter temporarily established his Third Army headquarters in Luxembourg and moved into my hotel. Throughout the entire Battle of the Bulge crisis, we worked in closest contact and saw each other daily, either at his headquarters or mine. We dined together and planned together. We had never been closer or worked in greater harmony.[29]

When Patton arrived, I said, "You won't like what I'm going to do, but I fear it is necessary." I briefed him on the extent of the German penetration. I outlined my strategy. We had to break off our attacks eastward, turn Hodges' army south and Patton's army north. My fears turned out to be groundless. Patton grasped the necessity for the change in the strategy at once and immediately became its most unrestrained champion. I asked what he could do immediately to help Middleton. His answer astounded me. He could have three divisions—the 4th Armored, 80th and 26th Infantry—moving northward within about twenty-four hours. He left, already mentally making plans for swinging his entire Third Army northward.[30]

I intended to fly to Spa that day to see Hodges and brief him on the change in strategy. But Hodges' First Army had been hit by the full weight of the Sixth Panzer Army. Gerow's V Corps, as well as Middleton's VIII Corps, was under severe attack. Hodges himself was in the process of retreating, moving his headquarters rearward from Spa to Chaudfontaine, outside Liège. It became clear in several telephone conversations with Hodges and Bill Kean that part of the First Army was in a bad way. Its veteran units, some committed piecemeal, were digging in at Bastogne and fighting heroically at St. Vith and a dozen other points, but many units were surrounded and cut off or rolling back with the punch. Hodges was in no shape to mount a counterattack. It would take all of his planning and resources merely to hold the northern shoulder. For the moment, Patton alone must mount the counterattack.[31]

On the following day, December 19, Ike convened an emergency meeting at my Eagle Main headquarters in Verdun. We met in a dank stone barracks heated by a single potbellied stove. Present were Ike, Tedder, Pink Bull, Kenneth Strong, Patton, Devers, various staff officers and myself. Ike opened the meeting on exactly the right note: "The present situation is to be regarded as one of opportunity for us and not of disaster. There will be only cheerful faces at this conference table." Patton responded: "Hell, let's have the guts to let the sons of bitches go all the way to Paris. Then we'll really cut 'em up and chew 'em up." His bravado evoked smiles, a note of comic relief.

By that time the German bulge in our line was large and deep. Hodges appeared to be hanging on by his fingertips. Ike had two choices: a general withdrawal to the Meuse River line or my plan for a quick, massive attack in the southern flank of the German salient by Patton's army. All present favored the second choice. The crucial question was: Could Patton get his attack organized in sufficient strength in time to take the pressure off Hodges? Prior to this meeting, we had already primed three of his divisions to strike north.

Ike said to Patton, "When can you attack?"

Army historian Martin Blumenson wrote, correctly, that this was "the sublime moment" of Patton's career. Patton replied grandly, "On December 22, with three divisions." That was a mere three days hence.

Ike's initial reaction was extreme annoyance. "Don't be fatuous," he snapped, as Patton's aide Charles Codman logged it. We were facing a potential disaster. Ike did not want any more bravado, but rather careful, reasoned response. Patton's attack was crucial. Three divisions was clearly not adequate.

But there was more to the plan than that. Patton's three divisions would be organized into a new corps, III, commanded by John Millikin. In addition, I had made the decision to temporarily transfer Middleton's VIII Corps from Hodges to Patton. We did not then know Middleton's 106th Division had been overrun. We believed that Middleton still had three infantry divisions (106th, 28th, 4th) plus elements of the 9th Armored and the full 10th Armored Division already dispatched. That gave Patton a total of six-plus divisions.

When Ike heard the full details, he approved the attack, which would be carried out under my closest supervision. Disbelieving that Patton could attack on the 22nd, he set the date for the 23rd or 24th. The next day, when we learned that Middleton's VIII Corps was so badly shattered that little of the infantry could be used offensively, we assigned Eddy's XII Corps to the offensive, taking most of Walker's XX Corps troops, but leaving his headquarters behind. Jake Devers moved Haislip's XV Corps northeast to defensively man most of the old Third Army front.[32]

In the meantime, Hodges and Bill Kean, a tower of strength, had got a firmer grip on the northern shoulder. The two airborne divisions, operating as XVIII Airborne Corps under Matt Ridgway, had come into the line: the 101st to help at Bastogne and the 82nd near Werbomont, to help at St. Vith. In addition to the 7th Armored Division, Simpson had sent Hodges Hobbs's bulldog 30th Infantry Division, which went into the line as an element of Ridgway's corps. At the crucial corner of the northern shoulder, Hodges had dug in the veteran 1st, 2nd and 9th Infantry divisions, backing up the green and wobbly 99th. Now, at every point of contact with the enemy, our soldiers were fighting with utmost courage and resourcefulness. The "Battling Bastards of Bastogne" and, later, Patton's Third Army, would garner most of the publicity for "winning" the Battle of the Bulge; but the defenders of St. Vith and the veteran First Army on the northern shoulder contributed no less and, in many instances, more.

The truth of the matter was that Hodges had received a terrific blow, but within four days, by December 20, he and his veteran corps commanders, Middleton, Gerow, Ridgway and Collins, had recovered and regrouped to the point that the German offensive was doomed. Had Hodges been a more "colorful" and forceful character, inspiring unbounded confidence in the high command, and had Ike and SHAEF not been so relentlessly pessimistic and fearful, I believe the Allied high command would have perceived much sooner that the offensive was doomed.

THIRTY-NINE

The story of the military action in the Battle of the Bulge has been vividly and fully told many times and I shall not repeat it here. Rather, I shall concentrate on the vital high-level political and strategic battles that the German attack precipitated. These battles violently shook, and very nearly shattered, the Allied high command.

Immediately prior to the German offensive, Montgomery, Alan Brooke and Churchill had expressed the gravest misgivings about Ike's long-term strategy for the defeat of Germany. They disagreed with his broad-front offensive approach and his timetable of May 1, 1945, for the final crushing blow. They argued for a narrower, massive thrust, led by Monty, to the north of the Ruhr, to begin much sooner. Prodded by Alan Brooke, Churchill had requested a meeting of the Combined Chiefs to present the British view, but Roosevelt had begged off. In the meantime, Alan Brooke's staff had begun a paper designed to demolish Ike's plans.

Until the Bulge, I do not believe the British held much hope of forcing a change in the strategy. American forces outnumbered the British by more than three to one. The American public would not tolerate a British commander leading our massive forces to final victory. President Roosevelt, who was weak and ill, now deferred almost completely to Marshall on military decisions involving our land forces on the Continent. Marshall and the U.S. Army General Staff unequivocally backed Ike's broad-front strategy.

Our temporary setback in the Bulge provided the British a potent new excuse to fault U.S. leadership and strategy and advance their own ideas. They did not hesitate to use it. Montgomery, Alan Brooke and Churchill all came at us like sharks at a shipwreck. Montgomery was the first to scent blood and attack. He led the pack. He would continue to be the most vicious and ravenous.

In his obsessive campaign to name himself land commander, Monty had earlier proposed that he be named commander of forces north of the

Ardennes and I be named commander of forces south of the Ardennes. As it happened, the German attack through the Ardennes had split my front more or less along Monty's proposed dividing line. When Monty became aware of this, he at once moved to gain control of all forces north of the Ardennes on the spurious grounds that I had been physically separated from Hodges and Simpson and was therefore unable to properly communicate with them and exercise command. Beyond that lay a larger dream. "It is probable," his chief of staff, Freddie de Guingand, conceded, "that he felt this crisis had produced the opportunity to introduce a land force commander into the Allied High Command system."[1]

To reinforce his case, it was in Monty's interest to paint the darkest possible picture of what was going on. While Ike, Patton, Devers and I were meeting at Verdun on December 19, planning Patton's counteroffensive, Monty got off a scathing and wildly distorted telegram to Alan Brooke: "The situation in the American area is not repeat not good . . . great confusion and all signs of a full-scale withdrawal. There is a definite lack of grip and control and no one has a clear picture as to situation. . . . There is an atmosphere of great pessimism in First and Ninth Armies due, I think, to the fact that everyone knows something has gone wrong and no one knows what or why. Bradley is still in Luxembourg but I understand he is moving, as his Headquarters are in danger. I have no information as to where he is moving. I presume Ike is at Rheims but I have heard nothing from him or Bradley. . . . I have myself had no orders or requests of any sort. . . . The command setup has always been very faulty and now is quite futile, with Bradley at Luxembourg and the front cut in two. I have told Whitely that Ike ought to place me in operational command of all troops on the northern half of the front. I consider he should be given a direct order by someone to do so. This situation needs to be handled very firmly and with a tight grip."[2]

Later, when I read this letter, I was stunned by its self-serving inaccuracies and exaggerations, its insulting and deprecating tone and most of all by its arrogant display of disloyalty to Ike. As Monty knew well, only the Combined Chiefs of Staff could give Ike a "direct order" to place Monty in operational command of the northern land forces, which included my armies. By suggesting to Alan Brooke (a member of the Combined Chiefs) that such an order be promulgated, Monty had gone behind Ike's back in a manner that in the American Army would probably have caused a severe reaction. It was tantamount to my asking George Marshall directly and privately to have the Combined Chiefs order Ike to place Monty's forces under my command.

The "Whitely" Monty referred to in his letter was British General John F. M. Whitely, Pink Bull's assistant G-3 at SHAEF. To Whitely and others at SHAEF, Monty likewise painted the darkest possible picture. Monty later wrote of that day, December 19: "I could see little to prevent

German armoured cars and reconnaissance elements bouncing the Meuse and advancing on Brussels." Monty was then in process of redeploying his most powerful striking force, Horrocks' XXX Corps, *behind* the Meuse in front of Brussels, to save that city from possible recapture.[3]

These dire reports from Monty, together with fragmentary and alarming reports from American units at the front, caused panic at SHAEF. When Ike's G-2, Kenneth Strong, returned from our meeting at Verdun, Whitely cornered him to relay Monty's dark appreciation of the situation—and Monty's suggestion that Ike appoint him commander of northern land forces. The two British generals agreed this was a good idea, then took the proposal to Bedell Smith. According to official U.S. Army historian Hugh M. Cole, "Smith, famous in the headquarters for his hair-trigger temper, first reacted negatively and with considerable heat, then cooled off and admitted the logic of the proposal."[4]

Bedell called me later that evening to sound me out. His basic argument was that "it may save us a great deal of trouble, especially if your communications with Hodges or Simpson go out." I was completely dumbfounded—and shocked. I had only left Ike a few hours before. He had not expressed concern over my communications with Simpson and Hodges or even remotely intimated that Monty might take command of their armies. Nor was there any real reason for concern about communications. I had been in closest telephone conversation with Hodges and Simpson. As a precaution, we were already laying auxiliary circuits west of the Meuse.

There was an Alice-in-Wonderland air about this telephone call. Bedell Smith had been one of Monty's toughest critics and one who had consistently and vehemently opposed Monty's push to promote himself land commander. Now he was urging a vastly increased responsibility for Monty, apparently momentarily oblivious of the repercussions and the heavy complications that would ensue. Nor do I think he realized at the time what a slap in the face this proposal was to me—and by extension my staff and commanders.[5]

One important factor in determining Smith's position, I believe, was a sudden temporary loss of confidence in Courtney Hodges. Hodges had been under immense pressure for four days and he was exhausted. He was not a man like Patton, who naturally radiated unbounded confidence and dogged determination. In fact, even in the most optimistic circumstances he had an air of caution. Now, as I knew, Hodges was sounding more and more depressed at a time when we needed Pattonesque bravado. Perhaps Smith felt that Monty might provide that missing ingredient.[6]

I now made one of my biggest mistakes of the war. Instead of standing up forthrightly to Smith, telling him that SHAEF was losing its head, that I had things under control, and reassuring him that Hodges was performing magnificently under the circumstances and would continue to do so, I knuckled under. I believe it was partly the shock of the proposal, partly my deep reluctance to blow my own horn. All I could manage was a lame "I'd question whether such a changeover is necessary."

Smith pressed his case. He assured me the arrangement was merely *temporary*. When the crisis was over, the First and Ninth armies would be returned to me. Ike wanted me to give my full attention to Patton's offensive, now the key to turning disaster into triumph. We wanted to be sure Patton did not go off half-cocked. Monty would merely be *temporarily* (he repeated) relieving me of a lot of headaches in the north. So far, Monty had contributed nothing to the battle; as northern land commander he might be more willing and eager to commit British forces to help Hodges and Simpson.[7]

The latter point was not minor. Monty had not volunteered so much as a platoon to help Hodges. As I related, he had ordered Horrocks' splendid XXX Corps (the equivalent of two armored divisions plus three infantry divisions) to withdraw to a defensive line behind the Meuse between Liège and Brussels. This backstopped Hodges and freed Hodges to commit all his reserves to the front, but I was still thinking *offensively*. If Monty would commit Horrocks' corps, it could help carry out a strong counterattack, complementing Patton's attack, cutting off the German salient at its base.[8]

Here I was guilty of wishful thinking. In the rush of events, I had momentarily forgotten Monty's innate caution. A moment's reflection would have reminded me that he would never move quickly in a fluid situation. He would not commit XXX Corps until the battlefield had been "tidied up," lines properly drawn, supplies massed—until there was only minimal risk.

"Bedell," I interrupted impulsively, "it's hard for me to object. Certainly if Monty's were an American command I would agree with you entirely. It would be the logical thing to do." With that one last warning about the political problems that might lie ahead, I let the matter drop, hoping that by morning Bedell and Ike would come to their senses.[9]

The next morning, December 20, Patton arrived at my headquarters at 0900 to discuss his forthcoming offensive. While he was present, Ike called to confirm the decision to put Monty in charge of the northern sector, to obtain my approval and to reassure me. Although Ike, too, stressed that the arrangement was merely temporary (owing to telephonic difficulties between Simpson, Hodges and me, he claimed) he did not get my approval. Patton, who overheard my end of the conversation, summed it up nicely in his diary: "As a matter of fact, telephonic communications were all right, and it is either a case of having lost confidence in Bradley or having been forced to put Montgomery in through the machinations of the Prime Minister or with the hope that if he gives Monty operational control, he will get some of the British divisions in [the fight]. Eisenhower is unwilling or unable to command Montgomery."[10]

In the meantime, Alan Brooke was taking steps that day in London to boost Monty's appointment. There was no time to raise the matter with the Combined Chiefs; he did the next best thing. He took Monty's scathing telegram to Churchill and asked Churchill to call Ike and urge him to place Monty in command of the "Northern Wing." Churchill needed no prodding. The short and long-term political advantages and the prestige that would accrue to Britain were entirely obvious. When Churchill called, Ike was able to say he had already made that decision and issued the orders. With no real help from London, Monty had scored a political triumph.[11]

Ike's first written notice to Monty, composed that same day, reflected the panic at SHAEF. "Please let me have your personal appreciation of the situation on the north flank of the penetration particularly with reference to the possibility of giving up, if necessary, some ground on the front of the First Army and to the north thereof in order to shorten our line and collect a strong reserve for the purpose of destroying the enemy in Belgium." Based on Monty's lugubrious reports of the day before, SHAEF was almost reconciled to a need for full retreat to behind the Meuse. Later that day, Ike telegraphed Monty and me in a defeatist tone: "This is just to remind you of the vital importance of insuring that no repeat no Meuse River bridges fall into enemy hands intact."[12]

That same day, December 20, Monty and Freddie de Guingand set off to meet with Simpson and Hodges at Hodges' headquarters. A British officer recalled that Monty arrived "like Christ come to cleanse the Temple." Horrocks wrote: "It was a situation which required immense tact—but this is a quality for which high-ranking soldiers are not noted, and Monty was no exception."[13] Monk Dickson wrote with great restraint:

> This change of command created undercurrents of unhappiness at First Army Headquarters. We were all Bradley's boys, some of us from Tunisian days, and we hated to see him hurt in any way. We also felt that, although he gave no sign of favoritism, First Army was closest to his heart. Monty's cocky mannerisms and his orders in cricket terms like "Hit him for a boundary" and "See him off with a clean bowl" were apt to rouse the old South Boston Irish in us.[14]

After reviewing the situation with Hodges and Simpson, Monty's immediate decision was to give up ground. He thought it best to "sort out the battlefield and tidy up the lines." He recommended that St. Vith, still valiantly holding out like Bastogne, be abandoned and that the northern shoulder be pulled back. "After all, gentlemen," he said, "you can't win the big victory without a tidy show." Hodges was dismayed. Though he was sagging from lack of sleep and a Niagara of bad news, he stubbornly refused to yield a yard of ground. Giving up St. Vith and pulling back the northern shoulder for the sake of "tidiness" seemed imprudent, if not inane. Monty backed off. U.S. Army historian Charles MacDonald put it this way: "When Hodges and his staff reacted as if he had proposed to strip them of their ranks, Montgomery desisted."[15]

Even though Hodges was hard pressed at every turn, he and Bill Kean were actually thinking *offensively*. They had conceived a plan to have Collins and his VII Corps make a southward counterattack on the German salient, complementing Patton's northward attack on December 22 or 23. Monty conditionally approved this plan, claiming later in his memoir that the idea was his own and that he had personally chosen Collins to lead it. But Monty insisted on an important modification in the plan which actually crippled it. Hodges believed that Collins should attack the German salient at its waist, relieving the garrison at St. Vith and linking up with Patton near Houffalize. From Ultra dispatches, Monty had formed the opinion that the German offensive would swing northwest near Marche and attempt to cross the Meuse between Namur and Liège. Since there was no organized First Army front at Marche, Monty insisted that Collins should first move west and form a front there, blunt the German attack, then launch his counterattack from the Marche area.[16]

This was a poor and timid decision, reminiscent of Monty's ill-advised and timid decision in the Falaise Gap battle. During that critical period, instead of reinforcing the Canadians in their faltering drive on Falaise from the north, Monty had launched Dempsey's Second Army from the west. His plan for Collins to move west to Marche was a near duplicate of that plan but on a larger scale. It was the wrong way to do it—and it would take far too much time.

In retrospect, Troy Middleton was bitterly critical of Monty's decision: "The leadership up there was poor. Montgomery should have moved in and launched a counterattack long before he turned his troops loose. Joe Collins would have attacked the Germans long before he was allowed to, if he had his way."[17]

Significantly, there was no offer of real help from Monty, as Ike, Bedell and I had hoped and banked on. Horrocks' large, powerful and aggressive XXX Corps, deployed behind the Meuse River between Namur and Liège, was far closer to Marche than Collins. It would have been a relatively simple matter, tactically and logistically, for Monty to move Horrocks forward some thirty miles to Marche to form a front and blunt the anticipated German swing to the northwest, making an aggressive rather than passive defense of the Meuse. This commitment would have left Collins free to strike the German salient in the waist, as Hodges originally planned. Had the plan taken this shape, I believe we could have inflicted an absolute slaughter on the Germans and, ultimately, saved many American lives. But Monty, as usual, played it safe, apparently content to let the Americans take all the punishment. His actual commitment to the Bulge crisis, finally, was a single token force of one armored brigade, the 29th, consisting of sixty tanks, sent to Dinant on Collins' right flank.[18]

Upon conclusion of this meeting, Monty got off another arrogantly self-serving telegram to Alan Brooke: "Neither Army Commander had seen Bradley or any of his staff since the battle began. . . . There were no reserves anywhere behind the front. Morale was very low. They seemed delighted to have someone give them firm orders. . . . It will take a day or two to get American front reorganized and in better shape and we may have a few more shocks before that is completed. . . . But it is necessary to realize that there was literally no control or grip of any sort of the situation and we shall never do any good so long as that goes on."[19]

That same day Monty telegraphed Ike, filling him in on the plans for Joe Collins and his VII Corps. "I have every hope," he wrote reassuringly, "that we shall be able to restore the situation and I see no need at present to give up any of the ground that has been gained in the last weeks by such hard fighting."[20]

Monty had come away from his meeting with Hodges convinced that Hodges was in danger of a heart attack and ought to be relieved of command. He conveyed his impressions to Bedell Smith by telephone, stating that he, Monty, was unwilling to personally relieve U.S. commanders. Fortunately Smith, and later Ike, had the good sense to realize what a calamitous impact Hodges' relief would have on American morale. Ike hastened to write Monty: "I know you realize that Hodges is the quiet, reticent type and does not appear as aggressive as he really is. Unless he becomes exhausted he will always wage a good fight." Ike also sent both Hodges and Simpson a letter of encouragement: "Now that you have been placed under the Field Marshal's operational command I know that you will respond cheerfully and efficiently to every instruction he gives. The slogan is 'Chins up.' "[21]

Ike had a reassuring word for me as well. The day after Monty took over my First and Ninth armies, Ike wrote Marshall stating that "this would be a most opportune time to promote Bradley." Marshall apparently agreed with the suggestion but replied that it was not feasible to promote me at the moment, because Congress had adjourned for the holidays.[22]

True to his boast at Verdun, Patton, having turned his Third Army ninety degrees, attacked on December 22. His generalship during this difficult maneuver was magnificent, one of the most brilliant performances by any commander on either side in World War II. It was absolutely his cup of tea—rapid, open warfare combined with noble purpose and difficult goals. He relished every minute of it, knowing full well that this mission, if nothing else, would guarantee him a place of high honor in the annals of the U.S. Army. Chet Hansen logged his mood: "He is boisterous and noisy, feeling good in the middle of a fight." Patton himself wrote: "Give us victory, Lord."[23]

Patton's objective was to inflict maximum damage on the German salient. Equally important was a subsidiary mission: to relieve our forces at Bastogne, which were still holding out with magnificent courage. On the day Patton launched his attack, the temporary commander of the 101st Airborne at Bastogne, Anthony C. McAuliffe (Max Taylor was in Washington), gave his legendary one-word reply to German demands for surrender: "Nuts."

Bastogne was in John Millikin's III Corps sector. Millikin and his staff were new, untried in combat. We were naturally concerned about Millikin; it was a tough test for him. At the end of the first day, III Corps had done well to advance seven miles in a snowstorm. Patton logged: "John Millikin is doing better than I feared. I told him he had to go up and hear them [the shells and bullets] whistle. I think he will."

The weather broke fair the next day, December 23, and remained fair for three days. Fighters and bombers swarmed into the air in Patton's support; transports dropped supplies to our troops in Bastogne. Even so, Millikin managed to inch ahead only two to five miles. On the next day, Christmas Eve, Millikin's veteran 4th Armored Division met a violent German counterattack and was thrown back several miles. In the late afternoon, Patton and I attended Christmas Eve services at the Episcopal church in Luxembourg.[24]

This was the darkest of times for me. Giving Monty operational control of my First and Ninth armies was the worst possible mistake Ike could have made. Owing to Monty's caution and conservatism, it practically assured that we would fail to cut off the German salient with a bold thrust from the north. The enemy would escape in force as it had escaped from the Falaise Gap. We were going to lose a golden opportunity to utterly destroy the German war machine west of the Rhine. I prayed for the souls of the dead American GI's, whose stubborn courage had already doomed the German offensive.[25]

FORTY

I kept in close touch with Simpson and Hodges by telephone. What I learned from Hodges about Monty's plans in the northern sector confirmed my worst fears. Although initially Monty had assured Ike that he saw no need to give ground, he was now giving it. Against strong objections from Ridgway, Monty had ordered a withdrawal from St. Vith. Against equally strong objections from Jim Gavin, Monty had ordered the 82nd Division, which was assisting in the evacuation of St. Vith, to withdraw farther to the north and ''tidy up'' the battle line. Even worse, he had ordered Joe Collins' VII Corps into an indefinite defensive role at Marche. The planned VII Corps offensive had been postponed indefinitely—at a time when Patton was on the verge of reaching Bastogne.[1]

On Christmas Day Monty telephoned, suggesting an immediate conference to coordinate our maneuvers. I welcomed the invitation, hoping it might give me an opportunity to build a fire under him. I flew to his headquarters near St. Trond, Belgium. There was no aide at the airport to meet us—not even a car and driver. This I took to be a calculated insult. I was so put out I told my aide Chet Hansen we should go home. But Hansen found one of Hodges' staffers, who offered his car. After a fumbling search through unfamiliar ground, we located Monty's headquarters. Neither Monty nor anyone else offered us anything to eat or drink. I determined to make my visit as short as possible and, in fact, it lasted a mere thirty minutes.[2]

Monty was more arrogant and egotistical than I had ever seen him. He began by lecturing and scolding me like a schoolboy. That night he wrote Alan Brooke: ''I was absolutely frank with him. I said the Germans had given us a real 'bloody nose'; it was useless to pretend that we were going to turn this quickly into a great victory; it was a proper defeat and we had better admit it . . . I then said it was entirely our own fault; we had gone much too far with our right [Patton]; we had tried to develop two thrusts at the same time, and neither had been strong enough to gain decisive results. The enemy saw his chance and took it. Now we were in a proper muddle." He went on to add that I "looked thin, and worn and ill at ease" and that I "agreed entirely" with all he said. "Poor chap," Monty concluded, "he is such a decent fellow and the whole thing is a bitter pill for him. But he is man enough to admit it and he did."[3]

Never in my life had I been so enraged and so utterly exasperated. It required every fiber of my strength to restrain myself from an insulting outburst. Somehow I remained silent, seething inside, nodding as Monty imperiously rattled on. I admitted to nothing. In fact, I silently disagreed with every word he uttered. However, to avoid a potentially crippling breakdown in the Allied command, I kept my counsel.

Even more dismaying was Monty's view of future courses of action. Far from being beaten, the Germans had sufficient strength for another blow, he believed. Hodges' First Army was too weak to do anything but hold. Hodges desperately needed replacements. It would be *three months* before Hodges would be ready for a major offensive. Patton's offensive was futile; it was too weak and would accomplish nothing. Patton should break off the attack and withdraw to defensive positions along a line the Saar River–Vosges Mountains or even the Moselle River and supply Hodges with more divisions. In sum, Monty's view was that all Allied armies should go completely to the defensive, regroup and gear up for a single-thrust offensive led by him, some time in the distant future.[4]

Although Monty's penchant for tedious planning, the massive build-up and the "set piece" battle were only too well known, it seemed to me that he talked like a man who had lost touch with reality. Every scrap of intelligence we had available, including a mountain of Ultra, indicated beyond doubt that owing to our rapid and effective countermeasures and the courage of the individual American soldier, Hitler's last great, ill-advised gamble had failed. His panzers had run out of gas and ammo. He had suffered enormous casualties. His air power had not been effective in the slightest; with the coming of favorable weather, we were now in a position to savagely apply our own overwhelming air power. *Now* was the time to hit back. Not three months from now.[5]

I flew back to my headquarters in a dark mood. Later that evening I had a long talk with Patton, relaying the substance of Monty's views. Patton was apoplectic. He wrote in his diary: "I feel this is disgusting. . . . If ordered to fall back, I think I will ask to be relieved."[6]

The next morning I got Bedell Smith on the telephone. This time I was no shrinking violet. I let him have it with both barrels. I told him Monty insisted on going over to the defensive and was throwing away an opportunity to inflict a devastating defeat on the enemy. I asked in no uncertain terms that the First and Ninth armies be returned to my operational command so that I could get some action in the north. I would move my headquarters to Namur to assure coordination of all U.S. forces. I stressed that we *had to act now*.[7]

So disturbed was I by Monty's "stagnating conservatism" (as Chet Hansen put it) that same day I took the extraordinary step of writing a formal letter directly to Hodges. While making clear that I had no control over First Army and that my letter was not to be considered a directive, I said that I did not see the situation "in as grave a light as Marshal Montgomery." Moreover, I viewed "with alarm" any plan to give up terrain which might be favorable to future operations. I went on to say that while I was aware that the First Army had been hard hit, I nevertheless believed that the Germans had also suffered heavily and were now weaker than First Army forces. As I saw it, "If we could seize the initiative, he would have to get out in a hurry." I advised Hodges to study the battle with an eye to pushing the enemy back "as soon as the situation seems to warrant."[8]

Two galvanizing military events that day, December 26, strengthened my hand. Advance elements of Patton's Third Army broke a thin corridor to Bastogne and began the relief of that brave band of soldiers and a strengthening of that vital road hub. Equally important, Joe Collins, in the face of Monty's orders to the contrary, ordered Ernie Harmon's 2nd Armored Division out of defensive positions near Dinant to assault von Rundstedt's leading westbound panzer elements. In one of the most brilliantly conducted operations of the war, Harmon utterly destroyed the 2nd Panzer Division and ground the German attack to a final, humiliating halt. Believing the enemy thrust was fully spent, Collins again began drafting plans for vigorous counteroffensives to cut the German salient at the waist.[9]

My pressure on SHAEF compelled an immediate reconsideration of future planning. Tedder noted that I was "very disturbed" at Monty's "purely defensive view." My own views could no longer be ignored or dismissed. Accordingly, Ike called for a meeting in Brussels for the next day, December 27, with Monty and me. That evening I telephoned Ike to again stress the need for vigorous offensive action in the north. He had already left for his train, so I talked to Bedell Smith again. "Damn it, Bedell," I said with undisguised heat, "can't you people get Monty going in the north? As near as we can tell the other fellow's reached the high-water mark today. He'll soon be starting to pull back—if not tonight, certainly by tomorrow." I *demanded* prompt action in the north.[10]

The Brussels meeting had to be postponed by one day, to December 28, because the train Ike was scheduled to take had been bombed by the Luftwaffe. Owing to that development, Ike suggested that I meet him at SHAEF on the 27th. I welcomed the opportunity to see Ike before he saw Monty. It would give me a further opportunity to stress the urgent need for quick and decisive action. Patton wrote in his diary: "Bradley left at 1000 to see Ike. . . . If Ike will put Bradley back in command of the First and Ninth Armies, we can bag the whole German Army. I wish Ike were more of a gambler, but he is certainly a lion compared to Montgomery, and Bradley is better than Ike as far as nerve is concerned. . . . Monty is a tired little fart. War requires the taking of risks and he won't take them."[11]

I flew to Paris, then motored to SHAEF headquarters in Versailles. This was my first meeting with Ike since Verdun on December 19—since he had given Monty my First and Ninth Armies. Fortunately I arrived on the wave of good news from Dinant and Bastogne. Chet Hansen logged: "Ike was gloriously cordial when Brad came in, shook hands heartily and Brad smiled shyly as he always does." I had a long session with Ike, Tedder, Smith, Strong, Bull and Whitely. Tedder reported that I "exuded confidence."[12]

My presentation included both short-term and long-term strategy proposals. For the short term I urged an immediate pincer attack against the waist of the German salient. Patton, reinforced, should attack out of Bastogne northeast toward Houffalize and St. Vith. Hodges should attack southeast toward Houffalize and St. Vith, with two corps, Collins' VII as the spearhead and Ridgway's XVIII Airborne Corps covering Collins' left flank toward St. Vith. This would put the cap on the toothpaste tube and trap the bulk of the German Army. I would move my Twelfth Army Group headquarters to Namur or Dinant in order to coordinate operations of both Patton and Hodges. I urged that this attack begin *at once*.[13]

For the long term, I proposed a substantial change in Allied strategy, designed to quickly exploit Hitler's blunder of the Bulge. Instead of putting our main effort to reach the Rhine in the north under Monty as originally planned, I proposed that we now put our main effort through the center under me. The armies of Hodges and Patton would advance eastward abreast, on a north-south line commencing just south of the Roer dam area and extending farther south into the Ardennes. This great mass would follow in hot pursuit of the retreating Germans through the Eifel to the Bonn area, cross the Rhine and proceed toward the good open tank country lying between Frankfurt and Kassel. At the same time Monty, with his British and Canadian armies, would cross the Rhine and go north of the Ruhr, protecting our left flank. Devers would remain on the defensive in the Saar area.

My long-term proposal, which became known in our headquarters as the "hurry up" offensive, had several advantages. It could be launched immediately—almost as an extension of the short-term assault on the waist of the German salient. Pursuit without pause would insure mounting pressure on the Germans, denying them a chance to build up a defensive line against us. An attack through the Eifel, south of the Roer dams, would eliminate the need to take the dams and would unhinge German defenses in the dam area. A deep thrust into Germany itself would unhinge German defenses in the Ruhr area, making Monty's task of going north of the Ruhr easier. A main attack in the center would catch the Germans off guard; Ultra told us they were expecting it in the north, as Monty intended.

Finally, a bold, successful large-scale purely American attack would regain us prestige lost in the Bulge.

Ike was more forceful and commanding than I had ever seen him. "Calamity acted on Eisenhower like a restorative," Alan Brooke wrote, "and brought out all the greatness in his character." This was true and the change was remarkable. I soon saw that Ike was not going to rubber-stamp my plans as he had so often done in the past. From now on, Ike would run the war; he would make the major decisions.

He would not make any formal decisions until he met with Monty. However, he did agree with me completely on the short-term strategy: cutting the German salient in the waist at Houffalize. Monty, I then learned, was also now apparently swinging to my point of view. Earlier in the day he had telephoned Ike to say that he was now ready to consider a definite counterattack, leading Ike to comment, "Praise God from Whom all blessings flow." He likewise agreed that I should shift my headquarters to the Namur area. But he refused to return control of Hodges to me until his forces and Patton's had screwed the cap on the tube at Houffalize. That was a sharp personal disappointment.

As to my long-term proposal for a "hurry up" offensive through the center, Ike was less enthusiastic. He now held the view that nobody was going to jump the Rhine on the run, as we had jumped the Seine. He would risk no more Bulges; he wanted a strong, easily defended line from which we would plunge into the heart of Germany. The most easily defended line was the Rhine River. Ike believed we must wipe out German forces west of the Rhine along its entire length, then all draw up to the Rhine abreast before the final big push. For that big push, he still favored putting the bulk of our weight in the north under Monty, with Simpson's Ninth Army reinforcing him.

At the same time, however, he saw the advantages of my "hurry up" offensive. If successful, it could at least get the Allied center to the Rhine. It would keep pressure on the Germans until Monty regrouped from his Bulge redeployment. Ike approved it, informally, with sharp limitations. If my attack failed to achieve early promise of "decisive success" he would halt it. He did not want it to develop into another ghastly war of attrition. Moreover, the plan was subject to review at any time, and if Ike so decided, I was to go on the defensive without question or objection.[14]

There was one final sticky point. Under my plan, Simpson's Ninth Army would assist in the "hurry up" offensive by taking over the First Army front in the Roer dam area. Although I had long since reconciled myself to the fact that Monty would keep the Ninth Army, I thought it would be advantageous for U.S. morale if the Ninth Army returned to my command temporarily for the "hurry up" offensive. If Hodges bogged down in the Eifel, I could use Simpson to put pressure on the Düren area. But Ike was adamant on this point. Now that Monty had the Ninth Army, it would remain under his command. He said that he had "fought the propaganda to put Marshal Montgomery in command [of all ground forces] so long it was wearing him out." By leaving the Ninth Army under Monty, "he might be able to shut up the element that was trying to put everything under Marshal Montgomery." I was extremely disappointed in this decision, angered that political decisions were adversely affecting tactical operations.[15]

The next day, December 28, Ike went by train to confer with Monty. Poor weather conditions compelled them to meet in Hasselt, Belgium. Since I had already made my views quite clear, there was no need for me to attend this meeting. When they sat down to talk, Ike was keenly disappointed to learn that Monty's apparent willingness to go immediately to the offensive against the German salient was not quite true. Based on Ultra reports, Monty was now convinced that the Germans would stage one last great attack in the north against Hodges. He thought the best strategy was to absorb this attack, *then* counterattack.[16]

We all had access to the same Ultra reports. It was by no means absolutely certain that these reports foreshadowed a last great attack. Hitler had ordered such an attack—an advance to the Meuse—but intercepted reports filtering back from the individual German divisions in combat indicated a lack of resources to carry out such an attack. There was a possibility that the proposed German attack might be a deception. While Monty lay back waiting for the mythical assault, the Germans could use the time gained to substitute infantry for panzer divisions, thus freeing up the panzers for offensive operations elsewhere, or to be held in reserve to counterattack our counterattack.[17]

Heretofore Ike had been reluctant to impose his operational ideas and plans on Monty, leaving him a free hand. But this time he was not. He compelled Monty to commit to a quick, definite plan. If the German offensive did not materialize within three days, by January 1, Monty was to "start driving." That is, launch Collins' VII Corps in a counteroffensive, with Ridgway's XVIII Airborne Corps supporting his left flank. If the German attack did come, Monty was to absorb it and then "drive in on him on the rebound." Under no circumstances was there to be a typical long Montgomery-type buildup followed by a set-piece battle.[18]

Beyond that, Ike and Monty discussed long-term strategy. Ike described my plan for the "hurry up" offensive and stated his own desire to have everybody draw up to the Rhine before launching the final big push. This news apparently came as a shock to Monty, leading him to lecture and scold Ike as he had me. Brooke noted in his diary: "Monty had another interview with Ike. I do not like the account of it. It looks to me as if Monty, with his usual lack of tact, has been rubbing into Ike the results of not having listened to Monty's advice." Monty took sharp exception both to my "hurry up" offensive and Ike's broad-front approach to the Rhine

River. My offensive would be a waste of precious resources. He insisted that it be canceled, that all fronts other than his go on the defensive so that he could lead a single massive assault into Germany's heartland. For best results, I should come completely under his command. Monty later wrote Alan Brooke to say that Ike had agreed with his strategic concepts, but this was either another gross misunderstanding or a deliberate distortion on Monty's part.[19]

On returning to SHAEF, Ike, having now conferred with both Monty and me, drew up an "outline plan" for short- and long-term operations. The plan approved two of my major proposals: a short-term offensive to close pincers on the waist of the German salient and my long-term "hurry up" offensive with the aforementioned restrictions. To prod Monty and make it clear that he expected an all-out effort from the north on the short-term strategy, Ike specified to Monty that we would utilize "everything consistent with minimum security requirements." Following that operation, I would resume command of the First Army (but not the Ninth) for my offensive, which would go northeast toward Bonn and "eventually to the Rhine." When all enemy forces west of the Rhine had been destroyed, we would prepare to cross the Rhine with the *main effort north of the Ruhr*.[20] (Ike's italics.)

Monty clearly lost this round. I had not had my way completely, but at least Monty had been ordered to go all-out on the short-term effort to cut the German salient at the waist; and, against Monty's counsel, Ike had approved my limited offensive.

Before Ike could cable this plan to us, Monty composed and sent to Ike a formal letter summarizing his views on long-term operations. This letter was an arrogant and unequivocal *demand* that my "hurry up" offensive be canceled, that I and all my armies be placed under Monty's operational control (making Monty, in effect, land commander) for a single massive Allied thrust north of the Ruhr, and that Ike's plan to draw all armies up to the Rhine be scrapped.

"I think we want to be careful," Monty wrote, "because we have had one very definite failure. . . . I therefore consider that it will be necessary for you to be very firm on the subject, and any loosely worded statement will be quite useless." He went on to say that since Ike "cannot possibly" be land commander himself, "you would have to nominate someone else." That person, Monty said, should be "C in C 21 Army Group"—Monty. He would have "full operational direction, control and coordination of" all operations in the north. "I put this matter to you again because I am so anxious not to have another failure," he continued. He was "absolutely convinced" that *all* offensive power had to be thrown behind his northern operation and that "a sound set-up for command" had to be established. "I am certain," he concluded, "that if we do not comply with these two basic conditions, then we will fail again."[21]

Monty's letter arrived at SHAEF at the height of an unprecedented anti-American press campaign in England. British newspapers were unbridled in their criticism of Ike, me and the Allied command setup. As though the media campaign were being orchestrated from Monty's headquarters, Fleet Street was praising Monty to high heaven for his magnificent battlefield management of the Bulge crisis and demanding that he be named overall land commander. The media campaign was so intense that it had prompted Marshall to cable Ike, warning him not to leave any substantial American forces under Monty. "Under no circumstances make any concessions of any kind whatsoever," Marshall said. "You not only have our complete confidence but there would be a terrific resentment in this country following such action. . . . You are doing a fine job and go on and give them hell."[22]

At the time Monty sent this letter, I was in process of making final arrangements with Patton for his onward attack from Bastogne toward Houffalize. This was to be a strong attack of three corps: Middleton's VIII, Millikin's III and Eddy's XII. The attack jumped off on December 30, a mere four days after Patton's advanced elements reached Bastogne. I had counted on Monty to complement Patton's attack by launching Collins' VII Corps and Ridgway's XVIII Airborne Corps southward, but Monty was dragging his feet as usual and we had to go it alone. Monty was still holding back awaiting the possible last-ditch all-out German attack on Hodges. The defensive posture Monty had assumed, together with the British anti-American press campaign, had absolutely infuriated everyone in Twelfth Army Group. When Monty's liaison officer, Thomas Bigland, came to my office on December 30 to inquire if I had any word for Monty, I responded with utmost restraint: "I wish the hell he'd attack up there, but I can't tell him that." The word from Monty now was that he could not possibly attack before January 3.[23]

Monty's letter, the pro-Monty and anti-Ike press campaign in Britain, and the news that Monty would not launch Collins and Ridgway until January 3 (five days behind Patton's attack), sent Ike and Bedell Smith into a towering rage and precipitated a command High Noon. Ike, now reassured of his position by Marshall, began drafting a letter to the Combined Chiefs of Staff in which he, in effect, asked them to choose between him and Monty. Inasmuch as the United States now had the preponderance of military power on the Continent, there would be no question about the outcome: Monty would be sacked.

That same day, December 30, Monty's chief of staff, Freddie de Guingand, after talking to Bigland and Bedell Smith, realized that an "extremely dangerous situation had developed." Determined to seek peace, he flew through a snowstorm to Paris, raced to SHAEF by car, and hurried on to Bedell Smith's office. Smith told de Guingand that "the matter had practically reached a stage where nothing more could be done about it." Nonetheless, Smith escorted him to see Ike.

Ike was in conference with Tedder, editing the me-or-Monty cable to the Combined Chiefs. De Guingand recalled: "The Supreme Commander looked really tired and worried. He very quietly started to explain how serious matters were. He told me that Bradley's position had become intolerable, and that there was every chance that he would lose the confidence of his troops. This would be most unfortunate and might mean his losing one of his ablest commanders. He asked me whether my Chief fully realized the effects of the line taken up by the British Press, and how Monty himself had helped to create this crisis by his campaign for a Land Force Commander and by the indiscreet remarks he had passed. Eisenhower went on to say that he was tired of the whole business, and had come to the conclusion that it was now a matter for the Combined Chiefs to make a decision. It was quite obvious that with Montgomery still pressing for a Land Force Commander it was impossible for the two of them to carry on working in harness together." Ike then gave de Guingand the cable to read. De Guingand saw that Ike had gone so far as to propose Alexander as Monty's replacement.

De Guingand was "stunned." He implored Ike to delay the cable twenty-four hours to give him an opportunity to "solve the impasse." He was "absolutely convinced" Monty had no idea "things had become so serious." Neither Ike nor Tedder was inclined to delay, stressing the "damage which had already been done." But Bedell Smith, to de Guingand's "intense relief," advised giving de Guingand a chance, and after "quite a time," Ike and Tedder relented.

The next day, December 31, de Guingand, racing against time, and suffering "a very bad attack of nerves," flew back through heavy weather to Monty's headquarters. He briefed his boss on his impending professional catastrophe, pointedly showing him a copy of Marshall's cable to Ike, and mentioning that Alexander had been proposed as Monty's replacement. Monty appeared to be "genuinely and completely taken by surprise" and found it "difficult to grasp" what de Guingand was saying, and "extremely hard to believe it possible" that he might be relieved of command. When Monty did at last grasp the gravity of the crisis, de Guingand recalled, "He looked completely non-plussed—I don't think I had ever seen him so deflated. It was as if a cloak of loneliness had descended upon him."

"What shall I do, Freddie?" Monty asked helplessly.

De Guingand had already anticipated that question and drafted a letter of apology and retreat to Ike. Monty read the signal, marked it "most immediate," "top secret," and "personal for Eisenhower, for his eyes only," and sent it off. The letter:

> Dear Ike, Have seen Freddie and understand you are greatly worried by many considerations in these very difficult days. I have given you my frank views because I have felt you like this. I am sure there are many factors

> which have a bearing quite beyond anything I realize. Whatever your decision may be you can rely on me one hundred per cent to make it work, and I know Brad will do the same. Very distressed that my letter may have upset you and I would ask you to tear it up. Your very devoted servant, Monty.

The letter did the trick. With it, de Guingand pulled Monty's chestnuts out of the fire. Ike apparently destroyed his own letter to the Combined Chiefs; no trace of it was ever found. De Guingand met with a committee of British war correspondents, frankly described what had happened and pleaded with them to ask their editors to cool the pro-Monty, anti-American propaganda and the campaign to make Monty land commander. There followed an abrupt silence on the matter in most responsible Fleet Street organs.[24]

On December 31, Ike forwarded his "outline plan" to Monty and me. In a covering letter to Monty, he wrote, tactfully but firmly:

> You know how greatly I've appreciated and depended upon your frank and friendly counsel, but in your latest letter you disturb me by predictions of "failure" unless your exact opinions in the matter of giving you command over Bradley are met in detail. I assure you that in this matter I can go no further. . . . For my part I would deplore the development of such an unbridgeable gulf of convictions between us that we would have to present our differences to the Combined Chiefs of Staff. The confusion and debate that would follow would certainly damage the good will and devotion to a common cause that have made this Allied Force unique in history.[25]

I have the greatest admiration for the firm manner in which Ike handled this episode, the most taxing command crisis of the war. But the attack was not yet over. In the distance, Alan Brooke and Churchill were preparing for another assault on the U.S. command.

FORTY-ONE

Roosevelt, Churchill and Stalin had decided to confer at Yalta, in early February 1945. In preparation for that meeting, Roosevelt and Churchill together with the Combined Chiefs would meet in Malta to discuss world strategy, including Allied strategy on the Western Front for the final drive into the heart of Germany.[1]

It was no secret within the Allied high command that Churchill and Alan Brooke had now become outspoken advocates of Monty's view of strategy on the Western Front. They believed with Monty that Allied strategy should take the form of a single massive thrust north of the Ruhr, led by a single land commander, Monty, while the remainder of the front, from Aachen to Switzerland, went over to the defensive. Like Monty, they disapproved of my offensive in the center as a wasteful dispersion of effort and, likewise, Ike's determination to have all Allied forces reach the Rhine before Monty cut loose. Both Churchill and Alan Brooke were priming for Malta, where they hoped to persuade the Combined Chiefs to adopt the British view.[2]

Ike was pleased to learn that Churchill and Alan Brooke would visit his headquarters at Versailles on January 3 and 4, then go on to see Monty. It provided Ike opportunity to try to swing them to his views before the Malta conference. In preparation for this visit, he flew to Etain for a short airport visit with me on January 2. We talked in my car, a map spread on our laps, and munched caramel candy from a box of K rations. He was in absolute command and determined that his strategy was sound. The British were *not* going to dictate to him or, if he could possibly help it, to the Combined Chiefs and Roosevelt at Malta. Monty would get the lion's share of our resources for the main offensive north of the Ruhr because that was where Ike wanted to put the big effort. But first we would all reach the Rhine on a broad front. Toward that end my "hurry up" offensive had now become vital, and Ike was most anxious that it go off right and achieve a breakout like the one at St. Lô. He would support me to the utmost, but if the offensive showed no real promise within a week, he would close it down and begin transferring U.S. divisions to Monty for the first phase of his operations, ordering me to go on the defensive.[3]

Ike, Bedell Smith and the SHAEF staff laid out the strategy for Churchill and Brooke at Versailles. But they met a stone wall; the impasse was total. Churchill and Brooke would place the issues before the Combined Chiefs at Malta. They went on to visit Monty, gathering further ammunition for the assault.[4]

During these sessions, Churchill drew Ike aside with a novel proposal. The Prime Minister confided that the British Air Ministry was anxious to get Tedder to serve as number two under Air Marshal Portal. If Alexander could be sprung from the Mediterranean, how would Ike look upon having Alexander in place of Tedder as deputy supreme commander? Ike, who was fond of Alexander, replied unthinkingly and incautiously that he would be more than happy to have Alexander as his deputy. Tedder was "splendid," but it might be helpful to have a man who better understood ground operations. Monty also approved Alexander for Tedder at first blush, writing Brooke that such a plan "might go some way towards putting the matter straight."[5]

Ike did not realize it at first, but this was a British ploy to insert a land commander under Ike who would be acceptable not only to Ike but also to Monty and probably to me. When he heard about the proposal, Marshall astutely raised warning flags from Washington, pointing out to Ike that replacing airman Tedder with ground soldier Alexander would mean two things: "First, that the British had won a major point in getting control of the ground operations . . . and second, the man being who he is and our experience being what it has been, you would have great difficulty in offsetting the direct influence of the P.M." Ike, belatedly seeing the light, then made it clear to Marshall that he would "seriously object to any officer being named deputy for ground operations," and that "I do not repeat do not believe any single individual could or should exercise a greater measure of control over this extensive front than is now being exercised." However, Churchill and Brooke would continue to press for Alexander to replace Tedder for the next several months.[6]

The temporary Allied command setup during the Battle of the Bulge had been classified top secret. War correspondents were prohibited from writing that Monty temporarily commanded the First and Ninth armies on the northern shoulder, while I commanded the southern shoulder. But in early January, an unauthorized leak in a publication compelled SHAEF to confirm what had happened. The brief SHAEF announcement of January 5 was one of the most ill-considered and mindless of the war:

> When the German penetration through the Ardennes created two fronts, one substantially facing south and the other north, by instant agreement of all

concerned, that portion of the front facing south was placed under command of Montgomery and that facing north under command of Bradley.

The release went on to say that command of my two armies had passed from me to Montgomery because communications with my armies had been cut. Nowhere in the release was it said that the command setup was *temporary,* that the First Army would soon revert to my control. The unintended effect of the release was to promote Monty to the status of Hero of the Bulge.[7]

Freddie de Guingand's efforts to cool the Monty-for-land-commander campaign were completely undone by this witless SHAEF release. The British press wildly extolled and exaggerated Monty's role in the Bulge and asked, in effect, if he was good enough to command that many Americans in an emergency then why not all Americans all of the time? As Chet Hansen put it: "The effect has been a cataclysmic Roman Holiday in the British press, which has exulted over the announcement and hailed it as an increase in the Montgomery command." Hansen went on bitterly: "Many of us who were avowed Anglophiles in Great Britain have now been irritated, hurt and infuriated by the British radio and press. All this good feeling has vanished under these circumstances until today we regarded the people we once looked upon as warm and sympathetic friends, as people whom we must instead distrust for fear of being hoodwinked. . . . Their press is building a well of resentment among our American troops that can never be emptied, a distrust that cannot be erased."

Even our quasi-official *Stars and Stripes* newspaper fell in with Fleet Street's line. Headlining Monty's takeover, the story contained this belittling aside: "It is presumed that Bradley continues to command 12th Army Group, which now consists of only Third Army."[8]

This new wave of anti-Ike, pro-Montgomery publicity in the British media was so vitriolic that it prompted Churchill to write Roosevelt on January 7: "I hope you understand that, in case any troubles should arise in the press, His Majesty's Government have complete confidence in General Eisenhower and feel acutely any attacks made on him. He and Montgomery are closely knit and also Bradley and Patton, and it would be a disaster which broke up this combination which has, in nineteen forty-four, yielded us results beyond the dreams of military avarice. . . . I most cordially congratulate you on the extraordinary gallantry which your troops have shown in all this battle, particularly at Bastogne."[9]

That same day, January 7, Monty, who professed in his memoirs to be perturbed "about the sniping at Eisenhower which was going on in the British press," held a press conference to "put in a strong plea for Allied solidarity." He cleared his plans in advance with Churchill, who, taking Monty at face value, naturally thought such a conference would be "invaluable."[10]

Monty's press conference may have been well intentioned, but in execution it was a disaster. It did more to undermine Anglo-American unity than anything I can remember. Eisenhower wrote in his memoirs: "This incident caused me more distress and worry than did any similar one of the war." Fourteen years afterward Monty wrote in his memoirs: "I should never have held that press conference." To that I say, Amen.[11]

The overall impression Monty projected was that of St. George come to slay the dragon. His tone, aptly described by Freddie de Guingand in his memoirs, was "What a good boy am I." Excerpts:

> When von Rundstedt attacked on December 16 [Monty said] he obtained a tactical surprise. He drove a deep wedge into the center of the United States First Army and the split might have become awkward; the Germans had broken through a weak spot and were heading for the Meuse. As soon as I saw what was happening I took certain steps myself to ensure that if the Germans got to the Meuse they would certainly not get over that river. And I carried out certain movements so as to provide balanced dispositions to meet the threatened danger; these were at the time merely precautions, i.e., I was thinking ahead.
>
> Then the situation began to deteriorate. But the whole Allied team rallied to meet the danger; national considerations were thrown overboard; General Eisenhower placed me in command of the whole Northern front. I employed the whole available power of the British Group of Armies; this power was brought into play very gradually and in such a way that it would not interfere with the American lines of communications. Finally it was put into battle with a bang and today British divisions are fighting hard on the right flank of the U.S. First Army. . . .
>
> The battle has been most interesting; I think possibly one of the most tricky battles I have ever handled, with great issues at stake. . . . the battle has some similarity to the battle that began on August 31, 1942, when Rommel made his last bid to capture Egypt and was "seen off" by the Eighth Army.

In his concluding remarks Monty paid high tribute to the bravery and professionalism of the American GI and asked the British press to stop picking on Ike. "The captain of our team is Eisenhower," Monty said. "I am absolutely devoted to Ike; we are the greatest of friends. It grieves me when I see uncomplimentary articles about him in the British Press; he bears a great burden, he needs our fullest support."[12]

The British press had an absolute field day with Monty's remarks. The *Daily Mail* headlined:

MONTGOMERY FORESAW ATTACK
HIS TROOPS WERE ALL READY TO MARCH
ACTED "ON OWN" TO SAVE DAY[13]

We first learned of Monty's press conference through a BBC broadcast, whose tone and content were much the same. My staff exploded with indignation. One of them, Ralph Ingersoll, founder of the New York newspaper *PM*, wrote: "Gentle Omar—for the first, last and only time in the campaign—got all-out right-down-to-his-toes mad." That was not quite accurate, but it was one of the few times that I allowed my staff to see my anger.[14]

My staff interpreted this latest Montgomery outrage as another move to promote himself into the position of land commander. I did my best to reassure them: "There will be no Deputy [Land] Commander for General Eisenhower," I told them. "Ike has assured me of this. General Marshall has assured me of this. I am absolutely certain that General Marshall will not stand for it."[15]

In the heat of the moment, I telephoned Ike to register my strong disapproval about the way SHAEF and Monty had handled the account of the Bulge and the command situation. I felt absolutely certain that Monty would not be named land commander, but knowing that the Combined Chiefs would soon meet in Malta and anything might happen, I took this opportunity to make my position on one point very clear: "After what has happened," I said to Ike, "I cannot serve under Montgomery. If he is to be put in command of all ground forces, you must send me home, for if Montgomery goes in over me, I will have lost the confidence of my command. . . . This is one thing I cannot take." I also told him that Patton would not serve under Montgomery. Ike was clearly upset by my ultimatum. He assured me that he would call Churchill himself and request that the British press clarify the Bulge story and the command setup.[16]

Hansen and Ingersoll urged me to issue a factual statement on the Bulge and the command setup to set the record straight. I was hesitant; I had never done anything like that and was concerned that a statement from me might be interpreted as mudslinging or be used by the German propagandists to crow about discord in the Allied high command. (They had used Monty's press conference for that purpose.) However, after careful thought, I decided that the need to build or restore confidence in our soldiers and commanders outweighed the objections, and I told Hansen and Ingersoll to draft a low-key conservative statement.

Ike, meanwhile, was taking steps to soothe my feelings. As promised, he called Churchill and said that "Bradley was very seriously upset by what Monty had said in his interview with the Press." Ike told Churchill that in view of the excellent job I had done in the Bulge, he was preparing to present me with a Bronze Star and he asked Churchill to telephone and congratulate me. Alan Brooke talked Churchill out of telephoning me, but Churchill nonetheless sent a telegram.[17]

Hansen and Ingersoll completed a satisfactory statement and arranged a press conference for January 9. I did not clear the statement with Ike or SHAEF. I defended my strategy, explaining that in "leaving the Ardennes line lightly held," I took a "calculated risk." I stated that "had we followed more cautious policies we would still be fighting west of Paris." I detailed the roles played by Simpson, Hodges and Patton and praised the "heroic resistance" of our troops. I deliberately used the word "temporary" three times when describing how and why Monty took command of the First and Ninth armies, and went out of my way to be nice, stating that "Field Marshal Montgomery has made a notable contribution" to the battle. I concluded on an optimistic note, which led *The New York Times* to headline the story OUR RISK MAY WIN, BRADLEY DECLARES.[18]

There was only one misstatement in the document and that was deliberate. I said that Twelfth Army Group would resume command of the Ninth Army when the Allied lines were rejoined. I still had hopes that Ike, for the sake of American morale, would reconsider and return the Ninth Army to my command, even for one day. The misstatement was designed to prod him in that direction, but it did not work.[19]

At the conclusion of the press conference, my staff distributed the statement, along with a separate document I had composed praising the GI's who had fought so magnificently in the Bulge, the citation for my Bronze Star medal, and the text of Churchill's telegram of congratulations.[20]

Churchill apparently had some considerable influence over the British press. Fleet Street and the BBC, as Hansen put it, were "judiciously fair" in their treatment of my statement. We heard no more from those quarters about Monty being the hero of the Bulge, and the British press clamor to nominate him land commander abruptly ceased. Churchill himself undertook to set matters aright with a final word to the House of Commons on January 18:

> I have seen it suggested that the terrific battle which has been proceeding since December 12 on the American Front is an Anglo-American battle. In fact, however, the United States troops have done almost all the fighting and suffered almost all the losses. . . . The Americans have engaged 30 or 40 men for every one we have engaged and they have lost 60 to 80 men for every one of us. . . . Care must be taken in telling our proud tale not to claim for the British Army an undue share of what is undoubtedly the greatest American battle of the war and will, I believe, be regarded as an ever famous American victory. . . . The gap was torn open as a gap can always be torn open in a line a hundred miles long. General Eisenhower at once gave command to the north of the gap to Field Marshal Montgomery and to the south of it to General Omar Bradley. Judging by the result, both these highly skilled commanders handled very large forces at their disposal in a manner which I think I can say without exaggeration may become a model for military students in the future. . . . Let no one lend themselves to the shouting of mischief makers when issues of this momentous consequence are being successfully decided by the sword.[21]

Our attempt to exploit the Bulge militarily finally moved into high gear on January 3, when Monty at long last released Collins' VII Corps and

Ridgway's XVIII Airborne Corps. Collins had our two best armored divisions in his beefed-up five-division corps: Harmon's 2nd and Rose's 3rd. But the weather was foul: subfreezing temperatures, heavy overcast, icy roads, fog, drifting snow. The Germans, fighting a skillful withdrawing action, were shrewd in their resistance. It was slow going. Too slow.[22]

Coming up from the south, Patton's tankers and infantrymen fought through the same miserable weather. Patton diaried on January 9: "The ground and the snow and the brief period of daylight are a greater menace than the enemy. . . . I wish that great soldier Sir B. [Bernard Montgomery] would do a little more." James Van Fleet, now commanding one of Patton's divisions—the 90th—more than justified our faith in him, but even his fiery leadership could not melt ice and snow. Patton looked forward to the juncture and my resuming control of the First Army, he wrote, "as Bradley is much less timid than Montgomery."[23]

As the two armies drew ever closer, Monty got off a letter to me. Its tone was considerably more sincere than his press conference remarks, and he gave credit where credit was due:

> My dear Brad:
>
> It does seem as if the battle of the "salient" will shortly be drawing to a close, and when it is all clean and tidy I imagine that your armies will be returning to your operational command.
>
> I would like to say two things:—
>
> First : what a great honour it has been for me to command such fine troops.
>
> Second : how well they have all done.
>
> 2. It has been a great pleasure to work with Hodges and Simpson; both have done very well. And the Corps Commanders in the First Army (Gerow Collins, Ridgeway [sic]) have been quite magnificent; it must be most exceptional to find such a good lot of Corps Commanders gathered together in one Army.
>
> 3. All of us in the northern side of the salient would like to say how much we have admired the operations that have been conducted on the southern side; if you had not held on firmly to BASTOGNE the whole situation might have become very awkward.
>
> 4. My kind regards to you and to George Patton.
>
> Yrs very sincerely,
>
> /s/ B. L. Montgomery[24]

Our forces met at Houffalize on January 16, cutting the German salient at the waist, exactly one month after von Rundstedt launched the Bulge offensive. But we were too late to trap the mass of Germans. They had withdrawn toward the West Wall, maneuvering skillfully under difficult circumstances. U.S. military historian Russell F. Weigley assessed the outcome accurately: "The slow progress of Patton's wide-front attack along the southern flank, the lateness of Montgomery's attack in the north

—perhaps unavoidable but with the field marshal offering no stimulus toward an earlier start—and the admirably stubborn resistance of the German Army everywhere, all combined to permit the bulk of German forces and equipment to escape eastward before the trap closed."[25]

On the day our armies joined, I met with Ike in Versailles. Hansen noted that I was "plainly dressed, wearing only the Bronze Star which General Ike had given him several days before." Hansen went on to say that Ike appeared "unusually buoyant" but that I looked "a trifle constrained." That was certainly true. The link-up of our forces at Houffalize had taken much longer than planned; I was deeply concerned that, owing to the delays, Ike might find it necessary to cancel my "hurry up" offensive.

Fortunately this was not the case. Ike was in the process of drafting a new directive for Monty and me. My offensive was included. Ike ordered: "The Central Group of Armies will continue its offensive to take advantage of the enemy's present unfavorable position in the Ardennes, inflict the maximum losses on him, seize any opportunity of breaching the Siegfried Line, and, if successful, advance northeast on the axis Prüm-Euskirchen. This attack will be pressed with all possible vigor so long as there is a reasonable chance of securing a decisive success. However, as an alternative, we must be prepared to pass quickly to the defensive in the Ardennes sector, and to attack in the sector of the Northern Group of Armies."

Monty, meanwhile, would continue with the planning for his offensive, which would be a two-phase operation, "Veritable" and "Grenade." Under Veritable, which would jump off first, Crerar's First Canadian Army would attack southeast from Nijmegen and the Reichwald Forest to clear the Germans from the area west of the Rhine in Monty's northern sector, opposite Düsseldorf. Under Grenade, Simpson's Ninth Army would jump off from the Aachen area and strike northeast, and having cleared the Germans from the area west of the Rhine in Monty's southern sector, link up with the Canadian Army. Thereafter Monty would prepare a massive crossing of the Rhine and thrust into the north German plain with Dempsey's Second British, Crerar's First Canadian and Simpson's Ninth U.S. armies.[26]

It had generally been assumed that Monty would launch Veritable and Grenade about February 1. But Ike pushed that back, setting no definite date, giving priority to my "hurry up" offensive. Veritable and Grenade would be launched, Ike wrote vaguely, "with the minimum of delay if and when I decide not to continue with the offensive in the Ardennes." Moreover, Ike made a significant reduction in the U.S. troop commitment to Monty. Originally Monty was to directly command sixteen American divisions in Simpson's Ninth Army. Ike reduced this to twelve divisions, making up the slack by directing that Hodges support the Ninth Army's right flank with Joe Collins' VII Corps under operational control of Hodges.[27]

I could not have been more pleased. My offensive was to take priority over Veritable and Grenade; it was not to be "weakened" by preparations for those operations. No definite time limit had been placed on my offensive; it would continue as long as it was successful. I was hopeful that we might go all the way—be the first to reach the Rhine.

Knowing that the Malta conference was forthcoming and that the Combined Chiefs could force a change in strategy, I was determined to jump off as quickly as possible. By Ike's command, at midnight January 17-18 Hodges' First Army reverted to my operational control. On January 18, I called on Hodges, who had re-established his headquarters at Spa, to give him his orders—and to build a fire under him.

Unfortunately, Monty arrived that same day for a ceremonial leave-taking. He described our meeting to Alan Brooke as "a fine conference with Bradley." It was hardly that. I was civil but cold and purposefully made no mention of Ike's forthcoming directive, which was certain to infuriate Monty. Since I had urgent work to attend to, and no desire to pass the time of day with Monty, I did not encourage him to stay.

Monty received Ike's directive a day later and he was predictably furious. He complained to Alan Brooke about my offensive, stating that Bradley was once more "going off on his own line" and that "instead of one firm, clear and decisive plan, there was great indecision and patchwork." He ranted on: "Both Ike and Bradley are emphatic that we should not repeat not cross the Rhine in strength anywhere until we are lined up along its entire length from Nijmegen to Switzerland. If we work on this plan we shall take a long time to get anywhere."[28]

One matter that impinged continuously on our new planning, needlessly I thought, was Ike's undue concern about possible German threats in Jake Devers' southern sector. Devers, commanding the Sixth Army Group, still had two armies: Sandy Patch's Seventh and the First French under de Lattre de Tassigny. After taking Strasbourg in November, the French had lazily and ill-advisedly failed to clear about 50,000 Germans west of the Rhine in a thirty-by-fifty-mile area we called the Colmar Pocket. "It affected Eisenhower like a burr under a saddle," Charles MacDonald wrote.

Ike insisted that the Colmar Pocket be eliminated. Like all of us, Devers was shorthanded, trying to do much with too little. Devers ordered de Tassigny's First French Army to clear the Colmar Pocket. But when it soon became apparent the French were bogging down, Devers began pleading with Ike to assign him more U.S. divisions. Ultimately Ike decided that he must give Devers a corps—five divisions, plus 12,000 service troops—to help the First French Army get the job done.[29]

Where was this corps to come from? One division, the 35th, was siphoned out of Patton's army. On January 23, when I received these orders from SHAEF, I was furious, as was, needless to say, Patton. The loss of the division weakened our proposed "hurry up" offensive. Patton angrily wrote in his diary: "It is too bad that the highest levels of command have no personal knowledge of war. . . . The elimination of the Colmar Pocket seems to have developed into a fiasco." What was even more disastrous was that SHAEF insisted on taking four more divisions from us! I thought this draft might be met by asking Monty to temporarily take over Simpson's Ninth Army front, but Ike and SHAEF would not even entertain such a proposal.[30]

I don't think I have ever been so angry in my life. I sat down and composed a memorandum for the record, railing at Montgomery in what was for me strong language. "In an endeavor to satisfy the British propaganda for putting Monty in command of the whole thing," I wrote, "we have arrived at a command setup which adversely affects our tactical operations. Everything we do now is colored by our desire to keep our operations tactically sound and at the same time to meet nationalistic requirements. There are many conflicts and, in my opinion, the command setup is definitely detrimental to efficiency."[31]

Learning what was afoot, Monty railed too—at Ike. He wrote Alan Brooke: "SHAEF are very worried about situation in South about Colmar and Strasbourg. . . . Whitely tells me that they may have to send considerable strength down there to get that area well in hand. If this is done it will mean that Grenade will be put back indefinitely. That would put Veritable back, as the two operations are interdependent. The prospect of getting by degrees sufficient numbers of really good fresh divisions for Grenade is fading away. . . . I fear that the old snags of indecision and vacillation and refusal to consider the military problems fairly and squarely are coming to the front again. . . . The real trouble is that there is no control and the three Army Groups are each intent on their own affairs. . . . One has to preserve a sense of humor these days, otherwise one would go mad."[32]

I called Ike to protest the stripping of our front to favor Devers, stressing that the loss of a full corps would cripple my offensive. I thought I talked him out of it, but on the following day, while conferring with Patton and Hodges on the final details of the offensive, Pink Bull's British assistant, Whitely, telephoned, interrupting our conference to insist that the four divisions be sent to Devers.

Patton described my reaction: "For the only time to my knowledge he lost his good humor and told Whitely that if he wanted to destroy the whole operation he could do so and be damned, or words to that effect, and to take *all* the corps and divisions. . . . Bull got on the phone and Bradley repeated his statements, adding that much more than a tactical operation was involved, in that the prestige of the American Army was at stake. We were all very pleased with Bradley's attitude and told him so."

Patton's chief of staff, Hobart Gay, who was present, recalled in his diary more exactly what I said to SHAEF:

> I want you to understand that there is more at stake than the mere moving of divisions and corps, and of a certain tactical plan. The reputation and the good will of the American soldiers and the American Army and its Commanders are at stake. If you feel that way about it, then as far as I am concerned, you can take any goddam division and/or corps in the Twelfth Army Group, do with them as you see fit, and those of us that you leave back will set on our ass until hell freezes over. I trust you do not think I am angry, but I want to impress upon you that I am goddam well incensed.

Gay went on to write: "At this time, practically every officer in the room stood up and clapped and the Army Commander [Patton] stated in a voice that could well be heard over the telephone: 'Tell them to go to hell and all three of us will resign. I will lead the procession.' "[33]

SHAEF backed down. No more divisions were taken from us. Four divisions from SHAEF reserve were sent to Devers, formed into a new American corps, which joined de Tassigny. A week later the Allied forces split the Colmar Pocket. However, by that time Hitler had already ordered the Germans to withdraw. By February 9, the Colmar Pocket had evaporated and the west bank of the Rhine south of Strasbourg was free of Germans.[34]

There was an unfortunate aftermath involving my old outfit, the 28th Division, commanded by Dutch Cota, which had been sent to Colmar to help the French. On the night of February 5, in Colmar, Cota's signal company officers foolishly left unguarded a two-and-a-half-ton truck containing top-secret cryptography equipment, including a SIGABA (akin to the German Enigma) machine and all the paraphernalia that went with it. The truck and all the top-secret gear it contained was stolen, probably by French civilians wholly unaware of the truck's contents. Nothing like this had happened before. A great panic ensued throughout the entire ETO as MP's, halting every truck in sight, tried to find the stolen vehicle and the cryptographic gear.

In time, the truck and two of three safes were found abandoned in the woods and, luckily, none of the cryptographic gear fell into German hands. An official investigating officer found that almost everybody concerned had behaved irresponsibly. He recommended that Cota, his chief of staff and his G-2 be relieved from command and that the four signal officers responsible be tried by court-martial. In forwarding the official report, Devers suggested that the punishment for Cota, his chief of staff and his G-2 be reduced to an official "reprimand." Fortunately, his recommendation was accepted by Ike and Marshall, sparing Cota, who had fought superbly from Omaha Beach to the Ardennes, utter disgrace and professional ruin.[35]

The Colmar Pocket episode had not enhanced Jake Devers' already middling standing in my eyes or in Ike's. In an evaluation of his principal field commanders prepared for George Marshall, Ike placed Devers far down on the list. (I was number 1, Devers number 24.) He damned him professionally with this evaluation: "Enthusiastic but often inaccurate in statements and evaluations. . . . The proper position of this officer is not yet fully determined in my own mind. The over-all results he and his organization produce are generally good, sometimes outstanding. But he has not, so far, produced among the seniors of the American organization here that feeling of trust and confidence that is so necessary to continued success."[36]

The central offensive thus became a matter of utmost urgency, a last chance for the American forces to prove their mettle before the weight shifted to Monty. On January 26, as Ike had requested, I transferred my tactical headquarters to Namur on the Meuse River in order, as Ike believed, to better coordinate the First and Third armies and to keep in closer touch with Monty. My aides chose an overly splendid palace for my quarters. I thought it all a bit grandiose and ridiculous—and much too far to the rear—but I was too busy planning the offensive to overturn their decisions.[37]

Hodges and Patton would attack, more or less abreast, on an irregular twenty-five-mile north-south front through the Ardennes into the Eifel. Hodges had three corps: Ridgway's XVIII Airborne and Collins' VII and V corps, now commanded by Clarence Huebner, replacing Gee Gerow, whom we had promoted to command the new U.S. Fifteenth Army. Ridgway's XVIII Airborne Corps would spearhead the assault, with two of our best infantry divisions in the lead: the Big Red One, now commanded by Clift Andrus, and Jim Gavin's 82nd Airborne. Huebner's V Corps would attack on Ridgway's left flank; Collins' VII Corps would be held in reserve to exploit a breakthrough. Farther south, Patton had two corps: Middleton's VIII and Eddy's XII. In sum: there were five corps of twenty-one divisions, plus supporting units, comprising some 400,000 men.[38]

Ridgway jumped off first, on January 28. Middleton followed on the 29th, Huebner on the 30th. Official Army historian Charles MacDonald wrote: "The story of all these first attacks could be told almost in a word: weather. By the end of January the month's unusually heavy snowfall and low temperatures had left a snow cover one to two feet deep everywhere and in some places drifts up to a man's waist. Snow glazed the hills, choked the valleys and the roads, and hid the enemy's mines. On the first day, it snowed again all day and into the night." Even so, the Big Red One and the 82nd Airborne gave their all. Ridgway wrote: "I don't think any commander ever had such a magnificent experience as to see those two splendid divisions, both veteran outfits at their highest state of combat effectiveness, attacking side by side. It was a joy to see . . . like watching two great racehorses, driving head and head to the finish line."[39]

And yet, it was slow, slow going. By February 1, we had advanced only an average six miles along the whole twenty-five-mile front. We were back again at the West Wall. But foul weather precluded a significant breakthrough. We were not able to commit Joe Collins and his VII Corps.[40]

En route to the Malta and Yalta conferences, George Marshall met with Ike in Marseilles on January 28. Prior to the meeting, Ike had cabled Marshall his views on strategy. Marshall was well aware that Churchill and Alan Brooke disagreed with these views and were still intent on kicking Ike upstairs and naming an overall land commander, perhaps Alexander. In Marseilles, Marshall backed Ike to the hilt. After their meeting, Ike dictated a memo summing up Marshall's views. In part: "General Marshall will not agree to any proposal to set up a Ground Commander-in-Chief in this theater. If this is done he says he will not remain as Chief of Staff. . . . He agrees that crossing the Rhine in force should be preceded by well-conducted campaigns to eliminate the German forces west of the Rhine."[41]

At the Combined Chiefs' meeting in Malta, Ike was represented by Bedell Smith and Pink Bull. They formally laid out Ike's overall plan: to first clear the west bank of the Rhine of Germans, then launch a heavy assault in the north (thirty to thirty-six divisions) under Monty, with a secondary attack in the center toward Frankfurt-Kassel, led by me. As expected, Alan Brooke viciously attacked Ike's plan, especially Ike's insistence that everybody first draw up to the Rhine before Monty launched the final big drive and my secondary offensive in the center. Marshall, in "a very acid meeting," leaped to Ike's defense. The discussion became so heated that Marshall demanded a "closed session" with only the principals present and no stenographers to keep notes.

It was, Marshall recalled later, "a terrible" session which quickly devolved into scathing criticisms of personalities. As Marshall recalled it, Alan Brooke said, "The British Chiefs of Staff were much worried by the influence on General Eisenhower by General Bradley." Marshall rejoined coldly, "Well, Brooke, they are not nearly as much worried as the American Chiefs of Staff are about the immediate pressures . . . of Mr. Churchill on General Eisenhower." Marshall pointed out that at his suggestion President Roosevelt practically never saw Ike, because Ike was not merely an American but an Allied commander. Marshall was "deeply concerned" by the way that Churchill and the British Chiefs of Staff brought direct "pressures" on Ike. Moreover, Marshall, believing that much of Brooke's distrust of Ike and his strategic plan stemmed from Monty, took this occasion "to express his full dislike and antipathy for Monty." He made it absolutely clear that he would not accept Monty or Alexander or anyone else as a "land commander."

In the face of Marshall's ire, Alan Brooke retreated. There was no more discussion about naming a British general overall land commander. After obtaining assurances orally from Bedell Smith and in writing from Ike that Ike did not literally mean clearing every single German from the west bank of the Rhine before crossing it, that Monty's offensive in the north would have highest priority on all our resources (up to thirty-five divisions), and that my secondary efforts in the center would not be turned "into a major operation capable of stifling the main offensive," Brooke accepted Ike's strategic plan in much the same form that Ike had originally drafted it.[42]

Malta was a clear-cut victory for Marshall—and Ike. Marshall had forcibly put both Monty and Alan Brooke in their place. The scheme to kick Ike upstairs and name a British general land commander was brought to an end. Most important to me, and to my commanders, he blocked the British demand that my center armies go over completely to the defensive. Monty would get the major resources for the big push, but my long-term plan to advance on Frankfurt-Kassel as a secondary effort was approved. We would not sit idly by while Monty marched on Berlin.

The tensions and pressures raised at Malta had a direct impact on my offensive in the Ardennes. To show good faith to the British and to get Monty moving, on February 1, Ike ordered me to cancel my offensive. "It is of paramount importance," he wrote, "to close the Rhine north of Düsseldorf with all possible speed." The first phase of Monty's attack, Veritable, should be launched "at the earliest date," and "not later than 8 February." Grenade should go no later than February 10. I was to transfer U.S. divisions to Simpson's Ninth Army, building his strength to a total of eleven divisions. In addition, I was given the responsibility of seizing the Roer dams in direct support of Simpson. Until we seized those dams, the Germans could flood Simpson's sector and stop his advance.

As to immediate operations on my front south of the Roer dams, Ike was deliberately vague. We were to assume a posture of "aggressive defense." Short of another major offensive, that could be interpreted almost any way I wanted. I chose to view it as an order to "keep moving" toward the Rhine with a low profile.

Patton, of course, viewed the directive in the bitterest possible terms. "Damn this political war. . . . I feel, and I believe Hodges also agrees, that our present attack, which is moving, has a better chance of getting to the Rhine first than has a new attack which will not start until February 10, if then. . . . Neither of us has a very high opinion of the offensive value of British troops. . . . Personally I think that this is a foolish and ignoble way for the Americans to end the war."[43]

FORTY-TWO

Montgomery's Veritable and Grenade offensives, designed to clear out all Germans west of the Rhine in his northern sector, setting the stage for his massive thrust into the heart of Germany, were to proceed in three stages.

Step one was the seizure of the Roer dams so the Germans could not flood the river and critically impede the Allied crossing. This vital task was our job. I gave it to Hodges, who delegated it to his V Corps, commanded by Clarence Huebner. The operation was launched on February 2. Owing to the wholesale transfer of U.S. divisions to Simpson, and to other factors, Huebner had to assign the job to the relatively inexperienced 78th Division, reinforced by elements of the veteran 5th Armored Division. The attack was neither well planned nor well executed, and it soon became necessary to throw in more experienced infantry to help. This was one time when the First Army staff flagrantly fell down on the job.

Step two was Veritable, to commence on February 8. This was Crerar's First Canadian Army attack southeast from Nijmegen. Actually, this offensive would be as much (or more) British as Canadian. Monty had assigned Brian Horrocks' XXX British Corps, beefed up to near-army size (seven regular divisions, three armored brigades), to spearhead Crerar's attack. After Horrocks broke through, the II Canadian Corps of three Canadian divisions, commanded by G. G. Simonds, would join the assault. In all, it was a massive force of 400,000 men.

Step three was Grenade, to commence on February 10. This was Simpson's Ninth Army assault to the northeast, to link up with Crerar's army. Simpson would command three corps: Gillem's XIII, McLain's XIX and a new corps, XVI, commanded by John B. Anderson. In all, Simpson had ten divisions for the assault and one in reserve, a total of 303,000 men. In addition, Joe Collins' VII Corps of four divisions, comprising some 100,000 men, would jump off simultaneously with Simpson, covering Simpson's right flank. Thus in Veritable and Grenade Monty would directly command a total force of nearly 800,000 men organized into the equivalent of twenty-seven divisions, fifteen of them American.[1]

During the final preparations for Veritable and Grenade, Ike summoned Monty to a meeting at my headquarters in Namur on February 5. Ike arrived the night before. By this time my "hurry up" offensive had wound down with inconclusive results; Monty was center stage, controlling fifteen U.S. divisions, and I was not in the best of spirits. However, I conceded to Ike that from a purely military standpoint Veritable-Grenade was the best possible plan at the moment. It was the political side that still worried me. With Monty commanding so many U.S. divisions, there was real danger that his megalomania would lead him to repeat the disgraceful performance of his January 7 press conference, touching off more crowing on Fleet Street that Monty had saved the Allies again. Ike assured me that he had already specifically warned Monty that if anyone in his Twenty-first Army Group fired up Fleet Street again, he would return Simpson's Army to me![2]

On the day following, no one at my headquarters looked forward to Monty's visit. He was coldly received. Kay Summersby, afraid that she might lose control and insult him, asked to be seated at another table for the luncheon. During lunch I was civil but cool, having nothing to say to this arrogant egomaniac who had publicly demeaned me and attempted to destroy my usefulness as a commander. Hansen logged in a hostile tone that Monty's "ego" remained impervious to the coolness and that he "joked . . . and gesticulated . . . and talked too loudly throughout the meal."

Fortunately, Ike and I had previously made plans to tour the fronts. Hansen wrote: "The luncheon ended quickly when Bradley suddenly arose, left Montgomery seated at the table and excused himself to start his trip with Ike." The truth of the matter was that I could not get out of there fast enough. Before he left, Ike, as he later wrote Marshall, "warned" Montgomery that "he must use his entire influence" to prevent a repetition of the Fleet Street xenophobic outbursts of January.[3]

We drove to Bastogne to confer with Patton, who had come up from his headquarters in Luxembourg. Ike's February 1 orders had restricted Patton's Third Army to an "aggressive defense." He was full of plans to keep moving toward the Rhine. Patton and his biographers would imply that Patton carried out these operations in secret, without my knowledge or Ike's, but that is nonsense, yet another Patton myth. Both Ike and I were fully apprised at all times of Patton's operations and approved all of them within reason and always providing that he maintained a low public profile during Veritable and Grenade. Too much limelight on Patton at this time could wound Monty's monumental ego or, worse, again evoke charges from Monty that we were not going all out to help him.[4]

We went on to Spa to confer and spend the night with Hodges, who had re-established his headquarters there. We found Hodges less than satisfied with Huebner's progress toward the Roer dams. Indeed, the 78th Division was encountering the same sort of fierce resistance we had met in the Roer dam area in November and December. Hodges had already borrowed Jim Gavin's 82nd Airborne Division from Ridgway to assist the 78th. After touring the area, Gavin was bitterly contemptuous of Huebner's battle plan, and rightly condemned it in his memoirs. Almost too late, we saw that our effort on the Roer dams was too little. Hodges subsequently was compelled to commit elements of Craig's 9th Division to help.[5]

The next day Ike and I visited big, bald, enthusiastic Bill Simpson and all the corps commanders who were or would be involved in Veritable and Grenade: Huebner, Collins (tanned and fresh from a quick leave on the French Riviera), Anderson, Gillem, McLain. We were immensely impressed with Simpson and his staff and the planning they had done. Simpson's chief of staff, James E. Moore, was one of the least-known yet ablest officers in the ETO. I had taught him math at West Point, remembered him well and determined to keep an eye on him in the future. Moore "minded the store" while Simpson toured his corps and division headquarters. Owing to Moore's intelligence and talent for administration, Ninth Army's staff, although least experienced in battle, was in some respects superior to any in my command. Moreover, both Simpson and Moore got along remarkably well with Monty and the British staffs. Ike and I left Simpson's headquarters convinced that the Ninth Army was destined for outstanding performance, and we were not disappointed. As Ike put it in his memoirs: "If Simpson ever made a mistake as an Army Commander, it never came to my attention."[6]

Veritable jumped off on schedule on February 8. Horrocks and his immense XXX Corps attacked with the thunder of 1,400 guns. The weather was foul, bitterly cold and rainy. Horrocks wrote: "The main trouble was mines—and mud, particularly mud. I am certain that this must be the chief memory of everyone. . . . Mud and still more mud. It was so bad that after the first hour, every tank going across country was bogged down, and the infantry had to struggle forward on their own." Progress was very, very slow, enemy resistance strong, and it mounted daily as von Rundstedt rushed troops to block Horrocks. In his memoirs, Horrocks recalled that the fight was "unquestionably the grimmest battle in which I took part." Later Ike, in a letter to Crerar, stated that "probably no assault in this war has been conducted in more appalling conditions of terrain than was that one."[7]

To make matters much grimmer, Huebner's troops failed at the Roer dams. Craig, taking command of the operation, broke through to the dams, but not before German engineers had set off demolitions. The demolition of the floodgates was cleverly arranged to cause us the worst possible trouble downstream: not a sudden and brief Niagara-like cascade, which we would have welcomed, but a steady slow flow calculated to create a long-lasting flood in the Valley of the Roer, and one that we could not stop. Simpson's big Ninth Army "right hook" could not be swung across the flooded Roer River for two long, utterly maddening weeks. Meanwhile, Horrocks and Simonds absorbed the full fury of the German counterattacks.[8]

At Malta, Marshall had made it crystal clear that he would not accept Monty or Alexander or anyone else as a land commander interposed between Ike, Monty and me. However, in a private meeting with Roosevelt, Churchill and Alan Brooke, Marshall agreed to reconsider the Churchill–Alan Brooke proposal to have Alexander relieve Tedder as deputy supreme commander. This was a concession on Marshall's part, following his conference with Ike in Marseilles. Ike had assured Marshall that Alex would not become a land commander. Alexander had been serving faithfully as Allied commander in Italy all this time; now that difficult campaign was drawing to a close and Italy had become a subordinate theater. Ike was extremely fond of Alex and wanted him to share some of the prestige of the final kill in Germany. I think Ike also believed that Alex could help keep Monty in line—curb his megalomania—and I agreed. But Marshall insisted that any change must be postponed for at least six weeks, so that, as Alan Brooke put it, it would not look as though "Alex was being put in to support Ike after his Ardennes failure."[9]

After Malta and Yalta, Marshall went on to Italy to tour the battlefront and did not return to Washington for some time. The first word Ike had that it had officially been decided to replace Tedder with Alexander came from Pink Bull on his return to SHAEF from Malta on February 11. Ike, taken completely by surprise, was resentful that the Combined Chiefs had not formally notified him, that he had learned the news by the back door, so to speak. Furthermore, the news had come at a most inopportune time. Monty had jumped off with the usual clamor and headlines; the Americans, owing to the Roer dam flooding, were helplessly stuck behind the Roer River. To name Alexander deputy supreme commander at this point might be ballyhooed by Fleet Street as another British general coming to the rescue of the inept Americans.[10]

On the day after my fifty-second birthday, February 13, Ike arrived at Namur to confer with me and spend the night. He had his son John in tow. John had been assigned as a rifle platoon leader in the newly arrived 71st Division, which was moving up to the front. But I was opposed to Ike's son serving in so risky a slot for two reasons. Sandy Patch's son had been killed in the fall while serving in Patch's Seventh Army. The psychological effect on Patch had been so devastating as to impair his effectiveness as army commander. If John were killed, the psychological impact on Ike might seriously jeopardize our operations. Secondly, if John were captured in action, Hitler could make great propaganda of the fact or subject John to extraordinary humiliation—or worse. Ike and I had arranged that John would be assigned to me as a staff officer.[11]

Ike was in low spirits. His knee was giving him great pain again. The day before, at SHAEF, he had had a "minor" operation on the leg; a physiotherapist was treating him nearly full-time. He was very much disturbed by the Alexander-for-Tedder proposal, could not understand Marshall's about-face at Malta, and Marshall's failure to notify him of his reasons for his change of views. He suggested that Monty might have had a hand in engineering the scheme. He was fully aware of the damaging impact Alexander's appointment could have on American morale at this point.[12]

Ike decided that he must confront Monty about the Alexander matter. One of his staff officers telephoned Monty to ask that he come to my headquarters the following day. But Monty declined; he had already made other plans and would not change them. This further infuriated Ike. Even though he was in great pain, Ike was compelled once again to drive to Monty's headquarters.[13]

The next day I gave Ike my car, and Chet Hansen served as his guide. They found Monty in his CP. Two years after the event Hansen recalled: "I have never seen a man as angry as he [Ike] was at that time. He was furious. He was going to have a showdown. As soon as he got there he stalked out of the car with a great scowl on his face and he walked in and started talking to Monty—no affability at all." In his diary for that day, Hansen discreetly wrote: "Our meeting was ended within the hour after some slight table thumping and General Eisenhower returned immediately to our headquarters for luncheon with Bradley."[14]

Ike laid it squarely on the table. Under the circumstances, Ike no longer wanted Alex to replace Tedder. He suspected Monty was intriguing against him toward that end, or so Ike had gathered from what went on in Malta. That night, Monty wrote in his diary: "I was sorry this was said at Malta. It got back to Ike very quickly and was no doubt attributed to me; he is such an awfully decent chap that I hate to see him upset." Monty, who like Ike had previously approved the Alexander-for-Tedder switch, now also backed off. He wrote: "I understood that he [Ike] himself wished to handle the land operations and to command the three Army Groups; he did not want a land force commander between him and the Army Groups. . . . I therefore considered that the command set-up was now satisfactory . . . having arrived at the present command situation I hoped it would remain unchanged till the war was over. . . . As soon as I had said I was very well satisfied with the situation about command, he became a different man; he drove away beaming all over his face."[15]

After discussing this matter with me further that afternoon, Ike returned to SHAEF, leaving John in my care. The next day he sent a letter to Alan Brooke, firmly and clearly setting forth his views on Alexander's possible appointment. He wanted Brooke to know that "there can be no question whatsoever of placing between me and my Army Group Commanders any intermediary headquarters, either official or unofficial in character." He had seen Monty and Monty was "most emphatic in insisting that command arrangements I have made are nearly perfect as circumstances, including diverse nationalities, will permit." Alexander should be told this, otherwise he might feel his new job is "one of less influence than he should properly have." In fact, Ike stressed, Alexander would probably be detailed to spend most of his time dealing with the urgent problems of the economies of the various liberated nations—strictly routine matters in rear areas.

Ike went out of his way to stress the "unfortunate burst of publicity" on Fleet Street which ensued when Monty temporarily took command of the First and Ninth armies during the Bulge. "No single incident that I have encountered throughout my experience as an Allied Commander has been so difficult to combat as this particular outburst in the papers." He warned: "Should there be any attempt on the part of any newspaper to interpret Alexander's appointment here as the establishment of a ground headquarters or the interposition of any kind of intermediate control between myself and my Army Group Commanders, I would find it immediately necessary to make a formal announcement setting forth the facts." Ike suggested that Alan Brooke show his letter to both Churchill and Alexander, and he sent a copy to Marshall.[16]

The matter dragged on for another two or three weeks. Churchill and Alan Brooke were miffed. With Alan Brooke's help, Churchill wrote Ike a snippy letter in which he said (in part), "I was not aware that your British Deputy was relegated to such non-military functions" as "setting up a decent living standard in liberated and conquered countries." Ike tactfully replied that he had not meant to restrict Alex solely to such matters. "The intent of my letter," he said, "was to point out that the tendency of the press to give its own interpretation of every move we make, particularly whenever such moves touch upon the delicate question of command, might compel public announcements that would injure Alexander's feelings."

On March 1, Monty declared unequivocal opposition to Alexander's appointment, writing: "If Alexander were now appointed Deputy Supreme Commander, it would be resented in certain American quarters; a further great storm would arise and all the old disagreements would be revived. For goodness sake let us stop any further causes of friction at all cost." Lacking support from Montgomery, Churchill and Alan Brooke had to give up the campaign. Alex remained in Italy; Tedder finished the war as Ike's deputy. Churchill, Monty wrote, "was not very pleased" to have lost this battle.[17]

I was filled with admiration for the resolute manner in which Ike dealt with this delicate matter involving our old friend Alex. Monty was right. No matter how skillfully the appointment was handled it was bound to raise another storm which would reflect adversely on or discredit me and other American commanders. Ike first got Monty on his side, then forthrightly faced down Churchill and Alan Brooke. It was the most emphatic demonstration yet that Ike had taken full command of the war on the Continent.

I soon found a job for young John Eisenhower. We had decided to copy one feature of the British Army's command structure, the so-called Phantom Service. This was a network of young officers attached to almost all major British outfits who reported daily or, more often, directly to Monty on what was happening in the units. These reports gave Monty a quick and excellent "feel" for the whole battlefront independent of the slower official channels, and in some cases provided a cover for Ultra reps. We would call our new outfit "SIAM"—for Signal Information and Monitoring. While waiting for his orders to SIAM, John spent considerable time at my headquarters.[18]

Crerar's massive offensive, Veritable, had bogged down in mud after several days. The Germans had concentrated against him in force. In two weeks of the toughest kind of fighting, Crerar advanced only seventeen miles, barely a third of the way toward his final objective. Owing to the flooding of the Roer, we were unable to help him, unable to move. Each day that dragged by was a terrible agony for me and all of the Americans in the fifteen divisions of Simpson's Ninth Army and Collins' VII Corps.[19]

Finally, on February 23, after a two-week delay, our troops were able to jump off and cross the Roer. They went off with a tremendous bang. In many respects, our breakout and the subsequent campaign resembled our campaign in Normandy. Although Monty had not planned it so, Crerar's Canadian Army had drawn the Germans on him just as Monty had drawn the Germans on him at Caen. Simpson broke through on the right as we had broken through at St. Lô, then wheeled counterclockwise as the First Army had wheeled in Normandy.

Simpson's attack, supported on the right flank by Collins' VII Corps, was one of the most perfectly executed of the war. In a mere two weeks the Ninth Army drove about fifty-three miles from the Roer to the Rhine at Wesel. Simpson cleared thirty-four miles of the west bank of the Rhine from Düsseldorf to Wesel, capturing some 30,000 German troops. His attack unhinged German defenses in front of Crerar, enabling the British-Canadian army to drive forward another twenty-three miles to link up with Simpson at Wesel, capturing another 22,000 German troops.

Ike and I visited Simpson on March 1, remaining overnight at his headquarters in Maastricht. We found Simpson and his chief of staff Moore and the Ninth Army staff confidently in command of the situation. Moreover, they were certain they could seize a bridge over the Rhine or force a crossing of the Rhine with their own bridging equipment. Ike, the Ninth Army historian wrote, "evidenced . . . intense interest" in these plans. Such a crossing was not part of Monty's battle plan—far from it. However, we believed that if a crossing of the Rhine could be obtained at small cost and risk, it would be a great shot in the arm for the American forces, provide a bridgehead that might be exploited later, or open up a singular opportunity to radically change the course of the war.

Ike's "intense interest" was apparently interpreted by Simpson and his staff as a green light to cross the Rhine. Simpson and his corps commanders—notably Ray McLain—made a close study and detailed plans for a crossing between Düsseldorf and Mundelheim, aimed at a drive on Hamm, a key Ruhr rail hub. But when Simpson took these plans to Monty for approval, Monty flatly turned them down. There would be no impromptu American crossing of the Rhine. Monty, planning his set-piece crossing, would decide the time and place and lead the attack. Simpson and his staffers were bitterly disappointed. The Ninth Army historian wrote: "So the course of history as it might have developed had Ninth Army leaped the Rhine early in March will never be known. Of one point, Ninth Army men are certain—it could have been done, and done successfully." Monty made no comment on this matter in his memoirs.[20]

No less remarkable was the performance of Collins' VII Corps. After crossing the Roer and escorting Simpson as far as the Erft River and Canal, Collins, with scarcely a pause, crossed the Erft and drove east toward Cologne. By March 3, with two major river crossings behind him, Collins encircled the city from the west and prepared to seize it. In this spectacular drive to the Rhine, Collins captured another 13,000 German troops. Collins had proved himself the ablest of all our five corps commanders. Had we created another ETO army, Collins, despite his youth and lack of seniority, would certainly have been named to command it.[21]

It will be recalled that Ike's directive of February 1 had placed the First Army (less Collins) and the Third Army on "aggressive defense" during the Veritable and Grenade offensives. Over the period from February 10 to February 23, while waiting for the Roer River waters to abate, I developed, in consultation with Hodges and Patton, a battle plan called "Lumberjack" which would immediately follow Veritable and Grenade. Lumberjack was designed to advance Hodges and Patton to the Rhine River, clearing out all Germans north of the Moselle River and west of the Rhine in the triangle formed by Cologne-Coblenz-Trier. Lumberjack clearly exceeded even the loosest definition of "aggressive defense." But it advanced our strategy of drawing all armies up to the Rhine before Monty made his set-piece Rhine crossing and, by my reckoning, it could be carried out while Monty was staging his crossing without interfering or delaying him. Ike authorized Lumberjack on February 20 and orally approved my final plans on March 1, in a meeting with Monty and me at Eindhoven.[22]

I issued orders for Lumberjack to commence on March 3. It was executed with drill-hall precision. No other campaign of the war brought me greater professional pride.[23]

The main thrust of the offensive was assigned to Hodges, who, with the return of Collins' VII Corps, commanded three corps comprising twelve (plus) divisions. After securing Cologne, Collins drove south along the west bank of the Rhine toward Bonn. Immediately to the south of VII Corps, Millikin's III Corps pushed southeast toward Bonn and Remagen. South of Millikin, Huebner's V Corps struck southeast through the Eifel toward the Ahr River, which was the army boundary line. Patton, commanding three corps comprising ten (plus) divisions, drove northeast from Trier in the narrow corridor between the Ahr and Moselle rivers. The attack was carried out by Middleton's VIII Corps abutting Huebner's V Corps on the Ahr and Eddy's XII Corps on Middleton's right. Walker's XX Corps remained anchored in the Trier area.

Lumberjack was very nearly flawless, the kind of campaign generals dream about but seldom see. All five corps of both armies advanced according to plan, with dazzling speed and elan. The German armies opposing us were utterly routed, the men falling back in confusion and disarray, leaving a trail of weapons and equipment behind. Within a mere four days —by March 7—advance elements of our armor had pushed up to the Rhine, from Cologne to Coblenz.[24]

On March 2, Churchill and Alan Brooke returned to the Continent to congratulate Monty, Crerar and Simpson on the success of Veritable and Grenade and to discuss final operations for the defeat of Germany with Monty, Ike and me. While touring the battlefields in Simpson's sector between Maastricht and Aachen on March 3, the procession came upon a section of the Siegfried Line. Simpson recalled: "Churchill ordered the procession to halt so that he could look at a German pillbox. When he got out of the car, he smiled and said to me and Alan Brooke, 'Let's all go piss on the West Wall.' Whereupon, Churchill proceeded to execute his suggestion. Photographers jostled for vantage points to record this historic act of contempt but Churchill barred pictures, saying, 'This is one of the operations connected with this great war which must not be reproduced graphically.' "[25]

Ike had sent his private train to Holland, and on March 5 it delivered Churchill and Alan Brooke to Ike's headquarters in Reims for lunch and an afternoon session on strategy. Churchill, dressed in the uniform of an army colonel, with a large cigar in his mouth, greeted Ike and me affably.

Alan Brooke, Hansen recorded, was "a severe man who says little but looks querulously out from behind his horn-rimmed glasses." Hansen judged that Ike and I, "country boys both of them, fitted well into the severe professionalism, the amazingly articulate conversation of the British generals." Churchill flattered me with glowing recollections of my military decisions in Normandy.[26]

By now, Allied armies had drawn abreast of the Rhine from Nijmegen to Coblenz. The strategy talks focused on crossing the Rhine and plunging into the heart of Germany and a secondary operation in the south to clear the Germans south of the Moselle River in the Saar and bring Devers forward to the Rhine.

Monty's massive Rhine crossing was code-named "Plunder." It was scheduled to jump off on March 24. In scope and weight it rivaled our D-day assault on Normandy. Monty would command the equivalent of thirty-two combat divisions (thirty divisions and six brigades) for the operation; twelve of the divisions American, twelve British and eight Canadian. Dempsey's Second British Army, comprising nine divisions, with Horrocks' veteran XXX Corps in the van, would make the main assault in the area between Xanten and Rees. Matt Ridgway's XVIII Airborne Corps, consisting of the British 6th and the U.S. 17th Airborne divisions, would jump or be landed across the river from Horrocks. Crerar's First Canadian Army would cross behind the British. Farther south, in a secondary effort, Simpson would cross the river with one five-division corps, Anderson's XVI, at Rheinberg, backed up by Gillem's XIII and McLain's XIX. In total, Monty would command nearly a million men.

In Monty's original plan, the American forces had virtually been squeezed from sight. He planned to incorporate only one U.S. Corps (of two infantry divisions) within Dempsey's Second Army, leaving the other two corps and nine divisions of the Ninth Army in reserve. Simpson would have no command responsibility in the crossing whatsoever. The official Army historian wrote: "Ninth Army was flabbergasted!" Simpson and Moore, working in harmony with Dempsey, were eventually able, by dint of diplomacy, to persuade Monty to let the Ninth Army make an independent crossing at Rheinberg.

There was still one unsettled, highly controversial question about Plunder. In Ike's original plan, Hodges' First Army was to "hold" in the center, with twelve divisions, on the west bank of the Rhine in the Cologne-Bonn-Remagen area. But as the planning progressed, Monty requested that no fewer than ten divisions of the First Army be placed in reserve, in case he suffered a reverse, or to exploit a major breakthrough. These ten extra divisions (totally stripping the First Army) would give Monty control of some forty-two divisions and leave me with nothing but Patton's Third Army. The total force envisioned by Monty much resembled his original "full-blooded" thrust proposal, long since shelved by

SHAEF. And yet Ike did not categorically disapprove Monty's request. He told Monty that should he take the bulk of First Army, it would go to him as a fully organized field army (rather than individual divisions) and that my Twelfth Army Group headquarters would be sent with it and I would be given command of both First and Ninth armies. This prospect gave Monty pause—but no final decision had as yet been made. Our standing orders from SHAEF were to maintain "readiness to employ the First Army in strength of not less than ten divisions for exploitation of the bridgehead north of the Ruhr."[27]

The operation in the south to clear the Saar and bring Devers' Sixth Army Group to the Rhine was code-named "Undertone." As originally planned, the main effort was to be made by Sandy Patch's Seventh Army, supported by de Tassigny's French First Army. Patch would bear the burden of the attack, which would first have to crack the Siegfried Line in the Saar. Patch's Army was to be built up to three corps comprising a total of fourteen divisions—several of these to be borrowed from my ever-shrinking Twelfth Army Group. Patton, in a feinting move, would cross the Moselle River to the south to draw Germans from Patch's front. Undertone was to commence on the heels of Lumberjack, about March 15, but in any event, before Plunder.

I had grave doubts about Undertone. Because of the ineptitude he had shown in the so-called Colmar Pocket operation, I had little confidence in Devers and even less in de Tassigny's French First Army. The Germans were dug in deep at the Siegfried Line with insane orders from Hitler not to yield a foot. I foresaw a long bloody campaign going nowhere at great cost to us, and further requests to shift my dwindling divisions to the south. I therefore proposed that Patton's feints south across the Moselle be enlarged to a major offensive which would sweep behind the Siegfried Line, trapping the Germans between Patton and Patch. Although Devers caviled, worrying about the two U.S. armies colliding, Ike approved the plan without qualification. As designed, Patton would hold Middleton's VII Corps at Coblenz, laying siege to the city (and seeking a foothold across the Rhine), while Eddy's XII and Walker's XX Corps carried the weight of the campaign. Patton was delighted.

We did not advertise the point to the British, but we believed that Undertone could well develop into the fulfillment of my long-standing goal of sending a strong thrust into Germany via Frankfurt-Kassel. Once Patton and Patch had cleared the Saar-Palatinate of Germans, we intended to merge the Third and Seventh armies (twenty-six U.S. divisions plus the French army) for a massive sweep to Frankfurt and beyond. The sweep would unhinge German defenses in front of Hodges and enable him to cross the Rhine and join us, adding another twelve divisions to our force, assuming that Ike would give me, rather than Monty, the First Army. If so, that would give us a total force of three U.S. armies, plus the French (comprising in all some forty divisions), driving on Kassel. If Monty's offensive failed or slowed, as his offensives usually did, our massive drive on Kassel would unhinge the Germans confronting him and enable him to go forward.[28]

Even though Monty's Plunder was to be the main event and Undertone a sideshow, I do not believe Churchill and Alan Brooke were satisfied. They did not say so that day, but there is no doubt that mainly for the sake of British prestige they would have preferred that Hodges' First Army be formally assigned to Monty and Undertone canceled, in effect reverting to Monty's original strategy of a single "full-blooded" thrust north of the Ruhr to Berlin. That day, Brooke carped in his diary about Ike. "There is no doubt," he wrote, "that Ike is a most attractive personality and, at the same time, a very, very limited brain from a strategic point of view. This comes out the whole time in all conversation with him."[29]

Coincidental with the Churchill visit and wholly unrelated, Ike renewed his campaign to have me promoted to four stars. This time he was successful. Marshall decided to recommend Devers, Clark and me for promotion to full general. Ike was not happy about promoting Devers, but since he and Clark and I were all army group commanders, it would be a slap in the face to omit Devers. Ike wrote me: "At last the President has sent your name to the Senate for four-star promotion. As you know, I have long felt such action was overdue and it is almost needless for me to say 'Congratulations.' I am truly happy, the more so because I believe that this action on the part of the President and the War Department will do much to re-establish a proper understanding at home as to the effectiveness of American leadership in this theater." The promotion was approved on March 29, 1945, to date from March 12, 1945.[30]

FORTY-THREE

Early in the evening of March 7, Pink Bull arrived at Namur on a raiding mission. SHAEF had once again decided that the Twelfth Army Group should supply Devers' Sixth Army Group reinforcements. This time it was for Undertone. Bull wanted the moon: one armored division, two infantry divisions, seven battalions of artillery and other miscellaneous units. Bull knew that Simpson's Ninth Army was committed to Monty's Plunder, that Patton's Third Army was committed to Undertone, and that the reinforcements could only come from Hodges' First Army. By a standing SHAEF directive, "not less than ten divisions" of the First Army had been placed in the rather nebulous "reserve" for Plunder. Bull's request for reinforcements for Devers would take all the rest of the First Army.[1]

I was furious. Patton and his Third Army got most of the headlines, but the truth was that ever since Normandy, Hodges' First Army had borne the brunt of the really tough fighting. Man for man, unit for unit, they were superior to any army on the Western Front. In the real clutches, such as Mortain and the Bulge, they had performed magnificently. It infuriated me to have the First Army placed first in the "reserve" for Monty and now raided by Bull for reinforcements. Hodges and his army deserved better treatment than that.

As Bull and I were arguing this matter, I received a telephone call from Hodges. He had electrifying news. Troops of his 9th Armored Division, commanded by my classmate John W. Leonard, had captured the Ludendorff railway bridge at Remagen![2]

I was stunned and exhilarated. "Hot dog, Courtney," I exclaimed, "this will bust him wide open. Are you getting stuff across?"

"Just as fast as we can push it over," Courtney said in his quiet way. He had already ordered up U.S. Navy landing craft, which we had stockpiled for a possible Rhine crossing. Army engineers had been summoned forward with pontoon bridges.

"Shove everything you can across it, Courtney," I said, "and button up the bridgehead tightly."

I hung up, turned to Pink Bull with a big grin and said, "There goes your ball game, Pink. Courtney's gotten across the Rhine on a bridge."

This was one of the most rewarding moments of my life. I was engulfed with euphoria. Monty had been preparing his massive Plunder for weeks. It was not to jump off for another two weeks. Our American troops had completely upstaged him, grabbing a bridge on the fly. Beyond that purely human reaction, and far more important, the opportunities that now lay before us were immense. If the crossing could be properly exploited, I could realize my long-sought strategic goal of a strong right hook into Germany—the old "two-thrust" concept.

The terrain opposite Remagen was less than ideal for military maneuver. There lay the Westerwald, a dense, mountainous forest, good for defense, poor for offense. We would have to go around the Westerwald. Fortunately, the north-south Ruhr-Frankfurt autobahn lay only six miles beyond the Rhine. If Hodges could establish a strong bridgehead opposite Remagen, resist the inevitable counterattack and fight to the autobahn, we could send his troops south on the highway to Limburg, then swing east along the Lahn River Valley to Giessen.

Patton's role in Undertone was designed to take him southeast to the Rhine at Mainz and Worms. Hodges' drive up the Lahn River valley would unhinge German defenses on the east bank of the Rhine at Mainz, thus making it possible for Patton to cross the Rhine without strong opposition. Once across the Rhine, Patton could turn due north, striking through Frankfurt to Giessen, linking up with Hodges. Together, Hodges and Patton, forming the strong right hook, could advance on Kassel.

It would be very, very difficult to gain approval for such a plan. Although Ike had always favored a strong right hook through Frankfurt, he was now firmly committed to a "main effort" in the north and no more than "aggressive defense" in the center and south. The British had consistently opposed the right hook. If Ike approved one now, they were certain to interpret it as not only an egregious breach of faith with the deal struck at Malta, but another dangerous dispersion of effort. The ten divisions of Hodges' First Army would no longer be in Monty's reserve—but headed for Kassel. From the standpoint of prestige, Monty's "show" might be massively upstaged.

But I had one big factor in my favor. Hodges was already across the Rhine! The feat had incalculable psychological value. Hodges' crossing *had* to be exploited. Not to do so would be almost criminally negligent. I therefore decided that the best way to get my right-hook strategy approved was to get Hodges so heavily committed in the Remagen bridgehead that he could not be pulled back. This was not my usual straightforward way of doing business, but the circumstances compelled me to resort to a little duplicity.

I was certain that my old and good friend Pink Bull would support me. But when I had outlined my plan, he looked at me as though I were a heretic. He scoffed: "You're not going anywhere down there at Remagen. You've got a bridge, but it's in the wrong place. It just doesn't fit the plan. Ike's heart is in your sector but right now his mind is up north."

I was angry. Pink Bull had become either so inflexible or so pro-British, or both, that he was blind to the opportunities that lay open to American forces. I demanded: "What in hell do you want us to do, pull back and blow it up?"[3]

I now decided to telephone Ike. He was at dinner with Ridgway, Gavin, Taylor and other airborne generals. When I gave Ike the news, he was ecstatic. He later wrote: "I could scarcely believe my ears." He said, "Brad, that's wonderful." I told him I wanted to push everything I had in the vicinity across—four divisions. Ike was completely supportive. He said, "Sure, get right on across with everything you've got. It's the best break we've had." He authorized me to put five divisions into the bridgehead if necessary, saying, "Make sure you hold that bridgehead." I fixed my eyes on Pink Bull and told Ike that Bull was opposed to exploiting Remagen because it did not fit The Plan. Ike replied, "To hell with the planners. Sure, go on, Brad, and I'll give you everything we've got to hold that bridgehead."[4]

When he gave these orders, Ike had no intimation of what my real intentions were. He initially perceived a Remagen bridgehead solely as an aid to Monty's Plunder, a limited thrust that would draw German forces from Monty's area. The next day he cabled the Combined Chiefs the news, adding: "Bradley is rushing troops to secure adequate bridgeheads with the idea that this will constitute greatest possible threat as supporting effort for main attack." That same day Ike telephoned Monty to give him the news. Monty wrote Alan Brooke: "I was consulted by Eisenhower by telephone this morning as to my opinion on this matter and I said I considered it to be an excellent move, as it would be an unpleasant threat to the enemy and would undoubtedly draw enemy strength on to it and away from the business in the north."[5]

The Remagen bridgehead was not easily exploited. Hitler was naturally furious that it had been taken. He used it as an excuse to again relieve von Rundstedt of command, bringing Albert Kesselring from Italy to replace him. Kesselring's immediate subordinate, Walther Model, employed every possible means to eject us and destroy the bridge. The Germans rushed elements of some twelve divisions (including four panzers) onto the bridgehead, but most of these units were undermanned and undergunned or green to combat. The Germans brought up heavy artillery, aircraft, floating mines, frogmen. They even fired eleven V-2s at the bridge—the first and only tactical use of either V-weapon in the war. But Hodges held on stubbornly, deterred as much by the rugged terrain as the enemy. The bridge, already damaged, soon collapsed, but by that time Hodges had a firm foothold on the east bank and six pontoon bridges spanning the river.[6]

When the troops of Leonard's 9th Armored had captured the bridge, the division had been assigned to Millikin's III Corps. Millikin had only recently come from Patton's Third Army to Hodges' First, and Hodges was disappointed in Millikin's leadership—even more so than Patton. Hodges faulted almost every move Millikin made to exploit the Remagen bridgehead. The friction grew so intense between them that Hodges felt compelled to relieve Millikin of command, owing to his "bad leadership" and timidity in the bridgehead. I had to agree with Hodges, and with Ike's approval I chose our classmate Jim Van Fleet to replace Millikin. In a matter of nine months, I had promoted Van Fleet from regimental commander to corps commander, thus setting to right the grave injustice done him in the past. Millikin retained his rank and was shifted to command the 13th Armored Division until the end of the war.[7]

On March 9, French General Alphonse Juin came to Namur to bestow French decorations on Hodges, Simpson, Patton, Gerow, some air generals and me. After the ceremony, I met privately with the four U.S. army commanders, our first get-together. After swearing them to secrecy, I revealed my desire—and plan—to exploit the Remagen bridgehead into a full right hook at Kassel. They could not have been more pleased. But I also warned them I did not yet have approval for this plan, that Monty would make the main effort in the north and that "not less than ten divisions" of the First Army were still earmarked for Monty's reserve. I confided to them my political strategy of gradually increasing the Remagen commitment until it could not be pulled back. Patton summed it up this way in his diary: "It is essential to get the First and Third Armies so deeply involved in their present plans that they cannot be moved north to play second-fiddle to the British-instilled idea of attacking with sixty divisions on the Ruhr Plain."[8]

Later that same day Pink Bull called from SHAEF with momentous news. He had discussed my right-hook plan with Ike. Ike had approved it. According to a memo Bull made for the record, Ike directed him "to call and inform you that he wants the Remagen bridgehead firmly held and developed to secure it with a view to *an early advance to the southeast*. He authorizes the employment of five divisions for this purpose immediately." (Italics added.) Bull's memo noted that I told him I "may eventually need one more division" and that I planned "to push the bridgehead out ten kilometers from the bridge, to include a section of the *Autobahn*." Four days later, March 13, Ike put the orders in writing. "The capture of a footing east of the Rhine at Remagen offers an opportunity to exploit this success in order to assist Operations Plunder and Undertone without detracting from the effort already allocated to them. Twelfth Army Group will firmly secure the bridgehead at Remagen and *launch a thrust therefrom towards Frankfurt*."[9] (Italics added.)

This order, often overlooked by the historians, was actually one of the most important of the war on the Continent. It signaled that Ike, with no consultation with the Combined Chiefs or Monty, had made a significant change in the strategy. He had formally approved my right-hook plan and in so doing had declared in favor of a two-thrust movement into Germany beyond the Rhine. The order made it clear that Monty's Plunder would still be the main effort, ours secondary. To reassure the British, Ike had even labeled our effort an "assist" to Monty's Plunder and specified that the First Army must still be ready to give Monty "not less than ten divisions." But this was all window dressing. In authorizing me to thrust the First Army "towards Frankfurt," where, by my plan, it would link up with Patton, Ike knew that the operation would develop into a major offensive and that the transfer of ten divisions to Monty was becoming less and less feasible or likely.

In fact, Ike was already making plans to expand my right hook with a major airborne assault in the Kassel area. At that time our 82nd and 101st Airborne divisions were being held in reserve for Operation Eclipse, a contingency plan in the event of a sudden collapse of the Hitler dictatorship. Under Eclipse the 82nd and 101st divisions would parachute into Berlin and take control of the city. This was a somewhat distant and uncertain mission, and the airborne generals were urging Ike to give them a more immediate task. On March 13, Ike proposed that the U.S. 82nd, 101st, and a British airborne division jump at Kassel and secure an airhead into which we would air-transport another four to seven regular divisions. This air operation—on a par with Market-Garden—was designed to prevent the Germans from forming a strong defensive line in the Kassel area as Hodges and Patton advanced toward it with ever-lengthening supply lines.[10]

Although the airborne forces had no greater champion than I, and I well understood Ike's desire to employ them whenever and wherever possible, I stoutly opposed the Kassel airborne operation for three compelling reasons. First, I intended to break out and run fast. Owing to the limited number of pontoon bridges we could throw across the Rhine, I could foresee another logistical logjam. I preferred to earmark the huge number of aircraft required for the Kassel operation to airlifting gasoline and other supplies to my divisions. Secondly, I believed that (as at Tournai) we would probably move so fast that we would overrun Kassel before the paratroopers could get there. Thirdly, I doubted that Ike could find enough spare divisions to successfully launch the operation. Owing to my strong opposition, the plan was ultimately shelved, much to the disappointment of Ridgway, Gavin, Taylor and others.[11]

From March 9 to March 16, we slowly enlarged the Remagen bridgehead and prepared to break out to the southeast. Collins' VII Corps and Van Fleet's III Corps took on the burden of fighting in the bridgehead while Huebner's V Corps was held in reserve on the west bank of the Rhine. Ike and I were criticized then, and later, for moving too slowly and too cautiously. I do not believe the criticism is warranted. There was no need to rush. My closely held plan to break out of Remagen was tied directly to Patton's part in Undertone. We would not break out of Remagen until Patton had swept southeast to Mainz and crossed the Rhine, otherwise the First Army would have no flank support on the right and might go too far too fast and get chopped up for its pains. Moreover, it seemed more prudent to launch the Remagen breakout immediately after Plunder, when Hitler's attention was focused on the north.[12]

Much now depended on Patton. He launched his part of Undertone on March 13, with Walker's XX Corps, swollen to six divisions. A day later, Eddy's XII Corps, likewise swollen to six divisions, crossed the Moselle. Walker, close to the Siegfried Line, met initial heavy resistance; Eddy, farther north, met only light resistance. Eddy's forces—notably Hugh Gaffey's 4th Armored Division—made spectacular advances toward Worms and Mainz. By March 20, his troops were on the outskirts of both cities and the German defenses at the Siegfried Line were unhinged. Patton's chief of staff, Hobart Gay, aptly wrote in his diary: "It can be safely said that . . . [this] has been the greatest campaign of Third Army. . . . Students of military history will study this campaign for many years to come."

Patch, jumping off on March 15, commanded three corps comprising fourteen divisions. Wade Haislip's XV Corps, beefed up to six divisions, spearheaded the attack on the Siegfried Line. At first it was a bloody yard-by-yard fight. But as Patton's troops advanced behind the Siegfried Line, the Germans realized they were trapped and Albert Kesselring authorized a withdrawal. Thereafter, Patch's troops drove steadily north, through the Siegfried Line and Saar. Between them, Patton and Patch captured 90,000 Germans, but the withdrawal was conducted with exceptional skill, and all too many Germans slipped through and crossed the Rhine to safety.[13]

On March 18, I flew to Reims for a conference with Ike. Ike was beginning to sag badly from the weight of his responsibilities. He looked terrible—exhausted. Kay Summersby wrote: "Beetle [Bedell Smith] and I were very much worried. The General's physical and emotional condition was worse than we had ever known it. . . . Beetle was positive that he was on the verge of a nervous breakdown." Bedell Smith had insisted that Ike take some time off. He and Kay had arranged the use of a villa in Cannes, and Ike was leaving for there the following day. He insisted that I take a vacation with him. He could not have found a more receptive and willing subordinate; ever since Joe Collins returned from Cannes, I had been determined to go there for a brief rest.[14]

This was my first meeting with Ike since our lunch with Churchill and Alan Brooke on March 5. I took the opportunity to press for further enlargement of my right-hook offensive, now called "Voyage." Ike agreed that I could increase the Remagen bridgehead forces from five to ten divisions by bringing Huebner's V Corps across the river. Since Patton was then outstripping our rosiest estimates, I also received permission from Ike for Patton to cross the Rhine on the run near Mainz and continue north to link up with Hodges near Giessen, from which area both armies would advance on Kassel abreast. The one remaining uncertainty was the still-standing order to provide Monty with "not less than ten divisions" of the First Army for a reserve. Hodges clearly could no longer provide the reserve. Ike was reluctant to formally rescind this commitment to Monty lest he stir up a political storm. We agreed—vaguely—that if Monty called for the ten divisions we would take them not from Hodges' First Army, but "from the south"—meaning from Patton or Devers—more likely Devers. On March 21, Ike formalized our agreements with this order: "Operations Undertone and Voyage will be pushed vigorously with the object of establishing a firm bridgehead across the Rhine in the Frankfurt area from which an advance in strength can be made at a later date in the general direction of Kassel."[15]

After remaining overnight at Ike's headquarters, I sent word for Hodges and Patton to meet me at Patton's headquarters in Luxembourg that day—March 19. There we discussed final plans for Voyage. I told Hodges to bring Huebner across, increasing his force to ten divisions, to keep expanding the Remagen bridgehead so the Germans could not dig in, and to be prepared to break out from March 23 onward "on my order." Gee Gerow's diminutive Fifteenth Army (a mere six divisions), heretofore consigned to training duties, would move up to the west bank of the Rhine in the Cologne area to take over defensive (and occupational) responsibilities. I told Patton to keep driving and to cross the Rhine in the vicinity of Oppenheim "on the run" and head for Giessen, where he and Hodges would link up. I stressed to Patton the urgency of getting across the Rhine and up to Giessen at full speed. If he got held up at the Rhine, the ten divisions still technically in reserve for Monty could conceivably come from his army.[16]

That done, I went to Cannes the following day for my brief vacation. I found Ike, Bedell Smith, Kay Summersby and others in the SHAEF party, including two other WAC's, ensconced in a fabulous seaside villa, Sous le Vent, owned by an American and reputed to have cost more than three million dollars. Kay recalled in her book, *Past Forgetting,* that for the first two days Ike slept, waking up only to eat lunch on the terrace, that after forty-eight hours "he began to look somewhat human," and they worried less about the possibility of a nervous breakdown. I cooperated in the therapy by avoiding any serious discussions of the war and filling in at the bridge table. After forty-eight restful hours, and reassured that Ike was recovering nicely, I returned to my headquarters at Namur on March 22.[17]

The following morning, March 23, while I was at breakfast, Patton telephoned. "Brad, don't tell anyone but I'm across." I gulped and replied, "Well, I'll be damned. You mean across the Rhine?" He went on: "Sure am. I sneaked a division over last night. But there are so few Krauts around they don't know it yet. So don't make any announcement. We'll keep it a secret until we see how it goes." The division that got across—at Oppenheim—was one in Eddy's XII Corps, the 5th Infantry, commanded by S. LeRoy Irwin. Hugh Gaffey's 4th Armored Division was going over right behind it. In accordance with the Voyage plan, I authorized Patton to put ten divisions into the Oppenheim bridgehead.

Later that evening, when Patton was absolutely certain his foothold across the Rhine was firm, he telephoned again. "Brad," he shouted, his high-pitched voice full of triumph, "for God's sake tell the world we're across. . . . I want the world to know Third Army made it before Monty starts across." [18]

I knew from Ike that Marshall had recently expressed grave concern about the paucity of press coverage of the U.S. Army. In the American press, Marshall complained, there was an "overdose of Montgomery." In order to offset the focus on Monty and put the limelight on U.S. commanders, Marshall had urged various steps and had sent Ike a personal message for me, designed to be released to the press: "I am filled with admiration over your handling of the operations involved in the development of the Remagen bridgehead and the clearing of the Saar basin. I want General Hodges and General Patton and their corps and division commanders to know that their great military successes of the past few weeks have registered a high point in American military achievement." [19]

Upon receipt of Marshall's complaint and message to me on March 23, Ike telephoned and directed that I hold a press conference to emphasize American achievements. Marshall's timing could not have been better. Patton's troops had just crossed the Rhine at Oppenheim. Now both Hodges and Patton had crossed the river before Monty's grandiose Plunder, scheduled to go the following day. I was more than happy to hold a press conference—to steal some of Monty's thunder. I reviewed the Lumberjack and Undertone operations in considerable detail, then turned to the Remagen bridgehead, and finally I released the news of Patton's crossing at Oppenheim. I complimented Hodges and Patton and pointedly stated that American forces were capable of crossing the Rhine at practically any point without aerial bombardment and without airborne troops. In fact, I said, sticking the needle in Monty, Patton had jumped across without even so much as artillery preparation.[20]

All eyes now turned to Monty's Rhine crossing. Ike, much rested, flew from Cannes to Simpson's headquarters to be with the American troops. They went forward to Anderson's XVI Corps headquarters in Rheinberg to watch the assault. Churchill and Alan Brooke flew from

London to Monty's headquarters in Venlo to be with the British troops. They watched from positions in Dempsey's Second British Army area. I spent the day refining future plans for the encirclement of the Ruhr and the final destruction of Germany.[21]

Monty's mammoth crossing has been well described elsewhere and I shall not attempt to recreate it here. In sum, he crossed without exceptional difficulty and with the usual roar of publicity and fawning acclaim. The Germans opposing his British troops put up a stiff but brief fight and were soon disorganized and overrun. Farther south, Simpson crossed with consummate ease and few casualties, proving to my satisfaction that his earlier contention that the Ninth Army could have crossed on the run was correct. One item in the barrage of British publicity that day amused us. The BBC released a prerecorded Churchill speech praising the British for carrying out the "first assault crossing of the Rhine in modern history." Of course, that historic feat had already been carried out by both Hodges and Patton; in reality, Monty was third.[22]

Later that afternoon Ike left Simpson and flew to my headquarters at Namur. He had not slept the night before, but he was full of energy and optimism about the future. I brought Ike up to date on plans for Voyage. Both Hodges and Patton were poised to plunge. Ike gave his final approval. I relayed word to Hodges to launch his attack from the Remagen bridgehead on the following day, March 25, and told Patton to strike for Frankfurt.[23]

That same day Ike drafted and sent from my headquarters a historic message to the Combined Chiefs. The message, in effect, announced Voyage and repudiated the Malta agreements. The wording was deliberately low key and vague in the extreme. "The dash and daring in First and Third Army sectors have gotten us two bridgeheads very cheaply which can be consolidated and expanded rapidly to support a major thrust which will assist the northern operation and make our exploitation more effective. . . . There is already deployed in the north all the strength that can be effectively maintained east of the Rhine for the next few weeks and I am directing the most vigorous action on all fronts. I intend to reinforce every success with utmost speed."[24]

Churchill now wished to visit American troops. On the following day —as Hodges and Patton jumped off—Ike and I flew to Anderson's XVI Corps headquarters at Rheinberg for a ceremonial gathering with the Prime Minister, Monty, Simpson, Anderson and others. Churchill was ebullient. He said to Ike, "My dear general, the German is whipped. We've got him. He is all through." Churchill wanted to board a landing craft and cross the Rhine, but Simpson and Ike and I strongly disapproved.

Simpson recalled that after Ike and I left, Churchill turned to Monty and said, "I'm now in command. Let's go over." Monty responded, "Why not?" Churchill hailed a passing American landing craft. He, Monty,

Simpson, Anderson and others climbed aboard and went to the far shore of the Rhine, disembarked for a half-hour, then returned to the west bank. Simpson, who technically bore the responsibility for Churchill's safety, privately pleaded with Monty to "get him out of here."[25]

During this visit, Ike and Alan Brooke held a significant exchange. Alan Brooke at last gave his approval to our two-thrust strategy. As he recalled it, Ike wanted to know if Alan Brooke agreed with Ike's plans "of pushing in the south for Frankfurt and Kassel." Brooke recalled that he said, "I told him that, with the Germans crumbling as they are, the whole situation is now altered. Evidently the Boche is cracking and what we want now is to push him relentlessly, wherever we can, until he crumbles. In his present condition we certainly have the necessary strength for a double envelopment strategy, which I did not consider applicable when he was still in a position to resist seriously." In a letter the next day to Marshall, Ike took note of Alan Brooke's about-face, stating: "Yesterday I saw him on the banks of the Rhine and he was gracious enough to say that I was right and that my current plans and operations were well calculated to meet the current situation." Ike added: "I hope this does not sound boastful, but I must admit to a great satisfaction that the things Bradley and I believed in from the beginning and have carried out in the face of some opposition both from within and without, have matured so splendidly."[26]*

I was not privy to that brief but historic discussion, so I cannot shed light on who said what to whom. But the import was clear: Alan Brooke now approved Voyage and our two-thrust strategy. That put an end, once and for all, to the prospect of Monty leading a more massive thrust into Germany north of the Ruhr and incorporating the ten U.S. divisions still in technical reserve. In my eyes it was an immense concession. It opened the way for me to draw a wholly new plan for the final conquest of Germany in which American commanders and forces would play the leading roles. I was immensely pleased. The prolonged British domination of our continental strategy was coming to an end; henceforth Monty's role would sharply decline.

Voyage, my drive on Kassel, proceeded with extraordinary dash and success. With Collins' VII Corps and Van Fleet's III Corps in the van, Hodges' First Army broke out of the Remagen bridgehead and drove up

* In *Crusade in Europe,* published three years later, Ike recalled that what Brooke had said to him was: "Thank God, Ike, you stuck by your plan. You were completely right and I am sorry if my fear of dispersed effort added to your burdens. The German is now licked. It is merely a question of when he chooses to quit. Thank God you stuck by your guns." In *his* memoir, published fourteen years later, Alan Brooke wrote: "I am quite certain that I never said to him, 'You were completely right' as I am still convinced that he was 'completely wrong.' " To his death, Alan Brooke held to the belief that a single "full-blooded" thrust to Berlin would have ended the war much sooner.[27]

the Lahn Valley with breathtaking speed. Within three days, Rose's 3rd Armored Division blasted beyond Giessen to Marburg. Patton's forces, spearheaded by Eddy's XII Corps, broke out and reached Giessen on the same day, March 28, linking up the First and Third armies as planned. Walker's XX Corps came up fast to join Eddy, and the two corps drove onward toward Kassel with dazzling speed.[28]

One incident marred this brilliant display of American arms. Patton had learned from the U.S. Military Mission in Moscow that a group of American prisoners of war had recently been shifted from a camp in Poland to a camp in Hammelburg, fifty-five miles due east of Frankfurt. Patton wanted to send a small task force to liberate the prisoners, one of whom was his son-in-law, John K. Waters, who had served under me in the tactical department at West Point and who had been captured in Tunisia. Most of Patton's senior officers advised him against the mission. A force large enough to accomplish the job safely would divert too much of Patton's strength off on a tangent; the small task force he envisioned was too risky. He did not consult me. Had he done so I would have forbidden it. Overriding all advice, Patton ordered the mission. It was a disaster; the rescue party was virtually wiped out. (Waters, severely wounded in the rescue attempt, survived and was later liberated by other forces.) In the aftermath, Ike severely reprimanded Patton orally, but took no official action. In writing Marshall of the incident, Ike said, "Patton is a problem child, but he is a great fighting leader in pursuit and exploitation."[29]

FORTY-FOUR

The final plan for the conquest of Germany evolved in the hours following the meeting at Rheinberg between Churchill, Alan Brooke, Ike, Monty and me. In his memoirs, *On to Berlin,* Jim Gavin has labeled it the "Bradley Plan." While it is true that my contribution to the plan was substantial, it is not accurate to grant me sole authorship. The major features of the plan were jointly conceived by Ike and me, and accepted without major dissent by Hodges and Patton in a meeting with Ike and me at Remagen on March 26.[1]

The plan did not at all please the British. In the postwar years it would become the subject of intense controversy. In arriving at the plan, Ike and I had to consider a number of major military factors. Two of the most important were the following.

The Russians. On January 12, the Russians, who by then had advanced west to the Vistula River in the vicinity of Warsaw, launched an all-out offensive designed to take them some 300 miles farther west to the Oder River—and then forty miles beyond the Oder to Berlin. To mount this ambitious offensive, Stalin had amassed ten armies comprising some seventy divisions, supported by two air armies. A great many of the infantry brigades in the ten armies were motorized, equipped with lend-lease U.S. two-and-a-half-ton trucks. The terrain through Poland into Germany to the Oder was highly favorable for open, mobile warfare. The two principal Russian field commanders were Georgi K. Zhukov and Ivan S. Koniev.

The Russian offensive was awesome not only in its mass and scope but also in its effectiveness and speed of advance. In a mere six weeks—January 12 to February 24—the Russians swept almost unchecked to the Oder, and in the south, the Neisse. But here they were compelled to stop. The German front, running north-south along the Oder and Neisse rivers between the Baltic Sea and the mountains of Bohemia, had constricted to only two hundred miles in length. The Germans, believing we had been severely mauled by the Ardennes offensive, weakened their western front to strengthen their eastern front, concentrating heavily along that two hundred miles. They had orders from Hitler to fight to the last man. An unseasonal thaw melted the Oder and Neisse, making the river fronts easier for the Germans to defend. The same thaw turned the already greatly overextended Russian supply roads to quagmire. Even so, Zhukov's forces in the center forced a Remagen-like bridgehead across the Oder and pushed to within thirty-five miles of Berlin. But the Russians could go no farther.[2]

Owing to this remarkable military achievement by the Russians, the capture of Berlin, a secondary objective after the Ruhr, now seemed, from a strictly military point of view, not only far less desirable, but probably impossible. As we pressed on into the heart of Germany, it seemed inevitable that we would relieve the pressure on the Russian bridgehead on the Oder, unhinging the German defenses. Zhukov had but a mere thirty-five miles to go to take Berlin. He commanded a force of 768,000 men. On his left flank, Koniev commanded another 432,000. Barring an unlikely Russian reverse, Berlin would be in Russian hands long before we got there. Moreover, a move toward Berlin would require that we concentrate heavy forces in the north for a power crossing of the Elbe River, which lay between our forces and Berlin. This could only be carried out at the expense of Hodges and Patton farther south; as we moved beyond the Rhine into Germany, logistics would again be controlling. To immobilize most of our front for a power crossing of the Elbe and a run to Berlin, which would in all likelihood already be in Russian hands, seemed unwise or, as Ike later put it, "stupid." Even in the unlikely event the Russians failed to take Berlin, it would be no easy job for us. The terrain between the Elbe and Berlin is not ideal for mobile warfare. Hitler had deployed a fresh new army, the Twelfth, on our front. I estimated that a run from the Elbe and the fight for Berlin itself would cost us 100,000 casualties and advised Ike that this was "a pretty stiff price to pay for a prestige objective."[3]

At this time there was another important military consideration with respect to the Russian forces. At some point in the near future we would meet head-on. How was this juncture to be carried out? If we did not have an absolutely foolproof plan, there was the real possibility of a disastrous collision of our armies and more men killed by friendly fire. All sorts of plans to effect a safe meeting had been submitted to me, but they depended on radio and visual signals that could be misinterpreted or confused by the formidable language barrier. I insisted on a clear-cut line of demarcation, such as a large unmistakable north-south river that neither side would cross. Even though it lay 220 miles east of the Rhine, and seemed hopelessly far away at the time, I chose the Elbe as the best halting point for my armies.[4] *

Finally there was the matter of zones of occupation. It had been decided by various Allied authorities that, after the victory, occupied Germany would be split into four zones, each of these administered by one of the Allied powers: the United States, Russia, Britain and France. The Russian zone would encompass eastern Germany to a point about ninety miles west of the Elbe. Berlin, which was to be divided into four sectors administered individually by the four powers, lay well *within* the Russian occupation zone. It seemed cruel and absurd to me to spend American lives or incur injuries to capture German territory which we would then turn back to the Russians. I believed that if we could reach the Elbe, that was help enough for the Russians.[5]

The Redoubts. For some time a group within the Allied command, influenced in part by OSS reports from Switzerland and Washington and to a lesser extent by cryptic Ultra fragments and other vague intelligence reports, had held the view that as the end of the war drew near Hitler and his Nazi government, together with a large force of loyal SS troops, would retreat to a "redoubt" in the Austrian Alps for a final suicidal stand. Hitler's edenic retreat, Berchtesgaden, would serve as the command post. As time progressed, this belief took such firm hold in the minds of its adherents that it became gospel. All other evidence to the contrary was discounted, even in the face of highly skeptical or ambivalent intelligence estimates from SHAEF on down.

Both Ike and I were early converts to the "redoubt" gospel. On March 9, Chet Hansen logged in his diary: "Bradley believes, and is convinced, that we shall have to fight the Germans in the mountain fastness of Southern Germany and there destroy the core of the SS units which are determined to carry on the battle." If we did not head off the retreat to the redoubt, I could foresee a difficult struggle, rooting fanatical suicide troops out of strongly fortified positions, with heavy casualties to our side. The war might drag on for months. If so, it would significantly delay the transfer of American forces from Europe to the Pacific for the final defeat of Japan, prolonging that conflict as well. Conceivably, Hitler and the Nazi government might elude us forever, bringing the war in Europe to a murky end with no formal surrender, perhaps leaving cadres of Nazis to rise again.

Concern over the Alpine redoubt had a decisive impact on my thinking and planning. My concern intensified in mid to late March, when Ultra indicated that certain German military headquarters were moving from the

* We used the term "Elbe" loosely. In the center of our projected line, the Elbe runs south-north. However, at Dessau, the Elbe flows west-east before turning north. For this reason, our line of demarcation below Dessau would be the Mulde, which flows south-north to the Elbe. On a map, the Mulde appears to be a south-north leg of the Elbe.

Berlin area to the Bavarian Alps, and certain German ministries to the Erfurt-Leipzig region. It now seemed imperative to me that we drive east through the center of Germany with all possible power and speed to link up with the Russians, splitting Germany and thus preventing a further migration of German military and civilian agencies to the southern Alpine areas. I believed we should also direct forces to the southeast to seize the Alpine passes and Berchtesgaden.

Coupled with the concern over the southern redoubt was a growing concern over the possibility of a northern redoubt. The Germans still maintained sizable forces in Norway. There was no indication that Hitler intended to abandon Norway and bring those forces home to defend Germany. This led to a belief in some Allied quarters that Norway, too, had been earmarked as a redoubt; that when the end drew near, Hitler would order German forces in Holland and northern Germany to retreat through Denmark—and Sweden—to Norway, there to fight to the last man. Rooting fanatical German troops from the mountain fastnesses of Norway would be no less difficult and costly than rooting them from the Austrian Alps. It might ultimately require another amphibious assault. Ike and I therefore deemed it imperative that Denmark be "sealed off" at the Kiel Canal, which forms the border between Germany and Denmark, at the earliest possible date.[6]

So Ike and I, in drawing our final plan, were far more preoccupied with military objectives than political or prestige objectives, such as Berlin. Our principal military objective was the complete and utter destruction of the German armed forces. From a strictly military point of view, our plan, at the time, appeared to be the quickest and cheapest way to achieve our assigned mission in the ETO and redeploy forces earmarked for the war against Japan. I still think so.

The final plan itself was as follows: First, we would complete the encirclement and destruction of German forces in the Ruhr. This would be achieved by swinging Simpson's Ninth Army south and Hodges' First Army north in a giant pincer movement designed to link up in the Paderborn-Kassel area. Some units of Simpson's and Hodges' armies would be detailed to mop up the Ruhr; others would be detailed from Gerow's Fifteenth Army, which would be brought across the Rhine. Second, with as little delay as possible, I would form up (north to south) the Ninth, First and Third armies in the Kassel area for a massive all-out drive through the center of Germany toward the Leipzig-Dresden area, halting at the Elbe River, face to face with the Russians. For this purpose, Simpson's Ninth Army would revert to my command immediately after Simpson and Hodges linked up at Paderborn. Monty's remaining forces (British Second Army, Canadian First Army) would protect my left, or northern, flank, driving toward a northern crossing of the Elbe and a dash to the border of

Denmark. Devers' Sixth Army Group would protect my right flank, meanwhile making plans for a southeasterly drive toward Austria.[7]

This plan put the American forces at center stage and reduced Monty to a supporting role in the north on a par with Devers' supporting role in the south. We knew very well that neither London nor Monty would like it, that for prestige and political reasons the British would howl to high heaven and insist on a thrust at Berlin. But Ike believed he had fulfilled our obligations to the British, agreed to at Malta, by his all-out support of Monty's Rhine crossing. Operations beyond the Rhine had not been specified in detail. This time we had drawn a plan based not on nationalistic considerations but on strictly military grounds. And this time Ike intended to hold to it no matter how strenuously the British opposed it.[8]

As it happened, on March 27, when we were putting the final touches on the plan, Ike received a cable from Marshall which indicated generally that all of us saw eye to eye on the question of where to put the main push. Marshall made no mention of Berlin whatsoever. He suggested Ike might want to consider pushing heavy columns eastward on a broad front on either a Nuremberg-Linz or Karlsruhe-Munich axis. This was a more southeasterly drive than we contemplated and probably reflected Marshall's concern over the redoubt rumors, but it was assurance to Ike that Marshall would approve of our general plan. Ike replied: "My views agree closely with your own, although I think the Leipzig-Dresden area is of primary importance. Besides offering the shortest route to present Russian positions, it would divide the German forces roughly in half and would overrun the one remaining industrial area in Germany to which also the high command headquarters and ministries are reported to be moving." To deny the Germans an Alpine redoubt, Ike told Marshall, he would make a drive on Linz and Munich "as soon as circumstances allow."

I gave orders for launching the first phase of the plan—the encirclement of the Ruhr—on the morning of March 28. By that time, Joe Collins' VII Corps was in Marburg and Van Fleet's III Corps was coming up on his right flank. I told Hodges to swing Collins north and go all-out for Paderborn. Rose's 3rd Armored Division led this drive, one of the most electrifying of the war. In one day Rose covered ninety miles, the longest gain on any single day of the war, exceeding even Patton's longest drive. Paderborn was a German tank training center. The instructors and students gave Rose's men a brief tough fight, but by April 1, Paderborn was ours. However, the stunning victory was marred by tragedy: Rose, one of our ablest armored division commanders, was killed in action.[9]

On the day I turned Hodges north on Paderborn, March 28, Ike received a message from Monty outlining his forthcoming plans. Monty would "drive hard for the line of the Elbe" at "utmost speed" with Dempsey's and Simpson's armor in the van. At the same time, Monty told Alan

Brooke that he hoped to take the autobahn to Berlin! Ike elected to unveil our new plans to Monty in a reply to Monty's message. Ike wrote: "As soon as you have joined hands with Bradley in the Kassel-Paderborn area, Ninth U.S. Army will revert to Bradley's command. Bradley will be responsible for mopping up and occupying the Ruhr and with the minimum delay will deliver the main thrust on the axis Erfurt-Leipzig-Dresden to join hands with the Russians. The mission of your Army Group will be to protect Bradley's northern flank. . . . Devers will protect Bradley's right flank and be prepared later when the situation permits to advance to join hands with the Russians in the Danube Valley."[10]

On that same day, Ike, now believing it imperative that he be fully apprised of Stalin's military plans, so that we could arrange the joining of hands, sent a personal message to Stalin through our military mission in Moscow, outlining our new strategy and requesting information on Russian plans. He told Stalin that after we had destroyed enemy forces in the Ruhr, we would make our "main effort" in a drive to Erfurt-Leipzig-Dresden, "the area to which the main German governmental departments are being moved," with a secondary advance on the Regensburg-Linz area, "thereby preventing the consolidation of German resistance in a redoubt in Southern Germany." Ike sent copies of this message to the Combined Chiefs of Staff. This was his first official notification to that body of our new strategy.[11]

The new strategy evoked the anticipated howls from London. Under Alan Brooke's guidance, the British Chiefs composed a cable to Marshall first criticizing Ike for communicating directly with Stalin, then faulting his strategy militarily because it downgraded the need to capture German seaports in the north. When he read the cable, Churchill criticized the military objections as exaggerations or irrelevancies and lifted the British dissent to a higher plane. As Churchill saw it, the main flaws were two: Ike's new plan might condemn Monty's Twenty-first Army Group "to an almost static role in the north" and Ike's supposition that Berlin was largely devoid of military and political importance "may be wrong." He expanded: "The idea of neglecting Berlin and leaving it to the Russians to take at a later stage does not appear to me to be correct. As long as Berlin holds out and withstands a siege in the ruins, as it may easily do, German resistance will be stimulated. The fall of Berlin might cause nearly all Germans to despair."[12]

Beyond that, Churchill was deeply concerned about the geopolitics of postwar Europe. He had never really trusted Stalin. Events since his meeting with Stalin at Yalta had revived the distrust. The Big Three had agreed that liberated European countries would be guaranteed free elections. The Russians had already violated that agreement in Rumania, where a communist puppet regime had been imposed under the guns of the Red Army. There were indications that Stalin was imposing another puppet regime in

Poland, in specific violation of a Yalta agreement to form a temporary coalition government. On March 27, Churchill had cabled Roosevelt, "I am extremely concerned at the deterioration of the Russian attitude since Yalta." Churchill believed that wherever the opportunity existed to limit Soviet advances in Europe it should be taken. On April 1, he cabled Roosevelt again: "The Russian Armies will no doubt overrun all Austria and enter Vienna. If they also take Berlin will not their impression that they have been the overwhelming contributor to our common victory be unduly imprinted in their minds, and may this not lead them into a mood which will raise grave and formidable difficulties in the future?" He urged that "should Berlin be in our grasp we should certainly take it."[13]

The controversy boiled along for a full week. Ike stuck by his guns. As to our decision to leave Berlin to the Russians, Ike expressed himself in no uncertain terms. To Marshall he wrote: "Berlin itself is no longer a particularly important objective. Its usefulness to the Germans has been largely destroyed." To Monty he wrote: "[Berlin] has become, so far as I am concerned, nothing but a geographical location and I have never been interested in these." To the Combined Chiefs he wrote: "Berlin as a strategic area is discounted as it is now largely destroyed and we have information that the ministries are moving to the Erfurt-Leipzig region."[14]

In tactful, patient, but firm letters to Churchill, Monty, Marshall and the Combined Chiefs, Ike explained in detail the reasons for reassigning the Ninth Army to me and making the drive in the center on Leipzig. He reassured the British that he was not neglecting Monty and the north; that it was most vital that Monty not only seize the northern German ports but also cross the lower Elbe, take Lübeck and seal off Denmark at the Kiel Canal. To assist in that effort, Ike even offered to give Monty "an American formation" again "once the success of the main thrust is assured." He told Churchill that he was "disturbed, if not hurt" that Churchill would think he had deliberately relegated Monty to a lesser role for any reasons other than strategic.

Ike emerged from the controversy a clear winner. Marshall backed him to the hilt, as did Roosevelt in a letter to Churchill on April 4. The British backed down and the issue was closed. Ike proceeded with our plan exactly as we had designed it.[15]

After Simpson crossed the Rhine at Wesel, his bridgehead, in the words of the Ninth Army official historian, "was not expanding with outstanding rapidity." One important reason was that by Monty's order Dempsey's Second British Army had been given priority on the bridges, most of them built by U.S. engineers. Dempsey was allotted use of the bridges nineteen hours a day; Simpson a mere five hours a day. Owing to this restriction, not until March 31, a full week after the assault crossing, did Simpson get his full army across the Rhine.[16]

Simpson coiled his army into the bridgehead—then sprang. Ray

McLain's XIX Corps led the breakout, with Isaac D. White's 2nd Armored Division in the van. White drove due east, along the north bank of the Lippe River toward Padenborn, where Joe Collins had been consolidating his positions for several days. At Lippstadt, White angled southeastward. On Easter Sunday, April 1, at 4:00 P.M., White's advance units linked up with elements of Collins' 3rd Armored Division. The pincers were closed; the Ruhr was now encircled, however thinly.[17]

As planned, two days later, at one minute past midnight April 4, Ike ordered Simpson's Ninth Army to revert to my Twelfth Army Group. This was a happy day for me. The four U.S. armies under my command then comprised twelve corps of forty-eight divisions numbering 1.3 million men, by far the largest ground force commanded by any U.S. or British general in World War II, or any general in U.S. history. Because there was no longer need for me to maintain a close physical relationship with Monty, I moved my tactical headquarters from Namur back to Luxembourg, temporarily, then forward to Wiesbaden, Germany.[18]

My most pressing task was to mop up the Ruhr. Intelligence estimated that some 150,000 Germans, commanded by Walther Model, were encircled. I ordered Simpson and Hodges to assign three heavily reinforced corps to the mopping up: Ridgway's XVIII Airborne, Anderson's XVI and Van Fleet's III. In the meantime, my remaining forces prepared to drive east to the Elbe and Mulde. Fortunately, almost all the German forces inside the Ruhr pocket surrendered without a fight. The total bag by April 18 was double the intelligence estimate: 317,000. This was a larger German force than the Russians had captured at Stalingrad or than we had captured in Tunisia. One man did not surrender: Walther Model. When he saw that he was utterly defeated, he walked into a forest and shot himself. Matt Ridgway presented me with a souvenir: Model's giant Mercedes-Benz staff car.[19]

We lost not an hour in gearing up for the last main eastward offensive, the 120-mile drive from Kassel to the Elbe. I deployed the Ninth, First and Third armies on a 140-mile north-south line. There were seven corps: Gillem's XIII and McLain's XIX of the Ninth Army; Collins' VII and Huebner's V of the First Army; Walker's XX, Middleton's VIII and Eddy's XII of the Third Army. The starring role in the offense was assigned to Hodges, whose objective was Leipzig and twelve miles beyond to the Mulde River. Simpson had orders to move to the Elbe, seize a bridgehead across it and "be prepared to continue the advance on Berlin or to the northeast." I doubted that Ike would approve going to Berlin. However, in case he changed his mind the bridgehead would provide a springboard. Simpson interpreted my orders broadly and optimistically set his staff to work on plans for an advance on Berlin—just in case. Patton's objective was the Mulde in the area of Chemnitz.

The offensive was scheduled to jump off on or about April 14, when I was confident the Ruhr pocket would no longer present a threat to our rear. Here, however, I took another calculated risk. Long before the Ruhr pocket was eliminated, I launched the offensive, with many units simply moving on eastward without pause or a formal jump-off. By April 6 or 7, most of the corps designated for the attack were on the way. From time to time I halted one corps or the other to maintain some semblance of armies marching abreast, but for the most part I let them run free. Generally, resistance was light and progress phenomenal, but a few units encountered daunting groups of Germans who seemed determined to fight to the death. One group of about 70,000 Germans, burrowed in the Harz Mountains in Joe Collins' VII Corps sector, held out for a full week before surrendering under pressure. By April 12 or 13, advance elements in all three armies had reached the Elbe and/or the Mulde.

Simpson's Ninth Army, spearheaded by McLain's XIX Corps, turned in another magnificent performance. White's 2nd Armored Division troops were first to reach the Elbe—at about 8:00 P.M. on April 11, at Schönebeck, south of Magdeburg. The next day troops of Gillem's XIII Corps reached the Elbe at Wittenberg and Tangermunde, a mere fifty-three miles from Berlin. Only nineteen days had passed since Simpson first crossed the Rhine. His Ninth Army traveled 226 miles in that time. "It was truly 'the blitzkrieg in reverse,' " wrote the Ninth Army historian. "The only thing that moved faster than the Ninth Army in those nineteen days were a few fleeing remnants of the broken, battered and beaten German Army."

Simpson was still under orders from me to seize a bridgehead across the Elbe. White's 2nd Armored Division troops crossed the Elbe on April 12, and promptly ran into fierce resistance. The next day, elements of the 30th Infantry Division crossed the Elbe to reinforce the besieged bridgehead. That same day, spearhead units of the 83rd Infantry Division crossed the Elbe a few miles farther south, at Barby. Heavy German pressure on the 2nd Armored Division bridgehead compelled McLain to abandon it (with light losses) and withdraw to the west bank of the Elbe, but the 83rd Division's bridgehead at Barby held firmly and they expanded against strong opposition.[20]

In the advance from Kassel to the Elbe, my forces in the center and the south came upon the first shocking evidence of Nazi atrocities. In the center, Joe Collins' VII Corps troops found a slave labor camp near Nordhausen. In the south, troops found a similar camp at Ohrdruf. The slaves at Nordhausen had been employed in a nearby underground V-weapons factory; those at Ohrdruf in a neighboring munitions factory.

The Americans who first saw these camps were stunned, horrified and sickened. An Army medic who visited the Nordhausen camp wrote:

> Rows upon rows of skin-covered skeletons met our eyes. Men lay as they had starved, discolored, and lying in indescribable human filth. Their striped coats and prison numbers hung to their frames as a last token or symbol of

> those who enslaved and killed them. . . . One girl in particular I noticed: I would say she was about seventeen years old. She lay there where she had fallen, gangrened and naked. In my own thoughts I choked up—couldn't quite understand how and why war could do these things. . . . We went downstairs to a filth indescribable, accompanied by a horrible dead-rat stench. There in beds of crude wood I saw men too weak to move dead comrades from their side. One hunched-down French boy was huddled up against a dead comrade, as if to keep warm. . . . There were others, in dark cellar rooms, lying in disease and filth, being eaten away by diarrhea and malnutrition. It was like stepping into the Dark Ages to walk into one of these cellar-cells and seek out the living.

To add to the horror at the Nordhausen camp, Allied bombers had recently—and unknowingly—bombed some of the buildings where the slaves were held. Joe Collins recalled:

> The one building . . . I entered, which had not been hit by bombs, was a scene of utter horror. Hundreds of men in their striped prison uniforms were scattered about on the damp, dirt floor, the dead and dying intermingled in the straw, the only cover afforded them. As we looked in with a medical officer to weigh the problem that confronted us, wails and piteous pleas for food came from the living, while the stench of the dead filled the air.

As Collins wrote later, his troops found "almost three thousand" bodies in the buildings, "most of whom had died of starvation or disease prior to the bombings." About 650 persons were still alive, but "scores of them" died in spite of immediate and intense medical assistance. Scarcely able to contain his outrage, Collins ordered that the so-called "best people" of the town carry the emaciated bodies, one by one, to a burial plot overlooking the town. There they were interred with proper services.[21]

FORTY-FIVE

Having reached the Elbe, we were now ready to begin the second phase of our plan, which was to block the Germans from moving to the redoubts in the Alps and Norway. Ike flew to my headquarters at Wiesbaden on April 11 to finalize these plans. Hodges joined the discussions, which were to be continued on the following day at Patton's headquarters.

The big problem now was Monty. Having amassed some twenty British and Canadian divisions and 1,500 tanks into his Rhine bridgehead, Monty struck to the northeast on a line Wesel-Hamburg. But, contrary to his vow to drive to the Elbe with "utmost speed," he was moving at turtlelike pace. Horrocks put it this way: "Slowly—too slowly for my liking—we penetrated deeper into Germany." By April 11, when Simpson's spearheads reached the Elbe, Dempsey's advanced units had only reached Celle, sixty miles short of the Elbe. Monty, who was upset over losing the Ninth Army, no longer seemed to have a sense of urgency about his mission.[1]

Early on, we had perceived his lack of enthusiasm. On March 28, to spur Monty, Ike had volunteered to return Simpson's Ninth Army to Monty's operational control to "facilitate" his crossing of the lower Elbe and his strike toward Lübeck and the Danish border. But Monty did not now appear to want our help. On March 31, Ike again volunteered "an American formation" to assist Monty and tactfully prodded him: "Manifestly, when the time comes, we must do everything possible to push across the Elbe without delay, drive to the coast at Lübeck and seal off the Danish peninsula." On April 6, Ike set off for Monty's CP to see him face to face, but bad weather forced a cancellation of the meeting. On April 8, Ike sent Monty another prodding letter and two days later, April 10, asked me to fly up to see Monty to find out how we could get him moving.[2]

Monty, Dempsey, Simpson and I had a luncheon meeting that day. Monty was in a curious, diffident mood. He believed the decision to leave Berlin to the Russians and drive on Leipzig was a "terrible mistake." He thought that when he reached Lübeck, it would be "comparatively easy" for him to pivot southeast and come on Berlin from an unexpected direction. I believed he viewed his primary mission of sealing off the Danish border as demeaning. I made it clear that Ike had ruled out Berlin and asked Monty how we might assist him in his primary mission. I relieved him of all responsibility for protecting the Twelfth Army Group's northern flank and offered him Simpson's Ninth Army to help him cross the Elbe. But Monty proudly refused any U.S. troops or logistical support. If I would move Simpson's Elbe front slightly north, relieving Monty of some responsibilities there, he could get the job done. I readily agreed to that and departed with the feeling that Monty, denied the glory of taking Berlin, had lost all heart for the fight.[3]

In my meeting with Ike and Hodges at Wiesbaden on April 11, I conveyed my impressions of Monty's state of mind and his refusal to accept any help from us other than the boundary line shift. At the same time, I expressed strong doubt that Monty could carry out his Lübeck mission without our virtually forcing U.S. troops on him. This gave rise to the idea of placing a U.S. corps on standby to come to Monty's aid—when Monty would finally see that he needed it. For this purpose, we designated Matt Ridgway's XVIII Airborne Corps, which was then winding up the Ruhr operation. No one could build a fire under Monty better than Ridgway. Several days later, Ike tactfully notified Monty that he had "a very small SHAEF" reserve available "in case you run into some unanticipated need." But Monty still equivocated, making elaborate plans for his Elbe crossing.[4]

Berlin once again intruded into our discussions. By April 11, the Russians had not yet launched their expected offensive on the city. Simpson had a bridgehead over the Elbe at Barby, sixty miles southwest of Berlin. Farther north at Tangermunde, fifty-three miles due west of Berlin, a bridgehead seemed easily obtainable. Simpson's Ninth Army then mustered a total force of three corps of thirteen divisions, comprising 330,000 men. Two of his corps, McLain's XIX and Gillem's XIII, were at the Elbe. The third, Anderson's XVI, assigned to the Ruhr mop-up, was no longer required there and could quickly be brought to the Elbe as reserve. Simpson was absolutely convinced that he could launch McLain's and Gillem's corps at Berlin on April 15, that McLain could reach the outskirts of the city by nightfall April 17, and Gillem by noon April 18, at the latest. And was he raring to go![5]

It was tempting—very tempting. It required the utmost restraint on my part not to urge it simply for the glory and prestige it would bring Simpson and, by extension, the U.S. Army. But militarily it still did not seem prudent. Simpson had just dashed 226 miles from the Rhine. While he insisted that his logistics would permit a further run to Berlin, I wondered. A dash yes, but what happened when he met the fresh German Twelfth Army, with its panzer division? As yet we had no gasoline pipeline to the Elbe or even a Red Ball Express. Everyone had squandered gasoline in the dash to the Elbe. His Elbe bridging would be minimal, barely enough to get his three corps across in a hurry, let alone gasoline and ammo sufficient for a heavy fight. Moreover, I still believed that we would suffer 100,000 casualties. Even so, I kept Simpson primed until the last minute.

Ike made the final decision on Berlin. We would leave Berlin to the Russians. Only in the remote event they failed to move on Berlin would we go, and only if, in our judgment, German resistance would be "light."[6]

We next turned our attention to the south and our plans to deny Hitler the Alpine redoubt. I had originally hoped to launch Hodges' First Army on that mission, but by this time Patton's Third Army had drawn up to the Mulde. If we sent Hodges southeast, he would have to cross in front of Patton's army, a needlessly complex maneuver. We made the decision to send Patton southeast, toward Linz and the Danube River. Devers would protect Patton's right flank, attacking southeast through Nuremberg and Munich.[7]

On the following day, April 12, Ike and I flew to Patton's headquarters at Herzfeld to assign and discuss his new mission. For several reasons, it was a day I would never forget.

Two helpful German women had led troops of VIII Corps to an astonishing Nazi treasure in a deep salt mine south of Gotha near Merkers. Here troops found $250 million in gold ingots and coins together with a great amount of gold and silver plate and art treasures which had been looted from museums and private homes in Nazi-occupied countries. Patton took us to the mine. Ike and I descended two thousand feet into the earth on an elevator to inspect the hoard, an awesome sight. Patton joked that we should keep it secret and in the peacetime years ahead, when the Army was cut back to bare bones, we could take a little bit out each year to pay our soldiers and buy weapons. I would have good reason to recall that joke in a few years.[8]

Patton had another exhibit of a far different kind. He escorted us to the slave labor camp at Ohrdruf. Of that visit I wrote:

> The smell of death overwhelmed us even before we passed through the stockade. More than 3,200 naked, emaciated bodies had been flung into shallow graves. Others lay in the streets where they had fallen. Lice crawled over the yellow skin of their sharp, bony frames. A guard showed us how the blood had congealed in coarse black scabs where the starving prisoners had torn out the entrails of the dead for food. . . . I was too revolted to speak. For here death had been so fouled by degradation that it both stunned and numbed us.

Ohrdruf and Nordhausen were merely the beginning of the horror story. Within the following week our forces overran camps where we found equal or greater depravity and bestiality—Belsen, Buchenwald, Dachau and elsewhere. I need hardly add that what was discovered at those places shocked the world. I hope the world will never forget.[9]

That evening we discussed our final strategy. Inevitably the matter of taking Berlin arose. Well knowing that Patton, like Monty, was thirsting to lead his army to Berlin and had often boasted publicly that he would do so, Ike attempted to persuade Patton that Berlin had "no tactical or strategic value." He might as well have been talking to the wall. Patton distrusted the Russians as much as or more than Churchill. With utmost restraint Patton rejoined: "Ike, I don't see how you figure that one. We had better take Berlin and quick and [then go eastward] to the Oder [River]."[10]

We talked late into the evening and finally went to bed at midnight, Patton to his trailer, Ike and I to a house Patton had commandeered. Patton turned on his radio, which was set on the BBC frequency, to get the correct time. An announcer was broadcasting a shocking bulletin: President Roosevelt had died. Patton immediately came to the house, told me the news and then together we went to Ike's room.

The three of us were saddened and depressed. We talked for nearly two hours. It seemed an irreplaceable loss. I was distressed by this cruel turn that denied Roosevelt the satisfaction of seeing this great war to the finish. We were concerned about Roosevelt's successor, Harry S. Truman. He had had no experience in dealing with Churchill and Stalin. None of us knew Truman or much about him. He came from my home state, Missouri, but I had to confess almost complete ignorance. I knew only that he had served in the Army in World War I and had risen to political prominence through the ranks of what I regarded as a somewhat unsavory political machine in Kansas City, Missouri. From our distance, Truman did not appear at all qualified to fill Roosevelt's large shoes. Patton wrote: "It seems very unfortunate that in order to secure political preference, people are made Vice President who were never intended, neither by Party nor by The Lord to be Presidents."[11]

At this uneasy time, it was most reassuring to know that George Marshall was on hand in Washington to help guide Truman in his new responsibility. The grand strategy for the windup of the war in Europe and the final defeat of Japan in the Pacific had already been set. It had its own logic and momentum. Marshall was one of the chief architects of that strategy and could be relied on to see the war to its conclusion.

One of Truman's first official acts earned him gratitude within the ETO high command. Under pressure from Ike, Marshall had decided to recommend promotion of Hodges and Patton to four-star general. This, in turn, opened the way to promote several corps commanders to three-star general. Without hesitation, Truman approved Marshall's recommendations and sent the list to the Senate. Hodges and Patton were promoted in mid-April; the corps commanders—Walker, Haislip, Collins, Gillem and Middleton—shortly afterwards.[12]

Following our conferences with Hodges and Patton, Ike issued orders for the final campaigns on April 15. In the north, Monty would continue his advance to the Elbe, cross it and strike for a line Kiel-Lübeck. In the center, I would hold the First and Ninth armies on the Elbe and Mulde. I was to retain our bridgeheads but go no farther without specific orders. In the south, I would launch Patton on a "powerful thrust" to link with the Russians in the Danube Valley and Salzburg. Devers would also attack southeastward to protect Patton's right flank. The order to hold on the Elbe dismayed Simpson and forever after he argued—unrealistically in my opinion—that he could have taken Berlin with ease.[13]

On the very next day, April 16, the Russians commenced the assault on Berlin. Zhukov broke out of the Oder bridgehead; Koniev forced a crossing of the Neisse. The two army groups converged on the city, encircled and isolated it, then closed toward the center, yard by yard, supported by thunderous artillery which reduced the city to a pile of rubble. By this time, most of the Nazi ministerial staffs had fled to the south. Hitler intended to leave his Berlin bunker on his fifty-sixth birthday, April 20, and carry on the fight from Berchtesgaden. On April 24, as though he were reading our minds, he issued orders that an inner fortress be established in the Alps as a last bulwark of fanatical resistance, and he included a long list of specific instructions to insure it was done. But it was too late and too complicated to do it then, and no German general could take the order seriously. Hitler then decided that "as a soldier" he must obey his own command and defend Berlin to the last. On the afternoon of April 30, when Russian troops reached the Tiergarten, Hitler and Eva Braun committed suicide—Braun by taking poison, Hitler by firing a Walther pistol into his mouth. Cornelius Ryan in his book *The Last Battle* estimated that 100,000 Russians died in taking Berlin. The British military historian John Keegon estimates that the Russians suffered 200,000 casualties—twice my estimate at the time.[14]

My attention focused on Patton's Danube offensive, which was to be the last great U.S. Army effort in the war. I made two major changes in the composition of his corps and corps commanders. Ever since Sicily, Troy Middleton had been suffering severely from arthritis in his left knee. Army doctors had advised him against further field service, but Marshall and Ike had persuaded him to take VIII Corps. ("I would rather have a man with arthritis in the knee than one with arthritis in the head," Marshall quipped.) Middleton still suffered great pain and had told me he intended to retire from the Army as soon as possible. He planned to return to an important job at Louisiana State University in Baton Rouge, where the climate was relatively warm. To spare Middleton further discomfort and to give Jim Van Fleet, who clearly had a promising future in the postwar Army, greater command experience and exposure, I switched Middleton's VIII Corps to Hodges' First Army and sent Van Fleet and his III Corps from the Ruhr mop-up to Patton. Manton Eddy, who suffered from high blood pressure, had a heart attack and was returned to the States for medical care. LeRoy (Red) Irwin, the outstanding commander of the 5th Armored Division of Eddy's XII Corps, was promoted to take his place.[15]

Patton, resplendent in four-star insignia, jumped off piecemeal on April 19. His army, composed of three corps—Walker's XX, Van Fleet's III, Irwin's XII—had been beefed up to fifteen divisions. Over the next week, it sped southeast with ease. By April 26, all three corps had reached the Danube. Irwin's XII Corps remained on the north side of the river. Walker and Van Fleet crossed to the south bank and drove toward Linz and Salzburg, respectively.[16]

On Patton's right flank, Devers' Sixth Army Group—Patch's Seventh Army and the French First Army—attacked southeastward through Nuremberg toward the Austrian border. Patch commanded three corps of ten divisions. He had a stiff fight in Nuremberg, the shrine of Hitler's National Socialist Party, but it fell, ironically, on April 20, Hitler's birthday. Haislip's XV Corps drove on Munich. Among his divisions was the new 20th Armored, commanded by Orlando Ward, whom I had reluctantly relieved on Patton's orders in Tunisia. South of Munich, Haislip's troops uncovered one of the most notorious of the concentration camps, Dachau. Amid great piles of grotesque starved cadavers, our medics found 30,000 prisoners clinging precariously to life. On Patch's right, de Tassigny's French First Army, often in violation of orders and going its own way, broke out of the Black Forest and drove through Stuttgart to the Swiss and Austrian borders.

Inasmuch as Patch's forces had a shorter distance to travel, they were first to reach the Austrian border to the west of Salzburg. To keep up the momentum, we hastily altered army boundaries to permit Haislip's XV Corps, rather than Van Fleet's III Corps, to capture Salzburg and Hitler's hideaway nearby at Berchtesgaden. At the latter place, Haislip had to compete with elements of Frank W. Milburn's XXI Corps for the honors in capturing the last shrine of Nazism in the assigned U.S. zone of occupation. A few days later, Mark Clark's Fifteenth Army Group forces driving from Italy linked up at the Brenner Pass.[17]

We soon discovered, to our chagrin, that the Alpine redoubt was a myth. With the benefit of hindsight, some historians and military analysts have chastised us for pursuing it. They argue that our preoccupation with the redoubt led us to turn away from Berlin and leave that prestigious objective to the Russians. While it is certainly true that the redoubt weighed heavily in my decision to strike due east toward Leipzig for an early link-up with the Russians in order to split the German forces and close off a southerly retreat to the redoubt, that strategy did not per se preclude the capture of Berlin. It was never a case of "either/or." As the tactical picture evolved, we could have launched simultaneous attacks on

Berlin and the southern redoubt. The capture of Berlin was still under active consideration by us as late as April 15, the day before the Russians jumped off. Simpson had thirteen divisions, Hodges twelve, sufficient force to move on Berlin while Patton and Devers, with a combined total of thirty-four divisions, carried out the drive on the redoubt. We rejected Berlin as a military objective for all the reasons enumerated earlier, not because we were foolishly pursuing a mythical redoubt.[18]

Nor was the southern campaign without benefit to us. It was carried out swiftly and decisively with light casualties. It wiped out all German forces in southern Germany, part of our assigned area of occupation. It delivered us Munich, Stuttgart and two important Nazi shrines, Nuremberg and Berchtesgaden. It enabled us to link up with our forces moving up from Italy to consolidate our front.

The link-up of our forces and the Russians now became a matter of utmost concern to our troops. In the minds of the soldiers and the war correspondents, the link-up rather than the complete collapse of German forces became the symbol of final victory. Since it would be a "historic event," every unit in the First and Ninth armies wanted to be "first" to join hands.

The first link-up came in Hodges' First Army area. On April 23, the burgomaster of Wurzen, a city on the east bank of the Mulde directly east of Leipzig, initiated surrender negotiations with units of Emil F. Reinhardt's 69th Infantry Division. Reinhardt cleared the negotiations with his V Corps commander, Clarence Huebner, and on the following day, the 69th's 273rd Infantry Regiment crossed the Mulde and took possession of the city.

The Elbe and Mulde rivers join at Dessau, forty miles north of Wurzen. In our initial exchange with the Russians we had specified the Elbe as the line of demarcation. Later, because the Mulde runs more north-south from Dessau than the Elbe, we asked that the Mulde be the line of demarcation below Dessau. The Russians were slow in getting this word to their front line units and these stopped at the Elbe, twenty-five miles east of Wurzen.

The commander of the 273rd Infantry, Charles M. Adams, was puzzled not to find the Russians approaching Wurzen. On the afternoon of April 24, he sent a patrol, commanded by Albert L. Kotzebue, east from Wurzen to find the Russians, but not to go farther than seven miles east. Finding no Russians, Kotzebue turned in for the night and resumed the search on the following day. Going far beyond his seven-mile limit, at 1130 that morning Kotzebue spotted a lone Russian cavalryman on a horse, surrounded by foreign laborers. Kotzebue approached the Russian with one of his men, Stephen A. Kowalski, who spoke Russian, and asked where he could find his commander. The Russian seemed reserved and suspicious. He waved his arm eastward and suggested that one of the laborers, a Pole, could lead them better than he, and he galloped off.

Led on by the Pole, Kotzebue advanced to Strehla, on the Elbe. Through binoculars he could see Russians on the opposite bank. He fired green flares (the agreed signal), then, in further violation of all orders, crossed the Elbe with five of his men in a commandeered sailboat. A Russian major and two other Russians met Kotzebue on the east bank, making them the first real link-up. Later that day, several other patrols from the 273rd Infantry made contact with the Russians near the Elbe. The next day, April 26, at Torgau, Reinhardt met Russian General Vladimir Rusakov, commander of the Russian 58th Guards Infantry Division, to make the link-up official. I was extremely pleased that the link-up honors —and publicity—went to Hodges' First Army.[19]

The British, meanwhile, had expressed concern over leaving the conquest and occupation of Czechoslovakia entirely to the Russians. Would not important political advantages accrue to the Allies if we took Prague? When Ike passed this question on to Marshall, he replied that he would be "loath to hazard American lives for purely political purposes." From a military point of view, Prague, like Berlin, had no strategic significance. Militarily, Ike too was content to leave Czechoslovakia to the Russians.

To join with the Russians in that area, two days after the official link-up at Torgau, I ordered Hodges to move Huebner's V Corps south to the 1937 Czechoslovakian border on a line Karlsbad-Pilsen. Since this was more properly Patton's area of command, a few days later, on May 4, I officially transferred V Corps to the Third Army. This gave Patton a total of four corps, comprising eighteen divisions, in all, some 540,000 men. As Patton proudly noted in his diary, it was the largest single U.S. Army formation employed in World War II. Patton was bitter that Ike held Huebner at Pilsen. Patton wanted desperately to liberate Prague, both for political reasons and, I am certain, for the headlines.[20]

In the north, Monty continued plodding onward, all too slowly. Dempsey's southernmost VIII Corps, adjacent to Simpson's Ninth Army, reached the Elbe on April 19, opposite Lauenberg—one week behind Simpson—and stopped. His XII Corps, in the center, reached the Elbe opposite Hamburg on April 23. On his left flank, Horrocks' XXX Corps invested Bremen, a pile of rubble, on April 24. Three days later, the city fell.

The capture of Bremen had required considerable ammunition which, in turn, further delayed Monty's plans to cross the Elbe and strike for Lübeck. On April 20, Ike had flown to Monty's headquarters to again urge him on—and to offer Ridgway's XVIII Airborne Corps in the Elbe crossing. By this time the Russians were encircling Berlin and advancing rapidly toward Lübeck and the Danish border. If Monty did not move faster at the Elbe, there was a real possibility that the Russians would beat him there —and keep going into Denmark. Ike sent Monty yet another prodding letter on April 27, stressing "the tremendous importance of anchoring our flank on Lübeck as quickly as possible." The same day he sent Alan Brooke a detailed summary of his efforts to spur Monty onward, designed to enlist Alan Brooke's aid in pushing Monty.[21]

Monty finally and reluctantly agreed to accept Ridgway's XVIII Airborne Corps. Ridgway, in a remarkable maneuver, sped the corps some 250 miles from the Ruhr to the Elbe in a matter of a few days. His force included Gavin's 82nd Airborne and the 7th Armored and 8th Infantry divisions, to which was added the British 6th Airborne Division. On April 29, the British VIII Corps crossed the Elbe almost unopposed. Instead of waiting to use the British bridges (as was the plan), Ridgway ordered hastily arriving units of Gavin's airborne troopers to force an American crossing near Bleckede and build a bridge. On April 30, Gavin's men crossed and Ridgway was on his way, full speed. In this little-known but astonishingly effective drive, Ridgway's corps sprinted sixty miles northeast to Wismar, firmly blocking the oncoming Russians and capturing 360,000 Germans, including fifty generals. When I learned that an entire army group—some 150,000 Germans with all their impedimenta—had surrendered to Jim Gavin's 82nd Airborne Division, my old outfit, I was pleased.

With Ridgway providing this strong flank support and German resistance utterly collapsing on the news of Hitler's death, Monty's forces finally got going. Dempsey's VIII Corps raced to Lübeck and on to Kiel. On the left, his XII Corps broke across the Elbe and drove forward to Kiel. Meanwhile, in a courteous gesture, Ridgway positioned the British 6th Airborne in the van of his XVIII Airborne Corps so the British could have the honor and public acclaim of greeting the Russians at Wismar. As it turned out, Gavin's troops actually linked first, but we downplayed that union in order not to upstage the British.[22]

Monty's last campaign, from the Rhine to Lübeck, was, on the whole, one of the most cautious and uninspired of the war. It began with flamboyant overkill at the Rhine in a typical Monty set-piece battle and petered out to his usual desultory pursuit and reluctance to go for the jugular, to make the kill, to take risks. Had we not primed Ridgway in advance and then rushed him to help Monty, the Russians would surely have reached the Danish border first and perhaps gone on to Copenhagen with possibly damaging consequences in the postwar world.

During these last days of the Third Reich, Ike and I were less concerned about ceremonial link-ups with the Russians than we were about our remaining enemy, Japan. MacArthur had taken the Philippines; Nimitz had taken Iwo Jima and Okinawa. Ahead of them lay the biggest job of all, the invasion of the Japanese home islands, for which MacArthur had been named commander in chief. The massive assault would consist of two steps: an invasion of Kyushu by some 800,000 men on November 1 (Operation Olympic), followed by an invasion of Honshu (Operation Coronet) on March 1, 1946. At Yalta, the Russians, in return for certain concessions, had agreed to declare war on Japan several months after the collapse of Germany and to invade Manchuria, pinning down Japanese forces that might otherwise be used to defend the home islands. Even so, MacArthur had estimated that the Allies would incur a million casualties in these final two invasions.[23]

We had known for a long time that some of our ETO forces would be redeployed to the Pacific to participate in the invasion of Japan. On April 25, Marshall cabled Ike that he had offered Hodges and his First Army headquarters to MacArthur, "who has accepted him gladly." It will be recalled that in Normandy I had asked Marshall for duty in the Pacific. Subsequently Marshall had recommended me to MacArthur. At the end of his cable to Ike, Marshall appended: "MacArthur does not anticipate army group commanders in Japanese homeland operation other than himself. Would Bradley care to go out as an army commander with present group staff, all at a later date?"

Inasmuch as going to the Pacific as army rather than army group commander amounted to a demotion for me, Ike was completely infuriated by the suggestion. He began writing Marshall a steamy letter in which he said that to relegate me to army commander "would make it appear to all soldiers in this theater and to the public that this war was rather a minor league affair and would have the further effect of diminishing Bradley's stature in the postwar Army and public opinion." In mid-letter, he stopped and telephoned to ascertain my personal feelings about the matter. He then resumed the letter: "His only answer was: 'I will serve anywhere in any position that General Marshall assigns me.' Nevertheless, I distinctly got the impression that he feels that to go to the Pacific as an army commander would be belittling in the American mind the magnitude of American accomplishments here, and the services of more than 3,000,000 U.S. soldiers. However he did not—repeat not—express any opinion as to his personal desires."

Marshall replied on April 27: "My intention was not to move Bradley to the Pacific unless he desired to go. In view of your message he will no longer be considered for such an assignment."[24]

I was a soldier. We had defeated one enemy, but from our distance, Japan still loomed large. Hodges, Patton, Simpson—a great many of us—were eager to join in the final conquest of Japan. No U.S. soldier had commanded large Army forces against both Germany and Japan. It would have been an unusual, if not unique, honor. But Ike was right in his assessment. I did not want to go to the Pacific in any job lower than army group commander.

Russian General Koniev invited me to a victory banquet at his army group headquarters near Torgau, on the east bank of the Elbe, on May 5. In the interest of goodwill and out of curiosity, I accepted and took along a brand new jeep as a gift. Koniev, a powerfully built man with a huge bald head, entertained us with a lavish spread of food, vodka and wine and a female ballet troupe. After the banquet he presented me with a Don Cossack stallion and a Russian pistol with a carved handle. In turn, I gave him the jeep.[25]

By this time, Hitler's former U-boat Commander, Karl Doenitz, had taken legal command of the Third Reich government and had sent General Alfred Jodl and Admiral Hans von Friedeburg to Ike's headquarters to sign the formal surrender documents. The Germans stalled for time, seeking to transfer as many German soldiers and civilians as possible from the Russian front to areas within our lines. Ike refused any further delays and at 2:41 A.M. on May 7, Reims time, the Germans signed the unconditional surrender documents in SHAEF's war room.

At about 0500 that same morning, Ike telephoned me at my quarters in the Hotel Furstenhof in Bad Wildungen, where we had located Eagle Tac headquarters. "Brad," he said, "it's all over. A TWX is on the way."

I notified my four army commanders. I found Patton in his trailer near Regensberg, Hodges in a private home in Weimar, Simpson in Luftwaffe quarters near Brunswick and Gerow in quarters near Bonn. I told each that the terms of the surrender would go into effect at 0001, May 9, to hold firmly in place and risk no more casualties.[26]

The war against Germany was over. The Third Reich lay pulverized beyond recognition. It was hard to grasp. My mind was awash with images and sensations. Omaha and Utah beaches. Avranches. St. Lô. Mortain. Argentan-Falaise. Bastogne. St. Vith. Aachen. The Roer dams. Metz. Cologne. Remagen. Across that large, blood-drenched swath of Europe, 586,628 American soldiers had fallen—135,576 to rise no more. The grim figures haunted me. I could hear the cries of the wounded, smell the stench of death. I could not sleep; I closed my eyes and thanked God for victory.[27]

PART FOUR

★★★★★

WASHINGTON

FORTY-SIX

In the days following the victory, our contacts with the Russian soldiers opposite us were frequent but cautious. As a military courtesy, I repaid General Koniev's hospitality by inviting him to my headquarters in Kassel. Army Special Services provided the entertainment: renowned violinist Jascha Heifetz, comedian Mickey Rooney and the Glenn Miller Orchestra. Not to feel outdone by the Russian ballet troupe, we added a jitterbug demonstration, superbly executed by five nurses and WAC's and five GI's. After the ceremonies and dinner, Koniev, on the personal instructions of Stalin, awarded me a Soviet medal reserved for high commanders, the Order of Suvorov, First Class.[1]

During this busy day, May 17, Ike called from Reims. He said, "Brad, I know you're entertaining Koniev today, but as soon as he leaves, come on back to Reims and spend the night with me. I've got something to take up with you." Ike's tone led me to believe the matter was more than routine and that it pertained to a new assignment for me.

Soon after Koniev and his party left, I flew to Reims. I found Ike seated in a comfortable chair in his quarters, having a drink with his British aide, James Gault. Ike waved a telegram at me and said, "Brad, before I show you this, you had better pour yourself a good stiff drink."

I poured a bourbon and sat down to read the cable. It was an "eyes only" from Marshall to Ike and it was full of jolting news.

First in importance, Marshall stated that he intended to "urge" that President Truman release him "from active duty" within the next two months. Since we had all assumed Marshall would stay at his post at least until Japan was defeated, this was flabbergasting. The further implication was that Ike would be recalled from Europe to replace Marshall as Chief of Staff. This news had devastated Ike. He wanted no part of the Chief of Staff job. His sole desire was to go to "a remotely situated cottage in a state of permanent retirement" and write his memoirs.

Secondly, and most important personally, Marshall had a new job in mind for me. He wrote that Truman was having a problem with the Veterans Administration and that he wanted "an outstanding Army figure" to head it up for "probably a year or two." The President had asked for me. Marshall had endorsed the idea. He wrote that while he realized this news would come as a "shock" and "great disappointment" to me, he thought I would do a "superb job in a very difficult position" and would thereby "enhance" my military career "instead of harming it."

Marshall correctly anticipated my reaction. I, too, was devastated. I knew absolutely nothing about the Veterans Administration. I was reluctant to go to any desk job in Washington before the war with Japan was over, especially one outside the Army and one which seemed on first blush so inconsequential and demeaning. I would much rather have gone to the Pacific, demoted to army commander. The only job in Washington I wanted was Chief of Staff of the Army. And yet I could not refuse the assignment. A suggestion from the Commander in Chief, especially one with Marshall's positive endorsement, was tantamount to an order.[2]

Later, when we were alone, Ike and I had a frank discussion which considerably lifted my spirits. He assured me that he would do everything within his power to see that sooner or later I was named Chief of Staff. If, upon Marshall's retirement, Truman asked Ike to be Chief of Staff (as seemed inevitable), Ike would attempt to decline the job unless Truman expressed a "positive desire" that he take it. If Ike could get out of it gracefully, he would recommend me. If Truman insisted he take the job, Ike would serve not the customary four, but only two years, making an arrangement in advance with Truman that I would be named to succeed him. By serving Truman in the thankless Veterans Administration job, Ike argued (echoing Marshall), I would gain Truman's gratitude and confidence, increasing the probability that Truman would follow Ike's recommendations.

The next day Ike cabled Marshall stating that since I believed the VA job "represents a field where much service could be rendered the country and particularly to returned soldiers," I was "quite ready . . . to undertake the task."[3]

When this news hit me, I was already scheduled to return to the States temporarily, on June 2, to participate in victory parades in Philadelphia and St. Louis. It was eventually arranged that I would proceed with those plans, then return to Europe for several weeks while Ike went home for victory parades. I would then take a month's leave with Mary and report to the VA about mid-August.[4]

On June 2 and 3, I flew from Paris to the Azores to Bermuda to New York. Mary, who came from Washington, was waiting at the airport, and we went directly to the Waldorf-Astoria Hotel. Twenty-one long months had passed since our last reunion. There was much to talk about, not least my new—and still top secret—assignment to the Veterans Administration. Neither of us was happy about it. Within an hour we left the Waldorf and drove to West Point for the thirtieth reunion of the Class of 1915, staying with the Beukemas.[5]

The next several days were a dizzy whirl. On June 4, we flew to Philadelphia for a massive downtown victory parade, which was led by Governor Edward Martin, the man I had relieved as commander of the Pennsylvania 28th National Guard Division in 1942. After the parade we returned to West Point to attend graduation ceremonies on the following day, June 5. I made the main speech and presented diplomas to the 852 graduates. On the next day, June 6, the first anniversary of D-day, we went to New York for a radio interview with Mary's friend and sorority sister Mary Margaret McBride. After that we unwound and took in an Olson and Johnson show and went to the Plaza to see Hildegarde.[6]

The next day I flew to Washington to see Marshall and President Truman about my new job. By this time I had learned that the Veterans Administration and its administrator, retired Army Brigadier General Frank T. Hines, who had been in the job for twenty-two years, were under severe attack. The assault had been launched earlier in the year by writer Albert Deutsch in an eleven-part series in Ralph Ingersoll's New York newspaper *PM*. This was followed by a two-part article in *Cosmopolitan* magazine by Albert Q. Maisel. Deutsch wrote that the VA was a "vast dehumanized bureaucracy, enmeshed in mountains of red tape, ingrown with entrenched mediocrity, undemocratically operated under autocratic control centered in Washington, prescribing medieval medicine to its sick and disabled wards, highly susceptible to political pressures, rigidly resistant to proposed reforms."

General Hines, a colorless but scrupulously honest, conservative and conscientious administrator, had refuted the charges and even invited a House investigation, but the public furor had overwhelmed him and he had lost his effectiveness. On Truman's suggestion, "elder statesman" Bernard Baruch had made a thorough study of the VA and found it deficient in many areas. At a press conference on May 15, Truman had been compelled to concede that the VA would have to be "modernized" to accommodate the large numbers of returning veterans. The Washington press corps, scenting blood, speculated that Hines would soon be fired.[7]

On the day I arrived in Washington, June 7, Hines, at Truman's request, had submitted his resignation. Truman held another press conference to announce that I would take his place. On hearing the news, the reporters were as stunned as I had been. The official transcript of the conference notes "low whistles and exclamations." Later that same day, I saw Marshall, who took me to the White House for a very brief meeting with the President. Both assured me that my tenure at VA would be no more than two years, that legislation would be introduced into Congress to assure that I would retain my four-star rank and pay ($13,000) and my place on the Army's seniority list. In our brief meeting, Marshall again expressed the belief that the VA job would "enhance" my career. I took this to mean that if I did a good job I would succeed Ike as Chief of Staff of the Army.[8]

One purpose of my trip home was to focus attention on the outstanding job the Army had done in Europe. This I was more than happy to do. The next day, June 8, Secretary of War Stimson presented me at a press conference. I said proudly, "American troops are the best ever put in the field by any nation in the history of the world." I extolled the individual worth of the American GI, stating that I knew of many cases "where one or two would hold up fifty to one hundred Germans just by their initiative and bravery." My remarks were dutifully reported, but the reporters were far more anxious to question me about my new VA job. However, Stimson, seeking to keep the focus on the Army, turned these questions aside.[9]

The next day, Saturday, June 9, Mary and I flew to Missouri for a statewide victory celebration. First stop was my "home town," Moberly. On the personal orders of Marshall, my son-in-law, Lieutenant Hal Beukema, and Lee flew from his Air Corps base in Roswell, New Mexico, to Moberly to join us. Hal and Lee had celebrated their first wedding anniversary three days before. This was my first opportunity to know Hal as a man, and I was very much impressed—even if he had chosen the Air Corps over the infantry![10]

I had not been to Moberly in twelve years, but the town turned itself inside out for me and my family when we landed at the Omar N. Bradley Airport. It was "General Bradley Day," a warm and moving occasion. All my Bradley relatives welcomed me like a long-lost son. The governor of Missouri, Phil M. Donnelly, headed a legion of dignitaries who descended on Moberly for a large and enthusiastic parade and some extended speech making at Tannehill Park. (In my brief remarks I described the terrible havoc of war, frankly stated I never wished to see another and heartily endorsed the new United Nations Organization as one method of preventing future wars.) That night the redoubtable Moberly High School Class of 1910 held a reunion in our honor, a lively fried chicken dinner at the Masonic Temple, to which our relatives and others were invited. One astonishing fact revealed at the dinner was that all members of the 1910 class were still living. We attributed that to "hearty Missouri stock." When an old friend and hunting companion, Cook Hickerson, prodded me into giving a quail whistle, it brought down the house and established a perfect home-town, if not hayseed, air to the proceedings. Next day, Mary, Hal, Lee and I attended services at the Central Christian Church, where Mary and I had been baptized. Later on that quiet and reflective Sunday, we visited the Oakland and Log Chapel Cemeteries to see the graves of our departed loved ones.[11]

Then on to St. Louis and another massive victory parade on June 11. The city pulled out all the stops, declaring a school holiday in my honor.[12]

Then back to Washington on June 12. I paid courtesy calls on President Truman, General Hines and Congressman John E. Rankin (Democrat, Mississippi), chairman of the House Veterans Affairs Committee. Rankin said, "General, remember you have only been through a war up to this time. It may look like a sewing circle by the time you get through with this job." Truman told me that the VA job was the "biggest one he had" (I'm certain he meant biggest headache) and promised me his fullest support, thanking me for taking the job. I replied, "I'm a soldier, sir, and I do whatever my Commander in Chief orders."[13]

I saw Marshall again that day and he had wonderful news. He had designated that a house—Quarters Seven—on "Generals' Row," at Fort Myer, Virginia, be assigned to me. These old-shoe brick houses on a bluff overlooking the Potomac were much coveted by Washington-based Army generals. Off-base housing was scarce and expensive. Official housing was not only free but staffed with orderlies and servants. Fort Myer had a commissary, PX, laundry, movie and other amenities. Old friends lived all over the post. Our private life would be as comfortable, congenial and economical as Marshall could make it, and for that we were deeply grateful.[14]

Leaving my aide Chet Hansen on duty at the VA to find out what made it tick, or fail to tick, I flew back to Europe aboard Truman's plane, *Sacred Cow,* on June 14 and reported to Ike. He was in a swivet, preparing to return on the plane to the States for an address to a joint session of the Congress and for victory parades in Washington, New York, Kansas City and Abilene. Then he was going for a week of R and R to the fabulous Greenbrier resort (which the Army had taken over and temporarily named Ashford General Hospital) in White Sulphur Springs, West Virginia. I relieved Ike, temporarily, and became Acting U.S. Theater Commander—but not Supreme Commander.[15]

My duties over the next three weeks proved to be so arduous that I never could find time to visit the corps and divisions as I had intended. Everything was in flux. Courtney Hodges and his First Army staff had already gone to the Pacific to arrange for redeployment. Simpson was preparing to redeploy his Ninth Army to China. Patton was on a month-long trip to the States for victory parades. Devers was on the way home for parades and to become chief of Army Ground Forces, Lesley McNair's old job. I became burdened with problems of U.S. troop rotation and redeployment, refugees, emergency food supplies, disarmament of German military forces, occupying our assigned zones, and other matters, all very complicated and time-consuming.[16]

The Big Three—Truman, Churchill, Stalin—had agreed to meet in Potsdam, a suburb of Berlin, on July 15, to discuss questions regarding postwar Europe and the war in the Pacific. In Ike's absence, it fell to me to make many of the arrangements for this meeting, especially those relating to the security of Truman, the U.S. Joint Chiefs of Staff and others in the presidential party. Ike returned to his SHAEF headquarters in Frankfurt on July 12, and on the following day disbanded SHAEF. Ike met Truman when he arrived in Antwerp on July 15 on board the cruiser *Augusta*. The President was driven to Brussels and flew in the *Sacred Cow* to Berlin. Churchill arrived the same day. Stalin, who had suffered a mild heart attack before leaving for the conference, came by train, arriving two days late on July 17.[17]

Neither Ike nor I was invited to participate in the Potsdam conference. However, Truman, through his military aide National Guardsman Harry H. Vaughn, invited Ike and me to attend a ceremony in Berlin on July 20. We had lunch with the President at his quarters in Babelsberg. This was my third meeting with Truman, but the first at which I had an opportunity to take the measure of the man. I liked what I saw. He was direct, unpretentious, clear-thinking and forceful. His knowledge of American history, particularly U.S. military history, was astonishing. I found him to be extremely well informed about the battles we had fought in Africa, Sicily, Italy and on the Continent.[18]

During our lunch, the talk focused on our strategy for the defeat of Japan and the use of the atomic bomb, which had been successfully tested at Alamogordo, New Mexico, four days earlier. Truman had already decided to use the two available "operational" A-bombs on Japan. I silently agreed with the decision. I had heard of MacArthur's estimate of one million Allied casualties for the invasion of the Japanese home islands of Kyushu and Honshu and did not doubt the estimate. Ike was not asked his opinion, but he volunteered it that day and later, rather forcefully, to Stimson. Curiously, Ike, almost alone among senior military men, opposed using the bomb. He believed Japan was already defeated, that dropping the bomb was "completely unnecessary" and that we should avoid "shocking world opinion" by dropping such weapons on people who were at that very moment attempting to seek surrender with minimum loss of face.[19]

After lunch, we proceeded toward the ceremony for which we had come to Berlin: raising an American flag that had flown over the U.S. Capitol on December 7, 1941, at the U.S. Control Council headquarters in the Teltower district of Berlin. Our auto procession was joined by cars transporting General Lucius D. Clay, Ike's civil affairs expert, George Patton, Henry Stimson and his assistant secretary John McCloy. As we drove along in Truman's car, the President was very much at ease and in a generous mood. He astounded Ike and me when he turned to Ike and said, "General, there is nothing that you may want that I won't try to help you get. That definitely and specifically includes the presidency in 1948."

I kept a poker face, wondering how Ike would reply to *that*. Ike laughed heartily and said, "Mr. President, I don't know who will be your opponent for the presidency, but it will not be I."[20]

After the ceremony, I rushed back to my headquarters prepared to leave for the States on the following day, July 21. When I reached my plane the next morning, a messenger arrived with a letter from Ike wishing me well.[21]

FORTY-SEVEN

Following the atomic bombing of Hiroshima on August 6 and Nagasaki on August 9, Japan sued for peace on August 10. Hostilities with Japan ceased on August 14. The next day, as the nation was recovering from V-J Day celebrations, I reported to VA headquarters, located in an old building across Lafayette Park from the White House. Associate Justice Harold M. Stephens of the District of Columbia Appeals Court administered the oath of office. Mary, General Hines, whom Truman had appointed ambassador to Panama, Congressman Rankin and a host of senior VA officials crowded into the office for the brief ceremony. Later, at an even briefer press conference, I told reporters: "I don't think there's any job in the country I'd sooner not have nor any job in the world I'd like to do better. For even though it is burdened with problems, it gives me the chance to do something for the men who did so much for us."

In a written statement to all VA employees, I said: "Frankly this work is new to me. I will learn the job as quickly as possible. I am greatly concerned with the lot of our veterans. I have personal knowledge of what they have done. I will do everything I can to see they receive promptly every benefit, help, and opportunity to which they are entitled. I expect you to do the same."[1]

Since the founding of our country, it had been the policy of the Congress to reward the civilian-soldiers of our wars—the veterans—with certain benefits. Veterans with war-incurred injuries or disabilities had been provided medical care and compensation pensions commensurate with the extent of the disability. In event of death, the pensions went to widows or dependent children. In many instances Congress had enacted laws granting pensions to non-disabled veterans of various wars and had made provisions for their care in VA hospitals. In World War I, government-subsidized, or "GI," insurance for veterans had been added to the benefits. In addition, Congress had passed a slew of "private" laws granting modest benefits to individual veterans suffering unusual hardships. More recently,

Congress had enacted the "GI Bill of Rights," granting World War II veterans a sweeping new array of financial benefits to help them readjust to civilian life.[2]

The Congress, through John Rankin and his Veterans Affairs Committee, kept an eagle eye on the VA. Before World War II, the nearly five million living veterans, mostly from World War I, formed a political constituency far more powerful than their numbers. They had created highly visible—and vocal—national organizations such as the American Legion and Veterans of Foreign Wars. Countless communities across the land had established Legion or VFW posts, which at election times were useful stumps for politicians. Members of Congress unashamedly curried favor with organized veterans groups and lived in fear of antagonizing them. In those days, the national commander of the American Legion had as much political clout on the Hill as any major union leader, and he was not bashful about exercising it.[3]

Every politician in the country knew that with the onset of demobilization, the veteran constituency would swell to four times its pre–World War II size: nearly 20 million men and women; 43 percent of the adult male population would be veterans. In every family, every community—and every congressional district—the voice of the veteran would now be a formidable political force and the national veterans organizations more powerful than ever. Thus both Democrat and Republican politicians were gearing up to court the "veteran vote" with unreserved zeal. From July 1, 1944, to June 30, 1945, a staggering 2,868 bills pertaining to increased or broadened veterans benefits had been introduced into Congress. The most important of these, notably the GI Bill of Rights, had been vigorously lobbied for by organized veterans groups.[4]

By the time I was sworn in as Administrator, the Veterans Administration, with some 65,000 employees, had grown to be the largest independent agency within the government. The VA operated some ninety-seven hospital facilities in forty-five states and the District of Columbia. There were then some 71,000 patients in these hospitals, including eight from the Civil War, 2,800 from the Spanish-American War and 45,000 from World War I. More than half of these patients were being treated for non-service-connected disabilities. The VA pension operation was already enormous: some 1.5 million veterans, widows or dependents were receiving $740 million a year in monthly benefits. About one-third of the pensions grew out of World War I, one-third from World War II, the other third from wars in the distant past. Astonishingly, checks were still going out to one eighty-eight-year-old dependent of a veteran of the War of 1812, fifty-five dependents from the Mexican War of 1848, and 229 living veterans of the Civil War (average age ninety-eight). The GI insurance operation was colossal: 18 million policy holders with $135 billion of insurance in force. With the enactment of the GI Bill of Rights, the VA, one journalist aptly wrote, had become "the world's largest social welfare agency, the biggest life insurance agency, the biggest dispenser of pensions, the biggest medical agency, and a huge bank, guaranteeing loans to veterans for homes, businesses and farms and providing funds for rehabilitation and education."[5]

Because of all these factors, the post of VA Administrator had rapidly become the focal point of diverse and intense political pressures. I soon perceived that every decision I made, however small, was bound to antagonize one political faction or another. It was going to be a no-win proposition for me. No matter what I did, someone would throw a brickbat. Inevitably I would antagonize many powerful men on the Hill, possibly jeopardizing my chances for approval as Army Chief of Staff, should Truman nominate me to that post at a later date. Thus there was a good chance the VA job could very well ruin my professional career and send me to early retirement.

This was not a pleasing prospect. And yet, even if I wanted to, there was no way I could change overnight into some kind of political chameleon. I discussed this frankly with President Truman in a brief meeting on the day I was sworn in. I told him that the only way I could do the job at all and maintain my self-respect was to remain, as I had always been, completely "apolitical." I would make my decisions in the best interest of the veterans, regardless of the political consequences.[6]

Truman himself was at that time far from politically entrenched. He had been sitting in the Oval Office only four months. The public did not yet know him well; he lacked the charisma of Roosevelt. In the words of one journalist: "He seemed to be a cardboard cutout; a dapper prairie-state politician in a bow tie and double-breasted suit who spoke flippantly in a twangy, earthy vernacular that contrasted gratingly with the cultured elegance of F.D.R." Many political seers were beginning to doubt Truman had sufficiently broad appeal to run for the presidency in 1948 and win.

He was then presiding over a troubling transition in the history of the nation. The economy had been geared for total war production. Everybody not in the armed forces who could or wanted to had been working, making good money. But what lay ahead when the war production suddenly stopped and 15 million veterans came home looking for jobs? Some economists were predicting economic chaos: rampant, uncontrollable inflation, crippling unemployment, perhaps even another Great Depression. Not many had faith that Harry Truman could safely steer the country through these turbulent economic waters.[7]

Beyond that, there was widespread discontent and unease, a letdown following the vast national effort to win the war. People were simply fed up with wartime red tape—rationing, price controls and all the rest. In England, the same fed-up attitude had unseated Churchill and the Conservatives in July while Churchill was at Potsdam. There were some signs that the same pattern was emerging in our country. The Democrats had controlled both houses of Congress since 1933. But the widespread discontent and unease led many political sages to predict a Republican sweep in the 1946 off-year elections, followed by another Republican sweep in the 1948 presidential elections.

Truman was in a unique situation to use the vast veterans benefits programs for the advancement of his own political interests and those of the Democratic party. But he would not. He agreed with me completely that my decisions should be made in the best interests of the veteran, regardless of political consequences. Moreover, he assured me that he would back me all the way. He kept his word, even when the heat was fierce. This decision required a measure of political courage you do not often see in Washington.[8]

I met with Truman four more times that fall. Each time my admiration for the man, and the job he was doing, increased. He may not have had charisma, but in private he was an impressive executive. He did his homework. His wide reading in U.S. history gave him a panoramic viewpoint not held by many politicians. He was determined to learn from our past mistakes and, if possible, to avoid repeating them. He was utterly devoid of pretension and pomposity. He had a quick mind, the ability to cut straight through to the heart of any complex issue. He was not afraid of responsibility. The sign on his desk, soon to become famous, spoke volumes about the man: THE BUCK STOPS HERE.[9]

We got along very well personally. We had much in common. Though he was about ten years older, we were of the same generation. His forebears, like my own, migrated west from Kentucky to Missouri. He had grown up in a small town in Missouri not very far from Higbee and Moberly. He had served as a captain in the Army in World War I in a National Guard outfit—Battery D, 129th Field Artillery, 35th Division—which saw considerable front-line action in France. He had remained close to and sympathetic toward the Army and, in that sense, he was a welcome change from the staunchly pro-Navy Roosevelt. He shared my admiration for George Marshall, believing, as did I, that Marshall was destined to become a towering figure in U.S. history. Although I had never registered to vote and did not consider myself either Democrat or Republican, I found myself increasingly sympathetic to Truman's prairie-state populist outlook, his concern for the "little man."[10]

The war with Japan had ended far sooner than most officials in Washington had believed possible. Already there was a mounting clamor to "bring the boys home." You did not have to be a political seer to divine that the Democrats in Congress, deeply concerned about the 1946 off-year elections, would hasten to respond to that clamor. It was soon apparent to me that the Pentagon's well-drawn demobilization plans, designed to extend over two or three years, would be scrapped. And so they were. Pell-mell demobilization commenced in October 1945. By June 1946, some 12.8 million men and women were returned to civilian life—all veterans. In my first eight months in office, the "veteran population" zoomed from nearly 5 million to nearly 17 million.[11]

The VA was unprepared to cope with this onrushing horde. Owing to Hines's antiquated management policies, control of VA had been tightly centralized in Washington. Every operation, no matter how large or small, was administered by the Washington staff, which had grown hidebound and old. When I took office, the chief lieutenants were already overwhelmed. The home office force could process 75,000 pieces of mail a day—no small feat in itself—but mail was coming in on some days at four times that rate. My most vivid memory of my first days in office is the sight of unopened canvas mail bags stacked to the ceiling in the hallways: hundreds of thousands of letters from veterans or dependents unanswered. Many tens of thousands of these letters were not answered for months.[12]

I had managed to persuade a dozen-odd members of the Twelfth Army Group staff to come with me to VA to help me. Notable among this brave, selfless band of administrative experts were Brigadier General Henry B. (Monk) Lewis, Colonel Edwin K. Wright, Colonel Eldon L. Bailey, Colonel Richard T. McDonnell, Lieutenant Colonel Ralph P. Bronson (our mail distribution expert) and Lieutenant Colonel Chet Hansen, who not only continued as my aide, but also served as unofficial chief of VA public relations. Thanks to the President, my C-47 aircraft, the *Mary Q,* remained in my custody and Robbie Robinson continued as chief pilot.[13]

After we had thoroughly inspected VA organization and digested the Baruch report and other similar studies, it was clear to all of us that the best way to prepare the VA for the oncoming rush of veterans was to decentralize its operations. We tackled this job on a crash basis. One month after taking office—on September 15, 1945—I announced the creation of thirteen branch offices, each a small-scale VA in itself, supervised by a deputy administrator with broad powers to make decisions. These branches were located in accessible downtown areas of our largest cities (New York, Philadelphia, Atlanta, Denver, Seattle) and staffed by personnel recruited locally, with hiring preference going to returning veterans. Each branch, in turn, established a network of regional and contact offices in the outlying smaller cities and towns. Within two years, the number of VA employees increased from 65,000 to 200,000. To house our decentralized operations we had to lease over 10 million square feet of office space.

Although decentralization was logical, even mandatory, it proved to be intensely controversial. It was, of course, opposed by the old entrenched VA bureaucracy, which was critical of any new approach. In many cities we could only get office space by resorting to condemnation proceedings which forced the eviction of existing tenants. Many did not leave happily. The vast increase in VA employee rolls was reviewed by some critics as a huge government boondoggle. My appointment of some ex-Army colonels and generals to run branch offices was not universally viewed with favor, even though the appointees were executives of exceptional ability. The brickbats came thick and fast but I learned to duck.[14]

The VA budgets were colossal for those days—in fiscal 1946, $4.5 billion and in fiscal 1947, $6.3 billion. These budgets were as much as, or more than, the budgets of the then forty-eight states combined. If monies for national defense and service of the United States federal debt were excluded, the VA was spending nearly one-third of the federal budget.

The principal economic assistance programs VA administered under terms of the GI Bill of Rights were in education; jobs and job training; disability pensions; loans; and insurance.

Education. World War II had interrupted the education of millions of men and women. We estimated that of the 15 million World War II veterans, about half—some 7 million—had either never had jobs at all or had had merely part-time "schoolboy" jobs of no real consequence. In order to prepare these men and women for a more useful and remunerative role in society, Congress enacted legislation to pay their way—$500 per year tuition plus subsistence—to college or vocational schools. Before I came into VA, Congress had ill-advisedly put an age ceiling on this program of twenty-five years, arbitrarily excluding the "older" veterans, who, it was assumed, already had sufficient education or job skills. I thought this age ceiling was discriminatory. Many older veterans who had been working in routine jobs before the war had had their eyes opened to the value of college or specialized training and wanted it. At my request, Congress repealed the age ceiling, opening the educational benefits to all 15 million World War II veterans.[15]

The response to the GI Bill educational program far exceeded all estimates. Our colleges and universities were swamped with veterans. Before the war, the total U.S. college student population was about 1.3 million. By 1947, the college student population stood at 2.3 million, of whom 1.25 million were veterans on the GI Bill. In other words, the postwar veteran student population almost equaled the entire prewar student population. Harvard ballooned from a prewar enrollment of 8,000 to a postwar enrollment of 12,200; Stanford from 4,800 to 7,200. Three-quarters of all students at Harvard and Stanford in 1947 were veterans, typical of many campuses.[16]

The college program ran raggedly the first two years. No college or university had foreseen the magnitude of veteran response. The institutions were compelled to throw up makeshift substandard (sometimes freezing cold) housing and classrooms (trailers, surplus wartime barracks) and to hire instructors by the busload. At VA, we, too, were swamped and fell inexcusably behind in our tuition payments to the institutions and subsistence payments to the veterans, causing untold hardships. But after two years, both the teaching institutions and the VA got the program on track and the complaints fell to a tolerable roar.[17]

Soon after the program was launched it became apparent that the subsistence level was inadequate. Originally it was fifty dollars per month for a single veteran and seventy-five for a married veteran. (Disabled veterans received about twice those amounts.) By January 1, 1946, I had persuaded Congress to raise this to sixty-five dollars for single and ninety for married veterans, with commensurate increases for disabled veterans. Moreover, I also got Congress to repeal a provision that denied students any subsistence if they took an outside job. However, the brutal inflation of 1946–47 soon ate up these modest increases, and most veterans or their wives (or both) had to take jobs to stay afloat. For those who could not get additional financial help from parents or relatives or other sources, it was a tough struggle all the way.[18]

Even so, most veterans applied themselves with extraordinary diligence. Going to college was serious business. They were mature, eager to learn. A study at the University of Wisconsin revealed that veterans made better grades than non-veterans, that married veterans made better grades than single veterans and that married veterans with children made the best grades of all. One veteran suggested an unscientific amendment to that report. He told me, "General Bradley, you will find that married veterans with children, *who live in trailers,* make the best grades of all."[19]

GI education benefits were not limited to colleges and universities. The same benefits were open to veterans seeking vocational training in approved technical schools.[20]

The GI educational programs cost probably $5 billion. To my mind it was one of the most notable social programs our nation has ever offered its veterans. It enabled about 1.5 million men and women, most of whom probably could not otherwise have afforded it, to complete four years of college and get degrees. This substantially raised the educational level of our citizenry. Those mature, well-educated men and women went forth into our society with great benefit not only to themselves but to the country as a whole. In communities all across the land they rose to be the leaders of the postwar generation, setting higher standards in every walk of life.

Jobs and job training. The majority of returning veterans—some 10 million—returned to the labor pool. To assist them in readjusting to civilian life, finding a job and improving skills on the job, the VA, working with state employment agencies, funded several programs.

The first, and perhaps most famous (or infamous), was a "readjustment allowance" of twenty dollars a week for a maximum of fifty-two weeks. This was intended to be somewhat like unemployment compensation or, in today's jargon, welfare. A veteran applied at a state employment office for a job and until the job came through he received twenty dollars a week subsistence. Between September 1944 and February 1947, more than 7 million veterans received readjustment allowances amounting to almost $2 billion.

VA records showed that the average veteran, conscientiously seeking a job, drew this compensation for eight weeks or less. But there were widespread abuses. Younger, unambitious or lazy veterans with no responsibilities and living at home with parents found that twenty dollars was adequate for beer and movies for a week. (Beer was then ten or fifteen cents a glass, movies twenty-five to fifty cents.) They were content to idle away their time in what became known, derisively, as the "52-20 Club." Fortunately, there were not many of these.

For some veterans who found jobs, the VA provided subsistence equal to college or vocational school subsistence for what was called "on-the-job training."[21] This well-intentioned program soon became much abused and highly controversial. By law, the individual states were responsible for determining what constituted a "job training" program. That meant that there were forty-eight different standards. Moreover, the states did not have the manpower to police the programs; almost any veteran so inclined could make a deal with his boss or company to "qualify" him for "on-the-job" training, provided the boss or company was willing. For example, in one large retail store, we discovered that the president's son, on a salary of $700 a month, had entered job training for the job of "president." In that same store, the sales manager, making $600 a month, entered job training for "vice president." We disallowed these claims, but many tens of thousands of trainees in less flagrant (and detectable) violations of the spirit of the program drew VA subsistence.[22]

We repeatedly urged state governments to more closely police job training programs, and I got money from Congress to assist them. But to small avail. It was simply too complicated a program to supervise or standardize. The only possible solution to the widespread abuses was for VA to limit a trainee's total earnings. I finally browbeat a reluctant Congress into passing such a ceiling, touching off a storm of controversy. About three-quarters of a million veterans enrolled in job training programs at a cost of several billion dollars.[23]

Disability pensions. Any veteran who was injured or disabled while on active duty in World War II was by law entitled to a pension, commensurate with the disability. Based on past experience, VA had estimated that about 10 percent of all World War II veterans would apply for pensions. We were astonished to find that the actual figure came to about 25 percent. This was due in part to the length of service of the average World War II veteran, the much higher casualty rate and, sad to say, a gross misunderstanding on the part of veterans as to what qualified him or her for a pension. The higher than expected rate of applications together with pell-mell demobilization soon swamped us. We had geared up for about

60,000 applications a month. They came in at the rate of about 400,000 a month. By February 1, 1946, we had received over 2 million pension claims from World War II veterans.[24]

The adjudication of pension claims was a tedious task which could only be carried out by highly trained personnel well versed in medical matters. We created some 500 "rating boards" to review and certify—or deny—the claims. The great majority of the cases—men and women with medical discharges that specifically denoted the disability—were routinely disposed of by well-established and legal formulas. But many tens of thousands of cases fell into a gray area: veterans with "temporary" medical discharges, or veterans with non-medical discharges who now claimed that a backache or a real or imagined psychiatric disorder had been service-incurred. These veterans had to be carefully examined by VA-appointed doctors, and we had to get their service jackets and medical records from the individual services. The latter job was made infinitely more difficult because the Army was in the process of shifting its records from North Carolina to St. Louis.

The result was that, although I added 7,000 personnel, doubling the number of rating boards to 1,000, VA fell far behind in adjudicating pension claims. By February 1946, we had cleared 1.5 million claims but had amassed a backlog of half a million. This backlog was of utmost concern to all of us. It took until July before we finally got pension claims under control. By then, 3.5 million World War II veterans had filed claims. Altogether, nearly 4 million World War II veterans filed pension claims; VA approved about half of these, or 2 million. These pensions have already cost countless tens of billions and will go on for a long time to come, figures that are not usually remembered when adding up the total cost of World War II.[25]

Loans. To assist veterans in the purchase of homes, farms or small businesses, the GI Bill of Rights specified that the VA would guarantee lending institutions all or a portion of the mortgage or loan, within certain specific limits. Originally the guarantee limit was $2,000, but at my request Congress raised it to $4,000. The VA did not actually lend money (a point often confused), but issued "certificates of eligibility" to veterans which "guaranteed" $4,000 of the loan to lenders in the event of default. Most of our guarantees were earmarked for low-cost housing loans. The VA housing loan guarantee fully protected the lender and enabled builders to offer a veteran a house for "nothing down."

This home loan guarantee program gave the housing industry a powerful shot in the arm. In the first year, we guaranteed some 200,000 home loans. All over the nation GI housing tracts sprang up, helping to ease the acute housing shortage and providing tens of thousands of new jobs for returning veterans. Our VA field representatives inspected the tracts to insist that GI housing meet certain building standards so the veteran was not cheated. In a few instances we slipped up and shoddy housing received VA approval. But on the whole, the veteran got good value for his money. The equity accrued in these GI houses enabled many veterans to move upward to more expensive homes.

The business loan guarantee program was less successful, in part owing to the inexperience of the veterans and in part to the impracticality of some of the ideas. I recall one category that was illustrative. Many pilots returning from the war believed the era of air freight had arrived and set about establishing air cargo services with war surplus C-46s and C-47s bought dirt cheap from the government with VA guaranteed loans. One scheme I recall was to air-ship oranges from Florida to New York. But air freight turned out to be an idea at least a decade ahead of its time. The woefully undercapitalized air cargo companies failed by the hundreds. Less than a half-dozen or so survived.

During my first year in office, VA guaranteed some 228,537 veteran loans of all kinds, amounting to about a billion dollars, and had processed certificates of eligibility amounting to another half-billion. The rate of default on most VA loans was negligible. Hence, the cost of the loan program to the government was not great. The chief expense was administrative—processing the applications and issuing certificates of eligibility.[26]

Insurance. Before World War II, the VA had issued about a half-million GI insurance policies, mostly to veterans of World War I. Some 95 percent of all members of the armed forces in World War II took advantage of this cheap insurance. While on active duty, the premiums were paid to VA by means of an automatic payroll deduction. Congress had enacted legislation which enabled World War II veterans to continue their GI insurance in civilian life.

When I came to VA, insurance operations were centralized in New York City. In those days there were no electronic computers; everything was done by hand. Every GI insurance policyholder had a folder or file. The half-million World War I veterans sent in their monthly premiums; receipt of these premiums was noted by hand. Outgoing payments to beneficiaries were also processed by hand. The 17.5 million new policies issued in World War II required the creation of that many folders or files, an enormous task which demanded a staff of some 8,000 employees. But the wartime servicing of these 17.5 million new policies was relatively simple. The premiums were automatically paid to VA via an intergovernment exchange of funds. There was little or no correspondence from the policyholder. Beneficiaries were limited to immediate relatives.

The big problem came with demobilization. If a veteran elected to continue the GI insurance, he or she now had to communicate with VA, sending checks for the premiums, home address, or new address, and so on. At the same time, the VA now had to send out monthly premium notices to the policyholders. All of this created the most mind-boggling mail logjam I have ever seen. In my first six months in office, we received 1.5 million letters from veterans regarding insurance. During that same period, we sent out 5 million premium notices.

The mail problem was further complicated by the failure of many veterans to include their full name or insurance policy number. They might simply sign a letter, "Sincerely, Bill Kelly." By June 1946, we had 28,000 policyholders with a Kelly surname. (And 17,000 Cohens, 16,000 Schultzes, 12,000 Bradleys, including two Omars and two Omers, and 825 George Washingtons.) Each "Bill Kelly" letter required a painstaking hand search through the files and folders or a letter from VA requesting more specific identification.

In time we straightened out this colossal insurance mess. But no less worrisome to me was the widespread indifference the veterans displayed toward their insurance. In August 1946, we estimated that the majority—10 million—of veterans had let their GI insurance lapse. Moreover, less than one out of four who elected to keep it was current on premium payments. The veterans had, as I put it then, thrown away "90 billion worth of economic security." In a series of national radio broadcasts (there was no TV) I appealed to veterans everywhere to reinstate their insurance. But the response was tepid. It is difficult to convince a twenty- or twenty-two-year-old single man that life insurance is important. Congress came to my help by greatly liberalizing the regulations regarding lapsed policy reinstatement. As the veterans grew older, married and assumed greater responsibilities and recognized the value of GI insurance, millions reinstated their policies and have kept them in force to date.[27]

It would be comforting from this perspective to boast that despite all the handicaps we worked miracles in gearing VA for the millions of World War II veterans. Regrettably, this was not the case. There was simply too much to do and not enough time. My staff and I—and most VA personnel—worked like slaves. A seven-day week was commonplace. I flew tens of thousands of miles in the *Mary Q,* meeting with branch and regional office personnel, making speeches to veterans groups, holding press conferences. But for all that we were only able to work near-miracles.

FORTY-EIGHT

The most urgent challenge we faced at VA was that of drastically upgrading the quality of VA medicine. It was not literally "medieval," as Albert Deutsch had described it, but it was—and always had been—mediocre. Moreover, owing to the demands of World War II, VA medicine now suffered from a critical shortage of doctors and hospitals. I became absolutely dedicated to the goal of providing our veterans medical care second to none. This proved to be the most difficult task of all.

Fortunately for the veterans and me, I was able to draft an extraordinarily able man to spearhead this crusade. He was Paul R. Hawley, Ike's chief surgeon in the ETO. Born in Indiana in 1891, Hawley, son of a doctor, had obtained his medical training at the College of Medicine at the University of Cincinnati. Finding practice with his father not to his liking, Hawley obtained a commission in the Regular Army and in World War I went to France with the 34th Division. He remained in the Army medical corps, rising to major general. In the ETO, Hawley had 16,000 doctors under his command. Ike thought the world of him. He was an outspoken iconoclast with a great distaste for red tape—an able and forceful administrator. When I asked for his help, he came, with considerable misgivings, bringing one of his chief assistants, Elliott B. Cutler, chief consultant with the surgery-medical section of ETO, who had had experience before the war with VA medicine in Massachusetts.[1]

There were many medical problems to solve, but none was more pressing than the shortage of VA doctors. We could not even care properly for our existing hospital population let alone the oncoming horde of World War II patients who would soon be transferred to us from military hospitals. There were then 2,300 full-time doctors in VA, of whom 1,700 were on "loan" from the Army and Navy, almost all of them recent graduates of wartime military college programs (the Army's Specialized Training Program, the Navy's V-12) who were obligated to serve out two years' active duty. Since these temporaries would be leaving VA as their duty tours expired, in reality we had only about 500 full-time career VA doctors. We had immediate need for over seven times that number—3,600—and in future years perhaps 7,000.[2]

At that time, any doctor the VA hired had to come to us through the U.S. Civil Service. When Hawley received a list of available doctors through Civil Service he was appalled. There were some eighty names on it, arranged by seniority. They seemed to be the dregs of the medical profession. Number one on the list was a man eighty-seven years old; number two was a seventy-six-year-old woman. Sixty percent of the people on the list were over age sixty. Digging deeper, Hawley found that some doctors on the list had been committed to mental institutions for insanity or alcoholism. He could not hire the few qualified doctors near the bottom of the list without elaborate paperwork to "show cause" why he could not hire those at the top. Moreover, few new young doctors worth their salt were attracted to Civil Service. It carried the connotation of "state" or "socialized medicine"; the pay was minimal; the seniority system and red tape were discouraging to the ambitious and able.[3]

After he had immersed himself in the problem for some days, Hawley brought me a broad-gauge plan designed to lure able doctors to VA, incorporating his own ideas, those proposed in the Bernard Baruch study of VA and those of many professional friends he consulted. There were two chief features to the plan. First, he proposed the creation of an elite non–Civil Service VA medical corps, roughly akin to the Army and Navy medical corps or the U.S. Public Health Service. We would offer pay and retirement benefits commensurate with those of the services, plus premium pay for specialists. Second, he proposed that existing and planned VA hospitals be formally affiliated with class-A medical teaching institutions. This would not only enable the VA to benefit from the know-how, talent and prestige of those institutions but also to gain the services of hundreds of interns and residents who could treat veterans under supervision of the teaching staffs.[4]

These were radical and revolutionary proposals. Removing VA medicine from Civil Service was bound to draw heavy opposition and a rain of brickbats from entrenched Civil Service bureaucrats and their boosters in Congress. Inherent in the "affiliation" proposal was the need to build new VA hospitals adjacent to existing medical schools. There were few issues more politically sensitive than the location of VA hospitals. And yet it was the best possible solution. I unhesitatingly approved it, buttoning up for all-out bureaucratic and political warfare.

Fortunately I was now blessed with an important ally—the national media. My new job had evoked interest among reporters in the Washington press corps and writers for the national magazines; they backed me almost 100 percent. Flattering stories about me—and my man-killing job—appeared in *The Saturday Evening Post, Look,* the Sunday supplement *Pa-*

rade, Ingersoll's *PM* and elsewhere. Even Henry Luce's *Time* magazine, which was unblushingly Republican and preparing to back Thomas E. Dewey against Truman, had unstinting praise for me. *Time* editors put me on the cover for the third time.[5]

Having thoroughly prepared ourselves with facts and figures General Marshall–style, Hawley and I proved to be effective lobbyists in Congress for our bill. The bill passed the House on Pearl Harbor Day, December 7, 1945, and the Senate on December 20. It then went to the White House for Truman's signature, which I thought would be routine.[6]

On New Year's Day 1946, while out of the city, I received an urgent telephone call from a VA associate. He said, "You better come down here, we're in trouble on the bill. The Civil Service is trying to get the President to veto it." I located Hawley, gave him the word, and we both returned to Washington. On the following day we met at the White House in the office of Raymond R. Zimmerman, an administrative assistant to Truman for personnel matters, among other things. The president of the U.S. Civil Service Commission, Harry B. Mitchell, was there, insisting that now that the war was over, Civil Service could recruit and provide VA with the doctors we needed. He urged that the bill be vetoed.

Mitchell made an impressive bureaucratic case, but it was nonsense to Hawley and me. We knew very well we could not recruit able doctors until VA medicine was removed from Civil Service. But Zimmerman was a personnel bureaucrat and appeared loath to bring down the wrath of the vast Civil Service network on the White House. He was not impressed with our case. He said, "I'm going to recommend that the President veto this bill."

I was livid. We had worked long and hard for that bill. It was a vital cornerstone for upgrading VA medicine. I had to assume that Zimmerman had already talked to the President, that the decision to veto had already been made, that Truman was reneging on his support for me. I contained my anger and said to Zimmerman coldly, "Before you do that, will you let me have five minutes with the President?"

"Yes. Why?" Zimmerman asked.

"Well," I replied, "I'm going to resign. I can't operate without this bill." I was not bluffing.

Zimmerman was stunned. He retreated like a scared rabbit. "In that case," he said, "I'll recommend the President sign it." I then decided that Zimmerman had not talked to the President, that he was acting on his own in an attempt to spare Truman a headache.

Truman backed me all the way, causing no small displeasure within the Civil Service. He signed the bill into law on January 3, 1946. The VA department of medicine and surgery became a reality, and I named Hawley chief medical director. The news immediately drew hundreds of applications from high-caliber young doctors, including many returning veterans.

Within six months Hawley had recruited 4,000 full-time VA physicians, plus nurses, technicians and other paramedical personnel.[7]

The second phase of Hawley's plan, affiliating old and new VA hospitals with class-A teaching institutions, proved to be far more difficult. The medical profession, the individual institutions, the Congress and the public had to be persuaded that it was a sound idea.

One big problem in achieving affiliation between VA hospitals and class-A schools was geography. VA hospitals had traditionally fallen into the category of pork barrel legislation. Like military bases, they were expensive to build and later became stable long-term government employers. Every Congressman wanted one in his district not only for the local economic benefit but also because he could wield some influence over who was hired at the hospital, giving him a small avenue of patronage for his local political machine. One result was that in the past all too many VA hospitals had been located in the boondocks to provide local industry for a deprived area and patronage jobs. They were, as Chet Hansen aptly put it, "handsomely landscaped Siberias," too far from medical schools to establish the kind of close ties we wanted.[8]

Before and during World War II, the VA had proposed various plans for the construction of new hospitals and substantial additions to many of the existing ninety-seven hospitals to meet anticipated demands both for World War I and World War II veterans. But the Army and Navy departments had higher priorities on building materials, and nothing much had been achieved during the war. Only two new VA hospitals were under construction when I arrived. Typically, they were in the boondocks—Tomah, Wisconsin, and Lebanon, Pennsylvania. Plans for seventy more new VA hospitals and as many hospital additions were in various stages of development. Some sites for new hospitals had already been negotiated through Congress and approved. Others were pending. All too many locations for the new hospitals or major additions to old hospitals were far removed from the medical schools and thus in conflict with our plans.[9]

If we were to achieve our goals for affiliation, there was only one solution: We had to remove VA hospital construction from the pork barrel category. Hawley bluntly put it this way: "To hell with the scenery. We want the best doctors."[10]

Well aware that the matter was politically explosive, I discussed it with Truman in considerable detail. His position was that we could not renege on all the commitments Hines had made. Some had to be honored, otherwise we would run the risk of antagonizing the whole Congress. An angry and aroused Congress might well disapprove or hack to pieces out of spite any new program we proposed. But generally he backed our concept and gave me a free hand, assuring me once more that I had his full support.[11]

The creation of the VA medical corps and the hospital construction and affiliation program were big, noisy, highly visible steps to upgrade VA medicine. But all the while, behind the scenes, Hawley and other dedicated public servants were quietly pushing along other programs too numerous to list here, but no less vital to our purpose. Two in particular deserve special mention.

Prestige advisory boards. In order to attract interest in VA medical problems, obtain the very best counsel, and at the same time improve our image within the medical profession, Hawley and his assistants created a VA special medical advisory group, a sort of august medical board of directors to VA. They persuaded the distinguished Dr. Charles W. Mayo of the Mayo Clinic to serve as chairman. Mayo, in turn, was able to recruit many able and renowned physicians to serve with him on the group, or on satellite specialty advisory groups, such as the council of chief consultants. These boards proved to be far more valuable than mere window dressing. At slight cost to us, they diligently reviewed all VA medical plans, made countless sound suggestions, helped us in our affiliation program with the medical schools and enabled us to attract a wide range of able consultants and specialists. These men selflessly gave us untold thousands of hours of conscientious service with almost no public recognition or reward. Somewhere a statue should be erected in their honor.[12]

Research and rehabilitation. In the past, VA had been more prone to warehouse than to rehabilitate wounded or disabled veterans. In my early tours of our hospitals, I had seen all too many men simply languishing away. If not encouraged to help themselves, a certain curious hopelessness overcomes many war wounded and they gradually become inured to institutionalization and take it for granted. Early in the game, Hawley and I decided we would place the strongest possible emphasis on patient physical and mental rehabilitation, if possible returning a much higher percentage of disabled veterans to society fully capable of taking care of themselves. Toward this end Hawley recruited hundreds of therapists skilled in rehabilitation and with VA funds stimulated research leading to new prosthetic appliances (artificial limbs) and special automobiles for amputees.

One outgrowth of this emphasis on rehabilitation was a VA program designed to encourage private industry to train and hire disabled veterans. One of the most successful of these was the Joseph Bulova School of Watchmaking, which was founded in 1944 by Arde Bulova, chairman of the board of the Bulova Watch Company of New York. The Bulova school was tuition-free and designed for veterans who had suffered at least a 70 percent disability. Its graduates were absorbed into the Bulova Watch Company and performed outstandingly.

Owing to its success, I took a special interest in the Bulova school, frequently holding it up as an example of what industry could do to help rehabilitate disabled veterans. I visited the school often, gave diplomas to the twenty members of the first graduating class in 1946 and became close friends with Arde Bulova and the man who had married his sister, Harry D. Henshel, vice chairman of the company. Henshel had served as a lieutenant colonel in the G-4 section of the Twelfth Army Group. He was an active member of the armed services division of the National Jewish Welfare Board and, like Arde Bulova, an ardent champion of the watchmaking school. The close association I formed with Arde Bulova and Harry Henshel led me to join Bulova when I retired from public life in 1953.[13]

We were not able to magically upgrade VA medicine overnight, but I believe it is fair to say that within two years we had launched it on the right track. Besides creating and staffing the VA medical corps, we placed most of the seventy new hospitals, and many additions, in places where we wanted them. We established affiliation with sixty-three of the seventy-seven class-A medical schools. (The other fourteen were willing but we had no VA facilities near them.) Meantime, we treated 882,000 hospital patients—three-quarters of them World War II veterans. In addition, we provided medical care or services for 6 million other veterans with less severe problems through direct payments to private physicians. No veteran was refused care, even if his illness was non-service connected, and the care veterans received was immeasurably improved.[14]

I was gratified when the VA's most exacting gadfly, Albert Deutsch, writing in *Look* magazine and elsewhere, pronounced that VA medicine had undergone a "revolution," that Hawley had "infused the whole hospital program with a spirit of modern, scientific medicine." Similarly, medical journalists Lois Mattox Miller and James Monohan, in a *Reader's Digest* article entitled "Veterans' Medicine: Second to None," wrote: "In two years General Omar N. Bradley has transformed the medical service of the Veterans Administration from a national scandal to a model establishment."[15]

By reason of my position in the U.S. Army in World War II, I had been compelled to send hundreds of thousands of men into battle. I had heard the mournful cries of the wounded on the battlefield. In countless Army field hospitals, I had seen the maimed stoically enduring nearly unbearable pain. Nothing I have done in my life gave me more satisfaction than the knowledge that I had done my utmost to ease their way when they came home.

FORTY-NINE

Truman deeply admired George Marshall and was reluctant to see him leave government service. He prevailed on Marshall to remain as Army Chief of Staff at least four months longer than Marshall had intended—to November 26, 1945. On November 27, Truman asked Marshall to return to government service as a special emissary to China with the rank of ambassador. Marshall accepted.[1]

Ike assumed the duties of Chief of Staff on December 3. I feel certain that no man in the history of the U.S. Army tackled the job with greater reluctance. As he promised me he would, he first tried to get out of it, proposing me in his place. However, Truman wanted me to stay at VA for at least two years. Ike then followed through on his other promise to me: he would take the Chief of Staff job for only two years; Truman agreed that I would succeed Ike. Our classmate, Joe McNarney, Marshall's deputy, replaced Ike in Europe as commander of U.S. forces.[2]

Ike and Mamie moved into Quarters One at Fort Myer. For the first time in our Army careers, we were neighbors. But we saw little of one another. Mamie and Mary didn't get along, and Ike was busy in his new job while I was busy in mine. Only rarely did our paths cross professionally. On a few occasions I saw Ike out near the parade ground flagpole with a nine iron practicing chip shots and I joined him.[3]

Owing to various circumstances, some "political," some tragic, only one of the senior World War II ETO commanders joined Ike in the Pentagon: Tooey Spaatz, who replaced Hap Arnold as commanding general of the Army Air Force. Ike wanted Bedell Smith for an important job, but Secretary of State James F. Byrnes named Smith ambassador to Moscow. Sandy Patch died suddenly in November 1945. Patton was in the doghouse again for some public comments he made comparing the Nazis to Republicans and Democrats. Within a short time he would be dead. Bill Simpson developed an ulcer and hernia and retired. Courtney Hodges, worn out and typically reclusive, returned his First Army headquarters to Governors

Island, New York, and remained virtually isolated in that sinecure until retirement. Ike was content to leave Jake Devers in command of Army Ground Forces. Gee Gerow, who was also worn out, became head of the Command and General Staff School at Fort Leavenworth. Mark Clark remained in Vienna, commanding U.S. occupation forces.[4]

Patton's death on December 21, 1945, was a great shock. It seemed the height of irony or ignominy that, having fearlessly courted death in three wars, he would die as the result of an automobile accident. It may be a harsh thing to say, but I believe it was better for George Patton and his professional reputation that he died when he did. The war was won; there were no more wars left for him to fight. He was not a good peacetime soldier; he would not have found a happy place in the postwar Army. He would have gone into retirement hungering for the old limelight, beyond doubt indiscreetly sounding off on any subject any time, any place. In time he probably would have become a boring parody of himself—a decrepit, bitter, pitiful figure, unwittingly debasing the legend.[5]

Ike turned to the "younger" officers—many of them corps or division commanders from the ETO—to help him run the postwar Army. He promoted Tom Handy from chief of OPD to deputy chief of staff. Joe Collins took over the important position of chief of information (public relations). Matt Ridgway became Ike's representative on the United Nations Military Committee. Max Taylor was made superintendent of West Point.[6]

Ike was terribly unhappy in his job. After a mere two weeks, he wrote his son, John, that the office "was a sorry place to light after having commanded a theater of war." He privately memoed: "This job is as bad as I always thought it would be." A year later he logged: "It has been a most difficult period for me, with far more frustrations than progress." He complained to Bedell Smith that the job was "irritating and weary." He wrote a friend: "While the shooting was going on I always thought that I would be able to retire the second the Japanese war was over. I was counting on Bradley serving as Chief of Staff while I could take Mamie off to some cabin in the woods and do a lot of high-powered resting. The more time goes on the more anxious I am to begin such a program."[7]

The problems Ike faced were large and depressing. None was more depressing than the helter-skelter demobilization of the magnificent U.S. Army that on V-J Day numbered about 8.2 million men. Within about a year, the Army's total manpower level, including the Air Force, had shrunk to about 1.5 million, and Truman had announced further cuts to about one million. On March 31, 1947, the draft was allowed to expire, and Army and Air Force manpower levels sank below one million. All too few of our ablest and battle-hardened officers and noncoms elected to make the Army a career. Army and Air Force budgets were slashed.[8]

At the same time Ike had to deal with the most complex and heated political issue the War and Navy departments had ever confronted: "unification" of the armed forces. Although I was wholly absorbed in my VA duties, as a senior military officer still on active duty I was never far from the turbulent center of this postwar debate. My future professional career would be profoundly influenced by it.[9]

The story of the battle to unify the armed forces is long and complicated, but extremely important. In the pre–World War II years, air-power zealots, chafing at being under Army control, launched a propaganda drive to create a "separate" Air Force department, which would be co-equal with the Army and Navy and would include all land- and sea-based air power. The British and Germans adopted this concept with the establishment of the Royal Air Force and the Luftwaffe, but the United States did not. American air-power advocates usually coupled the argument for a separate Air Force with a proposal for a higher, unified military-governing establishment to preside over all three "co-equal" military services. For decades the U.S. Army and U.S. Navy were opposed to both unification and a separate Air Force. President Roosevelt refused to consider the idea.

During the war, Marshall had a change of heart and began to urge both a separate Air Force and a unified national military establishment to govern the three services. One reason was the Pearl Harbor disaster, which might have been prevented had we had closer interservice coordination. Another was the chaotic war production planning, which had led to such calamities as the grave shortage of LST's in the ETO, forcing the postponement of Overlord. Still another reason was that the Air Force had simply grown too large and unwieldy for the Army to administer.

As early as November 1943, Marshall began urging a unified military establishment for the postwar period, to include a fourth branch—Supply. A committee chaired by retired Admiral James O. Richardson was created to study the problem and conducted world-wide interviews with senior military commanders, including me. A majority of senior Army officers (including me) approved "unification" but "exactly half" of all naval officers were opposed, principally because they feared losing control of Navy and Marine Corps aviation, and possibly the aircraft carriers. In April 1944, Congress conducted hearings on the matter, but they came to nought and the issue was shelved for the time being.

After the war President Truman, who had spent much of the war as chairman of a special Senate committee investigating national defense programs, emerged absolutely dedicated to military unification. On December 19, 1945—a couple of weeks after Ike took over as Chief of Staff—Truman sent Congress a special message urging an armed forces unification plan based, more or less, on proposals that had been developed by the Army. His proposal coincided with the congressional investigation of the Pearl Harbor debacle, which each day seemed to uncover further shocking examples of the need for service unification. Truman's unification proposal thus rode on a groundswell of favorable public opinion.[10]

Truman's proposal led to lengthy congressional hearings in the spring of 1946. These hearings broadened to examine such questions as "Why do we need a Navy at all? "Why do we have separate ground forces in the Marine Corps and Army?" "Why do we have three air forces—Army, Navy and Marine Corps?" By that time, the Navy and Marine Corps, sincerely fearing they would be diminished to ceremonial forces, were passionately and publicly opposing unification. The admirals made sensational anti-Army and anti–Air Force charges in the hearings. For example, it was revealed that Ike wanted to reduce the Marine Corps to a few lightly equipped regiments for "minor operations" and Spaatz wanted control of all guided missiles in the future. The new Chief of Naval Operations, Admiral Chester Nimitz, charged that "the ultimate ambition of the Army Air Force [is] to absorb naval aviation in its entirety and set up one large air force." The Navy and Marine Corps testimony was so heated and controversial that Truman was forced to fall back and regroup. He asked the new Secretary of the Navy, James V. Forrestal, and the new Secretary of War, Robert P. Patterson, to seek a compromise solution for presentation to Congress the following year.[11]

Forrestal and Patterson produced a greatly watered down compromise unification plan. New congressional hearings commenced in the spring of 1947. Although many Navy and Marine Corps witnesses continued to oppose unification, this time around Forrestal and Nimitz supported the President. The Republicans had won control of both the Senate and House in the November 1946 off-year elections. A majority of the Republicans, believing unification would save money, supported the bill. It was overwhelmingly approved on the last two days of the session, July 24 and 25, and Truman signed it into law on July 26.

This act created what was called the National Military Establishment, with a Secretary of Defense presiding over three co-equal services: Army, Navy, Air Force. Truman asked Bob Patterson to become the first Secretary of Defense, but when he declined, Truman gave the job to Navy Secretary James Forrestal. The act established secretaries of the Army (instead of War), Navy and Air Force, and for the first time gave the Joint Chiefs of Staff legal standing. It also created the National Security Council (NSC) and Central Intelligence Agency (CIA).[12]

I had supported and testified for Truman's original unification plan and was not very happy with the final outcome. The act had been so watered down to mollify the Navy that the end result was not truly "unification" but rather a loosely structured "federation." One part of the act stripped the three service secretaries of cabinet status, greatly diminishing their prestige. At the same time, the act deliberately denied the Secretary of Defense a staff or principal military adviser. Thus the sole representative of the National Military Establishment in the President's innermost circles had no support in formulating policy papers and positions, making his job nearly impossible to carry out. Another weakness of the act was that the creation of the NSC tended to degrade and diminish the power and policymaking role of the Joint Chiefs of Staff.[13]

All this time Ike was slowly developing his future personal plans, to which my own future was so closely tied. His dream of retirement to a "remotely situated cottage" had evaporated. He very wisely avoided being drawn into the 1948 presidential political race and instead accepted a position as president of Columbia University. The final plan was that he would leave the Army about November 1947, at which time, Truman agreed, I would relieve him as Chief of Staff. In the meantime, Ike had made a deal with the book publishers Doubleday and Company to write his memoirs (*Crusade in Europe*) in the interval between leaving the Army and assuming his duties at Columbia. Doubleday paid him the then astounding sum of $635,000 for all rights to the book, making Ike a rich man in one stroke.[14]

Commencing in April 1947, Ike took several steps to pave my way toward his relief. At his urging, on April 17 Truman submitted to Congress a special bill, soon passed, which made me and Tooey Spaatz permanent four-star generals. On May 23, Ike decorated me with a third Distinguished Service Medal for services in the ETO. Thirdly, he arranged with Truman that I be recalled to active Army duty for a period of six weeks (August 1 to September 15), in order that I (and Mary) might make an extended inspection of U.S. Army forces in Europe. We looked forward to the trip for both professional and personal reasons. Hal and Lee, who now had a son, Henry, Junior—our first grandchild—were stationed in Berlin.[15]

We launched our trip with a lovely weekend at Perle Mesta's Newport, Rhode Island, mansion, "Mid-Cliffe." We had previously met Perle, the Washington "hostess with the mostest," at gatherings in her Washington home. From Newport we traveled to New York, where we were entertained by, among others, Ike's and Bedell Smith's good friend, the famous toy tycoon and financier Louis Marx. On August 15, we sailed for Germany on the Army transport *E. B. Alexander*. After twelve pleasant and restful days at sea, we reached Bremerhaven on August 26.[16]

By this time, Joe McNarney had returned to the States to help organize the fledgling United States Air Force. His deputy, Lucius D. Clay, now a four-star general, had ascended to the post of commander in chief of the European Command and military governor of the U.S. zone in Germany. Clay (Class of 1918) was one of the brightest, most quietly forceful generals in the Army. An engineer in peacetime, during the war he had been Marshall's chief of procurement, an awesome job with horrendous political ramifications, which he had carried out brilliantly. Although Clay was something of a maverick and iconoclast, he had a keen political antenna and was an ideal choice for this international hot spot.

Clay had performed very ably in a near-impossible job. West Germany and Berlin had become focal points of Allied and Cold War tensions. Not only had he to deal with conflicting British, French and American occupational policies, but also with the Russians, who had become increasingly hostile and disruptive. On top of that, our own State Department was making new policy decisions which were in conflict with Clay's policies. Clay was worn down. He had several times threatened to resign. One of my unofficial tasks was to buck him up and encourage him to stay on the job.[17]

Clay could not have been a more gracious host. He assigned Hal, who worked on his staff, to serve as my aide during our trip and arranged that Lee could accompany us everywhere. For some time, most U.S. occupational troops in Germany had been serving as clerks and policemen. But recently, in reaction to Soviet saber rattling, Clay had fielded a new regimental combat team from troops of the Big Red One. He asked me to review it. I did and praised him to the heavens. This team signaled the rebirth of Army combat forces in Germany.[18]

We spent six days with Clay and his staff in Berlin, becoming thoroughly reacquainted with the situation there. I shall not attempt to recount the numerous and vexing military and political problems Clay was then facing. The main impression I carried away was that trouble—serious trouble—loomed with the Russians. When it came with a rush the following year, I was far better prepared to deal with it, thanks to this visit.

Over the next several weeks we traveled far and wide through Europe: Austria, Italy, Sicily, Switzerland, France, England. By that time Monty had returned from the British zone in Germany to replace Alan Brooke (now Field Marshal Lord Alanbrooke) as Chief of the Imperial Staff. Monty could not have been more hospitable. He had a dinner in our honor and his staff made our travel arrangements in the British Isles. This included a side trip to the Isle of Wight, where Mary looked up some distant cousins. Finally, ten days later than planned, on September 25, we boarded Clay's personal aircraft, a four-engined C-54, and flew home via the Azores and Bermuda.[19]

I returned to the VA grind for another eight weeks. Truman, meanwhile, had been searching for my replacement.[20]

The man he finally selected was Carl R. Gray, Jr., a railroad executive and major general in the Army Reserve.[21] Ike knew Gray and admired him. I thought Gray was a poor choice. I had known Gray in Africa and Europe and I did not share Ike's high opinion of him. Gray certainly did not have a sympathetic attitude toward the GI, which I thought was essential to the VA job. Upon learning that Gray was Truman's choice, Hawley, who also knew Gray, made plans to leave the VA when I did. He became chief executive officer of the National Blue Cross–Blue Shield medical plans.[22]

Truman announced my appointment to Army Chief of Staff on November 21, together with Gray's nomination to succeed me at the VA. I submitted my letter of resignation on November 26, to date from November 30.[23]

As it turned out, Ike could not yet step down. There were too many loose ends he had to attend to. He postponed the changeover to the first of the year, then later to early February. These postponements left me at loose ends for over nine weeks. Mary and I spent that time in glorious utter relaxation: almost three weeks at Fort Benning, where I played golf and hunted; Christmas in Quarters Seven; then a round trip by train to Los Angeles with Chet Hansen and his wife, where on January 1, 1948, I was grand marshal of the Rose Bowl parade.[24]

Had I known far enough in advance that my relief of Ike would be postponed as long as it was, I would most certainly have planned a tour of the Pacific and the Far East in January to confer with MacArthur and his Army subordinates. My knowledge of the problems in those areas was limited to what I had read or heard from others. I had not traveled west of California since I returned from Hawaii in 1928. Moreover, a trip to the Far East would have been politically beneficial, helping to allay the whispers and suspicions and growing paranoia that since the "ETO clique" had taken over the Army the Far East sphere was being neglected. I was particularly anxious to establish a relationship with MacArthur, who had rejected me for army group commander and who would now be, in a manner of speaking, my subordinate. A Far East trip remained near the head of my list of priority items.

When the 80th Congress, second session, reconvened in January 1948, the Senate Armed Services Committee routinely approved my appointment. Ike and I planned a simple, unceremonious turnover in his office on February 7, but Truman wanted to be present and so it became a more elaborate proceeding than we wished. At exactly noon, we all gathered in the office of the new Army Secretary, Kenneth Royall—Truman, Royall, Ike, Mary and I. Mamie was ill with flu and a penicillin reaction and could not attend, but her mother, Mrs. Doud, who was visiting the Eisenhowers, was present. Truman decorated Ike with a fourth Distinguished Service Medal and gave him a silver cigarette case, a gift from the JCS. Ike administered the oath of office to me and then said simply: "You have a job." It was all over in five minutes.[25]

FIFTY

When I assumed the post of Chief of Staff, I looked forward to a tour of four years, then retirement at the end of 1951. As it turned out, I was promoted out of the job within eighteen months, making my tour probably the shortest in Army history. But every moment of that tour was demanding and filled with drama.

The leading characters were diverse and fascinating. None was more fascinating than Secretary of Defense James V. Forrestal, who sat in lonely, uneasy splendor at the pinnacle of the National Military Establishment. He was Irish. Not glad-handing or hard-drinking Irish, but rather reclusive, brooding, intense. He was Princeton and Wall Street. He wore the Ivy League uniform: double-breasted pin-striped suits, button-down Brooks Brothers shirts and regimental ties. He had been an amateur boxer at Princeton and afterwards, until someone flattened his nose. During World War I, he was a naval aviator. Between the wars he had amassed a comfortable fortune at the New York investment-banking house Dillon, Read and Company. In 1940, Navy Secretary Frank Knox drafted Forrestal into the then prestigious post of Undersecretary of the Navy, and during the war Forrestal had supervised the purchasing and constructing of the vast U.S. Navy. Upon Knox's death of a heart attack in April 1944, Roosevelt had promoted Forrestal to Secretary of the Navy.[1]

Soon after I became Chief of Staff, Forrestal invited me to play golf with him at the Chevy Chase Club in a nearby Maryland suburb. I accepted gladly, not only because I liked golf but also as a way of getting to know Forrestal better. It was a bizarre experience. He arrived in his usual state, wound tightly as a clock spring. We literally raced around nine holes in one hour and ten minutes flat. Then he rushed back to the Pentagon to work. I shook my head in disbelief. I felt certain that Forrestal, who was one year older than I, was going to work himself to death very soon.[2]

In spite of his cold intensity and inability to let his iron-gray hair down, I admired Jim Forrestal. He was a totally committed public servant, giving his life to his nation. He had been handed a monumental job—to truly unify the services—and he was doing his utmost to carry it out. He was a Navy man and yet in his new job he was shedding his bias. He was trying to be a fair-minded and entirely objective Secretary of Defense with no axes to grind. He had good instincts. He was one of the first to perceive that Stalin should not be trusted, that Moscow intended to capitalize on the wreckage of the war to impose communism wherever it could.[3]

Down one peg in the civilian chain of command in my bailiwick stood Army Secretary Kenneth Royall, a man of far different character, roots—and size. He was a genial giant: 6 feet 5 inches, 250 pounds. Scion of a noted Southern family, Royall came from Goldsboro, North Carolina. A Phi Beta Kappa graduate of the University of North Carolina (1914) and Harvard Law School (1917), he had served in the field artillery in France in World War I, where he was wounded in action. Between the wars he built a lucrative law practice in Goldsboro and Raleigh, served in the state senate and was president of the North Carolina Bar Association. Six months after Pearl Harbor, at the request of Undersecretary Patterson, Royall returned to the Army as a reserve colonel in the Army service forces' fiscal and legal branches. Stimson and Patterson soon saw that Royall's charm, talent and ability outweighed his job. They promoted him to brigadier general, moved him to Stimson's staff and put him in charge of the Army's congressional relations. In November 1945, when Patterson replaced Stimson as Secretary of War, Royall was named Undersecretary, and when Patterson returned to his New York law practice in 1947, Truman promoted Royall to Secretary. He had a relaxed, patrician air, was an unstinting champion of the Army and, like Forrestal, was dedicated to making unification work.[4]

The Army General Staff, over which I presided, had been in the throes of reorganization ever since the war. Several plans had been proposed, endlessly debated and discarded. These debates continued during my first few months in office. Central to all these plans was the compelling need to relieve the Chief of Staff of onerous and routine detail so that he would have more time for high-level consultation on strategy, weapons and budgets with the Secretary of Defense, the Joint Chiefs of Staff and other joint bodies that unification had spawned. The setup I finally chose was one that had a vice chief of staff and, beneath him, two deputy chiefs of staff, one for plans and operations, one for administration. I named Joe Collins, who had replaced Tom Handy as Ike's deputy the previous September, to the post of vice chief of staff; Albert Wedemeyer to deputy for plans and operations; and Wade Haislip as deputy for administration.[5]

Joe Collins had grown enormously during his two and a half years in postwar Washington. As chief of information, he had met and charmed the Washington press corps. As the War Department's leading planner and spokesman on unification, he had become widely acquainted on the Hill. As Ike's deputy chief of staff for six months, he had become thoroughly acquainted with internal Army policy and problems. Joe was not a deep thinker or strategist. He was a "doer," an action man; and, on occasion, he was all too apt to live up to his nickname, "Lightning," and go chasing off as if he were still commanding VII Corps in the ETO. But on the whole, he was an excellent executive, and I let him handle most matters with complete confidence that he would make the right decisions. He thus lifted a great weight of detail from my shoulders, becoming, in effect, chief executive officer of the Army, while I presided like a chairman of the board.

This reorganization greatly reduced the need for me to maintain a large personal staff. Chet Hansen and my secretary, Mary Pitcairn, moved with me from the VA. Chet remained my chief letter and speech writer and unofficial public relations counsel, Mary my personal secretary. For my chief aide, executive officer and general factotum, I chose Willis Matthews, who had served with me in the tactical department at West Point, at Fort Benning when I was commandant and, later, as G-3 with the 82nd and 28th divisions. I had tried and failed to get Matthews into the ETO. He had become "lost" in the Southwest Pacific, first on Walter Krueger's Sixth Army G-3 staff, then on MacArthur's staff and elsewhere. Unfairly, I thought, MacArthur had not given him a major combat command, and thus he was still a colonel and not going anywhere. I found him buried in the job of professor of military science and tactics at the University of Wisconsin and was very glad to have him at my side again. An old Tennessee country slicker, Matthews had an uncanny ability to smell a rat. As matters soon developed, it was the right time to have a rat smeller on your side in the Pentagon.[6]

By the time I assumed my duties, the Soviet Union was undeniably and unequivocally the main enemy of the United States and free men everywhere. Moscow had brazenly vowed to communize the world. Stalin had ruthlessly imposed puppet governments in every nation in Eastern and Central Europe save one, Czechoslovakia, and that nation was soon to be doomed. Three weeks after I was sworn in, Stalin's political operatives, tunneling from within, overthrew the Czech government and seized control of the country, brutally suppressing opposition.

This shocking event was one more highly visible success. Stalin's minions in Berlin, deep inside the Soviet occupation zone, were doing their utmost to wreck any reasonable plan for a postwar German settlement and to drive the Western powers out of the city altogether. Moscow had engineered a communist government in Yugoslavia, which, but for the stubborn chauvinism of Marshal Tito, would have long since gone behind the Curtain. Stalin leered hungrily over the prostrate carcass of Western Europe, initiating intense political action programs designed to expand the growing communist blocs in the French and Italian assemblies into majorities. He was backing Greek insurgents in open warfare against the established Greek government and bringing pressure to bear in Turkey, Iran and other areas in the Middle East. In the Far East, he was backing communist leader Mao Tse-tung in the Chinese Civil War, which each day saw another defeat for the corrupt Nationalist regime of Chiang Kai-shek. In Indochina, another of his puppets, Ho Chi Minh, had launched guerrilla warfare against the established French colonial government. In North Korea, he was laying plans for yet another puppet government, backed by a growing Moscow-equipped army.

This was the Cold War, a wholly new and different kind of threat to the United States. It took some little time to perceive its character and to evolve a policy to cope with it. For two years, the Truman administration had groped along uncertainly, placing a great deal of sincere but misguided faith in the United Nations and other diplomatic forums, hoping to arrive at some kind of peaceful co-existence or détente. Gradually and haltingly, a new policy, which the historians have called "containment," began to evolve. The United States would "contain" Soviet expansionism by unilaterally shoring up anti-communist governments with economic and military aid. The first public manifestation of the emerging policy, ambitiously labeled the "Truman Doctrine," was a combined $400 million aid package to Greece and Turkey, launched with great fanfare in March 1947.

By this time, Truman had appointed George Marshall Secretary of State. Marshall's State Department planners, headed by Soviet expert George Kennan, in further defining and refining the so-called containment policy, hit upon the idea of a massive economic aid program for destitute Western Europe, which Churchill had aptly described as "a rubble heap, a charnel house, a breeding ground of pestilence and hate." The plan, as it finally emerged—an electrifying and radical notion—was to give Western Europe $17 billion in economic recovery aid over a period of four years. At Truman's suggestion, the program was called the Marshall Plan. Marshall himself unveiled it at Harvard University on June 5, 1947, in a historic speech which I was privileged to hear.

It seemed to me there was a fundamental dichotomy in the containment policy. No one had fully thought through its long-term military implications. Getting tough with the Russians, holding them in check around the globe, fighting fire with fire, clearly demanded a concurrent buildup of our conventional military forces, especially the U.S. Army. It may seem hard to believe, but exactly the opposite was taking place. Truman had placed a firm ceiling on military spending. By 1948 our armed forces had shrunk to a mere 1.6 million men, desperately trying to make ends meet on a total budget of about $10 billion a year.[7]

Several major economic considerations had led Truman to impose tight ceilings on defense spending. World War II had swollen the national debt to a then staggering $280 billion. In addition, indirect war costs, such as the $8 billion a year in veterans benefits, were continuing. Truman's goal was not only to maintain a balanced federal budget but, if possible, to *reduce* (!) the national debt to $200 billion, thereby curbing the huge (and inflationary) interest payments required to service the debt. One way to hold down federal spending was to put a tight ceiling on military expenditures, and that was the course Truman chose. The situation was further aggravated when in 1948 the Republican 80th Congress, in an attempt to curry favor with voters in the forthcoming presidential elections, passed, over Truman's veto, a substantial tax cut. In order to keep the federal budget balanced, Truman chose to cut military expenditures even further.[8]

The military spending ceiling had reduced the Army to a shockingly deplorable state. Congress had authorized a force level of 669,000 officers and men, but Truman's budget bureau, in turn, had reduced that figure to 560,000. Owing to the termination of the draft and to rampant inflation, which had severely eroded Army pay scales, bringing a sharp drop in reenlistments, we had not even been able to reach that modest force level. When I took over as Chief of Staff, our actual strength was 552,000 men. There was small prospect that we could hold very long at that level; we were still shrinking.

The Army had almost no combat effectiveness. Ike had left me an administrative rather than a military force. Half of the 552,000 officers and men were overseas on occupation duty, serving as policemen or clerks. The other half were in the States performing various administrative chores. In theory, there was an "Army Reserve" in the United States for emergencies. On paper, it consisted of two and a third divisions. But in truth, only one division—the 82nd Airborne at Fort Bragg, North Carolina—could be remotely described as combat ready. The Army was thus in no position whatsoever to backstop a get-tough policy of containment vis-à-vis the Soviets. Actually, the Army of 1948 could not fight its way out of a paper bag.[9]

The grave weakness of our conventional military forces—the Army in particular—was dramatically driven home to me during the first few months of my brief tenure as Chief of Staff by the intensification of trouble in three major crisis areas. These were:

Greece. Greece had been savaged first by Italy, then Germany. The principal postwar task, as everywhere in liberated nations, was to restore a freely elected government to power, backed up by a constabulary force of sufficient strength to maintain law and order. The task in Greece was greatly complicated when Stalin underwrote a communist guerrilla force dedicated to the overthrow of the government. Britain wished to help the Greeks—and had tried—but it was soon clear that she had neither the money nor the troops required to fight the guerrillas. In early 1947, she had appealed to us for help and this appeal had led to our allotting Greece $300 million under the Truman Doctrine. Later in the year—in August—London dismayed Washington with the news that she would be compelled to begin a gradual troop withdrawal.

This news touched off a major uproar in Washington. The Truman Doctrine had committed us to saving Greece. Our prestige as a great power was on the line. The Greek government was forming a seven-division army to combat the guerrillas, but it was far from ready to go it alone. Some Washington planners believed that when London pulled its troops out, Greece would fall to the guerrillas. Still others believed that if Greece fell to communism, so, in time, would the whole of the eastern Mediterranean and possibly the Middle East. A State Department planning council urged that the United States send ground forces to Greece.

This proposal was referred to the JCS for recommendation at about the time I was replacing Ike, and he naturally drew me into the discussions. I was shocked. Our Army was so weak and already spread so thin worldwide that even if the JCS deemed it strategically advisable to send appreciable numbers of ground troops to Greece we could not have done so, the JCS reported, without at least a partial national mobilization—a call-up of National Guard and Army Reserve units. In his usual direct, simple, concise way, Secretary of State George Marshall told the NSC on February 12—five days after I was sworn in—that "we are playing with fire while we have nothing with which to put it out."

Fortunately, the Greek crisis had a happy ending. In lieu of ground forces, we sent a substantial military advisory group to hurry the Greek Army into operational status and guide it in combat with U.S.-supplied weapons. Knowing that we would need a prestigious and forceful leader to head the advisory group, Marshall proposed that Jim Van Fleet, who had done so well as a corps commander in the ETO, be appointed. Ike and I heartily concurred. Van Fleet was worth two American divisions. He worked miracles in Greece, completely routed the communist guerrillas, and insured the stability of the government.[10]

Korea. In the closing days of World War II, when Russia entered the war against Japan, Japanese-occupied Korea had been arbitrarily divided at the 38th parallel. The Russians occupied the industrial north, we occupied the rural south. Our high-minded postwar goal for Korea was a unified democratic nation with a popularly elected government. Stalin had other ideas. He closed off North Korea at the 38th parallel and turned it into a puppet state, thus thwarting a nationwide election. In order to prevent North Korea from taking over South Korea—to contain the North—the U.S. proceeded with a plan to help the South Koreans set up a democratic nation and form a constabulary of sufficient strength to keep law and order and stop any military incursions from the north.

We had occupied Korea but we did not want to stay any longer than we had to. As a military operations zone, Korea—mountainous and bitterly cold in winter—had no appeal. In the very remote event we would be compelled to launch military operations on the Asiatic mainland, Korea would certainly be bypassed. Should the Soviets occupy South Korea and threaten Japan, it was believed we could destroy her military bases with air power. The military lack of interest in Korea was clearly and officially defined several months before I became Chief of Staff. In September 1947, the JCS (Ike, Nimitz, Spaatz, Leahy) had informed Forrestal and Forrestal in turn had informed Marshall that "from the standpoint of military security, the United States has little strategic interest in maintaining the present troops and bases in Korea." Marshall and his State Department advisers had concurred, stating that "ultimately the U.S. position in Korea is untenable even with the expenditure of considerable U.S. money and effort." In sum, from September 1947 onward, U.S. policy toward South Korea was to get out as soon as possible, withdrawing our occupational forces as the South Korean constabulary grew in size and effectiveness. I agreed entirely with this policy.

When I took over my new Army duties, the South Korean elections were originally scheduled to be held within about two months—before the end of March 1948. This was believed to be a delicate and dangerous period. Intelligence feared that the North Koreans might mount a major operation to disrupt or even prevent free elections in South Korea, or that a civil war might erupt between left and right political organizations in South Korea. If the elections were fouled by either event, it would be a major setback for the South Koreans and for us. We could not begin to withdraw our troops from Korea until a stable government and a constabulary were in place.

The original plan was to maintain a force of 40,000 U.S. Army troops in South Korea until after the elections and installation of a government. Owing to the acute shortage of personnel in the Far East, the Korean occupation force had shrunk to about 20,000 men. The U.S. Army commander in Korea, General John P. Hodge (one of MacArthur's World War II corps commanders), warning that his command was "approaching an impossible situation without the manpower and means to carry on," appealed to MacArthur in Tokyo for reinforcements. But MacArthur responded that he himself was so short of manpower that his headquarters was "virtually powerless to take effective action of any kind short of abandoning the occupation mission."

Here was a potentially explosive situation. Our long-term national policy required that we guarantee elections in South Korea. Hodge did not have sufficient troops to insure that the elections could take place. MacArthur had so few troops in Japan that he could barely perform his occupation mission. If he further reduced his forces to reinforce Hodge by

20,000 men, there was grave danger that Japanese dissident groups could overwhelm MacArthur's remaining forces, causing widespread unrest in Japan with grave consequences.

This crisis was one of the first that I took to the JCS for resolution. My recommendation was that we split the difference and hope for the best. I urged that MacArthur be ordered to send Hodge 10,000 men, bringing the Korean occupation force to 30,000. That was 10,000 short of his stated requirement, but we could not strip Japan further. The JCS agreed with my recommendation and MacArthur was so notified.

For the moment, the Korean story had a happy outcome. Hodge got his 10,000 extra men in time to put them into effective positions. The delayed elections went forward on May 10, 1948. Communist guerrillas killed more than one hundred Koreans near the polling booths, but no major riots occurred. The American-sponsored candidate, seventy-two-year-old former Korean exile Syngman Rhee, was voted in as President. With the help of Hodge, Rhee began forming a constabulary force, and we made plans to commence withdrawing U.S. forces. But the Korean story was far from over.[11]

Berlin. Hard on the heels of the February 1948 communist coup in Czechoslovakia, grave trouble arose in Berlin. It came as a shock. On March 5, Lucius Clay cabled a message that lifted me right out of my chair:

> FOR MANY MONTHS BASED ON LOGICAL ANALYSIS, I HAVE FELT AND HELD THAT WAR WAS UNLIKELY FOR AT LEAST TEN YEARS. WITHIN THE LAST FEW WEEKS I HAVE FELT A SUBTLE CHANGE IN SOVIET ATTITUDE WHICH I CANNOT DEFINE BUT WHICH NOW GIVES ME A FEELING THAT *IT MAY COME WITH DRAMATIC SUDDENNESS*. [Italics added.][12]

As if bearing out Clay's lugubrious assessment, Soviet authorities in Germany suddenly got very, very belligerent. They began a campaign of harassment designed to restrict our ground access to Berlin. For a while, the ultimate objective appeared to be to force the Western occupying powers out of the city altogether.[13]

Owing to the danger of air collision in the restricted air space over Berlin, the Western powers had long since entered into a formal written agreement with the Soviets guaranteeing our right of access along certain air lanes. Ground access by highway, railway and canal had been implied by the very fact of our occupation status, but some errant diplomat or general had failed to get it guaranteed from the Soviets *in writing*.

On March 30, the Soviet authorities clamped down hard on our ground access. Henceforth, they pronounced, vehicles, trains and barges en route to Berlin through the Soviet occupation zone would be subjected to a mountain of red tape, designed to slow down our logistics of operations, which were not only supplying our own forces in Berlin, but the entire civilian population (some 2.25 million) as well. Clay was properly outraged and determined to face down the Russians. He believed our most effective response to be a show of military toughness—to meet fire with fire. On March 31, he cabled me that it was his intent "to instruct our guards to open fire if Soviet soldiers attempt to enter our trains."

Had I had enough hair on my head to react, this cable would probably have stood it on end. I could sympathize with Clay's instinctive gut reaction, but this was neither the time nor place to open fire on the Russians. If, as Clay had warned, the Soviets could launch a general war with "dramatic suddenness" this could be a provocation to justify it. I counseled caution. As I have said, we were far from ready to fight a general war with Russia then, and owing to the frank and public disclosures we were compelled to make on the Hill in defense of our military budgets, the Russians knew precisely how weak we were.

The National Security Act had established the National Security Council specifically to formulate policy for a crisis of this kind, but it was not convened. Our response was generated in a series of informal emergency meetings between Forrestal, Undersecretary of State Robert Lovett (Marshall was away), Ken Royall, Ike (who happened to be in town), the JCS and others. The upshot was a cable from Royall to Clay ordering him to employ restraint. We urged him to try to keep the trains moving but not to increase guards or their arms, and under no circumstances to fire on the Russians unless they fired first. Clay sent a train across the Soviet-zone border but the Russians, who seemed to mean business, shunted it to a siding, where it remained for a few days. Finally Clay, angry at Washington timidity, was compelled to withdraw it.

Were the Russians moving toward general war? The CIA, recently established for the purpose of answering such questions, was no help whatsoever. It had not even hinted that the Berlin crisis was brewing. The best it could do was provide a hedging guess that there would be no war within sixty days. On April 1, we received a long cable from Bedell Smith in Moscow that was reassuring. Smith concluded that "the Soviet Union will not deliberately resort to military action in the immediate future but will continue to attempt to secure its objectives by other means." Clay himself, upon reflection, now believed that the chances of general war were only "one in four."[14]

For a few weeks the Berlin crisis abated. Reacting to tough U.S. diplomatic notes, the Soviets relaxed some restrictions, and some trains began to move, if slowly. But the crisis exploded again on June 18, after Clay introduced a badly needed currency reform in the Western occupation zones, which the Soviets had opposed. Moscow retaliated with an absolute clamp-down on all our ground access to Berlin. Nothing was to pass across the Soviet-zone border. In addition, the Russians shut off most electrical power to Berlin. Western occupation forces and Berliners alike were sealed inside the city with a mere thirty-day supply of food and coal. It was a total ground blockade, a raw show of military force, designed, I'm sure, to compel the Western powers to abandon the city once and for all.

The onset of the Berlin Blockade coincided with the dramatic opening acts of the 1948 presidential campaign: the Republican and Democratic party conventions in Philadelphia. The Republicans, convening on June 21, nominated Thomas E. Dewey on the third ballot, and he picked Governor Earl Warren of California for a running mate. The Democrats, meeting in the same hall three weeks later, chose Truman on the first ballot, and he picked Senator Alben Barkley for his running mate. The Dixiecrats, who bolted the Democratic party, held a separate convention in Birmingham, Alabama, and nominated South Carolina's Governor Strom Thurmond for President. The left-wing Progressives also held a rump convention, nominating Henry Wallace. So it was Dewey vs. a three-headed Democratic split: Truman, Thurmond, Wallace. Clare Boothe Luce summed up the opinion of the pollsters and the pols when she wrote off Truman as "a gone goose."[15]

Truman was thus in a desperate fight for his political life. Possibly because of this enormous distraction, the Berlin Blockade in its early stages did not receive his fullest attention. Again, the NSC was not convened, and as in the Berlin trouble of late March, our response was arrived at through a series of hastily arranged emergency meetings. The most important of these was held in Ken Royall's office on Sunday, June 27, from 2:45 P.M. to 7:00 P.M., with Forrestal, Lovett, me and a half-dozen others from the Pentagon and the State Department.

In my opinion, the NSC should have long since drafted a policy paper with respect to Berlin. But it had not. One consequence was that we attempted at this meeting under the worst possible circumstances—everybody talking at once about a very complicated situation—to formulate a national policy. The choices were basically three: get out; fight; or try to stand on quicksand, hoping for a diplomatic solution or another sudden change in Soviet policy.

We had a stack of cables from Clay and his State Department counterpart, Robert Murphy. Both men talked tough. Clay believed that "a determined movement of convoys with troop protection" toward Berlin would succeed in breaking the blockade and force the Soviets to back down all the way. Clay recognized the risks entailed. Once launched, such an application of military force could lead straight to general war. Clay's views became known as the "shoot our way into Berlin" policy.

As in March, I counseled caution. It was my opinion that sending armed convoys to Berlin should be attempted only as a last resort, and only if the U.S. government was prepared to move to all-out war. If the armed convoys led to gunfire between our troops and Soviet troops, and we won the encounter, the Soviets could not take it lying down. They would reinforce and counterattack until they won. If we lost the initial encounter, we could not take it lying down, either. We, too, would escalate to the extent our limited ground forces permitted. And then what? Sooner or later, probably sooner, we would face the likelihood of all-out war.

To me, this meeting was a disturbing experience. Many options were discussed but nothing could be firmly planned or decided without guidance and decisions from the President. We broke up on that note. Forrestal, Lovett and Royall would meet with Truman the following day, review the options and find out what he wanted to do. Meanwhile, we would explore further the extent of the various options—consulting with the British about basing our B-29s in England, for example.

One option that was not raised was the possibility of creating an airlift to bring food and supplies into Berlin over our legally guaranteed and thus far unchallenged air lanes. But Clay had thought of that and, in fact, had already ordered his theater Air Force commander, Curtis E. LeMay, to mobilize every air transport at his disposal for the job. This was merely intended as a temporary expedient, not the ultimate Berlin solution, but as is so often the case, the man on the spot hits on the best ideas. In time, Clay's airlift would turn out to be not only the best but the only solution, short of general war, to the Berlin Blockade.[16]

Forrestal, Lovett and Royall met with Truman on the following day, June 28. What was our policy to be: Get out? Stay and fight? Or . . . ? Forrestal wrote: "The President interrupted to say that there was no discussion on that point, we were going to stay, period." But at what price? Royall asked. Shooting our way into Berlin? General war? Truman grew vague: we would have to "deal with the situation as it developed." He approved sending two B-29 squadrons to Germany, but when Lovett casually raised the delicate matter of sending two groups of B-29s to England, Truman (perhaps preoccupied with other matters) made no comment, which was later assumed to mean approval.[17]

Little by little Clay and LeMay increased the airlift capacity. Berliners pitched in willingly to unload the planes—the beginning of our historic postwar alliance with the German people. The Russians—at least for the moment—made no attempt to interfere with our heavy air traffic. Clay, a logistical genius, realized that if he imposed food rationing, he might keep Berlin supplied by airlift alone. Clay importuned Washington to send him every available Air Force transport, and the bigger the planes the better. Inasmuch as the airlift was emerging as a possible non-confrontational solution to the Berlin problem, many officials received these requests favorably and bucked them to the Pentagon.

The President called Clay and Murphy to Washington for discussions with the NSC. The decision was made to vastly increase the airlift. A special airlift organization was created and placed under command of Air Force General William H. Tunner, then commander of the unified Military Air Transport Service. Nine MATS squadrons totaling eighty-one C-54 four-engine transports were sent to Germany, and bulldozers cleared rubble to build a second Berlin airfield, Tegel. Later, still more C-54s were sent to Berlin.

In the meantime, the JCS had generated a series of papers raising many questions on Berlin, the purposes of which were to force the government and the NSC to arrive at a clear-cut policy. In fact, we never did get an answer to our questions or any other clear-cut policy statement from the NSC. Truman's view seemed to be that he would keep postponing the decision until faced with the necessity to fight or get out. The JCS historian Kenneth W. Condit wrote that to the JCS "such a postponement was understandably unsettling." In fact, it was outrageous. During the critical phase of the Berlin Blockade, when we were nose to nose with massive Soviet military power, the JCS were so poorly advised that we could not draw contingency war plans. Our exposure was enormous.[18]

The Berlin crisis raised a personal family problem—reminiscent of that caused by John Eisenhower's assignment to the ETO during the war. Lee, Hal and the grandchildren, Henry, Jr., and a new baby, Mary Elizabeth, were still in Berlin. If the Russians overran the city and captured them, the personal blow to me might well be incapacitating. As in the case of John Eisenhower, I made the decision to remove them from danger. I asked the Air Force to order Hal to duty in the States. The Air Force willingly consented, assigning Hal to the Air Staff in the Pentagon. Mary and I were delighted to have our family reunited in Washington—and to see our newest grandchild—but Hal was not very happy about being pulled out of the front lines to a Pentagon desk job.[19]

I have always felt that we were very, very lucky in the Berlin Blockade. Clay's brainchild, the airlift, worked out far better than anyone dared hope. The Russians did not interdict it. Ultimately, Bill Tunner's planes were able to bring in some 5,600 tons of food and fuel a day. This was sufficient to keep our beleaguered troops and the Berliners warm and fairly well fed on a diet of 1,880 calories a day. The common effort created a close bond between us and the West German people, who, in time, became staunch allies. Thus the airlift turned out to be our single greatest triumph in the Cold War.

It seemed clear to me that if the United States were to pursue a policy of containment, drastic steps must be taken to upgrade the size, caliber and combat readiness of the U.S. Army. Royall, Assistant Secretary of the Army Gordon Gray, Joe Collins and I became determined to press hard for a reform. These were the major courses we decided to pursue:

Universal military training. This concept had been discussed ever since my cadet days as an alternative to a large and expensive standing Army. Many European countries had some form of UMT. The idea was that every physically and mentally able young man in the country would be conscripted to serve about six months' military service. During that period, he would receive full basic training and some specialized training. This great pool of trained military manpower would enable us to create a truly viable Army Reserve entirely free of the political entanglements of the National Guard. In an emergency, Army Reserve units under direct Army control could spring into action almost overnight.

Almost everybody in the government with any military background or responsibility favored UMT. In December 1946, the President, who was an ardent advocate of UMT, had appointed a "blue ribbon" committee to study the issue. After six months of exhaustive analysis and hearing some two hundred witnesses, the committee resoundingly recommended UMT as the most sensible, logical and inexpensive form of national preparedness.

But we knew full well that there was not a prayer of getting UMT passed by the 80th Congress, or any other Congress. Full-scale peacetime military training was widely opposed by most educators, many religious organizations and by the doves and pacifists. The Senate's "Mr. Republican," Bob Taft, opposed UMT, as did Congressman Leo Allen, chairman of the powerful House Rules Committee. Any congressman who voted for UMT was not likely to return to his seat in the next session. I knew of only one or two who had the courage even to discuss it. As Joe Collins relates in his memoirs, Dewey Short, chairman of the House Armed Services Committee, would get up and walk out of the committee room when the discussion turned to UMT.[20]

Selective Service. Knowing that UMT would not get through Congress, we prepared a fallback position. We would ask that the draft be resumed. The machinery and director, Lewis B. Hershey, who had been my classmate at the Army War College, were still in place. It was merely a question of persuading Congress to start it up again. Drafting in peacetime was likewise a radical proposal and likely to be vastly unpopular. Owing to the various deferments which were bound to be included in the law, I did not think it could be an equitable system. Inevitably the more affluent—college students and the like—would escape the draft and the poor would bear the burden. Many would elude the draft by joining the National Guard. But I was compelled to lay aside these misgivings. We were absolutely desperate for manpower. The draft was our *only* means of getting necessary personnel.[21]

Here, Truman helped immeasurably. Following the Czech coup and Clay's electrifying cable from Berlin, on March 17 he addressed a special session of Congress, outlining in tough terms the nature of the communist threat to the security of the free world. The speech was, in effect, a tremendous boost for the U.S. Army. Truman not only asked for enactment of UMT, but also for "temporary re-enactment of Selective Service legislation in order to maintain our armed forces at their authorized strength." I thought then, and still think, that given the shape of the political landscape in 1948, it was an act of extraordinary courage for Truman to ask Congress for the first peacetime draft in our history. In another time and circumstance, that gesture alone might have assured his defeat at the polls in November.[22]

Federalization of the National Guard. World War II had proven without a scintilla of doubt that the National Guard was virtually useless in a major national crisis. The divisions we had created from scratch and manned with draftees were in every instance superior to Guard divisions. My experience with preparing the draftee 82nd Division and the National Guard 28th Division was typical. General Lesley McNair, who had borne the great burden of the Guard training problems, had recommended in no uncertain terms that the Guard be abolished. "Dependence on this component as a part of the initial protective force of our nation," he wrote in 1944, "was a distinct threat to our safety because of the belief of our people that the National Guard could enter a war and act with combat efficiency."

Unfortunately, there was no hope of abolishing the National Guard. It was too deeply entrenched politically within the states and in the U.S. Congress. But something drastic had to be done. One justification for our small postwar standing Army was that we had a National Guard ostensibly ready to leap to arms. With our very survival seemingly at stake in the Cold War, I for one could not continue to support the fiction that the National Guard could be relied upon for anything more than local riot control.

Gordon Gray headed a study group designed to explore the Guard problems and recommend solutions. The outcome—the Gray Report—was one of the best studies ever produced on the subject. (It should be republished and read today.) The basic conclusion of the Gray Report was that if we were to depend on the National Guard as a viable component of our National Military Establishment in time of grave external emergency, it had to be brought directly under U.S. Army control. That is to say, the U.S. Army (in place of the states) should be given direct and full responsibility for its organization and training and for the selection of its officers and NCO personnel. We would also have the right to "call up" Guard units as we saw fit without interference from state authorities.

Unfortunately, the recommendations of the Gray board got nowhere. The issues were too complex and the Guard simply too powerful politically to allow such drastic change. The Guard continued more or less as it had been before World War II: an expensive boondoggle, lending a false sense of security to our military establishment. And so it remains to this day.[23]

Morale building. When I took over as Chief of Staff, the morale in the U.S. Army was—understandably—about as bad as I had ever seen it. I took two important steps to improve it.

First I put out the word that both the old hands and the new recruits and draftees must be offered a greatly improved moral, intellectual and social climate. World War II had taught me one important lesson in leadership: the most valuable soldier was one who was well informed, encouraged to use his head, and treated with respect. I was convinced there was no longer any place in the American Army for a "treat 'em rough, tell 'em nothing" policy toward our junior officers and noncoms. Some of the old-timers griped that this was "coddling," that soldiers so trained and treated would not fight. But I stuck by my guns and the overall morale of the Army improved substantially.

Secondly I mounted an all-out effort to gain an across-the-board Army pay raise. The crippling postwar inflation had drastically eroded the purchasing power of our soldiers' pay. Many of those who were married and living off base on the "civilian economy" suffered grave hardship. They lived in shacks and had to moonlight in menial jobs to make ends meet. Not many of those Army wives wanted to go on living that way. One result was that the re-enlistment rate of our most experienced noncoms was falling off sharply. Fortunately, I was able to persuade the President and Congress to see it my way, and in 1949 the military pay scale was overhauled and brought into line with civilian pay scales for the first time in forty-one years.[24]

I cannot leave the subject of Army morale without taking note of what was for me a painful and difficult issue during my tour as Chief of Staff. In 1948 the Army, like much of the nation, followed a policy of strict segregation; black soldiers were assigned to all-black units. By and large, these units were noncombatant service units, because there was a deep and widespread belief in the Army that "Negroes could not fight." Even though blacks were segregated, the Army had instituted policies to assure that blacks had "separate but equal" facilities and were not discriminated against with respect to pay, advancement and retirement benefits.

President Truman, a sincere proponent of civil rights, was determined to do all in his power to break down the color barrier and to set the nation on a course of desegregation. He made it clear that in the 1948 presidential campaign he would run on a strong civil rights platform. He launched this drive with a special civil rights message to Congress on February 2, 1948 (five days before I relieved Ike), in which he stated his belief that desegregation should begin in the federal government by executive order. He revealed that he had instructed Defense Secretary Forrestal "to take steps to have the remaining instances of discrimination in the armed services eliminated as rapidly as possible."

It is difficult today to believe the furor this statement caused in the

Army and the problems it presented me. A very high percentage of Army volunteers and career soldiers came from the Deep South, where segregation was the ordinary way of life. Many of our large and important bases —such as Fort Benning—were located in the Deep South. To have desegregated the Army overnight as Truman wished would have caused utter chaos, not only within Army ranks but also within the Deep South communities where our bases were located.

I was not a racist, nor did I accept the slander that "Negroes could not fight." To the contrary, on several occasions in the ETO when we had been compelled to utilize black service troops for emergency individual reinforcements, I had seen them fight as well as white men. But if I had encouraged Truman to create "instant integration" in the U.S. Army in 1948, I believe it would have utterly destroyed what little Army we had. We would also have lost the support of the many senior Southerners in Congress who held important positions on the Armed Services and Appropriations committees.

Behind the scenes, we in the Army did our utmost to discourage "instant integration" of the armed forces and were, to a certain extent, successful. When Truman finally issued the executive order on July 27, 1948, it was much watered down: "It is hereby declared to be the policy of the President that there shall be equality of treatment and opportunity for all persons in the armed services, without regard to race, color, religion, or national origin. This policy shall be put into effect as rapidly as possible having due regard to the time required to effectuate any necessary changes without impairing efficiency or morale."

I inadvertently got in some public hot water on this issue. On the day Truman issued his executive order, I was in Fort Knox on an inspection trip. While addressing an assembly of officers I was asked, in effect, what Truman's order would mean to the Army in practical, everyday terms. For example, should they build separate service clubs for white and black soldiers? Unknown to me, there were newspaper reporters in the assembly. My frank but generalized responses to questions were interpreted and reported as "stubborn resistance" to desegregation in the U.S. Army "until it had been totally achieved by the American people." Of course, these stories generated headlines embarrassing to me and to the President.

I was compelled to write a letter of explanation to the President. I assured him that my remarks had been misconstrued, that the Army would not "stubbornly" resist integration until first it had been totally achieved by the American people. "I assure you," I wrote, "nothing is farther from our intent. While I do believe it would be hazardous for us to employ the Army deliberately as an instrument of social reform, I do likewise believe the Army must be kept fully apace of the substantial progress being made by the civilian community in race relations."

The hue and cry continued for some months. Inasmuch as the executive order had not specifically required desegregation in the armed services as Truman had originally implied, civil rights leaders were livid. They judged the outcome a severe setback and a "victory" for the "racist" U.S. Army. They demanded Royall's resignation and castigated me. Regrettably, some senators, congressmen and editors from the Deep South felt the need to rush to my defense. They heaped praise on me for "resisting integration" in the Army and used me as a club to thrash the President. To placate the civil rights blocs, Truman had to come forward and state that, even though it had not categorically ordered it, his policy statement was *intended* to end segregation in the armed forces. But true integration of the armed forces would not come for another ten years, following the general pattern in the civilian community.[25]

FIFTY-ONE

The fundamental dichotomy in our Cold War "containment" policy persisted: Truman was determined to do his utmost to stop the worldwide march of communism, but he was unwilling to spend money on a powerful military establishment to enforce the policy. He continued to believe that a sound national economy was more vital than any other factor.

Many people, including not a few military men, shared Truman's views on military spending. Ike was one; I was another. In a personal letter to army commanders, I made my views crystal clear: "It is the general feeling here [in Washington], *in which I concur,* that a sound national economy is just as important as a large military establishment in our current situation." (Italics added.) Of course I wanted sufficient funds to field a viable Army to meet our growing worldwide commitments. But my view was that military spending should not exceed a *reasonable* level and that the money should more or less be divided equally to provide a "balanced military force."[1]

What was a "reasonable" level of military spending? Truman's original target was somewhere between $10 or $12 billion a year. (In 1981 dollars these figures seem absurdly small, but in 1947–48 dollars they seemed huge.) However the rampant inflation in 1947–48 severely eroded our military purchasing power, forcing Truman, much against his will, to raise the military spending ceiling to about $14 billion. He adamantly held to that figure. I thought it was a bit too low, but I supported the President.

From this distance, I must say that this decision was a mistake, perhaps the greatest of Truman's presidency. My support of his decision—my belief that significantly higher defense spending would probably wreck the economy—was likewise a mistake, perhaps the greatest mistake I made in my postwar years in Washington. From childhood I had been tight-fisted. I had lived through the terrible Depression of the 1930s. I was a dedicated fiscal conservative. I sincerely believed in those economists who were advising Truman to sharply limit defense spending.

I held to that viewpoint throughout what was the most difficult and taxing period of my postwar public service. This was the eighteen-month period between March 1948 and October 1949, when the Joint Chiefs of Staff attempted to draw up a "unified" war plan and military budget to support Truman's containment policy, at the same time having sufficient military forces, based around the A-bomb, to defeat the Soviet Union in an all-out war. This planning led to the bitterest "interservice war" in our history. It resulted in a revolt of the Navy and a near-revolt of the Air Force. The acrimony and pressures led many distinguished military men and top defense civilians to commit career suicide, and the taxing battle helped bring on Forrestal's real suicide. The pressures felled others—Ike for one—with severe illnesses. There were times when I was ready to abandon the effort, to retire and go fishing.

The drama of postwar unification and interservice planning divided into three acts or phases, the "Forrestal Phase," the "Ike Phase" and the "Louis Johnson Phase."

The Forrestal Phase. Soon after I was sworn in as Chief of Staff, Forrestal, who had been Secretary of Defense about five months, decided that the Joint Chiefs should draw up a unified short-range emergency war plan and, for the first time in our history, a "unified" military budget. His decision was made shortly after the Czech coup in February 1948, and was lent a sense of urgency by Lucius Clay's hair-raising telegram (war may come with "dramatic suddenness") and the Berlin Blockade.

In order to free ourselves of day-to-day routines for this task, the Joint Chiefs met with Forrestal at Truman's "Little White House" at the Key West naval base, March 11 through March 14. Tooey Spaatz was on the point of retirement; his replacement as Air Force Chief of Staff, Hoyt S. Vandenberg, then vice chief, accompanied him. Van, as we called him, was a nephew of the distinguished senator Arthur H. Vandenberg, and a graduate of the West Point class of 1923. (I had taught him math.) In World War II he first entered combat in North Africa. Later, in the ETO, he rose to lieutenant general and command of the Ninth Air Force, whose principal mission was to provide tactical air support to my Twelfth Army Group, a task he had carried out with extraordinary competence.

The Chief of Naval Operations was Louis E. Denfeld, Naval Academy Class of 1912, a personnel expert who had spent the greater part of the war in Washington. Van, who looked ten years younger than he was (forty-nine), was as handsome as a movie star and cool as a cucumber. Denfeld was an affable glad-handing Washington bureaucrat with only minimal naval combat experience and no grasp at all of large-scale land warfare.[2]

Coincidental with the Forrestal-JCS discussions in Key West, JCS planners in Washington were completing a unified short-term emergency war plan called "Halfmoon." (Later refinements were called "Fleetwood" and "Doublestar.") This was the first formal and comprehensive enunciation of what later became known as a strategy of nuclear "massive retaliation." If Russia launched all-out war, its huge Army overrunning Western Europe (as we assumed), we would respond by dropping atomic bombs on the Soviet homeland—mainly population centers—with the aim of destroying the Soviet government and breaking the Kremlin's will to wage war. The bombs would be carried to Soviet targets by our B-29 and B-50 heavy bombers, staging from bases in England and Egypt and, in the Far East, Okinawa. Air Force studies had suggested that 133 atomic bombs dropped on seventy Soviet cities would be required. Since we then had only about fifty bombs, the plan was to launch the strategic air attack against Russia on D plus 9 with twenty-five bombs, follow up with another twenty-five, then continue the attack with bombs coming right off the production line.[3]

The Army's role in Halfmoon was to support the strategic air offensive. Our main job would be to protect our air bases at home and abroad (notably Okinawa) and, in order to prevent "one-way" Soviet bombing attacks on the United States, deny the Soviets potential air bases in Greenland, Iceland, Spitsbergen, Alaska and the Azores. (It was assumed that British ground forces would protect air bases in Britain and Egypt.) Much later, following a World War II–type general mobilization, the Army would occupy Western Europe and Russia in order to help restore law and order and stable governments.

Army war planners calculated that to carry out our Halfmoon missions we needed a standing Army of a million men, nearly double our size at the time, with a fully equipped "ready" combat arm of eighteen divisions. Inasmuch as there was no conceivable way of maintaining a million-man standing Army within the $14 billion military budget ceiling, it was decided that the Army would build to only about 800,000 men, fielding twelve Regular Army divisions, backed up by six elite fully equipped National Guard or Reserve divisions which could be mobilized "instantly" on D-day. Of the twelve Regular divisions, seven would be deployed overseas and five in the United States as a "strategic reserve."

This was not altogether a satisfactory solution to the Army's responsibilities as envisioned in Halfmoon. For example, I knew from experience that we could never count on "instant" mobilization of National Guard or Reserve divisions. However, a build-up to an 800,000-man Army with twelve ready combat divisions was a substantial improvement over the 552,000-man administrative Army we then had. Such an Army would also greatly enhance our ability to cope with Cold War crises. I accepted this plan because I thought we could find a way to live with it. For this reason the Army's planned program remained, at least in public, largely noncontroversial.[4]

As it turned out, new military budgetary limitations—which I shall come to—sharply limited the buildup of the Army, and we actually grew nowhere near 800,000 men. No one in the Army was more displeased at what actually transpired than Douglas MacArthur, who was still serving as "proconsul" in Tokyo. Nor was he hesitant about expressing his displeasure to me. Later in the year he sent me a blistering cable complaining about the critical shortage of soldiers in the Far East. Blaming the situation in part on "a dangerous and risky subordination of operational requirements to administrative convenience," he concluded: "I am deeply disturbed by the apparent failure of military planners to recognize the necessity for maintaining the essential security of the Far East."[5]

I was furious at his "localitis" and the insulting tone of his cable. In response, I let MacArthur have it with both barrels. I told him his conclusions had been "evidently drawn without complete knowledge of the factors involved." I explained some of the factors and said "we must therefore accept calculated risks, in fact what might be termed dangerous risks in some areas, in order to provide reasonable chances of success in attaining vital national objectives in others." I went on to say that his charge that carefully analyzed minimal requirements for his theater were being "brushed aside" was "unjustified" and that his further charge that we were subordinating operational requirements to administrative convenience was "deemed erroneous and inappropriate." I heard no more from MacArthur directly on this subject.[6]

Initially within the Joint Chiefs of Staff there were no major disagreements on the fundamental Halfmoon strategy of "massive retaliation." Neither we nor the prostrate nations of Western Europe could match Russia's massive land army man-for-man and tank-for-tank on D-Day without total peacetime mobilization, which was patently out of the question. Given the military spending limits, we were forced to rely principally on our atomic monopoly. However, within the JCS (and elsewhere), two major problems arose early and became points of extreme controversy for longer than I care to remember.[7]

The first was the question of what size the Air Force should be to carry out the main task of Halfmoon. The Air Force then had a total strength of about forty-five first-line groups. An Air Staff study had concluded that a minimum of seventy first-line groups would be required to carry out the Halfmoon mission.* This estimate had been generally seconded by two independent study groups, one headed by a New York lawyer-writer, Thomas K. Finletter, the other by a Republican senator from Maine, Owen D. Brewster. In fiscal year 1949, the Air Force budget then being considered by Congress, Truman had approved an Air Force increase to fifty-five "limited strength" groups plus fifteen "skeleton" groups, considerably less than the Air Staff minimum requirement.[8]

* An Air Force bomber group consisted of thirty planes; a fighter group, seventy-five planes. A seventy-group Air Force would comprise a total of 6,869 first-line combat aircraft, including both bombers and fighters.

In open defiance of Truman, the Air Force, led by its handsome, articulate and persuasive Secretary, Stuart Symington, launched an all-out public campaign to persuade the nation to adopt a seventy-group Air Force. Promising the usual cheap-easy-victory-through-air-power-alone, the Air Force quickly gained impressive support in the media and in the Congress. Inasmuch as a seventy-group Air Force would consume a disproportionate share of the defense budget, or compel an undesired increase in defense spending (or both), Truman and Forrestal were furious. Forrestal even considered firing Symington. Truman noted disdainfully in his private diary: "The Congress can't bring itself to do the right thing—because of votes. The air boys are for glamor . . . I want a sensible defense for which the country can pay. If the glamor boys win we'll have another 1920 or another 1941. God keep us from that!"[9]

The Air Force won a substantial, though not complete, victory in Congress in 1948. Both the House and Senate voted overwhelmingly for an Air Force of sixty-six groups, eleven of which were to be immediately but temporarily equipped with World War II planes that had been mothballed. To make certain its wishes were carried out, Congress tacked an extra $1 billion onto the defense budget for the specific purpose of purchasing aircraft to upgrade these eleven groups. However, the force of this rider was diluted by a "hooker" that allowed Truman to spend the money at his own discretion. Truman hastened to invoke the hooker, thus putting a brake on Air Force expansion. But Truman had suffered a sharp defeat in Congress. He blamed Forrestal for not being more forceful at countering this brazen Air Force end run, and without doubt he lost considerable confidence in Forrestal.

Neither the Air Staff nor its legions of supporters was satisfied with the victory. Air zealots continued to campaign for a minimum force of seventy groups. This campaign, mounting in intensity, would continue through 1949, vastly complicating the JCS job of producing unified war plans and budgets.

The second controversial issue, which arose early and likewise refused to go away, was to what extent, if any, the U.S. Navy should participate in the primary task of Halfmoon, the strategic air offensive against Russia.

Ever since its impressive campaigns in World War II, particularly its carrier battles in the Pacific, the U.S. Navy had been losing public esteem in almost the same proportion the Air Force was gaining it. Navy critics argued that the atomic bomb had rendered aircraft carriers and large-scale amphibious landings obsolete. Other than some old coastal defense submarines, which had achieved nothing of note in the war, the Soviet Union had no navy worth discussing. Why then, the critics asked, should we maintain a U.S. Navy at all? And why should we have a Marine Corps with its substantial and expensive aviation arm?

The naval construction program in World War II had been vast. It had produced hundreds of major warships, including about thirty large aircraft carriers. Most of these ships had been mothballed after the war, but when the JCS met with Forrestal in Key West, the Navy still had eleven large aircraft carriers in active service, plus a substantial array of supporting warships. Moreover, ever since the war, the Navy had continued building new warships. The ongoing program included a new "super" aircraft carrier of 65,000 tons, which Forrestal had approved while still Secretary of the Navy and which Truman had agreed to fund.

Navy critics—notably the Air Force generals—asked: What was the point in building this expensive and vulnerable new carrier? The Navy argued, all too vaguely, that it was vital for maintaining freedom of the seas. The carrier would have a big strong "flush" deck, which was necessary to accommodate the larger, heavier jet aircraft on the drawing boards. The truth of the matter was that the supercarrier had been conceived to accommodate large heavy aircraft capable of carrying the atomic bomb.

Naval planners had divined that without a supercarrier the Navy would have no major offensive role in an all-out war with Russia. Without such a role, the Navy would soon wither away, reduced to pedestrian and dull missions such as hunting for Russian submarines and escorting supply convoys. The supercarrier was thus more than just another ship. It was the Navy's only hope for getting its hands on atomic bombs. If the Navy had its way, the new carrier would merely be the first step in creating a new and vital strategic role for a nuclear-age Navy.

Naval critics were quick to perceive the flaws in the Navy's plan. The biggest, of course, was that the strategic air mission the Navy envisioned for itself would duplicate the primary mission of the Air Force. It would be an expensive duplication. For the cost of a supercarrier and its aircraft and supporting vessels, we could buy a lot of Air Force bombers. Allotting the Navy atomic bombs for ill-defined carrier missions would gravely reduce the power and shock of the Air Force "massive retaliation" mission. Moreover, carriers were highly vulnerable to Soviet counterattack. Where, the critics asked, could they operate safely while launching a nuclear strike at the heartland of Russia?

The JCS discussed these issues with Forrestal in Key West. Contrary to some later assertions, Forrestal did not ask the JCS to "vote" for or against the Navy's supercarrier. The carrier was already in the Navy's shipbuilding program, approved by Forrestal and Truman. Had we been asked to vote in a formal sense, Spaatz, Van and I would probably have spoken against it for all the reasons enumerated. It was my view that the Navy was already getting far too much of the defense budget, and a large Navy with fleets of supercarriers was a luxury we could ill afford.[10]

Public opposition to the supercarrier mounted that spring as a by-product of the Air Force's drive for seventy groups. The Navy, believing that it might be on the threshold of a fight for its very existence, struck viciously at the Air Force. In a long memo leaked to columnist Drew Pearson, one admiral brazenly argued that the Air Force was simply incapable of carrying out the strategic air mission, that it should be limited purely to continental defense, and that the massive retaliation mission should be left entirely to carrier-based aircraft. Stunned by this outrageous attack on its integrity, the Air Force counterattacked with leaked assaults on the vulnerability, shortcomings and expense of the supercarrier. An unseemly semi-public Air Force–Navy brawl ensued.[11]

This brawl greatly disturbed Truman. On May 13 he called Forrestal and the Joint Chiefs to the White House for a general review of ongoing military plans and budgets, which still included funds for the supercarrier. He distributed a memo recapping the defense program, which concluded: "As Commander in Chief I expect these orders to be carried out wholeheartedly, in good spirit and without mental reservation. If anyone present has any questions or misgivings concerning the program I have outlined, make your views known now—for once this program goes forward officially, it will be the administration program, and I expect every member of the administration to support it fully, both in public and *in private*." (Italics added.)[12]

By this time both Vandenberg and I had grave reservations about the Navy's supercarrier—and all that it entailed—which was still in the military program. However, at this time neither of us spoke against it. This was a very complicated issue which required infinitely more study than we had been able to give it during my three months and Van's two weeks as members of the Joint Chiefs of Staff. Moreover, until then it had not been the custom for the chief of one service to criticize or raise questions about weapons another service was buying. To put the shoe on the other foot, it would have been grossly out of place had Denfeld raised questions about what kind of tanks I was buying for the Army. So we both remained silent.

But the supercarrier issue would not go away. Congress wanted to know if the Joint Chiefs of Staff approved or not. In sworn testimony, Denfeld misleadingly implied that the JCS had "approved" it at the Key West meeting. Spaatz, in a press club speech, properly denied this was so. The conflicting statements, in turn, led to a congressional demand that the matter be cleared up. In response, on May 26, Forrestal addressed a memo to the Joint Chiefs asking if we approved the supercarrier.

I still had not had time to give this complicated matter the study it deserved. Nor had Van. He returned a "non-voting" memo in which he reminded Forrestal that heretofore military budgets had been submitted unilaterally and had never been coordinated or examined in detail by the JCS. "Hence," Van wrote, "I cannot at this time approve or disapprove of one particular part of the budget of one service without the thorough consideration of the programs and budget requirements of all three services." Since I had not earlier raised a question at the White House military budget meeting and was thus pledged to support Truman's program (even "in private"), and since I shared Van's view that the issue was one that ought to be and *would* be thoroughly studied in the JCS, and for the sake of expediency and of avoiding yet more public controversy, I imprudently joined Denfeld in returning a nonqualified "yes" vote.[13]

By this time Forrestal had reached the decision that he needed more high-level military advice in the office of Secretary of Defense. In approving the National Security Act, Congress had expressly limited the power and scope of the Defense Secretary so that no single Chief of Staff or "man on horseback" could emerge, possibly acquiring so much power he might overthrow the government and create a dictatorship. However, Forrestal concluded that he could appoint a "principal military adviser" without violating existing law, serving him somewhat in the capacity that Admiral Leahy had served President Roosevelt. He chose me for the post and requested that Ken Royall make the necessary arrangements. I am not certain why he chose me. Perhaps to help fill his obvious gap in Army matters, or because I supported the balanced-force concept and had not yet become involved in the Navy–Air Force feud and could be a dispassionate referee.

When Royall raised the matter with me, I was both flattered and dismayed. I had only been Chief of Staff of the Army about three months. I had made a good beginning at drawing plans for rebuilding the Army, but there was still much to be done and I was reluctant to leave it after so short a time. Moreover, considering the uncertainty of the 1948 political picture, I was a little leery of what might happen to me after the elections. If, as seemed likely, Truman lost, Forrestal would be replaced; and there was not much likelihood that I would be asked to stay on as a principal military adviser to the new (probably Republican) Secretary of Defense. Having no legal status, the post might even be abolished. If I left the Army Chief of Staff's job it would be filled by another man. Since I could not return, I would have to retire.

There was another point, not minor. By now I was absolutely convinced the Navy's budget should be cut substantially and ultimately that the supercarrier be canceled. As Forrestal's chief military adviser, I could scarcely conceal those views. If I were successful in persuading him that I was right, there was little doubt that the Navy would launch a vicious attack on me and probably on the Army. One main reason the Navy had opposed unification was the fear that the Army would emerge on top with a single chief of staff, to the ultimate detriment of the Navy. In effect, I would be serving in that post without legal portfolio. A Navy assault on me or the Army or both would undermine, or possibly even destroy, what little progress we had made on unification.

After discussing the many pros and cons, Royall and I decided the cons outweighed the pros. In a delicate letter to Forrestal, Royall asked that my name be withdrawn from consideration because I could not be "spared" at this crucial point in the Army's history. Royall also tactfully alluded to the career risk involved for me by raising, in passing, "the possibility of a change in Administration next November."

I heard no more from Forrestal on this subject. Perhaps upon reflection he had second thoughts about naming me or anyone else to this "informal" job. However, I believe it reinforced his view that we should have a formal "chairman" of the Joint Chiefs of Staff, both to preside over that body and to serve as principal (and statutory) adviser to the Secretary of Defense and the President. Others had the same, or a similar, idea and these ideas would loom importantly in my future.[14]

In the summer of 1948, during the height of crisis created by the Berlin Blockade, Forrestal and the Joint Chiefs received the first hard cost estimates for Halfmoon. We were stunned. The projected military budget for the following fiscal year, 1950, would be $30 billion, or about two and a half times the fiscal 1949 military budget!

Clearly that would never do. Truman was now willing to go to about $15 billion, but only very reluctantly and not a dollar more. Since some $600 million of that sum had by law to be earmarked for stockpiling strategic materials, the fiscal 1950 military budget was thus fixed at $14.4 billion. It was obvious that the Joint Chiefs would have to drastically revise the Halfmoon war plan and the weapons and force levels to stay within that limit.

This realization led to a second extended out-of-town meeting of Forrestal and the Chiefs. These meetings were held at the Naval War College in Newport, Rhode Island, August 20 through August 22. One of our first decisions was to appoint a tri-service committee to whack away at the impossibly big military budget. We named my tough-minded classmate Joe McNarney to chair this committee, which became known (and in some quarters reviled) as the "McNarney Board."[15]

The Navy's role in the strategic air mission once again entered our discussions. When we turned to this matter we had for consideration a new two-man study which had been carried out at Forrestal's request by Tooey Spaatz and one of the Navy's leading aviators and carrier experts, Vice Admiral John H. Towers. To my utter astonishment, I saw that Spaatz had completely reversed his position on the supercarrier. He now believed the Navy should be equipped with carrier-launched atomic bombers that could be utilized to attack strategic targets.[16]

One factor that may have influenced Spaatz to reverse his stand was a technological breakthrough in atomic bomb design. Earlier that spring the Atomic Energy Commission (AEC) had conducted a series of new A-bomb tests at Eniwetok in the Pacific, called "Sandstone." These tests had demonstrated that the AEC could now produce A-bombs with twice the power (forty kilotons) of the Hiroshima and Nagasaki bombs, using considerably less fissionable material per bomb. Owing to this breakthrough and improved efficiency in producing fissionable material in the plants, it now appeared likely that by the end of 1950—a little more than two years hence—the United States could have as many as 400 A-bombs in the stockpile. This was more than sufficient to give the Navy an A-bomb capability, and Spaatz had agreed with Towers that the Navy should have it. That is, we should employ every available means we could devise to drop atomic bombs on Russia.[17]

Despite the misgivings Vandenberg and I had about the vulnerability and cost of the supercarrier, we did not formally oppose it at Newport. To the contrary, guided by the Spaatz-Towers report, we endorsed a written statement that in effect gave the Navy the green light to proceed with development of a nuclear bombing capability. To forestall any further public brawling—or speculation that could possibly lead to disclosure of our new A-bomb design breakthrough—we also signed a paper stating that none of us would publicly describe the decision as a "victory" or "defeat" for the Navy or Air Force and that we would all do our utmost to encourage unification and harmonious relationships between the services.

A third important decision reached at Newport was to more closely integrate our Halfmoon war plan with plans being developed by potential allies. Earlier that year, British pressure had resulted in the creation of the so-called Brussels Pact, linking the United Kingdom, France, Belgium, the Netherlands and Luxembourg in a military alliance. Three months later, on June 11, 1948, the U.S. Senate passed the famous Vandenberg Resolution, which urged the United States to pursue "collective arrangements" with other nations for national security purposes. Foreseeing the evolution of the North Atlantic Treaty Organization (NATO), we discussed in considerable detail the creation of a Western Europe headquarters and the appointment of various high-level field commanders, including a supreme Allied commander in chief.[18]

The McNarney Board met virtually nonstop from mid-August to October 1948. It started with the initial budget estimates of $30 billion and hacked relentlessly. But it could pare to nowhere near $14.4 billion. On October 1, the board passed its final report up to the JCS. For all its immense and tedious work, the board could not reduce the budget below $23.6 billion. It passed the buck back to the JCS.[19]

We Chiefs, knowing full well that Truman would approve no more than $14.4 billion, spent the next two full months in bloody committee combat. I cannot recall a time in my life when I felt greater frustration. During these tense, bitter meetings, for the first time I made no secret of the fact that I thought the Navy budget was simply too far out of line. I bluntly proposed elimination of one expensive naval feature of Halfmoon: the carrier task forces in the Mediterranean, designed in part to protect SAC staging bases in Egypt. From that point forward I was the Navy's sworn enemy.[20]

The Chiefs were unable to reach agreement. Accordingly we sent Forrestal what was called a "split decision." The split had Van and me in agreement on a $15.8 billion budget; Denfeld holding out for $16.5 billion, a figure which included the Mediterranean carrier forces. Forrestal took our figures to the President, who promptly rejected them. Forrestal then all but ordered us to return a "unanimous" JCS budget of $14.4 billion. On November 8 we complied, splitting the money as follows: $5 billion to the Air Force, $4.8 billion to the Army and $4.6 billion to the Navy. These figures drastically limited our Halfmoon force levels to an Air Force of forty-eight groups, an Army of about ten and two-thirds divisions, and a Navy of 282 combat ships and funds for the supercarrier.[21] *

Forrestal staged a final military budget presentation for the President on December 9. Fortunately, I was away. I had taken ten days' leave and was resting with Mary at the National Golf Club in Augusta, Georgia. Accompanied by most of the senior Pentagon officials, Forrestal presented two budgets to the President: the "Navy budget" of $16.9 billion and our compromise at $14.4 billion. According to those present, Forrestal urged the higher "Navy budget" figure. But Truman, jaunty and confident after his astonishing political upset of Tom Dewey, held adamantly to the $14.4 billion figure and after a mere thirty minutes dismissed the group. Army Undersecretary Bill Draper recalled that Forrestal was "greatly shocked" and "seriously troubled" and "more concerned than I had ever seen him in my life."[22]

The Ike Phase. Truman realized his fiscal 1950 $14.4 billion defense budget would be highly controversial. Congressional air-power zealots, still insisting on a seventy-group Air Force, would fiercely resist a reduction to forty-eight groups. At the same time, Truman was now leaning toward cancellation of the Navy's expensive supercarrier. If that were done, it would cause a furor in the Navy camp. The prospects were good that Truman's defense budget would evoke an unprecedented public brawl and possibly a mutiny in the Pentagon.

The newly elected Truman administration was not strongly manned for such a fight. Truman had lost his "tower of strength," George Marshall. Following the removal of a kidney in December, Marshall had retired as Secretary of State, replaced by Dean Acheson. Truman's confidence in Forrestal had greatly diminished for a variety of reasons, not least Forrestal's increasingly irrational behavior. He had sunk into a deep depression and was on the verge of a nervous breakdown.[23]

Truman, gearing for the fight, made the decision to bring two strong military allies into his camp. The first, to replace ailing Jim Forrestal, was millionaire lawyer Louis Johnson, who had cannily supported Truman in 1948 and almost single-handedly raised $2 million for the famous Truman

* We could not agree on how many carriers the Navy should keep on active service. I voted for six, Van four, Denfeld nine. Forrestal resolved the matter, fixing the number at eight.

whistle-stop campaign. The second was Ike, whom Truman persuaded to take a leave of absence from Columbia University and come to Washington to serve "temporarily" as "Presiding Officer" of the JCS. (Ike was often and erroneously described as JCS Chairman.) Truman's view was that Louis Johnson would provide the administrative stability and muscle in the Pentagon that Forrestal lacked; Ike would exercise his legendary conciliatory magic over the JCS, persuading us to agree unanimously on war plans, weapons, and budgets, thus heading off a brawl in Congress.[24]

Replacing the mentally ill Forrestal was a delicate problem, which Truman kept to himself and deferred for several months. When Ike came to Washington in January 1949, he was shocked at seeing Forrestal. He noted in his private diary: "Jim is looking badly. He has a conscience and a sense of duty. These, coupled with his feelings of urgency and his terrific, almost tragic, disappointment in the failures of professional men to 'get together' lead him to certain errors. Among these none is worse than the way he treats himself. He gives his mind no recess, and he works hours that would kill a horse. Except for my liking, admiration, and respect for his great qualities, I'd not go near Washington, even if I had to resign my commission completely. To a certain extent these same feelings apply to H.S.T., but he does not see the problems so clearly as does Jim, and he does not suffer so much due to the failure to solve the problems. I like them both."[25]

By this time there was a move afoot in Washington to "strengthen" unification of the armed forces. One of the proposals was to establish a legal post of "Chairman" of the Joint Chiefs. Ike, absolutely determined not to stay in Washington very long, asked me if I would consider succeeding him as "Chairman" of the JCS if and when the post was formally legislated. I replied, as Ike wrote in his diary, that I "wanted no part of [the] job." My reasons for demurring were the same as those I had advanced for declining Forrestal's invitation to become his principal military adviser. There was still much to be done to salvage the Army. Moreover, I did not relish the prospect of winding up my professional service moderating bitter debates between the Air Force and Navy. I thought that Joe McNarney, who apparently relished these endless hassles, would be the ideal candidate. Ike and Truman agreed with me and for several months we proceeded on the assumption that McNarney would be the nominee.[26]

By the time Ike rolled up his sleeves, the Air Force and Navy were once more going at it tooth and nail. Air Force propagandists (notably William Bradford Huie in four articles in *Reader's Digest*) were shrilly denouncing the Navy and the supercarrier. Navy propagandists, in turn, were denouncing the Air Force. Symington and Vandenberg were almost openly lobbying the Hill in another drive toward a seventy-group Air Force; the Navy was mobilizing its powerful lobby.

Ike was dismayed by the intensity of the controversy and by the near-insubordination of Air Force and Navy leaders. He registered his concern in his diary: "I believe the President has to show the iron beneath the pretty glove. Some of our [military] seniors are forgetting that they have a Commander in Chief. They must be reminded of this, in terms of direct, unequivocal language. If this is not done soon, some day we're going to have a blowup. . . . [The President and Secretary of Defense] are going to have to get tough—and I mean tough!"[27]

The President had laid down guidelines for the fiscal 1951 defense budget: another ceiling of about $14.4 billion. Ike saw his job as drawing up a new war plan that could be implemented within the budget limits, and resolving once and for all the Air Force–Navy dispute over strategic air power.

Ike, ever the diplomat, was determined to be fair-minded. Denfeld would later write accurately that "his effort to be an impartial presiding officer met with success." But privately, Ike brought some of his own long-standing biases to the conference table. He still thought the Marine Corps was an unwarranted and expensive duplication of the U.S. Army. He shared my view that the Navy's budget should be cut. In an early meeting with Truman, Ike told the President that we should "cut certain of [the] Navy's assumed missions in order to obtain more money for air" and "support [the] strongest possible air force."[28]

This is not to say that he agreed with Air Force zealots that all fleet carriers should be eliminated from the war plan. To the contrary, Ike believed, as he wrote, "that in the first months of war a few big carriers might be our greatest asset." His view was that we should keep ten fleet carriers in active service so that in event of war "six to eight" would "always be in operation." However, Ike did not believe we should spend hundreds of millions on the new supercarrier program. He had in mind using carriers already built (active or mothballed), which could be strengthened and modernized to handle heavier jet planes.[29]

The JCS first met with Ike on Janaury 24, 1949. He laid down the fiscal 1951 budget ceiling of $14.4 billion and gave us a pep talk. The prestige of the JCS was on the line—again. We had to be tough on ourselves as well as our sister services. We would evolve a new emergency and long-term strategy that could be sustained at about $15 billion a year, which, he said, "is all that this country need spend for security forces." He did not tell us, but he privately wrote that the JCS had better get the job done or he would "quit and begin criticizing," even though that might be "repugnant and out of character." We Chiefs agreed to work within the $14.4 billion budget.[30]

We commenced work on a new emergency war plan, which was called "Offtackle," perhaps in deference to Ike's football background. (Later refinements were called "Shakedown" and "Crosspiece.") By this time, due in large part to Forrestal's prodding, the NSC had drawn up and distributed (on November 24, 1948) Paper No. 20/4, which was the first definitive statement of American policy vis-à-vis the Soviet Union in the Cold War, and it would remain the basic policy for about a full year until the distribution of NSC 68 in April 1950. In essence, NSC 20/4 was a codification and formalization of our "get tough" or "containment" Cold War policy. The JCS responsibility was set forth in a single sentence: "Develop a level of military readiness which can be maintained as long as necessary as a deterrent to Soviet aggression, as indispensable support to our political attitude toward the USSR, as a source of encouragement to nations resisting Soviet political aggression, and as an adequate basis for immediate military commitments and for rapid mobilization should war prove unavoidable."[31]

Offtackle contained many of the assumptions on which we had based Halfmoon, with one notable difference. Owing to the European military alliances in being (Brussels) or in the works (NATO), we would now make every conceivable effort in concert with our allies to prevent the Soviet Army from overrunning Western Europe and to establish a defensive line "preferably no farther west than the Rhine." The principal American retaliatory attack would consist of a massive nuclear and conventional strategic air assault (292 atomic bombs, 17,000 tons of conventional explosives) in the first ninety days. The air attack would be launched from the States (with the new long-range B-36), the British Isles and Okinawa (with B-29s and B-50s). Owing to our inability to sustain a naval defense of Egypt on a $14.4 billion budget, the SAC launching platform was shifted far west to the "Western Africa" area, meaning Morocco.[32]

The problem now—the same old problem—was how to tailor American armed forces required for Offtackle to a $14.4 billion budget. This procedure, in spite of Ike's good intentions, once more led to blood in the scuppers. In our first go-round, we all generally agreed on the size of the Army at about ten and two-thirds divisions. But we split sharply over the composition of the Air Force and Navy. For the Air Force, Vandenberg recommended seventy-one groups; I sixty-seven; Denfeld forty-eight. For the Navy, Denfeld recommended ten carriers; I four; Van none. Van and I also proposed eliminating all Marine Corps aviation and halving the Marine Corps ground forces from eleven battalion landing teams to six. This divergence in proposed military forces was so great as to nearly defy reconciliation. Ike diaried: "The situation grows intolerable."[33]

We worked diligently to find a compromise, but got nowhere. Then, in the midst of our debates, in early March, Ike became gravely ill. On March 21, he was forced to take to his bed. The pressure had brought on a recurrence of a problem in his digestive system from which he had suffered for years. (He did not discover until 1956 that it was ileitis.) It scared him so badly that he gave up smoking for life—not easy, since he consumed four packs a day. After a thorough checkup at Walter Reed, at

Truman's suggestion he took a rest at the Winter White House in Key West until April 12. Thereafter he moved to the Augusta National Golf Club, where he remained another full month. The JCS met with him once in Key West, April 7 to April 12, and individually talked often to him by phone. But in truth the onset of this illness almost completely negated Ike's effectiveness during his brief tenure as "Presiding Officer" of the JCS.[34]

The JCS debates on Offtackle were greatly complicated by the completion of a new military study of the probable impact of a nuclear offensive against the Soviet Union. The study group, composed of two senior officers from each of the three services, was chaired by my classmate Air Force General Hubert R. Harmon. The Harmon Report was a well-done nonpartisan study, but its general conclusions were maddeningly ambiguous. On one hand the report was pessimistic and negative. It stated that our planned A-bomb assault on seventy Soviet cities would not inflict massive death or casualties (2.7 million deaths, plus an additional 4 million casualties) or bring about capitulation or destroy the Russian government or seriously impair its ability to overrun Western Europe. On the other hand, the report stated, the A-bomb would constitute the only means of rapidly inflicting "shock and serious damage" to vital elements of the Soviet war-making machine and that "from the standpoint of our national security, the advantages of its early use would be transcending." Despite the generally deflating tone of the report, it concluded: "Every reasonable effort should be devoted to providing the means to be prepared for prompt and effective delivery of the maximum numbers of atomic bombs to appropriate target systems."

The air-power zealots were shocked and stunned by the report and felt betrayed by their own, Hubert Harmon. Van mounted a vigorous effort to have the report suppressed or altered to eliminate its pessimistic tone. Denfeld gleefully seized upon the report because in one sense it could be read as a justification of the Navy position that the Air Force could not get the job done and carriers (and supercarriers) were therefore needed more urgently than ever.[35]

The Johnson Phase. Louis Johnson relieved Jim Forrestal as Secretary of Defense on March 28—one week after Ike took to his sickbed. By this time Forrestal was so ill he was barely able to attend the change-of-command ceremonies in the Pentagon courtyard. He went to Hobe Sound, Florida, to rest, broke down completely and on April 2, entered the psychiatric ward of the Naval Hospital in Bethesda, Maryland. On the morning of May 22, he climbed through an unguarded window on the sixteenth floor and leaped to his death.

Louis Johnson, fifty-eight, was a big 250-pound bear, whose major goal was to work a miracle in the Pentagon. That is, bash heads, cut budgets, stop the interminable wrangling and truly unify the services. He was the direct opposite of the shy, introverted, intellectual, apolitical Forrestal. Johnson was flamboyant, outspoken and, rumor had it, had his eyes on the White House. His first appointee to the newly created post of Undersecretary of Defense, Stephen T. Early, President Roosevelt's press secretary, fueled speculation that Johnson had "Potomac fever." I doubt seriously if Johnson knew much about military strategy or weapons systems. He was probably the worst appointment Truman made during his presidency. In a little more than a year, he too would be gone, a victim of his own ambition and excesses.[36]

An unstinting air-power advocate, Johnson was determined first and foremost to remove the Navy from the strategic air mission. He could best do that by canceling the Navy's new supercarrier, now named the U.S.S. *United States,* whose keel was laid only days after Johnson took office. After checking with Ike by telephone (apparently obtaining Ike's approval), on April 15 Johnson sent the JCS a memo asking for our opinion. On April 22, the JCS responded with a formal "vote": Van and I against the carrier, Denfeld for. In my remarks, I concluded that "it is militarily unsound to authorize at this time the construction of additional aircraft carriers or to continue expenditure on the U.S.S. *United States.*" The very next day, April 23, Johnson ordered construction of the carrier canceled.[37]

When this broadsword fell on the Navy's neck, Navy Secretary John L. Sullivan and the admirals were literally stunned. Johnson had not forewarned a soul—not the President, not Sullivan, not Denfeld. The Navy turned on Johnson as though he were a madman—or worse. Truman's naval aide Robert L. Dennison, who had not been forewarned either, later summed up the Navy's reaction to Louis Johnson: "He was just a criminal." Outraged, Navy Secretary Sullivan resigned in protest, an idealistic gesture that dismayed not only Johnson but the whole military establishment. Sullivan asked Denfeld to resign with him—to increase the impact—but Denfeld thought he could help the Navy more by staying on.[38]

Johnson soon replaced Sullivan with Francis P. Matthews, a prominent Omaha Catholic layman and Democrat who had helped swing the Nebraska delegation to Truman at the Democratic convention and who had subsequently contributed substantial sums to the campaign. By his own public admission, Matthews, who had never served in the armed forces, knew nothing about the Navy or the military. He was a sincere, devout and decent man who could not have taken over the Navy at a worse time. The admirals, judging Matthews' appointment another slap in the face, angrily derided Matthews as "Johnson's errand boy" or "Rowboat Matthews."[39]

By pure coincidence, at about this same time the top leadership of the Army became vacant. Ken Royall returned to North Carolina to enter politics and Bill Draper to the New York business world. That left only the two assistant secretaries—Gordon Gray and Tracy Voorhees—and

Gray was on the verge of leaving to take the post of dean of the University of North Carolina School of Business. At Truman's request, Gray agreed to stay on as Undersecretary of the Army for a "decent interval"—at least until Johnson could find a replacement for Royall.[40]

Ultimately, Johnson offered Gray the job of Army Secretary. Gray, who preferred the deanship in North Carolina, declined. There then ensued the most bizarre episode I had ever seen in Washington. While Gray was away on a trip, Johnson went to the White House and dishonestly told Truman that Gray wanted the Army Secretaryship so badly "he could taste it." Truman, who was absolutely "delighted" at that news, forthwith sent Gray's nomination to the Senate without consulting Gray. When Gray returned to Washington, he was stunned to find out what had happened. He went immediately to the White House to explain he had not sought—and did not want—the job. Truman, somewhat dumbfounded, said he'd "take the rap"—tell the Senate he had made a "mistake"—and withdraw his name.

I had the highest regard for Gordon Gray. It soared even higher when I heard what happened next. As Gray recalled, "Suddenly it dawned on me that you don't do that kind of thing to the President of the United States." In order not to embarrass Truman, Gray changed all his personal plans, gave up the cherished deanship and agreed to serve as Army Secretary for a "respectable time." Truman, who was "grateful" to Gray for his decision, must have certainly had some second thoughts about Louis Johnson's integrity and methods.

I was certainly happy to have Gordon Gray as my civilian boss but immensely disquieted about the way it came about. What it boiled down to was that Johnson, for whatever reason, had lied to Truman and thereby placed the President in an extremely awkward position. As time passed, there were many in Washington who sincerely believed Louis Johnson was mentally ill. Truman was one. He wrote in his private diary: "Something happened. I am of the opinion that Potomac fever and a *pathological condition* are to blame. . . . Louis began to show an inordinate egotistical desire to run the whole government. He offended every member of the cabinet . . . He never missed an opportunity to say mean things about my personal staff." Secretary of State Dean Acheson was another who felt this way. In *Present at the Creation* he wrote that Johnson's conduct became "too outrageous to be explained by mere cussedness," and he was not surprised when some years later Johnson had a brain tumor removed. Unwittingly, Truman had replaced one mental case with another.[41]

It seems difficult to believe in retrospect, but in mid-May, two months after Johnson took over, he informed the JCS that we must cut yet another $1.4 billion from the fiscal 1951 military budget—down from $14.4 to $13 billion. This order, of course, came as a profound shock and forced us yet again to review our already exhaustively reviewed plans. Van and I agreed the time had come to drastically cut the Navy and Marine Corps budgets and we so recommended to Ike (still technically the JCS Presiding Officer) in separate memos. The final budget of $13.132 billion and force levels of 1.5 million men were set by Johnson himself. They were divided this way: Air Force, $4.433 billion for forty-eight groups; Army, $4.018 billion for ten divisions; Navy, $3.881 billion for 238 combat ships, including (probably on Ike's recommendation) seven aircraft carriers, plus about $800 million to cover certain costs that had been consolidated in the Office of the Secretary of Defense. A substantial portion of the Air Force budget would be earmarked to fund fifteen strategic bombardment groups, eleven equipped with the older B-29s and B-50s, four with huge new intercontinental-range B-36s, which were in the test stage.

This new budget limitation marked the end of the Army build-up we had so hopefully embarked upon the year before. Our compromise goal had been to expand from 552,000 to about 800,000 men. In fact, during 1949, we reached a peak strength of only 660,473 men. Thereafter, owing to the newest budgetary restrictions, we began to shrink again.[42]

That spring, as expected, Congress enacted several laws modifying the 1947 National Security Act, designed to intensify unification. One of these laws changed the name of the National Military Establishment to the Department of Defense. Another had established the formal post of Chairman of the Joint Chiefs of Staff, who would serve a two-year term (and be eligible for reappointment to a second term in time of peace) but who would not have a formal "vote" in the JCS.

We were still operating under the assumption that Joe McNarney, then working closely with Louis Johnson on budgets and force levels, would be named the first Chairman. But McNarney was an Air Force general. To have named him to the Chairman's job at this time would have heavily stacked the JCS against the Navy—two Air Force generals, one admiral, plus me. Moreover, given the anti-Navy bias of Louis Johnson, McNarney was a politically injudicious choice. Besides that, the Air Force was the "junior" service, and upon reflection it did not seem fitting that the Air Force should have first crack at this prestigious job. All in all, the best bet appeared to be a neutral Army general of some public stature.[43]

The best bet, of course, was Ike. But when Johnson offered him the job, Ike flatly turned it down, noting in his diary: "Louis Johnson wants me to come to Washington as Chairman of the Joint Chiefs of Staff, permanently, or at least indefinitely. It is queer, but people in political life consider that anyone not in Washington is a lost soul, lost to ambition, to public regard, to any public usefulness. Of course I'll not do it—there are more able men available for that job than possibly any other in government. But he'll think I'm running out on him."[44]

Probably on Ike's recommendation, Johnson then turned to me, even though I had told Ike earlier in the year I did not want the job. I now changed my mind. I agreed to serve in the job one term—two years. The main reason for my change of heart was my deep concern about the state of the military establishment. Owing to the cancellation of the supercarrier, there was a vicious mutiny afoot in the Navy. With his crazy bull-in-the-china-shop approach, Johnson was in no way fitted to deal with it. Nor was his decent but weak and inexperienced Navy Secretary, Frank Matthews. A Navy mutiny could conceivably tear apart the Department of Defense, possibly tempting the Kremlin to capitalize on our military disarray. A firm but fair JCS Chairman, assisted by a neutral Army general (my replacement as Army Chief of Staff), might be the moderating force that could prevent a crippling brawl.

I was extremely reluctant to leave the Army. I had served as Chief of Staff but a year and a half of the traditional four-year tour, and I was far from satisfied with the progress we had made in reshaping an administrative Army into a crack fighting force. The one consolation was that my vice chief of staff, Joe Collins, had continued to grow. He was now more than qualified to carry on the work I had begun and was willing to continue the work in the post of Chief of Staff. Joe was also an ideal choice to represent the Army on the JCS—not passionately for or against the Navy or the Air Force, and an ardent believer in unification.[45]

My last major official act as Army Chief of Staff was a JCS trip to Europe, July 29 to August 9. The North Atlantic Treaty had been signed in Washington on April 4, 1949, and after extensive hearings, approved by the Senate on July 21. This historic treaty—still in force today—bound a dozen nations into a mutual defense pact. The purpose of my trip was to lay the groundwork for integrated war planning and military assistance which the United States would provide, to gather ideas for a NATO military command structure and, generally, to get the Europeans cracking. Flying in the President's plane, *Independence,* the JCS blitzed through nine countries in as many days, an exhausting though very worthwhile trip, during which I saw many old comrades-in-arms from the war, including Monty, who had not changed in the slightest.[46]

On August 12, Louis Johnson and I went to the White House, where President Truman announced my nomination as Chairman of the Joint Chiefs of Staff. The Senate approved the nomination at once, and at 0900 on August 16, in a modest ceremony in Johnson's office, I was sworn in. The reaction to my appointment generally was positive. I was still blessed with a "favorable press." However, to the Navy I was still an enemy. With the JCS now officially enlarged to four men—Denfeld, Vandenberg, Collins and me—the Navy felt that even though I had no official vote, its voice would be further weakened.[47]

FIFTY-TWO

I moved into a fancy new office decorated with a new "Chairman of the JCS" flag. I brought my faithful, hardworking aides with me: Willis Matthews and Chet Hansen, and my secretary, Mary Pitcairn. In order to "unify" the office, I took on a naval aide recommended by Denfeld: the distinguished World War II submariner Edward L. Beach. Later I added an Air Force aide. The office clerical staff was deliberately composed of members of all three services. To further mollify the Navy, and ostensibly give it a larger voice in JCS planning, a Navy admiral, Arthur C. Davis (USNA 1915), replaced Al Gruenther as director of the 100-man JCS joint staff, which operated under my supervision.[1]

I soon wore two other hats. It had been decided to establish a NATO military committee consisting of the chiefs of staff of all NATO nations, a sort of super Combined Chiefs of Staff. I served as chairman of this committee, which met periodically to consider strategy. It had also been decided to establish, within the military committee, a standing group (somewhat akin to the executive committee of a board of directors) consisting of representatives of the United States, the United Kingdom and France. I was chairman of the standing group, which was based in Washington and met weekly to work on details of NATO military strategy.

My office thus became a focal point and clearing house for all the military problems and plans of the free world. My desk was soon piled high with top-secret JCS and NATO papers. I usually met once a day with Louis Johnson, who used me as a sounding board or as a conduit to the JCS. The Secretaries of the Army, Navy and Air Force consulted me frequently. I maintained a continuous liaison with the AEC, which had responsibility for producing and storing our nuclear weapons. Senators and congressmen concerned about military matters large and small called on me or invited me to the Hill to testify. High-ranking foreign military chiefs visiting Washington stopped first in my office. My working days were long and tedious, and every night I carried home a briefcase full of papers. Only occasionally could I get away for a golf game or a weekend of hunting. Ike commiserated: "Brad, you have got the hardest job in all Washington and my heart is all with you."[2]

Meanwhile all hell was breaking loose in the Navy. The pent-up rage and frustration exploded in public. The trouble began in June, when a Navy speechwriter and propagandist leaked a document deriding the Air Force's newest intercontinental bomber, the B-36, as a "billion dollar blunder." Not only that, the memo charged, the bomber was kept in production only because Louis Johnson and Stuart Symington had a financial interest in it, and because they owed personal and political favors to Floyd Odlum, head of Consolidated-Vultee Aircraft, which had the B-36 contract.

The leak was a shocking charge and it generated screaming headlines nationwide. Navy supporter Congressman James E. Van Zandt demanded a congressional investigation. Carl Vinson, chairman of the House Armed Services Committee, reluctantly took on the chore but broadened the scope of the inquiry. On June 9, Vinson's committee voted to launch a sweeping investigation of the national military establishment, its decision-making process, its strategic doctrine and the roles and missions of the services. The hearings would begin in August and resume after a recess in October.

It was clear from the outset that these hearings were going to be more than routine. The Navy would use them as a platform to attack not only Johnson, the B-36 and the Air Force, but the whole concept of strategic bombing. It would be a long and bitter fight.

The Navy's revolt soon dominated all else. Never in our military history had there been anything comparable—not even the Billy Mitchell rebellion of the 1920s. A complete breakdown in discipline occurred. Neither Matthews nor Denfeld could control his subordinates. Most naval officers despised Matthews. Denfeld, in my judgment, had abandoned, or at least grossly neglected, his disciplinary responsibilities in an apparent, and unwise, effort to straddle the fence. Denfeld gave lip service to unification, yet he allowed his admirals to run amok. It was utterly disgraceful.

The leader of the Navy's mutiny was Arthur W. Radford, a distinguished and brilliant naval aviator. He was assisted by many other admirals and senior captains, notably aviators Ralph A. Ofstie and John G. Crommelin, and a destroyerman, Arleigh A. (31 Knot) Burke, hero of the Pacific war. Burke and Crommelin, both skilled propagandists, attempted, with varying degrees of success, to enlist the media in the Navy's cause. In any event, they kept the pot boiling with leaks or rebellious public statements, attacking Johnson's budget cuts, the Air Force, the B-36 and the nuclear retaliatory strategy.[3]

At the commencement of the Vinson hearings in August, Symington and Vandenberg and other Air Force witnesses utterly demolished the

Navy. After hearing all the testimony, the committee reported officially: "There has not been . . . one iota, not one scintilla of evidence offered . . . that would support charges or insinuations that collusion, fraud, corruption, influence, or favoritism played any part whatsoever in the procurement of the B-36 bomber."

The more important and sweeping Navy charges attacking our strategy, military budgets and weapons and the concept of unification were investigated in October. Arthur Radford was the principal Navy witness. He was followed to the stand by a dozen other admirals, Marine Corps generals and senior Navy captains who supported one aspect of his case or another.

The gist of the Navy's case was as follows: that our military establishment was being wrongly tailored to a single strategy of an "atomic blitz." That strategy was wrong because an atomic blitz would neither deter nor win a war and, moreover, the use of atomic weapons was immoral. Dependence on the B-36 to deliver the atomic blitz was a bad gamble because the plane had so many deficiencies it would be "useless defensively" or "inadequate offensively" and was thus an unwise investment. Even if some B-36s managed to reach the target areas, Air Force pilots would not be able to drop bombs close enough to be effective, and anyway the destructive power of atomic bombs was far less than advertised and not likely to inflict decisive damage on the enemy or break his will to resist.

The Navy men further argued that concentration of funds for the B-36 had forced the Air Force to dangerously neglect aircraft for other missions, such as interception of enemy bombers, tactical air support and troop lift, while cancellation of the supercarrier and reduction of naval and Marine Corps aviation units had gravely impaired the Navy's ability to carry out its wartime mission. They maintained that a plan was afoot to completely "abolish" the Marine Corps. They asserted that neither Vandenberg nor Collins nor I had a true understanding of sea power or how to properly plan for war. Finally, owing to the foregoing, morale in the Navy and Marine Corps was at a dangerously low ebb.

I was profoundly shocked and angered by the Navy's case. The main thrust of it was completely dishonest. As the Navy knew very well, we were *not* gearing our entire military strategy to a single strategy of an atomic blitz. Our strategy, as embodied in Offtackle, now envisioned massive conventional air, sea and ground operations in concert with our NATO allies. The atomic strategic offensive, which Denfeld had agreed to, was a vital element—perhaps *the* vital element—of that strategy, but not by any means the sole element. Moreover, while no one claimed the B-36 to be the perfect weapon, it was the best we had at the moment, and Denfeld himself had approved, without reservations, the inclusion of funds for four groups of B-36s in the Air Force budget. The Navy knew very well that better, all-jet bombers (the B-47 and B-52) were in the works.

The most dishonest and disturbing aspect of the Navy's testimony was the denigration of the power of the atomic bombs. The testimony was based on unclassified data on the impact of the twenty-two-kiloton Hiroshima and Nagasaki bombs. The Navy knew very well that the Sandstone tests had proved out new atomic bomb designs which had yielded twice the power of the original bombs, and that with further refinements in design we could build fission bombs with even greater yields. Unfortunately, owing to the highly classified nature of this data and the value its disclosure would have for the Russians, no one could rebut the dishonest impression Navy witnesses had created.[4]

For the Navy to raise public doubt about the effectiveness—or morality—of atomic bombs was the height of hypocrisy. Ever since I had been a member of the JCS the Navy had been fighting relentlessly not to be excluded from utilizing nuclear weapons. The principal purpose of the supercarrier was to accommodate aircraft large enough to carry atomic bombs. The cancellation of the supercarrier had, in effect, denied the Navy a decisive role in nuclear bombardment. This denial, in fact, was the main cause of the Navy's revolt.

The charges that a plan was afoot to "abolish" the Marine Corps were likewise dishonest, designed to incur the sympathy of the millions who regarded the Marine Corps as sacrosanct as motherhood. As the Navy well knew, the Marine Corps was "protected" under the 1947 National Security Act and could not be abolished without congressional repeal of that portion of the act. As I have written, Ike, Van and I, believing the Marine Corps was far too large (the equivalent of two reinforced divisions) and a wasteful duplication of the Army's mission, had proposed deep cuts in its size. But these cuts were more or less proportional to the cuts proposed for the Army and did not represent an attempt to abolish the Marine Corps. Moreover, Marine Corps aviation was still wildly out of balance, consisting as it did of twenty-one squadrons, which was the equivalent of seven Air Force tactical support groups. At the peak of Twelfth Army Group operations in the ETO, we never had more than fourteen groups supporting twenty-eight to thirty divisions in the line.

Quite apart from the blatant dishonesty of the Navy's attack, I was furious about the grievous psychological damage it was bound to cause. It was, in effect, an all-out assault on the credibility of our deterrent, our capability for waging nuclear war. Conceivably it could completely undermine public trust both at home and abroad in our weaponry and military leaders. This at a time when we were doing our utmost to coax our allies to support a NATO military force.

I had hoped that Navy Secretary Matthews and CNO Denfeld would seize the occasion and take drastic measures to restore order and discipline in the Navy. But neither man seemed capable of dealing with the crisis. Matthews was far out of his depth. His testimony on the Hill and other measures merely served to intensify the rebellion. Denfeld tried to talk out of both sides of his mouth at once, supporting both Radford and Louis Johnson. Of course he failed, antagonizing both sides and leaving the impression that he lacked integrity.

After the Navy had had its day, the Air Force took the stand. As in August, both Symington and Vandenberg made superb witnesses, rebutting Radford's case point by point, insofar as it could be rebutted. Symington was forceful and passionate; Vandenberg icily cool and precise. I thought their combined testimony went a long way toward restoring public confidence in our strategy and weaponry.

Knowing I would soon be called to the witness stand, I thought long and hard about what I would say. I could be lofty, vague and "statesmanlike" or I could be down to earth and hard-hitting. It seemed to me that it was time to be hard-hitting. The crybaby attitude of the naval aviators and Marines had been, in my opinion, gravely damaging both at home and abroad. The admirals were insubordinate, mutinous. No one had publicly censured them for the insubordination, and it did not seem likely anyone would. I therefore took it upon myself to administer the lash. It was the most forceful and controversial speech I ever made.

Having prepared my statement with the help of a new speechwriter, Chester V. Clifton, and not having shown it to anyone in advance, I took the stand on October 19. I began by trying to set our military strategy in proper perspective, paraphrasing the key features of Offtackle, in order to show how the plan was dependent on conventional NATO forces and not solely on an American B-36 atomic blitz. In broad and general terms, I refuted the Navy's principal charges about the immorality and ineffectiveness of atomic strategic bombardment, pointing out the Navy's glaring discrepancies in logic and distortion of truth.[5]

Going on, I stressed these points:

- That inasmuch as the surface navy of the Soviet Union was "negligible," it was grossly wasteful to fund a U.S. Navy beyond what was needed to cope with the growing Soviet submarine threat.
- That inasmuch as the Air Force had been assigned the primary responsibility for strategic bombing, it was militarily unsound to build supercarriers when the money was required for "other more vital needs."
- That aircraft carriers could not be justified to support future amphibious operations. I predicted that "large-scale amphibious operations" such as those in Sicily and Normandy "will never occur again." I added: "Frankly, the atomic bomb properly delivered almost precludes such a possibility. I know that I, personally, hope that I shall never be called upon to participate in another amphibious operation like the one in Normandy."[6]
- That no one could abolish the Marine Corps without congressional approval. I did not recommend that it be abolished but directly and indi-

rectly I challenged the need for a large Marine Corps. I pointed out to those who believed that a "tremendous Marine Corps" was essential for amphibious operations that at Sicily and Normandy, "two of the largest amphibious assaults ever made in history," no Marines were present. I described the bloated size of Marine aviation air tactical support, comparing it to Air Force ETO operations.

Having quietly dealt with the moral, technical and strategic aspects of the Navy's charges, I then got out the lash. I turned first to the insinuations Navy witnesses had left that neither Vandenberg nor I (nor Collins) had an adequate grasp of war or war planning. I sketched in the considerable war experience that we had had, then pointedly raised a question about Denfeld's qualifications: "I was not associated with Admiral Denfeld during the war and I am not familiar with his experiences." I went on lashing, stating: "The truth of the matter is that very few Navy men on the staff of the Chief of Naval Operations have had any experience in large-scale land operations." I said that "high-ranking Navy men" had appeared before the JCS with conclusions "that showed they had no conception whatsoever of land operations."

I turned next to the much-publicized matter of low Navy and Marine Corps morale. I blamed that on Denfeld and his senior admirals: "It would seem . . . that Navy leaders have lost sight of the fact that men, not machines, win wars and protect the peace. Senior officers decrying the low morale of their forces evidently do not realize that the esprit of the men is but a mirror of their confidence in their leadership. Confidence in leaders is an accepted ingredient of organizational esprit. However, dissensions among the top command, like a single drop of poison in wine, can destroy all partakers."

Finally I got down to the heart of the matter. The fundamental problem, I said, is that "many in the Navy are completely against unity of command and planning as established in the laws passed by the Congress of the United States. Despite protestations to the contrary, I believe the Navy has opposed unification from the beginning, and they have not, in spirit as well as deed, accepted it completely to date. As a policy, yes, but as the final and authoritative vehicle for planning our collective defense, no." World War II, I went on, "should have taught all military men that our military forces are one team—in the game to win regardless who carries the ball. This is no time for 'fancy Dans' who won't hit the line with all they have on every play, unless they can call the signals. Each player on this team—whether he shines in the spotlight of the backfield or eats dirt in the line—must be All-American."

My statement was beyond doubt the frankest and toughest delivered before Vinson's committee. Those who had come to perceive me as the "amiable Missouri schoolteacher" or "the nicest guy in Washington" were astonished. *New York Times* reporter William S. White called it "one of the most extraordinary tongue lashings ever given to high military officers in such a forum." Naval Academy graduate Hanson Baldwin, the *Times'* special military correspondent, wrote: "The vehemence and vigor of the statement, and the bitterness that seemed to mark some of it, astounded and amazed most of the listeners. . . . Here was no patient, calm and tolerant Bradley, but an aroused old soldier, smarting under the long tension of friction and the Navy's attacks of the last ten days. . . . The Bradley statement did the Navy no good but it has not added to General Bradley's past reputation for tolerance, breadth and patience."

My remarks generated headlines and editorial comment nationwide. The phrase I employed to characterize the admirals—"fancy Dans"—was quoted endlessly.[7]

That hit the nail on the head, but elsewhere I made an imprecise, or misleading, statement in my remarks which I was compelled to correct in a brief appearance the following day. In his testimony before the committee concerning the supercarrier, Denfeld had said that "It is no secret that General Bradley reversed his earlier approval of the project." He was referring to my May 26, 1948, "yes" vote to Forrestal and my April 22, 1949, "no" vote to Louis Johnson. In my remarks I said that Denfeld was "carelessly misinformed," that the JCS had not been asked "to pass on the matter" until the April 22, 1949, vote requested by Johnson. This was, of course, imprecise. In my "clarification," I explained to the committee that I had not considered the May 26, 1948, vote a "formal decision" of the JCS, that the vote of April 22, at least as I construed it, was the first. Technically, in my mind, I had not reversed myself.

Hanson Baldwin, unblushingly pro-Navy in his coverage of the hearings, wrote a follow-up article in *The New York Times,* headlined: "BRADLEY'S CHARGES UPSET WASHINGTON / General's Future Usefulness and That of Denfeld Called Affected by Testimony." In this long article, Baldwin asserted: "It was generally felt that his [Bradley's] testimony, piled upon Denfeld's prior charges, had made impossible a continuation of the present relationships in the Defense Department. Admiral Denfeld, it was thought, might well be superseded as the Chief of Naval Operations. . . . General Bradley's position, too, was not without complications; his testimony had put a great gulf between him and the Navy, had supported the Navy's charges of bias and partisanship and had certainly lessened somewhat, even his friends agreed, the general's future usefulness and his past stature."[8]

Despite Baldwin's biased reporting, my position was not in jeopardy. Most people supported me, including Baldwin's superiors on the *Times,* who, in an editorial, called my speech "powerful and persuasive." Louis Johnson applauded me both in private and in public, when he testified before the committee. Among the many letters and phone calls of support, none cheered me more than a note from Ike, who wrote, in part, that

Allied convoys massed offshore at Omaha Beach after the invasion. For longer than I liked the Normandy landing beaches continued to be our main source of supply.

The city of St. Lô, reduced to rubble, was the scene of our historic breakout in July 1944.

4

45

Generals Lesley McNair, Courtney Hodges and Wade Haislip (left to right). McNair was tragically killed by an American bomb near St. Lô. Hodges commanded First Army. Although he received far less publicity than Patton, in many ways he was a more reliable army commander. Haislip's XV Corps spearheaded Patton's electrifying dash across France.

47 48

British General Brian Horrocks (46). Severely wounded in North Africa, he recovered to lead XXX Corps to Antwerp and then on into Germany. General Raymond McLain (47), an outstanding National Guard officer, rose to command XIX Corps. General James Gavin (48), a fearless and brilliant commander, succeeded Matt Ridgway as commander of the 82nd Airborne Division.

With Patton and Monty in a rare moment of levity. 49

50

51

52

Corps commanders Manton Eddy (50), Walton Walker (51) and Charles (Pete) Corlett (52).

53

With General Troy Middleton, commander of VIII Corps in Patton's Third Army. An outstanding soldier, Middleton fought with me in Sicily and Europe.

54

55

56

General Leonard (Gee) Gerow (54), commander of V Corps in the heroic assault on Omaha Beach and later commander of the Fifteenth Army. General William Simpson (55), another fine commander, led Ninth Army to the Elbe. General Jacob (Jake) Devers (56) commanded Sixth Army Group from Marseilles to Munich.

57

In September 1944, American and British chiefs of staff met in Quebec to plan the final stages of World War II. Seated from left to right are Marshall, Admiral William Leahy, Roosevelt, Churchill, Brooke, and British Field Marshal John Dill. Standing left to right are British General Hollis, British General Hastings Ismay, Admiral Ernest King, British Air Marshal Charles Portal, General Henry (Hap) Arnold, and British Admiral Andrew Cunningham.

58

59

The Battle of the Bulge produced some of the most difficult fighting of the war (58). It shook and nearly shattered the Allied high command. The famous bridge at Remagen (59). The capture of this bridge by troops in Courtney Hodges' First Army led to a major shift in Allied ground strategy.

60

My aides Major Lewis Bridge (left) and Major Chester Hansen pin on my fourth star in April 1945.

61

A toast to the Allied victory with Russian Marshal Koniev in Germany, May 1945.

Victorious Allies.

62

63

A formal portrait of the victorious American generals. Seated left to right are William Simpson, Ninth Army commander; Patton; airman Carl (Tooey) Spaatz; Ike; myself; Hodges; and Gerow. Standing left to right are Ralph Stearley; Hoyt Vandenberg; Bedell Smith; Otto Weyland; and Richard Nugent. Except for Bedell all the generals in the second row are airmen.

My homecoming victory parade in Moberly in June 1945.

64

65

66

A favorable press assisted me invaluably in the difficult job of modernizing the Veterans Administration from 1945 to 1947.

67

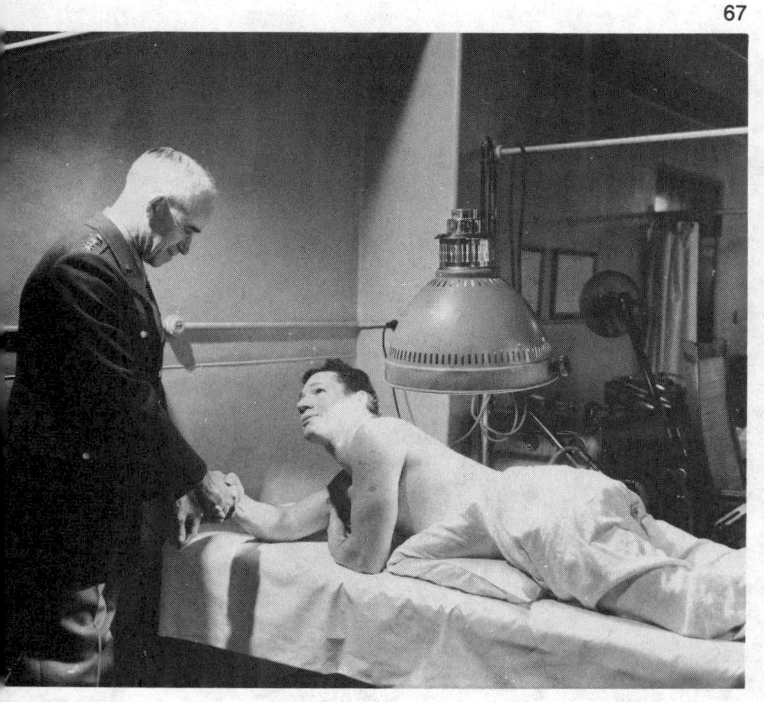

68

One of the greatest challenges I faced was improving the quality of VA medical care (67). Ike's wartime Surgeon General, Paul R. Hawley (68), deserves much of the credit for our success. I had sent hundreds of thousands of men into battle. Nothing gave me more satisfaction than easing their way home.

69

I succeeded Ike as Army Chief of Staff in February 1948. President Harry Truman and Army Secretary Kenneth Royall were present at the brief swearing-in ceremony.

70

The civilian and military leadership of the Army in January 1949: Seated with me are Undersecretary William Draper (on the left) and Secretary Royall. Standing left to right are General Albert Wedemeyer, Assistant Secretaries Tracy Voorhees and Gordon Gray, and Generals Joe Collins and Wade Haislip.

71

Conferring with my principal Army area commanders. Seated beside me are Generals Thomas Handy (left) and Mark Clark. Standing left to right are Generals Courtney Hodges, Walton Walker, Gee Gerow, and Alvan Gillem.

73

72

I had been Army Chief of Staff only a few months when the Russians closed ground access to Berlin, precipitating a major Cold War crisis. General Lucius Clay (73) conceived the Berlin airlift, which was a major victory for the West.

74

George C. Marshall served as Truman's Secretary of State.

75

Upon Marshall's retirement these men became the principal architects of Cold War foreign policy during Truman's second term. Left to right: presidential advisor W. Averell Harriman, Secretary of State Dean Acheson, Secretary of Defense Robert Lovett, and myself.

76

77

Our first two Secretaries of Defense James Forrestal (76) and Louis Johnson (77). Forrestal was mentally unstable and many people thought the same was true of Johnson.

78

79

80

81

Navy leaders during the "Admirals' Revolt" of 1948–49. Admiral Louis Denfeld (78), who was fired as Chief of Naval Operations by Truman; Admiral Arthur Radford (79), who led the revolt; Secretary of the Navy John Sullivan (80), who resigned in a dispute over the Navy's proposed supercarrier; and his successor, the decent but ineffectual Francis P. Matthews (81).

82

83

Opposing the rebellious Navy were air power zealots Stuart Symington (82), first Secretary of the Air Force; Hoyt Vandenberg, Air Force Chief of Staff (see photo 87); and Symington's successor, Thomas Finletter (83).

84

Five months before the outbreak of war in Korea, I finally got to the Far East, where for the first time in twenty-eight years I met with General Douglas MacArthur, our Far East commander.

85

MacArthur's Inchon landing, one of the riskiest military operations in history, proved to be brilliantly successful. After that victory, MacArthur's strategy in Korea was unsound and led to a humiliating rout of United Nations forces.

86

Matt Ridgway took command of Eighth Army and through sheer force of personality turned it into a magnificent fighting force. After Truman fired MacArthur, Ridgway was named Far East commander, and Jim Van Fleet, pictured behind Ridgway in this photo, took command of Eighth Army for the frustrating positional warfare that ensued.

The Joint Chiefs of Staff during the crucial stages of the Korean War. From left to right: Admiral Forrest Sherman, Chief of Naval Operations; myself; General Hoyt Vandenberg, Chief of Staff of the Air Force; and General Joe Collins, Army Chief of Staff. Our greatest concern was that the Soviets would overrun Western Europe. We therefore disagreed with MacArthur's proposals to enlarge the war in the Far East.

87

At home with my family. I'm holding my grandson Hank Beukema, the oldest of my grandchildren. Mary is beside me. Standing are my son-in-law, Hal Beukema, and my daughter, Lee.

89

After Mary's death I married Kitty Buhler on September 12, 1966.

90

Revisiting Fort Benning with Kitty.

91

At the Academy Awards ceremonies with actor Karl Malden, who played me in the film *Patton*. Kitty and I served as senior advisors to the film.

"your standing is too high, your place in public opinion too secure to be materially damaged by any carping criticism." He added: "Don't defend yourself—don't explain—don't worry!!"[9]

It turned out that in spite of the prolonged hullabaloo, nothing substantial emerged from these so-called B-36 hearings. The official committee report deplored the way the supercarrier had been canceled, but did not recommend that it be restored. Johnson went right on wielding the economy ax. Shortly after the hearings concluded, Congress finally voted on the fiscal 1950 military budget, which had been shelved pending the outcome of the hearings. As in 1948, the House tacked on an extra $800 million for aircraft, but the Senate refused to pass the budget until another "hooker" had been inserted to again enable Truman to impound the money, which he did later. In sum: The 1950 military budget emerged from Congress in almost exactly the shape Truman had submitted it.

The principal outcome of the "Admirals' Revolt" was the professional death of Louis Denfeld. At a press conference on October 27, one week after my testimony, Truman announced that Matthews had requested that Denfeld be relieved of his CNO post and transferred to other duty. Truman released a terse letter approving the request. Denfeld asked for retirement and it was swiftly approved by Matthews. Although Matthews had lost all effectiveness as Secretary of the Navy, Johnson kept him in the post because he had been loyal to him and the administration.

The choice of CNO to replace Denfeld was a fortunate one—Forrest P. Sherman, one of the most impressive military officers I ever met in any service. Urbane, intellectual, diplomatic and smart as a whip, he was a well-known naval aviator and veteran of the Pacific war. After the war he had been a Navy negotiator in the 1947 unification fight, opposed to unification but faithfully accepting the final outcome. He then went on to take over the Navy's Sixth Fleet in the Mediterranean, where he had served closed-mouthed during the "Admirals' Revolt." He was the perfect man to restore discipline in the Navy—particularly among his peers in naval aviation—and a welcomed face in the JCS. The great pity was that Sherman had less than two years to live. In August 1951, he would die of a heart attack.[10]

The revolt of the admirals dominated the headlines for months. But behind the scenes a military event occurred that would soon shove that controversy to the back pages and cause a profound reappraisal of our military strategy and an abrupt reversal of the Truman-Johnson military economy drive. On or about August 29, 1949, a mere two weeks after I assumed my duties as Chairman of the Joint Chiefs of Staff, the Soviets exploded an atomic bomb, ending forever our "atomic monopoly," which had lasted only four short years.[11]

The question of *when* the Soviets would break our atomic monopoly had always been uppermost in the minds of the JCS. Various estimates were floating around. The official JCS estimate in force at the time of the Soviet explosion, based on the best guesses from scientists advising the three services, had been drawn a year and a half earlier, on March 22, 1948. It stated that the "earliest date" would be mid-1950, but the "probable date" was mid-1953. Thus the Russians had beaten the "earliest date" by one full year and the "probable date" by four full years.

Sound and reliable intelligence on Soviet nuclear activities was almost impossible to come by. We had no spies inside the Russian nuclear community to my knowledge. Some fleeting and incomplete breaks into various Soviet codes provided nothing on the subject that I can recall. We depended entirely on an airborne "detection" net, designed to scoop up telltale signs of nuclear explosions in the atmosphere.

This detection net was first proposed—*urged,* I should say—in 1947 by Atomic Energy Commissioner Lewis L. Strauss, a hawkish Wall Street millionaire who had served in the Navy in World War II, rising to the rank of rear admiral. Responsibility for operating it had been delegated to the Air Force. It was satisfactorily tested during our Sandstone nuclear tests in 1948 in the Marshall Islands and thereafter put into operation. It had been in full-time service barely one year when one of its aircraft, a B-29 operating under the guise of a "weather plane," picked up signs of the Soviet atomic explosion (radioactivity in the atmosphere) near Alaska on September 3, 1949. This was assumed to be the first Soviet atomic explosion, but as Strauss pointed out then and later, they could very well have set off an atomic test before our detection net was in place.

The detection of these radioactive samples electrified the military establishment. The Air Force sent aloft additional aircraft to collect samples and asked the British to do likewise. The samples were carefully analyzed by Air Force and AEC scientists. Some scientists doubted that the Soviets could have exploded a bomb. Perhaps, they argued, the radioactivity had been caused by a laboratory accident or a reactor explosion. But on September 19, a panel of distinguished AEC scientists, including Vannevar Bush and Robert Oppenheimer, concluded that "the origin of the fission products was the explosion of an atomic bomb." Truman made the news public on September 23, using the phrase "atomic explosion" rather than "explosion of an atomic bomb" in deference to those who still doubted.

This news came as a terrible shock to Louis Johnson. It caught him with his economy ax poised in midair for yet another blow. He swung and continued to swing for some months, but it was almost immediately obvious that he was embarked on the wrong course; the balance of power had profoundly shifted. With our atomic monopoly slipping away,* it was

* The JCS estimated the Soviets would have ten to twenty bombs by mid-1950, twenty to forty-five by mid-1951 and forty-five to ninety by mid-1952.

clearly a time to build our military forces, not pare them. His plans to ride a defense-cutting program to the presidency were dashed.

One immediate result of the Soviet explosion was that on October 19 —the day I made my tough anti-Navy speech before the House Armed Services Committee—Truman approved a long-standing JCS recommendation for an acceleration in American fission materials production. Our recommendation had been made after the Sandstone tests had proven out the bombs with twice the yield of the Nagasaki and Hiroshima bombs. These tests had also proved that a smaller, lower-yield warhead was feasible, opening the way for utilizing atomic bombs against military targets on the battlefield—"tactical" atomic bombs. Following Sandstone, we had asked for a broad increase in fission production for warheads of all types —both strategic and tactical—but until the Soviet explosion, our requests, which required expensive new production facilities, had been pigeonholed. Truman's approval of this expansion program enabled us for the first time to seriously plan for tactical battlefield atomic weapons dropped from tactical aircraft, or fired from a large (280-mm) cannon, or as warheads for medium-range ballistic missiles such as the Redstone.

A second immediate result of the Soviet atomic explosion was a proposal from Commissioner Strauss and nuclear physicist Edward Teller and other hawks in the scientific community that the United States make a "quantum jump" in nuclear weaponry, by embarking on a program to build a thermonuclear or "hydrogen bomb," which might yield 1,000 times the power of the Nagasaki bomb. This concept had been explored at the AEC Los Alamos weapons laboratory during and immediately after the war. No one was quite sure that it would work or could be done, but Strauss, Teller and others were very anxious to give it a try. However, a large segment of the scientific community, led by Robert Oppenheimer, immediately rose up to oppose the hydrogen bomb on the grounds that it was immoral or not feasible or would interfere with the accelerated fission production program, or for other reasons.

A bitter internal debate ensued for several months, from October 1949 to January 1950. The Joint Chiefs were asked their opinion. On November 23, we forwarded a memorandum to Johnson, unanimously declaring in favor of attempting the hydrogen bomb. We argued that "available information indicates" that making a hydrogen bomb was "within the capability of the USSR" and that "possession of a thermonuclear weapon by the USSR without such possession by the United States would be intolerable."[12]

Behind the scenes, representing the JCS, I was an active lobbyist for the H-bomb program, or "Campbell," as it was code-named. On October 14, I appeared before a secret session of the Joint Congressional Committee on Atomic Energy, chaired by Senator Brien McMahon. The majority of the committee was hawkish; McMahon himself was a zealous H-bomb advocate. I also appeared before the five-man Atomic Energy Commission, whose chairman was a noted liberal, David Lilienthal. The AEC's Scientific Advisory Committee, chaired by Robert Oppenheimer, had voted against the H-bomb. Among the five commissioners, only Lewis Strauss favored it at that time, although Gordon Dean soon sided with him. Lilienthal was actively opposed. My lobbying at the AEC was resented by him and the two other commissioners who opposed the H-bomb.[13]

An important new factor influenced the debate. As a result of an American break in Soviet codes, we had learned that German-born Dr. Emil Klaus Julius Fuchs, a naturalized British subject who had worked on nuclear weapons at Los Alamos during and after the war, was a Soviet spy. The investigation of Fuchs was proceeding cautiously during the fall of 1949 with the hope that if confronted in the proper manner, Fuchs might confess. A confession was mandatory. We would not bring him to public trial with evidence based on codebreaking, because that would reveal we had read or could read some Soviet codes, giving away an important source of intelligence.[14]

FBI investigation revealed that Fuchs had been well situated to deliver atomic secrets to Russia. He was a leading participant in the work on atomic bombs at Los Alamos during the war. In addition, he had toured all American fission production facilities and experimental laboratories. In April 1946 he had attended a special conference at Los Alamos led by Edward Teller, the purpose of which was to prove that a hydrogen bomb was probably technically feasible. After the war he had taken a position at the main British atomic energy establishment at Harwell. In 1947 he had revisited American atomic research facilities.

The British security services (MI-5) assigned a top agent, William J. Skardon, to the Fuchs case in October 1949. His job was to elicit the required confession, which he managed to do on January 13, 1950. Fuchs told Skardon that he had spied for the Russians for seven years—from 1942 through 1948. Working through couriers, Fuchs had not only told the Russians how to make an atomic bomb, but also had passed along all available information on Teller's April 1946 Los Alamos conference on the hydrogen bomb.*

The Fuchs confession was profoundly shocking news. It meant that in 1946 both the United States and the USSR had the same technical data on the hydrogen bomb. Even though Teller believed the hydrogen bomb was probably feasible, the United States had shelved the project for more than

* Fuchs identified Harry Gold as one of his couriers. When the FBI subsequently arrested Gold, he implicated David Greenglass, an Army machinist who had worked at Los Alamos. Greenglass, in turn, implicated his sister's husband, Julius Rosenberg. The FBI had already decoded Soviet messages confirming the existence and operations of this Soviet courier ring, but did not use the messages in the trials of Gold, Greenglass, or Julius and Ethel Rosenberg.[15]

three years. But what if the Russians had not shelved it? What if they had proceeded with development of atomic and hydrogen bombs on parallel tracks? (An A-bomb was required to trigger an H-bomb.) If so, it was possible the Russians were even then only a step or two away from exploding a hydrogen bomb. Even in the face of the Fuchs confession, Oppenheimer and his colleagues who opposed the hydrogen bomb were not persuaded to change their minds. They continued to actively oppose it.

While Truman was weighing the decision in January 1950, I visited him in the White House on three occasions. We discussed the H-bomb privately, man-to-man. Truman was deeply troubled because AEC Chairman David Lilienthal was a humanitarian whom Truman greatly respected. But Truman had a way of seeing things clearly and going to the heart of the matter. If the Russians proceeded with the H-bomb and we did not, and if it worked, we would find ourselves in an intolerably inferior military posture. To Truman, it was as simple as that.[16]

On January 31, 1950, one day after Klaus Fuchs signed a full confession in the War Office in London, Truman, in one of his smartest and most courageous decisions, publicly directed that the United States pursue a program to construct the H-bomb. Owing to some brilliant work by Edward Teller and his chief assistants, we were able to test our first H-bomb in November 1952. The Russians tested an H-bomb nine months later, in August 1953. In terms of nuclear weapons development, we beat them by an eyelash.

The explosion of the Soviet A-bomb coincided with a final series of smashing communist victories in China, which forced the Nationalist government to retreat to a mountain redoubt in Chungking. On October 1, 1949, in Peking, the victorious Mao Tse-tung proclaimed the establishment of the People's Republic of China. In December, after further humiliating defeats and defections, the Nationalist government and what was left of their army and air force retreated to the island of Formosa.[17]

The Joint Chiefs of Staff had had very little involvement in the Chinese situation. When I was appointed Chief of Staff in February 1948, there were several plans floating around proposing various ways that we could help the Nationalist government militarily. I viewed all these military plans with profoundest skepticism, believing that the worst possible mistake we could make would be to involve ourselves in a land war on the Asian continent. The administration's position was that we could help Chiang most by providing economic support, just as we intended to help Western Europe with the Marshall Plan. Such economic support might conceivably prop up the Nationalist government long enough for it to get its house in order, cleanse the military forces of corruption and incompetence, and thereafter mount effective counterattacks against the communist forces. This idea was formalized on February 18, 1948, when Truman asked Congress to provide $570 million in economic assistance to China, to extend over a fifteen-month period ending June 30, 1949. None of this aid was to be in the form of military assistance.

The China Lobby members on the Hill were not happy with the exclusion of military aid. They set machinery in motion to modify the bill, which was known as the China Aid Act of 1948. The upshot was that Congress insisted that about one-fourth ($125 million) of the aid package be military assistance. To supervise the distribution of this hardware, the JCS laid plans to beef up the joint military advisory group in China to about 1,000 men under supervision of Army General David G. Barr. In contrast to Van Fleet's role in Greece, the Barr advisory group was specifically instructed to stay away from the battlefields, lest the Chinese blame us when the inevitable defeat came.

These decisions with respect to aid to China were taken without meaningful advice and direction of the JCS. On two or three occasions our views were sought on an ad hoc basis. Our position was similar to that of the China Lobby: "Limited" military assistance in the form of hardware was necessary to provide "the National Government some means with which to improve the present situation of internal conflict." In sum, we wrote, the *"buying of time"* with limited military hardware seemed advisable.

As it turned out, before Barr's group could make any appreciable contribution to the Nationalist military posture, or distribute any of the $125 million in military hardware, the communist forces won several decisive battles. In mid-October 1948, Chinchow and Changchun fell. Two weeks later, November 2, the communists captured Mukden, the capital of Manchuria, concluding the Manchurian campaign, which cost Chiang, in total, some 300,000 troops. With the fall of Mukden, we could see the end was near. We all but shut down Barr's advisory group and began to withdraw its members from China.

The final collapse of the Nationalist government and the retreat to Formosa was a deplorable but, in my opinion, unavoidable turn of events. There was never any realistic hope of "saving" China. I agreed entirely with General Barr's final report: "The Nationalist military collapse stemmed primarily from a weak and unstable government which was overcentralized, which had little or no popular support, and which had as a primary interest the protection of the privileged class."

These two events—the Russian explosion of an A-bomb and the communization of China—set in train a government-wide reappraisal of our foreign and military policy in the winter of 1949–50. Prolonged behind-the-scenes discussions resulted, in April 1950, in a new "posture paper," NSC-68, which replaced NSC 20/4 as the basic United States Cold War policy document. In the words of one historian, NSC-68 "was the most elaborate effort yet made to integrate political, economic and military considerations into a comprehensive statement of national security policy." Basically, NSC-68 was a ringing "call to arms" designed to eliminate the dichotomy in our Cold War policy. Henceforth we would back up containment with military force. The paper argued, in effect, that Truman's $15 billion ceiling on military forces was grossly inadequate; that the United States should be spending perhaps three times that much and could probably do so without wrecking the economy.[18]

Louis Johnson, whose obsessive aim was to reduce military expenditures, was caught out in left field, and of course he vigorously opposed NSC-68. Its principal supporter in the NSC was Secretary of State Dean Acheson, who was an uncompromising hawk. The JCS unequivocally supported NSC-68, creating a rare, awkward and ironic situation in which the three military chiefs and their chairman were more closely aligned with the views of the Secretary of State than with the Secretary of Defense.[19]

PART FIVE

★★★★★

THE KOREAN WAR

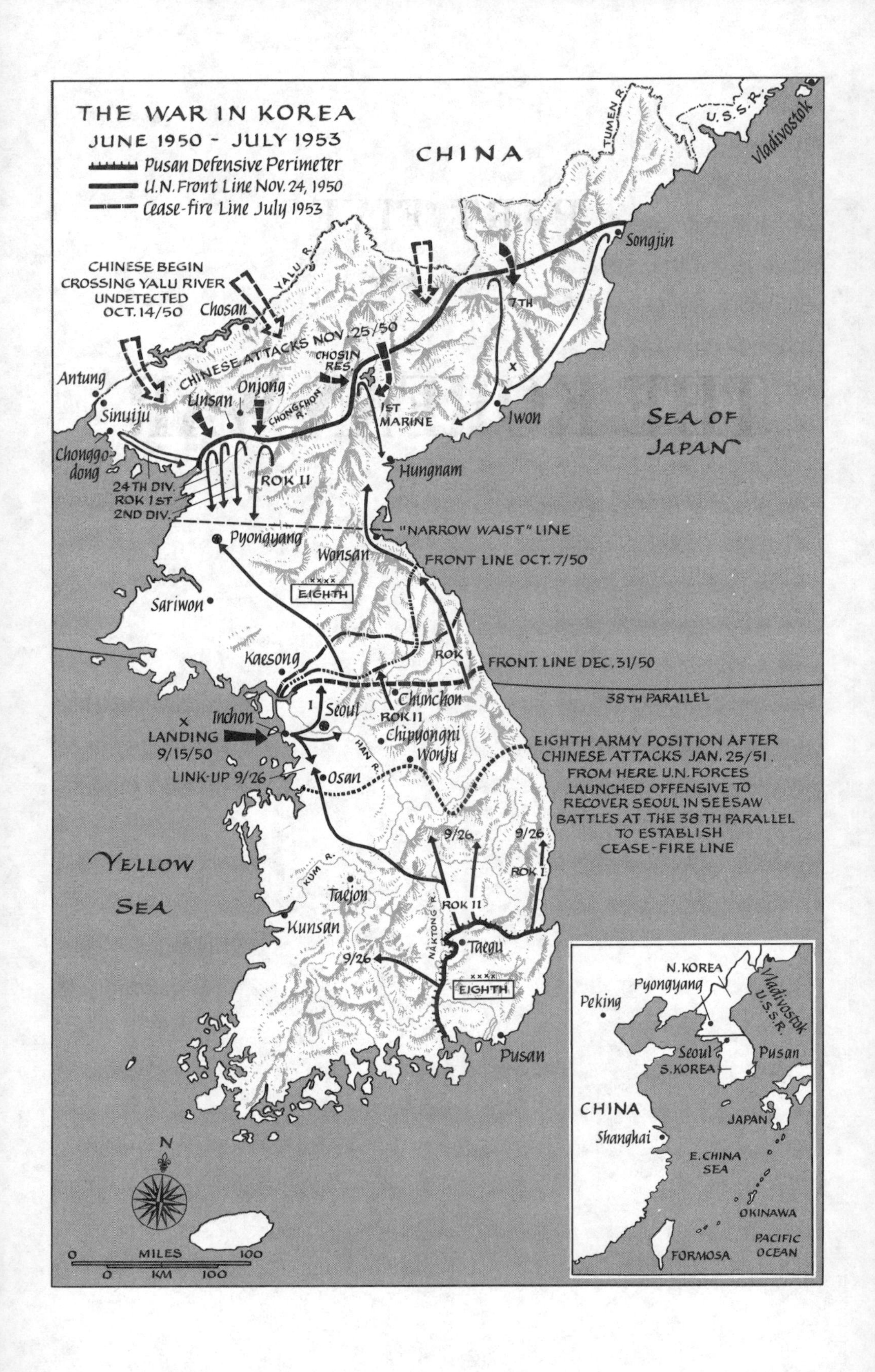
THE WAR IN KOREA
JUNE 1950 - JULY 1953
Pusan Defensive Perimeter
U.N. Front Line Nov. 24, 1950
Cease-fire Line July 1953
CHINA
TUMEN R.
U.S.S.R.
Vladivostok
Songjin
YALU R.
CHINESE BEGIN CROSSING YALU RIVER UNDETECTED OCT. 14/50
Chosan
7TH
CHINESE ATTACKS NOV 25/50
CHOSIN RES.
Antung
Unsan
Onjong
Sinuiju
CHONGCHON R.
1ST MARINE
Iwon
SEA OF JAPAN
Chonggo-dong
Hungnam
ROK II
24TH DIV.
ROK 1ST
2ND DIV.
"NARROW WAIST" LINE
Pyongyang
Wonsan
FRONT LINE OCT. 7/50
EIGHTH
Sariwon
ROK I
Kaesong
FRONT LINE DEC. 31/50
38TH PARALLEL
Chunchon
I
Seoul
Inchon
ROK II
LANDING 9/15/50
Chipyongni
HAN R.
Wonju
LINK-UP 9/26
Osan
EIGHTH ARMY POSITION AFTER CHINESE ATTACKS JAN. 25/51. FROM HERE U.N. FORCES LAUNCHED OFFENSIVE TO RECOVER SEOUL IN SEESAW BATTLES AT THE 38TH PARALLEL TO ESTABLISH CEASE-FIRE LINE
9/26
9/26
YELLOW SEA
KUM R.
ROK I
Taejon
ROK II
NAKTONG R.
Kunsan
Taegu
9/26
EIGHTH
Pusan
N
0 MILES 100
0 KM 100
N. KOREA
Pyongyang
Vladivostok
U.S.S.R.
Peking
Seoul
S. KOREA
Pusan
CHINA
JAPAN
Shanghai
E. CHINA SEA
OKINAWA
FORMOSA
PACIFIC OCEAN

FIFTY-THREE

Owing to circumstances entirely beyond my control, my relationship with MacArthur had remained distant. During my eighteen months as Chief of Staff of the Army, on at least a half-dozen occasions I had made plans to visit MacArthur. Regrettably, the urgency of the JCS budget and force level battles had compelled me to cancel each of these plans. This was awkward. Not since Ike's visit in May 1946 had the Army Chief of Staff called on MacArthur; nor had MacArthur been to Washington. On my last day as Chief of Staff, I wrote MacArthur praising his "faithful and invaluable service" and apologized for not having visited his headquarters. He responded that he had been "disappointed" and hoped that in my new assignment as Chairman of the Joint Chiefs I could find time for a visit.

A week after Joe Collins assumed the duties of Chief of Staff, he flew to Tokyo. I made plans to follow him there as quickly as possible. However, because of the "Revolt of the Admirals," the urgent and prolonged governmental conferences following the explosion of the Soviet A-bomb and the fall of China, I was again forced to postpone my trip to Tokyo.[1]

In January 1950, at long last, I finally got to Japan. This trip—January 29 to February 10—was made by the entire JCS—Collins, Forrest Sherman, Hoyt Vandenberg and myself. We flew from Washington to Alaska to Tokyo. This was the first time I had laid eyes on MacArthur since West Point in 1922—some twenty-eight years. Privately, he congratulated me on my "fancy Dan" speech, remarking, "Somebody had to say it," and he was glad I had.[2]

Five days before we arrived in Japan, MacArthur had celebrated his seventieth birthday. Even so, he was remarkably vigorous and keen and could not have been a more gracious host. For the first time I had an opportunity to take the measure of the man. He was awesomely brilliant; but as a leader he had several major flaws: an obsession for self-glorification, almost no consideration for other men with whom he served, and a contempt for the judgment of his superiors. Like Patton and Monty, MacArthur was a megalomaniac.[3]

His chief of staff was a man of entirely different character. He was Edward M. (Ned) Almond, a man I had known and respected for years. Then fifty-seven, Almond was a graduate of VMI (1915) and a hero of the AEF in World War I. He was a career officer of extraordinary ability, in a class with Wade Haislip, Gee Gerow, Tom Handy and Manton Eddy. Almond was not the usual yes-man or sycophant that seemed to gravitate to MacArthur's staffs and, of course, not one of the "Bataan crowd."[4]

MacArthur's chief ground commander in Japan was Walton Walker, who had commanded XX Corps in the ETO under Patton. After serving briefly as commander of the Fifth (paper) Army in Chicago, Walker had relieved the retiring Bob Eichelberger as commanding general of the Eighth Army in Japan in 1948. Walker was getting on in years (sixty-one), and was nearing retirement. His chief of staff was my former chief of staff at Twelfth Army Group, Lev Allen. The Eighth Army consisted of four Japan-based divisions: the 7th, 24th and 25th Infantry and the 1st Cavalry Division. My old First Army chief of staff, Bill (Captain Bligh) Kean, commanded the 25th Infantry Division. These divisions were understrength (generally two instead of three battalions per regiment), and in crowded Japan lacked proper space to train. The draftees manning these divisions were green and, for the most part, flabby. Many—too many—had Japanese servants.[5]

Over the next several days we held detailed discussions with MacArthur, Almond, Walker, Allen and others on Far East strategy, covering these major points:

War plans. In Offtackle, the JCS had agreed that if Russia launched a global war, we would conduct a "strategic offensive" in Eurasia and a "strategic defense" in the Far East. In this respect, the thrust of our plan was similar to that of global strategy in World War II: first priority to Europe.

Our principal Offtackle goals in the Far East were to defend Japan and Okinawa to the utmost for use as platforms for mounting the strategic air offensive, and for naval bases in support of the Navy's general mission of maintaining control of the seas. The Philippine Islands, where we had air and naval bases, were regarded as supporting elements of this strategy and were to be defended to the greatest extent possible, although first priority would go to Japan and Okinawa. Other islands of the Ryukyus ringing Okinawa were to be denied the enemy insofar as possible in order to preserve the integrity of Okinawa SAC bases.[6]

MacArthur expressed no disagreement with the main thrust of the Offtackle strategy. However, I feel certain that privately he disagreed. To MacArthur, Asia—the Far East—was the crucial battleground in the war against communism. Vast China, swallowed up by communism, was close at hand, threatening the fragile balance of power in the Far East; and to MacArthur it loomed as a greater immediate threat than communism in

Europe. From Tokyo, Europe seemed quiescent, while the Far East flamed. Had he had his way, I'm sure MacArthur would have reversed our strategy, giving first priority to the Far East, second to Europe.

There was a weakness and complication in our Far East strategy. Japan, the centerpiece of the strategy, and a nation of 80 million people, was utterly supine. Under the terms of her surrender and her new constitution, she was prohibited from organizing armed forces, even for maintaining internal order or for self-defense. She was thus entirely dependent for her security and safety upon the armed forces of the United States. We, in turn, could guarantee her safety only by maintaining military forces and bases in Japan and some of her former possessions, such as Okinawa.

These considerations had become intertangled with the question of arranging a Japanese peace treaty. As early as March 1947, MacArthur had declared that Japan was ready for a conciliatory peace treaty and urged that the United States pursue the matter with our former allies and the Soviet Union. At first the Department of State agreed with MacArthur's views; but, influenced by George Kennan's hawkish policy planning staff, which pointed to the "great risks" entailed in withdrawing our military presence from Japan, State reversed itself. By late 1948, the National Security Council, adopting Kennan's position, had put the Japanese peace treaty on a back burner.

The Joint Chiefs of Staff, not wishing to leave Japan wide open for military conquest or internal overthrow by infiltrating communists, consistently opposed an early Japanese peace treaty. We insisted that for our own safety, as well as Japan's, we must maintain a U.S. military presence in Japan and have indefinite rights to certain bases, such as the naval base in Yokosuka (near Yokohama), as well as Okinawa and the surrounding islands. One interim solution proposed by the JCS in the spring of 1949 was that plans be drawn "in highest secrecy" for the "eventual establishment of limited Japanese armed forces for the purpose of maintaining internal security and for local defense against external aggression." We suggested that "the question should be explored of obtaining an amendment to the Japanese constitution with a view to permitting eventual Japanese military armaments for defense." MacArthur, still supporting an early peace treaty, agreed with us on the need for a military presence and base rights, but he strongly opposed our scheme for the secret rearming of the Japanese. He wrote that such secret planning was both undesirable and premature and that if it became known, it "would destroy the character and purpose of the occupation." Nor did our proposal find much favor at State.

In fact, by the summer of 1949, State had again reversed itself and on Dean Acheson's insistence was once more pressing for an early Japanese peace treaty. Truman, who favored the treaty, encouraged Acheson to pursue it despite the continuing objections of Louis Johnson and the Joint

Chiefs. Seeing the handwriting on the wall, the Chiefs began drawing up position papers which would insure our indefinite base rights, and we explored the possibilities of a bilateral military treaty with Japan which would continue our "military presence" until such time as Japan could defend herself.

One proposed short-term solution to part of the problem was to do in Japan what we had done in Germany. By the spring of 1949, we had more or less solved the West German postwar occupational and governmental problems by urging the Germans to create a popularly elected government and the appointment of a United States high commissioner, John McCloy, to replace Military Governor Lucius Clay. McCloy would be responsible and report to the Secretary of Defense until the German government was in place, thereafter to the State Department.

On June 3, 1949, I wrote MacArthur, in part: "For some time our trend of thought here is that we should try to get the State Department to take over the Military Government in Japan in a similar manner [to that in Germany] as soon as the State Department is organized to handle it. We hope to take up this matter again with the President and the Secretary of State as soon as the German Government is established and functioning."

Inasmuch as MacArthur was still urging a Japanese peace treaty, thus allying himself with State against Defense, I thought this was a fairly reasonable proposal to which he would probably have no objections. How wrong I was! Back came a scathing diatribe the like of which I have seldom read. I did not know until later the deep distrust with which MacArthur viewed our State Department in general and Dean Acheson in particular. He must have viewed me as a traitor too, "selling out" to State. He wrote that if State replaced the military in the governing of Japan through a high commissioner setup, "no move could be more calculated to destroy the remaining prestige of the United States in the Far East." He maintained that it would foreshadow a weakening of our purpose and "give greater impetus to the communist drive to bring all of Asia under control." He insisted that before any such proposal went further, he be permitted to place his views before Acheson and Truman.

By the time we met with MacArthur in Japan, the high commissioner proposal, perhaps owing to MacArthur's heated objections, had been buried and the Japanese peace treaty, pushed along by Acheson, was back on the front burner. We Chiefs still believed the treaty was "premature," but we were softening in our opposition. MacArthur assured us that in forthcoming discussions with State representatives (W. Walton Butterworth and later John Foster Dulles), he would see that our insistence on base rights and the military security of Japan had a full hearing and would make certain provisions for insuring that they would be incorporated in the final settlement, whatever form it took.[7]

Korea. As we have seen, the JCS and NSC had little strategic interest in Korea. Following the 1948 elections in South Korea, by mid-1949 all but a handful of American military advisers had been withdrawn. To counterbalance the growing Soviet-supplied North Korean Army, the JCS and MacArthur supported a plan urged by Syngman Rhee to build a South Korean Army. By the time we visited Tokyo, this Army had grown to some 100,000 men, organized into eight understrength infantry divisions. The United States had provided minimum military assistance to the Republic of Korea (ROK) Army. Owing to the fact that Korea was not considered "good tank country" and to our own acute shortages, we had not provided the ROK Army with tanks. It was short of artillery and ammunition and had not conducted large-scale unit training. Nonetheless, American military advisers considered the ROK Army capable of maintaining internal order and, if it came, repelling a North Korean invasion.[8]

Formosa. In our Offtackle planning, no specific provision had been made for the defense of the island of Formosa. Bypassed by the United States Pacific campaigns in World War II, Formosa had been given to the Chinese Nationalists after the war. As long as they held out on the mainland, Formosa was protected; but when they retreated to Formosa, it introduced a new complication in our war planning. It seemed likely that in order to wipe out all vestiges of Chiang and his Nationalist government, the Chinese communists would invade and overrun Formosa.

Formosa in communist hands would seriously threaten our war plans. MacArthur aptly likened the island to an "unsinkable aircraft carrier," and an important geographical link in our defensive offshore island perimeter, running from Japan to the Philippines. Formosa had a large network of airfields built by the Japanese in World War II. The Nationalist government took over and began refurbishing these fields. If the communists, in turn, captured these airfields, they could be used to threaten our bases in the Philippines and, more important, our SAC bases on Okinawa.

On May 29, 1949, when Chinese Nationalist forces were in full retreat and eyeing Formosa as a redoubt, MacArthur warned Washington of the danger of Formosa in communist hands. After the full collapse of the Nationalists in the fall of 1949, the JCS, on the recommendation of Joe Collins, began a reappraisal of our Formosa policy, based in part on MacArthur's recommendations. The upshot was that on December 23, 1949, the JCS unanimously recommended that while American forces should not be employed in the defense of Formosa, the United States should help Chiang with a "modest, well-directed and closely-supervised program of military aid" and send a fact-finding group to the island to see what was needed most.[9]

This proposal had touched off another bitter high-level debate within the administration, pitting Johnson against Acheson. Johnson supported the MacArthur-JCS view on Formosa, but Acheson, usually hawklike on such matters, assumed an implacable stand in opposition. Basically, Acheson wanted the United States to wash its hands of the Chinese Nationalists. He believed Chiang was doomed, that the Nationalists would not fight for Formosa any harder than they had fought for the mainland, and that if we continued to support Chiang, however modestly, when Formosa fell it would do "further damage to our prestige and to our whole position in the Far East."[10]

Acheson won this battle. On December 29, 1949, the NSC adopted his views and on January 5, 1950, Truman issued a public policy paper on Formosa in which he stated that "the United States Government will not provide military aid or advice to Chinese forces on Formosa." He also denied Chinese communist propaganda charges that we were on the threshold of militarily occupying the island. Our basic policy remained "hands off" Formosa.[11]

Nor was our strategy regarding Korea kept secret. On March 1, 1949, MacArthur, in an on-the-record interview with British journalist G. Ward Price, said that "our line of defense runs through the chain of islands fringing the coast of Asia. It starts in the Philippines and continues through the Ryukyu Archipelago, which includes its main bastion, Okinawa. Then it bends back through Japan and the Aleutian Island chain to Alaska." On January 12, 1950, Acheson, in a speech before the National Press Club in Washington, said the same thing, but reversed the geography: "This defensive perimeter runs along the Aleutians to Japan and then goes to the Ryukyus. We hold important positions in the Ryukyu Islands, and these we continue to hold. . . . The defensive perimeter runs from the Ryukyus to the Philippine Islands."

In these public statements, both MacArthur and Acheson had drawn our defensive line well to the east of Korea. Our indifference to Korea was further emphasized one week after Acheson's speech when the House voted (193 to 192) to kill a small ($60 million) economic aid bill to Korea. (The administration rescued the Korean aid the following month only by combining it with a small economic aid bill for the Chinese Nationalists.)[12]

Indochina. Russia and her satellites had recognized the communist government of Ho Chi Minh; the West was allied with the French-sponsored government of Bao Dai. The JCS believed it probable that the Chinese communists would intensify aid to Ho Chi Minh in order to seize the rice bowl in southern Indochina. The JCS advanced the "domino principle," although it was not yet called that: "If Indochina succumbs to Soviet-dominated Communism, the weak Thai and Burmese governments would probably take immediate steps to orient themselves with Communist China and the USSR. If this occurred, the Communists could advance next on Malaya, where terrorism is now increasing, on Indonesia and on India." The JCS agreed that if Indochina fell to communism, "The United States will be forced to strengthen its present position in Japan and Okinawa, to develop its position in the Philippines into a front line base instead of a supporting one, and, in all probability, to seek bases in Indonesia." To avert such a possibility, the JCS had urged, on December 22, 1949, that "assistance" be given French Indochina.[13]

The JCS and MacArthur were in nearly full agreement on most specific Far East matters. We shared the view that Korea was still of little strategic interest and that in the event of "trouble," the ROK Army could handle North Korea. We shared the view that the possible fall of Formosa would be a devastating blow to our strategic position in the Far East, to be avoided if possible, Acheson's views notwithstanding. The JCS assured MacArthur that we would continue to press for a reversal of American policy and aid to the Nationalists. We shared the view that we should continue to urge aid for the French in Indochina. The single point of disagreement I can recall was over the Japanese peace treaty; and, owing to MacArthur's reassurances on our base rights and the military security for Japan, it was not major.

We concluded our visit to the Far East with side trips to some U.S. military units and, on the way home, Okinawa, where we were briefed for seven hours by the local Army, Navy and Air Force commanders. I am certain that each member of the JCS benefited greatly from the trip. I know I did. What stands out above all in my mind was the general amity established between MacArthur and the JCS. We had spent enough time together to get to know one another on a personal basis. All of us left the Far East considerably less awestruck by the man and his theatrical style.[14]

I made a second trip to the Far East several months later—June 11 to June 24—in the company of Louis Johnson. Mary and Mrs. Johnson went with us. On the way over, we stopped in Hawaii for several days, where Admiral Arthur Radford, commanding the Pacific Fleet, entertained and briefed us. We flew from Hawaii to Manila, where we spent two days in company of our ambassador, Myron Cowen, and military officers, then flew on to Tokyo, where the briefings of the previous January were more or less repeated. We remained in Tokyo five days, sightseeing and being briefed, then visited Okinawa (for two hours), Osaka, returned to Tokyo for one day, then flew back to the States via Alaska. I arrived home exhausted and coming down with an intestinal infection.[15]

Three items stand out from that visit:

The Japanese peace treaty. By this time, John Foster Dulles was energetically working in State's behalf to hammer out the provisions of a treaty that would satisfy State, Defense, our Allies and others concerned. Dulles was in Tokyo during our visit. Johnson, MacArthur and I met with him collectively and individually. It was now clear that a peace treaty was going to be arrived at, no matter what, and our talks were fruitful. They led to various memoranda from MacArthur that, Dulles said later, "provided the bridge which subsequently brought together all the branches of our Government in agreement as to the desirability of a peace treaty, provided we could get arrangements necessary for the security of the U.S." Of the many points incorporated in MacArthur's memos, the "most important," Dulles noted, was the right of the United States "to maintain forces in Japan." We were also assured of our base rights in Japan and Okinawa. With this general assurance, thereafter Defense and JCS opposition to an early Japanese peace treaty diminished rapidly.[16]

Korea. There were persistent reports from various sources that the North Koreans were on the verge of invading South Korea. It happened that Brigadier General William L. Roberts, an old friend (West Point 1913) and veteran of the 4th Armored Division in the ETO, and who had been chief of the Korean military advisory group for the last two years, was passing through Tokyo en route to the States—and retirement. I met privately with Roberts in MacArthur's headquarters in the Dai Ichi Building for forty minutes on the morning of June 20. I questioned Roberts closely about the reports of a North Korean invasion and the ability of the ROK Army to repel it if it came. Roberts was completely reassuring. The ROK Army could meet any test the North Koreans imposed on it. Since I knew Roberts to be a professional soldier of good judgment, I took his word on it, feeling greatly relieved that we had no cause for concern in Korea.[17]

Formosa. The JCS had not changed their views on the need to help Formosa militarily. Following the fall of Hainan Island, we had again recommended (May 4, 1950) that a fact-finding group be sent to Formosa to see what needed to be done.

While in Tokyo, MacArthur gave Louis Johnson and me a persuasive top-secret memorandum on Formosa which he had drafted on June 14, 1950, in anticipation of our visit. This paper reiterated the threat to our Far East strategy should Formosa fall into communist hands—using the "unsinkable aircraft carrier" analogy. MacArthur urged that the "United States should initiate measures to prevent the domination of Formosa by a communist power." He was "unable to recommend the exact political, economic and military measures which should be taken" to prevent the fall of Formosa, but urged that the JCS recommendations of December 23, 1949, and May 4, 1950, to send a fact-finding group to Formosa be approved.

This paper made the case for helping Formosa more eloquently than anything the JCS had produced, and I was very glad to get it. After reading it, Johnson and I agreed that it should be forwarded to the President with a recommendation from me in the name of the JCS, that the United States change its hands-off policy toward Formosa and render aid to the Nationalists, as recommended by a fact-finding group.[18]

After we landed in Washington on June 24, Mary and I went immediately to Quarters One at Fort Myer. I climbed into bed feeling awful. At 10 P.M. that Saturday night, United Press reporter Dayton Moore telephoned my quarters to ask if I had a comment on the situation in Korea. He had received a fragmentary report that the North Korean Army had invaded South Korea. I was stunned speechless and, of course, had no comment.[19]

FIFTY-FOUR

Although I was still sick, and getting worse, I forced myself out of bed on Sunday, June 25. The Navy had staged an aircraft carrier orientation in Norfolk aboard the USS *Midway,* to which Louis Johnson and I had been invited. Too many men in the Navy already viewed me as the enemy; to have canceled this visit at the last minute owing to illness would have been awkward, further alienating the admirals.

The reports from Korea were still maddeningly fragmentary. Admiral Sherman, who was in his Pentagon office and who would be our escort to Norfolk, telephoned at 0930 to ask if the JCS would meet that day on Korea. I thought no purpose would be served in a JCS meeting until we had more information. John D. McCone, assistant secretary of the Air Force, came in at 0945 for an eighteen-minute discussion of Korea. Joe Collins, also in his office, came by a little after 1200 and we talked for twenty-four minutes. Collins had no real hard information either. Based on my talks in Tokyo with General William Roberts, I was confident that the ROK Army could handle the situation. Collins shared that view.[1]

My thoughts that morning were on Formosa. MacArthur's eloquent memo had fired up Louis Johnson. He was determined to make an all-out assault within the NSC to reverse American policy on Formosa. He wanted unanimous JCS support for his position. I drafted a memo to Vandenberg, Collins and Sherman:

> From my discussions with Secretary Johnson both before our trip and during our trip to the Far East, I am sure he will want to take up the question of Formosa again with the President. For the basis for discussion, I submit herewith a draft of a memorandum for the Secretary [of Defense] to send to the President. I suggest that we discuss the matter at our meeting Monday afternoon.
>
> After my talk with General Roberts, I am of the opinion that South Korea will not fall in the present attack unless the Russians actively participate in the operation. Therefore, if Korea falls, we may want to recommend even

stronger action in the case of Formosa in order to offset the effect of the fall of South Korea on the rest of East Asia.

The suggested memo from Johnson to the President

On December 29, the National Security Council decided that no further action would be taken to assist the Chinese Nationalists to hold Formosa.

Since that time conditions have changed to such an extent that the Department of Defense feels it [is] its duty to ask you to reopen the question for further study and consideration.

Since the first of the year, Hainan and the islands just off the coast near Shanghai have fallen to the Communists. Communist China has signed a military agreement with Russia. During the last few days the situation in Korea has become acute. While Formosa is not essential as a base for U.S. troops, its occupation by an unfriendly power would seriously affect our position in Japan, Okinawa and the Philippines. It has many prepared air fields which move any unfriendly combat planes sufficiently close to our positions and routes of communication to increase their effectiveness many fold. For example, our present fighter planes have just enough range to permit their movement between the Philippines and Okinawa. Any detour to avoid interference from Formosa makes this lateral movement impracticable or extremely hazardous. In December, the Department of Defense recommended that the Commander-in-Chief, Far Eastern Command [MacArthur] be directed to send a survey team to Formosa to obtain firsthand information on what might be done to prevent Formosa from falling into the hands of an unfriendly power.

I again recommend that you take this action. The Joint Chiefs of Staff and General MacArthur concur in this recommendation.[2]

I had these documents typed and put them in my briefcase, along with a copy of MacArthur's memo on Formosa. Johnson, Sherman and I left for Norfolk at 1445 and returned to Washington at 1800, having cut our visit short in order to meet with the President that night. Sherman and I went immediately to my Pentagon office, where we remained for an hour and a half, trying to get the latest information from Korea. Then, at 1945, as requested, we left for our meeting with the President, who had just flown back from Independence, Missouri. The meeting took place at Blair House because the White House was then undergoing drastic interior remodeling.[3]

There were fourteen people at the Blair House meeting, including the President. These were Acheson, Undersecretary of State James E. Webb, and three others from State: Dean Rusk, John D. Hickerson and Philip C. Jessup. The Pentagon contingent outnumbered the group from State eight to five: Johnson, the three service secretaries and the four members of the JCS.

Collectively, the civilian leadership from the Pentagon was not the strongest team: erratic Louis Johnson, whom Truman had already decided to fire; earnest but discredited Navy Secretary Frank Matthews, still hanging in there; and two brand-new men, Army Secretary Frank Pace and Air Force Secretary Thomas K. Finletter. Only the JCS had substantial military expertise: Hoyt Vandenberg, steady and cool; Forrest Sherman, emerging as a gifted strategist; Joe Collins, a "can do" administrator and advocate; and I. On this historic night I was so ill that all I wanted to do was crawl in bed.[4]

This crisis meeting on the Far East provided Johnson with what I assumed he believed to be the ideal forum for launching his campaign to reverse our position on Formosa. He commenced by seizing the floor and insisted that I read aloud to the group MacArthur's long memo on Formosa and the draft letter I had prepared for Johnson to send the President.

Some historians have suggested this was neither the time nor place to discuss Formosa. In one sense they are correct. Korea was obviously the more urgent matter, the reason for the meeting. But in another sense, they are wrong. Strategically, the military considered Formosa far more important than Korea. We believed Korea could well be a diversion to distract us from an imminent attack on Formosa. In the last several weeks, the Chinese communists had massed some 200,000 troops opposite Formosa. If the communists were going to continue shooting in the Far East in earnest, we had to protect Formosa with the greatest possible speed. In Korea, we could depend on the ROK Army, or so we believed; but Formosa lay nearly bare, ripe for plucking. As I indicated in my draft letter, the loss of Formosa would be a severe setback to our strategic position in the Far East.

After I read my papers, we had dinner. When the dishes were cleared away, we got down to a detailed discussion of Korea—what it meant, what our response should be. The reports from Korea were still fragmentary, but there were some signs that the ROK Army was not holding as stoutly as expected, and the situation could turn out to be "serious in the extreme." Nonetheless, we continued to have faith—too much faith as it turned out—that the ROK Army, after its initial blooding, would rally and repulse the North Koreans.

The U.S. Army had long since been delegated executive responsibility for Korea. Earlier in the day Pace, one of his assistant secretaries, Karl Bendetsen, Joe Collins and his operations chief, Thomas S. Timberman, had met with Acheson and his advisers at the State Department. They had agreed on certain courses of action, which Acheson, and to a lesser extent Collins, now presented to the war council. These were to rush military equipment to the ROK Army; employ U.S. Air Force planes to cover the evacuation of American women and children, destroying North Korean tanks and aircraft if necessary; deploy the Navy's Seventh Fleet to Formosa to prevent a Chinese communist invasion and to prevent Chinese

Nationalists from launching operations against the mainland, but not to "tie up" with Chiang or have MacArthur go to Formosa; order MacArthur, who then had no executive or administrative responsibility for Korea, to send a military fact-finding group to South Korea to find out what was going on and what was needed; increase aid to Indochina to help offset possible Chinese communist military intervention on Ho Chi Minh's side; continue efforts in the United Nations, begun earlier in the day, to secure a cease-fire and/or help for South Korea from other nations.[5]

Underlying these discussions was an intense sense of moral outrage, even more than we had felt over the Czechoslovakia coup in 1948. We had experienced coups, subversion, the Berlin blockade and a dozen other steps short of outright military hostilities in the Cold War; but Korea was raw, naked aggression, a communist nation invading a peaceful nation—given and guaranteed its free status by the UN—with blazing tanks and artillery. It was an affront not only to us but to the UN itself, an arrogant challenge to all the UN stood for.

Although Korea had been "written off" and we were now in the process of drastically changing our policy with respect to her, there was not a single dissenting voice to the suggested proposals at the table. As I later wrote Truman (as documentation for his memoirs): "Everyone present seemed to be of the opinion that the failure to take action to protect South Korea would be appeasement and History proves that one appeasement leads to another and this inevitably leads to war." As one historian, Glenn D. Paige, aptly wrote: "The real basis of the Korean decision had almost nothing to do with Korea. It had to do with aggression." At the meeting, I put it this way: "We must draw the line somewhere," and Korea "offered as good an occasion for action in drawing the line as anywhere else."[6]

In those days we held the rather simplistic belief that *all* communist moves worldwide were dictated from Moscow by Stalin personally. The guessing that night was that Stalin had temporarily set aside his designs on Europe and the Middle East for an all-out push in the Far East conducted by his satellites. Korea might only be one phase of this push. Formosa could be another. Indochina might well be still another. The Philippines could also be a target. But we did not believe Stalin wanted all-out global war.

"Russia," I said, "is not yet ready for war." But, I said, she was "obviously testing" us. Korea was a "limited challenge," but one which showed a willingness by Moscow to take bigger risks than heretofore. Sherman said, "The Russians do not want war now, but if they do, they will have it." Van was not so sure. He advised that we "not base our action on the assumption that the Russians would not fight." The President ordered us to make a "careful calculation" as to the "next probable place in which Soviet action might take place."[7]

We discussed the possibility of sending American ground forces into Korea to backstop the ROK Army. I was opposed to this idea, as were Louis Johnson, Frank Pace, and Joe Collins. For the time being, at least, our military moves in the Far East would be restricted to air and sea power.

Acheson dominated the meeting. Louis Johnson was strangely subdued. He had very little to say other than press for military aid to the Nationalists on Formosa. However, he did make one specific suggestion which was uncannily prescient. He urged that any instructions to MacArthur "should be detailed so as not to give him too much discretion," and he expressed the view that "there should not be a real delegation of presidential authority to General MacArthur." Truman agreed, adding that "he was not yet ready to put MacArthur in as Commander-in-Chief in Korea."

I was still ill on Monday, June 26, and getting worse. It was a long, busy, tedious day during which the reports on the ROK Army grew gloomier and gloomier. Late in the afternoon, Dr. C. L. Hedberg from the Pentagon dispensary came to my office to look me over. He advised me to go to bed and stay there. But Truman had called a second meeting of the war council at Blair House for that night, and I felt that if I could still walk I should attend.[8]

The second Blair House meeting co-joined the same thirteen men, with the exception of Navy Secretary Frank Matthews, who arrived as we were adjourning but who was not missed, and Dean Rusk, who was replaced by Elbert G. Mathews. By then we realized the ROK Army was in full rout and there seemed little hope that it could rally. Soviet-built North Korean tanks were already on the outskirts of Seoul, the South Korean capital. Again Acheson dominated the meeting. He now proposed a step-up in our military action, that we give an "all-out order" to our air and naval forces to "offer fullest possible support" to the ROK Army—south of the 38th parallel—and specific orders to the Seventh Fleet to prevent an attack on Formosa. He further proposed an increase in aid to the Philippines, the southern anchor of our offshore defensive perimeter.[9]

No one expressed anything but approval of these measures. The President went further. He said he had done everything he could for five years to prevent "this kind of situation," and now that it was here, "we must do everything we can" for the Koreans. Considering the situation, this *implied* deployment of American ground forces to Korea to backstop the ROK's. I was still reluctant to commit ground forces, as was all the military, and told the President that if we committed our ground forces to Korea, we would have to have a mobilization, at least a call-up of some National Guard divisions. Collins agreed with me. I suggested that we wait "a few days" before deciding on this drastic step. The President and Acheson agreed, the President adding, "I don't want to go to war." Louis

Johnson "hoped those steps already authorized will settle the Korean question."

The rest of the meeting was taken up with a discussion about briefing congressional leaders on the situation and the details of a public statement Truman was to issue the following day. I returned to the Pentagon from 2200 to 0015 for a telecon* talk with MacArthur and his staff, to pass along the new orders about the use of our air and naval forces in Korea and Formosa.[10]

When I arrived at the office the following morning, Tuesday, June 27, I went immediately to the dispensary to see Dr. Hedberg. He again advised bed. But this was an important day for the President—his congressional briefing and public statement—and he asked that I come to the White House. I went there twice during the morning to advise him on the statement and to be present for the briefing of congressional leaders. At 1250 I returned to the Pentagon dispensary to see Dr. Hedberg, who emphatically ordered me to bed. I went home immediately and remained in bed for the next forty-eight hours, not returning to the office until 1430 on Thursday, June 29, for a JCS meeting and, later, at 1645, for a trip to the White House. But the whole time I was in bed I kept in close contact with my office by telephone, and my aides came to Quarters One to brief me on important developments.[12]

On Wednesday, June 28, while I was out sick, Ike, who had a routine appointment at Walter Reed Hospital, came by the Pentagon and talked with the Army's top team: Collins, Haislip, Ridgway and Gruenther. Afterwards he dictated a memo (no carbons were made) for me which I was to read and destroy. The thrust of Ike's message that day is summarized in a personal diary entry he made two days later:

> (Couldn't see Brad, he was sick) I went in expecting to find them all in a dither of effort, engaged in the positive business of getting troops, supplies, etc., that will be needed to settle the Korean mess. They seemed indecisive, which was natural in view of the indecisiveness of political statements. I have no business talking about the basic political decision (to support or not to support South Korea). It happens that I believe we'll have a dozen Koreas soon if we don't take a firm stand, but it was not on that basis that I talked to my friends. My whole contention was that an appeal to force cannot, by its nature, be a partial one. This appeal, having been made, for God's sake, get ready! Do everything possible under the law to get us going. Remember in a

* A teleconference was conducted in the Pentagon communications room between participants, each of whom had a large TV-like screen on the wall. In a telecon, each series of questions and answers appeared in full on the screens at both ends and remained visible while the conferee considered the content. In addition, a teletype machine fed out a typed copy of the exchanges. The system was secure from enemy penetration, much faster than coding and decoding radio messages and informal—like a conversation. The only problem with telecons with Tokyo was the time zone differences: one party or the other had to be up at ungodly hours.[11]

> fight we (our side) can never be too strong. I urged action in a dozen directions and left a memo for Brad. We must study every angle to be prepared for whatever may happen, even if it finally came to the use of the A-bomb (which God forbid).

In sum, Ike believed that the Pentagon was not moving fast enough, that we did not grasp the gravity of the situation, that the United States must immediately go to all-out mobilization. A week later (July 5), he and George Marshall lunched with the President and urged these views. Afterwards Ike saw Louis Johnson and was disappointed that Johnson wasn't doing enough. "There seems to be no disposition to begin serious mobilizing," Ike complained in his diary. "I think that it is possible that the military advisers are too complacent when talking to HST." [13]

The most important development in the wind during those forty-eight hours I was out sick was the mounting pressure to commit ground forces to Korea. MacArthur had sent Brigadier General John H. Church, whom Collins had described as "an able and dynamic officer," to South Korea on a fact-finding mission as per Washington's instructions. Church, trying desperately to rally the ROK Army, reported to MacArthur that U.S. troops would be required to restore the original boundary line at the 38th parallel. In my absence on June 28, the JCS, still opposed to using our ground forces in Korea, met to discuss what other action, "in lieu of committing ground troops," could be taken. Admiral Davis, in assembling and passing on the paperwork to the Joint Staff, added a handwritten note which emphasized that the JCS "do *not* want to commit troops." [14]

By the time I returned to the office on the afternoon of Thursday, June 29, the JCS had reached the decision that American ground troops must be introduced in South Korea—but in a very limited way. The JCS recommended two specific ground force roles: service forces to maintain communications and other essential services, and combat and service troops to ensure the retention of a port and air base at Pusan, on the southern end of the peninsula. The latter mission was deemed essential to facilitate the evacuation of our military advisory group and other U.S. nationals. The JCS did *not* envision use of ground forces along the "front" farther north.

These decisions, and others relating to the intensification of naval and air support to the ROK's, were approved by the President at a meeting in the White House that afternoon between 1645 and 1816. Upon return to the Pentagon, the JCS met again (for the third time that day) to send MacArthur detailed instructions relating to employment of American forces. These included authorization to launch air attacks on military targets above the 38th parallel in Korea, taking "special care" to "stay well clear of the frontiers of Manchuria and the Soviet Union." [15]

In the meantime, MacArthur had gone to South Korea for a firsthand inspection, courageously driving right up into the confused front lines.

Late that same night—June 29-30—he got off a message to Washington in which he said, "The only assurance of holding the present line, and the ability to regain later lost ground, is through the introduction of U.S. ground combat forces into the Korean battle area." He wanted to send one regimental combat team immediately, followed by two full divisions "for an early counteroffensive."[16]

Joe Collins was "so concerned" about the deteriorating situation in Korea—and MacArthur's radical proposal—that he hurried to the Pentagon for an 0300 (June 30) telecon with MacArthur. He told MacArthur that his proposal would "require presidential decision which will take several hours," but that meanwhile Collins (still the JCS executive agent for Korea) authorized movement of the regimental combat team to Pusan, in accordance with earlier authorization and instructions to deploy combat forces to defend the port. That did not satisfy MacArthur. He wanted to put the regimental combat team into the front lines. "Time is of the essence," he said. "And a clear-cut decision without delay is imperative."

Collins, possibly influenced by Ike's exhortations on June 28, then made a very large military decision all on his own. Ignoring JCS recommendations to the contrary, Collins now decided that MacArthur was right, that U.S. combat troops should be sent at once to the front. He told MacArthur that he would "proceed immediately" to request the necessary permission from the President, going up through the chain of command to Army Secretary Pace. Collins called Pace, who called Truman at 0500. Truman, "already up and shaved," authorized the deployment of the regimental combat team, but deferred decision on the commitment of the two divisions MacArthur had requested. Collins then sent MacArthur this historic message: "Your recommendation to move one regimental combat team to combat area is approved. You will be advised later as to further buildup."[17]

Having taken these steps, Collins then telephoned Vandenberg, Sherman and me about 0530 to tell us what he had done. I had mixed reactions. In a sense it was unavoidable and inevitable. Air and naval power obviously could not stop the North Koreans. But I was deeply concerned over getting into a fight with Asiatics on the Asian mainland. As Sherman put it later, it was a step he had grown up to believe "should be avoided if possible." If the two divisions failed to stem the North Koreans, MacArthur would surely ask for two more—and so on. We would have to go to mobilization, possibly sending more divisions to the Far East. We had no war plan for Korea. The gravity of the situation would demand piecemeal commitment of our ground forces, the worst possible way to enter a fight. Our available troops in the Far East were green and flabby and had not trained in divisional maneuvers. Walton Walker, who would lead them, had been on the verge of retirement. Rugged Korea seemed to me a job for a younger, more vigorous man—a Van Fleet or a Ridgway.[18]

After we reached our offices that morning, June 30, the JCS joined

Louis Johnson, the three service secretaries and State Department representatives for a war council meeting at the White House at 0915. Truman approved MacArthur's request to commit two divisions to the front lines. In addition, at Sherman's suggestion, he approved a naval blockade of North Korea. By this time, Chiang had offered 30,000 troops, but we all agreed that the offer should be declined for various reasons. We went back to the Pentagon and relayed these orders to MacArthur, then returned to the White House for a Cabinet meeting, to which congressional leaders had been invited, at 1100. I gave a briefing on the situation in Korea, and the President revealed his decisions. That afternoon in my office, I saw Dr. Hedberg twice, and each time he brought along a consultant. I left the office at 1740 and went back to bed.[19]

The die was cast. For the fourth time since I entered West Point, the U.S. Army was gearing for a shooting war.

FIFTY-FIVE

I shall not attempt here to tell the story of the Korean War. That job has already been well done by the official service historians and by numerous other writers. I only got to Korea twice during the fighting; most of what I know about it is secondhand. I shall confine this account to the major events and decisions in Washington which I had a role in or was close to, and to the unfolding controversy which developed between Truman and MacArthur about our Far East policy and the way the Korean War should be fought.

As our military commitment to Korea grew, MacArthur was named United Nations commander as well as commander in chief of all U.S. forces. It was unfortunate but true that Truman had never liked MacArthur and he distrusted him. Truman was insulted that MacArthur had refused a presidential invitation (virtually an order) to return to the United States after the war for victory parades and consultations. Truman was also well aware that MacArthur had encouraged Republican political supporters in 1948, and he suspected that MacArthur might try politics again in 1952. Truman viewed MacArthur as actively allied with his political enemies on the Hill.

Soon after assuming the presidency in 1945, Truman blew off steam about MacArthur in his private diary, labeling him "Mr. Prima Donna, Brass Hat, Five Star MACARTHUR."

> He's worse than the Cabots and the Lodges—they at least talked with one another before they told God what to do. Mac tells God right off. It is a very great pity we have to have stuffed shirts like that in key positions. I don't see why in Hell Roosevelt didn't order Wainwright home [from Corregidor in 1942] and let MacArthur be a martyr. . . . We'd have had a real general and fighting man if we had Wainwright and not a play actor and a bunco man such as we have now. Don't see how a country can produce such men as Robert E. Lee, John J. Pershing, Eisenhower and Bradley and at the same time produce Custers, Pattons, and MacArthurs.[1]

These sentiments—in different words or expressions—continued down through the years to the Korean crisis. Thus Truman launched the Korean War with a Secretary of Defense (Louis Johnson) whom he believed to have a "pathological condition" and was determined to fire, and a field commander whom he deeply mistrusted and whom he may have been determined to fire at the first opportunity. He would have saved himself a lot of grief had he relieved both men at the onset of the war on one pretext or another. A commander in chief in a tough military situation should not be compelled to rely on men in whom he has no faith.

When the Korean War came, Truman instinctively turned to the military man he trusted most: George Marshall. By that time Marshall had assumed the post of head of the American Red Cross at which he was working very hard, and was living the life of a country squire at his modest home in Leesburg, Virginia. Truman's luncheon for Ike and Marshall on July 5—which Sherman and I attended—was, I believe, Truman's opening move to entice Marshall back into the government as Secretary of Defense, replacing Johnson. Certainly by that time Truman was determined to engineer that switch as early as possible, and he followed up by occasionally visiting Marshall at his place in Leesburg.[2]

By this time, too, the President's confidence in me had substantially increased. Until the Korean War, I had seen the President in my official capacity as Chairman of the JCS only infrequently (seven times in 1950 prior to the outbreak of the war). By July 1950, fully recovered from my "bug," I saw him daily (or more often) to brief him on the war and other pertinent military matters. On his insistence, all orders to MacArthur were personally approved by him and I usually hand-carried these messages between the Pentagon and White House. In a short space of time, I became Truman's chief and most trusted military adviser. Although he gave me no inkling of it, the President had already decided that should it become necessary to relieve MacArthur I was his choice to replace him.[3]

There was also talk of recalling Ike to full-time military service. The job Truman had in mind—and which I resoundingly approved—was to name Ike Supreme Commander of NATO forces in Europe. This would put the "winning team" of "Ike and Monty" back into harness in Europe. The original idea was to name Ike to the job after NATO had fielded substantial land, sea and air forces and sorted out various controversial matters—such as rearming the Germans. But after the onset of the Korean War, we began to talk in terms of naming Ike much sooner so that he could bring his prestige to bear in the massive task of rearming Western Europe. When Truman discussed the job with Ike, he responded typically that "I am a soldier and I am ready to respond to whatever orders my superiors in the defense forces and the President, as Commander in Chief, may care to issue to me."[4]

As I had feared, the war in Korea went badly for us at first. Our garrison troops, committed piecemeal, took a terrible pounding and were gradually driven south toward a defensive perimeter at Pusan. The principal ground forces rushed into battle were William F. Dean's 24th Division and Bill Kean's 25th Division—Kean's first combat command. In a heroic delaying action, Dean's division suffered dreadful casualties—about 30 percent. When Dean was captured by the North Koreans, John Church took command of the decimated division. One regiment in Kean's division, the 24th Infantry, which in keeping with the Army's segregationist policy was all black, broke and ran on several occasions.* Owing to these losses and reverses, MacArthur was compelled to commit a third infantry division, the 1st Cavalry (actually an infantry division), commanded by Patton's World War II chief of staff, Hobart Gay. MacArthur's "strategic reserve" in Japan, the 7th Infantry Division, commanded by David D. Barr, was stripped of half its strength to provide replacements for the 24th and 25th divisions. The 29th Infantry Regiment was rushed to Korea from Okinawa.[5]

Walton Walker assumed tactical command of all UN forces in Korea, including the ROK's, on July 13. Not for nothing had he been nicknamed "Bulldog." He was tenacious, imperious, demanding, and dismayed that his green and flabby troops could not or would not hold against the North Koreans. He relentlessly chewed out his subordinate commanders. On July 29, Walker gave Bill Kean and other commanders his famous and controversial "stand or die" order:

> There will be no Dunkirk, there will be no Bataan, a retreat to Pusan would be one of the greatest butcheries in history. We must fight until the end. Capture by these people is worse than death itself. We will fight as a team. If some of us must die, we will die fighting together. Any man who gives ground may be personally responsible for the death of thousands of his comrades.[6]

As I indicated earlier, I did not believe Walker was the ideal commander for the situation. MacArthur quickly lost faith in him; but instead of relieving him, he made the mistake of trying to second-guess him and run the tactical ground war from Tokyo, some seven hundred miles away, which only made Walker's job all the tougher. When the President's troubleshooter Averell Harriman, accompanied by General Lauris Norstad and Matt Ridgway, returned from a quick trip to Korea and Tokyo on August 9, Harriman (with Norstad's concurrence) recommended to Truman, Johnson, Collins and me that Walker be relieved and Matt Ridgway

* More than any other factor, the disgraceful performance of this regiment led to integration of the U.S. Army.

be sent out to replace him. Collins agreed that Ridgway would be an ideal replacement, but he had earmarked Ridgway for promotion to vice chief of staff of the Army when Wade Haislip retired in 1951 and did not want to lose him. He thought Van Fleet, who had done such an excellent job in Greece, was the natural choice.[7]

Despite the stand or die order, UN forces were pushed ever southward into the Pusan perimeter. We rushed additional U.S. ground troops: the 5th Regimental Combat Team from Hawaii, the 2nd Infantry Division from Tacoma, Washington, the 1st Provisional Marine Brigade (principally the 5th Marines) from Southern California. In addition, Collins and Vandenberg established a replacement airlift, which in July ferried some 5,300 officers and men to Korea, a great many from the newly activated 3rd Infantry Division at Fort Benning. By early August, we had about 50,000 U.S. troops in the Pusan perimeter, plus about 45,000 ROK's, organized into five divisions—a total UN ground force of almost 100,000 men.[8]

In the meantime, MacArthur had conceived a strategy for winning the war. He would hit the enemy in the rear with an amphibious landing at Inchon (on the west coast near Seoul), while simultaneously Walker's Eighth Army would break out of the Pusan perimeter. The North Koreans would thus be trapped in a giant pincer movement and, MacArthur predicted, annihilated. His plan for the amphibious assault at Inchon envisioned the use of two infantry divisions and an airborne regiment, the latter to be dropped (as in Sicily and Normandy) inland of the invading amphibious forces. For this operation he would need additional forces. He requested we send him the full 1st Marine Division and the 3rd Infantry Division, which would relieve the 7th Infantry Division in Japan, freeing the latter for use in the Inchon landing.[9]

MacArthur was secretive about the Inchon operation, reluctant to divulge details to Washington or the JCS. We did not learn the full scope of the plan until Collins and Vandenberg flew to the Far East for conferences on July 13 and 14. At that time MacArthur, Almond and others laid out the plan to Collins. It was bold—and very risky. Inchon was probably the worst possible place ever selected for an amphibious landing. The channel into Inchon was long, narrow, shallow, easily blocked and dominated by a fortified island, Wolmi-do. The huge tides would be favorable only a few days each month. Inchon itself was protected by a twelve-foot seawall.[10]

When Collins returned to Washington, he briefed the JCS on the plan, expressing gravest doubt that it would work. After hearing the details, I had to agree that it was the riskiest military proposal I had ever heard of. At that time we were not certain MacArthur could even hold the Pusan perimeter. It seemed imprudent that a large portion of his staff be preoccupied with a blue-sky scheme like Inchon rather than with the immediate and grave threat at Pusan. Not only that, MacArthur wanted to launch Inchon no later than mid-September! Even had we wholeheartedly approved Inchon, it appeared impossible that we could assemble and ship the requested forces to the Far East in time.[11]

The JCS found themselves in an awkward position. Traditionally the JCS had delegated broad responsibility to theater commanders and let them work out the tactical details. But Inchon was an extremely risky maneuver, absorbing most of our military reserve, and a failure could be a national or even international catastrophe, not only militarily, but psychologically. For this reason and because Truman was relying on us to an extraordinary degree for military counsel, we determined to keep a close eye on the Inchon plan and, if we felt so compelled, finally cancel it.[12]

Meanwhile, practical matters intruded. Sherman, in response to a July 19 cable from MacArthur iterating his need for the full 1st Marine Division by September 10, told the JCS it would be impossible to provide it before November without depleting Marine Corps forces in the Atlantic and Mediterranean to an "unacceptable degree." When we passed that word to MacArthur, he replied on July 21 that it was "absolutely vital" that he have the division, adding loftily: "There can be no demand for its use elsewhere which can equal the urgency of the immediate battle mission contemplated for it."[13]

This led to a request from the JCS on July 22 for MacArthur to "justify" his need for the Marine division and the airborne regiment. This was a not-so-subtle signal to MacArthur that the JCS wanted a formal outline of his Inchon plan. On the following day, July 23, MacArthur conceded and sent along a vague description of the plan, stressing the need for haste. An "early and strong effort" in the North Korean rear, he said, would "sever his main line of communication and enable us to deliver a decisive and crushing blow. Any material delay in such an operation may lose this opportunity." In a follow-up telecon the next day, the JCS asked MacArthur—again pointedly—whether in light of enemy pressures on the Pusan perimeter he was really sure a mid-September operation at Inchon was feasible? He replied that if he were given the Marine division, "the chances to launch the movement in September would be excellent."[14]

MacArthur's request for additional U.S. Army ground forces (the 3rd Division and the airborne regiment) to implement Inchon presented equal difficulties. Collins ingeniously solved the problem of the now depleted 3rd Division by proposing that we pull a regiment and a battalion from Puerto Rico and Panama, respectively, and send the whole lot piecemeal to the Far East. However, he was unable to work out a plan to get the airborne regiment to MacArthur in time. The JCS insisted that the 82nd Airborne—the only ready mobile division left in General Reserve—be retained in the United States. Collins was thus compelled to turn to the unready 11th Airborne Division, which could not get a regiment combat-ready in time for Inchon but sent it later.[15]

MacArthur's Inchon plan got a decisive boost in early August when Averell Harriman, Ridgway and Norstad returned from the aforementioned trip to Korea and Tokyo. In Tokyo on August 8, in a two-and-a-half-hour briefing, MacArthur had unveiled his complete plan. Ridgway, in a memo, described MacArthur's presentation as "brilliant." MacArthur, Ridgway wrote, spoke "with utmost earnestness, supported by every logical military argument of his rich experience, and delivered with all of his dramatic eloquence." Harriman said later that "the three of us were enthralled by General MacArthur"; and they strongly endorsed the plan.[16]

Returning to Washington on August 9, Harriman went directly to the White House carrying Ridgway's memo. Harriman persuaded the President that Inchon could be our salvation. Truman said: "You better get over to the Pentagon as fast as you can and talk to Johnson and Bradley." The JCS spent most of that day in conference with Johnson, Harriman, Ridgway, Norstad and others, discussing the plan. Harriman would later give the impression that the JCS "recommended" Inchon, but that is not true. We approved the concept of an amphibious assault to the rear of the North Koreans on the Korean west coast, but we still had gravest doubts about Inchon as the site.[17]

The following day, August 10, in a series of White House briefings, culminating with an NSC meeting in the afternoon, the JCS exhaustively reviewed MacArthur's plan. The JCS and NSC formally approved MacArthur's amphibious plan in principle but expressed our misgivings about Inchon and hoped MacArthur could be persuaded to settle on a less risky site. The President authorized the dispatch of the Army's 3rd Division and the Marines' 1st Division to the Far East. He also approved the sending of the battleship *Missouri* and the carrier *Leyte* to the Far East. Sherman expressed the view of the JCS when he said that MacArthur would undoubtedly make good use of these forces but "the Joint Chiefs of Staff would have to pass on his plans for an amphibious assault." That is, finally approve the site.[18]

All told, we had in a very short time virtually doubled MacArthur's forces in the Far East, from four-plus U.S. divisions to the equivalent of eight-plus. In so doing, we had stripped bare the United States, Puerto Rico, Panama, Hawaii and Okinawa. In order to fill the gaps, the JCS recommended mobilization of certain Army, Navy, Air Force and Marine Corps reserves. Although we were reluctant to do so, we also soon recommended the mobilization of four National Guard divisions and two regimental combat teams, together with Air National Guard units. By September 1, these call-ups had brought about 256,000 additional men into the three services.[19]

We had still not received a detailed plan from MacArthur about Inchon. On August 19, we sent a JCS delegation to Tokyo to get the details.

The group consisted of Sherman, Collins and Vandenberg's deputy chief of staff for operations, Idwal H. Edwards. During the briefings that ensued in Tokyo, both Sherman and Collins expressed gravest misgivings about the Inchon plan and suggested less risky landing sites on the west coast of Korea. Almost all the admirals and Marine Corps generals in the Far East agreed with Collins and Sherman. But MacArthur, in another famous, mesmerizing briefing, insisted on the original plan for Inchon and would not be talked out of it.[20]

Upon return to Washington, Collins and Sherman laid out the Inchon plan and stated their misgivings. Subsequently, I briefed Louis Johnson and the President on the plan, conveying the doubts of Collins and Sherman, and adding a few of my own. By that time (August 26), the situation at the Pusan perimeter appeared grimmer than ever. A failure at Inchon could very well so inspire the North Koreans that they would overrun the Pusan perimeter. The JCS inclined toward postponing Inchon until such time that we were certain Pusan could hold. But Truman was now committed. "It was a daring strategic conception," he wrote. "I had the greatest confidence it would succeed."[21]

On August 28, the JCS sent MacArthur "approval for an amphibious landing," although the "approval" was highly qualified as to Inchon:

> We concur in making preparations and executing a turning movement by amphibious forces on the west coast of Korea either at Inchon in event that enemy defenses in vicinity of Inchon prove ineffective or at a favorable beach south of Inchon if one can be located. We further concur in preparation . . . for an envelopment by amphibious forces in the vicinity of Kunsan. We understand that alternative plans are being prepared in order best to exploit the situation as it develops. We desire such information as becomes available with respect to conditions in the possible objective areas and timely information as to your intentions and plans for offensive operations.[22]

In the meantime, a different problem concerning MacArthur was arising on an entirely different front: Formosa.

The JCS were still gravely concerned that the Chinese communists might invade Formosa, thereby seriously undermining our strategic position in the Far East. Mao Tse-tung had massed some 200,000 troops on the mainland opposite Formosa, and Peking had publicly stated that it would take the island. Although Truman had ordered the U.S. Seventh Fleet to "neutralize" Formosa, the JCS did not believe the Seventh Fleet was strong enough to repel an invasion. Many of its ships had been detailed to support the Korean War. Moreover, we did not believe the Nationalist troops on Formosa had the will or equipment to stop the invasion.

Accordingly, in the last week of July, the JCS, with Louis Johnson's unequivocal support, urged a further modification of our Formosa policy to insure the island would be denied to the Chinese communists. Our recommendations were rather drastic: that Chiang be furnished "materiel and supplies" at once; that the often-recommended military fact-finding mission be sent; that the Nationalist Air Force be permitted to make air strikes against the massing Chinese troops on the mainland and mine the waters in the mainland ports. In keeping with our past policy, we did not recommend using any American forces, other than the Seventh Fleet, for the defense of Formosa.[23]

These recommendations were presented to a meeting of the NSC on July 27. Truman and Acheson now fully recognized the need to deny Formosa to the Chinese communists, but continued to lean toward a more conservative policy. Neither man wanted any sort of close relationship with Chiang and his corrupt government or even the appearance of a close relationship. Moreover, they feared that if we gave Chiang too much military aid he might use it to attempt a return to the mainland or provoke the Chinese communists into major moves, such as an attack on Britain's colony of Hong Kong or support to the North Koreans. It was an excruciatingly delicate situation.

That day Truman approved some, but not all, of our recommendations. He agreed to send at once to Chiang all-out military aid and to put an American fact-finding mission on Formosa. However, owing to strong opposition from Acheson, he refused to authorize the Nationalist Air Force to attack Chinese troops on the mainland. Acheson believed mining operations would be "acceptable if suitable precautions" (such as notification to international shipping) were taken. But no firm decision on this was reached. In the meantime, Nationalist Air Force operations in the vicinity of the mainland would be restricted to the ongoing reconnaissance overflights for purposes of determining the imminence of an invasion.[24]

Two days later, July 29, the JCS, believing that the danger to Formosa should be sharply called to MacArthur's attention, sent him what amounted to a "war warning." We pointed out the presence of the 200,000 Chinese communist troops massed on the mainland, estimated that some 4,000 sea craft had been assembled, and told him Peking had announced the intention of capturing the island. Owing to the short distance to Formosa and the "limited" U.S. naval forces available, we went on, "it appears that Communist craft and military personnel might reach the coast of Formosa in sufficient numbers to jeopardize seriously the political and military stability of the Nationalist Government and to cause major defection of its ground forces, and thus to cause the loss of Formosa." We informed MacArthur that we had recommended that the Nationalist government be authorized to "employ its military forces in defensive measures to prevent Communist amphibious concentrations directed against Formosa or the Pescadores" and that such "defensive measures should include attacks on such concentrations on the mainland and mining of those mainland water areas from which such an assault could be staged." We concluded: "Any comments you may have are requested soonest."[25]

When Collins and Vandenberg had visited MacArthur in mid-July, he had indicated an intent to visit Formosa soon, but events in Korea had forced a postponement of this trip. Perhaps jogged by our war warning, MacArthur cabled that he planned "a brief reconnaissance" of Formosa on July 31. Because of the delicacy of the situation—and the as yet unresolved issues—we attempted to dissuade MacArthur from going personally to Formosa at this time. On July 30 we cabled: "There are certain policy matters with respect to Formosa which are now being considered by State and Defense which should be worked out within the next few days. Pending receipt of new instructions on these matters you may desire to send a senior officer to Formosa . . . and go later yourself." But we added this qualification: "However, if you feel it necessary to proceed personally on the 31st, please feel free to go since the responsibility is yours."[26]

While MacArthur was en route to Formosa, we received a cable from him that was disquieting. In the event Formosa were attacked, he said, he intended to transfer three squadrons of U.S. Air Force F-80C jet fighters to the island. As he later reported, he had already authorized "familiarization flights for small groups of U.S. fighter aircraft to Formosa," whose landings were to "be of a temporary and refueling nature only."[27]

These steps far exceeded any measures the JCS had proposed and were in strict violation of JCS-NSC policy of not using American forces, other than the Seventh Fleet, for the defense of Formosa. Furthermore, owing to an erroneous report from a State official on Formosa, Acheson got the impression MacArthur had already issued orders to move the fighters to Formosa and Acheson naturally went through the ceiling. The JCS hastened to get off a cable to MacArthur stressing that such action would have "strong political implications" and should not be undertaken until it had been considered at the "highest levels" in Washington. MacArthur replied that he had had no intention of moving the aircraft except in case of attack.* [28]

As things developed, it would no doubt have been better had Truman himself ordered MacArthur to postpone his trip to Formosa. MacArthur arrived there like a visiting head of state, and was entertained accordingly. Naturally, Chiang Kai-shek made propaganda hay of the visit. The net effect of the Nationalist propaganda was to give the impression that the United States was, or was going to be, far more closely allied with Chiang militarily in the struggle against communism in the Far East; that we might even arm him for a "return to the mainland." This impression was dis-

* Acheson incorrectly wrote in his memoir *Present at the Creation* that MacArthur "ordered three squadrons of jet fighters to Formosa without the knowledge of the Pentagon."

tinctly at odds with the Truman-Acheson hands-off policy and the JCS view, which was merely to help Chiang deny Formosa to the communists.

The fallout from this meeting naturally infuriated Truman. Even though MacArthur technically had not gone beyond JCS directives in his promises to Chiang, the overwhelming impression was that he had. Some of our allies, such as the British, who had already recognized the Chinese communist government, were appalled. The China Lobby in Washington (together with some right-wing senators and congressmen) crowed that MacArthur might yet save the China that Truman and Acheson had "lost." Truman was certain that MacArthur himself was encouraging the China Lobby. To make certain MacArthur clearly understood our policies, Truman instructed Averell Harriman on his early-August Tokyo trip to spell them out in detail. At the same time, Truman ordered Johnson to send MacArthur a sharp message advising him that "the most vital national interest requires that no action of ours precipitate general war or give excuse to others to do so." MacArthur replied that he fully understood the President's policy and that his headquarters was "operating meticulously in accordance therewith." He hoped that Truman had not been misled by "false or speculative reports from whatever source, official or nonofficial."[29]

In Tokyo on August 6 and 8, Harriman stressed to MacArthur the main point: that we must "not permit Chiang to be the cause of starting a war with the Chinese Communists on the mainland, the effect of which might drag us into a world war." Harriman noted that MacArthur replied "that he would, as a soldier, obey all orders that he received from the President." But Harriman was not convinced of that. In his report to the President he wrote: "For reasons which are rather difficult to explain, I did not feel that we came to a full agreement on the way we believed things should be handled on Formosa and with the Generalissimo. He accepted the President's position and will act accordingly, but without full conviction."[30]

To make doubly certain that MacArthur clearly understood our Formosa policy, the President instructed the JCS on August 14 to send MacArthur another directive. We informed him that United States policy was to limit our defense of Formosa to operations that could be carried out without committing any U.S. forces to the island. Specifically we stated that MacArthur was not to promise Chiang that we would transfer jet fighters to the island in event of attack. In any case, no U.S. forces were to be based on Formosa without specific JCS approval.[31]

We all assumed that surely that was the end of the matter, but unfortunately it wasn't. Two weeks later, MacArthur sent a "message" to the annual encampment of the Veterans of Foreign Wars. The theme of his message was, of all things, Formosa, which, he wrote, was the subject of "misconceptions currently being voiced." His long message was a recapitulation of his June 14 memo I had brought back from Tokyo, stressing the strategic importance of Formosa, with two paragraphs tacked on the end that could be read as an attack on the Truman administration's conservative policy on Formosa. "Nothing," he wrote, "could be more fallacious than the threadbare argument by those who advocate appeasement and defeatism in the Pacific that if we defend Formosa we alienate continental Asia." The tenor of the entire message was that the United States wanted—or should want—Formosa as a military base, and anyone who advocated other than all-out defense of Formosa did not understand the Oriental mind.[32]

Truman was absolutely furious, and with good reason. He called a meeting of Acheson, Johnson, Harriman and the JCS for 0915 Saturday, August 26. (Sherman and Collins had only just returned from Tokyo.) Acheson was "outraged at the effrontery and damaging effect at home and abroad" of the MacArthur message and believed "that this insubordination could not be tolerated." Truman, "lips white and compressed," dispensed with "the usual greetings." He had a copy of MacArthur's statement; he read it and asked if any of us had any prior intimation or knowledge of it. No one had. I was shocked. To me, the message seemed the height of arrogance.[33]

Even though the message was to be published in *U.S. News & World Report* magazine, and had already gone out over the wire service tickers, Truman insisted that MacArthur be ordered to "withdraw" the statement. He assigned this chore to Louis Johnson. Johnson was reluctant to send the order to MacArthur, and he spent most of the day trying to weasel out of it. After several phone calls between Acheson, Harriman and Johnson, Truman himself finally called Johnson and dictated the message that was to go to MacArthur: "The President of the United States directs that you withdraw your message for the National Encampment of Veterans of Foreign Wars because various features with regard to Formosa are in conflict with the policy of the United States and its position in the United Nations." MacArthur complied with the order, although the damage was already done. The "officially withdrawn" VFW message was published worldwide.[34]

These episodes led to an irreparable break between Truman and MacArthur. Truman wrote: "I gave serious thought to relieving General MacArthur as our military field commander in the Far East and replacing him with General Bradley. I could keep MacArthur in command of the Japanese occupation, taking Korea and Formosa out of his hands. But after weighing it carefully I decided against such a step. It would have been difficult to avoid the appearance of a demotion, and I had no desire to hurt MacArthur personally." He did not discuss this idea with me. Had he, I would have advised against it on a number of grounds, the main one being that MacArthur's offense, serious though it was, was not grave enough to warrant such a drastic step.[35]

Meanwhile, Truman had finally decided that Johnson had to go. He had learned through Averell Harriman that Johnson was now secretly conniving with and encouraging Truman's—and Acheson's—political enemies on the Hill. Johnson's attempt to weasel out of sending the order to withdraw the VFW statement, Margaret Truman wrote, was "close to the last straw."

Truman turned immediately to Marshall, only to discover he was on vacation in Michigan. He asked Marshall to come in to see him when he returned. I suspect Marshall knew what was in the wind. When he called at the White House later, he was perfectly willing to take the job of Secretary of Defense. But by that time, Marshall was under severe public attack from the China Lobby and the right wing for the "loss of China" and other supposedly traitorous acts while he had been Secretary of State. For that reason, Marshall thought he might be a political liability. Truman dismissed this without a second thought and told Marshall he wanted him.[36]

Truman immediately sent Marshall's name to Congress for confirmation as Secretary of Defense. The Republican leadership in both houses had decided to make the administration's "loss of China" and "softness on communism" a major campaign issue in the forthcoming November off-year elections. Since Marshall's mission to China in 1946 had recommended a coalition government for China composed of Nationalists and communists, he became—as he had feared—a target when the bill reached the floors of both houses on September 15.

The attacks on Marshall were brutal. But despite the Republican opposition, Marshall was confirmed. He was sworn in on the morning of September 21.

Another salutary and important change in command took place at about this same time. Ike's World War II chief of staff, Bedell Smith, was named to head the Central Intelligence Agency. The CIA had not matured as we had hoped under the administration of Director Admiral Roscoe H. Hillenkoetter. It had failed us badly on Korea and in other areas. Following Smith's three years as ambassador to Moscow, I had appointed him to relieve Courtney Hodges as commander of First Army on Governors Island, New York, in 1949. Knowing that the CIA required a thorough housecleaning, Smith had twice refused the job. He wrote Ike: "As you know I wanted to avoid the Intelligence job if possible, but in view of the general situation, and particularly in light of the Korean affair, I did not feel I could refuse for a third time." To a friend, Smith wrote: "I expect the worst and I am sure I won't be disappointed." Smith wielded a firm broom at CIA and greatly improved the quality of its intelligence gathering and analysis.[37]

At the beginning of September, the President decided to promote me to the five-star rank of General of the Army. A bill authorizing my fifth star was introduced into Congress. It passed both houses and reached Truman's desk on September 18. That day Truman signed the bill while

Vice President Alben Barkley and Speaker Sam Rayburn and I looked on. Later that day Truman sent the fountain pen he used to sign the bill to Mary "as a souvenir of such deserved recognition." On September 22—the day after Marshall was sworn in as Secretary of Defense—in a White House ceremony attended by the JCS, the Cabinet and some members of Congress, Truman swore me in as General of the Army. He then pinned my new five-star insignia on both epaulets with "obvious pleasure and a great deal of effort," a *New York Times* reporter wrote. However, the *Times* account continued, "sartorially it was a failure." Truman pinned the insignia on askew. The *Times* account concluded: "A certain colonel who had accompanied General Bradley viewed the pinning job with a drillmaster's eye and disapproved. He was a man of caution, however. When General Bradley got out of the President's office he persuaded him to halt. He unpinned the emblems and realigned them, straight as a squad of West Pointers."[38]

I thus became the "last" and youngest of the five-star World War II generals of the Army—after Marshall, Arnold, MacArthur and Ike. My salary was raised to $17,000 a year. Eisenhower telegraphed: "I just this morning heard of your long deserved promotion. Congratulations and best wishes from your devoted and admiring friend. Ike."[39]

FIFTY-SIX

To command the amphibious assault at Inchon, code-named "Chromite," MacArthur established X Corps and gave it to his chief of staff, Ned Almond. Doyle O. Hickey, deputy chief of staff, moved up to become acting chief of staff, temporarily replacing Almond. It was my understanding that when Korean operations were concluded, Ned would return to Tokyo and resume his prior duties.[1]

Ned Almond had never commanded a corps—or troops in an amphibious assault. However, he and his staff, mostly recruited from MacArthur's headquarters, were ably backstopped by the expertise of the Navy and Marines, notably that of Oliver P. Smith, who commanded the 1st Marine Division, which would spearhead the assault.

Ned's other unit for the Inchon operation, David Barr's 7th Infantry Division, cannibalized to provide reinforcements for Church's 24th and Kean's 25th divisions, was in terrible shape. To rebuild it, MacArthur assigned it many artillery and most infantry reinforcements and replacements arriving in the Far East in August. But this was still not enough. To flesh it out to final assault strength—25,000 men—MacArthur resorted to the extraordinary step of recruiting 8,600 civilians from the cities and farms of Korea. Official Army historian Roy E. Appleman wrote that these non-English-speaking Korean volunteer-conscripts arrived in Japan "stunned, confused and exhausted." They were integrated individually into the existing company units and "paired" with American soldiers in a "buddy system." It was hard to believe that MacArthur would assign this jerry-built untrained division to a risky operation like Inchon.[2]

Receiving such reports indirectly, our concern over the feasibility of Inchon mounted. We had not yet received a detailed plan. On September 5, we sent MacArthur this request for information: "The JCS desire to be informed of any modification which may have been made in your plan for a mid-September amphibious operation." MacArthur's reply was insultingly evasive: "The general outline of the plan remains as described to you." He said he was sending an officer courier with a detailed description of the plan who should arrive in Washington by September 11. This was an act of arrogance unparalleled in my military experience. MacArthur knew very well that the courier would arrive too late for the JCS to make a sensible evaluation of his plan.[3]

In the meantime, reports from the Pusan perimeter continued grim. In spite of an artful defense by Walker, the North Koreans appeared to be on the threshold of throwing us out of Korea. To us, the Inchon plan seemed to increase that danger, because MacArthur ordered one of Walker's toughest and most dependable outfits—the 5th Marines—out of the Pusan perimeter and assigned it to the Inchon landing force. He would replace the Marines with two Army regiments, one from the 7th Division and one from the 3rd Division (still en route to the Far East) but both these Army regiments were unblooded and had had little training.[4]

On September 7, after carefully weighing what little we knew about Inchon, the JCS sent MacArthur a final warning of the disastrous consequences that could ensue if Inchon miscarried and failed to produce a quick victory:

> While we concur in launching a counter-offensive in Korea as early as is feasible, we have noted with considerable concern the recent trend of events there. In light of all factors including apparent commitment of practically all reserves available to Eighth Army, we desire your estimate as to feasibility and chance of success of projected operation if initiated on planned schedule. We are sure that you understand that all available trained Army units in the United States have been allocated to you except the 82nd Airborne Division and that minimum of four months would elapse before first of partially trained National Guard Divisions could reach Korea in event that junction of main Eighth Army Forces with Tenth Corps bridgehead should not quickly be effected with forces now available to Far East Command.[5]

MacArthur wrote in his memoirs, *Reminiscences*, that the message "chilled me to the marrow of my bones." He said it "expressed doubt of success and implied the whole movement should be abandoned. . . . Had someone in authority in Washington lost his nerve? Could it be the President? Or Marshall . . . or Bradley?"[6]

On September 8, back came a long rosy reply from MacArthur, justifying the operation and explaining his strategy with these conclusions and judgments. In part:

> There is no question in my mind as to the feasibility of the operation and I regard its chance of success as excellent. I go further and believe it represents the only hope of wresting the initiative from the enemy and thereby preventing an opportunity for a decisive blow. . . . I repeat that I and all of my

commanders and staff officers, without exception, are enthusiastic and confident of the success of the enveloping operation.[7]

The closing sentence was not true. A majority of MacArthur's staff—especially the naval and Marine officers—held gravest reservations about Inchon. It was the wildest kind of military plan—Pattonesque. Even General Courtney Whitney, MacArthur's fawning shadow, conceded as much in his book. On the eve of the invasion, he depicts MacArthur as a bundle of nerves, agonizing over his Inchon decision, worried that it "could go down in history as one of the great United States military disasters." Whitney recalls MacArthur as saying: "No, there was no doubt about the risk. It was a tremendous gamble."[8]

We had one final round of conferences on Inchon on September 8, a full JCS meeting with the President that morning to review MacArthur's rosy appraisal. It was really too late in the game for the JCS to formally disapprove Inchon. We did not yet even have facts enough on which to base a disapproval.* We told the President that we now formally approved Inchon. He already well knew the tremendous risks entailed; there was no need to rehash them. Later that day we sent MacArthur a final message: "We approve your plan and the President has been so informed."[10]

Inchon proved to be the luckiest military operation in history. Astonishingly, it caught the North Koreans completely by surprise. The 1st Marine Division, spearheading the attack on September 15, performed magnificently. The jerry-built 7th Division came ashore three days later and deployed to the right, or south, of the Marines. Both forces moved inland quickly against ineffectual resistance. In a speech in Detroit on September 20, I described the operation with only slight exaggeration as a "military miracle."[11]

Walker's Eighth Army had been instructed to attack out of the Pusan perimeter on D plus 1, September 16. However, the North Koreans were apparently slow to grasp the fact that they were trapped, and they fiercely resisted Walker's attack. For a full week the North Korean Army held. Then, on September 22, it buckled and Walker broke out at full speed. With little or no concern for his flanks, he ordered his men to race north and west and destroy the routed enemy. On September 26, units of the 1st Cavalry and the 7th Division linked up near Osan. Seoul fell to the Marines on September 26 and 27. Meanwhile, the I ROK Corps dashed up the east coast of Korea virtually unopposed. The decimated North Korean Army fled north, helter-skelter.[12]

The swiftness and magnitude of the victory were mind-boggling. We had been at the point of despair, bracing for a "Dunkirk" at Pusan and/or

* The officer-courier, Lieutenant Colonel Lynn D. Smith, perhaps by design, did not arrive in Washington until 2300 on September 13. He briefed the JCS—less me, on leave—at 1100 September 14 (Washington time)—six and a half hours before the invasion.[9]

a disaster at Inchon. A mere two weeks later the North Korean Army had been routed and all South Korea had been regained. MacArthur was deservedly canonized as a "military genius." Inchon was his boldest and most dazzling victory. In hindsight, the JCS seemed like a bunch of nervous Nellies to have doubted.

What to do next? Militarily, should MacArthur's forces continue in pursuit of the fleeing remnants of the North Korean Army, if necessary crossing the 38th parallel? Stop at the 38th parallel, restoring the *status quo*? Politically, should we be satisfied with merely restoring the Rhee government to office in Seoul? Or should we attempt to "unify" all of Korea—North and South—with a single popularly elected government as the UN had originally intended? Since it was impossible to answer any of these questions without reference to the others, Korea ceased being a purely military problem and became a politico-military problem with manifold and delicate nuances.[13]

Throughout the summer of 1950 when decisions about Korea were being considered, JCS eyes were fixed on Moscow. We believed Stalin had equipped and trained the North Korean Army. It seemed inconceivable to us that the North Koreans had invaded South Korea without the active support and encouragement of the Kremlin. We saw the war in Korea as Moscow-inspired. Why, no one could be sure. One possibility was that it was a tactical or strategical diversion—tactical to cover a Chinese communist invasion of Formosa, strategical to cover a Soviet invasion of Western Europe. Although we did not believe Russia was ready for global war, it was possible it could occur, either by design or accident. It was our job to weigh all the possibilities.

As we have seen, owing to the postwar military budget ceilings, the United States was not militarily prepared for global war. The explosion of the Soviet atomic bomb and the fall of China to the communists had resulted in NSC-68 in April 1950, urging a substantial military buildup, and we had entered into a military alliance with our European allies through NATO. These were promising steps to be sure, but in the summer of 1950 they were still largely paper proposals which would not bear fruit for several years. (Nor would our increased fission-bomb production and the H-bomb program.) We were thus a long way from being in a position for a military showdown with the USSR. Under the circumstances, the overall JCS position was, as I described it at the time, "one of steadfast patience and determination in opposing communist aggression without provoking unnecessarily a total war," while at the same time we "improved our military power."

Our greatest concern militarily was the possible loss of Europe. That fear was clearly reflected in our various war plans, culminating in Offtackle. Should Russia overrun Western Europe, the vast technical and industrial potential of the area would then be hers and could ultimately be directed against us. As I put it at the time: "From a global viewpoint—and with the security of our nation of prime importance—our military mission is to support a policy of preventing communism from gaining the manpower, the resources, the raw materials and the industrial capacity essential to world domination. If Soviet Russia ever controls the Eurasian land mass, then the Soviet-satellite imperialism may have the broad base upon which to build the military power to rule the world."

While the JCS had unstintingly supported the President's reversal of policy toward Korea and had stripped the United States, Puerto Rico, Panama, Hawaii and Okinawa to provide MacArthur necessary forces for defeating the North Koreans, we still believed our greatest potential for danger lay in Soviet aggression in Europe. Accordingly, our general view of Korea was to get it over with as soon as possible, get our troops and naval forces out, return some Army divisions to the United States as a mobilization base and send some to Europe to help put backbone in NATO.

Above all, we did not want the war in Korea to "spread" into a war with communist China or with Soviet forces in the Far East. In particular, a war with Red China was to be avoided. To risk widening the Korean War into a war with China, I said, "would probably delight the Kremlin more than anything else we could do." I said that "frankly, in the opinion of the Joint Chiefs of Staff, this strategy would involve us in the wrong war, at the wrong place, at the wrong time, and with the wrong enemy."[14]

On July 17, Truman queried the NSC about how to wind up the Korean War. The State Department was divided in its views. Its two foremost Soviet experts, George Kennan and Charles (Chip) Bohlen, urged utmost restraint. They were opposed to crossing the 38th parallel. Their views strongly influenced State's policy planning staff, headed by Paul Nitze, which on July 23 produced a position paper recommending that the United States "should make every effort to restrict military ground action to the area south of the 38th parallel." The reason? "It is extremely unlikely that the Kremlin would accept the establishment in North Korea of a regime which it could not dominate and control." As our troops approached the 38th parallel, the paper stated, "the danger of conflict with Chinese Communists or Soviet forces would be greatly increased." The risks of bringing on such a conflict "appear to outweigh the political advantages that might be gained."[15]

Read in retrospect—some thirty years later—this paper is full of good sense. It did not get a wider reading at the time because Dean Acheson and his chief Far Eastern advisers, Dean Rusk and John Allison, had adopted a hawkish stance on crossing the 38th parallel. As Acheson put it: "Troops could not be expected . . . to march up to a surveyor's line and stop. . . . No arbitrary prohibition against crossing the parallel should be imposed. As a boundary it had no political validity." Acheson dismissed dissenting State views as "negative" and impractical.[16]

The military was unanimous in its view about what to do in Korea, and the view never wavered. When Collins and Vandenberg visited MacArthur in mid-July, MacArthur said: "I intend to destroy and not [merely] to drive back the North Korean forces. . . . I may have to occupy all of North Korea." The JCS agreed that in order to preclude another North Korean invasion of South Korea, the North Korean Army should be utterly destroyed. It was our hope that the North Korean Army could be destroyed in South Korea, but we believed that MacArthur should not be restrained at the 38th parallel. We urged that the whole country be occupied and guaranteed free elections. However, in order to minimize the possibility of Soviet or Chinese communist intervention, we felt that ground operations north of the 38th parallel should be conducted mostly by ROK forces, with continued American air and naval support.[17]

The NSC position paper on all these important questions gestated slowly. Numbered 81, it was finally promulgated on September 1. In final form it was a masterpiece of obfuscation, designed, I believe, as much to reconcile the conflicting views in State as to provide the President with clear-cut options. Joe Collins has described NSC-81 as a "long, somewhat rambling paper." It was long, but I would not describe it as rambling. Rather, it was dense and cogent, like a fifteen-page legal contract, and no less difficult to understand. Owing to the fact that this paper was classified until recently, historians have had to guess at its contents. One result was that much misinformation about it has been published. Now that it has been declassified, historians would be well advised to give the paper the analysis and emphasis it deserves.[18]

I saw it like this. On the one hand it argued the Kennan-Bohlen-Nitze dovish view that crossing the 38th parallel was certain to provoke a Soviet or Chinese communist reaction, perhaps armed intervention, and appeared to recommend not crossing it. On the other hand, it categorically recommended that MacArthur "should be authorized to conduct military operations, including amphibious and airborne landings or ground operations in pursuance of a roll-back, north of the 38th parallel, for the purpose of destroying North Korean forces," provided there was no indication of major Soviet or Chinese communist intervention. It urged the "unification of Korea" by free elections, held under the auspices of the United Nations.

The JCS had less than one week to analyze NSC-81 and send our comments to the Secretary of Defense. This was the five-day period from September 2 to 7, when we were much distracted by the grave crisis in the Pusan perimeter, the risky forthcoming Inchon landing and a great many other pressing matters. Joe Collins took strong exception to NSC-81, inasmuch as in his view, it seemed to argue militarily for "stabilization of the front on the 38th parallel" and put too many restrictions on MacArthur with respect to crossing the parallel and follow-up operations in North Korea designed to destroy the North Korean Army. He wanted NSC-81 redrafted.

At an NSC meeting on September 7, I presented Joe's reservations, in the name of the full JCS, taking care to say that I "had not had time to study the paper closely." The brief JCS letter I read stated that the JCS, after consultations with MacArthur, agreed with MacArthur's goal of complete destruction of the North Korean forces. The JCS believed such destruction would occur south of the parallel but that "subsequent operations must take place both north and south of the 38th parallel." It was anticipated that these "subsequent operations" would "probably be of a guerrilla character" and that ROK forces "should be adequate at the time to cope with this situation." We went on to say that occupation of Korea by UN forces after hostilities ceased should be limited to the "principal cities south of the 38th parallel," that such occupation be terminated as early as possible and that American forces should be removed from Korea "as early as practicable." We made no recommendations on the political aspects, but added that it was our understanding that the Rhee government was to be re-established in Seoul and a general election held to "set up a single government for all Korea."[19]

Dean Acheson dismissed the JCS objections, saying we had undoubtedly misread NSC-81. I think Acheson was probably right, since paragraph 15 clearly recommended that MacArthur should be authorized to conduct amphibious, airborne or ground operations north of the parallel to defeat the North Korean Army. There was nowhere any suggestion that the front should be "stabilized on the 38th parallel." In fact, paragraph 15, as written, gave MacArthur such a free hand that Acheson, on second thought, insisted that a sentence be added requiring MacArthur to clear operations north of the 38th parallel with the President. After this was inserted and some other minor changes in wording were made, we all informally approved this paper, which was shortly reissued as NSC-81/1. On September 11, the President formally approved the slightly revised version.

In sum, although NSC-81 was complex and ambiguous, it provided the basis for the two major American decisions with respect to winding up the war in Korea. It authorized MacArthur to conduct various military operations north of the 38th parallel on approval from Washington, and it urged the political unification of all of Korea by free elections. On September 1, in a wide-ranging foreign policy speech, Truman pronounced our political aims: "We believe that Koreans have a right to be free, independent and united." Having publicly announced the latter policy on September 1, Truman informally but secretly approved crossing the 38th parallel on September 7, and formally approved it on September 11, four days before Inchon. It should be noted that the President, Acheson, the JCS and MacArthur were in full agreement on these fundamental policies.[20]

Among its many caveats, NSC-81 urged that the United States obtain United Nations approval for military or political operations in North Korea. This goal was pursued by our UN ambassador, Warren Austin, with strong support from the British. As Acheson has written, the proposed resolution, specifically designed to avoid too much discussion about crossing the 38th parallel, was ambivalent, vague and "not thought through." In effect, it revived the original but long-dormant UN plan to create a unified, independent and democratic government in Korea by first insuring "conditions of stability throughout Korea"; followed by an economic aid program and free elections under UN auspices. Insuring "conditions of stability throughout Korea" gave wide latitude to MacArthur—far more so than did NSC-81.[21]

NSC-81/1 reflected a drastic change in our concept of the Korean War. Our initial intervention had been launched as an effort to "save" South Korea. Now we had broadened our war aims to include complete destruction of the North Korean Army and political unification of the country. This was a bold and aggressive step on the Far East stage. I might even say that, given the possibility of Chinese communist or Soviet intervention, it was an extremely dangerous step. Later it struck me as tragically ironic that Truman and Acheson would be charged with "appeasement" in the conduct of the Korean War.

The JCS and everyone else committed one cardinal sin. We seriously misjudged Chinese communist reaction to our plans to cross the 38th parallel. It is the duty and responsibility of military advisers to gauge a potential enemy's *capabilities* rather than his *intentions*. In this case, we Joint Chiefs allowed ourselves to be overly influenced by various estimates of Chinese communist intentions. As historians have now shown, those who drew those estimates ignored too many obvious warning flags and miscalculated badly.

Solid intelligence on Red China was not easy to come by. It was especially difficult to sort out real intentions from propagandistic threats. (Ironically, our earlier orders to MacArthur not to violate Chinese and Soviet borders or air space had grounded our intelligence overflights and cut off our most reliable means of information.) Collins has written correctly that about 90 percent of our intelligence came from MacArthur's headquarters. A substantial percentage of that, in turn, came from the Nationalists on Formosa, who were running agents into Red China. However, the Nationalists had a big propaganda ax to grind too, and much of what they gave MacArthur was unreliable or canted.[22]

Early in the war—July 6—the joint intelligence committee estimated that there were 565,000 Chinese communist troops in Manchuria (of whom about 70,000 were Korean), plus 210,000 more farther south near Peking and Tientsin. MacArthur's intelligence chief, General Charles A. Willoughby, more or less agreed with these figures, although he trimmed them by a total of about 100,000 men. He estimated 489,000 in Manchuria and 176,000 in North China. He reported that about a quarter of these troops (115,000) were "regulars," the other three-quarters "militia." Significantly, in late August and early September, Willoughby reported a large movement of "regular" troops to Manchuria. By August 31, the total of regulars had doubled from 115,000 to 246,000. By September 21, the number had nearly doubled again to 450,000. While it was believed that most of these increases were due to the Chinese Fourth Field Army returning home after its successful campaign against the Nationalists, there was also evidence of non–Fourth Army units massing in Manchuria. Neither the JCS nor MacArthur gave sufficient weight to these increasing numbers or to the presence of the outside units.[23]

Our intelligence agencies, both military and CIA, monitored Chinese public and private statements for clues to their intentions. Official JCS historians James F. Schnabel and Robert J. Watson write that in July and August most of the information collected "suggested that Communist China had relatively little interest in the Korean situation." But in mid-August, after our UN ambassador made a tough speech advocating the unification of Korea, a gradual change took place. Foreign Minister Chou En-lai declared that China was deeply concerned about Korea's future and endorsed a Soviet proposal that communist China be represented in the UN when Korean problems were under discussion.[24]

Despite the significant movement of troops to Manchuria and increasingly belligerent assertions from Peking, the consensus of the intelligence community in Washington and Tokyo was that Red Chinese intervention in Korea was, in Acheson's words, "improbable, unless the Soviet Union started a global war." We thought the Chinese were mostly bluffing. Nonetheless, Truman sent a message through Indian diplomats to Peking warning the Red Chinese to stay clear of Korea. In his September 1 foreign policy speech, he delivered a public warning: "We hope in particular that the people of China will not be misled or forced into fighting against the United Nations and against the American people."[25]

It took the JCS no little time to draft specific orders to MacArthur. Part of the delay can be attributed to the general Pentagon standstill that occurred during the Johnson-Marshall switchover, part to the week-long delay in the Eighth Army Pusan perimeter breakout, which created temporary uncertainty, and part to delays at State, which was in turn awaiting action on the UN resolution. On September 15, we sent MacArthur a copy of NSC-81/1 for guidance and to alert him to what was coming. After I obtained approval from the President, Marshall and Acheson, the orders, which were drafted by the JCS joint staff, went out on September 27—twelve days after Inchon.[26]

These orders to MacArthur were based on NSC-81/1 and in some cases used the exact language of the paper. NSC-81/1 had laid heavy stress on the likelihood of a strong Soviet or Chinese communist reaction to our crossing the parallel. In such an event, the paper had recommended more cautious and detailed measures, which would be determined in Washington. Thus at the outset of the orders we pointedly alluded to NSC-81/1 and stated: "You will continue to make special efforts to determine whether there is a Chinese Communist or Soviet threat to the attainment of your objective, which will be reported to the Joint Chiefs of Staff as a matter of urgency."

The thrust of our order was broad: "Your military objective is the destruction of the North Korean armed forces."

There followed immediately language from NSC-81/1: "In attaining this objective you are authorized to conduct military operations, including amphibious and airborne landings or ground operations north of the 38th parallel in Korea, provided that at the time of such operations there has been no entry into North Korea by major Soviet or Chinese Communist forces, no announcement of intended entry, nor a threat to counter our operations militarily in North Korea."

In our original discussions of NSC-81/1, it had been our hope that most of the North Korean Army would be crushed in South Korea. By the time we issued the orders, we knew that a third of the Army had escaped and that it was going to take more than "mopping up" or guerrilla actions by ROK forces to wipe it out. We therefore realized that significant numbers of U.S. ground forces would have to cross the 38th parallel. We placed no restrictions on MacArthur on these troops crossing the parallel. However, we stated that "as a matter of policy" no non-Korean ground forces would be employed in the Northeast Provinces bordering the Soviet Union or in the area along the Manchurian border. We also stated that "under no circumstances" would any of MacArthur's forces cross the Soviet or Manchurian border, nor should his air or naval forces take action against Manchuria or USSR territory.

We then turned to questions of what MacArthur should do if the Soviets or Chinese communists threatened intervention or if the Soviets intervened. If either the Soviets or Chinese announced in advance their intention of reoccupying North Korea, he should "refer the matter immediately to Washington." If the Soviets intervened with major forces, overtly or covertly, either north or south of the 38th parallel, he was to "assume the defensive, make no move to aggravate the situation and report to Washington." It was our view that such intervention probably meant a Soviet move to total war. If so, we would withdraw our forces from Korea and prepare to execute Offtackle.

One of the curious omissions in NSC-81/1 was what instructions should be given MacArthur in event the Chinese communists intervened in North Korea. This occurred, I believe, because of our view that North Korea was a Moscow-inspired operation and hence a Russian problem, not a Chinese communist problem. Thus we believed Soviet intervention in North Korea was far more likely than Chinese intervention. If the Chinese communists were going to make a decisive military move, Formosa was a more likely target. We did not believe the Chinese communists were likely to rush in to help solve Russia's problem in North Korea, taking on well-organized American ground, air and naval forces. It was "possible that Chinese Communist forces might be used to occupy North Korea," NSC-81/1 stated, but "politically unlikely."

However, in the early stages of Korea, when NSC-81 was drafted, we believed there was a possibility that the Chinese communists might intervene in South Korea, possibly in concert with an invasion of Formosa, while we were hanging by our fingertips in the Pusan perimeter. If they intended to invade Formosa, as they said, it was in their own best interest to help the North Koreans keep our air and naval power pinned down in South Korea for as long as possible. Thus NSC-81/1 had stated that in the event of major Chinese intervention *south* (emphasis added) of the 38th parallel, the United States should continue the action as long as there was a "reasonable chance of successful resistance" and take "appropriate air and naval action outside Korea against Communist China." Under no circumstances should the United States "permit itself to become engaged in a general war with Communist China."

We viewed the possibility of Chinese intervention in North Korea as we did the possibility of Soviet intervention in North Korea: a probable signal that the Russians were moving toward global war. In the event of Chinese intervention, our reaction would be the same. We would withdraw our forces from Korea and prepare to launch Offtackle. In a meeting with the British Chiefs, I stated our policy plainly and succinctly. The JCS, I said, "all agree that if the Chinese Communists come into [North] Korea, we get out."[27]

By the time our orders went out to MacArthur, Inchon had reduced the chances of Chinese communist intervention in South Korea to near zero. Nonetheless, whoever drafted the order paraphrased NSC-81/1 and stated: "In the event of open or covert employment of major Chinese Communist units *south* of the 38th parallel, you should continue the action for as long as action by your forces offers a reasonable chance of successful resistance." (Emphasis added.) This pointless order should have been deleted, but it slipped by all of us, from the President on down. It was not an error; we did not mean to say *north* of the parallel.

Having dealt with these important matters (excepting Chinese communist intervention in North Korea), our orders to MacArthur continued for seven more paragraphs, all reflecting recommendations in NSC-81/1. He should make an all-out propaganda effort, blaming the war on the communists. He should attempt to brainwash North Korean POW's. ROK forces should take the lead in disarming remaining North Korean forces and conducting guerrilla activities. In conclusion, we alerted him that State was preparing guidance documents relating to a public surrender ultimatum he would deliver, and courses of action to be followed in the post-hostility period. We concluded by asking him to submit his plans for "military operations north of the 38th parallel" and "occupation of North Korea" to the JCS "for approval."

Before these orders were finally approved in Washington, Acheson had added a paragraph of "political guidance"—a clear demonstration of how the political and military problems of Korea had become irrevocably intermixed. Acheson advised that as soon as practical, MacArthur should "facilitate the restoration" of the Rhee government in Seoul. ROK forces should cooperate in military and occupational duties in North Korea, but "political questions such as the formal extension of sovereignty over North Korea should await action by the United Nations to complete the unification of the country."

MacArthur's orders, together with the copy of NSC-81/1 I had sent him for guidance, amounted to the most extraordinarily detailed and limiting set of instructions ever sent a military field commander. We had made clear our belief that the situation was exceptionally delicate, that we were walking on eggshells, that it was highly likely to provoke a Soviet reaction, and every major move in Korea had to be cleared in Washington. There can be no question that MacArthur was fully apprised of our policies and the reasons behind them.

After receiving his orders from the JCS, MacArthur replied on September 28 as follows:

> If the North Korean Armed Forces do not surrender in accordance with my proclamation to be issued 1 October 1950, dispositions will be made to accomplish the military objective of destroying them by entry into North Korea. Briefly my plan is:
>
> a. 8th Army as now constituted will attack across the 38th parallel with its main effort on the Kaesong-Sariwon-Pyongyang axis with the objective of capturing Pyongyang [capital of North Korea].
> b. X Corps as now constituted will make amphibious landings at Wonsan, making juncture with 8th Army.
> c. 3rd Infantry Division will remain in Japan in GHQ Reserve, initially.
> d. ROK Army forces only will conduct operations north of the Line Chungjo-Yongwon-Hungnam.
> e. Tentative date for the attack of 8th Army will be not earlier than 15 October and not later than 30 October.
>
> You will be provided detailed plans later. There is no indication at present of entry into North Korea by major Soviet or Chinese Communist forces.[28]

Shortly after this exchange, news dispatches quoted Walker as stating he would halt at the 38th parallel, presumably to await permission from the UN to cross. This was an awkward development inasmuch as our UN diplomats were then attempting to get the UN resolution through without a specific vote on crossing the 38th parallel. Accordingly, I conferred with Marshall on September 29 and together we composed the following message:

> Message for General of the Army Douglas MacArthur
> (FOR HIS EYES ONLY)
>
> Reference present report of supposed announcement by 8th Army that ROK divisions would halt on 38th parallel for regrouping: We want you to feel unhampered tactically and strategically to proceed north of the parallel. Announcement above referred to may precipitate embarrassment in UN where evident desire is not to be confronted with necessity of a vote on passage of 38th parallel, rather to find you have found it militarily necessary to do so.
>
> [Signed] G. C. Marshall[29]

MacArthur replied September 30. He doubted Walker had made any such statement, nonetheless he would caution him against "any involvement connected with the nomenclature of the 38th parallel." He went on to interpret his authority in the broadest possible terms:

> Parallel 38 is not a factor in the military employment of our forces. The logistical supply of our units is the main problem which limits our immediate advance. In exploiting the defeat of enemy forces, our own troops may cross the parallel at any time in exploratory probing or exploitation local tactical conditions. My overall strategic plan for North Korea is known to you. Unless and until the enemy capitulates, I regard all of Korea open for our military operations.[30]

He also said he intended to publicly release these views. Since this would intensify the very controversy we had cautioned Walker against, the JCS hastened to advise him we felt it "unwise" to issue such a statement. Instead, we urged, he should proceed with his operations "without further explanation or announcement and let action determine the matter." We emphasized again that "our government desires to avoid having to make an issue of the 38th parallel until we have accomplished our mission of defeating the North Korean forces."[31]

These latest messages from MacArthur were disturbing. They indicated either an insensitivity to an extremely delicate politico-military situation or a brazen contempt for our restrictions or perhaps some of both.

However, he was basking in the sunshine of a big victory, his reputation soaring to the heavens and his ego beyond that.

What was most disturbing to me was his plan of operations. To me it didn't make sense.

By October 1 (two weeks after Inchon), it was clear that MacArthur's victory in South Korea had not been as decisive as we had hoped or been led to believe. Too many North Koreans had slipped through the trap, perhaps a third of the 90,000 North Korean troops in South Korea, including most of the senior commanders. Moreover, we knew that a substantial number of reserves—perhaps 125,000 partially trained men—were mobilized in North Korea. The combined North Korean forces would represent a formidable enemy. Given time to regroup, the combined forces, fighting on "home soil," might well put up a prolonged and costly fight.

The military textbook solution to the existing problem was "hot pursuit." That is, to drive forward at utmost speed with all the UN forces at hand before the North Koreans could dig in defensively. Since the Eighth Army had been under exhausting siege for weeks and had just made a 200-mile dash from the Pusan perimeter, outrunning and overstretching its supply lines, and was strung out from Pusan to Inchon, the logical solution was to get Almond's fresh X Corps, which had suffered few casualties and was being supplied through Inchon, cracking north under command of the senior man on the scene, Walton Walker. Most of the senior commanders and staffers (Walker, Allen, Hickey) had simply assumed this would be the plan. But they were overruled by MacArthur, who personally conceived his own.

In my book, MacArthur had arrived at the worst possible solution. Instead of driving north with X Corps in hot pursuit, he had detailed it to make a second amphibious landing on the east coast of Korea at Wonsan. This meant stopping all pursuit, pulling X Corps from the line, reloading it aboard ship and sending it on a long sea voyage at what was in reality a secondary target. That decision, in turn, left the main pursuit north to the primary target (Pyongyang) to Walker's tired and strung-out Eighth Army, which would have to be regrouped and resupplied before it could resume the offensive. Moreover, on our maps, the Wonsan operation seemed to be completely unnecessary. The ROK I Corps, then dashing up the east coast of Korea virtually unopposed, was certain to take Wonsan long before X Corps could land there. Finally, the Wonsan maneuver would continue a division in our forces, both physically and in terms of command. MacArthur would direct X Corps operations from Tokyo.

MacArthur's rationale for this plan was logistics. He argued that Inchon did not have the facilities both to support X Corps operations in "hot pursuit" and replenish the Eighth Army. It was too difficult at that stage to bring sufficient supplies all the way from Pusan. If he removed X Corps from dependence on Inchon (getting its resupply for Wonsan through

Pusan), everything coming into Inchon could go to the Eighth Army, thus speeding up its replenishment.

That sounds quite logical on the surface, but in reality the rationale was unsound. In the first place, the 1st Marine Division had to be outloaded through Inchon. This required literally days, during which time the Marines had top priority, so that only a trickle of supplies could come *into* Inchon for the Eighth Army. So congested was Inchon that MacArthur had to march the 7th Division 200 miles south and outload it through Pusan. The 7th went southward over clogged roads, taking priority over other northbound supplies for the Eighth Army. When the division reached Pusan, its outloading took priority over incoming supplies destined for the Eighth Army. The end result was that in the name of improving logistics, MacArthur created a logistical nightmare at Inchon, on the southern highways and at Pusan. The enemy himself could not have concocted a more diabolical scheme to delay our pursuit.

I think the truth of the matter was that MacArthur's vanity got in the way of good sense. There was an aura of glamour about an amphibious landing, far more so than tedious footslogging overland. A sudden bold and decisive strike in the enemy's rear made big headlines and generated editorials about "military genius" at work. In the first act, MacArthur had overridden staff objections and pulled it off at Inchon, bringing down the curtain amid thunderous applause. A second-act curtain would generate even more headlines, editorials and applause.

In sum, MacArthur threw away an opportunity for decisive hot pursuit, bringing operations to a standstill for almost three weeks; sent X Corps off on a secondary mission of doubtful value, assigning the primary mission to the least prepared of his two forces; divided his force and command; and created an unnecessary logistical logjam of monumental proportions at a time when logistics were crucial to operations. Had a major at the Command and General Staff School turned in this solution to the problem, he would have been laughed out of the classroom.

The JCS shared my reservations; nevertheless we did not raise any formal objections. At that point, any further questions about MacArthur's tactical operations from the JCS in all probability would have been viewed as carping. Field operations were still the responsibility of the theater commander. Accordingly, we cleared the plan with Marshall and Truman and sent out formal approval on September 29.[32]

What a terrible mistake this would prove to be. If only we had cabled: CANCEL WONSAN. SEND X CORPS IN HOT PURSUIT. CONSOLIDATE X CORPS AND ITS SUPPORTING TACTICAL AIR INTO EIGHTH ARMY.

If . . .

FIFTY-SEVEN

The war in Korea proceeded full tilt. ROK forces in central and eastern Korea continued driving north with remarkable speed. On the east coast, advance elements of the ROK I Corps crossed the 38th parallel on October 2 and sped on toward MacArthur's X Corps objective, Wonsan. In central Korea, advance elements of the ROK II Corps crossed the 38th parallel on October 6. On the west coast, Walker's Eighth Army, regrouping and replenishing, sent elements of the 1st Cavalry Division across the 38th parallel on October 7. MacArthur set X Corps D-day at Wonsan for October 15, but owing to various outloading problems, D-day had to be postponed to October 20.[1]

In the meantime, Washington began receiving ominous signals from Peking, channeled through the Indian ambassador to China, Kavalam Madhava Panikkar, who in turn relayed them to British diplomats. On September 27, we received a report from the British that Red China's high military officials were apparently threatening intervention in Korea. These reports were not at first taken seriously, because the British believed Panikkar to be a "volatile and unreliable reporter" and a mouthpiece for Chinese communist propaganda. But messages we received from British diplomats via London and New Delhi on October 3 caused far deeper concern. Foreign Minister Chou En-lai had called in Panikkar and told him (according to our London ambassador) that if UN armed forces, other than ROK's, crossed the 38th parallel, "China would send troops across the frontier [to] participate in defence [of] North Korea."[2]

Was this for real? State's Far Eastern expert Alexis Johnson cranked out an immediate appraisal that same day: "Although the statement attributed to Chou En-lai undoubtedly contains a large element of bluff . . . I do not feel that we can assume it is entirely bluff." He recommended that in order to reduce the "grave risk of calling the Chinese bluff," it would be "well worthwhile further to explore the possibility of using entirely ROK forces for the subjugation of North Korea," maintaining an "umbrella" of tactical air and naval support.[3]

Unfortunately, Johnson's sound appraisal did not get the consideration it deserved. The weight of opinion of the higher-ups at State was that Chou's statement was bravado—part of a joint Soviet-Chinese diplomatic effort to save the North Korean regime. This tragically erroneous view was—again unfortunately—reinforced by Bedell Smith's analysts at CIA, who reported to the White House:

> Despite statements by Chou En-lai [and] troop movements to Manchuria . . . there are no convincing indications of an actual Chinese Communist intention to resort to full-scale intervention in Korea. . . . From a military standpoint the most favorable time for intervention in Korea has passed. . . . While full-scale Chinese Communist intervention in Korea must be regarded as a continuing possibility, a consideration of all known factors leads to the conclusion that barring a Soviet decision for global war, such action is not probable in 1950. During this period, intervention will probably be confined to continued covert assistance to the North Koreans.

Nor did CIA analysts believe the Soviets wanted global war. They wrote: "It is believed that the Soviet leaders will not consider that their prospective losses in Korea warrant direct military intervention and a consequent grave risk of war."[4]

Our thinking was that Russian or Chinese communist intervention in Korea risked global war; the Russians were not ready to risk global war over Korea; and China was not militarily capable of unilateral intervention. Therefore, there would be no Soviet or Chinese communist intervention in Korea.

There were two flaws in this logic. The first was our belief that Red China was a Soviet satellite under tight Moscow control. Not enough consideration was given the view that Red China could, or might want to, act independently of Moscow or that a dramatic Red Chinese military rescue of North Korea could, in effect, turn North Korea into a Chinese communist satellite, greatly enhancing Red China's power and prestige in the Far East. The second flaw was the all too widespread belief that Red China acting alone could not make a decisive difference; in fact, might even suffer a humiliating defeat; and further, that the most favorable time militarily for intervention (when we were hanging on in the Pusan perimeter) had passed.[5]

I would very much like to write that the military establishment had seen the flaws in this logic and held a different view. Such was not the case. Our military intelligence estimates had contributed substantially to the CIA's conclusions. We wrongly continued to focus too much emphasis on enemy intentions and not enough on his capabilities. The military view continued to be that neither Red China nor the USSR was likely to intervene in Korea and that operations, as set forth in NSC-81/1, should continue.

Nonetheless, in view of Chou En-lai's statement, the JCS now had to consider Chinese intervention in North Korea "possible." We then realized that our orders to MacArthur of September 27 had dealt only with the possibility of Chinese intervention in *South* Korea. Accordingly, on October 7, we drafted a letter for Marshall to the President suggesting that MacArthur's orders be revised to specifically provide for Chinese intervention in North Korea. The proposed language:

> Hereafter in event of open or covert employment anywhere in Korea of major Chinese Communist units, without prior announcement, you should continue the action as long as, in your judgment, action by forces now under your control offers a reasonable chance of success. In any case you will obtain authorization from Washington prior to taking any military action against objectives in Chinese territory.

This amendment to MacArthur's orders was approved by the President on the following day, October 8, and radioed to MacArthur on October 9. Truman's implication in the second volume of his memoirs, *Years of Trial and Hope,* that this message was conceived at his suggestion is not accurate.[6]

On the day that order went out, October 9, MacArthur broadcast a surrender ultimatum (which had been cleared by State) to the North Koreans. Unless they laid down their arms and cooperated fully in establishing a "unified, independent and democratic government," MacArthur said, "I shall at once proceed to take such military action as may be necessary to enforce the decrees of the United Nations." The following day, October 10, in a broadcast from Pyongyang, North Korean Premier Kim Il Sung rejected the ultimatum, saying the Korean people "are not standing alone in our struggle and are receiving the absolute support of the Soviet Union, the Chinese people," and so on.

That same day the Foreign Ministry in Peking issued a grave warning: "The American War of invasion in Korea has been a serious menace to the security of China from the very start. . . . The Chinese people cannot stand idly by with regard to such a serious situation—created by the invasion of Korea by the United States and its accomplice countries and to the dangerous trend toward extending the war. The Chinese people firmly advocate a peaceful solution to the Korean problem and are firmly opposed to the extension of the Korean War by America and its accomplice countries. And they are even more firm in holding that aggressors must be answerable for all consequences resulting from their frantic acts in extending aggression."[7]

Four days after that statement, October 14, huge numbers of Chinese troops began crossing the Yalu River from Manchuria into North Korea. These were well-trained regular units of the Chinese Fourth Field Army, which three months earlier had moved into Manchuria. Official Army historians estimate that some 180,000 Chinese troops crossed the Yalu within the next two and a half weeks. In spite of all the warnings from Peking, the movement of these troops was not detected by military intelligence units or by aircraft reconnaissance operating under MacArthur's command. They melted into the mountains, concealed as thoroughly as Hitler's troops massing for the Battle of the Bulge.[8]

The possibility of Red Chinese intervention in Korea had deeply concerned Truman ever since Chou En-lai's October 3 threat. Soon after that, he decided that he and MacArthur should have a face-to-face meeting to discuss that possibility and a whole range of Far East matters. The President and MacArthur, Truman wrote, "had never had any personal contacts at all," and Truman naturally felt they should know one another better. Truman did not believe MacArthur fully understood his thinking on foreign policy matters and believed that he should. Later speculations, fostered by the MacArthur camp, that Truman connived to meet MacArthur in order to associate himself with the expected victory in Korea to help Democrats at the polls in the November off-year elections, were, I believe, sheer nonsense.[9]

Many at the State Department opposed this meeting. Acheson wrote: "I begged to be excused. While General MacArthur had many of the attributes of a foreign sovereign, I said, and was quite as difficult as any, it did not seem wise to recognize him as one. . . . The whole idea was distasteful to me." Ambassador-at-large Philip Jessup was also leery. He feared the meeting "would be interpreted to foreshadow some major new move in the Far East" that might provoke an already tense situation.[10]

Truman would not be dissuaded. He first considered meeting MacArthur in Korea itself. But that was ruled out as too dangerous from a security standpoint. He then chose Hawaii, but at Marshall's suggestion, the site was shifted to Wake Island in order to minimize MacArthur's absence from command of operations—in particular the X Corps landing at Wonsan, scheduled for October 20. Truman wanted to take along the whole JCS; but since they were heavily burdened and didn't want to go, at my suggestion I represented the JCS. Others in the Washington party would include Dean Rusk and Philip Jessup from State, Averell Harriman from the White House and Army Secretary Frank Pace.[11]

That trip to Wake was a complicated operation requiring three aircraft. Truman and his White House advisers left first, October 11, on the *Independence,* accompanied by a separate plane for the press. The next day, October 12, Pace, Harriman, Rusk, Jessup and I, together with various aides and secretaries, left Washington on a third plane, a Constellation named *Dewdrop*. We joined the Truman party that night at Fairfield-Suisan Air Force Base in California. This was a debarkation point for Korean wounded who had been airlifted back to the States. We visited some wounded at the base hospital, then left for Hickam Air Force Base, Hawaii, shortly after midnight. On the long night flight to Hickam, Truman wrote a letter to his cousin, Nellie Noland, in which he said he was en route "to talk to God's righthand man."[12]

Admiral Radford, still commander in chief of the Pacific Fleet, was our host for the day. After the usual military briefing, he took us on a boat tour of Pearl Harbor which included a brief pause at the battleship *Arizona*, capsized in the Pearl Harbor attack and now a memorial. Following an afternoon tour of military installations on Oahu, we went swimming, had dinner, then took off for Wake Island about midnight, having survived Friday the 13th with no private disasters or misfortunes. Unknown to us, this was the day that units of the Chinese Fourth Field Army were massing to cross the Yalu River on the morrow, so the day would prove unlucky after all.[13]

During the long flight to Wake, we crossed the International Date Line, "losing" October 14. We had a good strong tail wind, which pushed us far ahead of schedule. Our plane and the press plane landed early. However, to avoid throwing everybody into a tizzy with a premature arrival, Truman's *Independence* slowed down, then circled Wake, trying to stick to the original schedule. This perfectly ordinary procedure would later lead to a misunderstanding, fostered principally by Truman's physician, Major General Wallace Graham, who was on the *Independence*. Merle Miller, in his book on Truman, *Plain Speaking*, quoted Graham as saying that MacArthur, "a showman type . . . deliberately tried to hold up his landing so that we would go in and land ahead of them" but that Truman "caught it right away" and ordered MacArthur to land first.[14]

In fact, MacArthur, flying in from Tokyo on his plane, *SCAP*, had arrived on Wake the night before and had had a nap. Since he had received no detailed information from any source on what the meeting was about, he was mystified, somewhat apprehensive and a little suspicious that it was purely "political."

After the *Dewdrop* landed, Harriman, Pace, Radford and I met MacArthur. He was dressed in freshly pressed khakis, the effect of neatness somewhat diminished by the fact that he was wearing his ancient, faded, stained World War II garrison cap. He said to Harriman: "What's this meeting all about?" Harriman told him it would concern a whole range of issues: political plans for Korea following the victory, the Japanese peace treaty—all matters affecting the Far East. MacArthur appeared to be relieved. "Good," he said, "then the President wants my views?" Harriman replied, "Yes."[15]

Harriman took MacArthur in tow—arm-in-arm—and led him to the place on the runway where the *Independence* would taxi to a halt. Pace and I and others, including the press, followed behind. When Truman came down the ramp at 0630, MacArthur did not salute (as I thought would have been proper etiquette), but he greeted the President with (as the *New York Times* reporter said) "every appearance of warmth and friendliness." They shook hands heartily. MacArthur, pumping Truman's right hand, said, "Mr. President." Truman smiled and said, "How are you, General? I'm glad you are here. I have been a long time meeting you." MacArthur replied, "I hope it won't be so long next time, Mr. President." On this cordial note the meeting began. But as it turned out, there would be no "next time." This was the one and only meeting between Truman and MacArthur.[16]

There was no military on Wake other than a temporary honor guard of twenty-one Marines Radford had flown from Hawaii. The only government people on Wake were some officials from the Civil Aeronautics Administration who provided their battered car and pickup truck and offices for our use. The President and MacArthur first climbed in the old car and went off for an hour's private conference in a beachside Quonset hut.

Truman wrote of that meeting: "We discussed the Japanese and Korean situations. The general assured me that the victory was won in Korea. He also informed me that the Chinese Communists would not attack and that Japan was ready for a peace treaty. Then he brought up the subject of his statement about Formosa to the Veterans of Foreign Wars. He said that he was sorry if he had caused any embarrassment. I told him that I considered the incident closed. He said he wanted me to understand that he was not in politics in any way—that he had allowed politicians to make a 'chump' (his word) of him in 1948 and that it would not happen again."

MacArthur recalled that Truman "radiated nothing but courtesy and good humor." He had an "engaging personality, a quick and witty tongue, and I liked him from the start." MacArthur wrote that he "rather impertinently" asked Truman if he intended to run for re-election. Truman sidestepped this query and asked MacArthur if *he* had any ambitions along that line. "None whatsoever," MacArthur said he replied. "If you have a general running against you, his name will be Eisenhower, not MacArthur." MacArthur said Truman replied, "Eisenhower doesn't know the first thing about politics. Why, if he should become President, his Administration would make Grant's look like a model of perfection."[17]

The formal meeting lasted from 0736 to 0912—one hour and thirty-six minutes. At least seven people took notes, including Jessup's secretary Vernice Anderson, who sat in a smaller room off the main room. MacArthur's camp would later imply that note taking was not encouraged and that Vernice Anderson had been surreptitiously "planted" in the room. This is ridiculous. There was no prohibition against taking notes and I took them myself. So did Harriman and Dean Rusk. Later, at Truman's request, I compiled a "transcript" of the proceedings based on all the notes I could collect, including Anderson's. Five days after the meeting, October 19, I sent five copies of this transcript to MacArthur for amending if necessary. His aide received and signed for the five copies on October 27. MacArthur suggested no corrections whatsoever, indicating complete concurrence with the record, later charges to the contrary notwithstanding.[18]

This brief conference was broad-ranging. MacArthur did most of the talking—usually in response to questions. The chief points were:

- MacArthur said that "formal resistance will end throughout North and South Korea by Thanksgiving." It was his hope "to be able to withdraw the Eighth Army to Japan by Christmas," leaving X Corps, composed of the 2nd and 3rd U.S. Army divisions and some UN detachments. He hoped Korean elections could be held by the first of the year, after which he expected to pull out "all occupying troops." He said, "Nothing is gained by military occupation. All occupations are failures." He would leave a well-supplied ROK Army of ten divisions, and a "small but competent" ROK Navy and Air Force to secure Korea and serve as a "tremendous deterrent to the Chinese Communists moving south," which was "a threat that cannot be laughed off."
- In response to a question from Truman ("What are the chances for Chinese or Soviet interference?"), MacArthur replied, "Very little. Had they interfered in the first or second months it would have been decisive. We are no longer fearful of their intervention. We no longer stand hat in hand. The Chinese have 300,000 men in Manchuria. Of these probably not more than 100,000 to 125,000 are distributed along the Yalu River. Only 50,000 to 60,000 could be gotten across the Yalu River. They have no air force. Now that we have bases for our air force in Korea, if the Chinese tried to get down to Pyongyang there would be the greatest slaughter."
- As to the possibility of Soviet intervention, MacArthur said, "With the Russians it is a little different. They have an air force in Siberia and a fairly good one, with excellent pilots equipped with some jets and B-25 and B-29 [type] planes. They can put 1,000 planes in the air with some 2,000 to 3,000 more from the Fifth and Seventh Soviet [Navy] Fleets. They are probably no match for our air force. The Russians have no ground troops available for North Korea. They would have difficulty in putting troops into the field. It would take six weeks to get a division across [the border] and six weeks brings the winter. The only other combination would be Russian air support of Chinese ground troops . . . but the coordination between the Russian air and Chinese ground would be so flimsy that I believe Russian air would bomb the Chinese as often as they would bomb us . . . it just would not work with Chinese Communist ground and Russian air."
- In a discussion on the need to get American troops to Europe to put backbone in NATO, I asked MacArthur if the U.S. Army 2nd or 3rd Division could be made available for Europe by January. He replied, "Yes. I will make one available by January." He recommended the 2nd Division as "better trained" and hence it would make a "better impres-

sion." He repeated that he hoped to get the Eighth Army back to Japan "by Christmas."

- In response to a question by Harriman about the situation in Indochina, MacArthur said, "The situation in Indochina is puzzling. The French have 150,000 of their best troops there with an officer of the highest reputation in command [M. M. Carpentier]. Their forces are twice what we had in the perimeter and they are opposed by half of what the North Koreans had. I cannot understand why they do not clean it up. They should be able to do so in four months, yet we have recently seen a debacle. . . . What is the capacity and caliber of the French Army? In the first World War they were excellent. In the second World War they were poor. The present French soldier is doubtful. . . . They have the flower of the French Army in Indochina and they are not fighting. If this is so, no matter what supplies we pour in they may be of no use. The loss of territory in itself is nothing, but the French failure is broader than this. I cannot understand it."[19]

Throughout the meeting the atmosphere was one of utmost cordiality. There was not one discordant or negative note until the very end. Our schedule called for a day-long stay on Wake, with further conferences scheduled for the afternoon. But MacArthur declined lunch or a prolongation of the conference into the afternoon, indicating a desire to return to Tokyo as quickly as possible—to get back to the war. Whether intended or not, it was insulting to decline lunch with the President, and I think Truman was miffed, although he gave no sign. However, we had covered a broad range of subject matter very quickly; and, in truth, there was no further need for talks between Truman and MacArthur.

Truman left, going back to the seaside Quonset hut to get cool and rest while we continued conferring with MacArthur in the hot shack for another hour and forty-five minutes. In these talks, Dean Rusk mentioned that the Chinese communists had "privately" threatened to enter the Korean War if UN forces crossed the 38th parallel. According to Rusk's notes, MacArthur "said he did not fully understand why they had gone out on such a limb and that they must be greatly embarrassed by the predicament in which they now find themselves."[20]

We all reassembled at the aircraft at about 1130. There, Truman decorated MacArthur with a Distinguished Service Medal—his fifth. In his farewell to Truman, MacArthur remained cordial. "Goodbye, sir. Happy landing. It has been a real honor to talk to you." To me he said, "Goodbye, Omar. Don't let them get you down, up there." In response to a question from a reporter as to how things shaped up, Truman beamed and said, "Perfectly. I've never had a more satisfactory conference since I've been President."[21]

This was my third meeting with MacArthur, all in 1950. He could not have been friendlier. He thanked me privately for the tremendous support the JCS had given him during the almost four months of the Korean War. Although by then I knew he deeply and fervently believed the Far East to be the crucial battleground in the fight against communism, he appeared to understand fully and appreciate our need to reduce his forces in order to build NATO and professed that he would cooperate to his utmost.

Truman's *Independence* took off first, MacArthur's *SCAP* five minutes later. The presidential party and the press stopped in Hawaii for a leisurely second October 15, a Sunday. We swam and toured my old stomping grounds: Blowhole, Diamond Head, Waikiki Beach. We had lunch at the Kailua Officers' Club and dinner with the President, who was preparing a speech to deliver in San Francisco on the way back to Washington. I have seldom seen him in better spirits. It was a relief to all of us that the Korean War would soon be over. Now we could proceed with the vital task of building NATO. There was a very long way to go in that area.[22]

I accompanied the President back to San Francisco on October 16. The following night I was present when he gave his speech at the San Francisco Opera House. He explained at some length why he had gone to Wake Island. He stressed one point: "I also felt there was a pressing need to make it perfectly clear—by my talks with General MacArthur—that there is complete unity in the aim and conduct of our foreign policy." He sent Peking another signal: "Our sole purpose in Korea is to establish peace and independence. Our troops will stay there only so long as they are needed by the United Nations for that purpose. We seek no territory or special privileges in Korea or anyplace else. We have no aggressive designs in Korea or in any other place in the Far East or elsewhere. And I want that to be perfectly clear to the whole world."[23]

We arrived back in Washington on the morning of October 18. Believing that the Korean crisis was at long last over, I turned my attention to the mounting problems of NATO. It was not going well. We wanted to rearm the Germans, but the French were imposing many difficult restrictions. The question of the size of the American ground force commitment to NATO had not been resolved and was going to be politically controversial, since no American troops had ever been sent to Europe in peacetime.[24]

Prior to my departure for Wake Island the JCS had agreed that we could no longer postpone drafting Ike for the job of Supreme Commander of NATO. Truman personally offered the job to Ike, and Ike accepted. But I don't think he was wildly happy. It would be a wrench to leave Columbia University, even though there were men there who could carry on. Although it was hardly a secret, Ike was not formally appointed to the job of Supreme Commander until December 19, following a vote from the full North Atlantic Council in Brussels. Not long afterward, Montgomery, who had been working tirelessly to build an allied European defense force since 1948, was appointed deputy supreme commander.[25]

On his return to Tokyo, MacArthur resumed direct command of Korean military operations, designed, as he promised at Wake, to wipe out all resistance by Thanksgiving and get the Eighth Army back to Japan by Christmas. His first moves were to increase United States troop commitments to Korea—North Korea, in fact. He ordered the 187th Airborne Regimental Combat team, which had finally arrived in the Far East, to assist the Eighth Army in the capture of Pyongyang (and North Korean officials) by jumping north of the capital on October 20. In addition—to our surprise and concern—he ordered his theater reserve, the Army's 3rd Infantry Division, to land at Wonsan, following behind X Corps, in early November.[26]

However, operations soon began to turn sour. Owing to the long delays imposed on the Eighth Army by MacArthur's decision to deploy X Corps to Wonsan, the pursuit of North Korean forces had bogged down. By the time the Eighth Army closed on Pyongyang, October 20, and the 187th jumped, most North Korean units and governmental officials had fled far to the north, escaping the trap. The Wonsan amphibious landing proved to be anticlimactic and failed to provide MacArthur a dramatic second-act curtain. The ROK I Corps took Wonsan on October 11—nine days ahead of the proposed X Corps assault. Then it was discovered that Wonsan harbor was more heavily mined—with Russian mines—than had been anticipated. Clearing out those vast Russian-laid minefields delayed the X Corps landing by six days. The 1st Marine Division walked ashore, to be greeted by ROK I Corps troops and Marine aviators already operating from nearby airfields, on October 25. Even the Bob Hope USO show beat X Corps to Wonsan![27]

As these events were unfolding, MacArthur, on October 24, issued a new battle order that stood Washington on its ear. His commanders were "enjoined to drive forward toward the north with all speed and with full utilization of all their force." This order ignored the spirit of the September 27 JCS directive to MacArthur that he should "as a matter of policy" use only ROK forces in the Northeast Provinces as he moved toward the borders of Manchuria and Russia.[28]

Up to this point, MacArthur had not actually violated or ignored standing orders or suggested policy. His trip to Formosa and his message to the VFW had been ill-advised and unfortunate, creating needless headaches for the administration. His decision to keep the JCS in the dark about Inchon plans was an act of arrogance. But his October 24 order, while not technically insubordinate, came very close. Owing to the extreme delicacy of the issue, the use of non-ROK forces in the Northeast Provinces should have been cleared in Washington.

After many top-level conferences, the JCS got off a message to

MacArthur that same day, pointing out the policy set forth in our September 27 instructions and questioning his plan. We expressed confidence that he had "sound reasons" for his order, but asked him to tell us what they were, inasmuch as his action was "a matter of concern here." Acheson criticized this message—long after the fact—as "timorous" and our expression "concern here" as "magnificent understatement." To my knowledge, this was the first time that anyone in Washington had ever directly questioned MacArthur's plans or orders in writing; and I for one favored caution and understatement, as did the President. Only nine days had gone by since the amicable Truman-MacArthur meeting on Wake, and the JCS had no desire to tear down what had been built by landing on MacArthur with both feet. At the time the message was drafted (and cleared by State and the White House) there was no suggestion from Acheson that we employ tougher language.[29]

MacArthur's reply the following day was a brief but shocking message. His orders were a matter of "military necessity," he said. ROK forces were too few and their commanders too "emotional" to do the job. More "seasoned and stabilized" commanders were essential. He saw "no conflict" with his September 27 instructions, since those instructions clearly stated they were not "final" and could "require modification in accordance with developments." Moreover, Marshall's message of September 30 ("We want you to feel unhampered tactically and strategically to proceed north of the 38th parallel") gave him latitude beyond his September 27 instructions. Finally, he concluded with a touch of asperity, "This entire subject was covered in my conference at Wake Island."[30]

This was an evasive, if not untruthful, response. While it was true that his September 27 orders were not considered final and were subject to modification, such changes were to come from Washington, not to be made unilaterally in the field. Marshall's order of September 30 pertained only to localized action near the 38th parallel, not to a sweeping drive to the borders. To my knowledge, no one at Wake Island discussed a change in policy to allow United States forces to go into the Northeast Provinces. I am certain the subject was never raised. Collins later correctly said that this exchange with MacArthur led the JCS "to fear that just as he violated a policy in this case without consulting us, perhaps the thing might be done in some other instance of a more serious nature."[31]

As in the case of the Inchon plan, it was really too late for the JCS to do anything about the order. On the west side of Korea, MacArthur had already sent a strong mixed force of American (Church's 24th Division), British (27th Commonwealth Brigade) and ROK's (1st, 6th, 7th and 8th divisions) fanning north and west toward the Yalu River.* On the east coast he canceled the U.S. 7th Division landing at Wonsan and put it

* Elements of the 24th Division reached Chonggo-dong—eighteen miles from the Yalu River at Sinuiju—the closest any American units got to the Yalu River on this drive.[32]

ashore 105 miles farther northeast at Iwon, about 160 miles southwest of the Soviet border. Due west of Iwon, the Marines from Wonsan were advancing northward toward the Chosen reservoir area, which was about seventy miles south of the Yalu River. In sum, major U.S. ground forces—the 24th Division in the west, the 1st Marine Division in the center and the 7th Division in the east—were advancing ever closer to the Chinese communist and Soviet borders.[33]

For a while—a very little while—it appeared that MacArthur would get away with it and have a stirring third-act curtain. However, on October 25, the day after MacArthur issued his order to drive north with all speed and force, units of both the Eighth Army and the X Corps took a few Chinese POW's. These POW's were from "regular" Chinese units and under interrogation revealed that the Chinese had intervened in large numbers. At first Willoughby, MacArthur's intelligence chief in Tokyo, scoffed and discounted the intelligence, arguing that "the auspicious time for intervention has long since passed."[34]

Then disaster struck. On October 26, the Chinese regulars hit the ROK 6th and 8th divisions near Onjong. The divisions collapsed and fled. About the same time, the Chinese struck the ROK 1st Division, advancing with the U.S. 24th Division, near Unsan. Confusion reigned. The 1st Cavalry Division, in reserve, was ordered forward. On November 1, elements of the 8th Cavalry Regiment were cut off and annihilated. Walker wisely ordered the general advance halted and got the bulk of his forces into a defensive position behind the Chongchon River, keeping a small bridgehead.[35]

If ever there was a time for military caution, it was now. The drive by non-Korean forces toward the Yalu had been blunted by savage attacks from what were obviously well-trained and well-led Chinese communist regulars. How many Red Chinese had actually been committed to North Korea was not known. Nor did we have any idea what their military objective might be.

FIFTY-EIGHT

The next sixty days—the months of November and December 1950—were among the most trying of my professional career, more so than the Bulge. The war in Korea abruptly turned from victory to humiliating defeat, one of the worst in our history. MacArthur lost control of the battle and his emotions, leading Washington to lose all confidence in him. Throughout the ordeal we believed it likely that a global war with Russia could erupt at any hour, that the free world was poised on the brink of catastrophe.

The JCS and NSC met in almost continuous session, weighing alternatives and options, drafting directives or discussing the unthinkable prospects of nuclear war. Armageddon. Our deliberations over those sixty days would make a book in itself.[1]

Dean Acheson has written that during this period "none of us, myself included," served the President "as he was entitled to be served." He went on to say that "all the President's advisers . . . civilian and military, knew that something was badly wrong, though what it was, how to find out, and what to do about it they muffed." He is archly critical of the military, especially the JCS. He wrote that we "hesitated" and "wavered" and lost the chance of averting the military disaster in Korea. In one instance he is right.[2]

The news that Chinese Regular Army forces had been employed in combat in North Korea initially caused far graver worry in Washington than it did in Tokyo. MacArthur and his staff were principally concerned with tactical assessments. How many? How effective? We were concerned on a higher and broader level. What did it mean strategically? Was it unilateral or had Moscow ordered the Chinese to intervene? Would the Kremlin support the Red Chinese with air or naval power—submarines perhaps? Would the Soviets themselves overtly intervene in North Korea? Would they overrun Berlin and then all of Western Europe? Was this, in fact, the beginning of World War III?

With little or no solid intelligence to guide them, strategists and analysts at State, CIA and Defense began drawing up new appraisals and recommendations. All agencies agreed that Chinese communist intervention in North Korea had dramatically increased the risk of global war with the Soviets. A CIA-generated "National Intelligence Estimate" of November 8 concluded with these somber words: "The fact that both the Chinese Communists and the USSR have accepted an increased risk of general war indicates that the Kremlin is ready to force a showdown with the West at an early date or that circumstances have forced them to take that risk."[3]

We still believed that unilateral action by Red China in North Korea was improbable. Moscow had dictated the intervention. Hence Moscow, for whatever reason, was now willing to run the risk of global war. Inasmuch as we were still militarily unprepared for global war—we still could not save Western Europe—our overriding concern was to avoid global war with the Soviets. Facing the prospect of global war at any hour, to the JCS Korea was comparatively a minor irritation. We still held to the view that the sooner we got out the better and that, above all, we should not let the war "spread" to involve us in a general war with Red China. Moscow was the real enemy. Korea was a diversion; a war with China would be the ultimate diversion.

We thus took a cautious and conservative view of Korea. We did not want to send more troops there, and only those machines and equipment that were absolutely needed to wind it up. Every infantryman, round of ammunition or aircraft that went to Korea meant a delay in the far more important task of arming NATO to defend Western Europe. To prevent the war from "spreading," we continued to insist that our air and naval forces steer well clear of Chinese communist and Soviet borders.

A major consideration during this period was the outlook of our allies, in particular Britain, which had made a strong commitment to NATO—indeed, had initiated the mutual Western European defense system. Britain was no longer the powerful nation of the old days, yet she had been our strongest ally in World War II and the ties were still close. We needed the British Isles for a place to base our nuclear retaliatory force and, if it came down to it, as a staging base for the ultimate invasion of a Soviet-overrun Europe. Thus, as in World War II, we viewed Britain as an equal partner, and at all times her views were given full consideration in Washington.

The British had supported our decision to commit military forces in Korea. Even though she was hard pressed economically to meet commitments to NATO, she had contributed an infantry brigade to the Korean War. The British military chiefs shared the JCS view that the war should not spread to Red China. In fact, if anything, they were more insistent on that point than we were. War with Red China was not only war with the wrong enemy, it could very well lose Britain her Hong Kong colony, a vital cog in the wheels of her economy.

These views on Korea ran counter to those of MacArthur. He was a local theater commander. He had a war on his hands. His aim was victory. He quite naturally wanted all the power at our disposal to complete his job. He resented any restrictions that interfered with his goals. Because of the new situation in Korea, it was difficult for him to understand the need for building NATO. There was no war in Europe—yet. He thought, as he did in World War II, that the British had too much influence in Washington. I could understand his point of view. In the ETO, I had wanted almost everything directed to the Twelfth Army Group, even at Monty's expense. On a lower level, Patton had demanded everything for *his* army. It is a remarkable field commander who can rise above "localitis."

When the Chinese intervened, MacArthur was still operating under JCS orders of September 27 to destroy the North Korean Army. Our follow-up orders of October 9 had authorized him in the event of intervention of major Chinese communist units in North Korea to continue the action as long as there seemed "a reasonable chance of success." By November 2, he and Willoughby had concluded that while the Chinese had the *capability* of committing huge numbers of forces in North Korea they had in fact sent only about 16,500 across the Yalu. In Peking's words, these were "volunteers" to "protect" the hydroelectric plants along the Yalu, which provided electricity to Manchuria. As we have seen, unknown to MacArthur, there were already some 180,000 regular Chinese communist troops in Korea.[4]

Considering the damage inflicted on the Eighth Army, MacArthur's estimate of 16,500 "volunteers" seemed to be a casual and rosy picture of what was going on. Accordingly, on November 3, the JCS queried him: "Request earliest your interim appreciation of the situation in Korea and its implications in light of what appears to be overt intervention in Korea by Chinese Communist units." The next day MacArthur replied in a "don't worry" tone. While it was "impossible at this time to authoritatively appraise" the exact extent of Chinese communist intervention in Korea, he said, he doubted the communists had made or would make a major commitment of ground forces. Full-scale overt intervention would "represent a momentous decision of the gravest international importance." It was a "distinct possibility," he said. However: "There are many fundamental logical reasons against it," and there was not "sufficient evidence" to confirm it. More likely, MacArthur said, the Red Chinese intervention was merely a low-key covert or "volunteer" operation designed only to fight ROK's and to "salvage something from the wreckage." He concluded by recommending against "hasty conclusions which might be premature."[5]

This message was so utterly reassuring that the JCS temporarily dropped their guard. I continued with a brief leave: two days hunting in Connecticut, followed by two days of work (Sunday, November 5 and

Monday, November 6) on my long-overdue book on World War II, *A Soldier's Story,* which was then scheduled to be serialized in *Life* in the spring of 1951 and published in book form later in the year.[6]

So self-confident was MacArthur that he continued with plans to drive all communist forces from North Korea. The plan was as follows. Commencing about November 5, he would launch a massive air attack in North Korea, an all-out two-week effort in which, he said, "combat crews are to be flown to exhaustion if necessary." His purpose was to "isolate the battlefield" and destroy every "installation, factory, city and village" within it. In addition, to prevent any more Chinese communists from entering Korea, his aircraft would destroy "the Korean ends" of international bridges over the Manchurian border, but without crossing the border itself. Hard on the heels of the two-week air attack, about November 15, he would launch a ground offensive that would take his UN forces (including U.S. troops) to the Yalu River and finish the war.[7]

This plan in its entirety was not formally submitted to the JCS for approval. It came in bits and pieces via lower level telecon exchanges between the Army Department and Tokyo. Had the plan been formally submitted all of a piece, as it should have been, the JCS would have been compelled to examine it in detail. Without doubt, the JCS would have raised the strongest reservations about bombing the "Korean ends" of the Yalu bridges. This aspect of the plan violated the spirit of our previous instructions to MacArthur to stay well clear of all borders. It was certain to draw a strong protest from the British and was likely to evoke an unwanted retaliatory response from the Chinese and possibly the Russians.

Without formal notification to the JCS, on November 6 MacArthur gave orders to his air commander, George E. Stratemeyer, to commence the air offensive with a B-29 bombing attack on the bridges at Sinuiju-Antung on the Yalu River. Recognizing the extreme sensitivity of the orders, Stratemeyer had the good sense to telephone Hoyt Vandenberg in the Pentagon to alert him. Thunderstruck at the news, Van immediately conveyed the word to Air Secretary Finletter, who in turn went immediately to Undersecretary of Defense Bob Lovett. Lovett raced to the State Department to consult with Acheson and Rusk. Acheson was appalled and determined at once that the mission be canceled. Among other reasons, the United States was at that very moment trying to get the UN to pass a resolution calling for a halt to Chinese communist aggression in Korea. If American bombs fell into Manchuria, it would surely jeopardize the resolution.

Acheson called the President, who had gone to Independence, Missouri, to vote on the next day, Tuesday, November 7. Truman, and then Marshall, agreed the order was unwise. Truman would only approve the bombing if there were an immediate and grave threat to the safety of MacArthur's forces. The President directed that the attack be canceled and that MacArthur be asked to explain why he found this dangerous step so necessary. A mere one hour and twenty minutes before the bombers were to take off from Japan, the JCS, acting on Truman's instructions, sent MacArthur the following blunt message: "Until further orders postpone all bombing of targets within five miles of Manchurian border. Urgently need your estimation of situation and reason for ordering bombing Yalu River bridges."[8]

I was still on leave that day in Quarters One working on my book. Aides called to keep me informed on what was transpiring and to read the text of the message to MacArthur. I concurred entirely with the action taken, but I knew it was bound to elicit a protest from MacArthur and I mentally braced for it. This was the first time Washington had ever directly (or even indirectly) countermanded a MacArthur order. It may have been the first time the JCS had ever overridden a theater commander on a tactical operation.

Neither I nor anyone else in Washington was in any way prepared for the ferocity of the blast that came back from MacArthur about eight o'clock that night. In the first place, the first two sentences of his message amounted to a complete about-face of his forces estimate of November 4 and caused the most profound shock in Washington: "Men and material in large force are pouring across all bridges over the Yalu from Manchuria. This movement not only jeopardizes but threatens the ultimate destruction of the forces under my command." Hearing this, I was stunned. This was a whole new kettle of fish: massive Chinese communist intervention. I immediately left for the Pentagon.[9]

The rest of the message was no less disturbing in tone and substance. "The only way to stop this reinforcement of the enemy is the destruction of these bridges and the subjection of all installations in the north area supporting the enemy advance to the maximum of our air destruction. Every hour that this is postponed will be paid for dearly in American and other United Nations blood. The main crossing at Sinuiju has to be hit within the next few hours and the mission is already being mounted. Under the gravest protest that I can make, I am suspending this strike and carrying out your instructions. . . . I cannot overemphasize the disastrous effect, both physical and psychological, that will result from the restriction which you are imposing." He insisted that the matter be brought to the immediate attention of the President, "as I believe your instructions may well result in a calamity of major proportion for which I cannot accept the responsibility without his personal and direct understanding of the situation."

Apart from the shocking news that his complete command might now be destroyed by Chinese communists, this message said, in effect, that the JCS were a bunch of nitwits and that MacArthur would not accept orders from anyone but the President on this matter. The way the message was phrased, it was not insubordinate, but it was a grave insult to men who were his legal superiors, including George Marshall.

This message led to an extraordinary meeting that very same night in the JCS war room. By nine-twenty, present were: Marshall, Lovett, the JCS (with Haislip substituting for Collins), Al Gruenther and four other admirals, generals or colonels; from State: Acheson, Rusk, H. Freeman Matthews and John D. Hickerson. Inasmuch as the minutes of this meeting remain classified, little or nothing has been written about it. Yet I think it was one of the most important meetings of the Korean War.[10]

When we met we also had on hand another of MacArthur's public "communiqués," issued that day from Tokyo. It was typical MacArthur bombast, unnecessarily belligerent in tone and, in my view, better left unsaid. He reported, quite prematurely we thought, the defeat and destruction of the North Korean armies, then went on to deal with the Chinese communist intervention. He charged that the communists had "committed one of the most offensive acts of international lawlessness of historic record by moving, without any notice of belligerency, elements of alien Communist forces across the Yalu River into North Korea and massing a great concentration of possible reinforcing divisions with adequate supply behind the privileged sanctuary of the adjacent Manchurian border." Whether these reserves would be committed to battle, he said, remained to be seen and was a matter of gravest international significance. (This was the first time I saw the phrase "privileged sanctuary" but not by any means the last.)[11]

First we had to deal with MacArthur's cable as a matter of urgency. Since he had said he must bomb the bridges or face destruction of his forces, in lieu of Truman's earlier guidance on the matter we had little choice but to authorize the mission, whatever the consequences. I telephoned the President to get his approval, reading him the complete text of MacArthur's message. Truman agreed that we should give MacArthur a "go-ahead." The conferees at the table then drafted a message to MacArthur which, as Acheson later noted, was tinged with polite skepticism.[12]

We noted first and pointedly that the "situation depicted" was now "considerably changed" from his last (rosy) report of November 4. We went on to say: "We agree that the destruction of the Yalu bridges would contribute materially to the security of the forces under your command unless this action resulted in increased Chinese Communist effort and even Soviet contribution in response to what they might well construe as an attack on Manchuria. Such a result would not only endanger your forces but would enlarge the area of conflict and U.S. involvement to a most dangerous degree. However in view of your first sentence [troops pouring in] . . . you are authorized to go ahead with your planned bombing in Korea near the frontier including targets at Sinuiju and Korean end of Yalu bridges provided that at the time of receipt of this message you still find such action essential to the safety of your forces. The above does not authorize the bombing of any dams or power plants on the Yalu River."

We then iterated the diplomatic delicacy: "Because of necessity of maintaining optimum position with United Nations policy and directive and because it is *vital in the national interest of the U.S. to localize the fighting in Korea*, it is important that extreme care be taken to avoid violation Manchurian territory and airspace and to report promptly hostile action from Manchuria. It is essential that we be kept informed of important changes in situation as they occur and that your estimate as requested in our [November 3 message] be submitted at once." (Italics added.)[13]

Having drafted this message, we then turned to a generalized discussion of the Korean situation. I can say with hindsight that this night we committed the worst possible error. As Acheson said, we sensed that something was badly wrong. MacArthur had exceeded his authority in ordering the bombing of the Sinuiju bridges and had first tried to do it without Washington clearance. It was an indication that he was going off willy-nilly on his own in defiance of established policy. Had it not been for Stratemeyer's back-door alert, we would have been caught completely unaware. The language of his protestations, the complete about-face on the estimate of Chinese forces, indicated instability. Here Acheson was justified in criticizing the JCS. Right then—that night—the JCS should have taken firmest control of the Korean War and dealt with MacArthur bluntly.

We did not. There were two principal reasons. The first was the traditional and customary reluctance of the JCS to meddle in the tactical operations of the theater commander. The second was the lack of clear-cut information on the extent of the Chinese communist threat; the actual situation was still unknown.

Some have argued that in the face of JCS equivocation, Marshall himself should have stepped in with a firm hand. He did not, some say, because he was old and sick and did not have his heart in the job and wanted to quit. I saw not the slightest evidence of this. Marshall withheld action, I am sure, pending decisions of the Chiefs. He did not believe that service secretaries should interfere with field operations or orders. As his biographer Forrest Pogue commented: "If Secretary Stimson had sent 'firm messages' to Ike and MacArthur [in World War II] Marshall would have exploded."[14]

That night we examined what ought to be done in the "worst possible case": massive Chinese intervention. This led to a discussion of the possibility of a pullback of MacArthur's forces to the narrow "waist" of Korea, along a line roughly Pyongyang-Wonsan, together with a concurrent diplomatic drive to arrange a cease-fire. Militarily, this would remove MacArthur's advance elements from immediate danger of a severe, perhaps decisive, Chinese onslaught and enable him to consolidate X Corps into the Eighth Army. Although the line across the waist would be thinly held, it would eliminate the then considerable gaps between Eighth Army and X Corps and establish a single unified and cohesive ground force, which might be deployed in a more conventional defensive posture, backed up with proper corps and army artillery, reserves, and a consolidated tactical air force.

There were, of course, several major negatives inherent in this plan. First, it would surrender territory gained at considerable cost. No military man likes to surrender territory he has paid for in blood unless he is absolutely compelled to. Second, it would be surrendering territory before we were absolutely certain the Chinese communists had the power and skill to overpower us, regardless of numbers. There was still considerable doubt about the fighting quality of the lightly equipped Red Chinese soldier in the face of massed and coordinated artillery and tactical air support. Third, it would be a "retreat," with all the psychological disadvantages entailed, both within our own forces and worldwide. We had vowed to unify Korea and hold democratic elections. A retreat would be admission of failure, backing down to communism. In the Far East and elsewhere, we would lose face among those peoples not under communist control, with perhaps dire long-term consequences. We were particularly concerned about the impact of a retreat on the ROK Army, which had ultimately to assume military responsibility for a free Korea. We knew the ROK's to be irrationally afraid of the Chinese. If they saw us retreating in the face of the Chinese, they might forever lose the will to fight, presenting us with a nearly insoluble long-range Korean security problem. Finally, ordering MacArthur to retreat from 7,000 miles away was certain to evoke another burst of outrage, perhaps a tumultuous resignation and angry public charges of appeasement.

The official JCS historians wrote that we conferees reached "a consensus in favor of a withdrawal to the 'waist' of Korea followed by a search for a political solution," but that "no formal recommendations to this effect were made." That is the way I recall it. Assuming massive Chinese intervention, the positives of a withdrawal outweighed the negatives. Thus our initial instincts were correct: pull back and seek a diplomatic cease-fire at the earliest possible date, regardless of the consequences. But beyond reaching a "consensus," we did nothing about it. It was 11:35 P.M. when we broke up, and everybody was punchy from a long and taxing day. Many times later I wished that we had had the stamina that night to put that recommendation in writing to the President and get the orders out to MacArthur.[15]

On the following day, November 7, I again remained at Quarters One on leave to work on my book, keeping in close touch with the situation by phone. We received several messages from MacArthur that day. The first had a note of hysteria, like the one the day before:

> Hostile planes are operating from base west of the Yalu River against our forces in North Korea. These planes are appearing in increasing numbers.

> The distance from the Yalu to the main line of contact is so short that it is almost impossible to deal effectively with the hit and run tactics now being employed. The present restrictions imposed on my area of operations provide a complete sanctuary for hostile air immediately upon their crossing the Manchurian-North Korean border. The effect of this abnormal condition upon the morale and combat efficiency of both air and ground troops is major. Unless corrective measures are promptly taken this factor can assume decisive proportions. Request instructions for dealing with this new and threatening development.[16]

We learned subsequently that the aircraft he was referring to were Soviet-made Migs, piloted by Russian-trained Red Chinese pilots. The appearance of these aircraft represented an "escalation" of the Korean War into a new and dangerous dimension. What MacArthur wished us to do was to lift the restrictions on crossing the Manchurian border so that his pilots could counter the threat with "hot pursuit." This presented us with a difficult dilemma. In this instance, militarily, hot pursuit seemed justified. No communist seeking to kill Americans should have been granted the advantage of a "sanctuary" (or "privileged sanctuary"). But hot pursuit might ultimately lead to that which we feared most: a gradual widening of the war with China or even global war with Russia.

The JCS agreed with MacArthur that the communists should not be provided a sanctuary. In our deliberations we decided that MacArthur's planes should be permitted to pursue enemy planes "six or eight" miles inside Manchuria. This was sufficient distance for our planes to react to a hit-and-run attack and have a good chance of bringing the enemy down or of shooting up their planes on the advance airfields. We felt that if enough kills could be made on the as-yet small and unskilled Red Chinese Air Force, it might discourage them and compel a general withdrawal. But this was a matter of profound sensitivity, which only the President (still in Missouri) could resolve. The JCS cabled MacArthur: "Situation and urgent necessity corrective measures being presented for highest United States level consideration."[17]

Two other messages that day from MacArthur were far less hysterical. In fact, they seemed to indicate that things were not so bad after all. In response to our request of the night before for new estimates of the situation, he replied that his optimistic estimate of November 4 had been "confirmed." That is, rather than massive open Chinese communist intervention, the intrusion was more likely to be on a smaller covert scale. However, he went on, the intervention thus far had been of sufficient magnitude to have "seized the initiative" in the Eighth Army sector and "materially slowed" X Corps operations. If the "augmentation" continued, he concluded, it could well make further "advance" impossible and even force a "movement in retrograde" (retreat). That was why it was so "essential" to bomb the Yalu River bridges.[18]

Suddenly there was no more scary talk of men and materiel "pouring" over the Yalu bridges in force sufficient to destroy MacArthur's command. In fact, he appeared so confident of his ability to handle the situation that he was planning to go ahead with the planned ground offensive to take the measure of enemy strength. "An effort will be made in the west [Eighth Army] sector in due course of time, possibly within ten days, to again assume the initiative provided the flow of enemy reinforcements can be checked." As we were later to learn, he had already brought such strong pressure to bear on Walker to get the Eighth Army moving again by this date, that Walker had been compelled to defend his pullback in a letter, stating in part, "There has never been and there is now no intention for this Army to take up or remain on a passive perimeter or any other type of defense."[19]

That same day another dispatch from Tokyo reported a startling development, baffling but somewhat encouraging. Chinese and North Korean troops, in a "surprise maneuver," had completely broken contact with Eighth Army and X Corps. They had withdrawn and disappeared. This report, together with MacArthur's estimate, tended to foster the conclusion that the Chinese had only intervened in moderate numbers and that these few had suffered such a bloody nose that they may have lost the taste for battle.[20]

Marshall felt compelled to repeat to MacArthur the extreme delicacy and potentially explosive nature of the Korean War. In a message that same day, he skillfully cloaked his punch in velvet, telling MacArthur that we understood the difficulty of his situation in far-off Korea and reassured him that we were all behind him. But he added: "The discussions and decisions here are heavily weighted with the extremely delicate situation we have before the Security Council of the UN at the present time whose meeting tomorrow may have fateful consequences. . . . We are faced with an extremely grave international problem which could so easily lead to a world disaster." MacArthur's reply was equally velvety. In his message, he reassured Marshall that he was in "complete agreement with the basic concept of localizing, if possible, the Korean struggle."[21]

It had been decided to defer all major decisions on the Korean War for a day or so more, pending an NSC meeting on Thursday, November 9. I returned from leave the day before and, in between a full day of appointments and meetings, reviewed all the messages from MacArthur and the data we had received from Tokyo via telecons. Discounting the two hysterical messages about bombing the bridges and the Manchurian aircraft sanctuary, which could be interpreted as spur-of-the-moment overreaction, the situation as reported by MacArthur seemed to be as follows:

- An undetermined number of regular Chinese communist Army units had come into North Korea to help North Korean units without a declaration of war. MacArthur's guess was that the total number of Chinese was less than 25,000.

• The Chinese troops had hit hard at mostly ROK units, causing panic and forcing Walker to pull the Eighth Army back behind the Chongchon River and slowing Almond's X Corps in the east.

• MacArthur had launched a massive air offensive, designed to isolate the battlefield and flatten everything within it. Additionally, at his insistence, we had given him permission to bomb the Korean ends of the Yalu bridges in order to stop the flow of Chinese reinforcements.

• MacArthur's confidence in his ground forces to handle the Chinese was so high that he was planning to resume the ground offensive by about November 15 and go all the way to the border with both Eighth Army and X Corps.

Influenced by MacArthur's assessment of the situation, I now decided in my own mind that our "consensus" at the Monday night "crisis" meeting to order a pullback to the narrow waist of Korea would be premature and perhaps unwise. All the negatives I enumerated earlier now seemed outweighed by the positives. Although I did not by any means share MacArthur's optimism about what the air offensive could achieve, it seemed to me the actual physical threat to Eighth Army and X Corps had substantially diminished or, on the evidence presented, had not been that great in the first place. There seemed to be more than a reasonable chance of success. It should not be abandoned by "timidity" in Washington. We had to back the man on the scene.

However, the JCS staff was taking a more cautious view. While the planners did not necessarily advocate a pullback to the waist, they had deep reservations about the forthcoming offensive. Their consensus was that MacArthur's forces ought to stay where they were (if they could), avoiding the risk of further and massive Chinese intervention, while our diplomats pursued a cease-fire. Accordingly, on November 8, the JCS cabled MacArthur to request his final views for the NSC meeting on the next day. The message stated that the Chinese intervention had created a new situation and that his mission to destroy the North Korean Army might have to be "reexamined" by the NSC and that "discussion is certain to occur as to what further political approaches can be made toward solution of this new problem."[22]

Back from MacArthur came the most withering blast yet. "I cannot agree," he wrote.

> In my opinion it would be fatal to weaken the fundamental and basic policy of the United Nations to destroy all resisting armed forces in Korea and bring that country into a united and free nation. I believe that with my air power . . . I can deny reinforcements coming across the Yalu in sufficient strength to prevent the destruction of those forces now arrayed against me in North Korea. I plan to launch my attack for this purpose on or about November 15th with the mission of driving to the border and securing all of North Korea. Any program short of this would completely destroy the morale of my forces

> and the psychological consequences would be inestimable. It would condemn us to an indefinite retention of our military forces along difficult defense lines in North Korea and would unquestionably arouse such resentment among the South Koreans that their forces would collapse and might even turn against us. It would therefore necessitate immediately a large increment in foreign troops. That the Chinese Communists after having achieved complete success in establishing themselves in North Korea would abide by any delimitations upon further expansion southward would represent wishful thinking.[23]

He digressed for three paragraphs to vehemently denounce the British, perhaps because of press reports that the British had proposed a *cordon sanitaire*—a narrow demilitarized strip along the border. This proposal, he said, would "appease the Chinese Communists," and "finds its historic precedent in the action taken at Munich." He aimed a barb at Acheson by quoting a U.S. State Department historical study which concluded that Munich had unmistakably demonstrated "the weakness of peaceful efforts towards just settlements in the face of determined aggression." Such action, MacArthur argued, "would carry within itself the germs of its own ultimate destruction" and would be a "tribute to aggression."

The penultimate paragraph was, I presume, addressed to the President:

> To give up any portion of North Korea to the aggression of the Chinese Communists would be the greatest defeat of the free world in recent times. Indeed, to yield to so immoral a proposition would bankrupt our leadership and influence in Asia and render untenable our position both politically and militarily. We would follow clearly in the footsteps of the British who by the appeasement of recognition lost all the respect of all the rest of Asia without gaining that of the Chinese segment. It would not curb deterioration of the present situation into the possibility of general war but would impose upon us the disadvantage of having inevitably to fight such a war if it occurs bereft of the support of countless Asiatics who now believe in us and are eager to fight with us.

He concluded by recommending that the United States press for a UN resolution condemning Chinese communist aggression in Korea and demanding that they withdraw behind their borders "on pain of military sanctions" by the UN if they failed to do so. "I recommend," he signed off, "with all the earnestness that I possess that there be no weakening at this crucial moment and that we press on to complete victory which I believe can be achieved if our determination and indomitable will do not desert us."

We gathered at the White House for the NSC meeting on November 9 at 2:43 P.M. Unfortunately, the President was still in Missouri. The principals in attendance were Acheson, Marshall, Bedell Smith and I. We had a mound of paperwork: State, CIA and JCS position papers, as well as a complete file of MacArthur's dispatches for the last week.[24]

The JCS position paper, as finally drawn, examined three possible courses of action in Korea: "(a) force the action to a successful conclusion in Korea, (b) continue the action on a defensive line short of the Korean border; or (c) withdraw." The first course, the JCS paper went on, "may require some augmentation of military strength in Korea even if the Chinese Communist scale of effort is not materially increased. The second course is apparently feasible now and it might be a temporary expedient pending clarification of the military and political problems raised by Chinese intervention which are as yet unanswered. The third course, withdrawal, if conducted voluntarily would so lower the worldwide prestige of the United States that it would be totally unacceptable."

The JCS recommended as follows:

> Every effort should be expended as a matter of urgency to settle the problem of Chinese Communist intervention in Korea by political means, preferably through the United Nations, to include reassurances to the Chinese Communists with respect to our intent, direct negotiations through our allies and the Interim Committee with the Chinese Communist Government and by other available means. Pending further clarification as to the military objectives of the Chinese Communists and the extent of their political commitments, the missions assigned to the Commander in Chief, United Nations Command, should be kept under review, but should not be changed.[25]

The discussion which followed was discursive. It more or less centered on the courses of action and recommendations in the JCS paper, which I read to the council. I expressed the view that "we should be able to hold in the general area of our present position," but that "there would be an increasing question of how much pressure we could stand without attacking Manchurian bases." Acheson, referring back to our Monday night meeting, asked if there was a better line than the present one. I replied that from a purely military point of view "the farther back the line was the easier it would be to maintain." I added, however, that I "realized that any backward movement of our forces would lose us support and might lose us the South Koreans' will to fight." Marshall expressed concern about how our Korean front "was widely dispersed and thinly spread." I replied that MacArthur had done this "in order to carry out his directive that he was to occupy the whole country and conduct elections." * [26]

* This was, of course, an error on my part, a MacArthurian interpretation of MacArthur's orders, which, thus far, still limited him to destroying the North Korean Army.

The NSC that day approved the recommendations of the JCS. MacArthur would "continue military operations in accordance with current directives." These should be "kept under review, but should not be changed for the present." At the same time, we would continue political and diplomatic action in the UN and elsewhere to demand a prompt withdrawal of Chinese forces from North Korea. We would also intensify our efforts, overt and covert, to find out exactly what the Chinese were up to. Finally, the United States should "develop plans to make its preparations on the basis that the risk of global war has increased." These recommendations were never formally approved by Truman but all were put into effect.[27]

The sensitive issue of "hot pursuit," which the JCS favored, was not discussed at this time. The JCS paper had noted that the communists were permitted to use Manchuria as a "privileged sanctuary," but made no formal recommendation that the restriction be removed. Marshall and Acheson agreed with the unwritten JCS position that our planes should be permitted "hot pursuit" of six to eight miles inside Manchuria. The matter was later followed up privately with our allies and inside the UN, but opposition to it was so overwhelming that Truman ultimately ruled against it, making the policy public on November 16. MacArthur did not like the decision, nor did the JCS.[28]

I have gone to some length to describe what went on from November 2 to November 9 because some historians have overlooked the importance of those days. We read, we sat, we deliberated and, unfortunately, we reached drastically wrong conclusions and decisions. Our initial instincts in the November 6 Monday night Pentagon meeting were correct. Take charge of the war. Order MacArthur to pull back to the waist while our diplomats sought a political solution. At the very least, the Chiefs should have canceled MacArthur's planned offensive. Instead, we let ourselves be misled by MacArthur's wildly erroneous estimates of the situation and his eloquent rhetoric, as well as by too much wishful thinking of our own. And we had adhered too closely to the established tradition of giving the theater commander the utmost latitude.

FIFTY-NINE

In Korea, the fateful military operations proceeded. The all-out air assault pulverized or flattened a great sector of northwest Korea but, as it turned out, missed the massing Chinese troops who were hiding in the hills. Owing to the difficulty of bombing just the Korean ends of the Yalu bridges, only four of twelve were completely severed. This proved to be small hindrance to the Chinese. They quickly threw across pontoon bridges. In any case, the river soon froze over, rendering any bridges unnecessary. The attack of Eighth Army and X Corps, originally scheduled for November 15, was delayed by logistical difficulties.[1]

MacArthur oozed optimism. In a Tokyo meeting on November 17 with the U.S. ambassador to Korea, John J. Muccio, MacArthur stated that he was sure "the Chinese Communists had sent 25,000, and certainly no more than 30,000, soldiers across the border." He went on to say that "they could not possibly have got more over with the surreptitiously covert means used. If they had moved in the open, they would have been detected by our Air Force and our Intelligence." He predicted that the area of North Korea under air assault would unfortunately be "left a desert." The upcoming ground offensive to the border would clear out all North Korean and Chinese communist troops "within ten days." The Eighth Army would soon be on its way back to Japan, leaving X Corps, the ROK's and other UN elements to "stabilize the situation."[2]

The fact of the matter was that by then, according to official Army historian James F. Schnabel, the Chinese communists had moved a total of some 300,000 battle-hardened regular troops of the Fourth Field Army into North Korea. As we have seen, most of them had come over long before MacArthur urged bombing the bridges. In addition, some 65,000 North Korean soldiers had been regrouped and re-equipped and were ready to enter the fighting. Total enemy strength was 365,000. However, Willoughby's final estimate of enemy forces before the attack was 83,000 North Koreans and 40,000 to 80,000 Chinese communists. The failure to detect the true size of the enemy forces was our greatest battlefield intelligence blunder since the Bulge.[3]

There was a final, notable meeting in Washington to review the Korean situation on November 21. It took place in Marshall's private dining room, adjacent to his office, from 12:52 to 2:25 P.M. Present were Marshall, Lovett, Pace, Finletter, Matthews and the JCS, and from State, Acheson and Jessup. Averell Harriman represented Truman. This was our last real chance to stop MacArthur's proposed ground offensive. But by now, although duly apprehensive, we were unanimously in favor of letting him go ahead. MacArthur's most recent estimates reflected the optimism and confidence he had exhibited to Ambassador Muccio three days before. Collins and I expressed concern about the "gap" between Eighth Army and X Corps, as did Acheson, and as had Marshall at our earlier NSC meeting on November 9. But we were still reluctant to meddle in the theater commander's job, leaving the tactical problems to MacArthur. There was a brief and inconclusive discussion of what would happen if the offensive "bogged down," but "no consensus" as to alternative courses.

Most of our discussion focused on how far north MacArthur should be permitted to go in the west and east sectors. Our concern was to avoid a clash at the border which might widen the war. We more or less agreed that in the west—where the Manchurian border lay—he should stop a few miles south of the Yalu and occupy the high ground dominating the river (thus offering a buffer zone or *cordon sanitaire*). In the east—where the Soviet border lay—he should go no farther north than Chongjin, a coastal city about sixty miles south of the Russian border.[4]

On the eve of the offensive, Collins sent out a careful message to MacArthur which had been cleared by State, wherein these proposals were suggested, along with our reasons for them, requesting his comments. This message indirectly amounted to JCS "approval" for the offensive, although this was not specifically stated. Back from MacArthur came another searing blast. He had flown over the Yalu the day before. The terrain dominating the Yalu was "utterly impossible" for the proposed stop line in the west sector. It was imperative to go all the way to the river. In familiar purple prose he warned us of the "disastrous consequences" of failing to push the war to a successful conclusion. The Koreans would regard it as a "betrayal" and other Asians as "weakness reflected from the appeasement of Communist aggression." He dismissed the possibility of Chinese communist intervention in force, repeating the Tokyo view that the time for such intervention was long past: "Had they entered at the time we were beleaguered behind our Pusan perimeter beachhead, the hazard would have been far more grave than it is now that we hold the initiative and have a much smaller area within which to interdict their hostile moves."[5]

Despite our deeply felt concern, we took no further action with regard to this message. The theater commander had flown over the disputed area

—at considerable personal risk—and had arrived at a tactical plan that seemed suitable for the safety of his forces. Once more we adhered to the custom of yielding to the recommendation of the man on the scene.

The ground offensive jumped off on November 24, the day after Thanksgiving. MacArthur launched it with another bombastic—and unnecessarily provocative—communiqué from Tokyo. He spoke grandly of a "massive" UN "compression envelopment" against "the new Red Armies." He boasted that his air forces had "successfully interdicted enemy lines of support . . . so that further reinforcements . . . have been sharply curtailed." The X Corps had been steadily advancing "in a brilliant tactical movement," cutting in two the enemy's territory. Now the Eighth Army would move forward "in an effort to complete the compression and close the vise." He concluded: "If successful this should for all practical purposes end the war." According to his confidant, Courtney Whitney, he told IX Corps commander John B. Coulter what he had told us at Wake Island: "If this operation is successful, I hope we can get the boys home by Christmas."[6]

It is one matter to make a prediction like that in a top-secret meeting with the President and his advisers, quite another to make it on the battlefield with the media close at hand. Inevitably word leaked to reporters, and unfortunately MacArthur's "home by Christmas" made headlines worldwide. The prediction later made MacArthur the subject of considerable ridicule. In his memoirs he attempted to weasel out of it and shift the blame for "home by Christmas" to me: "I told them of General Bradley's desire and hope to have two divisions home by Christmas."[7]

At first all went well. In the Eighth Army, Church's 24th Division moved ahead against little or no resistance a distance of three or four miles in the first few hours. However, shortly after dark on November 25, Chinese regulars hit the ROK II Corps, which was on Eighth Army's right flank. The corps broke and fled, exposing the U.S. 2nd Division. On the left of the front, the ROK 1st Division wavered, endangering the 24th Division. Far to the east in X Corps sector, Red Chinese hit the Marines in force near the Chongjin reservoir. Within forty-eight hours it was clear to Walker and Almond that they had been ambushed by massive Chinese forces and that the entire UN ground force was in danger of piecemeal envelopment.[8]

The gravity of the situation was not immediately clear to the JCS. Press reports on the morning of November 27 were not unnecessarily alarming. *The New York Times,* for example, merely stated that the UN offensive was "stalled." The JCS spent the afternoon going over official reports from Korea and Tokyo. These were not unduly alarming either. That night I proceeded with a long-planned dinner party at Quarters One for French Ambassador and Madame Henri Bonnet.[9]

During the night of November 27-28, we received a rather hysterical message from MacArthur. "The developments resulting from our assault movements have now assumed a clear definition. All hope of localization of the Korean conflict to enemy forces composed of North Korean troops with alien token elements can now be completely abandoned. The Chinese military forces are committed in North Korea in great and ever increasing strength." He once again changed his view of Chinese commitment: "No pretext of minor support under guise of volunteerism or other subterfuge now has slightest validity. We face an entirely new war." He estimated Chinese forces as "approaching 200,000" and North Korean "fragments" at approximately "50,000." (As we now know, he was short of actuality by 115,000 men.) He guessed that the "ultimate objective" of the Chinese was "undoubtedly a decisive effort aimed at the complete destruction of all U.N. forces in Korea."

In an uncharacteristically modest closing paragraph, MacArthur conceded:

> It is quite evident that our present strength of force is not sufficient to meet this undeclared war by the Chinese with the inherent advantages which accrue to them. The resulting situation presents an entirely new picture which broadens the potentialities to world-embracing considerations beyond the sphere of decision by the Theater Commander. This command has done everything humanly possible within its capabilities but is now faced with conditions beyond its control and strength. . . . My plan for the immediate future is to pass from the offensive to the defensive with such local adjustments as may be required by a constantly fluid situation.[10]

I called the President at 0615, November 28, to read him this cable. The morning papers were now screaming disaster. As Truman wrote, I reported to him that while the JCS regarded the situation as "serious," we were "doubtful that it was as much a catastrophe as our newspapers were leading us to believe." I did, however, express one of our gravest concerns. We knew that by then the Chinese communists, with Soviet help, had amassed at least 300 aircraft—including 200 twin-engine bombers—on nearby Manchurian airfields. If the Chinese mounted an all-out air attack, they could inflict heavy damage on our ground and air forces, particularly the latter. Every American airfield in Korea was crammed with planes of all types.[11]

During that morning, the official reports from Korea grew darker and more disturbing. Truman called an extraordinary expanded session of the NSC for the afternoon. In addition to the President and Vice President Barkley, those in attendance were Marshall, Lovett, Pace, Finletter, Matthews, the JCS, Acheson, Rusk, Nitze, Jessup, Stuart Symington (now head of the National Security Resources Board) and Bedell Smith. I sketched in the military situation and referred to MacArthur's message, an indirect appeal for a new directive—now that we were facing "an entirely new war." It was the JCS opinion that since MacArthur had gone on the defensive he needed no immediate new directive. We had to wait and see what happened in the next forty-eight to seventy-two hours. I stressed the Joint Chiefs' greatest concern: a Chinese air attack. As Sherman put it, we could not stay in Korea under air attack without retaliating across the border. But I said the JCS did not believe we should make a pre-emptive strike on the Manchurian airfields. We would have to wait and see what happened.

There were no real decisions made at this meeting. All felt, as Acheson expressed it, that we had moved much closer to danger of general war with the Soviets and that, above all, that war had to be avoided. There was general agreement that we should not make a pre-emptive air attack on Manchuria lest such action provoke the Soviets into intervening in Korea or starting a big war elsewhere on the globe. We should not commit more troops to Korea. On the contrary, as Marshall put it, we should "avoid getting sewed up in Korea" and find a way we could get out "with honor."

In retrospect, I think the most important consensus reached at that meeting was a realization that the long-pending recommendations of the April NSC-68 paper must be implemented. That is to say, the United States must rearm on a fairly grand scale, even if the citizenry "had to give up such things as refrigerators and television," as Stu Symington put it. From this day forward, the momentum for general rearmament gathered steam, and the JCS, while keeping a sharp eye on Korea, submitted and discussed papers calling for ever-greater force levels.[12]

Now, for the first time, the JCS began moving to exercise more direct control over MacArthur's tactical operations. In a JCS meeting the following day, November 29, Sherman, deeply concerned about the Marines in the Changjin reservoir area, virtually demanded that MacArthur be ordered to withdraw the badly exposed X Corps to a "consolidated defense line." What he meant, of course, was a continuous line across the narrow waist of Korea. But Collins and I were still reluctant to give MacArthur direct tactical orders. I kept thinking, What utter confusion could have resulted, for example, if during the Bulge, Marshall, King and Arnold had sent Ike orders to move this corps or that here or there. In a message that day we handled it in this indirect but pointed way: "What are your plans regarding the coordination of operations of the Eighth Army and X Corps and the positioning of X Corps, the units of which appear to us to be exposed?" That we were suggesting a consolidation across the narrow waist was implicit.[13] *

* That same day, Truman called Marshall and instructed that all further messages from the JCS to MacArthur "must be processed through the Secretary of Defense to the President personally." Up to now, I had been informally clearing all important JCS messages to MacArthur with the President, but not always with Marshall. This was the first message to go through the new formal procedure. In almost all cases, I hand-carried these messages to Marshall, who "cleared" most of them by telephone with the President.[14]

The response we received to this message was so utterly absurd and insulting that my faith in MacArthur's ability to deal with the military situation eroded sharply. He argued grandiosely that "X Corps geographically threatens the main supply lines of the enemy forces," and that he had diverted some six to eight divisions from the enemy attack on the Eighth Army. He loftily dismissed any "concept" of joining X Corps and Eighth Army in a line across Korea as "quite impracticable," owing to the thinness of his forces, logistical difficulties and the north-south mountain ranges. Instead, he would withdraw X Corps into a perimeter in the Hamhung-Wonsan sector. In sum, MacArthur rejected out of hand any discussion of a line across Korea. I was outraged by this message and felt that MacArthur treated the JCS as if we were children.[15]

Before we could even draft a response to this insulting dispatch, another arrived from MacArthur. More hysteria. His message stated that Chinese communist troops continued to flow into North Korea, "despite all interdiction of our air command." He said that owing to this fact, "it is quite evident that the 8th Army will successively have to continue to replace to the rear" and that "everything leads to the conclusion that the Chinese forces have as their objective the complete destruction of United Nations forces and the security of all of Korea."[16]

We set about responding to both these messages in one. Our reply was the strongest possible suggestion to unite Eighth Army and X Corps that we could make, short of a direct order:

> Your plan for withdrawal of X Corps into the Hamhung-Wonsan sector as enemy pressure develops and your anticipation of probable further successive displacements to the rear by the 8th Army are causing increased concern here. Experience to date in Korea, particularly during the last few days, indicates that enemy can operate strong forces through difficult mountain terrain. The development of a progressively widening gap between your forces on the east and west coasts would afford the enemy opportunity to move considerable forces southward between the 8th Army and X Corps. We feel that the elements of the X Corps must be extricated from their exposed positions as soon as practicable and that then the forces on the two coasts should be sufficiently coordinated to prevent large enemy forces from passing between them or outflanking either of them.

We unfortunately diluted the force of the message by adding: "The JCS hope you will take the foregoing into consideration in the formulation of future plans." However, when I cleared this with Marshall, he reinforced our suggestion to unite Eighth Army and X Corps by adding a sentence telling MacArthur that he could now "ignore" trying to hold the "entire region northeast of the waist of Korea." (In other words, he was free to withdraw X Corps to the waist and unite it with Eighth Army.)[17]

At this time, we received another message from MacArthur that disturbed all of us profoundly. It suggested that MacArthur was monumentally stupid, had gone mad or had rejected the JCS and administration policy to keep the war localized and was willing to risk an all-out war with China, regardless of the consequences. He urged that we accept a long-standing offer from Chiang Kai-shek to send some 33,000 troops to Korea. "The Chinese Armies on Formosa," he said, "represent the only source of potential trained reinforcements available for early commitment. Troops drawn from this source could be landed in Korea in approximately 14 days and a much larger force than originally offered would undoubtedly be made available if desired." He "strongly recommended" that he be authorized to deal directly with Chiang Kai-shek to arrange the movement and incorporation of these units into his command.[18]

This message came at a time when our allies in the United Nations were nearly panicked, both over the dire prospect of a general war with China and the even more dire prospect of a global holocaust. Both the British and the French were opposed to any step that would exacerbate the situation in the Far East vis-à-vis China. A proposal to bring Chiang's troops to Korea would surely provoke the Chinese communists, perhaps to the point of launching an air attack on our forces in Korea. This in turn would compel us in self-defense to cross the borders with aircraft to defend our troops, all of which could widen the war and perhaps even lead to Soviet intervention. Moreover, the appearance of Chiang's troops in Korea might very well invite a Chinese communist invasion of Formosa, which, considering our dire circumstances, had a very good chance of success.[19]

Our response to this suggestion was deliberately moderate:

> Your proposal . . . is being considered. It involves world-wide consequences. We shall have to consider the possibility that it would disrupt the united position of the nations associated with us in the United Nations, and leave us isolated. It may be wholly unacceptable to the Commonwealth countries to have their forces employed with Nationalist Chinese. It might extend hostilities to Formosa and other areas. Incidentally our position of leadership in the Far East is being most seriously compromised in the United Nations. The utmost care will be necessary to avoid the disruption of the essential allied line-up in that organization.[20]

Then—almost unbelievably—MacArthur launched a public attack on administration policy. In a long question-and-answer interview in the conservative anti-administration newsweekly *U.S. News & World Report,* dated December 1, MacArthur criticized the limitations Truman had placed on "hot pursuit" and bombing Manchurian bases as "an enormous handicap, without precedent in history." On the same date, in a message to Hugh Baillie, president of United Press, he came close to impugning the motives of our allies, suggesting that their "selfish" and "short-sighted" vision had been responsible for withholding support for his forces.[21]

These shocking public utterances absolutely infuriated Truman. For the second time in three months, he considered relieving General MacArthur of command. He later wrote: "I should have relieved General MacArthur then and there. The reason I did not was that I did not wish to have it appear as if he were being relieved because the offensive failed. I have never believed in going back on people when luck is against them, and I did not intend to do it now. Nor did I want to reprimand the general, but he had to be told that the kinds of public statements which he had been making were out of order."[22]

Truman's mood was registered more pungently in a desk calendar entry on November 30: "General MacArthur as usual has been shooting off his mouth. . . . I must defend him and save his face even if he has tried on various and numerous occasions to cut mine off. But I must stand by my subordinates."[23]

To muzzle MacArthur, Truman drafted an extraordinary order, which would also apply to almost everyone in government. In light of the present critical international situation, he wanted all officials to take immediate steps to "reduce the number of public speeches pertaining to foreign or military policy." No speech, press release or other public statement pertaining to foreign policy was to be released without prior clearance at State and the White House. The purpose, Truman stated, was to insure that "information made public is accurate and fully in accord with the policies of the United States Government." State and Defense officials overseas, he continued, were to be ordered "to exercise extreme caution" in public statements and to "refrain from direct communication" with newspapers, magazines or other media in the United States.

We relayed this presidential directive to MacArthur through military channels on December 6. Almost immediately he appeared to challenge it by sending us a long, bombastic communiqué for formal clearance in which he denied media assertions that his command had suffered a rout and blamed the intelligence failure on others. "Losses inflicted on the enemy have been staggering," he said. The JCS believed this communiqué was far out of line and killed it with this sharp rebuke: "Discussions of foreign and military policy, references to press comments, and comments relative to political or domestic matters should not be included in military communiqués issued in the field."[24]

These instructions did in fact muzzle MacArthur for a good three months. But it was a subsequent violation of this presidential directive that led to his dismissal.

By December 1, it was clear that we faced a grave situation in Korea. In the west sector, Walker's Eighth Army fell back to the Chongchon

River, paused briefly, then began fighting its way farther south toward Pyongyang. The U.S. 2nd Division—that which we had earmarked for early redeployment to Europe—was so badly shattered it had to be sent to the rear for reorganization. In the east sector, the U.S. 7th Division fell back toward Hungnam, while the Marines commenced a heroic retreat from the Changjin reservoir area toward the east coast. As we feared, the Chinese began infiltrating the gap between Eighth Army and X Corps, and threatening Wonsan.[25]

Press reports continued to give the impression that UN forces had suffered a major catastrophe. The impression was far from accurate. The ROK II Corps and the U.S. 2nd Division had been badly mauled; but, as Ridgway observed later, both Eighth Army and X Corps had "performed a magnificent withdrawal in the face of unremitting attacks by overwhelmingly superior forces" and "thanks to some extremely gallant fighting, particularly by the 1st Marines and the U.S. 2nd Division," losses had been kept to a minimum.[26]

On December 3, in response to our strong suggestion that MacArthur unite Eighth Army and X Corps, we received a long and gloomy reply. He refused to consider the unification of those forces, repeating the arguments he had put forth earlier. "There is no practicability, nor would any benefit accrue thereby, to unite the forces of 8th Army and X Corps," he pronounced grandly. He said he did not believe we fully comprehended what basic changes had been wrought by the Chinese intervention. He now faced twenty-six Red Chinese divisions with a minimum of 200,000 men in reserve, plus the North Korean Army "remnants."

He went on to paint the darkest possible picture. "The situation with 8th Army," he said, "becomes increasingly critical." He thought Walker would have to retreat all the way to Seoul. The X Corps was being withdrawn into the Hamhung area as rapidly as possible. He said that unless ground reinforcements "of the greatest magnitude" were promptly supplied him, the UN command, which was "mentally fatigued and physically battered," would be forced into successive withdrawals or forced into beachhead bastions, with little hope of anything but defense. Unless there was some positive and immediate action on our part, he could only foresee "steady attrition leading to final destruction."[27]

To those of us who had fought in the ETO and who had weathered the massive Bulge counterattack, this message and all it conveyed was profoundly dismaying. It seemed to say MacArthur was throwing in the towel without the slightest effort to put up a fight. From other reports, we knew that after Walker abandoned Pyongyang the Chinese, as Ridgway put it, "broke contact and showed no immediate appetite for pursuit." Why then was the Eighth Army running to the rear so hard and fast? Why hadn't MacArthur gone to Korea to steady Walker and to rally the troops with his famous rhetoric? It was disgraceful.[28]

The State Department shared our dismay. At a meeting of Acheson, James Webb, Rusk and others, Rusk wondered if "the military were in the frame of mind for the best possible effort which we could make" in Korea. He thought that the military in Korea "all appear to be extremely dejected." Could we not "muster our best effort and spirit together to put up the best possible fight" in one or two points in Korea? The British in World War II had held when the odds seemed overwhelmingly against them. Why couldn't we? We should, at minimum, make the Chinese communists pay a high price for throwing us out of Korea. He suggested that perhaps Joe Collins ought to take over as the field commander, leaving MacArthur to spend full time on matters in Japan.[29]

Here again Marshall, the JCS and I failed the President. Rusk was right. MacArthur had obviously lost control of the battlefield and possibly his nerves. A new hand was needed on the battlefield—not Joe Collins but a Van Fleet or a Ridgway. It would have been a cruel thing to do, but we should have relieved Walker and *ordered* MacArthur to consolidate X Corps into the Eighth Army. At the very least we should have sent MacArthur a firm and ringing directive telling him to find a line—possibly the waist—and hold. The Chinese were not supermen. As they moved south, their supply lines were extending while ours contracted, giving us a growing logistical advantage. We also still had the incalculable advantage of complete air supremacy over all of Korea. In the Eighth Army, we had enormously superior firepower in our artillery and tanks.

Ridgway, a blunt and outspoken soldier, had been harshly critical of JCS failure at this point. The problem, he thought, was that the JCS held MacArthur in "almost superstitious awe." He was a "larger than life military figure who had so often been right when everyone else had been wrong" that we were afraid to challenge him. Ridgway put it this way: "Too much blame cannot be attached to his superiors and his colleagues who, after the blazing success at Inchon, hesitated to question MacArthur's military judgment or even the hazardous disposition of his forces."[30]

At the time, Ridgway did not hesitate to express his own views. During one very long meeting he boiled over. He later wrote that everyone was talking the subject to death, "with no one willing to issue a flat order to the Far East Commander to correct a state of affairs that was going rapidly from bad to disastrous. Yet the responsibility and authority clearly resided right there in the room, and my own conscience finally overcame my discretion. Having secured permission to speak I blurted out—perhaps too bluntly but with deep feeling—that I felt we had already spent too damn much time on debate and that immediate action was needed. We owed it, I insisted, to the men in the field and to the God to whom we must answer for those men's lives to stop talking and to act." The director of the joint staff, Arthur Davis, slipped Ridgway a note which said, "I am proud to know you." Later, Davis told Ridgway that Sherman had had virtually the same reaction and wanted Ridgway to know it.

After that meeting, Ridgway recalled, he approached Hoyt Vandenberg, whom he had known since West Point days. "Why don't the Joint Chiefs send orders to MacArthur and *tell* him what to do?" Van shook his head and said, "What good would that do? He wouldn't obey the orders. What *can* we do?" Ridgway exploded and said, "You can relieve any commander who won't obey orders, can't you?" Van looked at Ridgway "both puzzled and amazed" and silently walked away.[31]

Ridgway was absolutely right that we did indeed talk the subject to death. On Friday, December 1, and Sunday, December 3, we held joint State-Defense crisis meetings in the JCS War Room, which totaled some six hours of steady talk.* These discussions ranged worldwide in scope and subject and became very complicated and discursive. (It was at the four-hour December 3 meeting that Ridgway had exploded.)[32]

The upshot was that militarily we more or less accepted MacArthur's defeatist outlook of the situation and his proposed plans, which by then were to withdraw his forces into three "beachheads": Hamhung, Seoul-Inchon and Pusan. Following the December 3 meeting, we drafted this brief message: "We consider that the preservation of your forces is now the primary consideration. Consolidation of forces into beachheads is concurred in." I took it to the White House for Truman's approval, which he gave without modification.[33]

This was the low point of the Korean War—lower even than the grim days in the Pusan perimeter. Instead of giving MacArthur firm and ringing orders to try to turn things around, we had merely "concurred" in his beachhead perimeter plan. In the meantime, we would attempt to arrange some kind of cease-fire—if the price wasn't too high. If forced into a "Dunkirk" at our three beachheads, we would make an orderly fighting evacuation, taking the ROK's and all our equipment with us, even if the evacuation required striking at Manchurian air bases.[34]

At a November 30 press conference, Truman had inadvertently put his foot in his mouth, causing universal consternation. In response to a reporter's question, Truman said that "we will take whatever steps are necessary to meet the military situation, just as we always have." Another reporter asked, "Will that include the atomic bomb?" Instead of ducking, Truman said, "That includes every weapon we have." Another reporter chimed in: "Does that mean that there is active consideration of the use of

* On Saturday, December 2, the President and I and many other high military officers kept a long-standing commitment to attend the Army-Navy football game in Philadelphia. On the train to and from Philadelphia, we met with Truman to discuss Korea, and that night, on return to Washington, Marshall, Acheson and I met with the President for two hours more at the White House.

the atomic bomb?" Truman replied, "There has always been active consideration of its use." In response to further probing on the use of the atomic bomb, Truman said, "It is a matter that the military people will have to decide. . . . I am not a military authority that passes on these things. . . . The military commander in the field will have charge of the use of weapons, as he always has."[35]

This statement caused a worldwide furor. Much of what Truman said was wrong. We had indeed studied the possibility of using the atomic bomb in Korea, but the JCS had ruled against it for many reasons. But Truman had created the impression that the decision on whether or not to use the bomb was up to the military field commander—MacArthur. In fact, by law, only the President could authorize the use of the atomic bomb. Later in the day the White House issued a "clarification" on that point. But it was too late. Worldwide headlines proclaimed that the United States was considering using the A-bomb in Korea, and it was up to MacArthur to make that decision.[36]

This caused renewed panic among our allies—especially in the British House of Commons. It brought British Prime Minister Clement R. Attlee and a British delegation winging across the Atlantic for urgent conferences. Attlee was, as Acheson has written, "persistently depressing," a "Job's comforter." Briefing, entertaining and reassuring the British party (among whom was my wartime comrade-in-arms Arthur Tedder, now Lord Tedder, head of the Air Ministry) absorbed the better part of my week from Monday, December 4, to Thursday, December 7.[37]

Fortunately for all concerned, on December 1 Marshall had asked Joe Collins to fly to Tokyo and Korea to make an assessment of the situation. Collins reached Tokyo on December 4, conferred with MacArthur, flew on to Korea and met with Walker and Almond. He found that while the military situation "remained serious, it was no longer critical." The Eighth Army and X Corps were "calm and confident." The Eighth Army was "skillfully executing its planned withdrawal" toward Seoul-Inchon and was in "no immediate danger." He anticipated "no serious trouble" in concentrating and evacuating X Corps. Apart from the ROK's, in the Eighth Army only the U.S. 2nd Division had been "hard hit" and it was being rapidly reconstituted. The three other U.S. divisions (24th, 25th, 1st Cavalry) were in "good shape." In X Corps, the Marines were taking casualties in the withdrawal, but the U.S. 3rd and 7th divisions were also in good shape.

After consultations with Walker and Almond, Collins concluded that the best solution to the existing military problem was to evacuate X Corps from the east coast, land it at Pusan, whence it would (at last!) join the Eighth Army. The latter should not "beachhead" at Seoul-Inchon for a stand or evacuation (owing to the unfavorable tides and other factors) but rather should be gradually withdrawn toward Pusan, linking up with X

Corps. Walker believed that the Eighth Army, reinforced by X Corps and a rebuilt U.S. 2nd Division (giving him a total of the equivalent of eight U.S. divisions) "could hold the old Pusan perimeter indefinitely." Collins reached the same conclusion.

Returning to Tokyo, Collins met with MacArthur, Doyle Hickey and others. In these talks, Collins sought MacArthur's views on three purely hypothetical possibilities:

• Chinese communists continued to drive south; UN forces were not reinforced; and limitations on border and on "hot pursuit" remained in force.

In reply, MacArthur was utterly defeatist. He told Collins there could be no alternative but "surrender." Collins hastened to say that "what he unquestionably meant was not surrender but complete evacuation of the peninsula." Although by now Collins did not think we could be thrown out, he did not challenge MacArthur's views.

• Chinese communists continued the drive south; UN forces were reinforced; border limitations were removed to permit bombing of Manchurian and Chinese cities; naval blockade of China coast.

In reply to this possibility, MacArthur perked up. He believed he "could maintain forces in Korea and ultimately if properly supported restore our position."

MacArthur strongly urged that we adopt this course. He wanted UN forces increased by not less than 75,000 men; iterating his suggestion that we accept Chiang Kai-shek's offer to send the 33,000 troops to Korea. If he did not receive these reinforcements quickly, Collins later wrote, MacArthur believed "the United Nations command should pull out of Korea."

• Chinese communists voluntarily stopped at the 38th parallel.

In reply, MacArthur felt that the United States should accept an armistice, with a United Nations commission to oversee implementation.[38]

Collins arrived back in Washington on December 8. The thrust of his report—that things were not all that dire—was like a ray of sunshine. We now had options to discuss other than catastrophe. We hastened to agree with Collins that as a first step X Corps should be evacuated from the east coast, landed at Pusan and joined with the Eighth Army. Orders approving this step went out to MacArthur immediately, urging him to carry it out "as early as practicable."

From Hungnam, X Corps (108,600 troops plus 98,000 Korean refugees) was skillfully evacuated by air and sea with 350,000 tons of its equipment. The Eighth Army pulled back to a line roughly along the 38th parallel, reinforced on the east coast by the ROK I Corps, which landed there from Hungnam. Curiously, the Chinese armies did not interfere with the X Corps evacuation, nor did they immediately continue the pursuit of the Eighth Army. For a time, at any rate, the Eighth Army was stabilized and further retreat was temporarily halted.[39]

The question of whether or not Walker should be relieved was resolved by a deus ex machina. On the morning of December 23, he was killed in a motor accident eerily reminiscent of Patton's death. His jeep was hit by a truck driven by a Korean. The jeep flipped over and Walker died almost instantly. Frank Milburn, commanding the U.S. I Corps, assumed temporary command of the Eighth Army.[40]

On one of his trips to Tokyo, Collins and MacArthur had agreed that in the event Walker became a casualty Ridgway should replace him. Upon learning of Walker's death, MacArthur telephoned Collins directly to report the accident and request Ridgway. After clearing the request through Truman, Marshall and Pace, Collins notified Ridgway by telephone. Ridgway left immediately for Tokyo, arriving there near midnight on Christmas Day. (Van Fleet was put on alert to take over in case anything should happen to Ridgway.)

Ridgway and MacArthur had known one another since West Point days. MacArthur had utmost confidence in Ridgway. He willingly gave him the free hand he had withheld from Walker. The X Corps would be landed at Pusan and integrated into the Eighth Army. "The Eighth Army is yours, Matt," MacArthur said. "Do what you think best. . . . Use your own judgment. I will support you. You have my complete confidence." Ridgway left immediately for Korea, determined to hold as far north as possible and already mentally planning an offensive![41]

It is not often in wartime that a single battlefield commander can make a decisive difference. But in Korea, Ridgway would prove to be the exception. His brilliant, driving, uncompromising leadership would turn the tide of battle like no other general's in our military history.

SIXTY

Although the tactical military crisis in Korea had absorbed a great deal of our time and effort, it did not divert us from the central and more vital question: Did Chinese communist intervention in Korea signal the onset of World War III with the Soviet Union? For a time we had to assume it might. The JCS declared in a position paper:

> The United States faces today one of the greatest dangers in its history. The Korean War could be the first phase of a global war between the United States and the USSR. No areas of agreement which might lessen or end this global struggle are apparent, except those based on appeasement of the Soviets.[1]

On December 6, we sent a personal "war warning" to all theater commanders:

> The JCS consider that the current situation in Korea has greatly increased the possibility of general war. Commanders addressed take such action as is feasible to increase readiness without causing atmosphere of alarm.[2]

On December 11, the National Security Council resumed ongoing discussions of implementing the recommendations of NSC-68 for a massive rearmament. These discussions led the Joint Chiefs to recommend a minimum Army of eighteen divisions, a Navy of 397 major combatant vessels and an Air Force of ninety-five wings. The military budget for fiscal year 1952, then in preparation, would be about $55 billion—more than four times the pre-Korean ceiling of $13 billion.[3]

At this same NSC meeting, it was decided that the President should declare "a state of national emergency." He did this on the evening of December 15 over both radio and television. Communist rulers, he asserted, "are now willing to push the world to the brink of general war [in order] to get what they want." In response, he said, the United States' armed forces would expand to 3.5 million men and women "as rapidly as possible," and production of military aircraft, electronic components and military vehicles would be increased by some 400 to 500 percent. To prevent crippling inflation, he would impose selective price and wage controls and take other measures. "No nation," he said, "has ever had a greater responsibility than ours has at this moment."[4]

In the meantime, the JCS were formulating a new war plan to replace Offtackle. The new plan, called "Reaper," was similar in most respects to Offtackle but placed far greater stress on holding Western Europe with NATO forces in what was termed a "forward strategy." The goal was to defend Western Europe "as far to the East as possible," along a line Rhine-Alps-Piave. That was the plan Ike inherited on December 19, when he took over as NATO Supreme Allied Commander.[5]

All the while, we continued the search for a solution to the Korean War. Truman made two fundamental decisions: We would not *voluntarily* leave Korea or abandon the ROK government and the ROK Army. We would keep on fighting until forced out, and if forced out we would take the ROK's with us. Based on the report of Joe Collins, holding a Pusan perimeter "indefinitely" now seemed a possibility, but we still had to consider that if the Chinese communists committed overwhelming manpower to the war the odds were good that we could be thrown out. This much was certain: Short of a massive commitment of new forces, probably leading to all-out war with Red China and possibly the Soviet Union, there was no way on earth we could militarily clear all the communists out of North Korea and unite the country with free elections. Thus, by the first week in December, we had been compelled to abandon that high-minded goal and hope that we could arrange a *status quo*, an armistice along the 38th parallel.[6]

The problem was how to get an armistice without paying too high a price or, as Marshall had put it, how to get out "with honor." For the moment, the Chinese held the strong hand. They might very well demand a whole range of unacceptable concessions: unification of Korea under a communist regime, a seat in the UN, cessation of American aid to Indochina and, worst of all, physical occupation of Formosa.

The British were no help. In his Washington visit in early December, Prime Minister Attlee urged that in return for an armistice we more or less give Red China whatever she wanted. The British thought China was ripe for "Titoism," that she could be split away from Moscow. Attlee wanted to encourage that split and have Red China, the emerging giant in the Far East, as a friend of the West. He believed that we should formally recognize Peking, support a Red China seat in the UN and dump Chiang, leaving

Formosa to the Chinese communists. Truman, Acheson, Marshall and I very patiently explained why these steps were out of the question.[7]

The British ultimately agreed to help us seek a cease-fire on our terms through the UN and other diplomatic channels. The decision to seek the cease-fire was formally ratified by the NSC in its December 11 meeting. On that same day, the JCS notified MacArthur and asked for his views on the terms a cease-fire should include. His views, which generally were in agreement with ours, were incorporated in a memo to Marshall on December 12. Generally, the JCS urged a cease-fire along the 38th parallel, to include a twenty-mile-wide buffer zone and certain safeguards.[8]

Peking vehemently rejected our proposal. This pronouncement came directly from Foreign Minister Chou En-lai in a December 22 radio broadcast. He said the 38th parallel had been "obliterated forever" by the UN invasion of North Korea. Peking would not consider a cease-fire until Red China had a seat in the UN and all UN troops had been withdrawn from Korea and Formosa. From this broadcast and other information reaching us, we concluded that the Chinese communists now intended to launch an all-out drive to throw us out of Korea.[9]

We then had to urgently consider what would happen if the Chinese communists threw us out. Would that be the end of China's ambitions? There was a good possibility it might not be. She had recently moved south into Tibet. She was aggressively supporting Ho Chi Minh against the French in Indochina. She had vowed to throw Chiang out of Formosa. Was it possible that Japan was on her list? It was a mere 115 miles by water from Pusan to the principal Japanese home island of Honshu, about the same distance as from Amoy, China, to Formosa. If she took all of Korea, her battle-hardened Fourth Field Army would be in a good position to launch an assault on Japan.

How the Soviets might view this scenario was not known. Perhaps not favorably. If so, a threat of a Chinese invasion of Japan might impel the Soviets to get there first, invading the northernmost Japanese home island, Hokkaido, by staging from Soviet military bases in Sakhalin. A mere thirty miles of water—the Soya Strait—separated Sakhalin and Hokkaido. On the other hand, the Kremlin might have its own scenario: a Chinese communist attack, or threat of an attack, on Honshu, designed as a diversionary move to cover a Soviet invasion of Hokkaido, then Honshu, from Sakhalin. Or the scenario might call for a Soviet attack on Japan while the Chinese had the Eighth Army pinned down in South Korea.

At that point, Japan was naked. MacArthur had stripped her bare to reinforce the UN command in Korea. We had sent him the U.S. 3rd Division to serve as "theater reserve" and provide an American "presence" in Japan. Without clearing it with us, he had sent the 3rd Division to Korea. There was not even one U.S. regiment in Japan, no military means (other than the Air Force and Navy) to resist either a Chinese or Soviet invasion.

An invasion of Japan by either Chinese or Soviets would, of course, ignite World War III and probably compel nuclear retaliation. Although there was still doubt that Russia was ready for World War III, as I have said, we all believed that we had moved very much closer to it, that Russia appeared more willing to risk it. We kept constantly in mind that more wars than one had been started by miscalculation or mistake.

Renewed urgent concern over the vulnerability of Japan arose almost simultaneously in Tokyo and Washington. On December 19, Marshall convened a meeting of the three service secretaries and the JCS to discuss this problem, inviting Dean Rusk from State. According to Rusk's notes: "Marshall opened the discussion by stating that he has been concerned for a week or ten days about the extreme vulnerability of Japan in event of a sudden Russian onslaught." A Russian attack on Japan "would disclose a degree of vulnerability which would produce a very serious situation."[10]

In the midst of this meeting—the timing was uncanny—a message arrived from MacArthur to the JCS on the same subject. A messenger brought the cable to the meeting. MacArthur proposed that in order to provide "emergency protection" for Japan, the four National Guard divisions we had mobilized in September be sent to Japan as quickly as possible. He realized these divisions were not yet fully trained. His idea was that the divisions could complete training in Japan and at the same time provide some reassurance to the Japanese people, who were voicing fears over a Soviet invasion. He would not send these divisions to Korea.[11]

No member of the JCS wanted to comply with this request. In the first place, the four divisions had only been in camp a few weeks. They had been beefed up with thousands of draftees, who, as Wade Haislip (sitting in for Collins) put it, "had not yet learned how to be a basic soldier." The divisions would not even complete basic training until March 1. It would be extremely unwise—downright crazy in fact—to send them to Japan. Moreover, it would cause chaos in our overall training and expansion plans and disrupt and delay our vital need to send U.S. troops to Europe. Subsequently, the President and the State Department agreed with our general view that no more U.S. divisions be sent to the Far East. On December 23, we, in effect, disapproved MacArthur's request for the four Guard divisions, telling him that pending other decisions regarding Korea, "no additional divisions will be deployed to the Far East."[12]

This decision was far more important than it would seem at first glance. It meant that the security of Japan, which was then more important in the strategic sense than the security of Korea, would depend on the Eighth Army. It thus became all the more vital that the Eighth Army not be destroyed in Korea. And this, in turn, led to a pronounced caution in the JCS about courses to follow in Korea.

We had to bear in mind that a military evacuation is one of the most complex maneuvers in the book. We had been lucky with X Corps, the Chinese had let it alone. But we might not be so lucky at Pusan. Now that we had integrated the Eighth Army and X Corps, the Chinese might elect to attempt to annihilate all our forces in one fell swoop. A withdrawal could turn into a Dunkirk, a frantic, desperate affair in which we had to leave masses of equipment behind, all of which would fall into the hands of the Chinese armies. We might save some men for the defense of Japan, but they would have no equipment. If the Chinese decided to commit air power, the evacuation might turn into a disastrous and bloody operation, costing tens of thousands of lives.

Given the strategic importance of Japan and its vulnerability and the threat then posed to the Eighth Army, from a strictly military point of view one sensible course to follow would have been to evacuate the Eighth Army from Korea then and there, before the Chinese had time to renew the assault. This is the course that Sherman and Vandenberg advocated at that meeting. Sherman said that "Western Europe" would be "delighted" to see us withdraw from Korea. "There might be some loss of prestige and some adverse effect in Asia," he went on, but "we might have to accept that and balance it off against our increased capacity to deal with the overall situation."[13]

I did not think we should withdraw the Eighth Army from Korea, at least not until we had clear evidence that the Chinese communists had advanced in great strength south of the 38th parallel. MacArthur had the equivalent of eighteen divisions in the Eighth Army (seven American, ten ROK, one Turkish and two British brigades), some 300,000 men. Except for the initial Chinese assaults, our forces had not "seriously engaged" the Chinese armies, I said. As Collins had suggested, the Eighth Army might be able to put up a stronger fight than it had so far. Depending on the weight of the Chinese offensive, if it came, it might even be possible that the Eighth Army could "spare one or two divisions from Korea" to protect Japan. The Chinese had the capability, in terms of manpower, to drive us from Korea if they were "really intent" on it, but I suggested we wait and see if they came below the 38th parallel in strength. In the meantime, we would prepare a series of defensive lines and a heavy defensive perimeter around Pusan.[14]

In sum, the military situation was quite complex. From a strategic point of view, the security of Japan was "paramount." Only the Eighth Army could guarantee the security of Japan. It was thus strategically vital that it not be trapped and annihilated in Korea and that when or if it were forced out, it take its equipment, both to prevent the Chinese from getting it and to have it on hand for the defense of Japan. For these reasons, Sherman and Van thought we ought to get the Eighth Army out immediately. Collins and I thought we should wait until the Chinese intention to force us out was unambiguous, meanwhile preparing such defensive lines as would absolutely assure orderly evacuation of the Eighth if it came down to it.

Acheson and Rusk fully agreed that the safety of Japan was "paramount." Rusk said, "If there is a clear choice as between Japan and Korea, priority must go to Japan." State also agreed that we should not send the four Guard divisions to Japan. Rusk said, "The dispatch to Japan of the divisions now in training in the U.S. would have a disastrous effect upon the program for the defense of Europe." Rusk thought that one way to increase the security of Japan would be to send the U.S. 3rd Division back there, rather than landing it at Pusan. Another way might be an "increase of Japanese constabulary capability."

At the same time, State wanted to make the strongest possible stand in Korea for as long as possible. Rusk thought that we should attempt to stabilize a position at the 38th parallel "by political means" and "reinforce this effort by military means" if this could be done "without risking the destruction of U.S. forces." Thereafter, Rusk believed, we should "find a means honorably to withdraw U.S. forces from Korea at the earliest opportunity," in the meantime using whatever time we might buy "to strengthen Japanese and Korean ability to contribute to their own defense." He would not urge holding a specific position in Korea "regardless of cost" but rather attempt to stabilize a position wherever there was a "reasonable chance of success," making maximum use of all our forces to punish the Chinese. If all that became "impracticable," then as a last resort, Rusk would withdraw to Pusan and evacuate "as a matter of military necessity."[15]

Collins and I were more or less in agreement with these views on Korea. However, I do not believe that either Acheson or Rusk fully appreciated the complexities and risks entailed in a military evacuation under heavy enemy fire, possibly including hostile air power. One result was that they displayed some impatience with JCS caution during this period. Some historians and writers who have not given sufficient weight to the strategic risks entailed have unfairly depicted the JCS as timid and foot-dragging. Considering the stakes involved in Japan and Korea, I cannot imagine a time in our history when caution was of more overriding importance.

These discussions and others that took place just before and after Christmas led up to the drafting of a new directive for MacArthur. Technically, he was still operating under the September 27 orders we had sent him, plus various amendments, some of which, given the situation, might be construed as conflicting or obsolete. Still pending was his oral request to Collins for 75,000 reinforcements and his formal request for Chiang's troops. He had told Collins that without reinforcements evacuation was inevitable. He had also told Collins that if we were to hold in Korea, bombing and blockading Red China would be necessary. All these matters, plus others, had to be dealt with without further delay.

The new directive to MacArthur was the product of close collaboration between Acheson, Rusk, Marshall, Lovett and the JCS. It was cleared by the President and sent through the JCS on December 29, at a time when evidence of an all-out Chinese communist offensive below the 38th parallel had mounted to the point that it appeared it could come at any hour. In fact, it did come forty-eight hours after our directive reached Tokyo.[16]

The text read:

> This message has been handled here with the ultimate of security and it is suggested that the contents thereof be confined, for the present, to you and your Chief of Staff and to General Ridgway and his Chief of Staff. Message follows:
>
> It appears from all estimates available that the Chinese Communists possess the capability of forcing United Nations' Forces out of Korea if they choose to exercise it. The execution of this capability might be prevented by making the effort so costly to the enemy that they would abandon it, or by committing substantial additional United States Forces to that theater thus seriously jeopardizing other commitments including the safety of Japan. It is not practicable to obtain significant additional forces for Korea from other members of the United Nations. We believe that Korea is not the place to fight a major war. Further, we believe that we should not commit our remaining available ground forces to action against Chinese Communist Forces in Korea in face of the increased threat of general war. However, a successful resistance to Chinese-North Korean aggression at some position in Korea and a deflation of the military and political prestige of the Chinese Communists would be of great importance to our national interests, if this could be accomplished without incurring serious losses.
>
> Your basic directive to furnish such assistance to the Republic of Korea as may be necessary to repel the armed attack and to restore international peace and security in that area requires modification in the light of the present situation.
>
> You are now directed to defend in successive positions, as generally outlined in your CX 50635, inflicting such damage to hostile forces in Korea as is possible, subject to the primary consideration of the safety of your troops. Every effort should be continued to mobilize the maximum Korean contribution to sustained resistance, including both conventional and unconventional means.
>
> Since developments may force our withdrawal from Korea, it is important, particularly in view of the continued threat to Japan, to determine, in advance, our last reasonable opportunity for an orderly evacuation. It seems to us that if you are forced back to positions in the vicinity of the Kum River and a line generally eastward therefrom, and if thereafter the Chinese Communists mass large forces against your positions with an evident capability of forcing us out of Korea, it then would be necessary, under these conditions, to direct you to commence a withdrawal to Japan.

> Your views are requested as to the above-outlined conditions which should determine a decision to initiate evacuation, particularly in light of your continuing primary mission of defense of Japan for which only troops of the Eighth Army are available.
>
> Following the receipt of your views you will be given a definite directive as to the conditions under which you should initiate evacuation.

MacArthur has written that he was dismayed by this new directive. Courtney Whitney put it more melodramatically: "I have seen MacArthur in moments of great sorrow and distress; but I cannot recall when I have seen heartache so vividly on his countenance." MacArthur and Whitney both assert that the message signaled to them one overriding conclusion: Washington had lost the "will to win" in Korea, a "shameful decision."[17]

MacArthur's reaction arose, I feel certain, at least in part from the fact that his legendary pride had been hurt. The Red Chinese had made a fool of the infallible "military genius." By then, it must have been clear to him that his failure to send X Corps in pursuit of the North Korean Army after Inchon and to split up his forces and send X Corps around to Wonsan was an error of grave magnitude. He must also have realized that this error was compounded by his airy dismissal of objections about the strategy from his own subordinates and, later, pointed questions from the JCS. Furthermore, the Chinese had made a mockery of his intelligence estimates, of his vainglorious boasts that his all-out air assault (including bombing the Korean ends of the Yalu bridges) would make northwest Korea a "desert" and of his assertion that our men would advance to the Yalu and be "home for Christmas."

The only possible means left to MacArthur to regain his lost pride and military reputation was to now inflict an overwhelming defeat on those Red Chinese generals who had made a fool of him. In order to do this, he was now perfectly willing to propel us into all-out war with Red China and, possibly, with the Soviet Union, igniting World War III and a nuclear holocaust.[18]

MacArthur's response to our directive, according to Whitney, was composed "late in the evening of December 30," and it amounted to his "most important single comment on the Korean War." By this time, there were unmistakable signs that the Red Chinese armies were on the verge of an all-out offensive below the 38th parallel and that it could jump off at any hour. (It came twenty-four hours later.)[19]

MacArthur had told Collins in early December that if he did not get substantial ground reinforcements quickly, including Chiang's troops, and was not permitted to bomb and blockade Red China at will, he saw no alternative in Korea but complete evacuation. He more or less hewed to that view in his lengthy response and was contemptuous of our decision not to support his views. He thus blindly chose to view our directive as tantamount to an order to commence evacuation. He completely ignored our statements that if he could mount "successful resistance" to the Red Chinese, "inflicting such damage to hostile forces in Korea as possible," but "without incurring serious losses," it would be of "great importance to our national interests." To me those instructions said the opposite of MacArthur's interpretation: Stand and fight as hard as possible, "subject to the primary consideration of the safety of your troops," bearing always in mind his "continuing primary mission of defense of Japan."

He then urged that we:

- Blockade the coast of China.
- Destroy through naval gunfire and air bombardment China's industrial capacity to wage war.
- Secure reinforcements from the Nationalist garrison on Formosa to strengthen our position in Korea.
- Release existing restrictions upon the Formosa garrison for diversionary action (possibly leading to counterinvasion) against vulnerable areas of the Chinese mainland.

He did not believe these measures would widen the war. Red China was so fully committed to Korea that "nothing we can do would further aggravate the situation as far as China is concerned." He casually dismissed the possibility of Soviet intervention in Korea or global war as "a matter of speculation." He explained: "I have always felt that a Soviet decision to precipitate a general war would depend solely upon its own estimate of relative strengths and capabilities with little regard to other factors."

In conclusion, MacArthur dealt with the tactical plan for evacuation we had proposed, in the event it proved necessary. He thought it "would seem to be sound." But he alarmed us with his closing sentence: "In the execution of this plan it would not be necessary for you to make an anticipatory decision for evacuation until such time as we may be forced to that beachhead line." That could indicate he was not going to commence evacuation until the Red Chinese were knocking on the gates of Pusan, which could be disastrous. We exchanged several messages on this point without achieving a meeting of the minds. Finally, in near-exasperation, the JCS made the decision for him. If and when his troops were pushed to a point roughly thirty miles north of Pusan (the so-called Davidson Line, named for Garrison H. Davidson, an engineer who devised it), the time for a "final decision" on withdrawal would have arrived. As Collins observed, this was the "first time that the Chiefs stepped in" and gave MacArthur "a specific order on a matter of seeming detail."[20]

On New Year's Eve, the Chinese communists attacked in force, hitting several ROK divisions with awesome manpower. Much as Ridgway disliked it, he was forced to order a withdrawal to the Han River near Seoul. As Collins wrote, the withdrawal was not without some disorder, but by then Ridgway had a firm grip on the Eighth Army, and his firmness was everywhere evident. There was no rout; and as it fell back, the Eighth Army killed Chinese by the "thousands." Very reluctantly Ridgway was compelled to abandon Seoul on January 4 and pull behind the ice-choked Han River. Fifteen miles to the south he stopped, turning the Eighth Army to meet the enemy from strong, well-prepared positions Ridgway had had the foresight to have constructed. To the east, near Wonju, X Corps, only recently arrived from Pusan and now including the newly rebuilt 2nd Division, had a tougher time. In the ensuing confusion, Wonju was lost to the enemy and Almond was compelled to relieve the 2nd Division's commander, Robert B. McClure, giving the outfit to his chief of staff, Clark L. Ruffner. Thereafter X Corps dug in and fought stubbornly.[21]

In Washington, we held our breath. Ridgway was pushed back an average of sixty miles along the front. An important political position, Seoul, had again been yielded, along with our supply base at Inchon. However, by January 5, the Red Chinese attack appeared to be running out of steam. We received encouraging reports from Ridgway, who was then working miracles to restore the spirit and fighting ability of the Eighth Army.

Could Ridgway withstand yet another concerted Chinese attack? We were not certain. The Chinese attacks showed a distinctive pattern: hard initial charge, limited pursuit, followed by a lull during which more men and supplies were brought forward. We had to assume that yet another attack was in the works and that the Eighth Army might this time be compelled to fall back as far as the Kum River line near Taejon. And after that . . .[22]

On January 9, the JCS replied to MacArthur's December 30 message urging that we widen the war to include bombing and blockading the Red Chinese and utilizing Chiang's troops. This amounted to a second revised JCS directive for the conduct of the war. We formally rejected all three principal proposals. The only new steps under active consideration at that time were sending two of the four National Guard divisions to Japan; expediting the arming of Japanese constabulary forces; and intensifying an *economic* blockade of China by discouraging trade. We then restated his directive:

> Defend in successive positions as required by JCS 99935, inflicting maximum damage to hostile forces in Korea, subject to primary consideration of the safety of your troops and your basic mission of defending Japan. Should it become evident in your judgment that evacuation is essential to avoid severe losses of men and materiel, you will at that time withdraw from Korea to Japan.

To the JCS, these orders were as clear as crystal. MacArthur's forces were to fight as hard as possible, inflicting utmost possible damage on the enemy but avoiding *severe* (i.e., catastrophic) losses, so that the Eighth Army would be able to defend Japan. In a previous message we had made it equally clear that if pushed back as far as the Davidson Line, thirty miles north of Pusan, the time would have come to order evacuation.[23]

Courtney Whitney wrote that Tokyo saw this message as a "booby trap." That is to say, by leaving it up to MacArthur to decide what exactly was meant by "severe losses," we were shifting to MacArthur the onus for making the decision on evacuation, thereby, Whitney implied, cravenly avoiding the distasteful decision ourselves. "MacArthur refused so easily to be taken in," Whitney wrote with typical paranoia. "He shot a query right back asking for clarification."[24]

In fact, the query was childish quibbling over the connotation of "severe losses" and yet another long, involved argument for widening the war. MacArthur brazenly tweaked our noses by stating that he was in "full agreement" with the JCS position expressed in our December 29 message that unless the war were widened the position of the UN forces would eventually be rendered "untenable." Of course, we had said no such thing; we had urged him to fight on as hard as possible, defending specific lines, suggesting only that "developments may force our withdrawal from Korea."

But what was most disturbing in this message was a negative and defeatist tone about the Eighth Army, which came in sharp contrast to the upbeat reports from Ridgway. It indicated that MacArthur might well be completely out of touch with the battlefield:

> The troops are tired from a long and difficult campaign, embittered by the shameful propaganda which has falsely condemned their courage and fighting qualities in misunderstood retrograde maneuver, and their morale will become a serious threat to their battlefield efficiency unless the political basis upon which they are asking to trade life for time is clearly delineated, fully understood, and so impelling that the hazards of battle are cheerfully accepted.[25]

When I had testified at the B-36 hearings after Admiral Denfeld had complained about deteriorating morale in the Navy, I had said, "Senior officers decrying the low morale of their forces evidently do not realize that the esprit of the men is but a mirror of their confidence in their leadership." Acheson wrote that Marshall now echoed this sentiment to Dean Rusk: "When a general complains of the morale of his troops, the time has come to look into his own." Truman wrote that upon reading the message he was also "deeply disturbed."[26]

Acheson has described this message as a "posterity paper," designed to absolve MacArthur of all blame if things went wrong and to exert maximum pressure on Washington to reverse itself and adopt his proposals for widening the war. He was now utterly convinced that MacArthur was "incurably recalcitrant and basically disloyal." Putting it another way, Admiral Sherman believed that "the normal relationships which are desirable between one echelon of command and another had been seriously impaired." Marshall said, "We were at our lowest point." At a JCS meeting on January 12, it was decided that the JCS would draft what now amounted to a *third* military directive to MacArthur, while the President, independently, would send him a personal letter describing our overall political position.[27]

Acheson was right. MacArthur had become incurably recalcitrant and basically disloyal. Our first directive had been quite clear and so had the second. It was absurd that we were now required to send MacArthur a third. He had every official right to express his views and to ask for clarifications, but his messages had taken on a "do it my way or it can't be done" character. Washington was thus being placed in the position of *convincing* a subordinate commander that our orders should be carried out. While MacArthur had not been technically insubordinate, he was skating on very thin ice indeed.

Our third directive went out to MacArthur at noon on January 12. By this time, Ridgway had stabilized his defenses, but all signs indicated yet another Chinese communist offensive would be launched. We could not know from our distance that by that time Ridgway had thoroughly indoctrinated the Eighth Army with his own aggressive spirit. Ridgway was so supremely confident of his ability to hold that he had his staff drawing up plans for a limited offensive designed to throw the Chinese off balance and disrupt their plans for offensive action. Unaware of this change, we told MacArthur:

> Based upon all the factors known to us, including particularly those presented in your recent messages, we are forced to the conclusion that it is infeasible under existing conditions, including sustained major effort by Communist China, to hold for a protracted period a position in Korea.
>
> However, it would be to our national interest, and also to the interest of the UN, to gain some further time for essential diplomatic and military consultations with UN countries participating in Korean effort before you issue firm instructions for initiation of evacuation of troops from Korea.
>
> It is important also to United States prestige worldwide, to future UN and NATO organizations, and to efforts to organize anti-communist resistance in Asia that Korea not be evacuated unless actually forced by military considerations, and that maximum practicable punishment be inflicted on communist aggressors.

We went on to say that it was "not possible in Washington to evaluate present state of combat efficiency and morale of UN forces." However, we did express concern over the possibility that if it learned of plans to evacuate, the ROK Army might collapse, endangering U.S. forces. Meanwhile, our instructions of January 9—the second directive—to hold out if possible, otherwise to withdraw to Japan, remained in force.[28]

Because Ridgway's and MacArthur's reports on the morale of the Eighth Army were at such wide variance, at Marshall's suggestion, immediately after that message was cleared, Collins and Vandenberg left for consultations in Tokyo and Korea. While they were en route, Truman drafted and sent, via JCS channels, his personal letter to MacArthur. It was, as Acheson wrote, an "imaginatively kind and thoughtful document," once more patiently spelling out our Korean War policy. Rarely in our history has a President been compelled to draft such a document. Truman listed ten reasons why it would be in our interests to fight as long and as hard as possible in Korea. He went on to say that we must "act with great prudence in so far as extending the area of hostilities is concerned." Truman said we would not leave Korea unless militarily forced to, and if we were forced to, "we shall not accept the result politically or militarily until the aggression has been rectified."[29]

Collins and Vandenberg reached Tokyo on January 15, at about the same time Truman's letter arrived there. In a meeting with Collins and Vandenberg, MacArthur read the letter aloud and said that he had interpreted it as a "directive" to remain in Korea "indefinitely." (Or, as Whitney quoted MacArthur: "That, gentlemen, finally settles the question of whether or not we evacuate Korea. There will be no evacuation.") How MacArthur gained that interpretation from the President's letter remains a mystery. Collins rightly pointed out that it was not a "directive" (it specifically stated it was not), nor did it say anything about staying in Korea "indefinitely." To the contrary, Truman had said "we recognize of course that continued resistance might not be militarily possible with the limited forces" in Korea.[30]

What lifted MacArthur's spirits that day, I believe, was an unfortunate misconception created first by the President's letter and then by Collins and Vandenberg that the administration might be swinging around to his views. The President had said that if we were forced out of Korea we would "not accept the result politically or militarily." He did not say what we might do militarily to rectify the aggression, but it seems clear from Whitney's account that MacArthur believed the administration would widen the war—impose a naval blockade, permit bombing of China and perhaps "unleash" Chiang Kai-shek.[31]

MacArthur's views of future courses we might take were unfortunately strengthened by a document that Collins and Vandenberg took along to Tokyo. This was a JCS joint staff "study paper," prepared at Truman's request, exploring possible courses of action in the event of total or "open war" with Red China, or in the event we were thrown out of Korea, for consideration at a National Security Council meeting scheduled for January 17. The JCS approved this document on January 12 and forwarded it to Marshall, who in turn sent it to the NSC staff without comment. It had not been approved by the NSC and was not official policy. The courses proposed were in response to a hypothetical situation far more drastic than that we now faced!

The JCS document recommended the following:

- Consider sending two partly trained Guard divisions to Japan if we could "profitably" hold Eighth Army in Korea.
- Expedite the build-up of Japan's defense forces.
- Continue and intensify now an economic blockade of Red China.
- Prepare now for a naval blockade of Red China, to be imposed whether or not we were thrown out of Korea, "depending on circumstances then obtaining."
- Remove now restrictions on air reconnaissance of Manchuria and coastal area of China.
- Remove restrictions on Chiang's forces and give them logistical support.
- Send a military mission to Formosa and increase military aid.
- Furnish all practicable covert aid to effective Nationalist guerrilla forces in China.
- In the event of Chinese communist attacks on any of our forces outside of Korea (in Okinawa, Japan, etc.), initiate damaging naval and air attacks on objectives in Communist China.

The JCS favored two of the three recommendations in MacArthur's December 30 message: blockading and bombing Red China. His third, the use of Chiang's troops in Korea, was rejected. It should be noted that both the naval blockade and the bombing recommendations were contingent on a rather drastic change in the situation and were by no means being urged as a course of action then and there.[32]

Collins and Vandenberg flew on to Korea for talks with Ridgway, his subordinate commanders and GI's in the field. Although Ridgway felt it was necessary to make several changes in his commanders, he was now optimistic and said, "There is no shadow of doubt in my mind that the Eighth Army can take care of itself." Touring the battlefields (Van foolishly flew deep over enemy front lines), Collins and Vandenberg were tremendously impressed with the job Ridgway had done. Even then the Eighth Army was conducting a limited offensive, "Operation Wolfhound" —named for my old outfit in Hawaii, the 27th Infantry Regiment, which spearheaded the attack.[33]

After returning to Tokyo, Collins got off a brief interim flash report to me on January 17. This message would mark a turning point in our views of the Korean War. For the first time we began to think that the Chinese could not throw us out of Korea, even with the self-imposed limitations under which we were fighting. It was a tremendous relief to all. The report:

> Eighth Army in good shape and improving daily under Ridgway's leadership. Morale very satisfactory considering conditions. ROK forces lack confidence and instinctively fear Chinese but are still capable of resistance against North Korean troops. No signs of disaffection or collapse though this could change quickly in event of serious reverses. Barring unforeseen development Ridgway confident he can obtain two to three months' delay before having to initiate evacuation. Does not want to do this before Army is back in old beachhead.
>
> Chinese have not made any move so far to push south from Han River. When counter-attacked they have usually fled. They are having supply difficulties and there are many indications of low morale . . . On the whole Eighth Army now in position and prepared to punish severely any mass attack.[34]

Upon reaching the office that day, January 17, I took this cheering message to Marshall, who telephoned the President and read it to him. As the word spread through the upper levels of government that day, you could almost hear the sighs of relief. In the afternoon, the NSC met to consider, among other items, the JCS January 12 staff study outlining options should we find ourselves facing a much more drastic situation. Because of the Collins report, most of our proposals—blockading and bombing China, for example—were not approved and were sent back for further study.[35]

Collins and Vandenberg arrived back in Washington on January 18. On the following day they submitted an official report that was thoroughly optimistic. In a separate memo to Marshall on the morale of the Eighth Army, which MacArthur had decried, Collins wrote: "There is no cause for alarm over the present state of morale and fighting efficiency of the Eighth Army and ROK forces." On the same day, January 19, Collins and Vandenberg formally briefed the President and the full Cabinet.[36]

The dramatic change of fortune that had occurred in Korea, Collins later wrote, was due entirely to Ridgway's leadership on the battlefield. This fact was soon realized in Washington, and thereafter we looked beyond MacArthur to Ridgway for reliable military assessments and guidance. Although we continued to address JCS messages and directives to MacArthur, there was a feeling that MacArthur had been "kicked upstairs" to chairman of the board and was, insofar as military operations were concerned, mainly a prima donna figurehead who had to be tolerated.[37]

SIXTY-ONE

Under Ridgway's magnificent leadership, the Eighth Army continued aggressive operations in Korea. On January 25, he launched a larger probing action, "Operation Thunderbolt," which soon graduated into a major sustained offensive, "Thunderbolt-Roundup." In the west sector, the Eighth Army advanced about thirty-five miles north and on February 10 recaptured Inchon. In the east sector, X Corps found the going tougher but recaptured Wonju and helped crush a determined five-division Chinese attack in the seam between IX Corps and X Corps near Chipyongni.

These operations, together with the infusion of new faces in key command jobs, made the Eighth Army the equal of any army in the ETO in World War II. By February 18, Ridgway was ready to launch a major army-wide offensive, "Operation Killer," designed primarily to destroy Chinese and North Korean forces east of the upper reaches of the Han River. D-day was set for February 21.[1]

MacArthur had twice visited Ridgway, in January and February. He came a third time on February 20, the eve of Operation Killer. When Ridgway briefed MacArthur on his plan, MacArthur approved it without change, then strode forward to meet the press at the X Corps tactical command post and said grandly, "I have just ordered a resumption of the offensive."

Ridgway, who looked on from the back of the room, was dismayed. "There was no undue emphasis on the personal pronoun," Ridgway wrote, "but the implication was clear: He had just flown in from Tokyo, had surveyed the situation, discussed it with his subordinates, and had then ordered the Eighth Army to attack. There had, of course, been no orders at all concerning any part of the operation from CINCFE [MacArthur] or from GHQ staff in Tokyo. . . . Neither he nor his staff had had any part in the conception or in the planning of Operation Killer."[2]

Unfortunately Operation Killer did not live up to its name. Foul weather, an early spring thaw and other factors disrupted air operations and road and rail movement. Undaunted, Ridgway planned yet another offensive, "Operation Ripper," designed to keep the Chinese off balance, and take the Eighth Army close to the 38th parallel. Owing to the fact that MacArthur's much-ballyhooed visits in Korea could now be identified by the enemy as presaging a new offensive, Ridgway asked MacArthur to stay away for security reasons. Ripper jumped off on March 7. By March 15, troops of the Eighth Army had recaptured Seoul—never to be lost again—and Chunchon to the northeast and forced the Chinese communists and North Koreans back into North Korea. These aggressive moves cost the Chinese tens of thousands of casualties.[3]

The question of the 38th parallel arose once again. Should we cross it or not? This question led to endless talk and debate in Washington, Tokyo and Korea. The Defense and State departments were soon involved in an Alphonse and Gaston routine. As Collins points out, State preferred not to express political objectives with respect to Korea until military capabilities had been established. On the other hand, the JCS believed that a political decision was necessary before there could be a suitable determination of military courses of action.

As we have seen, the initial "political" decision by the United States and United Nations had not barred UN forces from crossing the 38th parallel. This policy was technically still in force, even though, as the JCS knew well, our friends and allies were now warning that we should not cross it again and State generally shared that view. The JCS position was that until the policy was changed, Ridgway should have complete freedom of military maneuver—not be prohibited from crossing the 38th parallel. The parallel itself had few natural terrain features to provide good defensive lines. Moreover, unless there was a legal cease-fire or armistice, arbitrarily stopping Ridgway at the parallel would provide the communists with a "sanctuary" (i.e., North Korea) in which to build up for another ground offensive below the parallel. The JCS formally declared: "Until this governmental decision is reached there should be no change in that part of the directive to General MacArthur which now permits him to so dispose his forces north or south of the 38th parallel as best to provide for their security."[4]

As military historian James Schnabel put it, we finally arrived at a policy "almost by default." Encouraged by Ridgway's tremendous ground advances in Korea, which had inflicted severe damage on the Chinese communists and robbed them of the initiative on the battlefield, Washington decided to focus efforts on a negotiated or "political" settlement with Red China. Since the Chinese communists had rejected negotiations in December, it was decided that the opening move in the new diplomatic campaign should be a moderate, direct appeal from President Truman himself.[5]

The proposed presidential statement was a carefully conceived document, worked out in consultations between State and Defense representatives. The JCS sat down with Marshall and Acheson on March 19 to approve the final draft. The following day, March 20, after clearing it through Marshall and the President, the JCS sent this message to MacArthur:

> State planning presidential announcement shortly that, with clearing of bulk of South Korean aggressors, United Nations now prepared to discuss conditions of settlement in Korea. Strong UN feeling persists that further diplomatic effort towards settlement should be made before any advance with major forces north of the 38th parallel. Time will be required to determine diplomatic reactions and permit new negotiations that may develop. Recognizing that parallel has no military significance, State has asked JCS what authority you should have to permit sufficient freedom of action for next few weeks to provide security for UN forces and maintain contact with enemy. Your recommendation desired.[6]

MacArthur seized upon this message to once more needle us about the restrictions placed on his forces. He cabled:

> Recommend that no further military restrictions be imposed on the United Nations Command in Korea. The inhibitions which already exist should not be increased. The military disadvantages arising from restrictions on the scope of our Air and Naval operations coupled with the disparity between the size of our command and the enemy ground potential renders it completely impracticable to attempt to clear North Korea or to make any appreciable effort to that end. My present directives, establishing the security of the command as the paramount consideration, are adequate to cover the two points raised by the State Department.[7]

I do not know what went on in MacArthur's mind at this time. His memoirs and the memoirs and books of his associates shed little light. He had been made a fool of by the Chinese communist armies; now, as all the world had seen, Ridgway's brilliant leadership had bailed him out. In January, as I explained, he may have convinced himself that Washington might adopt his views on widening the war. Our cable indicating that Truman was going to ask for a "settlement" doubtless shattered that hope. There would be no all-out war with China directed from Tokyo. Perhaps this realization snapped his brilliant but brittle mind. What lay ahead now was merely a diplomatic search for the *status quo* and unrestricted praise for his subordinate, Ridgway.

Or, as has been suggested, perhaps at this time MacArthur decided that he would come home and run for the presidency in 1952. He still had considerable popularity and substantial support among the right-wing politicians on the Hill and in some state houses. Perhaps he believed that a sharp break with Truman, whose popularity was slipping badly, would redound to his credit and build such a massive groundswell of support that he could knock Republican front runner Bob Taft aside. I don't know; I can only speculate. However, it is noteworthy that the events that were to transpire would fit this scenario.

Whatever the reason, on March 24, MacArthur committed an unforgivable and irretrievable act. Knowing that the President was on the threshold of releasing his statement to the Chinese communists, MacArthur, in violation of the December 6 presidential order forbidding him to speak out without clearing his statements in Washington, released his own proclamation to the Chinese communists disguised as a "communiqué." Its defiant, mocking tone seemed calculated to sabotage any chance for a settlement. It directly and forcibly challenged the United States policy of limited war in Korea. The JCS historians wrote: "Had he deliberately sought to do so, the UN Commander could hardly have found a more effective way to arouse the President's wrath."[8]

In a sharp reversal of his former estimates of Red China's power which he had sent to the JCS, he began by ridiculing the fighting ability and stamina of her soldiers and her industrial capacity to wage war. "These military weaknesses," he went on, "have been clearly and definitely revealed since Red China entered upon its undeclared war in Korea. Even under the inhibitions which now restrict the activity of the United Nations forces and the corresponding military advantages which accrue to Red China, it has shown its complete inability to accomplish by force of arms the conquest of Korea."

Then, unbelievably, he raised the possibility of a widened war:

> The enemy, therefore, must by now be painfully aware that a decision of the United Nations to depart from its tolerant effort to contain the war to the areas of Korea, through an expansion of our military operations to his coastal areas and interior bases, would doom Red China to the risk of imminent military collapse. These basic facts being established, there should be no insuperable difficulty in arriving at decisions on the Korean problem if the issues are resolved on their own merits, without being burdened by extraneous matters such as Formosa or China's seat in the United Nations.

Then, upstaging the President's planned statement, he proposed that the Chinese communists might contact *him* if they wanted a settlement:

> Within the area of my authority as the military commander . . . it should be needless to say that I stand ready at any time to confer in the field with the Commander-in-Chief of the enemy forces in the earnest effort to find any military means whereby realizations of the political objectives of the United Nations in Korea, to which no nation may justly take exception, might be accomplished without further bloodshed.[9]

MacArthur's statement began moving on the press service wires and by radio on the evening of Friday, March 23, Washington time. At eleven o'clock that night Bob Lovett, Dean Rusk and others gathered at Acheson's home to discuss its implications. Acheson recalled that Lovett, "usually imperturbable and given to ironic humor under pressure, was angrier than I had ever seen him." Acheson recalled that Lovett said that MacArthur must be removed and removed at once. After reading the statement, Acheson wrote, "I shared his sense of outrage." Acheson thought it was "defiance of the Chiefs of Staff, sabotage of an operation of which he had been informed, and insubordination of the grossest sort to his Commander in Chief." They discussed the matter until 1 A.M.[10]

On the following day at noon, Acheson, Lovett and Rusk met with the President. Truman was "deeply shocked." He wrote that MacArthur's statement was "extraordinary" and it had been issued "totally disregarding all directives to abstain from any declarations on foreign policy." And it was, Truman wrote, "open defiance of my orders as President and Commander in Chief. . . . By this act MacArthur left me no choice—I could no longer tolerate his insubordination. . . . I realized that I would have no other choice myself than to relieve the nation's top field commander."[11]

Although he had made up his mind, Truman did not act hastily. That Saturday he merely dictated a restrained message designed principally to shut off further damaging statements from Tokyo. I sent the message to MacArthur.

> FROM JCS PERSONAL FOR MACARTHUR
> The President has directed that your attention be called to his order as transmitted in JCS 98134 of 6 December 1950. In view of the information given you in JCS 86276 of 20 March 1951 any further statements by you must be coordinated as prescribed in the order of 6 December. The President has also directed that in the event Communist military leaders request an armistice in the field, you immediately report that fact to the JCS for instructions.[12]

In the meantime, another MacArthur time bomb was ticking away. On March 8, Congressman Joseph Martin, minority leader of the House, had written MacArthur to get his "views" on Far East policy "on a confidential basis or otherwise." Martin, along with many other Republicans, had expressed concern over building up NATO at the expense of what he termed weakening our position in the Far East. He had recently delivered a speech, which he enclosed, in which he suggested that Chiang's troops "might be employed" to open "a second Asiatic front to relieve the pressure on our forces in Korea."

MacArthur wrote in his memoirs that he had always felt "duty-bound" to "reply frankly" to every congressman who made an inquiry into matters related to his official responsibility. He said he "attached little importance" to the letter and drafted a "polite response" on March 20 and put it in the mail to Martin. It said in part:

> My views and recommendations, with respect to the situation created by Red China entry into the war against us in Korea, have been submitted to Washington in most complete detail. Generally these views are well known and clearly understood, as they follow the conventional pattern of meeting force with maximum counter-force as we have never failed to do in the past. Your view with respect to the utilization of the Chinese forces on Formosa is in conflict with neither logic nor this tradition.
>
> It seems strangely difficult for some to realize that here in Asia is where the Communist conspirators have elected to make their play for global conquest, and that we have joined the issue thus raised on the battlefield; that here we fight Europe's war with arms while the diplomats there still fight it with words; that if we lose the war to Communism in Asia the fall of Europe is inevitable. Win it and Europe most probably would avoid war and yet preserve freedom. As you point out, we must win. There is no substitute for victory.[13]

This bomb exploded on the afternoon of Thursday, April 5, during a House debate to extend the draft. Martin got the floor and released the text of MacArthur's letter to support his continuing argument for using Chiang's troops. A few moments later alert wire service reporters were telephoning bulletins. The AP lead was "House Republican Leader Martin of Massachusetts told the House today General MacArthur favors use of Chinese Nationalist troops in Korean fighting."[14]

I did not need a crystal ball to see what was coming now. The Martin letter was another clear violation of the December 6 directive and another public challenge to administration policy. Soon after I got word of the Martin letter, I called the JCS into a thirty-one-minute session. I did not know that Truman had already made up his mind to relieve MacArthur, but I thought it was a strong possibility. Collins did not attend this meeting. He had left that day for a two-day trip to the South. As was customary, Haislip sat in for him. I told Van, Sherman and Haislip that the President was "quite disturbed" by a "series of incidents" concerning MacArthur, including the Martin letter, and suggested they think the matter over, since it was possible the JCS might be called upon for recommendations. We discussed the possibility that Truman might relieve MacArthur, or, alternatively, Sherman's proposal that Marshall might go to Tokyo to explain to MacArthur what difficulties his public statements were causing the government, or my suggestion that Marshall might write MacArthur a letter to that effect. No decisions were reached.[15]

This matter could not have arisen at a more inopportune time. We had recently received alarming intelligence information (from a classified source) that the Soviet Union was preparing for a major military move;

where, we did not know. One suggestion, taken with utmost seriousness, was that they would intervene in Korea. Another was that they might attempt to overrun Western Europe.

The intelligence had led the JCS that same day to forward a paper to Marshall, for consideration by the NSC, proposing various courses of action in the Far East under certain assumptions. We recommended that if the Soviets precipitated a general war, UN forces should be withdrawn from Korea as rapidly as possible and deployed for service elsewhere. If the Soviets committed "volunteers" to Korea in sufficient numbers as to be critical to the safety of UN forces, the UN should withdraw and the United States "should then mobilize in readiness for general war."

Assuming that there would be no global war with the USSR or significant Soviet intervention in Korea, we then turned to the realities we were left facing. A Korean armistice that would leave communist armies in North Korea would not be in our best interests, inasmuch as it would compel us to keep offsetting forces in South Korea, a tremendous drain on our military resources, particularly in light of Japan's vulnerability. We concluded:

> *a.* United States forces in Korea must pursue their current military course of action there until a political objective for that country appears attainable without jeopardizing United States positions with respect to the USSR, to Formosa, and seating the Chinese Communists in the United Nations;
>
> *b.* Dependable South Korean units should be generated as rapidly as possible and in sufficient strength to take over the major part of the burden from the other United Nations forces;
>
> *c.* Preparations should be made immediately for action by naval and air forces against the mainland of China; and
>
> *d.* Action should be taken as a matter of urgency to ascertain the policies and objectives of our allies toward Korea specifically and the Far East in general, and also to discover the degree and nature of the support which we would expect from them if, while continuing our present military course of action in Korea, operations against the mainland of China are initiated.[16]

In view of the possibility of Soviet intervention in Korea, which might well include air attacks on Japan and Okinawa, we approved this same fateful day—April 5—a draft order to MacArthur authorizing him in event of a "major" air attack on UN forces originating outside Korea, to attack air bases in Manchuria and on the Shantung Peninsula of China. Ordinarily we would have sent this order to MacArthur for contingency planning. However, I was now so wary of MacArthur that I deliberately withheld the message and all knowledge of its existence from him, fearing that he might, as I wrote at the time, "make a premature decision in carrying it out."

I discussed this proposed order on the following day with British ambassador Oliver Franks and Arthur Tedder, who were in town for consultations. The British were absolutely opposed to granting Tokyo this advance authority to bomb China and insisted they be consulted in advance. However, over the next few days Marshall, Acheson and Truman approved the plan. It was agreed that if time permitted, the President would give the final approval for the attack; if not, the JCS were authorized to give it.[17]

Against this somber background, on the day after Martin released MacArthur's letter, April 6, the President called Marshall, Acheson, Harriman and me to the White House to discuss the MacArthur problem for about one hour. This meeting took place immediately after the regular Friday Cabinet meeting. Giving no inkling that he had made up his mind to fire MacArthur, Truman asked what, in our opinion, should be done? Truman, as Harriman has stated, proceeded in this matter with greatest care and delicacy, far more so than would be indicated by his private diary entries or his memoirs.[18]

Some accounts of what took place at this meeting, including Truman's, are at variance with my notes and recollections. Truman reports that Harriman advised that Truman should have fired MacArthur two years before. Harriman more recently said that that was a misquote and that what he had actually said was: "Mr. President, this was a problem which you faced last August and which you decided you would not deal with until later." Truman correctly wrote that Marshall advised caution, particularly in light of the adverse effect a relief of MacArthur might have on the huge military appropriations bill then before Congress. Marshall asked for more time to reflect; Truman asked if Marshall would read all the key messages between the JCS and MacArthur over the last two years and, of course, Marshall did. Although Acheson clearly favored firing MacArthur—he did not attempt to conceal his position—he, too, advised caution. "If you relieve MacArthur," Acheson said, "you will have the biggest fight of your administration." Acheson believed that before the President acted it was essential that he have unanimous and unshakable backing from all his top civilian and military leaders, particularly Marshall and the JCS.[19]

As to my position, Truman is in error. He wrote: "General Bradley approached the question entirely from the point of view of military discipline. As he saw it, there was a clear case of insubordination and the general deserved to be relieved of command." Truman added that I first wished to consult the JCS. This is not true. On the contrary, there was considerable doubt in my mind that MacArthur had committed a clear-cut case of military insubordination as defined in Army Regulations. Ultimately I concluded that he had not. My advice that morning was to go slow; I did want time to reflect and talk it over with the JCS. Collins was still down South on a busy schedule and not due back until Saturday evening. To call him back prematurely would cause possible alarm and possibly harmful speculation.[20]

The upshot of this meeting was to defer any hard and fast decisions until Collins returned and the JCS could meet unhurriedly. The President asked all of us to think it over, talk among ourselves and meet with him later.

That afternoon—after the meeting with British ambassador Franks and Tedder—Marshall, Acheson, Harriman and I met in Marshall's office for two hours. Marshall did not want to fire MacArthur outright. He suggested we first call him home for consultations. Acheson was opposed to this idea, as were Harriman and I. Acheson thought that to bring MacArthur home "in the full panoply of his commands" would be the "road to disaster." He foresaw a public alliance between the Republican "primitives" and MacArthur that might be ruinous to Truman and impair his freedom of decision. Marshall saw the wisdom of Acheson's point of view and withdrew his suggestion. We decided that when we met with the President on the following day we would recommend deferral of any action until Collins had returned. This would give all of us a full weekend to think it over.[21]

That same night Truman vented his feelings in his diary: "MacArthur shoots another political bomb through Joe Martin. . . . This looks like the last straw. Rank insubordination. . . . I call in Gen. Marshall, Dean Acheson, Mr. Harriman and Gen. Bradley . . . to discuss situation. I've come to the conclusion that our Big General in the Far East must be recalled. I don't express any opinion or make known my decision."[22]

We four met again with the President at 8:50 A.M. on Saturday, April 7, for about an hour and ten minutes. Here it was revealed that MacArthur had made yet another public statement on the Korean War without clearing it beforehand. This one appeared in a now-defunct right-wing magazine, *The Freeman*. The editor had written MacArthur citing a news report that the ROK Army was releasing young ROK draftees because the United States would not give them equipment. Why, the editor asked, had not the United States supplied enough equipment to arm them? MacArthur's published reply was that the question "involves basic political decisions beyond my authority." In sum, it was Washington's fault. The truth was that MacArthur himself had recommended on January 6 against creating or arming any more ROK groups, owing to the abysmal performance of the existing units.[23]

Truman wrote that at this meeting Marshall reported that he had read all the messages between the JCS and MacArthur and he had now concluded that "MacArthur should have been fired two years ago." That is not true either. As planned, we merely advised the President to postpone any action until Monday, giving us all another two full days to cogitate and me time to meet with the full JCS. Truman agreed.[24]

After the White House meeting that Saturday, I met with Marshall in his office for a little more than an hour. By that time it seemed obvious what course Truman would pursue. Marshall and I were not certain that it was the wisest course, for a number of reasons, certainly not on a charge of military insubordination as defined in Army Regulations. That could lead to myriad legal entanglements, perhaps even—God forbid!—a Billy Mitchell–type court-martial. I again discussed the possibility of a letter in effect telling MacArthur to shut up. The two of us actually tried our hand at drafting a letter on a pad. But this grew too complicated and we tore it up. I went home to think.[25]

This was an especially difficult decision for Marshall and me. Marshall had agreed to serve as Secretary of Defense for only a year. More and more he was delegating responsibilities to the extraordinarily able Bob Lovett, whom he was grooming as his successor. He had only about five months to go before retiring. Firing MacArthur was certain to cause an unprecedented furor and provoke yet another savage right-wing political assault on Marshall personally, hardly a pleasant way to wind up his long and distinguished public career. Moreover, although untrue, there was a widespread belief in military circles (and some media) that Marshall had long had it in for MacArthur, and a recommendation to fire him might be construed as an act of revenge.

I was in a somewhat similar position. I had been appointed to a two-year term as JCS Chairman. My term would expire in four months, after which I expected to retire from public life. In my nearly six years of Washington duty I had been spared attack by the right-wing primitives on the Hill and had always endeavored to be scrupulously apolitical. Endorsing Truman's decision to fire MacArthur might be construed as a political act. It might provoke the primitives and subject me to the kind of savage mauling they were giving Acheson and Marshall. Personally, I did not relish going out on that sour note either.

There was a larger point. If the JCS endorsed Truman's decision to fire MacArthur and if the firing was construed as mainly political, this could have the effect of "politicizing" the JCS. This, in turn, could lead to a drastic erosion in the standing of the JCS as objective advisers to any and all presidents, whatever the political party. Conceivably we might ultimately find ourselves in the position of changing the membership of the JCS with every change of administration, a prospect I viewed as calamitous.

At that time Army Secretary Frank Pace was on an inspection trip in the Far East. We knew that he had been cordially received by MacArthur in Tokyo and had no inkling of what was transpiring in Washington. Marshall and I decided that if Truman was actually going to relieve MacArthur, the best way to handle it would be for Pace to do it personally. However, this presented a problem. If we cabled Pace's instructions to Tokyo, the message was certain to be intercepted in MacArthur's headquarters before reaching Pace, leaking to MacArthur. To avoid that possibility we decided to use State Department communications channels to Ambassador Muccio in Pusan, Korea. Accordingly Marshall got off a personal message to Pace which utterly baffled him: "This is explicit. Repeat this is explicit. You will proceed to Korea and remain there until you hear from me."

That night I thought long and hard. Truman, as President and Commander in Chief, had established our policy for the conduct of the Korean War. MacArthur was clearly opposed to that policy and had openly and defiantly challenged it to the point where there was a serious question that he would carry out that policy. It was not a question of who was right or wrong. As the ultimate in civilian control over the military, Commander in Chief Truman had every right to replace a general who defied his policy and in whom he had lost confidence.

On the following day, Sunday, April 8, at my request, the full JCS met from 2 to 4 P.M. I told them that Truman was considering relieving MacArthur and that Marshall wanted JCS views "from a strictly military viewpoint." We discussed every conceivable aspect. We even considered proposing that MacArthur be left in his Tokyo post with no direct control over Ridgway and the Eighth Army. But owing to the close interrelation of the defenses of Japan and the war in Korea, this idea was rejected. In the end the JCS agreed unanimously that MacArthur should be relieved.[26]

Because of the legal complexities that could arise, we avoided the term "insubordination" as a reason. In point of fact, MacArthur had stretched but had not legally violated any JCS directives. He had violated the President's December 6 directive, relayed to him by the JCS, but this did not constitute violation of a direct JCS order.

I wrote our reasons for declaring for the relief of General MacArthur in a memo sixteen days later, on April 24. Later, on May 16, I prepared a revised memo, which was distributed to Collins, Vandenberg and Sherman. They approved it without change. This is that second memo:

> 1. By his public statements and by his official communications to us, he [MacArthur] had indicated that he was not in sympathy with the decision to try to limit the conflict to Korea. This would make it difficult for him to carry out Joint Chiefs of Staff directives. Since we had decided to try to confine the conflict to Korea and avoid a third world war, it was necessary to have a commander more responsive to control from Washington.
>
> 2. General MacArthur had failed to comply with the Presidential directive to clear statements on policy before making such statements public. He had also taken independent action in proposing to negotiate directly with the enemy field commander for an armistice and had made that statement public,

despite the fact that he knew the President had such a proposal under consideration from a governmental level.

3. The Joint Chiefs of Staff have felt, and feel now, that the military must be controlled by civilian authority in this country. (The Congress itself was very careful to emphasize this point in the National Security Act of 1947 and in its amendment in 1949.) They have always adhered to this principle and they felt that General MacArthur's actions were continuing to jeopardize the civilian control over the military authorities.[27]

After the JCS meeting on the afternoon of April 8 we went immediately to Marshall's office, arriving at 4:05. We were, as Collins wrote, "a sad and sober group." After we took seats, Marshall asked each of us individually for our views and we gave them orally. He then asked for our conclusions. I spoke for the group: If it should be the President's decision to relieve MacArthur, the JCS concurred. Marshall made no comment other than to ask that I state the views of the JCS to the President at a meeting scheduled at the White House the following morning.[28]

In the meantime, that same Sunday, Truman was reaching outside his inner circles for advice and counsel. He separately invited Chief Justice Fred Vinson, a longtime close friend and adviser, House Speaker Sam Rayburn and Treasury Secretary John Snyder to the White House for talks. He spoke by telephone to Vice President Alben Barkley, who was in the hospital. Truman still did not disclose his intentions. Exactly what Vinson, Snyder and Barkley advised I never knew.[29]

On Monday, April 9, Marshall, Acheson, Harriman and I met with the President at the White House after the Cabinet meeting to give him our counsel. At Marshall's suggestion, I conveyed the views of the JCS. Although technically by law I could not vote on JCS matters, it was clear to Truman that I concurred with the JCS views, as did Marshall. Acheson and Harriman were still emphatic that MacArthur should be relieved. After all had spoken, Truman then revealed—for the first time—his view that MacArthur should be relieved.

That done, we then dealt with the question of MacArthur's successor. Marshall, Collins and I had already decided that Ridgway was the logical man for the job and so told the President. At the same time, we recommended that Van Fleet replace Ridgway as commander of the Eighth Army. Truman forthwith approved these choices and asked me to handle the various official messages to effect MacArthur's relief and the transfers of Ridgway and Van Fleet. I returned to the Pentagon at 11:38 and delegated the preparation of the paperwork to Collins.[30]

On the following day, Tuesday, April 10, Marshall, Acheson, Harriman and I met again with the President at 3 P.M. Presidential press secretary Joseph Short sat in on this meeting at Truman's invitation so that he could prepare a press release on MacArthur's relief. The President approved the idea of having Army Secretary Frank Pace return from Korea to Tokyo and deliver the news to MacArthur. As we planned, a cable would go to Pace via Muccio in Pusan telling Pace to meet with MacArthur at his home in Tokyo at 8 P.M., April 11, Washington time. I did not envy young Pace his assignment.[31]

This careful plan went awry in a most curious and unfortunate way. Later that day, a *Chicago Tribune* radio reporter in the Far East telephoned the *Tribune*'s managing editor in Chicago to say he had it on good authority that MacArthur was to be fired. The *Tribune* notified its Washington correspondent, Walter Trohan. Trohan got busy checking White House sources and mobilized his able Pentagon correspondent, Lloyd Norman, to "nose around." Trohan confronted Joe Short, Truman's press secretary. "I got a double talk, so I knew there must be something to it," Trohan recalled. Meanwhile, Norman contacted my press aide, Ted Clifton, and, as Norman later put it, "could not get a denial."

In the meantime, Trohan recalled, the *Tribune*'s radio reporter in the Far East called Chicago to say he thought he was in error. Trohan recalled: "With that the managing editor decided to kill the story. I protested. It was a stupid decision. Although Norman and I did not have a solid confirmation, by that time we thought we had enough to go with a speculative story."

The inquiries from Trohan and Norman convinced Joe Short and Clifton that there had been a leak somewhere. They believed the *Tribune* would break the story in its editions of the following morning. This fear—groundless, as it developed—led to a tremendous flap. A concern developed that MacArthur might beat Truman to the punch and resign. Truman, in part to head off that possibility, decided the orders should go out immediately through JCS channels directly to MacArthur. Frank Pace should be told to disregard his instructions. Truman called an extraordinary press conference for 1 A.M., April 11. When Trohan arrived at the White House, correspondent Merriman Smith said, "What's up, Walt?" Trohan, correctly divining the reason for the press conference, replied knowingly, "They're going to fire MacArthur." When the official documents were released, Trohan sprinted eleven blocks to his home on R Street. Owing to the time difference in Chicago, he was able to phone in the story but it only made the *Tribune*'s final editions.[32]

The JCS communications channels were slower than we calculated. Before the orders reached MacArthur, radio reports of the White House press conference were broadcast in Tokyo. One of MacArthur's aides heard it, tearfully told Mrs. MacArthur, who told her husband. He was at lunch with Senator Warren Magnuson and others. Courtney Whitney wrote that "MacArthur's face froze." Then he stood up and with no trace of emotion said to his wife, within the hearing of his luncheon guests, "Jeannie, we're going home at last." Privately he was justifiably furious at the manner in which the news reached him.[33]

In Korea, owing to a communications breakdown in Pusan, Frank Pace did not receive his original instructions to go to Tokyo and fire MacArthur. His first intimation of what was transpiring came when Lev Allen gave him a personal message from Marshall telling Pace to disregard his earlier unreceived instructions, find Ridgway and tell him he was now Supreme Commander Allied Powers in the Pacific. Pace took Ridgway outside into a raging hailstorm and gave him the news. Ridgway was thunderstruck. He found it hard to believe. Pace was worried about the live grenades that Ridgway wore on a shoulder harness. He later recalled thinking that if a "hailstone hits one of those live grenades, they're going to need a new Supreme Commander *and* a new Secretary."[34]

Ridgway flew to Tokyo and met with MacArthur for an hour in the late afternoon of April 12. Ridgway has written that the meeting was cordial and that MacArthur "was entirely himself—composed, quiet, temperate, friendly, and helpful to the man who was to succeed him." What amazed Ridgway most was MacArthur's "apparent lack of rancor or resentment."

In a private memo for the record, however, Ridgway noted: "He stated that he had been told by an eminent medical man who had gotten it from General [Wallace] Graham, the President's physician, that the President was suffering from malignant hypertension; that his affliction was characterized by bewilderment and confusion of thought; that it was because of this he had written both the letter to the music critic and the one about the Marines; that according to the medical man, he wouldn't live six months." MacArthur went on to say that he had a "hankering" to go to New York to live, not having seen it since the 1930's. He alluded to various offers he had received, "one for $150,000 for some unstated purpose, another for $300,000 to write 50 lectures and 'raise hell' . . . and one for a million, which again he did not enlarge upon."[35]

That night Truman delivered a speech to the nation designed to explain and defend his dismissal of MacArthur. It was a complete flop. Instead of specifically explaining the reasons for MacArthur's dismissal, Truman, partly on Acheson's advice, chose a loftier (and duller) theme: Defense of his Korean War policy. The 84,000 letters reaching the White House after the speech were 55 percent pro-MacArthur. A great opportunity had been lost. Having made this courageous political decision, Truman failed to mobilize the country behind him and, by this default, helped pave the way for MacArthur's triumphant return.[36]

MacArthur left Tokyo on April 16. His first stop was San Francisco, where his party was mobbed by tens of thousands of frenetic admirers. There, he said, "I was just asked if I intended to enter politics. My reply was no. I have no political aspirations whatsoever. I do not intend to run for political office, and I hope that my name will never be used in a political way. The only politics I have is contained in a single phrase known well to all of you—'God bless America.' "[37]

By sheer coincidence, that day, April 17, I fulfilled a long-standing commitment to address a group of radio and television broadcasters in Chicago. Believing that the public must by now be somewhat confused by our Korean War policy, I chose that as my subject. I frankly outlined our policy as I have described it, stressing that our goal was to limit the war. Although not intended to be, my speech was widely interpreted as a public "rebuttal" of MacArthur's views, and reports on it became intermingled with reports on his return. The front-page headline in *The New York Times* the following day was:

> M'ARTHUR IS HAILED BY SAN FRANCISCO;
> GREAT CROWDS ROAR HERO GREETING;
> BRADLEY OPPOSES WIDENING KOREAN WAR

My speech thus became controversial. Absurd suggestions were made that the State Department had inserted material into the speech. Questions were raised as to why I could speak out on foreign policy while MacArthur could not. It did little good to explain that unlike MacArthur's statements, my speech had been cleared and, in any case, my views were not in opposition to government policy.[38]

Adding to my public relations problems, the April 9 issue of *Life* magazine had just come out. It featured me on the cover decked out in my ETO battle jacket and helmet, and contained the first installment of a four-part excerpt of my book, *A Soldier's Story*. The timing was purely coincidental. However, inasmuch as I had not "cleared" the book and in some instances it was critical of Montgomery, questions were raised as to why I was permitted to publicly criticize an important NATO ally like Monty when MacArthur had been fired for speaking out. (One of the ironies of this contretemps was that *Life* was editorially one of MacArthur's most ardent supporters.)[39]

These attacks were merely the beginning of a concerted campaign by right-wing primitives who were determined to punish me for my role in firing MacArthur. The attacks upon me never became as vicious as those leveled at Truman, Acheson and Marshall; nonetheless, as I had feared, my long Washington "honeymoon" was over.[40]

From San Francisco, MacArthur flew directly to Washington, where he had been invited to address a joint session of Congress. At the President's suggestion, Marshall and the full Joint Chiefs met his plane, the *Bataan,* which arrived at National Airport thirty-two minutes past midnight on April 19. The White House was represented by Truman's Army aide, Harry Vaughan; "Skinny" Wainwright also joined our official greeting party. Congressman Joe Martin was on hand as well. An estimated 12,000 Washingtonians turned out to cheer MacArthur. Security broke down and a hysterical crowd rushed the plane as it came to a stop. We welcomed MacArthur with strained but proper military courtesy and he, in turn, was courteous. "Hello, George," MacArthur boomed, as he clasped hands with Marshall. "How are you?" Marshall's reply went unheard as the crowd and media (some photographers wearing football helmets) engulfed us.[41]

Later that day, April 19, MacArthur spoke before the joint session of Congress. Neither Marshall nor the Joint Chiefs attended. However, after the speech there was a ceremony to honor MacArthur on the grounds of the Washington Monument at which Marshall and the Chiefs were present. I watched MacArthur's address to Congress on television in the Pentagon before leaving for the Monument. It was quintessential MacArthur, the most effective presentation of his views possible and one of the most moving speeches I had ever heard. His concluding lines touched me deeply: "I now close my military career and just fade away—an old soldier who tried to do his duty as God gave him the light to see that duty. Goodbye."

There was one quite disturbing aspect about the speech. Once again he advocated intensification of the economic blockade of Red China; the imposition of a naval blockade against Red China; removal of "restrictions on air reconnaissance" of China's coastal area and Manchuria; and removal of restrictions on Chiang's forces "with logistical support to contribute to their effective operations against the common enemy." He then said that those views were "fully shared" by the Joint Chiefs of Staff. As we have seen, this was not true. The JCS "fully approved" only the first of these four proposals and had emphatically rejected the fourth. We favored proposals two and three, as stated in our January 12 study, only in the event of a much more serious situation.[42]

After MacArthur finished his triumphal visits to various cities throughout the country, he returned to Washington on May 3 to become the first witness before a special Senate committee, convened ostensibly to investigate his dismissal. The committee was composed of thirteen members of the Senate Armed Services Committee and thirteen members of the Senate Foreign Relations Committee. The hearings were "closed," but at the end of each day a transcript, censored by Arthur Davis of the JCS joint staff, was released to the media. Senator Richard B. Russell, a Democrat from Georgia, served as chairman. Most of the testimony was taken in May and June, but the committee did not complete its final reports until August.[43]

MacArthur appeared first, for three days. Marshall followed him to the stand, testifying for six consecutive days. I came next, for another six days (May 15, 16, 21, 22, 23 and 24). Then came Collins, Vandenberg and Sherman for two days each. Acheson was the final major administration witness. He spent eight full days on the stand.[44]

With some twenty-six senators on hand asking questions, the hearings wandered all over the place. And they became repetitious—the same questions again and again in different forms. In the first week or so there was tremendous excitement, but after that the affair, in my opinion, became a great bore.[45]

It was during my opening statement, on May 15, that I said that enlarging or widening the war with Red China would be a mistake. "Frankly, in the opinion of the Joint Chiefs of Staff, this strategy would involve us in the wrong war, at the wrong place, at the wrong time, and with the wrong enemy." Subsequently, many careless writers have misconstrued this statement as JCS views on the Korean War itself.[46]

Much of our time was spent in denying MacArthur's assertion to the joint session of Congress that the JCS "fully shared" his views on widening the war. The JCS "study" of January 12 was introduced as "proof" that we did indeed share MacArthur's views. All five of us from Defense spent countless hours explaining that our recommendations to bomb and blockade China were based solely on the contingency that we would be facing a far more serious situation.[47]

Early in my testimony, one of the hostile senators, Alexander Wiley, asked me to divulge what was said at the April 6 White House meeting with the President. I refused, saying, "At that time I was in a position of a confidential adviser to the President. I do not feel at liberty to publicize what any of us said at that time." This led to a prolonged parliamentary debate on executive privilege, with veiled threats to cite me "for contempt." In my absence on May 17, the committee finally put the question of whether or not I could be compelled to testify (or be held in contempt) to a vote. My position carried by eighteen to eight, and the matter was put to rest.

The great MacArthur Hearings finally wound down. The committee reached no conclusions. Acheson put it well: "Senator Russell piloted the two committees into safe haven with great skill and wise judgment. Aware that any reference to the committee's terms of reference would only open partisan rifts and bickering, he treated those terms with intelligent neglect. Instead of a majority report, which would have invited a minority report, he dealt with those gloriously broad generalities to which the wise and just could repair, thus turning the committees from unhappy differences to universal agreement."[48]

In the meantime, the war in Korea went on. Ridgway had moved to Tokyo, and Van Fleet assumed command of the Eighth Army. It was a great relief to finally have a man in Tokyo who was in agreement with the administration views on containing the war.

When Ridgway took over, we were still very much concerned about the intelligence reports indicating a Soviet move, either direct or through Red China. There had been a substantial build-up in the Red Chinese Air Force. This suggested the possibility of an all-out air assault on the Eighth Army, our supply bases in Inchon and Pusan, or perhaps on Japan. So far, the Chinese had not attacked our troops or bases in Korea by air—giving us, in effect, a reverse "sanctuary."

Such was our confidence in Ridgway that the JCS sent to him, for *contingency planning purposes,* that which we had withheld from MacArthur: authorization, in event of a "major air attack" on our Korean forces, to bomb enemy air bases in Manchuria and the Shantung Peninsula of China. We stressed that the message did not authorize such bombing; that would have to be cleared through the JCS.

We had asked Ridgway if this gave him sufficient latitude and flexibility to respond quickly enough to an enemy air attack. He immediately replied no. He requested that we delegate to him authority to carry out the mission without prior need to clear through the JCS. On April 28, after obtaining the President's permission, we not only delegated that authority but also authorized, by way of preparation and intelligence gathering, immediate air *reconnaissance* of enemy air bases in Manchuria and the Shantung Peninsula, to be "made at high altitude and as surreptitiously as possible."[49]

Fortunately for us, this crisis soon passed; neither the Soviets nor the Red Chinese launched air attacks on our forces or bases in Korea. Nor did Red China attack Indochina or Formosa. The Chinese restricted air activity principally to large flights of Migs into northwest Korea. Our Air Force F-86 fighters engaged the Migs in dogfights, scoring many kills.

On the ground, Van Fleet, a fine soldier and leader, ably filled Ridgway's shoes. He did not have long to wait for real action. On April 22, the Chinese launched a massive attack (some 337,000 men) against the Eighth Army. Under the weight of this attack, a ROK division in the center broke, compelling Van Fleet to fall back some thirty-five miles in the west—to a mere five miles north of Seoul. But under Van Fleet's steady hand, the Eighth Army held, inflicting slaughter on the lightly armed Chinese. The attack soon beat itself out on the ironlike Eighth Army front.[50]

A second massive Chinese attack hit the Eighth Army on May 16. Five Chinese armies attempted to drive a wedge between IX and X Corps. Van Fleet met this attack, then counterattacked along his whole broad front, enveloping and killing Chinese by the thousands with massed artillery, tanks and air support. This Eighth Army counteroffensive resulted in the capture of huge quantities of enemy weapons and 10,000 dispirited POW's, indicating morale was falling badly. Van Fleet's northward momentum took the Eighth Army back to where it had been on April 22, roughly along the 38th parallel.[51]

The absolute defeat of these two massive enemy offensives in as many months was another notable milestone in the Korean War. The combined enemy numbered nearly half a million men. Even that was not enough to push us out of Korea. To do so would require the commitment of even greater numbers of men and ever larger losses. Were the Chinese willing to pay the price? We began to doubt it.

The time was ripe to draw up a blueprint for a final solution to the Korean problem. It appeared now that neither side could win a decisive victory in Korea. In our memorandum of April 5, the JCS had said that the Korean War could not be resolved "by military action alone." On May 1, the NSC met to consider that paper and others, and subsequently generated a blueprint which Truman approved on May 17. With due allowance for certain military maneuvers to obtain a more favorable defensive line, the United States would now go all out to reach a solution to Korea, as Collins put it, "primarily by political negotiations."[52]

Thus we arrived at a military stalemate in Korea. The fighting would continue along the 38th parallel—some of it fierce—for two more bloody years, costing thousands more American lives, as we sought to force the Chinese communists to the negotiating table.

SIXTY-TWO

The task of achieving a negotiated armistice in Korea consumed no little time and effort of the JCS over the next two years. But I prefer to return here to a matter which throughout the Korean military crisis had burdened the JCS no less, NATO.

Ike had accepted the post of Supreme Commander in December 1950. His first step was to make an "exploratory" trip to visit NATO governments. The JCS saw Ike off at the Washington Military Air Transport Service airfield on January 6, 1951, and greeted him, in company with the President, on his return, January 31. In bitter cold, snowy winter weather, Ike had visited eleven European capitals. He wrote: "I was favorably impressed by the governments with which I conferred. Each was prepared, more or less, to do its part. Of course, each wanted more American strength in Europe than we then had and I agreed to strive to attain reinforcements, but only on a temporary, emergency basis. I had to point out over and over again that the United States would be providing a strong Navy and Air Force for the benefit of all of us and at the same time we would always have to be one of the principal arsenals of democracy in the event we got into trouble." In other words, Europe should provide the bulk of the manpower, the United States would provide the weapons.[1]

In the meantime there was arising among Old Guard Republicans a new, intense wave of isolationism. This had begun in the dark days of December 1950, when we feared we were on the brink of World War III. On December 20, ex-President Herbert Hoover in a major address had decried our involvement in both the Far East and Europe. He urged a total military pullback, letting the Atlantic and Pacific oceans serve as our protection, making the "Western Hemisphere the Gibraltar of Western civilization." His ideas were seconded by a conservative Democrat, former ambassador to England, Joseph P. Kennedy, whose son John was a representative then preparing to run for the Senate. Although Joseph Kennedy held no official governmental position, his views carried weight in some circles. These public pronouncements would touch off what came to be known as the "Great Debate."[2]

Congress soon leaped into the debate. On January 3, 1951, on the eve of Ike's trip to Europe, conservative representative Frederic R. Coudert, Jr., of Manhattan, introduced into the House a resolution declaring that "no additional military forces" be sent abroad "without the prior authorization of the Congress in each instance." This was followed by a similar resolution, introduced into the Senate by Kenneth Wherry, a conservative Republican from Nebraska, which declared that "no American troops shall be sent to Europe for the purpose of the Atlantic Pact without the approval of Congress." These resolutions called into question the President's constitutional powers to deploy troops in peacetime where he saw fit without the express approval of Congress.[3]

Up to this point Republican Senator Arthur Vandenberg, an isolationist in pre–World War II days but a determined internationalist in the postwar period, had strongly supported Truman's foreign policy. He had helped pass the Truman Doctrine and NATO. Unfortunately, Vandenberg was now gravely ill (he would die on the day MacArthur arrived in Washington to make his speech to the joint session) and no longer a force in the Senate. Senator Robert Taft, who had voted against NATO and who had generally deferred to Vandenberg, now began to assume a leading foreign policy role in the Senate.[4]

It was not easy to discern exactly where Taft stood on foreign policy. Some have declared him a pure isolationist, but I believe that oversimplifies. He initially supported the administration on Korea. In time, his views would very nearly coincide with MacArthur's. Taft was now the front runner for the Republican nomination in 1952 and the leader of the opposition. It often appeared to me that his foreign policy was more muleheaded reactionary opposition to whatever Truman did rather than any clearly defined policy of his own.

After Coudert and Wherry introduced their resolutions in the House and Senate, Taft, in major speeches, supported both resolutions. Senator Wherry called for hearings on sending troops to Europe. The Great Debate was on.[5]

The JCS had taken the position that in addition to air and naval power, and the atomic bomb backup, the United States should furnish six divisions to Europe. There were already the equivalent of two divisions in Manton Eddy's Seventh Army in Germany; we should send four more: one armored and three infantry. We did not delude ourselves that six American divisions could stop the Russians. The hope was that our six divisions in full battle regalia would inspire other NATO nations to get cracking and put troops in the field. (We hoped to quickly deploy a total of some forty divisions.) Ike returned from his tour convinced that our position was correct and, not incidentally, passionately committed to the concept of NATO.[6]

Ike appeared before an informal gathering of Congress in the Library of Congress auditorium and made a speech on television espousing his views. He then testified for NATO—and a six-division U.S. force—in closed sessions before various House and Senate committees. In these sessions he began to sense the deep-seated opposition to NATO. This in turn led to an extraordinary private meeting with Taft at the Pentagon, which Ike described in his book *At Ease*.

By this time, there was widespread speculation that Ike would be a nominee for the presidency in 1952. Both Democrats and Republicans were urging him to run. If he decided to run, as Democrat or Republican, he represented a potent threat to Taft's ambitions to gain the White House. Ike wrote that before his private Pentagon meeting with Taft he reached the conclusion that if Taft would support the concept of NATO, Ike would issue a statement renouncing any political ambitions, so strong in tone that it would be "impossible" for him to have "any political future." Ike jotted down his statement and stuck it in his pocket: "Having been called back to military duty, I want to announce that my name may not be used by anyone as a candidate for President—and if any do I will repudiate such efforts."

Ike wrote that Taft arrived at the meeting "a bit suspicious" of Ike's motives. Ike put it to Taft bluntly. He said if Taft would agree to the principle that "collective security is necessary for us in Western Europe," Ike would spend his "next years" attempting to carry out his great responsibilities. If Taft would not agree, if there was to be a continuing serious division between Congress and Truman on NATO, then, Ike told Taft, "I would probably be back in the United States."

Taft, perhaps still suspicious, refused to change his position. He was not sure what he would do, he said. After he left, Ike took the statement out, tore it up and threw it away. Ike wrote: "I gained the impression—possibly a mistaken one—that he and some of his colleagues were interested, primarily, in cutting the President, or the Presidency, down to size."[7]

This little-known meeting was a milestone in our history. Ike was absolutely a man of his word. If Taft had made the deal, I am certain that Ike would have stood by his statement and would not have been a presidential candidate in 1952. Taft could then have had the Republican nomination in a walk, and he probably would have beaten Adlai Stevenson. Since Taft declared that if nominated he would name MacArthur as his vice presidential running mate, that would have meant that in mid-1953, when Taft died of cancer, MacArthur would have become President. I still cringe every time I think about how close we came to having MacArthur in the White House.[8]

The Great Debate absorbed a good deal of our time in February 1951. Marshall, Acheson and I came to bat on the Hill. Acheson wrote that Marshall mounted a counterattack with "devastating effect." I certainly agree. This was one of Marshall's finest hours. Acheson also wrote, apropos of this debate, that "General Bradley was one of the best colleagues in a fight I have ever known." Acheson was a brilliant man and I admired him tremendously. Sad to say, he was *not* a good ally in a fight on the Hill. There Acheson was imperious and professorial and invariably talked down to senators and congressmen, an unwise posture that often needlessly antagonized them.[9]

We squeaked through, but the victory was somewhat murky. In our favor, no inhibiting legislation emerged. However, one provision of a Senate resolution (passed by a close vote of forty-nine to forty-three) specified that "no ground troops in addition to . . . four divisions should be sent to Western Europe . . . without further congressional approval." The JCS got the NATO force levels we had recommended, but Truman, in effect, got a slap on the wrist.*

Ike returned to Europe in mid-February 1951 to take up his duties as SACEUR (Supreme Allied Commander Europe) at SHAPE (Supreme Headquarters Allied Powers in Europe), which was formally opened for business on April 2. He located SHAPE at a site near Versailles. Montgomery moved into SHAPE as deputy supreme commander. On paper, as chairman of the NATO standing group, I was now Ike's military boss.[11]

Ike had his hands full launching SHAPE. There were many growing pains. His first personal letter to me, of March 30, was a gloomy litany of problems. In response, I tried to cheer him up: "I know that you must at times feel very frustrated in trying to get things done. However, I know of no one who is as well qualified to get things going or who would command the respect of the European people as much as you do. I must confess that at times during the war some of our allies sorely taxed my patience, but you always seemed to straighten them out."[12]

After my testimony before the MacArthur hearings, I flew to Europe on June 1 to give Ike a little moral support. Mary accompanied me. We spent four busy working days in Paris with Ike, his chief of staff, Al Gruenther, U.S. ambassador David K. E. Bruce and others, including my old friend and Twelfth Army Group G-1, Red O'Hare, all of whom wined and dined us royally. On the night of June 4, I met with a group of American correspondents at the home of journalist Theodore H. White, a one-time China hand for Henry Luce and, much later, author of *The Making of the President* series.

These correspondents were, of course, avid for background on the Far East and the firing of MacArthur. I candidly spelled out the JCS policy views on the Far East and Korea, but ducked all personal questions on

* The divisions sent over were the 4th Infantry (in May 1951), the 2nd Armored (in July) and two of the four National Guard divisions mobilized in September 1950: the 43rd Infantry Division (in October) and my old outfit, the 28th Infantry Division (in November). Six tactical air groups were deployed with the troops.[10]

MacArthur. Later, my press aide, Ted Clifton, discussed the MacArthur firing with them, saying, according to C. L. Sulzberger, that while MacArthur commanded in Korea, his mood ranged from "hysterical optimism" to "deepest pessimism." In a lengthy review of the situation, Clifton said that MacArthur had made three big mistakes: He had split his forces unnecessarily; he misinterpreted the intelligence on the Chinese communists; and he predicted we couldn't hold in Korea. Ridgway, he concluded, had accomplished what MacArthur had said was impossible.[13]

On June 6, we flew from Paris to London, crossing the English Channel. As I looked down on the choppy waters, it was hard to believe that seven years had passed since D-day on Utah and Omaha beaches. Seven years and yet another war unresolved, blood still spilling on battlefields far away.

Our five-day stay in England was memorable. In addition to full days of working meetings with the British Chiefs and others on NATO problems, we enjoyed many elegant social functions: a dinner in honor of Lord Tedder at Cambridge; a luncheon in our honor in London given by Field Marshal William Slim; a garden party at the home of Lady Astor, where we met the Queen; a dinner party in our honor in London given by Field Marshal Wilson; a luncheon in our honor at Norman Tower, Windsor Castle, by Viscount and Viscountess Gowrie.[14]

After we returned to Washington, I received the most shocking news. While on a NATO inspection trip, Admiral Forrest Sherman died of a heart attack in Naples, Italy, on July 22. His body was returned to Washington on July 25 for a funeral on July 27, with full military honors. His was a great and sad loss. Sherman had grown into an outstanding strategist and, in contrast to his predecessor Denfeld, a cooperative JCS partner. He had ably led the Navy from its 1949 nadir to a position of strength and confidence. History should not forget this outstanding statesman-sailor.[15]

The leading candidates to succeed Sherman as Chief of Naval Operations were the two senior fleet commanders: Arthur Radford in the Pacific and William M. Fechteler in the Atlantic. I do not believe Truman ever seriously considered Radford. The sores Radford had opened in the "Admirals' Revolt" of 1949 had not yet healed. Fechteler was chosen and approved by the Senate on August 9. After I got to know Fechteler, I felt the loss of Sherman even more keenly.[16]

When this change in CNO took place, Truman took steps to strengthen the Navy's civilian leadership. Kindly, ineffective Frank Matthews was eased out and named Ambassador to Ireland. Navy Undersecretary Dan A. Kimball, a Missourian (St. Louis) and World War I Army aviator, moved up to replace Matthews. A positive personality like Symington and an adroit bureaucrat, Kimball had provided exceptional strength and continuity through Sullivan's resignation, the Admirals' Revolt, the firing of Denfeld, and Matthews' lackluster term. I liked Kimball and was glad to see him get the job. He made no pretense at being a military strategist. His strengths lay in his managerial ability, his technical background (he was a rocket and jet propulsion expert) and his knowledge and contacts in the aerospace industry.[17]

The Kimball-Matthews relief took place on July 31, and the Fechteler swearing-in on August 16.

August 16 was also the day I was sworn in for my second term as Chairman of the Joint Chiefs of Staff in a small ceremony in my office, attended by Mary, Lee and Hal (still on the air staff and shortly to be promoted to major) and my grandson, Hank. Truman had privately told me some time before that he wished me to serve a second two-year term as JCS Chairman. Since his wish was tantamount to a command, I had to postpone my retirement another two years.[18]

Less than one month later Marshall retired as Secretary of Defense, and Bob Lovett moved up to succeed him on September 17, 1951, as planned. No man was more deserving of full retirement than George Marshall. He had served in the highest positions of responsibility in Washington virtually uninterrupted since 1939. He had mobilized our Army for World War II, helped direct Allied global strategy, served ably as Secretary of State in the Cold War and returned to help direct us through the Korean War and the rearmament that ensued. He was one of the authentic giants in our history, towering far above the much-publicized MacArthur and Patton.

With these changes, the top team at Defense would remain constant for the rest of Truman's term. After Marshall, Lovett, our fourth Secretary of Defense, was the best we had during my five and a half years in the Pentagon. He was a self-effacing but clear-headed and tough administrator who steered us through some very complex and delicate waters (Korean armistice, Japanese peace treaty, NATO build-up, rearmament) with a firm and wise hand. Unlike Acheson, Lovett was esteemed on the Hill and never became a target of the Old Guard primitives. During his term, there were no notable public Pentagon controversies. This alone, I think, speaks volumes about his administrative talents. He took us a long way toward true unification and deserves more credit than he has received.[19]

During my second term as Chairman of the Joint Chiefs, I became a world traveler. I made seven long trips to Europe and two to the Far East. Most of these trips were to attend NATO meetings. Because of its intricate top-heavy structure, there were scads of NATO committees. Since a committee cannot function without meeting, I was kept very busy. Most of these meetings were tedious and dull affairs, often dealing with the most trivial matters. There was constant wrangling as to who was to contribute what forces and who would pay for them and who would command this or that area. No one I know, other than Ike, could have brought all these diverse people together and made NATO work. He did a magnificent job.[20]

At a meeting of the NATO council in Ottawa, Canada, September 16 to 20, 1951, we resolved a very important and highly controversial matter. Greece and Turkey were invited to join NATO, bringing the participating nations to fourteen.[21]

After the Ottawa meeting, I flew out to the Far East, September 26 to October 3. By this time, Van Fleet's Eighth Army had more or less reached a line that seemed satisfactory for defense. In the west sector, it was anchored at Panmunjon, just south of the 38th parallel. From there it ran northeasterly to Chorwon, then straight east across the waist about twenty-five miles north of the parallel, and then, on the east coast, still farther northward to Kosong. This line had been achieved at great cost in American and ROK casualties in brutal World War I-like battles at Porkchop Hill, the Iron Triangle, Heartbreak Ridge, Bloody Ridge and the Punch Bowl. All the while, negotiations were proceeding at a glacial pace, the communists milking them of maximum anti-West propaganda.

Van Fleet's mission, carefully monitored from Tokyo by Ridgway, was frustrating in the extreme. It was to keep sufficient pressure on the communists to make them negotiate in a meaningful way. Few army commanders have ever been called upon for such a delicate and exacting task while paying such a high cost in casualties at the same time. Van Fleet was like a caged lion. He was certain he could punch through to the Yalu and destroy the opposing armies. I felt great sympathy for him—and those men who were killed, wounded or missing—but an armistice, roughly along his battlefield, was the administration's goal. We had to suffer patiently until the communists were ready to end the war.[22]

One dire possibility we had constantly to consider was that the Chinese would suddenly change their strategy, break off the truce talks and attack us with enormous forces brought down from Manchuria. If this occurred, it was not likely the Eighth Army could hold in Korea without extraordinary measures, that is, use of atomic weapons.

Our atomic bomb production lines were now turning out weapons in such great numbers that in the summer of 1951 the JCS, in response to a request from Lovett, began the first serious study of their use in Korea. On August 14, we forwarded the results of our study to Lovett. We recommended that "under current conditions atomic weapons should be employed in the Far East ONLY in the event our forces in that area would otherwise be faced with military disaster." Quite apart from moral and other considerations, such as Soviet reaction, we urged that a decision to use atomic weapons not be taken prematurely, "thus giving present and potential enemies opportunity to develop defenses against what would be a new employment of an existing weapon."

We went on to point out that we had forces in the Far East capable of delivering atomic weapons (we meant our SAC bases on Okinawa), but the "weak link" was that these forces had no experience in "providing tactical atomic support of engaged land forces." We therefore recommended that "simulated" tactical atomic strikes be staged in Korea. Actual atomic weapons (shorn of their nuclear components) would be used in all phases of the tests except "actual flights over enemy territory." There conventional munitions would be employed. These tests commenced in utmost secrecy in September 1951, and were still in progress on my visit to the Far East.[23]

The general American rearmament program, recommended in NSC-68 and given vast impetus by the Korean War, continued at a high level of urgency all through 1951. A new NSC study (No. 114), circulated on July 27, 1951, warned that NSC-68 had underestimated the Soviet threat. Intelligence now indicated that the Soviet Union was increasing its military forces substantially and estimated that by mid-1953 the Russians would have a stockpile of 200 atomic bombs—enough to launch a devastating nuclear attack on the United States. NSC-114 recommended that our defense production be stepped up and military force levels be increased substantially.

During the summer and fall of 1951, the JCS, responding to NSC-114, entered into extended debate over the composition of the increased force levels. These debates were reminiscent of the force level debates in 1948 and 1949. I wrote Ike in September 1951: "Our Chiefs have been meeting every day this week trying to arrive at recommendations for forces for the [fiscal] 1953 budget. We are going through part of the process that you went through with us two years ago. Things seem to get more complicated all the time instead of simpler."[24]

By comparison to 1948–49, the numbers we were now batting back and forth were awesome. Collins wanted an immediate Army of 1.5 million men organized into the equivalent of twenty-seven divisions, which would grow to the equivalent of thirty-three divisions in two years. Sherman (and then Fechteler) wanted a Navy of one million men manning 421 major combatant vessels (including twelve heavy aircraft carriers) and a Marine Corps of three divisions. But they were pikers compared to Vandenberg, who demanded an immediate Air Force of 1.2 million men organized into eighty-seven groups (now called "wings"), growing within two years to an "interim" level of 143 wings. In public testimony, Van had described his service as a "shoestring air force." All this would cost about $70 billion a year.[25]

During the fall of 1951, the JCS, working with Lovett, pared these figures somewhat, but generally the force levels we recommended were approved. The Air Force emerged from these debates a clear winner, programmed for a major buildup to 143 wings—twice the size of the "seventy-group air force'' so passionately debated in 1948–49. These force level decisions in the fall of 1951 laid the groundwork for our strategy of ''massive retaliation'' that prevailed through the 1950s.[26]

By December 1951, when these requests reached the White House, global tensions had eased and general war with the Soviet Union seemed less likely. The Korean peace talks were proceeding, albeit at a snail's pace, in Panmunjon. Truman approved the increased force levels but, conflictingly, disapproved the budget of $70 billion. He set a ceiling of about $45 billion, declaring that he would ''stretch out the build-up.'' (Based on this ceiling, the JCS estimated that the Air Force build-up to 143 wings would be delayed until 1956.) The military budget finally submitted by Truman in January 1952 represented the end of the ''balanced force'' concept which had governed our planning since World War II. Of the $48.1 billion requested, the lion's share ($20.7 billion) went to the Air Force. The Army got $14.2 billion; the Navy $13.2 billion.[27]

This hefty military budget was decried in Congress and elsewhere. Without a commensurate tax increase, it was estimated that it would cause a $14 billion federal deficit, a figure many considered calamitous. Even Ike deplored it. He wrote in his diary that he was ''astonished'' that we could have produced such a monstrous budget. ''The only justification for the imposition of an expenditure program that foresees a minimum $14 billion deficit is an immediate prospect of war—an emergency which removes all normal limitations upon maximum financial, industrial and military effort.'' He had read newspaper speculation that our military budgets would continue at a high level until 1954. ''If this is true (and I cannot believe for a moment that it is) then we are headed for worse than trouble. The effect will be disastrous.''[28]

It was a presidential election year. No one in Congress wanted to raise taxes to cover the deficit. Out came the pruning shears. Bob Taft suggested that an even greater reliance on air power might make possible a $20 billion cut in the defense budget. Fortunately, that proposal went nowhere. Nor were there, finally, any major slashes. In the end, Congress cut about $2 billion, mostly out of the Army and Navy budgets.[29]

The force level debates continued inside the administration throughout 1952. Generally, Truman favored further cutbacks, again stretching out the Air Force build-up. His final military budget, completed in December 1952, and submitted to Congress in January 1953, totaled $40.3 billion, with $16.8 billion for the Air Force, $12.1 billion for the Army and $11.4 billion for the Navy.*

* Actual U.S. forces in being on December 31, 1952, were: Air Force, ninety-eight wings; Navy, 401 major combatant ships (including fourteen heavy carriers, five light carriers and ten jeep carriers) and three Marine divisions; Army, twenty divisions (six of reduced strength), sixteen regiments (four of reduced strength). Manpower: 3.5 million.[30]

All during 1951, a steady stream of Republicans called on Ike at SHAPE, urging him to take a hand in the 1952 presidential race. They argued that the Democrats—Truman in particular—had made a "mess" in Washington which had to be cleared up urgently. Communists had infiltrated the highest levels of government. Truman was surrounded by crooks. Truman was leading the United States down the road to pure socialism and was spending the nation into economic ruin. Some wanted Ike to support Taft and become Secretary of Defense in Taft's Cabinet; others wanted him to run against Taft so that the nation would not be saddled with an isolationist administration should Taft win. To all these callers, Ike at first said no; he would stay right where he was and do the best job he could for the nation.[31]

Two of these callers, both with Army backgrounds, made a difference. One was Lucius Clay, by now retired and working in the private sector, a man in whom Ike had utmost confidence. The other was Senator Henry Cabot Lodge from Massachusetts. Lodge had joined the Army Reserve in the late 1920s and had always been an active and enthusiastic Army backer. As a Reservist, he had participated in the Louisiana and Carolina maneuvers in the early part of the war and had briefly served with a tank outfit in North Africa. In 1944, he had taken the extraordinary step of resigning his Senate seat to go on full-time active Army duty in Italy and, later, France.[32]

In early September 1951, Lodge called on Ike at SHAPE to urge him to run for the presidency on the Republican ticket. Lodge's motive may not have been all that pure. Re-elected to the Senate in 1946, Lodge now faced a tough campaign in 1952 against a rich and popular challenger: three-term congressman John F. Kennedy. One possible way for Lodge to beat Kennedy would be to have Ike, not Taft, heading the ballot in Massachusetts. Lodge was also a man Ike respected, and that day, as Ike told it, Lodge was very persuasive. For the first time, rather than a blunt refusal, Ike wavered and said he would "think the matter over."

For his part, Lodge returned to the States convinced that Ike would not campaign, but would respond favorably to a "bona fide draft." The problem was to create a "draft" for a man who would not even publicly encourage, let alone endorse, it. Lodge joined forces with Lucius Clay, Tom Dewey, Senators James H. Duff (Pennsylvania) and Frank Carlson (Kansas), Herbert Brownell and others to form an advisory group to achieve this political miracle. The group elected Lodge "campaign manager," and he commenced an all-out effort to mobilize the citizenry behind Ike.

In the meantime, Truman had long since decided not to seek re-election. "In my opinion," he wrote in his diary on April 16, 1950, "eight years as President is enough." By December 1951, he thought he might go back to Missouri and run for the Senate. He sent Ike a handwritten personal note revealing this possibility and then appeared to offer Ike (as he had before) the Democratic presidential nomination. He asked what Ike's plans were. "My own position is in the balance. If you decide to finish the European job (and I don't know who else can) I must keep the isolationists out of the White House."

Ike's reply on January 1, 1952, was cautiously noncommittal. His desire—still—was to live a semi-retired life and do some writing on current affairs. He did not feel "any duty to seek a political nomination." He would remain silent. Having insisted on that position, he told Truman, "The possibility that I will ever be drawn into political activity is so remote as to be negligible." If Truman's letter was meant to offer Ike the Democratic presidential nomination, Ike's letter amounted to a polite refusal.

Meanwhile, Lodge, having been assured by Ike that Ike would not repudiate his efforts, decided to enter Ike's name in the New Hampshire primary. On January 6, Lodge announced that he would do this. This bombshell dominated the headlines for days, almost blanking out the January 5–8 visit to Washington of Winston Churchill, back in office as Prime Minister. All this compelled Ike to issue a public statement confirming that he was a Republican and that if he got a clear-cut call to duty he would not duck it. He wrote in his diary that he was willing to go this far ("part way") in "trying to recognize a duty" but "I still do not have to seek one, and I will not."

One event that profoundly impressed Ike was a gigantic Ike rally that Lodge staged in Madison Square Garden late on the night of February 9. Some 30,000 frenzied fans turned out in the freezing cold. The whole affair was filmed. After Ike saw it he said, "The incident impressed me more than had all the arguments presented by the individuals who had been plaguing me with political questions for many months." A week later, Ike saw Lucius Clay in London at the funeral of King George VI and told him that he was committed in his mind "to run if nominated" but he still would not seek the nomination.[33]

I had seen Ike in Paris during this period. I'm certain I had no influence whatsoever on his decision, but on one occasion I told him quite forcefully that he had to make up his mind and say yes or no. "I know a man who gave up his job to work full-time for you," I said. "You can't do that to people. If you're not going to run, then say so." Perhaps owing to my close relations with Truman, Ike did not confide his plans to me as he ordinarily would have. Politics had begun to intrude into our close relationship of ten years.[34]

I was thrust into the political campaign in a peripheral way. On February 12, 1952—my birthday, of all days—Bob Taft, campaigning in Seattle, Washington, attacked the Joint Chiefs of Staff. He had done this before, but never so harshly. The thrust of his remarks was that the JCS were merely lackeys and errand boys for Truman and Acheson. This time he directed a personal attack at me. As *Saturday Evening Post* writer Demaree Bess reported it, Taft said he had lost confidence in my judgment and, if elected, would replace me as Chairman.

Truman and others rushed to my defense. The President said that the Joint Chiefs were not political appointees and were therefore not a "proper issue" in a campaign. Republican Wayne Morse of Oregon (an Ike backer) declared in the Senate that it was a "great disservice" to make political attacks like that "which shake confidence in the leadership of our military men." Unperturbed, Taft responded by saying he did not question my "military ability" but rather my political and economic judgments.

I was in Lisbon at a NATO meeting when this attack was leveled at me. Of course, I did not respond directly. Ten days after my return to the States, I had a speaking engagement in Pasadena, California. I took that occasion not only to defend our military policies in Europe and the Far East, but also to stick a needle into the Taftites and Hooverites who were espousing the "Fortress America" concept:

> Some prefer the dramatic vision of American power sitting securely in the Gibraltar-nest of the North American continent, with our eagles flying out to defend the nest and to attack the enemy if war should occur. This Gibraltar concept is a selfish and defensive one. The American spirit would tire of it right after the first atomic bomb dropped on an American city. Our chagrin and shame would be unbounded if we saw the enemy making slave camps out of Paris, Brussels and Berlin. It is not in the American nature to invite war by backing away from a difficult situation. Our greatest chance for peace in Western Europe and the world—and our greatest hope for the security of the United States—lies in continuing steadfastly and strongly our collective forces in a forward strategy against the Iron Curtain.

Taft pulled in his horns publicly and so far as I know did not again attack the JCS or me personally. But in private he made no secret of his contempt for me, even questioning my integrity. The JCS had been "politicized," too closely identified with Truman's foreign and economic policies and the firing of MacArthur, whom Taft was now courting as a running mate.[35]

After a smashing victory in New Hampshire and a strong showing in Minnesota (where Ike was not on the printed ballot), the Ike bandwagon got rolling full steam. On March 29, Truman added spice to the campaign by announcing that he would not run again. At this time, Truman wanted his friend Chief Justice Fred Vinson to be the Democratic candidate, but Vinson declined for several reasons, one being his poor health. Thereafter Adlai Stevenson, governor of Illinois, emerged as the leading candidate. About this same time, Ike wrote Truman requesting relief from his NATO post on June 1 and, should he be nominated, transfer to the retired list without pay. Truman approved this request on April 11 and made the exchange of letters public.[36]

The question of who would replace Ike at SHAPE was not easy to answer. Ike and Monty wanted Al Gruenther, Ike's chief of staff, to move up. But the British Chiefs of Staff were opposed to Gruenther because he had always been a staff officer and had never held a major command. The JCS felt the same way. Accordingly, the decision was made to name Ridgway to the post. I do not think Ike fully approved of Ridgway's appointment, but he wrote that he found it "satisfactory," since Gruenther would remain as chief of staff. Mark Clark, then commanding Army Field Forces, was named to succeed Ridgway in Tokyo.[37]

The Republican convention was held in Chicago the week of July 7–12. It was no shoo-in for Ike. Taft, who had not been idle, arrived with a reported hundred-vote lead. He had also made a deal with MacArthur, who was to make the keynote address to the convention, that if Taft won, MacArthur would be his vice presidential running mate and if elected, MacArthur would serve as his "deputy commander in chief of the armed forces." But Taft was outmaneuvered at the convention. MacArthur's keynote speech was widely regarded as a flop. Lodge and his floor-fighting lieutenants swung delegates to Ike. At the end of the cliff-hanging first ballot, with 604 votes needed to win, Ike had 595, Taft 500, Earl Warren 81. Minnesota, which had cast its nineteen votes for favorite son Harold Stassen, switched its vote to Ike and put him over with 614 votes.

It has always struck me as perfectly fantastic that history worked out so that MacArthur and Ike were pitted at this convention and that it was Ike—MacArthur's former aide and speechwriter—who finally buried MacArthur's hopes for a political career.[38]

I could find little to admire in Ike's campaign against Adlai Stevenson. Nor in Stevenson's campaign. Both men ran against Truman and the "mess" (communism and corruption) in Washington. Ike unwisely forged a political alliance with Taft, which in turn brought Ike into league with the Old Guard primitives, who needed Ike's coattails infinitely more than Ike needed theirs. With Ike's tacit approval, the Old Guard and Ike's running mate, Richard M. Nixon, conducted a reprehensible smear campaign, one of the worst I'd seen. Ike himself, holding to a loftier level, used our foreign and military policy as political footballs, hypocritically calling into question policies that he himself had helped formulate or approved or had carried out.

Three episodes in Ike's campaign especially angered me.

- Campaigning in Indianapolis, Ike appeared on a platform in support of Senator William Jenner, the man who had viciously vilified George Marshall as "a living lie." To insure an image of a close bond, Jenner embraced Ike several times. When I saw photographs of this I could hardly believe my eyes. It turned my stomach. No man was more beholden to Marshall than Ike.

• Perhaps in atonement, when Ike campaigned through Wisconsin, he asked one of his speechwriters, Emmet John Hughes, to write in a paragraph praising Marshall. Hughes wrote: "I know that charges of disloyalty have, in the past, been leveled against George C. Marshall. I have been privileged for thirty-five years to know General Marshall personally. I know him, as a man and a soldier, to be dedicated with singular selflessness and the profoundest patriotism to the service of America. And this episode is a sobering lesson in the way freedom must *not* defend itself."

This passage was included in a speech Ike would make in Milwaukee. Senator Joseph McCarthy, running for re-election, had joined the Ike campaign party. McCarthy had earlier denounced Marshall as "a man steeped in falsehood." Ike not only embraced McCarthy as he had Jenner but also, under pressure from Wisconsin Republicans, agreed to delete the passage about Marshall in his speech. Aides had already shown advance texts of the speech to newsmen. When the final version appeared with no mention of Marshall, the story made the rounds. When I heard about it I was furious.

• Throughout the campaign the Korean War, still in unresolved stalemate, was a major issue. Ike and the Old Guard blamed Truman. Ike went so far as to say that America henceforth "must avoid the kind of bungling that led us into Korea." Campaigning in Detroit on October 24, close to election day, he stunned the world—and me personally—with this statement: "Where will a new administration begin? It will begin with its President taking a simple, firm resolution. That resolution will be: To forgo the diversions of politics and to concentrate on the job of ending the Korean War—until that job is honorably done. That job requires a personal trip to Korea. I shall make that trip. Only in that way could I learn how best to serve the American people in the cause of peace. I shall go to Korea."

Politically, this was a stroke of genius, not Ike's, but most likely that of a *Newsweek* senior editor who passed the idea to Ike's camp. But in reality, it was pure show biz. Ike was well informed on all aspects of the Korean War and the delicacy of the armistice negotiations. He knew very well that he could achieve nothing by going to Korea. Furthermore, this new element could weaken our hand at the negotiating table. "No man," Truman aptly wrote in his memoirs, "had less right to use this crisis for political purposes."[39]

Truman was deeply hurt by the campaign, especially the fact that Stevenson avoided him. One day he said to me in utter seriousness: "I wish I'd known you better, earlier. I'd have made you President." I believe he meant that he would have groomed me for the Democratic ticket in 1952 and backed me fully. This was a high compliment, but had circumstances worked out so that he had asked me, I would have declined, thus sparing the country an ''Ike-Brad'' campaign. I did not—and still do not—believe in generals in the White House. Nor, having seen Truman close up for almost eight years, did I desire in the slightest to be President. It is a thankless, killing job.[40]

Ike, of course, won a great political victory. On November 5, I sent him a Western Union telegram at his home on Morningside Drive in Manhattan: ''Dear Ike. Congratulations on your victory. We shall be very happy to have you and Mamie back in Washington again. I am proud that this great honor has been bestowed upon a classmate from West Point by the American people, and it will be a privilege and honor to be serving under you again. Your job will probably be tougher than Overlord. Best regards and good luck. Omar Bradley.'' On November 9, Ike replied from Augusta, Georgia, where he had gone to rest: ''Many thanks for your telegram. . . . I too am delighted that we shall be working closely together again and look forward to seeing you at the earliest possible moment. Warm regards. Ike.''[41]

These were pure formalities. The fact of the matter was that Ike, under heavy pressure from Taft and the Old Guard, was already thinking in terms of a complete new set of military chiefs. Politics was further widening our close personal relationship.

Ike had promised to go to Korea, and now he was stuck with fulfilling that promise. The proposed trip entailed considerable personal risk. Should his itinerary be known in advance, the Chinese communists could launch an air attack on the airports where Ike landed or took off or attempt to assassinate him with undercover teams. Thus the trip was made under the tightest security I have ever seen. Nothing would be revealed until Ike had gone to Korea and come back.[42]

The official party was purposely kept small: Charles E. Wilson, the ex-chief of General Motors whom Ike had nominated for Secretary of Defense; Herbert Brownell, who would be Attorney General; press secretary James Hagerty; and retired general Wilton B. (Jerry) Persons, a longtime Army friend, a specialist in congressional relations whom Ike had recruited for the campaign as an adviser. At Ike's request, I came along, bringing various JCS studies on Korea and recent proposals from Mark Clark. A small press ''pool,'' which would not file stories or photographs until we left Korea, joined us for takeoff from New York.

We flew from New York to the Pacific. At Iwo Jima, Admiral Radford joined the official party. On the long trip out, I had briefed Ike and Wilson on the military situation in Korea and the steps in the armistice negotiations, which were now completely stalled.

My briefing also included a rather detailed picture of our swelling nuclear arsenal, about which neither Ike nor Wilson was well informed. There were two items of major importance.

• By now, scientific improvements in the yield of fission weapons and the dramatic increase in production had given us an enormous stockpile of atomic warheads. We were producing a great number of so-called tactical atomic bombs for use against military targets. Joe Collins even had a battlefield "atomic cannon" in the works. Further improvements in yields were anticipated. We had so many atomic bombs now that we could spare a considerable number for the Korean War, should it be deemed advisable to use them.

• On October 31, 1952, less than a week before the election, we had successfully tested our first fusion or hydrogen bomb on a Pacific island. The yield had exceeded all forecasts: 10,400 kilotons, or about ten megatons. This bomb was not a military weapon but rather an enormously complicated "laboratory device." The significance of the test was that it proved the H-bomb would work. Already Dr. Edward Teller and his associates were following up another approach which promised a simplified, smaller (air-transportable) H-bomb which could be produced relatively cheaply. The perfection of the latter weapon would give us an enormous strategic edge vis-à-vis the Soviet Union.[43]

We landed in Korea on December 2. Mark Clark and Jim Van Fleet met the plane. Clark and Van Fleet had cooked up a new, powerful, "victory" plan (Oplan 8-52) to so severely punish the Chinese communist armies that they would give up. The plan was MacArthuresque. Clark wanted to advance the Eighth Army to the narrow waist (Pyongyang-Wonsan) of Korea and at the same time launch sea and air operations against Red China. To carry out the ground operation would require about eight additional divisions and they wanted to use some of Chiang's troops. They also urged that "serious consideration" be given to using atomic weapons.[44]

Mark Clark had long since briefed the JCS on this plan. Since two of its key features—sea and air operations against Red China and use of Chiang's troops—had often been considered and rejected by Truman, we put it on the back burner for Ike's consideration. On the way to Korea I fully briefed Ike on the plan. When he asked me what I thought about it, I was not very enthusiastic. There was still the grave risk of widening the war. I still opposed using Chiang's troops in Korea.

Ike expressed no opinion one way or the other, except to say that he, too, was opposed to using Chiang's troops in Korea. In Korea, Clark and Van Fleet tried—in vain—to find the opportunity to present this plan, but Ike, deliberately I'm sure, avoided any discussion of it. Clark and Van Fleet were quite naturally miffed. Clark got the impression that Ike wanted no part of the plan and that Ike's solution to Korea was to go on trying to arrange an honorable truce.

We spent two full days in Korea. We toured the various military headquarters and many front-line units. We had a long talk with aged

President Rhee, who wanted "victory" and not an armistice that would leave North Korea in communist hands. Before leaving Korea, Ike conceded at a press conference that he had "no panaceas, no trick solutions" for the war. He later wrote: "My conclusion as I left Korea was that we could not stand forever on a static front and continue to accept casualties without any visible results. Small attacks on small hills would not end this war."

On this trip, I privately discussed with Ike the touchy question of changing the Joint Chiefs, as Taft was continuing to demand. I urged him not to concede to this request. If he did, it would tend to confirm that the JCS had been "politicized" and it could lead to the deplorable practice of changing Chiefs with each administration. Ike agreed that that would be a bad precedent.

I explained to him that in any case, with one exception, normal attrition would take care of "changing" the Chiefs. Vandenberg had taken office as Air Force Chief of Staff on April 30, 1948. The normal tour was four years. He was already beyond that by half a year, was ill (cancer of the prostate) and *wanted* to retire. My second and final two-year tour as Chairman would be over in mid-August 1953. Joe Collins would complete his normal four-year term as Army Chief of Staff at the same time. The only "problem" was Fechteler, who had been on the job as CNO only a year and four months. But in the postwar years, Nimitz had only served two years and Denfeld nearly two, so there was not yet a Navy four-year-term tradition. Fechteler could be handled by permitting him to serve out a full two years.

Who, then, would replace me as Chairman of the JCS? The understanding had always been that the chairmanship would "rotate." It was the Navy's turn. That seemed even more appropriate inasmuch as a five-star general would be sitting in the White House. One possibility was to elevate Fechteler. I did not think he had the prestige, war experience, strategic grasp or personality to be Chairman of the Joint Chiefs of Staff. Besides that, Ike felt that with his own considerable background in the ETO and NATO, his chief military adviser ought to be a man with extended experience in the Pacific and Far East.

In terms of seniority, prestige and Pacific–Far East background, the logical Navy candidate was Arthur Radford (Naval Academy 1916). At first it was hard for me to agree that my arch-foe in the B-36 hearings, a man I had publicly castigated, should succeed me. But I had to concede that Radford was the best-qualified admiral the Navy had. Moreover, since 1949 he had broadened and matured; he clearly had the potential to grow into the job and shed his service bias.

Who then would replace Collins as Army Chief of Staff (a matter dear to both Ike and me)? We had many outstanding possibilities, high among them Ridgway. Ridgway was not proving to be the ideal choice for NATO.

Matt was a field commander without peer but not a diplomat. Since taking over SHAPE, he had been putting relentless pressure on our allies to do their part with more alacrity and enthusiasm. Some of this pressure was needed—indeed, had been endorsed by the NATO Council—but in his zeal, Ridgway had antagonized many politicians among our allies.

Ike, all along, had wanted Al Gruenther to succeed him at SHAPE. Now the opportunity arose to kill three birds with one stone. With his prestige, background and energy, Ridgway would be an inspiring Army Chief of Staff. If he got overzealous, as he tended to, Ike would be right there to restrain him. It would remove a burr from SHAPE and make room for Gruenther. So it was decided.

Later, in the spring of 1953, when Ike announced the changes in the JCS, some of the media interpreted the moves as a fulfillment of Ike's pledge to Taft. In fact the White House, for political purposes, slanted it that way in public and private briefings. However, no Chief other than Fechteler (and his case was arguable) was removed prematurely. For this I give Ike a great deal of credit.[45]

Ike was inaugurated on January 21, 1953, the first Republican President to sit in the White House since Hoover. I had occasion to telephone him shortly after he assumed his duties. I properly addressed him as "Mister President." He wrote later that my formality helped drive home to him the fact that his life was going to be very, very different from now on. "To a very definite degree," he wrote, he would be "separated from all others, including my oldest and best friends."[46]

Thanks to Ike's decision, the Joint Chiefs continued on as before for several months, advising the new administration on defense plans and policies. Although these were grandly packaged as the "New Look" and "massive retaliation," they were in reality outgrowths of JCS decisions in the fall of 1951 to build up the armed forces and lay heavy stress on air power—decisions that were reinforced by the development of Dr. Teller's air-transportable H-bomb.

All during that spring the JCS, in response to Ike's directives and suggestions, produced various studies on possible ways to end the Korean War. These studies, based on Clark's Oplan 8-52, gradually assumed a much more aggressive stance. In March, the JCS took the unprecedented step of recommending that "the timely use of atomic weapons should be considered against military targets affecting operations in Korea" and "planned as an adjunct to any possible military course of action involving direct action against Communist China and Manchuria."[47]

That same month, Joseph Stalin died. Georgi M. Malenkov replaced Stalin in the Kremlin. Soon afterwards we began to get signals that the new Soviet leadership (as Ike put it) "no matter how strong its links with the Stalin era, was not completely bound to blind obedience to the ways of a dead man." Would Malenkov exert influence on Chou En-lai to end the Korean War?[48]

In the meantime, Ike had independently reached the decision the JCS were now voicing: If necessary, use atomic weapons in Korea. His reasoning was that it would be impossible for the United States to go on maintaining all its worldwide military commitments if we did not possess "the will" to use atomic bombs "when necessary." Accordingly, Ike and Secretary of State John Foster Dulles decided to let the communists know that if the Red Chinese would not negotiate and "put an end to these intolerable conditions," we would "not be limited by any worldwide gentleman's agreement" and intended "to move decisively without inhibition in our use of weapons, and would no longer be responsible for confining hostilities to the Korean Peninsula." It is now well known that Dulles conveyed this view to Nehru, knowing that it would be relayed to Peking. But as Ike wrote, we also "dropped word, discreetly, of our intentions" in "the Formosa Straits area" and at the truce tent at Panmunjom.[49]

In late March we received two extraordinary signals indicating that the communists might be coming around. North Korean Premier Kim Il Sung and Red China's Premier Chou En-lai both agreed to a preliminary exchange of sick and wounded POW's, long one of the hitches in the negotiations. Chou En-lai went further. He said the time was now ripe for settling the "entire question" of POW's "in order to insure the cessation of hostilities in Korea and to conclude the armistice agreement."[50]

We did not know if these words were sincere. Accordingly, the JCS went on making tough military plans. We recommended to the NSC that if the negotiations fell through again, we hit the communists with an all-out effort. This included "extensive strategical and tactical use of atomic bombs" against China and Manchuria, coordinated with a massive Eighth Army ground offensive to achieve a position along the "waist." The NSC voted to adopt our proposals "as a general guide" should conditions arise "requiring more positive action in Korea."[51]

Full talks resumed at Panmunjom on April 26, after a freeze of six months. President Rhee did everything in his power to sabotage the talks, so much so that we planned a military coup ("Plan Everready") to overthrow him if necessary. Fortunately, we were able to keep Rhee in line. The armistice was signed on July 27. The Korean War had cost America 142,091 casualties: 33,629 dead, 103,284 wounded, 5,178 captured or missing.[52]

Until the Chinese open their archives to scholars, we shall never know with certainty why they finally agreed to an armistice in Korea. It may have been at Malenkov's suggestion. It may have been Chinese reaction to our diplomatic threats to widen the war with atomic bombs. Or maybe, like us, the Chinese communists simply tired of the war and its pointless bloodshed. Whatever the reason, it gave me the greatest sense of satisfaction to see it end while I was still Chairman of the Joint Chiefs of Staff. And still more satisfaction to see that for all the years since, South Korea has remained a free nation.

My last major job for Ike was to serve as a member of the small American delegation to the coronation of Queen Elizabeth II. George Marshall was the head of the delegation.[53]

When we returned to Washington on June 10, I was weak and had a high fever. I went immediately to a doctor, who diagnosed bronchial pneumonia. I checked into Walter Reed Army Hospital for two weeks and was an outpatient until July 9. Several more weeks—my last in full-time government service—elapsed before I fully regained my strength.[54]

Now it was time for the Chiefs to step down. First came Van. I attended his official retirement service at Bolling Air Force Base (across the Potomac River from the Pentagon) on June 30. It was a moving experience. Van was still youthful-looking and movie-star handsome. But, as we knew, the cancer was spreading uncontrollably. Nine months later he died at Walter Reed Hospital, age fifty-five.[55]

Collins and I came next, in joint ceremonies. On August 5, at the White House, Ike presented Collins, Fechteler and me with Distinguished Service Medals—my fourth. Mary, Hal (now a major) and Lee attended the ceremony. On August 13, Secretary of the Army Robert T. Stevens honored Collins and me with a late afternoon retirement parade and garden party at Fort McNair. Earlier that day I had been invited to drop in at the 159th meeting of the National Security Council, presided over by Vice President Richard Nixon in the absence of the President, who was in Denver on vacation. I was embarrassed almost to tears by the kind things each member of the NSC had to say about my public service. As I departed, the NSC stood in a mark of respect.[56]

From Denver that same day, Ike sent a letter which I treasure:

> Dear Brad:
>
> You are probably so worn out with dinners and ceremonies to salute you as you leave your post of active duty that you are glad you have to go through the thing only once in a lifetime. Nevertheless, I hope you never forget that each of those occasions is merely an effort on the part of others to express to you something of their appreciation of a long, useful and brilliant career in the service of our common country.
>
> The purpose of this note is simply to assure you once again—as I have so many times in the past—that I have always counted your approval to be almost the certification of the value of any proposal or project; your disapproval to be equally conclusive that the matter had better be discarded without further to-do.
>
> You well know that my admiration and continued affection go with you to your new occupation—I sincerely trust you will find it interesting and rewarding.

With love to Mary and your family, and, as always, with the very best to yourself,

As ever,

[s] Ike[57]

Mary and I packed our possessions and turned Quarters One over to the Ridgways, not without a deep sense of loss. It had been our home for five and a half uninterrupted years, longer than we had ever lived in one place. As we walked away for the last time, it occurred to me that it had been forty-two years, almost to the day, since I checked in at the main gate at West Point. Now I was a mere sixty years old; an entirely new and quite different life lay ahead.

Collaborator's Afterword

General Bradley lived on for twenty-eight more years. After stepping down from the job of Chairman of the Joint Chiefs of Staff, he was not again recalled to full-time active duty. Since by law, no five-star general ever retires in the usual sense, from 1953 until his death he remained on the "active" list, drawing a salary of about $20,000 a year until the mid-seventies, when it was raised to a little more than $30,000. In addition, he was entitled to such perquisites as government office space, travel and military aides. To all intents and purposes Bradley was "retired" from military service. However, from time to time he was called upon to represent the President or Department of Defense at D-Day anniversaries on the beaches in Normandy or to make speeches on Veterans Day, Memorial Day and Independence Day. He thus became a sort of senior military statesman.[1]

That was not enough to keep him occupied. He accepted a position with the Bulova Watch Company, initially as head of its research and development laboratories at a salary of $25,000 a year. Later, in 1958, following the death of Bulova's chairman, Arde Bulova, Bradley was elected chairman of the board of Bulova with a salary of $75,000 a year plus stock options. These were not figurehead jobs; Bradley worked at them diligently. He also became a director of a half-dozen other companies.[2]

When Bradley "retired" from full-time government service in 1953 he and Mary were uncertain whether they wanted to live in Florida or Southern California, but eventually they settled on the latter. In December, they rented a house on South Rodeo Drive in Beverly Hills that once had been owned by movie star Loretta Young. While in the midst of this move, they received tragic news. On January 19, 1954, Hal Beukema, age twenty-nine, was killed when his Air Force F-86 jet fighter crashed into the James River near Langley, Virginia, leaving Lee and four children: Henry ("Hank"), Mary Elizabeth, Omar Bradley (Brad) and Anne. He was buried at West Point.[3]

Hal's death significantly altered the Bradleys' life-style. In the spring of 1954, Lee and the grandchildren came to live with the Bradleys in Beverly Hills, thus creating a need for a larger house. They gave up the Rodeo Drive house and bought one—the first they owned—on Saltair Avenue in Brentwood. Two orderlies, including Frank E. Stewart, who had been with the Bradleys since 1948, completed the "family."[4]

The Bradleys remained in Los Angeles for a little more than three years. Lee and the grandchildren moved back to Washington, where Lee married an attorney, Benjamin H. Dorsey, and had a fifth child, Melanie. Bradley was kept busy with Bulova matters and his other corporate directorships. But he had plenty of time for golf, fishing and hunting with a new set of California friends, mostly from the business world, and old Army friends passing through. He also devoted no small amount of time to a passion he had developed in Washington in the postwar years, horse racing. Drawing on his mathematical talents, he became a handicapper, approaching every race as if it were another battle. He rarely won, but he never gave up trying.[5]

In the spring of 1957, the Bradleys returned to Washington. "Proximity to our daughter and our . . . grandchildren is our most compelling motive," Bradley wrote George Marshall. The Bradleys bought a comfortable six-bedroom house on Indian Lane in the Spring Valley section of northwest Washington. Lee and Ben Dorsey had a second child together, Benjamin Dorsey III, giving the Bradleys a total of six grandchildren close at hand.[6]

For eight years the Bradleys settled into a "retired" social routine, seeing their many old Army friends living in retirement. They often wintered in Miami, taking in the horse racing there. Owing to his bad knee stemming from the West Point football injury, and which ultimately required an operation to remove the kneecap, Bradley was forced to curb his golfing and hunting. The general kept a firm and steady hand in Bulova, traveled, delivered speeches, and collected honorary degrees and awards of all kinds.

By the fall of 1965, Mary, then seventy-three, was not well. She had ulcers, a chronically bad back and not much stamina. "She got tired easily," the faithful family orderly Stewart recalled, "and had to lie down a lot." In late November she entered Walter Reed Hospital. Four days later, December 1, one year shy of her golden wedding anniversary, Mary died of virulent leukemia. A private service was held at the Fort Myer chapel, and she was buried in Arlington National Cemetery.[7]

In the next few months, callers found General Bradley in the big Spring Valley house, a lonely, grief-stricken man of seventy-two, completely at loose ends. "He was just lost when Mrs. Bradley died," Stewart said. Friends recall that when visiting the general, they "had never seen a man so utterly alone."[8]

Some months after Mary's death, Bradley embarked on a new and different life-style. The catalyst was a vivacious, twice-divorced forty-three-year-old Hollywood screenwriter, Kitty Buhler. Born in New York City, Kitty had taken writing courses at Kansas Wesleyan University in Salina, Kansas, and afterwards had launched her career as a writer in Hollywood. In the late 1940s she served in Japan and Okinawa as a reporter and feature writer for *Stars and Stripes* and local base service papers. She recalled that she was working in the latter capacity on Okinawa in February 1950 when Bradley came through and she interviewed him. After that she returned to Hollywood. During the 1950s, Kitty Buhler grew up with television, turning out both comedy and melodrama as well as dramatic specials starring various Hollywood notables. Between writing assignments Kitty attended classes at the University of Southern California and the University of California at Los Angeles and spent her weekend afternoons at various racetracks, becoming a skilled handicapper.

Kitty acquired the rights to the life story of General Bradley and met with him at the Astor Hotel in New York for extended taped interviews. After Mary's death, when business brought Bradley to Southern California, further interviews were conducted in Beverly Hills and at Del Mar, where Kitty was spending the summer. Somewhere along the way they fell in love and on September 12, 1966, they were married at the courthouse in San Diego. They spent the afternoon of their wedding at the Del Mar Race Track, had a wedding reception that evening and left for Washington, D.C., the following morning.[9]

Kitty Bradley greatly enlivened Bradley's life. She redecorated the Indian Lane house, installing a glass-encased solarium with a heated pool and whirlpool so Bradley could exercise his "football" knee. She opened the house for parties for the general's West Point classmates and government officials. When she found his medals and decorations stuffed in tuxedo pockets and old shoe boxes, she set in motion the creation of the Omar N. Bradley Museum, on the grounds of the Army War College, at Carlisle Barracks, Pennsylvania, where the general's uniforms, awards, decorations and memorabilia were housed.[10]

In the summer of 1967, at Kitty's suggestion, she and the general went to Vietnam on assignment for *Look* magazine to collaborate on a situation report on the war. After a grueling two-week tour of the battlefront, Bradley came away convinced (as he and Kitty jointly wrote in *Look*) that Vietnam was "a war at the right place, at the right time and with the right enemy—the Communists."[11]

The general became increasingly restless living on the edge of official Washington without an official assignment. After a winter at the races in Southern California, where the gentler weather was kinder to the general's arthritis and allergies, in 1968, the Bradleys put the Spring Valley house on the market and bought a new custom-designed home on a hilltop in Trousdale Estates in Beverly Hills.[12]

For the next several years Omar Bradley had the time of his life. Kitty was well connected in Hollywood; the general's five stars and reputation brought almost anyone of filmland note to their home. They entertained the Bob Hopes; the Jimmy Stewarts; the Gregory Pecks; Greer Garson; Esther Williams; Efrem Zimbalist, Jr.; Pat O'Brien; Elvis Presley; Jane Wyman; Karl Malden; a former actor turned politician, Ronald Reagan and his wife Nancy; and countless other celebrities. Bradley, somewhat in awe of film stars, genuinely relished rubbing elbows with them, and they, in turn, enjoyed the company of this famous war hero.[13]

The marriage was also financially profitable. Kitty had good instincts for making money. Now she brought Omar Bradley into the game. When producer Frank McCarthy (Marshall's wartime assistant) sought the general's advice for the enormously successful film *Patton,* starring George C. Scott, Kitty persuaded McCarthy to lease Bradley's war memoir, *A Soldier's Story,* for background material and to put the general and her on the film as senior advisers. The contract called for a guaranteed down payment and for a percentage of the profits, an arrangement which would ultimately generate a sizable income for the Bradleys. Kitty's careful investment of the income, together with the appreciation of their home and other deals, made the Bradleys financially comfortable.

They drew wills, leaving everything they owned to the Omar N. Bradley Foundation and Museum and to the Omar N. Bradley Library, which was established at West Point in 1974 to house part of the general's papers. They also established the Omar N. Bradley Fellowships in mathematics and military history.[14]

In July of 1973, at age eighty, Bradley resigned as chairman of the Bulova Watch Company, remaining on as honorary chairman and consultant to the corporation. One month later, in the early hours of August 13, General Bradley awoke in severe pain. Kitty found him sheet-white and perspiring heavily. He thought he was dying of a heart attack and told Kitty goodbye. She responded resolutely: "You die and I'll kill you!" She called the paramedics, administered mouth-to-mouth resuscitation and pumped his chest until the paramedics took over. At UCLA medical center, doctors diagnosed a massive blood clot in the lungs. In the next week, hovering near death, General Bradley developed four more life-threatening clots. A newly developed operation was performed, and the General's life was saved. Bradley survived this close call without apparent grievous after-effects, and the Bradleys resumed their lives.

Then, in January 1975, at age eighty-two, Bradley struck and gashed his head while debarking from a commercial aircraft in New York. At the Waldorf Astoria a doctor stitched the gash. Two months later, perhaps as a result of that bump, Bradley developed a blood clot in the brain. Rushed to UCLA medical center in convulsions, he again very nearly died. One of his aides, Major Brian W. Brady, recalled: "We almost lost him for sure. He was very depressed and didn't want to depend on other people. Kitty kept him alive. She *ordered* him not to die and brought him out of the depression." He emerged from this ordeal confined to a wheelchair.[15]

Fearing that Bradley might again give up the will to live if his life became too sedentary and dull, Kitty encouraged activity. She kept his days busy with physical therapy and events, many of them therapeutic inventions. They traveled to West Point football games, to Army Association reunions, to presidential inaugurations. She invited his old hunting pals and friends to special dinners and poker games. Her life was devoted entirely to keeping him alive, managing their financial affairs, shipping historic materials and papers to the Omar N. Bradley Foundation and the Omar N. Bradley Library, and to answering every one of the tens of thousands of personal letters he received over the years. Partly as therapy, she encouraged Bradley to resume his autobiography, which he had begun in 1971 before the first clots struck.[16]

The increased medical attention required became too complicated to manage from a private residence. In November 1977, the Bradleys left Beverly Hills and moved to Army quarters at Fort Bliss in El Paso, Texas. The quarters were nearby the base hospital, where a special intensive care room was set aside specifically for Bradley. Ultimately, the Fort Bliss "Bradley Family" grew to sixteen: Kitty, five medical corpsmen, five house orderlies, four commissioned aides and a clerk. The government also provided a secretary for Bradley's Pentagon office.[17]

In the late summer of 1979, as he began taping sessions for this autobiography, General Bradley, then age eighty-six, had settled into a routine at Fort Bliss. This consisted of physical therapy several times a day plus numerous "outings" during the week at which he mingled with the troops at Fort Bliss and gave a lighthearted and humorous speech on leadership to the senior noncoms at the various Fort Bliss schools. The Bradleys went out often into the El Paso community and spent many lazy afternoons at the Sunland Race Track ten minutes over the border in New Mexico. The general spent other afternoons dozing off in his wheelchair by the piano, giving Kitty "moral support" as she practiced her music. When the team of doctors supervising the general's health gave their blessing, the Bradleys periodically undertook trips to Israel, England and France, always accompanied by the aides and medical corpsmen.

Considering all he had been through since 1973, General Bradley was remarkably vigorous and mentally keen. Interview sessions, which were scheduled around his therapy exercises, usually began at lunchtime and, with a brief midafternoon break, continued straight through dinner to nine or ten o'clock at night. He was so enthusiastically dedicated to the project that at times it seemed he wanted to keep going indefinitely. When sessions ended, it was not because the general had run out of steam.

Wearing a lamb's wool golfing sweater, poised in his wheelchair with a bourbon cocktail before the burning logs in the fireplace, the Bradley of old came through remarkably. He was charming, tranquil and modest—the perfect country slicker. Like many older people he could remember more about his younger years than his later years and could recall with uncanny precision the details of almost every hunting trip he had ever made. Kitty Bradley, who sat in on the interviews, proved to be an excellent and demanding goad, prodding out important events or conversations which the general had earlier shared with her and forgotten.

The Bradley "family" continued to travel. One trip, April 8, 1981, took them to New York to accept the Gold Medal Award from the National Institute of Social Sciences in the Winchester Room at the "21" Club.

Less than ten minutes after receiving the award, as he was being wheeled onto the elevator, Bradley, age eighty-eight, died while Kitty, his aides and about one hundred guests looked on helplessly. He died instantly of a clot in the brain. He apparently felt no pain; there were no convulsions or seizures, merely a quiet passing from life into death.

Six days later, *Air Force One* transported Kitty and Omar Bradley to Washington, D.C. There, on April 14, he was buried with full military honors at Arlington National Cemetery.[18]

Sources and Acknowledgments

A substantial portion of this book was based on the papers of Omar N. Bradley. These papers are in two locations: the Omar N. Bradley Library in the special collections division of the U.S. Military Academy Library, West Point, N.Y., and at the U.S. Army Military History Institute (USAMHI), Carlisle Barracks, Pennsylvania. While there is some duplication of papers, anyone researching Omar Bradley must visit both locations. The papers at West Point, for which a computerized index exists, are mostly "personal"; those at Carlisle Barracks mostly concern World War II. The USAMHI also has the papers of Bradley's wartime and postwar aide, Chester B. Hansen. The Hansen Papers are, in reality, mostly additional Bradley papers and should not be overlooked.

While we were at work on this book, the Bradley papers at West Point were in the care of Robert E. Schnare, Jr., assistant librarian for the special collections division, USMA Library; those at Carlisle in the care of Dr. Richard J. Sommers, archivist-historian. One would be hard-pressed to find two more helpful, obliging and intelligent individuals. We remain eternally grateful for the assistance provided by both men and the members of their staffs, as well as Schnare's assistant, Pat Anthony Dursi.

Additional Bradley papers, all official, may be found in the National Archives. These are filed under various commands or positions Bradley held: II Corps; First Army; Twelfth Army Group; Chief of Staff, U.S. Army; and Chairman of the Joint Chiefs of Staff. The last-named papers, on file in the Modern Military Branch of the National Archives in downtown Washington, were particularly useful, especially a series labeled "Chairman's File." We are grateful to Archivist John E. Taylor for his assistance during our research at the National Archives.

Whenever material from these collections was utilized, it is identified in the chapter notes. The papers at West Point are abbreviated as BP, WP; those at Carlisle, BP, Carlisle. The Chester B. Hansen papers are identified as Hansen papers, USAMHI. Papers from the National Archives are abbreviated as NA or Chairman's File. Because of the duplication of papers, many that are identified as being at West Point may also be at Carlisle, and vice versa.

The noteworthy unpublished or published writings of Omar N. Bradley, on file at West Point or Carlisle, are: "As I Remember," 1971, an original draft of Bradley's autobiography (both places); *A Soldier's Story,* his World War II memoirs, published in 1951 by Henry Holt and Company, New York (both places); "The Collected Writings of Omar N. Bradley," photocopied and bound in six volumes (both places). These selectively edited volumes contain many speeches, public statements, magazine articles, radio interviews and excerpts of congressional testimony. (Additional unbound material of this kind may be found in the Hansen papers at the USAMHI.) Useful adjuncts to these works are "Magazine Articles by and about Omar Bradley," collected in five volumes, photocopied and bound (both places). The Bradley scrapbooks, some thirty-eight albums of photos, newspaper and magazine clips and memorabilia, are at West Point. There are also photo and clipping albums at Carlisle.

Four other valuable sources of information on Bradley are: 1) Bradley's personal diary, which is divided into two parts, pre-war and World War II. It might be more aptly called a "log" since it contains mostly one-line entries of dates and major events and only rarely a personal comment. Nonetheless it is a valuable tool for establishing Bradley's whereabouts at key moments in his life. 2) The World War II diaries of Bradley's aide Chester Hansen. 3) The so-called "VA diary." 4) Bradley's desk calendars from February 1948 to August 1953. The enormously long and thorough Hansen war diaries (on file at Carlisle) contain virtually day-by-day accounts of Bradley's activities in North Africa and Europe from February 1943 to June 1945. The "VA diary," on file at both places, is less complete but gives a fairly good picture of Bradley's activities at the Veterans Administration from June 1945 to November 1947. The desk calendars, also on file at West Point, contain astonishingly thorough (hour-by-hour) records of Bradley's activities (including detailed trip itineraries) throughout his five-and-a-half-year tour as Chief of Staff of the U.S. Army and Chairman of the Joint Chiefs of Staff. Given these four sources, amounting to thousands of pages, it is possible to trace Bradley's every important move or appointment during ten and a half years of his most important public service.

Additional primary source material—mostly official letters or reports —was derived from the Bradley file at each of the following: the MacArthur Archives, MacArthur Memorial, Norfolk, Virginia; the George C. Marshall Research Foundation, Lexington, Virginia; the Harry S. Truman Library in Independence, Missouri; the Dwight D. Eisenhower Library in Abilene, Kansas. The Truman and Eisenhower libraries also provided pertinent diaries and oral histories of men who knew or served closely with Bradley. Materials utilized from these institutions are identified at the appropriate place in the chapter notes. We are grateful to the directors of these institutions and their staffs for all assistance and suggestions.

Owing to Bradley's innate shyness and reticence, available transcribed interviews with him are all the more valuable. Notable among these are: a massive oral history conducted by Lieutenant Colonel Charles K. Hanson of the Army Military History Institute (thirteen sessions, 12-2-74 to 10-12-75); an interview by William Hillman and Francis E. Heller as background for Truman's memoirs (3-30-55); an interview on Bradley's younger years conducted by Colonel George S. Pappas of the Army Military History Institute as background for creating the Bradley Museum at Carlisle (8-14-69); several interviews by Kitty Buhler (Bradley), as background for her proposed film *Breakout* (in 1965); extended interviews by Chester B. Hansen, 1946–49, as background for Bradley's war memoir, *A Soldier's Story;* my own interviews with Bradley, 2-1-80 to 2-13-80, which in turn led to supplemental interviews with Bradley in 1979–80 about his dogs, guns, automobiles and other personal matters, kindly conducted on my behalf by his staff—Lieutenant Colonel Allan G. Little, Lieutenant Colonel Courtney M. Rittgers and Major Thomas A. Hansen. Transcripts of these interviews are located as follows: Charles K. Hanson, Chester B. Hansen, George S. Pappas and Kitty Buhler (Bradley) at USAMHI; Hillman-Heller at the Truman Library; my interviews and the follow-up staff interviews by Little-Rittgers-Hansen at West Point. Wherever use is made of these interviews in this book, the material is identified in the chapter notes by the name or initials of the interviewer.

Published secondary sources—memoirs, biographies, histories—were used extensively. Space limitations prohibit the inclusion of a formal bibliography. Where such material was used, it is described in the chapter notes. Even so, I would like to pay special tribute here to several particularly outstanding and indispensable works of military scholarship. *The Papers of Dwight D. Eisenhower,* nine volumes, Johns Hopkins University Press, Baltimore, 1970–1978. This collection spans the years 1942 to 1948. The first five volumes were edited by Alfred D. Chandler, the second four by Louis Galambos. *The Patton Papers,* edited in two volumes by the distinguished military historian Martin Blumenson. Dr. Forrest C. Pogue's biography of General of the Army George C. Marshall, of which, to date, three volumes have been published by the Viking Press, New York: *Education of a General: 1880–1939; Ordeal and Hope: 1939–42; Organizer of Victory: 1943–45.* Two works by Russell F. Weigley: *History of the United States Army,* Macmillan, Inc., New York, 1967; and his brilliant *Eisenhower's Lieutenants,* Indiana University Press, Bloomington, 1981. The diaries of Field Marshal Alanbrooke, edited in two volumes by Arthur Bryant: *The Turn of the Tide,* 1957, and *Triumph in the West,* 1959, both by Doubleday, New York. *The Mighty Endeavor* by Charles B. MacDonald, a brilliant one-volume account of United States military operations in North Africa and Europe, Oxford University Press, 1969.

I would also like to pay special tribute to the official American and British military historians of World War II and the Korean War. By now it is a commonplace that no one should attempt a serious history of either war without these superb volumes close at hand. As can be seen in the chapter notes, I have made extensive use of numerous volumes. I salute the indefatigable and gifted authors and editors on both sides of the Atlantic: G. R. G. Allen, Roy E. Appleman, Martin Blumenson, J. R. M. Butler, Ray S. Cline, Hugh M. Cole, John Ehrman, Lionel F. Ellis, Albert Garland, Kent R. Greenfield, Gordon A. Harrison, Walter G. Hermes, Michael Howard, George F. Howe, Eric Linklater, Charles B. MacDonald, Maurice Matloff, C. J. C. Molony, Samuel E. Morison, Lewis Morton, I. S. O. Playfair, Forrest C. Pogue, James Robb, James F. Schnabel, Howard McG. Smyth, Edwin M. Snell, A. E. Warhurst, and Mark S. Watson.

Finally, another salute to a little-known but indispensable official history of the U.S. Joint Chiefs of Staff, of which, to date, four volumes comprising some 2,600 pages have been completed, declassified and released. Owing to budgetary restrictions, these books have not been published in the traditional sense; they are merely single-spaced typescripts. However, photocopies may be obtained from the Modern Military Branch of the National Archives or from Michael Glazier, Inc., Wilmington, Delaware. The volumes constitute a complete official history of American military and foreign policy from the years 1945 to 1952 and include carefully annotated excerpts of the principal JCS, National Security Council and State Department documents generated during the period. Volume three is the most comprehensive official history we have of the Korean War from the Washington point of view. The authors of this valuable series are Kenneth W. Condit, Walter S. Poole, James F. Schnabel and Robert J. Watson. Schnabel and Watson jointly wrote the magnificent volume three (in two parts) on the Korean War.

A final word about the chapter notes. A very large number of books were utilized for general background, especially in the World War II period. Owing to space limitations, material derived from these sources is generally but not always specifically annotated. However, wherever Bradley is directly involved or quoted, I have endeavored to note the source. In the less well documented and less familiar post-World War II and Korean War periods, all source material is cited, whether directly involving Bradley or not. The Eisenhower quotation about Bradley in the front matter is from a letter to Paul A. Hodgson, 2/2/48, Eisenhower papers, vol. IX, p. 2234.

Throughout the three years this book was in preparation, my wife,

Joan, worked as a writer's collaborator in the fullest sense. She participated in the many interviews, including those with General Bradley, and thereafter handled the considerable correspondence, filing, typing, editing, travel arrangements and a thousand other chores with skill and thoroughness. In truth, the book is as much the product of her work as it is of mine.

PICTURE CREDITS

Frontis: Arnold Newman © 1982
U.S. Army Military History Institute: 1, 2, 3, 4, 6, 10, 11, 12, 14, 20.
Special Collections Division, USMA Library, West Point: 5, 7, 8, 15, 16, 65.
U.S. Military Academy Archives, West Point: 9, 31, 58.
UPI: 13, 17, 19, 22, 23, 24, 25, 26, 27, 32, 33, 34, 35, 36, 39, 41, 43, 44, 45, 46, 47, 48, 57, 59, 70, 72, 73, 74, 75, 76, 77, 78, 80, 81, 82, 83, 85, 86, 88, 89, 91, 92.
U.S. Army: 18, 30, 37, 40, 42, 49, 50, 53, 60, 61, 62, 63, 69, 71, 79, 84, 87, 90.
Omar N. Bradley Library, USMA, West Point: 21, 64.
National Archives: 28, 38, 51, 52, 54, 55, 56.
World Wide Photos: 29.

Veterans Administration: 67, 68.

Notes

PART ONE: EARLY YEARS

Chapter One

1. Bradley Family history: Bradley Family Tree (hereafter BFT) compiled by CB, based on family Bibles, Randolph and Howard County, Missouri, courthouse records, cemetery records and interviews with ONB relatives. CB was invaluably assisted by Missouri Secretary of State James C. Kirkpatrick and archivist Mrs. John A. Gross, who provided genealogical charts based on census data and other official state records. Construction of the BFT turned up two errors in ONB family legend or records: Bradley's paternal great-grandfather, who was also a private in the Confederate Army in the Civil War, was not, as believed, John Smith Bradley, but rather Thomas S. Bradley; and the date of birth—1868—on ONB's father's tombstone in Log Chapel Cemetery near Burton, Missouri, is in error by one year. The Civil War records of great-grandfather Thomas S. Bradley and grandfather Thomas Minter Bradley may be found in the National Archives, Washington, D.C. (hereafter NA), Confederate Records, cards, #45062139 and 44218554. A more detailed account of Bradley's ancestry and the Missouri Bradleys may be found in the original, uncut, version of this manuscript on file with the Bradley papers at the Omar N. Bradley Library, Special Collections Division of the U.S. Military Academy Library, West Point, N.Y. (hereafter BP, WP).
2. CB-Omar N. Bradley taped interviews, 2-1-80 to 2-13-80, conducted at Fort Bliss, El Paso, Texas (hereafter CB-ONB int.), on file with BP, WP. Here and below, I have also made liberal use of the typescript of ONB's "autobiography" entitled "As I Remember" (hereafter memoir), which is in the Bradley papers, United States Army Military History Institute (USAMHI), Carlisle Barracks, Pennsylvania (hereafter BP, Carlisle).
3. BFT; memoir; CB-ONB int.; CB-Glenwood Spurling int., 3-1-80, during which the Hubbard-Spurling family Bible, containing births, deaths, marriages, etc., was made available; NA, Union Records, Henry C. Hubbard, 62nd Reg't, E.M.M. Co. H.
4. Marriage license, J. S. Bradley and Bessie Hubbard, vol. 4, p. 259, Randolph City, Missouri, Courthouse. ONB's birth recorded in Bradley Family Bible, BP, WP.
5. BFT; CB-ONB int.; CB-Glenwood Spurling (son of Nettie Bogie) int. On Raymond Calvert: BFT and obit, *Higbee Weekly News,* 1-24-02, on microfilm at the State Historical Society, Columbia, Mo. Note: For further information on Nettie and Opal Bogie, see original manuscript, BP, WP.
6. On J. S. Bradley teaching posts and ONB early rural schools and homes: CB-Fred Bradley (ONB double cousin) int., 3-3-80, re Pemberton. The *Higbee News,* 6-17-43, published a photograph of Pemberton School body, dated 9-27-99. ONB, then age six, is in front row, J. S. Bradley in back row. Correspondence, 1981, with Mrs. Lois E. Davis, re Locust Grove School. CB-Otho B. Lynch int., 3-3-80, re Baldridge School. (Mr. Lynch, an ONB classmate at Baldridge, has written a brief unpublished history of the school.) CB-Truby Koenig (ONB first cousin) int. re Bradley homes, during which she provided a snapshot of

one. The interviews and records provided indicate that ONB attended Pemberton (first grade) 1899–1900, Locust Grove (second grade) 1900–1901, and (third grade) 1901–1902, an unknown school near Burton taught by Omar Robb (fourth grade) 1902–1903, the Baldridge School (fifth grade) 1903–1904 and (sixth grade) 1904–1905.

7. Memoir.
8. For further details on childhood in this vein, see George S. Pappas-ONB int. and Kitty Buhler (Bradley)-ONB int. both in BP, Carlisle.
9. Allan G. Little-Courtney M. Rittgers int. with ONB, 12-13-79, BP, WP.
10. Memoir; the World War II diary of ONB's aide Chester B. Hansen (hereafter Hansen diary) contains a few fleeting references to ONB's earlier years, including this "omelet" anecdote. The Hansen diary is in Hansen papers, Carlisle.
11. Memoir; CB-ONB int.; C. M. Rittgers-Thomas A. Hansen int. with ONB, 1-9-80, BP, WP.
12. Memoir; CB-ONB int.
13. Memoir; CB-ONB int.; real estate records, John S. and Bessie Bradley, Randolph City, Mo., Courthouse; CB-Fred Bradley int.
14. Higbee School records, collected by CB, 3-3-80.
15. C. M. Rittgers-ONB int., 1-7-80, BP, WP.
16. Memoir.
17. Memoir; CB-Fred Bradley int.
18. Higbee School records.
19. CB-ONB int.; obit, *Higbee Weekly News,* 1-31-08, State Historical Society.
20. Ibid., issue of 2-7-08.
21. CB-ONB int.

Chapter Two

1. CB-ONB int.
2. ONB Moberly High School records, at the school, the Moberly Historical and Railroad Museum, and BP, WP. In addition, CB is indebted to the following—some of them ONB classmates—for general background on Moberly, the high school and the early days: Mrs. Zada M. Kenoyer, J. Will and Ruth Fleming, Mrs. Ruth Stevenson, Mrs. Mary Lozier and Orville Sittler, Moberly journalist and local historian. Interviews conducted 3-2-80 and 3-3-80. Interviewees kindly loaned copies of the Moberly High School yearbooks, *Salutar,* for 1909 and 1910 and the 1910 humor magazine, *Foehn.*
3. CB-ONB int.; MHS yearbook *Salutar,* 1909.
4. The church is described in a privately published booklet *100th Anniversary, Moberly, Missouri 1866–1966,* and in another privately published booklet, *Moberly Art Souvenirs, 1896,* both on file at Little Dixie Regional Library, Moberly. ONB baptismal records from Central Christian Church, Moberly, courtesy the Rev. Donald Mattson, 6-16-80.
5. For more extended information on the Quayle family and antecedents, see original ms. Sources here: obit, Charles L. Quayle, *Moberly Daily Monitor,* 11-4-02; Probate Court, Moberly, "Charles L. Quayle, deceased"; Sittler, Orville, "Charley Quayle Unique Guardian of Law and Order at Moberly," *Moberly Monitor-Index & Evening Democrat,* March 22, 1981; obit, Eudora Goodfellow Quayle, *Moberly Monitor-Index-Democrat,* 9-5-39; death certificate, Eudora Goodfellow Quayle, 9-3-39, John Day, Oregon. Other documents and written material on the Quayle family kindly provided by ONB's daughter, Elizabeth Dorsey, in an interview 4-10-80.
6. Moberly High School records. Note: A casual reading of these records would not reveal that ONB was put back a year, then skipped ahead a year.
7. CB-ONB int.
8. *Salutar,* 1910. Some class standings (but not ONB's) are in the 1910 humor magazine, *Foehn.*
9. Memoir; CB-ONB int.
10. Ibid.; Mary Quayle Bradley scrapbooks, BP, WP. These numerous scrapbooks are crammed with valuable family memorabilia, photographs, newspaper clippings and some official documents.
11. CB-ONB int.; marriage records, Bessie Bradley and J. R. Maddox, and real estate records, Bessie Bradley, Randolph Co. Courthouse; obit Mrs. J. R. (Bessie) Maddox, *Moberly Monitor-Index-Democrat,* 6-24-31; obit Charles W. Maddox, *Columbia Tribune,* Columbia, Mo., 3-15-74; Moberly High School records for David Russell Maddox and Charles William Maddox provided corroboration of the boys' ages, courtesy counselor Roy Hedrick, 11-13-80.
12. The following account of ONB's decision to try for West Point is based largely on the memoir, supplemented by CB-ONB int.
13. Letter, Nannie C. Anderson (widow of Dempsey Anderson) to CB, 7-14-80.
14. Letter, W. W. Rucker to ONB, 7-23-11, BP, WP.
15. CB-ONB int.

Chapter Three

1. Much of the material on ONB's West Point years is derived from the memoir, CB-ONB interview and ONB West Point records, including an exact record of his demerits, BP, WP. Additional sources, all from the West Point Archives or Library: *Annual Report of the Superintendent,* 1912, 1913, 1914,

1915; *USMA Register of Graduates* (Association of Graduates USMA, West Point, N.Y.); *Official Register of Officers and Cadets, USMA,* 1912, 1913, 1914, 1915; The West Point yearbook, *Howitzer,* 1912, 1913, 1914, 1915; *Army Football 1890–1947,* a booklet published by the USMA, WP; *Army Baseball 1890–1947,* a booklet published by the USMA, WP; *Annual Report,* Army Athletic Council, 1913–14, USMA, WP; *Semi-Annual Report,* Army Athletic Council, winter-spring 1914–15, USMA, WP.

2. The quotation from ONB's card is from *Omar Nelson Bradley,* by Colonel Russell P. Reeder, Champaign, Ill., Gerrerd, 1969. This book, designed for juvenile readers and which was read and corrected by ONB before publication, contains other interesting—but brief—sidelights on ONB's athletics at West Point.
3. The existence of Omicron Pi Phi was a closely held secret until 1966, when Hanson W. Baldwin, military editor of *The New York Times,* found references to it while going through the personal papers of John S. Wood (Class of 1912). It developed that Charles L. Mullins, Jr., (Class of 1917) still had the fraternity charter and membership lists, which included, among others, Omar Bradley's signature. In 1967, Mullins turned these papers over to West Point Superintendent D. V. Bennett, who, in turn, placed them in the West Point Archives, along with some correspondence Baldwin's discovery had prompted. Baldwin apparently did not pursue the matter. General Bradley felt no harm would—or should—result from disclosing the existence of the fraternity. He insisted in CB-ONB interviews that no member later benefited in a career sense from membership.
4. For more detail on Ike's knee injury, see: Hatch, Alden, *General Ike,* N.Y., Henry Holt, 1944; and Davis, Kenneth S. *Soldier of Democracy: A Biography of Dwight Eisenhower,* N.Y., 1945.
5. MQB scrapbooks, BP, WP. These MQB-ONB letters, and others from later years, cannot be found.
6. Quote from *Semi-Annual Report,* Army Athletic Council, winter-spring 1914–15.
7. *Howitzer,* 1915. Eisenhower used ONB's 1914 batting average of ".383" (he meant .387) rather than his 1915 average, .325.

Chapter Four

1. For background on the U.S. Army in 1915, see: Ganoe, William A., *The History of the United States Army,* N.Y., Appleton-Century, 1943; Weigley, Russell, *History of the United States Army,* N.Y., Macmillan, 1967; Riker, William H., *Soldiers of the State: The Role of the National Guard in American Democracy,* Washington, D.C., Public Affairs Press, 1957; Millis, Walter, *Arms and Men: A Study in American Military History,* N.Y., 1956; *The Army Almanac.*
2. Eisenhower, Dwight D., *At Ease—Stories I Tell My Friends,* Garden City, N.Y., Doubleday, 1967; memoir; CB-ONB int.; C. M. Rittgers-ONB int
3. Memoir; CB-ONB int.; *Moberly Daily Monitor,* 6-24-15 and 7-18-15 Little Dixie Library, Moberly. The editor variously described ONB as 'an 18 karat ballplayer," an "outstanding" fielder and "one of the fastest fielders seen here in a long time."
4. CB-ONB int.; University of Missouri yearbook *Savitar,* 1914, 1915, 1916; MQB scrapbook, BP, WP.
5. For further information on the 14th Regiment, see original ms. and: Rodenbough, Theodore F., Brevet Brigadier General U.S.A., and William L. Haskin, Major, First Artillery (editors), *The Army of the United States, Historical Sketches of Staff and Line with Portraits of Generals-in-Chief,* N.Y., Maynard, Merrill, 1896; Sorley, Captain Lewis S., *History of the Fourteenth United States Infantry from January 1890 to December 1908,* Chicago, privately printed, 1909. Both at Army War College Library, Carlisle. Regiment, battalion and company personnel from "Chronological Statement of Duties, January 1, 1917, to December 31, 1918," BP, Carlisle, and from K Company Thanksgiving Day menu, 1915, MQB scrapbook, BP, WP.
6. Memoir; CB-ONB int.; Harding: *Register of Graduates,* op. cit.
7. Memoir; CB-ONB int.
8. Weigley, op. cit.; Ganoe, op. cit.; Tompkins, Frank, *Chasing Villa,* Harrisburg, Pa., 1934; Mason, Herbert N., *The Great Pursuit,* N.Y., Random House, 1970; Toulmin, H. A., Jr., *With Pershing in Mexico,* Harrisburg, Pa., 1935; Blumenson, Martin, *The Patton Papers,* vol. I, Boston, Houghton Mifflin, 1972.
9. ONB personal "diary," BP, WP. This "diary" consists almost exclusively of dates of major events or changes of duty in ONB's pre-WW II career, without comment.
10. *Moberly Democrat,* 5-15-16, Little Dixie Library, Moberly, Mo. The story stated that "Miss Quayle is one of Moberly's prettiest and most accomplished ladies."
11. ONB diary; ONB photo scrapbook "Early Days" has many pictures of vast tent encampments; album, BP, WP.
12. Weigley, op. cit.; Ganoe, op. cit.
13. ONB diary; memoir; CB-ONB int.; undated, unmarked newspaper clipping from

a Douglas, Arizona, paper, headlined "BRADLEY TO TRAIN 14TH TEAM," MQB scrapbook, BP, WP, gives some details about the baseball team. The photographs are in the album "Early Days."

14. ONB diary.
15. ONB diary; federal income tax returns, BP, WP.
16. Memoir; CB-ONB int.; marriage license ONB-MQB, Boone County Courthouse, Columbia, Mo., vol. 13, p. 225; photo MQB in wedding dress and the announcement, MQB scrapbook, BP, WP; letter to CB from Mrs. Helena W. Frank, sorority sister of MQB and niece of the F. P. Spaldings who attended the wedding, 3-16-80.
17. CB-ONB int.; ONB diary; memoir. Note: ONB's written request for Alaskan duty and the approved endorsement cannot be found.

Chapter Five

1. Weigley, *History of the United States Army,* op. cit.; Ganoe, *The History of the United States Army,* op. cit.
2. Memoir; CB-ONB int.; ONB diary.
3. Ibid.; ONB "Orders," BP, Carlisle.
4. CB-ONB int.; CB visit to Quayle plot, Oakland Cemetery, Moberly.
5. Accounts of the St. Patrick's Day "riot" in the *Anaconda Standard,* 3-18-18, and the *Butte Bulletin,* 3-18-18, both in MQB scrapbook, BP, WP. See also "Resolutions of Lincoln Comp. No. 5, Sons of Veterans," Butte, Montana, 3-20-18, BP, WP. ONB and Company F were lavishly praised in the press.
6. ONB "Promotions," BP, WP. News of ONB's promotion evoked further praise for him in the local Butte press.
7. ONB diary and "Orders"; Lasseigne: *Register of Graduates.*
8. CB-ONB int.
9. Marriage records, Wayne C. Stewart and Sarah J. Quayle, Randolph County Courthouse.
10. Memo in "Twenty Year Book, Class of 1915," USMA, 1935, WP Library. Some years later, a historian analyzed the Class of 1915's service in the war. He discovered that 102 out of 164—62 percent—had been sent overseas to Europe. Fifty-six—34 percent—saw action at the front. Thirty-two received decorations. Fourteen were wounded in action and two were killed—ONB's good friend Spec Reaney and Harry A. Harvey.
11. Memoir; CB-ONB int.; ONB diary; ONB "Orders", op. cit.
12. CB-ONB int.; ONB "Orders."
13. ONB "Statement of Preferences," 4-12-19, in ONB "Orders."
14. Weigley, op. cit.; Ganoe, op. cit.; Millis, *Arms and Men,* op. cit.; Pogue, Forrest C. (with the editorial assistance of Gordon Harrison), *Education of a General, 1880–1939,* N.Y., Viking Press, the first of a four-volume biography of General of the Army George C. Marshall. The Army strength figure is derived from Watson, Mark S., *Chief of Staff: Prewar Plans and Preparations,* Washington, D.C., Office of the Chief of Military History (hereafter OCMH), 1950 (see yearly strength table, page 16).
15. CB-ONB int.; ONB "Orders"; ONB diary; Van Fleet: *Register of Graduates.*

Chapter Six

1. James, D. Clayton, *The Years of MacArthur, 1880–1941,* vol. 1, Boston, 1970; Ambrose, Stephen E., *Duty, Honor, Country: A History of West Point,* Baltimore, 1966; Fleming, Thomas J., *West Point,* N.Y., 1969; Masland, John W., and Lawrence I. Radway, *Soldiers and Scholars,* Princeton, 1957; *Annual Report of the Superintendent,* 1919, 1920, 1921, 1922, WP Library; CB-David P. Page, Jr. (Class of 1924) int.; CB-Charles E. Hart (Class of 1924) int., 4-18-80. Note: The *Register of Graduates* explains how the wartime and immediate postwar West Point classes were disrupted and reorganized.
2. Memoir; CB-ONB int.; CB-Page int.; CB-Hart int.
3. Memoir; CB-ONB int.; life in the remodeled bachelor officers' quarters and at West Point in the early 1920s was described to CB in interviews with Page and Hart and on 2-11-80 with H. Crampton Jones (Class of 1916), who was a math instructor in 1920; with Mrs. J. J. (Bobbie) O'Hare, widow of Joseph J. O'Hare (1916) on 4-17-80.
4. CB-ONB int.; CB-Matthew B. Ridgway int., 4-25-80; Omicron Pi Phi records, West Point Archives; ONB's golf competition; Letter of commendation, 10-3-29, Col. Duncan K. Major, C/S IV Corps, with endorsements, BP, Carlisle; unidentified newspaper clip: *Lieutenant Baldwin Retains Army Golf Title, Beating Maj. Bradley,* BP, WP.
5. Memoir; CB-ONB int.; ONB "Promotions"; ONB federal income tax returns.
6. CB-ONB int.
7. Ambrose, op. cit.; Fleming, op. cit.; James, op. cit.; *Annual Report of the Superintendent,* 1923, 1924.
8. French: *Register of Graduates,* Class of 1924, n., p. 363.
9. Memoir; CB-ONB int.; ONB "Orders," BP, WP. Colonel Echols rated ONB "Above Average" in his first two years, "Superior" in his second two years, ONB "Efficiency Reports."

10. Memoir; CB-ONB int.; CB int. with James Ridpath, manager of Bear Mountain Bridge, 7-28-80.
11. CB-ONB int.; for a masterful study of Sherman, see: *Sherman: Soldier, Realist, American,* by British military historian Sir Basil H. Liddell Hart.
12. Warfield, A. B. "Fort Benning: The Home of the Infantry School," *Infantry Journal,* vol. XXXII, no. 6, June 1928; *History of Fort Benning, 1918–1968,* U.S. Army official monograph, both at the Army War College Library, Carlisle.
13. Roster, advanced class, Fort Benning 1924–25, BP, Carlisle; *Register of Graduates*; CB-Ridgway interview; CB-Mark Wayne Clark int., 4-7-80.
14. Fox and Chilton: *Register of Graduates.*
15. *Twenty-ninth U.S. Infantry, 1901–1926,* U.S. Army monograph, Fort Benning, Ga., 1926, Army War College Library, Carlisle; CB-Mrs. Charles Ryder int.; CB-Charles L. Bolte int., 4-20-80. Bolte was stationed at Benning during the early 1920s.
16. CB-ONB int.; Gerow: *Generals of the Army,* a cumulative biographical roster, Washington, D.C., Dunleavy, 1953.

Chapter Seven

1. Memoir; CB-ONB int.; ONB "Orders."
2. CB-ONB int.
3. ONB diary; ONB "Orders." On the N.Y.–California leg of the trip, ONB was "casual officer," in effect nominally in charge of the enlisted men, who were embarked as passengers.
4. Smith, Heintzelman, Halstead: *Register of Graduates.*
5. Memoir; CB-ONB int. ONB received two official letters of commendation during his tour with the 27th Infantry: Major General W. R. Smith to ONB, 10-19-26, Brigadier General S. Heintzelman to ONB, 5-19-27, BP, Carlisle. He was rated "Superior" throughout the tour, ONB "Efficiency Reports."
6. ONB "Orders."
7. Ibid.; ONB diary.
8. Charles K. Hanson-ONB oral history, in thirteen sessions conducted in Los Angeles, 12-2-74 to 10-12-75, BP, Carlisle, hereafter Hanson int. and not to be confused with Thomas A. Hansen or Chester B. (Chet) Hansen interviews. The latter were Bradley aides, the former, Charles K. Hanson, conducted the oral history for USAMHI. On nervous breakdowns and suicides, see also: Davis, Kenneth S., *Soldier of Democracy,* op. cit., p. 203–4; King: *Register of Graduates.*
9. Hanson-ONB int.; Brownell: C & GSS class roster, 1928–29, BP, Carlisle.
10. G. Pappas-ONB int.
11. Health problems: CB-ONB int.
12. Reflecting his casual attitude toward the school, officially ONB completed the course with a grade of "Satisfactory"—two ranks below "Superior" and "Excellent" —per student records, C & GSS, courtesy Major Carl Chun; ONB "Efficiency Reports." However, in interview, ONB told CB that "at least two of my instructors told me, informally, that had class standings been posted, I would have finished first." Eisenhower stood number one in his C & GSS class three years earlier: Davis, *Soldier of Democracy,* op. cit.
13. CB-ONB int.; ONB "Orders."

Chapter Eight

1. CB-ONB int.; ONB federal income tax returns; CB-Elizabeth Dorsey int.
2. CB-ONB int.; Pogue, *Education of a General,* op. cit.; Collins, J. Lawton, *Lightning Joe,* Baton Rouge, LSU Press, 1979; Warfield, "Fort Benning," op. cit.; Tuchman, Barbara W., *Stilwell and the American Experience in China, 1911–1945,* N.Y., Macmillan, 1977; Acheson, Dean, *Sketches from Life of Men I Have Known,* N.Y., 1961. Interviews: CB-Charles L. Bolte; CB-Matthew B. Ridgway; CB-J. Lawton Collins, 4-15-80.
3. Memoir; CB-ONB int.; Tuchman, op. cit.
4. G. Pappas-ONB int.
5. Ridgway oral history USAMHI; CB-Ridgway int.
6. CB-ONB int.
7. Ibid.; A. G. Little-ONB int., 12-31-79; C. M. Rittgers-ONB int., 1-9-80; CB-Elizabeth Dorsey int. Names of Tweed and Copass verified by CB in U.S. Army records, Fort Benning, 1980. According to ONB, who adored Tip, the dog's name was Tippecanoe Doughboy. He was the grandson of a dog named Doughboy, which had been a national champion in the Tennessee Field Trials.
8. ONB "Orders," "Efficiency Reports"; Tuchman, op. cit., is source for Stilwell's strict grading practice.
9. Weigley, *History of the United States Army,* op. cit.; Ganoe, *The History of The United States Army,* op. cit.; James, *MacArthur,* op. cit.; Eisenhower, *At Ease,* op. cit.
10. Memoir; CB-ONB int.
11. Smith: *Current Biography 1953;* CB-ONB int.; Chet Hansen-ONB int.; Hanson-ONB int.
12. Pogue, op. cit.; Marshall, Katherine Tupper, *Together: Annals of an Army Wife,* N.Y., 1946.

13. BFT; death certificate, Bessie Maddox, #22488, Missouri State Board of Health, Jefferson City; CB visit to Log Chapel Cemetery, 3-1-80; ONB diary.
14. Upon detachment, Marshall rated ONB "Superior" for the two years ONB directly served him and wrote: "Quiet, unassuming, capable, sound common sense. Absolute dependability. Give him a job and forget it. Recommended command: regiment in peace, division in war." There was a widespread rumor that owing to Marshall's faulty memory for names he carried a little black notebook into which he jotted names and assessments such as the above. ONB could recall no such notebook and seriously doubted its existence. The Marshall comments on ONB, which ONB deemed the most crucial of his entire prewar career, are in ONB "Efficiency Reports."
15. Marshall's assignments and speculation on the MacArthur-Marshall feud: Pogue, op. cit.; James, *MacArthur,* op. cit.
16. CB-ONB int.; G. Pappas-ONB int.; in approving ONB's application for the War College, Colonel Weeks wrote, "He is an officer of the highest type and is particularly suited for higher military education," ONB "Orders."
17. CB-ONB int.; on the Army budget and role in the CCC: Weigley, op. cit.; Ganoe, op. cit.
18. Pogue, op. cit.; Tuchman, op. cit.

Chapter Nine

1. Memoir; ONB diary; CB-ONB int. The Bradleys lived on the fifth floor of Woodley Park Towers, 2737 Devonshire Place, N.W.
2. For a different view, see Collins, *Lightning Joe,* op. cit. Collins, who graduated from the War College four years later (in 1938) and then remained there as an instructor, has high praise for the institution.
3. Memoir; CB-ONB int.; ONB "Topic" card file, Army War College Records, Carlisle. On the baseball team: memoir and Ernest N. Harmon Papers, USAMHI.
4. CB-ONB int.; White House invitation in MQB scrapbook, BP, WP.
5. *Annual Report of the Superintendent,* 1916–1938, WP Library; Dupuy, R. Ernest, *The Story of West Point, 1802–1943,* Washington, D.C., Infantry Journal Press, 1943.
6. Cullum, George W., *Biographical Register, Officers and Graduates, USMA,* Saginaw, Mich., Seeman & Peters, 1920 (and later editions), has bio on Conner and other superintendents.
7. *Annual Report of the Superintendent,* 1916, 1937, 1938. The controversial summer programs for first classmen are described in detail.
8. *Register of Graduates.*
9. Westmoreland, William C., *A Soldier Reports,* Garden City, N.Y., Doubleday, 1976.
10. *Official Register of Officers and Cadets, USMA,* 1936, 1937; ONB "Promotions," "Orders." Others in the department: Normando A. Costello; Leonard H. Rodieck; Lewis S. Sorley, Jr.; Carl F. Fritzsche; Edward H. Bowes; William M. (Bud) Miley; Clyde D. Eddleman. Helpful for this period in ONB's life were CB interviews with Matthews (4-9-80); Easterbrook (9-18-80); Sorley (9-18-80); Costello (9-17-80); Rodieck (3-18-80); Miley (9-18-80); Eddleman (4-10-80); and Elizabeth Dorsey.
11. CB-ONB int.
12. Pogue, *Education of a General,* op. cit.; letter GCM to ONB, 9-29-36, BP, Carlisle.
13. *Official Register of Officers and Cadets, USMA,* 1938; *Annual Report of the Superintendent,* 1938; CB-Willis Matthews int.; CB-Mrs. Charles M. Ryder int.
14. Watson, Mark S., *Chief of Staff,* op. cit.; Weigley, *History of the United States Army,* op. cit.; *Annual Report of the Superintendent,* 1916–1938.
15. ONB "Orders." Both McCunniff and Ryder were glowing in their praise of ONB.

Chapter Ten

1. Pogue, *Education of a General,* op. cit.
2. Memoir; CB-ONB int.
3. ONB "Orders"; CB-ONB int.
4. Here and below in this chapter, Army manpower expansion and other War Department problems: Watson, Mark S., *Chief of Staff,* op. cit.; Pogue, *Education of a General,* op. cit.; Weigley, *History of the United States Army,* op. cit.
5. General political and military developments in Europe, here and below: Liddell Hart, B. H., *History of the Second World War,* N.Y., Putnam, 1971; Churchill, Winston S., *The Second World War,* 6 volumes, Boston, 1948–53; Wilmot, Chester, *The Struggle for Europe,* N.Y., 1952; Calvocoressi, Peter, and Guy Wint, *Total War,* London, Penguin, 1972.
6. Watson, op. cit.; Pogue, op. cit.
7. CB-ONB int.
8. Pogue, op. cit. Volume II of Pogue's magisterial Marshall biography, *Ordeal and Hope 1939–1942,* N.Y., Viking Press, 1966, picks up the story with Marshall's appointment to Chief of Staff.

9. ONB "Orders"; memoir; CB-ONB int.; Ward: *Register of Graduates;* Mickelsen: official U.S. Army biography, provided by ONB staff, 1980; Pogue, *Ordeal and Hope,* p. 8.
10. Chester B. Hansen-ONB int. The Hansen interviews with ONB were conducted in 1946–49 as background for ONB's war memoir, *A Soldier's Story*. The interviews were recorded on a Dictograph or similar instrument. The actual recordings cannot be found. However, typed summarized transcripts of the recordings (sometimes containing direct quotes) may be found stapled to file cards in two wooden file boxes in the Hansen papers at USAMHI, Carlisle. Most of the material deals with the war. However, there are occasional prewar anecdotes or impressions, such as this.
11. Memoir; Hanson-ONB int.
12. Hanson-ONB int.
13. Hansen-ONB int.
14. Memoir; Hanson-ONB int.
15. See note 5.
16. Ibid; Watson, op. cit.
17. See note 5.
18. Obit, Eudora Quayle, *Moberly Democrat;* death certificate, Eudora Goodfellow Quayle, Moberly Probate Court records: "Estate of Eudora Quayle"; CB visit to Oakland Cemetery.
19. War Department budget, politics and other: Watson, op. cit.; Pogue, *Ordeal and Hope;* Weigley, op. cit.; MacDonald, Charles B., *The Mighty Endeavor,* N.Y., Oxford University Press, 1969; for European developments see note 5.
20. ONB diary; Watson, op. cit., has a good account of the 1940 Louisiana maneuvers.
21. CB-ONB int.
22. Reunion: ONB diary.
23. See note 19.
24. CB-ONB int.; Clark, Ronald, *The Man Who Broke Purple,* Boston, Little, Brown, 1977; Kahn, David, *The Codebreakers,* N.Y., Macmillan, 1973; Holmes, W. J., *Double-Edged Secrets,* Annapolis, Naval Institute Press, 1979; Lewin, Ronald, *The American Magic,* N.Y., Farrar, Straus, Giroux, 1982; Blair, Clay, *Silent Victory: The U.S. Submarine War Against Japan,* N.Y., Lippincott, 1975; "History of the Special Branch, MIS, War Department 1942–1944," Record Group 457 (SRH035), Modern Military History Branch, National Archives, 1979.
25. See note 5.
26. See note 19.
27. CB-ONB int.; on GHQ, see note 19 and Cline, Ray S., *Washington Command Post,* Washington, D.C., OCMH, 1951.

Chapter Eleven

1. Memoir; Hanson-ONB int.; CB-ONB int.; ONB "Orders" and "Promotions"; ONB diary.
2. Official Army biography, courtesy ONB staff, 1980. Rare are the biographical profiles of Hodges. The best is Murray, G. Patrick, "Courtney Hodges: Modest Star of WW II," *American History Illustrated,* vol. VII, no. 9, January 1973.
3. Correspondence between ONB and GCM re expansion of Benning schools (together with charts, etc.) in box 58, folder 9 and microfilm reel 27, item 1007, GCM papers, George C. Marshall Research Library, Lexington, Virginia (hereafter Marshall Library). Further on this subject in Watson, *Chief of Staff,* op. cit.; the *Army-Navy Register,* 1-25-41 and 5-10-41. See also memoir; Hanson-ONB int.; G. Pappas-ONB int.; CB-ONB int.; CB-Costello int.; CB-Matthews int.
4. Blumenson, Martin, *The Patton Papers, 1940–1945,* vol. II, Boston, Houghton Mifflin, 1974; Carver, Field Marshal Sir Michael, editor, *The War Lords,* Boston, Little, Brown, 1976 (see: "Patton," by Martin Blumenson); Farago, Ladislas, *Patton: Ordeal and Triumph,* N.Y., Obolensky, 1964; Essame, H., *Patton: A Study in Command,* N.Y., Scribner's, 1974. The superb short portraits of Patton by Blumenson in *The War Lords* and at the end of vol. 2 of *The Patton Papers* come as close as humanly possible to defining Patton.
5. Blumenson, *Patton Papers II,* p. 55.
6. Devlin, Gerard M., *Paratrooper!* N.Y., St. Martin's, 1979; Gavin, James M., *War and Peace in the Space Age,* N.Y., Harper, 1958; Gavin, James M., *On to Berlin,* N.Y., Viking, 1978; Ridgway, Matthew B., *Soldier: The Memoirs of Matthew B. Ridgway,* N.Y., Harper, 1956; Ellis, John T., Jr., "The Airborne Command and Center," Study No. 25, Historical Section, Army Ground Forces, 1946, unpublished monograph at Army War College, Carlisle; CB-James M. Gavin int., 4-29-80; CB-Ridgway int.; CB-William W. Miley int.
7. Memoir; Hanson-ONB int.; Hansen-ONB int.; CB-ONB int.
8. Memoir.

Chapter Twelve

1. Memoir; Hanson-ONB int.; Hansen-ONB int.; CB-ONB int.; additional data on the activities and training of the 82nd Division, here and below, based on CB interviews

with the following men who were there: Ridgway (see also his *Soldier*); Ralph P. Eaton, 9-26-80; Richard K. Boyd, 9-25-80; George E. Lynch, 9-25-80; Frank W. Moorman, 9-25-80; Alexander Stoute, 11-8-80; Chet Hansen, 11-8-80. On Eichelberger and Haislip: *Register of Graduates*. Note: Joseph T. McNarney, who was making a brilliant mark in the Air Corps, was the first 1915 graduate to be promoted to major general.

2. CB-ONB int.; CB-Chet Hansen int.
3. CB-Stoute int.
4. Ridgway, *Soldier,* op. cit.
5. ONB's talent as a teacher may have helped in the success of training the division. Ridgway's leadership and drive were also a prime factor. ONB was extremely proud of the job he did with the 82nd. In CB-ONB interview, he uncharacteristically boasted that on one visit McNair told him: "You are the best of the three new divisions—by far."
6. Letter, McNair to ONB, 6-18-42, BP, WP.
7. Memoir; CB-ONB int.; ONB "Orders"; CB-Ridgway int.; Ridgway, op. cit.; CB-Gavin int.; CB-Miley int.; Taylor: *Register of Graduates* and CB-Taylor int., 4-17-80.
8. For extended discussions of National Guard problems, see Watson, *Chief of Staff,* op. cit.; Riker, William H., *Soldiers of the State: The Role of the National Guard in American Democracy,* Washington, D.C., 1957.
9. Memoir; Hanson-ONB int.; Hansen-ONB int.; CB-ONB int. Additional data on the history, troubles and reorganization of the 28th Division from CB interviews with Hansen, Matthews, Stoute, Forrest Caraway, 9-25-80, and from numerous clippings in the Bradley scrapbooks, BP, Carlisle, and the MQB scrapbook, BP, WP.
10. Ord: *Register of Graduates;* CB-ONB int.
11. ONB diary; staff roster, 28th Division Headquarters, 12-1-42, BP, Carlisle.
12. Letter GCM-ONB, 12-23-42, box 58, folder 9, Marshall Library.
13. Beukemas: *Register of Graduates;* CB int. with Elizabeth Dorsey; CB int. with Mrs. Margaret Shaw (Peggy) Beukema, 4-10-80 and 9-30-80. Herman Beukema was born in Michigan, January 29, 1891, son of a postal worker. Like Eisenhower, he was twenty when he entered West Point. A track star, he graduated twenty-sixth in the class of 1915 and chose the Artillery. Upon graduation, he married Margaret Whitman Shaw, daughter of Henry A. Shaw, U.S. Army medical corps. They had three children—two girls, then Henry, the youngest, born February 16, 1924, two months after Elizabeth Bradley. Herman was wounded in France in World War I. In 1928, he reported to West Point for duty as an instructor. Two years later he was offered a permanent professorship. He resigned from the artillery and devoted the rest of his life to teaching. Hal and Elizabeth met at the West Point grammar school in the mid-1930s when both were ten years old. Hal gave her the nickname "Li" or "Lee."
14. Kean: *Register of Graduates;* official Army biography.
15. Here and below, to end: memoir; Hanson-ONB int.; Hansen-ONB int.; CB-ONB int.; early draft of *A Soldier's Story,* BP, Carlisle, and *A Soldier's Story;* ONB "Orders"; ONB diary.
16. Telegram, GCM to ONB, 2-12-43, Marshall papers, box 58, folder 9, Marshall Library.

PART TWO: OVERSEAS TO WAR

Chapter Thirteen

1. Here and below on grand strategy and Mediterranean military operations: Ambrose, Stephen, *The Supreme Commander: The War Years of General Dwight D. Eisenhower,* Garden City, N.Y., 1970; Blumenson, Martin, *Kasserine Pass,* Boston, 1967; Blumenson, Martin, *Patton Papers II,* op. cit.; Bryant, Arthur, *Triumph in the West* (based on the diaries of Field Marshal Alanbrooke), Garden City, N.Y., 1959; Buell, Thomas B., *Master of Sea Power,* Boston, 1980; Butcher, Harry C., *My Three Years with Eisenhower,* N.Y., 1946; Chandler, Alfred D., Jr. *The Papers of Dwight D. Eisenhower: The War Years,* 5 volumes, Baltimore, 1970 (hereafter Eisenhower papers); Churchill, Winston S., *The Second World War,* vol. III, IV, op. cit.; Clark, Mark W., *Calculated Risk,* N.Y., 1950; Cunningham of Hyndhope, Viscount, *A Sailor's Odyssey,* N.Y., 1951; de Guingand, Francis, *Operation Victory,* London, 1963; Eisenhower, Dwight D., *Crusade in Europe,* Garden City, N.Y., 1948; Essame, *Patton,* op. cit.; Fraser, David, *Alanbrooke,* N.Y., 1982; Hamilton, Nigel, *Monty: The Making of a General (1887–1942),* N.Y., 1981; Harmon, Ernest N., Milton MacKaye and William R. MacKaye, *Combat Commander,* N.Y., 1970; Horrocks, Sir Brian, *Escape to Action,* N.Y., 1960; Howard, Michael, *Grand Strategy,*

vol. IV, August 1942–September 1943, History of the Second World War, United Kingdom Military Series, J. R. M. Butler, editor, London, Her Majesty's Stationery Office, 1972; Howe, George F., *Northwest Africa: Seizing the Initiative in the West* (The United States Army in World War II, Mediterranean Theater of Operations), Washington, D.C., 1970; Irving, David, *The Trail of the Fox*, N.Y., 1977; Liddell Hart, Basil H., *History of the Second World War*, op. cit.; Loewenheim, Francis L., Harold D. Langley and Manfred Jonas, *Roosevelt and Churchill: Their Secret Wartime Correspondence*, N.Y., 1975; MacDonald, *The Mighty Endeavor*, op. cit.; Matloff, Maurice, and Edwin M. Snell, *Strategic Planning for Coalition Warfare 1941–1942*, Washington, D.C., 1953; Montgomery of Alamein, B. L., *El Alamein to the River Sangro*, N.Y., 1949; Montgomery, Field Marshal, the Viscount of Alamein, K. G., *Memoirs*, N.Y., 1958; Morison, Samuel E., *American Contributions to the Strategy of World War II*, London, 1958; Morison, Samuel E., *History of U.S. Naval Operations in World War II, Volume II, Operations in North African Waters*, Boston, 1958; Nicolson, Nigel, *Alex: The Life of Field Marshal Earl Alexander of Tunis*, N.Y., 1973; North, John, editor, *Alexander of Tunis: The Alexander Memoirs, 1940–45*, N.Y., 1963; Playfair, I. S. O., and G. J. C. Molony, *The Mediterranean and Middle East, Volume IV: The Destruction of Axis Forces in Africa*, London, 1966; Pogue, Forrest C., *George C. Marshall: Ordeal and Hope 1939–1942*, op. cit.; Tedder, Lord Arthur W., *With Prejudice*, Boston, 1966; Truscott, Lucian K., Jr., *Command Missions*, N.Y., 1954; Wilmot, *The Struggle for Europe*, op. cit.

2. Published literature on breaking the German codes in World War II is growing at a great rate. Volume I of the definitive official British history of that activity, which takes the story through June 1941, is now available: Hinsley, F. H., with E. E. Thomas et al., *British Intelligence in the Second World War: Its Influence on Strategy and Operations*, N.Y., 1979. Other, unofficial, accounts abound: Beesly, Patrick, *Very Special Intelligence: The Story of the Admiralty's Operational Intelligence Centre 1939–1945*, N.Y., 1978; Bennett, Ralph, *Ultra in the West*, N.Y., 1980; Brown, Anthony Cave, *Bodyguard of Lies*, N.Y., 1975; Calvocoressi, Peter, *Top Secret Ultra*, N.Y., Pantheon, 1980; Jones, R. V., *The Wizard War: British Scientific Intelligence*, N.Y., 1978; Lewin, Ronald, *Ultra Goes to War*, N.Y., 1978; Montagu, Ewen, *Beyond Top Secret Ultra*, N.Y., 1978; Stevenson, William, *A Man Called Intrepid*, N.Y., 1976; Winterbotham, F. W., *The Ultra Secret*, N.Y., 1974. Useful periodicals: Beesly, Patrick, "Ultra and the Battle of the Atlantic: The British View," *Cryptologic Spectrum*, vol. 8, no. 1, winter 1978; Boyd, Carl, "The Magic Betrayal of Hitler" (on Baron Oshima), paper at Citadel Symposium, April 24, 1980; Blumenson, Martin, "Will Ultra Rewrite History?" *Army*, August 1978; Deutsch, Dr. Harold C., "The Historical Impact of Revealing the Ultra Secret," *Parameters* (journal of the U.S. Army War College), vol. VII, no. 3, 1977; Deutsch, Dr. Harold C., "The Influence of Ultra on World War II," *Parameters*, vol. VIII, no. 4, 1978; Gores, Landis, "Princetonians in the Ultra Service," *Princeton Alumni Weekly*, 5-27-75, pp. 10–13; Rosengarten, Adolph G., "With Ultra from Omaha Beach to Weimar Germany—A Personal View," *Military Affairs*, October 1978; Spiller, Roger J., "Some Implications of Ultra," *Military Affairs*, April 1976; Spiller, "Assessing Ultra," *Military Review*, vol. LIX, no. 8, August 1979.

The National Archives has declassified and released hundreds of primary documents that are relevant. These are in the Modern Military Branch, Record Group 457NSA. Especially useful for this book were "History of the Special Branch," SRH 035; "Reports by U.S. Army Ultra Representatives with Army Field Commands in the ETO," SRH 023, part I and II; "Report of Brigadier E. T. Williams (G-2, Eighth Army) and British Group Captain R. H. Humphrey," SRH 037. (Humphrey is the source for the Auchinleck quote.)

3. Eisenhower papers I, pp. 1–109; Eisenhower, *Crusade in Europe*, op. cit., p. 31; Blumenson, Martin, "Ike and his Indispensable Lieutenants," *Army*, June 1980; CB-Mark W. Clark int., 4-7-80; Pogue, *Education of a General*, op. cit. Note: Ike's promotion to major general preceded ONB's promotion to the same rank by one day.
4. Eisenhower papers I, p. 427.
5. Williams quote from Williams Report, NA, op. cit. (see note 2).
6. Morison, *American Contributions to the Strategy of World War II*; Butcher, *My Three Years*, p. 387; Clark, *Calculated Risk*. Ike was well aware beforehand that a landing at Casablanca might cost an early victory in Tunisia. On August 25, 1942, he wrote Marshall, in part: "Though we may successfully occupy Casablanca and Oran and deny this section of the continent to the enemy, all calculations are flatly against re-

sulting chances to capture Tunisia either initially or eventually." (Eisenhower papers I, pp. 493–94.)

7. On Mockler-Ferryman "wrong call," see unpublished portion of Butcher diary, Eisenhower Library. Quoted in Lewin, *Ultra Goes to War,* pp. 273–74. Eisenhower, *At Ease,* p. 262, and *Crusade in Europe,* p. 147.
8. Truscott, *Command Missions.*

Chapter Fourteen

1. ONB diary; *Soldier's Story;* Eisenhower papers II, pp. 928–29; CB-ONB int.
2. See chapter 13, note 1.
3. Eisenhower papers II, p. 951; Marshall to ONB, 2-15-43, BP, Carlisle, and Eisenhower Library, #2312 cable file; Ike to Marshall #1086, 2-16-43, cable file, Eisenhower Library.
4. *Soldier's Story.*
5. Hansen diary; Hansen-ONB int. and notes; CB-ONB int.; *Soldier's Story.*
6. CB-ONB int.; *At Ease,* p. 261. Ike wrote of ONB at this point: "Bradley was not only a favorite classmate of mine at West Point, but a man whom I respected and admired throughout his military career. When he reached my headquarters, a close association began that has endured until this day—an association that was invaluable to me then and the memory of which is pleasurable now." He went on to say: "Of all the ground commanders I have known, ever, and of those of whom I've read, I would put Omar Bradley in the highest classification. In every aspect of military command, from the planning of an operation to the cleanup after its success, Brad was outstanding. I have yet to meet his equal as an offensive leader and a defensive bulwark, as a wielder of every arm that can be practically employed against an enemy. In the aftermath of the war, I'm surprised that he seems at times to be ignored or undervalued by those who write of the Mediterranean and European campaigns. Patton, for instance, was a master of fast and overwhelming pursuit. Headstrong by nature, and fearlessly aggressive, Patton was the more colorful figure of the two, compelling attention by his mannerisms as much as by his deeds. Bradley, however, was a master of every military maneuver, lacking only the capacity—possibly the willingness—to dramatize himself. This, I think, is to his credit."
7. Eisenhower papers II, pp. 969–70, 1034–35. Mockler-Ferryman was relieved by Kenneth W. D. Strong.
8. Miller, Merle, *Plain Speaking,* N.Y., 1973; Summersby, Kay Morgan, *Past Forgetting: My Love Affair with Dwight D. Eisenhower,* N.Y., 1976; *Letters to Mamie,* edited by John S. D. Eisenhower, N.Y., 1978, CB-ONB int.
9. Eisenhower papers V, chronology, 2-27-43.
10. Hansen-ONB int.; Hanson-ONB int.; CB-ONB int.; *Soldier's Story.*
11. Howe, *Northwest Africa,* op. cit.; Truscott, *Command Missions,* op. cit.; Blumenson, *Kasserine Pass,* op. cit.; Blumenson, *Patton Papers,* op. cit.; Harmon, *Combat Commander,* op. cit.; Hansen-ONB int.
12. Hansen-ONB int.; CB-ONB int.; *Soldier's Story.*
13. Eisenhower papers II, pp. 980–88, 1002; vol. V, chronology, 3-5-43.
14. Memoir; *Soldier's Story.*
15. Eisenhower papers II, p. 939; Ambrose, *Supreme Commander,* op. cit.; Butcher, *My Three Years,* op. cit.; *Patton Papers II.*
16. Hansen-ONB int.; *Soldier's Story;* "Orders," BP, Carlisle.
17. Eisenhower papers II, pp. 1016, 1019; Hansen-ONB int.; memoir.
18. Eisenhower papers II, pp. 1016, 1017; Marshall cable to DDE, 3-7-43, research file #1582, Marshall Library. In part, Marshall said of ONB: "His judgment, ability, and outstanding capacity as a trainer for HUSKY requirements and his selfless attitude make him a natural choice for this assignment."
19. Eisenhower papers II, p. 1022. That same day, in another cable (p. 1024), Ike told Marshall: "I cannot tell you how fortunate it was for me that Bradley arrived here at the time he did. He has been a godsend in every way and his utter frankness and complete loyalty are things that I count on tremendously." A little more than a week later, March 20, in a letter to OPD's Tom Handy, Ike said of ONB: "What a godsend it was to me to get that man!"
20. *Patton Papers II,* p. 188. Two days later, Patton diaried: "Omar Bradley is my deputy and is good. He will get the job when I have finished this phase. If I do" (p. 189).
21. Farago, *Patton,* op. cit., pp. 256–59. Farago reinforces his misconception of the Bradley-Patton relationship by misdating the DDE-ONB meeting as 3-22-43, twelve days later than it actually occurred.
22. CB-ONB int.; DDE, memorandum for personal file, 6-11-43, A472, Eisenhower Library.

Chapter Fifteen

1. Kitty Buhler (Bradley)-ONB int.
2. See note 1, chapter 13. Here and below in particular, Alexander, *Memoir,* op. cit.; Nicolson, *Alex,* op. cit.; Montgomery, *Mem-*

oirs, op. cit.; Montgomery, *El Alamein to the River Sangro*, op. cit.; de Guingand, *Operation Victory*, op. cit.; Howe, *Northwest Africa*, op. cit.; Howard, *Grand Strategy*, op. cit.; Playfair, *Mediterranean and Middle East*, op. cit.; Liddell Hart, *History of Second World War*, op. cit.; Eisenhower, *Crusade in Europe; Soldier's Story; Patton Papers II*.
3. Irving, *Trail of the Fox*, op. cit.
4. *Patton Papers II*, p. 190; Hansen-ONB int.
5. Memoir.
6. Hansen-ONB int.
7. *Patton Papers II*, p. 193 ("I may have to relieve a general").
8. Alexander, *Memoir*.
9. *Patton Papers II*, pp. 196–99.
10. Hansen-ONB int.
11. *Patton Papers II*, pp. 194–95; *Soldier's Story*.
12. Eisenhower papers II, pp. 1055–57; vol. V, "Chronology," 3-22 and 3-23-43; *Crusade in Europe*, p. 152 (the source Ike gives—chapter note 39—actually deals with entirely different matters several weeks later); Farago, *Patton*, p. 259; Hansen-ONB int.; *Soldier's Story*, pp. 56–9.
13. Liddell Hart, *Second World War*, pp. 418–19; Playfair, *Mediterranean and Middle East;* Montgomery, *Memoirs* and *El Alamein to the River Sangro;* Horrocks, *Escape to Action*.
14. Howe, *Northwest Africa; Patton Papers II*, pp. 196–97.
15. Hansen-ONB int.
16. Playfair, *Mediterranean and Middle East*, pp. 354–57.
17. Howe, *Northwest Africa*, p. 565; *Patton Papers II*, pp. 199–200; *Soldier's Story*.
18. Ibid., pp. 61–2; *Patton Papers II*, pp. 207, 209; memoir.
19. *Soldier's Story*, pp. 62–3; *Patton Papers II*, pp. 206–10; Howe, *Northwest Africa*, p. 573; Ambrose, *Supreme Commander*, p. 181; Tedder, *With Prejudice*, p. 411; Eisenhower papers II, p. 1071.
20. *Patton Papers II*, p. 210.
21. Eisenhower papers II, p. 1073.
22. *Patton Papers II*, p. 211; *Soldier's Story*, p. 65.
23. Ibid., p. 65.
24. *Patton Papers II*, pp. 212–13; Howe, *Northwest Africa*.
25. Playfair, *Mediterranean and the Middle East*, p. 375.
26. Ibid., pp. 358, 381–82; Howe, *Northwest Africa*, pp. 578–82; Eisenhower papers II, p. 1089; *Patton Papers II*, p. 218.
27. Howe, *Northwest Africa*, pp. 582–90; *Patton Papers II*, p. 218; *Soldier's Story*, pp. 67–8; memoir; Hansen-ONB int.
28. *Soldier's Story;* Eisenhower papers II, p. 1090; *Patton Papers II*, p. 220; "Orders," BP, Carlisle.
29. *Patton Papers II*, p. 232.

Chapter Sixteen

1. Churchill, *Hinge of Fate*, p. 780, op. cit.; Howard, *Grand Strategy*, p. 253, op. cit.
2. Liddell Hart, *Second World War*, pp. 424–25, op. cit.; *Soldier's Story;* Howe, *Northwest Africa*, op. cit.; Playfair, *Mediterranean and the Middle East*, op. cit.
3. *Patton Papers II*, pp. 217–18; *Soldier's Story*, p. 73; memoir.
4. Eisenhower papers II, pp. 1093–94; *Soldier's Story*, p. 71.
5. *Soldier's Story;* Dickson, Benjamin A., "Algiers to the Elbe," an unpublished journal, West Point Library; Eisenhower papers II, p. 1045; CB-Charles E. Hart int., 4-18-80; CB-William A. Carter int., 4-16-80; CB-John B. Medaris int., 3-19-80; CB-Andrew T. McNamara int., 4-14-80.
6. *Soldier's Story;* memoir; Dickson, *Algiers to the Elbe*, pp. 62–3, op. cit.
7. Playfair, *Mediterranean and Middle East;* Howard, *Grand Strategy;* Liddell Hart, *Second World War;* Nicolson, *Alex;* Alexander, *Memoirs*.
8. Howe, *Northwest Africa*, p. 614; *Soldier's Story;* Eisenhower papers II, pp. 1102–3.
9. Kitty Buhler (Bradley)-ONB int.; memoir, p. 139; Fletcher Pratt-ONB int., 10-21-46; Hansen papers, USAMHI; Pratt, Fletcher, *Eleven Generals*, N.Y., 1949.
10. Dickson, *Algiers to the Elbe*.
11. *Soldier's Story*, pp. 85–6.
12. Ibid.; CB-ONB int.
13. Howe, *Northwest Africa; Soldier's Story*.
14. Howard, *Grand Strategy;* Playfair, *Mediterranean and Middle East;* Nicolson, *Alex;* Horrocks, *Escape to Action;* Liddell Hart, *Second World War;* Howe, *Northwest Africa; Soldier's Story*.
15. Howe, *Northwest Africa; Soldier's Story*.
16. Howe, *Northwest Africa; Soldier's Story;* CB-ONB int.
17. Liddell Hart, *Second World War*, p. 429; *Soldier's Story*.
18. Howard, *Grand Strategy*, pp. 354–55; Playfair, *Mediterranean and Middle East*, p. 460; Liddell Hart, *Second World War;* Howe, *Northwest Africa*, p. 675; *Soldier's Story;* Eisenhower papers II, p. 1120; CB-ONB int.; the casualty figures in footnote are from Howe.
19. On April 30, Ike cabled Marshall: "I cannot speak too highly of Bradley. He is doing a great job and McNair's report states 'Bradley definitely impressive.' " In another cable to Marshall, May 8, Ike said: "The II Corps has been superb throughout the op-

eration and a great amount of the credit must go to Bradley. I recommend his promotion to the rank of lieutenant general." Marshall sent Ike's cable to the President. In response to ONB's "Mission Accomplished," Ike cabled ONB on May 10: "I am bursting with pride over you and the magnificent fighting team you are commanding." A month later, summing up ONB's professional ability in June, Ike memoed privately:

> *Omar N. Bradley*. This officer is about the best rounded, well balanced, senior officer that we have in the service. His judgments are always sound and everything he does is accomplished in such a manner as to fit in well with all other operations. He is respected by British and American alike. I have not a single word of criticism of his actions to date and do not expect to have any in the future. I feel that there is no position in the Army that he could not fill with success.

Ike passed along words of congratulations to ONB and II Corps from Prime Minister Churchill ("Warm congratulations on their brilliant advance"), President Roosevelt ("Personal congratulations for your remarkable leadership") and others, but the message that impressed ONB most came from George Marshall:

> Your leadership of the II Corps has inspired the entire War Department and will be greeted by acclaim and delight throughout the Army wherever you are known. Tell your division commanders and the leaders of your corps artillery, engineers and anti-tank units that we are very proud of what they have done and very grateful for the prestige they have brought to the American Army.

Eisenhower papers II, pp. 1104, 1110, 1114, 1116, 1117, 1120. Ike's assessment of ONB is from memo for personal file, 6-11-43, Eisenhower Library, and also published in Ferrell, *Eisenhower Diaries*, p. 94.

From George Patton came a personal letter: "Please accept my most sincere congratulations on your magnificent work. I am just as tickled as if I had been there myself. Everyone tells me what a magnificent job you have done. I spent yesterday with Ike who was loud in your praise, and I believe you will soon be promoted. I certainly hope you will, and in fact have ordered some stars for you." *Patton Papers II*, p. 242. "Go discover Bradley," Butcher, *My Three Years with Eisenhower*, op. cit., p. 298. The OSS agent report is from OSS Papers, NA, Record Group 226, Report #89525, courtesy John Taylor, Archivist.

20. Eisenhower papers II, pp. 119–120; Montgomery, *Memoirs*, p. 148; Nicolson, *Alex*, pp. 186–87.

Chapter Seventeen

1. Liddell Hart, *History of the Second World War*, p. 438; for Sicily planning see: Garland, Albert N., and Howard McG. Smyth, with Martin Blumenson, *Sicily and the Surrender of Italy*, Washington, D.C., OCMH, 1965; Matloff, Maurice, *Strategic Planning for Coalition Warfare 1943–44*, Washington, D.C., OCMH, 1959; Morison, Samuel E., *History of U.S. Naval Operations in World War II*, vol. IX, Boston, 1959; Howard, *Grand Strategy*, op. cit.; Linklater, Eric, *The Campaign in Italy*, London, H.M.S.O., 1951; Eisenhower, *Crusade in Europe;* Butcher, *My Three Years with Eisenhower;* Ambrose, *Supreme Commander; Patton Papers II; Soldier's Story;* Truscott, *Command Missions;* Bryant, *Turn of the Tide;* Montgomery, *Memoirs;* Nicolson, *Alex;* Cunningham, *Sailor's Odyssey;* Tedder, *With Prejudice*.
2. Garland and Smyth, *Sicily and the Surrender*, pp. 11, 420; Howard, *Grand Strategy*, p. 364; Eisenhower papers III, pp. 1420–24.
3. *Sicily*, p. 75; Greenfield, Kent Roberts, editor, *Command Decisions*, "Hitler's Decision on the Defense of Italy," by Ralph S. Mavrogordato, Washington, D.C., 1960; Lewin, *Ultra Goes to War*, pp. 280–81.
4. *Sicily*, pp. 80–1.
5. Mavrogordato, op. cit., p. 312; Baldwin, Hanson, W., *Battles Lost and Won*, N.Y., 1966, p. 460; Nicolson, *Alex*, pp. 206–11.
6. Morison, *History*, vol. IX, pp. 218–19.
7. *Sicily*.
8. Ibid., pp. 65–6; Eisenhower papers II, p. 1113.
9. Eisenhower papers II, pp. 1046–47, 1086.
10. *Grand Strategy*, p. 369; Tedder, *With Prejudice*, pp. 429–30.
11. *Grand Strategy*, p. 369; Eisenhower papers II, p. 1086.
12. Montgomery, *Memoirs*, pp. 157–58.
13. Ibid., pp. 159–61; *With Prejudice;* Cunningham, *Sailor's Odyssey;* Nicolson, *Alex*, pp. 194–96; *Patton Papers II*, pp. 235–37; *Sicily*, pp. 419–20.
14. Ike's assessment of Monty: DDE to GCM, 4-5-43, Eisenhower Library; Ambrose, *Supreme Commander*, p. 207; *Patton Papers II*, p. 237; *With Prejudice*, p. 432.
15. *Sicily*, p. 66; Clark, *Calculated Risk*, p. 166.
16. *Sicily*, pp. 19–23, 268–69; *Grand Strategy*, pp. 409–57; Churchill, *Hinge of Fate*, pp. 800–11; Bryant, *Triumph in the West*, p. 516; Loewenheim, *Roosevelt and Churchill*, pp. 331–34.
17. *Sicily*, pp. 234; Pogue, Forrest C., *Orga-*

nizer of Victory: 1943–45, N.Y., 1973, pp. 216–19; Eisenhower papers II, p. 1174; Butcher, *My Three Years,* p. 318; *Hinge of Fate,* pp. 818-19.

18. Pogue, *Organizer of Victory,* p. 217; *Triumph in the West,* p. 525.

Chapter Eighteen

1. *Register of Graduates; West Point Register 1920–22,* Eisenhower papers III, p. 1436.
2. *Patton Papers II,* pp. 248, 231; Eisenhower papers II, p. 1136.
3. Hansen-ONB int.
4. *Soldier's Story,* p. 102; *Patton Papers II,* p. 251.
5. *Soldier's Story,* p. 109; *Patton Papers II,* pp. 253–54; Cunningham, *Odyssey,* p. 540; Butcher, *My Three Years,* p. 312; CB-ONB int.
6. *Soldier's Story,* p. 108; "Orders," BP, Carlisle; Hansen-ONB int.
7. CB-Stoute int., 11-8-80; CB-Cekada int., 5-5-81; Hansen-ONB int.
8. *Soldier's Story,* p. 106–7; Garland and Smyth, *Sicily,* pp. 94–6.
9. *Patton Papers II,* p. 251; Hanson-ONB int.; CB-ONB int.
10. *Sicily,* p. 95; *Soldier's Story,* p. 116; *Patton Papers II,* p. 224; Pogue, *Organizer of Victory,* p. 224; Price, James F., *Troy H. Middleton: A Biography,* Baton Rouge, LSU Press, 1974.
11. ONB to Marshall, 5-29-43, BP, Carlisle; also in Bradley file, Marshall papers, Marshall Library; Truscott, *Missions,* p. 192.
12. *Soldier's Story,* pp. 109–10; *Missions,* pp. 205–6.
13. *Patton Papers II,* p. 255; Hansen-ONB int.
14. Gavin, James M., *On to Berlin,* op. cit., p. 10.
15. *Sicily,* pp. 103–4.
16. Morison, Samuel E., *The Two Ocean War,* Boston, 1963, p. 263; *Soldier's Story.*
17. *Patton Papers II,* p. 257; *Soldier's Story,* pp. 118–19.
18. *Soldier's Story,* p. 118.
19. *Sicily,* pp. 64–5; Montagu, *Beyond Top Secret Ultra,* op. cit.
20. *Sicily,* pp. 64–5, 81–2; On Ultra: Lewin, p. 280–81; report of E. T. Williams, op. cit.
21. Report of E. T. Williams; *On to Berlin,* p. 14.
22. Hansen-ONB int.; *Soldier's Story,* p. 120; *Dictionary of American Naval Fighting Ships,* vol. I, p. 44, vol. II, p. 471.

Chapter Nineteen

1. Garland and Smyth, *Sicily,* pp. 105–8; Tedder, *With Prejudice,* pp. 445–48; Eisenhower, *Crusade,* pp. 164–66; Morison, *Naval Operations,* vol. IX, pp. 56–8; Truscott, *Command Missions,* p. 205; CB-ONB int. On Ultra: Report of Group Captain R. H. Humphrey, NA, op. cit., p. 16.
2. Morison, vol. IX, pp. 167–69; Morison, *Two Ocean War,* p. 248.
3. *Soldier's Story,* p. 122; Hansen-ONB int.; Hansen diary, 7-10-43; Hanson-ONB int.; CB-ONB int.
4. *Sicily,* pp. 115–18; Morison, vol. IX, p. 94; Linklater, *The Campaign in Italy,* pp. 23–5; Gavin, *On to Berlin,* pp. 22–6; Ridgway, *Soldier,* pp. 68–72; de Guingand, *Operation Victory,* p. 290.
5. *Sicily,* pp. 91, 125–74, and battle maps; Morison, vol. IX pp. 71–147, 159; *Campaign in Italy,* pp 26–29; Montgomery, *El Alamein to the River Sangro,* pp. 81–111; Montgomery, *Memoirs,* pp. 153–88; Nicolson, *Alex,* pp. 199–200.

Chapter Twenty

1. Garland and Smyth, *Sicily and the Surrender of Italy,* pp. 147–201; Morison, vol. IX, pp. 71–169.
2. Hansen diary; memoir, pp. 144–48; Hansen-ONB int.; Hanson-ONB int.; CB-ONB int.
3. Hansen-ONB int. Troy Middleton, commanding the 45th Division, observed: "From the standpoint of the high commander who had something to do besides just fight, Bradley was much Patton's superior. Brad considered all the angles. He got along better with people. Patton's principal worth was that he kept things moving. He kept everybody else moving—not only his juniors but his seniors." Price, *Middleton,* op. cit., pp. 390–1.
4. *Sicily,* pp. 175–84.
5. CB-ONB int.
6. Butcher, *Three Years,* pp. 358–61; Morison, vol. IX, p. 123; Eisenhower papers II, pp. 1011, 1255; *Patton Papers II,* pp. 227–83; *Sicily,* pp. 184, 206; Cunningham, *Sailor's Odyssey,* p. 852; Lucas: *Register of Graduates;* Greenfield, editor, *Command Decisions,* op. cit , "General Lucas at Anzio," by Martin Blumenson; Lucas, John P., "From Algiers to Anzio," unpublished diary, USAMHI.
7. *Soldier's Story,* pp. 134–38; Morison, vol. IX, pp. 170–73; *Sicily,* pp. 201–9 (note: footnote 19, p. 209, and text p. 209 in error. Patton reports in diary, p. 285, that Alexander arrived in Gela at 1310 on 7-13.) and 236; Montgomery, *Memoirs,* pp. 168–69; Nicolson, *Alex,* p. 202; *Patton Papers II,* pp. 285–89; Eisenhower papers II, p. 865; Hansen-ONB int.; Gavin, *On to Berlin,* p. 48; Lucas, diary, pp. 74–6, USAMHI; Es-

same, *Patton,* p. 97; Dickson, *Journal,* p. 84; de Guingand, *Operation Victory,* p. 309.

Chapter Twenty-One

1. For the breakout and exploitation of Sicily, see: Garland and Smyth, *Sicily,* pp. 202–416; Morison, vol. IX, pp. 170–224; *A Soldier's Story,* pp. 134–64; Molony, Brigadier C. J. C. *The Mediterranean and Middle East,* vol. V, *The Campaign in Sicily 1943,* London, H.M.S.O., 1973; Linklater, Eric, *The Campaign in Italy,* pp. 29–47; Montgomery, *El Alamein,* pp. 90–103; Baldwin, *Battles Lost and Won,* pp. 215–35 and notes 447–66; Truscott, *Command Missions,* pp. 214–44; Liddell Hart, *History of the Second World War,* pp. 433–46; Blumenson, Martin, *Sicily: Whose Victory?,* N.Y., 1969, pp. 58–158; de Guingand, *Operation Victory,* pp. 300–10; Eisenhower, *Crusade,* pp. 174–78; John Lucas diary, pp. 53–123; Dickson journal, pp. 84–94; Hansen-ONB int.; Hanson-ONB int.; CB-ONB int.; memoir.
2. *Soldier's Story,* pp. 141–42; Hansen-ONB int.
3. Butcher, *Three Years,* p. 368; *Patton Papers II,* p. 290; *Sicily,* p. 236.
4. *Sicily,* p. 246.
5. *Soldier's Story,* p. 143; Hansen-ONB int.
6. *Three Years,* p. 384.
7. *Sicily,* p. 255.
8. *Three Years,* p. 387.
9. Ike's G-2, British General Kenneth W. D. Strong, was highly critical of Monty's follow-up attacks from his beachheads. In a special report, which Ike passed on to the Combined Chiefs, Strong expressed the view that had Monty made a bid for it, he could have taken Catania on the first or second day and if he had been "less conservative and his forces more mobile, he could probably have been to Messina during the first week." Ike's comment: "I did not sufficiently appreciate the situation." Curiously, in his memoirs, published twenty-four years later, Strong reversed himself. See: Ambrose, *Supreme Commander,* pp. 227–28; Eisenhower papers II, p. 1320; Strong, Kenneth W. D., *Intelligence at the Top,* N.Y., 1969.
10. *Sicily,* p. 304.
11. Slapping incident, here and below: *Sicily,* pp. 425–31; *Patton Papers II,* pp. 326–42; *Soldier's Story,* pp. 159–62; Eisenhower papers II, pp. 1340–41, 1350.
12. *Command Missions,* p. 228.
13. Blumenson, *Whose Victory?,* p. 156; Morison, vol. IX, p. 205 (Morison and Admiral Cunningham were also critical of Monty for failing to use amphibious forces more imaginatively); Cunningham, *Sailor's Odyssey,* p. 554; Morison, vol. IX, pp. 206–7.
14. *Sicily,* pp. 366–67; Morison, vol. IX, pp. 197–99.
15. *Sicily,* pp. 390–91; *Soldier's Story,* p. 158.
16. Hansen-ONB int.; *Sicily,* p. 404.
17. Farago, *Patton,* p. 337; *Sicily,* p. 404.
18. Hansen-ONB int.
19. The most complete account of the Axis withdrawal is Morison, vol. IX, pp. 209–18; see also *Sicily,* p. 410; Liddell Hart, *History,* pp. 445–46; Blumenson, *Whose Victory?,* pp. 130–47; Nicolson, *Alex,* p. 208; Gavin, *On to Berlin,* p. 52.
20. *Sicily,* p. 415; Morison, vol. IX, pp. 207–8.
21. Hansen-ONB int.
22. Lucas diary, pp. 114–18. Lucas wrote: "Bradley is one of our greatest soldiers. He is brilliant and imperturbable in action and possesses a determined spirit that refuses to be discouraged when things are black."
23. *Sicily,* pp. 416–17; *Command Missions,* pp. 243–44; Hansen-ONB int.
24. *Sicily,* p. 417; Morison, vol. IX, p. 223; Liddell Hart, *History,* p. 446. In response to a message from Marshall congratulating him on the "brilliant success" in Sicily, Ike wrote, in part: "For your personal information, on the American side of the ground organization, Generals Patton, Bradley and Keyes and each of the division commanders have been outstanding. Unit leadership throughout the command has greatly improved" (Eisenhower papers II, pp. 1341–42). In a letter to ONB, 8-19-43, Patton said: "My Dear General Bradley: I am writing you this letter to make a permanent record of my frequently expressed admiration for and appreciation of the magnificent loyalty and superior tactical ability you have evinced throughout the Campaign of Sicily. Beyond question, your capture of Troina is the outstanding tactical operation of the Campaign, and is so far as I am aware the most important military victory gained so far during World War II. Again thanking you, I am as ever, (signed) Devotedly yours, G. S. Patton, Jr." (BP, Carlisle).
25. Six-part Ernie Pyle series, Hansen papers, USAMHI. The long Pyle series, more than any other publicity, established Bradley as a household name and a prominent national figure. Pyle wrote in part:

   "General Bradley is a hard man to write about in a way, just because he is so damn normal. He has no idiosyncracies, no superstitions, no hobbies. There is absolutely no pretense about him in any way, and he hates ostentation . . . [he] is a tall man who seems thin, although he weighs 182 pounds. His legs are long and he is a terrific walker . . . The general is deeply tanned. He is balding on top, and the rest of his hair is short and speckled with gray. His head flares out above the ears more than the average man's, giving him a dome and an air of eruditeness. He wears faintly-tinted tortoise-shell glasses. It would be toying with the truth to call him handsome. Instead of good looks, his face shows the kindness and calmness that lies behind it. To me, General Bradley looks like a school teacher rather than a soldier.

"He can be firm, terribly firm, but never gross or rude . . . He is just the opposite of a 'smoothie.' His conversation is not brilliant or unusual, but it is constant with great sincerity. The general still has the Midwest in his vocabulary—he uses such expressions as 'fightin' to beat the band' and 'horse of another color' . . . He is not an orator nor a ringing speaker . . . He has complete confidence in himself and once he makes up his mind, nothing sways him. He is resolved as a rock. He is one of the politest men I ever met . . . I make no bones about the fact that I am a tremendous admirer of General Bradley. I don't believe I have ever known a person to be so universally loved and respected by the men around and under him . . ."

Chapter Twenty-Two

1. Slapping incident: see chapter 21, note 11; also Butcher, *Three Years,* p. 393; *Patton Papers II,* p. 337; Eisenhower papers II, p. 1353. In this same letter, Ike wrote of ONB: "There is very little I need to tell you about him because he is running absolutely true to form all the time. He has brains, a fine capacity for leadership and a thorough understanding of the requirements of modern battle. He has never caused me one moment of worry. He is perfectly capable of commanding an army. He has the respect of all his associates, including all the British officers that have met him. I am very anxious to keep him in this theater as long as we have any major operations to carry out."
2. Garland and Smyth, *Sicily,* pp. 435–40; Pogue, *Organizer of Victory,* pp. 241–62; Bryant, *Turn of the Tide,* pp. 563–95; Howard, *Grand Strategy,* pp. 559–80; Matloff, *Strategic Planning 1943–1944,* pp. 211–243.
3. On Italy, see Montgomery, *Memoirs,* pp. 171–78; Montgomery, *El Alamein,* pp. 109–16; Linklater, *Campaign in Italy,* pp. 48–76; Liddell Hart, *History of the Second World War,* pp. 447–68; Molony, *The Mediterranean;* Nicolson, *Alex,* pp. 212–18; Montgomery, *Memoirs,* p. 171.
4. Hansen-ONB int.; *Patton Papers II,* pp. 84, 87, 138.
5. Eisenhower papers II, p. 1358.
6. Marshall to Ike, August 25, EM, cable file 5968, Eisenhower Library; also Hansen papers, USAMHI.
7. Hansen-ONB int.; *Three Years,* p. 397.
8. Eisenhower papers II, pp. 1357–58. Ike also mentioned Patton as a possibility, but was somewhat lukewarm: "He has planned two amphibious operations but, as you know, he is not as strong in that phase of the work as he is in the actual attack." Of the three, Ike concluded: "Bradley is the best rounded in all respects."
9. Eisenhower papers II, p. 1364.
10. Marshall to DDE, 9-1-43, Hansen papers, USAMHI.
11. Hansen-Dickson int., Hansen papers, USAMHI.
12. *Three Years,* pp. 401–2; Eisenhower papers II, p. 1366; *Patton Papers II,* p. 341; Truscott, *Command Missions,* p. 247; memoir, p. 152; CB-ONB int.
13. Hansen diary, 9-2 and 9-3-43; *Soldier's Story,* pp. 1–11; *Patton Papers II,* p. 345; *Sicily,* p. 484.
14. Eisenhower papers II, p. 1391, note 10.
15. CB-ONB int.
16. Memoir, p. 152.
17. GCM to DDE, 9-1-43; Eisenhower papers II, pp. 1387–88; "Promotions," BP, Carlisle. In making his case for ONB, Ike elaborated: "You have already designated Bradley as an Army Commander and he is, in my opinion, the best rounded combat leader I have yet met in our service. While he possibly lacks some of the extraordinary and ruthless driving power that Patton can exert at critical moments, he still has such force and determination that even in this characteristic he is among our best. In all other things he is a jewel to have around and I cannot tell you with what real distress I see him leave this theater."
18. Hansen diary, 9-6-43; *Patton Papers II,* p. 347; Hobart R. Gay diary, Gay papers, USAMHI.
19. *Patton Papers II,* p. 350.
20. Hansen diary, 9-8-43; CB-ONB int.

Chapter Twenty-Three

1. *Soldier's Story,* pp. 165–71; memoir; Horrocks, *Escape to Action,* pp. 174–77; CB-Harriman int., 4-21-80; CB-ONB int.
2. *Register of Graduates;* West Point *Register,* 1921–24; Pogue, *Organizer of Victory,* p. 264; Ambrose, *Supreme Commander,* pp. 312–13; Hansen-ONB int.; *Patton Papers II,* p. 414.
3. *Soldier's Story,* pp. 173, 177–79; ONB diary, 9-15 to 9-24-43.
4. Ray, Max A., *The History of the First United States Army,* monograph published by the First U.S. Army Field Printing Plant, Fort Meade, Md., 1980; Colby, Elbridge,

The First Army in Europe, monograph, U.S. Senate, doc. 91-25, U.S. Government Printing Office, 1969; Pogue, *Ordeal and Hope,* p. 118.

5. *Soldier's Story,* p. 177; Hansen-ONB int.
6. *Soldier's Story,* p. 180; Ray, *History;* Colby, *First Army.*
7. Hansen-ONB int.
8. ONB diary, 10-2-43; *Soldier's Story,* pp. 180–81.
9. Memoir, p. 158; "Statement of ONB," 3-2-44, BP, WP; CB-ONB int.; CB-Stoute int.
10. *Soldier's Story,* p. 360; CB-Mrs. Richard M. Dudley int., 3-17-80.
11. Pogue, *Organizer of Victory,* pp. 263–78, 297–325; Pogue, *The Supreme Command,* Washington, D.C., OCMH, 1954, pp. 23–35; Eisenhower, *Crusade,* pp. 193–208; Ambrose, *Supreme Commander,* pp. 295–309; Butcher, *Three Years,* pp. 421–35; Eisenhower papers II, pp. 1502n., 1526n.; Harrison, Gordon A., *Cross-Channel Attack,* Washington, D.C., 1951, pp. 1–128; Matloff, *Strategic Planning,* op. cit., pp. 334–87; Ellis, Lionel Frederic (with G. R. G. Allen, Sir James Robb, A. E. Warhurst), *The Battle of Normandy,* H.M.S.O., London, 1962, 2 vols., vol. 1, pp. 1–24; Ehrman, John, *Grand Strategy,* vol. V, London, H.M.S.O., 1956, pp. 155–202.

Chapter Twenty-Four

1. On Ike's command ideas: see Eisenhower papers III, pp. 1605, 1609, 1611, 1614, 1622–24. On Ramsay: Morison, vol. IX, pp. 148–49; Morison, Samuel E., volume XI, *The Invasion of France and Germany,* p. 24; Woodward, David, *Ramsay at War,* London, 1957, p. 130; Eisenhower, *Crusade in Europe,* p. 211. On Montgomery, Tedder and air command problems: Ellis, *Battle of Normandy,* pp. 204–5; Harrison, *Cross-Channel Attack,* pp. 158–64, 207–24; Tedder, *With Prejudice,* pp. 490–526; Eisenhower, *Crusade,* pp. 221–23; MacDonald, Charles B., *The Mighty Endeavor,* op. cit., pp. 253–55; *Soldier's Story,* pp. 245–46; Morgan, Sir Frederick, *Overture to Overlord,* N.Y., 1950; Morison, vol. XI, pp. 36–8; Nicolson, *Alex,* pp. 226–27.
2. Eisenhower papers III, pp. 1609, 1622–24.
3. Ike's press conference: Butcher, *Three Years,* p. 479. Patton on ONB: *Patton Papers II,* pp. 398–99.
4. Hansen-ONB int.; *Soldier's Story,* p. 229; Parker, Theodore W., and William J. Thompson, *Conquer: The Story of the Ninth Army,* Washington, D.C., Infantry Journal Press, 1947, pp. 15–20; CB-Simpson int., 2-9-80.
5. The official history of Fortitude, written by Roger Fleetwood Hesketh of the U.K., has not yet been published. A reliable outline, based on the official history (but with the names of the turned spies changed) may be found in *The Counterfeit Spy,* by Sefton Delmar, N.Y., Harper & Row, 1971. Major General (retired) William A. Harris, who was chief U.S. Army representative on the Fortitude committee, granted CB an interview on 2-16-80 and lent his official reports on Fortitude. Professor H. Wentworth Eldredge of Dartmouth, another U.S. Fortitude director, granted CB an interview on 4-28-80. Fortitude is discussed briefly in the official British history: Ellis, Lionel Frederic, with G. R. G. Allen, A. E. Warhurst, Sir James Robb, *Victory in the West,* vol. I, pp. 103, 127–28, 323, 489. See also: *Patton Papers II,* pp. 437, 472; Eisenhower papers III, pp. 1978, 1991; Essame, *Patton,* p. 127; Lewin, *Ultra Goes to War,* pp. 314–15; Brown, *Bodyguard of Lies,* pp. 459–99; Haswell, Jock, *D-Day: Intelligence and Deception,* N.Y., 1979, pp. 105–6; Ambrose, *The Supreme Commander,* pp. 400–1; Farago, *Patton,* pp. 400–1.
6. *Patton Papers II,* pp. 288, 433–34; Wedemeyer, Albert C., *Wedemeyer Reports!,* N.Y., 1958, p. 226; Eisenhower papers V, chronology (McCloy dinner); Farago, *Patton,* pp. 414–16; McCloy letter to MQB, 4-25-44, BP, WP. McCloy said, in part: "Of all the men I saw and talked with in England, I think Bradley gave me the greatest sense of confidence. General Eisenhower has told me he was an absolute tower of strength to him and I can well imagine that he is. He is taking a mighty important part in all the thinking, planning and preparation that is going on."
7. *Patton Papers II,* pp. 439–53; Eisenhower papers III, pp. 1837–41, 1846–47; *Soldier's Story,* pp. 230–32.
8. Gerow bio in *History of the Fifteenth U.S. Army,* U.S. Army official publication, 1945; *Webster's American Military Biographies,* Springfield, Mass., Merriman; *Generals of the Army,* cumulative biographical roster, op. cit.
9. *Soldier's Story,* pp. 227–28; Eisenhower papers III, pp. 1665–67, 1694–95, 1715–16, 1718; Eisenhower papers IV, p. 2192.
10. *Soldier's Story,* p. 228; Collins, *Lightning Joe,* pp. 179–80. Collins wrote further: "Brad and I had served together at West Point in the twenties and later as instructors at the Infantry School under the then Colonel Marshall. I got to know him well there and to admire him greatly. His rough-hewn features bespeak a deep-seated integrity, along with an uncommon feeling for his associates and the men under him, and a rare

ability to gauge their fine qualities as well as their human frailties. He is one of the most genuinely modest men I have ever known, but back of his somewhat retiring nature is a keen mind and a toughness in making decisions that engenders confidence. I was delighted to be part of his American First Army."

11. Woodruff, Roscoe B., "The World War II of Major General R. B. Woodruff," unpublished memoir and diary, Eisenhower Library; letter, Woodruff to ONB, 10-25-49, and ONB to Woodruff, 10-28-49, BP, WP; *Patton Papers II,* p. 416; Corlett, Charles S., *Cowboy Pete,* Santa Fe, N.M., 1974, p. 88.
12. Ibid., p. 88.
13. *Register of Graduates; Soldier's Story,* pp. 236–37, 275, 558–59; Colby, *The First Army in Europe,* p. 12.

Chapter Twenty-Five

1. Harrison, *Cross-Channel Attack,* pp. 158–98; Morison, *History of U.S. Naval Operations,* vol. XI, pp. 27ff.; *Soldier's Story,* pp. 212–21; Ambrose, *Supreme Commander,* pp. 334ff.; Butcher, *Three Years,* p. 434.
2. *Soldier's Story,* pp. 232–36; Eisenhower, *Crusade,* pp. 245–47; Gavin, *On to Berlin,* pp. 92, 96, 102–3; Ridgway, *Soldier,* pp. 91–2. Gavin wrote: "I had a good meeting with General Bradley, and I believe we were both glad to see each other. He was an enthusiastic supporter of airborne operations and he insisted that the parachute troops be used. In fact, he told me that he would not make the amphibious assault without them in front of him. . . . Bradley had a real feel for what could and what could not be done, and it was always reassuring to plan such operations with him. . . . Even today, more than thirty years later, I feel fury rise in me when I realize that Leigh-Mallory was going to have us left behind . . ."
3. On the campaign in Italy: Molony, C. J. C., *The Campaign in Sicily* and *The Campaign in Italy,* pp. 219ff.; Linklater, Eric, *The Campaign in Italy,* pp. 48ff.; Morison, Samuel E., vol. IX, pp. 254–384; Greenfield, Kent Roberts, editor, *Command Decision,* chap. 13, "General Lucas at Anzio," by Martin Blumenson, pp. 323–50; Truscott, *Command Missions,* pp. 245–380; MacDonald, Charles B., *The Mighty Endeavor,* pp. 177–219; Liddell Hart, *History of the Second World War,* pp. 447–76; Churchill, *Closing the Ring,* Boston, 1951, pp. 380, 488. On the Anvil debate: Harrison, *Cross-Channel,* pp. 164–73; Ambrose, *Supreme Commander,* pp. 349–62; Morison, vol. XI, pp. 50–7; Montgomery, *Memoirs,* pp. 198–99. Monty wrote that Anvil "in my view was one of the great strategic mistakes of the war." ONB wrote in *Soldier's Story,* p. 219, "I hoped desperately that it not be ditched."
4. See chapter 24, note 1. Eisenhower, *Crusade,* pp. 232–34; *Soldier's Story,* pp. 244–46; MacDonald, *Mighty Endeavor,* pp. 253–55; Irving, David, *The War Between the Generals,* N.Y., 1981, pp. 81–4.
5. Eisenhower papers V, chronology; Bryant, *Triumph in the West,* p. 102; *Soldier's Story,* p. 242; memoir, p. 104.
6. Montgomery, *The Path to Leadership,* N.Y., 1961, pp. 112–32.
7. Eisenhower papers V, chronology; *Register of Graduates; Patton Papers II,* p. 420.
8. Collins, *Lightning Joe,* p. 190.
9. *Soldier's Story,* p. 242; memoir, p. 165.
10. Churchill, *Closing the Ring,* pp. 620–21; Cooke, Alistair, *General Eisenhower on the Military Churchill,* N.Y., 1970, pp. 38–40.
11. *Lightning Joe,* p. 191.
12. For the St. Paul's School meeting: Eisenhower papers V, chronology; de Guingand, *Operation Victory,* pp. 356–62; *Lightning Joe,* pp. 191–93; *Triumph in the West,* p. 131; *Patton Papers II,* pp. 433–34; *Soldier's Story,* pp. 239–42; Montgomery, *Memoirs,* pp. 225–29; memoir, p. 167; Hanson-ONB int. Note: The "phase lines" are shown on a map in de Guingand's *Operation Victory.* ONB's recollection that Monty boasted he would have tanks in the vicinity of Falaise on D-day is distinct. In a letter to Joe Collins three years after this briefing, ONB wrote: "Marshall Montgomery had often spoken of getting an armored group that far on D-day and having it 'knock about.' " (ONB to Collins 7-22-47, BP, WP.)

Chapter Twenty-Six

1. See chapter 13, note 2, especially NA documents "History of the Special Branch," "Reports of U.S. Army Ultra Representatives," and Carl Boyd on Oshima. In addition, CB had interviews with the following SSO's or others who were in the "Ultra picture": Bussey, Donald S., 3-21-80; Clarke, Carter W. (letter only), 3-31-80; Gardner, Warner W., 4-15-80; Ingersoll, Harold B., 4-18-80; Kindleberger, Charles P., 4-29-80; Kirkpatrick, Lyman, 4-29-80; Orr, Samuel M., 4-7-80; Rosengarten, Adolph G., 4-25-80; Saussy, William H., 4-7-80; Standish, Alexander, 3-21-80; Taylor, Telford, 4-26-80; Wilkinson, Glen A., 4-22-80; Weaver, William M., 4-30-80 (Weaver also provided his privately published memoir, *Never a Dull Moment,* N.Y., 1979). Note: In the

Richard Collins papers, USAMHI, there is a useful, twenty-page "List of Ultra Recipients" in the ETO, dated 3-25-45. Veterans of Special Branch have formed a club. In 1982, the secretary was James T. DeVoss, P.O. Box 765, State College, Pa. 16801.

2. Harrison, Gordon A., *Cross-Channel Attack,* pp. 230–67; Morison, vol. XI, pp. 39–49; Ellis, *Victory in the West,* pp. 53–6, 104–7, 115–20, 128; Jones, R. V., *The Wizard War: British Scientific Intelligence;* Carver, Sir Michael, editor, *The War Lords,* "Field-Marshal Gerd von Rundstedt," by Andreas Hillgruber; Liddell Hart, *History of the Second World War,* pp. 548–49; Bennett, Ralph, *Ultra in the West,* pp. 43–6.
3. Ike's Overlord review at St. Paul's School: Morison, vol. XI, pp. 69–70 (Deyo quoted); Eisenhower, *Crusade in Europe,* p. 245; Butcher, *Three Years with Eisenhower,* p. 538; *Patton Papers II,* pp. 455–56; Bryant, *Triumph of the West,* p. 139; Ambrose, *The Supreme Commander,* pp. 398–99; Cunningham, *A Sailor's Odyssey,* p. 602. On ONB Order of the Bath: *Triumph,* p. 139, and BP, WP. Note: The King's presentation of the second, higher Order of the Bath decoration occurred on October 14, 1944.
4. *Time,* 5-1-44 (cover story); *Life,* 6-5-44; *Newsweek,* 1-31-44.
5. Taylor, Maxwell D., *Swords and Plowshares,* N.Y., 1972, pp. 49, 747.
6. *Patton Papers II,* pp. 461–62; Hansen diary, 6-2 and 6-3-44; de Guingand, *Operation Victory,* p. 372.
7. Hansen diary, 6-3; *Achernar: Dictionary of American Naval Fighting Ships,* vol. I, p. 7; *Soldier's Story,* pp. 258–64.
8. CB-ONB int.; number of ships: Ryan, Cornelius, *The Longest Day,* N.Y., 1969, p. 81.
9. *Soldier's Story,* pp. 264–67; Hansen diary, 6-6.
10. *Soldier's Story,* p. 272; Dickson journal, p. 117; Bennett, *Ultra in the West,* pp. 45–6. Confusion exists about whether Ultra had identified and located the 352nd Division. Bennett says not. But Dickson is unequivocal that intelligence of some kind had alerted them at the eleventh hour.

PART THREE: THE WAR ON THE CONTINENT

Chapter Twenty-Seven

1. D-day: Harrison, *Cross-Channel Attack,* op. cit., pp. 269–335; Ellis, *Victory in the West,* op. cit., pp. 149–223; Morison, vol. XI, pp. 93–169, 180–87; Eisenhower Foundation, *D-Day: The Normandy Invasion in Retrospect,* Lawrence, University of Kansas, 1971, pp. 3–241; *Soldier's Story,* pp. 267–85; Collins, *Lightning Joe,* pp. 198–203; Ryan, *The Longest Day;* MacDonald, *The Mighty Endeavor,* pp. 265–80; Hansen diary, 6-6-44.
2. Eisenhower papers III, p. 1713; Weigley, Russell F., *Eisenhower's Lieutenants,* Bloomington, Indiana University Press, 1981, pp. 86–7; Wilmot, *The Struggle for Europe,* p. 265.
3. Ryan wrongly attributed the "They're killing us here" quotation to Canham and incorrectly wrote "murdering" for "killing." Jack Thompson, war correspondent for the *Chicago Tribune* at Omaha Beach who originally published the quote, attributes it to George A. Taylor, whom he could not name at the time for security reasons. Thompson also believes it was not Taylor, as Ryan writes, but Cota who said, "Two kinds of people . . ." CB-Thompson int., 6-13-81.
4. Hansen diary, 6-10-44.
5. Liddell Hart, *History of the Second World War,* p. 546.
6. *Victory in the West,* pp. 212–13.

Chapter Twenty-Eight

1. Hansen diary, 6-7-44; Eisenhower papers III, pp. 1916, 1919n.; Collins, *Lightning Joe,* p. 205; Harrison, *Cross-Channel Attack;* Ellis, *Victory in the West;* Morison, vol. XI.
2. *Soldier's Story,* pp. 280–81; Butcher, *My Three Years with Eisenhower,* pp. 571–75; Morison, vol. XI, p. 159.
3. Hansen diary, 6-7-44.
4. Ibid., 6-8-44; *Soldier's Story,* p. 282; int. with Elizabeth Dorsey and Mrs. H. Beukema; *Register of Graduates.*
5. *Cross-Channel Attack,* pp. 349–51.
6. Hansen diary, 6-9-44; CB-Hansen int.
7. Rosengarten, Adolph G., "With Ultra from Omaha Beach to Weimar, Germany—A Personal View," *Military Affairs,* October 1978; Rosengarten report to Telford Taylor, "Ultra Intelligence at First U.S. Army," 5-21-45, NA RG 457 (NSA), SRH023, PT. 1; CB-Rosengarten int.
8. Hansen diary, 6-10-44.
9. *Victory in the West,* p. 247.
10. Bryant, *Triumph in the West,* pp. 156–60;

My Three Years, pp. 175–79; Hansen diary, 6-12-44.

11. Hansen diary, 6-12-44; Marshall letter to ONB, 6-13-44, BP, Carlisle. Marshall wrote, in part: "You are certainly due great credit for the success of the early phases of the operation, and I congratulate you." Marshall's aide Frank McCarthy was even more effusive to ONB's aide Chet Hansen. McCarthy told Hansen that during the Sicily landings the atmosphere in Marshall's Washington office had been tense. But when a report came through that ONB had landed on Sicily, Marshall said, "All right, pack up and let's go home. There's no need to worry now." Later Hansen passed this story on to ONB, noting in his diary that ONB was "markedly embarrassed" to hear it and replied lamely, "That's a nice compliment."
12. *Soldier's Story,* pp. 293–94; Bennett, *Ultra in the West,* pp. 71–2; handwritten letter ONB-Gerow, 6-12-44, BP, Carlisle.
13. *Soldier's Story,* p. 294.

Chapter Twenty-Nine

1. Ellis, *Victory in the West,* p. 266.
2. Butcher, *My Three Years with Eisenhower,* p. 581; Eisenhower papers III, p. 1934.
3. Collins, *Lightning Joe,* pp. 208–9; Hanson-ONB int.
4. Hanson-ONB int.
5. On Ultra and Cherbourg, see Bennett, *Ultra in the West,* pp. 73–4.
6. *My Three Years,* pp. 593–95; Eisenhower, John S. D., *Strictly Personal,* N.Y., 1974, pp. 69–70; Hansen diary, 6-24-44.
7. Eisenhower papers III, pp. 1948–49.
8. Report by the Supreme Commander to the Combined Chiefs of Staff, G.P.O., 1946, p. 41; Smith, Walter Bedell, *Eisenhower's Six Great Decisions,* N.Y., 1956, p. 73 (excerpted ten years earlier in *The Saturday Evening Post;* see issue of 6-15-46 for relevant passage). See also following correspondence: Chester Wilmot to J. Lawton Collins, 6-13-47; ONB to Collins, 7-22-47, commenting on Wilmot letter, Hansen papers, USAMHI; DDE to Montgomery, 5-23-46, Eisenhower papers VII, pp. 1068–70.
9. Eisenhower papers III, p. 1950.
10. Harrison, *Cross-Channel Attack,* pp. 445–46.
11. Bryant, *Triumph in the West,* p. 170.
12. Tedder, *With Prejudice,* pp. 556-59; *My Three Years,* p. 605; Eisenhower papers, III, pp. 1982–83.
13. *My Three Years,* p. 601; letter ONB to DDE, 6-29-44; ONB to Montgomery, 6-29-44, BP, Carlisle; DDE to ONB, 7-1-44, Eisenhower papers III, p. 1968. Hansen diary, 6-28, 7-3-44; *Soldier's Story,* p. 320; Blumenson, Martin, *Breakout and Pursuit,* Washington, D.C., OCMHI, 1961, pp. 53 ff.; *Lightning Joe,* pp. 227–32.
14. Hansen diary, 7-1 to 7-4-44; *Triumph in the West,* p. 170; *With Prejudice,* pp. 556–57.
15. Hansen diary, 6-29-44.
16. Eisenhower papers V, chronology; *My Three Years,* p. 604; *Soldier's Story,* pp. 321–25.
17. Hansen diary, 7-3-44; *Soldier's Story,* pp. 297, 333; Eisenhower papers III, p. 1796; Hanson-ONB int.
18. *Breakout and Pursuit,* p. 125; Hanson-ONB int.; CB-Wm. C. McMahon int., 3-20-80.
19. *Lightning Joe,* pp. 228–30; *Breakout and Pursuit,* pp. 128–33.
20. Ibid., pp. 104–18; Pappas-ONB int.; Eisenhower papers III, pp. 2034–35; Corlett, *Cowboy Pete,* p. 92.
21. *Lightning Joe* p. 237.
22. Blumenson, *Patton Papers II,* pp. 477–82. ONB's badly sagging spirits were uplifted by a letter from Marshall, who wrote: "I have been on the verge several times recently of sending you and some of your people a special commendation, but for several reasons decided that the time was not quite ripe—though the Cherbourg campaign was a great feat and displayed a very high capacity of leadership, organization, and general battle management. Please have in mind my complete confidence in your ability. . . . The weather has treated you badly, particularly considering the character of the terrain you have been trying to break through. However, it seems to me that things have gone extraordinarily well and that the German dilemma must be a nightmare for them." Marshall to ONB, 7-12-44, Bradley file, Marshall Library.

Chapter Thirty

1. Casualty figures: Montgomery, *Memoirs,* p. 231; Hansen diary, 7-10-44.
2. Original date for Cobra (July 19) from Ellis, *Victory in the West,* p. 328. Details on Cobra plans: Blumenson, *Breakout and Pursuit,* pp. 197–228; *Soldier's Story,* pp. 330–45.
3. *Victory in the West,* pp. 327–34; *Breakout and Pursuit,* pp. 186–88; Eisenhower papers III, pp. 2002–4; letters DDE to ONB and Montgomery to ONB, BP, Carlisle. The letter from DDE to ONB is undated, as is letter from Montgomery to ONB, other than "July 1944." ONB initialed the upper right corner of Montgomery's letter and dated it 7-20-44, probably the day received. Eisenhower papers III, p. 2027, is

probably in error dating letter 7-24-44, the day Cobra began. For further on Goodwood, see Wilmot, *The Struggle for Europe,* pp. 336–65; Liddell Hart, *History of the Second World War,* pp. 552–57; Blumenson, "Some Reflections on the Immediate Post-assault Strategy," in *D-day: The Normandy Invasion in Retrospect,* pp. 201–16.

4. *Breakout and Pursuit,* p. 193; *Victory in the West,* pp. 338–53; Pogue, *The Supreme Command,* p. 188.
5. *Victory in the West,* p. 353; *The Supreme Command,* p. 189; Montgomery, *Memoirs,* p. 231.
6. Butcher, *My Three Years,* p. 617; Tedder, *With Prejudice,* pp. 562, 566, 571; *Breakout and Pursuit,* p. 194.
7. See note 2 above.
8. Eisenhower papers V, chronology; Ambrose, *The Supreme Commander,* p. 440; Bryant, *Triumph in the West,* p. 180; Hansen diary, 7-20-44.
9. *Breakout and Pursuit,* pp. 210–12; *Victory in the West,* pp. 361–75; *With Prejudice,* p. 565.
10. Eisenhower papers III, p. 2018.
11. *With Prejudice,* p. 567.
12. *Triumph in the West,* p. 181.
13. *Breakout and Pursuit,* pp. 210–12.
14. Hansen diary, 7-24 to 7-28-44. For Cobra operations and exploitation, see *Breakout and Pursuit,* pp. 228–339; *Victory in the West,* pp. 337–400; *Lightning Joe,* pp. 232–48; *Soldier's Story,* pp. 346–60.
15. Hansen diary, 7-25, 7-26-44; *Breakout and Pursuit,* p. 236; CB-Andrew McNamara int., 4-14-80.
16. *My Three Years,* p. 625; *Soldier's Story,* p. 349.
17. *Breakout and Pursuit,* p. 240.
18. Eisenhower papers IV, pp. 2080, 2298; Hanson-ONB int.; *Register of Graduates.*
19. Letter, ONB to DDE, 7-28-44, Bradley file, Eisenhower Library.
20. Hansen diary, 7-28, 7-29-44; *Patton Papers II,* pp. 486, 489. Monty's chief of staff, Freddie de Guingand, wrote in *Operation Victory:* "The time that Bradley impressed me most was during the vital battle of St. Lô. I happened to be staying with him in his advanced command post at the time. The opening stages were anything but easy and real drive was necessary to achieve the breakthrough. I liked the quiet and confident way he spoke to his commanders. How he was determined to force the battle his way, and encouraged them with simple words of praise. I was reminded of a passage in a book I had once read about the way Robert E. Lee encouraged his troops after Gettysburg. No wonder his staff liked working under him."

Chapter Thirty-One

1. *Soldier's Story,* p. 361; Weigley, *Eisenhower's Lieutenants,* p. 170.
2. De Guingand, Francis, *Generals At War,* London, Hodder & Stoughton, 1964, pp. 100–1.
3. *Soldier's Story,* p. 360; CB interviews with Hansen, Stoute, Cekada, Mrs. Dudley.
4. *Soldier's Story,* pp. 361–62 (ONB van photo opposite p. 365).
5. Ibid., p. 362; CB-Alvin E. Robinson int., 2-9-80.
6. Letter DDE to GCM, 8-2-44; letter GCM to DDE, 8-26-44, box 67, folder 11, Marshall Library; Blumenson, *Patton Papers II,* p. 536.
7. Blumenson, *Breakout and Pursuit,* pp. 345, 347.
8. Ibid., pp. 348–415.
9. See Liddell Hart, *History of the Second World War,* p. 557, where John S. Wood, CG 4th AD, is quoted as saying, "It was one of the colossally stupid decisions of the war." *Eisenhower's Lieutenants,* p. 186, refers to the "unwisdom of the turn into Brittany," stating that ONB was "inflexible about Brittany."
10. *Soldier's Story,* pp. 365–67; Ambrose, *The Supreme Commander,* p. 493; *Breakout and Pursuit,* p. 387.
11. Ibid., pp. 419–39.
12. Ibid., p. 630; *Patton Papers II,* p. 502.
13. *Breakout and Pursuit,* pp. 296–97; Hanson-ONB int.; Eisenhower papers IV, p. 2099.
14. Bryant, *Triumph in the West,* pp. 181–82; Tedder, *With Prejudice,* pp. 573–74; Eisenhower papers V, chronology.
15. Eisenhower papers IV, pp. 2041–42.
16. Montgomery, *Memoirs,* p. 234.

Chapter Thirty-Two

1. Blumenson, *Breakout and Pursuit,* pp. 410–24; Ellis, *Victory in the West,* pp. 395–99.
2. Montgomery, *Normandy to the Baltic,* Boston, Houghton Mifflin, 1948, p. 94; Eisenhower papers IV, p. 2049; Hansen diary, 8-6-44.
3. Eisenhower papers IV, p. 2050.
4. Hansen diary, 8-6-44.
5. Ibid.
6. *Breakout and Pursuit,* pp. 457–60.
7. Winterbotham, *The Ultra Secret,* pp. 214–19; Bennett, *Ultra in the West,* p. 119; CB-ONB int.
8. *Breakout and Pursuit,* pp. 458–59.
9. *Ultra in the West,* p. 119.

10. *Breakout and Pursuit,* p. 466; Collins, *Lightning Joe,* pp. 250–51. (Collins follows Winterbotham and Lewin but has no personal contribution on Ultra. He was not officially in the Ultra picture.)
11. *Breakout and Pursuit,* p. 472; Blumenson, *Patton Papers II,* p. 503.
12. Gavin, *On to Berlin,* p. 141.
13. Hansen diary, 8-7-44.
14. Ibid.; *Soldier's Story,* pp. 368–69.
15. *Breakout and Pursuit,* pp. 479–80; *Victory in the West,* pp. 419–25.
16. *Patton Papers II,* p. 504.
17. Hansen diary, 8-8-44.
18. Tedder, *With Prejudice,* p. 575; *Breakout and Pursuit,* p. 494; Hansen diary, 9-5-44.
19. Eisenhower, *Crusade in Europe,* p. 275; Eisenhower papers V, chronology; Butcher, *My Three Years,* p. 636; Hansen-ONB int.
20. *Normandy to the Baltic,* p. 99; *My Three Years,* p. 636; Farago, *Patton,* p. 532.
21. *Breakout and Pursuit,* pp. 492–94; Eisenhower papers IV, p. 2057; Pogue, *Supreme Command,* p. 209; *Crusade in Europe,* p. 498, note 16. ONB's formal orders to Patton and Hodges, 12 Army Group Letter of Instruction No. 4, went out the same day, August 8. Monty's confirming orders, 21 Army Group General Operational Situation and Direction M-518, were not issued until August 11.
22. *Patton Papers II,* p. 542.

Chapter Thirty-Three

1. Hansen diary, 8-7, 8-10-44.
2. *Soldier's Story,* pp. 375–76.
3. Blumenson, *Breakout and Pursuit,* pp. 497–98; Blumenson, *Patton Papers II,* pp. 506–11; CB-ONB int.
4. *Soldier's Story,* p. 377; Eisenhower, *Crusade in Europe,* p. 279.
5. *Breakout and Pursuit,* pp. 500–4; Bennett, *Ultra in the West,* pp. 120–21.
6. Hansen diary, 8-12-44.
7. Butcher, *My Three Years with Eisenhower,* p. 633; Eisenhower Papers V, chronology.
8. Collins, *Lightning Joe,* pp. 256–57.
9. *Breakout and Pursuit,* p. 504; Hansen diary, 8-13-44.
10. Hansen diary, 8-13-44; *Soldier's Story,* pp. 376–77.
11. Ibid.; *Breakout and Pursuit,* pp. 504–5. See also Blumenson, "General Bradley's Decision at Argentan," in *Command Decisions,* pp. 401–17.
12. Hansen diary, 8-13-44; *My Three Years,* p. 640. The rough outline of Monty's new strategic plan appears in Butcher's diary entry for the following day, August 14.
13. Letter, Montgomery to ONB, 8-14-44, BP, Carlisle; 12 AG Dir for Current Operations, 15 August 1944, quoted in *Breakout and Pursuit,* p. 524; Hansen diary, 8-14-44.
14. *Soldier's Story,* p. 377 ("Montgomery's blunder"); Hanson-ONB int.; Stacey (p. 276) quoted in Ellis, *Victory in the West,* p. 448; Wilmot, *The Struggle for Europe,* pp. 424–25.
15. *Breakout and Pursuit,* p. 522.
16. Hanson-ONB int.; *Breakout and Pursuit,* pp. 509–10; *Victory in the West,* pp. 429–34; *Soldier's Story,* p. 377; Montgomery, *Normandy to the Baltic,* p. 102.
17. Eisenhower papers V, chronology; *My Three Years,* p. 640.
18. *Patton Papers II,* pp. 508–9; Eisenhower, *Crusade in Europe,* p. 279; *Breakout and Pursuit,* p. 505; Farago, *Patton,* p. 539.
19. *My Three Years,* p. 640; Gavin, *On to Berlin,* pp. 143–45.
20. *Breakout and Pursuit,* pp. 523–27; *Lightning Joe,* p. 255.
21. *Patton Papers II,* pp. 509–10.
22. Ibid., p. 510.
23. Ibid., p. 511.
24. *Breakout and Pursuit,* p. 525; *Victory in the West,* p. 432.
25. *Breakout and Pursuit,* p. 527.
26. *Soldier's Story,* p. 379; Hansen diary, 3-28-45.
27. *Breakout and Pursuit,* pp. 528–58; *Victory in the West,* pp. 439, 448. Owing to the disorganization and loss of German records and to the subsequent free-for-all flight, an exact accounting of the number of Germans who escaped through the Falaise Gap is impossible. Canadian Major General Richard Rohmer, in *Patton's Gap* (Beaufort, N.Y., 1981), pp. 212–15, puts the figure much higher. He estimates that from August 12 to August 21, "200,000–250,000" Germans escaped through the gap. Official U.S. Army historians consider these figures far too high.
28. *Breakout and Pursuit,* pp. 573–83.
29. Total figures difficult to arrive at. Blumenson, pp. 557–58, is source for 10,000 killed and 50,000 captured in Mortain-Falaise. Blumenson, p. 700, is source for 500,000 German casualties since D-day. Figure of forty German divisions from Montgomery, *Memoirs,* p. 236. Figure of forty Allied divisions is estimate based on: 1) *Soldier's Story,* p. 361 chart (37 divisions on 8-1-44); 2) *Crusade in Europe,* p. 289 (37 divisions on 8-31-44, probably an underestimate); and 3) Blumenson, p. 700 (49 Allied divisions were landed by 9-11-44). The Air Force figure is from *Crusade in Europe,* p. 289. See also *Normandy to the Baltic,* pp. 112–13. The Allied casualty figures are estimates based on: 1) Montgomery, *Memoirs,* p. 235

(170,000 as of 8-11-44); and 2) Blumenson, p. 700 (224,000 as of 9-11-44).
30. *Breakout and Pursuit,* pp. 701–2.
31. Weigley, *Eisenhower's Lieutenants,* pp. 180–87, 283–86; *Patton Papers II,* p. 532.
32. *Soldier's Story,* p. 409.

Chapter Thirty-Four

1. Blumenson, *Breakout and Pursuit,* pp. 657–64; Greenfield, *Command Decisions,* "Logistics and the Broad-Front Strategy," by Roland G. Ruppenthal, pp. 419–27.
2. Tedder, *With Prejudice,* p. 584; Jones, *Wizard War,* pp. 438, 458.
3. Eisenhower papers IV, pp. 2072–73; Blumenson, *Patton Papers II,* pp. 519, 522–24; *Breakout and Pursuit,* pp. 583–89. Contrary to some reports, Patton's electrifying drive to the Seine was not of his own devising, but rather the result of meticulous planning and strict control on the part of ONB and Twelfth Army Group. The strict control can be seen in *Patton Papers II,* pp. 520–25. Six months later, when Patton was paid a visit by former justice James F. Byrnes, then director of the Office of War Mobilization, Patton gave a "very generous tribute" to ONB for (in Blumenson's words) "his part in planning Patton's summer campaign." Byrnes wrote Patton that he had passed along Patton's tribute to ONB to his former colleagues in the Senate and that everyone was pleased to know of the "affectionate regard" that the two generals had for each other. (*Patton Papers II,* p. 637.)
4. *Soldier's Story,* pp. 384–96; Weigley, *Eisenhower's Lieutenants,* pp. 249–52; Hansen diary, 8-25 and 8-26-44.
5. Liddell Hart, *History of the Second World War,* pp. 557–67.
6. Butcher, *My Three Years,* p. 642, has the first general outline of Monty's plan; Montgomery, *Memoirs,* p. 239, has a more detailed account. See also *Soldier's Story,* pp. 396–99; *Breakout and Pursuit,* pp. 657–61.
7. Pogue, *The Supreme Command,* pp. 263–64; Eisenhower papers IV, pp. 2074–77; *My Three Years,* pp. 647–49.
8. Hansen-ONB int.; *Patton Papers II,* p. 527.
9. *With Prejudice,* p. 584.
10. *Soldier's Story,* p. 399.
11. Montgomery, *Memoirs,* pp. 239, 243.
12. Hansen diary, 8-18-44.
13. Ike's position is set forth in *My Three Years,* p. 642.
14. Eisenhower papers IV, p. 2078.
15. De Guingand, *Operation Victory,* pp. 411–12; Montgomery, *Memoirs,* p. 240; Eisenhower Papers V, chronology.
16. Montgomery, *Memoirs,* p. 240.
17. Ibid., pp. 240–41.
18. *Patton Papers II,* pp. 526–27.
19. Hansen diary, 8-22-44.
20. Montgomery, *Memoirs,* p. 241; Eisenhower Papers IV, p. 2090; Ike's official order was issued August 29; Eisenhower Papers IV, pp. 2100–2.
21. Montgomery, *Memoirs,* pp. 241–42; Bryant, *Triumph in the West,* p. 196.
22. Hansen-ONB int.
23. Liddell Hart, *History,* pp. 566–67.
24. Hansen-ONB int. ("Patton could not have gone on to Berlin—that's silly. Doubt he could have gotten to the Rhine. He could have gone to the Siegfried Line and that's as far as he could have gone.")
25. For additional discussion of this decision, see Eisenhower Papers V, p. 39; "Eisenhower as Commander: Single Thrust Versus Broad Front," by Stephen E. Ambrose; also Ambrose, *The Supreme Commander,* pp. 504–8; *Victory in the West,* pp. 459–64.

Chapter Thirty-Five

1. Blumenson, *Breakout and Pursuit,* pp. 670–75, 676–84; Ellis, *Victory in the West II,* pp. 1–7; Montgomery, *Normandy to the Baltic,* pp. 123–28; Collins, *Lightning Joe,* pp. 260–67; Horrocks, *Escape to Action,* pp. 194–206.
2. *Breakout and Pursuit,* pp. 666–69; Blumenson, *Patton Papers II,* pp. 528–32; Weigley, *Eisenhower's Lieutenants,* pp. 263–66.
3. *Escape to Action,* p. 205; Liddell Hart, *History of the Second World War* (quoting North), p. 567; *Victory in the West II* (Ramsay cable), p. 5; Hansen-ONB int.; *Soldier's Story,* p. 425.
4. MacDonald, *Mighty Endeavor,* p. 332; *Escape to Action,* p. 204.
5. Rough estimates based on: Ruppenthal, in *Command Decisions,* p. 530; MacDonald, Charles B., *The Siegfried Line Campaign,* Washington, D.C., OCMH, 1963, pp. 10–14.
6. *Victory in the West II,* pp. 71–3; Ruppenthal in *Command Decisions;* Liddell Hart, *History,* p. 564; *Eisenhower's Lieutenants,* p. 271; *Soldier's Story,* pp. 403–5.
7. Ibid., pp. 402–3; Hansen diary, 9-1-44.
8. *Soldier's Story,* pp. 402–5; *Patton Papers II,* pp. 531–32; *Lightning Joe,* p. 263.
9. Eisenhower papers IV, p. 2110; *Patton Papers II,* p. 535.
10. Eisenhower papers V, chronology; Hansen diary, 9-2-44.
11. *Soldier's Story,* p. 415; Pogue, *The Supreme Command,* pp. 252–53; Hansen diary, 9-2-44.
12. *Patton Papers II,* p. 537; Hansen diary, 9-3-44.
13. *Patton Papers II,* pp. 537–38.

14. Eisenhower papers IV, p. 2116.
15. Eisenhower, *Crusade in Europe*, pp. 305–6; Butcher, *My Three Years*, p. 659.
16. Hansen diary, 9-3-44; Hansen-ONB int.; *Normandy to the Baltic*, p. 128 ("fresh" orders of 9-3-44).
17. Montgomery, *Memoirs*, p. 244.
18. Eisenhower papers IV, pp. 2120, 2122, 2144.
19. Montgomery, *Memoirs*, p. 246.
20. *Breakout and Pursuit*, pp. 692–96; *The Siegfried Line Campaign*, pp. 36–7.
21. Cole, Hugh M., *The Lorraine Campaign*, Washington, D.C. OCMH, 1960, pp. 52–70, 117–83; Hansen diary, 9-5-44.

Chapter Thirty-Six

1. Pogue, *The Supreme Command*, p. 280; MacDonald, *The Siegfried Line Campaign*, pp. 119–20.
2. Jones, *The Wizard War*, p. 459; Bryant, *Triumph in the West*, p. 200; Montgomery, *Memoirs*, p. 246.
3. Hansen-ONB int.
4. Montgomery, *Normandy to the Baltic*, p. 137; Ellis, *Victory in the West II*, p. 44 (facing map). Personnel figures estimated.
5. Total First and Third Army divisions: *Siegfried Line Campaign*, and Cole, *The Lorraine Campaign*. (Does not count the VIII Corps in Brittany.)
6. Hansen-ONB int.; *Soldier's Story*, pp. 416–18.
7. Eisenhower papers IV, p. 2144.
8. *Wizard War*, p. 459.
9. *Siegfried Line Campaign*, p. 119.
10. Eisenhower papers V, chronology.
11. Bennett, *Ultra in the West*, p. 153; *Siegfried Line*, p. 127; Hansen-ONB int.; ONB memoir, p. 202.
12. Blumenson, *Patton Papers II*, p. 548.
13. Eisenhower papers V, chronology; Montgomery, *Memoirs*, pp. 246–47; Wilmot, *The Struggle for Europe*, pp. 488–89; Ambrose, *The Supreme Commander*, pp. 515–16.
14. Ryan, Cornelius, *A Bridge Too Far*, N.Y., 1974, pp. 85–6.
15. Quoted in *The Supreme Commander*, p. 515.
16. *A Bridge Too Far*, pp. 88–9; Eisenhower, *Crusade in Europe*, p. 307; Tedder, *With Prejudice*, p. 591.
17. Montgomery, *Memoirs*, p. 247; Eisenhower papers V, chronology; Hansen diary, 9-10-44; Pogue, *The Supreme Command*, pp. 283–84.
18. *Siegfried Line*, p. 122.
19. Hansen diary, 9-12-44; letter, ONB to DDE, 9-12-44, BP, Carlisle.
20. Letter, DDE-ONB, 9-15-44, Eisenhower Library.
21. *Siegfried Line*, pp. 3–115; Corlett, *Cowboy Pete*, pp. 101–2; letter, ONB-DDE, 9-14-44, BP, Carlisle.
22. Eisenhower papers IV, pp. 2079–80, 2212.
23. *Patton Papers II*, pp. 548–50.
24. *Breakout and Pursuit*, p. 696.
25. Ryan, *A Bridge Too Far*, p. 599; Weigley, *Eisenhower's Lieutenants*, pp. 317–19.
26. *Triumph in the West*, p. 219.

Chapter Thirty-Seven

1. Dragoon: Weigley, *Eisenhower's Lieutenants*, pp. 221–37, 345. Allied and German Order of Battle: Ibid., p. 356.
2. Ibid., pp. 534–35; Montgomery, *Memoirs*, p. 253; Gavin, *On to Berlin*, p. 217.
3. Letter, ONB-DDE, 9-21-44, BP, Carlisle.
4. Montgomery *Memoirs*, pp. 250, 252–53.
5. Eisenhower papers IV, p. 2175; Ellis, *Victory in the West II*, pp. 79–80; letter, DDE-ONB, 9-23-44, BP, Carlisle; Pogue, *The Supreme Command*, pp. 294–95; *Soldier's Story*, pp. 422–23.
6. Eisenhower *Crusade in Europe*, p. 312; Hansen diary, 9-22-44.
7. Ibid., 9-23-44; Blumenson, *Patton Papers II*, p. 553.
8. *Conquer: The Story of the Ninth Army*, pp. 52–3; MacDonald, *The Siegfried Line Campaign*, pp. 213, 232; *Patton Papers II*, pp. 553, 557.
9. Montgomery, *Memoirs*, p. 254; Montgomery, *Normandy to the Baltic*, pp. 158–59; *Siegfried Line Campaign*, pp. 231–46; Eisenhower papers IV, pp. 2213, 2309.
10. Letter, ONB-DDE, 10-19-44, BP, Carlisle; Corlett, *Cowboy Pete*, pp. 103–7; Eisenhower papers IV, pp. 2233–34.
11. Pogue, *Organizer of Victory*, p. 474.
12. Hansen diary, 10-6 to 10-12-44; Hansen-ONB int.
13. Montgomery, *Memoirs*, p. 254; *Organizer of Victory*, p. 475.
14. *Victory in the West II*, p. 85.
15. Eisenhower papers IV, p. 2224.
16. Montgomery, *Memoirs*, p. 284.
17. *Siegfried Line*, pp. 207–30; *On to Berlin*, p. 209; Ridgway, *Soldier*, p. 111. (The 82nd Division was released on 13 November, the 101st on 27 November per *Siegfried Line*, p. 205.)
18. Montgomery, *Memoirs*, p. 266.
19. *Siegfried Line*, pp. 390–92; *Soldier's Story*, pp. 433–35.
20. *Conquer: The Story of the Ninth Army*, pp. 63–6; *Soldier's Story*, p. 437.
21. CB-Wm. H. Simpson int.; *Register of Graduates*.
22. *Siegfried Line*, pp. 323–74; *Soldier's Story*, p. 442. Hansen-ONB int.
23. *Soldier's Story*, pp. 496–97.

24. Cole, *The Lorraine Campaign,* pp. 311, 372; *Soldier's Story,* p. 438; *Patton Papers II,* pp. 567, 569–70.
25. *Patton Papers II,* pp. 572–77, 586–87; *Victory in the West II,* p. 165; *Lorraine Campaign,* pp. 311ff.
26. *Lorraine Campaign,* p. 525n; Eisenhower papers IV, p. 2333; *Patton Papers II,* pp. 586–87.
27. *Siegfried Line,* pp. 408–595 and maps; Collins, *Lightning Joe,* pp. 275–78; *Victory in the West II,* p. 164; *Soldier's Story,* p. 441.
28. Bryant, *Triumph in the West,* pp. 252–53.
29. Ibid., p. 253; Tedder, *With Prejudice,* p. 619.
30. *Triumph in the West,* pp. 255–57, 262.
31. Ibid., pp. 258–59; Ambrose, *The Supreme Commander,* pp. 546–47.
32. *Triumph in the West,* p. 259.
33. *Victory in the West II,* p. 166.
34. *Triumph in the West,* p. 260.
35. Ibid., pp. 260–61; *Victory in the West II,* p. 166.
36. Hansen diary, 11-28, 11-29-44.
37. Butcher, *My Three Years,* p. 718; Eisenhower papers IV, p. 2323.
38. Hansen diary, 12-6-44.
39. Montgomery, *Memoirs,* pp. 270–74; *Victory in the West II,* pp. 167–69.
40. Ibid., p. 169; *Triumph in the West,* p. 265.
41. Ibid., pp. 266–67; *With Prejudice,* p. 623. (Summary notes, November 28–December 16: Ellis, pp. 165–70; Tedder, pp. 616–23; Bryant, pp. 252–67; Ambrose, pp. 546–52; Montgomery, pp. 270–74; Eisenhower papers IV, pp. 2323–26, 2341–42; Eisenhower papers V, chronology; Butcher, pp. 717–20; Hansen diary, 11-28 to 12-9-44.)

Chapter Thirty-Eight

1. Cole, Hugh M., *The Ardennes: Battle of the Bulge,* Washington, D.C., OCMH, 1965, pp. 56–7; Eisenhower, John S. D., *The Bitter Woods,* N.Y., Ace edition, 1969, p. 214n.; *Soldier's Story,* p. 448.
2. NA, RG 331 HQ12AG, G-2 Sec., "Weekly Intelligence Summary No. 18"; 21 AG Intelligence Summary, 12-16-44, Hansen papers, USAMHI. (See also excerpts in Ellis, *Victory in the West II,* pp. 170–71.)
3. Hansen diary, 12-5-44.
4. Bennett, *Ultra in the West,* pp. 178–204; Hansen-ONB int.
5. HQ, First Army, office of AC of S G-2, "G-2 Estimate No. 37, 12/10/44," in Oscar Koch papers, USAMHI.
6. *Victory in the West II,* p. 171.
7. Williams and Rosengarten reports, NA; letter, Edwin L. Sibert to Hanson W. Baldwin, military editor, *The New York Times,* 1-2-47, Hansen papers, USAMHI.
8. *The Ardennes,* pp. 1–74; *Victory in the West II,* pp. 176–78.
9. MacDonald, *The Siegfried Line,* pp. 340, 374; letter, ONB-Montgomery, 12-3-44, BP, WP.
10. Dickson, "G-2 Estimate No. 37, 12/10/44."
11. Hansen diary, 11-8-44; Eisenhower papers V, chronology.
12. Eisenhower papers IV, p. 2417 and vol. VII, pp. 654–55.
13. Eisenhower, *Crusade in Europe,* p. 337; Blumenson, *Patton Papers II,* p. 582; *Soldier's Story,* p. 461.
14. "Extracts from G-2 Periodic Reports, HQ, Third Army, 20 November 1944–16 December 1944," Oscar Koch papers, USAMHI. See also relevant correspondence between Koch and S. P. Walker, 4-8-47, and Gordon B. Rogers, 10-6-50.
15. Pogue, *Supreme Command,* p. 365n.
16. Hansen-ONB int.
17. *Soldier's Story,* pp. 444–45.
18. Eisenhower papers IV, p. 2360; Hansen diary, 12-16-44.
19. Pogue, *Organizer of Victory,* pp. 365–66, 483–84.
20. *Soldier's Story,* pp. 449, 455; Hansen diary, 12-17-44.
21. Butcher, *My Three Years,* p. 723; Hansen diary, 12-16, 12-17-44.
22. Eisenhower papers IV, p. 2368; *Ultra in the West,* pp. 208–9.
23. *Soldier's Story,* p. 450.
24. Eisenhower papers IV, p. 2373; *Soldier's Story,* p. 465; *Patton Papers II,* p. 595.
25. Hansen diary, 12-17-44.
26. *Supreme Command,* p. 374; Eisenhower papers IV, p. 2374.
27. *Soldier's Story,* p. 466; Hansen diary, 12-17-44.
28. Ibid.
29. Ibid., 12-18-44.
30. *Patton Papers II,* pp. 596–97.
31. *Soldier's Story,* p. 470; Monk Dickson journal, pp. 178–79; Sylvan diary, 12-18-44, William C. Sylvan papers, USAMHI.
32. Hansen diary, 12-18-44; Tedder, *With Prejudice,* p. 625; *Crusade in Europe,* p. 350; *Patton Papers II,* p. 599; Codman, Charles R., *Drive,* Boston, 1957, p. 230; *The Ardennes,* pp. 486–89; Eisenhower papers IV, p. 2358.

Chapter Thirty-Nine

1. De Guingand, *Generals at War,* p. 106.
2. Bryant, *Triumph in the West,* pp. 270–73.
3. Cole, *The Ardennes,* p. 557; Montgomery, *Normandy to the Baltic,* p. 176.
4. *The Ardennes,* pp. 423–24.
5. *Soldier's Story,* pp. 476–77.

6. Hansen diary, 12-11-44.
7. *Soldier's Story*, pp. 476–77.
8. Ellis, *Victory in the West II*, p. 184; Horrocks, Sir Brian, with Eversley Belfield and H. Essame, *Corps Commander*, N.Y., 1977, pp. 236–41; *Soldier's Story*, p. 478.
9. Ibid., pp. 476–77.
10. Blumenson, *Patton Papers II*, p. 601.
11. *Triumph in the West*, p. 270.
12. Eisenhower papers IV, p. 2361; cable DDE to ONB, 12-20-44, BP, WP.
13. *Triumph in the West*, p. 272; Wilmot, *The Struggle for Europe*, p. 592; Montgomery, *Memoirs*, p. 276; *Normandy to the Baltic*, p. 176; *Corps Commander*, p. 239.
14. Monk Dickson journal, p. 180.
15. Toland, John, *Battle: The Story of the Bulge*, N.Y., 1959, pp. 146–47; Baldwin, Hanson, *Battles Won and Lost*, pp. 336–37; MacDonald, *Mighty Endeavor*, p. 384.
16. *The Ardennes*, p. 426; *Normandy to the Baltic*, p. 176; *The Struggle for Europe*, p. 593; Bennett, *Ultra in the West*, pp. 212–13.
17. Price, *Troy H. Middleton*, p. 391.
18. *The Ardennes*, pp. 433–34; *Soldier's Story*, p. 478.
19. *Triumph in the West*, p. 272.
20. Eisenhower papers IV, p. 2362.
21. Pogue, *Supreme Command*, p. 381; Eisenhower papers IV, p. 2369.
22. Eisenhower papers IV, p. 2367. Ike wrote: "Bradley has kept his head magnificently and has proceeded methodically and energetically to meet the situation. In no quarter is there any tendency to place any blame upon Bradley. I retain all my former confidence in him and believe that his promotion now would be interpreted by all American forces as evidence that their calm determination and courage in the face of trials and difficulties is thoroughly appreciated here and at home. It would have a fine effect generally."
23. *Soldier's Story*, p. 472; Hansen diary, 12-24-44; *Patton Papers II*, p. 604.
24. Hansen diary, 12-24-44; *Patton Papers II*, p. 606.
25. Two Christmas greetings uplifted ONB. Secretary of War Stimson wrote that he had faith in ONB's "quiet competence and effectiveness," adding, "I know that everything will come out to a victorious finish for our cause." George Marshall wrote: "Needless to say you have my complete confidence, the more so in these difficult days. The fact of your presence and leadership in this crisis is a great reassurance to me." (Letter, Stimson-ONB, 12-19-44, BP, WP; letter, Marshall-ONB, 12-25-44, BP, WP.)

Chapter Forty

1. Cole, *The Ardennes*, p. 413; Gavin, *On to Berlin*, pp. 264–65; Collins, *Lightning Joe*, p. 285; Wilmot, *The Struggle for Europe*, pp. 596–97; *Soldier's Story*, p. 480; Hansen diary, 12-25-44: "Monty has dissipated the VII Corps by committing them on a defense line that runs west to Givet and the river."
2. *Soldier's Story*, p. 480; Bryant, *Triumph in the West*, p. 279; Hansen diary, 12-25-44.
3. *Triumph in the West*, p. 278.
4. Pogue, *Supreme Command*, p. 383; Weigley, *Eisenhower's Lieutenants*, pp. 539–40; *Patton Papers II*, p. 606; *Soldier's Story*, p. 481.
5. Bennett, *Ultra in the West*, pp. 186–227.
6. *Soldier's Story*, p. 481; Blumenson, *Patton Papers II*, p. 606; Eisenhower, John, *Bitter Woods*, p. 430, note 22. In 1966, when John Eisenhower interviewed Montgomery for *The Bitter Woods*, Monty "categorically denied" estimating that the First Army could not attack for three months, and described the situation on Christmas Day as "a piece of cake." On Christmas night, after his talk with ONB, Patton wrote in his diary: "Monty says that First Army cannot attack for three months."
7. *Supreme Command*, p. 383.
8. Ibid., p. 383; *The Ardennes*, p. 610; Hansen diary, 12-26-44. (The letter to Hodges cannot be found in ONB papers.)
9. *The Ardennes*, pp. 611–13; *Soldier's Story*, p. 482; *Lightning Joe*, p. 290; *Patton Papers II*, p. 607.
10. *Soldier's Story*, p. 482; Tedder, *With Prejudice*, p. 629.
11. *Bitter Woods*, p. 473; *Patton Papers II*, p. 608; Hansen diary, 12-27-44.
12. Hansen diary, 12-27-44; *With Prejudice*, p. 629.
13. *The Ardennes*, pp. 611–12.
14. *The Ardennes*, p. 612; MacDonald, Charles B., *The Last Offensive*, Washington, D.C., OCMH, 1973, pp. 5, 55–7; *Triumph in the West*, p. 272; Hansen diary, 12-28-44.
15. ONB Memorandum for Record, 1-23-45, BP, WP.
16. Eisenhower, *Crusade in Europe*, pp. 360–61. (Ike is in error, p. 361, in stating Monty's offensive was to begin "January 3." It should be January 1. See Eisenhower papers IV p. 2384: "January first if the enemy does not make a prior attack.")
17. Eisenhower papers IV, p. 2384; Ambrose, *The Supreme Commander*, p. 572.
18. Eisenhower papers IV, p. 2384.
19. *Triumph in the West*, p. 279; Eisenhower papers IV, p. 2384; Butcher, *My Three Years*, p. 736.
20. Eisenhower papers IV, pp. 2388–89.

21. Montgomery, *Memoirs,* pp. 284–85.
22. Eisenhower papers IV, p. 2391; *My Three Years,* p. 737; ONB Memo for Record, 1-23-45; Hansen diary, 12-28-44; Pogue, *Supreme Command,* p. 386.
23. *Patton Papers II,* p. 609; Hansen diary, 12-27-44.
24. De Guingand, *Generals at War,* pp. 106–14; de Guingand, *Operation Victory,* p. 435; Eisenhower papers V, chronology; *Supreme Command,* pp. 386–87; Ambrose, *Supreme Commander,* pp. 571–76. De Guingand wrote in *Operation Victory:* "I felt very sorry for Bradley during this period for I had a great affection for this modest soldier. From Sicily days we had worked a lot together. Particularly during the months of planning before the landing in Normandy, Bradley had shown me the greatest kindness. I had admired the quiet way in which he tackled the great problems facing him, how he would never admit anything was impossible. This feeling towards the Commander of the 12 U.S. Army Group was shared by all of us at our headquarters."
25. Eisenhower papers IV, pp. 2386–87.

Chapter Forty-One

1. Churchill, Winston S., *The Second World War: Triumph and Tragedy,* Boston, 1953, pp. 331–45; Loewenheim, et al, *Roosevelt and Churchill: Their Secret Wartime Correspondence,* pp. 602ff.
2. Bryant, *Triumph in the West,* pp. 291–303; Pogue, *Supreme Command,* pp. 407–16.
3. Hansen diary, 1-2-45; Eisenhower papers V, chronology.
4. *Triumph in the West,* p. 284; Eisenhower papers V, chronology; Eisenhower, *Crusade in Europe,* p. 370.
5. Eisenhower papers IV, pp. 2420, 2422–23; *Triumph in the West,* p. 285.
6. Eisenhower papers IV, pp. 2419–23.
7. *Soldier's Story,* p. 484; Hansen diary, 1-6-45.
8. Hansen diary, 1-6-45.
9. *Roosevelt and Churchill,* pp. 645–46.
10. Montgomery, *Memoirs,* p. 278; *Triumph in the West,* p. 286.
11. *Crusade in Europe,* p. 356; Montgomery, *Memoirs,* p. 281.
12. De Guingand, *Operation Victory,* p. 434; Montgomery, *Memoirs,* pp. 278–81.
13. Eisenhower, John, *Bitter Woods,* p. 487.
14. *Soldier's Story,* p. 485; Ingersoll, Ralph, *Top Secret,* N.Y., 1946, p. 279.
15. Hansen diary, 1-8-45.
16. *Soldier's Story,* pp. 487–88; Hansen diary, 1-8-45; Blumenson, *Patton Papers II,* p. 614. On January 3, Patton wrote: "Montgomery got some fool Englishman in America to suggest that as Eisenhower had too much work, he (Montgomery) should be made Deputy Ground Forces Commander of all troops in Europe. If this occurs, I shall ask to be relieved. I will not serve under Montgomery and neither, I think, will Bradley."
17. *Triumph in the West,* p. 286; ONB "Awards," BP, WP. The citation for this medal—a Bronze Star—was designed in part to counteract Montgomery's "heroic role" in the Bulge. It stressed that ONB "quickly appreciated consequences" of the German attack and "made arrangements within his Group to meet the blow" and "instantly sensed the points at which the principal defensive measures should be concentrated." It also stressed, for the first time, that ONB turned his armies over to Monty for "temporary operational control." The citation concluded: "This award symbolized the appreciation of the Theater Commander of the great fighting qualities of the 12th Army Group and of the service rendered by General Bradley." At the same time, Ike renewed his request to Marshall to have ONB promoted to four-star general. He wrote Marshall that he hoped Marshall would consider ONB "at once" and that such a promotion would have a "fine general effect." In a follow-up letter, Ike said: "While true that the battle of the Ardennes is not over I should like to point out the fine record of solid accomplishment that is behind Bradley all the way from the time you sent him to me in February 1943. Moreover, the battle of the Ardennes is one of those incidents that is to be anticipated along a great line where contending forces are locked up in battle with varying fortunes in particular sections on the front. The real answer is the leadership exhibited by the Commander in meeting his problems. I consider that throughout this affair Bradley has handled himself admirably."
18. Hansen diary, 1-9-45; *The New York Times,* 1-10-45, for complete text.
19. ONB Memo for Record, 1-23-45, op. cit.
20. *The New York Times,* 1-10-45.
21. Hansen diary, 1-11-45; *Soldier's Story,* pp. 488–89.
22. Weigley, *Eisenhower's Lieutenants,* pp. 557–61; Collins, *Lightning Joe,* pp. 293–94.
23. *Patton Papers II,* pp. 620, 622.
24. BLM to ONB, 1-12-45, BP, WP.
25. *Eisenhower's Lieutenants,* p. 561. After the war, Raymond S. McLain defended ONB's role in the Bulge: "It has been suggested that Bradley was a good 'tactician' but not a profound 'strategist.' But where do we find more discrimination and sound strategic judgment than Bradley exhibited . . .

in the Ardennes . . . ? Bradley had judgment, determination, tenacity, courage, daring and general analytical capabilities equal to that of anyone in the field, and he will compare favorably with the top generals of history. He had the daring of a Stonewall Jackson and judgment comparable to a Robert E. Lee. His daring, though, is his one quality not usually recognized by the general public, or by many writers. It is a trait that history will reveal, of that I am certain. . . .

"[In the Bulge] General Bradley had made one of the decisive military decisions of the war and had triumphed. Truly, he was one of the greatest." Papers of Raymond S. McLain, edited by Albert N. Garland. This excerpt from *Assembly*, Spring 1970, a quarterly periodical published by the West Point Alumni Foundation, Inc., West Point, N.Y.

26. Eisenhower papers IV, pp. 2439, 2441; Hansen diary, 1-16-45.
27. Eisenhower papers IV, pp. 2440–41; *Triumph in the West*, pp. 292–3.
28. Ibid.
29. MacDonald, *Mighty Endeavor*, pp. 407, 417; *Supreme Command*, pp. 397–404.
30. *Patton Papers II*, p. 628.
31. Memo for Record, 1-23-45, op. cit.
32. *Triumph in the West*, p. 294.
33. Eisenhower papers V, chronology; *Patton Papers II*, pp. 628–29; Hobart Gay diary, 1-24-45, Hobart Gay papers, USAMHI.
34. *Mighty Endeavor*, p. 417.
35. NA, Record Group 165, WD General and Special Staffs, OPD 333.9 Case 520 (envelope), "Report of Investigation of Circumstances Surrounding the Disappearance of a 2½-ton Truck . . ." dated 3-7-45.
36. Eisenhower papers IV, pp. 2468–69.
37. *Patton Papers II*, p. 628; Hansen diary, 1-26-45.
38. *Soldier's Story*, p. 559 (Andrus); MacDonald, *Last Offensive*, pp. 60–3.
39. Ibid., p. 63; Ridgway, *Soldier*, p. 127.
40. *Last Offensive*, pp. 60–7.
41. Pogue, *Organizer of Victory*, pp. 511–13; Eisenhower papers IV, p. 2460, and vol. V, chronology.
42. *Organizer of Victory*, pp. 516–17; *Triumph in the West*, pp. 297–301; *Supreme Command*, pp. 407–16; Eisenhower papers IV, pp. 2463–65.
43. Ibid., pp. 2465–66; *Patton Papers II*, pp. 632–33.

Chapter Forty-Two

1. Ellis, *Victory in the West II*, pp. 255–56; Montgomery, *Normandy to the Baltic*, pp. 188–89; Horrocks, *A Full Life*, pp. 243–49; MacDonald, *The Last Offensive*, pp. 70–83, 135–37; Collins, *Lightning Joe*, pp. 298–99; Gavin, *On to Berlin*, pp. 293–96.
2. Eisenhower papers V, chronology, vol. IV, p. 2473; Hansen diary, 2-4-45; Ambrose, *Supreme Commander*, p. 613.
3. Hansen diary, 2-5-45; Eisenhower papers V, chronology, vol. IV, p. 2473.
4. Hansen diary, 2-5-45; *Soldier's Story*, p. 501.
5. Hansen diary, 2-5-45; *The Last Offensive*, p. 80; *On to Berlin*, p. 295.
6. Hansen diary, 2-6-45; *Soldier's Story*, p. 422; CB-ONB int.; Eisenhower, *Crusade in Europe*, p. 376.
7. *A Full Life*, pp. 249–55.
8. *The Last Offensive*, pp. 82–3; *Soldier's Story*, p. 499.
9. Bryant, *Triumph in the West*, p. 305; Tedder, *With Prejudice*, p. 662.
10. Pogue, *Organizer of Victory*, p. 536; Eisenhower papers IV, p. 2482.
11. Hansen diary, 2-13, 2-14-45; MacDonald, *Mighty Endeavor*, p. 407; Eisenhower, John, *Strictly Personal*, pp. 78–81.
12. Eisenhower papers V, chronology; *Strictly Personal*, p. 80.
13. Hansen diary, 2-14-45.
14. Hansen-ONB int.; Montgomery, *Memoirs*, p. 290; Hansen diary, 2-14-45; Eisenhower papers V, chronology. (Chronology is in error, stating ONB accompanied Ike to Monty's.)
15. *Triumph in the West*, p. 217; Montgomery, *Memoirs*, p. 291.
16. Eisenhower papers IV, pp. 2480–82, 2490.
17. Ibid., p. 2494; Montgomery, *Memoirs*, p. 292.
18. *Strictly Personal*, pp. 81–2.
19. *The Last Offensive*, p. 145; *Soldier's Story*, pp. 503, 504.
20. *The Last Offensive*, pp. 178, 183–84; Hansen diary, 3-1, 3-2-45; *Conquer*, pp. 184, 190.
21. *The Last Offensive*, pp. 185–91; Eisenhower papers IV, p. 2597; *Lightning Joe*, pp. 302–3.
22. Eisenhower papers IV, p. 2490, vol. V, chronology; Hansen diary, 3-1-45.
23. *Soldier's Story* p. 506.
24. *The Last Offensive*, pp. 185–207.
25. *Triumph in the West*, pp. 321–24; CB-Simpson int.
26. Hansen diary, 3-6-45; *Triumph in the West*, p. 324.
27. Eisenhower papers IV, pp. 2512, 2527; *The Last Offensive*, pp. 295–304; *Soldier's Story*, pp. 517–18; *Conquer: The Story of the Ninth Army*, pp. 209–11; *Normandy to the Baltic*, pp. 197–204; *Victory in the West II*, pp. 279–88; Pogue, *The Supreme Command*, pp. 430–31.

28. Eisenhower papers IV, p. 2512; *The Last Offensive,* pp. 236–41; *Soldier's Story,* pp. 516–17.
29. *Triumph in the West,* p. 324.
30. Eisenhower papers IV, pp. 2503, 2527; ONB "Promotions," BP, WP.

Chapter Forty-Three

1. Hansen diary, 3-7-45.
2. MacDonald, *The Last Offensive,* pp. 208–35; *Register of Graduates.*
3. *Soldier's Story,* pp. 510–13, 526; Hansen diary, 3-7-45; Hansen-ONB int.; Hobart Gay diary, 3-9-45, p. 776; Blumenson, *Patton Papers II,* p. 653.
4. Eisenhower, *Crusade in Europe,* pp. 379–80; *Soldier's Story,* p. 511; Butcher, *My Three Years,* p. 768; Gavin, *On to Berlin,* pp. 304–5.
5. Eisenhower papers IV, p. 2510; Bryant, *Triumph in the West,* p. 327.
6. *The Last Offensive,* pp. 221–22, 228, 232.
7. Ibid., p. 229, 367; Sylvan diary, 3-15-45, p. 231; *Register of Graduates.*
8. Hansen diary, 3-9-45; *Patton Papers II,* p. 653; Hobart Gay diary, 3-9-45, pp. 775–76.
9. Bull, Memo for Record, 3-9-45, Eisenhower Library; Eisenhower papers IV, p. 2526.
10. Ibid., pp. 2524–25, 2529, 2547–48; *On to Berlin,* p. 299.
11. *Soldier's Story,* p. 527.
12. *The Last Offensive,* p. 232; Colby, *The First Army in Europe,* pp. 148–52; Hansen-ONB int.
13. *The Last Offensive,* pp. 244–65; Hobart Gay diary, 3-20-45, p. 807.
14. Eisenhower papers V, chronology; Morgan, Kay Summersby, *Past Forgetting,* p. 217; ONB flight diary, 3-18-45, BP, WP. The "flight diary" appears to be a record kept for reimbursement for flight pay. It usually notes only where ONB has flown (hours in air) and whom he saw, but occasionally noteworthy events are tersely noted. ONB's movements in the period from March 9 to 26 are from this diary.
15. Eisenhower papers V, chronology; flight diary, 3-18-45, mentions expansion of Remagen bridgehead and ten divisions "from south"; Hobart Gay diary, 2-23-45; *The Last Offensive,* p. 266; Eisenhower papers IV, p. 2537.
16. Eisenhower papers V, chronology; flight diary, 3-19-45; Sylvan diary, 3-19-45, p. 235; *Patton Papers II,* p. 658; *Soldier's Story,* p. 519; *The Last Offensive,* pp. 266, 323.
17. Eisenhower papers V, chronology; flight diary, 3-20, 3-22-45; *Past Forgetting,* pp. 217–18.
18. *Soldier's Story,* pp. 521–22; Hobart Gay diary, 3-23-45, p. 813.
19. Marshall to ONB via DDE, 3-23-45, BP, WP. See Eisenhower papers IV for numerous Marshall letters re lack of U.S. Army publicity.
20. Eisenhower papers IV, pp. 2540–41; *The Last Offensive,* p. 273; Hobart Gay diary, 3-23-45, pp. 813–14.
21. Eisenhower papers V, chronology; *Triumph in the West,* pp. 338–42; Eisenhower, *Crusade in Europe,* pp. 389–90; *Soldier's Story,* p. 524; flight diary, 3-24-45. (There is conflict in Eisenhower papers V, chronology, *Crusade in Europe* (p. 390), *The Supreme Commander* (pp. 626–27), *The Last Offensive,* (pp. 310, 310n., 319–20) and elsewhere about Ike and ONB's movements and whereabouts and meetings with Churchill and Montgomery on March 24 and 25, 1945. Bryant, Churchill and ONB flight diary, believed to be the most accurate, are followed here.)
22. *The Last Offensive,* pp. 273, 294–320.
23. *Conquer: The Story of the Ninth Army,* p. 247; Eisenhower papers V, chronology; *The Last Offensive,* p. 234.
24. Eisenhower papers IV, p. 2539.
25. Churchill, *Triumph and Tragedy,* pp. 416–17; *Triumph in the West,* p. 333; CB-Simpson int.
26. *Triumph in the West,* p. 332; Eisenhower papers IV, p. 2544.
27. Eisenhower, *Crusade in Europe,* p. 372; *Triumph in the West,* p. 333.
28. *The Last Offensive,* pp. 279–80, 346–50, 373–74; Collins, *Lightning Joe,* pp. 311–13.
29. *The Last Offensive,* pp. 280–84; Toland, John, *The Last 100 Days,* N.Y., 1966, pp. 314ff.; *Soldier's Story,* pp. 541–43; Eisenhower papers IV, p. 2617. Patton continued to get most of the publicity. In an attempt to offset it and focus the limelight on Hodges and Bradley, Ike, on March 30, wrote Marshall expressing the hope that Army publicists could put their imaginations to work "to figure out some way of giving Hodges his proper credit and showing that Bradley's handling of 12th Army Group has been masterful." Buttressing his case, Ike wrote: "In our latest successes . . . Hodges has been the spearhead and the scintillating star. . . . Equally with Hodges the part that Bradley has played in this campaign should be painted in more brilliant colors. Never once has he held back in attempting any maneuver, no matter how bold in conception and never once has he 'paused to re-group' when there was opportunity lying in his front. His handling of his Army commanders has been superb and his energy, common sense, tactical skill and complete loyalty have made him a great lieutenant on whom I always rely with greatest confidence. I do not—repeat not—

decry or deprecate the accomplishments of the other Army commanders because all have performed in the finest fashion. What I am trying to say is that First Army's part in this whole campaign has been seemingly overlooked by the headline writers and others have received credit for things for which Hodges and Bradley were primarily responsible. I consider Bradley the greatest battle-line commander I have met in this war." (Eisenhower papers IV, pp. 2564–65.)

Chapter Forty-Four

1. Gavin, *On to Berlin*, pp. 306–7; Hansen diary, 3-26-45; Eisenhower papers V, chronology.
2. Liddell Hart, *History of the Second World War*, pp. 663–69; Eisenhower, *Crusade in Europe*, p. 396; *Soldier's Story*, p. 535.
3. Ambrose, *The Supreme Commander*, p. 632; *Crusade in Europe*, pp. 396–97; *Soldier's Story*, p. 535; Ziemke, Earl F., *Stalingrad to Berlin*, OCMH, Wash. D.C., 1968, p. 479.
4. Ibid., pp. 531–33.
5. For a comprehensive summary of the foregoing, see: Greenfield, *Command Decisions*, pp. 479–92, "The Decision to Halt at the Elbe," by Forrest C. Pogue. For a provocative view of the decision, see *On to Berlin*, pp. 331–357.
6. MacDonald, *Last Offensive*, pp. 407–42; Pogue, "Decision to Halt"; *Soldier's Story*, pp. 536–37, 546; Hansen diary, 3-9-45; Eisenhower papers IV, pp. 2560–61, 2569, 2604–5. On Ultra: Bennett, *Ultra in the West*, pp. 246, 257–62.
7. Eisenhower papers IV, pp. 2557–58, 2576–77.
8. *Crusade in Europe*, p. 403.
9. *Last Offensive*, p. 351, Collins, *Lightning Joe*, pp. 312–14.
10. Eisenhower papers IV, pp. 2552, 2555; Bryant, *Triumph in the West*, p. 337.
11. Eisenhower papers IV, p. 2551.
12. Ehrman, *Grand Strategy*, vol. V, pp. 131–51.
13. Churchill, *Triumph and Tragedy*, pp. 440–45, 465; *Grand Strategy*, pp. 137–38.
14. Eisenhower papers IV, pp. 2565, 2568–69.
15. Ibid., pp. 2559–63, 2566–67, 2572–74; Loewenheim, *Roosevelt and Churchill*, pp. 701–3. For full discussions of the controversy, see Pogue, *Supreme Commander*, pp. 441–47; *Last Offensive*, pp. 339–43; *Grand Strategy*, pp. 131–49; Ellis, *Victory in the West*, pp. 295–304.
16. *Conquer*, pp. 256–68; *Last Offensive*, pp. 357–59.
17. *Conquer*, p. 269.
18. Eisenhower papers IV, p. 2576; *Last Offensive*, p. 379; *Soldier's Story*, p. 528. (Note: Hansen diary skips 3-31 to 4-5-45.)
19. *Last Offensive*, pp. 362–72; *Soldier's Story*, p. 526.
20. Eisenhower papers IV, p. 2594; *Last Offensive*, pp. 379–406, map XV; *Conquer*, pp. 285–330; *Soldier's Story*, p. 537.
21. *Last Offensive*, pp 378, 391–92; *Lightning Joe*, p. 324; Blumenson, *Patton Papers II*, p. 683; Price, *Troy Middleton*, p. 287. (The camp at Ohrdruf was discovered on April 4; the camp at Nordhausen on April 12.)

Chapter Forty-Five

1. Ellis, *Victory in the West II*, pp. 308–9; Liddell Hart, *History of the Second World War*, p. 679.
2. Eisenhower papers IV, pp. 2552, 2567–68, 2593–94, 2650, chronology; ONB flight diary, 4-10-45. (Note: Hansen diary missing 4-6 to 4-16-45.)
3. Eisenhower papers IV, pp. 2594, 2650–52; Bryant, *Triumph in the West*, p. 340; letter ONB-DDE, 4-10-45, Eisenhower Library.
4. Eisenhower papers IV, pp. 2617–18, 2650–52.
5. *Conquer*, p. 304; letter Simpson-*New York Times Book Review*, 4-30-66, James E. Moore papers, USAMHI. (In S. L. A. Marshall's review of John Toland's *The Last 100 Days* and Cornelius Ryan's *The Last Battle*, he argued in the review that Simpson was unable, militarily, to capture Berlin; Simpson's letter, the best extant SITREP on Ninth Army, is in rebuttal.)
6. Eisenhower papers IV, p. 2615.
7. *Soldier's Story*, p. 543; Eisenhower papers IV, p. 2611.
8. *Soldier's Story*, pp. 539–41; Eisenhower, *Crusade in Europe*, pp. 407–8; Eisenhower papers IV, p. 2601, vol. V, chronology; Hobart Gay diary, 4-12-45, pp. 865–68.
9. *Soldier's Story*, p. 539.
10. Blumenson, *Patton Papers II*, p. 685; Hobart Gay diary, 4-12-45, p. 865.
11. *Soldier's Story*, p. 541; *Crusade in Europe*, pp. 409–10; *Patton Papers II*, p. 685.
12. Eisenhower papers IV, pp. 2595, 2600.
13. Ibid., pp. 2611, 2615; Ryan, *The Last Battle*, pp. 331–32; Toland, *The Last 100 Days*, pp. 385–86, 388; Mosley, Leonard, *Marshall*, N.Y., 1982, pp. 326–30.
14. *Last Offensive*, pp 405, 423; Liddell Hart, *History*, p. 680; *Victory in the West II*, pp. 429–32; Toland, *The Last 100 Days*, pp. 519, 592; Ryan, *The Last Battle*, p. 520; Keegan, John, *Six Armies in Normandy*, N.Y., 1982, pp. 323–24.
15. Price, *Troy H. Middleton*, pp. 169–71, 285; *Last Offensive*, p. 425; letters Middleton-

ONB 5-5-45, ONB to Middleton, 5-9-45, BP, Carlisle.
16. *Last Offensive*, pp. 425–26, 434.
17. Ibid., pp. 422–33, 436, 440–42.
18. Ibid., pp. 399, 422.
19. Ibid., pp. 445–56.
20. Ibid., p. 456; *Patton Papers II*, p. 696.
21. *Victory in the West II*, pp. 315–16; Eisenhower papers IV, p. 2649, vol. V, chronology; *Last Offensive*, pp. 460–61; Horrocks, *Corps Commander*, p. 264.
22. Ridgway, *Soldier*, pp. 141–46; *Last Offensive*, pp. 461–62; Eisenhower papers IV, p. 2650; Gavin, *On to Berlin*, pp. 316–21; *Victory in the West II*, pp. 337–38.
23. Matloff, *Strategic Planning for Coalition Warfare, 1943–1944*, pp. 536–37; Manchester, William, *American Caesar, 1880–1964*, Boston, 1978, pp. 436–38.
24. Eisenhower papers IV, pp. 2647–48.
25. *Soldier's Story*, pp. 547, 549–53.
26. Eisenhower papers IV, pp. 2694–96; *Soldier's Story*, pp. 547, 553; Hansen diary, 5-7, 5-8-45.
27. *Last Offensive*, p. 478 (casualties).

PART FOUR: WASHINGTON

Chapter Forty-Six

1. *Soldier's Story*, p. 553; KB-ONB int. *Atlas*, May 1966, published a translation of a portion of Koniev's memoirs from *Novy Mir*, Moscow, in which Koniev recalled the meeting. Koniev wrote:

   > Bradley himself made a favorable impression on me as a man and as a soldier at both our meetings. He was no longer a young man in May of '45 . . . A professional soldier, he was strong, calm and reserved. Judging from our exchange on military subjects, he analyzed the course of events accurately and in an interesting way and understood the importance that powerful artillery, tanks and aviation had acquired during the war. He understood the nature of modern warfare well and accurately separated the decisive from the secondary. I felt he also had a profound understanding of artillery matters and appraised our tanks, their armament, armor, engines, etc., with knowledge of the subject. In sum, I both felt and could see that the man beside me was well oriented in the use of all arms of the service, and this, in my opinion, is the primary mark of a highly qualified commander. I had the impression that here was a military man in the full sense of the word, an Army leader, worthy of representing American troops in Europe.

2. "Eyes Only" GCM to DDE, 5-16-45, box 67, folder 25, Marshall papers, Marshall Library. Ike's reaction—the remote cottage—is in Eisenhower papers VI, p. 310. See also Morgan, *Past Forgetting*, p. 232. ONB's reaction: ONB notes, dictated 12-31-64 and mislabeled "Interview with General Omar Bradley," BP, Carlisle; Hanson-ONB int.; CB-ONB int.
3. Ike's plans re taking Chief of Staff job and recommending ONB to follow him: Eisenhower papers IX, p. 2194; Ferrell, Robert H., editor, *The Eisenhower Diaries*, N.Y., 1981, p. 370; Eisenhower, *At Ease*, p. 316; Eisenhower, *Crusade in Europe*, p. 444. ONB's "acceptance," DDE to GCM, Eisenhower papers VI, p. 65. (See also below, chap. 49.)
4. Final arrangements on ONB victory tour and VA job: Eisenhower papers VI, p. 72; GCM to DDE, 5-20-45, box 67, folder 24, Marshall papers, Marshall Library; memorandum GCM to HST, 5-18-45, Truman Library.
5. Memoir, pp. 207–8; flight diary, 6-2, 6-3-45.
6. Flight diary, 6-4, 6-5-45; *Register of Graduates*, 1945, p. 485.
7. Flight diary, 6-7-45; *Medical Care of Veterans*, a carefully researched history produced by the VA, 1967, Washington, D.C., G.P.O., pp. 171–75; Deutsch quote from *PM*, 9-15-46 in another article, "General Bradley, a Veteran's Veteran," by Kenneth Stewart.
8. *Medical Care*, pp. 175–76; Hines to HST, 6-7-45, and HST to Hines, "Official File," Truman Library; William Hillman and Francis E. Heller int. with ONB as background for Truman's memoirs, 3-30-55, p. 41, transcript in Truman Library (hereafter Hillman-Heller-ONB int.).
9. *New York Times*, 6-9-45 (cited in Eisenhower papers VI, p. 72); AP dispatch in *Moberly Monitor-Index and Democrat*, 6-8-45.
10. Flight diary, 6-9-45; memoir, p. 207.
11. Flight diary, 6-9, 6-10-45; extended coverage in *Moberly Monitor-Index and Democrat*, 6-7, 6-8, 6-11-45; CB-ONB int.
12. Flight diary, 6-11-45; *St. Louis Globe-Democrat*, 6-10-45, which had the jawbreaking headlines: "HE'S THE NEAREST THING TO ABRAHAM LINCOLN IN UNIFORM THE AMERICAN ARMY HAS EVER PRODUCED / General Omar Bradley has Persistence of Grant, Likened to Lee, Jackson

—A Tough Knotty Fighter Who Strikes Sledgehammer Blows."

13. Flight diary, 6-12-45; Hanson-ONB int.; Hansen "log," 6-13-45, Hansen papers, USAMHI; *Medical Care,* pp. 177–201.
14. Hillman-Heller-ONB int.
15. Eisenhower papers VI, p. 163; Hanson-ONB int.; draft of Hansen ms. for *Soldier's Story,* unused chapter entitled "Veterans," p. 7, Hansen papers, USAMHI. On ONB temporarily relieving Ike as Theater Commander, see Hanson-ONB int. and Eisenhower papers VI, pp. 72, 145.
16. On Hodges: Murray, G. Patrick, "Courtney Hodges," *American History Illustrated;* on Patton: Blumenson, *Patton Papers II,* p. 728; on Simpson: official Army biography: "After the German surrender in Europe, General Simpson was preparing to take his Ninth Army to China." ETO problems during ONB's brief tenure as Theater Commander may be found in Eisenhower papers VI, May–July 1945.
17. Eisenhower papers VI, pp. 163, 184–86; Mee, Charles L., Jr., *Meeting at Potsdam,* N.Y., 1975, pp. 24, 49–50, 90.
18. Eisenhower papers VI, p. 204.
19. *Command Decisions,* pp. 493–518, "The Decision to Use the Atomic Bomb," by Louis Morton. The literature on this decision is, of course, vast but Morton's account stands up well. On Ike: Eisenhower papers VI, p. 205; *Crusade in Europe,* p. 443.
20. Eisenhower papers VI, p. 204; Daniels, Jonathan, *Man of Independence,* Philadelphia, 1950, p. 280; *Crusade in Europe,* p. 444; Truman, Memoirs, vol. I, *Year of Decisions,* N.Y., 1955.
21. Eisenhower papers VI, p. 207. Ike wrote, in part:

> I cannot resist the urge, upon your departure to the United States, to attempt once more to give some expression of the personal sense of gratitude and admiration I feel toward you.
>
> Since you first joined me in North Africa in early 1942 [1943] I have constantly depended, with perfect confidence, upon your counsel and advice. In the Allied Command you have successively and successfully commanded a Corps, an Army and an Army Group. In my opinion you are pre-eminent among the Commanders of major battle units in this war. Your leadership, forcefulness, professional capacity, selflessness, high sense of duty and sympathetic understanding of human beings combine to stamp you as one of America's great leaders and soldiers. I know that you are now going to a most important post and one that is fraught with possibilities for public criticism. These will be inevitable and the only word of advice I would like to submit is that you carry on that task with the same methods, the same objective attitude and the same devotion to duty that have made you so successful in the past.
>
> My personal thanks are due you for the way you have always made my own tasks the easier to accomplish. With good luck and best wishes. From your old friend, Ike.

Chapter Forty-Seven

1. *Medical Care,* op. cit., p. 189.
2. The full range of World War II veterans benefits and a description of enabling legislation may be found in VA Annual Report, June 30, 1945, on file at VA, Washington, D.C.
3. The "veteran population" is described in VA Annual Report.
4. On new legislation, see VA Annual Report, 1945, p. 30. A good many of ONB's postwar speeches, congressional testimony, radio talks, magazine articles and other writings have been reproduced and bound in six volumes, entitled "The Collected Writings of General Omar N. Bradley." These volumes are on file at West Point and Carlisle. Volumes I, III and IV contain several hundred pages of material on ONB's VA days. While by no means complete, these documents were invaluable and are cited hereinafter as "Collected Writings." Many other speeches, congressional testimony, etc., may be found in the Hansen papers, USAMHI. The 43 percent figure is from "Collected Writings III," p. 128.
5. VA Annual Report, 1945. The description of VA is from "General Bradley—A Veteran's Veteran," by Kenneth Stuart, *PM,* 9-15-46.
6. CB-ONB int.; HST appointment calendar, Truman Library.
7. Phillips, Cabell, *The 1940s: Decade of Triumph and Trouble,* N.Y., Macmillan, 1975, pp. 275–76.
8. An exchange between Truman and his budget director, Harold D. Smith, is pertinent. On November 20, 1945, Smith wrote Truman:

> I recently had a long and very satisfactory conversation with General Bradley. In conformity with my conversation with you we have agreed to go through with commitments of the previous Veterans Administration unless those commitments were completely incompatible with general plans. General Bradley, I am convinced, will thereafter develop his plans with complete objectivity and will not be pushed around by anyone. We have both agreed—and this is really the point in bringing this matter to

> your attention now—that if there are to be any changes made for political reasons the President is the only person who can make such changes and none of his subordinates should do so. . . . I did want you to know how pleased I am with General Bradley's attitude and unless I am very badly mistaken you have a good Administrator in that post and can rest assured that there will be no significant trouble on your hands from that direction.

Truman replied the following day:

> One of the first things I told General Bradley when he took over the Veterans Bureau [Administration] was that I wanted his program set up for the benefit of the veterans and, while some political commitments had been made by General Hines and in all probability will have to be carried out, I did not under any circumstances want him to feel that he had to confirm recommendations due to the political approach in the matter. General Bradley came to see me about two weeks ago and I reiterated that direction to him. I think he is really going to do a job with this program and I don't believe we will have any headaches trusting him with it. He has my complete backing and confidence.

Smith to Truman, 11-20-45; Truman to Smith, 11-21-45, Truman papers, secretary file, Truman Library. See also Hillman-Heller-ONB int.

9. After August 15, ONB saw HST on October 24, November 13, and December 17, HST appointment calendar, Truman Library.
10. Phillips, *The 1940s*, pp. 254–55; Phillips, Cabell, *The Truman Presidency,* N.Y., Macmillan, 1966; Daniels, *Man of Independence*.
11. VA Annual Report, 1946; "Collected Writings IV," p. 83; The initial demobilization plan envisioned a discharge rate of 250,000 to 600,000 a month, or by 7-1-47, 14 million veterans.
12. *Medical Care,* pp. 195, 204, 222–23; Hillman-Heller-ONB int.; CB-ONB int.
13. *Medical Care,* p. 188; cable, ONB-Hansen, 7-16-45, Hansen papers, USAMHI; Hansen ms. "Veterans," pp. 19, 25; CB-Robinson int.
14. On decentralization, see *Medical Care,* p. 195; "Collected Writings I," pp. 9–12, 53, 153; vol. III, pp. 76, 120, 133, 177, 192, 193, 217; Hillman-Heller-ONB int; Hansen ms. "Veterans," pp. 16–19, 25, 27, 29–30; Hanson-ONB int.; VA employment Annual Report, 1947.
15. "Collected Writings III," pp. 126, 134, 147, 155; vol. IV, pp. 72–73; Hanson-ONB int.
16. "Collected Writings I," pp. 161, 393–94, 428–29; vol. IV, p. 85.
17. "Collected Writings I," pp. 391–92; Hillman-Heller-ONB int.
18. "Collected Writings III," pp. 134, 158, 162–63; vol. IV, p. 72–73.
19. "Collected Writings I," p. 395.
20. Ibid., p. 390.
21. Ibid., p. 399.
22. "Collected Writings III," pp. 159–60.
23. "Collected Writings I," p. 399; vol. III, pp. 162, 170; vol. IV, pp. 72–74, 85.
24. "Collected Writings III," pp. 102, 190; Hillman-Heller-ONB int., pp. 36–37.
25. "Collected Writings III," pp. 102, 190; "Collected Writings IV," p. 91.
26. "Collected Writings III," pp. 135, 203; "Statistical Summary of VA Activities," 7-31-46, HST papers official file, Truman Library.
27. "Collected Writings III," pp. 101, 125, 151, 167, 188; Hanson-ONB int.; Hillman-Heller-ONB int.

Chapter Forty-Eight

1. *Medical Care,* pp. 206–7, contains a biography of Hawley and a full account of his role in VA medicine; Hansen ms. "Veterans," pp. 8–9, further describes Hawley.
2. *Medical Care,* p. 214; VA Annual Report, 1947, pp. 3–4; "Collected Writings I," p. 20; vol. III, p. 185.
3. *Medical Care,* pp. 210–12. The description of the Civil Service list is derived from Hawley's sworn testimony to a congressional committee.
4. *Medical Care,* pp. 210–13, 216–18; see also Baruch plan, p. 193; "Collected Writings I," pp. 14, 36–7.
5. For ONB profiles at VA see for example: *Look,* 4-2-46; *Saturday Evening Post,* 11-24-45; *PM,* 9-15-46; *Parade,* 11-24-45; and a *Time* cover story, 4-1-46.
6. *Medical Care,* p. 210–11.
7. *Medical Care,* pp. 210–14; Hanson-ONB int.; memoir, p. 209.
8. Hansen ms. "Veterans," p. 10; political sensitivity, Hanson-ONB int.
9. The VA hospital construction program underwent many changes. For 6-30-45 program, as approved, see VA Annual Report, 1945, pp. 7–9; for the program as approved on 7-31-47, see "Collected Writings I," pp. 440–46.
10. *Medical Care,* p. 219.
11. See Harold D. Smith-HST letters of 11-30, 11-31-45, Truman Library. (See note 8.)
12. *Medical Care,* pp. 220–21.
13. On Bulova school: "Collected Writings III," p. 181; *Nation's Business* int. with ONB, April 1969; "VA Diary," 8-14-46; Hanson-ONB int.; CB-Harry B. Henshel (son of Harry D. Henshel) int., 4-30-80; prosthetic research, *Look,* 4-2-46.
14. VA Annual Report, 1947, contains an excellent summary of achievements. See also

Medical Care, pp. 203–4; medical school affiliation, "Collected Writings III," pp. 179, 364.

15. Deutsch in *Look,* 4-2-46; *Medical Care,* p. 220; Miller and Monohan, *Reader's Digest,* September, 1947.

Chapter Forty-Nine

1. Eisenhower papers VI, p. 537, note 2; Truman memoirs II, op. cit., p. 86.
2. Eisenhower papers IX, chronology. Ike has explained his "deal" with Truman on the Chief of Staff job and ONB's succession in two places in similar words. In a memo for the record, 11-28-59, published in Ferrell, *Eisenhower Diaries,* p. 370, Ike wrote: "I was ordered back to Washington to become Chief of Staff of the Army. I informed the president of my hope to retire and unless he had a positive desire that I take the office for a period, I should like to decline the appointment. He told me that the only other individual he could consider to take General Marshall's place was General Bradley, who was at that time serving as head of the Veterans' Bureau [Administration]. He informed me also that he would need General Bradley in that post for at least two years but stated that if I was still of the same mind at that time, he would accept my resignation and appoint Bradley to the post of Chief of Staff of the Army." In *At Ease,* p. 316, Ike put it this way: "No personal enthusiasm marked my promotion to Chief of Staff, the highest military post a professional soldier in the United States Army can reach. When President Truman broached the subject I told him I'd much rather retire but he said he had a special need of me at the moment. He promised that my tour could be brief if I chose, lasting only until he found a replacement (as head of the Veteran's Bureau) for General Bradley who would succeed me." On McNarney, see *Register of Graduates.*
3. CB-ONB int.
4. On Spaatz, *Register of Graduates;* Smith: Eisenhower papers VII, pp. 582, 892; Patch: Eisenhower papers VI, p. 347; Simpson: letters, Simpson-ONB, 10-7-46 and ONB-Simpson 10-14-46, BP, WP, and CB-Simpson int.; Hodges: Murray, "Courtney Hodges," op. cit.; Devers: *Register of Graduates;* Gerow: Eisenhower papers VI, p. 330; Clark: CB-Clark int. For extended discussion of these and other proposed appointments, see Eisenhower papers VI, pp. 330–41 and 472–73, and other references in name index, vol. IX.
5. On Patton's death, see Blumenson, *Patton Papers II,* pp. 818–19, 821–24, 830–31, 835; on latest "doghouse" see Eisenhower papers VI, pp. 374, 394–95; *Patton Papers II,* pp. 760–87; Farago, *Patton,* pp. 812–32. For a detailed study of the postwar Patton see Farago, Ladislas, *The Last Days of Patton,* N.Y., McGraw-Hill, 1981. On December 12, when ONB first learned of Patton's accident, he telegraphed Patton: "Dear George, A truck can't do what the Germans tried so long to do and failed. Your friends everywhere pray for your recovery. I'm sure that if they could, the thousands of your men, now veterans, would join me in these greetings. My best to you always. Bradley." Patton's wife, Beatrice, who had flown to Germany to be at his side, dictated a reply to ONB on December 10: "Georgie has asked me to thank you for your telegram. He is improving slowly but steadily and I know the concern and sympathy of friends is helping him no end." She did not sign the letter. Patton took a sudden turn for the worse and died on the late afternoon of December 21, of pulmonary edema and congestive heart failure. He was buried in the American Military Cemetery at Hamm with a simple white cross. On December 21, ONB cabled Mrs. Patton: "My grief in George's death is lightened only by my memory of him as the great soldier on whom we could count when his country needed leadership. I am sure that if his troops could tell you today of their pride in his achievements you could understand completely how essential to the nation his life has been." (These documents in BP, WP.) That same day ONB released a statement to the media. In part: "He was strong in his devotion to his country. He did the jobs entrusted to him with tireless zeal and with unstinted courage . . . . He was an uncompromising fighter. He was greatest when the going was toughest. The word surrender was not in his vocabulary. He had a habit of victory." (In "Collected Writings, III," p. 90.)
6. Collins, *Lightning Joe,* p. 339; Ridgway, *Soldier,* p. 163; Taylor: *Register of Graduates* and CB-Taylor int.
7. Eisenhower papers VII, p. 637; vol. VIII, p. 1649; Ferrell, *Eisenhower Diaries,* p. 136–37.
8. Weigley, *History of the United States Army,* pp. 486, 596. On pages 566–69 there is a chart of yearly Army force levels from 1789 to 1966.
9. Here and below, Caraley, Demetrios, *The Politics of Military Unification,* N.Y., Columbia University Press, 1966; Hammond, Paul, *Organizing for Defense: The American Military Establishment in the Twentieth Century,* N.J., Princeton University Press, 1961; *The Evolving Role of the JCS in National Security,* pamphlet prepared by the

historical division, JCS; *Lightning Joe,* pp. 335–39; Vandegrift, Alexander A., *Once a Marine,* as told to Robert B. Asprey, N.Y., 1964.

10. Truman's views on unification are spelled out in memoirs I, pp. 63–6, and in an article devoted to the subject in *Collier's* magazine, 8-26-44.
11. Ike's views on limiting the Marine Corps—with which ONB agreed—may be found in Eisenhower papers VII, pp. 927–32; Spaatz's views on missiles, Eisenhower papers VII, pp. 789–91.
12. Patterson and Forrestal appointments: oral history, Marx Leva (special assistant to Forrestal), Truman Library, pp. 18–20.
13. For a critique on the act with which ONB was in substantial agreement, see Ike's long memo to Forrestal, 2-7-45, Eisenhower papers VIII, pp. 2242–56. During the 1945–47 unification fight, ONB became exasperated not only with Navy and Marine Corps witnesses, but also with Air Force witnesses who made shrill and wild claims about the efficacy of strategic bombing. Caraley, in *Military Unification,* p. 354, has an example. On November 15, 1945, Spaatz boasted in a congressional appearance that the Air Force had single-handedly defeated the German V-2 missile by bombing the launching sites and factories. Bradley followed Spaatz to the stand and said: "I've heard many statements as to what service won the war. In my opinion no one service won this war or is going to win any future war of any magnitude. It takes all our services together, plus the industrial effort of our nation to win any major war. The question was asked here a moment ago about the Air Forces knocking out the launching sites of the V-2. There is no doubt that the Air Forces had a good deal to do with cutting down the V-2s. However, I would like to call your attention to the fact that not until the Navy and the Army forces got together and went over and captured the launching sites did the V-2 attacks completely come to a stop. It was not until then that the V-2s stopped falling on England."
14. Dwight D. and Mamie D. Eisenhower, "Summary of Joint Federal Income Tax Returns for the Ten Years Ended December 31, 1951," dated October 15, 1952, Eisenhower Library. Owing to a special and highly favorable tax ruling, Ike and Mamie were able to declare the book money as "capital gains" and paid only $158,750 in taxes (netting $476,250). (See *The New York Times,* 10-15-52.) Ike wrote the book in a "blitz" of effort and it was published in the fall of 1948. At about this same time ONB entered into an agreement with Time Inc. to write his war memoirs, which emerged in 1951 as *A Soldier's Story*. Time Inc.'s *Life* magazine would first publish excerpts; Henry Holt & Co. would publish the book. In return for this arrangement, ONB received $75,000. He gave 25 percent of this sum to aide Chet Hansen, who actually wrote the book. Details in "Agreement" Hansen-ONB, 5-12-48, and "Agreement" ONB-Time Inc., 6-14-48, BP, Carlisle. Related documents in Hansen papers, USAMHI.
15. Permanent four-star rank: Eisenhower papers VIII, p. 1677; letter Harry S. Vaughan to Secretary Patterson, 4-17-47, Truman papers, official file, Truman Library. DSM: Eisenhower papers VIII, pp. 1653–54; ONB "Decorations." Designed to cover the period August to December 1944, the DSM citation read in part: "Under his brilliant leadership his 12th Army Group, through a series of skillfully conceived and boldly executed victories advanced from the Seine to the German border and effected the liberation of Northern France, Luxembourg, the southern part of Belgium and the Netherlands and breached the Siegfried Line. Through his coordination of the three armies under his command he made conspicuous contributions to the defeat of the German Army and the ultimate successful conclusion of the war." This was ONB's last U.S. decoration for World War II. In sum they were: three Army Distinguished Service medals, one Navy Distinguished Service Medal, two Legion of Merit medals, one Silver Star Medal (for D-day) and one Bronze Star Medal (for the Bulge). Trip to Europe: DDE memo to W. S. Paul, 4-23-47, EM, Eisenhower Library; White House press release, 7-18-47, Truman papers, official file, Truman Library.
16. "VA Diary," 8-15 to 8-26-47; letter ONB-Lucius D. Clay, 7-29-47; MQB scrapbooks, other documents relating to trip, BP, WP; on Louis Marx: Eisenhower papers I, pp. 536–37.
17. Clay, Lucius D., *Decision in Germany,* N.Y., Doubleday, 1950, pp. 1–19, 59–60; Smith, Jean Edward, editor, *The Papers of Lucius D. Clay,* 2 vols., Bloomington, Indiana, 1974 (for Clay bio, see "Foreword," vol 1); on Clay's threats to resign: Eisenhower papers VIII, pp. 1858–59; vol. IX, pp. 1870–71.
18. Clay, *Decision,* p. 230. Clay wrote of ONB: "I was proud of the combat team which he reviewed. I know of no greater soldier ever produced from our Army and to sense his satisfaction with our progress made all of us feel that our efforts had proved worthwhile."
19. Itinerary: "VA Diary" to 9-8-47, at which point the diary stops; Hanson-ONB int.;

thank-you letter, ONB-Montgomery, 9-30-47, BP, WP; MQB scrapbooks, BP, WP; return to States: DDE to Clay, 9-24-47, and Clay to DDE, 9-25-47, Bradley file, Eisenhower Library; Lord Alanbrooke: Fraser, David, *Alanbrooke,* N.Y., Atheneum, 1982; Monty: *Memoirs,* pp. 385ff.

20. Two candidates considered were Selective Service Director Lewis B. Hershey and former assistant secretary of war Louis Johnson. See: Millis, Walter, *The Forrestal Diaries,* N.Y., Viking Press, 1951, p. 325. ONB favored Paul Hawley, but did not campaign for him, CB-ONB int.
21. Gray biography, *Medical Care,* pp. 221–23; Eisenhower papers II, p. 1154, vol. IV, pp. 2472–73; profile, *St. Louis Post Dispatch,* 11-22-47.
22. Eisenhower papers IX, p. 1904; ONB attitude on Gray, Hanson-ONB int., tab C, p. 34; *Medical Care,* p. 220.
23. Eisenhower papers IX, p. 2130, note 4; letter ONB-HST, 11-26-47, and HST-ONB, 11-28-47, Truman papers, official file, Truman Library. In his "Dear Omar" letter accepting ONB's resignation from VA, Truman wrote in part: "I cannot overlook this opportunity to express to you my gratitude for the fine and loyal service you have rendered as Administrator of Veterans' Affairs. I fully realize that your problems have been arduous and complex, but you have filled this position with honor and distinction through your understanding and devotion to the tasks at hand. As you relinquish these duties for another important post you take with you my thanks for all that you have done for the Veterans Administration."
24. CB-Hansen int.; CB-ONB int.; MQB scrapbooks, BP, WP.
25. Eisenhower papers IX, p. 2257; *Newsweek,* 2-16-48.

Chapter Fifty

1. Millis, *Forrestal Diaries,* "biographical introduction," pp. *xvi–xxiv; Current Biography 1948.*
2. Hanson-ONB int.
3. CB-ONB int.
4. Eisenhower papers XVIII, p. 712; *Current Biography 1947.*
5. Hewes, James E., Jr., *From Root to McNamara: Army Organization Administration 1900–1963,* Washington, D.C., Center of Military History, United States Army, 1975, pp. 129–215; Collins, *Lightning Joe,* op. cit., pp. 344–45.
6. CB-Hansen int.; CB-Matthews int.; *Register of Graduates.*
7. For background on Cold War, military policy and containment, see: Gaddis, John Lewis, *The United States and the Origins of the Cold War,* N.Y., Columbia University Press, 1972; Kolodziej, Edward, *The Uncommon Defense and Congress,* Columbus, 1966; Etzold, Thomas H., and John Lewis Gaddis, editors, *Containment: Documents on American Policy and Strategy 1945–50,* N.Y., Columbia University Press, 1978; Bernstein, Barton J., and Allen J. Matusow, editors, *The Truman Administration: A Documentary History,* N.Y., 1966, pp. 158–266; Millis, Walter, *Arms and Men: A Study in American Military History,* op. cit., pp. 304–18; Kennan, George F., *Memoirs: 1925–50,* Boston, 1967, pp. 271–367.
8. On Truman economic policy see Truman memoirs II, pp. 53–4; on postwar military budgets see Huzar, Elias, *The Purse and the Sword: Control of the Army by Congress through Military Appropriations 1933–50,* Ithaca, N.Y., Cornell University Press, 1950, pp. 132–206; Kolodziej, op. cit., pp. 33–123. Weigley, *History of the United States Army,* pp. 485–504.
9. Millis, *Forrestal Diaries,* p. 375; "Collected Writings IV," pp. 112–128 (ONB testimony before House Armed Services Committee, 4-14-48, on status of Army); ONB memo to the JCS, 3-11-48, outlining world tensions, noted "the inability of the Army to back up our country's policies"; *Foreign Relations of the United States,* 1948, vol. 1, pp. 539–40.
10. Condit, Kenneth W., *The History of the Joint Chiefs of Staff,* vol. II, Wilmington, Delaware, Michael Glazier, Inc., pp. 25–58; Millis, *Forrestal Diaries,* p. 373 (Marshall quoted on playing with fire).
11. Schnabel, James F., and Robert J. Watson, *The History of the Joint Chiefs of Staff,* vol. III, part I, Wilmington, Delaware, Michael Glazier, Inc., pp. 1–20 (copy of vol. III also available in the Modern Military Branch of the National Archives); Truman memoirs II, pp. 360–76; Eisenhower papers IX, p. 2100; JCS Paper No. 1834 (with attachments), 2-17-48 (troop strength in Japan and Korea), Bradley file, Marshall Library.
12. Millis, *Forrestal Diaries,* p. 387; Smith, *Papers of Lucius D. Clay,* op. cit., p. *xxviii.*
13. On the Berlin crisis here and below, see Clay, *Decision in Germany,* pp. 358ff.; Condit, *History of the JCS,* vol. II, pp. 109ff.; Murphy, Robert D., *Diplomat Among Warriors,* N.Y., 1964, pp. 298ff.; Smith, Walter Bedell, *My Three Years in Moscow,* Philadelphia, 1950, pp. 230–36.
14. CIA failure: Millis, *Forrestal Diaries,* p. 395; Smith's encouraging cable, ibid., p. 409; Clay's "one in four," ibid., p. 460; Bradley's caution: Hanson-ONB int.
15. Phillips, *The 1940s,* op. cit., pp. 330–35, Luce quote, p. 330.

16. On the Sunday, June 27, meeting: ONB desk calendar, BP, WP; Millis, *Forrestal Diaries*, pp. 452–54.
17. Ibid., pp. 454–55.
18. On the various JCS problems and position papers on Berlin, see Condit, *History of the JCS*, pp. 131–47; Condit quote from p. 147.
19. CB-ONB int.
20. On UMT: Truman memoirs II, pp. 71–3; Collins, *Lightning Joe*, p. 346; Jacobs, Clyde Edwards, and John F. Gallagher, *The Selective Service Act: A Case Study of the Governmental Process*, N.Y., 1968, pp. 27–9.
21. Ibid., pp. 43ff.
22. Truman speech: Bernstein and Matusow, *The Truman Administration*, pp. 269–71.
23. On federalization of the Guard: Riker, William H., *Soldiers of the State*, pp. 67–100.
24. On ONB policy to improve GI self-esteem, see: Whitman, Howard, "What Every Draftee Should Know," *Reader's Digest*, November 1948. On pay raise, see, for example: ONB speech to nonpartisan political study club, Washington, D.C., 5-3-48, Hansen papers, USAMHI. In CB-Matthews int., Matthews said: "Bradley's drive to push the military pay raise through the White House and Congress was one of his great achievements as Chief of Staff." This statement is corroborated in a story in the *Army-Navy Journal*, 10-8-49, in part: "General Bradley is credited by personnel of all the Armed Forces with a major contribution to the recent congressional enactment of the Career Compensation Act. At several crucial points in the legislative processing of the Military Pay Bill when its adoption was in serious jeopardy, General Bradley's forceful enunciation of the needs for men of outstanding qualifications in the Services helped convince congressmen of the necessity for long overdue pay increases. And as the legislation, delayed in the Senate, faced a possible congressional adjournment, it was a letter from General Bradley to Senator Scott Lucas, Majority Leader, which helped speed the measure to a conclusive vote."
25. Dalfiume, Richard M., *Desegregation of the U.S. Armed Forces*, Columbia, Missouri, 1965, pp. 155–74. Letters ONB-HST, 7-30-48, and HST-ONB, 8-4-48, HST papers, secretary file, Truman Library. The incident did not rupture the HST-ONB relationship in the slightest. In his response, HST wrote: "You understand of course the newspapers generally are violently opposed to anything I undertake or try to do and they would magnify any statement that you would make on any subject where there is controversy. I understand the situation as it affects you very well and I know that you never would do anything that would stand to cut the ground from under me without first talking to me about it." See also HST press conference, 7-29-48: (Q: "Does your advocacy of equality of treatment and opportunity in the armed forces envision eventually the end of segregation?" A: "Yes."), transcript, Truman Library; story on press conference and related data in *The New York Times*, 7-30-48.

Chapter Fifty-One

1. Ike's views on military spending ceilings: Ferrell, *Eisenhower Diaries*, pp. 153, 156 ("We must hold our position of strength without bankrupting ourselves"), p. 157 ("I personally and very earnestly believe that $15 billion or $16 billion per year is all that this country need spend for security forces if it is done every year"); ONB's views: letter to army commanders, 7-9-49, copy to General MacArthur, Bradley file, MacArthur Archives. See also Collins, J. Lawton, *War in Peactime*, Boston, 1969.
2. Millis, *Forrestal Diaries*, pp. 389–90; ONB desk calendar, 3-11 to 3-14-48, BP, WP; Vandenberg: *Register of Graduates, Current Biography 1945*. Vandenberg relieved Spaatz on 4-30-48, per Condit, *History of the JCS*, vol. II, pp. 557–59. (A useful chart, listing principal military establishment people, jobs and dates of service.) Denfeld: *Register of Alumni, USNA; Current Biography 1947*. ONB's views on Denfeld: testimony, House Armed Services Committee, 10-19-49, p. 531; CB-ONB int.
3. The text of Halfmoon is in Etzold and Gaddis, *Containment*, op. cit., pp. 315–23. On evolution of Halfmoon, see Condit, op. cit., pp. 275–86. A-bomb numbers and other valuable background in: Rosenberg, David, "American Atomic Strategy and the Hydrogen Bomb Decision," *The Journal of American History*, vol. 66, no. 1, June 1979.
4. "Collected Writings IV," pp. 112–47. Other 1948–49 congressional testimony in this volume has useful information on Army war plan responsibilities, force levels and planned buildup. At one point ONB briefly strayed off the reservation and mounted a drive for 822,000 men. See testimony on 4-14-48, and Millis, *Forrestal Diaries*, pp. 414–15. But he soon pulled in his horns. See also ONB letter to army commanders, 7-6-48, copy to General MacArthur, MacArthur Archives.
5. MacArthur to ONB, 8-3-48, MacArthur Archives.
6. ONB to MacArthur, 8-7-48, MacArthur Archives.

7. Here and below, on military planning and budget controversies in 1948–50, see Stein, Harold, editor, *American Civil-Military Decisions: A Book of Case Studies;* "Super Carriers and B-36 Bombers," by Paul Y. Hammond, pp. 1–75, Tuscaloosa, 1963; a useful three-part analysis in the National Archives periodical *Prologue,* "The Defense Unification Battle, 1947–1950," spring, 1975. The Navy's position is related by Paolo E. Coletta, the Air Force's by Herman S. Wolk, and the Army's by Richard F. Haynes. See also Condit, *History of the JCS;* Kolodziej, *Uncommon Defense,* op. cit., and Huzar, *The Purse and the Sword,* op. cit.; Millis, *Forrestal Diaries,* pp. 382–450. Force level and budget figures are often in conflict in these accounts. Condit seems soundest, and his figures are used throughout.
8. Finletter chaired the President's Air Policy Commission, usually called the Finletter Commission; Senator Brewster chaired the congressional Air Policy Board. Finletter bio: *Current Biography 1948.*
9. On Forrestal almost firing Symington, see Millis, *Forrestal Diaries,* pp. 462–65; Truman on "glamor" boys: Truman, Margaret, *Harry S. Truman,* N.Y., 1973, p. 407. Truman's "1941" seems to be a reference to Pearl Harbor, but the "1920" is unclear. Perhaps a reference to Billy Mitchell's 1920 air-power propaganda or to the drastic reduction of the U.S. Army?
10. The Key West "agreements" are summarized in *Forrestal Diaries,* pp. 390–94. See also Hammond, *Organizing for Defense,* op. cit., p. 9. For the controversy over the Key West "vote" on the supercarrier, see note 13 below. For ONB's position on supercarrier and Navy budgets, see *Forrestal Diaries,* pp. 253–57; testimony to House Armed Services Committee, 10-19-49, and memo, ONB to DDE, 5-25-49, Bradley file, Eisenhower Library.
11. The Navy leaker was Rear Admiral Daniel V. Gallery, a skilled and persuasive writer. Drew Pearson summarized his memo in three columns. See Gallery oral history (no. 4), Naval Historical Center, Washington, D.C. The complete Gallery memo, copied from *Army-Navy Register,* 12-11-54, is appended. For impact of Gallery memo, see Hammond, *Organizing for Defense,* p. 9.
12. Truman's meeting and quoted memo: *Forrestal Diaries,* pp. 435–39.
13. Condit, *History of the JCS,* pp. 314–15. Admiral Leahy also voted yes.
14. On Forrestal's proposal to name ONB principal military adviser, see *Forrestal Diaries,* pp. 433–34.
15. Ibid., pp. 475–78; ONB desk calendar 8-20 to 8-22-48. On the McNarney Board, see *Forrestal Diaries,* p. 450. Other members were the Navy's Robert B. Carney (later CNO) and the Army's George J. Richards.
16. The Spaatz-Towers report, *Forrestal Diaries,* pp. 466–69, 475–76.
17. Rosenberg, "American Atomic Strategy," op. cit.
18. The "Newport Decisions" are summarized in *Forrestal Diaries,* pp. 475–78. See also "Newport Decisions," transcript of an extraordinary Forrestal-JCS mass Pentagon staff briefing held on 8-24-48, Bradley file, Marshall Library. In his remarks to the Army planners, ONB stated: "I think if every one of us would forget what service we belong to and think only of national defense, we won't have any trouble carrying out the decisions. I want you to enter into this thing the way I have outlined it and that is 'We all are working for national defense.' " Forrestal, Denfeld and Vandenberg spoke in a similar spirit of harmony.
19. Condit, *History of the JCS,* has a full and fascinating account of the fiscal 1950 budget battle, pp. 219–42. See also *Forrestal Diaries,* pp. 492–530; Hammond, "Super Carriers and B-36 Bombers," op. cit., pp. 18–23.
20. Condit, *History of the JCS,* pp. 226–27, describes ONB's proposal, and comments: "A sharp interservice debate ensued."
21. *Forrestal Diaries,* pp. 498, 504; Condit, *History of the JCS,* pp. 238–42.
22. *Forrestal Diaries,* p. 536; Condit, *History of the JCS,* pp. 244–75; on ONB's absence: desk calendar, 12-5 to 12-15-48; letter, ONB to DDE, 12-16-48, Bradley file, Eisenhower Library; Draper oral history, pp. 18, 23. The fiscal 1950 defense budget Truman finally submitted to Congress on January 10, 1949, asked for $14.24 billion. (Another $173 million had been trimmed from the Navy's shipbuilding funds—but not the supercarrier.) The budget proposed would provide a forty-eight-group Air Force, a ten-and-two-thirds-division Army and a 282-ship Navy, including eight carriers.
23. Truman, Margaret, *Harry S. Truman,* p. 407; Acheson, Dean, *Present at the Creation: My Years in the State Department,* N.Y., 1969, pp. 249–50; on Marshall's kidney removal and general health: *Present at the Creation,* letter ONB-GCM, 12-23-48, Bradley file, Marshall Library; on Forrestal's health, see various notes below.
24. On Louis Johnson fund raising, see *Harry S. Truman,* pp. 20–1, 42; Renfrow, Louis H. (Johnson aide), oral history, pp. 72, 136, Truman Library; Leva, Marx, oral history, p. 57; CB-John L. Sullivan (Navy Secretary) int., 5-6-80. The $2 million figure is

from Renfrow. On Ike's return to Washington, see *Forrestal Diaries,* p. 540; Ferrell, *Eisenhower Diaries,* p. 150. Ike's title "Presiding Officer" of the JCS is from letter HST-DDE, 8-1-49, Truman Library (upon Ike's termination of JCS duties).

25. *Eisenhower Diaries,* pp. 152–53. Ike's private notes on his first few weeks in Washington in 1949 are full and revealing.
26. Ibid., p. 158. The note re ONB wanting no part of the JCS chairmanship is dated 3-19-49.
27. Huie, William Bradford, *Reader's Digest,* December 1948, January, March, April 1949; *Forrestal Diaries,* p. 544; *Eisenhower Diaries,* pp. 152, 157.
28. Denfeld on Ike's impartiality, from *Collier's,* 3-25-50; Ike's views on carriers, *Eisenhower Diaries,* p. 157.
29. Ibid.
30. Here and below, the budget debates are fully described by Condit, *History of the JCS,* pp. 249–62. Ike's comments re quitting and criticizing, *Eisenhower Diaries,* pp. 157–58.
31. The complete text of NSC 20/4 is in Etzold and Gaddis, *Containment,* pp. 203–11, as is the Offtackle war plan, pp. 324–34.
32. The proposed atomic offensive is described in Poole, Walter S., *The History of the Joint Chiefs of Staff,* vol. IV, 1950–1952, Washington, D.C., 1979, pp. 163–70.
33. *Eisenhower Diaries,* p. 158.
34. Ibid., pp. 158–59; JCS meeting in Key West, ONB desk calendar, 4-7 to 4-12-49.
35. The Harmon Report is discussed at length in Rosenberg, "American Atomic Strategy"; a partial text may be found in Etzold and Gaddis, *Containment,* pp. 360–64.
36. Forrestal-Johnson changeover and Forrestal mental illness: *Forrestal Diaries,* pp. 548–55. See also: Draper, William, oral history, op. cit., p. 25; Renfrow oral history, pp. 106–106A; Johnson bio: *Current Biography 1949;* Steve Early: *Current Biography 1949.*
37. ONB's vote on the supercarrier: "Collected Writings IV," pp. 253–57.
38. Angry reaction to cancellation of the supercarrier—and some fascinating byplay—is contained in virtually every oral history of naval figures from this period. These are on file at the Naval Historical Center, Washington, D.C. See especially: Robert L. Dennison, Daniel V. Gallery, Malcolm Schoeffel, George Miller, John S. Thach (vol. II), Fitzhugh Lee, Walter W. C. Ansel, David McDonald, C. D. Griffin (vol. I), Charles Wellborn, Herbert Riley. For similar material see also the following oral histories at the Truman Library: Marx Leva, Louis H. Renfrow, John L. Sullivan. Additional data in CB-John L. Sullivan int., 5-6-80. The "criminal" quote is from Coletta in *Prologue,* op. cit. The complete text of Sullivan's letter of resignation is in Hammond, *Organizing for Defense.*
39. Matthews bio: *Current Biography 1949.* For Navy reaction to Matthews see sources cited in note 38. Some sources believed Johnson had deliberately chosen Matthews to please and court the Catholic vote should Johnson run for President.
40. Here and below: Gordon, Gray, oral history, pp. 30–40; CB-Gray int., 3-31-80; *Current Biography 1949;* CB-ONB int. The complete Gray appointment story, greatly condensed here, is a fascinating example of the inner workings of the erratic Louis Johnson regime.
41. Ferrell, Robert H., editor, *Off the Record: The Private Papers of HST,* N.Y., 1980, p. 192; *Present at the Creation,* p. 374.
42. Condit, *History of the JCS,* pp. 265–73; Weigley, *History of the United States Army,* p. 569 (chart on peak Army force levels). The Vandenberg (5-23-49) and ONB (5-25-49) memos to DDE are in Bradley file, Eisenhower Library.
43. CB-ONB int.
44. *Eisenhower Diaries,* p. 162.
45. Collins, *Lightning Joe,* p. 347.
46. On NATO and the trip, Condit, *History of the JCS,* pp. 372–99; ONB desk calendar 7-29 to 8-9-49; *New York Times,* 8-5-49; *Newsweek,* 8-15-49.
47. ONB desk calendar, 8-12 and 8-16-49. Typical of the flattering portraits was that written by *New York Times* Washington reporter William S. White, "Nicest Guy in Washington," *Collier's,* 10-28-49. Other reporters, seeking a means to identify ONB in his new job, described him as "Our Number One Military Man." This was not literally true. Truman, as Commander in Chief, was the Number One Military Man. By law, the five-star generals and admirals of World War II could not "retire" in the usual sense and were kept on the active list, subject to presidential recall. All outranked ONB. Of this group, one, Douglas MacArthur, was still serving in a full-time government post. ONB was thus merely the senior military officer on full-time active duty in Washington; and since he commanded no forces, he might have been more accurately described as "Washington's Number One Military Adviser."

Chapter Fifty-Two

1. Here and below, see Chapter Fifty-One, note 7; CB-Willis Matthews int.; CB-Hansen int.; CB-Edward L. Beach int., 4-16-80.

Chet Hansen, by then a full colonel, remained with ONB until *A Soldier's Story* was completed. Since he assumed ONB would serve only one two-year term, he took a job at the CIA. He was replaced by a new writer and press aide, Army Colonel Chester V. Clifton (West Point 1936). Mary Pitcairn soon married ONB's wartime Ultra rep Bill Jackson, who was a deputy director of CIA. (See letters, W. H. Jackson, to ONB, 1-8-51, ONB to Jackson, 1-17-51, and ONB to Pitcairn, 1-19-51, BP, WP.) A WAC warrant officer, Olive Marsh, replaced Pitcairn as office secretary. For further details on the start-up staff, see story in *Army-Navy Journal,* 10-8-49. Clifton: *Register of Graduates;* Davis: *Register of Alumni, USNA*. The "joint staff" is described by ONB in "Collected Writings IV," p. 203. The Chairman's flag, a rather pretentious creation (an eagle clutching three arrows, representing the three services, in his talons against a field of blue and white), is described in *The New York Times,* 1-27-50.

2. Poole, *History of the JCS,* vol. IV, pp. 179–85; chart on p. 181 shows NATO organization. The Ike quote is from a transcript of DDE-ONB telephone conversation, 10-10-49, BP, WP.
3. In addition to notes 7 and 38 (Chapter Fifty-One), see: Davis, Vincent, *Postwar Defense Policy and the U.S. Navy 1943–46,* Chapel Hill, N.C., 1962; and Davis, Vincent, *The Admirals' Lobby,* Chapel Hill, N.C., 1967.
4. See Chapter Fifty-One, note 17.
5. ONB's speech in "Collected Writings IV," pp. 222–72; published in *Hearings Before the Committee on Armed Services, House of Representatives 81st Congress, First Session, October 6 to October 21, 1949,* Washington, D.C., GPO, 1949, pp. 515–41 and 567.
6. Navy critics would unfairly needle ONB for this prediction after the carrier-supported Inchon, Korea, landing was made less than a year later. In his statement, ONB specifically said "large-scale" amphibious operations against an enemy armed with atomic bombs. Inchon was a small-scale landing against North Korean forces armed with conventional weapons. The two quotations here are from two separate parts of the speech. In the first, when ONB was discussing the possible course of a future all-out war, he said: "I also believe that after the initial phases are over, there will be little need for any campaign similar to the Pacific 'island-hopping' that took place during the last war, and as I will develop later on in my discussion, I also predict that large-scale amphibious operations, such as those in Sicily and Normandy, will never occur again." Later, returning to the subject, he said: "Undoubtedly, without Navy support, any amphibious operation is impossible. However, by appraising the power of the atomic bomb, I am wondering whether we shall ever have another large-scale amphibious operation. Frankly, the atomic bomb, properly delivered, almost precludes such a possibility. I know that I, personally, hope that I shall never be called upon to participate in another amphibious operation like the one in Normandy."
7. *New York Times,* 10-20-49, articles by William S. White, p. 1, and Hanson W. Baldwin, p. 6.
8. *New York Times,* 10-21-49, Hanson W. Baldwin, p. 5.
9. *New York Times* editorial, 10-21-49; Johnson testimony, *New York Times,* 10-22-49; letter DDE-ONB, 10-26-49, Bradley file, Eisenhower Library. Ike's letter in full:

> Dear Brad:
>
> Within a day or two after returning from Washington last week, I began to see a few barbed comments in the gossip columns speculating on your possible future usefulness at the head of the Defense Establishment because of your use of terms that were considered "belittling." I know that you are too level-headed to let such statements bother you. If you are going to do anything constructive someone is going to attack you; I do hope you will never let such inconsequential things worry you. Of course, at the time I testified, we had heard nothing but the most glowing comments concerning your statement. It did not occur to me at the moment that anything further needed to be said on that side and, frankly, it had escaped me that the term "fancy dan" might be whipped up into one of very violent derogatory meaning. Otherwise I might have thought of something helpful.
>
> In any event, your standing is too high, your place in public opinion too secure to be materially damaged by any carping criticism. This morning I was talking to Kenneth Royall and he stated in most emphatic terms what is the general consensus as I have found it ever since I left the Pentagon—"Bradley has more sense than all the rest of them combined. If anyone can make a success of unification he is the one to do it."
>
> The other night at a rather large dinner this opinion was not only unanimously expressed, but Helen Reid—publisher of the New York Herald Tribune—was even more emphatic. . . .
>
> Best of Luck.
>
> P.S. Don't defend yourself—
> Don't explain
> Don't worry!!

10. Hanson-ONB int.; CB-ONB int.; *Current Biography 1948*. Collins, *War in Peacetime*, op. cit., p. 38.
11. On the Soviet nuclear explosion and the aftermath, here and below, see: Condit, *History of the JCS*, pp. 515–48; Rosenberg, "American Atomic Strategy," op. cit.; Strauss, Lewis L., *Men and Decisions*, Garden City, N.Y., 1962; Truman, Margaret, *Harry S. Truman;* Acheson, *Present at the Creation;* Shepley, James R., and Clay Blair, Jr., *The Hydrogen Bomb*, N.Y., 1954.
12. The JCS position on the H-bomb is in *Foreign Relations of the United States, 1949*, vol. 1, pp. 595–96. For additional JCS views, see Rosenberg, "American Atomic Strategy."
13. Joint Atomic Committee: ONB desk calendar, 10-14-49; ONB and AEC: Hillman-Heller int.
14. The breaking of Soviet codes in the mid to late 1940s is described in *Newsweek*, 5-19-80, in an article based on two sources: a book, *Wilderness of Mirrors*, by *Newsweek* correspondent David C. Martin (Harper & Row, 1980) and an unpublished manuscript by Robert Lamphere, a onetime FBI counterespionage agent. See also: Hyde, H. Montgomery, *The Atom Bomb Spies*, N.Y., 1980.
15. Hanson-ONB int. Within the context of codebreaking, ONB told Hanson the United States had "hard evidence" that the Rosenbergs were guilty but "we couldn't use the information at the time."
16. ONB visits, 1-5, 1-10, 1-23-50, HST calendar, Truman Library; *Harry S. Truman*, pp. 416–19. See also Rosenberg, "American Atomic Strategy."
17. On China, here and below, the literature is vast. Condit, "History of the JCS," vol. II, pp. 429–72 has an excellent summary account from the JCS point of view.
18. The text of NSC-68 is in Etzold and Gaddis, pp. 383–442; see analysis, pp. 383–85.
19. See for example the bizarre story related by Dean Acheson in *Present at the Creation*, pp. 373–74.

PART FIVE: THE KOREAN WAR

Chapter Fifty-Three

1. Eisenhower papers IX, chronology; letters ONB to MacArthur, 8-16-49 and MacArthur to ONB, 9-3-49, RG-5, SCAP, Bradley file, MacArthur Archives; Collins, *Lightning Joe*, p. 348.
2. ONB desk calendar, 1-29 to 2-10-50; Hanson-ONB int.; CB-ONB int.
3. ONB views on MacArthur: Hanson-ONB int.; CB-ONB int.; MacArthur's birthday: James, *Years of MacArthur*, p. 24 (date of birth: January 26, 1880).
4. Almond: *Current Biography 1951;* professional appraisal: Eisenhower papers IX, p. 2252.
5. Walker: *Register of Graduates;* Eisenhower papers IX, p. 2226; Kean: *Register of Graduates;* Appleman, Roy E., *South to the Naktong, North to the Yalu*, Washington, D.C., OCMH, 1969, p. 108; Allen: Appleman, p. 177n.; U.S. Army Forces, Japan: Appleman, pp. 49–50.
6. Condit, Kenneth, "History of the JCS," vol. II, pp. 290, 294; Etzold and Gaddis, *Containment* (Offtackle text), p. 330.
7. "History of the JCS," vol. II, pp. 485–501; Acheson, *Present at the Creation*, pp. 426–35; McLellan, David S., *Dean Acheson: The State Department Years*, N.Y., 1976, pp. 265–70. JCS views on secretly rearming Japan: *Foreign Relations of the U.S., 1949*, vol. VII, pp. 671–73, 884–87, 922–29. ONB-MacArthur exchange over High Commissioner for Japan: letters, ONB-MacArthur, 6-3-49, MacArthur-ONB, 9-16-49, RG-5, SCAP, Bradley file, MacArthur Archives.
8. Schnabel and Watson, unpublished "History of the Joint Chiefs of Staff," vol. III, pp. 42–3 (in two parts; hereafter Schnabel and Watson I or II), NA; *South to Naktong*, pp. 12–8.
9. Schnabel and Watson I, p. 32; *Foreign Relations of U.S. 1949*, vol. IX, pp. 460–67. The MacArthur 5-29-49 memorandum on Formosa is alluded to in a 6-14-49 memorandum on Formosa in NA, RG 218, Records of the JCS, box chairman's file, folder CJCS 091, China 1950.
10. Schnabel and Watson I, pp. 33–4; *Foreign Relations of U.S. 1949*, vol. IX, pp. 461–67; *Present at the Creation*, pp. 349–52.
11. *Foreign Relations of the U.S. 1949*, vol. IX, pp. 463–67; Schnabel and Watson I, p. 34; *Present at the Creation*, pp. 355, 360.
12. G. Ward Price in *The New York Times*, 3-2-49; Schnabel and Watson I, pp. 37–8; *Present at the Creation*, pp. 357–58.
13. JCS position on Indochina in undated JCS "Enclosure Study," titled "Review of Current World Situation," Truman papers, President's secretary file, Truman Library. This document was probably drawn as background for NSC-68 and submitted to the NSC about mid-February 1950. For JCS

recommendation of aid to Indochina, 12-22-49, see brief mention in *Foreign Relations 1949,* vol. IX, p. 461.

14. ONB desk calendar; CB-ONB int.
15. ONB desk calendar, 6-11 to 6-24-50. *Pathfinder* magazine, 7-26-50, wrote that ONB's "stomach upset" was "caused by a piece of Boston cream pie he had eaten in Alaska." Liebling, A. J., "Five Star Schoolmaster," *The New Yorker,* two-part profile on ONB, 3-3 and 3-10-51. Liebling wrote that it was a "nasty touch of dysentery from eating lemon meringue pie in Anchorage, Alaska."
16. "Memo for the Record," 4-17-51, on a conference in Tokyo between Matthew B. Ridgway and John Foster Dulles in which Dulles sketched in the background of key steps in formulating the Japanese peace treaty, Ridgway papers, USAMHI.
17. Roberts: *Register of Graduates;* his views on ROK Army, *South to the Naktong,* pp. 18, 20–1; Hanson-ONB int.; place and date of ONB-Roberts meeting, ONB desk calendar, 6-20-50.
18. MacArthur, 6-14-49 memo on Formosa: NA, RG 218 (see note 9 above).
19. ONB desk calendar, 6-24-50.

Chapter Fifty-Four

1. ONB desk calendar, 6-25-50.
2. Text of all three documents in NA, RG 218, Records of the U.S. JCS, chairman's file, folder CJCS 091, China, 1950. Text of MacArthur memo also in *Foreign Relations of the U.S., 1950, Korea,* vol. VII, pp. 161–65.
3. ONB desk calendar, 6-25-50. The events and decisions of the first week of the Korean War here and below are based largely on the following sources: *Foreign Relations of the U.S., 1950,* pp. 125–270; Schnabel and Watson I ("History of the JCS"), pp. 57–130; Schnabel, James F., *Policy and Direction: The First Year,* OCMH, Washington, D.C., 1972, pp. 61–79; Appleman, *South to the Naktong,* pp. 1–48; Truman memoirs II, pp. 331–43; Collins, *War in Peacetime,* pp. 1–24; Acheson, *Present at the Creation,* pp. 402–13; Paige, Glenn D., *The Korean Decision,* N.Y., 1968, pp. 79–270; Haynes, Richard F., *The Awesome Power: Harry S. Truman as Commander in Chief,* Baton Rouge, 1973, pp. 154–83; Smith, Beverly, "The White House Story: Why We Went to War in Korea," *Saturday Evening Post,* November 10, 1951, p. 22 (an extraordinary piece of journalism, composed with White House and State Department assistance, therefore considered "authoritative"); Hillman-Heller int., Truman Library; Hanson-ONB int.; CB-ONB int. (There is no indication in these sources that ONB was ill from June 25 to June 30.)

   A valuable document on the Korean War from the JCS point of view is a 107-page summary, "Record of the Actions Taken by the Joint Chiefs of Staff Relative to the United Nations Operations in Korea from 25 June to 11 April 1951, Prepared by Them." This document, dated April 30, 1951, and originally classified secret, was drawn up by the JCS for distribution to members of the Senate Armed Forces and Foreign Relations committees as background for the so-called MacArthur Hearings in May 1951. It contains paraphrases of all important messages to and from MacArthur and the JCS from the outbreak of the war to MacArthur's relief, as well as brief summaries of some important meetings between the JCS and State and Defense representatives. We have used this document more or less as a guidebook and will not cite it hereinafter. The document may be found in NA, RG 218, CCS 01336, "Bulky Package" or "Misc. Correspondence, Bradley File."
4. On Truman firing Johnson: Ferrell, *Off the Record,* p. 192.
5. On Army-State meeting: *Korean Decision,* p. 109; recommended courses of action distilled from minutes of meeting, *Foreign Relations, 1950,* vol. VII, Korea, pp. 157–61.
6. Letter ONB-HST, 7-1-57, BP, WP; "had to do with aggression": *Korean Decision,* p. 298, cited in McLellan, *Dean Acheson,* p. 274; ONB quotes: *Foreign Relations, 1950,* vol. VII, Korea, p. 158.
7. *Korean Decision,* p 133; *Foreign Relations,* pp. 158–59.
8. ONB desk calendar, 6-26-50.
9. State Department representative Elbert G. Mathews, from ONB desk calendar; probably erroneously confused with H. Freeman Matthews or misspelled in *Foreign Relations* (p. 178), Truman memoirs (p. 337) and elsewhere. Recommendations distilled from minutes of meeting, *Foreign Relations,* pp. 178–84. See *Korean Decision,* pp. 162–79.
10. On use of U.S. troops and mobilization, *Foreign Relations,* p 183.
11. Telecon procedures described by Collins in *War in Peacetime,* p. 21.
12. ONB desk calendar, 6-27-50.
13. "Memo for Record" by Eisenhower's aide Robert L. Schulz, 6-29-50, Bradley file, Eisenhower Library; Ferrell, *Eisenhower Diaries,* pp. 175–77.
14. *South to the Naktong,* p. 43; *War in Peacetime,* pp. 17–8; Schnabel and Watson I, pp. 100–1.

15. *South to the Naktong,* pp. 46–7; Schnabel and Watson I, pp. 108–9.
16. *War in Peacetime,* pp. 20–4; *South to the Naktong,* pp. 46–8; Schnabel and Watson I, pp. 110–22.
17. *War in Peacetime,* pp. 20–3; *South to the Naktong,* p. 47; Truman "up and shaved," *Off the Record,* p. 185. Collins-MacArthur telecon texts are in Collins and also *Foreign Relations,* pp. 250–53; latter also contains other JCS-MacArthur telecons through 6-30-50.
18. Sherman views on troops: Schnabel and Watson I, p. 117.
19. ONB desk calendar; *South to the Naktong,* p. 47; *War in Peacetime,* p. 23; Schnabel and Watson I, pp. 118–20.

Chapter Fifty-Five

1. Ferrell, *Off the Record,* p. 47.
2. ONB desk calendar, 7-5-50; visits to Leesburg: Truman, Margaret, *Harry S. Truman,* p. 404.
3. Analysis: ONB desk calendar, 1950; Truman desk calendar, Truman Library. HST-ONB relationship: Hillman-Heller int., 3-30-55, pp. 10–12. On replacing MacArthur: Truman memoirs, vol. 2, pp. 355–56.
4. Ferrell, *Eisenhower Diaries,* pp. 178–79.
5. The tactical situation in Korea: Appleman, *South to the Naktong,* pp. 36–487. Depletion of 7th Division: Ibid., p. 481. Casualties, 24th Division: Collins, *War in Peacetime,* p. 46. Performance of 24th Infantry: *War in Peacetime,* pp. 90–1; Collins, *Lightning Joe,* pp. 356–58.
6. *South to the Naktong,* pp. 206–8.
7. On Walker: Heller, Francis H., editor, *The Korean War: A 25-Year Perspective,* Lawrence, Kansas, 1977, pp. 34–5; Flint, Roy K., "The Tragic Flaw: MacArthur, the Joint Chiefs, and the Korean War," Duke University Ph.D. dissertation, 1976, University Microfilms International, Ann Arbor, Michigan, pp. 198–99. In a "Memo for the Record," 8-15-50, Ridgway wrote that on return to Washington he met separately with Collins and Pace and told them of his "concern over General Walker's leadership, lack of force, acceptance of a mediocre staff, and an unsound base organization." Pace, Ridgway wrote, "indicated clearly his own conviction that a change ought to be made as early as possible." Pace, Ridgway recalled, suggested Ridgway or Gruenther as Walker's replacement (Ridgway papers, USAMHI).
8. Buildup: *South to the Naktong,* pp. 257–58, 264; Schnabel and Watson I ("History of the JCS"), pp. 199–200.
9. *South to the Naktong,* pp. 488–99; Schnabel and Watson I, pp. 201–2; *War in Peacetime,* pp. 114–16; Schnabel, *Policy and Direction,* pp. 139–54.
10. *War in Peacetime,* pp. 120–21; Schnabel and Watson I, p. 202.
11. Ibid., p. 116.
12. For a discussion on this point, see "The Tragic Flaw," p. 233.
13. *War in Peacetime,* p. 117; Schnabel and Watson I, p. 193.
14. Ibid., p. 204.
15. Ibid., pp. 196–98. For a detailed discussion on the problems and the debate over airborne regiment, see "Tragic Flaw," pp. 219–21.
16. Text of Ridgway memo in *Foreign Relations, 1950,* vol. VII, pp. 540–41.
17. Harriman quoted in Heller, pp. 26–7.
18. Schnabel and Watson I, pp. 206–7.
19. *War in Peacetime,* pp. 98–9; Schnabel and Watson I, pp. 188–89.
20. Ibid., pp. 207–11; *War in Peacetime,* pp. 121–29.
21. Schnabel and Watson I, p. 211; Truman memoirs II, p. 358.
22. Schnabel and Watson I, pp. 211–12; JCS-CINCFE, 89960, 8-29-50, MacArthur Archives.
23. Schnabel and Watson I, pp. 508–9.
24. Ibid., p. 509.
25. JCS-CINCFE 87401, 7-29-50, MacArthur Archives.
26. Schnabel and Watson I, pp. 507, 510; JCS-CINCFE 87492, 7-30-50, MacArthur Archives.
27. Schnabel and Watson I, p. 511; the familiarization flights described by MacArthur after visit to Formosa in CINCFE-DA C59569, 8-7-50, MacArthur Archives.
28. Schnabel and Watson I, p. 511; Acheson, *Present at the Creation,* p. 422.
29. What MacArthur committed to on Formosa is fully described in CINCFE to DA, 8-7-50; Schnabel and Watson I, pp. 512–13.
30. Harriman memo on talk with MacArthur printed in full in Truman memoirs II, pp. 350–52.
31. Schnabel and Watson I, p. 514; Truman memoirs II, p. 354.
32. Schnabel and Watson I, pp. 514–17.
33. ONB desk calendar, 8-26-50; *Present at the Creation,* p. 423.
34. Ibid., pp. 423–4; Truman memoirs II, p. 356.
35. Truman memoirs II, pp. 355–56; CB-ONB int.
36. Johnson conniving: *Present at the Creation,* p. 441; *Off the Record,* pp. 192–93; *Harry S. Truman,* p. 479.
37. On Smith: *Current Biography 1953;* letters Bedell Smith to Ike, 9-7-50, to asst. sec. of state John D. Hickerson, 8-23-50, both in Smith papers, Eisenhower Library.
38. ONB desk calendar, 9-18 and 9-22-50; HST

to Mary Bradley, 9-18-50 (enclosing pen), "President's Personal File," Truman Library; White House ceremony: *The New York Times,* 9-23-50.

39. ONB salary: Liebling, "Five Star Schoolmaster"; Ike to ONB telegram, 9-22-50, Eisenhower papers, Bradley file, Eisenhower Library.

Chapter Fifty-Six

1. Appleman, *South to the Naktong,* pp. 490–91.
2. Ibid., pp. 491–92.
3. JCS-CINCFE 90639, 9-5-50, MacArthur Archives; Schnabel, *Policy and Direction: The First Year,* pp. 152–53.
4. *South to the Naktong,* pp. 496–97.
5. Schnabel and Watson I ("History of the JCS"), p. 213.
6. MacArthur, Douglas, *Reminiscences,* N.Y., McGraw-Hill, 1964, p. 399 (Crest Book edition).
7. Schnabel and Watson I, pp. 213–14; *Reminiscences,* pp. 399–400.
8. Whitney, Courtney, *MacArthur: His Rendezvous With History,* N.Y., 1956, p. 358.
9. Schnabel and Watson I, p. 215; ONB desk calendar, 9-14-50.
10. ONB desk calendar, 9-8-50; Schnabel and Watson I, p. 214; Collins, *War in Peacetime,* p. 129.
11. Schnabel and Watson I, p. 217; ONB desk calendar, 9-20 and 9-21-50; speech briefly quoted in *The New York Times,* 9-21-50.
12. *South to the Naktong,* pp. 488–606.
13. Schnabel and Watson I, pp. 220 and n. 5.
14. Condensed from ONB's opening statement to the "MacArthur Hearings," May 1951, excerpted in Bernstein and Matusow, *The Truman Administration,* pp. 476–81. For additional views, see "The Collected Writings of ONB," vol. II, pp. 113–62 (general speeches in 1951).
15. Acheson, *Present at the Creation,* p. 451; the policy planning staff paper is in *Foreign Relations, 1950, Korea,* vol. VII, pp. 449–54.
16. *Present at the Creation,* pp. 445–46, 451.
17. *War in Peacetime,* p. 144. For a complete exposition of the military view, see DOD memo, 7-31-50, "U.S. Courses of Action in Korea," *Foreign Relations,* pp. 502–10.
18. Text of NSC-81, *Foreign Relations,* pp. 685–93; *War in Peacetime,* p. 144.
19. *Foreign Relations,* pp. 705–8; *War in Peacetime,* pp. 145–46.
20. *Foreign Relations,* pp. 706, 712n.; complete text of NSC-81/1, pp. 712–21; Truman memoirs II, pp. 358–59.
21. *Present,* pp. 454–55; text of the resolution, *Foreign Relations,* pp. 826–28.
22. *South to the Naktong,* pp. 752–59; *Policy and Direction,* pp. 196–99; *War in Peacetime,* p. 173.
23. Schnabel and Watson I, pp. 257–58; see also Flint, "The Tragic Flaw," pp. 259–60.
24. Schnabel and Watson I, p. 257; *Policy and Direction,* pp. 198–200.
25. Schnabel and Watson I, p. 259; Flint, p. 261.
26. *Policy,* pp. 181–82; complete text of JCS orders to MacArthur, *Foreign Relations,* pp. 781–82, 785.
27. ONB quote from Schnabel and Watson I, p. 263.
28. CINCFE to DA (JCS), 9-28-50, MacArthur Archives.
29. Message as sent, NA, RG 218, JCS records, chairman's file, 380.01, 1950.
30. Schnabel and Watson I, p. 243.
31. Ibid., p. 243.
32. MacArthur's plan is described in *South to the Naktong,* pp. 609–12; *Policy,* pp. 187–92. For an astute critique, see Flint, pp. 303–34. *War in Peacetime,* p. 158. Collins writes that the JCS, "perhaps somewhat awed by the success of Inchon," quickly approved the plan. His criticism of it is mild, limited here to one paragraph on logistical problems. But see also pp. 160–61. He and Bradley were "skeptical about the command arrangements." He also notes opposition to the plan in the Eighth Army.

Chapter Fifty-Seven

1. Appleman, *South to the Naktong,* pp. 615–19, 622–23.
2. Schnabel and Watson I ("History of JCS"), p. 260; *Foreign Relations, 1950, Korea,* vol. VII, pp. 793–94, 839, 850.
3. *Foreign Relations,* p. 849.
4. Schnabel and Watson I, p. 261; full text of the October 12 CIA estimate on Chinese intervention, *Foreign Relations,* pp. 933–34; full text of October 12 CIA estimates on Soviet intervention, ibid., pp. 935–36. (These documents were evidently prepared for Truman-MacArthur Wake Island meeting.)
5. Schnabel and Watson I, pp. 283–84.
6. *Foreign Relations,* pp. 911, 912, 915; Truman memoirs II, p. 362.
7. *Foreign Relations,* pp. 913–14, 931.
8. Schnabel and Watson I, p. 233; *South to the Naktong,* p. 687.
9. Truman memoirs II, pp. 362–63; Whitney, *MacArthur,* pp. 384–85.
10. Acheson, *Present at the Creation,* p. 456; *Foreign Relations,* pp. 915–16.
11. Schnabel and Watson I, p. 264.
12. Truman memoirs II, pp. 363–64; ONB desk calendar, 10-12, 10-13-50; Ferrell, *Off the Record,* p. 196.

13. ONB desk calendar, 10-13-50.
14. *The New York Times,* 10-15-50; Miller, *Plain Speaking,* p. 293.
15. *MacArthur,* pp. 384–86; Harriman recollections in Heller, *The Korean War,* pp. 31–2.
16. *The Korean War,* p. 32; *The New York Times,* 10-15-50.
17. *The New York Times,* 10-15-50; *MacArthur,* p. 387; MacArthur, *Reminiscences,* pp. 410, 412–13; Truman memoirs II, pp. 364–65.
18. ONB desk calendar, 10-14-50; who took notes, etc., explained by ONB in letter to Senator Richard Russell, 5-2-51, chairman's file, NA.
19. ONB transcript of Wake Island conference, chairman's file, NA; also in *Foreign Relations,* pp. 948–61.
20. ONB desk calendar, 10-14-50; Rusk in *Foreign Relations,* pp. 961–62.
21. *The New York Times,* 10-15, 10-16-50; Truman memoirs II, p. 367.
22. *The New York Times,* 10-16-50; ONB desk calendar, 10-15-50.
23. ONB desk calendar, 10-16, 10-17-50; Truman memoirs II, pp. 367–70; *The New York Times,* 10-18-50.
24. ONB desk calendar, 10-18-50; on NATO problems 1950, see Truman memoirs II, pp. 256–57; Poole, "History of the JCS," vol. IV, pp. 180–220.
25. *The New York Times,* 12-20-50. See Montgomery, *Memoirs,* pp. 460–61, re his assignment as deputy supreme commander.
26. Schnabel, *Policy and Direction,* pp. 215–16.
27. Ibid., pp. 205–8; Collins, *War in Peacetime,* pp. 178–79; Flint, p. 335.
28. Schnabel and Watson I, p. 274; *Policy,* p. 218; *South to the Naktong,* pp. 670–71; *War in Peacetime,* p. 180.
29. Schnabel and Watson I, p. 275; *Present at the Creation,* p. 462.
30. CINCFE to DA C67397, 10-25-50, MacArthur Archives.
31. Collins quoted in Schnabel and Watson I, p. 276.
32. Schnabel and Watson I, p. 278.
33. Ibid., p. 277; *Policy,* p. 219.
34. *Policy,* pp. 233–34.
35. *War in Peacetime,* pp. 183–84, 189.

Chapter Fifty-Eight

1. ONB desk calendar, 11-1 to 12-31-50.
2. Acheson, *Present at the Creation,* pp. 466–68.
3. "National Intelligence Estimate No. 2," 11-8-50, *Foreign Relations, 1950, Korea,* vol. VII, pp. 1101–6. See also draft memorandum, "Chinese Intervention in Korea," by John P. Davies of State policy planning staff, 11-7-50, *Foreign Relations,* pp. 1078–85; JCS to Marshall, 11-9-50, "Chinese Communist Intervention in Korea," Ibid., pp. 1117–21.
4. Willoughby estimate in Schnabel, *Policy and Direction,* pp. 239–40.
5. DEPTAR to CINCFE 95790, 11-3-50, and CINCFE to DEPTAR 68285, 11-4-50, MacArthur Archives. See also Schnabel and Watson I, pp. 289–90.
6. ONB desk calendar, 11-2 to 11-6-50.
7. *Policy,* pp. 241–42.
8. *Policy,* pp. 241–42; Schnabel and Watson I, pp. 290–92; memos by Lovett and Acheson, *Foreign Relations,* pp. 1055–57.
9. CINCUNC to JCS C-68396, 11-6-50, MacArthur Archives; text in *Foreign Relations,* p. 1058; Schnabel and Watson I, pp. 293–94.
10. ONB desk calendar, 11-6-50; Schnabel and Watson I, p. 295n.
11. Summary and partial text in *Foreign Relations,* p. 1051n.
12. Truman memoirs II, pp. 375–76.
13. JCS to CINCFE 95949, 11-6-50, MacArthur Archives; Schnabel and Watson I ("History of the JCS"), pp. 294–95.
14. Ike was one who thought Marshall wanted to quit. See Ferrell, *Eisenhower Diaries,* p. 181. Comment from Pogue in letter to CB, 8-19-82.
15. Schnabel and Watson I, p. 295n. on "consensus"; ONB desk calendar, 11-6-50, on breakup of meeting.
16. ONB desk calendar, 11-7-50; CINCFE to DA C68411, 11-7-50, MacArthur Archives.
17. *Policy,* pp. 249–50; Schnabel and Watson I, p. 299.
18. CINCUNC to DEPTAR "FLASH" C-68465, 11-7-50, MacArthur Archives; full text, *Foreign Relations,* pp. 1076–77.
19. *Policy,* p. 235.
20. Schnabel and Watson I, p. 299.
21. Ibid., pp. 296–97.
22. JCS to CINCFE 96060, 11-8-50, MacArthur Archives; Schnabel and Watson I, p. 301.
23. CINCFE to DA C68572, 11-9-50, MacArthur Archives; full text, *Foreign Relations,* pp. 1107–10.
24. ONB desk calendar, 11-9-50; Schnabel and Watson I, pp. 304–7; Truman memoirs II, pp. 378–80.
25. JCS papers in *Foreign Relations,* pp. 1120–21.
26. Truman memoirs II, pp. 378–80. (NSC minutes not published yet.)
27. NSC "Interim Report" on 11-9-50 meeting, *Foreign Relations,* p. 1150; *War in Peacetime,* p. 208.
28. Schnabel and Watson I, pp. 313, 315–16; *Policy,* pp. 249–50; *War in Peacetime,* p. 203.

Chapter Fifty-Nine

1. Schnabel and Watson I ("History of the JCS"), p. 298; *Foreign Relations, 1950, Korea,* vol. VII, p. 1149n.2.
2. *Foreign Relations,* p. 1175.
3. Schnabel, *Policy and Direction,* p. 275; Collins, *War in Peacetime,* pp. 218–19.
4. ONB desk calendar, 11-21-50; *Foreign Relations,* pp. 1204–8; Acheson, *Present at the Creation,* p. 467; *War in Peacetime,* pp. 210–11.
5. DEPTAR to CINCUNC 97287, 11-24-50, and CINCUNC to JCS C69808, 11-25-50, both in MacArthur Archives; *Foreign Relations,* pp. 1222–24, 1231–33; Schnabel and Watson I, pp. 326–29.
6. Schnabel and Watson I, p. 333; Whitney, *MacArthur,* p. 416.
7. MacArthur, *Reminiscences,* p. 433.
8. *Policy,* pp. 274–75; Schnabel and Watson I, pp. 334–35.
9. Schnabel and Watson I, p. 337; ONB desk calendar, 11-27-50.
10. CINCFE to DA "FLASH" C69953, 11-28-50; Schnabel and Watson I, p. 337.
11. Truman memoirs II, p. 385.
12. ONB desk calendar, 11-28-50; *Foreign Relations,* pp. 1242–49; Schnabel and Watson I, pp. 338–42.
13. ONB desk calendar, 11-29-50; Schnabel and Watson I, pp. 342–43; *Foreign Relations,* p. 1253.
14. Memo, GCM to ONB, 11-29-50, chairman's file, NA; Schnabel and Watson I, p. 343.
15. CINCUNC to DEPTAR C50095, 11-30-50, MacArthur Archives; *Foreign Relations,* pp. 1259–60; Schnabel and Watson I, pp. 345, 345n., 346.
16. CINCUNC to DEPTAR C50107, 11-30-50, MacArthur Archives; Schnabel and Watson I, pp. 346–47.
17. JCS to CINCFE 97772, 11-30-50, MacArthur Archives; Schnabel and Watson I, pp. 346–47.
18. CINCUNC to DEPTAR C50021, 11-19-50, MacArthur Archives; Schnabel and Watson I, pp. 343–44.
19. Schnabel and Watson I, pp. 347–48.
20. JCS to CINCFE 97594, 11-29-50, MacArthur Archives; Schnabel and Watson I, p. 344.
21. Ibid., p. 521; *Present at the Creation,* pp. 471–72.
22. Truman memoirs II, p. 384.
23. Truman, Margaret, *Harry S. Truman,* p. 493.
24. JCS to all Theater Commanders 98134, 12-6-50, Truman papers, secretary file, Truman Library; CINCUNC to DEPTAR C50736, 12-8-50, Ridgway papers, USAMHF; JCS to CINCFE 98410, 12-9-50, MacArthur Archives; Schnabel and Watson I, pp. 522–23.
25. Schnabel and Watson I, p. 350.
26. Ridgway, Matthew B., *The Korean War,* N.Y., 1967, p. 73.
27. CINCUNC to DEPTAR C50332, 12-3-50, MacArthur Archives; Schnabel and Watson I, pp. 356–58.
28. *Korean War,* pp. 72–3.
29. *Foreign Relations,* pp. 1345–46; *Present at the Creation,* p. 476.
30. *Korean War,* pp. 61, 74.
31. *Korean War,* pp. 61–2; re Davis and Sherman reaction: "Memo for Record," 12-8-50, Ridgway papers, USAMHI.
32. ONB desk calendar, 12-1 to 12-3-50; *Foreign Relations,* pp. 1310–13; *Korean War,* p. 61.
33. ONB desk calendar, 12-3-50; JCS to CINCFE 97917, 12-3-50, MacArthur Archives; *Foreign Relations,* pp. 1333, 1336–39; Schnabel and Watson I, p. 361.
34. Minutes 12-3-50 meeting in *Foreign Relations,* pp. 1323–34.
35. *Harry S. Truman,* pp. 495–97.
36. *Foreign Relations,* p. 1324; *Harry S. Truman,* p. 498; Schnabel and Watson I, pp. 372–73.
37. *Present at the Creation,* pp. 478–85; Schnabel and Watson I, p. 350; ONB desk calendar, 12-4 to 12-8-50.
38. *Foreign Relations,* p. 1278; *War in Peacetime,* pp. 229–33; "Memo for Record," 12-8-50, Ridgway papers, USAMHI; Schnabel and Watson I, pp. 366–69.
39. JCS to CINCFE 98400, 12-8-50, MacArthur Archives; *War in Peacetime,* p. 235; *Policy,* pp. 300–6; Schnabel and Watson I, pp. 386–87.
40. *Policy,* p. 305; *War in Peacetime,* p. 236.
41. *War in Peacetime,* pp. 236–37; *Korean War,* pp. 79–81; *MacArthur,* p. 432.

Chapter Sixty

1. Poole, "History of the JCS," vol. IV, p. 79.
2. Schnabel and Watson I ("History of the JCS"), p. 364.
3. Poole, pp. 82–3.
4. *Foreign Relations, 1950, Korea,* vol. VII, p. 1548; Poole, pp. 72–3.
5. Ibid., p. 171.
6. Truman memoirs II, pp. 400–2.
7. Ibid., pp. 396–413; Acheson, *Present at the Creation,* pp. 402–5.
8. Schnabel and Watson I, pp. 379–84.
9. Ibid., p. 385.
10. *Foreign Relations,* pp. 1570–76.
11. CINCUNC to JCS C51559, 12-18-50, Schnabel and Watson I, p. 389; *Foreign Relations,* p. 1588; *Foreign Relations, Asia*

and the Pacific, 1951, vol. VI, part 1 (hereafter *For. Rel. 1951*), pp. 780–81.
12. *Foreign Relations, 1950,* p. 1589; JCS to CINCFE 99616, 12-23-50, MacArthur Archives.
13. *Foreign Relations, 1950,* pp. 1572–73.
14. Ibid., p. 1573.
15. Ibid., pp. 1574–76, 1588–90.
16. Schnabel and Watson I, pp. 394–97, 406; Ridgway, *Soldier,* pp. 208–9; JCS to MacArthur (personal) 99935, 12-29-50, MacArthur Archives.
17. MacArthur, *Reminiscences,* p. 430; Whitney, *MacArthur,* p. 431.
18. Truman memoirs II, pp. 415–16.
19. *MacArthur,* pp. 432–33; *Soldier,* pp. 208–9.
20. CINCUNC to JCS C52391, 12-30-50, in *Foreign Relations, 1950,* pp. 1630–33. See also Schnabel and Watson I, pp. 399–402, and *MacArthur,* pp. 432–34; Collins, *War in Peacetime,* p. 247.
21. Schnabel, *Policy and Direction,* pp. 308–10; *War in Peacetime,* pp. 243–46; *Soldier,* pp. 211–15. McClure: *Army Almanac,* 1959 edition.
22. Schnabel and Watson I, p. 407; *War in Peacetime,* p. 252.
23. JCS to MacArthur (personal) 80680, 1-9-51, MacArthur Archives; Schnabel and Watson I, pp. 408–10.
24. *MacArthur,* p. 435.
25. CINCUNC to DEPTAR (personal for JCS) C53167, 1-10-51, MacArthur Archives; Schnabel and Watson I, pp. 410–11.
26. *Present at the Creation,* p. 515; Truman memoirs II, p. 434.
27. Schnabel and Watson I, p. 415; *Present at the Creation,* p. 515; Sherman and Marshall quotes: testimony in U.S. Congress, Senate Committees on Armed Services and Foreign Relations, *Hearings to Conduct an Inquiry into the Military Situation in the Far East and the Facts Surrounding the Relief of General of the Army Douglas MacArthur from His Assignments in That Area,* 82nd Congress, 1st Session, 1951, part 1, p. 329, part 2, p. 1601 (hereafter, MacArthur Hearings).
28. Schnabel and Watson I, pp. 415–16; see also MacArthur Hearings, part 2, p. 907 for paraphrase.
29. *War in Peacetime,* pp. 252–53; MacArthur Hearings, part 2, p. 907; *Present at the Creation,* p. 516. Full text of President's letter in Truman memoirs II, pp. 435–36.
30. *War in Peacetime,* p. 252; MacArthur Hearings, part 2, pp. 1227–28; *MacArthur,* p. 439.
31. *MacArthur,* pp. 438–39.
32. Schnabel and Watson I, pp. 416–19, has fullest account of the "famous" January 12 study. For other comments, see MacArthur Hearings, part 1, pp. 334–36 (Marshall), and part 2, p. 738 (Bradley). Bradley testified: "Well, Mr. Chairman, to us it was . . . perfectly apparent that it was a study and was never handled as a proposed directive."
33. *War in Peacetime,* p. 253.
34. Schnabel and Watson I, p. 437; *War in Peacetime,* pp. 253–54 (full text of message).
35. ONB desk calendar, 1-17-51; Schnabel and Watson I, pp. 436–38; *War in Peacetime,* p. 255.
36. ONB desk calendar, 1-18, 1-19-51; Schnabel and Watson I, pp. 438–39.
37. Collins on Ridgway: *War in Peacetime,* p. 255.

Chapter Sixty-One

1. Collins, *War in Peacetime,* pp. 257–61; Schnabel, *Policy and Direction,* pp. 333–40.
2. Ridgway, *Korean War,* pp. 108–9.
3. *War in Peacetime,* p. 262; *Korean War,* pp. 109–10, 111–16.
4. *War in Peacetime,* pp. 263–67; *Policy,* pp. 351–54.
5. Ibid., p. 357.
6. JCS to CINCFE 86276, 3-20-51, MacArthur Archives; Schnabel and Watson I ("History of JCS"), p. 525; Truman memoirs II, p. 438. (Text of Truman's *proposed* statement in memoirs II, pp. 439–40.)
7. CINCUNC to DA C58203, 3-21-51, in Schnabel and Watson I, p. 526.
8. Ibid., p. 526.
9. Full text of MacArthur "communiqué" in Truman memoirs II, pp. 440–41; *The New York Times,* 3-25-51; and MacArthur, *Reminiscences,* pp. 441–42. For ONB reaction to the communiqué—he deplored it—see testimony, MacArthur Hearings, part 2, pp. 1030–31.
10. Acheson, *Present at the Creation,* p. 519.
11. Truman memoirs II, pp. 443–44.
12. JCS to CINCFE (personal for MacArthur) 86736, 3-25-51, MacArthur Archives; edited text also in Truman memoirs II, p. 443.
13. Text of Martin letter and MacArthur reply in *Reminiscences,* pp. 439–40; text of MacArthur letter also in *Congressional Record,* 4-5-51, copy in Truman papers, secretary file, Truman Library.
14. AP story from Truman papers, secretary file, Truman Library.
15. Details of the various meetings that ONB attended 4-5 to 4-19-51 re firing MacArthur derived from six sources: 1) desk calendar; 2) undated handwritten ONB memo, "Meetings that Led to Relief," in chair-

man's file, NA; 3) undated typed memo, "Chronology of General Bradley's Part in the Relief of General MacArthur," chairman's file, NA; 4) ONB top-secret memos for the record, 4-11, 4-18, and 4-24-51, BP, Carlisle; 5) testimony of Marshall, ONB, Collins, Vandenberg and Sherman at MacArthur Hearings; 6) Collins, *War in Peacetime,* pp. 282–87. On Haislip for Collins, see Sherman, MacArthur Hearings, part 2, pp. 1571–75.

16. On the new intelligence, see Schnabel and Watson I, pp. 485–87; *Korean War,* pp. 121–22; on JCS response: memo ONB to GCM, 4-5-51, and GCM to HST, 4-9-51, Truman papers, secretary file, Truman Library.
17. Schnabel and Watson I, pp. 485–86, 535; ONB desk calendar, 4-6-51.
18. Harriman from Heller, *The Korean War,* p. 235.
19. Truman memoirs II, p. 447; Harriman quote in Heller, *The Korean War,* p. 235; *Present at the Creation,* p. 521.
20. Truman memoirs II, p. 447; ONB's position on insubordination is unequivocally stated in MacArthur Hearings, part 2, pp. 1042–43: "I do not say that General MacArthur was insubordinate." He thought that MacArthur "embarrassed" the President. Marshall (MacArthur Hearings, part 1, p. 341) testified that MacArthur violated the President's directive of December 6. However, Marshall says (p. 416), "He did not violate the [U.S.] policy by military action but he took issue with the policy before the world." On Collins' trip: *War in Peacetime,* p. 282.
21. *Present at the Creation,* pp. 521–22.
22. Ferrell, *Off the Record,* p. 210.
23. Schnabel and Watson I, pp. 393, 539.
24. Truman memoirs II, p. 448.
25. Schnabel and Watson I, p. 539. In ONB handwritten notes (see note 15 above), ONB says, "Gen. M. and I drafted letter." No trace of this draft has been found; Pace oral history, p. 104, Truman Library.
26. *War in Peacetime,* p. 283, has a good account.
27. Typed memo ONB to Vandenberg, Collins, Sherman, 16 May 1951, chairman's file, NA. Attached are several interesting prior drafts. (Collins has essence of this memo in *War in Peacetime,* p. 284.) For elaboration of JCS views, see MacArthur Hearings, part 2, pp. 1391ff.; Collins, part 2, pp. 1187ff.; Sherman, part 2, pp. 1577ff.
28. *War in Peacetime,* p. 283; ONB handwritten memo, "Chiefs stated fr. mil. pt. view —relieved."
29. *Present at the Creation,* p. 522; *Off the Record,* p. 211.
30. Truman memoirs II, p. 448; *Present at the Creation,* p. 522; *War in Peacetime,* p. 284; Schnabel and Watson I, pp. 542–43.
31. Ibid., p. 543; *Present at the Creation,* pp. 522–23.
32. Interview, CB-Walter Trohan, 4-20-80; int., CB-Lloyd Norman, 4-6-80; Truman memoirs II, p. 449; Trohan, Walter, *Political Animals,* Garden City, N.Y., Doubleday, 1975, pp. 252–53. Text of Truman's letter of relief, etc., in Truman memoirs II, pp. 449–50.
33. Schnabel and Watson I, p. 546; Whitney, *MacArthur,* p. 471.
34. Pace oral history, p. 105, Truman Library.
35. *Korean War,* pp. 158–59; Ridgway, *Soldier,* p. 223; "Memo for Diary," 4-12-51, Ridgway papers, USAMHI.
36. Ryan, Halford R., "Harry S. Truman: A Misdirected Defense for MacArthur Dismissal," *Presidential Studies Quarterly,* vol. XI, no. 4, fall 1981.
37. *MacArthur,* pp. 481–82.
38. ONB desk calendar, 4-17-51; speech in "Collected Writings," vol. II, pp. 120–24; *The New York Times,* 4-18-51.
39. *Life,* 4-9, 4-16, 4-23, 4-30-51; pro-MacArthur editorial in *Life,* 4-30-51.
40. Memoranda: "Statement re Your Speech on April 17," and "Statement re Your Book," chairman's file, NA. See also Marshall testimony re ONB book, in response to Senator Hickenlooper's questions, MacArthur Hearings, part 1, pp. 514–15.
41. *MacArthur,* p. 483; *The New York Times,* 4-19-51.
42. ONB desk calendar, 4-19-51; complete text MacArthur address, *Reminiscences,* pp. 454–60; *The New York Times,* 4-20-51.
43. MacArthur Hearings, vol. 1, p. ii. The censored testimony and various related documents were published by the government in 1951 in five volumes totaling 3691 pages. In 1973, the censored material was declassified and made available at the National Archives. The whole of it constitutes an astonishingly rich catalogue of United States Far Eastern and Korean War policies.
44. CB analysis of testimony; see also *Present at the Creation,* p. 525.
45. For a detailed analysis of these hearings, see Schlesinger, Arthur M., Jr., and Roger Bruns, editors, *Congress Investigates: A Documented History 1792–1974,* vol. V, "The MacArthur Inquiry," by John Edward Wiltz, N.Y., Chelsea House, 1975. For a brief account of the JCS point of view, Schnabel and Watson I, pp. 546–58.
46. ONB testimony, MacArthur Hearings, part 2, p. 732.
47. See, for example, ONB testimony, MacArthur Hearings, p. 738ff.

48. MacArthur Hearings, part 2, pp. 763, 869–72; *Present at the Creation*, p. 526.
49. JCS to RIDGWAY, "eyes only," WST-211, 4-26-51; CINCFE to DEPTAR for JCS "eyes only," WST-242, 4-27-51; JCS to CINCFE "emergency," WST-218, 4-28-51. All in Ridgway papers, USAMHI.
50. *Policy and Direction*, p. 379; *War in Peacetime*, p. 296.
51. *Policy*, pp. 387–90; *War in Peacetime*, p. 297.
52. *Policy*, pp. 390–406; *War in Peacetime*, p. 305.

Chapter Sixty-Two

1. Ferrell, *Eisenhower Diaries*, p. 185; Eisenhower, Dwight D., *The White House Years: Mandate for Change: 1953–1956*, Garden City, N.Y., Doubleday, 1963 (hereafter *Mandate*), pp. 12–3; Eisenhower, *At Ease*, pp. 366–67; ONB desk calendar, 1-6, 1-31-51.
2. Acheson, *Present at the Creation*, pp. 488–90; Radosh, Ronald, *Prophets on the Right*, N.Y., 1975 (hereafter *Prophets*), pp. 176–77.
3. Ibid., pp. 177–79.
4. Ibid., pp. 169–70; Vandenberg death: *The New York Times*, 4-20-51.
5. *Present at the Creation*, pp. 491–94; *Prophets*, pp. 178, 183–86; Poole, "History of the JCS," vol. IV, pp. 221–24; Paterson, J. T., *Mr. Republican*, Boston, 1972, pp. 392–93, 434–39, 454–55, 476–93.
6. Poole, "History of the JCS," vol. IV, p. 222.
7. Eisenhower, *At Ease*, pp. 368–69; *Mandate*, p. 14; Taft-Ike: *Eisenhower Diaries*, p. 373.
8. Hanson-ONB int.
9. ONB desk calendar, 2-16-51; *Present at the Creation*, p. 495; ONB on Acheson: CB-ONB int.
10. *Present at the Creation*, pp. 496, 755; Poole, pp. 221–24.
11. Ibid., pp. 225–26; *Eisenhower Diaries*, p. 187.
12. DDE to ONB, 3-30-51, and ONB to DDE, 4-12-51, BP, WP, and Bradley file, Eisenhower papers, Eisenhower Library.
13. ONB desk calendar, 6-1 to 6-4-51; Sulzberger, C. L., *A Long Row of Candles*, N.Y., 1969, pp. 638–39.
14. ONB desk calendar, 6-6 to 6-10-51.
15. Ibid., 7-22, 7-25, 7-27-51.
16. On Fechteler: USNA *Register of Alumni*; *Current Biography 1951*.
17. On Matthews being eased out: *Present at the Creation*, p. 478; Kimball: *Current Biography 1951*.
18. ONB desk calendar, 7-31, 8-16-51.
19. ONB appraisal of Lovett: CB-ONB int.
20. CB analysis of ONB desk calendar, September 1951 to August 1953.
21. ONB desk calendar, 9-16 to 9-20-51.
22. Collins, *War in Peacetime*, pp. 309–11; Ridgway, *Korean War*, pp. 185–204.
23. Memo (top secret—restricted data) JCS to Lovett, 8-14-51, in "Pertinent Papers on the Korean Situation," vol. VIII, pp. 1310–14, Truman papers, Truman Library.
24. Poole, pp. 92–3; ONB to DDE, 9-7-51, Bradley File, Eisenhower Library, also, BP, WP.
25. Poole, pp. 94–105.
26. Ibid., p. 101.
27. Ibid., pp. 109–10.
28. Ibid., p. 112; *Eisenhower Diaries*, p. 212.
29. Poole, pp. 112–13.
30. Ibid., pp. 116–33 ("Forces in Being" charts for 6-30-50, 6-30-51, 6-30-52 and 12-31-52 on p. 133).
31. *Eisenhower Diaries*, p. 197.
32. Lodge, Henry Cabot, *The Storm Has Many Eyes*, N.Y., 1973 (hereafter *Storm*), pp. 43, 57–61.
33. Eisenhower, *Mandate*, pp. 16–21; *Storm*, pp. 77–99; Ferrell, *Eisenhower Diaries*, pp. 209, 224; Ferrell, *Off the Record*, pp. 177, 220.
34. ONB desk calendar, 11-13-51; CB-ONB int.
35. Bess, Demaree, "Are Generals in Politics a Menace?" *Saturday Evening Post*, 4-26-52; Lisbon: ONB desk calendar, 2-8 to 3-10-51; "ONB Collected Writings," vol. II, p. 167 (speech of 3-20-52). For additional accounts of Taft's attack on ONB and the JCS, see White, William S., *The Taft Story*, N.Y., 1954, pp. 248–50; Donovan, Robert J., *Eisenhower: The Inside Story*, N.Y., 1956, p. 109; and *The New York Times*, 8-14-53.
36. *Mandate*, pp. 22–3; Truman memoirs II, pp. 490–92; *Storm*, p. 102.
37. Montgomery, *Memoirs*, p. 462; *Mandate*, p. 24; Ridgway, *Korean War*, p. 211; Collins, *War in Peacetime*, p. 348. Clark, Mark W., *From the Danube to the Yalu*, N.Y., 1954, pp. 29–30.
38. *Mandate*, pp. 41–7; CB-ONB int.; *Storm*, pp. 111–26; Whitney, *MacArthur*, pp. 523–29.
39. Truman memoirs II, pp. 497–500, 501–2; *Present at the Creation*, pp. 689–93. On Jenner and McCarthy: Martin, John Bartlow, *Adlai Stevenson of Illinois*, N.Y., 1976, pp. 712–13; Hughes, Emmet John, *The Ordeal of Power*, N.Y., 1963, pp. 41–3; Childs, Marquis, *Eisenhower: Captive Hero*, N.Y., 1958, pp. 151–54. On Korea and Ike's trip: Childs, *Eisenhower*, p. 151; Donovan, *Eisenhower*, p. 17; *Mandate*, pp. 72–3; Truman memoirs II, p. 501.
40. Hanson-ONB int.

41. Telegram ONB to DDE, 11-5-52, and letter DDE to ONB, 11-9-52, Eisenhower papers, Bradley file, Eisenhower Library. Also in BP, WP; ONB desk calendar, 11-5-52.
42. Here and below, details on Korean trip: *Mandate*, pp. 93–7; Schnabel and Watson II ("History of the JCS"), pp. 934–36; *War in Peacetime*, pp. 323–24.
43. Poole, pp. 142–49.
44. Oplan 8-52 is described more fully in Schnabel and Watson II, pp. 932–34.
45. CB-ONB int. In a press conference May 14, 1953, Ike said, "All of the men who have been on these Joint Chiefs of Staff; they are my old friends, they are my old associates. . . . I have found them to be loyal and dedicated men. I have no criticism of anyone that is going out. We do have a new approach. We feel that the United States has a right to think that there is a new approach, a study that is made without any real chains fastening to the past. The Secretary of Defense felt he should have an entirely new team, and I agreed with him. But I must assure you this: There is nothing that I can say, from my viewpoint as an old soldier, having served with these men, that would be too high praise for every single man on that Chiefs of Staff as I have seen him operate." (Public papers of Dwight D. Eisenhower, 1953.)
46. *Eisenhower Diaries*, p. 225; *Mandate*, pp. 107, 112–13.
47. Schnabel and Watson II, pp. 953–54.
48. Ibid., pp. 949, 963; *Mandate*, p. 189.
49. Ibid., pp. 180–81.
50. Schnabel and Watson II, pp. 964–65.
51. Ibid., p. 961.
52. Ibid., pp. 983–1034, 1045–48, 1050.
53. ONB desk calendar, 5-29 to 6-10-53; *Mandate*, p. 226.
54. ONB desk calendar, 6-10-53; Walter Reed Army Hospital, medical records of ONB.
55. ONB desk calendar, 6-30-53; Van's age: *Register of Graduates*.
56. ONB desk calendar, 8-5 and 8-13-53.
57. Letter DDE to ONB, 8-13-53, BP, WP.

Collaborator's Afterword

1. Bradley's salary, and that of all five-star generals or admirals, was frozen by the terms of a 1958 military pay bill. Since he long outlived all other five-star generals and admirals, the restrictive provision finally applied solely to him. In the mid-1970s, a new law keyed his military pay to inflationary indices like other military pensions.
2. CB-Harry B. Henshel int., 4-30-80. Henshel was Arde Bulova's nephew and president and chief executive officer of the Bulova Watch Corporation. Documents relating to ONB's Bulova service and other directorships in BP, WP.
3. CB-ONB int.; date of Hal's death: *Register of Graduates*. Documents relating to Bradley's Los Angeles houses in BP, WP.
4. CB-ONB int.; CB-Frank Stewart int., 4-19-80.
5. CB-ONB int.; CB-Elizabeth Dorsey int.
6. Letter, ONB to GCM, 12-26-56, box 224, folder 13, Marshall Library; CB-Elizabeth Dorsey int.
7. CB-ONB int.; CB-Stewart int. MQB obituaries, *The New York Times*, 12-2-65, and *Washington Post*, 12-2-65. Mary's death created financial complications. The Bradleys had assumed that Mary would outlive Omar and had put most of their assets in her name. In her will she left her assets to the grandchildren with Lee Dorsey as trustee.
8. CB-Stewart int.; CB-Hansen int.
9. CB-ONB int.; CB-KB int., 2-8-80; KB Scrapbooks, BP, WP.
10. CB-KB int.
11. *Look*, 11-14-67. In the article itself, ONB wrote: "My wife Kitty brought the trip about." The $8,000 payment for the article, *Look* stated, was donated to the USO.
12. CB-KB int.
13. CB-ONB and KB int.; KB-ONB "party books" and activities calendars, BP, WP. These detailed records amount to virtually a day-by-day record of travel, entertainment, etc.
14. CB-KB int.
15. Ibid., CB-Harry Henshel int.; CB-Brian W. Brady int., 3-12-80
16. CB-KB int.; party books and activities calendars, BP, WP.
17. CB-KB int.; roster, office of ONB, Fort Bliss, 8-15-79, BP, WP.
18. CB-KB int.; obituary, *The New York Times*, 4-9-81. Most wire services and newspapers erroneously reported ONB had died of a heart attack. For details on the burial, see *The New York Times*, 4-15-81; *Washington Post*, 4-15-81 and *Washington Star*, 4-15-81. Owing to his longevity and unique status as a five-star general who could not officially retire, ONB's total active military service, including his four years as a West Point cadet, came to sixty-nine years and eight months, a record.

Index